EUROPE 1979

STOP PRESS!

1. THREE CLASSES ON AIRPLANES. By "early 1979," *British Airways* will have inaugurated its revolutionary three-class passenger system on trans-Atlantic flights. The scheme, which some other airlines may imitate, is intended to give the higher-fare passenger something more for his money, in contrast to the old system, where a person paying full fare economy class received the same kind of treatment accorded someone paying only half as much money. Here are the new categories:

First class will remain the way it is now.

Club class will be rated higher in comfort than the old economy class, and will concentrate on maintaining high standards for businessmen and others paying full fare. (There *may* be free drinks and a better menu, for example, or more leg room.)

Discount class will include those on bargain fares, as well as standby and advance purchase budget (APEX) travelers. Some of the old economy-class features will be retained, such as the present international economy class legroom (or "pitch," as the airlines term it).

2. LAKER FROM LOS ANGELES TO LONDON. *Laker's Skytrain*, which pioneered the cheap air route from New York to London, is to begin service from Los Angeles to the British capital on Sept. 26, 1978. Fares announced were: Los Angeles-London $220, and London-Los Angeles $152 (latter subject to change as it is in pounds sterling). Peak season (summer) rates will be about $25 higher each way.

A comprehensive handbook
of 35 countries, 838 pages of text;
map of Europe; 7 city plans

FODOR'S MODERN GUIDES

Founded by Eugene Fodor

EDITORIAL STAFF

New York
ROBERT C. FISHER
editor-in-chief
LESLIE BROWN
managing editor
DOROTHY FOSTER
research director

London
RICHARD MOORE
executive editor

PRODUCTION STAFF

New York
C. R. BLOODGOOD
director
EILEEN ROLPH
managing director, Fodor's Modern Guides (U.K.) Ltd.

ADVERTISING STAFF

New York
E. W. NEWSOM
director
SANDRA LANG
assistant director

EUROPE 1979:

Editorial Contributors: BARBARA ANGELILLO, PETER BESAS, NED BLACKMER, JULIANNE DARROW, ERLING DUJARDIN, BRYN FRANK, AKE GILLE, PEG HOLDEN-PETERS, FRANCES HOWELL, HEIN DE JONG, ENID KIRCHBERGER, RICHARD LEAVITT, SUSAN LESTER, SUSAN LOWNDES, EDWARD F. MACSWEENEY, E. GEORGE MADDOCKS, ROBIN MEAD, VIVIENNE MENKES, NINA NELSON, PAUL NEUBERG, SYLVIE NICKELS, GLADYS NICOL, RICHARD PARIS, HELEN SCOTT-HARMAN, PETER SHELDON, HILARY STERNBERG, DAVID D. TENNANT, MICHAEL VON HAAG

Maps: DYNO LOWENSTEIN, RAYMOND XHARDEZ

Production: C.R. BLOODGOOD

FODOR'S

EUROPE 1979

ROBERT C. FISHER
editor-in-chief

RICHARD MOORE
executive editor

LESLIE BROWN
managing editor

**AND 145 AREA
SPECIALISTS**
correspondents

DAVID McKAY COMPANY, INC.-NEW YORK

The following Fodor Travel Books are current in 1979:

AREA GUIDES:

EUROPE
EUROPE ON A BUDGET
AUSTRALIA, NEW ZEALAND
  AND THE SOUTH PACIFIC
CANADA
CARIBBEAN, BAHAMAS
  AND BERMUDA

INDIA
JAPAN AND KOREA
MEXICO
SCANDINAVIA
SOUTH AMERICA
SOUTHEAST ASIA
SOVIET UNION
U.S.A. (1 vol.)

COUNTRY GUIDES:

AUSTRIA
BELGIUM AND
  LUXEMBOURG
BRAZIL*
CZECHOSLOVAKIA
EGYPT
FRANCE
GERMANY
GREAT BRITAIN
GREECE
HOLLAND

HUNGARY*
IRAN
IRELAND
ISRAEL
ITALY
MOROCCO
PORTUGAL
SPAIN
SWITZERLAND
TUNISIA*
TURKEY
YUGOSLAVIA

USA GUIDES:

NEW ENGLAND*
NEW YORK*
MID-ATLANTIC*
SOUTH*
INDIAN AMERICA
ONLY-IN-AMERICA
  VACATION GUIDE*

MIDWEST*
SOUTHWEST*
ROCKIES AND PLAINS*
FAR WEST*
HAWAII
OLD WEST*
OLD SOUTH*
SEASIDE AMERICA*

CITY GUIDES:

LONDON   PARIS   PEKING

SPECIAL INTEREST GUIDES:

CRUISES EVERYWHERE

RAILWAYS OF THE
  WORLD

LATEST ADDITIONS TO THE SERIES:

AMERICA ON A BUDGET
ANIMAL PARKS OF AFRICA
BERMUDA
HOW-TO-TRAVEL TRAVEL GUIDE*

JORDAN AND THE
  HOLY LAND
OUTDOORS AMERICA*
PEOPLES' REPUBLIC OF
  CHINA
WORLDWIDE
  ADVENTURE GUIDE

*Not available in Hodder and Stoughton editions
MANUFACTURED IN THE UNITED STATES OF AMERICA

CONTENTS

PLANNING YOUR TRIP

Charting a course to the New, Old World 2

SPECIAL INTEREST TRAVEL

Touring with a Purpose 17

HOW TO REACH EUROPE

CONTENTS
STAYING IN EUROPE

TRAVELING IN EUROPE

LEAVING EUROPE

CONTENTS

CONTENTS

CONTENTS

Editors' Foreword

We opened our Foreword for the 1978 edition with the words "there was a time, and not so very long ago either, when the world that confronted the traveler abroad did not change from one decade's end to another. Prices remained stable; beaches were free from pollution, except perhaps for the occasional stranded whale; historic houses could only be visited when the owners were far away; and, if you struggled on foot to the top of a mountain, you were not confronted by a motorway snaking up the other side. The situation is very different today and, to complicate matters, the thing that has changed most is the rate of change itself."

Those words were hardly out of our mouths when a new factor appeared that radically changed the scene once more. After years of struggle against entrenched interests, Freddie Laker, one of Britain's tenacious bulldogs, won his fight for the Skytrain. His victory set off a price-slashing war that has already brought trans-Atlantic prices tumbling, and will, there is little doubt, have its repercussions on routes all over the world.

Unfortunately the happier state of affairs above the Atlantic is not reflected in the skies over Europe. It currently costs almost as much to fly from Britain to Germany as it does from New York to London—over five times as far; while the normal fare from London to Paris is almost twice as much as that from New York to Washington, for roughly the same distance. This is a situation which badly needs remedying. It is not as if air travel is a luxurious novelty. For the most part it is a tiring and frustrating experience in which crowded airports, delayed flights and endless waiting for baggage all play their part. That it is needlessly costly into the bargain (to use entirely the wrong expression) only compounds the fault. We hope that our next *Foreword* will be able to record that the seeds sown by Freddie Laker have born fruit in a new approach by all the major airlines, who, after all, exist to serve the public, not, as it sometimes seems, the other way round.

One of the best ways to beat the cost of air travel is to take full advantage of the multitude of packages offered on both sides of the Atlantic, packages which can include hotels, theater tickets, cars, local tours and a multitude of other valuable extras, often for less than the cost of the regular airfare. It is also an idea to take one of the cheaper tickets across the Atlantic and then a tour from, say, a British-based firm. The ways around the airfare squeeze are legion. We give you a few useful hints in the *Planning Your Trip* section.

It is unfortunately not possible in a book of this size to deal with such a vast area, full of interest and variety, in as much detail as we would wish. The hotel and restaurant listings, for example, are only intended as a basic guide, not to be exhaustive coverages of the wealth of places available. In most cities, or deep in the heart of the countryside, there will be other establishments that you would enjoy every bit as much as those contained in these pages. If you wish to learn more about the background, culture and travel possibilities of most of the countries in this book, we also publish individual guides which will help you to explore them in greater depth. We intend *Fodor's Europe* to be exactly that, a guide to Europe as a whole.

It is a region that is constantly changing. We see this more, perhaps, than the ordinary traveler might. We find that we are overtaken by events at an alarming rate. No sooner have we passed an edition for the press than a country, through financial turbulence or political upheaval, totally changes its status as a tourist destination. Normally this does not mean that it is any the less attractive for the visitor, merely that conditions, and especially costs, will be different. Currently both Italy and Portugal are bargain destinations. Britain, which had a period of being the most sought-after country for the traveler with an eye on costs, is now regaining a certain balance in its economy and is therefore not the bargain it was. We can still recommend the countries of Eastern Europe for an unusual and fairly inexpensive holiday, though costs in Yugoslavia, for long a mecca for the beach buff, are rapidly rising.

But although the focus may shift, Europe remains a kaleidoscope of fascinating variety. It may be the Old World, but it has never been further from senility. If you keep an eagle eye on the exchange rates before you leave and while traveling; if you plan carefully ahead; if you are ready to enjoy the off-beat and intriguing when they happen—then you are in for a delightful time. And we will be very interested to hear of your experiences when you get home. We really do take note of suggestions you have to make. Our two addresses are:

In the U.S.A., Fodor's Modern Guides, 750 Third Ave., New York, N.Y. 10017; **in Europe,** Fodor's Modern Guides, 40 Long Acre, London WC2E 9JT, England.

In a book of this size, a few errors are bound to creep in, and when a hotel closes down suddenly, or a restaurant's chef has a migraine and produces an inedible meal, our comments seem suddenly out of place. Let us know, and we will redouble our efforts to investigate the establishment and the complaint. Your letters will help our correspondents on the spot throughout Europe to pinpoint trouble spots, and may help them in evaluating the results of their own research.

★

Acknowledgments to people and organizations which have helped us prepare this volume would consume far too much space, with the result that no one would be noticed in the mass. But in addition to thanking all the officials of the tourist organizations who have helped us, we want to pay special tribute to the legion of readers who have written to us with their suggestions, criticisms, and in a few cases, complaints. These letters have been most helpful and we welcome them all.

★

As faithful readers of the Fodor series know, merely listing an establishment merely in one of our books is sufficient recommendation. Needless to say, no establishment pays to be listed, and establishments will not know if they are listed, or dropped, until the book is published.

★

We accept advertising from a few firms representing the cream of the travel industry, but there is absolutely no connection between the advertising and the editor's recommendations. We have advertising for two good reasons, namely (1) the ads partially defray the high cost of producing this series yearly, something which we are the only guide book series in the world to do; and (2) the advertising itself carries useful information to readers, frequently containing information which we cannot include in our own text.

FACTS AT YOUR FINGERTIPS

FACTS AT YOUR FINGERTIPS

N.B.: We've tried to bring you latest price information throughout this book, but because of the continuing instability in world
currency markets, we have to point out that all prices herein are
subject to change without notice. We've used an approximate exchange rate of $2.00 to the pound sterling, and have tried to quote
prices in local currencies. But if governments, banks and speculators
can't get it all together, we'll just have to ask you to check prices
before starting out on your travels. Note that while some currencies
(Portugal, Spain, France, for example) have moved up or down,
others (Holland, Switzerland, West Germany) have remained firm
in themselves but have climbed for Americans because it is the
dollar that has deteriorated. See under money matters and individual country chapters for more information.

PLANNING YOUR TRIP

How to Use this Guide

For the reader's convenience and easy reference, we have organized this book in two streamlined sections:

Section I, *Practical Planning,* is designed to supply you with all
the information relevant to planning your trip in the broad sense.
This includes detailed indications as to necessary documents, travel
agents, how to reach Europe by air and sea; transporting your car
to Europe, hiring and buying cars abroad, and touring by car, bus,
train, plane or boat.

Section II, *Europe Up-to-Date,* comprises specific facts on *costs,
daily budgets* and other practical information for each nation, plus
a descriptive guide to the people, sights, hotels, restaurants, nightlife
and other attractions of 35 countries of Europe, alphabetically arranged.

An **index** to place names will be found at the back.

Charting a Course to the New, Old World

As Europe enters the supersonic era, new areas of tourist interest open up almost daily and the old attractions of the continent become more easily accessible to the traveler than ever before. Entirely revised, the 1979 edition of *Fodor's Europe* has been designed with the world economic situation in mind, and includes special new cost information, tables of hotel rates, and hints on budgeting, discounts and other money-saving devices.

In addition to the new material contained in this edition, five special sections in the *Practical Planning* pages will be helpful in charting your course:

1. What Will it Cost. The most important question is the hardest to answer, and we've had to tackle it on a country-by-country basis, as no two national sets of figures look alike. After an overall view in this section of the book, turn to the chapter on the country you're visiting for the latest (at presstime) details. In particular, tipping practices vary so much from country to country that they are given separately for each one.

2. Special Interest Travel helps you to avoid the overcrowded, run-of-the-mill tours by telling you where to find trips arranged for people with special interests—whether the interest be auto-racing, gardening, mountaineering or bird-watching.

3. Motoring in Europe reflects the latest information on the continent's good roads and where they can lead you. Especially designed for the man and woman who like leisurely travel with not-too-rigid a timetable, this chapter is full of helpful hints for charting your itinerary.

4. Rail Travel in Europe tells you what you already know—Europe has better trains than America. Luxury and comfort, plus incredible speed, are the keynotes. You'll be tempted to take the lazy man's way of traveling after seeing all the sleek trains and their routes listed here.

5. Bus Travel in Europe highlights the economy and ease with which you can enjoy some of the most beautiful scenery on the Continent from the depths of a comfortable seat—and without having to worry about filling the tank.

WHAT WILL IT COST?

Keeping the Price Within Reason

Important Note: *specific details of costs in each country are given in the individual chapter for that country later in the book.*

In approximating the overall cost of your trip it is helpful to check a number of the all-expense roundtrip tours currently offered from America and England to the continent.

Globus Gateways, a Swiss-based company, offers a number of charter-flight tours of Europe at prices such as the following, New York to Europe return: 6 countries in 16 days from $818; 4 countries in 16 days from $878; 9 countries in 16 days from $888; 7 countries in 16 days from $918; Portugal, Spain and Morocco in 16 days from $698, or First Class from $778. All of these prices include airfare. *Europacar* and *Lufthansa* offer a number of fly/drive package plans for the Germany-Austria-Switzerland area. The land portions alone of these plans include car rental, hotel accommodations, breakfasts, service charges and airport transfers at rates per day of about $25 to $47. Generally speaking, airfares in off-season (mid-September to mid-June) can be about $100 less than usual. However, if you decide to do the land portion of your trip independently, remember that most of the charter flights operate in summer. See "Getting to Europe" section, later, for more detailed air fares, including cheaper fares.

Travel expenses from Britain are suggested by the following air tours, London return: Athens and surroundings, 10 days from $319 (£160); to the Costa del Sol, 10 days from $159 (£80), or 17 days from $199 (£100), skiing in Switzerland, 7 nights from $284 (£142), or 14 nights from $417 (£208). You can have 2 nights in London and 14 in Majorca from $189 (£95). Fifteen days touring Italy by car from $277. This random sampling represents a medium price range—there are higher- and lower-priced package tours, depending a good deal on the class accommodation offered, and extent of the itinerary, and you can usually find something to suit your taste and pocket after studying the brochures of various tour operators.

As for the *communist countries,* although individual travel is possible, including even camping, most tourists prefer a package tour and the variety available is increasing. An 11-day air/coach tour of the Soviet Union and Poland costs from £175; a 15-day air holiday to Bulgaria or Romania, about £170; a 14-day air/coach tour of Albania, (not always open to Americans), about £180; of East Germany £105, of Hungary £130 for 8 days and £190, for 16 days, and of Yugoslavia £140 for 8 days, £200 for 16 days. For individual travel costs see country chapters.

When *booking a package tour* it is always wise to check with your travel agent on the extent of the "package". Some really are inclusive—down to tips and taxis, nightclubs and theaters; others cover all your transportation, accommodation and meals but leave you to pay on the spot for trips, excursions, etc.

Credit Travel and Credit Cards

A number of organizations in the United States and Britain make credit cards available which enable you to sign for hotel and restaurant bills, car rentals, purchases, and so forth, and pay the resulting total at one time on a monthly bill, either pay-as-you-go or in instalments after you return home. In these days of currency exchange rate fluctuations, cards save you the trouble of converting, as you'll be billed in dollars back home at current exchange rate on date of purchase. If you want to be certain of the rate at which you will pay, insist on the establishment entering the current rate onto your credit card charge at the time you sign it—this will prevent the management from holding your charge until a more favorable rate (to them) comes along, something which could cost you more dollars than you counted on. (On the other hand, should the dollar be revalued upward before your charge is entered, you could gain a little.) Some credit card organizations are the *Diners Club, American Express Card, Carte Blanche, Master Charge, Bankamericard, Eurocard, Access* and *Barclaycard.*

Speaking of credit, airline tickets can be bought on the instalment plan with a 10 percent down payment securing the reservations, the balance, plus interest, being paid in monthly instalments.

Finally, you can borrow money specifically for travel, from your bank or from special firms handling travel loans.

DEVALUATION-REVALUATION-"FLOATING"-INFLATION

The ups and downs of U.S., British, and European currencies make accurate budgeting long in advance extremely difficult. In addition, many of the Common Market currencies, and also that of Switzerland, are now allowed to fluctuate in value ('float') from day to day—a form of instant devaluation or revaluation—though this is kept within modest bounds. Prices mentioned throughout this book are indicative only of costs at time of going to press.

Keep a close eye on the exchange rates of the countries you are intending to visit—both when you are planning your trip and while you are on it. As things are at the moment, you may well find that Europe is a great deal cheaper than you imagined.

Money Matters

Travelers' checks are the best way to safeguard travel funds. They are sold by various banks and companies in terms of American and Canadian dollars, pounds sterling, German marks, Swiss francs and other foreign currencies. We recommend buying them in the local currencies you will be using, whenever possible. These are called *destination-currency* checks, and have the double advantage of being cashed free of service charge, and protecting you against loss on exchange rates. Those issued by *American Express, First National City Bank* and *Bank of America* are best known and their offices are most widespread. Note that in the US only *Barclays, Thomas Cook* and *Perera* do not charge commission for issuing checks. *The Bank of America* has 28,000 correspondent banks around the world; *Thomas Cook & Sons* has 20,000; *Barclay's Bank,* about 8,000. Best known and easily exchanged British travelers' checks are those issued by *Thos. Cook & Son* and the main banks *(Barclays, Lloyds, Midland, National Westminster)*.

It is usually advantageous to buy foreign currency up to the maximum permissible amount or in accordance with your anticipated expenses before entering the country. Sometimes you can do this at larger banks. There are a number of private firms that buy and sell foreign money; look under *Foreign Money Brokers and Dealers* in the Yellow Pages of large-city phone books. In New York, *Deak & Co., 29 Broadway, Perera Co.,* 630 Fifth Ave., and *Deak- Perera International* at Kennedy Airport are among the over two dozen listed.

CHANGING travelers' checks or cash is easiest at your hotel, but will cost you more (and it will be worse in shops and restaurants!). So change at banks, if you can afford the extra time, and try to avoid doing so at weekends, when rates are less advantageous. Rates at main downtown banks are often better than those at airport branches. So try to have on hand enough local currency for arrival at next port of call, to get you through the unnerving procedures at airports with porters, taxi drivers, bellhops at the hotel, etc. You can buy small packets for this purpose at many banks and at *Perera, Deak* and similar agencies.

Don't ever have any truck with characters who sidle up to you on the street with offers to change money.

It is now possible for *British* travelers to cash checks abroad for up to £30 each transaction, on production of a Barclaycard or one of many bank check cards participating in the scheme in over 19 countries. It is cheaper than exchanging travelers' checks. Enquire at your bank before starting out.

In Eastern Europe. You usually cannot bring any local currency with you into a communist country (except Yugoslavia and Hungary, small amounts). If caught you may be subject to a prison term (some tourists have been imprisoned), or at best, embarrassment, confiscation of your money, and expulsion from the country.

Roughing It

Europe is full of youth hostels and excellent camping facilities, providing the cheapest and in a sense the most intimate way of getting to know various countries. Hostels offer less privacy, of course; and for camping you need your own equipment, but camping can be especially advantageous if you rent a car in Europe. For more information on Europe's highly developed network of campgrounds see below the section on Motoring in Europe. For information write to the following:

U.S.A.

American Youth Hostels, Inc.,
National Campus, Delaplane, Virginia 22025;
  Campgrounds Unlimited,
  Blue Rapids, Kansas, 66411;
    National Campers & Hikers Association,
    7172 Transit Road, Williamsville, N.Y. 14221.

CANADA

Canadian Youth Hostels Association, National Office,
333 River Road, Vanier City, Ottawa, Ontario K1L 8B9.

GREAT BRITAIN

Camping Club of Great Britain and Ireland,
11 Lower Grosvenor Place, London S.W.1;
  The Youth Hostels Association,
  29 John Adam Street, Strand, London W.C.2.

Year-round Travel

In addition to the price differential indicated above, off-season travel has other advantages over touring during the peak summer months. In cases where prices remain the same, the pressure is off, and you will have a wider choice of accommodation.

The choicest hotel rooms, the very best tables in the restaurants, will not have been pre-empted by fellow tourists, and you will gain a more intimate knowledge of the countries you visit, seeing their inhabitants in their normal routine of making and enjoying a living. The great cities and capitals of Europe bloom in the fall and winter, rather than in the summer. The theaters open, the concert and opera seasons begin, the new shows are presented in the night clubs. The traditional balls and gala soirées are winter affairs. The celebrations of Christmas and the New Year are even gayer than they are at home, and the gaiety continues *crescendo* through the carnivals preceding Lent. Even if you are not a member of that mass movement that converges annually with the first fall of snow on the ski slopes of the Alps, think about "out-of-season" travel this year in Europe.

Practical Packing Tips

Always pack separately your passport, enough money (both Traveler's Checks and some local currency to use upon arrival) and any medications you may need, and have them readily available, preferably on your person. Take along copies of all medical prescriptions, including eyeglasses, in case you need a refill. Pack film separately or in special lined bags for protection against airport-security X-rays.

Don't buy cheap luggage. Borrow if you must, but have bags whose construction and locks you can trust. Never leave your luggage unlocked anywhere, anytime. Airlines will not take luggage that is not tagged with your name and home address. Put on your destination address as well, with dates of arrival and departure, in case your bags go astray and have to be forwarded. Put your identification inside, too; special stickers are free from any airline. Remove all old tags; they just confuse things. Near the handle put a piece of some bright-colored tape to help pick out your bag from all the similar models on your plane, train, or bus.

At airports, watch to be sure that your bags go on the conveyor belt, and keep your stubs until you have carefully compared the numbers; those stubs are your receipts. Lost luggage must be reported within four hours after arrival. Remember that the carrier's liability is limited, so carry extra baggage insurance if you need it. It's available from travel agents.

If your baggage is oversize on your return trip, get the rates for shipping the excess separately by Air Freight instead of paying the higher rates for excess baggage.

Traveling with Children

Traveling with children is always full of surprises, but the biggest one, for parents who haven't tried it, is that trips abroad with children are more enjoyable than those without. The peculiar curiosity of children, their enthusiasm about new lands and people and the special way they have of melting the reserve of strangers add a rewarding new dimension to travel.

Preparing the children should begin about two months prior to departure. Check the planned itinerary with their doctor to see what inoculations may be necessary and allow plenty of time to complete each series. He can also advise what special prescriptions or feeding formulas should be taken along. Each child should have a thorough physical and dental exam. Remember, too, that even children must be covered by passports. You can put them on a family passport, but then you must always travel as a group. Separate passports cost more initially, but give you far more freedom in planning and traveling.

Minor medical problems can easily be handled with a good first aid kit. Include the standard contents as recommended by the Red Cross, any special prescriptions required, spare glasses, (and the prescriptions for all the glasses the family uses), a cough syrup, a stomach-ache remedy, a laxative, children's aspirin, an opthalmic ointment and antidiarrheal tablets (they go down easier than the liquid.) One of the greatest triumphs of medical science, as far as traveling children are concerned, is the individually packaged gauze pads pre-treated with antiseptic and a mild local anesthetic (such as Clean and Treat, made by Pharmaco, Inc.). These are ideal for cleaning up the scrapes and scratches children can collect the world over. A tube of zinc-oxide is a versatile aid for sun and wind burn, diaper rash and minor abrasions. The dosage and directions for all medicines should be checked with the physician before departure. Pack the kit in a small shoulder bag so it can easily be kept handy.

The itinerary itself should take the children into consideration. Because children's "biological clocks" are more finely tuned than adults', long trips should be divided into segments as short as possible to allow the children to adjust to time zone changes. This also decreases the period of time in which children can repeat the age-old question, "Are we there yet?"

A day of sightseeing that doesn't include something of special interest to the children may be a day of turmoil. The public parks, zoos, and museums found in every major European city are perfect child-pleasers. Beaches, circuses, castles, forts, towers also are common in Europe and make big hits with tiny tourists. Nowadays many European centers, such as Copenhagen, have specially organized services for small fry including country camps, baby-sitting, baby carriage rentals and even children's theaters and restaurants. Museums fascinate children, but avoid guided tours. They will go either too fast or too slow for the children and you may have to stand apart to keep from disturbing the rest of the group.

Tours and excursions for children should allow as much freedom as possible. Probably the ideal way (though certainly not the only way) for a family with young children to travel would be in their own auto on their own schedule. The convenient locations of camping sites all across Europe offer children the space and freedom not found in hotels. Whenever possible, children should be able to set their own pace. A tightly scheduled and confined tour of more than a half-day in length is generally too restrictive.

Packing for children requires little extra effort. Clothing should be as simple, comfortable and versatile as possible. Wash-and-wear and stain-resistant fabrics will make life a little easier for mother. One of the handiest items will be a damp washcloth wrapped in a plastic bag for impromptu cleaning of hands and faces. If a child is not yet a good walker it is a good idea to pack him too—in one of the back carriers which allows a parent to carry a child while keeping their own hands free.

The times which try parents' souls (and their progeny's) do not usually occur at some major juncture of a trip, as one would expect, but at the scores of times each day when the family is waiting for a plane, waiting for a meal to be served, waiting for everyone else to get ready to leave for an outing. The solution is deceptively simple: toys. A few small cars such as the Corgi and Matchbox toys, a mini-doll a few inches high, small notebooks and pencils, small puzzles and games, should be kept on reserve in pocket or purse. If, when boredom rears its ugly head, the parent can produce a *passe temps,* it is like a bridge over troubled waters. Easily portable collections of stamps, coins, jacket emblems, seashells or minerals also can be called into the breach when needed. When you check in for your plane, ask for early boarding permission to get the children in ahead of the crowd. Also request the first row of seats in your compartment; they offer more leg room. Some airlines provide bassinets for infants; and in flight you can ask the stewardess to serve the children earlier than the other passengers. Once on the plane, check for airsick bags, too.

Hunger pangs have a way of striking children at the exact time when food isn't available. Carrying a small snack the children like will keep their sunny dispositions from suddenly clouding. Space sticks (designed for the astronauts) made by General Foods, for example, are nutritionally balanced and convenient. Packets of powdered, instant soup are easy to carry. Order hot water for tea and make your soup in the cup.

Another continuing need of itinerant children is for what the Greeks call *to meros,* "the place" (lavatory), and it is indeed *the* place for anyone traveling with children. If you learn no other word of the language of the country in which you are traveling, you should know the one for "the place". It will save anxious moments of sign language when you have a very fidgety youngster in tow. Remember that in many countries the public toilets do *not* supply paper. Carry a small supply of your own.

The languages themselves today prove little problem in all but the most out-of-the-way areas of Europe. Children have an innate ability to pick up foreign languages. It is not at all uncommon to see youngsters on tour acting as translators for their monolingual parents.

Most children adapt to foreign food more easily than their parents. However, spicy, rich foods and restaurants which appear unsavory should be avoided. Canned milk is widely available throughout Europe. Drinking water in large hotels and restaurants is usually reliable, but bottled water is best for baby formulas.

The most important need of all for children is something you'll find in every corner of Europe—love! Europeans adore children and enjoy catering to them, especially foreign ones. Wherever you go, you'll find your children are superlative ambassadors. Doors—and hearts—are opened to them that never would be to "unaccompanied" adults. *(By Alan Linn.)*

Languages

Perhaps you already know a smattering of Spanish, French, Greek or some other European language, and even if it's just enough to let you order a meal, ask directions, and say 'please' and 'thank you', you'll find that it makes your trip that much more enjoyable. But if your command of a foreign language needs some brushing up, or even if there's nothing there to brush up, it would be well worth your while to purchase a packaged course, or, better yet, attend a live one before you go. The *New School,* 66 West 12th Street, New York, NY 10011, will get you in shape with a vengeance. Their "One-Day Language Courses for Travelers" ($35) come in French, German, Greek, Italian, Portuguese, Spanish and other versions. The basics of polite conversation come first, followed by intensive practice in restaurant, shopping, currency and "How do I get to . . . ?" situations. These courses, 7½ hours each, are given only on weekends in June.

Britons can least expensively learn a language by attending classes at a school of further education run by their local education authority, or otherwise attend one of the numerous private language schools throughout the country. *Regent School,* 19–23 Oxford Street, London W1, offers intensive courses in French, German, Italian and Spanish.

Passports

There actually was a time when you could decide to go to Europe one day and leave the next. Before World War I, you didn't even need a passport. Those days are gone, presumably forever. Today every traveler, even an infant, needs a passport, or to be on a passport. The U.S. Government issues both individual and joint family passports. Individual passports cost more ($13 each) but they offer flexibility. It is not always convenient, or possible, to cross frontiers as a group. You may need to separate—for business, illness, or special-interest sightseeing. Plan for maximum freedom of movement. It may be a good idea, too, to have children wear identification bracelets listing their names and U.S. passport numbers. Another tip: keep extra photos on hand in case you change your plans and need visas for additional countries.

U.S. citizens. Apply several months in advance of your expected departure date. US residents must apply in person to the US Passport Agency in Boston, Chicago, Detroit, Honolulu, Houston, Los Angeles, Miami, New Orleans, New York, Philadelphia, San Francisco, Seattle, Stamford (Conn.), or Washington DC, or to their local County Courthouse. In some areas selected post offices are also equipped to handle passport applications. If you still have your latest passport issued within the past eight years you may use this to apply by mail. Otherwise, take with you: 1) a birth certificate or certified copy thereof, or other proof of citizenship; 2) two identical photographs 2 inches square, full face, black and white or color, on nonglossy paper and taken within the past six months; 3) $13 ($10 if you apply by mail); and 4) proof of identity such as a driver's license, previous passport, any governmental ID card. Social Security and credit cards are NOT acceptable. If you expect to travel extensively, request a 48- or 96-page passport rather than the usual 24-page one. There is no extra charge. US passports are valid for five years. If your passport is lost or stolen, immediately notify either the nearest American Consul or the Passport Office, Department of State, Washington, DC 20524.

If a non-citizen, you need a Treasury Sailing Permit, Form 1040C, certifying that Federal taxes have been paid; apply to your District Director of Internal Revenue for this. You will have to present various documents: 1) blue or green alien registration card; 2) passport; 3) travel tickets; 4) most recently filed Form 1040; 5) W-2 forms for the most recent full year; 6) most recent current payroll stubs or letter; 7) check to be sure this is all! To return to the United States you need a re-entry permit if you intend to remain abroad longer than 1 year. Apply for it in person at least six weeks before departure at the nearest office of the Immigration and Naturalization Service, or by mail to the Immigration and Naturalization Service, Washington, D.C.

British subjects must apply for passports on special forms obtainable from main post offices or a travel agent. The application should be sent or taken to the Passport Office according to residential area (as indicated on the guidance form) or lodged with them through a travel agent. Apply at least 3 weeks before the passport is required. The regional Passport Offices are located in London, Liverpool, Peterborough, Glasgow, Newport (Mon.) and Belfast. The application must be countersigned by your bank manager or by a solicitor, barrister, doctor, clergyman or justice of the peace who knows you personally. You will need two photos. The fee is £11: passport valid for 10 years.

British Visitor's Passport. This simplified form of passport has advantages for the once-in-a-while tourist to most European countries (Yugoslavia and eastern European countries presently excepted). Valid for one year and not renewable, it costs £5.50. Application may be made at main post offices in England, Scotland and Wales and at the Ministry of Health and Social Security offices in Northern Ireland. Identification and two passport photographs are required—no other formalities.

. **Canadian citizens** must have a valid passport (even for the U.K.), application forms for which may be obtained at any post office; these are to be sent to the Canadian Passport Office at 40 Bank Street, Ottawa, together with a remittance of $10.

Visas

Of the 35 countries covered in this guide, the following require a visa from *American* citizens: Albania, Czechoslovakia, East Germany, Hungary, Poland, Romania, U.S.S.R. and Yugoslavia (in Romania and Yugoslavia, you get a free visa on arrival). Since the U.S. has no direct diplomatic relations with Albania, Americans must apply for visas through Albanian embassies in Paris or Rome.

British subjects from the United Kingdom and Canadians must have visas for Albania, Czechoslovakia, East Germany, Hungary, Poland, Romania (issued immediately on arrival) and the U.S.S.R.

Note: American, British and Canadian tourists do not require visas for Bulgaria provided they stay longer than 48 hours and less than two months, as long as their stay is prepaid. Otherwise entry or transit visas are required. Nor are visas necessary for Romania if accommodation has been pre-paid through Carpati.

Tourists may now obtain a transit visa for most of the above countries at the frontier (see country chapters)—useful for impulse trips from adjoining countries. Some evidence of identity is required (with photograph), so always carry your passport and spare passport photographs. Also, Vienna is a particularly convenient jumping-off place for Eastern Europe and has a number of tour agencies specializing in package visits to places like Prague, Cracow and Budapest, and cruises down the Danube.

Potential visitors to communist countries should ask their passport agency to provide them with the addresses of consular offices of the countries they intend to visit in order to check on last-minute details concerning documentation, though visa regulations are considerably eased in some of these countries.

Commonwealth citizens sometimes require visas where United Kingdom "patrial" residents do not. Visas may usually be procured through the consulates of the countries you wish to visit, either in your country or abroad.

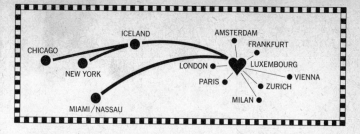

Rabies

Being an island, Britain is one of the few rabies-free areas in the world, and intends to stay that way. Dogs, cats, and other warm-blooded animals arriving from abroad must be put in quarantine for six months. Persons attempting to smuggle pets into Britain face unlimited fines and up to one year's imprisonment, and their pets could be destroyed.

Health Certificates

Not needed for entry to any European country covered in this book. However, any country may demand vaccination certificates periodically and temporarily, especially if there has been a minor outbreak of smallpox or cholera anywhere in Europe. Best check in advance of your trip.

Smallpox vaccination is no longer required for *US and Canadian citizens* returning from Western Europe, but it is "if you come from an infected area". So we suggest you have a vaccination, anyhow. *British residents* face the same kind of uncertain regulations, and we advise them to have a shot as well.

The wise traveler, however, will not be satisfied by complying with the minimum vaccination requirements of the countries he is visiting. If traveling in southern Europe, typhoid, paratyphoid, polio and cholera shots would be a good idea, even if these diseases are rare and the likelihood of contracting them is slight; and a tetanus shot is advisable wherever you go.

Travel Agents

Travel agents are experts in the increasingly complicated business of tourism. A good travel agent (and they are located everywhere) can save you time and money through his knowledge of details which you could not be expected to know about. He can help you take advantage of special reductions in rail fares and the like, save you *time* by making it unnecessary for you to waste precious days abroad trying to get tickets and reservations. In the all-important phase of planning your trip, even if you wish to travel independently, it is wise to take advantage of the services of these specialists. (Travel to certain eastern European countries can be arranged *only* through special tourist agencies—see below.) Whether you select *Maupintour Associates, American Express, Thomas Cook,* or a smaller organization is only a matter of your preference. But you should be sure he is reliable.

If you wish him merely to arrange a steamship or airline ticket or to book you on a package tour, his services should cost you nothing as he almost certainly has a commission from the tour operator.

If, on the other hand, you wish him to plan for you an individual itinerary he will make a service charge on the total cost of the work he does. This may amount to 10 or 15 percent, but it will *save* you money on balance. If your travel budget is limited, you should frankly explain this to your agent and he will work out an interesting itinerary accordingly.

If you cannot locate a travel agent near your home, write, if in America, to the *American Society of Travel Agents,* 711 Fifth Ave., New York, N.Y. 10022; in Canada, to *A.S.T.A.-Canada,* 130 Albert St., Suite 1207, Ottawa, Ontario K1P 5G4; and in Britain, to the *Association of British Travel Agents,* 53 Newman St., London W1P 4AH. Any agency affiliated with these organizations is almost sure to be thoroughly reliable.

Types of Travel

Between the all-expenses-paid-in-advance type of travel and the pay-as-you-go there are enormous variations and unless you are a widely experienced traveler you will be wise to consult a travel agent on the various possibilities. We list below the four principal ways of traveling:

The **group tour,** in which you travel with others, following a prearranged itinerary hitting all the high spots, and paying a single all-inclusive price that covers everything—transportation, meals, lodging, sightseeing tours, guides. These can range from two weeks to several months and can be taken on luxury or budget levels. Usually accompanied by experienced multilingual guides.

Furthermore, there are possibilities for special interest tours in which you are ensured of companions with similar interests or hobbies to your own. Whether you want to visit neolithic sites, or the outstanding opera houses, your travel agent is likely to be able to find you a specialist tour.

On some group tours, especially those from Britain, the total cost is less than the ordinary return (round-trip) air fare (perhaps only 50% of it). You can ignore the tour once you have arrived, even stay at a different hotel (provided you are willing to pay for it), and rejoin the group just before departure for home. You can thus have a completely individual tour for group-tour prices, plus your extras.

The **freelance tour** is now defined as following a set itinerary planned for you by the travel agent or by tour operators, with all costs in advance. You are strictly on your own, not with any group. This type of tour allows for a great deal of flexibility. Hotel reservations and transportation facilities are all taken care of by the travel agent, but no sightseeing is included—you do this on your own. If your arrangements are through one of the larger operators, their representative may meet you on arrival and help you with your luggage. This same rep can book you on sightseeing tours, if you want them, but you will pay extra for this.

The **FIT (foreign independent travel) tour** is the custom-made type of program, all arranged for you by your travel agent prior to your departure. The agent tailors the tour to your preferences. There's a charge for this type of service, so it's an expensive way to travel. You usually pay for everything prior to departure.

The **individual tour** is a do-it-yourself itinerary, but the travel agent makes transportation arrangements, hotel reservations, transfers and even sightseeing plans. This can sometimes involve a service charge. Except for your transportation, you pay your bills as you travel.

To visit certain of the **eastern European** countries you still must *plan* ahead and *pay* ahead. To obtain from them your tourist visa, you must first make all your hotel reservations. To secure a hotel reservation (foreigners being admitted to specified hotels only), you must pay in advance, in dollars or pounds, for your entire stay. You make this pre-payment to the accredited travel agent in your country acting for the various national tourist bureaux. (These, incidentally, are empowered to represent each other, so you may set up a multi-country tour through a single agent.)

You must pre-pay hotel rooms and meals, and may also pay in advance for guide and interpreter services, private cars or buses, even theater tickets. In exchange for your hard-earned hard currency, your travel agent will hand you a *tourist voucher,* which is simply a receipt itemizing the services you have paid for, at the prevailing legal rate of exchange.

But, as soon as you arrive, the local tourist bureau will redeem your voucher at a special favorable tourist exchange rate. This "bonus" varies from country to country (as do the details of the procedure itself). In most countries you get several times your money back; you can use this extra cash to order special dishes, upgrade your hotel accommodation, buy souvenirs, or alter your tour itinerary (if hotel space is available). Any travelers' checks or banknotes you cash inside the country will also be exchanged at the bonus rate. The U.S.S.R. does not offer these advantages.

Your voucher also enables your travel agent to obtain your *tourist visa.* This is more than a permit to cross the frontier and stay in the country. It is an official guarantee that fully paid-up hotel accommodation has been reserved in your name.

Even if you plan to move in with relatives, in some eastern European countries you must pre-pay a certain number of days of tourist hotel accommodation. If changed plans make it impossible to fulfil your entire pre-paid tour itinerary, apply for a refund at the nearest tourist bureau office. (It's usually 90% of your pre-payment.)

See country chapters for individual requirements in eastern Europe.

Sampling the Tours

From North America, a vast range of tours is available, and the situation changes constantly. Here, we can only show you a few of the possibilities to whet your appetite and to start your imagination working toward deciding what to ask your travel agent for.

Among the *best* are tours operated by *Maupintour,* whose reliability and careful handling of all arrangements has given the firm one of the best reputations in the travel business. Sample tour: 15 days in Spain and Portugal, for $1488 including air fare. A 23-day tour of France will run about $1800–$2360, fare included. *Maupintour,* 408 E. 50 St., New York, N.Y. 10021; 900 Massachusetts St., Lawrence, Kansas 66044; or 1780 Pacific Ave., San Francisco, Calif. 94109; or 2912 M St., N.W., Washington, D.C.

Among those offered by airlines are TWA's, ranging from budget tours to deluxe trips around the world. For a 7-day "London Theater" tour, figure about $400 for air fare plus anywhere from $96 to $266, depending on your choice, for hotel. For 14 days, hotels from $227–$267. In addition, you receive daily breakfast, all transfers, tickets to 4 or 6 shows, and special arrangements for shopping, cruises, excursions, car rental, casinos and sightseeing. Available through all TWA offices and through travel agents.

American Express, 65 Broadway, New York, N.Y. 10006, has about 90 different European vacation packages from 8 to 31 days long. "Carefree," a 15-day tour of Rome, Florence and Venice, is priced from $828 to $1048. "Europe Magnifique" covers France, Monaco, Italy, Austria, Switzerland, Germany, Holland and England for $1299–$1584. "Pageant" is a 17-day tour of England, France, Switzerland and Italy for $2098–$2199. Airfare is included in all of these prices.

Extra Value Travel, 5 World Trade Center, New York, N.Y. 10048 offer 15 days in Milan, Venice, Florence, Rome, and Naples for about $1500 including airfare in summer, about $1390 off-season.

From Great Britain, the variety of tours is tremendous. Just a few, in addition to prices mentioned previously:

15-day holiday at Torremolinos on the Costa del Sol from about £160; 11, 12 and 15 days at Lido di Jesolo from about £150; 15 days in many resorts in Greece from about £210; all from *Thomson Holidays,* Greater London House, Hampstead Road, London, N.W.1.

The same firm offers 8-day cruises round the Greek Islands, combined with 8-day resort stays, from £340.

4, 5 and 8 day Discovery Tours of the Rhine Valley, Provence and the Camargue, Seville and the Sherry Country and the Fjords of Norway to name a few, start at around £120 and are offered by *Inghams Travel* 329 Putney Bridge Road, London, S.W.15.

For the young and the not-so-young, there are adventurous treks by coach, Ford Transits and Land Rovers through France, Spain and Morocco (£130 for 17 days), Greece and Turkey (£225 for 22 days), or Russia and Eastern Europe (£270 for 30 days) from *Trail Finders,* 48 Earls Court Road, London, W8.

Official Tourist Bureaux

All the major tourist countries maintain official information bureaux in important cities—New York, San Francisco, London, Toronto and many others. They have a wealth of free printed matter to help you in planning your trip and they are at your service to give you any additional special information you may require. There is no charge for any of this. They do *not,* however, issue tickets or make hotel reservations.

Addresses of some of the principal European tourist offices in the United States, Canada and Gt. Britain are as follows:

UNITED STATES

Austrian National Tourist Office, 545 Fifth Ave., New York City 10017; 3440 Wilshire Blvd., Los Angeles, Calif. 90010; 200 E. Randolph, Chicago, Ill. 60601 1007 N.W. 24th Ave., Portland, Ore. 97210.

Belgian National Tourist Office, 720 Fifth Ave., New York City 10019.

British Tourist Authority, 680 Fifth Ave., New York City 10019; 875 N. Michigan Ave., Chicago, Ill. 60611; 612 So. Flower St., Los Angeles, Calif. 90017; 171 Commerce St., Dallas, Texas 75201.

Bulgarian Tourist Office (Balkantourist), 50 E. 42nd St., Suite 1508, New York City 10017.

Czechoslovak Travel Bureau (Cedok), 10 E. 40th St., New York City 10016

Danish National Tourist Office, 75 Rockefeller Plaza, New York, N.Y. 10019 3600 Wilshire Blvd., Los Angeles, Calif. 90010.

Finland National Tourist Office, 75 Rockefeller Plaza, New York, N.Y. 10019 3600 Wilshire Blvd., Los Angeles, Calif. 90010.

French Government Tourist Office, 610 Fifth Ave., New York City 10020; 645 N. Michigan Ave., Chicago, Ill. 60601; 9401 Wilshire Blvd., Suite 314, Beverly Hills, Calif. 90212; 323 Geary St., San Francisco, Calif. 94102.

German Tourist Information Office, 630 Fifth Ave., New York City 10020; 104 S. Michigan Ave., Chicago, Ill. 60603; 700 S. Flower St., Los Angeles, Calif. 90017.

Greek Nat. Tourist Organization, 5th floor, Olympic Tower, 645 Fifth Avenue, New York, N.Y. 10022; 627 W. Sixth Street, Los Angeles, Calif 90017; 168 N. Michigan Ave., Chicago, Ill. 60601.

Icelandic National Tourist Office, 75 Rockefeller Plaza, New York City 10019; 3600 Wilshire Blvd., Los Angeles, Calif. 90010.

Irish Tourist Board, 590 Fifth Ave., New York City 10036; 230 N. Michigan Ave., Chicago, Ill. 60601; 510 West 6th Street, Los Angeles, Calif.; 681 Market St., San Francisco, Calif. 94105.

Italian Government (ENIT) Travel Office, 630 Fifth Ave., New York City 10020; 500 North Michigan Ave., Chicago, Ill. 60601; 360 Post Street, San Francisco, Calif. 94119.

Luxembourg Tourist Information Office, One Dag Hammerskjold Plaza, New York City 10017.

Monaco Gov't Tourist Office, 115 East 64th Street, New York, N.Y. 10021.

Netherlands National Tourist Office, 576 Fifth Ave., New York City 10036; 681 Market St., San Francisco, Calif. 94105.

Norwegian National Tourist Office, 75 Rockefeller Plaza, New York City 10019; 3600 Wilshire Blvd., Los Angeles, Calif. 90010.

Polish Travel Bureau (Orbis), 500 Fifth Ave., New York City 10036.

Portuguese Tourist & Information Office (Casa de Portugal), 548 Fifth Ave., New York City 10036. 3250 Wilshire Blvd., Los Angeles, Cal. 90010; Room 500, The Palmer House, 17 E. Monroe Street, Chicago, Ill. 60603.

Romanian National Tourist Office, 500 Fifth Ave., New York City 10036.

Spanish National Tourist Office, 665 Fifth Avenue, New York, N.Y. 10022; 180 N. Michigan Ave., Chicago, Ill. 60601; 209 Post St., San Francisco, Calif. 94108; 338 Biscayne Blvd., Miami, Fla. 33132; Casa del Hidalgo, St. Augustine, Fla. 32084; Fortaleza 367, San Juan, Puerto Rico.

Swedish National Tourist Office, 75 Rockefeller Plaza, New York City 10019; 3600 Wilshire Blvd., Los Angeles, Calif. 90010.

Swiss National Tourist Office, 608 Fifth Ave., New York City 10020; 104 So. Michigan Ave., Chicago, Ill. 60603; 661 Market St., San Francisco, Calif. 94105.

U.S.S.R. (Intourist), 45 E. 49th St., New York City 10017.

Yugoslav State Tourist Office, 630 Fifth Avenue, Suite 210, New York, N.Y. 10020.

CANADA

Austrian National Tourist Service, 401 Bay St., Suite 2008, Box 21, Toronto, Ont.; 630 Dorchester Blvd., Montreal, 101, Quebec.

British Tourist Authority, 151 Bloor St. West, Toronto 5, Ontario.

French Government Tourist Office, 1840 W. Sherbrooke, Montreal, Quebec H3H 1E4; 372 Bay St., Suite 610 Toronto, Ontario M5H 2W9.

German National Tourist Office, 47 Fundy, P.O. Box 417, Place Bonaventure, Montreal, 114, P.Q.

Irish Tourist Board, 7 King St. East, Toronto, Ont.

Italian Government (ENIT), Travel Office, 3 Place Ville Marie, Montreal, Canada.

Netherlands National Tourist Office, Suite 3314, Royal Trust Tower, Toronto-Dominion Centre, Toronto, Ontario M5K 1K2.

Spanish National Tourist Office, 60 Bloor St., Toronto, Ont.

Swiss National Tourist Office, Commerce Court West, P.O. Box 215, Commerce Court Postal Station, Toronto, Ontario M5L 1E8; 44 Frontenac, Place Bonaventure, P.O. Box 1162, Montreal, P.Q. H5A 1G5.

GREAT BRITAIN

Austrian National Tourist Office, 30 George St., London, W.1.

Belgian National Tourist Office, 66 Haymarket, London, S.W.1.

British Tourist Authority, 64 St. James's St., London, S.W.1.

Bulgarian National Tourist Office, 126 Regent St., London W.1.

Czechoslovak Travel Bureau (Cedok), 17–18 Old Bond St., London, W.1.

Danish Tourist Board, 169 Regent St., London, W.1.

Finnish Tourist Board, 56 Haymarket, London, S.W.1.

French Tourist Office, 178 Piccadilly, London, W.1.

German Tourist Information Bureau, 61 Conduit Street, London, W.1.

Gibraltar Tourist Office, 15 Grand Bldgs, Trafalgar Square, London, W.C.2.

Greek Tourist Office, 195–197 Regent St., London, W.1.

Iceland Tourist Information, 73 Grosvenor St., London, W.1.

Irish Tourist Office (Eire), 150 New Bond St., London, W.1.

Italian State Tourist Office, 201 Regent St., London, W.1.

Liechtenstein (see Switzerland).

Luxembourg (see Belgium).

Netherlands Tourist Office, 143 New Bond St., London, W.1.

Norwegian National Travel Office, 20 Pall Mall, London, S.W.1.

Polish Travel Office (Orbis), 313 Regent St., London, W.1.

Portuguese National Tourist Office, 1–5 New Bond Street, London, W.1.

Rumanian National Travel Office (Carpati), 98 Jermyn St., London, S.W.1.

Spanish National Tourist Office, 70 Jermyn St., London, S.W.1.

Swedish Tourist Secretary, Swedish Embassy, 23 North Row, London, W.1.

Swiss National Tourist Office, 1 New Coventry St., London, W.1.

U.S.S.R., Intourist, 292 Regent St., London, W.1.

Yugoslav Tourist Office, 143 Regent St., London, W.1.

Many countries also maintain National Tourist Offices in principal cities within continental Europe, which may prove useful if you suddenly decide to change your itinerary and want to collect a few brochures and last-minute information.

SPECIAL INTEREST TRAVEL

Touring With a Purpose

More and more people are looking for unusual methods of travel and off-beat, but purposeful, pastimes. The standard Grand Tour of the continent's sights is still popular, particularly among those with limited time and those who expect to see Europe only once in their lives. But among younger holiday-makers, or anyone who plans to return, the special interest tour is rocketing in popularity. In 1976 alone, travel agents in the United States offered about 900 different tour arrangements, many of them with multiple departures, in 60 special interest categories, from anthropology to yachting. The problem is to select the right one from such an abundance of offerings.

For, no matter what your interests, somewhere there's a package holiday to suit you. If you don't like packages, you can still go it alone, putting purpose into travel by fixing up special visits before you leave, and if you don't want to plan ahead, you can even wait till you get to Europe before choosing a special interest tour.

To get the best from a holiday, try to live a life of complete contrast to your normal routine. Off-beat arrangements which bring an extra dimension to travel should be just the thing to give your vacation an added zip.

To be off-beat, you don't have to don oxygen bottles and flippers to explore bedrock beneath the ocean. It's just as off-beat to go hunting

Polar bears on Norway's Spitzbergen Island or trailering around Ireland in a horse-drawn gypsy caravan. If you are interested in comfort, how about the kind which you find in a European castle? Germany, France, Scotland, Portugal, Hungary and Ireland have castles where paying guests are welcome. Travel agents and the national tourist offices of those countries can provide details. Contentment can be found visiting European gardens or when listening to great music beautifully played or sung at one of Europe's international music festivals. Younger travelers wanting something less sophisticated should be happy on a bachelor's tour or at a house party, pony-trekking, cycling or working abroad in return for board and lodging.

The more ambitious of the special interest tours start and finish in the United States or Canada. Those you can book in Europe, though covering a wider range of interests, are usually shorter (seven or fourteen days being the popular length), which enables them to be slotted into a standard European touring itinerary for a few days' fun. While following a favourite hobby or pastime, share your vacation on these shorter tours with Europeans, who will extend a warmer welcome for no other reason than your interest in enjoying a European special interest holiday in their company in preference to one surrounded by fellow Americans.

Package tours booked in Europe are simpler than those arranged in the U.S.A.—most Europeans, for example, regard a private bath or shower as a luxury rather than as a necessity (there are always public ones for use). For a preliminary view of tours originating in Britain see Sampling the Tours earlier in this book.

Starting in North America

Fluctuating economic conditions have produced a major change in the European tour scene in that some highly-specialized, small-group tours originating in the U.S. have been discontinued in favor of more standardized package plans which either cater to larger groups or provide a more open schedule within which you are free to pursue your own special interest, at your own pace. British Airways, for example, offers holidays in London which give you a specific number of vouchers good at a large number of pubs, restaurants, theaters and shops, so that if you want a gourmet tour or a shopping holiday, the specific choices are up to you. On the other hand, many special-interest opportunities which originate locally are still available. Thus, for example, caravan tours, sailing, hunting, castles, etc. in Ireland. As always, the full range of activities is too great to list here. For the first kind of tour, a good travel agent is your most up-to-date source of information. For the second, the various national airlines and tourist offices can help you. Ask your travel agent to show you the "OAG Worldwide Tour Guide," published by Reuben H. Donnelley Co. A recent edition contained 70 pages of special interest tour listings. Enough to stimulate anyone's imagination.

Private groups such as churches, athletic clubs, cultural organizations, professional societies, business firms and sports or hobby groups who want to work out tours to fit their needs, tastes or incentives may do so through American Grand Circle, 555 Madison Avenue, New York, N.Y. 10022, a tour operator which has retained all its European contacts, although it is not at present running pre-prepared tours.

Remember also that the American Automobile Association, 28 East 78th Street, New York, N.Y. 10021, is a fully authorized travel agency which can arrange any type of foreign tour you may wish, from package or excursion to individually escorted.

Wine and Gourmet Tours

Wine Tour of France *(Hanns Ebensten Travel/Air France),* a 15-day trip costing $1,350 plus air fare (single room supplement of $100) and limited to 25 persons, includes visits to vineyards with wine tasting in Burgundy, Côtes du Rhône and Bordeaux areas. The tour is met at each château by the owner or his representative to explain the wine-making and help with the sampling. Only one departure—in September. This is an excellent package for the serious wine fancier. A similar tour, of 16 days, to the Rhine, Mosel and Rhone vineyards, leaves in June, for $1525. Folders from *Hanns Ebensten Travel, Inc.,* 55 W. 42nd St., New York City 10036.

Wine and Gourmet Tours of France are offered by *Travel Plans International,* 1301 W. 22 St. Oak Brook, Ill. 60521. Allows you enough time in Paris to do the gourmet bit at special restaurants. Also features tours through the vineyards of Champagne, Burgundy, Côtes du Rhône, Loire or Bordelais. Twenty-three days; land portion is about $1050. Cost covers two meals a day, sightseeing, wine tasting in the famous vineyards and more.

West Germany has eleven different wine-growing districts each of which offers Wine Seminars lasting from two to six days and combining lectures, wine sampling, visits to vineyards and cellars, sightseeing tours, local scenery and museums, city tours, etc. Prices and offerings vary from year to year and depend somewhat on enrollment. For a weekend, $50 to $75; for a full week, about $175. For details on the year and region you are interested in write to the German National Tourist Office (address above). During summer, 5-day general Wine Seminars in English are held at Kloster Eberbach on the Neckar River in the Rheingau region, all inclusive price around $500. Write to *German Wine Academy,* Reisebüro Bartholomae, D-62, Wiesbaden, Wilhelmstr. 8.

For those who love to cook, or want to try, the *Ecole de Cuisine La Varenne,* of Paris, offers bilingual courses in the full range of French cuisine. Short-term courses of 1, 2, or 3 weeks accept students at all levels of ability; fees are $250 per week. In the longer courses, of from 6 to 36 weeks, students are grouped by ability, from beginners to professionals, and the fees are about $1400 per six-week unit. Certificates and diplomas are awarded. A single demonstration is $11. The school's advisors include Anne Willan, James Beard and Julia Child. Students arrange their own travel and lodgings, although the school does have a list of nearby hotels, in the 7th Arrondissement. For details, contact *William Peter Kosmas,* 1841 Broadway, New York, NY 10023.

Arts, Antiques and Archeology

Kaleidoscope Tours, 1 News Plaza, Peoria, Ill. 61601, offers 15-, 18- and 22-day tours in England, Denmark, Belgium, France, Austria and Spain built around styles (baroque, Victorian etc.), or places (capital cities). Land portions are roughly $1,500–$1,950.

The leading Art Tour operator is *Esplanade Tours,* 14 Newbury Street, Boston, Mass. 02116, with about 30 different tours to art treasures the world over, including such lesser known parts as Macedonia, Transylvania and Sicily. Most European tours are 17 days.

In archeology a leading specialist is *Sunnyland Tours,* 166 Main Street, Hackensack, N.J. 07601, with packages around the Mediterranean, the Aegean and the Holy Land, lasting 10, 15 or 22 days. England and Wales are the special province of *Anglo American Travel Ltd.,* Hope Farm, Beckley, Rye, Sussex, England. They run tours of 14-21 days to 21 different sites, in addition to a three week summer course at Oxford University.

Pilgrimages

You may well find the great shrines of Europe far more peaceful and inspiring under less crowded conditions than if you were to visit them in a Holy Year. Certain travel agents specialize in pilgrimage tours, among them: *Fatima Travel,* 360 Belvedere Ave., Washington New Jersey 07882, *Catholic Travel Office,* 1730 Rhode Island Avenue, N.W., Washington, D.C.; *Guild of Catholic Travel,* 500 Fifth Avenue, New York, N.Y. 10036; *Catholic Travel Center,* 761 South Atlantic Blvd., Los Angeles, Cal. 90022; *Religious Tours Inc.,* 1180 6th Ave., New York, 10036. Major destinations are Portugal, Spain, Ireland, France and Italy. Departures are mostly between April and October, and a 15-day itinerary will cost around $1200.

Singles of all Ages

More and more people, of all ages and social situations, are choosing to travel by themselves. The great disadvantage is the punishing extra expense of the single supplement, a surcharge that can run up to as much as $200 on an overseas tour. Because most accomodation is still designed for couples, several travel agencies now specialize in finding ways to beat the extra expense and to introduce people of similar tastes and interests. The largest of these is *Gramercy Travel Systems,* Inc., 444 Madison Ave., New York City 10022, with its *Singleworld* Tours. Some others are: *Single Party Tours,* 1472 Broadway, New York 10036; *Travel Mates,* 574 Fifth Ave., New York 10036; *Travel Match,* (for women) at P.O. Box 22, Lenox Hill Station, New York 10021; *The Widows Travel Club,* 17 East 45th Street, New York 10017, with some 15,000 members; *Friends in Travel,* 9300 Wilshire Blvd., Beverley Hills, Cal., 90212; *Companions in Travel,* 1803 Avenue U., Brooklyn, N.Y. 11229; *Company To Go* (for women) at Suite 206 A, Benson East, Jenkintown, Pa. 19046; and *Gender-Blender Tours,* 216 East King St., Lancaster, Pa. 17602. Some of these agencies charge small membership fees ($5–$25).

Educational, Student, and Budget Youth Travel

To know a country well you must live with its people; and learning a foreign language is always easier on the spot. If you are a teacher, student, or young traveler going overseas for the first time, you have a wide and exciting range of possibilities ahead of you. Many American colleges and universities sponsor language and study programs abroad, although the logistical details are usually contracted out to commercial tour operators. If you are looking for any sort of specialized and/or credit-bearing study experience, it is important to choose a program that is well-organized, experienced, and responsible. Some good sources of general information and certain administrative services (scholarships, charter flights, I.D. cards, etc.) are:

The Council on International Educational Exchange, 777 United Nations Plaza, New York City 10017, for summer study, travel and work programs and travel services for college and high school students, and a free Charter Flights Guide booklet.

The Institute of International Education, 809 United Nations Plaza, New York, N.Y. 10017, provides information on study opportunites abroad and administers scholarships and fellowships for international study and training.

UNESCO Publications Center, P.O. Box 433, New York, N.Y. 10016, publishes a survey entitled *Study Abroad* (cost: $6.00) that includes vacation study.

Commission on Voluntary Service and Action, 475 Riverside Drive, New York, N.Y. 10027, publishes *Invest Your Self,* a 68-page pamphlet (cost: $1), listing voluntary service opportunities in the U.S. and overseas.

U.S. Student Travel Service, Inc., 801 Second Avenue, New York, N.Y. 10017, is a mine of information and help on all aspects of student travel.

A few of the many specific programs available are:

The Experiment in International Living, Brattleboro, Vermont 05301, offers high school students summer programs in 31 countries: a month with a foreign family and another month of travel around the country with the hosts. Costs in Europe are about $1300–$1500, all-inclusive. The *Academic Semester Abroad* program operates in six countries at a cost of $1800–$2400 for travel and independent study abroad for both high school and college students.

The American Field Service, 313 East 43rd Street, New York, N.Y. 10017, sends about 2200 students, ages 16–18, every year to live either a summer or a full school year with families in nearly 60 countries. Costs are about $1100–$1800.

Academic Year Abroad, Inc., 221 East 50th Street, New York, N.Y. 10022, arranges single semester or one-year study programs for pre-college and college-level students in London, Paris and Madrid. Students live with local families and attend a variety of cultural activities.

Academic Travel Abroad, (1346 Connecticut Avenue, N.W., Washington, D.C. and 280 Madison Avenue, New York, N.Y. 10016), arranges academic credit-bearing study tours year-round for teachers, students, and educational institutions such as museums; while *Teacher Group,* P.O. Box 809, Radio City Station, New York, N.Y. 10019 (or T/G Travel Service, 111 W. 57th Street., New York, N.Y. 10019), arranges 2- to 14-week charter flights to Europe and Asia, and 1- to 4-week tours of Europe, Asia, Africa, the Soviet Union, and Latin America, with special prices for student groups.

AIESEC (Association International des Etudiants en Sciences Economiques et Commerciales), U.S. National Commission, 52 Vanderbuilt Avenue, New York, N.Y. 10017, is a student-run organization which finds work (usually summer jobs) for college students majoring in business or economics.

IAESTE (International Association for the Exchange of Students for Technical Experience), American City Building, Suite 217, Columbia, Maryland 21044, does the same thing for engineering, science, architecture and agriculture majors.

The American Institute for Foreign Study, 102 Greenwich Avenue, Greenwich, Conn. 06830, offers tours, accompanied by lecturers, for high school and college students and teachers. One- and two-week mini-programs from $500; summer programs from $750. Academic credit offered.

The New York University World Campus Program, NYU School of Continuing Education, 2 University Place, New York, N.Y. 10003, offers 1- and 2-week intensive seminars, taught on the spot by leading national authorities in such fields as The Heritage of Russia, Italian Art, Music in Vienna, and Dutch Art. About seven trips per year, January-April.

Agencies offering inexpensive, non-academic travel possibilities include:

American Youth Hostels, Inc., National Campus, Delaplane, Virginia 22025, has low-cost overseas activity arrangements. Membership in AYH makes you eligible for the entire network of youth hostels in 50 countries all over the world. In addition to its Directory, AYH also handles hosteling and camping equipment, and runs conducted hosteling tours.

Worldtrek, 415 Lexington Avenue, New York, N.Y. 10017, runs 3-, 5-, 6- and 9-week camping/carvanning tours that cover all Western and Eastern Europe, plus Africa, Russia and South Asia. Travel is by motor caravan with professional driver, guide, and cook for the specialist jobs. Rates from about $450 to $1150 plus air fare.

University Travel Company, 44 Brattle Street, Cambridge, Mass. 02138, runs camping tours in Europe, and is U.S. agent for *Continental Coach Tours,* 139 Earl's Court Road, London. The range of tours includes Scandinavia, Russia, the Balkans and North Africa. Specifically for "the 18–30 generation."

Trek Adventures, 3 East 54 St., New York, N.Y. 10022, runs both European and Trans-Continental camping expeditions. Those in Europe cover Britain, the Arctic Circle, Western Europe, Greece and Turkey, Scandinavia and Russia, and Spain, Portugal and North Africa. Tours last from 21 to 62 days; land prices range from about $350 to $950.

The Biking Expedition, Inc., Hall Avenue, Henniker, New Hampshire 03242 conducts 3- to 6-week bicycle trips in England, Scotland, Ireland and Scandinavia for young people ages 13 to 17. Rates run about $800 to $1050 plus airfare.

The above is by no means a complete list, and what is available changes from year to year. The principal and central clearinghouses for information, the best places to start, remain the first two listed, the C.I.E.E. and the I.I.E. Begin by writing for free lists of all their publications in the field, then narrow your focus from there.

Sports, Sun-Worshipping and Naturism

Specialists in Irish fishing and shooting holidays are *Irish Multi-wheel Ltd.,* The Five Lamps, North Strand Road, Dublin 1, Ireland. A choice of weekly holidays of coarse, game and sea fishing, shooting holidays around the country and fishing for salmon or deep-sea angling at Westport, County Mayo. Prices range between around £36 and £85 for each of four persons, including meals, hotels and self-drive auto. Not included: air fares, fishing tackle, etc., or licenses and fees.

Horseback riding vacations are available in several European countries, notably Ireland, Spain and Hungary. In Spain they are conducted as treks into mountain areas, in Hungary as extended tours across the plains around Lake Balaton, and in Ireland around particular riding schools or castles, with 4- to 7-day stays costing from $150 to $300. Details on Ireland from the *Irish Tourist Board* (address above) or from *Lismore Travel,* 16 West 57 St., New York, N.Y. 10019. For Spain, consult *Hamilton Travel Service,* 630 Fifth Avenue, New York, N.Y. 10020. Hamilton also operates in Ireland, England and France. For

Hungary, write to: Hungarian Consulate General, 8 East 75 St., New York, N.Y. 10021.

Sun worshippers should look into the numerous summer cruises that sail the Adriatic, Dalmatian Riviera, Aegean, Greek Islands and coast of Turkey. *The Adriatica Line* covers this entire area, and in fact the entire Mediterranean, with year-round sailings. Enquire c/o Italian Line, General Passenger Agents, One Whitehall Street, New York, N.Y. 10004.

The leading operator of "summer villages" for sun-seekers is *Club Méditerranée International, Inc.,* 40 West 57th Street, New York, N.Y. 10019; 9481 Airport Boulevard Suite 730, Los Angeles, California; Place Ville Marie, Montreal, Quebec, Canada; and 5 South Molton St. London, W1Y 1DH, England. Situated all around the Mediterranean, including the Near East and North Africa, as well as the mountains of France and Switzerland. Tours include transfers, double occupancy rooms, three meals daily, wine with all meals, free use of sports facilities (water skiing, sailboats, scuba-diving, etc.), and evening entertainment.

A fast growing variant of this is the Naturist or Nudist tours offered by *Skinny-Dip Tours,* 30 East 42nd Street, New York 10017; and by *Lotus Travel* (V.I.B. Tours), 244 E. 46 St., New York City 10017. Vacation villages, yacht and cruise ship vacations are featured; the main areas are France, Corsica, Yugoslavia and Israel; and the Caribbean in the Western Hemisphere.

Golf and tennis packages are offered by *Atesa, Inc.,* 501 Madison Ave., New York City 10022, with Iberian Airlines. Features one or two weeks in Torremolinos with unlimited golf and tennis, free green fees and use of the tennis courts.

A leading specialist in golf vacations around the world is *International Golf,* 1650 Lincoln Ave., Montreal, P.Q., Canada H3H 1H1, currently operating in 7 countries, including Scotland, Ireland and Spain. Tours to Scotland are from 9 to 13 days, prices run about $700 to $950.

Golfing in Ireland is offered by *Gaelic Tours,* 465 Statler Office Building, Boston, Mass. 02116, and Irish Aer Lingus. A two-week package of golfing costs from $250 for land only. Features five nights in Killarney, three in Dublin and five in Connemara.

Skiing Trips

These have become very popular in the last few years; 7, 8, 9, and 14 day packages are offered by: *Continental Camping Tours,* 44 Brattle St., Cambridge, Mass. 02138; *Europe on Skis, Inc.,* 1414 Sixth Avenue, New York, 10019; and *Eurotop Tours,* So. Clinton St., Hempstead N.Y. 11550.

A week in Northern Italy, via TWA, would cost around $550, including air fare, transfers, hotel, two meals, taxes, but not lift tickets. To Austria by Pan Am, a week would cost around $369 for air fare, with choice of hotels at $130, $170 and $260. *Alitalia,* SAS, and American Express also offer interesting ski packages, some including "fly-drive" and other features.

Europacar Tours, 3 E. 54 St., New York, N.Y. 10022, in cooperation with Lufthansa offers skiing packages to Austria. For 7 days in Kitzbühel, the land portion is from $140 to $254, plus airfare of $391.

Photography

The leading specialist in this field is *Thru the Lens Tours,* 5301 Laurel Canyon Blvd., North Hollywood, California 91607, whose recent tours have included Switzerland, Greece, Iceland, Portugal, Morocco, France, Yugoslavia, Turkey, Norway, and Austria. To make sure everyone gets good results, the tour leaders are qualified in photography, so failures are few.

For the Handicapped

One of the newest, and largest, groups to enter the travel scene is the handicapped, literally millions of people who are in fact physically able to travel and who do so enthusiastically when they know that they can move about with safety and comfort. Generally these tours parallel those of the non-handicapped traveller, but at a more leisurely pace, with everything checked out in advance to eliminate all inconvenience, whether the traveller happens to be deaf, blind or in a wheelchair. Some specialists in the field to contact are: *Flying Wheel Tours,* 148 West Bridge Street, Owatonna, Minn.; *Rambling Tours,* PO Box 1304, Hallendale, Florida; and *Evergreen Travel Service,* 19429 44th Street, Lynwood, Washington. However, the definitive source of information in this field is the book, *Access to the World: A Travel Guide for the Handicapped,* by Louise Weiss, published in Nov., 1977 by Chatham Square Press, Inc., 401 Broadway, New York, N.Y. 10013, at $7.95. This book covers travel by air, ship, train, bus, car, recreational vehicle; hotels and motels; travel agents and tour operators; destinations; access guides; health and medical problems; and travel organizations. Another major source of help is the Travel Information Center, Moss Rehabilitation Hospital, 12th St. and Tabor Road, Philadelphia, Penn. 19141.

Black Europe

For the black traveler to Europe, and to any other part of the world, *Henderson Travel Service,* 931 Martin Luther King Jr. Drive, Atlanta, Georgia 30314, specializes in making up tours for individuals or groups small or large that combine Europe's traditional sights with little known black art, black theater, black history, black food and black people.

Music

Between May and October each year there are about 45 *major* music festivals in Europe. Most of them sell out well in advance. You can try your luck on the spot, but it is obviously wiser to plan ahead. Two agencies which have much experience in this field are:

Mayfair Travel Service, Inc., 119 W. 57th St., New York City 10019, offers tours for opera and music fans. The tours are timed so that tour members are able to attend various opera and music festivals in Europe. Tours are offered at opera time to Munich, Copenhagen, Berlin and Vienna. Most tours are 18–28 days, cost $1800–$2200.

Dailey-Thorp Travel Inc., 654 Madison Ave., New York City 10021, runs tours to all the major centers (Vienna, Budapest, Munich, Salzburg, Bayreuth, London, Edinburgh, Moscow, Leningrad) as well as many others. They offer a very wide range of tours particulary emphasizing opera. All accommodations are deluxe, seat reservations the best. Most tours are about 2 weeks, prices from around $1,600 up.

For general information, write to the European Association of Music Festivals, 122 rue de Lausanne, 1202 Geneva, Switzerland.

Starting in Great Britain

Though the selection of special interest tours in, and starting from, Great Britain is wide, arrangements are either in the hands of (almost) non-profit travel associations or a small number of specialist tour operators happy to concentrate on providing something a little different. Most British travel agents and operators, naturally, are happier featuring two-week package holidays to European bathing resorts and the like, for a reasonable profit. Because of this, it is best to send for a brochure from a specialist tour operator like *R.A.S. Holidays Ltd.* or the *Youth Hostels Association.* Their brochures list a wide range of special interest holidays probably featuring the kind of vacation you're looking for, from dinghy sailing along the Spanish coast to climbing the Austrian Alps in search of mountain flowers.

Note to American readers: Because of Britain's proximity to the Continent and the greater flow of tourist traffic between the U.K. and the rest of Europe, special interest tours here are more numerous (and often better organized) than those from the U.S.A. If you spot a tour in the following pages which you'd like to join from the U.S.A., therefore, ask your travel agent if it is possible . . . he may be able to arrange it for you.

There are some 3,000 youth hostels in Europe, including over 200 in England alone. If you are already an American Youth Hostels member you don't have to join any of the European associations—just show your AYH card. Every year the *Youth Hostels Association* offers a wide range of inexpensive and unusual adventure holidays, including a 7-day gliding holiday in Worcestershire for about £90, an 8-day holiday studying the industrial archeology of either the Tamar Valley in North Devon or the Peak District of Wales for £60.

Continental Coach Tours Ltd., 136 Earl's Court Road, London, and *University Travel Company,* 44 Brattle Street, Cambridge, Mass. 02138, run 3-, 5-, 6- and 9-week camping tours covering all of Western Europe plus Morocco, the Balkans, Scandinavia and Russia. Tours depart from London; fees are about $300-$750 plus air fare. Travel is by motorcoach; the general tone is more youth-and-fun-oriented than the *Worldtrek* or the *Trek Adventure* tours listed above. Most of the tours of all of these organizations start from London. Other agencies in this field are *Sundowners Ltd.,* 8 Hogarth Place, London SW 5, and *Trail Finders,* 48 Earl's Court Road, London W8. In the U.S., try *Anchor Travel,* 1324 Lexington Ave, New York 10028 for economical, "no-frills" bus tours from London to Athens.

For Art and Music Lovers

Mayfair Travel Service, Inc., 119 West 57th St., New York, NY 10019, and *International Travel Services Ltd.,* 7 Haymarket, London SW1Y 4BU, are agents for the *European Association of Music Festivals* and carry information on some 38 music festivals, from the major ones like Bayreuth to the smaller ones like Perugia and Bath. They also can help to arrange your visit.

More unusual is the same agent's cultural tours to Poland, in conjunction with Orbis, the official Polish travel agency. Prices, which include London-Cracow return air travel, are about £187 (15 days).

Painting tours, offering an opportunity for sightseeing in addition to the satisfaction of having individual tuition from an expert in the media of oils and water colors, are popular. Group numbers are kept down so everyone gets the maximum attention.

Specialists in this field are *Galleon World Travel Association Ltd.* (85 King Street, Maidstone, Kent ME14 1EG), who also arrange painting holidays on the continent. Choice of centers includes Cadaques, near Salvador Dali's home on the Costa Brava (15 days from £165), and Bruges, with its canals lined with old Flemish houses (8 days from £100). All prices include return air travel from London. They also offer innumerable painting holidays within Britain, including one week at Keswick in the Lake District for £77.

On the luxury side there is a splendid range of cultural holidays to view the art treasures of Tuscany, Provence, and Turkey, or to attend the music festivals at Prague, by *Heritage Travel* (22 Hans Place, London S.W.1). This firm is sponsored by Sotheby's of London and the London *Financial Times.* The tours are accompanied by distinguished experts and cost about £300 (1 week) and £450 (10 or 11 days).

W.F. and R.K. Swan (237-238 Tottenham Court Road, London W.1.) do a series of "Art Treasures Tours", guided by experts, and taking in some of the most glorious parts of Europe's heritage. Not all the tours follow the beaten track; for example a 15-day painting and appreciation tour of the Italian hill towns, or one visiting Thrace and Macedonia. Prices hover around £475.

For Winetasters and Gardeners

Autumn is the best time for wine and beer lovers, for then Europe resounds with the gaiety of drinking festivals. Many travel agents offer short tours of vineyards in Burgundy, Bordeaux, Alsace and the Rhine Valley, often coinciding with the fall festivals. Among them is *Inghams Travel, Ltd.* (329 Putney Bridge Road, London, S.W.15.), whose four- to six-day inclusive tours cost from about £120.

Heritage Travel arrange parties limited to 25 and accompanied by a wine expert, to the Champagne, Sherry and Bordeaux areas; up to a week's duration, costing between £210 and £295. Excellent way to gain expertise and enjoy wine and cooking on their home ground.

For just about £380 there's an 11-day tour of the finest stately homes and gardens of England and Wales (Burghley, Chatsworth, Berkeley Castle, Longleat and many others) by *Swan Hellenic Ltd.* (237-238 Tottenham Court Road, London W1P 0AL). The same firm also have a 12-day tour planned by distinguished British archeologist, the late Sir Mortimer Wheeler, costing around £410, which shows the best of Roman Britain.

Also, each spring the *National Trust for Scotland* (5 Charlotte Square, Edinburgh EH2 4DU) charter a boat for seven-day cruises to some of the fine gardens of Scotland's west coast and to the Hebrides.

Questers Tour and Travel, Inc., 257 Park Avenue South, New York, N.Y. 10010 conducts nature tours all over the world. Small groups visit not only nature reserves and wildlife sanctuaries but also study the culture and customs of the area, be it Switzerland or Greenland. Recent destinations in Europe include Switzerland, Norway, England, Wales, Scotland, Greenland and Iceland.

Bird-Watching

The British are great lovers of wildlife and natural scenery, so it is no surprise that you can select from numerous tours which concentrate on these subjects. Bird-watching is one way of combining an interest in wildlife with the enjoyment of beautiful and unusual settings. *Heritage Travel* (22 Hans Place, London, S.W.1) offers 12–15 day adventures to Provence and the Camargue, Montenegro, Majorca, the Spanish Sierras, and Austria's Lake Neusiedl from £260. All tours are accompanied by expert ornithologists. Less expensive programs within Britain are also available.

Cox and Kings, 46 Marshall St., London W1V 2PA, England, run many tours for people interested in ornithology, botany, gardens, and so on. They mainly take place between March and October, and range over most of Europe, from Russia to Majorca.

Life In The Raw

Whether you call yourself a naturist or a nudist, the up and coming place to take off your clothes is along Yugoslavia's sunny Dalmatian coast. *Yugotours* (150 Regent St., London, W.1.) will fly you there and back and cover you over with a tent or bungalow for as little as £135 for two weeks. (See also naturist tours originating in the U.S.)

Horses and Railways

The British love for horses is reflected in the variety of special interest riding and trekking holidays. Pony-trekking is carried out in all parts of scenic Britain. The *Youth Hostels Association* (Trevelyan House, St. Albans, Hertfordshire) look after younger travellers with 6-day pony-treks in Wales and Yorkshire for about £59, which includes a bed, food, riding instruction and pony hire.

Something more unusual is arranged by the *Jysk Ride-Institut* at Vejle, Denmark, whose parties ride the old Viking trails, luggage being moved in authentic prairie wagons. The tour features a stage coach, whose back opens up to make a kitchen. You sleep in tents and evening entertainment is provided around the camp fire. Just like the Wild West!

Switzerland is wonderful for touring, but an added dimension is given by *R.A.S. Holidays* (Wings House, Bridge Road East, Welwyn Garden City, Herts.), who have an annual tour for railway enthusiasts. It is designed to take in every aspect of the subject, in one of the world's richest railway countries. At about £250 for 15 days, costs are not cheap, but the interest content is remarkable and the tour so popular that you are advised to book early in the year.

Anchors Aweigh

One popular cruise is a coast-hugging journey from Bergen, Norway, up to the North Cape beyond the Arctic Circle in the land of the Midnight Sun. June departures are best and the cruise usually lasts 10 or 12 days. Cost averages around $750 (£375) from Bergen, more if you fly from London or go by sea from Newcastle. For details, try *Norwegian*

Travel Office (20 Pall Mall, London S.W.1), or *Fred. Olsen-Bergen Line* (229 Regent Street, London W1).

If you prefer less salty waters, an Irish firm called *Ryans* (4 Lower Abbey St., Dublin 1; also Ireland House, 150 New Bond St., London, W.1) lets you captain your own luxury cruiser (full briefing given) on the Shannon. The cost per person, including flight from London, is £115 per week.

For cruises along the canals of the English countryside—Oxfordshire, Warwickshire and Shakespeare Country—from £85 a week, try *Inland Waterway Holiday Cruises Ltd.* (Preston Brook, Runcorn, Cheshire).

More adventurous, and somewhat more energetic, is a 15-day holiday combining traveling by canoe through the gorges of the Ardèche, a tributary of France's mighty River Rhone; riding in the Gigondas (Europe's answer to the Rockies!) with sailing, underwater swimming and cruising near St. Tropez on the Mediterranean. This involves camping and plenty of excitement, variety and fun. The round trip from London costs around £160 by coach, £200 by air. *P.G.L. Adventure Ltd.* (Station Street, Ross-on-Wye (Herefordshire, England).

The Handicapped Traveler

Physically disabled people, and also diabetics, are offered a full service by *S.M. Sweiry & Co. Ltd.,* 35 Ashcombe Gardens, Edgware, Middlesex, when coming to Britain, or if wishing to enjoy Europe on one of the company's special holiday coach tours. The *Airline Users Committee,* Space House, 43–59 Kingsway, London WC2, publish a very useful booklet, *Care in the Air,* advice for handicapped passengers. The *Central Council for the Disabled,* 34 Eccleston Sq., London SW1, have several extremely good booklets for the disabled traveler, e.g. *Access in Norway,* giving details of hotels, theaters, restaurants etc, that cater for the handicapped.

But one of the very best guides is a book published by the *Royal Association for Disability and Rehabilitation,* 25 Mortimer St., London W1N 8AB, called *Holidays for the Physically Handicapped,* 556 packed pages for 75 pence. It covers Great Britain in detail, with valuable chapters on many other countries.

Sports in Europe

Golf. In this department, we once asked Tom Scott, editor of *Golf Illustrated,* to name the 12 best courses on the Continent. At the risk of being "decidedly unpopular" with his many European friends, he named the following links:

Three in *Belgium:* the Golf Club des Fagnes, at Spa; the Royal Zoute Golf Club, at Le Zoute-sur-Mer; the Royal Antwerp Golf Club. Two each in *France, Germany and Holland:* the clubs of Morfontaine and Chantilly in France; those of Wiesbaden and Frankfurt in Germany; the Haagsche Golf Club, The Hague, and the Kennemer Golf and Country Club at Zandvoort in Holland. Three other countries get one each—the Milan club for *Italy,* the Stockholm club for *Sweden,* and the Club Puerto de Hierro of Madrid for *Spain.*

Tom Scott obliged us again by listing what he considers the 12 best links in Britain. He names three in Scotland, St. Andrews, Carnoustie and Muirfield; three in the Cheshire-Lancashire area, Royal Liverpool, Royal Birkdale and Royal Lytham-St. Annes; one in Kent, Royal St.

George's; two in the London area, the West Course at Wentworth and the Old Course at Sunningdale; one outside of the main golfing areas, Woodhall Spa, in Lincolnshire; and two in Northern Ireland, Royal Portrush and Royal County Down.

As for golf in Eire, the 20-odd courses in and around Dublin include such internationally known venues as Portmarnock, Dollymount, and Woodbrook.

For Americans, the golfing tour of Britain and lately of Ireland, starting and ending in the States, is now a popular specialty with a number of travel agencies, including *Personal Golf Ltd.* (3 Fitzwilliam Place, Dublin 2, Ireland).

Golf in Scandinavia has made rapid strides in recent years and there are no less than 66 courses, most of them in Southern Sweden. Portugal's Algarve area is an up and coming golf center, and Greece has good courses in (conveniently!) the tourist centers of Athens, Rhodes and Corfu. *Global of London, Ltd.* (Glen House, 200 Tottenham Court Rd., London, W.1.), offers first class accommodation and round-trip jet flight from London to the Algarve, for example, costing from £175 for 8 days.

Hunting and fishing. When it comes to field sports, you will find splendid opportunities in almost every European country. Throughout eastern Europe, hunting ranks high on the list of tourist attractions—in price as well as quality (bear hunts in Poland and Romania, stag hunts in Hungary, and birds everywhere).

Best fishing regions for mountain-trout are Scotland, Iceland, Sweden, Norway, Austria, Yugoslavia, Czechoslovakia and France. *Yugotours,* 150 Regent Street, London W.1., offer trout fishing holidays in Croatia from £150 a week. Facilities for deep-sea fishing exist in Great Britain, South of France, Iceland, Norway, Sweden, Yugoslavia and Greece.

Skin diving flourishes wherever there's a Mediterranean coastline. *Club Méditerranée* provide excellent facilities and instruction at many of their centers. The following islands deserve a special mention: the Balearics (Spain); Corsica (France); Sardinia and the Aeolians (Italy); Rab, Hvar, Losinj and Korcula along the Yugoslav coast; the northern Sporades (Greece). The Club's offices are: 40 West 57th St., New York, N.Y. 10019; Suite 2422, Place Ville Marie, Montreal, P.Q. Canada; 5 South Molton St., London W1Y 1DH, England.

Sailing. The best areas are Belgium, France, Holland, Germany, Great Britain, Greece, Italy, Monaco, Scandinavia, Yugoslavia (Adriatic coast) and Spain, and also Austria and Switzerland where you can enjoy a brisk run under canvas on inviting sheets of fresh water. In the Eastern orbit Hungary offers Europe's largest, Lake Balaton. See later in this section for details of cruises and yacht chartering.

Pony trekking. Holidays on horseback are becoming more and more fashionable and there are over two hundred centers in Europe. Best are Norway, the Scottish Highlands, Ireland, France and Spain's Sierra Nevada.

Racing. As for the Sport of Kings, the great countries of Europe are Britain, France, Ireland, and Italy; some of the leading races are listed in the calendar of events later on in this introductory section.

Tennis. You will find tennis played everywhere in Europe where there's a flat space, and mountain climbing wherever there's a mountain and a climber.

Motor sport. If you're an addict of motor racing, you will see more of this thrilling sport in Europe than anywhere else in the world. The Big Four of European racing countries are Britain, France, Italy and Germany, but Sweden is right in there on the suicide circuit with its Rally of the Midnight Sun, and Austria with its Österreichring World Championship in Styria. Each year there are more than 100 racing events listed by the International Auto Federation (FIA) in Europe. Among the most exciting: The French Grand Prix at Rheims in early July; the Le Mans twenty-four hour classic; the British Grand Prix (in July); Italy's Grand Prix in September at Monza (near Milan); Monaco's Grand Prix for formula one cars only, in May, and the famous Monte Carlo Rally, held in January with several hundred drivers starting out from a dozen points between Paris and Athens and fighting through snow and ice to fame and glory on the Riviera.

Hang gliding. Those wishing to get the hang of this comparatively new and certainly exciting sport can practise 1000 metre glides down into the valleys of the Black Forest. Lessons, equipment, accommodation, and, of course, insurance can all be obtained from *Drachenfliegerschule Peter Uhlig,* D 7292 Baiersbronn, Murgtalstrasse 167, Germany.

Winter Sports. There are hundreds of beautifully-equipped resorts in the skiing centers of Austria, Switzerland, France, Germany and Italy. Switzerland probably leads the field in amenities, Austria in economies. Specific information will be found under the country chapters.

The Alpine areas of Europe—an 800-mile arc of majestic mountains—are bustling with hundreds of special events and competitions each winter and advance reservations in the smarter resorts are always advisable.

The Alpine winter playgrounds can be easily reached overnight by plane from the States. Accommodations for every taste and budget abound. Package ski tours are offered by most of the leading airlines such as *Swissair, Air France* and *Alitalia* as well as *American Express. Lufthansa* offers a special ski report service, giving details of snow conditions at more than 30 resorts in Germany, Austria and Switzerland to anyone telephoning their local or toll-free Lufthansa reservation number. Specialists are *Europe on Skis,* 1414 Avenue of the Americas, New York, N.Y. 10019; *Eurotop Tours,* 50 Clinton St., Hempstead, N.Y. 11550; and *Ski-O-Rama Tours,* 7 South Franklin, Hempstead, Long Island. Departures are frequent, accommodations usually simple, and the prices quoted low because meals and most extras may not be included. The season for ski tours is, at the outside, mid-October to late March. Starting from London, one of the leading British tour operators in this field is *Swans Tours,* 2 The Causeway, Bishop's Stortford, Herts., with inclusive holidays by air to all the top alpine resorts from around £90 for seven days. With as much emphasis on the *après* as on the *ski, Supertravel* (22 Hans

Place, London, S.W.1.) specialize in group chalet holidays, the cozy way to make new friends.

Here is a list of the best known winter-sports resorts in the five-country Alpine region:

Austria. Igls-Innsbruck, Kitzbühel, Seefeld, Bad Gastein, Saalbach and the Semmering, near Vienna. For would-be champions it's the Arlberg district: Lech, Zürs and St. Anton. For early and late season skiing, Obergurgl, Hoch-Sölden and the Dachstein region are recommended. Over 2,650 lifts and cable cars (about 25 of which take you to the heights between 8,200 ft. and 10,000 ft.), over 200 skating rinks and other amenities, spread throughout more than 450 resorts.

France. Chamonix, at the foot of the Mont Blanc, is an old favorite. New favorites include the futuristic resorts of Flaine, La Plagne and Avoriaz. Most fashionable are Courchevel, Megève, Val d'Isère, l'Alpe d'Huez, Flaine and La Plagne. For an unusual winter thrill you can sunbathe at Cannes in the morning and descend the slopes at Valberg or Auron in the afternoon. Lac de Tignes, along with Val d'Isere, provides the biggest and most varied skiing area in France. En route to Spain, one might sample the Pyrenees resorts of Barèges, Superbagnères and Font-Romeu, though they are "family and friendly", not for the international set. Metabief and Les Rousses are well-equipped and inexpensive Jura Mountain ski towns, though again these are mainly for the locals, not for sophisticates from abroad.

Germany. The Bavarian and Allgäu Alps are the best area. Garmisch-Partenkirchen, (where the Ski World Championships are being held in February 1978), Oberstdorf, Füssen, Mittenwald, Reichenhall and Bayrischzel, are well known resorts. The Black Forest offers good skiing at Hornisgrinde-Kandel, Feldberg and Blauen. Arnoldshain-Sandplacken in the Taunus Mountains is convenient to Frankfurt.

Italy. The southern slopes of the Alps offer the sunniest winter playground. The western spots are Sestriere, Courmayeur, Cervinia-Breuil while the foremost center in the Dolomites is Cortina d'Ampezzo. In the Trentino region, Madonna di Campiglio is noteworthy. Abetone is close to Florence, while Rieti-Terminillo is handy to Rome. Far south in Calabria is San Giovanni in Fiore, with a November-March season.

Spain. Marvelous slopes, long season and cozy hotels at the expanding center of Formigal in the Pyrenees. Farther south in the Sierra Nevada you can ski pretty nearly year-round, but accommodation is scarce. Baqueira-Béret, in the Aran Valley, is the newest developing ski spot. Access is not easy, but once there, two hotels, apartment for rent, etc.

Switzerland has over 125 resorts, so it's not easy to choose. Statistics of their equipment are impressive: nearly 1,200 assorted lifts and cableways, 175 places with ice rinks, about 3,000 licensed ski instructors, and around 7,000 hotels and pensions in every price range.

In the southwest our pick is Villars, Verbier and fashionable Gstaad. In the shadow of Matterhorn there are Zermatt and Saas-Fee, while Jungfrau dominates Wengen, Grindelwald and Mürren. The most fashionable spots in the Grisons are St. Moritz, Davos and Arosa, all world famous. Beginners are often referred to Crans, Lenzerheide, Pontresina, Saas Fee or Zweisimmen, to name but five.

Spring skiing is commonplace, and there are many places where you can ski throughout the summer. List from Swiss National Tourist Office.

For illustrated folders write to Alpine Tourist Commission, 60 East 42nd Street, New York 10017.

Non-Alpine Areas

Scandinavia. This is the home of cross-country ski-ing. You can ski in the parks of Helsinki, *Finland,* but an hour by bus to Nuuksio or by train to Hyvinkää gets you to popular and more extensive terrains. Many possibilities include reindeer safaris in Finnish Lapland. In *Norway,* the best-equipped ski resorts are Lillehammer, Voss and Geilo. Dalarna is the southern most skiing terrain of *Sweden* and the easiest accessible, with Sälen and Grövelsjon in the north. But Jämtland is the top skiing region for experts and long distance enthusiasts, and in Lapland you can ski under the rays of the Midnight Sun in May-June. You will not find a plethora of winter sports amenities in Scandinavia because the Scandinavians prefer overland, long distance skiing, now also called ski-touring.

Others. Yugoslavia is the best value, for little money. Kranjska Gora, Bled and Ratece Planica are nearest, in Slovenia. Some fine skiing awaits you on the Jahorina plateau near Sarajevo. *Czechoslovakia's* long established resorts are Spindleruv Mlyn in Bohemia; Strbské Pleso, Stary Smokovec and many others in the Tatra Mountains. On the *Polish* slopes of this chain Zakopane and Krynica are the best.

POLLUTION REPORT

Europe has serious pollution problems, but none which should cause you inconvenience if you plan your trip to avoid certain areas. In addition to the filthy Rhine in Holland and northern Germany, and the general dirtiness of the air in major cities (though London, for example, is quite clean), the worst place is some parts of the Mediterranean, particularly some spots in the western end. (The Aegean is mostly clean.) Here are the areas of worst pollution, but you should remember, of course, that beaches only a few miles apart may be quite different in character, with a heavily polluted stretch near a river's mouth and a very clean expanse just a short drive away. This listing, therefore, is not intended to condemn *all* the beaches in the area mentioned, but only to point out that many therein are badly polluted:

Worst: Venice-Trieste area in Adriatic, Provençal Basin off French Riviera; the Rhône; the Po; beaches near Rome and Naples; eastern Sicilian and Italian "toe" coastline; coastline near Bari.

Second worst: many parts of the Costa Brava, much of the French Mediterranean coast; Italian Riviera; southern Sardinia; the Athens beaches; Split and Rijeka in Yugoslavia.

Going it Alone

If you're looking for something different to liven your vacation, contact the national tourist office of the country you intend to visit and ask them for off-beat suggestions.

Meeting people at home gives the most conventional holiday a boost and it's not difficult to make contacts. Although there are enough museums, scenery, historic monuments and shops in Europe to keep the average tourist panting, many travelers want to penetrate beneath the surface and know what foreign people are really like in their own homes.

A number of organized meet-the-people projects exist to satisfy this natural and laudable curiosity.

Denmark set the pace back in 1945 with a state-sponsored program called "Meet the Danes". If you visit any of the local tourist offices outside Copenhagen, they will arrange for you to meet a family whose interests, which they list from acrobatics to zoology, correspond to yours. The families which open their homes do so as a gesture of hospitality and international cooperation; they expect no recompense except for the reciprocal advantages of sharing interests in common with you. These contacts cannot be arranged in advance of your arrival in Denmark, and you should allow 48 hours for the visit to be arranged.

"Sweden at Home", a similar program, was launched in 1954; details will be furnished by the *Swedish National Tourist Office* in New York (75 Rockefeller Plaza, New York 10019) or London (Swedish Embassy, 23 North Row, W.1). Or contact the Stockholm Tourist Information, Sverigehuset, Hamngatan, Stockholm.

A scheme called "Find the Finns", by the *Finnish Tourist Board,* Mikonkatu 13A, Helsinki 10, enables visitors to meet Finns with similar interests.

The *Irish Tourist Board,* 590 Fifth Avenue, New York, will supply a list of private homes which receive foreign tourists.

If you want to meet French people who share your professional interests, you can learn about the many contact organizations, such as the *Welcome Service of Paris,* in a comprehensive booklet on Paris available at the French Government Tourist Office, 610 Fifth Avenue, New York 10020; 178 Piccadilly, London W.1.; 8 Avenue de l'Opera, Paris.

"Amsterdam Receives" is a program of personal contact between foreign and Dutch women.

For information about meeting Italians at home, write to *Ente Nazionale Italiano per il Turismo,* Via Marghera 2, Rome.

The prototype of all these schemes for promoting closer international relationships among people is the celebrated *Experiment in International Living* (see earlier in this chapter).

Many factories and industrial plants welcome visitors, and the national tourist offices can also pinpoint those happy to see you. In Copenhagen, most travelers visit the *Carlsberg Brewery* or the *Royal Copenhagen Porcelain Factory.* Those holidaying on the French Riviera normally make the journey to the *perfume factories* at Grasse.

These are small things, true, but they can do much for anyone's holiday.

Looking Up the Family Tree

Visitors from the United States and Canada who might enjoy tracing their family history will find the *British Tourist Authority* (64 St. James's Street, London S.W.1; and 680 Fifth Avenue, New York, N.Y. 10019) publish a special leaflet telling you how and where to begin.

If your background's Finnish, the *National Travel Association of Finland* would most likely suggest you start by going to the village where you think your family came from. As it is necessary for every Finn to be registered in the local church book, and their subsequent movements recorded in the books, it's not difficult to find the answers.

In fact, most countries have some sensible starting point for anyone wishing to turn up his family history and the national tourist office staff are the people to tell you where it is.

One of the leading reasons for American travel to eastern Europe is the flow of visitors going to see relatives, in many cases to reestablish previously disrupted connections with their families. Those cousins and inlaws in Bialystok or Budapest to whom you sent packages all these years will now be thrilled to see you in the flesh, and their Communist regimes will be delighted to have you—for the hard American dollars you'll spend. You can stay in your relatives' house (provided you pay the ransom); you can leave gifts behind (now mostly duty free, unless grossly exaggerated, and depending partly on how you handle the customs officer at the frontier). For special procedures concerning such visits, see individual country chapters.

Exploring Eastern Europe

We were the first guidebook to explore the capitals of eastern Europe, long before travel there became even remotely popular, and we will continue featuring these countries now that a kind of detente has smoothed over the rough edges of the old cold war. In planning your trip to Europe, you no longer have to cut off the eastern countries, and we hope you will consider visiting one or more of them, particularly Czechoslovakia, Hungary, Poland, Romania and the USSR itself. Yugoslavia is, in general, so much freer and more open than these other countries that visiting it is a fairly simple and carefree matter. Your very presence indicates an interest by the "outside" and encourages the freer flow of ideas between countries through the conversations you will have with people in the street.

HOW TO REACH EUROPE

By Air from North America (see Fares map following)

The jet planes currently in service fly at the rate of 500 to 600 miles an hour, reducing the New York to London flying time, by Laker Skytrain, for example, to 5½ hours. Obviously this disrupts your normal daily body rhythms and produces the unpleasant and confusing feelings known as "jet lag." This may be impossible to avoid, but our advice can help minimize it: get a good sleep before leaving, go easy on food and drink in flight, try to sleep on the plane, and get plenty of rest the first few days in Europe. Time in Britain and Ireland is 4 hours earlier than U.S. EDST; in most of continental Europe it is 5 hours ahead; Bulgaria, Finland, Greece, Romania, and Turkey are 6 hours ahead; Moscow is 7. The supersonic Concorde and the jumbo Boeing 747 try to soften the present ordeal; Concorde by getting you there in less than half the normal time, the 747 by managing to carry 360-390 passengers, nine abreast, yet in seats which are a comfortable two inches wider than on ordinary jets (though the "pitch", the distance between your seat and the one in front, is the same).

Most airlines have first and economy class only. Children from two to 12 travel at half adult fare. A child under two not occupying a separate seat is charged 10 percent of full fare, when the child is accompanied by an adult passenger—a second infant must pay full fare unless there is a second adult passenger. The free baggage allowance is now based on *size* rather than weight: in First Class, 2 pieces up to 62 inches overall measure each piece; in Economy Class, 2 pieces, neither one over 62 inches, both together no more than 106 inches. Underseat baggage up to 45 inches.

Monday, September 26, 1977, was a milestone in the history of the travel business. At eleven P.M. that evening *Laker Airways* Flight GK20 rose off the runway of New York's Kennedy Airport and headed out over the Atlantic for London, leaving behind it an airline fare structure in utter collapse, in a shambles that is no way yet sorted out. New York to London for $135; Freddie Laker's six-year dream had become a reality.

For some, it looked more like a nightmare; but the safest thing to call it is probably—a revolution. Even before Skytrain's inaugural flight took off the scramble had begun; and the major scheduled airlines, which for years had fought first the charters and then Freddie Laker as hard as they could, were proudly announcing their "firm belief in the concept of low promotional fares" and that they were "pleased to be participating" as they came up with their own (almost) competitive new prices and a whole rash of plans and arrangements, some approved, some promptly disapproved, some pending, some merely applied for. If the public was (and is) confused, so were (and are) the airline and travel businesses as well. Everybody now has to run faster just to stay in place; and the best we can do here, because of our production schedules, is to give you an overview of the situation "at presstime," knowing only too well that it may have changed radically by the time you, the reader, begin to make your plans.

The repercussions of Freddie Laker's breakthrough can only be enormous. He estimated that there were 63,000,000 Americans alone who rarely if ever traveled by air because of the cost; and while the idea of all 63,000,000 of them descending on a dazed London, Paris or Amsterdam all at once is too dreadful to contemplate (and fortunately unlikely), clearly the ripple effect will extend into every area of life on both sides of the Atlantic, then the Pacific, ultimately the entire world. Demand for hotels, restaurants, theaters, trains, buses and rental cars will obviously grow. Beaches, mountains, forests, ski slopes—every kind of resort area and natural environment will feel the impact. Palaces, museums, cathedrals, monasteries, opera houses, all the noblest works of civilization will be familiar to millions who a few years ago would never have left their home towns and daily routines. And if tourists from Nebraska will experience the splendor and awe of Notre Dame on Easter morning, tourists from Poitiers will experience good telephone service and the immensity of a country 18 times the size of their own. Tastes and habits in clothing, cooking, music, architecture, subway design, childbirth techniques, medical care, urban planning, gymnastics and automobiles (to name but a few) will change even more radically than they already have when millions more people from all walks of life see for themselves how people in other cultures do things. Freddie Laker may well turn out to be one of the major cultural influences of the 20th century.

So where does all this leave you, the tourist? "At presstime," the North Atlantic fare structure is, more or less, like this:

1. The cheapest fare is Laker *Skytrain,* New York to London $135 (plus $3 departure tax), London to New York $103. This is strictly a standby flight; you cannot get reservations. Tickets, payable in cash or

traveler's checks only, are sold on a first-come first-served basis at the Laker Travel Center, 95–25 Queens Boulevard, Rego Park, New York (accessible by subway or city bus), starting at 4 A.M. each day for the flight which will leave at 11 P.M. that same evening. There are 345 seats daily, each way, on DC10s.

2. *TWA* and *Pan Am* offer both *Budget* and *Standby* passage for $146 (plus $3 tax) eastbound and $110 westbound. For Budget seats you must buy your ticket 3 weeks in advance and indicate the *week* you wish to leave in. Seven days before that week, the airline will assign you a *day* of departure. For Standby seats you wait at the airport on the day you want to leave to take your chances for one of a specific number of seats allocated to standbys.

3. APEX (Advance Purchase Excursion) fares vary according to the plan you choose. If you buy your ticket 45 days ahead of departure and agree to stay abroad from 14 to 45 days, the New York to London fare is $350. A regular 22- to 45-day excursion, purchasable any time costs $467. A 14- to 21-day excursion is $541. And an ordinary round-trip Economy Class ticket with no specified length of stay costs $626. Charter fares, where an entire planeload of passengers goes as a group, vary from about $290 to $350, depending on season, destination, and type of plan.

Thus, ABCs (Advance Booking Charters) require varying minimum stays and 60 days advance booking but no group membership nor ground arrangements. If you want a general tour package, ask about an ITC (three-stop Inclusive Tour Charter), which requires a 7-day minimum stay but no advance booking. If you want only one specific resort area, look for an OTC (one-stop Inclusive Tour Charter), which requires a 7-day minimum stay, 30-day advance booking and minimum hotel arrangements. For special events, such as a music festival, you want a SEC (Single Entity Charter), available to members of certain groups. And for basic air transportation with no strings attached, ask about TGCs (Travel Group Charters), which have neither group memberships nor ground arrangements. A New York-London round trip by TGC can be about $300, which is about half the normal Economy Class Fare. The whole situation is covered in the annually-revised *Charter Flight Directory* published by Travel Information Bureau, P.O. Drawer 100, Halesite, N.Y. 11743.

Fares and accommodations on the transatlantic air routes are subject to change and regulation by the International Air Transport Association. This important body of some 105 airlines recently reached agreement on reduced fares, but the structure is so complicated that ASTA compiled a special calendar to aid travel agents. Air fares mentioned in this volume are therefore merely indicative. *You may pay more, or less, depending on the dates of your trip.* If, for some reason of your own, you prefer to pay more, or the most, it has been estimated that the difference between Laker Skytrain's New York to London in 5½ hours for $135 and the Concorde's Washington to Paris, a comparable distance, in 3¾ hours for $868, comes to $418.80 per hour of time "saved." As you like it!

With the increasing sense of competition, special excursion rates and group-discount fares are continually being introduced. Check with your travel agent on these.

Fare Reductions: There are off-season economy rates from September to May (eastbound) and October to June (westbound), and special 14- to 21-day excursion fares between the U.S., Canada and Europe at certain periods of the year. Also available, at even lower prices, are the 22- to 45-day excursions which, however, do not permit stopovers enroute to or from your European destination. Again, the structure is so involved that only your travel agent can advise you on the cheapest time to travel.

Affinity Group Fares: These are offered to bona-fide members of established organizations or clubs. Minimum group size from the U.S. is 40 passengers. (Two children, each paying 50%, will count as one member of the group.) These fares are very reasonable—for example, New York-London off-season round trip is $467.

Armed Forces Rates: For U.S. or Canadian forces based overseas only. Dependants are not included. From Europe, round-trip rates are reduced up to 50 per cent in the economy class.

Since the transatlantic airline baggage allowance to most countries is now based on size and the number of pieces of luggage rather than weight, the charges for excess are rather high, about $40 to $50 for each additional piece. If you know in advance that you're going to be *really* overweight, check to make sure that your extra luggage can accompany you, or better, send it in advance. Carry with you anything you'll need in the plane while in flight. Umbrellas, cameras, binoculars, a reasonable supply of reading matter, a lap robe, etc., are not included in your weight allowance, so it's to your advantage to carry them instead of packing them. When you fly, remember that, in spite of claims to the contrary, airport security X-ray machines do in fact damage your photographic films in about 17% of the cases. Insist on their being inspected separately, or pack them in special protective bags. FilmShield is one such brand name.

Always keep your passport, money, special medications and immunization card with you.

Stopovers

Ask your travel agent or airline how many stopovers you are allowed on your ticket when you are planning to go to a certain destination. As your ticket is interchangeable with nearly all airlines in the world, regardless of who issued it, you may find it possible to fly to several different cities en route to your ultimate destination. There are "maximum allowable mileages" between any two given points, and you are entitled to all of them, even if it means a zig-zag itinerary.

By Sea from the U.S.A. and Canada

As air travel becomes more crowded, it's a pity that there is no alternative available, or not much of one. Each year, the number of ships crossing the Atlantic has declined. Most of the remaining passenger travel to Europe has been taken over by passenger-carrying freighters. These have very comfortable, one-class accommodations for 12 persons, and while they cannot provide the entertainment of a big liner, they replace it by informality, relaxation, inexpensiveness and friendliness. The cost factor is particularly attractive, for what you get, if your schedule permits, is in fact a leisurely cruise at rates of from $15 to $50 a day, whereas crossing the Atlantic on a liner, which is much faster, will cost you $75 to $125 a day for comparable accommodations. The popularity of freighter travel makes it advisable to reserve well in advance. To help you choose from the 70 or so lines available, consult

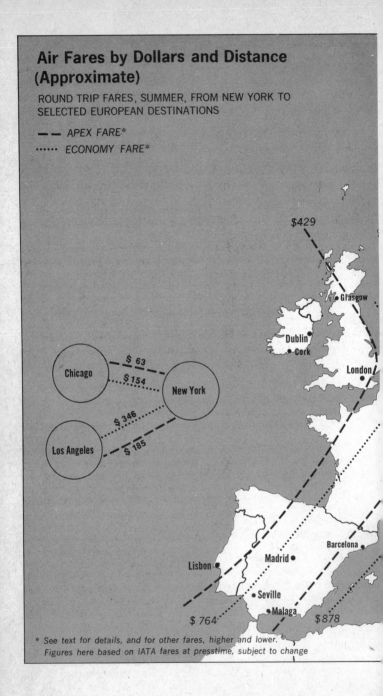

Air Fares by Dollars and Distance (Approximate)

ROUND TRIP FARES, SUMMER, FROM NEW YORK TO
SELECTED EUROPEAN DESTINATIONS

— — APEX FARE*

•••••• ECONOMY FARE*

$429

Glasgow

Dublin
Cork

London

Chicago

$ 63

$ 154

New York

$ 346

$ 185

Los Angeles

Barcelona

Lisbon

Madrid

Seville

Malaga

$ 764

$ 878

* See text for details, and for other fares, higher and lower.
  Figures here based on IATA fares at presstime, subject to change

specialist *Freighter Travel Service Ltd.,* 201 East 77th Street, New York 10021; *Traveltips Freighter Travel Association,* 163–09 Depot Road, Flushing, N.Y. 11358; or *Ford's Freighter Travel Guide,* P.O. Box 505, 22030 Ventura Blvd., Suite B, Woodland Hills, Calif. 91364.

Crossing time may take from 5 to 11 days, depending on the route and the speed of your particular vessel. This leisurely tempo affords a way of living that, for many, is equally as appealing as the land part of their trip.If you have any apprehension about motion sickness at all, provide yourself with Dramamine, Marzine, tranquilizing Nautamine, a French product, or one of the other well-known "stabilizers". All ocean-going ships with capacity for more than 12 passengers must by law carry a doctor, and the large liners have hospital and nursing facilities.

Luggage is far less of a problem to ocean travelers than to those who fly. Although you are limited to a specified number of cubic feet of baggage (the figure varies from class to class and line to line), the allowance is so generous that you are unlikely to exceed it. Pack the clothing you will use on shipboard in one or two bags and mark the rest of your luggage for storage in the hold; it's a nuisance to have your cabin cluttered with suitcases you don't need en route. Both Europeans visiting the U.S. and Americans going to Europe can store their cars with *Auto Baby Sitters,* c/o Intercontinental Parking Systems, 17 Radnor Road, Great Neck, N.Y. 11023.

Cost. When you travel by sea, your cost is an elusive quantity. Tips and incidentals will add to your expenses. There is usually a 5 percent discount on the round-trip fare, and further reductions for groups of 25 persons or more, and some lines offer much greater discounts in the intermediate and thrift seasons (eastbound, April 1-May 31; Aug. 1-Sept. 15, and Jan. 1-Mar. 31; Sept. 16-Dec. 31 respectively). It is also possible to buy an air/sea ticket, traveling one way by ship, the other by air. Cunard/Pan Am, for example, offer attractive two-week tours from about $500, inclusive. Fares vary according to route and season, so check with your travel agent when planning your trip.

Tipping on board. Don't be overawed by the problems of tipping at the end of the voyage. Treat it exactly as you would in a hotel—tip for service. The cabin steward and the dining room steward will have helped you most, and perhaps the deck steward. The ship's officers, from the purser up, are not for tipping, of course.

Port taxes. These vary from year to year and from country to country, like airport exit taxes, know that they exist, be prepared for them, and check to see whether they are or are not included in the fare. Figure roughly $5–$10.

SHIPPING LINES SERVING WESTERN EUROPEAN PORTS

CUNARD LINE. The Cunard Line is the company with the longest experience on the North Atlantic, since 1839. On the route New York-Cherbourg (France)-Southampton (England) is the superbly equipped *Queen Elizabeth 2.* Fares are subject to change, but it is always cheap in thrift season. Newest promotion is an air/sea combination offering free travel one way. In addition there's a 15 percent reduction each way on regular round trip sea rates. These roundtrip sea "specials" enable travelers to stay at least one month in Europe. Tour programs and special land arrangements may be made through Cunard. For up-to-date information write to *Cunard Steamship Co.,* 555 Fifth Ave., New York 10017.

JOHNSON LINE operates cargo passenger ships from Vancouver, Seattle, Portland, San Francisco and Los Angeles to Liverpool, Le Havre, Rotterdam, Antwerp, London, Gothenburg. Sails every six or seven weeks from the West Coast. Two ships, the *MSS Axel Johnson* and *Annie Johnson,* completely air-conditioned, take six passengers each. Goes via the Panama Canal. Swedish cuisine. Details: General Steamship Corporation, Ltd., 400 California St., San Francisco, Calif. 94104.

POLISH OCEAN LINES. Has a monthly service between Montreal, Southampton or London, Rotterdam and Gdynia, with the 15,000-ton *Stefan Batory.* Stabilized and fully air-conditioned. Details: McLean Kennedy Ltd., 410 St. Nicholas St., Montreal, Canada H2P 2P5.

In addition, the Gdynia America Line, Inc., general agents for Polish Ocean Lines freighters, can book passage from New York (sailing from Port Newark, N.J.), Philadelphia, Baltimore, Wilmington, N.C., Savannah, Ga., and sometimes from Jacksonville, Fla. to Europe. Monthly eastbound sailings go to Le Havre, Rotterdam, Bremen, Hamburg and Gdynia. Westbound trips from Poland call at either Bremen or Bremerhaven, Germany, returning to New York only. It is also possible to book passenger on semi-container ships from New York via Baltimore and Wilmington, N.C. to Europe. All ships accommodate 12 passengers. Modern facilities include private bath and shower. Cabins are located in midship and are outside. Contact: Gdynia America Line, Inc., One World Trade Center, Suite 3557, New York, N.Y. 10048.

BALTIC SHIPPING CO., c/o March Shipping Services, 1 World Trade Center, Suite 5257, New York, N.Y. 10048; 159 Bay Street, Suite 816, Toronto, Ontario M5J 1J7, Canada; and 400 St. Antoine Street West, Montreal, P.Q., Canada, has a May, June, Sept. service from New York and Montreal variously to Le Havre, London, Bremerhaven and Leningrad; and a June sailing to the Mediterranean and the Black Sea. Fares from $390 up to Le Havre, with varying rates to other ports of call. Special student fares and 20% discount excursions featured. Automobiles and campers accepted. *Mikhail Lermontov,* 20,000 tons, and *Alexandr Pushkin,* 19,860 tons.

CRUISING AROUND EUROPE. Apart from the main shipping lines above, innumerable cruises are operated from British and European ports throughout the year by smaller companies. Many of these are part of a fly/cruise package, originating in the US. Some possibilities are mentioned under "Ships, Ferries, Yachts and Boats" further on in this chapter.

By Air from the Commonwealth and South Africa

Not only London, but most other European capitals are linked by many airlines to all parts of the Commonwealth and South Africa. Fortunately, the air fares which made European travel too expensive for many people have recently been supplemented by attractive Advance Purchase Excursion Fares (APEX) and other low-cost rates, finally making it possible to visit relatives in Europe and have a cultural holiday at the same time.

As we go to press, South Africans can travel from Johannesburg to London and back for as little as SAR483,30. This is an Apex fare for which booking and full payment must be made three months prior to travel. Passengers must stay a minimum of 14 days and a maximum of 90 days, and no stopovers are permitted. However, on the 19–75 day excursion to London, you can make four stopovers anywhere in Europe as far north as Amsterdam. Points farther north, Israel, and even Iran can be included on the itinerary for a slight surcharge. The normal economy-class return fare is SAR1128,40, which may include many more stopovers.

Australians have similar Apex fares, but are allowed to stay in England for up to 270 days. From Sydney to London and return (without stopovers) the fare is A$850 to A$1150, depending on dates of travel. If they want to break the long journey, they can take the 270-day excursion which costs between A$1,000 and A$1,300 and permits one stopover in each direction (in Asia) at the cost of A$75 per stop. Of course, on the normal economy-class return fare of A$1,880, Australians may stop in a great many exciting places, ranging from Singapore and Bangkok to Kathmandu, Nepal, at no extra charge. There is even a one-way fare from Sydney to London, which is A$695.

New Zealanders can fly around the world, stopping in many places of interest, for the economy-class return fare from Auckland to London of NZ$1,900. For NZ$1,200, they can take the 180-day excursion fare (valid for 180 days), which permits one stopover to and from London, at Hong Kong, Los Angeles, Singapore, or San Francisco, for not more than two nights. The one-way fare from Auckland to London is NZ$697.

By Sea:

Several lines link South Africa, India, Australia, New Zealand and the Far East with European ports, usually in the Mediterranean. One way fares are from about £350 (Sydney to Naples, high season by Lloyd Trestino). Ask your travel agent for information about latest routes and lines. Since the re-opening of the Suez Canal the picture has been changing rapidly.

By Air from Britain to the Continent

Britain is particularly well served from the Continent, with frequent flights not only to all European capitals (except Tirana, Albania) from London's Heathrow and Gatwick airports, but also with many excellent routes from Birmingham, Manchester, Yorkshire, Scotland, Wales, the West Country, and Ireland to several Continental centres. (For more information and samples of fares, stopovers, etc., see "Jetting Around Europe's Air Network" later in this section.)

By Hovercraft:

This is the quickest way across the Channel. These air-cushioned craft skim across the water in 35 to 40 minutes, carrying up to 250 passengers and 30 cars. *Hoverlloyd* operate between Ramsgate and Calais, *Seaspeed Hovercraft* between Dover and Boulogne, also Calais. Frequent daily services. Seaspeed fares are from £31 for a 14-ft. car and 2 passengers, Hoverlloyd £30 up to 4 passengers. There is also the new P & O Jetfoil, 4¾-hour service London–Bruges from £27. No cars on this one. Both lines offer London-Paris inclusive tickets, about £13 (Hoverlloyd by bus) or £17 (Seaspeed by train), return. London to Brussels inclusive ticket, about £14.50 (Seaspeed, by train), return. Less direct, but more varied and very pleasant and leisurely are the various car ferry services to a number of points in Normandy and Brittany listed below ("By Car").

By Train:

Best train linking London and Paris is an express which leaves Victoria Station daily at 10:30 A.M. (9:30 in winter), and arrives at the Gare du Nord at 5:25 P.M. This is a two-class train that goes by way of Folkestone-Calais, using new and "luxurious" *Sealink* ferries. From Paris (Nord), the train goes on to Paris (Lyon), where it connects with the Blue Train, Rome Express, etc.

The cheapest and most direct London-Paris route (but with a longer sea crossing) is via Newhaven-Dieppe, leaving Victoria at 9:48 A.M., arriving Paris (St. Lazare) at 6:07 P.M. For those in a hurry, there are two choices: the *Seaspeed Hovercraft* services connecting with trains from London (Charing Cross) or Paris (Nord), with a total travel time of around 6 hours, or Rail-Air: the *Silver Arrow service* (twice daily), taking just over 4 hours, station-to-station. It goes by rail from Victoria to Gatwick, air to Le Touquet, then rail to Paris (Nord).

If you prefer to travel while you sleep, the Night Ferry, which leaves Victoria Station at 10 P.M. (9 P.M. in winter), provides through sleeping car service via Dover-Dunkirk to Paris, where you are deposited before 9 A.M. The sleeper charge makes this the most expensive train. (First and second class coaches, 1st-class sleepers.)

The channel crossing taken is largely dependent on your ultimate destination. Generally speaking, for Paris, the rest of France and countries south, the best routes are Dover to Calais/Dunkirk/Boulogne, or Folkestone to Calais/Boulogne or Newhaven to Dieppe and Southampton-Le Havre-Cherbourg. For Belgium, Germany, and countries eastwards, cross from Dover or Folkestone to Ostend. A through-coach service from London to Cologne and Frankfurt leaves Victoria Station at 9 P.M., arriving Cologne 10:00 A.M. and Frankfurt at 1:30 P.M. Longer sea crossing, but with excellent connecting trains, is the Harwich-Hook of Holland route for Scandinavia, Russia, Germany, Austria, Yugoslavia. See also "By Car", below.

Fares vary according to the route taken. For example, the return first class fare London-Paris is about £50 via Calais, Boulogne or Dunkirk; to Copenhagen, about £125 via Ostend or via Hook of Holland.

By Car:

Some of the larger ferries on the longer crossings have very comfortable accommodation, including French cuisine, classical music, reserved seating, and comfortable cabins, and are, in fact, mini-liners even offering 4- to 6-day cruises at certain times of the year, at most reasonable prices. It is also possible to hire camping equipment, even a tow-caravan when booking your passage. All ferries these days have drive on/off systems for cars, and the fares listed below are the cheapest on each service for adult passengers, single journey, and for a 14-ft. car.

FRANCE *Dover-Calais.* Sealink or Townsend-Thoresen 1¾ hrs. crossing, or Seaspeed Hovercraft 30 mins., all frequently throughout the day. Car and 2 passengers, £31.20.

Dover-Boulogne, as above, plus Normandy Ferries, 2 passengers and car £30; much the same frequencies.

Dover-Dunkerque. Sealink 4 hrs. 3 day 1 night crossing. Same rates as above.

Ramsgate-Calais. Hoverlloyd. 40 mins. up to 20 a day. Car fare £30.50 includes 4 passengers.

Folkestone-Calais/Boulogne. Sealink. 2-3 crossings daily. Otherwise as from Dover.

Newhaven-Dieppe. Sealink 3¾ hrs. 4 daily and once nightly. Car and 2 adults, £37.80.

Weymouth-Cherbourg. Sealink 3½ hrs. 4 by day, 2 by night. Car and 2 adults, £39.90.

Southampton-Le Havre. Normandy Ferries. 2 day crossings, 7 hrs. 2 nightly 8 hrs. Car & 2 Pas. £43. Townsend-Thoresen 6½ hrs. 3 daily. £41.

Southampton-Cherbourg. Townsend-Thoresen. As to Le Havre.

Portsmouth-Cherbourg and *Le Havre.* Townsend-Thoresen 4 hrs. Car and 2 Pas. £29.20.

Portsmouth-St. Malo. Brittany Ferries 8½ hrs. Car, 2 Pas. £45.

Plymouth-Roscoff. Brittany Ferries. 6½ hrs. Daily. Same fares as to St. Malo.

Plymouth-St. Malo. Brittany Ferries. 7½ hrs. daily. Fares as to Roscoff.

BELGIUM *Dover-Ostend.* Sealink 4 hrs. 9 daily. Rates as to Boulogne.

Dover-Zeebrugge. Townsend Thoresen. 4 hrs. 6 daily. Rate as Sealink.

Felixstowe-Zeebrugge. Townsend-Thoresen 5 hrs. 3 daily. Car & 2 Pas. £32.20.

Hull-Zeebrugge. North Sea Ferries. 15 hrs. nightly. Car & 2 Pas. £59.60. Includes couchette & meals.

HOLLAND *Hull-Rotterdam.* North Sea Ferries. 15 hrs. nightly. Fares as for Zeebrugge.

Sheerness-Flushing Olau Line. A successful new line with easy access to the Continent. 7 hours, twice daily sailings. Car & 2 Pas. £35.

Harwich-Hook of Holland. Sealink. 6½ hrs day. 8 hrs. night. Pas. £11.50. Car £17.60.

GERMANY *Harwich-Hamburg.* Prins Ferries. 20 hrs. Alternate days. Car & 2 Pas. £96.45.

Harwich-Bremerhaven. Prins Ferries. 16 hrs. Alternate days. Car & 2 Pas. £88.80.

DENMARK *Harwich-Esbjerg.* DFDS 19 hrs. Daily. Car & 2 Pas. £84.

Newcastle-Esbjerg. DFDS. 17 hrs. 2 weekly, May-Sept. only Pas. £30.50. Car £22. & 2 Pas. £56.50.

SWEDEN *Felixstowe-Gothenburg.* Tor Line. 23½ hrs. Thrice weekly. Car & 2 Pas. £79.50.

Newcastle-Gothenburg. DFDS Seaways/Tor Line. 25 hrs. twice weekly. Car & 2 Pas. £97.50 by DFDS, £79.50 by Tor Line.

NORWAY *Newcastle-Stavanger/Bergen/Kristiansand* Olsen-Bergen Line. 16.-20. hrs. 3 per week. Car & 2 Pas. £91.

Newcastle-Oslo. Olsen-Bergen. 39 hrs. once weekly. Car & 2 Pas. £109.

Harwich-Kristiansand/Oslo. Olsen-Bergen. 22 hrs. 2 weekly. As above.

SPAIN *Plymouth-Brittany Ferries-Santander.* 25 hrs. Twice weekly. Cars & 2 Pas. £80.

Complete tariff information is obtainable from the AA, RAC, and London office of the AAA, and Continental Car Ferry Centre, 52 Grosvenor Gardens, London, S.W.1. For Townsend-Thoresen Car Ferries: 127 Regent Street, London W.1. For Normandy Ferries: Arundel Towers, Portland Terrace, Southampton. For Brittany Ferries: Millbay Docks, Plymouth.

For reservations in North America, write to *BritRail Travel International* at 270 Madison Ave., New York 10016; Room 513, 333 North Michigan Ave., Chicago, Ill. 60601; Room 1215, 510 West Sixth St., Los Angeles, Calif. 90014; 55 Eglinton Ave. East, Toronto 12, Ontario; Suite 815, United Kingdom Bldg., 409 Granville St., Vancouver 2, B.C.

STAYING IN EUROPE

Customs upon Arrival

Thanks to the efforts of the United Nations, this vexatious problem has been eased by an agreement among most tourist-receiving nations on a standardized list of items which travelers may bring into their territories without paying duty. It includes portable typewriters, radios or phonographs, cameras with a reasonable amount of film, sports equipment and new as well as used clothing, provided it is only imported in such quantities as would be normal for personal use. The amounts accepted are minimums; thus the countries which have signed the convention all agree to permit tourists to bring in 200 cigarettes, but actually most of them individually set larger quotas—for France, for instance, it is 400 for North American visitors. For these variations, see individual chapters of this book, following. In general, the rule is that you can bring in almost anything for normal personal use while traveling, and it is unlikely that you will have any difficulty with such belongings.

The Sunshine Calendar

A rough guide to maximum sunshine from May through September is given here for sun-worshippers. In each case, you will find, based on averages from past years, a minimum of 8 hours of sunshine per day in the following areas:

May: Denmark, Finland, Riviera of France, northern Germany, Greece, southern Italy, Portugal, Spain (except the Atlantic coast), Sweden, Switzerland, southern Yugoslavia.

June: the same as May, plus France's Atlantic coast, all of Italy, Norway's southern coast, all of Yugoslavia.

July: Finland, France, Greece, Italy, Portugal, Spain (except Atlantic coast), Sweden, Switzerland, Yugoslavia.

August: France (except Channel coast), Greece, Italy, Portugal, Spain (except Atlantic coast), Sweden, Switzerland, Yugoslavia.

September: French Riviera, Greece, southern Portugal, southern Spain, and best of all, *everywhere* in the Alps.

If you prefer to winter on a beach rather than a ski slope, we suggest two areas in Europe. In the Greek islands winter temperatures are in the upper 50s and 60s, and spring begins around the end of January. Rhodes claims 300 days of sun a year and to its treasure house of Greek, Roman,

Byzantine, Arabic and Crusader art and architecture has added luxury hotels open year round and with heated swimming pools.

Portugal's southernmost province, the Algarve, has over 100 miles of coast where a warm-water current keeps mid-winter temperatures in the 60s, flowers out year round and spring beginning in late January, when the almond trees bloom. Golf, tennis, water sports and deep sea fishing add to the natural attractions of this area.

Shopping

Shopping will be one of the thrills of your trip, and you'll find European stores full of beautiful things and impressive bargains.

Here's a tip for tourists resident *outside* the Common Market countries of Britain, Denmark, France, Germany, Holland, Belgium, Luxembourg, Italy and Ireland that could save you up to 11% on most of your purchases. In these countries, VAT (value added tax) is tacked onto most prices. You can avoid this tax by having the shop send your purchases home, or by having them delivered to your point of departure, or by promising that you will leave that particular country within three months. Since the shop will have to pay the tax until you have actually left the country, when it will receive a refund from customs, your promise will sometimes have to be a deposit on the tax, which will be returned to you when you have filled out the customs declaration at the point of departure. Some countries are more generous, allowing you to remain with them six months before VAT is payable, and all Common Market countries will allow you one year in the case of car purchase.

This is the time to warn you about those duty free, tax free shops. While they *can* offer bargains, especially in liquor, cigarettes, cosmetics and perfume—because of the huge taxes these attract in the normal shops—the "DUTY FREE" signs can often be unpleasant hoaxes. Some airport shops charge up to 50%, sometimes even 100%, above the prices charged for exactly the same goods in not only their own cities but in New York as well. In general, a country's own specialty products are good buys (woolens in Britain, cheese in Holland). Since Amsterdam's Schiphol and Ireland's Shannon are the two most important duty-free-shopping airports, you can plan ahead by ordering their catalogs. Write to Netherlands National Tourist Office, 576 5th Avenue, New York, N.Y. 10036; and to Shannon Free Airport Co., 590 5th Avenue, New York, N.Y. 10036; then compare prices on the articles you want. You may be surprised. Cameras, radios, calculators are among the goods which fall into the "Think Twice" category. Of all the airport shops we have sampled, only Amsterdam's Schiphol seems to offer its customers a really even break. You had better remember, too, the restrictions of your own customs laws. Don't buy more than you can legally take in to your country of residence, and keep sales receipts as proof of what you have paid.

Vacation Travel Insurance

Generally speaking, you can insure: yourself and your family, your baggage, and your travel expenses. For personal accident insurance, "family" usually means a spouse and dependent children aged 14 days through 21 years. Some policies also cover siblings, in-laws, grandparents and grandchildren. Benefits are paid for loss of life, hands, feet, eyesight, for total disability, and for some medical expenses, unless any of these are due to suicide, war, or military maneuvers. Top limit is usually $200,000.

Baggage and personal possessions can be insured up to $2,000 against loss or damage anywhere in the world. Usually covered are clothing, luggage, jewelry, cameras and recreation equipment. However, a long list of things not insured includes animals, cars and other vehicles (except bicycles), cash and securities, business and professional papers and property, artificial teeth and limbs, household effects; loss due to government seizure; and damage from war, vermin, normal wear and tear, illegal acts and nuclear contamination.

Trip cancellation insurance, up to about $5,000, covers the nonrefundable parts of your transportation and hotel expenses that you may lose from having to cancel because of death, illness, injury or complications of pregnancy either before you leave or while traveling, except in case of suicide, war, or illegal activity (smuggling, for example). Here again, "family" always includes your spouse and children, and *may* extend to siblings, in-laws and other generations.

Specific conditions, coverage and limitations vary so much from one company to another and one policy to another that is is impossible to describe them all here. Premiums vary even more. So far, travel insurance has not had the benefit of the kind of standardization-plus-comparison-shoppers' guide that occured a few years ago in Pennsylvania for life insurance. You just have to ask one or several travel and/or insurance agents and try to find a good deal for yourself.

Medical Services

The *I.A.M.A.T.* (International Assoc. for Medical Assistance to Travellers), offers you a list of approved English-speaking doctors who have had postgraduate training in the U.S., Canada or Gt. Britain. Membership is free; the scheme is world-wide with many European countries participating. An office call costs $15; house and hotel calls are $20; Sunday and holiday calls are $25. For information apply in the U.S. to Suite 5620, 350 Fifth Ave., New York 10001; in Canada, 1268 St. Clair Ave. W., Toronto; in Europe, 17 Gotthardstrasse, 6300 Zug, Switzerland.

Travelers from Britain can avail themselves of the unlimited medical assistance provided by *Europ Assistance Ltd.,* 269/273 High Street, Croydon, Surrey. When you need help, there is a 24-hour, seven days a week (all holidays included) telephone service staffed by multilingual personnel. Medical advisors and casualty surgery specialists, plus air and road ambulances, are on call throughout Western and Eastern Europe, Turkey, Morocco, Tunisia, the Mediterranean islands, the Canary Islands and Madeira. Medical expenses insurance of £2,000 is also included. Both individual and group travelers are eligible at a basic price of £3 per person for 23 days, 75p for each additional week.

Physically disabled travelers have had trouble in the past in arranging the most normal forms of travel insurance. Usually the process has involved an exacting questionnaire resulting at best in severely restricted cover. But now, under a special master policy arrangement with Britain's Central Council for the Disabled, British travelers can obtain standard insurance cover at a premium in line with normal market rates. Travelers should either directly or through their travel agents contact *J. Perry &*

Co. (Holiday Insurances) Ltd., 27 Cockspur Street, London SW1 (Telex 917377).

Certain countries, Gt. Britain and Sweden, for instance, offer free treatment and hospitalization to visitors, provided the problem arose, or became severely exacerbated, during your stay there.

Free medical services in urgent cases are available for British travelers in other EEC countries. Provided you are neither unemployed nor self-employed (all employed people, pensioners and their dependents *are* eligible), you can go to any local office of the Department of Health and Social Security or any employment exchange and obtain form CM1. Post it to the nearest social security office and a form E111 will be issued to you by post. It is essential to take it with you when you go abroad: it is your certificate of entitlement to medical benefits during your stay in other EEC countries (Belgium, France, West Germany, Italy, Luxembourg, The Netherlands, Denmark and Ireland).

Conversion Charts

Simplified: 1 inch = 2.54 centimeters; 1 foot = 12 inches = 30.48 centimeters; 1 yard = 3 feet = 0.9144 meters.

Simplified: 1 ounce = 28.35 grams; 1 pound = 453.5924 grams. 2.2 pounds = 1 kilo.

Simplified: 1 U.S. gallon = 3¾ liters; 1 English gallon = 4½ liters.

Length		Weights	
centimeters	inches	gram(me)s	ounces
5	2	100	3.33
10	4 (under)	200	6.67
20	8 (under)	250	8.03
30	11¾	500	16.07
40	15¾	1 kilogram (kilo) = 2.2046 lbs.	
50	19¾		

1 meter = 39.37 inches

CLOTHING

Although you may see several charts with comparative U.S.-British-Continental sizings, in our experience these are not truly standardized. Best take along a tape measure, or rely on the shop assistant's assessment (in the first place) of your sizing. Always try on a garment before purchasing: an apparently correct sizing may prove to have arm-holes too wide or too narrow, sleeves too long or too short. After all, each country sizes according to the average measurements and proportions of its nationals, just as in the States and Gt. Britain. Dress fabrics, usually 1 meter (100 cm.) wide.

KILOMETERS INTO MILES

This simple chart will help you to convert to both miles and kilometers. If you want to convert from miles into kilometers read from the center column to the right, if from kilometers into miles, from the center column to the left. Example: 5 miles = 8.046 kilometers, 5 kilometers = 3.106 miles.

Miles		Kilometers	Miles		Kilometers
0-621	1	1-609	37-282	60	96-560
1-242	2	3-218	43-496	70	112-265
1-864	3	4-828	49-710	80	128-747
2-485	4	6-347	55-924	90	144-840
3-106	5	8-046	62-138	100	160-934
3-728	6	9-656	124-276	200	321-868
4-349	7	11-265	186-414	300	482-803
4-971	8	12-874	248-552	400	643-737
5-592	9	14-484	310-690	500	804-672
6-213	10	16-093	372-828	600	965-606
12-427	20	32-186	434-967	700	1,126-540
18-641	30	42-280	497-106	800	1,287-475
24-855	40	64-373	559-243	900	1,448-409
31-069	50	80-467	621-381	1,000	1,609-344

TIRE PRESSURE CONVERTER

Pounds per Square Inch	16	18	20	22	24	26	28	30	32
Kilogrammes per Square Centimeter	1.12	1.26	1.40	1.54	1.68	1.82	1.96	2.10	2.24

GALLONS INTO LITERS

U.S. Gallon	Liters	Imperial (British) Gallon	Liters
1	3.78	1	4.54
2	7.57	2	9.09
3	11.36	3	13.63
4	15.14	4	18.18
5	18.93	5	22.73
6	22.71	6	27.27
7	26.50	7	31.82
8	30.28	8	36.36
9	34.07	9	40.91
10	37.85	10	45.46

There are 5 Imperial (British) gallons to 6 U.S. gallons.

TRAVELING IN EUROPE

Jetting Around Europe's Air Network

Every country in Europe with an airport has an airline linking its major cities with other European and world capitals. There are also many charter companies which operate frequent services between major points. But European air fares are a great muddle, and travel agents and the public are applying pressure on the International Air Transport Association (IATA), governments, and the airlines themselves to simplify matters.

Until quite recently, visitors going to Europe from other continents were usually advised to take an excursion fare to the farthest destination in their itinerary, which would allow them free stopovers in a number of cities. These fares have become less attractive in view of the variety of new low-cost fares that, in effect, usually require the traveller to fly to and from a single destination. (On the North Atlantic, we are referring to Advance Purchase Excursion Fares, Advance Booking Charters, stand-by fares, *Laker Skytrain,* etc.)

Most agree that on many short and medium routes in Europe, air fares have long been excessively high. The normal economy-class one-way and return fares on scheduled airlines are, however, now supplemented with a variety of excursion fares, while inexpensive charter flights and package holidays continue to draw hundreds of thousands of holiday makers away from high fares and scheduled carriers.

We sincerely hope that a realistic air-fare structure which most travellers can understand will soon become standard procedure. It is possible, however, that competition will be even more fierce and the variety of fares even greater and more confusing!

Whatever happens, soaring fuel prices and general inflation will prevent anyone from accurately predicting air fares more than a few months in advance. For this reason, we are quoting just a few sample fares from London to various points in Europe on both scheduled airlines and charter carriers; as you will read, the latter can be booked only at certain travel agents. Remember that while the normal economy-class return fares seem high, they are the only fares within Europe for which stopovers are permitted at no extra charge. For example, on the normal, £ 235, Y-class (economy) return fare between London and Rome, you could stop in Paris, Geneva, and Nice one way, and other cities as far north as Amsterdam on the way back.

Samples Of Return Air Fares From London To European Cities—Mid-1978

Amsterdam: (first) class £123; Y (economy) class, £82. Instant Purchase, £49. Conditions: Reservations and tickets must not be made prior to 9 P.M. local time on the day before departure, and return travel shall not commence prior to 12:01 A.M. local time on Sunday following the day of outward travel.

Athens: F class, £402; Y class, £316. One-Month Excursion, £162.50–£218, depending on time of year. Conditions: minimum stay six days, maximum stay one month, and stopovers allowed only in Greece. Charter flight, £58.50–£81.50, depending on time of year.

Copenhagen: F class, £309; Y class, £206. One-Month Excursion, £119. Conditions: minimum stay six days, maximum stay one month.

Madrid: F class, £252; Y class, £188. One-Month Excursion, £109.50–£140. Conditions: check with travel agent.

Malaga: F class, £275; Y class, £208. One-Month Excursion, £125.50–£161, depending on time of day and year. Conditions: minimum stay six days, maximum stay one month. Group Two Excursion, £62.50–£97.50, depending on time of day and year. Conditions: applicable for groups of two persons or more; see travel agent. Charter flight £57.50.

Moscow: F class, £534; Y class, £377. One-Month Excursion, £213. Conditions: minimum stay ten days, maximum stay one month.

Paris: F class, £117; Y class, £78. Instant Purchase, £47.50. Conditions: Reservations and tickets may not be made prior to 2 P.M. local time on the day before departure, and return travel shall not commence prior to 12:01 A.M. local time on Sunday following the day of outward travel. Weekend Excursion, £47.50. Conditions: valid for travel between 12:01 A.M. Saturdays and 2 P.M. Sundays; maximum stay one month.

Venice: F class, £283; Y class, £202. One-Month Excursion, £145. Conditions: minimum stay six days, maximum stay one month. Advance Purchase Excursion, £79.50. Conditions: minimum stay fourteen days, maximum stay three months; reservations, ticket issue, and full payment of fare must be made at the same time, and not less than one month prior to commencement of travel. Charter flight, £53.50–£73.50, depending on time of year.

Rome: F class, £339; Y class, £235. One-Month Excursion, £165.50. Conditions: minimum stay six days, maximum stay one month. Advance Purchase Excursion, £85. Conditions: same as for Venice. Charter flight, £58.50–£78.50, depending on time of year.

In spite of glossy advertisements to the contrary, flying today is neither an exciting adventure nor an elegant form of transportation. Within Europe, where most flights are between 50 minutes and three hours, it is just a way of getting from one point to another fairly quickly, so the differences between one airline and another are, to many passengers, negligible. Efficiency in handling passengers on the ground, and punctual aircraft arrivals and departures, are what count most. Reputations vary, but few can be said to be totally and consistently reliable; nor are most of them, and we say this with regret, as good as they used to be.

The problems created by the phenomenal development and growth of air travel are only accentuated by the stringent security precautions, the industrial disputes and strikes, and by the nonchalant attitude of employees whose desire to please for the sake of a satisfied customer is, more often than not, an oddity rather than the rule. Of course, airlines are not entirely to blame for falling standards; nor is their performance worse than that of today's other service industries.

You can almost always choose between the national airline of the country you are flying *from* and that of the country you are flying *to*. There usually are others, on the short hops within Europe at the beginning or end of the long routes of intercontinental airlines. These services are less frequent, and there is the risk of delays, particularly when the plane is coming from the other side of the globe. What really matters with scheduled flights is, of course, which one is flying when you want to fly or when the excursion fare you have chosen permits you to fly. Charter flights are fine, but they can be restricting. One disadvantage is that they often leave from airports which are not as conveniently situated as those of scheduled carriers, although there is always some form of public transportation available.

Whether scheduled or charter, all European airlines fly modern jets and take about the same time to cover the same distance. Few serve proper meals on flights under two hours, and what you get usually varies little from one airline to the next, so do not expect great national dishes while aloft. American cocktails are seldom available. While we do not suggest that you avoid flying on the airlines of Eastern Europe, it must be said that the Russian planes which most of them use are noisier and less comfortable than the British, American, or French planes used by other airlines.

Charter flights, student flights, and package tours are seldom available on very short (less than a week) notice. They should be booked as far ahead as possible. Unfortunately for visitors from other continents, this must usually be done from the country of departure in the local currency. Your travel agent will know the exceptions. For cheap charter flights from Britain, look at the prominent advertisements in the national press, particularly *The Times,* the Sunday papers, and the London weekly entertainment magazine, *Time Out.* Student travel is well organized in Europe. Holders of an internationally recognized student card should investigate the agencies in London and other European capitals that cater to them. On the Continent, the English-language and local press should also be helpful.

Accredited travel agencies can offer the whole range of summer and winter package tours, most of them directed at the person with a limited budget. They offer the best value for money in the world of travel today. For example, as we go to press, it is possible to have seven nights in Majorca with three meals a day, for as little as £77; this rate is for May, a splendid time of year anywhere in the Mediterranean. Or you can have a week in Jerusalem or Istanbul, on a bed and breakfast basis, in January, for just £99. Among the well-known and reliable tour operators are *Laker, Cosmos, Thomson's, Thomas Cook,* and *British Airways Sovereign Holidays.* New in the British market is *Tjaereborg* (7–8 Conduit Street, London), a Danish tour operator which sells, direct to the public and not through travel agents, a number of destinations at cut-rate prices.

Rail travel is worth considering for distances of less than 250 miles. It usually is cheaper, just as fast, and much more convenient. As obvious as it may seem, the most aggravating thing about flying in Europe is the door-to-door time your journey actually takes, compared with the brief flying-time quoted in the timetable. An hour's flight can involve a day's expedition, starting with the taxi ride from the hotel to the air terminal.

To make your journey easier, we suggest that you take a minimum of luggage (not more than 44 lbs. in Europe, even though North Atlantic travelers are restricted now only by the size of their suitcases, not by their weight), and that you comply with the regulations concerning hand luggage (one piece per person), though they are seldom enforced. Duty-free shopping can be time consuming when the terminal is crowded, so check in early if you want to stock up. Once on board, try to remain seated throughout a short flight. Order more than one drink at a time if you want it, as crews rarely have time to do the rounds again. Above all, relax and don't allow yourself to get unduly annoyed about delays. After all, you're supposed to be on holiday!

RAIL TRAVEL IN EUROPE

by
DAVID TENNANT

The author is travel correspondent for Thomson Regional Newspapers in the U.K. and travel editor of The Illustrated London News. *He is co-author of a major book on world railways and has written extensively in many publications on rail travel.*

Throughout Europe today rail travel for business and pleasure is better placed than it has ever been to provide the public with a service that is second to none, though the over-all mileage of passenger-carrying track is considerably less than it was in the immediate post-war years. Many of the main lines have been completely re-built for today's high speeds and greater use. International co-operation in just about every aspect of railway management is more intensive than ever and is reflected in a highly efficient railway network. Increased electrification and other technical advances, such as the excellent turbo-trains operated by French Railways on a number of long distance routes, have resulted in higher speeds with averages of well over 80 m.p.h. being quite usual.

But the search for even greater speeds coupled with the ultimate in rail safety is being actively pursued. The Italians have completed a large part of their very fast *direttissima* line, which when finished next year will link Florence with Rome. Meanwhile, with most expresses running over the completed section, substantial time savings have been made. Construction is proceeding rapidly in France of a new, super high-speed railway between the suburbs of southeast Paris and the nation's second city, Lyon. In the U.K. the High Speed Train of British Railways (it travels at 125 m.p.h. over long stretches) is now well established, having been introduced on the routes from London (Paddington) to Bristol (and on to the resort of Weston-super-Mare) and south Wales, and more recently on the main line East Coast route from London (Kings Cross) to York, Newcastle, and Edinburgh. And in Germany there are other high speed lines being brought into service.

But comfort is just as important as speed, perhaps slightly more so to the leisure traveler. In the last few years there have been remarkable strides in this direction with all the railways of Europe progressively introducing new rolling stock for both day and night services. This new rolling stock offers comfort and spaciousness which a decade ago was restricted to the deluxe first class only trains. Under the UIC agreement second class coaches now have only three seats aside in compartments, as against four previously. Corridors are slightly wider allowing for easier access.

Air conditioning is becoming more common, mainly in first class but increasingly in second class also. Although not visually noticed by the average traveler the "behind the scenes" technical advances in coach design are of equal importance giving smoother and quieter riding all round. Multi-professional teams, including even psychologists and interior decorators, have been employed to make these new coaches more efficient and more attractive for the traveler.

These advances cannot be achieved in a short period, and you must not expect to find new coaches everywhere. However, in the course of thousands of miles of European rail travel each year, I am constantly impressed with the ever-rising standards, not only in first class (which is now quite luxurious in many cases) but also in second class.

Class Consciousness

The question of which class to choose is one that is often put to me, and the answer is both easy—and difficult. The easy part is "travel first when you can" for there is no doubt at all that it does give substantially more comfort, spaciousness, and generally a more relaxing atmosphere. But it is anything from 30% to 50% dearer than second class. Therefore, if economy is all important, then stick to second class. Where you want to economize but not sacrifice too many of life's comforts, then I would recommend traveling second class throughout Scandinavia, on the Benelux expresses in the Netherlands, Belgium and Luxembourg, on the TALGO, ELT and TAF trains in Spain, on "DC" trains in Germany, on the Transalpin express from Basle to Vienna (and also "TS" trains in Austria), on the fast inter-city expresses in Switzerland and on the turbo-trains and *Rapides* in France.

In the high summer season (and at peak traveling periods such as Christmas and Easter) second class travel is always very busy indeed, particularly on long-distance international trains. I advise first class travel then, if possible. It is also important to remember that in many European countries (but not all) supplementary fares are required for travel on certain express trains. The amount varies according to the distance traveled in most cases, and it is best to check this before departure. Holders of the full Eurailpass do not require to pay this extra supplement except on Trans Europ Expresses.

For Daytime Travel

One of the biggest advances in European rail travel had its beginnings 22 years ago when the first Trans Europ Expresses (known by their initials TEE) started operating, designed to give the business and holiday traveler the best available in rail travel. A success from the start this system now connects over 130 cities in no fewer than ten west European countries. Its smooth, stainless steel coaches are now a familiar part of the European rail scene.

There are at present six different types of these trains in operation. But they all share certain characteristics—entirely first class, luxuriously equipped, full restaurant services (some with restaurant cars, others serving meals at every seat), fully air-conditioned and high speeds. Some travel entirely within one country such as the "Aquitaine" (Paris—Bordeaux) or the "Vesuvio" (Milan—Naples) while others connect two or more countries. The "Edelweiss" and "Iris", for example, link Brussels and Zurich serving Belgium, Luxembourg and France en route. One or two have secretarial services and telephone links.

All the TEE trains require a special supplementary fare which varies according to the distance traveled. However, this surcharge is comparatively modest when one considers the extras one gets. All are also daytime-only trains, their high speeds enabling them to connect cities far apart without the need for overnight travel.

However, the TEE system does not have a monopoly of European deluxe train travel, for many excellent international expresses operate all over the continent. Unfortunately the legendary Orient Express from Paris to Istanbul, synonymous with intrigue, spies and elegance since 1883, is no more. Now you must change enroute at either Munich or Belgrade. In the U.K., where there are no TEE trains, all main line expresses have modern rolling stock with much of it now being air-conditioned in both 1st and 2nd class.

For Overnight Travel

Overnight travel by sleeping car on most of Europe's railways is as popular as ever, though many journeys which once required night travel no longer do, because of the faster trains. Night traveling can greatly extend many holiday or business trips—and in comfort. The majority of long-distance overnight trains carry both first- and second-class sleeping cars, and often "couchettes."

In the last two years, there has been a complete re-organization of the sleeping-car system in western Europe. The various railway systems (excluding those of the U.K. and Ireland) formed the International Sleeping-Car Pool to operate on routes that link two or more countries. Sleeping-cars are staffed and operated by the Wagons-Lit company, by the DSG sleeping-car and dining-car company in Germany, and by the respective railways in Scandinavia. The majority of these sleeping-cars now carry the logo and initials TEN, which stands for Trans Europ Nuit or Nacht or Notte, depending on the language of the country in which they originated.

From the traveller's viewpoint, they offer much the same facilities. Beds are full size, with one, two, or three in each compartment, the last found in the special second-class ("tourist") coaches. Each compartment has a washbasin with hot and cold running water, electric shaving points, coat hangers, mirrors, baggage space, and other amenities. During the day they usually make up into sitting compartments, although this is not always the case. All have toilet and full washroom facilities in each coach. In Germany, around 50 such sleeping-cars also have showers.

The sleeping-cars are all fully staffed, generally with multi-lingual attendants who often can provide refreshments. Each passenger is also provided with a towel and soap. Most trains also carry bottled water.

In the U.K., the first-class sleeping-cars have single berths; second-class has two berths. All have full wash-hand basin facilities, electric shaving points, foot mats, additional blankets, and several lights, as well as individually controlled heating and air ventilation. Most British Rail sleeping-cars can provide limited alcoholic beverages, and all supply morning tea and biscuits as part of the inclusive service.

If you wish to travel overnight more cheaply, many trains (except in the U.K.) have "couchette" cars. These are more or less simple sleepers with blanket, pillow and small towel provided. In first class, each compartment takes four couchette passengers. In second class, six passengers. Couchettes are certainly more comfortable than sitting up overnight and in the newer coaches—and particularly in first class—they are excellent value for money. But if you require a degree of privacy then opt for a standard sleeper. Apart from the romantic appeal of overnight travel you can save on hotel bills by traveling overnight. Incidentally almost all sleeping car attendants will provide you with a cup of coffee or tea and many also now carry alcoholic refreshments as well.

Always make sleeping car and couchette reservations in advance, but sometimes one can get a last minute cancellation. The cost varies according to the class, the type of sleeper or couchette and the distance traveled. First class single occupancy of sleeper compartments is expensive. For two traveling together, the cost is more or less halved. There are no single sleepers in second class. On many routes where couchettes are used, a standard charge is made whether one is traveling first or second, but of course the appropriate first or second traveling ticket is required.

Meals on Wheels

Every railway system in Europe operates dining cars or refreshment cars of one kind or another. In addition to the standard and traditional dining cars (meals here are always expensive, being anything from £6 to £10 per head), there are buffet cars (which provide simpler meals from one third to one half the cost of a full dinner meal), self-service "grill" cars, mini bars and *vendes ambulantes.* The last is a traveling salesperson going through the train with a trolley selling sandwiches, coffee, soft drinks, beer and so on. This is the most economic way of having a meal en route. In some trains you can now get "pre-packed" cold meals at about the same price as on the cafeteria cars. These can be pre-booked or purchased at certain station buffets.

For formal meals in the dining car always book ahead—enquire about this as soon as you get on the train. In many cases you are given a "place card" and told what time the meal starts, or alternatively a dining car attendant comes along the train announcing the meal time.

The tendency on most European railways today is to replace the formal dining-car with a buffet, self-service, or grill car. All TEE trains, however, and most of the prestige expresses in individual countries, will continue to carry full diners for the next few years. But more and more expresses will be providing the simpler eating facilities. Labor costs coupled with the higher speeds of trains (which shorten travelling times) have brought this about. However, be assured that you won't go hungry while travelling by rail.

At most stations, even quite small ones, all over the continent, there are good buffets (some have top-grade restaurants as well). At all main line stations, trolleys with food and drinks meet most trains. Payment is generally required in the currency of the country, although at frontier stations it has been my experience that they will take several currencies.

"The Union Internationale des Chemins de Fer (European Railway Union) issues a timetable with diagrammatic maps covering the main international routes in Europe. This is valid for the period June to September inclusive each year. In addition to the T.E.E. and other international and main line expresses it also gives details of the car train (Motorail) services both on the continent and in the U.K. The timetable which is called "Through Europe by Train" is in English as well as several other languages and is scheduled to be available free of charge from Centre de Publicite, UIC, Via Marsala 9, 1 001185, ROME, Italy from around the beginning of April onwards. In addition some international railway offices will have it available for distribution.

Scenic Routes

Many of Europe's top-line expresses pass through some of the continent's finest scenic areas in daylight. It is not possible to list all of these (there are around 200 all told), but we have selected a number which are particularly outstanding. In every case these trains complete all (or the major part) of their journey in the daytime during the summer holiday season, and operate all the year around unless otherwise stated. Those which are T.E.E.-operated are so marked. Each has a dining car and, where necessary, sleeping cars. All trains listed other than the T.E.E. services carry both first and second-class coaches. Some require supplementary fare for all or part of the way.

Arlberg Express. Paris—Zurich—Innsbruck—Vienna. Leaves French capital in the evening, travels overnight to Switzerland. Goes through Swiss and Austrian Alps in daylight. Total traveling time 21 hours approx.

Barcelona Talgo. Madrid—Guadalajara—Zaragoza—Taragona—Sitges—Barcelona. Departs from the Spanish capital mid-morning, travelling through some of the most interesting parts of Spain to arrive in the country's second city and main seaport in time for dinner. Approx. 9 hours. Similar service in the afternoon, and about one hour earlier in opposite direction. Full diner throughout.

Blauer Enzian (T.E.E.) Hamburg—Hannover—Munich—Salzburg—Klagenfurt. Through the heart of Germany and Austria with much of the southbound route being in the daylight hours in summer. From mid-October to mid-December and again from mid-April to mid-May this train operates to and from Munich only. Total traveling time is 13 hours (5 hours less when it terminates at Munich).

Cisalpin (T.E.E.). Paris—Dijon—Lausanne—Milan—Venice (last named, summer months only). Leaves Paris at lunch time, arrives Milan mid-evening, Venice just after midnight. Total traveling time to Milan, 9 hours, to Venice under 12.

Cornish Riviera. London—Exeter—Plymouth—Penzance. One of Britain's longest established expresses. Very scenic route, especially after Exeter. Connections for many resorts in Devon and Cornwall. Does not operate on Sundays. 5½ hours' travel.

Edelweiss and **Iris** (T.E.E.). Brussels—Luxembourg—Strasbourg—Basel—Zurich. Twin trains which run twice daily in each direction linking four countries. Includes the attractive Ardennes country in south Belgium. Total traveling time approx. 7 hours.

Flying Scotsman. London—Newcastle-upon-Tyne—Edinburgh. Perhaps Britain's most famous train; rural scenery for much of way, passing many historic sites. Limited accommodation, reservations advisable. Nearly 400 miles in about 5 hours. Now a High Speed Train.

Glasgow-Mallaig. Twice daily (three times May to September), route is through the West Highlands and along the banks of Loch Lomond. One of the most scenic in Britain. Buffet car on all trains. About six leisurely hours for the 165 miles.

Gottardo (T.E.E.). Basel—Zurich—Lugano—Como—Milan. A very scenic route passing through the famous St. Gotthard tunnel. Southbound route always in daylight. Northbound terminates at Zurich but immediate connection for Basel. Total time approx. 4½ hours.

Henrik. Bergen—Voss—Finse—Geilo—Oslo. An early (but not too early) start from Norway's second city takes this express through some of the finest of the country's scenery reaching the capital in the early afternoon. Its "twin" the *Pernille* operates at similar timings in the other direction. Dining car on both trains.

Le Catalan (T.E.E.). Geneva—Chambéry—Grenoble—Avignon—Narbonne—Perpignan—Barcelona. This is a Talgo train and one of only two to operate outside Spain on an interesting and largely scenic route. Connections at Barcelona to/from Madrid and at Geneva for Lausanne, Berne, Zurich and Basle. Approx. 10 hours Barcelona-Geneva.

Le Mistral (T.E.E.). Paris—Dijon—Lyon—Avignon—Marseille—Cannes—Nice. Perhaps the most luxurious train in Europe—secretarial services, boutique, beauty salon, speeds up to 100 m.p.h. Reservations advisable. Approx. 9 hours travel.

Foguete —Lisbon—Coimbra—Oporto. Three times daily express between Portugal's two major cities calling at the ancient University city of Coimbra en route. Travels through the heartland of the country. First class only. Reservation strongly advised.

Mediolanum (T.E.E.). Munich—Innsbruck—Verona—Milan. Through the Tyrolean Alps and the famous Brenner Pass. Northbound route entirely in daylight throughout the year. Approx. 6 hours.

Peloritano. Palermo—Messina—Salerno—Naples—Rome. Connects the Italian capital with the leading city in Sicily (through coaches also to Catania for Taormina). Runs beside the sea for much of the way. Limited accommodation. Reservation essential. Approx. 11 hours, including train ferry crossing of Straits of Messina.

Rheingold (T.E.E.). Hook of Holland/Amsterdam—Dusseldorf—Cologne—Mainz—Mannheim—Basle. Runs up the Rhine Valley for much of its route. Through coaches go to Geneva via Lausanne, and to Milan via Lucerne and Lugano. Direct connections at Basle for Zurich.

Rhone-Isar. Geneva—Berne—Zurich—Lindau—Munich. Through Switzerland and part of Bavaria by day most of the way. Dining car in Switzerland. About 9 hours for nearly 400 miles.

Norgepilen and Sverigepilen. Oslo—Stockholm. Twin trains connecting the two Scandinavian capitals—lake and woodland scenery most of the way. Approx. 6½ hours.

Mare Nostrum. Barcelona—Tarragona—Valencia—Alicante. Down much of Spain's Mediterranean coast and then inland. A Talgo train with a buffet car runs throughout the year, daily. Approx. 10 hours for the journey.

Transalpin. Basel—Zurich—Innsbruck—Salzburg—Linz—Vienna. One of the best trains in Europe for mountain scenery, most of which is in daylight throughout the year. Limited accommodation. Reservation essential. Approx. 10 hours.

Vesuvio (T.E.E.). Milan—Bologna—Florence—Rome—Naples. A varied route from northern to southern Italy. Runs south in daylight all the way throughout the year, leaving Milan mid-morning and arriving in Naples late afternoon. Traveling time about 7½ hours.

City to City Expresses

In addition to the "scenic routes" mentioned above, there are also many excellent fast expresses connecting most of Europe's main cities, including those in Great Britain and Ireland. Here are a few that are of particular interest to the holiday traveler:

Aberdonian. London—York—Newcastle—Edinburgh—Dundee—Aberdeen. Daily restaurant car train linking the national capital with the "oil boom" city of Scotland. Total journey takes about eight hours for the 535 miles. Also the "Night Aberdonian" on the same route with first- and second-class sleepers but not serving Newcastle.

Blue Train. Paris—Marseille—Cannes—Nice—Ventimiglia. One of the most famous trains on the continent—all sleeping car-dining cars—dining car all the way—overnight journey.

Brabant (T.E.E.). Paris—Brussels. Non-stop (passports checked en route) between the two capitals—one of several similar expresses—very fast—2 hours 25 minutes.

Nymphenburg. Munich—Frankfurt—Wiesbaden—Bonn—Cologne—Dortmund—Hannover. One of Germany's "Inter-City" first-class-only expresses. Dining car throughout the entire journey. Takes just under nine hours for the 596 miles. Runs daily.

Enterprise. Belfast—Dublin. Several-times-daily expresses connecting the two cities. One in the morning and one in the early evening each way are non-stop —buffet car on each one.

Etoile du Nord and **Ile de France** (T.E.E.). Amsterdam—Rotterdam—Antwerp—Brussels—Paris. Twin trains running in each direction—no stop at frontiers (passports checked on board). Five hours' travel.

Freccia della Laguna. Rome—Florence—Bologna—Venice. Fastest rail service connecting these cities. Leave Rome at lunch time, arrive Venice for dinner. Runs daily. Reservation essential. Total time under 6 hours.

Le Capitole (T.E.E.). Paris—Limoges—Cahors—Toulouse. Twice daily fast *rapides* linking the French capital with the city of Toulouse within sight of the Pyrenees. One departs breakfast time, the other early evening. Opposite services at approx same times. Takes around 6 hours for the 445 mile journey, one of the fastest in Europe.

Palatino. Paris—Rome. Leaves each city in the early evening, arrives just after breakfast—sleeping cars all the way—dining car attached for dinner and breakfast. Inclusive tickets can cover journey, sleeper and meals.

Royal Scot. London—Glasgow. A long-established daylight express running every day in the year. Takes 5 hours for the 400-mile journey. Slower on Sundays.

Parsifal (T.E.E.). Paris—Cologne—Dortmund—Hamburg. A daylight express connecting several important cities. Also stops at Bremen. Total time 9½ hours.

Prinz Eugen (T.E.E.). Vienna—Nurnberg—Hannover—Bremen. Only T.E.E. go to the Austrian capital. Dining car all the way. Northbound route in daylight throughout most of the year. Takes about 10½ hours.

Puerta del Sol. Paris—Madrid. Sleeping cars on this train go through all the way—day coach passengers change at frontier—dining car all the way. Fastest service between the two cities. Under 15 hours. Inclusive ticket can cover journey, sleeper and meals.

Car Trains

Parallel with the development of the vast network of fast motorways throughout much of western Europe, the various railway systems have built up a service of "car trains". These fall into two categories—day travel and night travel. In both cases the car travels with you on specially constructed wagons. By night you have the choice of ordinary coaches, couchette cars or full sleeping cars. By day there are both first and second class coaches. Where timings are appropriate these trains carry a dining or buffet car or on some services "mini-bar" facilities.

Some of these trains are international connecting two or more centres while others run entirely within one country such as France and Germany. offers around 115 routes in Europe and about 25 in the U.K. Advance booking is advisable and essential in high season although in the offpeak periods places can often be found on the day of travel. Please note that most of these services run once or twice or in some cases three times a week. A very few offer daily services. All are in full swing in summer while many operate throughout the year. Bookings can be made through the appropriate railway offices in the U.S.A., Canada and Britain or from main travel agents. Last minute bookings are best made at the station of departure.

General Information

It is not possible to generalize with any degree of accuracy about cost of rail travel, as rates vary from country to country and according to the type of ticket issued. As a guide rule however, the farther you go, the cheaper the cost per mile becomes. It is more economic to book for long distances, then break your journey en route, than to buy individual tickets for each section of the journey. For example, if you bought a first-class ticket from London to Vienna, this would cost approx. $130 for the entire journey, including the North Sea ferry crossing. With this ticket, you could stop over, for example, in Amsterdam, Cologne, Frankfurt, Munich and Salzburg, all at no extra cost. But if you took individual tickets between each of these places, the total could be nearly half again as much. As you can see, there is a saving!

There are, however, certain restrictions on breaking your journey in some countries, and you should always enquire about these from a travel agent or main line railway station. Certain high-speed expresses such as all the T.E.E. trains require supplementary fares varying according to the distance traveled. But in no cases are these very high. All are clearly marked in the timetables and the supplementary tickets should be purchased before getting on the train, although in some cases this can be done after boarding.

Alas, with increased fares during the last two years the cost of first-class rail travel has gone up noticeably. This now is coming close to economy-class excursion return air fares on many routes and indeed in some cases first-class rail travel (on a return basis) is actually dearer than the equivalent economy air fare. It is however very much cheaper than first-class air travel (but then what is not?). As I stated earlier, second class fares are anything from 30% to 50% cheaper than first-class, but because of the big fare differential in different countries and on different types of tickets this is a wide generalization. Reservations are required on many trains and I would certainly advise it whenever possible, particularly during the busy periods. The amount is small, being between the equivalent of 65p. and £1 depending on the rate of exchange. Reservations can be made at main line stations and many travel agencies.

Concessions on fares are also given to children, the rates varying according to age and from one country to another. Roughly speaking, children under 3 (under 4 or 5 in some countries) travel free and those up to 10, 12, 14 or 15 (according to the country) for half price. On international tickets, travel is usually free under 4 and half rate between 4 and 11 years, inclusive.

The free baggage allowance again varies, but is always very substantial. You can send registered baggage on ahead of you even through international customs. We advise this if you are traveling a long distance by rail and have a lot to carry. Enquire at the station of departure.

In some cases, too, train tickets are interchangeable for bus travel over certain sectors. This also applies to some river steamer services, such as on the Rhine. With the last mentioned, for example, if you had a ticket from Dusseldorf to Frankfurt, you could sail on the Rhine for part of the way. Full information about interchanges (which, of course you must arrange in advance) can be got from the mainline stations and leading rail ticket agencies.

In all countries there are special cheap tickets for holiday travel. These sometimes involve using certain trains or traveling at certain times or going by certain routes. In other cases, they allow you unlimited travel within a certain period. Enquire locally on your arrival in the country.

Money-Saving Rail Passes

If you plan to do a lot of traveling around in western Europe, we suggest that you get a *Eurailpass*. This is a convenient, all-inclusive ticket that can save you money on over 100,000 miles of railroads and railroad-operated buses, ferries, river and lake steamers, hydrofoils, and some Mediterranean crossings in 15 countries of western Europe (excluding the United Kingdom, and Ireland) It provides the holder with unlimited travel at rates of: 15 days for $180; 21 days for $220; 1 month for $270; 2 months for $380; 3 months for $450; and 2nd-class Youthpass (anyone up to age 26) fare of 2 months for $250. Children under 12 go for half-fare, under 4 go free. These prices cover first-class passage for the Trans Europe Express and other services. Available only if you live outside Europe or North Africa. The pass must be bought from an authorized agent in the Western Hemisphere or Japan before you leave for Europe. Apply through your travel agent; or the general agents for North America: French National Railroads, Eurailpass Division, 610 Fifth Avenue, New York, N.Y. 10020; the German Federal Railroad, 630 Fifth Ave., New York 10020 and 45 Richmond Street, W., Toronto, Ontario M5H 1Z2, Canada. Also through the Italian and Swiss railways. To get full value from your pass, be sure not to have it date-stamped until you actually use it for the first time. For complete details, write to Eurailpass, c/o WBA, 51 Ridgefield Ave., Staten Island, N.Y. 10304.

Excellent value as the Eurailpass is it should be remembered that it is essentially for those who plan to do a lot of traveling. If you only want to make say two or three journeys it is best to purchase the tickets as required. In some countries if you travel a certain distance on a return trip or circular trip basis and stay a minimum length of time (generally just a few days) you can get reductions on the standard fares. For example in France if you travel more than 1500 kms. and spend five days or more in the country you get a 20% reduction on the normal fare.

For travel in Great Britain (England, Scotland and Wales only), you can purchase a *Britrailpass*, which again allows you unlimited rail (and associated ferryboat and bus) travel for certain periods. For 2nd-class travel the cost for 7 days is $65, for 14 days $95, for 21 days $125, and for one month $150. For 1st-class travel, the cost for 7 days is $85, for 14 days $120, for 21 days $150 and for a month $170. Reduced rates for children. In addition to these, young people (ages 14-22) can also obtain *Britrail Youth Passes,* which cost $55 for 7 days, $85 for 14 days, $100 for 21 days and $125 for one month, all for unlimited mileage in 2nd class.

All of these passes and coupons must be purchased in North America or Japan and are for Western Hemisphere and Japan residents only. Apply to BritRail Travel International Ltd., 270 Madison Ave., New York, N.Y. 10016; or 510 West Sixth Street, Los Angeles, Calif.; 333 N. Michigan Ave., Chicago Ill. 60601; or U.K. Building, 409 Granville Street, Vancouver 2, B.C.; or 55 Eglinton Avenue East, Toronto 4, Ontario, Canada. *Please note that these British arrangements are subject to review.*

Young people with a desire to travel extensively in Europe by rail should purchase an *Inter-Rail Card.* This is available to anyone under 23 years of age and the holder is entitled to unlimited second-class rail travel (along with connecting ferry and in certain cases bus services) in no fewer than 18 countries in western and central Europe plus Morocco. The card also allows half-fare travel on all rail services in the U.K. and Ireland and on the Sealink ferries connecting the British Isles with the continent. The Inter-Rail Card is valid for one calender month and can be purchased at most mainline stations, rail ticket agencies and travel agents. You must show evidence of age on purchase and the card is NOT transferable.

A *Senior Citizen Pass,* entitling older travelers to discounts of from 1/3 to 1/2, is now offered by many West European countries, with others expected to follow suit; check with each country's tourist bureau. A passport-size photo is required for the card, which must be applied for in each individual country.

Most of the European railways issue free informative brochures about their networks. These can be obtained from the addresses given or from the appropriate national tourist offices. All, of course, also issue various timetables, some publishing special condensed tourist editions. These again can be got from the addresses given.

Alternatively, students of any age and young people up to the age of 21 wishing to purchase their tickets one at a time should contact *Transalpino,* 224 Shaftesbury Avenue, London WC2, where, upon proof of age or student status, rail travel can be booked from one to any other of 14 European countries at reductions of up to 50% on normal fares.

If you want to be really knowledgeable about train times in Europe (including Gt. Britain and Ireland), then you should purchase *Cook's Continental Timetable.* Packed with details and lots of information, it is issued monthly. Available in the U.S.A. from: Travel Library, P.O. Box 249, La Canada, Calif. 91011. In Britain, order from: Thomas Cook Ltd., Timetable Publishing Office, P.O. Box 36, Peterborough, England PE3 6SB. Or the timetable is available from any Cook's branch for £3.20, including postage.

USEFUL ADDRESSES: Full information on rail services within the under-mentioned countries can be got from the following addresses (in all other cases, contact the national tourist office of the country concerned):

Austrian Federal Railways, 545 Fifth Avenue, New York City 10017.

Belgian National Railroads, 720 Fifth Avenue, New York City 10019.

BritRail Travel International Inc., 270 Madison Avenue, New York City 10016

French National Railroads, 610 Fifth Avenue, New York City 10020.

German Federal Railroad, 630 Fifth Avenue, New York City, 10020

Italian State Railways, (CIT Travel Service, Inc. Official Pass. Agent), 500 Fifth Avenue, New York City 10036.

Netherlands Railways, 576 Fifth Avenue, New York City 10036.

Norwegian State Railways, 21 Cockspur St., London S.W.1.

Scandinavian Travel Bureau, Inc., 75 Rockefeller Plaza, New York, N.Y. 10019.

Swiss Federal Railways, 608 Fifth Avenue, New York City 10020.

MOTORING ON THE CONTINENT

by
FRANCES HOWELL

(A member of the British Guild of Motoring Writers, Frances Howell has driven all the major European highways and thousands of miles of its byways in pursuit of material for her regular column in Homes and Gardens *and her many other articles on traveling by car.)*

Even people who don't much care for motoring agree that it is the best way to travel in Europe. In other continents, where the distances are greater, the road system perhaps not so extensive or the climate less kindly, other forms of transport may well be preferable—but in Europe, going by car is the thing to do.

The chief reason for this is, in a word, freedom. Freedom from the discipline of public transport schedules; freedom to stop and stare wherever and whenever you wish. Freedom to follow your own, maybe insane, route and at your own speed; to choose your own hotels; freedom from the tyranny of a suitcase which will hold and must weigh just so much and no more. With a car everything goes, even if it has to be carried loose, nor is there any limit set upon your buying something big and bulky if you wish.

This freedom is, however, something more than just a word. Auto travel really does offer the best value in pleasure travel, for in no other way can you see so much for your money. Fly to your destination and you save time and energy, but you see nothing of the land en route. Go by train and you will see much more but will still be moving too fast and are tied to the track, which invariably goes through the seamier side of cities. In a car, you can go by one pleasant route and return by another.

What is possibly more important, you can escape from noise and encourage economy by searching out country hotels away from main roads. Even if your interest lies in a city, it is increasingly worth while on both counts to find accommodation just outside it. Anyone who has never endured a night in a room overlooking a narrow street forming a part of some continental highway route can have no conception of the misery this can mean.

Economy and Convenience

Many people question the costs of taking a car abroad, but this need be no barrier, providing that the journey is more than just a short hop. Clearly, to take a car from London to Paris would be an extravagance, and to take it to Italy if your one idea is to get there as fast as possible would be boring and foolish. It used to be possible to make a reasoned comparison between traveling by road or 2nd-class rail, and to find that a journey of, say, 900 miles in a 14 ft. car would be more expensive than rail with one or two people but less expensive with three or four passengers. (This would be allowing for two overnight stops but no sleeping accommodation on the train, and not including meals which have to be eaten somewhere in either case.) If you elevate the train travel to something approaching the comfort of car travel, say by going 1st-class sleeper, then the differential is immediately reduced almost to nil. But it is very risky to make comparisons of that sort now, because apart from the surprise fare supplements that are liable to be levied on public transport, higher petrol prices knock the motorist and the speed limits at present operating almost throughout Europe must add, perhaps critically, to journey times. But there remains the money-to-value ratio, which must be subjective.

Then there is the question of parking—what to do with the car when you are not actually using it? This does not often present a problem. If you are staying in a smart hotel in the center of town, it is probable that the porter will be able to direct you to a garage, possibly belonging to the hotel, or take the car himself to park for you. This, of course, always costs a little money. Small hotels in side streets seem to have a facility for producing parking space whenever it is wanted, and naturally, country hotels are surrounded by space, though not always free. When using a car for sight-seeing, there is sometimes a temporary difficulty, but most places of tourist interest have parking places beside them, and arrivals and departures are more or less incessant. It is, naturally, wise to lock the car when leaving it—more so in some countries than others.

Some people also feel that driving long distances is very tiring and not their idea of a holiday. It is, of course, possible to reduce the long distance driving by taking the car on a train.

Package Tours

For either the first-timer or the idle and luxury-loving, this mode of motor travel has much in its favor. *Thos. Cook,* who were the first travel agency to accept that the motoring loner has come to stay and to cater for him, are probably holding their lead in this particular business. From them, a motorist can buy a complete holiday consisting of documents, special insurance, get-you-home service, channel transportation, en route and destination hotel bookings, maps and a planned route. Everything except fuel and personal extras is paid in advance, thus relieving the motorist of any financial anxiety and most of the need to struggle with foreign currencies and languages.

Such a trip will be custom built. So also can it be by *Erna Low, Ltd.,* which specializes in individual arrangements; but operators such as *Inghams Travel* and *Cosmos,* who sell holidays through almost any travel agent, are not prepared to deviate from the scheduled packages published in their brochures. Several of the car ferry companies also offer inclusive holidays, as for example the *Bergen Line* in Norway, *DFDS* in Denmark, *Tor Line* in Sweden. The *AA* will also provide travel assistance, while the *RAC* has its own complete travel service.

On the whole, the pre-paid motoring holiday works out well. It is not the cheapest way to travel, but neither is it by any means the most expensive. It deprives the real pioneer of the pleasure of making horrible discoveries, but it saves time and makes everything beautifully easy.

Car Hire

Car hire is possible in every country, with *Avis* and *Hertz* operating in all west European countries, plus Yugoslavia (Avis also in all East Europe), and *Godfrey Davis* in all of Western Europe, plus Yugoslavia, Hungary, Turkey, Israel etc. Local hire firms and their rates are mentioned under each country heading in this book. Some London firms, notably *Lane's Travel Service, Ltd.,* 251 Brompton Road, S.W.3, offer a most economical fly- and self-drive holiday package consisting of air fare to one city, return from another, use of hire car for 14 days and bed-and-breakfast hotel accommodation.

The cost of car hire with unlimited mileage, for cheapest cars, including insurance, varies from around £59 per week in Britain to 420 SF in Switzerland, often with special rates in capital cities. Island cars no longer come cheaper. The hire tax, if included, can be so high that it is worth planning to hire in a low levy country whenever possible. Some firms also offer reduced "holiday hire" rates for 14 days. Each firm has its own ideas about rental terms, and they may vary between countries. The minimum age may be 21 or 25, the max. 69, 70, or no limit. In Britain, a license must have been held for 12 months; in Germany, 6 will do. Endorsed licenses are accepted at the discretion of the company. Notice that insurance cover provided is usually pretty basic and could be costly. Lists of accredited car hire firms can be had from the *AAA* at 28 East 78th Street, New York, N.Y. 10021; Grosvenor Square, London W.1., or 9 rue de la Paix, Paris; *RAC,* 83–85 Pall Mall, London S.W.1., the *AA,* Fanum House, Leicester Square, London W.C.2 or from branches of *Thos. Cook.*

Car Purchase

For Americans taking, say, a two to eight week vacation the cheapest method is to rent a car. If you're staying longer, it would be better to buy a car abroad. Renting or buying a car and later selling it back are the methods preferred by most long-term motoring tourists. There are various types of car purchase plans, which also apply to motor caravans: Outright Purchase; Guaranteed Repurchase in which the full price of the car is paid but the company guarantees to buy back the car after a certain period of time for a predetermined price in dollars; Budget Plan, in which only the depreciation, financing and interest charges, cost of licensing and registration, documentation and insurance are paid for the period of time you use the auto. European cars are excellent, constructed for fine performance on European roads and mountains. They consume about half as much gas as U.S. cars. One piece of advice: don't buy a used car from a local citizen, as you will be paying for the taxes which the original owner had to cough up as a local buyer.

Here are firms who have cars for rent and/or purchase:

Auto-Europe Inc., 770 Lexington Ave., New York 10021.
Avis Rent A Car System, 1114 Avenue of the Americas, New York, N.Y. 10036.
British Leyland Motors, 600 Willow Tree Rd., Leonia, N.J. 07605.
Car-Tours in Europe, Inc., 516 Fifth Ave., New York 10036. (Also Century City, Los Angeles; 209 Post St., San Francisco; 6 N. Michigan Ave., Chicago.)
Europe by Car, 291 Geary St., San Francisco, Calif. 94102; 45 Rockefeller Plaza New York 10020, Chicago, Honolulu, Seattle, Washington D.C., Los Angeles, Calif., Northfield, Minn., and Coral Gables, Fla.
Fiat-U.S. Representatives, Inc., 375 Park Ave., New York 10022.
Renault Inc., 100 Sylvan Avenue, Englewood Cliffs, N. J. 07632.
Volkswagen of America, Tourist Delivery Dept. F-1, 818 Sylvan Ave., Englewood Cliffs, N.J.

European Road Conditions

Going in search of way-out hotels leads drivers onto secondary, and even lesser, roads. There is no need to fear excursions of this sort in most west European countries; in fact, secondary roads in many are now preferable to their trunk or "A" roads on account of the heavy commercial traffic the latter carry. Apart from the east European countries, where first-class roads tend to be second-class and second-class better left alone, the only countries where unclassified roads should be treated with respect are Spain, Yugoslavia, Greece, Finland and the north of both Sweden and Norway. In mountainous regions such as Austria, Switzerland, the French Alps and the Italian Dolomites, secondary roads are slow, often narrow, but the surfaces are usually good.

When planning a route, it is convenient to know that on good, open continental roads, it is generally accepted that one kilometer per minute (60 km./hour or 37 mph.) is a reasonable average to maintain. When there are long motorways, as in Holland, Germany, France, Austria and Italy, the speed will be higher, particularly in Germany, where the Autobahn net is extensive, although often heavy with traffic in summer, particularly on week-ends. The Belgian motorway network remains patchy and although the gap between Brussels and Liege is now plugged, it is probably still best when motoring eastward across Belgium from the coast to avoid Brussels—unless you want to visit the capital—by using the new motorway which starts east of Ghent to pass south of Antwerp, there to join up with the old E 39 to Liege and thence into Germany. Rush hour traffic can, however, be heavy.

The great north-south French autoroute is now fully operative between Lille and Marseille, a total distance of 642 miles. This motorway is very fast and could be covered from end to end in just under eight hours' driving before the 87 m.p.h. speed limit was introduced; that included circling Paris on the new Boulevard Périphérique, which is now completed. However, the roads leading into Paris, and the Boulevard itself, are often choked with traffic in the rush hours. Tolls for the whole trip would amount to over £20. In the southern half of France, many of the roads are winding and not very wide, which, of course, also applies to all mountainous countries, such as Norway, Switzerland, Austria and Northern Italy, which all now have speed limits.

All over Europe, there is now a network of International Highways, designated with the letter "E" and then the road number, in black on green. E5, for instance, runs from Ostend, Belgium to Istanbul, Turkey, by way of Germany, Austria, Hungary, Yugoslavia and Greece. Other "E" roads of interest to motorists starting out from Britain or Western Europe are E1, from the UK to Italy; E2, UK to Brindisi (for car ferries to Greece); E8, UK to Poland. These roads are not, by any means, all expressways or motorways or all of the same standard, but the various countries are concerned to see that they eventually become so.

British roads are not so atrocious as many Americans fear. There are now a couple of thousand miles of excellent motorways; the trunk roads have been greatly improved and the "B" roads, provided that you are not in a hurry, are delightful. They can boast the smoothest surfaces in Europe, and that goes for the wilds of Scotland and Wales as well. The British, Irish, and Cypriots drive on the left; all the rest on the right.

Road maps are available, free, from every national tourist office, or are on sale in offices of the AA, RAC and the AAA. Several petroleum companies also supply maps cheaply.

MOTORING ROUTES

Here are some outline routes with some idea of the *mileages*. In conjunction with good touring maps, they will enable you to plan a rough touring timetable. To reap the maximum enjoyment from your trip, do not hesitate to make detours from these routes to sample what takes your interest. The suggested time schedules provide ample time for such detours. In most cases, these times can be reduced if you exceed an *average* speed of 30 m.p.h.

PARIS—RIVIERA. This is probably the most popular holiday journey in Europe. There are three separate routes through widely differing regions or auto-route throughout.

(a) *Via Rhône Valley.* One night en route. Fontainebleau via Auxerre, Tournus, Lyon, Bollène, Avignon, Marseille—or Pont St. Esprit, Nîmes, Marseille—St. Raphael, Nice, Menton. Total distance Paris-Marseille, about 495 miles.

Note: to by-pass Sens and Auxerre you can take a section of the Autoroute du Sud, cutting the distance by about 25 miles and driving time by over an hour.

(b) *Massif Central Route.* About 515 miles. One night. Via Moulin, Vichy, Le Puy, Pont St. Esprit, Remoulins, Avignon, Les Baux, Marseille.

(c) *Route des Alpes.* Two nights. Troyes, Dijon, Geneva, Grenoble, Sisteron, Cannes. Distance about 615 miles.

PARIS-PYRENEES-ANDORRA-COSTA BRAVA. Mileage about 660. Three nights. Via Orleans, Limoges, Toulouse, Foix, Bourg Madame, frontier, Ripoll, Barcelona or eastwards from Toulouse via Carcassone, Perpignan, Côte Vermeille and Rosas.

PARIS-BIARRITZ-PORTUGAL OR MALAGA. Four nights, Chartres, Tours, Bordeaux, Biarritz, Burgos, Salamanca, Ciudad Rodrigo, frontier, Guarda, Coimbra, Lisbon. For Malaga go south at Burgos through Madrid, Cordoba or Granada to Malaga. Mileage about 1200 and 1100.

PARIS-FRANKFURT. About 480 miles. One night. Nancy, Strasbourg, Baden-Baden, Stuttgart, Frankfurt.

PARIS-CHERBOURG. Mileage 200. Autoroute to Evreaux, then Liseaux, Caen, Bayeux, Cherbourg.

PARIS-BRUSSELS. Mileage 185. Via Soissons, Laon, Maubeuge, frontier, Mons, Brussels, or autoroute all the way—170 miles.

CHANNEL COAST-PYRENEES (Touring Route). Two nights. Approximately 685 miles. Start from Rouen, thence Evreux, Chartres, Vendôme, Blois, Châteauroux, Tulle, Albi, Carcassone, Aix-les-Thermes.

CHANNEL PORTS-SWITZERLAND. One night. Calais, Arras, Cambrai, St. Quentin, Rheims, Châlons-sur-Marne, Chaumont, Vesoul, then to Basel. Approximately 535 miles.

BLACK FOREST ALTERNATIVE. From Rheims to Nancy, St. Die, Colmar, Freiburg, Basel. 260 miles.

CHANNEL COAST-AUSTRIA. 2 nights, About 700 miles. As to Basel, then Zurich, Liechtenstein, Feldkirch, Innsbruck. Alternatively, Motorway throughout from Ostend via Germany.

HOOK OF HOLLAND-FRANKFURT (Touring route). One night. The Hague, Amsterdam, Utrecht, Arnhem, frontier, Wesel, Duisburg, autobahn to Cologne and cross to west bank of Rhine, Bonn, Koblenz, Mainz, Frankfurt. 357 miles.

FRANKFURT-ROME (Touring route). Six nights. Karlsruhe, Freiburg, Titisee, Waldshut, Radolfzell, Konstanz, Meersburg, Füssen, Garmisch, Innsbruck, Brenner Pass, Bolzano, Trento, Verona, Bologna, or Verona, Venice, Bologna, Florence, Siena, Viterbo, Rome. Or motorway all the way.

ROME-CANNES. Two nights. Pisa, Rapallo, Genoa, San Remo, Nice, Cannes 478. *Alternatively,* autostrada throughout.

ROME-BRINDISI-ATHENS. Travel-while-you-sleep route requires one night only and reduces the overland distance by about 1/3. Rome-Naples-Brindisi 370. Overnight car ferry, to Igoumenitsa, continue to Gulf of Corinth ferry (or arrive by longer Brindisi-Patras ferry) then motorway to Athens. Total about 800 miles.

PARIS-BARCELONA-MADRID-MALAGA. Four nights. Route 20 from Paris to Barcelona 630, thence to Zaragoza, Madrid, Malaga. Total mileage: 1,158.

CHANNEL COAST OR PARIS TO SCANDINAVIA. Two nights. Lille, Antwerp, Breda, Arnhem, Hamburg, Flensburg, Kolding, Odense, Copenhagen, 780 miles. Alternative route Hamburg: Lubeck-Puttgarden ferry. On to Stockholm via Halsingborg ferry, Jonkoping and Norrkoping, 400. Ferry direct to Helsinki or via Turku (Abo).

COPENHAGEN-OSLO-BERGEN. Two nights. Ferry to Hälsingborg, Göteborg, Halden, Oslo, Geilo, Bergen. About 655 miles.

ARCTIC HIGHWAY-MIDNIGHT SUN-HELSINKI. Ten nights. Oslo, Lillehammer, Dombas, Trondheim, Namsos, Grong, Mosjøen, Arctic Circle,

Bodø, Mörsvik, Narvik, Tromsø, Skibotn 1225. Finnish frontier, Kilpisjärvi, Muonio, Tornio, Oulu, Vaasa, Pori, Turku, Helsinki 2180; or **TROMSØ-STOCKHOLM.** Four nights. To Tornio, Swedish frontier bridge to Sundsvall, Söderhamm, Gävle, Stockholm 1124.

The average speed is rather lower in northern Norway than in most countries owing to ferries across fjords.

LONDON-NORTH WALES. Touring route—Aylesbury, Stratford-on-Avon, Worcester, Rhayader, Aberystwyth, Dolgellau, Caernarvon, Betwys-y-Coed, Llangollen, Ludlow, Hereford, Gloucester, Oxford, London. About 500 miles.

LONDON TO WEST AND SOUTHERN ENGLAND 3 nights touring. Motorway to Taunton, then Exeter, Dartmoor, Plymouth, Torquay, Exeter, Salisbury, Winchester, Tunbridge Wells, Canterbury, London. About 600 miles.

LONDON TO SCOTLAND. Motorway to Doncaster, A1 to Darlington, A68 to Edinburgh. 370 miles. Alternatively, by rail night car sleeper, 7½ hours.

EDINBURGH TO LONDON (Touring route). Two nights. Carlisle, Chester, Shrewsbury, Ludlow, Hereford, Gloucester, Oxford, London 400; or Shrewsbury, Stratford-on-Avon, Oxford.

IN EASTERN EUROPE

VIENNA-BUDAPEST-BELGRADE-BUCHAREST. Enter Hungary at Nichelsdorf/Hegyes Halom, Gyor, Budapest, Szeged, Novisad, Belgrade, 450 miles, 2 nights. Alternatively, continue across Hungary to Oradea in Romania, then Cluj, Brasov, Polesti, Bucharest. 525 miles, 3 nights.

VIENNA-CRACOW-WARSAW. Three nights. Cross into Czechoslovakia at Bratislava. Then Zilina into Poland at Cieszyn 232. On to Cracow, Kielce, Radom, Warsaw 490.

BERLIN-WARSAW. One night. Frankfurt-on-the-Oder, cross into Poland at Slubice, then via Poznan to Warsaw. 341 miles.

NUREMBERG-PRAGUE-WARSAW-MOSCOW. Follow International Route E12 into Czechoslovakia and to Prague, then E14 into Poland and to Warsaw, then E8 to the Russian frontier at Brest, thence to Minsk, Smolensk to Moscow. About 1300 miles slow going.

BELGRADE-SOFIA-ISTANBUL. Two nights. Belgrade (Beograd), Nis, Sofia, Plovdiv, Edirne, Istanbul. Total: 600 miles.

Mountain Passes

There are close to a hundred mountain passes in Europe, some of them fantastic feats of road engineering, rising to heights of 9,000 ft. and more. Many of them are obstructed well after the snow season. Below we list some of the more scenic and useful highways, and the annual periods when they may be closed and ascent should not be attempted. Their opening depends on the weather, and local guidance should be sought before starting the drive. Asterisks show passes where alternative road or railroad tunnel transportation is available. "Closed occasionally" refers mainly to the winter months.

Austria	Route	Closed to traffic
Arlberg.........	St. Anton-Langen................	not closed*
Grossglockner ...	Heiligenblut-Bruck *alternative* by always-open Felbertauern toll tunnel..	Oct. 15-end of May*
Katschberg......	Villach-Mautendorf *alternative* road tunnel (toll)....................	intermittently closed*
Plöcken.........	Carnic Alps.....................	closed occasionally
Tauern	Radstadt-Mautendorf.............	closed occasionally

France (French Alps)

Allos...........	Barcelonette-Colmars.............	early Nov.-late May
Galibier	Valloire—Monetier-Les-Bains	Oct.-June
Iseran	Val d'Isère-Lanslebourg...........	mid-Oct.-late June
Izoard..........	Briançon-Arvieux.................	late Oct.-late June
Larche	La Condamine-Argentera (Italy)....	closed occasionally
Lautaret	Briançon-La Grave...............	closed occasionally
Mont Cenis	Lanslebourg-Susa (Italy) *alternatively,* rail through tunnel.	Nov.-closed occasionally
Petit St. Bernard	Bourg-Saint-Maurice—Aosta (It.)...	mid-Oct.-late June*

Road tunnel under Mont-Blanc between Chamonix and Courmayeur (It.) takes traffic all year. Toll.

France (Pyrénées)

Pourtalet........	Laruns-Sallent (Spain)	Nov.-June
Puymorens......	Aix-les-Thermes—Bourg Madame ..	closed occasionally*
Quillane	Formiguères-Mont Louis..........	occasionally closed
Somport	Oloron-Sainte-Marie—Jaca (Spain)..	not closed

Italy

Costalunga......	Bolzano-Vigo di Fassa............	seldom closed
Falzagero	Cortina d'Ampezzo-Andraz........	closed occasionally
Monte Croce (Plöcken)	Kötschach-Paluzza...............	closed occasionally
Pordoi..........	Canazei-Cortina d'Ampezzo	closed occasionally
Stelvio..........	Bormio-Gomagoi	usually mid-Oct.-early July
Tre Croci	Cortina d'Ampezzo-Pelos..........	not closed
Gran San Barnardo (Alps)	Aosta-Martigny (Switz.)...........	late Oct.-mid June*
Spluga..........	Chiavenna-Splügen (Switz.)........	Nov.-May

Spain

Navacerrada.....	Madrid-La Granja	mid-Nov.-mid-April

Switzerland

Albula..........	Filisur-La Punt..................	Nov.-early June*
Bernina.........	Pontresina-Tirano (Italy)..........	sometimes closed Winter toll
Flüela..........	Davos-Süsch	not closed, small winter toll

Forclaz.........	Martigny-Chamonix (France)......	not closed
Furka..........	Gletsch-Andermatt..............	mid-Oct.-mid-June
Great St. Bernard	Martigny-Aosta (Italy)............	late Oct.-mid-June

(St. Bernard *Tunnel* takes all-year road traffic—toll charge.

Grimsel.........	Gletsch-Meiringen	mid-Oct.-mid-June
Klausen........	Altdorf-Glarus Canton (east of Lucerne).........................	early Nov.-early June
Lukmanier......	Disentis-Biasca	Nov.-mid-June
Nufenen........	Ul Richen-Airolo	Oct.-mid-June
Oberlap.........	Andermatt-Disentis	mid Oct.-mid-May
Pillon..........	Le Sepey-Gstaad	not closed
San Bernardino..	Hinterrhein-Mesocco	mid-Oct.-mid-June*
St. Gotthard.....	Altdorf-Bellinzona	mid Oct.-mid-May*
Simplon........	Brigue-Domodossola (Italy).......	not closed

Traffic Regulations

For the most part, the old rule, "priority of traffic from the right" (*priorité à droite*), is no longer practised on country roads, but is still maintained to varying degrees in cities. Never, however, rely on a car, cart or bicycle to refrain from darting out in front of you if its driver has a will to do so. Where two country roads of equal importance cross one another, traffic from the right *usually* has right of way, but most such cross roads have signs to indicate who has priority. In France, however, it is *always* priority of traffic from the right, country roads or not, *unless* the road coming from the right has a stop signal (or obviously unless a small secondary road crosses a main thoroughfare, but there are *always* signs). For detailed instruction on such matters see the AAA, RAC or AA handbooks. Priority from the right is not accepted in Britain except on roundabouts (rotaries), and then it *is* from the right even though the British drive on the left.

In many countries, it is now obligatory to carry a portable, red reflective triangle, which must be put out on the road well behind a car which has broken down and is in danger of causing an obstruction. Such triangles can be hired at frontiers, but it is cheaper and less trouble to buy one for about $3.

In some European countries CB radios are completely forbidden, in others they are subject to very strict regulations and limits. Regulations vary so much from one country to another that your best bet is to give up completely any idea you may have had of using a CB in Europe.

Any regulations differing from the usual, including speed limits, are mentioned in this book's motoring sections under the countries concerned.

Police Fines. In several countries, police are authorized to make on-the-spot fines for infringements of the traffic regulations. These may be as low as $4 or as high as $80, depending on country. *This goes for jay-walkers, too, in some places.* Among countries with spot-fining are: Andorra, Austria, Denmark, France, Germany, Holland, Italy, Luxembourg, Portugal, Spain.

Drinking and Driving. Laws on this are strict in many continental countries, with heavy fines or imprisonment. Scandinavia is particularly strict. The legal limits of the blood alcohol level vary according to country. In Czechoslovakia it has to be nil. So check with your motoring association before setting out. *Better still, don't drink and drive.*

Petroleum

Most of the brands familiar to both American and British drivers are to be found on the continent at widely differing prices. Very few countries have more than two octane ratings—*super* (or premium) and *ordinary* (or regular)—and only super is recommended for most American or British cars. Owners of cars which will go on lower octane ratings are always aware of it, and will know that their petrol will cost slightly less than the prices quoted under each country. Oil brands are also common to all countries but invariably cost more than they do in Britain; so best take a can with you. Tourist petrol coupons, giving a discount, are available for some countries. See under country chapter.

Documentation for Driving

For yourself, of course, a passport, and a driving license. Most countries will accept a national driving licence, but some require an *International Driving Permit* (cost, $3, £1.50). For details write to the American Automobile Association, 28 E. 78 St., New York, N.Y. 10021. Take your money and national license, and two passport type photographs to the AAA, AA or RAC for the Permit. In the U.S. you may go to any office of the AAA or you may apply by mail, for which allow about 2-3 weeks in your scheduling. For the car, a national mark plate (USA or GB for example), and an international motor insurance card, known as the *Green Card,* are necessary. The latter, not required in the UK, is valid in all west European countries and some in the east. For particulars, see the country chapter concerned. Yugoslavia does not require any documents at all. A Green Card is issued by the car owner's insurance company, at differing rates starting from £5 (app. $15 in U.S.), according to type of car and record of driver. Insurance bought at a frontier is for minimum legal cover only, and usually works out to be rather expensive. For Spain, it is advisable to have also a *Bail Bond,* in case of a serious accident, which might otherwise result in the car being impounded. Experts advise against relying on the EEC form of inter-Community car insurance.

For taking a caravan to the continent, you need an *International Camping Carnet,* 60¢ (25p), and *Customs Carnet,* $3.60 (£1.25), from the motor associations or the Caravan Club (Foreign Touring Service), East Grinstead House, W. Sussex.

Transportation to Europe

Americans: If you go to Europe on a ship that will take your car as *accompanied baggage* (as, for example, Cunard's QE 2) the rates go by weight. New York to Cherbourg, one way: up to 1500 lbs. for $525; 1501-2500 lbs. for $620; 2501-3500 lbs. for $710; 3501-4500 lbs. for $845; 4501-5500 lbs. for $940; all rates plus a $15 New York Port Authority surcharge for handling. If you ship your car separately, as *freight,* multiply the length, width and height to get the *volume in cubic feet,* then figure, for New York to Rotterdam, $0.67 per cubic foot plus a handling charge of about $12 per long ton (2240 lbs.). A number of companies handle such arrangements, among them: *Auto Overseas Ltd.,* 230 W. 41st St., New York, N.Y. 10036; *Ship-A-Car,* 219 W. 40th St., New York, N.Y. 10018; *Overseas Expediters, Inc.,* 90 Broad St., New York, N.Y. 10004; *General American Shippers,* Inc., 450 7th Avenue, Suite 307, New York, N.Y. 10001; *Transcar GMBH,* 205 West 34th Street, New York, N.Y. 10001. For car rentals in Europe, see earlier in chapter.

For the **British,** or Americans stopping off in Britain, there are numerous *sea* car ferry services and several *air* car ferries operating across-channel. All of these now have drive on/off facilities.

Car Ferries to the Continent.

There is an exhaustive list of ferries earlier in this section. All of them now have drive on/off systems. Prices range somewhat, depending on the length of voyage. In some cases return trips are cheaper, or the car rate becomes progressively lower with the number of passengers accompanying it. There are sometimes reduced off-season rates, when there are fewer crossings. *Olau* (Sheerness to Flushing) and *Brittany Ferries* (Portsmouth-St. Malo, Plymouth-Roscoff and Santander) offer some of the most competitive prices around as well as some of the best service.

Continental Transportation

There are now rail car-sleeper services operating between every major city and many provincial ones all over the continent to carry the car and its human cargo the first few hundred miles of their journey. This saves time and energy, but not money. It is possible in this way to transport a car from Scotland to Greece without touching it, except to drive it on and off ships and trains. Many of the trains start from towns on or near the English Channel and go to Switzerland, Austria, southern Germany, Italy (north and south), Yugoslavia and points in southern France stretching from the Côte d'Azur to the Atlantic, many serving as springboards to Spain and Portugal. They are mostly all night services.

Sea ferries also play a prominent part in European motor travel. There are around thirty Mediterranean ferries that carry cars to the islands, or between countries, as for example, Italy to Greece or over to Yugoslavia, or from one end of Italy to the other. In Scandinavia, there are two sorts of ferries: the small ones, which virtually form part of a road, particularly in Norway and Denmark, and the inter-country ferries, which connect Norway with Denmark and Sweden, Denmark with Sweden and Finland, Sweden with the other three, and Germany with all of them. Particulars can be had from the motoring associations and the countries concerned (through their tourist offices).

Motels

Practically every European country lays claim nowadays to possessing motels, but their ideas on what a motel *is* vary considerably. If a motel is thought to be a place where comfortable but fairly simple accommodation is offered, with cars parked alongside, and with constant availability of inexpensive meals, such places can be found in Sweden, Denmark, Switzerland, Holland and Austria. In France, they are luxurious and expensive (and to some extent in England also). In Germany, Italy and Yugoslavia, they are of high standard and reasonably priced, but in many cases it is difficult to see wherein lies the difference between such a "motel" and a "hotel".

Reputable motels are associated with the European Motel Federation, whose booklet giving details of member establishments can be had from E.M.F., Daxelhofersr. 18, 3000 Berne, Switzerland.

Hotels for the Motorist

There is possibly a wider selection of hotels on the continent of Europe than anywhere else in the world, because they range from the universally common palaces to mountain inns offering no more than two rooms, but perfectly clean and respectable. Obviously, there are some which are neither, and these may be small or large. The point is that in some other parts of the world it simply is not possible to stay in cheap hotels and enjoy it. In Western Europe, you can. For this reason, the motorist can safely go off into the unexplored areas to make his own discoveries. (This advice cannot, however, apply to hotels in eastern Europe, where the standard is not quite so high, and there is in any case a shortage of accommodation.)

One such discovery is castles. In 17 countries of Western Europe some 500 castles have been converted into castle-hotels. In period and style they range from feudal fortresses complete with moats and drawbridges to elegant, spacious chateaux of the Renaissance and Baroque periods. Rates equally range from the surprisingly modest on upwards. One thing that all these castles are likely to have in common, however, is that they were not located so as to be served by modern mass transportation. Hence they are ideal for the motorist, whose car allows him to seek the quiet, out-of-the-way spot that may have the most to offer. Most individual countries' national tourist offices can furnish lists of castle-hotels; but the whole subject is thoroughly covered in Robert Long's book *Castle Hotels of Europe,* published by the author at 634 Bellmore Avenue, East Meadow, L.I., N.Y. 11554. The 5th edition contains 465 photographs and costs $4.95, paperbound.

Out of season (that is, other than from mid-July to the first week in September), it is not necessary to pre-book hotel accommodation en route to your holiday destination, and not even when you arrive (unless it happens to be one of exceptional tourist popularity, or such a city as Strasbourg, which is almost permanently occupied with conferences). An exception to this rule has to be made when motoring in winter if the chosen holiday location is a sports center. En route hotels always have plenty of room in winter, but it is as well to check that there will be one open in the place where you are likely to want it. In summer it is advisable to start looking for overnight accommodation not later than six o'clock.

Villas

In some countries, it is possible to rent villas or apartments in resort areas by the week or two, or by the month. This does entail doing your own shopping and cooking but usually maid service is included in the rental. For more details in the U.S. on how to rent a villa or chalet contact:

At Home Abroad, Inc., 136 East 57th St., New York, N.Y. 10022, which has properties in England, Scotland, France, Italy, Spain, Majorca, Portugal, Greece,

Tangiers and Tunisia; or the national tourist office of the country in which you are interested. It will have material on organizations existing in that country but which do not have representives in the U.S.

Interchange, 888 Seventh Avenue Suite 400, New York, N.Y. 10019, and 26 Omaha Avenue, Toronto, Ontario M5J 1Z8 Canada, has nearly 2,000 privately owned rental properties available, from simple cottages to villas with pools and servants, many of them along the Mediterranean or Atlantic coasts of Europe, or in Britain and Scotland, where rates run from $100 to $200 a week. In Spain, a villa for 6 could run $160–$200 a week depending on the season. Interchange also arranges exchanges between property owners in North America and in Europe, as well as air travel and car rentals.

Rent Abroad, Inc., 300 Madison Avenue, New York, N.Y. 10017, both rents and sells villas, chalets and apartments in France, Spain, Portugal, Austria, Switzerland and Italy. Prices vary according to season, and in off-season villas and apartments are available for less than one month at a time.

Another possibility is to *exchange* holidays in your caravan, boat, chalet or home with Britons who want to visit the U.S.A. For details write to: *International Holiday Exchange,* 47 Hatherleigh Road, Rumney, Cardiff, Sth. Glam., United Kingdom. A similar organization is *Homex,* working in co-operation with British Airways, P.O. Box 27, London NW6. The fee for an entry in the Homex directory, published twice a year, is £6.

Tayling's Holiday Cottages, 14 High Street, Godalming, Surrey, England have over 850 properties from cottages to castles in Britain.

The following British agencies are members of the National Villa Association, 139 Strand, London W.C.2., who can recommend you to other reliable agencies.

Holiday Villas Ltd., 357 Strand, London W.C.2.
OSL (Owners' Services Ltd.), Broxbourne, Herts.
Swiss Chalets InterHome, 10 Sheen Rd., Richmond, Surrey.

Facts about Camping

If going by car is for two or more people the most economical way of traveling, camping is in many respects the most rewarding one, especially if you are the outdoor-type. Some of Europe's favorite camping regions (Scandinavia, the Mediterranean shores, the Alps) have highly organized camps with electricity, shower baths, playgrounds, restaurants and even dancing. You find a new and different world here, with interesting people and leisurely living. Also it offers the healthiest and cheapest vacation for families with children.

Logistics of Camping

To pitch your tent in a European camp—owned more often than not by a club—you will have to produce the *International Camping Carnet* which is also your third party (public liability) insurance. If you wish to obtain your carnet before leaving home, write to the National Campers and Hikers Association, 7172 Transit Road, Williamsville, N.Y., 14221 or Camping Club of Great Britain, 11 Lower Grosvenor Place, London S.W.1. In Europe, try the Federation International de Camping et de Caravanning, 78 rue de Rivoli, Paris. If you intend to camp with your family apply for a family carnet, which is more economical (cost varies from country to country: in Britain it costs 50p for members). Enclose a passport size photo of the head or a small picture of the whole family and quote the number of your passport and driver's license. You can also become a member on arrival at the local branch of one of European camping clubs (apply in person) and receive the carnet which entitles your party to use camps anywhere in Europe—at reduced rates.

You are probably an old hand at camping and know what to take on a trip abroad. Remember however that your free baggage allowance is now limited to two pieces, neither one more than 62 inches overall, and totaling 124 in. in First Class, 106 in. in Economy Class, plus underseat baggage up to 45 inches. Excess baggage charges to Western Europe can run $40–$50. Pan Am, TWA and Northwest Orient offer special rates for bicycles. Tents are cheaper to buy in the U.S. than in Europe (there are facilities for renting, including from several of the Channel car ferry operators) and you might like to bring your well-tried insect bomb or mosquito repellent, your medicine for diarrhoea and antibiotics for dysentery.

Your daily budget—excluding car hire or purchase—covering *all* your expenses, should not exceed $6.75-$9 per person.

Your best way to start planning is write to a country's national tourist office; most countries publish directory/guides to their campgrounds. The one for Belgium, for example, lists over 170 sites, with maps and details of equipment, capacity, and classification for each. *European Campgrounds and Trailer Parks,* published by Rand McNally Co., 10 E. 53 St., New York, N.Y 10022, is a 300-page guide to over 3,000 selected sites in all of Europe, including the eastern countries and Turkey, 29 countries in all, with maps, access instructions, and complete listings of equipment and facilities. For individual countries you may wish to write directly to the national camping clubs, some of whose offices are listed below:

Austria: Österreichischer Camping Club, Schubert Ring 8, Vienna.

Belgium: Royal Camping et Caravanning Club de Belgique, 51 Rue de Namur, Brussels 1.

Denmark: Densk Camping Union, G1 Konegevej 74, 1850 Copenhagen.

Finland: Camping Committee, Finnish Travel Association, Uudenmaankatu 16A, Helsinki.

France: Federation Française de Camping et de Caravanning (FFCC), 78 rue de Rivoli, Paris.

Germany: Deutscher Camping Club, Mandlstrasse 28, Munich 23.

Great Britain: Camping Club of Great Britain and Ireland, 11 Lower Grosvenor Place, London S.W.1.

Italy: Federazione Italiana del Campeggio e del Caravanning, Via G. Mameli 2 (Casella Postale 255), Florence.

Netherlands: Koninklijke Nederlandse Toeristenbond, 220 Wassenaarseweg, The Hague.

Portugal: Federacao Portugesa da Campismo e Caravanismo, Rua da Madelena 75, 2 Lisbon.

Spain: Agrupacion Nacional de Campings de España, Calle de Duque de Medinaceli 2, Madrid 14.

Sweden: Swedish Camping Committee, Vasagatan 16, 111 20 Stockholm.

Switzerland: Swiss Federation of Camping, Hapsburgerstrasse 42, Lucerne.

Yugoslavia: Turisticki Savez Jugoslvije, M. Pijade 8 (P.O.B. 595), Belgrade.

Camp and Caravan Sites

These are to be found in all European countries. They vary from the extremely good to the absolutely horrible; from highly organized camps with electricity, showers, restaurants, shops, playgrounds and even dancing, to a field with one standpipe. But for the most part they fall between these extremes, are well run and inexpensive. Most state tourist offices can provide lists of sites in their own countries. Germany even operates a radio service for campers and caravaners. During the main holiday season, signs along the motorways tell which radio frequencies to tune in to for details of space available at sites in that region. Canvas Holidays, Parkway Chambers, Welwyn Garden City, Herts, also has its own ready erected tents or canvas villas, for renting on sites in France, Switzerland, Italy, Austria and Portugal, offered as a package to people who have not or do not wish to be bothered with their own tents.

In Central and Northern Europe the camping season lasts from mid-May to mid-September; around the Mediterranean some of the camps are open all year.

SHIPS, FERRIES, YACHTS AND BOATS

Touring Europe by boat isn't the quickest way to see the sights, but it's about the most relaxed. There are many possibilities, ranging from river steamer trips and organized cruises to the joys and expenses of doing it yourself in a chartered sail or motor boat. The elaborate network of Europe's inland water ways covers some of the loveliest scenery on the Continent. The Rhine trip is one of the great classics. You can steam your way from Rotterdam all the way to Basel and back, but the most popular sector is between Cologne and Bingen or Wiesbaden. You can arrange to have your car driven ahead while you relax aboard a Rhine steamer, and there are a number of places on the Rhine journey where you can switch from ship to railway (see Germany). Another floating-hotel cruise on "botels" cruises up the Rhine from Amsterdam and goes into Switzerland. There is a sightseeing service between Rotterdam and Stuttgart up the Rhine and the Neckar, stopping off in the afternoons to enable passengers to take excursions. A delightful river trip is the one from Passau or Linz down the Danube to Vienna. For idyllic scenery and a sense of intimate contact with the countryside, you can't beat the three-day voyage Gothenburg to Stockholm on the Göta Canal. Specialists in these cruises are *European Yacht Cruises,* 15 Denmark Hill, London S.E.5, and *Cornelder's,* Bath House, 52-60, Holborn Viaduct, London, E.C.1.

Barge holidays on the canals and rivers of Burgundy and the south of France are offered by *Continental Waterways Ltd.,* 22 Hans Place, London SW1. Gourmet meals and bicycles on board for shore excursions are included. Cruises in central France are offered by *Inland Voyages,* Guildford Boat House, Millbrook, Guildford, Surrey, England.

In the U.S. a company specializing in *all* types of European waterway travel is *Floating Through Europe, Inc.,* 501 Madison Ave., New York, N.Y 10022 (in the U.K., Hemingway P.R., Barclay House, Chapel Ash, Wolverhampton). In addition to operating its own luxury hotel barges in Britain and Holland, this company offers information, books, waterway maps, and booking services to individuals and groups. Its president, Stanley Kroll is the author of *Cruising the Inland Waterways of Europe* (Harper and Row, 1978).

Among lake excursions, those on Lake Geneva and the Lake of Lucerne are very popular. The Swiss have schedules so well planned that you can combine boat and rail travel so as to avoid repeating any part of your itinerary. Lake Constance (the Bodensee), between Switzerland and Germany, offers a number of pleasant excursions and so do the famed Italian lakes, Como, Maggiore, Lugano, and Garda. Also popular: Lake Balaton in Hungary. In Finland, cruises from several hours to several days (cabins available) are to be had on some of Europe's most extensive lake systems.

You can float down the river Shannon in Ireland, calling at places along the way, including Limerick, or take a day trip on the historic Thames.

Cruises within Europe

For those who like leisure cruising, but do not want it to form the whole of the trip, there are almost endless opportunities when once in Europe. Cruises operate out of England, Italy, Holland and Greece in particular, visiting scenic European and island ports in the course of 6 to 22 days, sometimes taking in several countries. Almost every shipping line, and even the larger ferries, mentioned in the *Practical Planning* section of this guide, run cruises at some time during the year. Best consult your travel agent for full prospects well in advance of your trip, as berths are quickly booked up.

Costs vary according to length of cruise and class of accommodation, but a 7-day cruise around the Greek islands and along the coast of Aegean Turkey, calling at Istanbul before returning to Piraeus, the port of Athens, cost from £380 (*Sovereign Holidays*).

A typical cruise from Southampton might take in Lisbon, Madeira and Casablanca (12 days); Lisbon and Ceuta (6 days); Copenhagen, Visby and the Kiel Canal (12 days). From Venice or Athens there are various cruises of the Greek Islands, the Adriatic, etc.

It is almost invidious to mention shipping lines that now operate cruises out of England or European ports (since they almost all do, so consult your travel agent), and most offer individual or package air/ cruise tours. Therefore see above under "Shipping", or consult your travel agent.

Sampling the Cruises

The water routes around Scandinavia are full of possibilities, from various Danish ports to points in Norway and Sweden, from Stockholm to the island of Gotland and Visby, and to Helsinki in Finland. Small excursion boats explore the intricate archipelago of Stockholm, while their Norwegian counterparts cruise through the Oslofjord. Larger boats cruise the fabulous fjords of Norway's western coast and take you to the Land of the Midnight Sun.

In southern Europe you can sail to the Balearic Islands from Barcelona and Valencia, see the Bay of Naples by boat on your way to Ischia or Capri, explore the island-studded waters off Yugoslavia's Dalmatian coast or follow the path of Ulysses and Lord Byron to the splendid Isles of Greece.

In a minor key, you'll enjoy a 2- to 4-day cruise visiting places in the Bay of Naples (Sorrento, Ischia, Capri) and along the rugged coast of Amalfi (Positano, Amalfi, Ravello), stopping overnight where your fancy takes you and changing boats at will.

Eastern Europe by Water

Polish and Soviet ports on the Baltic Sea are less than a week away from British and French channel ports by luxury ocean liners or more modest cargo vessels. The Soviet motor ships touch at London and Le Havre about every week, and the Polish Steamer, *Stefan Batory,* calls at Southampton about once a month on the way to Gdynia.

Cruise lovers will enjoy the Vienna-Yalta journey by the Soviet motor vessels which convey passengers from the heart of Europe to the Crimea. During the 6-day trip these ships traverse Czechoslovakia, Hungary, Yugoslavia, Bulgaria, Romania and finally the Black Sea. Calls are made en route at Bratislava, Budapest and Belgrade.

Greek Odysseys

The Greek luxury cruiser *Jason* (1967) is a sister ship to the earlier *Argonaut* (1966). Both are luxurious, designed by an American, Michael Bailey, with impeccable taste. Seven-day cruises on the gentle Aegean take you to Crete, Santorini, Rhodes, Ephesus, Istanbul, Delos and Mykonos. Good food, friendly service. From $365 (£228) to $840 (£525). All shore excursions extra.

Worldtrek, 415 Lexington Ave., New York City 10017, offers a 15-day yacht cruise of the Greek islands; groups limited to 16, numerous departures, flexible itineraries and stops, sailing and water-skiing. About $620.

For about $86 (£45) each per week you can board a traditional Greek *caique* with your party and do some island hopping by day. It's a simple life (the sailors prepare meals) but an exhilarating experience. For details write: *Dolphin Line,* 4 Nikis Street, Athens.

Both *Peter Storm Charters,* Smith Street, Norwalk, Conn. and *Bring Sailing Back Inc.,* 14 Pearl Street, New York 10004 have intriguing offers over a wide range.

Private Yachts

Private yacht cruises and cruiser hire (sea or inland waterways) are possible in most countries. *World Yacht Enterprises Ltd.,* 14 West 55th St., New York, N.Y. 10019, and 80 York St., London, England, offers private yacht cruises of any duration, in the Aegean and Mediterranean, with professional crew, from about $350 (£218) per person weekly, all-inclusive, for a party of 5. They also have short-term charters for special business and social events of any Mediterranean resort and major cities such as Paris and London. *Boat Enquiries Ltd.,* 12 Western Road, Oxford, runs a comprehensive information service on all types of hire.

Touring Europe by Bus

Europe's bus lines and bus touring companies have brought travel by motor coach to a peak approaching perfection. The physical comfort plus the wide choice of routes accounts for the increasing popularity of exploring Europe by bus. There is an almost equally wide choice of bus companies.

Almost all of them offer inclusive tours lasting as long as 30 days, and a single payment covers transportation, hotels, meals, and tips. Many of them operate regular services that you can pick up or leave at any point, in which case you pay only for transportation. Rates are slightly more than second-class railway fares. As for comfort, you may find yourself in a luxury coach with reclining seats, a hostess to look after you and point out sights, a refrigerator for refreshments, and even a toilet. Generally there are two drivers, who relieve each other periodically. Most tours are offered only in summer.

On long, trans-European bus journeys, it is a good idea to bring along a blanket, soap and towel, and a large supply of sandwiches and reading matter.

Apart from trans-European services, the French have introduced the Relais Bus Pass for those who want to see a good deal of the country at reasonable cost. The pass allows unlimited mileage for a period of 15, 21, 30 or 60 days, enabling the traveller to go where he wishes, when he wants, at his own pace. The 60-day pass, for example, with maps and guidebook, costs approximately $375. For details, write to the *Federation Inter Jeunes France Europe,* 218 Rue St. Jacques, Paris 75005.

EUROPABUS. Although it might at first glance look like "cutting off their noses to spite their faces" the railway organizations of much of Europe operate fast, long distance coach (that is bus) services on a network of routes, many in direct competition to the train. The system is known as *Europabus* and there are over 65,000 miles of routes, many in some of the most scenic parts of the continent.

In extent, Europabus services range from the Netherlands to southern Spain and from France through to Istanbul as well as going right down to Athens and Sicily. On some routes there are connecting services by train while in West Germany there is the alternative of Rhine steamer travel. You can break your journey at any of the scheduled stopping points although you must make advance arrangements for this and these stop-overs do not involve any extra cost. In other words whether you go right through or elect to stay a night or two at any of the en route halts, the fare is the same.

Although the type of bus varies from one country to another, all are of the latest design, many now being fully air conditioned. On the longer routes there are English speaking hostesses on board. At frontiers the buses receive priority treatment with customs and passport formalities, thus enabling them to keep to their timetables even in the very busy season. Most of the routes are summer only, but the starting and stopping dates vary considerably. A few operate throughout the year.

In effect travel by Europabus enables you to plan your own bus tour without the restrictions of a fully inclusive holiday. However on some routes (such as Brussels to Barcelona or Brussels to the French Riviera) overnight accommodation and meals can be included in the overall price. On other routes you make your own hotel and eating arrangements. This means that there is great flexibility in the operation. But if you want a fully inclusive "tour" then Europabus have also a wide selection of these.

Some routes connect two or more countries while others operate entirely within one nation. The longest through service (but with a change of bus in Belgium and at Munich) is between London and Athens crossing the Channel by ferry.

As far as fares go these vary according to the route. In many cases they are around the second class rail fare although on others they are higher. Of course although the buses do travel at high speeds particularly on the motorways they are slower over-all than the trains. On certain routes however there is not all that great a difference.

Advance booking is more or less essential although in the off peak season it is usually possible to get last minute reservations. All stop-overs must be notified beforehand so that the suitable seat reservations can be made. The free baggage allowance is the same as for first class air travel, namely 66 lbs. per person. And for children there are reduced fares according to age and route.

Each year Europabus issue a special tourist edition of their timetable giving details and costs of their main services as well as a selection of some of their inclusive tours. This brochure can be obtained from many travel agents or from the main European railway offices. And all British Rail main offices have copies.

SOME EUROPABUS ROUTES

London-Ostend-Rotterdam-The Hague-Amsterdam.

Leaves London's Victoria Station by rail in the mid morning, travelling by cross Channel ferry to Ostend where you board the bus for the Dutch cities, reaching the destinations in the mid and late evenings. Total travelling time 10-12 hours. Operates Mondays and Saturdays. Fare London-Amsterdam approximately $40 (£20).

Brussels-Dijon-Figueras- Barcelona.

Leaves the Belgian capital at breakfast time and journeys via northern France and Burgundy for overnight at Dijon. Then via the Rhone Valley and Perpignan across the Spanish border to Figueras. On the next day reaches Barcelona at lunch time. Operates southbound Saturdays and Sundays April to September. Northbound on Mondays and Tuesdays. Fare Brussels-Barcelona including two nights with full board approximately $120 (£60).

Wiesbaden-Frankfurt-Wurzburg-Rothenburg-Augsburg-Munich.

Leaves at breakfast time and travels by the famous "Romantic Route" through Bavaria to Munich. Lunch stop at historic Rothenburg. Total journey time 12 hours including lunch. Fare Wiesbaden-Munich approximately $36 (£18).

Florence-Siena-Perugia-Assisi-Spoleto-Rome.

Leaves at breakfast time and travels down through central Italy, partly on the "Autostrada del Sole" and partly on other main roads. A 90 minute lunch stop is at Perugia. Rome is reached in the early evening. Total time about 10 hours. Operates both directions (timings more or less the same) daily April to October inclusive. Fare Florence-Rome approximately $21 (£10.50).

FRAMES' TOURS operate out of London, offering a wide range of sightseeing tours including 6-day tours of the Shakespeare country for £140, with longer tours covering Gt. Britain and Ireland. There is also a 7-day, "Fine Capitals" tour, covering Belgium, Holland, Germany, Luxembourg, and France, for £195. Addresses: 25 Tavistock Place, London WC1H 9SG; 185 Madison Ave., New York 10016.

EUROPEAN EXPRESS operate a year-round service between London and Athens which is faster, and very much cheaper, than the train. An open-ended round trip ticket costs £70 more or less (depending on season). Address: 60 King Street, Twickenham, Middlesex.

GENERALCAR, a Belgian company, started its *Orientbus* service in 1964; it takes you from Brussels to Istanbul with stops in Germany, Austria, Yugoslavia and Bulgaria. Address: 10 Rue de la Montagne, Brussels.

WALLACE ARNOLD: This long-established British company have been operating coach and bus tours in the U.K. and on the continent for many years. Last year they added two long-distance express-bus services in Europe, operating these in conjunction with continental companies. One route goes from London via France to Barcelona and Alicante, stopping at various places in Spain en route. The journey takes around 36 hours, with no overnight stop. Reduced rates for children and students. Their other route, started on a trial basis, is from London to Moscow via Ostend, Germany, Berlin, and Poland. It takes four days, and three nights (two of them spent in hotels en route, and one spent travelling), with the same coach all the way from Ostend. As we went to press, there was every hope that it would operate in 1979 from May to September, probably on a weekly or twice weekly service. Details from *Wallace Arnold Tours Ltd.,* 8 Park Lane, Croydon CR9 1DN. tel. 01–462 7711.

In Eastern Europe

The Eastern Europe coach tour specialists *Maupintour Associates* 900 Massachusetts St., P.O. Box 807, Lawrence, Kansas 66044, and 270 Park Avenue, New York 10017, suggest air-bus trips from New York or the West Coast. You can choose a 15-day thrift tour or a 49-day grand tour, or various possibilities in between. You travel by latest-type jet planes, see Russia, Poland, Czechoslovakia the Balkans and parts of Central Europe at a leisurely pace in comfortable sightseeing coaches at an all-inclusive daily rate of about $60, according to length of journey and type of tour.

The Eastern European tourist bureaux all arrange local bus tours, many of them covering several countries. Their coaches are usually more modern and comfortable than their railroad rolling stock. These tours may be booked through accredited travel agents in the West.

LEAVING EUROPE

Paying to Leave the Country

One of the minor forms of taxation madness afflicting the bureaucrats of too many European nations is the "Airport Tax", a nuisance tax which is levied on all travelers, tourist or otherwise, just before they step aboard their aircraft. (This usually is a surprise to the traveler, and inevitably comes just after he has spent his last penny of the appropriate foreign currency. He is then obliged to go back and change another travelers' cheque, pay his ransom to get out of the country, and frequently swears never to come back again.)

Some countries only make you pay to get out; a few make you pay to get in; and even fewer, thanks for small favors, make you pay coming and going. This last category includes, sad to report, the U.S.A. (in the form of International Transportation Tax of $3 added to ticket price). Canada and Australia have no such charges, and New Zealand does only on outgoing passengers.

Psychologically, the ransom is a disaster, and breeds nothing but ill will. Hopefully, the authorities of countries not yet having this form of punishment will refrain from adopting it . . . it is probably too much to ask the offending nations to give it up.

Customs on Returning Home

If you propose to take on your holiday any *foreign-made* articles, such as cameras, binoculars, expensive timepieces and the like, it is wise to put with your travel documents the receipt from the retailer or some other evidence that the item was bought in your home country. If you bought the article on a previous holiday abroad and have already paid duty on it, carry with you the receipt for this. Otherwise, on returning home, you may be charged duty (for British residents, Value Added Tax as well). In other words, unless you can prove prior possession, foreign-made articles are dutiable *each time* they enter the U.S.

At this writing, **American residents** who are out of the USA at least 48 hours and have claimed no exemption during the previous 30 days are entitled to bring in duty-free up to $100 worth of bona fide gifts or items for their own personal use. Do not think that *already used* will exempt an item. If you buy clothing abroad and wear it during your travels it will nonetheless be dutiable when you reenter the U.S. (**Note:** Congress *may* raise the limit to $250 or $500 by the time you read this!)

The $100 duty free allowance (years ago, it was $500!) is based on the full fair *retail* value of the goods (previously, the customs' estimation was on the wholesale value). You must now list the items purchased and *they must accompany you when you return.* So keep all receipts handy with the detailed list, and pack the goods together in one case. The $10 mailed gift-scheme (see below) is also based on the retail value. Every member of a family is entitled to this same exemption, regardless of age, and their exemptions can be pooled. Infants and children get the same exemptions as adults, except for alcoholic beverages and tobacco.

One quart of alcoholic beverages and up to 100 cigars (non-Cuban!) may be included in the exemption if you are 21 years of age or older. There is no limitation on the number of cigarettes you bring in for your personal use, regardless of age. Alcoholic beverages in excess of one quart are subject to customs duty and internal revenue tax. Approximate rates are (1/5 gallon); brandy or liquor, $2-$3; champagne, 90¢; wine, 15¢. The importation must not be in violation of the laws of the state of arrival. Furthermore, your tobacco and alcohol may be reported to the authorities in your own home state, to be taxed by them.

Only one bottle of certain perfumes that are trademarked in the United States (Lanvin, Chanel, etc.) may be brought in unless you can completely obliterate the trademark on the bottle, or get written permission from the manufacturer to bring more. Other perfumes are limited by weight or value. The specialized Paris houses will give you the complete list.

Foreign visitors to the U.S. (nonresidents), and US military personnel returning from duty abroad should inquire separately about regulations and exemptions pertaining to them.

American rates of customs duty may change, so it is best to check the regulations with the nearest American Embassy during your visit. There are special Customs advisors at the U.S. embassies in London, Paris, Rome and Bonn and at the Consulate in Frankfurt. In general, of course, narcotics, pornography, seditious materials, and dangerous articles (fireworks, poisons, switchblades) are forbidden in the U.S. as everywhere.

You do not have to pay duty on art objects or antiques, provided they are over 100 years old. Remember this and ask the dealer who sells you that Sheffield plate or that 17th-century Dutch landscape for a certificate establishing its age. But when you buy, remember also that some countries regulate the removal of cultural properties and works of art.

Gifts which cost less than $10 may be mailed to friends or relatives at home, but not more than one per day (of receipt) to any one addressee. Mark the package: Unsolicited Gift—value less than $10. These gifts must not include perfumes costing more than $1, tobacco or liquor; however, they do not count as part of your $100 exemption.

Since 1976, under the GSP (Generalized System of Preferences) plan some 2,700 items from *developing* countries may be brought into the U.S. duty free. The purpose of this is, of course, to help the economic development of such countries by encouraging their exports; 98 countries and 40 dependent territories are currently considered to be developing. In this book, GSP countries are: Cyprus, Malta, Portugal, Romania, Turkey and Yugoslavia; the dependent territory is Gibraltar. Because the lists are reviewed annually, write to: Department of the Treasury, U.S. Customs Service, Washington, D.C. 20229 and ask for the latest edition of the leaflet *GSP & the Traveler.* GSP articles must be acquired in their country of origin.

Bringing a foreign car back to the U.S. is another matter covered by a special pamphlet. In this case, write to: The Department of the Treasury, U.S. Customs Service, Washington, D.C. 20229 and ask for the pamphlet, *Importing a Car:.*

Recently a number of endangered species of fish, marine mammals, wildlife and plants have come under government protection and may no longer be taken in or out of the U.S. For details write to the Director, U.S. Fish and Wildlife Service, Department of the Interior, Washington, D.C. 20240.

Do not bring home foreign meats, fruits, plants, soil, or other agricultural items when you return to the United States. To do so will delay you at the port of entry. It is illegal to bring in foreign agricultural items without permission, because they can spread destructive plant or animal pests and diseases. For more information, read the pamphlet "Customs Hints", or write to: "Quarantines", Department of Agriculture, Federal Center Bldg., Hyatsville, Maryland 20782, and ask for Program Aid No. 1083, entitled "Traveler's Tips on Bringing Food, Plant and Animal Products into the United States."

British residents, except those under the age of 17 years, may import duty-free from *any* country the following: 200 cigarettes or 100 cigarillos or 50 cigars or 250 grams of tobacco; 1 liter of spirits over 38.8% proof or 2 liters of other spirits or fortified wine, plus 2 liters of still table wine. Also 50 grams of perfume, ¼ liter of toilet water and £10 worth of other normally dutiable goods.

Returning from any *EEC country,* you may, *instead* of the above exemptions, bring in the following, provided you can prove they were not bought in a duty-free shop: 300 cigarettes or 150 cigarillos or 75 cigars or 400 grams of tobacco; 1½ liters of strong spirits or 3 liters of other spirits or fortified wines plus 3 liters of still table wine; 75 grams of perfume and ⅜ liter of toilet water and £50 worth of other normally dutiable goods.

Canadian residents: In addition to personal effects, the following articles may be brought in duty free: a maximum of 50 cigars, 200 cigarettes, 2 pounds of tobacco and 40 ounces of liquor, provided these are declared in writing to customs on arrival and accompany the traveller in hand or checked-through baggage. These are included in the basic exemption of $150 a year. Personal gifts should be mailed as "Unsolicited Gift—Value Under $15". Canadian customs regulations are strictly enforced; you are recommended to check what your allowances are and to make sure you have kept receipts for whatever you have bought abroad. For details ask for the Canada Customs brochure, "I Declare."

EUROPE UP-TO-DATE

ALBANIA

Drop the highest highlands of Scotland down into an area the size of Maryland (10,000 square miles) and sprinkle with a million feuding Kentucky mountaineers. Season with twenty centuries of warfare against invading Goths, Greeks, Serbs, Turks, Italians and Germans—all of whom have coveted this little country of high mountain passes and sweeping plains. Stir in 450 years of Turkish occupation. Top off with more than thirty years of communist control, first by the Soviets, then by the Chinese. If the resulting mixture of scenery, suspicion and somnolence is your dish, you will find a visit to Shqipëria ("Land of the Eagles," the Albanian name for Albania) an offbeat holiday of tremendous interest.

There is more to see than you might think: the Moslem mosques and bazaars of Shkodra (Scutari) and Tirana, the capital city; the fine sand beaches of Durrës (Durazzo), Vlora and Saranda; the romantic ruins of Kruja and Elbasan; beautiful lakes such as Ochrid, and numerous archeological sites—many still being excavated, including Apollonia, near Fier. Digs at Durrës and Butrint are among the highlights of an Albanian tour, though not the main attractions.

Albania is unique for its fierce tribal people, a race apart with a language apart. Descended from the original Illyrians, these rugged individualists go their own way. Under Soviet influence in the Krushchev era, they clung to Stalinist Marxism; today, they are loyal to the Leninist brand of Marxism, as practised by China, which now provides Albania with aid, technology, technical experts and increasing trade.

Lord Byron compared the Albanians to Scottish highlanders, not only because of the craggy mountains which roughen the land but also because of the religious and tribal differences that divide the population into a patchwork of clans and families whose customs and costumes are older than recorded history. The Party of Labour, which the Albanians now call their Communist Party, is undoubtedly doing its best to bring all these factions together, encouraging them, for example, to wear western clothes. But the past dies hard in Albania; you will still see farm workers in the fields in traditional dress.

In former days the law of the land was the *gjak,* or blood feud. If you struck a man, even by accident, only your death could avenge his honor; then only his death could avenge your family's honor, and so on. The *gjak* tradition was not without its mercies: if your avenging enemy found you with a woman or child, you were safe. To this day, Albanian chivalry protects women—who, incidentally, have constitutionally assured equal rights. And a tour group need have no fear if its bus breaks down in the high mountains; hospitality is a fierce obligation. One Albanian Moslem sect declares that "It is evil to be full when others are empty."

Most Albanians (70 percent) are Moslem; the Christian remainder is split into two groups, the Catholic *gegs* to the north and the Orthodox *tosks* to the south. Though the 1976 Constitution bans all religion, beautiful mosques and Byzantine churches are proudly displayed to tour visitors.

Albania's eternal passion for independence is embodied in its national hero, Skanderbeg, whose real name was George Kastriot. For over 20 years he fought the Turks and defeated them in 21 pitched battles, thanks to his light cavalry. When Skanderbeg died in 1468, the Albanian resistance movement collapsed and the Turks made courage-giving charms from the hero's bones. Longfellow celebrated Skanderbeg's saga in his *Tales of a Wayside Inn.* In modern Albania his statues are often seen, and modern industrial products bear his name.

Five hundred years after Skanderbeg's death, during World War II, 70,000 Albanian guerrillas, led by a handsome young communist schoolteacher named Enver Hoxha, bedeviled the Axis forces. In November 1945, the United States, Britain and the Soviet Union decided to recognize General Hoxha's government. The next year the United States and Britain broke off diplomatic relations with Hoxha's Albania.

During the postwar period and up to 1960 the People's Socialist Republic of Albania was a forward Adriatic bastion in the Soviet system and a thorn in the side of the Western alliance. Development of Albania's economy was coordinated with that of the Soviet bloc. But differences between Tirana and Moscow began to surface in the late fifties, when Albania remained loyal to Stalin, statues of whom are still prominent. Finally, the historic switch to Mao Tse-tung occurred, after which Albania was ostracized—in fact, boycotted—by members of the Soviet camp. All Soviet-bloc aid was withdrawn. Red China has not been able to fill the country's needs, and thus Albania, while remaining communist, shows some willingness to trade with western countries, particularly Italy. This development may speed up interchange with the West, even though Enver Hoxha is still the country's political leader.

Some Places to Visit

Durrës. This ancient seaport, has a medieval fortress, a Roman amphitheater dating from the 2nd century and still being excavated, ancient mosaics under a house, and an archaeological museum. From Durrës you can visit a large state dairy farm with glass-house unit and hear a talk on how the farm is worked. The beach, crowded with Albanian holidaymakers, is a good place to mix with local people.

Tirana. The capital city has wide streets with little traffic, flanked by imposing Italian-built structures, as well as an old town. There are a film institute, university, several sports stadiums and an intriguing old mosque. In high season demonstrations of national dancing and music are given. On Liberation Day there is a huge parade.

Kruja. This attractive little mountainside town with narrow winding cobbled streets can be visited as part of a day excursion from Durrës to Tirana. It is the birthplace of Skanderbeg, and there is a fine equestrian monument to him as well as the ruins of the dramatically located castle he defended. There is also a fine museum devoted to his memory.

Elbasan, Pogradec, Korga. These comprise a two-day tour from Durrës, the bus moving through magnificent mountain scenery for much of the way. Each corkscrew bend provides another view for photographers. You'll pass shepherd boys with their herds and isolated mountain villages with inhabitants in the ancient national dress, cross the dramatic Krebba Pass, and see hardly any traffic except for a few official cars, some Chinese trucks, and cyclists and donkeys. Your progress is more likely to be delayed by a wild tortoise blocking the road than by a motor vehicle. Korga, once a Greek city, now has a new *Albturist* hotel. Elbasan is the center of some industry. You will pass a new stretch of Albania's short railway which, until recently, ran only between Tirana, Durrës and Elbasan. Built by volunteer workers, the line today goes through the iron ore town of Prenjas on to Pogradec on Lake Ochrid. There is sometimes a lunch stop for a swim in the lake.

Fier. Two *Albturist* hotels serve this industrial town, which has a chemical fertilizer plant and an oil refinery. More interestingly, it is only seven or eight miles from ancient Apollonia, a Greek colony overlooking a fertile plain. By the 1st century B.C. it had a population of around 60,000. The magnificent ruins date in some cases back to the sixth century B.C. You can see a house with mosaics from the Roman period, a small *odeon* (performing hall) and an ancient portico, and there is more still under excavation. There is also a museum.

Butrint. This fishing port with Greek atmosphere is reached from Saranda in south Albania. There are archaeological sites nearby, including an amphitheater and mosaics. The Baptistery is one of the finest religious buildings remaining in the country. Not far away are rice paddies irrigated by Chinese methods.

Shkodra, once the capital of the ancient country of the Arians, is an interesting old town beside a huge, sinister lake of the same name. You can explore a marvelous medieval bridge at nearby Misi, and the ancient fortress of Rozafat, which can be seen for miles across the fertile plains covered with orchards, vineyards and tobacco fields. Shkodra has an ancient market and an anti-religion museum. The corniche road between Vlore and Saranda is particularly beautiful, rivaling any in the south of France.

PRACTICAL INFORMATION FOR ALBANIA

CAPITAL. Tirana.

LANGUAGE. Albanian—unlike anything you've ever heard. *English-Albanian Conversation Handbook* available with official guidebook, about $2.75 for both from Collet's Bookshop, 129 Charing Cross Road, London, England W.C.2. Some Italian is spoken and, due to continued cultural links with France, some French, especially by younger people. Guides assigned to English-speaking groups are bilingual.

CLIMATE. Coastal regions are very hot in summer, with cool breezes; warm, humid *sirocco* wind in spring and fall. However, since two-thirds of Albania is mountainous, and the towering peaks and deep valleys make for rapid and dramatic changes over a relatively short distance. Temperature sometimes soars to over 90°F. on coast. Average maximum and minimum daily temperatures for Durrës are as follows:

	Jan.	Feb.	Mar.	Apr.	May	June	July	Aug.	Sept.	Oct.	Nov.	Dec.
	51	53	56	63	71	77	83	82	76	68	58	53
	42	43	47	55	63	70	74	72	65	58	51	46

HOW TO GET THERE. U.S. passports are valid for travel to Albania, but the Albanian government seldom allows Americans into the country. (Russians, Portuguese, Greeks, and Yugoslavs are also unwelcome.) Britons are occasionally admitted, but only in groups of 15 or more, not individually. All foreign tourist travel to Albania is handled by *Albturist,* the national tourist bureau, Skanderbeg Square, Tirana, through their agents abroad. Albturist also organizes all internal travel and dispatches all official guides. In New York, apply to Cosmos Travel Bureau, 45 West 45th Street, New York, N. Y. 10036, or ask your own travel agent about the nearest Albturist representative. In Great Britain, Albturist is represented solely by Regent Holidays (I.O.W. Ltd), Regent House, Shanklin, Isle of Wight, P037 7AE, phone Shanklin 4212. Neither Britain nor the U. S. has diplomatic relations with Albania. For Britons, the nearest embassy for information about Albania is Embassy of the People's Socialist Republic of Albania, 131 rue de la Pompe, Paris 16, France. The French Embassy in Tirana looks after British interests in Albania.

Visas are compulsory for all nationalities. In Britain, Regent Travel makes all arrangements for their groups. You fill out and return their visa form with four passport photographs. (Do not send your passport). They do the rest, obtaining a visa for the whole group. No individual visas are issued, and journalists are often refused even as group members. There has been talk of day trips by air or bus from Yugoslavia, with temporary visas issued there; but the situation varies with the state of Albanian-Yugoslavian relations.

MONEY. Foreign currency in cash or travelers' checks may be exchanged at the current rate of approximately 4 *lek* to the U.S. dollar, 6 *lek* to the pound sterling. No local currency is allowed in or out, so take small denomination travelers' checks in order not to be left with a pocketful of *leks* at the end of your journey.

The *lek* is hardly used at all by tourists. All transactions are in hard currency, dollars or pounds. The only place that one might buy anything with a *lek* is in a country shop. The rate of exchange quoted here is the *commercial* rate, used by the very few firms who do business with Albania. The *tourist rate* is *approximately* 12 *lek* to the £ sterling (6 to the dollar).

13.06
5:34
2400
£2:30

WHAT WILL IT COST? The following indicates the cost of all-inclusive tours (fares, hotels, meals, museum visits, guide/interpreter, and so on).

From New York, a 15-day package tour for about $1,-150. No refund for tourists who may be visiting relatives and do not wish to use the services provided, but *Albturist* may arrange to furnish meals and hotel accommodation in the locality where visitors' relatives live.

From Britain, Regent Holidays tours of 9 to 13 days from March to October inclusive, cost from about £156 to £192, according to length and season. These rates, which may change with the floating pound, are based on Durrës, where accommodation is in the huge holiday center. In April, June and October accommodation is usually in the center's class A Hotel Adriatik. Departures at other times may mean staying in one of the center's four class B hotels. Tours are routed via Belgrade, with one night there included on return journey. Costs for children are about 20% less than the basic price. If the holiday starts at the Belgrade airport, there is a £35 reduction. Extra costs: visa, mandatory insurance and optional excursions.

OPTIONAL EXCURSIONS. Must be booked through *Albturist* during your stay. There is a choice, though not all excursions are always available, and a minimum of 15 persons is required. It is often possible to join a group from another country, though the guide will of course speak that language and may not know much English. Examples of local excursions: half-day, Durrës Town, about $1.25; two-day tour of Elgasan, Pogrades, Korga (overnight), about $27; three-day tour to southern Albania, taking in Gjirokastra, Saranda, Butrint with overnight stops at Gjirokastra and new resort at Saranda, about $40.

WHAT TO TAKE. Travel light, with informal clothes for hot weather, slacks and a sweater for the mountains. Women should take one or two cotton dresses for Tirana. Albanians are not used to tourists from the West, so avoid striking or extreme clothes or they will stare at you even more than usual—though always in a friendly way. No miniskirts, bathing suits or bikinis except at resorts. All exaggerated styles are generally frowned upon.

No long hair for males, and make sure a large shaven area separates your sideburns from the start of your beard, if you have one. Otherwise the authorities may decide you don't conform and call in the airport barber to rectify things right on the spot.

Take insect repellent and any medicines you need, for though the doctor's medical attention is free, prescriptions must be paid for and not all drugs are available.

DRINKING WATER. Don't drink tap water except in main hotels and restaurants, and preferably not even there. Beware of local ices.

CUSTOMS. When you enter Albania customs may confiscate books they don't approve of; they will be returned when you leave. Camera and photographic equipment are allowed, but be sure they are recorded on entry.

PHOTOGRAPHY. Do not take photos of docks, military establishments or military personnel. Because Albanians, especially in rural areas, are unused to tourists with elaborate cameras, ask their permission before you take their pictures, though they seldom object. If doubtful, ask your guide to explain before you shoot. Near resorts like Durrës and Saranda or in Tirana the populace is more sophisticated.

GUIDES. Official guides provided by *Albturist* accompany groups throughout the tour, from arrival to departure. On optional excursions, your guide will be an expert on the area and ready to answer questions in fluent English. He may give you more statistics on state farms and cooperatives than you want to know, and his answers may be a little stereotyped, since many guides have not been abroad themselves. He will want you to keep with the group as much as possible, though in resorts you are allowed to circulate freely and talk to the other tourists. When stopping overnight in towns, you can visit cafes and converse with local people if you can find any who speak English. Guides realize that most western tourtists come because they are interested in Albania's unique position in politics as well as its culture, history and sights. They are prepared to help whenever possible.

WHAT TO SEE. Guided tours take in mosques, bazaars, medieval castles, archeological sites. In addition, they emphasize signs of recent Albanian progress under the communist regime, including visits to collective farms, state fruit farms, carpet and knitwear factories, film studios. Museums display prehistoric and Illyrian artifacts and folk art from every region of Albania; partisan museums tell the story of the fight for liberation.

Women still dress in the baggy-trousered Moslem fashion, and mountain menfolk wear white skullcaps, brocaded Skanderbeg jackets and homespun breeches riding low on the loins with no visible means of support. They are adorned with heavy black embroidered designs whose fertility symbolism dispels any possible doubt about what the pants cover.

Music is all around. At folklore displays in resorts, strange instruments play oriental-sounding music from the tribal past. In the cities, students sing ancient as well as modern songs accompanied by an accordion. In remote country areas and in the mountains, young shepherds watching their flocks play tunes on primitive pipes.

Schools and kindergartens are open to visitors. Or, you may care to investigate more closely the intensive farming which uses every square foot of fertile ground. A good deal of modern machinery is used; it was provided first by the Soviets during their period of influence, then by the Chinese, who taught the Albanians methods of growing rice. Nevertheless, much work is still done with primitive implements.

HOTELS. All are operated by Albturist in main towns or near them, and they are clean and comfortable. No tipping. In **Tirana,** the modern *Dajti* is almost deluxe, all rooms with bath or shower, pleasant decor, spacious public rooms, marvelous views over the impressive main street.

Durrës, the main coast resort, has miles of sandy beaches and a complex of five tourist hotels: the *Adriatik,* class A, with private toilet and/or shower; the others (*Durres, Kruja, Butrinti and Apollonia*) are class B. Built during the Soviet period they have high ceilings and pillars and are reminiscent of Black Sea resorts. The complex is fenced off from the general public on the long beach, but guests mingle with Albanian and other tourists on the sands and in the beautiful warm sea. Hot and cold water in all rooms; showers and toilets on all floors. The hotels in this complex jointly provide ballroom, popular and folk dancing, bars, television, chess, souvenir shop, post office, outdoor cinema and other facilities in the high season.

The *Apollonia* is the new Albtourist hotel in **Fier.** This is a completely modern town, intended as an industrial center. The hotel is a little spartan, but quite adequate for a stopping-off point when traveling further south.

Gjirokastra is a very central spot for those wishing to explore southern Albania. The *Çajupi* is a new hotel, simply decorated and furnished, but comfortable.

A new resort hotel with modern convenience is located near the Greek border at **Saranda.** It is on the beach but adjoining the town, so guests can walk there alone, away from their group.

Pogradec's tourist hotel is set in a garden with orange and lemon trees; it has charm and atmosphere. Built in a more traditional form (less barracks-like than most others), it lies on the shores of Lake Ochrid, has good bathing and fishing and excellent food, frequently featuring fish fresh from the lake.

 FOOD AND DRINK. Much Balkan food, such as Kebabs, delicious soups, including a yogurt soup with sliced cucumbers. Soft boiled eggs for breakfast and cold omelette (better than it sounds). Fresh fish from sea or lakes. Good light, local beer; fiery *raki* (plum brandy). Wines from several districts. Sweet liqueurs in different colors—if you are entertained by officials you will drink many toasts in these liqueurs. Sweet Turkish coffee and weak tea.

SHOPPING. Carpets, filigree silver, earthenware pots, souvenirs from hotel shops. The old markets in towns like Shkodra are well worth exploring.

ANDORRA

The midget republic of Andorra, perched high in the Pyrenees between France and Spain (about 80 miles west of the Mediterranean), has managed to remain independent, largely because of sheer inaccessibility. But today a good tarmac road crosses Andorra from Spain to France. The impressive route from France branches off the Ax-les-Thermes—Bourg-Madame road and crosses the highest Pyrenean pass, the Envalira, at 7,897 feet.

Few countrysides are more romantic than this rugged mountain landscape, dotted with Romanesque towers. The ancient houses have jutting roofs and wooden or wrought-iron balconies. The Andorran national holiday, September 8, is a colorful festival honoring La Verge de Meritxell, a fierce-eyed wooden figure discovered under an almond tree, miraculously blooming in the middle of winter.

Andorra exerts a strong attraction for philatelists: both France and Spain maintain post offices and produce frequent changes of stamps. Between Andorran villages, postal services are free, so no stamps are required.

PRACTICAL INFORMATION FOR ANDORRA

CAPITAL. Andorra la Vella.

LANGUAGE. Catalan. Castilian (Spanish) and French also spoken.

CLIMATE. Mild in summer, but cold at nights (remember the altitude is some 3,300 to 8,000 ft.).

Average maximum daily temperatures in degrees Fahrenheit and centigrade:

Les Escaldes	Jan.	Feb.	Mar.	Apr.	May	June	July	Aug.	Sept.	Oct.	Nov.	Dec.
F°	43	45	54	57	63	73	79	75	72	61	50	43
C°	6	7	12	14	17	23	26	24	22	16	10	6

SEASONS. High season, July-Aug.; May-June less crowded and lovely; winter sports mid-Nov., to mid-May.

FESTIVAL HOLIDAYS. At *Canillo*, 3rd Sun. and Mon. in July; at *Les Escaldes*, 25–27 July; at *Sant Julià de Lòria*, last Sun., Mon., Tues. in July; at *Andorra la Vella*, first Sat., Sun., and Mon., in August; at *Encamp* and *La Massana*, 15–17 Aug.; at *Ordino*, 16–17 Sept.

 SPORTS. *Trout fishing*, roughly March to Aug./Sept. daily until sunset; rod only, max. 18 trout per day, min. size 15cms—6". *Chamois hunting*, Sept. to Jan. periods (one week) chosen by authorities. Permits from Sindicat d'Iniciativa. *Ski-ing* information from Andorra National Ski-ing School, Urbanitzacio Babot, Andorra. tel.20010. Pas de la Casa, 8 ski lifts: Soldeu, 1 cable chair and 5 ski lifts: Arinsal, 1 cable chair, 3 ski lifts: Grau Roig, 4 ski lifts: Vall d'Incles, 3 short ski lifts for beginners: Encamp village, cable cabin lift (all year).

MONEY. French *francs* and Spanish *pesetas*.

 WHAT WILL IT COST. It is possible to have full board at a small hotel for about 450 pesetas a day but around 550 is average, and at the best hotels about 1,200 pesetas. Good restaurant meals cost 400, a moderate one from 200.

TIPPING. Hotels and restaurants usually add 10–15% service charge; in small spots where service is not included, add 5–10%.

HOW TO REACH ANDORRA. *By car:* Barcelona to Andorra via Igualada, Calaf, Pons, Seo de Urgel. Madrid to Andorra via Zaragoza, Lerida, Seo de Urgel. *Private taxis* from any town in France and Spain. *By coach:* daily service between Barcelona (Ronda Universidad, 4) and Andorra (Co. Hispano-Andorrana). Puigcerda (Spain) bus to Seo de Urgel, change bus to Andorra. *By train:* From Paris (Gare d'Austerlitz) overnight via Toulouse. Get on through carriages to Bourg-Madame, Perpignan, so you don't change trains at Toulouse. At Ax-les-Thermes (early morning) train connects with afternoon bus to Andorra (1st May—31st Oct); at l'Hospitalet and La Tour de Carol, bus to Andorra connects direct; Bourg-Madame, walk through customs (International Bridge) to Puigcerdá, (see above).

Timetables change, so check before departure.

By air: nearest points are Toulouse, Perpignan, or Barcelona (autocar, bus and taxi services available).

CUSTOMS. None. French customs at Bourg-Madame and Pas de la Casa. Spanish customs at Puigceda and La Farga de Moles.

DOCUMENTS. No visas required, but if you wish to have the Andorran Coat of Arms stamped on your passport, the officials at Casa de la Vall, or the Sindicat d'Iniciativa Head Office in Andorra would be only too glad to oblige.

WATER. Try the mineral waters, French Vichy or Vichy Catalan. The thermal springs at Les Escaldes are sulphuric and sulphydric treatment for rheumatism and skin diseases.

RADIO & T.V. Sud-Radio 367 meters Medium Wave, 818 KHz—45–58 meters Short Wave 6–805 KHz. Radio Andorra: 428 meters Medium Wave 701 KW, 50 meters Short Wave 25 KW 4–995KHz. T.V. programs from France and Spain.

ELECTRICITY. 125 volts, 50C. A.C. and 220 volts A.C.

TRAVEL IN ANDORRA. By car: green card necessary; parking in towns is very difficult.

USEFUL ADDRESSES. In Andorra la Vella, *Sindicat d'Iniciativa de les Valls d'Andorra* (National Tourist Office), 1 Place Princep Benlloch; *Clinic,* Dr. Vilanova, tel. 20214; Automobile Club, Urbanització Babot, Tel. 20890; *Clinica Meritxell,* tel. 21521; *police* tel. 21222; ambulance and fire services, tel. 20020.

 HOTELS AND RESTAURANTS. Over 175 hotels and inns cater for the summer influx of tourists to Andorra (book well in advance for July-Aug.), and some stay open year round. In Andorra la Vella and Les Escaldes, try for rooms away from the main street.

ANDORRA LA VELLA. *President,* 88 rooms, restaurant has magnificent views. *Park Hotel,* 90 rooms, with bath, swimming pool. Almost deluxe and away from the noise. *Andorra Palace,* 140 rooms, with bath. *Pyrénées,* 81 rooms, 53 with bath, fine cuisine. *Florida,* 37 rooms, and *Internacional,* 50 rooms, with bath, are good. Recent is the *Eden Roc,* 55 rooms, all with bath.

Slightly out of town, *La Roureda* at Santa Coloma; 40 rooms with bath or shower, first class; swimming pool.

For dining try *Els Fanals.*

CANILLO. The fine *Pelisse,* 40 rooms, and *Armany,* 78 rooms, 61 with bath.

ENCAMP. The *Rosaleda,* 72 rooms, 28 with bath, has swimming pool, nightclub. Also *Hotel de France,* 50 rooms, 40 with bath.

LES ESCALDES, spa, many hotels. The best are *Comtes d'Urgell,* 200 rooms with bath, and *Roc Blanc,* 100 rooms, most with bath, pool, and a fine restaurant.

LA MASSANA. The restaurant at *Parc les Costes* is worth a visit, also has a few rooms.

PAS DE LA CASA. On the Franco-Andorran frontier, the *Refugi "deis Isards"* is excellent, 39 rooms with bath. The small *Vendeval* is also good, 14 rooms, 6 with bath.

SANT JULIA DE LORIA. *Pol,* 65 rooms, is highly recommended. The *Coma-Bella,* 3 miles out, finely situated, has 28 rooms with shower and toilet, good cuisine.

AUSTRIA

Austria, a pint-sized republic in the very heart of the continent, is one of the top tourist countries of Europe. The reasons? High mountains, gorgeous scenery and a historically high-spirited population who, many say, are "the most charming people in Europe".

Austria is not a cheap country, but the Austrians are conscious of this and do everything they can to help the visitor enjoy his stay—and not feel financially stretched. It is a country proud of its reputation for hospitality. There is a new "Skiers' Best Friend" program to help visitors on the slopes, and many other official schemes to smooth the tourist's path.

Scenery and charm in solid comfort may be enough for most visitors (and why not?), but Austria has much more to offer. It has one of Europe's best complexes of winter sports facilities—more than 500 places to go skiing, most of them not too crowded. You can drive down smooth roads through country scenery that looks like chocolate-box cover paintings to villages that are nearly too-perfect in their well-scrubbed quaintness. Tarry a while in the friendly atmosphere of the local inns' dining rooms, and then, perhaps, head for an Austrian musical interlude. Whether it be the Salzburg Festival, the opera in Vienna, or a local band blasting its way through the street, it will be good and appropriate music.

Tops among the highlights of Austria is the opening of the Spanish Riding School. The fascinating combination of beautiful horses, a display of unequalled equestrian ability and romantic music, all set in a glittering baroque hall, make it a once-in-a-lifetime event for any visitor.

Food . . .

The specialties of Austria include such delights as: *Leberknödlsuppe,* a meat broth with liver dumplings; *Fischbeuschlsuppe,* a thick, piquant, Viennese soup made from the lungs of freshwater fish, *Gulaschsuppe,* a hot soup with Hungarian overtones, highly seasoned, full of paprika and onions; *Fogosch,* pike, and *Krebs,* succulent little crawfish, all from the lakes and rivers of Austria; *Wiener Schnitzel* —no need to explain. Try any kind of schnitzel, *Holsteiner, Pariser, Natur;* you won't taste such veal anywhere else in the world. Pork is beautifully prepared. Try *Schweinscarrée,* a very special cut, or that tender strip, called *Schweinsjungfrau* (pig's virgin) on the menu. Skip lamb; the Austrians do.

Rehrücken (venison) should be ordered with avidity and so should other game dishes, usually served with cranberries. Beef is overcooked from the American and English point of view; if you want a medium steak, specify very rare. Austrian *Tafelspitz* (boiled beef) is delicious.

Noodles and dumplings are a national institution, and so are sweet desserts: the well known fruit *Strudel,* made here with a crust as light as gossamer; *Palatschinken,* thin dessert pancakes, rolled around a stuffing of fruit jam or nuts; *Salzburger Nockerl,* a delicious soufflé; *Torte,* rich Austrian cakes of which *Sachertorte,* created at the Sacher Hotel, is the most celebrated—chocolate cake coated with jam and iced with more chocolate. Try also *Dobosch, Linzer, Malakoff* and *Nusstorte.* Less rich is the fine-textured sponge cake called *Guglhupf,* wonderful with coffee.

. . . and Drink

Gumpoldskirchner, Grinzinger and *Nussberger* are good white wines grown in the suburbs of Vienna. You may find them a little too fruity. In the spring and summer, the Austrians make excursions into the suburbs to drink the new or *heurigen Wein* *(heuriger).*

The dry white wines of the Wachau area along the Danube, especially the selected types of *Kremser* and *Dürnsteiner,* are of very high quality, and the wines of Vöslau and Burgenland are perfectly potable. In fact, ordinary wine in Austria is usually good and cheap.

PRACTICAL INFORMATION FOR AUSTRIA

WHAT WILL IT COST. An inflation rate of about 10%, plus the added-value tax, increased to 18% in 1976, *plus* the luxury tax, introduced in 1978, keep Austrian prices up, particularly in Vienna, which has become one of Europe's more expensive capitals. In spite of efforts during the past 3–4 years to hold down prices directly concerned with tourism (hotels, restaurants, ski lifts, etc.), in order to protect one of Austria's main sources of income, prices in hotels and restaurants rise slowly, but steadily (only 3.3% in the last 2 years), in an effort to keep pace with the increasing taxes.

For deluxe restaurant meals, count on paying at least 120 Sch. per person without wine; 65 Sch. in an average restaurant; less if you take the *table d'hôte* meals (daily special menus), which are offered *only* at noon (the main meal in Austria). A bottle of wine ranges from 85–130 Sch. but the open wines are very good and cost, per ¼ liter carafe, about 18–25 Sch.

Budget Tips. To encourage tourism, the government has introduced *Visitor's Cards,* good for price reductions on many facilities in 375 resorts. This card must be obtained in Austria itself.

Visit less expensive, less frequented cities, such as Linz, Graz and Klagenfurt; smaller towns throughout the country, but particularly in Burgenland, Styria,

Lower and Upper Austria; cheaper and less-known resorts in Styria, Carinthia, Lower Austria and East Tyrol (see more complete list in text). Smaller summer lake resorts on Faakersee and Millstättersee are just as charming as the more expensive ones on Wörther Lake. And remember that in Austria simple inns are almost invariably clean and comfortable, particularly in the country.

Hotel prices (in Austrian schillings)

Category	Vienna, Salzburg, major resorts*	Provincial capital	Budget resort*	Small towns and country
Deluxe				
Single	300–1100	250–800		
Double	500–1700	450–1300		
1st Class				
Single	250–700	200–500	150–450	130–450
Double	400–1200	300–1000	250–700	250–900
Moderate				
Single	200–500	160–400	140–350	120–300
Double	300–800	250–700	200–500	150–500
Inexpensive				
Single	150–300	150–250	70–150	60–140
Double	260–600	200–450	140–350	100–300

Pension prices do not vary greatly from the above, but are sometimes 10–20% less.

* Peak seasonal prices are given here. Off-season charges (room and board) are about 20–40% cheaper.

Take advantage of the cheaper weekly rates offered by most winter and summer resorts and several hotels in the various cities including Vienna and Salzburg. The Austrian National Tourist Office provides a list, in English, of such places and also notes where ski resort prices include ski lift expenses.

The public transportation systems in all larger towns and cities are very adequate and eliminate taking the quite expensive taxis. Tickets (in Vienna only) can be bought in blocks of five at a cheaper rate at most tobacco shops (tabak trafik). If you plan to do a lot of traveling in Vienna in one day, buy a day's ticket, which entitles you to limitless riding within that day.

Costs for a typical day

	(AS)
Moderate hotel, with breakfast and tax and service charges: per person in double room	350
Lunch at moderate restaurant, with coffee, table d'hôte	65
Dinner at moderate restaurant, with coffee	90
Transportation (1 tram, 1 taxi)	30
One theater ticket, middle-range	300
One coffee in popular café (could be as low as 12AS)	25
One beer in popular café	20
Miscellaneous (10% for contingencies)	88
	968

CAPITAL. Vienna.

LANGUAGE. German. English understood almost everywhere.

CLIMATE. Moderate, the air clear and crisp at all seasons.
Average maximum daily temperatures in degrees Fahrenheit and centigrade:

Vienna	Jan.	Feb.	Mar.	Apr.	May	June	July	Aug.	Sept.	Oct.	Nov.	Dec.
F°	34	37	46	59	66	73	77	75	68	57	45	37
C°	1	3	8	15	19	23	25	24	20	14	7	3

SEASONS. Summer: May 15 to Sept. 30. Winter: Dec. through April. Skiing in high altitudes to late June and in some places later.

SPECIAL EVENTS: *January/February,* Salzburg Mozart Week; "Fasching" (Carnival) with music and gala balls in Vienna and the Austrian provincial capitals from New Year and lasts until Ash Wednesday; in the country, "Carnival on skis"; international ski races in Kitzbühel, Badgastein, Schruns and Schladming etc.; ski jumping events in Innsbruck and Bischofshofen; long-distance and cross-country ski races in various places. *Spring:* Salzburg Easter Festival and Whitsun Concert Cycle. *May/June,* Vienna Festival, Schubertiade in Hohenems; Mid-summer Day bonfires, particularly in Wachau section of Danube. *July/August,* Bregenz and Salzburg Festivals; Baden, Bad Ischl and Mörbisch (Neusiedler See) operetta weeks; Formula-1 automobile race for the Grand Prix of Austria on Graz/Zeltweg race course; *November,* International Riding and Jumping Event in the Vienna Stadthalle, *December,* Christmas celebrations, carol singing ("Sternsingers"), mobile Christmas cribs; pre-season ski "wedel courses" in the Alpine regions; New Year's Eve events including torchlight skiing in the mountains, Strauss Concert by the Vienna Philharmonic, Imperial Ball in the Vienna Hofburg etc.

CLOSING HOURS. Stores open from 9 to 6, close 12:30 or 1:00 on Saturdays. Banks (main offices), open from 8–3; branches from 8–12:30, 1:30–3:30; both til 5:30 on Thurs., closed on Sat. Some shops close for lunch, so best check. Barbers and hairdressers close Mondays, but are open all day Sat.

SPORTS. Austria is a great country for sports, particularly *winter sports:* facilities and amenities are highly developed. *Mountain climbing* terrains are numerous, and there are over a dozen mountain climbing schools. *Hunting* and *fishing* are rewarding, but strictly controlled. Lake *swimming* (particularly in Carinthia) and there are swimming pools in all resorts. There are also numerous possibilities for *sailing* and *water skiing. Saddle horses* are for hire throughout the country; there are numerous *tennis* courts and about a dozen *golf* courses.

MONEY. Monetary unit is the Austrian Schilling (AS), subdivided into 100 Groschen. There are *about* 14.50 Sch. to $1US, 27.50 to the pound sterling. Foreign currency and Austrian Schillings may be brought into Austria in unlimited quantities. Officially you must not take out more than 15,000 AS.

TIPPING. Most hotels and restaurants (among the few exceptions are smaller country inns) include service charges in their rates. For restaurants this includes 10% service and all the various taxes, but it is customary to give a little extra (about 5%). Coffeehouses do not include service in their prices, so a 10% tip is expected.

HOW TO REACH AUSTRIA. By Air. You can fly directly from New York to Vienna and there are direct flights from London and all major European cities.

By Train. Numerous routes (see *Practical Planning* section).

By Car. Most scenic route to Vienna, which covers almost the entire length of Austria, is from Switzerland via Bregenz, Innsbruck, Salzburg; from Salzburg on you can drive via the autobahn or through Salzkammergut on the main road. The fastest way to reach Vienna from Germany (and beyond from Paris, Belgium, Holland and Scandinavia) is via the German autobahn net and the autobahn Salzburg-Vienna; this is a very scenic and interesting route. When traveling to Tyrol, branch off the Munich-Salzburg autobahn; traveling to Carinthia and Styria, branch off near Salzburg.

By Bus: *Europabus* connects Frankfurt with Innsbruck, Salzburg and Vienna.

CUSTOMS REGULATIONS. Liberal. You may bring in almost anything for your own personal use, but only 400 cigarettes, 80 cigars, or 500 grams of tobacco duty free (visitors from Europe can bring only half of these quantities), two liters of wine and one liter of liquor.

MAIL. For the first 20 grams (about ¾ ounce) letters cost 3 Schillings for local and all other domestic destinations; 6 for destinations abroad; postcards to Austrian destinations 2.50 Sch., abroad 4, and airmail to U.S. and Canada 5.50 Sch.; regular-size letters (20 grams) and postcards are forwarded within Europe automatically by airmail (with no extra charge); airmail charges for letters (up to 5 grams) to U.S. and Canada 7.50 Sch.

ELECTRICITY. Generally 220 volts, 50 cycles A.C.

DRINKING WATER is delicious and safe everywhere in Austria. Vienna's, ice-cold from a natural underground reservoir in the mountains, is famous.

TRAVEL IN AUSTRIA. By Car: Drive to the right. Gasoline (petrol) costs 6.60 Sch. per liter regular, 7.00 for premium. There is a 130 kph (80 mph) speedlimit on autobahns; on all other roads 100 kph (62 mph); in built-up areas 50 kph (31 mph). All main roads are in good condition. Most secondary roads are paved and constantly being improved. Check condition of mountain roads in winter before setting out. Railroad tunnel ferries operate when the Arlberg Pass is snowbound and all year round through the Tauern Tunnel. Several mountain toll roads, notably Grossglockner and Felbertauern, scenically glorious but heavily trafficked during high summer season. There are four autobahns: West Autobahn (Salzburg-Vienna), Süd Autobahn (Vienna-Wiener Neustadt, the rest under construction with two more sections already open near Graz and near Klagenfurt), Tauern Autobahn, leading south of Salzburg, is now completed beyond the Pass Lueg tunnel, as well as a 44-mile stretch, including the Tauern Tunnel, between Eben and St. Michael and the Katschberg Tunnel further south; and Brenner Autobahn (Kufstein-Innsbruck-Brenner); last part of latter and the Tauern and Katschberg tunnels are toll roads, the others are free. Car pilot service is available for motorists wishing to use Danube steamers between Passau and Vienna.

By Train: The rail system is extensive and there are various forms of reduced fare tickets. Inquire at the railroad stations. All rail routes are now electric. Most scenic routes are via the Transalpin Express (Vienna-Basel), through Salzburg,

Tyrol and Vorarlberg, and Vienna-Klagenfurt-Villach, through Styria and Carinthia.

By Bus: Postal and local buses link up nearly every village, even in the Alps.

By Boat: You can travel by Danube river boats, large and comfortable, between Passau (on the German-Austrian border) and Vienna; the most scenic sections are between Passau and Linz and the Wachau (between Melk and Krems).

CAR HIRE. *Hertz Rent-a-car,* Rotenturmstr. 5–9; *Avis,* Operngasse 3; *Carop,* Mollardg. 15; and *Inter-Rent Austria,* Kärntner Ring 6—all in Vienna. Branch offices in other cities. A number of firms provide you with chauffeur-driven cars, among them: *Hellmut Schwarz,* Kempelengasse 12; *Franz Mazur,* Leebgasse 35; *Mosel,* Horlgasse 6.

GUIDES. Inquire at *Austria-Information* at Josefsplatz 6, Vienna, or contact *Sektion Fremdenverkehr* (Tourist Section) of the Chamber of Commerce in Vienna, or ask at the hotel desk.

CAMPING. Large sites with all facilities are in strategic locations around larger cities, in the vicinity of summer lake resorts, as well as in numerous other places, for instance along the Danube. Altogether about 350 camp sites. Also about 33 winter camp sites.

 USEFUL ADDRESSES. Embassies: *Australian,* Concordiaplatz 2; *British,* Reisnerstr. 40; *Canadian,* Obere Donaustr. 49; *S. African,* Reisnerstr. 48; *United States,* Boltzmanngasse 15, all in Vienna.

Austrian National Tourist Office, Hohenstaufengasse 3, *Austria-Information,* Josefsplatz 6, *Vienna City Tourist Office,* Opernpassage, *American Express,* Kärntnerstr. 21; *Wagons Lits/Cook,* Kärntner Ring 14 in Vienna; also at Innsbruck and Salzburg.

Nationwide emergency first aid telephone: 144; police: 133.

Vienna's Viewpoints

There are four ways to get a good bird's-eye view of Austria's great capital of nearly two million souls: (1) take one of the four-seater plane sightseeing tours at the Vienna Airport; (2) climb the 458 steps of the "Old Steffel", the south steeple of Saint Stephen's cathedral (or take the elevator to the observation platform at the top of the uncompleted and much smaller second tower if you prefer the easy way); (3) take the elevator to the observation platform of the Donauturm (Danube Tower), a supermodern structure which serves as a TV tower and soars to a height of 826 feet in the Danube Park across the river from the city; (4) take the half-hour street car ride to Grinzing plus the 15-minute bus trip to the Kahlenberg, Cobenzl or Leopoldsberg. From any one of these hills in the Vienna Woods, you will get a very good idea of the layout of the city.

Vienna does not really lie on the Danube; only the northern outskirts of the city touch it. The heart of Vienna, the Innere Stadt (Inner City) is bounded by the handsome Ringstrasse (Ring), built in the 19th century on the site of the moats and ramparts of medieval Vienna. The Danube Canal, diverted from the main river just above Vienna and flowing through the city to rejoin the parent stream just below it, completes the Ring. About a mile beyond the Ring runs the roughly parallel line of the Gürtel (Belt), which until 1890 formed the outer fortifications, or Linienwall. It was at the height of Vienna's imperial prosperity that the Ringstrasse became one of the handsomest streets in Europe, studded with such imposing buildings as the Opera House, Art Gallery, Museum of Natural History, the "New Wing" of the Hofburg, Parliament, the Rathaus, the Burgtheater, the university, and the Votivkirche.

Around and beyond the Gürtel lie the residential districts, some of them old, interesting, and having their own tradition, but many, if not most, consisting of functional and uninspiring apartment blocks constructed by the Vienna communal administration.

Vienna's weather is pleasantest from spring to about halfway through the fall, but the old three-quarter time rhythm is perhaps a little more marked in winter in the glittering interiors of baroque theaters and palaces. Outstanding event of the winter season is Fasching (carnival time), which lasts from New Year's Eve until Mardi Gras. During January and February there are often as many as 10 formal balls in a single evening, the greatest and most gala being the Opernball. White tie and *grande robe de gala* are required for this and the other major balls.

The most prominent spring event is the Festival of Vienna, featuring concerts and performances in the theaters, concert houses and palaces of the city during four weeks from the second half of May. In July and August you'll hear plenty of Strauss waltzes in palace and park concerts, and these are the best months for excursions on the "Beautiful Blue Danube".

Sightseeing in Vienna

One of the best ways to orientate yourself, especially if you are in a hurry, is to take a guided city bus tour. You can also take a boat tour along the Danube and the Danube Canal (see also *Practical Information*). However, the best way to explore the Inner City, that vital square mile that includes Vienna's greatest treasures of art and architecture, her leading hotels and her best shops, is on foot. The main artery is the three-quarter-mile of the Kärntnerstrasse-Rotenturmstrasse that runs from the Opera to the Danube Canal. Halfway down, where the street changes its name, is Saint Stephen's Cathedral, the main landmark of Vienna. Left of the cathedral is the square-like street of Graben with its famous Plague Column, and if you turn left again at the end of Graben, you proceed through the Kohlmarkt to the Michaeler Platz, where you see the main entrance to the Hofburg (Imperial Palace). All of this is an attractive pedestrian mall.

See by all means a performance of the Spanish Riding School in the beautiful baroque manège of the Hofburg. Here, under the glittering chandeliers, the famous white stallions, called Lipizzaner (originally from the stud farm at Lipizza, Slovenia, but now from Piber in Styria) go through their courbettes, levades, and caprioles to the music of Mozart, Schubert and Johann Strauss.

In the Hofburg, historic central palace of the Austrian Empire, visit the imperial apartments of Emperor Franz Josef and Empress Elizabeth, and the Schatzkammer (Treasury) to see the fabulous crown jewels of the Holy Roman and Austrian empires, the cradle of Napoleon's son, and other secular and religious relics.

The Kunsthistorisches Museum (Museum of Fine Arts) ranks as one of the most important art museums in the world. It is especially remarkable for its collection of antiquities, its huge range of paintings, from

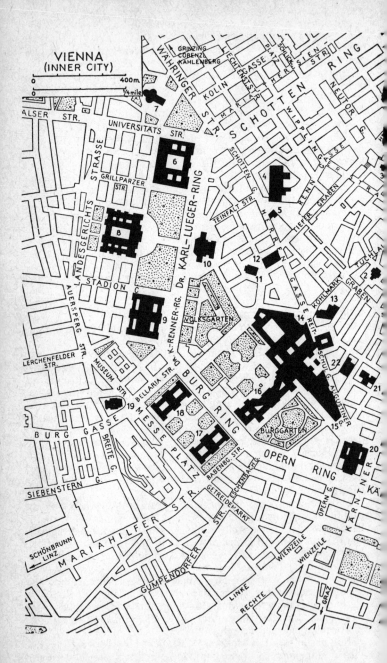

VIENNA
(INNER CITY)

1 St. Stephen's Cathedral
2 St. Peter's Church
3 St. Maria-am-Gestade
4 Scottish Church
5 Harrach Palace
6 University
7 Votive Church
8 City Hall (Rathaus)
9 Parliament
10 Burgtheater
11 Minoriten Church
12 Landhaus
13 St. Michael's Church
14 Hofburg
15 Albertina
16 New Burg Museum
17 Museum of Fine Arts
18 Natural History Museum
19 Volkstheater
20 Opera Haus
21 Capuchin Church
22 Dorotheum
23 Franciscan Church
24 Konzerthaus
25 Karlskirche

Breughel and Dürer to Titian, and the famous salt cellar of Benvenuto Cellini.

Go to Schönbrunn Palace, designed by Fischer von Erlach to rival Versailles, for a tour of the gardens, superb view from the Gloriette, and visit to the imperial apartments. Forty of the palace's 1,400 rooms are sumptuously furnished in baroque and rococo style.

The baroque Belvedere Palace, built by Lukas von Hildebrandt for Prince Eugene of Savoy, houses three museums: Medieval Austrian Art (in the Orangerie); Austrian Baroque (in the Lower Belvedere); Austrian 19th-and 20th-Century Art (in Upper Belvedere).

The Albertina Collection of Graphic Arts (near the Opera) is world-renowned, and the Gallery of the Academy of Fine Arts is equally well known for its collection of paintings by Hieronymus Bosch, Titian, Rembrandt and others. You can also visit the Herzgrüfterl der Habsburger, the small crypt in the Loretto Chapel of the Augustine Church where the hearts of the Hapsburgs are enclosed in 54 urns; or the Kapuzinergruft, crypt of the House of Hapsburg, containing 144 sarcophagi.

Even if your visit to Vienna is a short one, you should see the Austrian National Library at Josefplatz 1. Built by Fischer von Erlach, it is a masterpiece of baroque architecture, possibly the most beautiful library in the world. Among other baroque monuments typical of this theatrical Austrian specialty are the elaborate Pestsäule (Plague Column) in the Graben; the nearby Peterskirche with its patinated copper dome; and the Karlskirche, ecclesiastical masterpiece of Fisher von Erlach.

PRACTICAL INFORMATION FOR VIENNA

 HOTELS. Unless you are motorized, and particularly if you plan to spend only a short time in Vienna, you will probably want to stay in the famous Inner City (First District) within walking distance of most museums, restaurants and the fashionable shops. From May to mid-October it is advisable to make hotel reservations well in advance (Vienna is an international congress center). If you have no reservation, consult the room information office in Opernpassage, tel. 43 16 08 or the West or South station office, open from early morning to late night. Hotel reservations also can be made at the airport, and in summer at information offices near the West and South Autobahn approaches to Vienna. There are over 200 hotels so you should be able to find something.

DELUXE

Imperial, Kärntner Ring 16, continues to rate top position. About 100 years old, several suites have antique furnishings, though most room décor is modern. The 200 spacious rooms have bath with heated floor. Elegant restaurant and café with Viennese music, cozy bar.

Hilton, next to City Air Terminal and the City Park in central location; 622 air-conditioned rooms in different styles, antique and modern; color TV; fine dining in *Prinz Eugen* restaurant, *Vindobona* wine tavern, café and bar; large garage.

Vienna Intercontinental, modern, all 500 rooms with bath, some overlooking skating rink, is quietly located at Johannes Gasse opposite the City Park; several restaurants, bar, large underground garage.

Sacher, Philharmoniker Strasse 4. A house of great distinction. Still has many treasures of the old days. 80 rooms, most with bath. Two bars, several café rooms, and one of the best restaurants in town.

Bristol. Kärtner Ring 1. Opposite the Opera, has 80 rooms with bath, several plush suites. American bar, and a glittering dining room. Garage.

Ambassador. Neuer Markt 5, Modernized, but old traditions and contemporary facilities are happily combined. A favorite of diplomats, it has a long tradition of catering to important personalities. All 60 rooms with bath.

Parkhotel Schönbrunn, next to Schönbrunn Palace, with new (1976) Erzherzog Maximilian annex. Large, with indoor pool, sauna, bar and restaurant.

Palais Schwarzenberg. Exclusive hotel in a wing of baroque Schwarzenberg Palace. All rooms with bath, period furnishings. Excellent restaurant, delightful bar.

Modul. Peter-Jordan-Str. 78, 19th District. Modern luxury in green surroundings; 40 rooms and 3 apartments.

FIRST CLASS SUPERIOR

Europa. Neuer Markt 3. In heart of city, modern. The best of its 101 rooms (all with bath) are located in the corners of the building. Evenings there is musical entertainment in the restaurant. There's a small bar upstairs. All rooms air-conditioned.

Prinz Eugen. Wiedner Gürtel 14. Opposite Südbahnhof (South Station), completely modern. All 110 rooms have bath or shower.

Hotel am Stephansplatz. Stephansplatz 9. Across from St. Stephen's Cathedral. Offers modern rooms (120 beds), majority with bath; the best are on upper floors with magnificent view of St. Stephen's. Pleasant breakfast room, but no full restaurant service.

Royal. Singerstr. 3, near Graben and St. Stephen's. About 130 beds, spacious rooms, most with bath; on top floors.

Mailbergerhof, Annag. 7 in center; in modernly adapted late-Baroque building, with quiet courtyard; small and new (1976).

Erzherzog Rainer. Wiedner Hauptstr. 27 in 4th District near Karlsplatz. Fine restaurant; ask for quieter rooms at back.

Grinzingerberg. In Grinzing suburb. Small, new (1976), with pool and suana.

Astoria, Kärntnerstr. 32 in center (entrance from Führichg.). Old tradition, modernized facilities, many rooms with bath, very good restaurant.

De France, Schottenring 3. House of old tradition, but completely modernized; large, restaurant with fine French specialties, bar.

Albatros, Liechtensteinstr. 89 in 9th District. Recent, all rooms with bath and air-conditioned; swimming pool.

President. Wallg. 23 in 6th district near West Station. Recent, all rooms with bath, radio and TV.

FIRST CLASS REASONABLE
Alpha, Boltzmanng. 8, near US Embassy. All rooms with bath.

Regina, Roosevelt Platz 15, near University and next to Votive Church, 75 rooms with bath and shower, good restaurant.

Westminster, Harmoniegasse 5, not far from U.S. Embassy. About 140 beds and 50 baths. Extensively renovated and modernized.

Amadeus, Wildpretmarkt 5, near St. Stephen's. Garni; new in 1976.
In nearby Klosterneuburg, **Martinschloss** is a baroque castle-hotel in lovely park overlooking the Danube.

MODERATE
The hotels in this category often will charge first class prices for a few of their best rooms, which they will try to sell you first. However, they do have good medium accommodations.

Inner City. Two quiet, small hotels in the charming old streets near the Central Post Office are *Austria,* Wolfengasse 3, and *Kärntnerhof,* Grashofgasse 4. *Wandl,* Petersplatz 9, near Graben, has balconied rooms facing St. Peter's Church. *Römischer Kaiser,* Annagasse 16, just off Kärntnerstrasse, in a baroque-style building, recently modernized. *Terminus,* Filgraderstr. 4, is near museums and Opera.

INEXPENSIVE
City. *Carlton,* Wiedner Hauptstr. 23, about a 5-minute walk from the Opera. Also in the same area is *Schweiger,* Schikandergasse 4, in a reasonably quiet side street. *Wolf,* Strozzigasse 10, and *Graf Stadion,* Buchfeldg. 5, quiet side street, are in the 8th District, near Parliament; *Kugel,* Siebensterng. 43, in the 7th District. *Goldene Spinne,* Linke Bahng. 1a, on quiet side street, is near city air terminal.

 RESTAURANTS. The *Vienna Gastronomic Festival* is held twice yearly: during the Fasching season, and during the Vienna Festival in late May and the first weeks of June. You can recognize participating establishments by the red-white-red "G" displayed, symbol of Austrian hospitality.

TOP, WITH IMPERIAL ACCENT
Sacher (see *Hotels*) provides a handsome setting for dining with *Tafelspitz* being the best selection. The main restaurant sparkles as it did in the red plush era of the Hapsburg archdukes, and so do the alcoved, intimate dining rooms on the upper floor. This is of course, the home of *Sachertorte* chocolate cake.

Drei Husaren, Weihburggasse 4, just off Kärntnerstrasse. Candlelight, antique style furnishings, and soft music. Superb bill of fare. Chicken paprika or *Rahmbraten* with dumplings and lentils are two specialties: also mouth-watering Husaren soufflé. Very good selection of wines and first class bar. Frequented by the social set. Dinners only. Fills up rapidly, so reserve.

Imperial (see *Hotels*). Superior Viennese and international specialties, accompanied by music in the evening. Pleasant bar with wide selection of drinks; afternoon music in the café.

USUALLY EXPENSIVE

Salut, Wildpretmarkt 3, French cuisine in small, attractive rooms, evenings only, except for Sat. lunch.

Kervansaray, Mahlerstr. 9 near the Opera. Turkish specialties from various *kebabs* to fresh Bosphorus fish, including lobster. Pleasant bar upstairs. Reservations advisable.

Rotisserie Coq d'Or. Führichgasse 1. The grill dishes are excellent, usually the wisest choice is the daily special.

VIENNESE SPECIALTIES, REASONABLE PRICES

Wegenstein "Zum Weissen Schwan", Nussdorferstr. 59. Renowned for its game dishes, particularly fowl and wild boar. Closed Sat.-Sun. Must reserve.

Weisser Rauchfangkehrer (White Chimneysweep), Rauhensteingasse 2, near Graben. A series of rooms, mostly in Tyrolean Stuben-style, 100-year-old wine bar. Excellent beef and pork dishes. Delicious chocolate cream puff, Brandteig Krapfen.

Eckel. Sieveringerstr. 46, on the way to Sievering. Not dressy, but serves some of the best all-round food. Specialties are sweet-water crayfish (in season), *Backhendl,* and delicious fluffy, hot soufflé-type desserts. Pleasant garden.

Schubertstüberl, Schreyvogelg. 4 on Mölkerbastei. Pleasant evening dining grill and game specialties.

Hauswirth. Otto Bauer Gasse 20, in the Sixth District, just off Mariahilferstrasse. Classic Viennese specialties and spicy grill dishes. A pleasant courtyard garden in summer.

Rathauskeller. A colossal operation in the basement of Vienna's over-elaborate city hall. Vaulted rooms. One of the longest, most comprehensive menus, with Schnitzel a specialty.

Marhold, Fleischmarkt 9, in the old section near main post office. Small wood-decorated rooms on two floors of a 16th-century house. Some of the best food in this category, including game. Good wines and original Budweiser (from Bohemia) beer on tap.

Fenstergucker. Stephansplatz 4. Behind the cathedral, in the *Deutschordenshaus* (House of the German Order of Knights), erected in mid-17th century. In the summer, eat in the pleasantly cool courtyard garden.

Winter, Albener Hafenzufahrtstr. 262 in 11th District. A bit out of the way, but the food, particularly the fish specialties, are worth it.

Stiedl's Gösser Bierklinik. Steindlgasse 4, in a narrow street in the oldest part of the center. One of the oldest taverns in the city, founded in 1566; trout in season, Gösser beer.

PAPRIKA AND FLAMING SWORDS

The prices in these restaurants vary. It is usual to tip the Primás (pronounced "primash"), the gypsy orchestra leading violinist who plays your favorite song.

Balkan Grill. Brunnengasse 13. You must reserve. Spicy Balkan specialties (mostly Serbian and Bosnian) from grill and spit. Particular gastronomic attraction is Genghis Khan's Flaming Sword. In summer an attractively arranged garden. Dinner only. Expensive.

Pataky. Spiegelgasse 10, off Graben. Old-time Hungarian restaurant with very good gypsy orchestra. Many types of *gulyas,* good chicken paprika, and stuffed peppers. Attractive décor. Dinner only. Moderate.

Csardasfürstin. Schwarzenbergstr. 2, about two blocks from the Opera. Excellent gypsy orchestra and good selection of Hungarian food. It is a small place and very crowded, so reserve a table. Dinner only. Moderate to expensive.

INEXPENSIVE

Stadtbeisel, Naglerg. 21. Small, cozy and crowded at noon. New and popular.

Ilona, Bräunerstr. 7. Small and jammed at lunchtime. Hungarian dishes.

Goldener Hecht, Waagg. 5 (4th District), about 10 minutes from the Opera. Wood-paneled interiors. Fish, veal and pork the best bets.

Gösser Bierhaus, Wollzeile 38. Large beer restaurant with simple, but good, food.

Weisshappel Stüberl, Petersplatz 1 (upstairs), near Graben. Small, simple, but owned by the large meat store downstairs.

PANORAMIC VIEW

Kahlenberg Café-Restaurant. Higher up on the Höhenstrasse, with the best view of all. Three types of restaurant: expensive, with large terrace, piano music; a moderate tavern-type; and an inexpensive self-service. Also hotel.

WINE TAVERNS AND HEURIGERS. Although existing in honor of Bacchus, you can always get at least a bite (usually a large one) and sometimes dinner. Most have Viennese music and are often called *Nobel-Heuriger* by the Viennese. Real Heurigers, where the new (*heuriger*—"this year's") wine is served, abound in the wine-growing suburbs of Grinzing, Nussdorf, and Sievering.

Urbanikeller. Am Hof 12. A centuries-old wine cellar with antique décor. The atmosphere is still genuine.

Paulusstube, Walfischg. 7 near Opera. Sidewalk garden in summer, music in the evening; fine bottled wines, but variable service.

Piaristenkeller, Piaristeng. 45, in the 8th District; also a restaurant.

Augustinerkeller. Augustinerstr. 1 (under the Albertina). A rambling establishment where the countryside atmosphere prevails.

Zwölf-Apostelkeller. Sonnenfelsgasse 3 (not far from St. Stephen's). Frequented by students, and so deep below the street level that some walls are covered with straw to diminish dampness. No music.

SNACKS AND KONDITOREI. The Konditorei or pastry shop is thoroughly Austrian, and the most famous name in this field is *Demel's* at Kohlmarkt 14, near the Hofburg gates. Their pastry, ice-cream and *schlagobers* are among the gastronomic wonders of Europe, and you can also have such delicacies as tiny roast squabs, stuffed mushrooms, vegetable soufflés, all served up with the best coffee or hot chocolate on little marble-topped tables. You pick out the delicacies you want from a staggering array. Don't miss it! (Incidentally, both Demel's and the Sacher Hotel will ship the famous *Sachertorte* anywhere the mail goes.)

Also recommended: *Lehmann,* Graben 12, and *Aida* at Stock-im-Eisenplatz and Opern Ring 7; *Heiner,* Wollzeile 9 and Kärntnerstr. 21; along with Demels, former imperial purveyors of pastry.

For a quick lunch, try *Rôtisserie Palffy,* Josefsplatz 6, *Perle Josefinum,* Währinger Str., *Carrousel,* Krugerstr., with music; or *Trzesniewski Buffet,* Dorotheerg. 1 just off Graben, for mouth-watering, spicy canapés.

NIGHTCLUBS. The prices in the Viennese nightclubs have gone up considerably in the last few years. Champagne is obligatory in some of the floorshow nightclubs. *Eden-Bar* in Liliengasse 2, and *Splendid Bar,* Jasomirgottstr. 3, both near St. Stephen's, are the leading spots for dancing. Among the more popular dance bars are *Chatanooga,* Graben 29, *Scotch* at Parkring 10, and *Café Volksgarten* in park of same name; outdoor dancing in summer. *Fledermaus,* Spiegelgasse 2, is literary cabaret plus dancing. *Safari,* Singergasse 13, has professional hostesses. Floor shows, with the accent on striptease, cater primarily to the foreign and out-of-town customer. *Eve,* Führichg. 3, is probably best, followed by *Maxim,* Marco d'Aviano Gasse 1 and *Moulin Rouge,* Walfischg. 11.

OPERA AND THEATER. The Vienna Opera, installed in its carefully-reconstructed old home, is one of the top operas of the world. What with a pre-season in September, the Vienna Festival in June and other productions, performances go on continuously from 1 Sept. to 1 July. There are summer chamber opera productions in the *Schlosstheater* of Schönbrunn. The tradition of light opera and operetta continues at the *Volksoper.* The world-famous *Burgtheater* maintains its great reputation as one of the leading centers of German theatrical arts. There is a series of other drama theaters, headed by *Akademietheater* in the Academy of Dramatic Arts, and a number of experimental theaters, such as the new *Künstlerhaus* theater and *Courage. Theater an der Wien* performs mostly operetta and musicals.

MUSIC. Vienna remains one of the greatest cities in the world in this department, supporting two superb orchestras, the *Vienna Philharmonic* and the *Vienna Symphony.* There are also innumerable chamber music and choral groups, including the celebrated *Wiener Sängerknaben* (the Vienna Boys' Choir). There are summer concerts in the Arkadenhof of the Rathaus and in several palaces, including Schönbrunn, Schwarzenberg and Pallavicini, the latter offering baroque music by candlelight and performers dressed in period costumes and powdered wigs.

Operas and concerts are usually sold out, so to reserve seats, it's best to order them through your hotel desk, or one of the many ticket agencies. If you're on a budget, go to the city ticket office for the federal theaters, situated in a courtyard near the Opera, with entrances from Goetheg. 1 and Hanuschg. 3. If you're young and hearty, standing room is available for a few schillings. Most of the concerts are given in various halls of *Musikverein,* Dumbastrasse 3 and *Konzerthaus,* Lothringerstrasse 20, both with own ticket offices.

MUSEUMS, GALLERIES. *Kunsthistorisches Museum,* Burg Ring 8, large collection of paintings. *Schatzkammer,* Hofburg, entrance from Schweizerhof, has brilliant display of historical jewelry. *Kaisergruft* (Imperial Crypt) under Capuchin Church, Tegetthoffstr. 2 (guided tours only). *Albertina,* Augustinerstr. 1, huge collection of graphic arts from the Middle Ages to the present day. *Gallery of the Academy of Fine Arts,* Schillerplatz 3, upstairs; select collection of paintings. *Museum des XX Jahrhunderts,* Schweizergarten 3, modern art.

SHOPPING. Austrian prices are fixed, except in some antique shops. The rough triangle formed by Kärntnerstrasse, Graben and Kohlmarkt (all a pedestrian zone) is the center for discriminating Viennese. The less moneyed shop on Marihilferstrasse, where the large department stores are located. (Where no district number is mentioned in the address in the following list, it means that the shop is located in the First District.) *Note:* you may get a refund on Value Added Tax you have paid if your purchase was in a "Tax Free" shop and was more than 2,000 Sch. Ask for details when shopping.

Blouses. *Gretl Sieder,* Kärntnerstr. 2. *Hilde Kral,* Kohlmarkt 7. *Rositta,* Kärntnerstr. 17. *Gertrude Sikl,* Stephansplatz 6.

Dirndls and Trachten. *Lanz,* Kärntnerstr. 10. *Tostmann,* Schottengasse 3a. *Gill,* Brandstätte 8. *Loden-Plankl,* Michaelerplatz 6. *Modell-Dirndl,* Tegetthofstr. 6; *Resi Hammerer,* Kärntnerstr. 29–31.

Handcrafts, Gifts and Souvenirs. *Österreichische Werkstätten,* Kärntnerstr. 6. *Niederösterreichische Heimatkunst,* Herrengasse. *Souvenir in der Hofburg,* Hofburg arcade. *Venuleth,* Kärntnerstr. 16, Graben 17 and lobby of Hotel Intercontinental. *Tiroler Werkkunst,* Mariahilferstr. 89, 6th District.

Jewelry. *A. E. Köchert,* Neuer Markt 15. *Jul. Hügler,* Freisingerstr. 4 and Kärntnerstr. 12. *Carius & Binder,* at No. 17. *Heldwein,* Graben 13.

Leather Goods. *Förster,* Kohlmarkt 5. *Nigst,* Neuer Markt 4. *Popp & Kretschmer,* Kärntnerstr. 51 *Illenberger,* Kärntnerstr. 8. *Schultz,* Führichg. 6.

Lederhosen. *Loden-Plankl,* Michaelerplatz 6. *Adolf Remesberger,* Freisingerstr. 4. *Georg Richter,* Mariahilferstr. 169 (15th District). *Albion,* Hoher Markt 4.

Petit Point. *Jolles Studios,* Andreasgasse 6 (7th District). *Berta Smejkal,* Operngasse 13 and Kohlmarkt 9.

Sports Equipment. *Hans Schwanda,* Bäckerstr. 7 (equipment and clothing, especially for mountain climbing and skiing).

Sports Shoes and Clothing. *R. Mörtz,* Windmühlgasse 9 (6th District), for ski and mountain boots. *Resi Hammerer,* Kärntnerstr. 29–31 (ski and après-ski clothing).

SIGHTSEEING TOURS. *Wiener Rundfahrten,* Stelzhammerg. 4, offer daily sightseeing tours of the city and its vicinity, as well as "Vienna by night" tours, and tours of the Austrian countryside. Vienna sightseeing tours are also offered by *Cosmos,* Kärntner Ring 15, and *Cityrama Sightseeing,* Scholzg. 10.

From April through October, the *Danube Shipping Company (DDSG)* provides sightseeing boat trips along the main Danube stream within the city limits and along the Danube Canal. The starting point is at Schwedenbrücke on the Canal; there are several daily trips, ranging in length from a one-hour quickie to a 2½ hour tour.

An old-timer (1909) trolley tours the city on Summer Sundays; 9 A.M. from Opernring-Eschenbachgasse.

Salzburg's Music Festival

Salzburg is the biggest tourist attraction of Austria after its charming capital. A baroque jewel in a perfect mountain setting on both banks of the Salzach River, the city and the surrounding countryside are dominated by the magnificent Festung Hohensalzburg, a 12th-century fortress 500 feet above the town at one end of the Mönchsberg. Accessible by cog railway or by an easy zig-zag climb, this mighty, siege-proof seat of the powerful archbishops of Salzburg is one of the most impressive sights in Europe.

Its floodlighted silhouette is familiar on summer evenings to tourists who flock to Salzburg for the annual Salzburg Music Festival, which honors the city's most famous son, Wolfgang Amadeus Mozart, from the last week in July to the end of August.

Sightseeing in Salzburg

Although there are conducted tours of the castle, you can get an excellent feel for the place by wandering round it alone. Don't miss St. George's chapel, added to the ensemble in 1501. Its 16th-century 200-pipe barrel organ plays daily during the summer. Not far away from the fortress is the Nonnberg convent, founded in the 8th century.

Virtually everything in Salzburg is within a few minutes walk of the old center of the city. The very heart of things is the handsome Residenzplatz, with its 40-foot-high fountain. The Residenz itself, a 17th-century palace of the archbishops, provides guided tours of the state rooms. From another side of the square, carillon concerts chime out at 7 and 11 A.M. and at 6 P.M. from the 35 bells in the Glockenspiel tower. Nearby is the colorful Alter Markt, with another fountain and an old chemist's shop.

The 17th-century Dom (Cathedral) on Dom Platz, was the first, and remains one of the finest, baroque buildings north of the Alps. Among a host of lovely city churches is the Universitätskirche (University Church), an outstanding example of the ubiquitous Viennese architect, Fischer von Erlach, who also began the work on the lovely Mirabell Gardens. Visit the Benedictine abbey of St. Peter, begun in 847, with its romanesque interior and gothic cloister.

The Grosse Festspielhaus is the focus for the Salzburg Festival. Designed by Holzmeister, it holds 2,400 people, has the largest stage in the world and splendid acoustics. The Festival complex also contains the Felsenreitschule, the winter riding academy, now used as an open-air theater; and a beautiful, small, 17th century auditorium which was once a stable, with a frescoed ceiling by Rottmayer. All these have interesting guided tours.

Mozart's birthplace is now a museum with his clavichord, hammerklavier, family pictures and intriguing exhibits including small models of settings for his operas. The tiny house where he is reputed to have composed the *Magic Flute,* the Zauberflötenhäuschen, is also a museum. The Mozarteum music academy has two excellent concert halls and is also responsible for housing the Bibliotheca Mozartiana, a library with about 1,500 works by Mozart, another couple of thousand about him, and quantities of other books and musical works. Although the mortal remains of the immortal Mozart were buried in a common grave in Vienna, his family lies in St. Sebastian's cemetery, Linzergasse 41.

Across the river in the newer town, the Schloss Mirabell and Mirabell Gardens should not be missed, especially the lovely marble Angel Staircase, whose carved angels look more like cupids. There are often candle-lit chamber music concerts here, even when the festival is not on. The north part of the Mirabell Garden is now called the Kurgarten, since it encloses the very modern Kurmittelhaus, where all kinds of cures can be taken, as well as the Kongresshaus, Salzburg's up-to-date convention hall. Try to see a performance of the famous Salzburg Marionettes in the Marionette Theater, which is headquarters for Professor Hermann Aicher, whose family has been making and exhibiting these fabulous puppets for 200 years.

About 20 minutes by car from town is 17th-century Hellbrunn palace, summer residence of the archbishops. The baroque park has marvelous fountain displays, a natural rock theater and fine sculptures. In the grounds, Monatsschlösschen has a folklore museum.

If you wish to have a splendid view over the city and over the Alps, drive up to Gaisberg (sightseeing buses also take you up there) or, even better, take the daringly-constructed aerial cable car to the top of Untersberg (over 5,800 ft.), the valley station of which can be reached by bus from the city.

PRACTICAL INFORMATION FOR SALZBURG

SALZBURG FESTIVAL. This is the most celebrated festival in Europe, and securing tickets for its many events as well as hotel accommodations is a major problem. The demand for tickets always exceeds the supply, so get them early through your travel agent or at the official Austrian tourist office in your country. The only thing you can count on in Salzburg itself is standing room for the serenade concerts and for outdoor presentations where the space is more or less unlimited.

 HOTELS. It is unwise to come to Salzburg during the Festival season without hotel reservations. If you haven't time to write to individual hotels and wait for replies, try the *Landesverkehrsamt,* Mozartplatz 1, or the *Stadtverkehrsbüro,* Auerspergstr. 7. The latter is a clearing house for placing visitors in rooms in private houses. If you are willing to accept this sort of accommodation, you can bank on clean rooms and a friendly reception.

Students who want to take a summer course at the Mozarteum music school and attend the Festival incidentally, can find living quarters through the school if they register early.

If you can't find a place to stay in Salzburg, you can do what many do—find a place nearby. If you have a car, it's fairly simple. One good spot is Fuschl. Other lake resorts where you can stay are on the Wolfgangsee and Mondsee, both serviced by buses to Salzburg, about 18 miles away. Or you can stay at Bad Gastein, which has a large number of hotels, and commute by autorail (the trip takes an hour and a half). (See subsequent regional information for hotels.)

In May, June and September, excellent months in the Salzburg region, you will have no trouble in finding accommodations in Salzburg itself. Rates during the summer season (June 1-Sept. 30) and especially during the Festival may be as much as 50 percent higher than during the rest of the year, which often makes them higher than those in Vienna.

DELUXE

Gastschloss Mönchstein, on the Mönchsberg, in a magnificent location above Salzburg, is a small exclusive castle hotel. 11 elegant suites, each with bath. Superior service; open summer only.

Österreichischer Hof, Schwarzstr. 5–7, on bank of Salzach River near Mozarteum; 200 beds, most rooms with bath. Three restaurants with excellent cuisine; panoramic views.

Goldener Hirsch, Getreidegasse 37, 800-year-old house, an inn since 1564, transformed after extensive reconstruction into a charming hotel in the old Salzburg style but with modern comfort. Modern appliances ingeniously hidden; all rooms with bath; outstanding food and service.

Mirabell, Auerspergstr. 4, at the Mirabell Park, 100 rooms (70 with bath or shower); restaurant, bar, roof terrace, café, indoor pool, teleprinter service.

Schlosshotel St. Rupert, Morzgerstr. 31. Delightfully located near Hellbrunn Castle; 55 beds, very good restaurant, café, bar; summer only.

Schlosshotel Klessheim, a section of the Klessheim Castle in Siezenheim, on the city outskirts; 45 beds, 16 baths; in a large park with golf course, tennis courts, swimming pool; open mid-June through August.

FIRST CLASS SUPERIOR

Fondachhof, in large park at foot of Gaisberg. Castle-hotel with heated pool, open summer only.

Maria Theresien Schlössl, in Hellbrunn, 30 beds, 12 baths, good restaurant.

Grand Hotel Winkler, Franz Josefstr. 7, modern, 200 beds, all rooms with bath; restaurant, café, bar; about 2 blocks from Mirabell Platz.

Kobenzl, 7 miles and 2,700 ft. up on Gaisberg mountain (also bus). Small, most rooms with bath, pool, restaurant, crisp mountain air and marvelous view over Salzburg. Open March-September.

FIRST CLASS REASONABLE

Kasererhof, Alpenstr. 6, in Nonntal near river; 110 beds, quiet location, garden restaurant.

Europa, Rainerstr. 31, next to railroad station; modern 15-story building spoils the city's baroque beauty; 156 beds, all rooms with bath or shower. Roof café and restaurant; unique view of Salzburg and Alps.

Pitter, Rainerstr. 6, near station; large, restaurant, café, beer cellar with music, garden.

Stieglbräu, Rainerstr. 14, 80 beds, all rooms with bath or shower; large restaurant divided in several sections, garden in summer, parking for 70 cars.

Stein, at main bridge (Staatsbrücke); 130 beds, 40 rooms with bath; good restaurant, roof terrace café.

Bayerischer Hof, Elisabethstr. 12, near station; 90 beds, 50 baths; many rooms with view of Gaisberg; very good restaurant.

Gablerbräu, Linzerg. 9, near main bridge, 85 beds, 40 baths.

Kasererbräu, Kaig. 33, not far from Mozartplatz; small, furnished in old Salzburg style.

Auersperg, Auerspergstr. 61, 95 beds, located between station and Kapuzinerberg.

MODERATE

Traube, Linzerg. 4, near main bridge; 80 beds. *Elefant,* Sigmund-Haffner-Gasse 4, 70 beds, recently renovated. *Eder,* Gaisbergstr. 20, 60 beds, renowned for its Austrian cuisine. *Meran,* Plainstr. 14, and the smaller *Markus Sittikus,* Markus-Sittikus-Str. 20, are near the main station; *Germania,* Faberstr. 10, is near Mirabell Garden.

INEXPENSIVE

Gasthof Blaue Gans, 100 beds, Getreideg. 43. *Alter Fuchs,* Linzerg. 47, 55 beds.

PENSIONS. Salzburg has a better selection of pensions than any other city in Austria. They are of all categories and usually well appointed.

Superior. These should be classified higher than superior and perhaps would best be defined as superior-luxurious: *Dr. Wührers Haus Gastein,* Ignaz Riederkai 25. *Haus Arenberg,* Blumensteinstr. 8, under the Kapuziner Berg. *Haus Ingeborg,* Sonnleitenweg 9, small, with heated outdoor pool. *Fuggerhof,* Eberh.-Fugger-Str. 9, about same size, also heated pool.

Moderate. *Koch,* Gaisbergstr. 37, in the upper brackets of this category. *Am Dom,* Goldg. 17, all rooms with bath, in center.

Inexpensive. *Goldene Krone,* Linzerg. 48, 50 beds. *Adlerhof,* Elisabethstr. 25, near station, 45 beds, restaurant, bar.

RESTAURANTS. Salzburg has many good restaurants but it's wise to make reservations, and to check on the closing days. See also "Hotels".

Glockenspiel (E), Residenzplatz, 2 floors, both with terrace, particularly for lunch.

Flughafenrestaurant, at the airport; not the usual airport misery, but a first-class restaurant, especially for grills, game and fish; expensive.

Grand-Café Winkler, on the Mönchsberg. Very expensive food with a view. Too bad the former isn't up to the latter.

Festungsrestaurant, a really high-perched one, at the fortress. Inexpensive to moderate.

Stiftskeller St. Peter, in St. Peter's Abbey. This is the traditional spot to eat in Salzburg. Good white Praelaten wine from the abbey's own vineyards. Moderate.

Café Restaurant Glockenspiel, on the Residenzplatz, two stories, both with terrace, expensive.

Gewürzmühl, Leopoldkronerstr. 1, grill specialties, moderate to expensive.

Bacchus Stuben, Rudolfskai 16, wine tavern with good grill dishes, music in the evening.

Weinhaus Moser, Wiener Philharmoniker Str. 3, has good South Tyrolean wines, tasty food and moderate prices.

Eder, Gaisbergstrasse 20 in Parsch section; excellent Austrian dishes at reasonable prices.

Beer restaurants: *Stiegelbräu,* Rainerstr. 14; *Sternbräu,* two ways in at Getreideg. 25 or Griesg. 23, self-service garden and semi-covered garden restaurant, own butcher and sausage shop, weekend music; *Mundenhammer Bräu,* Rainerstr. 2; and *Zipfer Bierhaus,* Universitätsplatz 19, also good wines; all moderate.

Stieglkeller, Festungsgasse 10, the seat of the Stiegl Brewery, is very popular, has excellent beer and low prices.

 SHOPPING. Many fine stores: don't miss the *Salzburger Heimatwerk* on the Residenzplatz, a magnificent treasure trove of hand-made peasant artifacts; and world-renowned *Lanz,* at the end of the Staatsbrücke, for dirndls and trachten. Try also *Schaller,* Judengasse 6; *Fritsch,* Getreidegasse 42–44 for petit point and leather goods.

Upper Austria

Northeast of Salzburg lies the federal state of Upper Austria (Oberösterreich). Its capital is Linz, the third largest city in Austria, an important industrial center (steel, chemicals) and a busy port on the Danube. However, Linz harbors also much charm in the old town streets around the main square, in the shadows of the baroque Old Cathedral, and in the splendidly arranged Upper Austrian State Museum located in the former fortress towering over the Danube. Not far from Linz are the famous baroque abbeys of St. Florian (where composer Bruckner was organist) and Kremsmünster (founded in 777).

Most of the scenic beauty in Upper Austria is displayed in its southern part, the Salzkammergut region, a delightful summer and winter playground of lakes, streams and mountains.

Among the many charming resorts are Bad Ischl, former summer residence of Emperor Franz Josef; Fuschl on the lovely lake of the same name; and, of course, St. Wolfgang on Wolfgangsee, the stage of the famous White Horse Inn operetta. There are marvelous views of the Salzkammergut region from the 5,900-foot Schafbergspitze, reached from St. Wolfgang by cogwheel railway, and from Feuerkogel (about 5,400 ft.), ascended by cable car from Ebensee at the southern tip of Traun Lake, not far from Bad Ischl at the northern end of Traun Lake in Gmunden, an old lake town with swans, sailboats and two lake castles.

In the eastern section of Salzkammergut is the deep Hallstätter Lake, majestically enclosed by the steep mountains that rise straight out of its depths; here is the picturesque little town of Hallstatt, known mostly for the fact that it gave its name to the prehistoric Hallstatt Period (see the museum with finds from the 11th century B.C.). From the nearby Obertraun, you can take an aerial cable car to Krippenstein, on the Dachstein Plateau, stopping off also at the middle station for a visit to the Dachstein Ice Caves (some of whose fantastic formations have been here since the glacial period).

Grossglockner Alpine Highway

One of the thrills of Austria is driving over one of the most spectacular mountain highways in existence. You can do it by bus or private car, and this is a toll road. The road is normally open from mid-May until mid-November, but check on conditions before starting out, and don't drive it at night—fog can make it very dangerous. The road starts at Bruck, and there are a number of parking places and rest houses on the ascent. At the Edelweiss spitze, nearly 8,500 feet up, you can sit on a terrace, sip a beer, and gaze out over a view that comprises 37 peaks higher than 10,000 feet, and 19 glaciers. At Tauerneck, the road sweeps around a curve and suddenly the Grossglockner, highest peak in Austria, bursts on your vision for the first time. The impact of this glittering, snowcovered 12,461-foot giant silhouetted against the sky is thrilling. The road now turns westward, heading straight for the majestic peak, and stops at the dead end of the Franz-Josefs-Höhe, where you can have lunch on the open terrace of the Franz-Josefs-Haus (or stay overnight) nearly 8,000 feet high, with a view across the Pasterzen Glacier to the Grossglockner.

REGIONAL HOTELS

BAD ISCHL. *Post,* old imperial style; *Kurhotel,* large and new; both first class (1). *Golfhotel,* next to 9-hole course, and *Freischütz,* a little outside in Rettenbach, are second class (2). *Goldener Stern* (good food) and *Goldener Ochs* are moderate.

BAD HOFGASTEIN. *Palace Gastein,* indoor pool, is best, followed by *Grand,* both superior. *Kärnten, Moser,* and *Astoria* are (2); *Germania, Alpina, Tirol,* and *Austria* all third class (3).

HALLSTATT. *Grüner Baum,* on lakefront with fish dishes in terrace restaurant, is reasonable; *Seewirt,* with wine tavern, is moderate.

LINZ. Two superior motels in suburbs: *Tourhotel, Crest Hotel,* near Autobahn. *Drei Mohren,* since 1595, and the colorful *Wolfinger,* with wine tavern, are reasonable. Moderate are *Ebelsbergerhof* and *Goldene Krone. Pöstlingberg,* across the Danube, small, good restaurant and wine tavern, is (2).

ST. WOLFGANG. *Weisses Rössl* of operetta fame is superior. *Post,* with its *Schloss Ebenstein* annex, and *Cortisen* are reasonable. *Belvedere* and *Wolfganger-hof* are moderate.

Badgastein, Spa and Winter Resort

Badgastein is back in Land Salzburg (the federal state of Salzburg, of which the city of Salzburg is the capital); it is one of the most attractive resort towns in Austria. Famous ever since its "miraculous spring" cured Duke Frederick of Styria of a gangrenous infection in the 15th century. Even without its radioactive hot springs, Badgastein would attract visitors because of its incomparable mountain setting on both sides of a rushing torrent which cascades through the center of the town. The town, together with Bad Hofgastein down the valley, and Sportgastein, up the mountain, is also a well-equipped ski resort.

Not far from here, in a northwest direction, is Zell am See, a lake resort gem and a winter sports center, with a magnificent view of the surrounding mountain ranges and deep valleys from Schmittenhöhe, reached by cable car. West of here, on the border of Tyrol, are the Krimml Waterfalls, highest in Europe.

BADGASTEIN HOTELS

Deluxe: *Elisabethpark,* has panoramic view, fine restaurant, and indoor thermal pool. *Der Kaiserhof,* in private park, cure facilities, full board only. *Parkhotel Bellevue,* near center; under same management, less expensive *Bellevue-Alm,* reached by chair lift, only a few rooms, swimming pool, outdoor grill, and night-club.

First Class Superior: *Habsburgerhof,* modern, on edge of town; *Salzburgerhof,* near station; *Germania,* in green surroundings; *Grüner Baum,* in nearby Kotschach valley, about ½ hr. on foot from town; all have pools.

First Class Reasonable: *Straubinger,* where Emperor Franz Josef used to stay, at the waterfall; 100 beds, 10 baths, tavern. *Mozart,* with wine tavern, café, is near tennis courts.

Moderate: *Krone,* near station; *Alpenblick,* on road to Kötschach Valley; and the small *Pension Haus Gerke.*

Among the **inexpensive** hotels, *Moser* (65 beds) is right next to waterfall; *Münchnerhof,* on the way to Böckstein.

Vorarlberg's Panoramic Peaks

If you enter Austria from the west, you are literally 'before the Arlberg'. It is the smallest of Austria's nine federal states. Few things in Europe are more charming than the Bregenz Forest, in whose villages the Vorarlbergers still wear their shiny, starched folk costumes, peculiar to this region.

Capital of Vorarlberg is Bregenz, a picturesque little town at the eastern end of the Bodensee (Lake Constance). It has a delightful annual music festival, featuring light opera and ballet on a unique water stage in the lake. The festival starts in mid-July and lasts until mid-August, and, since the 30-tier amphitheater on the shore can accommodate 6,000, this is one festival where you don't have to know the president of Austria to get seats.

A funicular from the heart of Bregenz will take you in 10 minutes to the 3,200-foot top of Pfänder Mountain and one of the finest panoramic views. It includes the old town at your feet, the 40-mile sweep of the Bodensee, the German frontier and Bavarian town of Lindau to the right, the Rhine and Switzerland to the left. Unbeatable on a sunny day.

See the medieval town of Feldkirch and its Schattenburg Castle, the idyllic high mountain village of Gargellen, and the spectacular Flexen Pass road with Zürs and Lech. At Dornbirn, textile capital of Austria, there is the famed textile fair in August.

REGIONAL HOTELS

Bregenz. Best is *Messmer* (1), with excellent restaurant. *Weisses Kreuz* and the modern *Central* are (2). *Berghof Fluh,* with fine food and view; *Schwärzler,* indoor pool; *Bodensee* (garni) are (3). *Adler* and *Schwedenschanze,* Pfänder mountain above town, reached by cable car, are (4). The Gebhardsberg restaurant in fortress above town offers excellent food and a marvelous view.

Gargellen, mountain resort. *Madrisa,* local color in the tavern; *Feriengut Gargellenhof* and *Silvretta,* indoor pool, are (2). *Alpenrose* and *Edelweiss* are (3).

Lech, ski resort. *Post* (1), with old tradition, leads. *Arlberg, Schneider-Almhof, Tannbergerhof,* and *Krone,* all with pools, are (1–2). In Oberlech, *Sporthotel Sonnenburg* and the small *Montana* are (2).

Schruns, ski resort. *Kurhotel Montafon,* with cure facilities, and *Löwen,* both with indoor pools, are (1). *Messmer* and *Krone* (3).

Zurs, ski resort. *Zürserhof,* restaurant, bar, dancing, and *Albona* (garni), are (D). *Alpenrose-Post,* sun terrace and evening entertainment, is (1). *Flexen* is (2) and *Mara,* small, is (3).

Tyrol, Home of Skiers

Across the spectacular Arlberg Pass from Vorarlberg is the best winter sports area in Austria and one of the best skiing centers in the world. This is the country of skiing masters Hannes Schneider, Toni Seelos and Toni Sailer. The region has over 200 ski schools. Going from west to east in the Tyrol, the top sights are: St. Anton am Arlberg and the view from the top of Valluga above it (cable car); Wiesberg Castle and Trisanna Bridge at the entrance into the Paznaun Valley; the Silvretta group scenery at Galtür; the old Inn bridge and fort ruins at the Finstermünz Gorge on the Tyrol-Swiss border; the castle of Landeck; the Fern Pass area with lakes and castle ruins; Reutte with picturesque houses and Plansee; Zugspitze; Schemenlaufen masks in the museum of Imst; the lower Ötz Valley, with the typical Tyrolean village of Ötz, and the Stuiben Waterfall near Umhausen; the upper Ötz Valley, with mountain and skiing resorts of Sölden, Hochgurgl and Obergurgl (the latter is also the highest village in Austria) and with the magnificent panorama of glaciers and mountain peaks, seen especially from the cable car trip from Sölden to Gaislachkogel (about 10,000 feet) and from the chair lift from Hochgurgl up to Wurmkogel (also about 10,000 feet); here you can also ski all year round.

The 13th-century abbey at Stams, rebuilt in baroque style; Seefeld and the view around it; the mountain scenery seen from the left side of the train when riding from Innsbruck to Seefeld and Scharnitz; Stubai and Gschnitz valleys.

The medieval streets and buildings, Mint Tower and mining museum of Solbad Hall; Fuggerhaus, Freundsberg Castle (museum), Enzenberg Palace, the parish church, and the old streets of Schwaz; Tratzberg Castle, between Stams and Jenbach; the lake of Achensee; Mayrhofen, with the view of Zillertaler Alps from Penken (cable car) and old farmhouses in Tuxertal; Alpbach Valley; the medieval town of Rattenberg.

The castle-fortress of Kufstein, with huge outdoor organ and an interesting museum; the roundtrip of Kaisergebirge: from Kufstein to Walchsee, Kössen, St. Johann, Ellmau, Scheffau, and back. Kitzbühel, one of the top society winter resorts in the Alps.

Innsbruck, Capital of the Tyrol

Innsbruck, venue of the 1964 and 1976 Winter Olympics, is one of the most beautiful towns of its size (100,000). This 700-year-old university city is bounded on the north by the shimmering wall of the Nordkette Range of the Alps, on the south by the Tuxer Range, rising to heights of 10,000 feet. Hence, the world-famous view from Innsbruck's main street, the Maria-Theresienstrasse. The Empress Maria Theresia loved the Tyrol and Innsbruck, and so did the powerful Emperor Maximilian, which accounts for the city's many beautiful buildings, especially the Roman-style Triumphal Arch, built for her in 1767; the Goldenes Dachl (Golden Roof), an ancient mansion whose ornate stone balcony is covered by a roof of heavily gilded copper shingles; the Hofburg, imperial 18th-century palace, with its wealth of paintings and elaborate furniture; the 16th-century Imperial Church, containing the immense and magnificent tomb of Maximilian I, with its heroic bronze statues of the emperor's ancestors, including the celebrated effigy of King Arthur of England; and the Silver Chapel, with its beautifully executed silver altar. Don't miss a visit to the Tiroler Volkskunstmuseum (the Tyrolean Folk Art Museum), which has a complete collection of folk costumes, antique rustic furniture and delightfully furnished Tyrolean interiors.

There are various fine excursions to make: you can visit sites of the 1976 Winter Olympics at Axamer Lizum and Igls, both a part of Innsbruck's winter sports area. Or take a cable railway to the Hungerburg, 2,800 feet, and thence by two-stage cable car to the Hafelekar, at 7,500 feet. The view over Innsbruck and the southern Alps is beyond praise.

PRACTICAL INFORMATION FOR INNSBRUCK

HOTELS. Best are the luxurious *Tyrol, Holiday Inn,* the new *Innsbruck,* and *Europa,* with fine restaurant. *Grauer Bär, Roter Adler,* and *Maria Theresia* are first-class, reasonable, and well appointed. First class also is the historic *Goldener Adler,* founded in 1390 and once frequented by such eminent personages as Goethe and Andreas Hofer. 76 beds, atmosphere. Moderately priced atmospheric hostelries are *Goldene Rose* and *Greif.* Inexpensive: *Sailer,* with good restaurant; *Weisses Kreuz* (garni); *Goldene Krone* and *Neue Post;* pensions *Elisabeth* and *Stoi,* at the station.

On the Hungerburg plateau, with panoramic view, is the recent *Bellevue,* modern with terrace café, restaurant, and *Maria Brunn,* terrace restaurant and bar, both reasonable. There are a number of pleasant inns and pensions, among them *Zur Linde* and the recent *Alpina,* all rooms with shower, both moderate. If you can't find rooms, *Tiroler Landesreisebüro* will find you accommodations.

RESTAURANTS. During the season they are crowded by tourists but they still retain their typical, old atmosphere. Among them: *Ottoburg,* Herzog-Friedrich-Str. 1, moderate; *Goldene Rose,* same street at No. 39, moderate; *Alt Innsprugg,* Maria-Theresien-Str. 16, moderate to inexpensive, as is the *Stiftskeller,* Burggraben 21. *Goethestube* (in Hotel Goldener Adler), and *Altes Haus Delevo,* Maria-Theresien-Str. 9, both have dinner music and are moderate to expensive. *Stiegl-Bräu,* Wilhelm-Greil-Str. 25, is inexpensive.

SHOPPING. For skiing and mountain climbing equipment *Witting,* Maria-Theresien-Str. 39, *Gramshammer,* Wilhelm-Greilstr. 19, and *Schirmer,* Maria-Theresienstr. 32. For dirndls and other Tyrolean folk dress *Trachten-Konrad,* Maria-Theresien-Str. 27, and for Tyrolean handicrafts *Tiroler Heimatwerk,* Meranerstr. 2. Leather clothes at *Obholzer,* Herzog-Friedrich-Str. 32, and *Schwammenhöfer,* Burggraben 1.

SKI RESORTS

Igls. *Sporthotel Igls,* with its *Schlosshotel* annex, is deluxe. *Gulfhotel* and *Parkhotel* are superior; *Maximilian,* reasonable, and *Stettnerhof,* moderate.

Kitzbühel. Deluxe are *Grand* and *Schloss Lebenberg.* Superior: *Goldener Greif* (since 1274); *Tennerhof,* antique furnishings, *Schlosshotel Münichau,* with lovely garden, is reasonable.

St. Anton. *Post* is best and superior. *Berghaus Maria,* in nice location and with good food, is reasonable. *Gasthof Reselehof* and *Goldenes Kreuz* are inexpensive.

Seefeld. *Karwendelhof,* with old collar tavern, is deluxe. *Astoria, Schlosshotel Klosterbräu,* and *Tümmlerhof* are superior. *Philipp* is reasonable; *Waldruh,* moderate.

Forested Styria

Styria is Austria's second largest federal state, an area of large, dense forests, rife with game. Some places, like Mariazell, offer all the fashionable amenities of winter resort life plus local flavor, at lower prices than elsewhere in Austria. Towering above the historic old town of Schladming is Dachstein, the highest peak of Styria (almost 10,000 feet), which can be reached by cable car. Styria has the longest chair lift in the world at Tauplitz and one of the biggest ski jumps near Mitterndorf, where jumps longer than 140 yards are not uncommon. West of Mitterndorf is one of the most romantic areas of Styria, the Ausseer Land around Bad Aussee, with a string of lakes nestled among the mountains and forests; this is the Styrian section of the Salzkammergut.

The capital of Styria is Graz, a university town (second largest in Austria) with an old world atmosphere, one of the oldest museums in the world, the Joanneum; a fascinating folklore museum with Styrian folk costumes dating all the way back to the Hallstatt and Celtic periods; Schloss Eggenberg, a superb 17th-century castle, housing a unique hunting museum; and the Styrian Armory, which contains the greatest collection of ancient armor in Europe.

REGIONAL HOTELS

In **Graz** the leading hotel is *Steirerhof* near the Opera with fine food and Styrian wines in its wood-paneled rooms; deluxe. *Daniel,* at railroad station, modern and functional, and *Parkhotel,* near City Park, are superior. *Wiesler,* on the Mur river bank, offers a fine view of the river, the old town and the castle hill, as well as a good restaurant and a Styrian wine tavern; first class reasonable. *Weitzer,* in similar position, is a bit less. The old-fashioned *Erzherzog Johann* is moderate.

In **Altaussee** *Am See,* beautiful lakeside location, and *Tyrol* are superior. *Kitzer,* with fine food and pastries, is reasonable; *Dachstein,* moderate. The baroque *Schloss Rabenstein* near **Frohnleiten** is a small, superior castle-pension. In **Irdning** in the Enns Valley, the deluxe *Schloss Pichlarn,* one of Austria's finest castle-hotels, offers a variety of sports.

Carinthia, Austria's Lakeland

Carinthia is the lovely southern state with warm lakes, rocky peaks, and a vintage history going back to the Stone Age, whose graves have yielded rich prehistoric finds. This federal state is at its best between mid-May and early October, when a fine climate, the mildest in Austria, makes it possible to swim in the emerald lakes. Of these, the most renowned is the lovely Wörthersee, with its internationally famed resorts, Velden and Pörtschach, and its outstanding landmark, almost completely surrounded by water on a small peninsula, the picturesque village of Maria Wörth, with two ancient churches. The Carinthians are also proud of their great Romanesque cathedral of Gurk, and their many castles, of which the famous Schloss Hochosterwitz is perhaps most like something out of a fairytale. The best excursion center for these two attractions is Klagenfurt, the capital of Carinthia, founded in the 13th century and capital since 1518. Another well-located excursion center is the historic town of Villach, with the nearby spa, Warmbad Villach, which has been in existence since Roman times.

REGIONAL HOTELS

FAAKER SEE. *Karnerhof,* marvelous location, pool, first class reasonable; at Egg, *Strandgasthof Trink,* with good food, *Faakersee* and *Sonnblick* are inexpensive.

KLAGENFURT. First class reasonable are: *Sandwirt,* with old tradition and good food; the small *Musil,* with cozy period-furnished rooms, fine cuisine and renowned Konditorei; and the recent *Europapark* and *Porcia. Janach,* with atmospheric, good restaurant, is moderate. Outside the city, near Wörthersee, is the moderate *Schloss Freyenthurn,* a small castle-hotel.

MARIA WÖRTH. First class superior; *Linde,* 100 beds, restaurant terrace on lake; *Post Astoria,* indoor pool; and *Golfhotel* in nearby Dellach.

MILLSTATT, beside warm water Millstättersee. *Forelle* is first class superior; *Postillion,* reasonable.

PÖRTSCHACH. *Park,* large, and the highly recommended *Schloss Leonstein,* a converted castle on the main road, antique décor, candlelight dining in courtyard, are superior. *Werzer-Astoria,* a complex of 16 buildings in a park, moderate to reasonable.

VELDEN. *Schloss Velden,* a converted baroque castle, antique décor in public rooms, lakeside terrace restaurant and bar, superior.
Seehotel Veldnerhof-Mösslacher, 240 beds, garden restaurant on lake front, tennis and water sports, and *Yacht Hotel,* in large park, own beach, tennis, are superior. *Carinthia, Kleines Hotel,* and *Seehotel Hubertus,* are reasonable. Moderate are *Frank* and *Michaela,* with good restaurant.

VILLACH, a historic town on the Drau. The best hotels are *Parkhotel* and *City,* first class reasonable; *Post,* in 15th-century patrician house on main square, is moderate.

Lower Austria and its Castles

Largest of the nine federal states, Lower Austria with some 500 castles and abbeys, of which the following are outstanding: Seitenstetten, Benedictine abbey founded in 1112; Melk, one of the most beautiful baroque churches and abbeys on the right bank of the Danube; the renaissance castle Schallaburg near Melk; Dürnstein, romantic ruined castle where Richard the Lionhearted was imprisoned in 1193; Klosterneuburg, Augustine abbey from 12th century, just outside Vienna; Heidenreichstein, one of the most remarkable water castles; Heiligenkreuz, treasure-filled Cistercian abbey, 10 miles west of Baden.

Baden, very close to Vienna, is a gay spa, whose Roman spring has been in use for 2,000 years, curing people of rheumatic and skin afflictions. South of Vienna, the resort center known as the Semmering is a favorite summer and winter weekend spot for the Viennese.

The 20-mile stretch of magnificent scenery along the Danube known as the Wachau is best seen by Danube boat. From mid-May to mid-September, there are daily steamers to take you nine hours downstream from Linz to Vienna, 17 hours upstream from Vienna to Linz. If you are going by car, take the road on the left bank between Emmersdorf (opposite Melk—cross by ferry) and the old town of Krems, founded in the 10th century, the wine capital of Austria.

HOTELS

BADEN. *Clubhotel, Gutenbrunn, Herzoghof, Parkhotel,* and *Kongress* are all superior and have own cure facilities. *Papst,* near Kurpark, and *Josefsplatz,* are reasonable.

Five miles west, in wooded quiet spot, is the *Neue Krainerhütte,* good food (trout), superior. *Schlosshotel,* is moderate and the small *Bausch,* Pergerstr. 11, pleasant restaurant and garden, inexpensive to moderate.

Restaurants include *Stadtkrug,* in the Kongresshaus in Kurpark, with nice outdoor terrace facing the park; *Krebs,* near station, moderate; *Badener Stadtkeller,* rustic atmosphere in cellar, pleasant courtyard garden, moderate.

SEMMERING. Best is *Südbahnhotel,* luxurious, 200 beds, 70 baths, on hill above railroad station; beautiful view of mountains; well appointed rooms; first class food; glassed-in pool, tennis, 9-hole golf course, superior service.

First class superior *Alpenhof,* south of the pass on the Styrian side, modern chalet-style, all rooms with bath, dancing, heated swimming pool. First class reasonable *Silvana,* 32 beds, most rooms with bath. *Park-Villa* and *Pension Belvedere* are moderate. *Stefanie, Waldruhe* and *Landau,* all in quiet locations, inexpensive.

Miniature Burgenland

This tiny federal state is sandwiched between Lower Austria and the Hungarian border. Its principal natural curiosity is Neusiedler Lake, whose shallow expanse of salt water expands and contracts at the caprice of the wind. Fourth largest lake in Europe, it is pleasant for summer swimming. The chief tourist attraction of Burgenland and its capital is Eisenstadt, in whose church the composer, Josef Haydn, lies buried in an elaborate tomb of white marble built by his grateful patron, Prince Esterhazy. Esterhazy Palace may be visited, and the composer's home is now a museum. The Vienna Philharmonic Orchestra gives an annual Haydn concert on Good Friday in the Eisenstadt Church. Bad Tatzmannsdorf, in south Burgenland, has been a health resort for hundreds of years, with treatment for heart and circulatory troubles.

HOTELS. In **Eisenstadt** Parkhotel (garni) is reasonable; *Schwechaterhof,* moderate; 13 miles south is the superior *Schlosshotel Drassburg.* In BAD TATZMANNSDORF, *Parkhotel* is reasonable; *Zum Kastell* and *Kurhotel,* moderate; *Jormannsdorf,* a castle hotel nearby, is reasonable. At **Bernstein,** *Schlosshotel,* a converted castle complete with ghost, is first class, with swimming pool and game hunting facilities.

WINTER SPORTS

Austria definitely vies with Switzerland as the Number One skiing country of Europe; you can ski virtually anywhere. *Fodor's Guide to Austria* carries a com prehensive section on this subject, or you can ask any branch of the Austrian National Tourist Office for the folder *Winter in Austria,* which lists over 450 winter sports centers and what they have to offer, and for their new listing of special all-inclusive bargains. There is year-round skiing (reached by cable cars and with all facilities including ski teachers) on Wurmkogel above Hochgurgl in Tyrol; on Kitzsteinhorn above Kaprun and Weissee above Utendorf, both in Salzburg; and on Dachstein, the highest peak of Styria.

BELGIUM

Often overlooked by travelers intent upon more distant goals in Europe, or dismissed for study "after the big, important nations", Belgium is, in fact, a perfect model-in-miniature of much of Europe, its treasures and its troubles. It is, moreover, the perfect setting in which to investigate the castles of your imagination. Conscious of its splendid heritage in this field, the Belgian government is vigorously promoting "open house" at the country's many stately homes, and some have now been converted into hotels or restaurants.

This stampsized country has tourist attractions out of all proportion to its territory. Old world charm, a great cuisine, golden beaches, and the scenic forest of the Ardennes—these are a few. The rest is art, to which Belgium, at the cultural crossroads of Europe, has been one of the supreme contributors. And all this is crammed into an area small enough to cover thoroughly in a week, or superficially in a few days. Basing yourself in Brussels (which you should be prepared to find an expensive city), you can head for the splendid beaches in summer, for the lush green of the Ardennes in any season, or for the art cities of Ghent and Bruges whenever the spirit moves you.

Belgium Today

Belgians are among the most enterprising people in Europe, as anyone will testify who saw them snap back from two catastrophic military occupations within the space of 30 years. The country's rapid recovery after World War II astonished the world. This was the "Miracle of Belgium". By 1948, production exceeded pre-war levels, exports exceeded imports in value, and the national budget was balanced; all this while, Belgium's larger neighbors were barely stirring from the stillness of exhaustion. Today, taking exports per-head of population, Belgians sell more to foreign countries than any other nationals.

Most recently of all, Belgium has re-discovered its international vocation. For some time it has been the headquarters for SHAPE and NATO and, as capital of the EEC, from 1973 controls the enlarged community of nine. Three separate diplomatic corps are accredited to Brussels, which thus has every right to call itself the "Capital of Europe". It is said that there are some 158 ambassadors in the city.

On Flemings and Walloons

It is a paradox that the focal point of European integration, namely Brussels, should be the remaining subject of contention between the Dutch-speaking Flemings and the French-speaking Wallons in Belgium —a country whose national motto is "Unity is Strength." However, the Bruxellois themselves are a distinct bilingual community (further conditioned by an influx of Anglo-Saxon and other non-Belgian residents). At all events, the occasional domestic quarrels pale in comparison with others in the world, and the good old "Belgic compromise" owes much to political and social currents that cut across ethnic lines.

Although both groups have a strong sense of Belgian nationality, a lot of ethnic rivalry and suspicion between them. Remember that a lot of Flemings resent any assumption that their language is or ought to be French, and even if your French is quite good, you may find that they prefer to answer you in English.

Off the road and away from the tax office, the Belgians are conservative, law abiding, and dignified, even a little sedate and staid, as befits good solid burghers. There is, however, general agreement on one fact: the Belgians are industrious. In this country, as in all fundamentally bourgeois societies, trade is King, work is a cardinal virtue and sloth is the deadliest of the sins.

Food and Drink

"French cooking is superb," said a Belgian gourmet, "but Belgian cooking is divine." This is carrying patriotism too far. But Belgian cooking is not to be sniffed at. Or rather, it is. And eaten. But watch your waistline. Belgian cooks are even more lavish with the butter and cream than their French counterparts.

Try sampling some typical Belgian dishes: *Anguilles au vert* are young eels served hot or cold with a green sauce of shredded herbs, sorrel, mint, sage and verbena. They taste wonderful. *Witloof,* which is Flemish for white leaf, is endive in America, chicory in Britain. The Belgians grow it and cook it better than anyone else in the world.

The Belgians are very fond of *moules* (mussels) which are served in R months in about thirty-five different fashions and always in enormous portions.

There is a wide selection of French and German wines available everywhere. But the national drink of Belgium is beer. In fact, the Belgians rival the Germans as beer drinkers. Try *Gueuze* (bottled), which is known as *Lambic* when it's on tap. This is a wheat and barley-based beer, slightly vinous in flavor. *Kriek-Lambic* is the same thing, with a flavoring of cherries, not so grim as it sounds. *Orval,* brewed by the Trappist monks, is different, and tastes like a soft drink, but look out for those monastery brews; they're loaded. Visit the cellar of the tavern *Roi d'Espagne* in Brussels. Here you might start with *Faro,* the famous wheat-based beer that has already celebrated its 1,000th birthday. Beer is a venerable institution, and differences of brew and origin are deeply respected.

PRACTICAL INFORMATION FOR BELGIUM

WHAT WILL IT COST. For a single room with bath: *deluxe,* about 2,300 francs; first class 1,900 francs; moderate 1,250 francs; inexpensive 500; these are all-inclusive and must be shown in room; local visitors' tax is rare nowadays; modest meal 400 francs; gastronomic meal 900 francs. Hotels in Brussels and other places promote weekend and off-peak packages.

Most towns levy a small visitors' charge which comes on your hotel bill. There are no beach charges. Value added tax (VAT) applies to most goods and services, but is usually included in the price.

CAPITAL. Brussels.

LANGUAGES. Flemish (Dutch) in north and French in south Belgium are the official languages. Brussels is bi-lingual. English widely spoken and understood, especially in Flanders. German on the eastern border.

CLIMATE. Moderate. Bring a raincoat; it drizzles frequently.
Average maximum daily temperatures in degrees Fahrenheit and centigrade:

Brussels	Jan.	Feb.	Mar.	Apr.	May	June	July	Aug.	Sept.	Oct.	Nov.	Dec.
F°	39	45	50	57	64	72	73	72	70	59	48	43
C°	4	7	10	14	18	22	23	22	21	15	9	6

SEASONS. The main tourist season runs from early May to end September, with the peak (school holidays) in July and August.

SPECIAL EVENTS. *February,* start of carnival season, best at Eupen and Malmédy, climax on Shrove Tuesday at Binche, with the procession of the Gilles. *April,* International Fair, Liege. *May,* Procession of the Holy Blood at Bruge (Ascension Day); Festival of the Cats at Ypres. Queen Elizabeth International Music Competition for young artists in Brussels. *June,* Festival of the Lumeçon, Mons (Trinity Sunday); Carillon concerts in Bruges and Malines (through Sept.); Grand Prix automobile race at Zolder. *July,* Ommegang, an historical cavalcade in Brussels Grand' Palace (not every year); nightly sound and light performances in front of Tournai Cathedral and at nearby Beloeil Castle; Music Festival, Bruges. *August,* Begonia Festival at Lochristi, six miles from Ghent. *September,* Beer Festival, Wieze. *November,* St. Hubert Festival.

HIGHLIGHTS OF BELGIUM. The three big cities are Brussels, Antwerp and Liège, all of them commercially and industrially very active and all with claims as museum cities. Belgium has more echoes of the past than most areas of comparable size, especially in picturebook towns, such as Bruges and Tournai or the more active Ghent. Even its chief watering place dates from Roman times and gave its name, Spa, to all the water-cure towns of the world. This "cockpit of Europe" too, has many battlefields, the chief commemorations of which are at Waterloo (1815), Ypres or Ieper (1915–18) and Bastogne (the Battle of the Bulge, 1944).

The centuries have left here a great deal to be seen in the way of painting, sculpture, religious and civic architecture, including the many Béguinages built in the Middle Ages for communities of lay sisters of humble origin. The mother of all carillons is at Malines (Mechelen), and the most widely reputed (if you know your Longfellow) at Bruges; but you will find them, either in churches or in special bell-towers, in at least a dozen other towns.

Besides all this, you will find modern achievements such as the world's biggest sea lock (Zandvliet, Antwerp) and the world's biggest barge-lift (Ronquières). There are 40 miles of fine sandy seaboard, with all the amenities of summer holidays, whether on the beach or at the green tables of sophisticated casinos. Further south you have the ancient Meuse and the idyllic scenery of the Ardennes.

CLOSING TIMES. Banks open usually from 9 to 15:30 hrs (sometimes till 16:30). Shops must close for 24 consecutive hours once a week and they post a notice to say which day this will be; the usual opening hours are 9 to 18:00 or 18:30, but a number of smaller shops stay open later. For shopping centers and many supermarkets, the hours are 9 to 20.00 hours.

SPORTS. There are two good *golf* clubs near Brussels at Tervueren (Royal Golf Club de Belgique—expensive and rather exclusive) and Waterloo. There are three along the coast at Ostend, Klemskerke (Le Coq) and the Royal Le Zoute, and others around Mons, Antwerp, Ghent, Liège and, the best of all, the Golf Club des Fagnes at Spa. There are plenty of *lawn tennis* clubs everywhere and it is usually possible to arrange temporary membership.

For *shooting* you need a license and should write to the Société Royale St. Hubert, 25 Ave. de l'Armée, 1040 Brussels, and for *fishing* you should get information from the National Tourist Office. In neither case does the mere possession of a license give you automatic access to preserved shoots or streams. For *water sports* there are two Belgian federations from which you may need information— for canoeing, at 21 Bogaardenlaan, Aarschot; and for yachting, 5 Rue du Chêne, 1000 Brussels. *Horseback riding* is easy and inexpensive. There are a number of good stables in the Brussels area, especially around the Bois de la Cambre, and opportunities for trek outings across the Ardennes foothills.

MONEY. The Belgian *franc,* divided into 100 *centimes,* is the monetary unit. There are about 38 francs to the $US, about 63 to the pound sterling. The money comes in coins of 25 and 50 centimes, 1, 5, 10 and 50 francs. There are 20, 50, 100, 500, 1,000 and 5,000 franc banknotes. You can bring in and take out unlimited foreign currency and Belgian francs.

TIPPING. A 15% service charge is usually included in your hotel bill, so that you needn't give any of the staff more than a token tip. Restaurants also include service charge. So do nightclubs. If they don't, you add it. Tip Brussels hatcheck girls and washroom attendants 5 francs. Taxi fares are expensive but at least the tip is included.

HOW TO REACH BELGIUM. By air: Sabena, the Belgian airline company, has direct services with New York, Montreal, London, and most European cities. Most international airlines have direct or connecting services to Brussels. BA flies 5 times daily from Heathrow, London to Brussels. Sabena has 6 daily flights from London to Brussels and also from Heathrow direct flights to Antwerp, Liege, and Charleroi. British Caledonian Airways, operate regularly between London/Gatwick and Brussels. British Air Ferries links Southend and Ostend. British Midland Airways services between Birmingham/Derby and Brussels. For getting there by sea, train, or by car, see *Practical Planning* section.

CUSTOMS. Simple and painless; you may never be asked to open a suitcase. You can bring in 400 cigarettes, one pound of tobacco or 100 cigars duty free (visitors from U.K. only half of these quantities), also one bottle of wine or liquor with seal broken.

MAIL. Surface letters to US cost 14 francs; postcards 10 fr. Airmail letters to US are 14 frs. for first 5 grams; postcards 9.50 frs. All letters and postcards to Britain and other European countries go airmail automatically.

ELECTRICITY. Nearly (but not quite) all Belgium has 220 volts A.C. Check before plugging.

DRINKING WATER. Town water is potable everywhere in Belgium, unless temporary notices are posted to the contrary. Restaurants and cafés seldom serve tap water, however, and a request for water brings a small bottle of *Spa, Spontin* or *Chaudfontaine* mineral water.

 TRAVEL IN BELGIUM. By car: Belgium's big motor highways are Antwerp-Liège bypass-German frontier, Brussels-Ostend, Brussels-Antwerp, the Wallonie (E 41), Brussels-Paris (E 10), Brussels-Liège (E 5), and Antwerp-Lille (E 3). There is a new ring-road to the north of Brussels, which links the motorway from Ostend to the cities of Antwerp, Liege, and Namur. There is much construction in progress, so best get the most recent road map and supplement it by up-to-date information from AAA, AA, or RAC. Many of the secondary roads are extremely good and make interesting drives.

Gasoline (petrol) prices vary, but at presstime it's 13.62 and 16.14 frs. per liter.

Car hire: If you arrive by air, you can arrange in advance for a self-drive car to meet you at the airport, and there is a similar arrangement with Belgian Rail for arrival at the chief stations. *Avis,* 145 Rue Américaine, Brussels. *Hertz,* 8 Blvd. Maurice Lemonnier, Brussels. Bicycles can be hired at railway stations.

By rail: frequent, efficient services. Fares run about 2.05 francs per km. first class, 1.39 second class, but various types of season tickets available, which also operate on the rail company's bus services.

By bus: Particulars at rail stations or travel agents.

By boat: trips on the River Meuse from Namur, Dinant and other towns. Launch tours from Antwerp port (even to Rotterdam, Holland).

GUIDES. Knowledgeable guide-escorts can be obtained from Brussels Hostesses, I Rue du Chêne, or from International Hostesses, 158 Circulaire Avenue, Brussels.

CAMPING. Many sites. Information from the Royal Camping and Caravanning Club of Belgium, 51 Rue de Namur, Brussels, or from the National Tourist Office (see below).

USEFUL ADDRESSES. *American Embassy,* 27 Blvd. du Regent; *British,* 28 Rue Joseph II; *Canadian,* 35 Rue de la Science. *National Tourist Office,* 61 Rue Marche-aux-Herbes; *American Express,* Place Rogier; *Wagons Lits/Cook,* 17 Pl. de Brouckère and 41 Ave. de la Toison d'Or. All in Brussels. *Emergency:* dial 900 (throughout the country).

Brussels, Lively Capital

Whether you call it Bruxelles (French), Brussel (Flemish), or Brussels (Anglo-American), it all adds up to the same thing—Belgium's busy, bustling capital, one of the more expensive cities of Europe. It's a vigorous, neon-lighted boom town, bursting at the seams, and at the same time paradoxically enclosing its quietly dreaming heart of long ago. That heart, one of the most beautiful and impressive squares in Europe, is the Grand' Place. Completely surrounded by flamboyantly-decorated 17th-century guild houses, it is dominated by the Hôtel de Ville or town hall, which, with its 320-foot belfry, is one of the finest gothic structures in northern Europe. After you've had a beer or two in one of the many outdoor cafés in this superb *place,* you may feel ambitious enough to climb the 420 steps to the tower's summit. The view over Brussels and the green surroundings of Brabant is worth all the huffing and puffing.

Not far away in the Rue de l'Etuve is another symbol, but on a smaller scale. This is the ancient symbol of the Rights of Man, the Manneken-Pis, the famous bronze statue of Brussels' oldest inhabitant. In the Maison du Roi, back in the Grand' Place, you can see a collection of beautifully tailored costumes which various admirers of the Manneken-Pis have bestowed upon him, including a gold-embroidered suit from Louis XV of France. On September 3, you can see the Manneken himself dressed in the uniform of the Welsh Guards, who liberated Brussels on this date in 1944, and on October 27, this spoiled brat wears an American sailor suit in honor of United States Navy Day.

Brussels is both old and new, and, for some years at least, you cannot avoid the signs of its becoming still newer. The new jostles the old; and, in the narrow Rue Neuve, you will step straight out of the Eglise du Finistère, after contemplating the wood statue of Our Lady of Aberdeen (whose original owner, a bishop of Aberdeen, was a contemporary of Macbeth), to see the bold lines of Brussels' grand department store, *Innovation,* rebuilt on the site of the old fire-destroyed store. A minute's walk to the right brings you to two modern triumphs—the Philips Building (backing onto the last relic of the city's earliest fortification) and the splendid Post Office Building, opposite the Opera House (Théâtre Royal de la Monnaie), where the 1830 Revolution started and the Belgian nation was born. Had you gone, instead, to your left, a minute would have brought you to the foot of the Rogier Building, Brussels' first skyscraper, and Manhattan Center with its various restaurants, shops, conference and exhibition halls.

The shops are wonderful, and you cannot fail to be impressed with the large number of small boutiques now in covered galleries on the ground floor of many modern buildings, through which you find your way from street to street. From the coffee shop in the Hilton, you pass out into the gardens of a Renaissance palace, past the Peter Pan statue (a gift to the children of Brussels from the children of London) and so through the one-time stables and the great courtyard to the gem-square of the Petit Sablon, with its 48 elegant bronze statues of the medieval craft guilds.

Facing you is the church of Notre Dame du Sablon, one of the city's many ecclesiastical masterpieces, the most important of which is the 13th-century Cathedral of St. Michael, with its impressive tapestries and glass and its great west window floodlit at night. On your way there from the Sablon, you will have passed the Museum of Ancient Art (an impressive collection of Flemish masters) and the temporary quarters of the

Museum of Modern Art; turned downhill from the 18th-century Place Royale, leaving on your left the Palais des Congrès.

Close on the other side of the Hilton, and the only challenge to its lofty stature, is the massive Palais de Justice. Its 19th-century architect, Poelaert, intended its dome (now the technical home of the Eurovision relays) to be a pyramid; and you will have to choose, as do the locals, whether to call it Greco-Roman or Assyro-Babylonian. It is larger than St. Peter's in Rome, dominating Brussels from the summit of the one-time Gallows Hill.

Though much of the central city (old and new) is apt to be congested, it is traversed by wide streets and surrounded by a spacious boulevard with underpasses and side lanes for local traffic. Among the open spaces, there are four parks deserving special mention. The Parc de Bruxelles stretches between the Royal Palace and the Palais de la Nation (Parliament), with the Rue Royale on one side and the Rue Ducale (residences of the US and British ambassadors) on the other. Just outside the boulevard, at the Rue Royale level, the Jardin Botanique stretches downhill towards the back of the Palace Hotel. Leaving the central area eastwards by the (one-way only) Rue Belliard, you come to the Parc Léopold; and from here an underpass brings you into the majestic Parc du Cinquantennaire, with its *gloriette* and complex of buildings which include the Musée de l'Armée and the Musée Royal d'Art et d'Histoire. Nearby, in Place Schuman, at the end of Rue de la Loi, is a huge glass building called Berlaymont, seat of the European Community (EEC).

PRACTICAL INFORMATION FOR BRUSSELS

HOTELS. Brussels has developed rapidly as the Common Market business and administrative center and it is advisable to make hotel reservations ahead. Some hotels offer reductions and vouchers for free access to the main sites (including Boitsfort racecourse) during the weekend. Most hotels are concentrated in the downtown area near the World Trade Center.

DELUXE

Hyatt Regency, Rue Royale, 322 deluxe rooms and gourmet restaurant. Brussels' newest.

Sheraton, Place Rogier in high-rise building; rooftop restaurant.

Hilton, Blvd. de Waterloo, has 373 rooms and panoramic restaurant.

Holiday Inn, next to the airport, 300 rooms, pool, sauna.

Ramada, near Ave. Louise, 202 rooms, garden restaurant.

Royal Windsor, conveniently located near air terminal and main station has 300 rooms, underground parking.

Brussels Europa, Rue de la Loi, is a short walk from EEC headquarters; 245 rooms; restaurant (closed Sundays).

Mayfair, Ave. Louise. Rebuilt; excellent decor.

Arcade Stephanie, 91 Ave. Louise, offers smallish but comfortable apartments for weekly, monthly or yearly rental.

FIRST CLASS SUPERIOR

Park, 21 Ave. de l'Yser, is also near EEC headquarters, 46 rooms.

Arenberg, close to Grand'Place, 160 rooms, elegant bar, parking facilities.

FIRST CLASS REASONABLE

Vendome, 98 Blvd. Adolphe Max, 38 rooms with bath; reader recommended.

Mirabeau, Place Fontainas, 29 rooms is a good choice.

Bedford, 135 Rue du Midi, 220 rooms in quiet setting.

La Madeleine, located near air terminal, is small.

MODERATE

Central-Bourse, opposite stock exchange, is central, large. **Scheers,** Blvd. Adolphe Max, 63 rooms. **La Vielle Lanterne,** Rue des Grands Carmes.

INEXPENSIVE

Albergo, Ave. de la Toison d'Or across the street from the Hilton, is a series of old houses joined together; good Italian restaurant. **Cecil,** 13 Blvd. Jardin Botanique and **Duc de Brabant et du Rhin,** 19 Rue St. Lazare, both handy for the Nord rail station.

RESIDENTIAL HOTELS

Smaller, more intimate and less impersonal than the bigger hotels, these usually expect visitors to book on pension, or half pension terms. Among the best is **Résidence Richmond,** 21 Rue de la Concorde, half of rooms with bath. **Lancaster Résidence,** 114 Rue du Cornet, breakfast only, is near EEC.

 RESTAURANTS. For an evening in quest of culinary adventure, go to the Rue des Bouchers, a street of restaurants—mostly small—which climbs the hill between the Galerie du Roi and the Galerie de la Reine. Every restaurant here has its own style and its own specialties, and you are quite sure to find something utterly satisfying and enjoyable. Mussels, in season, are a favorite choice.

Practically all restaurants offer a fixed menu as well as *à la carte*. The menu is usually exhibited at the entrance or in one of the windows, but does not, however, cover wine or extras; so the price of your meal could be considerably augmented. You can eat modestly but well for 140 frs. at one of the department store restaurants, in pleasant surroundings.

TOPS IN CUISINE AND ELEGANCE

Epaule de Mouton, in the narrow Rue des Harengs, has been a hostelry for 300 years and is still a great restaurant.

In the nearby Grand' Place, outstanding restaurants include *Maison du Cygne* (entrance under the archway) and *La Couronne*.

Also downtown, near Opera House, the *Londres* in Rue de l'Ecuyer is most comfortable for business lunches (best book). Not too expensive. *L'Ecailler du Palais Royal,* Rue Bodenbroek, specializes in fish dishes. All these are expensive.

MODERATELY EXPENSIVE

On Blvd. Emile Jacqmain is the *Rôtisserie d'Alsace,* which is the spot to sample fois gras. At the other end of the lower town, in the Place Rouppe, *Comme chez Soi* is a prize winner. Closed Sun., Mon., and second half July. *La Petite Auberge,* Rue des Harengs, is a family-type place in ancient building just off the Grand'-Place.

Uptown the choice is between the Burgundian atmosphere of the *Ravenstein* opposite the Palais des Congrès and the Mediterranean *En Provence. La Villa Lorraine* in the Bois de la Cambre has an excellent reputation. *Peppino's,* 86 Rue du Marais, an attractive paved garden. In the Rue du Grand Cerf, is *Lobert,* an outstanding place for seafood.

Rather further out, but quite outstanding, are *Swiss Grill* on the Chaussée de Waterloo, with first-class Swiss food; and *Henri I,* Avenue Messidor, excellent food. Moderate. Book ahead.

INEXPENSIVE

Aux Armes de Bruxelles, 13 Rue des Bouchers.

Trattoria, 58 Ave. de la Toison d'Or in Albergo hotel has good Italian cooking. In Rue des Dominicains *Stans* or *Vincent* for atmosphere and excellent food.

OUTSKIRTS

Showplace number one is the *Atomium Restaurant,* a vestige of the '58 World Exhibition, panoramic view, music. Quite nearby, at Wemmel, *Le Kam* (terminal of "W" bus) offers good dinner by candlelight: so does *Le Vieux Dielegham, chez Pierrot,* in the same neighborhood, with fine wine cellar. To the south, near the university, *Le Parc Savoy,* presently very fashionable. *Le Châlet de la Forêt,* on forest fringe, is pleasant in summer. All fairly expensive.

 NIGHTCLUBS. You can dance at the Hilton's *En Plein Ciel,* and at *Cub Room* in the Brussels Residence. *L'Interdit* and *The Funny Horse,* both in Rue de Livourne, are fashionable at cocktail hours.

The best floorshows in town are at Le Crazy, 15 Rue Captain Crespel (Porte Louise) and *Chez Paul au Gaity,* 18 Fossé-aux-Loups, near Place de Brouckère. You can dine, too, in a Spanish décor with dancing and show at *Las Cuevas del Tio Pepe* in Marché-aux-Fromages.

For latest discos inquire at City Information Center, 61 Rue Marché aux Herbes near Grand' Place. *New Pols,* 23 Rue de Stassart, is a jazz club.

BOTTLE CLUBS. Here is a thriving branch of the catering industry that calls itself *club privé.* You must comply with the statutes by becoming a member for a nominal fee. In the Galerie Louise there is *Le Bivouac,* highly atmospheric under a Napoleonic tent. On the Grand' Place *Le Cerf* and *Le Cygne* (below restaurant) serve drinks in attractive settings. At the other end of the square, *La Brouette* is very pleasant. The *Manhattan* at the Carlton restaurant, is currently the smartest bottle club in town.

 ENTERTAINMENT. Opera and ballet may be seen at the *Théâtre Royal de la Monnaie,* which is the home of the world-famous Ballet du 20ème Siècle, directed by Maurice Béjart. Except for the *Flemish Theater,* all theaters play in French.

Classical music is provided by the *Palais des Beaux Arts* and the *Conservatoire* concert halls.

MUSEUMS. The important fine arts collections are in the *Museum of Ancient Art*, Rue de la Régence, and *Museum of Modern Art*, temporarily at 1 Place Royale (10–17 hrs., closed Mons.). The spacious *Museum of Art and History* is in the Parc du Cinquantenaire. Half its collection is shown on alternate days (9:30–17 hrs., closed Fri.). A full list of museums can be obtained from the Tourist Information Center, 61 Rue Marché aux Herbes near Grand-Place. A museum, exclusively for children, is located in a mansion at 32 Rue Tenbosch (off Avenue Louise) and is open each Wednesday and Saturday afternoon from 2 to 6 p.m.

TOURS. Two-hour tours with multi-lingual guides operate daily from Apr.-Oct., arranged through travel agents.

SHOPPING. Brussels has been called the shopwindow of the world, there are enough Belgian specialties to keep you broke for years. For an overall view of Belgian products, visit the permanent Design Center, at 51 Galerie Ravenstein, near the Central Station and Sabena Air Terminal. The big stores, *Au Bon Marché, Galeries Anspach,* and *A l'Innovation* all have a variety of Belgian specialties.

LACE. Stay out of the souvenir shops, and try any one of the following for good solid buys: *Antoine,* 26 Grand' Place. *Real Lace Manufactory (Louise Verschueren),* 16 Rue Watteau. *Mme. Foiret,* 29 Place de Brouckère (near Metropole Hotel). *Manufacture Royale des Dentelles,* Passage du Nord. *Maria Loix,* 54 Rue d'Arenberg.

LINEN. One of the best tourist buys. Try the *Biot-Belièvre,* 8 Rue de Naples, for exclusive trousseaus. And *Tissages Réunis de Courtrai,* 107 Rue Royale.

SHOTGUNS. World famous, hand-wrought firearms from Liège, which has been making them for 500 years. In Brussels, at *Christophe,* 11 Galerie de la Reine; *Maison du Chasseur et Mahillon,* 413 Ave. Louise.

WROUGHT IRON. Another outstanding Belgian craft. *Les Fils Costermans,* 5 Place du Grand Sablon. *La Forge de Vulcain,* 3 Rue de la Perche, offers a vast choice in the medium price range.

JEWELRY. Antwerp is a world center for diamond cutting. Among the leading shops: *Maison J. Teldonck,* 121 Blvd. Adolphe Max; *Wolfers,* 82 Ave. Louise; *Leysen Frères,* 28 Marché aux Poulets and 53 Blvd. de Waterloo. The Rue au Beurre, by the Grand'Place, is the spot for moderately-priced jewelers.
Note: If you are leaving Belgium by air for any destination other than a Benelux country, see the guarantee-backed diamonds, cut at Antwerp, at the tax-free Brussels Airport Sky-Shop, where you get 20 percent price reduction.

ANTIQUES. *Le Brun,* 12–14 Blvd. de Waterloo; *Galeries Reding,* 18 Ave. de la Toison d'Or, often stage interesting auctions. And don't forget all the wonderful junk at the *Foire des Antiquaires* in the Gallery Louise. The Antiques and Book Market is held in the Place du Grand Sablon from 10 a.m. until 6 p.m. on Saturdays and from 10 a.m. until 1 p.m. on Sundays.

Environs of Brussels

The Brabant countryside around Brussels offers a delightful atmosphere of historic interest and rural calm. A good introduction is the Bois de la Cambre, a 20-minute tram ride from the heart of the city. The forest is full of smart restaurants and modest inns, and offers a perfect setting for a picnic under its centuries-old trees.

Twelve miles south, accessible by the "W" bus, is the famous field of Waterloo. The conventional tourist activity here is to climb the lion memorial. The Wellington Museum was recently installed in Wellington's old headquarters, which contains some of his furniture. Here you can reconstruct the battle with the aid of models and phase maps. It is open 10–12 and 2–7, except Mondays. In winter, 4–6 only. The Battle Panorama near the Lion Monument is open all year. Hougoumont farm is still privately owned, but you can visit the tiny, mutilated chapel where the British wounded were brought. Along the road to Charleroi, visit the farm Le Caillou, now a museum, where Napoleon spent a restless night before the battle.

Other things worth seeing near Brussels: In Anderlecht, you can visit the house where Erasmus lived; it is now a museum, and contains a library with many of his works. Genval has a pretty lake with hotels and lakeside restaurants; don't go on Sundays—too crowded. Beersel: Shakespeare and folk plays are presented outdoors here in summer at this interesting moated brick castle. Gaasbeek, a beautifully-furnished castle; don't miss it. Nivelles, a town of great historic importance, reduced almost to rubble by World War II. The one rose in the bed of thorns was the discovery of Merovingian and Carolingian remains, now being restored. Tervuren, only 20 minutes from Brussels on the Louvain road, is the site of the very authoritative African Museum (largely angled on the Congo). It has a beautiful large park. For the sports-minded, there is a good swimming pool (Beausoleil) nearby and the links of the Ravenstein Golf Club.

PRACTICAL INFORMATION FOR ENVIRONS OF BRUSSELS

BOIS DE LA CAMBRE. Vast park: *Châlet de la Forêt,* one of Belgium's best restaurants, also seven rooms with bath, first class superior. The *Pavillon de l'Horloge,* on the road to Waterloo. Excellent but quite expensive. *Villa Lorraine,* on the road to La Hulpe. Fabulous food, fabulous prices.

GENVAL. Charming lake. *La Perle du Lac,* moderate, with good restaurant. Restaurant: *Chalet Normand,* moderate.

GROENENDAEL. Gourmet's paradise in the forest of Soignes. *Château de Groenendael;* 7 rooms, 4 with bath, first class reasonable. *La Forêt,* near Groenendael station, a small deluxe hotel with famous restaurant, *Le Père Mouillard. Romeyer,* expensive, has an enviable reputation: located near Hoeilart.

MEISE. Ten miles from the city center, along the Brussels-Antwerp highway. Three fantastic places: *Chateaubriand,* where you can sample moambe, straight from the Congo; *De Molen,* smaller but just as expensive, Hungarian. *Auberge Napoléon,* atmospheric.

NIVELLES. Historic city, full of good eating places. Hotels: *Aigle Noir,* small, moderate, good cuisine. *France,* inexpensive.

Restaurants: *Pascall,* offers in season grouse in wine sauce. *Restaurant de la Collégiale,* noted for first class cuisine. Both moderate.

TERVUREN. Hotels: *Beausoleil,* small, first class reasonable; swimming pool. *La Vignette,* moderate.

Restaurants: The excellent little *Petit Moulin,* offers lobster paella and Algerian couscous. *La Laiterie* pleasant tea on a château terrace.

WATERLOO. Restaurants: *Le Bivouac,* near Waterloo Lion. Historic setting, and grills on open fireplace. *Solarium Rossome,* moderately priced, fine swimming pool; on the Charleroi road. On the same side, *Auberge du Caillou,* converted farmhouse, next door to Napoleonic Museum, the emperor's former H.Q; reasonable.

Catholic Bastions, Malines and Louvain

To understand fully the profound Catholicism of Belgium, you should visit the picturesque old town of Malines (the Flemings call it Mechelen) and the university town of Leuven (better known abroad as Louvain, its French name).

In the tower of Malines' Saint Rombaut's cathedral (13th and 14th century) you will see and hear the most famous bells of Belgium, for this is the place where Jef Denijn revived the art of carillon. Malines is also noted for its beautiful tapestries whose fame has spread as far as the bells. You can still see the ancient art of tapestry weaving practised here with new methods and design adapted to contemporary tastes.

The University of Louvain dominates an attractive town, many of whose treasures have miraculously escaped the holocausts of two world wars. The outstanding one is the Hôtel de Ville (Town Hall), built in 1448, one of the handsomest secular buildings in Belgium. See also the 13th-century church of Saint Jacob; the Béguinage with its early 14th-century church in the Brabant style (many of its buildings have been converted for married students), and the Grand' Place, with its 15th-century nave of Saint Peter's church.

PRACTICAL INFORMATION FOR MALINES AND LOUVAIN REGIONS

LOUVAIN (LEUVEN). Hotels: *Royale,* opposite station, 25 rooms, about half with bath, and University Inn, 20 Naamsestraat. first class reasonable. Slightly less expensive is *Majestic,* with 14 rooms (some with showers).

At nearby Heverlee, the excellent *Hof Terbank,* 55 rooms with bath, and *AC Motel* on E5 motorway, 41 rooms.

Restaurants: Best is *Maison des Brasseurs.*

MALINES (MECHELEN). Hotels: *De Drie Paardekens,* 20 rooms, a few with bath, has a first class restaurant. *Europe,* 10 rooms, some with bath, is less expensive.

Restaurants: *Pekton,* is good and not expensive. *Bavaro,* less expensive. Next to *Bavaro* is the delightful *'In De Beer'.*

Antwerp—Seaport of Yesterday and Today

Antwerp, locally called La Métropole, has long been a great commercial city. It bears the mark of every period, most of all the baroque 17th century, and its boom-town period in the last decade with the great new industrial development in the port area.

The earlier period found much of its expression in religion. Apart from the museums, the cathedral and churches, such as St. Charles Borromeo,

St. James, St. Augustin and St. Andrew, are treasure houses of the work of great masters, including Rubens and Van Dyck. A modern masterpiece is the Kennedy Tunnel, carrying road and rail traffic beneath the Scheldt, a triumph of prefabrication engineering. For the rest, "if you want a monument, look around"—and do not neglect the port area, which you can best see by the steamer service. Do not forget, too, that Antwerp is the world's biggest diamond market and cutting center, and most of the big firms arrange group visits (ask the tourist office).

PRACTICAL INFORMATION FOR ANTWERP

HOTELS

First class superior: Eurotel 350 rooms, Theatre 63 rooms; *Quality Inn,* 180 rooms (some adapted for handicapped people) with bath, TV, air conditioning, swimming pool and garage; *Plaza,* 79 rooms, no restaurant; *Waldorf,* 96 rooms, restaurant.

First class reasonable: *Terminus,* 42 rooms, *Drugstore Inn,* 26 rooms, and *City Park,* 67 rooms; all in town center; none have restaurants.
Rivierenhof in Middelheim park is a chateau transformed into a hotel-restaurant; only 15 rooms, tennis.

Moderate: *Columbus,* Frankrijklei 4, 29 rooms, restaurant. *Florida,* De Keyserlei 59, 15 rooms, no restaurant. *Residence Rubens,* Amerikalei 115, 25 rooms, no restaurant.

Inexpensive: *Hotel des Sports,* 31 Astridplein; *Old Tom,* 53 De Keyserlei, good restaurant.

Motels: *Londerzeel,* halfway between Brussels and Antwerp; *Dennenhof,* 10 miles from Antwerp on the Breda road. A 300-room *Crest Hotel* is conveniently sited on the E3 3 miles from both Antwerp city center and the central station. *GB Motor Hotel* at Aartselaar is on the Antwerp-Brussels highway and has an indoor/outdoor heated swimming pool and restaurant.

RESTAURANTS. *St. Jacob in Galicie,* 14 Braderijstraat, best restaurant in town. *La Pérouse,* highly recommended. Located on a ship pontoon near Steen, it's closed in summer, Sun. night and Mon. *Rade,* Van Dyckkaai 8, has an excellent reputation. Closed Sat. and Sun. night. Both expensive, book ahead.
Criterium, De Keyserlei 25, is popular. Closed Mon. and holidays. *Lindenbos,* Boomsesteenweg 91, is very good, in park setting. Closed Mon. and August. Both fairly expensive.
More moderate restaurants are *Commerce,* Koningin Astridplein 30; *Le Relais,* Kelderstraat 1; *Terminal,* Leopolddok 214 for a fine view of the port.
Rooden-Hoed, Oude Koornmarkt 25, is ancient and specializes in eels and mussels; *De Perel,* Mechelsesteenweg 231, tavern style. Both inexpensive.

MUSEUMS. Free admission. The most representative collection among Antwerp's rich art museums is the *Gallery of Fine Arts,* Leopold de Waelplaats. Rooms with the most famous paintings are specially marked. Closed Tuesdays.
The *Rubens House* is off the Meir, at 9 Rubensstraat. The great master provided the plans for this opulent patrician dwelling, erected in 1610. Paintings by Rubens and his pupils. Open daily 10–17 hrs. (except Mon.).

Plantin-Moretus Museum, 22 Vrijdagmarkt. An enchanting patrician house of the 16th century; original printing press. Open daily 10–17 hrs. (except Mon.).

The *Mayer van den Bergh Museum,* 19 Lange Gasthuisstraat, contains works by Breughel the Elder, Jordaens, etc., sculptures, fine furniture, china, and ancient lace. Open even number days.

Open-Air Museum of Sculpture, Middleheim Park, a vast expanse. Contains over a hundred sculptures by Rodin, Maillol, Moore, and others. Open daily 10 to sunset.

Folklore Museum, 2–6 Gildekamersstraat. Open daily 10–17 hrs., except Mon. Access to the *Cathedral* is in the afternoon only.

EXCURSIONS. The Steenplein is the main embarkation point for various cruises, some over to Holland. Those with a sweet tooth might want to see how the excellent Belgian chocolate is made and visit the plants of *Meurisse* or *Martougin,* or *De Beukelaer's* biscuit factory.

SHOPPING. For diamonds, what else, at: *Int'l. Diamond Sales,* Huidevetterstr. 51.

USEFUL ADDRESSES. Consulates: *American,* 64–65 Frankrijklei; *British,* 6 Van Schoonbekeplein; *Ireland,* 14 Schermerstraat, *American Express,* 87 Meir; *Wagon-Lits/Cook,* 5 Teniersplaats. Guides: *Antwerpse Gidsenbond,* 19 Lange Altaarstraat, also at *City Tourist Office,* 19 Suikerrui. (Helps you find a hotel room.)

The Belgian Coast

An unbroken belt of golden sand stretches for 40 miles along Belgium's coast from the French to the Dutch frontiers. The English Channel is less glacial here than usual because of the Gulf Stream. Given the variety of vacation attractions and the shortness of the northern summer, it is not surprising that this fringe of beaches is very popular.

PRACTICAL INFORMATION FOR THE BELGIAN COAST

HOTELS AND RESTAURANTS. There are over a thousand hotels and pensions, from the simplest to the most luxurious, along the coast. You should experience no difficulty in finding accommodation at short notice, except during the peak periods, July-Aug., and weekends. Prices may be up nearly 30% in full season.

KNOKKE HEIST. Recently for administrative purposes five closely connected resorts have been regrouped as *Knokke-Heist.* They comprise *Albertstrand, Duinbergen, Heist, Knokke,* and *Zoute.* Of the hotels, *La Réserve* is the most luxurious and was recently enlarged. The *Memlinc Palace* is also deluxe. First class superior, *Residence Albert, Claridge's, Astoria* and *Normandy.* The *Cecil* and *Nouvel Hotel* are first class reasonable; *Mayfair, Simoens* and *Miramar* moderate.

Among the many restaurants, *Flots Bleus* is a good one. *Breughel,* in an ancient setting, features grills, *Relais du Comte Jean,* top cuisine, rustic interior. *Le Perchoir* is reasonable.

Knokke Casino arranges "Evasion Weekends": hotel accommodation and breakfast, with voucher book for choice of eating spots and entrance to private bars. Check with the city tourist office.

BLANKENBERGE. Small fishing port grown into noisiest of the beach resorts. All hotels on the Zeedijk have seaview.

First class superior: *Hotel Asdic,* expensive. *Idéal,* Zeedijk, followed by nearby *Laforce.* First class reasonable: *Petit Rouge,* 60 rooms.

DE HAAN. *Astel,* new, *Joli Bois* and *Beach* are first class superior. *Hotel des Dunes,* and *Belle Vue,* are moderate.

An outstanding restaurant *Hostellerie au Coeur Volant,* expensive. Also has 6 rooms, 4 with bath.

OSTEND (OOSTENDE). Has Europe's largest casino. The *Palais des Thermes* is the leading deluxe hotel with 157 rooms with bath, thermal springs and covered swimming pool.

First class superior: *Ter Streep,* 38 rooms some with bath; no restaurant. The newer 60-room hotels in the same class are *Imperial,* facing casino, and *Belle-Vue-Britannia,* also near casino on seafront. First class reasonable: *Royal Astor,* 15 Hertstraat, 94 rooms; *Ambassadeur,* 24 rooms, restaurant; *Viking,* 25 rooms. *Europe,* 65 rooms, inexpensive restaurant; and *Die Prince* are moderate.

Among the numerous inexpensive hotels are *Mondial,* and *Prince Albert,* facing yacht harbor, 10 rooms, with excellent moderately expensive restaurant.

Restaurants: *Freddy's Grill,* is well worth a visit. *Bel Air,* is delightful and also lets rooms. *Prince Albert,* has an excellent kitchen. All fairly expensive.

More moderate are *Beau Site,* and *Host. Bretonne.*

ZEEBRUGGE. Popular with day trippers from UK. Beach on the left of harbor. British Memorial to St. George's Day raid, 1918.

Le Chalut, excellent restaurant.

WHAT TO SEE. Nature lovers will visit the Zwijn marshes covered with sea lavender that blooms in July and August. This is a site of 370 acres, more than 100 species of birds assembled at the Zwijn Aviary outside Le Zoute for the benefit of amateur ornithologists.

An excursion boat will take you up the canal from Zeebrugge to Bruges, or you can visit the tiny Dutch township of Sluis, near Knokke. A fast car-ferry will bring you across the Scheldt to picturesque Walcheren, where traditional costumes are a feature of everyday life.

SPAS AND CASINOS. The Palais des Thermes at Ostend offers mineral baths for the treatment of rheumatism with water from a well sunk to over 1,000 feet, along with electrotherapy and other cures.

You can buy chips of 10 to 1,000 francs at the casinos of Ostend, Knokke-Heist, Blankenberge, and Middelkerke, and pray.

Flanders Art Towns

The Art Cities of Flanders is a phrase which conjures up images of Ghent, "the Florence of the North", of fabulous Ypres and medieval Bruges, "the northern Venice", contemplating its weathered beauty in the dark mirror of its calm canals. In the 15th century, these were among the proudest and richest cities of Europe, and the aura of that golden age still seems to emanate from their cloth halls, castles and cathedrals. It doesn't take long to fall under the spell of these lovely towns. It was at Ghent that John Quincy Adams and Henry Clay met the British representatives in 1814 and, after five months of negotiations, signed the treaty ending the War of 1812. And from Ghent University, over a century ago, Leo Hendrik Baekeland emigrated to America and there invented bakelite—the forerunner of plastics.

PRACTICAL INFORMATION FOR FLANDERS ART TOWNS

BRUGES (BRUGGE). Part of the excellent *Holiday Inn* was converted from a convent with great taste. Good food. The intimate *Portinari* has 50 rooms with bath. Almost deluxe. *Park Hotel* has 37 rooms with bath and TV. *Grand Hôtel du Sablon*, 48 rooms, 22 with bath, first class superior. *Au Duc de Bourgogne*, (overlooking waterway), is small, atmospheric, all rooms with bath, restaurant. *Bryghia*, (no restaurant). Both moderate. Best among the pensions: *Rembrandt-Rubens*.

Restaurants: In full view of the magnificent belfry, you can eat at *Civiére d'Or*, *Panier d'Or*. A good place is the *Comte de Flandre*, open until midnight; another, the *Central*. *Duc de Bourgogne* is excellent and expensive and so is the superb *Weinebrugge*, 4 kms out on the autoroute south.

COURTRAI (KORTRIJK). *Damier*, Grand'Place, first class reasonable, *Continental*, inexpensive.

GHENT (GAND, GENT). *Holiday Inn* on the E3 motorway, 5 kms from town center. Two good modern hotels are *Europa*, 40 rooms with bath, and *Carlton*, 25 rooms with bath; the *Park*, is leader of the older hotels. All first class superior. *St. Jorishof* claims to be the oldest hotel in Europe, though the service is happily modern; 71 rooms, 31 with bath, first class reasonable. An excellent small residential hotel is the *Grand Vatel*.

Wilson, and *Britannia*, moderate.

Restaurants: *Vieux Strasbourg*, offers good food at moderate prices. *Cordial*, also rates. *Patijntje*, is reasonably priced, and *Lido*, is inexpensive. For medieval atmosphere and excellent beer visit the *Raadskelder*.

YPRES (IEPER). Hotels: *Regina*, has 22 rooms, restaurant, moderate. *Hostellerie St. Nicolas*, delicious food.

Eight miles away, the *Hostellerie Mont Kemmel* is one of the temples of Belgian gastronomy; also good overnight stop.

MUSEUMS

BRUGES. Bruges, the purest of medieval towns in Northern Europe, has several important art collections. *Groeninge Museum*, on the Dyver Canal, has masterpieces by Jan van Eyck, Memling, and Hieronymus Bosch.

Gruuthuse Museum, originally the palace of the lords whose name it bears today, shows lace, pottery, goldsmith's art, etc.

Memling Museum, a one-time chapter-room in St. John Hospital's precincts. A unique collection of the master's paintings is exhibited. Insist on being shown the medieval pharmacy in use until recently.

Museum of the Holy Blood. Contains the gold and silver reliquary made in 1617, wrought copperwork, and paintings.

The Archers Guild of St. Sebastian is a unique architectural complex in Cermerstraat; remarkable collection of paintings and silver.

Folkloric Museum, converted from eight adjoining cottages. Situated on a little street down to the left of the Church of the Holy Sepulcher.

GHENT. *Fine Arts Museum* in the Citadel Park. Fine collection of Breughel, Rubens, Tintoretto, Reynolds, etc.

Museum of Decorative Arts, former De Coninck mansion (1752). Rich collection of furniture of the period. Exhibitions of modern arts and crafts.

Folklore Museum, customs and traditions in the city of Ghent.

CARILLON CONCERTS. The principal concerts given by the carillonneurs take place in the following localities. *Bruges:* year round from 11:45 to 12:30 on Sun., Wed., and Sat., from mid-June through Sept., 9–22 hrs., Mon., Wed., and Sat. *Ghent:* less regularly, enquire at City Tourist Office.

The Wooded Ardennes

This rolling forest region, full of fast-flowing streams and wooded glens, is a perfect vacationland. Reputedly the Forest of Arden of Shakespeare's *As You Like it,* it offers the double charm of quaint villages and towns and a beautiful landscape, still only half discovered. Whatever your budget, you will find accommodation here to suit it, from the excellent hotels of Spa and La Roche to modest, hospitable inns, manor houses transformed into youth hostels, and ideal campsites.

This is the land of Ardennes ham, smoked over sweet-smelling gorse branches, of walnut groves, fresh, hot bread, cold beer and other basic joys of life. When you explore this countryside, you'll find it hard to imagine the tragic Battle of the Bulge. Yet the world still remembers General McAuliffe's classic reply to the Nazi summons to surrender at Bastogne, and the citizens of that city still tend with loving care the graves of the American boys who died here.

If you're looking for wonderful scenery, food, and people, off the beaten track, try the Ardennes.

PRACTICAL INFORMATION FOR THE ARDENNES

Ardennes hotels are noted for comfort and good food, although rates are reasonable, probably the lowest in Belgium.

ARLON. *Arly,* first class superior, recent, followed by *Hôtel du Nord* and *Ecu de Bourgogne,* antique furnishings, moderate.

BASTOGNE. Leading hotel is *Lebrun,* moderate; 24 rooms, 11 with bath. In season their young wild boar is delicious. *Prince Baudouin, Luxembourg,* and *Elite,* are inexpensive.

BOUILLON. Historic city and castle. *Panorama* which does live up to its name; 65 rooms, 14 baths. *Le Tyrol,* beautiful view, nice furnishings, 16 rooms, moderate, has excellent restaurant.

At nearby Herbeumont is *Prieuré de Conques,* a former priory, with fine antique furnishings. Recommended, expensive. Reserve.

At nearby Noirfontaine is marvelous restaurant, *Auberge Moulin Hideux,* one of Europe's best. Very expensive.

HAN-SUR-LESSE. *Bellevue et Grotte,* 60 rooms, half with bath, first class reasonable. On the road to Rochefort you can eat well, and not too expensively, at *Hostellerie Henri IV.*

LA ROCHE. *Air Pur,* small, has gourmet cuisine and panoramic view. Very good is *Belle-Vue. Les Merlettes,* is charmingly situated; swimming pool, miniature golf. All moderately expensive.

Restaurant: Excellent *Le Chalet,* specializing in mountain game; moderate.

SPA. *Balmoral* and *Eurotel,* first class superior. Right in the heart of town, *Cardinal* has 36 rooms, most with bath, first class reasonable, nice restaurant.

Rosette, 34 rooms, 12 with bath, has well-known restaurant. *Hostellerie Ardennaise,* central, next to post office.

Near the Francorchamps road is the *Château Sous-Bois,* 20 rooms with bath, first class superior. Set in large park and gardens. Golfers will patronize *La Charmille,* 4 miles out, at Tiège.

ST. HUBERT. In legendary forest. The *Hotel de l'Abbaye;* inexpensive.

WHAT TO SEE. There is a whole cluster of grottos, notably Han in the Lesse valley; also the historic castle of Bouillon and the ancient town of Durbuy. The archaic charm of Spa will remind you that it was for three centuries the playground of Europe's nobility. Cheerful little towns and rustic villages, and elegant manors all add an attraction of their own to the landscape of rivers and wooded hills. From December to March, it is possible to ski in the Ardennes at about 2,200 ft.; ski runs at Bévercé (Malmedy), Butgenbach, Francorchamps, Jalhay, Robertville-Ovifat, and Spa.

SPAS AND CASINOS. The original *Spa,* and *Chaudfontaine,* close to Liège, excellent mineral springs. Both these resorts have casinos open all year. The casinos at *Dinant* and *Namur* are open all year round, also. While the former is on a more modest scale, *Namur* casino is the last word in luxury and entertainment. Its weekend gourmet dinners and dances are worth attending.

The Southwest—Hainaut, Sambre-Meuse

Here, in the southwest of Belgium, you are in the cradle of Walloon history. It is a proud old country, the nursery of French kings, the dowry of dynastic marriages, and for centuries the buffer between expansive France and quarrelsome Flanders. Today Hainaut is one of the most progressive parts of Belgium, a region of contrast between industry and a smiling countryside. You will see model farms, and in the Borinage (around Mons), though you will see many mine-tips, these are progressively giving place to modern factories. Six miles from the city are SHAPE's headquarters and while French is the language of the region, English is fast becoming current parlance as a result of this international presence.

The Carnival of Binche

You will find plenty to divert you in the art town of Tournai and in Mons, the city of coal and carillons, but the most unusual attraction of this whole area is the Carnival of Binche, a Shrove Tuesday festival which is so vigorous that it added a word to the English language: *binge.* It is a binge, too. The climax of the show is the procession and dance of the Gilles, said to stem from an Inca dance witnessed by the Spaniards after the conquest of Peru. Oranges are brought into Binche by the truckload for this annual carnival, and the crowd is pelted with these and water-inflated sheep bladders. The costumes of the Gilles, replete with ostrich feathers and the tallest hats you ever saw, are absolutely fantastic, and so is the entire celebration. See it if you can. The museum here rates a visit.

PRACTICAL INFORMATION FOR THE SOUTHWEST

BELOEIL. Louis XIV-style château, with beautiful park. *La Couronne,* close to entrance, has 12 rooms, 6 with bath. Good value, inexpensive.

BINCHE. Has no proper hotel, but you can eat well at *Philippe II,* and *Bernard* without spending too much.

At nearby Mariemont is a fine restaurant, *Mairesse,* in park setting, expensive. You can eat less expensively at Morlanwelz at *Château des Arondes.* Restaurant is open till midnight.

CHIMAY. Famous château. Hotel: *Commerce,* is small, inexpensive; has a moderate restaurant.

Restaurant: *Edgard et Madeleine,* is reasonable.

MONS. Capital of province and art city. Has some 20 hotels, all small. *Europe Hotel,* 9 Rue Leopold II. *Raymond,* 70 rooms, no restaurant, first class reasonable; *St. Georges* and *Residence H.* both small, without restaurants and moderate.

In Casteau is the *Crest Hotel,* comfortable, with restaurant. Close to Casteau at Masnuy St. Jean, the *Amigo* of Brussels has a 58-room hotel, same deluxe category.

Restaurants in Mons: *Devos,* good food, moderate. *Robert,* inexpensive.

The *Auberge du Caillou-qui-Bique* near Roisin, which is about 20 miles southwest of Mons, is well worth a visit. Good food served in the house was once owned by the celebrated poet Verhaeren.

TOURNAI. One of Belgium's important art towns. *Armes de Tournay,* 23 rooms, reasonable, and *Neuf Provinces,* 14 rooms, expensive. *Ecu de France* is a former stagecoach halt, a delightful example of Flemish Renaissance, reasonable.

Two good restaurants: *Trou Normand* on the Grand' Place (closed for two weeks in early August) and *Trois Pommes d'Orange* near the belfry. Both moderately expensive.

 WHAT TO SEE? There are two historic and art cities— Mons and Tournai. Plans are afoot to turn Vincent Van Gogh's home at Mons into a museum. Tournai is delightful and merits leisurely exploration on foot. Beloeil, which the Belgians fondly call their Versailles, and Chimay, farther to the south, are late French Renaissance châteaux housing innumerable treasures. You will spot additional castles as you roam the countryside: Ecaussinnes, Attre, Ham-sur-Heure, Antoing, Chièvres, Moulbaix, Le Roeulx etc.

The Meuse Valley and Liege

What the Loire is to France, the Meuse is to Belgium. There are numerous châteaux and the whole countryside is redolent of history. Signs of the great Belgian craft of metalwork are everywhere, especially in Dinant. Another local craft is the manufacture of *couques,* those gingerbread cakes baked in beautiful wooden moulds. Don't bite too hard—they are of a tooth cracking consistency.

A visit to Namur, at the confluence of the Meuse and the Sambre, is rewarding, and so is a stopover at Huy. But the living symbol of Walloon independence and progress is Liège, one of the most vital cities of Belgium. You will see the old traditions amply illustrated in the Museum of Folklore and in the extraordinary puppet shows in the Rue Féronstrée, where all the heroes of local legend appear, one of the major attractions of the city.

PRACTICAL INFORMATION FOR LIEGE

HOTELS. First class superior: *Ramada,* 105 rooms. *Holiday Inn,* 200 rooms, is linked to Palais de Congrès by covered arcade, has restaurant, heated pool, parking; good value. *Couronne,* 79 rooms most with bath.

First class reasonable: *Ramada,* 105 rooms.

Moderate: *Cygne d'Argent,* 23 rooms, good restaurant; *Britannique,* 60 rooms, no restaurant; *Angleterre,* 45 rooms, restaurant.

Inexpensive: *Duc d'Anjou,* 30 rooms, good restaurant.

RESTAURANTS. *Clou Doré,* and *Vieux Liège* in 16th-century house are both expensive. Also in gourmet class but less expensive *Chez Septime* and *La Coquille.* Candlelit dining at *Le Seigneur d'Amay; Le Rouet, Rôtisserie Dinantaise* and the small *Capri* are recommended moderates. *Les Mas* and *Maison Basque* are inexpensive.

 WHAT TO SEE. Museum of Fine Arts, Churches of Saint-Martin, Saint Jean, Saint Jacques, and Sainte Croix. Cathedral of Saint Paul. Museum of Walloon Folklore. Curtius Mansion (Archeological Museum). Baptismal font (12th-century) in Church of Saint Barthelemy is one of Belgium's greatest treasures. Weaponry Museum, contains 8,000 arms, ranging from daggers to howitzers. At nearby Herstal, there is an Industrial Archeology Museum situated in a modern small-arms factory.

SHOPPING. Guns. Liège has been famous for them for centuries. Best stores for firearms and hunting and fishing equipment: *Antoine Masereel,* 15 Rue St. Hubert; *J. Fissette Debor & Fils,* 172 Rue de Visé, Cheratte; *Manufacture Liègeoise d'Armes,* 54 Rue du Vertbois. You will find a number of good gunsmiths in Herstal. Liège also has a large selection of Val de Lambert crystal.

RIDING IN THE ARDENNES. *Hippotour,* a non-profit making association, promotes equestrian tourism in Belgium. Address: 12 Rue du Moulin, 1331 Rosières Saint-André. Near Dinant at Ciergnon is the *Cercle Equestre d'Herock* where you can have riding holidays on a residential basis.

PRACTICAL INFORMATION FOR THE MEUSE VALLEY

DINANT. Hotels: *des Postes,* 60 rooms, 25 with bath, first class reasonable. *Henrotaux,* only a few rooms with bath, and *Hostellerie Thermidor,* 8 rooms, 6 with bath; has the best restaurant in town. Also good for a meal, *Central.*

NAMUR. Hotels: *Amigo,* at the citadel, has 34 rooms, deluxe. *Queen Victoria,* 20 rooms, first class superior (but some cheaper rooms available). *Grand Hotel Flandre,* 32 rooms and an excellent restaurant is moderate.

Restaurants: *Moulin de Provence,* moderate. *Rôtisserie,* and *Wepion* with a few rooms; both inexpensive.

Nearby, at Yvoir, *Hostellerie Vachter* has a magnificent menu and the owner is chef. Has a few rooms. Expensive.

WHAT TO SEE. Capital of the province, Namur offers easy access to the whole region and, as a city, has a wide range of attractions. From there you can visit not only the Meuse valley but parts of the Ardennes as well, all within a day's motor trip.

If you are interested in medieval religious art, you will find rewarding collections at Namur, Dinant, Hastière, and Walcourt. This is Belgium's château country, with such remarkable edifices as Spontin, Walzin, Freyr, and many others, all in a fairytale setting. Citadels of more recent construction overlook the cities of Huy, Namur, and Dinant. You will find remarkable grottos at Dinant, Hastière-Lavaux and Rochefort; also, farther inland on a much vaster scale, at Han-sur-Lesse.

BULGARIA

Known in the world for its attar of roses and for its great bass singers, Bulgaria has only become a tourist attraction in recent years, despite the beauty of its landscape and the friendliness of its people. It is a sunny land, with excellent fruit and vegetables, a splendid coastline with wide sandy beaches, and a sea warm enough to swim in from late May onwards. At the height of summer, Germans and Scandinavians abound among Western visitors, though Bulgaria is also a favorite with tourists from the socialist countries including the Soviet Union.

New hotels built along the Black Sea coast in the past decade or so are ideal for package tour travelers, and indeed Bulgaria is a country where a package trip is recommended. Apart from being a bargain, package deals get priority in service at hotels and also include firm bookings, a thing to value in this delightfully, but sometimes excessively, happy-go-lucky land.

In the old days the great east-west road, which now cleaves its way through Bulgaria as a modern highway, was an important trade route between Europe and Asia Minor. Being a transit station contributed much to the wealth of the country, founded as a kingdom in the seventh century and grown to something of an empire by the ninth when, under Boris I, it adopted Christianity. Nowadays Bulgaria is thought of as something of a backwater. This is not how its proud people see the country, but its unswerving loyalty to Moscow in the communist camp has certainly deprived it of the international publicity which Romania, next door, keeps earning through its independent moves.

A country of 43,000 square miles, about the size of Tennessee, Bulgaria has benefited from its close relationship with the Soviet Union and today it offers its eight million people an unquestionably better life than the pre-war generations knew. But rapid industrialization has still not overcome its agrarian character with over half the cultivated land given over to cereal growing and vineyards in the southern valleys. Bulgaria is a major exporter of wine and its canned tomatoes and jam are much appreciated abroad. Nor have the Bulgars, whose name originally meant "man with a plow", wholeheartedly become city dwellers. Even in the capital Sofia most people are no more than a generation or two from the soil.

The Current Scene

Bulgaria's paternal communism expects hard work and discipline from the people, but in recent years it has gone a good way towards making life more enjoyable. Western pop music, a taboo in earlier times, is now heard everywhere; the annual pop festival at Sunny Beach attracts singers from all over Europe. The consumer drive of the past few years, general to Eastern Europe, has some way to go before reaching the levels attained by Bulgaria's more developed neighbors. But the leadership is undoubtedly making an effort not just to raise real wages but to offer people better quality and wider choice in consumer goods. Prices have remained remarkably stable in the face of adverse global trends.

Food and Drink

Bulgarians eat their one big meal in the middle of the day; supper is a snack, with wine. Bulgarian food is heavy, hearty and good, its wine light and cheap, its world-famous fruits and vegetables delicious.

Bulgarian national dishes are closely related to their Greek, Turkish and Yugoslav counterparts—basic Balkan cookery relies mainly on lamb and potatoes. You should try cold yogurt soup with cucumbers, *moussaka* and *kebabtcheta*. Bulgarian melons, apples and pears are in a class by themselves, as are the rich amber-colored *bolgar* grapes and orange-red apricots. All are cheap and plentiful the year round. Particularly popular is the traditional Turkish coffee, heavily sweetened, and served in small cups. *Banitsa* is a pastry eaten with fruit or cheese, very sweet and sticky.

Bulgarians drink a fragrant infusion of dried lime leaves. Water, found in fountains along the road, is good anywhere. Sofia's citizens are downright patriotic about their city's drinking water, which they believe to be the best in the world. Milk bars are popular throughout the country. Bulgaria of course, is the original home of yogurt—fermented sheep or goat's milk turned thick and creamy by well-disposed bacteria, *Lactobacillus bulgaricus.* The result is good, and good for you. The real national drink is a thickish, greyish brew of fermented sesame seed, called *boza.* The thirsty tourist can buy it by the jugful, and drink it by the hour. White wines *(bialo vino)* are of the hock type, best among them *Tcherpan* and *Evsinograd;* the red ones *(tcherveno)* on the heavy side: ask for *Trakia* or *Mavroud.*

PRACTICAL INFORMATION FOR BULGARIA

WHAT WILL IT COST. Package tours are available through accredited travel agents (see below). From the U.S.A., several multi-country tours visit Bulgaria: a 14-day tour, including roundtrip air fare, would be from about $1070, 22 days about $1500. From London a 2-week tour costs from about

£100. Individual travel, of course, works out at a higher rate, though there are seasonal hotel reductions. Independent travellers, in any case, are well advised to make pre-paid arrangements through a travel agent as far as possible, for they will gain from advantageous hotel rates and benefits such as free petrol, referred to below. An excellent system of vouchers still leaves them with plenty of freedom of movement.

Hotels in the capital and major resorts charge as follows per person for room with full board: deluxe single 42 leva, double 37; first-class single, 20–24 leva, double 16–20 leva; moderate single 14–17 leva, double 12–14 leva. Children of 2–12 years get an excellent discount of 50% if sharing adult accommodation (see also section on Black Sea beaches for further discounts for children at certain resorts).

Private accommodation is also available from the *Tourist Bureau* in Sofia and elsewhere; categories range from deluxe to downright cheap. Bed and breakfast in a private home costs from 6 leva to 4 leva per person per day.

All the better hotels have restaurants which are quite expensive. Elsewhere an expensive (E) meal costs from 10–12 leva, moderate (M) from 7–10 leva, inexpensive (I) around 4 leva. A very good system of meal vouchers enables holidaymakers to eat where they wish, even if they have booked accommodation with full board. A voucher document is obtained from the tour operator through whom they have booked, and can be exchanged for vouchers at local tourist offices or at the hotel at which they are staying; they can also be purchased from Balkantourist offices at border points. The vouchers can be used in any restaurant in the country.

Some miscellaneous costs: glass of wine, soft drink from 0.30 to 0.50 leva; hairdresser 2 leva, barber 1 leva; tram or bus 0.06 leva; theater ticket 1.50 leva; foreign cigarettes 1–1.60 leva.

A TYPICAL MODERATE DAY		
Hotel room	16	leva
Lunch	7	
Dinner with wine	10	
Beer	.60	
Coffee	.30	
Tram	.06	
Taxi	1	
Theater	1.50	
Miscellaneous	1	
	37.46	leva

CAPITAL. Sofia, population about 1 million.

LANGUAGE. Bulgarian, nearest to Russian. English spoken by members of travel industry. German spoken and understood in major cities.

CLIMATE. Very warm (but not unpleasant) in summer. 2,240 hrs. of sunshine per year in coastal areas, nearly 30% more than southern England.

Average maximum daily temperatures in degrees Fahrenheit and centigrade:

Sofia	Jan.	Feb.	Mar.	Apr.	May	June	July	Aug.	Sept.	Oct.	Nov.	Dec.
F°	36	39	50	61	70	75	81	79	72	63	48	39
C°	2	4	10	16	21	24	27	26	22	17	9	4

SEASONS. Spring and summer are best for sightseeing, early fall for events and the fruit harvest. The main season for the Black Sea coast is May-Oct.

SPECIAL EVENTS. *May,* "Sliven Fires" Cultural Celebration, Sliven; Sofia Music Weeks. *May–June,* Sofia Music Weeks. *June,* Varna Summer International Festival of Music; "Golden Orpheus" international pop festival, Slunchev Bryag; Rose Festival, Kazanluk; Ten Days of Symphony Music, Slunchev Bryag. *July,* Neptune Carnivals, Black Sea resorts. *August,* Int'l folklore festival, Bourgas. *September 9th,* national holiday: Trade Fair, Plovdiv; Chamber Music Festival, Plovdiv; Bulgarian Film Festival, Varna.

SPORTS. The usual *water sports* on the Black Sea coast. Winter *skiing* in the Rila and Rhodope Mountains, prices among the cheapest in Europe. Possibilities for *hunting* trips.

MONEY. You may bring in any amount and kind of foreign currency including travelers' checks and freely exchange it at branches of the Bulgarian State Bank, at Balkantourist hotels and offices, at the main airports and at all the frontier customs offices. The import and export of Bulgarian currency is *not* permitted. Unspent amounts of leva can be exchanged at frontiers on departure, provided that counterfoils showing the leva to have been bought with foreign currency or travelers' checks are produced.

The monetary unit is the leva. Banknotes circulate in denominations of 1, 2, 5, 10 and 20 leva. The leva is divided into 100 *stotinki;* coins exist in denominations of 1, 2, 5, 10, 20, 25 and 50 stotinki.

The approximate rate of exchange is 0.96 leva to the US$, about 1.65 to the pound sterling. To this official rate, a bonus of 50% has been added, since the beginning of 1978, for all tourists exchanging foreign currency in Bulgaria.

Credit cards are accepted in larger stores, hotels, restaurants and nightclubs. They also can be used in border currency formalities.

TIPPING is officially discouraged, but acceptable; 10 percent is safe.

HOW TO REACH BULGARIA. By Air: From New York to London, then *Balkan Bulgarian Airlines* and *BA* fly to Sofia six days a week. Other connections from most European capitals. There is a bus from the airport to Sofia which costs 0.20 leva.

By Train: International trains include *Tauern Orient Express* from Munich to Belgrade, thence *Marmara Express* to Sofia; *Istanbul Express* (Frankfurt/Munich –Sofia); *Danube Express* (Moscow–Sofia); *Pannonia Express* (Berlin–Sofia). From London, basic 2nd-class return fare approx. £150.

By Car: Three international highways cross Bulgaria: E5N London-Vienna-Sofia-Istanbul, E20 Thessalonika-Sofia-Bucarest-Moscow, and E95 along the Black Sea coast from Romania to Turkey. There is a car ferry between Vidin and Kalafat in Romania. Five times daily in summer, the ferry crosses the Danube in half an hour.

Bulgaria demands only a national or international driver's license. Insurance is optional, and can be obtained at the border. International Green Card is valid.

By Ship: From Vienna, down the Danube, on the luxury vessels of the *Danube Steamship Co.,* or the *Navrom* (Romanian) *Co.,* or on Russian ships: about 4 days to Russe. Basically these are cruises, and you normally cannot join or leave the ship at intermediary ports, as on a regular service.

HOW TO GO. Foreign tourist travel to the People's Republic of Bulgaria is handled by Balkantourist, the national tourist bureau. Addresses: 126 Regent Street, London W.1.; Bulgarian Tourist Office, Suite 1508, 50 East 42nd St., New York 10017. Bulgarian Trade Mission, 1550 Blvd. de Maisonneuve West, Montreal, P.Q.

Balkantourist operates a growing chain of tourist hotels, runs sightseeing tours and excursions, arranges hunting parties, maintains information booths at frontier posts, Sofia railroad station and air terminal, and is responsible for such matters as foreign exchange.

In most Western countries Balkantourist is represented by accredited travel agents who take care of all transportation arrangements including hotel accommodation and payment. Some of these are:

In the United States:
Maupintour Associates, 900 Massachusetts St., Lawrence, Kansas 66044. Also 1780 Pacific Ave., San Francisco, Calif. 94109.
General Tours, 49 West 57th St., New York, N.Y. 10019.
Caravan Tours, 401 N. Michigan Ave., Chicago, Ill. 60611.
American Travel Abroad, 250 West 57th St., New York 10019.

In Great Britain:
Balkan Holidays, 126 Regent Street, London W1.
Sovereign, West London Air Terminal, Cromwell Rd., London SW7.
Cosmos, 1, Bromley Common, Bromley, Kent, BR2 9LX.
Peltours, 72 Wigmore St., London W1H 0DD.
Sovscot Tours, 8 Belmont Crescent, Glasgow G12 8EU.
Sunquest Holidays, 43/44 Church Road, Burgess Hill, Sussex.

 CUSTOMS. Personal belongings including sports equipment, musical instruments, radios, cameras may be brought in duty-free. 1 litre of spirits, 2 litres of wine and 200 cigarettes allowed. Valuable objects will be entered on your passport, and if left behind as gifts to relatives, require payment of import duty when you leave. Foreign currency purchases may be freely exported. Even attar of roses may now be taken out tax free. Customs and currency inspection is casual.

 TRAVEL DOCUMENTS. Valid passport, but no application or Bulgarian visa required for tourists with pre-paid services, staying from 48 hrs. to 2 months. If staying under 48 hours you must buy a transit visa, preferably from a Bulgarian embassy where it costs £4.30 single transit, £7.40 double transit, or at the border where it costs considerably more. Renewable in Bulgaria. It is important to retain the yellow immigration card as it is required when leaving the country.

MAIL. Airmail letter to the US costs 0.45 leva, postcard 0.35. To Great Britain a letter costs 0.38 leva, postcard 0.25 leva, but check before mailing.

PHOTOGRAPHY. No special restrictions, except for government installations or military zones. Photographing the Black Sea Coast from offshore is not recommended. Bring your own film.

ELECTRICITY. 220 volts, 50 cycles, A.C., 2-pin plugs.

DRINKING WATER is good everywhere and especially in Sofia. Drinking fountains are found along main roads.

TRAVEL IN BULGARIA. By Air: Balkan Bulgarian Airlines connect Sofia with the main cities and towns of Bulgaria. There is a shuttle service from Sofia to Varna and Bourgas on the Black Sea Coast, which takes under an hour. Sofia airport has a reputation for general chaos, so be warned.

By Train: Bulgarian State Railways connect Sofia with principal points of tourist interest.

By Boat: Danube River steamers run from *Vidine* to *Silistra;* coastal excursion boats on the Black Sea ply from main seaside resorts.

By Car: Traffic drives on right: usual continental rules of the road observed. Do not sound horn after dark and avoid using it at all in Sofia. Highways are good, sometimes stone-paved. There are an increasing number of gasoline stations on the 200-mile Bulgarian stretch of the Trans-Europe highway leading to Turkey, some open late into the night. Elsewhere they are few and far between. Bring a spare-part kit with you. Speed limits are 60 km in towns, 100 km outside. At border points, be prepared for a delay while your documents are deciphered and duly stamped.

Free petrol is available to motorists accommodated through Balkantourist and Shipka Hotels on full board basis, as follows: 10–13 day holiday, up to 50 litres, 14–20 days 100 litres, 21 days and over 150 litres. Otherwise, petrol can be obtained more cheaply with coupons purchased at the border: about $1.70 or 85 pence per gallon.

Self-drive cars can be hired through hotel reception-desks.

Motels: at Kalotina, on the Yugoslav-Bulgar frontier; near the village of Kapitan-Andreevo, on the Bulgar-Turkish frontier; east of Pazardjik, about 5 miles before reaching Plovdiv; two large residential motels south of Bourgas: at Arkoutino and the second at Kavatzite; Pravec is enroute between Sofia and Varna. A few other new ones along the Black Sea Coast, and other main roads.

Camping sites: There are about 100 sites throughout the country, a great many near the Black Sea beaches; all deluxe and first class sites have hot and cold water, showers, electricity, grocery stores and restaurants. Rates are from 0.60 leva per person per night. Situated close to most main roads and tourist areas. A map showing location of the sites and their facilities is available from Balkantourist.

SPAS. There are a number of good spas such as Pomorie, Hissarya, Kyustendil, Sandanski, and Velingrad where full board and treatment is available from about $17–$26 (£8.50–£13) per person per day.

USEFUL ADDRESSES. *Embassies:* American, Blvd. Stamboleesky 1; British, Blvd. Tolbuhin 18. *Balkantourist,* Lenin Square 1. *Emergency* telephone 150, motorist emergency telephone 146. All in Sofia.

Sofia, Capital City

For foreign tourists, Bulgaria's capital city is more a point of departure than a major resort or attraction in itself. First, however, it is a point of arrival, for all major land and air routes into Bulgaria funnel through Sofia. The city sprawls on a high fertile plain in the lee of the Balkan Mountains, or Stara Planina, a high range running eastward to the Black Sea. Sofia is a fast-growing metropolis of one million, with wide, straight, fluorescent-lit, tree-shaded streets paved with tan glazed brick, 384 parks and grassy squares, and a rash of recent architecture, much of it inspired by Moscow and unkindly described as "Stalinist Gothic".

The motto of ancient Sofia's coat of arms reads, "Grows, but grows not old". Modern Sofia grows, at a mushroom rate, not only in size but in stature. Some travelers still find it more provincial than other Eastern European capitals, but it is rapidly adding industrial suburbs and modern metropolitan amenities to its basic Balkan charm.

Unlike most European cities, Sofia's streets and boulevards run at neat right-angles, like a midwestern American town. Even the two little rivers that border the downtown section flow in straight lines.

The outstanding feature of Sofia is the Alexander Nevsky Memorial Church, erected in 1878 to celebrate Bulgaria's liberation from the Turks. Designed by a Russian architect, it was decorated jointly by Russian and Bulgarian artists. Excellent icons are in the crypt.

Oldest of all landmarks (and closest to the Balkantourist office) is the Church of St. Georgi, some of whose 14th-century frescos hint at western baroque influence. Alongside this handsome structure, excavations have discovered the remains of an even earlier church, dating back to the dawn of Balkan Christianity, and octagonal in shape.

One block west and a thousand years later, the Turks built Sofia's largest mosque, the Bouyouk. Its nine cupolas today shelter Bulgaria's archeological museum. Around the corner is Deveti Septembr (September Ninth) Place, which does for Sofia what Red Square does for Moscow. Here the towering red star atop the semi-skyscraper of the Bulgarian Communist Party headquarters dominates the city skyline. Across the large oblong square stands the massive tomb of Georgi Dimitrov, Bulgaria's leading communist figure until his death in 1949.

West of the square, on Moskovska Street, is Sofia's most typical church, St. Sophia—from which the city took its name. This stately Byzantine basilica, with its cruciform cupola-topped structure, dates from the sixth century. A short jog south brings you to the large and pleasant "Park of Liberty", which offers the pleasures of an open-air theater, cinema and restaurant, a sports stadium (or rather stadia, since there are three of them), as well as tennis courts and swimming pools (also three).

PRACTICAL INFORMATION FOR SOFIA

HOTELS. Latest is the deluxe *Novotel Evropa,* part of the big French group, with 1240 beds and every comfort. The deluxe *New Otani-Vitosha,* Japanese-owned, with nearly 1,000 beds, is due to open in 1979. The more traditional *Grand Hotel Sofia* is also deluxe, centrally located, good restaurant. *Bulgaria* is large, first class superior but located in noisy pedestrian-only precinct; very modern *Moskva-Park,* deluxe, is located in park away from city center; good restaurant on 20th floor. *Balkan,* in town center is also deluxe.

First class are *Hemus,* large; *Pliska,* enroute from the airport, and *Serdica* in the city center; all with good restaurants.

The *Preslav* (formerly Moskva) and *Lyulin* nearby are both first class reasonable. *Gorna Banya* in the suburbs is near famous mineral springs of same name; good rooms and first class restaurant.

Ten miles distant on Mt. Vitosha is the *Prostor* with ski school, swimming pool, sauna, garages. Nearby *Moreni* has no restaurant and is inexpensive.

There is a reasonable transit hotel at Vrajdebna airport 7 ½ miles from town.

Deluxe and first class furnished apartments and private rooms are available from the *Tourist Bureau,* 37 Dondukov Blvd., open day and night.

MOTELS AND CAMPSITES. *Tihiyat Kut,* cluster of modern buildings with good restaurant, on Mt. Vitosha can be reached by bus (61 or 62) from downtown area: *Goroublyane* is 9 kms from Sofia on the E5N, open all year.

All three campsites are within 10 miles of Sofia; *Vrana* off E5N has the best facilities; *Cherniya Kos* between Vitosha and Lyulin mountains; and *Bankya,* near mineral springs, has chalets for hire.

RESTAURANTS. Expensive *Russki Klub* serves good food. *Strandja Tavern* has folk decor and Bulgarian specialties; *Boyansko Hanche* has a good cold table, wines and floor show; and the *Loven Park* specializes in game dishes; all three moderate.

ENTERTAINMENT. As in other socialist countries, "culture" is emphasized. Opera and drama are on a year-round basis with companies moving to the open-air stages during summer months. A festival of classical music is held throughout June. Sofia has a national opera house, two national, and several other, theaters; Western visitors are invariably most attracted by the National Folk Ensemble programs of song and dance.

The Greek Orthodox Church service is a superb and moving experience, and the choir of the Alexander Nevski church an outstanding musical treat.

Original soundtrack foreign films are often shown at one of Sofia's 35 cinemas.

Cabaret standards are high: the *Astoria, Orient* and *Sofia* nightclubs have floorshows; open from 10 PM to 4 AM.

 MUSEUMS. Sofia's *Archeological Museum* (former great Bouyouk mosque) is unique in that is displays only material found within Bulgaria itself. The *Ethnographical Museum* shows folk art, particularly costumes, from every region of the country. The *National Art Gallery* shows Bulgarian art from medieval times to the present, while the crypt of *Alexander Nevsky Church* houses icons and other religious works.

Visitors who are curious as to the origins of Bulgaria's present-day socialist regime will be interested in the "Museum of the Bulgarian Revolutionary Movement", on the Boulevard Russki. The embalmed body of Georgi Dimitrov is on display in his great mausoleum on 9th September Square, and there is a museum devoted to the life of this revered Bulgarian leader at 66 Opulchenska Street.

SHOPPING. The main streets are Zhdanov St., Vitosha Blvd., Georgi Dimitrov Blvd. and Russki Blvd. Shops are generally open from 9am to 1pm and from 4pm to 7pm, closed Sundays. Bulgarian arts and crafts can be found centrally at 6 Russki Blvd., and original carpets and rugs at 7 Stamboliski Blvd.

LAUNDROMAT. There's one in Iskar Street, in the center of Sofia, where they'll do your laundry and dry cleaning for you; several others are around the town.

 TRANSPORTATION. Tickets for *trams, buses* and *trolleys* should be bought in advance from special kiosks and most grocery stalls. Trams and buses 6 stotinki. *Taxis* are inexpensive but rather scarce; quickest is to order one from your hotel or dial 142 for the central taxi service.

All tour transport facilities are provided by Balkantourist, which maintains regular bus tours from Sofia.

Bulgaria's Highland Wonderland

Western tourists in search of new outdoor stamping grounds are now discovering the rugged, unspoiled invigorating altitudes of Bulgaria's southwestern highlands. Just off the highway leading south from Sofia to Salonika lie the Rila mountains, with the famous monastery of the same name, and Mount Moussala, highest peak in the Balkans (9,596 ft.). Adjoining this range to the south is the magnificent snow country of the Pirin mountains, and to the east the beautiful untouched Rhodopes.

Rila

Shangri-la-like Rila Monastery is only 75 miles from Sofia (regular bus services). Its monastic brotherhood was founded by a holy hermit of the 10th century, Ivan Rilsky. During five centuries of Turkish domination, Rila Monastery remained a kind of oasis for Bulgarian Christian culture. To this day, it is considered the most remarkable monument to Bulgarian architecture, painting and woodcarving. Balkantourist has built an excellent hotel and restaurant on a panoramic site near the monastery. Rila is also the starting point for the seven beautiful lakes and for mountain climbing (several lodges).

Borovets and Pirin

Just off the Sofia-Plovdiv highway is Borovets, the starting place for the 9,596-foot summit of Mount Moussala. At 1,500 feet, Borovets is a well-known summer and winter mountain resort. Besides hotels and restaurants, it is well equipped for all winter sports.

South of Rila, tucked in the corner between northern Greece and eastern Yugoslavia, is the splendid upland wilderness of the Pirin mountains. Hunters and fishermen love its snug chalets and its 200 limpid lakes. Pirin has eagles and chamois, and the rare *balkanska zvezda* (Balkan star), a variety of Alpine edelweiss.

The Rhodopes

Between Plovdiv and the Aegean sea lies the storybook land of Thrace. Its southern half belongs to Greece and is flat farmland. The Bulgarian northern half is occupied by the fabled Rhodope mountains where Orpheus is said to have been born. Archeological treasures found in the area include a Thracian tomb, and the dead city of Tamrache. A recent object of tourist enchantment is the Convent of Batchkovo, near the village of Assenovgrad, just south of Plovdiv, which shelters remarkable ancient frescos and medieval manuscripts.

Many of Bulgaria's 360-odd mineral springs are to be found in the Rhodopes, which is also a skiing and mountain-climbing center, well equipped with tourist chalets. Many of its summits may be reached by good roads.

Plovdiv, Commercial Center

Exactly 100 miles east of Sofia, on the international highway to Istanbul, lies the busy city of Plovdiv, perched on the cliffs overhanging the Maritsa River. For over 2,000 years, it had been a commercial crossroads for caravans carrying goods between Europe, Asia and Africa. Today, it is the site of the Plovdiv International Sample Fair, which takes place annually during the last two weeks of September.

Plovdiv is Bulgaria's second largest city and an important industrial center. In the archeological museum you may see the famous Thracian treasure of solid gold household utensils. In the streets of the old town are some Roman ruins and charming medieval wooden houses.

Turnovo, Mountain Fortress

Bulgaria's turbulent history and typical art forms are strikingly summed up in the amazing city of Turnovo, midway along the Sofia-Varna highway, and about 30 miles south, on a good road. The city is in the shape of a mountain amphitheater, surrounded on all sides by steep rocks, rising over 70 feet above the Yantra River. This setting is a natural fortress, to which Turnovo owes its role as the cradle of Bulgarian history. When Bulgaria became independent in 1878, Turnovo was chosen as its first capital. It is today a museum city of marvelous church relics, works of art and fascinating panoramas.

In the environs is the impressive Preobrazhenski Monastery and a curious transplanted Albanian village, Arbanassi.

Pleven lies 115 miles east of Sofia on the road to Varna. The Kaylaka Park, on the outskirts of town, is a zigzag gorge three miles long, with a grotto that has been fitted up as a luxury restaurant, complete with dance floor.

Kazanluk, Valley of Roses

For a unique experience, go to the precise center of Bulgaria and get up before dawn on a day in May. You are in Kazanluk's "Valley of Roses", sheltered between the Stara Planina on the north and the Stred-na Gora Mountains to the south. The over-powering fragrance of millions upon millions of fresh pink roses reminds you that "smells are surer than sights or sounds to make your heartstrings crack". Next to tobacco, attar of roses is Bulgaria's single most valuable export crop.

Kazanluk Valley is thick with archeological and artistic treasures. Fully 400 Greek burial mounds have been discovered thus far. Kazanluk Convent contains frescos from the days of the Ottoman Empire, as well as old icons, ornamented with gold leaf and studded with precious stones. Balkantourist organizes frequent guided bus tours to Kazanluk.

PRACTICAL INFORMATION FOR THE REGIONS

ALEKO, mountain resort 20 miles from Sofia. Excellent ski runs. *Kopitoto* hotel and restaurant.

BOROVETS, 4,000 feet high in the Rila mountains. *Edelweiss,* 80 rooms with bath; orchestra in restaurant. *Bor, Moussala,* all first class.

KAZANLUK. In town, best hotel is the *Roza.*

PAMPOROVO, in the Rhodope mountains. Wonderful skiing Dec.-Apr., in summer warm breezes from the Aegean. Many splendid hiking routes. Hotels: *Mourgavets,* deluxe; *Rozen, Prespa, Orpheus* and *Panorama,* all first class; *Snezhanka,* moderate.

In nearby Devin, *Grebennets* hotel has 160 modern rooms.

PLOVDIV. Newest is the deluxe *Novotel Plovdiv,* part of the big French group, with over 700 beds and all comforts. Also deluxe is the *Trimontium. Maritsa, Asenovec* are first class, and there is a *motel* on the outskirts.

. Restaurant: *Pudlin.* reputedly the best in Bulgaria; reservations a must.

TURNOVO. Best hotel is the *Veliko Turnovo.* Also *Yantra, Trapezitsa,* with pleasant rooms and service, and a *motel.*

The Black Sea Beaches

If you're tired of Miami, Brighton and Cannes, but value your comforts, you and the Black Sea coast were meant for each other. Here, Balkantourist is busily developing a hundred-mile chain of fine sand beaches. This playground stretches from Sozopol north to Balchik. Of course, the Black Sea isn't black, it changes from blue to grey, depending on the weather. But swimming there has its share of problems. Tricky currents mean swimming in designated areas only, and there are occasional influxes of stinging jellyfish.

Just about one flying hour from Sofia, or 280 miles by road is Varna, a major industrial center and Bulgaria's main seaport with important shipyards; its tourist activity is largely limited to serving as an airport town for the popular resorts nearby. This is also the place from which to take the excursion boats up and down the coast.

North

Situated midway between Varna and Golden Sands lies the hospitable small coast resort of Drouzhba with its 18th century monastery. Another five miles up the coast is Zlatni Pyassutsi (Golden Sands), a two-mile-long gently sloping stretch of silky sand, 500 feet wide, the country's major resort, with very good amenities.

Nine kms north is Bulgaria's newest and second largest resort, the futuristic Albena, geared primarily to the young market with a varied choice of activities, skin diving, water skiing, riding, etc. Its beach, with water only knee-deep 100 meters out, is ideal for families with small children.

Ancient Balchik, 20 miles or so up the coast, terraces down from its hillside perch to a fine beach. The showpiece here is an extraordinary small palace mixing Christian and Moslem elements, which was built for the last queen of Romania when Balchik was Romanian.

South

About 60 miles south of Varna, Slunchev Bryag (Sunny Beach) is Bulgaria's largest resort and very popular, with a few comparatively luxurious facilities. A mile or two inland lies Aladja Monastery, built into the rocks and dating from the sixth century.

Near Sunny Beach and 25 miles north of Bourgas, Nessebar is an ancient and highly historic town on a little peninsula linked to the mainland by a 1,000-foot causeway. It has a beach, but its fame is due to its incredible collection of over forty ancient Byzantine churches, many displaying frescos and other items of considerable artistic value.

Pomoriye sits on a narrow rocky peninsula between the sea and a large salt lagoon. Its proudest produce is mud—dark, grey, greasy mud smelling of hydrogen sulphide (like rotten eggs). Special machines dredge it up from the bottom of the lagoon and people come from all over Bulgaria to wallow in the noisome substance, which is rich in iodine compounds and reputedly good for what ails you.

PRACTICAL INFORMATION FOR THE BLACK SEA BEACHES

 HOTELS. An ambitious hotel construction program has equipped most of the beach towns with comfortable modern facilities, ranging from deluxe through second class. Some hotels in Albena, Slunchev Bryag and Zlatni Pyassutsi are open all year round; rates are 40% less Oct. 1—May 31. Rooms in private homes are available for those interested in close contact with the local life-style. Note that an excellent discount of 50% applies to children of up to 12 years, and there is no charge—except for cots—for children under two. At Sunny Beach and Albena, children between 2–5 sharing an adult's room get a 75% discount all year round. At Sunny Beach, baby sitting up to midnight is free; small charge at other times or at other resorts.

ALBENA. Hotels: *Kamelia,* 53 rooms with bath, and *Tervel,* 150 rooms with bath, both facing beach; *Kaliakra, Bratislava, Gergana, Mura, Karvuna, Boryana,* are all modern first class. Note children's discounts above.

DROUZHBA. Hotels: *Varna,* deluxe, Swedish-built, 400 rooms, 2 swimming pools, saunas, nightclub, etc. *Prague* in converted 18th-century monastery, *Chaika, Prostor, Rubin, Bor, Lebed,* all first class; *Riviera,* hot mineral water spring and spa treatment. Restaurant: *Monastirska Ixba,* folk style in former monastery.

SLUNCHEV BRYAG (Sunny Beach). a couple of miles north of Nessebar. Hotels: *Chaika, Cuban, Bourgas* and *Globus,* deluxe. *Fenix, Europa,* both on sea. Restaurants right on the beach are the *Orféy* and *Dyuni.*

VARNA. Hotel: New deluxe *Cherno More* is near the Marine Gardens. First class *Varna* faces seaside park.

ZLATNI PYASSUTSI. (Golden Sands). Hotels: 11 miles from Varna; *Hotel International,* deluxe, nightclub, indoor swimming pool. *Metropole, Shipka, Astoria, Rodina, Ambassador, Morsko Oko, Moskva,* all first class and on or near sea. Restaurants: Rustic-style outdoor *Vodenitsa* (Water Mill) and *Koshara* (Sheepfold). Night clubs include *Indian Village, Gipsy Camp,* and *Koukeri.*
At Primorsko, the *International Youth Camp,* motel-style cabins in cool forest. Fabulous beach.

HINTS FOR THE BUSINESSMAN. Balkantourist, Lenin Square 1, Sofia, can help in arranging business contacts, and with secretarial and interpreter services.

CYPRUS

Aphrodite, the Greek goddess of desire, was not born but rose naked and fully formed from the sea near Paphos, on the beautiful south coast of Cyprus. That, at least, is the legend—and one which the Cypriots will never tire of telling you. But, at present, like almost all of the other evocative beauty spots in Cyprus, Petra tou Romiou, (Aphrodite's "birthplace") is comparatively unknown.

For Cyprus is still bedevilled by the communal problems between Greeks and Turks which have marred its history, and at the time of writing the north of the island, which includes the former resort areas of Kyrenia and Famagusta, is still under Turkish military occupation and *extremely difficult to visit*. It can be done, but only via Turkey and only by the adventurous. Tourism, which until a few years ago was a major industry on the island, is re-established in the Greek areas to the south centered on the towns of Limassol, Larnaca, and Paphos, and in the area around the magnificent beach of Aghia Napa.

In these places, Cyprus is once again taking on the appearance of a holiday island—and in that respect it has many natural advantages. The climate is ideal: spring flowers blanketing the fields in color in March, and summer lingering very late. Most people speak English; the food is of international variety and standard, as one might expect on an island which is geographically at the crossroads of Europe, Asia and Africa.

Nicosia, the island's capital, consists of modern urban sprawl built around the vast sixteenth-century walls of the historic Old City, but it is not a place in which to stay at present because of the demarcation lines drawn up between Greeks and Turks. A far better holiday base is Larnaca, which is rapidly developing into a major tourist resort. There are good hotels and restaurants, and such beauty spots as Petra tou Romiou are within easy reach by hired car, taxi, excursion coach or local bus. Alternatively it is an easy walk from Larnaca to the Great Salt Lake—dry and snowy white in summer, but tinted pink by the plumage of wintering flamingoes during the wetter months—or the attractively-situated Moslem shrine of the Tekke of Hala Sultan, tomb of the Prophet Muhammed's foster mother, on the shores of the lake.

A longer but very attractive trip can be made to Stavrovouni Monastery, 2,260 ft. up on the top of the most easterly peak of the Troodos Mountains. "Entrance prohibited for women with short sleeves, short trousers, mini and lipstick", warns an ungrammatical and faintly out-of-date notice outside the main door of the monastery, but the three monks who live there are welcoming enough. Their greatest treasure is a piece of wood said to be from the true cross, and now encased in silver to protect it from souvenir hunters.

Other worthwhile spots to see are the pottery-making village of Kornos, and the rather more commercialized lace-making village of Lefkhara, where the women lacemakers sit outside their doorways in the sun making their famous tablecloths, place mats, and gloves. But beware of the hard sell.

Limassol, also an easy spot from which to make the above-mentioned visits, is the second largest town in Cyprus, and makes up for what it lacks in loveliness by its liveliness. There are frequent festivals, including a spring carnival and the two-week September wine festival, and a varied night life catering in part for the nearby British military base. Colossi Castle, dating from 1454, is an interesting spot.

Paphos is perhaps the loveliest town in Cyprus now, and in many ways the most typical. The modern town lays behind an old Graeco-Roman port, which was once the island's capital. The rocky Tombs of the Kings, a third-century BC necropolis, are worth seeing, as are the many other remains—including the vestiges of a theater, the Frankish baths, the harborside Byzantine castle, and the "Pillar of St. Paul" to which the apostle is said to have been bound when being beaten for preaching Christianity on the island. The recently-discovered Roman mosaics are also very interesting, and explorers will find a warm welcome and plenty of typically Cypriot refreshments in a harborside restaurant.

Food and Drink

Many local dishes are of Greek and Turkish origin. Of these *kebab* comes first—bits of lamb or pork, skewered and roasted by slow charcoal fire, and eaten in an "envelope" of bread (*pitta*). *Patcha* is a thick lamb's stew, served with lemon, garlic and toast, while *tavas* consists of meat, onion and herbs, served in little earthenware bowls straight from the oven. *Zalatina* is boiled, jellied pork, flavored with laurel and pepper. Fresh fruit is plentiful. *Commandaria* is the rich sweet dessert wine of the Crusaders. Cyprus produces a whole range of wines, as well as sherries. Local brandy is excellent, as is lager beer. Coffee is served in Turkish style (*turkiko*) and English tea is also drunk.

PRACTICAL INFORMATION FOR CYPRUS

LANGUAGE. Greek, spoken by 80% of the population in the south; Turkish in the north. English widely spoken and understood.

CLIMATE. Summer heat tempered by a permanent breeze around the coast; temperatures about 10 degrees less in mountains. The tourist season is year-round, but specially recommended in winter.

Average max. and min. daily temperature in degrees Fahrenheit:

	Jan.	Feb.	Mar.	Apr.	May	June	July	Aug.	Sept.	Oct.	Nov.	Dec.
Nicosia	58	59	65	74	83	91	97	97	91	81	72	62
	42	42	44	50	60	65	69	69	65	58	51	45

CLOSING HOURS. Business hours are usually 8 to 13:00 hrs. and 14:30 to 18:00 hrs. in winter (19:00 hrs. in summer).

SPORTS. Cyprus offers superb *bathing*, officially from mid-April through October, but northerners will extend the season both ways. There are countless bays around the coastline. Among the most popular of beaches are those of Larnaca and Limassol, the Coral Bay beach at Paphos, and Aghia Napa in the southeast. The wonderful translucency of the sea makes *skin-diving* a special delight. Here the activities of frogmen are now part of the beach scene. If you are really good you might bring up a piece of ancient pottery or coinage of the Hellenistic or Roman period from a sunken Greek or Roman galley. *Sailing* is another of the main sports in Cyprus; there are clubs at the larger coastal towns. The Flamingo Club at Larnaca and all the other sailing clubs welcome visitors as temporary members. There are not many places where you can bathe in the morning and *ski* in the afternoon: in Cyprus you can. Troodos is used by skiers from January through March.

MONEY. The unit of currency is the Cyprus £, divided into 1,000 mils. There are notes of £5, £1, 500 mils, 250 mils. Coins are 100, 50, 25, 3 and 1 mils. At this writing there are about 710 mils to the £ sterling.

WHAT WILL IT COST. Full board at a five-star or four-star hotel costs from £5 to £9 per day, dependent on location and degree of comfort. Single room with bath and breakfast costs, on average, £6, while meals are relatively less expensive: 400 mils to £1 for breakfast, £1.50 upwards for lunch or dinner.

Taxis charge a fixed fare in towns of 300/500 mils, but are now being fitted with taximeters; long distance rates by arrangement. It is cheaper to reserve a seat in a fixed-departure, inter-city cab, sharing with others.

HOW TO REACH CYPRUS. By *Cyprus Airways* or *British Airways* from London direct (£211 for a day flight booked in advance).

By Sea: There are regular ferry sailings from Piraeus. Also sailings from Marseille by *HMW* and from Genoa by *Adriatica*.

All inclusive tours from Britain are the best bet. *Kypros Travel*, Euston Centre, 29-31 Hampstead Rd. London NW1 3JA offer two-week package tours from about £160. Other tour operators include *Amathus Holidays, Exchange Travel, Libra Travel, Meon Travel, Thomas Cook, Wings,* and *Sovereign (British Airways)*.

DRINKING WATER. Perfectly safe, though near the sea sometimes slightly brackish. You can buy bottled mountain water.

MOTORING. British and international driving licenses are acceptable, or visitors' permits are issued on presenting a national license and one passport-type photograph. You drive on the *left.* The main road system is unexpectedly extensive and well surfaced. There are service stations every few miles: premium fuel costs about 650 mils a gallon.

CAR HIRE. Self-drive cars cost from about £5 per day with unlimited mileage.

SHOPPING. Because Cyprus is considered a developing country, many of the things you buy there may be exempt from U.S. Customs duties under the G.S.P. plan, as explained in the section on Customs in *Facts at Your Fingertips,* at the beginning of this volume.

HOTELS. Hotels are classed five-star for deluxe; four-star and three-star for first class; and so on. State in advance or on arrival on what terms you wish to stay, i.e. full board, half board or bed and breakfast only. No reduction is granted for meals not taken.

LARNACA. *Sun Hall,* (four-star) 113 rooms; *Four Lanterns* (three-star), 37 rooms.

LIMASSOL. *Apollonia Beach,* (five-star), 156 rooms and suites, pool, 3 miles from center. *Miramare,* also on the sea, 60 rooms, and *Curium Palace,* 83 rooms, are both four-star, as also the *Amathus Beach,* 208 rooms, in large grounds, 2 pools, mini-golf. *Pavemar,* (three-star) on the outskirts, pleasant.
Alasia, Astir, Continental, Panorama, all (B).

NICOSIA. The *Cyprus Hilton,* (five-star) 149 rooms, out of town; the *Churchill,* (four-star).

PAPHOS. *Paphos Beach* (four-star), *Dionysus* (three-star), *New Olympus* (two-star); *Axiothea* (two-star).

CZECHOSLOVAKIA

The beautiful but ill-fated country called the Socialist Republic of Czechoslovakia is a shoe-shaped land about the size of North Carolina or half as large as the British Isles. The square heel of the shoe makes a dent in the map of Germany, and is called Bohemia. The narrowing instep, with Brno as its main city, is the province of Moravia; the slender mountainous, ankle and toe form Slovakia. The population of these three provinces is about 14,000,000.

Czechoslovakia means "land of Czechs and Slovaks". These two peoples were until recently about as different as English and Irish, or Texans and Yankees. The Czechs, in fact, were long ago nicknamed "the Yankees of Europe". They will probably impress you as a serious, sensible set of citizens completely absorbed by the problems of everyday life. Slovaks on the other hand, are farther removed from the Germanic influence of Bohemia and have an easier-going temperament. The country is now a federation politically emphasizing the equality and union of the two peoples.

Czechoslovakia is the nearest of the Eastern countries to get to and not expensive to visit. A land of natural scenic beauty with unspoiled forests, snowtopped mountains and ancient towns, it has over 3,000 medieval castles and furnished châteaux, old-world spas and a tradition of Central European culture.

Some Recent History

By the early sixties the country, through concentrating investment in the wrong areas of heavy industrialization, had achieved a thoroughly capitalist-type slump. This, combined with the general atmosphere of de-Stalinization of Eastern Europe, started the process which led, with some detours, to the heady months of 1968, when, under the leadership of Alexander Dubcek, the party tried to construct "socialism with a human face". The attempt to mix Communist ideology with democratic rights for the people stampeded the Russians and their Warsaw pact allies into invading Czechoslovakia in August 1968.

Gustav Husak replaced Dubcek in April 1969, and has kept the country on a tight rein since. But he and his regime have tried to compensate Czechs and Slovaks with consumer benefits for the loss of freedom. Prague has been having a face-lift (which is why you will see so much scaffolding around the historic buildings you may visit) and the new Metro, opened in 1974, is being extended. Every tenth family owns a car, food is plentiful—in fact, a third of the population is overweight—and private travel to the West is being allowed on a scale comparable to neighboring Poland and Hungary. All this has not made the regime popular, especially with the intelligentsia, but most people are prepared to forget about politics and concentrate instead on getting all they can out of the materially good life.

Regional Activities

If you're spoiling to go on a wild goose chase, then the Bohemian ponds or the Slovakian Danube regions are your hunter's paradise for this and kindred game birds. In the eastern Slovak woods you can try your luck on bear, wolves and wild boar. Angling in Czechoslovak mountain streams, lakes or rivers may net you trout and perhaps a 40-pound Danube salmon. (All arrangements, including permits, guides, organized hunts, stays at lodges or hunting castles, etc. are handled by Cedok, the National Tourist Bureau. Permit to import your own gun and ammunition must be obtained from a Czechoslovak consulate before your trip.)

Ski resorts generally agreed to be best are Spindleruv Mlyn in the Krkonose (Giant Mountains), and the Strbske Pleso winter sports complex (with bobsleigh run) in the High Tatras, locale of the 1970 World Ski Championship.

Slovakia has great stretches of virgin forest, hidden lakes and craggy mountains to climb, with here and there an ancient castle ruin to explore.

Moravia has gentler country in which to ramble, lovely Renaissance towns and painted wooden villages.

Bohemia has a wealth of art-historical treasure to discover as well as two international standard golf courses, famous spas and bathing and camping facilities on her lakes and rivers.

Food and Drink

A square meal starts off with a flourish of assorted cold meats—famous Prague ham, smoked tongue, Russian crab meat in mayonnaise, eggs with caviar—all garnished with plenty of pickles. As for meat, it is usually well-boiled, drowned in delicious thick gravy and accompanied by large dough *knedliky,* the Czechs' beloved dumplings. Roast pork, duck and goose all come carrying their cargo of knedliky and *zeli* or spiced red cabbage. Desserts are rich. But what is sadly lacking are fresh vegetables and salads.

Na zdravi! means "To your health!" in flawless Czech and best said to the music of two clinking mugs of *Pilsner* (Urquell) beer. *Slivovice,* a strong plum brandy, *borovicka,* a pungent gin, and *becherovka,* a herb brandy, are the local spirits. Pleasant table wines come from Melnik and Moravia. Excellent wines (even champagne) come from the Bratislava and Tokaj regions.

Regional Shopping

Bohemia: crystal and glass, porcelain, garnets, costume jewelry, cosmetics, old books; *Moravia:* lacework, embroideries; *Slovakia:* peasant pottery, woodcarvings. *Tuzex* stores throughout the country sell export quality items from Prague ham to oil paintings for hard currency, so don't change all your shopping money into local currency. Incidentally, a gift from Tuzex (or a Tuzex voucher) makes an appreciated gift for your host or hostess.

PRACTICAL INFORMATION FOR CZECHOSLOVAKIA

WHAT WILL IT COST. General costs remain much the same in Czechoslovakia, but fluctuating exchange rates naturally affect the visitor. Broadly speaking, costs are lower than in western Europe.

Prague continues to be relatively the most expensive place, followed by the Slovak capital Bratislava, the Moravian capital Brno, the High Tatra resorts (though these are good value for the budget-minded skier) and those in the Krkonose (Giant Mountains).

The country's spas seem to be rather reasonable: ex-London, for example, you can have a comprehensive 3-week stay in Piestany, including medical treatment for arthritis and related disorders, return flight and full board in a top hotel, for £370–£490, according to season. A similar package in Karlovy Vary costs £590–£640, and it can work out much lower at less expensive hotels or spas.

A TYPICAL DAY FOR ONE PERSON
(For hotel rates, see "Hotels" below)

Lunch in moderate restaurant	40 Kcs.
Dinner in first class restaurant (excl. wine)	80
Tram, anywhere in city	1
Taxi, approx. 2-mile ride	10
Theater, opera, good seat	20–30
Cigarettes, local	7
Coffee	3
Beer	2
Miscellaneous	18
	191 Kcs.

Other local prices are: Hairdresser, 30 Kcs.; haircut, barber (don't risk it!), 10 Kcs.; cinema, good seat, 15 Kcs.; bottle of Melnik Ludmila wine, 60 Kcs.; Scotch whisky, per drink, 30 Kcs.; beef, 40 Kcs. per kilo. First class train fare, Prague-Bratislava, is 200 Kcs.; roundtrip bus fare, Prague-Karlovy Vary, 150 Kcs.

The average monthly take-home pay in Czechoslovakia is 2,500 Kcs., and the rent for a modern 2-bedroom apartment (practically impossible to get) would cost a citizen 300 Kcs. per month.

CAPITAL. Prague (Praha). Bratislava is the regional capital of Slovakia.

LANGUAGES. Czech and Slovak. English spoken by members of travel industry and most younger people. German spoken and understood by all the older generation, Hungarian in southern Slovakia.

CLIMATE. Average maximum daily temperatures in degrees Fahrenheit and centigrade:

Prague	Jan.	Feb.	Mar.	Apr.	May	June	July	Aug.	Sept.	Oct.	Nov.	Dec.
F°	34	37	45	55	64	72	73	73	64	54	41	34
C°	1	3	7	13	18	22	23	23	18	12	5	1

WHEN TO GO. Spring or summer for sightseeing; mid-Dec. through April for winter sports. The hunting season generally lasts from Sept. through Dec.; permit required.

SPECIAL EVENTS. *May,* Prague Spring Music Festival; Dvorak Music Festival, Pribam; Summer Theater in Castle grounds, Karlstejn (through August). *June,* Bratislava Int'l Song Festival. *July,* Straznice Folk Art Festival; Brno Grand Prix Motor Rally; Karlovy Vary Int'l Film Festival (biennial); *August,* international Festival of Dance, Telc; *September,* Znojmo Wine Festival. *October,* Pardubice Grand Steeplechase.

HOW TO GO. All foreign tourist travel to Czechoslovakia is handled by *Cedok,* the national tourist bureau. Cedok has offices in New York (10 East 40 St., N.Y. 10016) and London (17 Old Bond St., W.1), as well as in major European capitals. Cedok manages the best hotels in Czechoslovakia, which are reserved for foreign tourists. It runs sightseeing tours and excursions, arranges hunting parties, and is responsible for all practical matters connected with your visit, including visas and guides. Package tours by air for both groups and individuals work out very much more cheaply than independent travel especially from London. The arrangements are also likely to proceed more smoothly, for in general the system is better geared to deal with pre-booked services. If you prefer to go-it-alone, this can also have its rewards, especially in terms of more contact with the people, but the bureaucratic machine and some language problems may at times test your patience! Cedok is represented abroad by over 100 accredited travel agents who can arrange for visas, hotel accommodation and prepayment, among them:

In America
American Express Company, 65 Broadway, New York, 10006.
General Tours, 49 West 57 St., New York 10019.
Maupintour Associates, 900 Massachusetts St., Lawrence, Kansas 66044.
American Travel Abroad, 250 W. 57th St., New York 10019.
Travcoa, 875 N. Michigan Ave., Chicago 60611.

In Canada
Kennedy Travel Bureau, 296 Queen St., W. Toronto, Ontario.
Globe Travel Service, 60 Dorchester Bldg., West Montreal.

In Great Britain
Thos. Cook & Son, Ltd., 45 Berkeley St., Piccadilly, London W.1.
Balkan Holidays, 130 Regent St., London W.1
Peltours, 72 Wigmore St., London W.1.

Inghams, 329 Putney Bridge Rd., London SW15 2PL.
Wings, Wings House, Welwyn Garden City, Herts.
Swans (Hellenic), 237–238 Tottenham Court Rd., London W1P 0AL (art treasure tours).
Wakefield Fortune, 176 Tottenham Court Rd., London W1P 0DE (spa holidays).

 HOTELS. Accommodation is officially classed Deluxe, A*, B* and B, and the following rates are for independent tourists, for a single room with bath or shower with half board: Deluxe, $48 or £24.20, A* $25–28 or £13–£14; B* $20–$24 or £10–£12; B $14 or £7 (without bath). Less for double occupancy and off season. Advance booking essential for all accommodation.

Student hostels, open summer only, charge about $10 or £5 per day for room without bath. Cheaper rooms may sometimes be available.

Motels: Cedok runs a number, generally modern, conveniently located, some with pools and tennis, rated A* or B and offering half board at comparable hotel rates. List from Cedok.

Campsites: There are many auto-campsites; Cedok runs some. Charges are from $1.20 or 60 pence per person per night. Equipment may be hired. Open May through Sept. Complete list from Cedok.

Mountain chalets: In well-located cottage camps, may be hired for about $15 or £8 for 4 persons per day; some have kitchens.

TIPPING. Tipping is expected of foreigners; 10% is safe. Hotels and restaurants include a service charge of 10% in better places, 5% in others.

\$P£ **MONEY.** Monetary unit is the *koruna* (Kcs.), divided into 100 *halir.* There are coins of 5, 10, 20 and 50 hellers and 1, 2 and 5 Kcs.; banknotes are in denominations of 10, 20, 50, 100 and 500 Kcs. You may bring in any amount of foreign currency and exchange it at all branches of the Czechoslovak State bank, some hotels, and in *Tuzex* stores in exchange for vouchers valid only in Tuzex; also at certain frontier customs offices. The import and export of Czechoslovak currency is *not* permitted. All exchanges should be noted on your visa as only surplus korunas from such exchanges, beyond the minimum required daily exchange rate, will be refunded to you in hard currency at your departure. (Larger amounts will be mailed to your home address.)

The tourist exchange rate is about 10 Kcs. to the US dollar, 17 to the pound sterling.

Travelers check and credit cards such as American Express, Diner's and Eurocard may be used to exchange currency and are also accepted in better hotels and restaurants.

Note: Visitors must exchange a sum representing the value of their living expenses in CSSR at a minimum rate of $10 or £5.50 per day per adult. Children under 6 pay nothing and up to 15 years half this amount.

Hotel accommodation including meals can be paid for in advance by means of vouchers. (Unused hotel vouchers may be exchanged for local cash.) Travelers with vouchers or other documents stating prepaid services are not obliged to exchange the daily required minimum amount, provided the prepayment covers at least $10 or £5.50 per person per day.

TRAVEL DOCUMENTS. A visa is required; obtainable from Czech consulates in person (processed while you wait) or through most travel agents. Fees are: single visa $8 for U.S. citizens, £3.30 for U.K. citizens; one-way transit visa $8 (£4); two-way transit visa $16 (£6); group visa $4 (£2) per person, though these are subject to increase. One copy of the 4 page application and two photographs are required. Visas can be extended in Czechoslovakia by Cedok. Visas are *not* issued at points of entry.

Visiting Relatives. If you wish to stay with relatives or friends, you must apply for visa permission from a Czechoslovak embassy and you must register with the local police authorities within 48 hours of your arrival. You will be required to exchange the full minimum daily amount of $10 or £5.50, unless you are staying with a first generation relative (i.e. parent, child, brother or sister), when it is reduced to half.

HOW TO REACH CZECHOSLOVAKIA. By Air: *Pan Am* and *CSA* (Ceskoslovenske Aerolinie) each have one flight a week from New York; *Air Canada* and CSA each one flight a week from Montreal; *British Airways* and CSA fly on alternate days except Sunday from London; all to Prague's Ruzyne airport.

By Train: International services with connections to London include expresses from Stuttgart and Nurnberg to Prague, and the Zapadni Express from Paris to Prague. The basic 2nd class return fare from London is approx. £105.

By Bus: Europabus connections from Frankfurt and Munich, Germany; Vienna, Austria; and other countries.

By Car: Czechoslovakia has a common border with 6 states and there are 33 crossing points. The major routes with border point in parenthesis are: from Austria: Vienna-(Pressburg-Bratislava)-Bratislava; Vienna-(Drasenhofen-Mikulov)-Brno; Linz-(Wullowitz-Dolni Dvoriste)-Ceske Budejovice; from W. Germany: Nurnberg-(Waidhaus-Rozvadov)-Prague; Bayreuth-(Eger-Cheb)-Karlovy Vary; Munich-(Eisenstein-Zelezna Ruda)-Plzen; Regensburg-(Furth im Walde-Folmava)-Plzen.

Documents essential for the vehicle's entry are a registration certificate and your national driver's license; the green card insurance is no longer necessary, but recommended, or visitors may insure their vehicle at border crossings. When in difficulty get in touch with the *Central Automobile Club* (*Ustredni Autoklub CSSR*), Opletalova 29, Prague. Tel. 22-35-47.

It has become much easier to get "super" gasoline, but it is still wise to fill up when you can if you have a long drive ahead. Filling stations are quite often closed in the evenings. Petrol coupons reduce the price (see below).

By Hydrofoil: Daily except Sunday from Vienna to Bratislava and return, about 2 hours each way down the Danube. May 5 to Sept. 22.

CUSTOMS. Personal belongings may be brought in duty-free. Also 250 cigarettes, 1 liter spirits, 2 liters wine, ½ liter (about 1 pint) of toilet water, three rolls of film, 325 ft. of motion picture film and up to 6½ lbs. of foodstuffs. Jewelry and other valuable objects should be entered on your customs declarations. Foreigners are permitted to import duty free up to $100 worth of gifts and souvenirs. Clothing may be left duty-free. Purchases up to 300 Kcs. may be freely exported; more valuable items purchased for officially exchanged currency, including articles from *Tuzex*, may be exported duty-free provided you have the bills.

MAIL. An airmail letter costs 5.60 Kcs., postcard 4.20 Kcs. to the U.S.; 3.60 and 2 Kcs. to European countries. 24-hr. service at the main post office, Jindrisska Ulice 24, Nove Mesto, Prague.

TELEPHONE. When placing a long-distance call from your hotel be sure to check the hotel's service charge, which can sometimes double the basic cost of the call.

PHOTOGRAPHY. Don't photograph railway tunnels, steam locomotives, or near the frontier or near barracks or military installations.

ELECTRIC CURRENT. 220 volts A.C., 50 cycles.

DRINKING WATER is safe in all main towns.

 TRAVEL IN CZECHOSLOVAKIA. By Air: Daily domestic flights connect Prague with Bratislava and Brno as well as with the Tatra Mountains and Karlovy Vary. Cedok arranges sightseeing flights over the Tatra Mts.

By Train: A dense rail network serves Czechoslovakia, including several express trains between Prague and main cities and resorts.

By Car: Cars drive on the right; usual Continental rules of the road observed, except that a right turn is permitted on a red light (watch for arrows). There is a 50 kph. speed limit in built-up areas.

It is advisable to purchase gasoline coupons from Cedok, or (most practically) at border crossings. This enables you to buy Super (96 oct.) or Special (90 oct.) gasoline for 30% less than when purchasing for Czech currency. The larger service stations can handle repairs but best bring a spare parts kit.

There are several new highways (Prague-Brno, Prague-Benesov); European roads, marked "E", are usually maintained in good condition. Secondary roads are also good and getting off the beaten track lets you in for some beautiful country and out-of-the-way finds.

Car Hire: Cars may be hired through *Avis* and *Pragocar* at Ruzyne airport and Stepanska 42, Prague, or pre-book through Cedok in all towns and resorts. Fly-and-drive is also available.

USEFUL ADDRESSES. Embassies: *American,* Mala Strana, Trziste 15; *British,* Mala Strana, Thunovska ulice 14; *Canadian,* Mickiewiczova 6. Tourist offices: *Cedok,* Na Prikope 18; *Balnea,* Parizska 11. All in Prague. Emergency telephone: 37-37-37.

Exploring Prague

The best way to get acquainted with Prague is to start with a bird's eye view of it from the corner of Hradcanske Namesti (Castle Square). From the parapet overlooking the city you will see a magnificent panorama before you. A high point is the cupola of the baroque St. Nicholas Church. All around it, between the Castle and the Vltava River lies the Mala Strana (Little Town) with the palaces and gardens built in the 17th and 18th centuries by the aristocracy, and the smaller but still beautiful houses constructed by burghers and artisans. To the right of the Little Town are a series of interlinked parks with promenades and the ruins of a medieval wall. Below you is the 14th-century Charles Bridge with its two watchtowers and baroque statues, which is open to pedestrians only. Across the river are the Stare Mesto (Old Town), the Nove Mesto (New Town) and much of modern Prague. To the right of the Old Town, just across May 1st Bridge is the domed National Theater; further down the embankment is Vysehrad Castle perched on a rock.

The Castle area, the Little Town and the Old Town are well worth a visit, preferably on foot. The Hradcany complex, once the seat of Bohemian kings and now the official residence of the president of the republic, is over a thousand years old. It includes every kind or architecture that Prague has known, from early romanesque (St. George's Church) to imitation gothic; the cathedral itself was only completed this century. Visit the enormous Vladislav Hall where indoor jousting tournaments were held, the mirrored Spanish Hall, and the storybook Zlata Ulicka (Golden Lane). On the righthand side of Castle Square is the National Gallery, on the left the former Schwarzenberg Palace which is now a military-historical museum. Farther along you will come to Loretto Square with its charming church housing the Loretto treasure of religious valuables.

From Castle Square you descend via the medieval Nerudova Street to the Little Town. Notice the beautiful old house signs signifying the trade of the original occupant. On Mala Strana Square is the 200-year old church of St. Nicholas, a perfect baroque structure. Inside, the frescos are so subtly blended with the structural elements its impossible to tell where architecture ends and art begins. Then take Mostecka Street with its attractive shops and walk across Charles Bridge, an ideal vantage point for Prague's timeless beauty. Turning left, after about six blocks you'll come to Parizska (Paris Street), a jewel of art nouveau architecture. On the left is the 20th-century Inter-Continental Hotel, on the right a 13th-century synagogue with an amazing cemetery. Continuing down Parizska, where most of the airlines have their offices, you will come to the Staromestske Namesti, the magnificent Old Town Square with its gothic Tyn Church. The Square, and the enchanting 500-year old clock with its hourly presentation, is a favorite meeting place. The tastefully-reconstructed Betlemska Kaple (Bethlehem Chapel) where John Huss used to preach is nearby. Beyond the Old Town lies Vaclavske Namesti (Wenceslas Square), commercial heart of the city.

The foregoing is perforce only a summary of the wealth of sights an ancient city like Prague offers. Cedok's half-day and day sightseeing tours, with English-speaking guide, provide a more comprehensive picture.

PRACTICAL INFORMATION FOR PRAGUE

WHEN TO GO. A year-round city, Prague is loveliest in the spring. The *Prague Spring Festival* (half of *May*—beginning of *June*) is an annual musical event that attracts outstanding soloists, ensembles, and orchestras.

TRANSPORTATION. Sections of Prague's modern *subway* (underground) are open; fare is 1 Kcs. Tokens for *trams* must be bought beforehand at hotels and newspaper kiosks; fare is 1 Kcs. per ride, no transfers. Trolley *buses* charge according to distance traveled. *Taxis* are marked with a broken white line and charge 2.50 Kcs. per km; they can be hard to get. Your own car is more convenient.

TOURS of Prague and environs, as well as longer excursions, are arranged by Cedok. There's also a panoramic night river cruise through the city. English-speaking guides accompany tours. Individual guide service available at moderate rates.

 HOTELS. Prague hostelries date partly from the Empire period and unfortunately show it. Others are ultrafunctional and lack charm. Unusual are the three floating *botels* anchored on the Vltava River. Most hotels are managed by Cedok; these are called Inter-hotels. Non-Interhotels are graded (B), but can be comfortable.

DELUXE

Inter-Continental, of the American chain, on the banks of the river in Old Town. Modern, 398 rooms with bath; roof-top restaurant, nightclub.

Jalta, Vaclavske Nam. 45, all 88 rooms with bath. Best chef, popular bar. Noisy, central location.

Alcron, Stepanska 40, 149 rooms with bath/shower, good restaurant, bar, garage. Lobby popular rendezvous for foreigners.

Esplanade, Washingtonova 19, 65 rooms with bath, famous Est Bar nightclub. Elegant, facing park near new Parliament building.

International, Praha-Dejvice, known to some as the Russian Ritz for its architectural pretensions, 375 rooms in all categories; mini-golf. In the outskirts.

A* HOTELS

Tri Pstrosi (Three Ostriches), magically located at Mala Strana end of Charles bridge, 17th-century atmospheric inn. Its 18 rooms are the most desirable in town, reserve months in advance. Excellent restaurant.

Ambassador, Vaclavske Nam., 115 rooms with bath. French restaurant, sidewalk cafe.

Park, Veletrzni 20, 228 rooms with shower; snackbar, garage. Modernistic decor.

Olympik, Sokolovska Trida 138, one of Prague's largest. 314 rooms with shower; restaurant, tennis.

B* HOTELS

Palace, 12 Panska, 136 rooms, many with bath or shower. Recently renovated. Attractive restaurant, centrally located.

Pariz, U Obecnino Domu 1, 105 rooms, many with bath. Recently renovated. Good Slovak restaurant.

Flora, Vinohradska 121, 209 rooms, many with bath or shower. Lively nightspot.

Garni, Invalidovna, opposite the Olympik. 270 rooms with bath, guests use the Olympik's restaurant.

BOTELS

Three botels anchored along the Vltava River: *Albatross* near Old Town, *Admiral* near Mala Strana, *Racek* out of town center; each with 82 double rooms, 4 apartments, open-air restaurants, bars, etc. All (B*). Popular despite cramped quarters.

MOTELS. *Club Motel* (A*) at Pruhonice near Prague, 92 rooms with bath, well designed, fun restaurant-club; *Stop* (B*), on the Plzen road, *Konopiste* (A*), 44 km. south of Prague near chateau of same name, all rooms with shower. Also a non-Interhotel (B*) in the chateau park's grounds.

RESTAURANTS. Your choice of typically Czech cooking, international cuisine or foreign specialties. Taverns are divided into better class *vinarny* (serving wine) and more earthy *hospody* (serving beer). Restaurants listed below are rated (E) expensive, (M) for moderate, or (I) for inexpensive (though prices are lower than comparable Western listings). They are open generally from 11:30 A.M. to midnight.

INTERNATIONAL CUISINE

Opera Grill, Divadelni 24 (E). Best in town, intimate, elegant décor with antique Meissen candelabra, French cuisine, piano. Closed Sat. & Sun. Reservations a must.

U Labuti, Hradcanske Nam. 11. (E). Exclusive dining in tastefully-remodeled stables. Closed Sun. Reservations a must.

Ozivle Drevo, Strahovske Nadvori 132. (E), Hidden away in gardens of a monastery, lovely view of city, excellent food, service. Reservations a must.

Vysocina, Narodni Trida 28. (E). Attractive rustic décor, top quality food. Closed Sun.

U Mecenase, Malostranske Nam. 10. (E). Medieval inn, elegant especially in the back room. Closed Sun.

Cinska Restaurace, Vodickova 19. (E). Mao-Tse style. Very popular, reservations a must.

U Zlate Ulicky Grill Bar, U Daliborky 8, (M). In the castle grounds, food served with care, delicious omelettes. Closes 7 P.M. and Mon.

REGIONAL CUISINE

Valdstejnska, Valdstejnska Nam. (M). Pleasant, good food, piano. Closed Thurs. Book ahead.

Rotisserie, Mikulanska 6. (M). Excellent kitchen, always crowded for lunch. Closed Sun.

Klasterni, Narodni Trida 8. (M). Good for lunch or an after-theater snack.

Chalupa in the Club Motel Praha (M). Farmhouse atmosphere and country cooking.

U Medvidku, Na Perstyne 7/345. South Bohemian food in a jolly atmosphere (I).

U Pastyrky, Belehradska 12. Slovak setting; simple and good (I).

OUTDOOR DINING

U Lorety, Loretanske Nam. 8. (M). Next to the baroque church of the same name with its carillon bells, an agreeable spot.

Ve Zlate Studni, U Zlate Studne 4. (M). A steep climb through secret courtyards but, the view's worth it. Cold kitchen only. Open 2 P.M.-10:30 P.M., Spring/Summer.

Espreso Kajetanka, (M). Just under the castle ramparts, gorgeous view. Closed Mon.

TAVERNS, BARS AND WINE CELLARS. Prague has many popular beer taverns and wine cellars. Among the most famous is *U Fleku,* Kremencova 11/183, which has been making its own 13° caramel-dark beer on the premises since 1499. Try their brew to the accompaniment of toasted garlic bread and hot sausages and sit in the garden.

U Zlate Konvice, Melantrichova 20. (E). Unusual underground Gothic labyrinth with tables set among huge wine barrels. Generous portions, but cold food only. Closed Sun. Reservations a must.

U Zelene Zaby, U Radnice 8. (M). Medieval home of a legendary hangman, popular with the young arty set. Cold snacks are overpriced. Closed Fri. and Sat.

U Maliru, Maltezske Nam 11. (M). 16th-century, in lovely old part of town. Relaxed, Bohemian atmosphere. Closed Sun.

U Zlateho Jelena, Celetna. (M). A newly restored ancient cellar serving White Burgundy wines.

Zelezne Dvere, Michalska (M). Specializes in Moravian wines; popular. Closed Mon.

U Tomase, Letenska 12. (M). Founded by Augustinian monks in 1352, serves super 12° dark ale.

U Bonaparta, Nerudova 29. (I). Packed with impoverished students. Not for the timid.

U Kalicha, Na Bojisti 12, (M). Packed with associations with the Good Soldier Svejk; Czech food.

U Radnice, Male Nam. 2. (M). Vaulted ceilings and pure Czech cooking.

NIGHTLIFE. Western-style nightlife is not one of Prague's specialties. You can enjoy dinner dancing at the better hotels' restaurants. Some night bars with music and, in some cases, cabaret, are: *Est Bar* in the Hotel Esplanade, *Jalta Club* in Hotel Jalta, *Embassy Bar, Havana Club Olympik, Park-Club,* and the Georgian atmosphere of *Gruzia.* All (E).

ENTERTAINMENT. Opera. The *National Theater (Narodni Divadlo)* is currently under reconstruction. Its opera, ballet, and theater teams can be seen at the elegant *Smetanovo Theater* near the National Museum and the *Tylovo Theater* near the Old Town Square.

Concerts: Held at the *House of Artists (Dum Umelcu)* and *Smetanovo Sin* (an extravaganza of turn of the century design). The Czech Philharmonic is first rate and so is the Smetana Quintet. Sunday afternoon chamber music sessions are held in a hall of the *National Museum* where you sit on the grand staircase. Go see any performance in the historic palaces or the *Strahov library;* the historic settings complement the music. Not to be missed are the marvelous organ recitals given in the magnificently appropriate settings of *St. Jacob's* (Old Town), *U Krizovniku* (near Charles Bridge) and *St. Nicholas* (Little Town) churches where choral Masses are also sung.

Theater: Best productions of Czech and foreign classics given at the *Divadlo Za Branou* home of the Laterna Magika, and at the *Divadlo Na Zabradli* where the mime Fialka, the Black Theater and the chanson singer Hegerova perform. You won't need to know the language to enjoy these.

Puppet shows: Brought to a high art form at the *Spejbl & Hurvinek Theater.* Adult-oriented performances. The *Ustredni Loutkove Divadlo* (Central Puppet theater) caters more to children.

Tickets may be bought at the box office, Cedok or through your hotel, but book well ahead especially during the spring festival.

Horse racing: at the Chuchle course outside town; open Sats. and Suns. from spring to autumn.

MUSEUMS. Generally open from 10 to 5, closed Mondays.

National, Vaclavske Nam. More of a landmark. Prehistoric, natural science and numismatic depts.

Military Historical (Vojenske historicke) Hradcanske Nam. 2. Housed in the former Schwarzenberg Palace, itself interesting. Exhibits of European arms up to World War I. Medieval jousting tournaments staged here in summer.

Jewish (Zidovske), Stare Mesto. Spread over several buildings and including an ancient cemetery, has the largest collection in the world of temple furnishings and everything related to Jewish customs and history in Bohemia.

Strahov Library (Pamatnik Narodniho pisemnictvi) Strahovske Nadvori 132. Beautifully preserved ancient manuscripts exhibited in gorgeous rooms of the former monastery. Contains a collection of bibles from every country in the world.

Amerika, Ke Karlovu 20, Nove Mesto. Former baroque summer palace, now Dvorak museum.

Hvezda, palace with large grounds; museum of Czech history, art gallery, summer open-air concerts.

Loretto, On Hradcany hill next to church of same name. Collection of antique religious jewelry; one piece with over 6,000 diamonds.

ART GALLERIES. Permanent collections of art are often housed in beautiful former palaces. Frequent exhibits by contemporary Czech artists. The recently opened *St. George's Monastery* in Prague castle is an ideal setting for its national collection of choice old Czech art, superb woodcarved Gothic madonnas and panel drawings. *Rudolfinska,* also in Prague castle, displays a recently discovered collection of Italian masterpieces. The *Wallenstein Riding School,* Valdstejnska Ul. 2, specializes in 18th- and 19th-century Czech art. All come under the aegis of the *Narodni Galerie* (National Gallery), Hradcanske Nam.15 outside the castle gate, which exhibits European art: Breughel, Durer, French Impressionists, etc. Graphics at the *Kinsky Palace,* Staromestske Nam. For modern Czech art, go to the *Prague Municipal Gallery* in the Old Town Hall. Sculpture is displayed in a Cistercian monastery in Zbraslav, 12 miles south of Prague.

SHOPPING. Prices are standardized throughout and there's no bargaining. Bohemian glass and porcelain from internationally renowned *Moser,* Na Prikope 12 (mostly for hard currency), who will ship purchases home for you. Folkloric handicrafts at *UVA,* Na Prikope 25. Best antiques are sold by *Tuzex,* Jungmannovo Nam., or at the *Starozitnosti* at Mikulanska 7, tucked away in a courtyard, and at the same store in the Uhelny Trh Square. Shops are open 9-12 and 2-6. Most close on Sat.

LAUNDROMAT. This is called "pradlenka;" there's a self-service one at Koruna House, Vaclavske Nam., and another, including dry cleaning, at Konevova 71, Prague 3. Others are not self-service and you should count on a wait of 1–2 days.

Environs of Prague

You should take advantage of several interesting one-day excursions and visit the castles of Karlstejn and Krivoklat, the chateaus of Konopiste and Veltrusy and the towns Lidice and Nelahozeves. Karlstejn, a massive old fortress, was built as a safety deposit vault for the Bohemian crown jewels in the 14th century by Charles IV. The lovely Chapel of the Holy Rood depicts the solar system in gold on its ceiling; the walls are adorned with Gothic portraits and studded with 1,000 polished semi-precious stones. Krivoklat is a pure Gothic castle from the 13th century, small, dark and dingy. Medieval banquets are held here for groups. The 19th-century chateau of Konopiste was the hunting residence of Austrian Crown Prince Ferdinand and it was from here that he went to Sarajevo in 1914. Surrounded by forests, it contains an overwhelming collection of hunt trophies and arms. Veltrusy is a baroque chateau situated in a park, noteworthy for its remarkable rococo furnishings and collection of oriental porcelain. Nearby is Nelahozeves, the birthplace of Dvorak, now a museum. Lidice is the village that was razed to the ground by the Nazis in retaliation for the assassination of Heydrich. A new village has been built, and the former is now only a peaceful meadow with a monument and flowers.

The Four Corners of Bohemia

West: You will want to see the three famous spas in this region, Karlovy Vary (Carlsbad), Marianske Lazne (Marienbad) and Frantiskovy Lazne. Karlovy Vary, has attracted Europe's crowned heads and ailing bodies for ages. The oldest and largest of the spas, its sulphurous waters taste so awful, they must be good for you! Just outside town are the world-famous Moser crystal works and arrangements can be made to visit the factory and watch the glass being made. Purchases may be made on the spot. Also worthwhile is a visit to the Brezova porcelain factory which has an interesting museum. Karlovy Vary plays host on even years to an International Film Festival. And, it has a challenging 18-hole golf course, as does Marianske Lazne, 30 km. (18 miles) away. This is the youngest and prettiest of the spas, admired by England's Edward VIII, Beethoven, Goethe and others. Its waters are only mildly salty. Frantiskovy Lazne dates its mineral spring back to the 11th century and is chiefly known for its nearby peat bogs. In the Chod region further to the southwest is the preserved town of Domazlice with arcaded houses in renaissance and baroque styles. The Slav Chods were the traditional guardians of Bohemia's frontiers and their villages and culture are ethnically interesting.

South: South of Prague, the Vltava river soon forms a chain of lovely lakes which offer many recreation facilities. South Bohemia is scenically a beautiful region of lakes and woods, and has many points of interest. The old part of Tabor was the seat of the 14th-century Hussite movement. Ceske Budejovice has a beautiful square and the Budvar brewery. Nearby is Hluboka Castle, a carefully maintained replica of Windsor Castle with a remarkable collection of gothic wood carvings. Cesky Krumlov is a preserved gem of a medieval town and has an historic open-air theater. Then there are the castles Rozmberk (13th century), Orlik (19th century) and Zvikov (13th century), the latter two reached by boat.

East: Near to Prague is Kutna Hora, the Czech equivalent of a ghost mining town and just as spooky. It's foundations are so heavily undermined that it is dangerously sinking; it was here that silver deposits were discovered in the 13th century which helped finance the splendor of medieval Bohemian kings; the *thaler* (or dollar) originated here in the Vlassky Dvur. The distinctively domed St. Barbara Cathedral is a sight to see, and for those who fancy the macabre, the church in Sedlec contains a famous ossuary entirely lined with human skulls. Hradec Kralove, old and new, may be seen on the way to Litomysl, an ancient town dating from the 10th century whose claim to fame is a renaissance chateau opposite which the composer Smetana was born. The Eagle Mts. (Orlicke Hory) running along the Polish border, are unspoiled, have clearly marked trails, and are ideal for camping.

North: The Giant Mts. (Krkonose) are one of the most popular holiday areas in the country and are best visited in winter. Spindleruv Mlyn and Pec pod Snezkou are picturesque ski resorts and the wooded hills are dotted with fairytale cottages out of Hansel and Gretel. A pilgrimage to Terezin can be a moving experience. The town's 18th-century fortress was turned into a concentration camp by the Nazis and the cemetery at the entrance bears mute witness to the many who perished here. Not far away is the summer resort of Stare Splavy on Lake Macha (Machovo Jezero) in a lovely woodland setting under the eye of Bezdez Castle, a fantastic 11th-century ruin. Unfortunately, the place is utterly over-crowded in summer. The castle restaurant in Melnik, overlooking the confluence of the Vltava and Labe rivers, is a good place for a lunch of fresh trout and local white wine. Farther in the north, rock climbing is popular in the Jizersky Mts. Novy Bor is the center of the unique painted glassmaking industry.

PRACTICAL INFORMATION FOR BOHEMIA

WHAT TO SEE. In addition to what is described in the preceding text, the Sazava Valley (Poric n/Sazavou, Sazava, Cesky Sternberk), Jicin and the Trosky Castle are also interesting.

SPAS. The main ones are: *Karlovy Vary,* 120 km. (75 miles) west of Prague; *Marianske Lazne,* 160 km. (100 miles) west of Prague; *Frantiskovy Lazne,* 150 km. (93 miles) west of Prague; *Podebrady,* 50 km. (31 miles) east of Prague. Open all year. Rates lower in off season (Oct.-end Apr.).

 HOTELS. Good hotels outside Prague are to be found mainly at the better spas and ski resorts. When possible, choose an Interhotel or one with at least a B rating, which should have hot and cold running water.

BABYLON u. DOMAZLIC. Chalet village (A) under management of Praha Hotel. *Praha* (B), 33 rooms, restaurant.

CESKE BUDEJOVICE. *Zvon* (B*), 8 rooms with bath; *Slunce* (B), 32 rooms. In nearby **Hluboka,** the *Park* (B) has 54 rooms, 15 with bath.

CESKY KRUMLOV. *Krumlov* (B*), 32 rooms, 8 with bath. Newer *Vysehrad* (B*).

CHEB. Motorists crossing late in the day will find the *Hvezda* (B), convenient.

FRANTISKOVY LAZNE. *Slovan* (B).

JABLONEC. *Corso* (B*) 37 rooms, 12 with bath or shower.

KARLOVY VARY. *Grand hotel Moskva-Pupp* (A* Deluxe) spa hotel, 170 rooms, 70 with bath, garage, nightclub. Where the action is. *Parkhotel* (A*), 117 rooms with bath; garage, central location. *Motel* (A*), 40 rooms with shower. Latest is the *Thermal* (A). *Atlantic* and *Central* are (B*).

LIBEREC, *Imperial* and *Zlaty Lev* (both B*), both large, many rooms with bath, several restaurants.

MARIANSKE LAZNE. *Esplanade* (A*). Very comfortable, 28 rooms with bath. *Golf* (A*), 30 rooms with bath, opposite golf course. Super dining seated in great armchairs around a blazing hearth, dancing. *Palace Hotel Praha* (A*), 60 rooms, some with bath. *Campanilla* (B*), 28 rooms alongside Esplanade. *Corso é* (B*) 69 rooms, central location, restaurant.

PLZEN (Pilsen). If you decide to stop over, try the *Ural* (A*), modern, well-appointed 83 rooms with shower; good restaurant. *Continental* (B*), 52 rooms with bath or shower or the *Slovan* (B*), 116 rooms; both with restaurants.

Since this is home of arguably the world's best beer, try it at two taverns outside the Pilsner Urquell *brewery* on the eastern outskirts.

SPINDLERUV MLYN. Winter resort. Modern is *Montana* (A*), all rooms with shower. More traditional is *Savoy* (B*), 58 rooms, a few with bath. *Alpsky* is (B). Very modern and in a fine mountain setting near the resort is *Labska Bouda* (B), 69 rooms with shower, two restaurants, ski equipment for hire.

Moravia

Moravia is the rich little agricultural and industrial region sandwiched between Bohemia and Slovakia, Brno, its capital, is a major textile city. Gottwaldov (formerly Zlin) is the site of the former Bata shoe factory. Kromeriz is a town with an attractive old section. Moravska Ostrava mines coal and refines metals. And Moravia offers sightseers a variety of wooded highlands, renowned vineyards, folk art, and castles.

Brno, a busy modern industrial city with beautiful parks and vestiges of the past, is situated on an open plain. Grim Spilberk Castle, which dominates the city's skyline, has an infamous history as a political prison. The Moravian Museum in the Dietrichstein palace has a folk-art wing where elaborate embroidered costumes, laces, folk pottery and shepherd woodcarvings give an impressive idea of how rural Moravians have traditionally spent their long winter evenings.

A few miles north of Brno are the famous grottos of Macocha and Sloup—where you can go boating on underground rivers. Northwest of Brno is the magnificent 13th-century Pernstejn Castle, a center of resistance against the Hapsburgs, and most famous of Moravia's castles. Nearby is Kninicska Dam, with sports and recreation, and the Napoleonic battlefield of Slavkov (Austerlitz). Telc, in southern Moravia, with its medieval city architecture of the late Renaissance, merits a detour. Znojmo stages wine festivals.

One of the most famous folk festivals in Czechoslovakia takes place the end of June-July at the village of Straznice, 11 miles from Brno. It attracts hundreds of folk singers and dancers from all over Czechoslovakia.

PRACTICAL INFORMATION FOR MORAVIA

WHAT TO SEE. Pernstejn castle, Telc, Slavkov (Austerlitz) and Bitov; archeological digs (Cro-Magnon, 30,000 BC); painted villages; wine festivals; Moravian Karst subterranean grottos; Kromeriz castle with gallery; in Hreske Hradiste the ethnographical museum.

 HOTELS. Regional hotels available to foreigners are few and far between. Best is to make Brno your base unless you are booked on a Cedok bus tour. All hotels have restaurants.

BRNO. Hotels: *International* (deluxe), 290 rooms with bath or shower; garage, nightclub. *Continental* (A*) 228 rooms with bath, open-air summer restaurant; *Grand* (A*) 118 rooms with bath, restaurants; another new (A*) hotel opened last year. Good (B)s are *Metropol, Morava, Slavia, Slovan. Motel Bobrava* (A*), 40 rooms with shower, in nearby Modrice.

Restaurants: *U Kralovny Elisky,* a restored ancient wine cellar in former cloister, with fireplace grill; *Castle Spilberk,* period decor, folk band and good wines; *Myslivna,* in outskirts, first class, good view of the city.

KRNOV, off the beaten track in the north. *Morava* (B*), converted abbey, 13 double rooms with shower, wine cellar.

OLOMOUC, university town. *Narodni Dum* and *Palace* (both B*), both have few rooms with bath.

OSTRAVA. *Imperial* (A*) over 100 rooms with bath; garage. *Palace* (B*), 37 rooms with shower.

ZNOJMO, wine harvest town. *Nadrazi* (B), has 7 rooms.

USEFUL ADDRESSES. The Cedok office is at 3 Divadelni ulice, Brno; branches in all towns and resorts.

Slovakia

Easternmost and most mountainous region of Czechoslovakia, Slovakia can claim to be the Switzerland of Central Europe, not only because it is similar in size, population and geography, but because like Switzerland, it is really three "countries" in one. Southwestern Slovakia is the vast bountiful monotonous plain of the Danube river, bordering on Hungary and rising northward to the Carpathian foothills. Its food, architecture, music and folkways recall the influence of centuries of Hungarian rule.

Bratislava, capital of all Slovakia, is the region's main city. This major river port, which dates from Roman times, became an important trading center in the Middle Ages, and is still developing. The town has few architectural sights, except perhaps the castle which overlooks the city and itself looks like an upside down table.

Central Slovakia's main city, Banska Bystrica, was the cradle of the 1944 Slovak uprising against the Nazi occupiers. Since the early Middle Ages, the Low Tatras, High Tatras and Slovak Ore Mountains have been a storehouse of mineral treasure. Today its ancient mining towns form a chain of medieval museum sites, alongside thoroughly modern and industrialized communities.

Eastern Slovakia includes along its northern rim one of the most exciting natural wonderlands in Europe—the High Tatra Mountain National Park. The main ridge of this imposing Carpathian arc is more than ten miles wide and 16 miles long, with side spurs forming the beautiful Tatra valleys and lakes. The region, snow-topped the year round, is alive with whistling marmot, rare chamois, eagle and bear, and has several good resorts. Gateway to this area is the town of Poprad. The best-known resorts here are Tatranska Lomnica with a funicular railway running to the summit of the stupendously scenic Lomnicky Stit (8,645 ft.), Stary Smokovec with very satisfactory skiing runs, and Strbske Pleso on the edge of a lake at 4,400 feet.

Farther south and west, Vychodna village puts on its annual folk-festival in August. Levoca, a 13th-century walled "museum" town a few miles east of Poprad, has a collection of rustic wood sculpture unique in Europe.

If you are fond of underground grottos, there is a full-color version in central Slovakia at Demanovske Jaskyne. The caves are lined with red, yellow and blue-tinged stalactites and stalagmites.

A 100-foot geyser can be seen at Herlany near the town of Kosice.

PRACTICAL INFORMATION FOR SLOVAKIA

 WHEN TO GO. Winter sports are from December to the end of April. Mountain resorts are open all summer as well and offer a variety of outdoor recreation. Spas are a year-round proposition with the "high season" usually running from May 1 to Sept. 15.

WHAT TO SEE. Spis, Trencin, and Orava castles, Vratna Dolina Valley, Zdiar, a completely wooden, painted village; tour the Tatra and Fatra mountains.

TRANSPORTATION. Cedok bus tours or your own car are best. Roads are well-marked, but often narrow. Speed is not recommended. The Liberty Highway (*Cesta Svobody*) connects all the resorts in the High Tatra National Park (*TANAP*). Main cities are linked with Prague by air and rail service. From Poprad, excursion flights over the Tatra Mts. are offered by Cedok.

HOTELS AND RESTAURANTS. Mountain and spa hotels are very comfortable, with good cuisine and central heating in winter. Most of them maintain varied sports facilities (tennis, golf, swimming, skiing, etc.) and offer reduced rates during off-season.

BANSKA BYSTRICA. *Narodny Dum* (B*) 42 rooms, restaurant and outdoor cafe. *Urpin* (B*) 33 rooms, no restaurant. Recent *Lux* (B*).

BRATISLAVA. *Devin* (deluxe) is the best, 102 rooms with bath; *Carlton* and *Kyev* (both A*), modern, 268 and 217 rooms respectively. *Bratislava,* 344 rooms, is (B*), as is *Krym,* 50 rooms, some with bath. On the Danube, the hotel *Javorina* has 80 rooms, restaurant, bar, and fine view.

Motel Zlate Piesky (A*), outskirts of town, 40 rooms with shower; garden restaurant; pool, camping facilities. Closed Nov. to Mar.

Nearly 300 wine-cellar restaurants include *Mali Frantiskani* in the heart of town; *Klastorna Vinaren,* 300-year-old former monastery serves Slovak specialties; *Pod Bastou* and *Ribarsky Cech.* There's a *rotating café* atop the new TV tower and the *Bystrica Café* perched on a pylon above Slovak bridge; both offer outstanding views. *Koliba,* farther out, gypsy music and heady wines.

KOSICE. *Slovan* (A), 212 rooms, some with bath; wine cellar, garage. *Imperial* (B*), 40 rooms, some with bath, restaurant.

PIESTANY. Famed spa. *Magnolia* (A*) 108 rooms with bath; air-conditioned; *Eden* (B*). Both comfortable. also Balnea = the best. 3

POPRAD. *Gerlach* (B*), 124 rooms, 2 restaurants. *Europa* (B*), 78 rooms, garage.

About 40 kms away is **Podbanske-Pribylina,** charming country spot. *Krivan* (B*) 70 rooms with bath or shower, wine cellar with music.

SLIAC. Spa in parkland setting. The *Lazensky Dum* (A), the state spa hotel.

SMOKOVEC, a triple High Tatra winter resort center. At **Stary Smokovec,** most famous of the group, is traditional *Grand* (A*), 55 rooms with bath, central heating; garage. Also has a deluxe chalet for hire.

At **Horny Smokovec,** *the Bellevue* (A*), 110 rooms with bath or shower, central heating; garage, indoor pool. Most comfortable. *Sport* (B), 59 rooms, restaurant, near Bellevue.

At **Novy Smokovec.** *Tokajik* (B*), 16 rooms, central heating. Modern *Park* (B*), 96 rooms, ski equipment for hire. *Bystrina* (B*).

STRBSKE PLESO. Probably the best High Tatra ski spot, splendid location. *Patria* (A*) is newest. *Panorama* and *Fis,* both (B*).

TATRANSKA LOMNICA. Winter resort. *Grandhotel Praha* (A*), 102 rooms, 36 with bath or shower, central heating, restaurants, sauna. *Lomnica* is (B*).

TRENCIANSKE TEPLICE. The *Lazensky Dum* (A), another of the state spa hotels. *Krym Sanatorium,* new spa hotel with therapeutic facilities, sauna, night-club.

USEFUL ADDRESSES. The Cedok office is at 9b Sturova ulice, Bratislava; branches in all towns and resorts.

DENMARK

The Danes have always been known as "the Latins of Scandinavia", quite different from their Swedish and Norwegian brothers, not to mention the phlegmatic Germans on their other border. As the nation which abolished its laws against pornography in the late 1960s, Denmark had the last laugh on a horrified Anglo-Saxon world when consumption of dirty books and blue films took a nosedive. But the Danes are not all beer-and-skittles, as it were, for despite their easy-going attitude towards life in general and sex in particular, they are a tough lot, devoted to hard work and the idea of progress. They're just lucky enough to be able to enjoy life with as much zest as they put into their pursuit of thrift and cleanliness.

As for tourist highlights, it can all be summed up in one long sentence: Denmark is a kind of miniaturized Scandinavia—Danish to be sure, but crammed with beautiful little villages, blessed with good food, midsummer sun and fresh air, and a people eager to greet the knowledgeable visitor, especially if he speaks English and comes armed with a smile.

The Country and the People

Denmark, like Norway and Sweden, started decades ahead of the rest of the world in social legislation. The citizens of this progressive monarchy have social security from the cradle to the grave. There are no real slums, and social injustice is at a minimum. "The last place in Europe," wrote Negley Farson, "where sanity survives." He meant of course: "The only place where sanity has as yet occurred."

As for efficiency, though Denmark's soil is among Europe's most infertile, she has for generations been a leading food exporter. Today the agricultural labor force is declining steadily by 10% a year, but production still rises, despite frantic efforts to curtail it because of marketing difficulties. Danish farming cooperatives have much to do with this super-efficiency. The mere fact of dealing with a cooperative gives a man a say in its running: he may even become its president. So farmers and produce dealers or suppliers do not fall out. Denmark, however, is no longer primarily an agricultural country. Today she exports more industrial than farm products, even though she possesses no natural source of power and no raw materials whatsoever, except china clay.

Educational standards are high. You can't, for instance, be a humble cop unless you speak a second language well enough to take evidence in it. Almost everyone speaks good English.

Finally, if there's one sound that typefies Denmark, it's laughter. Danes seem incapable of conversing without endless jokes and wisecracks. Something will have gone sadly astray if you don't thoroughly enjoy your contacts with this friendly and hospitable people, wherever you go and whatever the time of year.

Food and Drink

The normal Danish breakfast or *Morgen complet* consists of coffee and an assortment of breads and sweet rolls (try the butter cake), served with generous slabs of butter. Danish coffee is delicious. If you want it *very* strong, ask for *mokka*.

At many hotels and restaurants, particularly outside of Copenhagen, that astonishing institution known as "cold table" holds sway at lunch time. This consists of an enormous table groaning with an assortment of smørrebrød, made of small portions of fish, meat, fowl, cheese, etc., delicately garnished and spread on white or rye bread. They are very tasty, but don't charge into the fray too recklessly, because a hot dish usually follows if you are taking the set lunch.

There are hundreds of varieties of Danish beer made by a score of breweries: those from the *Carlsberg* and *Tuborg* firms (both in Copenhagen) are world-famous. Most popular is pilsner, a light beer, but there is also lager, a darker beer. (What is "lager" in Britain is "pilsner" in Denmark.)

The other national drink of Scandinavia is Akvavit, popularly known as *snaps:* neither an aperitif, cocktail nor liqueur, it is meant to be drunk with food, preferably with a beer chaser. Akvavit is served icy cold and should never be sipped or left to get warm. Knock it back and damn the consequences. Remember that snaps goes with cold food, particularly herrings and cheese, not hot.

Shopping

Jewelry and silverware, furniture and anything wooden for the home, candles, light fittings, ceramics, Christmas cards and Christmas decorations, fabrics, porcelain, wallpapers—these are a few of Denmark's high-quality specialties. Best place to appraise the general offerings is *Den Permanente* (The Permanent Exhibition) in the black Vesterport Building near the Central Station. Here you will find a large selection of the finest handwork in Denmark, chosen by a group of discriminating judges and plainly marked with the artist's name so that you can look for his work elsewhere (and probably buy it cheaper). Den Permanente is also expert at handling export problems.

PRACTICAL INFORMATION FOR DENMARK

WHAT WILL IT COST. Prices are expected to rise by about 8% to 10% in 1979. Hotel prices are considerably lower outside the capital and North Zealand, though they are rising at the North Sea coastal resorts. The cheapest areas are probably Funen and Jutland. A stay in a country inn is a good bet, and here you will have the best chance of meeting the Danes; rooms will be clean and comfortable, but there are no private bathrooms.

HOTEL ROOM (DOUBLE) PER PERSON
(including VAT and service)

	Deluxe	1st class	2nd class	Moderate
Copenhagen	250	215	170	120
Provincial town, resort	160	110	95	85
Rural		80	75	60

The budget hotel area in Copenhagen is near the Central Station, around Colbjørnsensgade-Helgolandsgade; best among the cheaper hotels are the unlicensed Mission hotels. Or try Roskilde, 20 miles out, with frequent train services to Copenhagen.

Hotels are graded Deluxe (L), first class superior (1), first class reasonable (2), moderate (3), and inexpensive (4).

A TYPICAL DAY FOR ONE PERSON

Room in moderate Copenhagen hotel	120 kr.
Breakfast	20
Lunch, popular restaurant	25
Dinner	60
Transportation (bus, taxi)	15
Theater ticket	35
Cigarettes (pack of 20)	14
Coffee (cafeteria)	8
Beer (bottle)	8
Miscellaneous	25
	330 kr.

CAPITAL. Copenhagen.

LANGUAGE. Danish. English widely understood and spoken.

CLIMATE. Moderate, evenings tend to be cool.

Average maximum daily temperatures in degrees Fahrenheit and centigrade:

Copen-hagen	Jan.	Feb.	Mar.	Apr.	May	June	July	Aug.	Sept.	Oct.	Nov.	Dec.
F°	36	36	41	50	61	66	72	70	64	54	48	39
C°	2	2	5	10	16	19	22	21	18	12	7	4

SEASONS. Mid-May to mid-September with extra hours of sunlight.

SPECIAL EVENTS. Carnival of Street Urchins throughout the country on Shrove Monday. *May,* the Tivoli Gardens opens from the first to second Sunday in September. *June,* Frederikssund's Viking Festival from Last week to first week in July. *July,* American celebrations on the 4th in Rebild Park, Aalborg; Odense commemorates Hans Andersen from mid-July to mid-August. *September,* Arhus has "festive weeks" during first half. *December,* Goblins' Week (16-24) at Toftlund near Ribe when everyone goes about in fairy-tale costume.

CLOSING TIMES. Shops open from 9:00 to 17:30 hrs. but are allowed to stay open until 19:00 on Thursdays, 20:00 hrs. on Fridays; closed Sat. between noon and 14:00. Post offices open from 10 to 17.00 hrs. Banks open from 9:30 to 16:00 hrs. weekdays, close Sat., but Thurs. open to 18:00. (Varies outside Copenhagen.)

SPORTS. Yachting extremely popular, with some possibilities of hiring craft. Riding and tennis clubs galore and many golf courses. The many watercourses are ideal for anglers, but license mostly necessary for lakes and streams: inquire at local tourist office or hotel.

MONEY. The monetary unit is the *krone* in which there are 100 øre. You may import and export unlimited non-Danish currency. If you wish to export more than 3,000 kr. you must show you brought the money in or exchanged foreign currency or traveler's checks for it in Denmark. *Note:* The smallest coin is 5 øre, so all prices are rounded to a multiple of 5 before charging.

There are about 5.80 kr. to the US$, 11.15 to the pound sterling.

TIPPING. Hotels and restaurants quote fully inclusive prices; you should tip only for special personal help. Washroom attendants get 1 kr. Taxi fares include the tip, so don't tip extra. Also, don't tip movie or theater ushers or in barbershops.

HOW TO REACH DENMARK. By Air. *SAS* or *Pan American* flights from North America. By *British Airways, SAS* or *Air France* from London or Paris. **Note:** air lines subject to change.

By Train: from London to Harwich/Hook of Holland, or Dover/Ostend.

By Sea: The *United Steamship Co.* (*DFDS*) operates drive on/off car ferries to Esbjerg from Harwich (daily in summer, otherwise thrice weekly). From Newcastle (twice weekly in summer).

By Car: All car routes from continental starting-points converge at Hamburg. From here the motorist has two choices: he can either travel north via Flensburg into Jutland or via Lübeck to Puttgarden and then by ferry to Rødbyhavn, shortest sea crossing and quickest route to Copenhagen. A ferry links Gelting (near Flensburg) to Faaborg on Funen. Another ferry-crossing is from Travemünde (nr. Lübeck) to Gedser. In summer, best reserve in advance for ferry space at any main rail station in Germany. Reservations are free.

CUSTOMS. The import of duty-free goods varies according to way of entry into Denmark, so check before your trip for full details. 1978 rates on entry from an EEC country are limited to 1½ liters of spirits *or* 3 liters of dessert wine plus 3 liters of table wine, and 300 cigarettes (400 for U.S. citizens).

Lesser amounts if entering from a non-EEC country, or if having stayed less than 72 hours in the EEC area. See also *Practical Planning* section.

MAIL. Surface letters are 1.50 kr. for 20 grams to US; airmail extra 40 øre per 5 grams; postcards 1.20 kr. Letters to UK and Europe cost 1.50 kr. and go airmail automatically.

ELECTRICITY. 220 AC.

DRINKING WATER. Safe everywhere.

TRAVEL IN DENMARK. By Air. *SAS* and private air companies offer daily services to Jutland, Odense, and to Rønne, capital of Bornholm. Note that, thanks to international regulations, if you fly from Britain or the States any air trip *westwards* from Copenhagen (i.e., not onwards to Rønne) and back is free. Return tickets for certain daily departures are sold with 35% discount.

By Car. Drive on the right side. Danish roads are excellent. Gasoline, super, is about 2.70 kr. per liter. Third party (Green Card) insurance obligatory for US registration vehicles. Take particular care of the many cyclists. Local speed limits must be strictly observed. *No excuse for driving while under the influence of alcohol is accepted.* Offenders are always severely punished.

By Train. Trains have two classes. *Intercity* and *lyntog* (express) trains connect major cities with the capital within hours. For weekends, make reservations early through your hotel. Family reduction and excursion tickets available.

By Boat. Day and night boats from Copenhagen or Ystad (Sweden) to Rønne are comfortable and carry cars. Separate train and car ferries shuttle across the Great Belt, separating the islands of Zealand (Sjælland) and Funen (Fyn) on the Copenhagen-Odense-Esbjerg route.

CAR HIRE. *Hertz,* Air Terminal; *Autourist,* Halmtorvet 11; *Avis,* Kampmanns-gade 1, and all at airport; *Pitzner Auto,* Trommesalen 4. All Copenhagen.

MEET THE DANES. Contact the local tourist office for information on the Meet the Danes program. You must apply in person and at least 48 hours before you wish to visit a Danish family at home (usually arranged for 8 P.M., after dinner). This scheme is operated only in some Jutland towns, Odense, and Nyborg.

SUMMER COTTAGES. You can rent a cottage by application to a regional Danish tourist office, or to *Dansk Centralkontor for Sommerhusudlejning,* Falkoner Allé 7, Copenhagen, minimum period, one week. Apply as far ahead as possible.

CAMPING. Denmark claims—with good justification—to have the best camp sites in Europe, if not in the world. Over 500 are officially recognized and graded for facilities and shelter. The best provide absolutely everything campers can need, (showers, washing-up, ironing, shop, etc.) even to central heating for the public rooms in winter, when 90 sites remain open. Consult yearly issued camping guide.

Membership of a national or international camping, caravanning, or motoring organization, with a "carnet de camping" that includes third-party insurance, or a Danish "camping pass" (7 kr. per year) is essential. The latter can be purchased on arrival at any camp site.

Charges are 8–10 kr. per person, per night, with half price for children under 14. Tents and trailer (caravans) are sometimes charged separately. Holders of the International AIT Camping Carnet get discount at some sites and may use the 25 FDM sites.

USEFUL ADDRESSES. *American Embassy,* Dag Hammarskjolds Allé 24; *British Embassy,* Kastelsvej 38; *Canadian Embassy,* Prinsesse Maries Allé 2; The *Danish Tourist Board* is at Banegaardspladsen 2. All in Copenhagen.

Copenhagen, Happy Capital

The center of Danish fun is Copenhagen, biggest and liveliest of the Scandinavian capitals and by almost unanimous agreement one of the gayest cities of Europe. More than a million Danes, a quarter of the country's population, live and let live here. The city, on the island of Zealand, is just as flat as the sea that embraces it, as flat as the rest of Denmark, which averages only 98 feet above sea level. (This is why every second inhabitant has a bicycle.)

When is the best time to come? Denmark is lovely in summer, autumn and spring. May marks the liberation from the bonds of the long northern winter. That incomparable pleasure garden of Tivoli throws wide its gates in Copenhagen, and the "season" has begun. The circus comes to Copenhagen, too, in May; the amusement park, Bakken, opens in the Klampenborg Forest, and Denmark begins to rock like the yachts between Elsinore and Copenhagen, warming up for that June water carnival known as "Sound Week". The Royal Danish Ballet concludes the Copenhagen season in May, and June comes to a climax on June 23 with Midsummer Eve, a night of outdoor dancing, singing, feasting, bonfires and fireworks, transforming the whole nation into one big carnival. Try to celebrate this night along the Sound. You'll never forget the unreal summer twilight, streaked with rockets, edged with a thousand fires along the shores of the Kattegat, as though Sweden and Denmark were both aflame.

With the end of June, everyone in Copenhagen goes to the country, and everyone in the country comes to Copenhagen, a most inconvenient arrangement, since it fills all the hotels at the height of the tourist season. This is the period of long, sun-flooded days and short, balmy nights in Denmark. Make your reservations early. The Danes will do the rest.

Sightseeing In Copenhagen

A good place to orient yourself is in the Raadhusplads or Town Hall Square. The huge red brick town hall was built in 1905, and from here there is access to the 350-foot-high tower with its fine view of the city and countryside. The City Museum is at Vesterbrogade 59. Behind Tivoli, visit the Glyptotek, a gallery with a remarkable collection of sculpture magnificently displayed. From the Town Hall Square a series of streets, collectively known as "Strøget", run eastwards (Strøget is a pedestrians-only area from 11 A.M. each day). South of Gammeltorv square a short walk will bring you to the Frederiksholms Canal and the splendid National Museum with its exhibits of Stone and Bronze age relics, Viking camps and ships, and all the fascinating panoply of old Scandinavian life, handsomely recreated. The museum sells interesting silver and bronze replicas of certain of the exhibits. Directly across the bridge from the National Museum is Christiansborg Palace, seat of the Danish Folketing (parliament). Nearby, set in an idyllic garden, is the Royal Library with a great collection including the earliest records of Viking expeditions to America and Greenland. On one side of the Library is Tøjhuset, Copenhagen's arms museum with outstanding displays of weapons, armor and uniforms. Flanking the Library on the other side is the red-brick Børsen, oldest stock exchange in the world still partly used for its original purpose, and a splendid example of Renaissance architecture. Opposite the quays of this island, Slotsholm, the flower vendors tie up their boats and sell their wares. Still on Slotsholm, but on the inland side of Christiansborg Palace, is Thorvaldsen Museum, containing the famous sculptor's tomb and works.

Behind and north of the Thorvaldsen Museum you recross the canal by the Højbro, or High Bridge. You will see the Knippelsbro drawbridge from here and the green and gold spire of Vor Frelsers Kirke (Our Saviour's Church); the view from the tower is worth the climb up the gilded spiral staircase which winds around it. There is a colorful fruit and flower market in the Højbro Plads. Four blocks from here is the Round Tower which Christian IV, warrior-architect-scholar king of Denmark, built as an astronomical observatory. Peter the Great of Russia mounted its internal spiral ramp in a horse-drawn carriage; you'll probably have to do it on foot. If you stroll up the Købmagergade from here you'll come to the University and the Vor Frue Kirke, Our Lady's Church, the cathedral of Copenhagen with its marble statues of Christ and the Apostles by Thorvaldsen. The church was restored in 1977–1978.

At the opposite end of Strøget from the Town Hall Square is Kongens Nytorv, the southern side of which is flanked by the Royal Theater, home of Copenhagen's opera, classical theater and internationally-famed ballet. Even closer to the square is the Dutch baroque building of Charlottenborg, which has housed the Danish Academy of Fine Arts since 1754. The Nyhavn Canal, which runs up to Kongens Nytorv, is lined with picturesque 18th-century buildings and sailors' cafés. Attractions in this "newer" part of Copenhagen are: Amalienborg Square with its four immense rococo palaces including the residence of Queen Margrethe II and Prince Henrik where the guard is changed every day at noon: the Museum of Applied Arts, and—definitely not to be missed—the Langelinie Promenade, where foreign navies moor their ships, all of Copenhagen strolls on Sunday afternoon, and the Little Mermaid of Hans Christian Andersen gazes across to Burmeister and Wain's vast shipyards as though in search of her prince.

An excursion you are sure to enjoy in Copenhagen is that to the Rosenborg Palace, a museum containing a dazzling display of all the Danish crown jewels together with fine furniture and other personal effects of Danish monarchs since the time of Christian IV, whose pearl-studded saddle is one of the palace's chief attractions. This charming, rather liveable museum still belongs to the royal family. Opposite it are 25 acres of botanical gardens at the north end of which is the Statens Museum for Kunst, the National Art Gallery, very fancy with a liveried doorman and a first rate collection, not only of Danish art, but of Rembrandt, Cranach, Rubens, Durer, the French Impressionists, and Matisse.

Sorgenfri, on Copenhagen's northwest outskirts and well-served by electric trains, is the site of the open air museum known as Frilandsmuseet. Here in a park covering 40 acres is a collection of reconstructed Danish farms, windmills and country houses, moved here from all parts of Denmark and furnished with authentic period pieces and utensils. Recommended.

PRACTICAL INFORMATION FOR COPENHAGEN

 HOTELS. Hotels in Copenhagen are almost always full during the summer season; so get a reservation. If you find yourself without a place to stay, go to the billeting bureau in the Airport or Central Station (Kiosk P.). For a small fee the bureau will find you a room.

Luxurious

Copenhagen Sheraton, Vester Søgade 6, has 440 air-conditioned rooms, central; restaurant overlooks lakes. Large ballroom.

Hotel d'Angleterre, Kongens Nytorv 34; 130 rooms. Ranks first among the older Copenhagen hotels. Aristocratic, spacious, with excellent food and service. Bar, restaurant with excellent food.

Over the Air Terminal, at Hammerichsgade 1, is the skyscraper *Royal,* with 300 rooms and suites. Panoramic lounge on top floor.

Scandinavia, Amager Blvd. 70. 534 rooms, rooftop restaurant, indoor pool, sauna. Facing old city moats.

First Class Superior

Penta, H. C. Andersens Boulevard 50; 200 rooms with bath. An ultramodern restaurant on the 18th floor.

Imperial, Vester Farimagsgade 9; 187 rooms. Has excellent restaurants and bar. Central. Facilities include a 250-car garage.

Marina, at Vedbaek, north of Copenhagen, 72 rooms with bath; sauna. Near beach and station.

Admiral, Toldbodgade 24, 366 rooms with Wiinblad decorations and modern Danish design, in 1780–framed former granary, with intact Pomeranian pine girders. Opened 1978.

Nyhavn 71 (the address), 123 beds, in former storehouse.

Plaza, Banegaardsplads 3; 110 rooms. Rivals the more expensive hotels for comfort and service. Its restaurant is among the best in town. Breakfast extra.

3 Falke, Falkoner Allé 7; 159 rooms. Situated in the charming Frederiksberg section, it's part of a complex. Every room has a shower and television.

First Class Reasonable

Alexandra, H. C. Andersens Boulevard 8; 80 rooms, close to Raadhusplads. Quiet and modest.

Astoria, Banegaardsplads 4; 90 rooms, most with bath. Near the Grand and close to Tivoli and central station. Restaurant.

Bel Air, Løjtegaardsvej 99; 430 beds, rooms with bath. Restaurant, bar, sauna, garden.

Danhotel, Kastrup Airport, 262 rooms with bath or shower; restaurant, 300-car service garage. Various room categories.

Globetrotter, near Kastrup airport; 244 beds, all rooms with bath; restaurant, sauna.

Kong Frederik, Vester Voldgade 25-27; 62 rooms. Restaurant, pub. Breakfast extra.

Opera, Tordenskjoldsgade 15; 100 beds, all rooms with bath. Sauna.
Park, Jarmers Plads 3, 45 rooms with shower or bath in 24. Breakfast extra.
Rossini, G1. Jernbanevej 27, 118 beds, free parking, bowling, sauna. Near Valby Station.

Moderate

Baltic, Borups Plads, 86 beds; restaurant, terrace.
Carlton, Halmtorvet 14, 100 beds, in the "naughty" district, but quiet, near Central Station.
Weber's, Vesterbrogade 11; 65 rooms. Practically next door to the Central Station. Modest but spacious and comfortable. Restaurant.
Østerport, opposite Østerport Station; 120 rooms, some with bath.
Skovriderkroen, at edge of Charlottenlund wood, near beach, in wonderful surroundings; 37 beds. Breakfast extra. Various room categories.

STUDENT HOSTEL-HOTEL

Minerva, Rektorparken 1, 307 beds; specially designed to serve as student dormitories for 9 months of the year and a tourist hotel in summer; very good value.
D.I.S. International Students' Club, Sankt Hans Torv 26, is a student dormitory open all year.

Like the other Scandinavian capitals, Copenhagen has a number of "mission" hotels. These offer comfortable rooms at reasonable prices; most serve no drink stronger than beer. Meticulously clean, they are ideal for the traveler on a limited budget. The largest one, *Missionshotellet,* has 200 rooms and is located at Løngangsstraede 27, close to the Town Hall. Almost next door to each other and behind the Central Station are the *Hebron* and the *Westend,* at Helgolandsgade 4 and 3. *Ansgar,* Colbjørnsensgade 29, *Nebo,* Istedgade 6.

MOTELS. *Wittrup,* 9 miles west on Hwy. 1 at Albertslund; 56 rooms with bath, snack bar. Reasonable. *Esso Motor Hotel,* 7 miles west on Hwy. 1 at Glostrup; 96 beds, first class. Neither includes breakfast.

RESTAURANTS. Among hotel dining rooms, the *Royal's* gets highest praise, then the *Angleterre's* and *Imperial's.* The *Plaza* has excellent cuisine, the *Palace's Viking* restaurant stays open till midnight. Below is a selection from over 100 restaurants.

Expensive

Syv Smaa Hjem (7 Small Homes), Jernbanegade 4, is a delightful, intimate restaurant sporting a first-rate wine cellar. French cuisine.
Fiskehuset, Gammel Strand 34, is famous for gourmet fish dinners and Victorian décor. Well worth the high prices. Not Suns.
Krog, another fish restaurant next door, serves up its fruits of the sea in plusher—and more expensive—surroundings. Not Suns.

Moderate

Langeliniepavillonen, housing the Royal Yacht Club, is excellent for lunches, teas, dinners, and there is a magnificent view of the harbor. Dancing in the evening.
The Carvery and *Piano,* Vesterbrogade 9. Slice what meat you want. *Piano* is less expensive but has no steak bar.
Oskar Davidsen's Søpavillonen, Gyldenløvesgade 24, is a "must". Its main attraction is the four-foot long *smørrebrød* list with over 500 varieties of open faced sandwiches. Come early.

Glyptoteket, Stormgade 35, is across the street from the museum by the same name, revives weary art-lovers with excellent cooking.

Baghuset, Gothersgade 13, has charcoal grilled steaks and fish. Best book.

Escoffier, Dr. Tvaergade 43. Serves meals as French as a meal can be outside France. Closed Sun.

Den gyldne Fortun, Ved Stranden. Reasonable prices in basement, more luxurious on first floor. Very good food. Closed Sun.

Tokanten, Vandkunsten. Atmospheric, food plain and fair.

Gyllen, Norre Voldgade 2. Good lunch spot with unpretentious fare.

Els, Store Strandstraede 3. Nyhavn lunch restaurant with some French specialties. Closed Sat.

The Tivoli Gardens (summer only) has a number of excellent but pricewise slightly overrated restaurants, of which the best is *La Belle Terrasse.* Other good ones: *Divan I* and *Divan II.*

 ENTERTAINMENT. Copenhagen is without doubt the happiest city in Scandinavia. The Royal Theater offers opera and outstanding ballet in addition to plays, and tickets are normally in great demand; ask your hotel porter to secure reservations for you 3-7 days before the performance you wish to see. Films are in their original languages with Danish subtitles. Performances begin at fixed hours, there is no smoking and seats are reserved. Do not tip ushers.

Tivoli Gardens. Don't miss this famous amusement park, probably the gayest and most beautiful in the world. It has everything: a superb pantomime theater, an ultra-modern concert hall offering symphony concerts each evening; open-air acrobatic shows; two bands, and the usual array of rides and amusements plus the popular Funny Kitchen where you can indulge in an orgy of smashing china: better than analysis! There are fountains, a lake to go boating on, the famous Tivoli Boy Guard of toytown soldiers all dressed up in the king's uniform, and fabulous fireworks on Wednesdays, Saturdays, Sundays and holidays.

Nightlife. There's plenty of it. *Montmartre,* Nørregade 41, is a restaurant mainly visited for the top jazz artists. For traditional jazz it's *De tre Musketerer* at Nikolaj Plads or *Vognporten* at Magstraede, latter mainly for young people. There are quite a few discos in the Strøget area; check the weekend papers.

At Allégade 7-9 are a cluster of places guaranteed to make anyone's evening full. They don't close until the sun comes up. Also at Allégade is the family cabaret, *Lorry Landsbyen,* a roofed beer-garden restaurant where there is a nonstop show with music, singers, and variety artists. In the same building is *Drachmann's Kro,* an ancient, atmospheric tavern recommended for quiet dining in authentic surroundings. In central city is *Den røde Pimpernel,* Kattesundet 4, always crowded.

If it's drinks you're after, nearby is *Vin og Ølgod,* Skindergade 45, with a German beerhouse atmosphere: communal singing and dancing until 2 A.M., except Sundays. *Solvang,* Vesterbrogade 97, has orchestra, singing, dancing; cold food, a small selection of hot dishes. Closed Sun.

In quite another class are the places patronized mainly by bachelors in search of wine, women, and song (not necessarily in that order): *Kakadu Bar,* at Colbjørsensgade 6, is sophisticated. Try *Wonder Bar,* Studiestraede 69.

At Tivoli Gardens are the everfull *Faergekroen* for drinking and singing, teenager-dominated *Taverna* for dancing, and *Vise Vers Huset* for modern folk song.

For erotic shows, mixed saunas etc. check the classified ads in the "Ekstrabladet" newspaper. Or ask your hotel porter.

TRANSPORTATION. *Taxi* transportation being expensive (tips included in the fare) it's best to use buses or trains. The number of fare zones decide the price. There is a maximum fare on long distance rides. Tickets are valid for any train or bus for one hour or longer, according to distance, and ticket coupons reduce the price. On the canals are *motorboats* with or without English-speaking guides. *Motor coach* tours through the city as well as to North and South Zealand start from Raadhusplads, the main square.

In the delightful Deer Park, closed to motorists, you can hire *horse cabs.* (Don't miss seeing Bakken fun-fair corner.)

If you really want to go Danish, you can hire a bicycle through the Københavns Cyklebørs Gothersgade 157, and many rail stations. Consult your hotel porter.

 SHOPPING. Copenhagen's main department stores are *Magasin du Nord,* Kongens Nytorv, and *Illum,* Østergade 52. Both carry a good, representative selection of the best that Denmark has to offer—Furnishings, fabrics, ceramics, silver, etc. *Illums Bolighus,* Amagertorv 10, is the Center of Modern Design in Scandinavia and is famous as such round the world.

CANDLES. *Asp Holmblad,* Østergade 61; and *Daells Varehus,* Norregade 12.

FURS. *A. C. Bang,* Østergade 27, is furrier to the Danish royal family, as is *Birger Christensen* at no. 38 on the same street.

HANDCRAFTS. *Haandarbejdets Fremme,* Vimmelskaftet 38; *P. Brøste,* Overgade 8, in the 18th-cent. Potter's House.

PORCELAIN AND CRYSTAL. *Bing & Grøndahl,* next door to the *Royal Copenhagen Porcelain Manufactory* (Amagertorv 6); *Holmegaard Glassware,* Østergade 15. *Rosenthal,* Frederiksberggade 21.

SILVER AND STEEL. *Georg Jensen Silver,* Østergade 40; *A. Dragsted,* Bredgade 17, also for jewelry; *A. Michelsen,* Bredgade 11; *Hans Hansen,* Amagertorv 16.

TOYS. *Kay Bojesen,* Bredgade 47, wooden toys a specialty. *Rigtigt Legetøj,* Lavendelstraede 5-7, sells only experimental and educational playthings.

Dyrehaven and Bellevue

Dyrehaven, the Deer Park near Klampenborg (less than half an hour by electric train from the capital) is the Copenhageners' favorite place to spend a few hours in the country. If you go by car, remember you are not allowed to motor within the park. Here nearly 2,000 deer wander freely about. There's a golf course, a summer fun-fair (mid-Apr. to Aug. 15) and several year-round restaurants in this beautiful 3,500 acre haven of forests, paths and ponds. Near the entrance to the park is the Bellevue bathing beach. If you travel to the Klampenborg station, or to any other by electric train (S-train), remember you have to cancel your ticket in the time-dating machine at the platform entrance.

Elsinore and Hamlet's Castle

After Copenhagen, Zealand is the part of Denmark most visited, and the classic tour is up the coast to Elsinore and Kronborg Castle, down to Frederiksborg Castle, back to Copenhagen.

The seaside drive from the capital to Elsinore is along one of Europe's most crowded highways in summer—pleasant if you're not the driver. The fine, recently-built Louisiana Museum at Humlebaek, devoted to modern art, is well worth visiting on the way; there is a good restaurant, too. Chamber music concerts are given here in summer.

Elsinore (Helsingør) is one of Denmark's oldest towns. Its medieval church of St. Mary and attached Carmelite monastery attest to its importance in the early 15th century; they are both architectural treasures. Kronborg Castle, popularly known as Hamlet's "Castle of Elsinore" was actually built by Frederick II between 1574 and 1585, about 600 years after Prince Hamlet lived, and is quite unlike the sort of castle we visualize as the setting of Shakespeare's play. Visit this central courtyard first, then the inner and outer ramparts, the splendid 200-foot long banqueting hall and the gloomy dungeons where the brooding figure of Ogier the Dane waits to unsheathe his sword in the hour of Denmark's danger. Remember to see the chapel, too. The castle occupies a magnificent position overlooking the Sound, with Sweden only a few miles away. Elsinore also houses Denmark's Technical Museum.

Frederiksborg and Fredensborg Castles

The beautiful Renaissance-style castle of Frederiksborg is at Hillerød. Built by Christian IV between 1602 and 1620, it was gutted by fire in 1859 and has been fully restored with money from the Carlsberg brewery and private subscriptions. It is Denmark's National Historic Museum. The kings of Denmark used to be crowned here; these days they're not crowned at all. The castle is handsomely situated on a lake, and you will enjoy strolling through the adjacent chapel and the French-style park.

Fredensborg, just six miles from its twin city, Hillerød, has two claims to fame; its palace and its inn. The palace, built between 1719 and 1726, is still a royal residence and has the charm of a place that is lived in. It can be visited when the royal family is not there on Sundays in July. The park is open to the public at all times.

West of Copenhagen

At Odsherred in the most northwesterly part of Zealand, the mortal remains of Mary of Scotland's impetuous lover, the Earl of Bothwell, are visible in a glass-topped coffin in the Faarevejle Church. Not far away is Dragsholm Castle where he died in 1578, completely insane.

At Traelleborg off the main road from Copenhagen to Korsør there's a famous, thousand-year-old Viking fortress, partly reconstructed to show the elaborate style of military construction which prevailed at the time.

Roskilde, second largest city of Zealand, is only 20 miles from the capital on the main road. Its red brick cathedral is the burial place of Denmark's kings and queens. In addition to the 37 royal tombs, there is a 500-year-old clock and a pillar on which numerous royal personages from Peter the Great to the Duke of Windsor have marked their heights.

Southern Zealand and the Southern Isles

Southern Zealand abounds in interesting towns with half-timbered houses and enough castles to make it one of Denmark's château regions.

Gavnø is among the castles open to the public. Near Køge is Vallø Castle, with fine gardens and a good restaurant, the *Slotskro.*

For idyllic natural beauty it would be hard to beat the southerly island of Møn, with its white cliffs towering 400 feet up from the blue sea in fantastic shapes and its forests of beech, one of the supreme natural sights of Denmark.

Funen and the Central Islands

Funen (Fyn), second largest of Denmark's 500 islands, is the garden of Denmark. Its capital is Odense, birthplace of Hans Christian Andersen, a journey of three hours by train from Copenhagen.

Odense's 13th-century Cathedral of St. Knud is one of the finest gothic buildings in Denmark. But the chief tourist attractions are the mementos of the great Hans Christian Andersen: the museum on Hans Jensensstraede presumably on the spot where he was born, and the house where he lived between the ages of 2 and 14, another museum which you may visit at Munkemøllestraede 3.

South Funen contains fine woods and hill scenery and the lovely old towns of Svendborg and Faaborg. Among the numerous old manors and castles, Egeskov is outstanding. The five superb gardens are open to the public, together with an excellent museum of old cars, planes and motorcycles, housed in the estate's former barn.

AErøskøbing, on AErø island (ferry from Svendborg), is the best-preserved and loveliest of all Denmark's ancient villages. From Svendborg, you can also drive by bridges to the islands of Taasinge and Langeland.

Jutland and Neighboring Islands

Jutland is the only part of Denmark attached to the continent of Europe. A spit of sand, where you can stand with one foot in the waves of the Skagerrak and the other in the Kattegat, forms its northern tip. From here a magnificent sandy beach, backed mainly by dunes but sometimes by limestone cliffs, stretches for some 250 miles down the west coast, all the way to Esbjerg and the lovely island of Fanø opposite it. Løkken, Blokhus and a number of smaller resorts are dotted along this stretch of coast, where thousands of Danish families spend their holidays in small wooden chalets.

The region's eastern half is much hillier and often attractive. Rold Forest (Rold Skov) and the Rebild Hills National Park, 15 miles south of Aalborg, are lovely in both summer and winter. If you're here on the 4th of July, you'll think you're in America because tens of thousands of Danes and Danish-Americans gather on the Rebild Hills to celebrate America's Independence Day with speeches and other festivities in the National Park, purchased by Danish Americans in 1911. The Lincoln Memorial Cabin in this park was built of logs from every state in the union, and houses mementos of Danish migration to the United States.

Ebeltoft, the Mols Hills and the broad bay on which Aarhus, Denmark's second largest city, stands are justly renowned for their scenery. So is the Silkeborg region, with its innumerable lakes fed by the River Guden and its hills, which include Himmelbjerget, Denmark's highest.

Many of Jutland's towns and villages are especially appealing. Skagen, near the northernmost tip, is a holiday resort, fishing village and artists' colony rolled into one.

Aalborg, the most important town of north Jutland, has a harmonious combination of old and new. Sights here include the magnificent Jens Bang's House, St. Botolph cathedral from ca. 1500, the early 16th-century Aalborghus Castle, and the early 15th-century Monastery of the Holy Ghost.

Aarhus, an attractive large town, boasts the oldest Danish university after Copenhagen's, as well as a thriving port and a good deal of heavy industry. The 13th-century cathedral, old city center and Den gamle By (the Old Town) open-air museum are especially worth visiting. The latter consists of authentic medieval town houses collected from all parts of the country and re-erected, complete with fittings and furnishings, like the Den fynske Landsby (Funen Village) outside Odense.

Ebeltoft, 30 miles from Aarhus, possesses fine medieval streets (like Ribe, Møgeltønder and other Jutland towns) and an excellent beach as well. Silkeborg and Skanderborg, 30 and 15 miles from Aarhus, are your bases for seeing the Lake District. Vejle is a small industrial town and major holiday center at the head of a deep, picturesque fjord, with lovely excursions.

Ribe's 800-year-old cathedral and medieval houses fascinate Danes and foreigners alike. Like Randers it used to be a favorite summer haunt of storks, but the birds have become scarcer in recent years. Sønderborg, on the island of Als, is delightfully situated and a favorite yachting center.

One of the world's most unusual attractions can be found at Billund, a tiny village near Vejle. In 1954, the Billund village carpenter's son invented the now world-famous construction toy called Lego, which also has many commercial uses today. He has kept his office and his Danish factory at Billund and has also established there a 10-acre amusement park. Legoland, as the park is called, also contains a magnificent museum of antique dolls and dolls' houses, a puppet theater and restaurants. It is served by a jet-sized airport with regular flights from Copenhagen. (Closed each year from October 1 to April 30.)

Bornholm

Bornholm (accent on the second syllable), Denmark's outlying Baltic island, 100 miles due east of Copenhagen but only 22 from the Swedish coast, is unique not only in Denmark but also in Europe. Its maximum dimensions are 23 miles by 18. Yet the scenery ranges from miles of fine white sand at Dueodde in the south, through smaller sandy beaches and low rocks from which you dive into 20 feet of water, to sheer granite cliffs and the towering Hammeren headland in the north.

The wooded Paradisbakkerne (Paradise Hills) in the east, the Almindingen region in the island's center, the cliffs at Helligdommen, and the cliffs and hills round the gaunt ruins of the medieval Hammershus fortress are all well worth visiting.

Herring fishing is an ancient occupation and the coast is dotted with tiny, pocket-handkerchief-sized harbors, of which Tejn is the minutest. Neksø, Svaneke, Gudhjem (where you can buy freshly-smoked herrings that you drink rather than eat), Allinge, Sandvig and Hasle are all picturesque. Rønne, the capital, has well-preserved medieval streets as well as attractive modern suburbs.

Bornholm possesses four of Denmark's seven surviving round church-es. Located at Nyker, Nylars, Østerlars and Olsker, all were built in the

12th century to provide defense against pirates as well as places of worship.

PRACTICAL INFORMATION FOR THE REGIONS

AALBORG. Hotels: *Hvide Hus* and *Phønix*, (1). *Central* and *Motel Aalborg*, (2).

Restaurants: *Hotel Phønix; Duus Vinkjaelder*, old, intimate wine cellar; *Stygge Krumpen*, old-fashioned cooking—today; *Faklen*, British-style, exclusive.

AARHUS. Hotels: *Marselis* and *Atlantic* (L).

Restaurants: Best is *Sjette Frederiks Kro*, just outside town at Risskov, beautifully located. *Varna*, Marselisborg Wood, has floorshow, excellent cuisine.

EBELTOFT. Hotels: *Hvide Hus*, (L) with pool, golf course. *Vigen*, (2).

Restaurants: *Mellem jyder; Motel Vibaek* (modern).

ELSINORE. Hotels: *Marienlyst* (1), fashionable, pool, gambling casino. *Meulenborg*, (2); both have saunas. *Skandia*, (3).

ESBJERG. Hotels: *Britannia*, all rooms with bath, (2); *Esbjerg*, (3).

Restaurant: *Bonbonnieren*, old-style, music, bowling.

FAABORG. Hotels: *Rasmussens*, (2). About 10 miles north on the Assens road, *Steensgaard* (L), a former manor.

Restaurant: *Falsled Kro*, (1), one of Denmark's best; expensive.

FREDENSBORG. Hotel: *Frederik IV & Store Kro*, (1), all rooms with bath, offers unrivaled food. Expensive, but rooms in the old inn are more modest.

HELLEBAEK. Hotel: *Hellebaek Kyst*, (2); private beach.

HORNBAEK. Hotels: *Trouville*, (L), *Hornbaekhus*, in a park, diet food (2).

KØGE Hotel: *Hvide Hus*, (L), sauna.

NAESTVED. Hotel: *Vinhuset*, (2), pleasant.

NYBORG. Hotels: *Hesselet* (L), modern, sauna and pool; *Nyborg Strand* (1), some moderately priced rooms; a sauna; *Nyborg* (2), with music.

ODENSE. Hotels: *Grand*, (1), fine cuisine; *Park* and *Ny Missionshotel*, (3). *Motel Odense*, on Hwy. 9, is one of Denmark's best, a converted farmhouse; (3).

Restaurants: *Den gamle Kro*, charming; *Bang* (with dancing); *Sortebro Kro* (in open-air museum). All Excellent, moderate.

RIBE. *Dagmar* (2) and *Munken* (3). *Weis'stue* is a charming 16th-century inn.

RØNNE. Hotels: Best are *Dams* (2), and *Fredensborg* (1), with sea view and sauna.

ROSKILDE. Hotels: *Prindsen*, with good restaurant, *Risø;* both (2). *Motel BP* on Hwy 1, fairly expensive.

SILKEBORG. Hotel: *Dania*, (2).

SKAGEN. Hotels: *Skagen,* (2), pool and sauna; *Brøndums,* good restaurant, (3).

SKANDERBORG. Hotel: *Skanderborghus,* (1), all rooms with bath, fine lakeside setting, pool.

SØNDERBORG. Hotel: Best are *Alssund* and *City Garni;* both (3).

SVENDBORG. Hotels: *Svendborg,* most rooms with bath, (2). Music.

VEJLE. Hotels: *Australia,* (1), all rooms with bath, has sauna and pool, *Grand,* (2); *Caleb,* (3), mission hotel.

HOW TO GET ABOUT. You can fly within the hour from Copenhagen to all main centers. Motorists can gain hours and avoid Great Belt congestion in summer by using the Kalundborg-Aarhus, Hundested-Grena. and Sjaellands Odde-Ebeltoft car ferries operating direct from Zealand to Jutland. Train addicts have comfortable Lyntog connections from Copenhagen.

SAS provide daily services to Rønne from Copenhagen (35 mins.), but the traditional way of reaching the island is by the comfortable large night boats (day boats also in summer) from central Copenhagen. A direct seasonal ferry links Travemünde, in West Germany, with Bornholm and there are other routes from Sweden.

FINLAND

Finland has long been famous for sunlit nights, patriotism, design and architecture, Sibelius, and saunas. It's also famous, among discerning visitors these days, for being among the first of European nations to promote tourism on the basis of ecological conservation. For Finland is a c-l-e-a-n country, with clean air, clear water, unspoiled forests and plenty of virgin land for "living free". Finland is also known, however, for the emotional extremes of its people. A healthy, handsome (and, yes, clean!) race, the Finns conceal, under the patina of Scandinavian polish and discipline, one of the greatest drinking problems in the world.

There are slightly more than 4,700,000 Finns. They are a fair-skinned, fair-haired, sometimes taciturn, but essentially poetic, people. The essence of their character may be summed up in a Finnish word, *sisu*, of which there is no exact English equivalent; it's a combination of unyielding courage, stamina and fortitude. Their language is like nothing you ever heard before, unless you happen to be familiar with Hungarian or Estonian, which it is related to. The Finns call their own country Suomi, from the Finnish word for swamp. The land is an exhilarating expanse of lakes, rapid streams and rivers, and woods and forests. About one-third of the land lies north of the Arctic Circle.

Swedish and Finnish are the official languages, though they are quite dissimilar. Swedish has always been the language of a minority, yet it was the language of administration and culture until the latter part of the 19th century. Today the Swedo-Finns account for 6.4 percent of the population, while only 15 percent of the entire population is considered bilingual.

The light of freedom burns fiercely in this country, which was ruled for seven centuries by the Swedes, for one by the Russians, and which has only been independent since 1917. Since the Second World War, Finland has maintained its independence in face of muttered threats from Russia, and is careful about its neutrality. It is a member of the United Nations, the Nordic Council, and is one of the sixteen countries of the free trade area of Western Europe as well as having free trade agreements with the smaller Comecon countries of eastern Europe and long established trade agreements with the USSR.

Food and Drink

You will meet Swedish *smörgaasbord,* with Finnish variations, in many restaurants, and as Finns are solid eaters, no one will be surprised if you return for two or three helpings. Finland also has some unusual dishes of her own—reindeer tongue, for instance (*poronkieltä*). You might also try the provincial *kalakukko,* a mixture of fish and pork baked in a round rye dough, *lihapullia,* meat balls, *Karelian hotpot,* beef, mutton and pork cooked together, and *Karjalan piirakka,* a rice-filled pasty. The season for crayfish, a great delicacy, begins about 20th July and lasts several weeks.

Two especially good Finnish liqueurs are *Suomuurain* and *Mesimarja.* Both are exceedingly sweet. There are no Finnish wines, but many French, Italian and German wines are available. Finnish vodka is particularly good.

PRACTICAL INFORMATION FOR FINLAND

WHAT WILL IT COST. The tables of hotel and restaurant prices, based on 1978 figures, will act as a guide, but it is estimated that prices will increase by about 10% in 1979. Generally speaking, hotel and restaurant prices in Helsinki are about 20% higher than in the provinces, where prices don't vary much as there are no large resorts and rarely low standards. Double rooms usually cost very much less per person than singles. Hotels are graded first class superior (1), first class reasonable (2), moderate (3), and inexpensive (4).

HOTEL ROOM (SINGLE) PER PERSON

(including service and Continental breakfast)

	1st class superior	1st class reasonable	Moderate	Inexpensive
Helsinki	150–180	110–140	70–100	55–80
Resort	120–150	80–120	40–80	30–60
Provincial town	100–140	80–110	50–80	35–50

The standard of living in Finland is high, as are costs. The average weekly wage is about 800 Fmk. a week in Finland: and the monthly rental for an unfurnished 2-bedroom flat in a good area of Helsinki would be 800–1000 Fmk.

Some further prices: bottle of good, moderate wine, 23 Fmk.; large measure of spirits, 8; haircut (man's) 20; woman's shampoo and set, 30–45; cinema, 9–13; opera, 10–35 Fmk.

RESTAURANT PRICES
(table d'hôte prices; à la carte costs at least twice as much)

	Deluxe	1st class	Moderate	Inexpensive
Lunch	30–35	20–30	15–25	10–15
Dinner	40–60	30–45	20–35	12–20

Budget accommodations: Self-catering in summer cottages is well organized: from 200-1500 Fmk. a week. Youth hostels have no age restrictions: from 14–35 Fmk. per person per night. There are over 300 camp sites; usually a special family-rate is available from 10–20 Fmk. per day (2 adults, 2 children, car, and tent or caravan). Very reasonable full-board rates apply to farmhouse holidays.

A TYPICAL DAY FOR ONE PERSON

Room, breakfast, 2nd class hotel, incl. tax and service	70 Fmk.
Lunch, moderate, with coffee	15
Dinner, moderate, with coffee	30
Public transport	7
Taxi (say 3 km.)	12
Theater ticket (middle range)	15
Pack of 20 cigarettes (local)	5
1 coffee, popular café	1.50
1 beer, popular café	5
Miscellaneous	10
	170.50 Fmk.

CAPITAL. Helsinki.

LANGUAGE. Finnish, which is unlike anything you've ever heard before. The Finns' English will certainly be better than your Finnish. Swedish is the second official language.

CLIMATE. Due to the Gulf Stream, can be warm in summer.

Average maximum daily temperatures in degrees Fahrenheit and centigrade:

Helsinki	Jan.	Feb.	Mar.	Apr.	May	June	July	Aug.	Sept.	Oct.	Nov.	Dec.
F°	27	25	32	43	57	66	72	68	59	46	37	30
C°	-3	-4	0	6	14	19	22	20	15	8	3	-1

SEASONS. From mid-June to mid-August is the warmest period, with daylight up to 24 hours long. Spring is fresh and green; the fall, from early September in the far north, produces fabulous coloring. Good skiing throughout winter, reaching its peak in March when the days are long and often sunny. Helsinki can be at its best in May.

 SPECIAL EVENTS. Salpausselka Int'l. Winter Games at Lahti, late February; Ounasvaara Int'l. Winter Games at Rovaniemi, late March. Midsummer Eve is celebrated during the weekend closest to *June* 24, a gay occasion throughout the country; Kuopio Dance and Music Festival, Vaasa Festival in June; Jyväskylä Arts Festival (with a different theme each year) begins end of June; Savonlinna Opera Festival, Pori Jazz Festival and Kaustinen Folk Music Festival are in *July;* Turku Music Festival and Tampere Theater Summer, both in *August.* The Helsinki Festival, a major event offering two weeks of music and drama of all kinds, begins late August.

CLOSING TIMES. Shops open from 8:30 to 17:00 hrs. on weekdays (can be later on Mon. and Fri.). Sat. close at 14:00 hrs. In the subway by Helsinki rail station, shops of all kinds remain open until 22:00 hrs. including Suns. Banks open Mon.-Fri. 09.15-16.15, Sats. closed. Additional exchange facilities at Helsinki railway station and airport 7 days a week.

SPORTS. Lakes and rivers form hundreds of miles of water-courses which are a paradise for *paddlers.* Best *fishing* June-August; the rivers richest in salmon, sea-trout and grayling are in the Kuusamo district and in Lapland. Autumn is the *shooting* time for moose and game-birds. There are *golf courses, water skiing, sailing,* and *riding* facilities in several centers. In Lapland the gentle slopes of the fells are excellent for *skiing.* Inclusive 10-day skiing holidays in tourist-class hotels with half board, from 1,000 Fmk. ex-Helsinki; lower rates for hostel or hut accommodation. Other winter arrangements include fishing through the ice and skidoo excursions; or you can do a once-in-a-lifetime 5-day reindeer safari with Lapp guide for from 2,550 Fmk. ex-Helsinki. Winter tour operators in Finland include Globaltravel, Yrjönkatu 8A; Finland Travel Bureau, Kaivokatu 10; Finnish Travel Association, Mikonkatu 25; Finntourist, Iso Roobertinkatu 26; Kaleva Travel Agency, Mannerheimintie 5. All in Helsinki.

MONEY. The unit is the *markka,* divided into 100 *penni.* There are about 4.00 Fmk. to the US dollar, 7.70 to the pound sterling.

TIPPING. The hotel service charge of 15 percent takes care of everything. Porters or bellhops expect a mark for handling your bags, as do railways porters (when you can find them). The 14% service charge in restaurants and nightclubs (15% on Suns. and holidays) is sufficient. Sauna attendant 2–3 Fmk. Taxi drivers, ushers, washroom attendants, barbers, and beauty salon attendants are not tipped.

HOW TO REACH FINLAND By Air: You can fly from New York to Helsinki by *SAS* and *Finnair;* from London by *British Airways* and *Finnair.*

By Sea: Numerous services (including car ferries) link England, Germany and the rest of Scandinavia with Helsinki and other Finnish ports (see *Practical Planning* section). Finnlines' mammoth new *Finnjet,* the largest and fastest ship on the Baltic, now operates on the Travemünde-Helsinki route, reducing the journey from 38 to 22 hours. It links with other services, such as Prins Ferries' Harwich/Hamburg/Bremerhaven route, through to the U.K.

By Car: Routes lead to northern Finland from Sweden and Norway and to Helsinki from Leningrad. Trains and air connections are also maintained between these two cities. **Trains** link Stockholm via Boden and Tornio with north Finland. From London, direct service twice daily via Hook of Holland and Stockholm, thence by sea to Turku or Helsinki; basic 2nd-class return fare, approx. £155.

CUSTOMS. Gifts up to a value of 400 mk., including up to (a) 2 liters of malt beverages, 1 liter of wines and ¾ liter of spirits or 2 liters of malt beverages and 2 liters of wines and (b) 200 cigarettes or ½ lb. of other manufactured tobacco. Visitors from non-European countries may bring in duty free twice the amount of cigarettes or tobacco mentioned, and 2 liters of malt beverages and 2 liters of wines or other alcoholic beverages. Tourists may bring in unlimited amounts of Finnish and foreign currencies and take out all the currencies brought in plus up to 3,000 Fmk. bought in Finland.

INFORMATION AND TOURS. Much vital, free information is available from the Finnish Tourist Board U.K. Office, Finland House Annexe, 53–54 Haymarket, London SW1Y 4RP; Finland National Tourist Office, 75 Rockefeller Plaza, New York, NY 10019; and Scandinavian National Tourist Offices, 3600 Wilshire Boulevard, Los Angeles, CA 90010.

As usual, the cheapest way to travel is by group or independent package tour. Some specialists in the U.K. are:

Bennett Travel Bureau, 229 Regent St., London W1R 8AP.
Argosy (Automobile Association), Fanum House, Basingstoke, Hants RG21 2EA (for motorists).
Finlandia Travel Agency, 49 Whitcomb St., London WC2.
E. Raymond & Co., 25 Prudential Buildings, 36 Dale St., Liverpool L2 5SW.
Scantours, 8 Spring Gardens, London SW1.

MAIL. Up to 20 grams, letters airmail to Britain, 1.20 Fmk.; to US and Canada, 1.70 Fmk. Postcards airmail to Britain, 90 penni; to US and Canada, 1.10 Fmk.

ELECTRICITY. Usually 220 volts, 60 cycles, A.C.

DRINKING WATER. Excellent.

TRAVEL IN FINLAND. By Car. The main road network is excellent, except for a few roughish sections in the far north. Some secondary roads may be temporarily closed during the spring thaw. Gasoline costs 1.89–1.98 Fmk. per liter.

By Train. Comfortable Diesel trains cover most parts of Finland. Tourist tickets for combined rail/air/coach/steamer travel at reduced prices are obtainable year round. Excellent modern sleeping cars connect Helsinki with Lapland. Car-carrying trains operate from Helsinki to Oulu, Kemi and Rovaniemi; and from Turku and Tampere to Rovaniemi. A Finnrail Pass allows holders unlimited travel on Finnish State Railways for 15 days for 360 Fmk. first class, 240 Fmk. second class (other durations available at proportionately varying costs). This is available to foreigners at points of arrival by air, sea or land, on production of a passport.

By Bus. The network is efficient and extensive, and in the far north is the principal means of transportation.

By Boat. Traffic on the inland waterways is maintained by comfortable lake steamers and motor ships; you can take a few hours' ride or have an eight-day cruise in this unique lake labyrinth. A hydrofoil links Lahti with Jyväskylä in a 1-hour trip that otherwise takes 9 hours. A pilotage scheme is available on several lake routes for the transfer of the motorist's car between terminals.

By Air. Finnair connects Helsinki with all large towns. Fares are among the cheapest in Europe with special holiday tickets, including unlimited travel for 15 days.

Tours. Many Finnish travel agencies have tours starting from Helsinki, ranging from one day upwards and visiting all main centers and regions, including Lapland, as well as a wide choice of professional study tours. Tours to Russia are also arranged, among them no-visa cruises from Helsinki to Leningrad, Tallinn or Riga (passengers sleep on board in port) or, with visa, cruises via the Saimaa Canal or regular coach trips from Lappeenranta to Leningrad. Apply to *Area Travel Agency,* Pohjoisesplanadi 2; *Finland Travel Bureau,* Kaivokatu 10; *Finnish Travel Assoc.,* Mikonkatu 25; *Travek Travel,* Eteläranta 16; *Finntourist,* Iso Roobertinkatu 26; *Globaltravel,* Yrjonkatu 8A; *Kaleva Travel Agency,* Mannerheimintie 5. All in Helsinki.

CAR HIRE. *Helsinki* firms include: *Avis,* Fredrikinkatu 36; *Hertz,* P. Rautatienkatu 15A; *Scandinavia Car Rental,* Mariankatu 24; *Finn Rent,* Hietaniemenkatu 6B; *InterRent,* Kulosaarentie 46. Self-drive cars are available in most main centers, and there are advantageous fly-drive schemes, such as the one operated by Finnair/Hertz.

USEFUL ADDRESSES. *American Embassy,* Itä Kaivopuisto 14A. *British Embassy,* Uudenmaankatu 16-20. *Canadian Embassy.* P. Esplanadikatu 25b. *City Tourist Office,* P. Esplanadikatu 19. Emergency telephone: 000. All in Helsinki.

Exploring Helsinki

Heart of the town is the Senate Square, designed in the 1820s and 1830s by the German-born architect, Carl Ludvig Engel, and his Finnish partner Johan Albrekt Ehrenström. Between them, they replanned the town which had been devastated by fire in 1808 and which now became Finland's capital (formerly Turku). Here stand the cathedral, the State Council Building, and the University Library (Engel's masterpiece), a group of majestic buildings composed in a pure classic style which certainly presaged the well-known work of such later Finnish architects as Eliel Saarinen and Alvar Aalto. Engel also designed the Town Hall in the Market Square, down by the south harbor. This has been called one of the most beautiful squares in the world. The best time to see it is before noon when the flower and fruit sellers are grouped around the fountain of Havis Amanda, the sea maiden who represents Helsinki rising from the waves. Notice the obelisk, known as the Empress Stone, which commemorates the 1833 visit to Helsinki of Czar Nicholas I and his consort Alexandra Feodorovna. This is a favorite Helsinki rendezvous. The harbor side of the square is literally flipping with the produce of the fish market, caught early in the morning and sold directly from the boats. That building along the edge of the square, facing the sea and patrolled by a sentry in field grey, is the President's Palace. Behind the Town Hall you will see once again the silhouette of Helsinki's most famous landmark, the cathedral, just a few steps away in Senate Square.

For further orientation, you might try the Hotel Torni for lunch at the top of the tower. Get a table by the window and survey the town while you eat. You will recognize the cathedral, the massive railway station designed by Saarinen, the Stadium Tower and the broad street running through the city center, Mannerheimintie, named after Finland's great hero, Marshal Mannerheim.

After lunch, here are some of the sights you should examine at closer quarters—the richly decorated Greek Orthodox Uspenski Cathedral with its gleaming "onions" towering above the rocky island of Katajanokka, east of the President's Palace; the Sederholm House in the Great Square, built in 1757, the oldest house in this modern town; the impressive red granite Eduskunta or Parliment House, with its peristyle of 55-foot columns and its lavishly-decorated interior; the National Museum, with ethnographical exhibits illustrating Finland's history; the National Art Gallery and its collections of work by Wäinö Aaltonen and the other leading sculptors and painters of Finland; the National Theater in the huge square before the railway station, and the station itself which, with its strong, massive lines and 155-foot-high granite tower, is one of Eliel Saarinen's most widely-known buildings.

Some good examples of Finland's famous modern architecture include the magnificent "Finlandia" Concert Hall and Congress Center, designed by Alvar Aalto, near the National Museum; the City Theater, Eläintarhantie; the busy shopping complex of the City Center opposite the railway station; the extraordinary Dipoli Hall at the engineers' suburb of Otaniemi, and the whole of the satellite town of Tapiola. One of Europe's most unusual churches is that of Taivallahti, built into the living rock in one of the older residential districts of the city.

Three highly recommended outdoor attractions are the Botanical Gardens and their Water Tower, if you want another splendid panorama; Linnanmäki, close to the water tower, Helsinki's permanent amusement park; and the Open Air Museum of Seurasaari.

You will also enjoy the island fortress of Suomenlinna, or Sveaborg if you prefer the Swedish name. Begun in 1748 this "Gibraltar of the North" was never taken by assault. The surrounding parks and gardens are lovely in spring and summer, and there's an excellent restaurant, Walhalla, in one of the forts. Good bathing facilities and sandy beach here too. Ferries leave for Suomenlinna hourly from a pier opposite the Empress Stone, Market Place.

PRACTICAL INFORMATION FOR HELSINKI

HOTELS. During the peak summer months reservations are necessary. The central room booking bureau in the rail station (weekdays 9-21, Sats. 9-19, Suns. 12-19) can assist you in case of need. Summer hotels (student hostels the rest of the year) offer comfortable rooms at reasonable rates, with reductions for groups (open June through Aug.). Hotels listed are licensed unless otherwise stated.

FIRST CLASS SUPERIOR

Inter-Continental, Mannerheimintie 46; 294 rooms with bath, saunas, nightclub, hairdresser, swimming pool.

Hesperia, Mannerheimintie 50; recent, 285 rooms with bath or shower, top class amenities.

Kalastajatorppa, Kalastajatorpantie 1; 235 rooms with bath, sauna, swimming pool, private beach, beauty salon, barber. Linked by underground passageway with the famous Kalastajatorppa restaurant and nightclub. Lovely shoreside location.

Palace. Eteläranta 10; 60 rooms with bath or shower. Restaurant, grill room, sauna, and barbershop. A stunning view over the harbor.

Marski, Mannerheimintie 10, has 162 rooms with bath. Air-conditioning, restaurant, grillroom, dancing, garage. Nightclub. Conveniently located.

FIRST CLASS REASONABLE

Vaakuna, Asema-aukio 2; 224 rooms with bath or shower. Sauna and barbershop. Central

Helsinki, Hallituskatu 12; 85 rooms with bath or shower; sauna, nightclub. Central.

Seurahuone (Societetshuset), Kaivokatu 12; 76 rooms, most with bath. Opposite station. Sauna, nightclub. Some moderate and 1st class superior rooms.

Torni, Yrjönkatu 26; 100 rooms, some with bath. *Spanish Grill, Balkan,* and *Chinese Restaurant.*

Merihotelli, Hakaniemenranta 4; 87 rooms with bath. Nightclub, cellar restaurant, pool.

Olympia, Brahenkatu 2; 100 rooms, all with bath or shower. Restaurant, dancing, pool.

Karpilampi (Forest Lake), 14 miles west of the city. Brand-new congress hotel in idyllic setting; 162 rooms with bath or shower; sports facilities.

MODERATE

Polar Espoo (motel), 8 miles from center of Helsinki-Turku highway. 94 rooms with bath or shower, saunas, pool, discothèque.

Haaga, Nuijamiestentie 10; part of the Hotel and Restaurant College, 40 rooms with bath or shower. Restaurant, saunas, pool.

Academica, Hietaniemenkatu 14, 226 rooms, 115 with mini-baths, restaurant, café, saunas, swimming pool. Summer only.

Kustaa Vaasa, Vaasankatu 10, 90 rooms with shower, saunas, restaurant, summer only.

INEXPENSIVE

Satakuntatalo, Lapinrinne 1A, 64 rooms, good bargain. Summer only.

Finn, Kalevankatu 3B, 28 rooms, half with bath. No restaurant.

Hospiz, Vuorikatu 17; 141 rooms, many with bath or shower. Restaurant, sauna. Unlicensed. Some moderate rooms.

Ursula. Paasivuorenkatu 1; 43 rooms, some with bath or shower; but outside downtown area. Restaurant, unlicensed.

Martta, Uudenmaankatu 24 has 36 rooms, 18 with bath; comfortable. Unlicensed restaurant.

Cheapest are the boarding houses, among them: *Erottajanpuisto,* Uudenmaankatu 9; *Lönnrot,* Lönnrotinkatu 16; *Omapohja,* It. Teatterikuja 3; *Tarmo,* Siltasaarenkatu 11B; *Viipuri,* Vuorikatu 6. You can book through the Central Booking Bureau at the rail station.

RESTAURANTS. English is spoken at all better places. Most restaurants offer set menus for lunch or dinner at reasonable rates. All are licensed unless otherwise stated.

EXPENSIVE

Adlon, Fabianinkatu 14, fine cuisine. Music, dancing, floorshow.

Kalastajatorppa (Fiskartorpet), in the suburbs (take tram to Munkkiniemi) is undoubtedly a show piece. Beautifully designed, this huge modern restaurant is set in lovely scenery. Tables should be booked well in advance. Cabaret.

Casino, in the Kulosaari district; can be reached by bus. Music, dancing, roulette.

On the island of Suomenlinna, a few minutes by ferry from the south harbor, is the *Walhalla.* Here you may dine in an authentic 18th century fortress atmosphere. Dancing; summer only.

In another picturesque location, Kaivopuisto Park looking out to the harbor, is *Kaivohuone.* Music, dancing, floorshow, roulette.

Mestaritalli, Toivo Kuulan Puisto, formerly stables, now an elegant restaurant in a seashore park.

White Lady, Mannerheimintie 93. Elegant.

MODERATE

Havis Amanda, Unioninkatu 23, near the south harbor market, fish specialties.
Karl König, Mikonkatu 4. First class food in subdued, sophisticated setting below ground.
Royal, P. Esplanadikatu 2; music, roulette, and an open-air terrace in summer.
Mobile, Pitkänsillanranta 3; intimate nightclub atmosphere.
Kappeli in the Esplanade gardens near the South Harbor. Renovated and with five sections including open air summer restaurant.
Savoy, Esplanadikatu 14. Favourite business lunch place. Music.
Troikka, Caloniuksenkatu 3, one of a chain of three small eating places specialising in excellent Russian food.
Parrilla Espanola, Eerikinkatu 4. Spanish food.
Punainen Hattu, Keskuskatu 7. Intimate atmosphere.
Tullinpuomi, Mannerheimintie 118; music and dancing.
Motti, Töölöntorinkatu 2, one of the best in this category.

INEXPENSIVE

Kellarikrouvi, P. Makasiininkatu 6, and *Kantakrouvi,* Ruoholahdenkatu 4, with cosy wine cellar atmosphere.
Pizzeria Rivoli, Albertinkatu 38. Italian food, good for a quick lunch.
Vanhan Kellari, Mannerheimintie 3. In cellar of Old Students' House; self-service or with service.

Many modern, attractive cafés dotted about town serve light snacks and hot meals. Other low-priced restaurants are run by the *Fazer, Go-Inn, Nissen, Colombia* and *Primula* chains.

ENTERTAINMENT. The National Theater gives plays in Finnish while the performances of the Swedish Theater are in Swedish. The ultra-modern City Theater is at Eläintarhantie and the beautiful Finlandia Concert and Congress Center near the National Museum. Standards are high. The National Opera on Bulevardi gives performances of Finnish and international operas and ballet. During summer when theaters are closed, there are special open-air performances, including on the islands of Suomenlinna and Mustikkamaa. Linnanmäki Amusement Park is a fun place on summer evenings (closed Mondays).

GETTING ABOUT HELSINKI. The city is served by a network of trams and buses; multi-ride cards give a good reduction. A section of Helsinki's first Metro (subway) is due to open soon. The No. 3T tram, which describes a figure-eight through and around the city center, provides a commentary in several languages on main points of interest. A 24-hour tourist ticket (10 Fmk.) can be bought on the tram or from the City Tourist Office, entitling you to unlimited travel for that period on any central bus or tram; included is a descriptive folder with map of the 3T route. Taxis are quite plentiful. The sign "Vapaa-fri" means that a cab is free.

MUSEUMS. The *National Musuem* is at Mannerheimintie 34; the main *Ateneum Art Gallery* on railway square. Two others worth finding time for are the *Open-Air Museum,* Seurasaari and the *Gallen-Kallela Museum* (the home and works of one of Finland's greatest painters) at Leppävaara, Tarvaspää. *Korkeasaari Zoo* is on an island reached by boat from the north harbor.

SHOPPING. Look for the splendid Finnish design in household items and fashion. Finland's largest department store is *Stockmann's,* on Aleksanterinkatu: here you will find selections of all the best in Finland, with English-speaking guides and clerks to help you. See also the *Finnish Design Center,* Kasarmikatu 19. *Hakaniemi Market Hall,* Hämeentie, with 50 shops above the covered food market, is varied and fun.

LAUNDROMAT. *Suomen Pesu,* Porvoonkatu 3, Helsinki 51.

HANDCRAFTS, TEXTILES. *Friends of Finnish Handicrafts,* Meilahti 7; *Poppana,* Liisankatu 19; *Aarikka, Bulevardi 7; Neovius,* City Center. All these also for the handwoven *ryijy* rugs. *Metsovaara,* Mannerheimintie 42. *Vuokko* and *Marimekko,* each with several shops (both including one on P. Esplanadikatu) design and sell unusual fabrics and fashions. Specialists in leather fashions include *Asu,* Aleksanterinkatu 15, and *Halonen,* Pohjoisesplanadi 37.

FURS. *Polar Turkis,* Yrjönkatu 1. *Fur Lyx,* Kristinkatu 11. *Turkistuottajat Oy* have an auction at Kutomontie 6 in the suburb of Pitäjänmäki.

JEWELRY. *Kalevala Koru,* Keskuskatu 4; *Galerie Björn Weckström,* Fredrikinkatu 24; *Kaunis Koru,* P. Esplanadikatu 29.

PORCELAIN AND CRYSTAL. *Arabia,* Esplanadikatu 25B; *Karhula-Iitala,* E. Esplanadikatu 14.

SPORTS. *Swimming* at Hietaranta; on Seurasaari island (accessible by bridge); at Uunisaari, an island opposite the diplomatic district of Kaivopuisto; Lauttasaari, in the suburbs; the island of Pihlajasaari, which has its own restaurant. All are sand beaches, and very pleasant, though inclined to be rather crowded at the height of the season. Ferry boats maintain a regular service to the small islands in the archipelago. There are also several indoor and outdoor swimming pools.

For *golf,* the Tali links at Munkkivuori. In winter there is *skating* at numerous public rinks, and *skiing,* Within easy reach by bus are the good skiing grounds and amenities of Nuuksionpää and Salmi; or by train, those of Hyvinkää.

Excursions from Helsinki

Numerous and pleasant excursions can be made from Helsinki, either as day trips or stopovers. Porvoo (Borga.), is on the coast east of Helsinki, three hours by boat or one hour by bus. This is one of the oldest towns in Finland, its narrow winding streets contrasting with the more rational gridiron pattern of the capital. The Hotel Aulanko, in the midst of a superb national park at Hämeenlinna, is one of the show places of Finland, 1¼ hours by train from Helsinki. There's a lake for swimming. Notable sights in the vicinity include the town of Hämeenlinna, birthplace of Sibelius and site of a castle which dates from 1249. See also the Hattula Church, built of stone about 1250. Both these places are accessible by bus.

West of Helsinki is the pretty town of Tammisaari (Ekenäs), notable for its narrow old streets and oak trees, which Finnish foresters consider exotic. Here there is a charming open-air restaurant in the island park of Ramsholmen. The islands of the archipelago around Helsinki are easily accessible by boat in summer.

Three other main centers are Lahti (1½ hours by rail), Jyväskylä (1 hour by air) and Savonlinna (1 hour by air), all on major lake systems with good sports facilities and surrounded by forests. Savonlinna on

Lake Saimaa has a glorious old castle; Jyväskylä has become an important center for holiday villages of luxury log cabins in the heart of wild forestland. Yachts can be rented by the week at Lappeenranta and Savonlinna on the shore of Saimaa, the most massive lake system of all; there is even a sailing school in Lapland.

The rest of Finland, including "industrial" cities like Turku and Tampere, is more of the same—a magnificent stretch of unspoiled fen and forest, interlaced with waterways and dotted by more than 60,000 beautiful lakes. Tampere's famous sights include Scandinavia's first planetarium, a fine aquarium, the world's first open-air theater with revolving auditorium, many old churches in the surrounding countryside, and a wide choice of lake excursions. Turku has an old castle, ancient cathedral, and is the gateway to thousands of islands on which there are many possibilities to rent cottages. Finally, there is Finnish Lapland in the north.

Finnish Lapland

This northernmost province of the country extends from just a bit south of the Arctic Circle to almost the edge of the Arctic Ocean. Rovaniemi, Finnish Lapland's administrative center almost on the Arctic Circle, is a thriving modern town with excellent accommodation and facilities. In fact, amenities throughout the province are expanding rapidly, with new and well-equipped centers such as Suomutunturi and Pyhätunturi and, a little to the south, Rukatunturi, all in wild and lovely landscapes. A fishing paradise in summer and ski paradise in winter, it is becoming one of the offbeat tourist goals par excellence. In the extreme north of the province, you can see the midnight sun for two months; in winter the sun is invisible for the same period. True seekers of the wilderness will find marked paths through some of the loneliest landscapes. There is one about 90 km. long linking Pallastunturi and Enontekiö across the fells. Wilderness huts (unattended log cabins) along such marked paths offer shelter and simple overnight accommodation, though you will need a sleeping bag. This is ideal camping country, too, and there are quite a few official camp sites. In summer, mosquito repellent is a *must!*

There are endless opportunities for swimming in the region. For salmon fishing, one of the best waters is the Teno River, which forms the natural border between Finland and Norway and flows into the Arctic Ocean. Boat trips with Lapp guides are arranged into the wilderness near Inari. Just off the main road, near Vuotso, you can try your hand at gold washing . . . for a nominal fee.

PRACTICAL INFORMATION FOR THE REGIONS

HÄMEENLINNA. The lakeside *Aulanko* (2/3) in a beautiful national park, 239 rooms, most with bath or shower; beach, saunas, tennis, golf, horse-riding, boating, nightclub. *Vouti* and *Cumulus,* both (2), respectively 40 and 50 rooms with bath or shower; night club; *Cumulus* has a pool.

HANKO. *Regatta,* (2/3), 35 rooms most with bath; sauna, indoor pool, music, dancing.

HYVINKÄÄ. *Rantasipi Hyvinkää* (1), 190 rooms with bath or shower. Night-club.

INARI. *Tourist Hotel,* (3) 22 rooms, sauna, lovely site beside rapids near vast Inari lake. Comfortable log cabin accommodation in the vicinity.

IVALO. *Tourist Hotel* (3), 37 rooms, sauna. At Laanila, 25 miles to the south, *Laanihovi,* (3), 20 rooms, sauna, summer only.

JYVÄSKYLÄ. *Cumulus* (1), 76 rooms with bath or shower; *Jyväshovi,* 121 rooms, and Milton, 35 rooms, unlicensed, both (2/3). *Rantasipi Laajavuori* hotel and sports complex (1), just outside town; 176 rooms with bath or shower. Also in this forested heart of Finland are splendidly equipped log cabin holiday villages. Details from Rantaloma, Sepänkatu 14, Jyväskylä. For general information on renting a summer cottage in central Finland, contact Keski-Suomi Loma-Suomi, Vapaudenkatu 38, Jyväskylä.

KALAJOKI. *Kalajoki Tourist Hotel,* (3/4), 20 rooms, some with bath or shower, and *Rantakalla,* (3), 15 rooms with shower; beautifully situated among sand dunes. Sports facilities; music, dancing. Also cottages.

KOLI. *Loma Koli* (½), 63 rooms with shower; *Koli* (2), recently renovated, 40 rooms with bath or shower, dancing, pool, saunas, superb hilltop site. Also bathing, boating and fishing in Lake Pielinen, where there is an attractive holiday village.

KUOPIO. *Cumulus* (2), 62 rooms with bath or shower. All (2/3) with dancing are *Atlas,* 44 rooms, all with bath or shower; *Puijonsarvi,* 52 rooms, most with bath or shower; *Kuopio,* 24 rooms, some with bath or shower; *Iso-Valkeinen,* 100 rooms with shower, sports facilities. *Savonia* (3), 20 rooms with bath, pool.

LAHTI. Both (1) are *Seurahuone,* 119 rooms with bath or shower, one of Finland's top hotels, nightclub, pool, and *Musta Kissa,* 72 rooms with bath or shower, dancing. *Lahti* (2), 90 rooms with bath or shower, no restaurant. *Muk-kula* (3/4), summer only, 80 rooms with shower, sports facilities.

LAPPEENRANTA. *Polar-Lappeenranta* (2), 40 rooms with bath or shower, nightclub, sports facilities. Both (3) are *Viikinkihovi,* 28 rooms with bath, night-club, pool, and summer hotel *Karelia-Park,* 121 rooms with shower, dancing. Several holiday villages in the vicinity; details from city tourist office, Valtakatu 23.

PORVOO. In town, the *Seurahovi* (2), 33 rooms with shower, dancing. A few miles to the southwest is *Haikko Manor Hotel* (1) on the seashore, a converted old manor house in lovely grounds, 138 rooms with bath or shower, sauna, excellent restaurant, dancing, pool, health treatment, sports facilities.

ROVANIEMI. All (½) are the *Polar,* 53 rooms with bath; dancing; *Pohjanhovi,* 149 rooms with bath or shower; dancing, roulette, pool, sports; *Polar* (motel) on Ounasvaara hill, 38 rooms with bath, beautiful hill top position. *Lapinportti,* 18 rooms, excellent sauna with pool, is (2). Summer hotels *Domus Arctica,* 190 rooms with shower, and *Rovaniemi Ammattikoulun Kesahotelli,* 36 rooms with shower, are (¾).

RUKATUNTURI, near Kuusamo. Holiday center in fells, including modern *Rukahovi,* 95 rooms, most with shower. Dancing, sports; shooting the rapids organized: excellent for hiking. In Kuusamo is *Kuusamo Hotel,* 42 rooms with bath, sports facilities. Both (1).

SAVONLINNA. Best, *Casino* (1), 79 rooms with bath or shower, saunas, indoor pool, spa treatment, roulette. *Tott* (1/2), 43 rooms, most with bath or shower. Summer hotels *Knut Posse,* 51 rooms, *Elefantti,* 68 rooms, and *Malakias,* 120 rooms, all with showers and all (2).

TAMPERE. New *Rosendahl* (1), 213 rooms with bath, pool, nightclub. All (2): *Grand Hotel Tammer,* 64 rooms, most with bath, dancing, pool; *Emmaus,* 240 rooms, most with bath or shower, pool, unlicensed; *Kaupunginhotelli,* 82 rooms, 50 with bath or shower; *Jäähovi,* 72 rooms with bath or shower. Summer hotels *Domus* (3/4), 200 rooms, some with bath or shower, and *Härmälä* (4), 95 rooms with shower.

TURKU. Top class and new are *Ikituuri Congress Center,* 150 rooms with bath, and *Marina Palace,* by river, 188 rooms with bath or shower, pool, nightclub. Also (1): *Seurahuone,* 63 rooms, most with bath or shower, and *Maakunta,* 106 rooms with bath or shower. (½) is *Hamburger Börs,* 11 rooms, most with bath or shower, music dancing, floorshow; *Turku* (2) has 36 rooms, 26 with bath, music, dancing. Summer hotel *Ikituuri,* 1,100 rooms with shower, is (3). About 3 miles out, in lovely setting, is *Ruissalo* (1), 136 rooms, most with bath, nightclub, pool, sports facilities. Ten miles from town is *Raadelma Manor Hotel,* a beautifully furnished converted manor, 40 rooms, saunas, pool.

HINTS FOR THE BUSINESSMAN. Many offices start work early and finish early—usually 4 P.M. and, in many cases, an hour earlier in summer. In fact, summer can be a difficult time for finding the Finns, who take their holidays and disappear for weeks into the countryside. If you're told some elusive contact is away *"maalla,"* that's just where he or she is! Otherwise, it's rather easier than in many countries to reach "top" people. On the whole, Finns are bad at answering letters and good at settling matters on the phone or face to face. Secretarial or interpreter services can be arranged through main hotels or a number of agencies specializing in these. There are now excellent conference centers, notably in or near Helsinki, Hämeenlinna, Jyväskylä, Tampere, and Turku. And up-to-date conference facilities exist on Finnlines' fine *Finnjet* on the Travemünde-Helsinki service and, for smaller conferences, on routes between Sweden and Finland. Details and addresses from the Finnish Tourist Board.

FRANCE

"Is France the same as ever?" Returning to France after being absent for a while, the visitor wants to know if he'll find the qualities which lured him there before. First-timers, if they've done their homework, will know what France should offer . . . and, for both, it's the same thing.

Well, the answer is "yes" *and* "no": affirmative because France still has *charm* as no one else has it; *style* as no one else *can* have it; and *beauty,* as no one but the French can make it. These assets were never more appreciated than they are today.

But the negative side is soon visible when the visitor spots the ugly new skyscrapers which have begun to ruin the Paris skyline, or finds his favorite bistro replaced by a flashy "drugstore". Not content with having torn up some of Paris' lovely chestnut-tree-lined squares to build underground garages, the City Fathers have allowed the construction of such controversial architectural monstrosities as the 56-story Tour Montparnasse, sticking up over the skyline like an overlarge cigar box, and the chilly cement-and-steel Centre Culturel Georges Pompidou in the heart of the 17th- and 18th-century buildings of the Marais.

Surrounded by larger and uglier technological monstrosities, by the pollution of our cities and by the noise of scientific development, man needs the positive Gallic qualities more than ever. The French have managed to hang on to these intangible qualities, keeping much from the past, but also transforming some of the ugliness of today by their skill in applying standards of good taste. What do the French drugstore and the Pierre Cardin blazer have that the originals lacked? Well, you come back to charm, beauty and style.

Despite their good taste, the French are all anarchists, said Jean Cocteau, but they are conservative anarchists. This Gallic paradox helps to explain the most interesting and the most complex people in Europe. In no other country will you find more respect and veneration for tradition and the glories of the past, still physically manifest everywhere in France, though De Gaulle and his successors seem to have decided to sacrifice some of the country's beauty in an effort to streamline the nation's infrastructure so that France may become a powerful industrial nation in Europe, even beating Germany by 2000 (or 1985 if you believe Herman Kahn and the Hudson Institute's "think tank"). The 1973 Yom Kippur war in the Middle East, with the subsequent enormous rise in oil prices, has, however, put a serious damper on these ambitions.

From the time when it was known as Gaul, France has been a pivotal state in the affairs of Europe. Its territory violated constantly by invading armies, and torn by civil war, plagues and revolution, France seemed always to alternate between unbearable chaos in her public life and magnificent esthetic order in her private pursuits. Up to and including World War II, the Anglo-Saxon could say (and frequently did, with some contempt) that one never quite knew where one stood with the French. And even after 1945, it seemed for a while that this not-quite-noble tradition would continue.

After years of post-war instability, however, France under de Gaulle, Georges Pompidou, and now President Valéry Giscard d'Estaing, has moved in a steady direction, and the country's economy, until the 1976 recession, had forged ahead.

Despite intellectual and political ferment (always closely allied in France) the country seems somehow to keep its balance, and the French passion for lucid rationalism will no doubt stand the country in good stead through coming years, as it did in the 1978 elections. Of the three principles on which the French Republic is based—liberty, equality and fraternity—in the hearts of her people, liberty always comes first.

The Country and the People

The French passion for individual liberty explains why so many expatriates have found their spiritual home in this country, and especially in that overgrown village of Paris, where in bistros, and student restaurants, in elegant cafés and bourgeois salons, the eternal discussions of art and life go on, constantly recharging that incandescent glow of the intellect that illuminates the City of Light. If you stay around long enough, you may actually hear, as we did, a waitress launching into a highly articulate criticism of the way in which a Comédie Française actress misinterpreted the character of Racine's Andromaque, or an auto salesman describing a car as "nervous, harmonious and ironical". But even if your stay in France is limited to a few days, you will be conscious of an endless babble of animated discussion, guaranteed to make the most verbal Anglo-Saxon feel almost taciturn by comparison. So brush up on your French if you want to enjoy the full flavor of this country. But you'll have a good time in France, even if your French is not quite as good as you might wish. Which leads us to that most difficult of rumors—the one that says the French are inhospitable, and sometimes even nasty, to the traveler (particularly, it is alleged, if he can't speak good French). To begin with, when it is true, it's almost always a Parisian who's the villain—out in the country, you'll find genuine hospitality the order of the day.

The Parisian is an odd bird, a mockingbird almost, for that's his favorite sport, indoors and out, mocking people all around him. He doesn't particularly dislike Americans or the British—he more or less doesn't like anybody, and it's the lack of his ability to communicate with you that tends to make you think he's being brusque, or even rude. If the Parisian and the traveler could manage to rail at each other on an equal linguistic basis, they'd soon be the thickest of friends.

Touristic Highlights

The whole of France is your target, and its recent stardom as a fantastically exciting winter sports center is just one good reason to visit France out of season. But to begin with, there are the natural wonders of the country. From the Alps to the Pyrenees, from the trout-filled torrents of the Vosges to the placid Lake of Annecy, from the windswept Breton coast to the sun-drenched Riviera, there is almost every kind of scenery that exists. Wherever possible, this scenery has been cultivated, tempered by the hand of man. The land seems to have been molded and trimmed with a strange, unerring instinct for proportion, and this celebrated sense of Gallic measure is visible in the most impressive cities, châteaux and cathedrals of Europe.

Creative France

A similar quality is apparent in most aspects of French creative life. The same unerring *sens du plastique* is evident in the anonymous sculpture of the Middle Ages and in the energetic realism of Auguste Rodin, who used to spend hours in fervent contemplation of the sculptures at Chartres. Despite frequent revolutions and reactions in the history of French art, literature and music, there is always a sense of continuity, of a grand tradition still evolving.

The average tourist will be more conscious of French achievement in the plastic arts than in the realms of music or literature. Art is France's sixth most important industry. If you think that French painting stopped with the Impressionists, now on view in Paris in the Jeu de Paume, or with Cubism and Surrealism, you need only drop in at the Musée d'Art Moderne de la Ville de Paris, Avenue Wilson; the Centre Georges Pompidou; or any one of the avant-garde galleries that line the rue de Seine, de Mazarine, Boulevard St. Germain to see what's happened since. There are 60,000 painters in Paris, striving in various ways to capture reality on canvas. By sheer weight of output—that of past masters, still to be viewed in the museums, and present apprentices, to be seen in every nook and cranny—Paris is still one of the capitals of the art world.

Food and Drink

There is almost complete unanimity of opinion that French food is the best in the western world; generally, despite supermarket distribution, it still is. The vegetables, cheese, butter and fruit you eat in a Paris restaurant are usually fresh: they were brought in from the farm that morning, although with the alarming mushrooming of cafeterias and quick eateries quality is no longer always perfect as it was a few years ago, and can at times be alarmingly poor. Stick to the old-fashioned *bistro* to find that simple delicious cooking for which France is famous. Generally speaking, you get much better value for your money in the provinces where the food you eat, even in a modest restaurant, is cooked for you while you are eating the *hors d'oeuvre*.

The beef, veal, lamb and chicken in France are all first rate, and so is the seafood (*les fruits de mer*). French oysters are excellent (eat them and other sea food only in specialized restaurants), but are horribly expensive. If you want a steak, there are four major kinds on French menus: a *châteaubriand,* which is sirloin; *tournedos,* which we Anglo-Saxons would call a filet mignon; *entrecôte,* a thin steak; and *bifstec,* a small minute steak. They are tops for quality, flavor, texture. If you want your steak rare, say *saignant* (literally, bloody); medium rare, *à point;* well-done, *bien cuit.* If you want it very rare, say *bleu,* blue. Don't hesitate to try the simple homely stews: *pot au feu, boeuf bourguignon, blanquette de veau.* In the provinces, look for the regional specialties.

A meal without wine is like a day without the sun, say the French, who are the greatest producers and the greatest consumers of wine; the general subtlety and quality of French wines do not have their equal elsewhere.

The best-known wines come from Burgundy, Bordeaux and the Rhône Valley. A very popular and inexpensive red wine, excellent with snails, red meat and most cheeses, is *Beaujolais.* For a reasonable dry white wine, good with seafood and white meats, we are partial to *Muscadet, Champagne Nature* (non sparkling) or *Chablis.*

PRACTICAL INFORMATION FOR FRANCE

WHAT WILL IT COST. With worldwide inflation, costs for 1979 are difficult to estimate: in 1978, consumer costs rose by just over 9%, and it is thought they will rise another 10% by 1979. And hotel prices rise in conjunction with other travel costs. But by sensible timing and budgeting, a stay in France need prove no more expensive than in some neighboring countries.

Prices are generally highest in high season (July-Aug.), and, in ski and Mediterranean resorts, at Easter and Christmas. Off-season, they can be 10-20% lower. However, remember that many small resort hotels in off-beat areas, such as Brittany, the Auvergne and the Basque hinterland, are closed out of season.

Generally speaking, it is safe to say that prices in regional capitals (Bordeaux, Marseille, Grenoble, etc.) are from 10-15% lower than in Paris; in rural areas, from 15-25% less. Fashionable resorts (Cannes, Nice, St. Tropez, Megève, Biarritz, etc.) are as expensive as Paris or even more expensive.

A TYPICAL DAY IN PARIS		
Moderate hotel room, breakfast, tax and service incl.	135	Frs.
Lunch, moderate restaurant	50	
Dinner, ditto	80	
Theater, middle-range price	40	
Transport, public, plus taxi (3 km. each)	25	
Pack of best local cigarettes	3.20	
One coffee in popular café	1.50	
One beer in local café	1.70	
Miscellaneous	35.00	
	371.40	Frs.

Other costs: bottle of good, moderate price-range wine 15–20 frs.; measure of whisky, gin, 12; opera ticket, 60; cinema, 15; haircut, 25; woman's shampoo and set, 30–35; 1 hr. parking meter, 3 frs.

HOTEL ROOM FOR TWO				
(in French francs)				
	Deluxe	1st cl. superior	1st cl. moderate	Second class	Inex- pensive
Major city	250–450	200–280	120–180	90–120	50–80
Major resort	250–500	220–300	120–200	100–150	70–100
Prov. capital	250–300	130–225	90–130	70–110	50–80
Budget resort	—	—	80–100	60–80	30–60

Some food prices: a half kilo (about 1 lb.) inexpensive steak, 18 frs., best is nearly 30 frs.; a *baguette* (long French bread), 1.15; croissant, 1.70; 1 liter milk, 2 frs.

RESTAURANT PRICES			
	Deluxe	First-class	Moderate	Inexpensive
Major city	150–220	100–150	70–100	30–60
Major resort	150–220	100–150	70–100	40–80
Major town	100–150	80–120	45–75	20–45
Budget resort	—	60–80	40–60	15–30

Money-saving Ideas. Over a hundred resorts, from elegant St.-Jean-de-Luz to tiny Chambon-sur-Lignon (Auvergne) offer 20–40% hotel and restaurant reductions in June and Sept., while maintaining all usual summer activities. For details of these and other bargains, apply to the French National Tourist Office (addresses in Practical Planning section). One enterprising hotel in Paris has reversed the trend and offers reduced prices in July and August.

CAPITAL. Paris.

LANGUAGE. French. English spoken in most major hotels.

CLIMATE. Varies considerably between north and south regions.
Average maximum daily temperatures in degrees Fahrenheit and centigrade:

Paris	Jan.	Feb.	Mar.	Apr.	May	June	July	Aug.	Sept.	Oct.	Nov.	Dec.
F°	43	45	54	61	68	73	77	75	70	61	50	45
C°	6	7	12	16	20	23	25	24	21	16	10	7

Riviera												
F°	54	55	57	63	68	75	81	81	75	68	61	57
C°	12	13	14	17	20	24	27	27	24	20	16	14

SEASONS. Main tourist season: Easter to Sept. 30, high season July-Aug. On the Riviera, Feb. is rather smart, Easter also popular, and summer the biggest season. Winter sports season is from Dec. through Mar., with Jan. the budget month: Christmas, Carnival and Easter, are sky-high. Height of the Paris season is May and June, but Easter is very popular with British tourists.

 SPECIAL EVENTS. *February,* Fête of Saint Bernadette (18th), Lourdes. *March,* Fêtes of the Mi-Carême (mid-Lent) in Paris, Nantes and other French cities, Mardi Gras Carnival and the Battle of the Flowers in Nice (depending on date of Lent). *April,* Provençal Easter festivities in Vence; Bullfights in the Roman arena, Arles; Horse Show and Int'l Riding Contest, Nice; Int'l Film Festival, Cannes; Basque folklore and Easter fête, Biarritz. *May,* Joan of Arc celebrations in Orléans; Bordeaux Festival of Music, Ballet and Theatre; beginning of fountain displays and Son et Lumière programs in Versailles and the Châteaux of the Loire (through Sept.); religious Festival and Fair of the Gypsies at Saints Marie-de-la-Mer. *June,* Grand Prix automobile race, Le Mans; Music Festival, Strasbourg, Festival at Angers. *July,* Bastille Day (14th), Music Festival, Aix-en-Provence; great Celtic festival, Quimper in Brittany. *October,* Int'l Auto Show, Paris (but it wasn't held in 1977—a much-publicized cost-saving measure). *November,* Les Trois Glorieuses, 3 days of celebrating in honor of Burgundy wine, with processions, meeting of the Knights of Tastevin, wine auction in the Hotel Dieu in Beaune. *December,* opera season opens at the Municipal Casino, Nice.

CLOSING TIMES. Some elegant boutiques in Paris, and virtually all provincial stores, close from 12:30-2 or 2:30, and at 6:30. Small food-shops in Paris close from about 12:30 to 3:30 or 4, but the capital's department stores stay open Mon. through Sat., opening some time between 9 and 9:45 and closing at 6:30 or 7, though Trois Quartiers closes on Mondays in July and August. Some of the big stores stay open until 9 or 10 P.M. one night a week (usually Wednesday). Most of Paris's ten "drugstores" (which sell everything from newspapers to prepared salads and take-away hot dishes) are open until 2 A.M. And Sunday isn't a problem: bakeries and other food shops can be found open all over Paris and major towns, usually mornings only.

 SPORTS. Most popular spectator sports are soccer and rugby football and cycling—the gruelling Tour de France cycle race in June/July lasts for a whole month. There are a dozen *golf* courses around Paris and many more all over the country. *Horse-racing* is very popular; Longchamp, Auteuil, Chantilly, Maisons Lafitte, St.-Cloud are world famous tracks. *Horseback riding* is becoming popular and increasingly available. Roland-Garros Stadium in Paris is the scene of the most important *tennis* events, in June. The Chamonix *mountain climbing* guides are among the world's best. Although *skin-diving* was developed on the Riviera, the island of Corsica is the place to go to. You can rent *yachts* and *sailing* boats practically everywhere. Le Mans, Reims and Monthléry *motor-racing* tracks are the scene of some of Europe's most important events. Occasional *bullfights* are held in the ancient Roman arenas of Nîmes and Arles in the South of France, in the Basque Country and the region around Bordeaux.

France has over a hundred *winter sports* resorts scattered about the Mont Blanc, Savoie, Dauphiné, Alpes-de-Haute-Provence, Pyrenees and Jura areas.

FRANCE

MONEY. The $ and £ exchange rates with the franc are so volatile, advance predictions are almost impossible. At this writing, there are approx. 4.80 francs to the U.S. dollar, 9.45 to the pound sterling. There are, incidentally, 100 centimes to the franc.

Some stores still give from 10% to 20% discount (usually 17%) on purchases with dollar or other foreign currency to persons residing outside France. Residents of Common Market countries must buy at least 690 francs worth of goods to qualify for this exemption; from non-Common Market countries, a minimum of 400 francs worth. The store must fill out a form in quadruplicate, giving three copies to the tourist, who gives two to customs on leaving.

TIPPING. The practice of adding 12 or 15 percent service charge to the bill is common in restaurants, hotels and cafés all over France. When added, there is no obligation to leave anything additional, but, in effect, most people leave a little "extra something" (from one to five francs, depending on the size of the bill). If the wine steward (*sommelier*) has been particularly helpful, you may wish to give him from 5 to 10 francs extra. Tip bellboys almost everywhere. In the international luxury hotels in Paris, the bellhops expect 2 francs for each service. Tip the doorman 2 francs for getting you a cab. Leave 10 to 50 frs. with the concierge depending on hotel category and length of stay; on leaving, tip chambermaids 2 frs. a day, or 10 per week. Two francs to hatcheck girls and washroom attendants, 2 francs per person (minimum) to theater ushers, 3–5 frs. if in very expensive seats; 1–2 fr. to cinema ushers; 15% of the fare to cabdrivers; 15% to barbers and beauticians. Rail or airport porters: the official minimum is 3 frs. per bag, but use your judgment.

HOW TO REACH FRANCE. More *air* routes link the U.S. with France than almost any other Continental country, while from the U.K. air flights, air-car ferries, and numerous cross-channel ferries maintain a virtual shuttle service throughout the summer. By *car:* it is sensible to choose your port of arrival according to your destination, although if your line lies diagonally across this huge country from the Channel to the Côte d'Azur, there is less than 80 miles difference between the shortest and the longest route; but if the trip is down the west coast, you can save 150 miles by starting from Le Havre instead of Ostend, to Biarritz. By *hovercraft:* from Ramsgate to Calais in 40 mins., carrying 250 passengers, 30 cars; from Dover to Boulogne, 35 mins., same size craft. Numerous car-ferry services from southern England to points in Normandy and Brittany provide more leisurely crossings in cruise-like comfort.

CUSTOMS. Everything obviously for personal use, not for resale, comes in duty free. Americans may bring 400 cigarettes, 100 cigars or 500 grams of pipe tobacco duty free. British: 300 cigarettes, or 75 cigars or 400 grams of tobacco. You may bring in 2 cameras of different makes duty free (if used), 10 rolls of film, a movie camera and ten reels of film.

You can bring in as many French francs and foreign bills as you wish, and can take out 500 francs both in francs and foreign exchange without declaration.

There are no take-out restrictions on travelers checks or letters of credit obtained outside France. All currency which was declared upon entry can be taken out.

MAIL. If you are staying in a large hotel, it is simple to hand your mail to the porter. Stamps may be purchased at tobacco shops as well as in post offices. Rates are: Letters not over 20 gr., 1 fr. within France and to Common Market countries (except Britain) and Canada, 1.40 frs. to most other foreign countries. Postcards with more than 5 words go for 0.80 francs within France, to Canada, and to all other Common Market countries except Britain; for 1 franc (or 0.80 francs for a maximum of 5 words) to all other countries. *Airmail* works like this: you start with the basic rate of 1.40 francs for 20 grams and then add a surcharge for each extra 5 grams. Examples of surcharges: 0.50 francs for the United States and Canada; 0.70 for Australia and New Zealand; 0.30 for Israel. Post offices do not accept anything for air or surface mail weighing over 2 kg., except books may go up to 3 kg. Telegram rates vary widely, best to check before sending.

ELECTRICITY. Most of France is now on 220 volts, 50 cycle, and you will find this in all modern hotels both in Paris and the provinces. Older hotels may still be on 110 volts, so check.

DRINKING WATER. Safe. If you prefer mineral waters: Evian (still), Badoit (a bit fizzy), Perrier, Vichy.

TRAVEL IN FRANCE. By Air. France is particularly well served internally by air, fares are reasonable and on the major carrier, *Air Inter,* there are a variety of discount fares between Paris and Nice, Bordeaux, Lyon, Marseilles and other cities. Where Air Inter does not go, there are smaller airlines, the principal ones being *Rousseau Aviation* (for Brittany and Eastern France); *Touraine Air Transport* (Southwest France); *Air Littoral* (Mediterranean coast); and *Air Alpes* (linking Paris to major Alpine resorts). Bookings for all flights can be made from any travel agent.

By Car. Drive on the right hand side; green card is obligatory unless cover is bought on entry. Super gasoline (essence) costs 2.42 frs. per liter. On the autoroutes there is a speed limit of 70 m.p.h. (130 km/h); 68 m.p.h. (110 km/h) on specially-marked fast roads and approach roads to motorways; on all other roads 50 m.p.h. (90 km/h) and in built-up areas it is 37 m.p.h., or occasionally less (50 or 60 km/h). Yellow lights are not obligatory for tourists driving at night, but to avoid unpleasantness it is better to have them with (especially) bulbs which dip to the right. *Safety belts are obligatory at all times outside built-up areas, and between 10 P.M. and 6 A.M. in built-up areas,* as is a black-and-white tag identifying country of origin. In some *départements* horns may be sounded only in moments of dire need. On the whole it is advisable to do your homework on French motoring regulations before setting out.

Parking: Increasingly difficult in towns. Discs for *zones bleues* are valid for all towns using this system. They're obtainable free from tourist offices, tobacco kiosks, police stations, customs offices, garages and hotels . . . so get yourself a supply. In Paris there are quite a number of paying garages. Maps indicating them are available from tourist offices. In Paris, as well as major provincial towns, carry a supply of 1 franc and 50 centime pieces handy for the parking meters.

Car hire. Available in all principal cities by Avis, Hertz, etc. Main Paris addresses: *Avis,* 5 Rue Bixio, 7e (550-32-31); *Hertz,* central reservations (by telephone only): 788-51-51; main office is at 27 Rue Saint-Ferdinand, 17e (574-22-62); *Europcars,* central reservations: 645-21-25; otherwise, 42 Ave. de Saxe, 7e (273-35-20).

By Train. Because of the relatively long distances involved in touring France, rail trips can save time and money. Roundtrip tickets for journeys of more than

1500 kilometers (roughly 930 miles) cost 20 percent less than twice the one-way fare, provided the trip lasts six days or more.

"Family tickets" are advantageous when three or more persons of the same family are traveling together; all but two of the family can get reductions of 75 percent. There are numerous other types of reductions and there are many interesting package tours run by the SNCF to smaller resorts, with accommodations varying from camp sites to modest, family-run hotels.

In addition to inexpensive fares, French long-distance train service is excellent and fast. The spectacular scenery of southeastern France can be seen to particular advantage from the panoramic autorails that run from Marseille to Nice, and from Digne to Geneva (Switzerland).

By Bus. A great variety of tours is offered by the *French National Railways* (SNCF), the *Régie Autonome des Transports Parisiens* (RATP), the *Union Nationale des Agences de Voyages* (UNAV), *Tour-France, Compagnie Française de Tourisme, Europabus, American Express,* and *Cook's.* Many special-interest excursions as well as SNCF combined-rail-motorcoach weekend circuits of art and literary centers are offered. In addition, every region is well supplied with a local and sightseeing bus network, making a visit to even the remote spots easy. A Relais Bus Pass allows unlimited mileage over 15-60-day periods.

By Boat. Cruising on France's scenic rivers and canals can be most pleasant. You can enjoy good food, marvelous scenery and peace in launches and cruisers operated by a large variety of French and English companies, of which a few of the better-known, and most reliable are: *S.A.I.N.T. Cruisers,* 77100 Poincy, France, by a British firm, *Dolphin Cruise Lines* (Supertravel Ltd., 107 Walton St., London S.W.3), who have leisurely cruises covering some 150 miles of inland waterways from Paris to Macon through the Burgundy country; by *Nautic-Voyage,* 8 Rue de Milan, 75009 Paris, whose cruisers ply the waterways of the Camargue and southwest France; or with Continental Waterways Ltd., 22 Hans Pl., London S.W.1. For luxury barges, complete with crew, contact *Holt Paris Welcome Service,* 12 rue du Helder, 75009 Paris.

Sightseeing in Paris

Paris is a city of vast, noble perspectives and intimate streets, parks and squares. This combination is one of the secrets of its perennial charm. For the first-time visitor with only a few days at his disposal, one of the half-day sightseeing tours organized by a reputable travel agency, such as Cook's or American Express, is recommended. After that, the best way to know this city is on foot with that *Plan of Paris,* which shows every boulevard, street and *place,* supplemented by a good *métro* and bus map. Tourist agencies, hotels, or the French National Tourist Office in your country will provide all these.

Here are some of the outstanding places and monuments which you should see, exclusive of the museums and parks we have listed:

The Place Charles de Gaulle, formerly the Etoile, the great circle at the western end of the Champs-Elysées, which is one of 12 avenues radiating like rays of light from the star. In the center is the colossal Arc de Triomphe (164 feet high), more than twice the size of the Arch of Constantine in Rome. Planned by Napoleon to honor his victorious army, it contains some magnificent sculpture, most notably "The Marseillaise" by Rude. A perpetual light to France's Unknown Soldier burns under the arch. Take the elevator to the top for an interesting exhibition of the history of the Arc and a splendid view of Paris.

At the other end of the Champs-Elysées is the Place de la Concorde. There is nothing in its present harmonious proportions to suggest that it was once the notorious Place de la Guillotine, splashed with the blood of Louis XVI, Marie Antoinette, Lavoisier and 1,340 other victims of the French Revolution. In the center of the Place is the Obelisk of Luxor, a 200-ton stone needle from Egypt, erected here in 1836 during the reign of Louis-Philippe.

Facing the Tuileries Gardens (with your back to the Champs-Elysées), you have a long vista, framed by the winged horses of Coysevox, down through the little Arc de Triomphe du Carrousel to the Louvre. On your left, the Rue Royale, leading to the classic Church of the Madeleine, is framed by two 18th-century buildings designed by Gabriel. The one on the right is the French Naval Ministry. Its western twin houses the Automobile Club of France and the Hôtel Crillon. The perspective toward the Seine is equally impressive, leading the eye across the Pont de la Concorde to the Palais Bourbon, home of the National Assembly.

The Place de la Concorde is further embellished by two splendid bronze fountains and eight rather formidable stone females symbolizing the cities of Nantes, Brest, Rouen, Lille, Strasbourg, Lyon, Marseille and Bordeaux. Even if you have only one summer night in Paris, don't miss seeing this square illuminated.

Iles de la Cité and St.-Louis

The best approach to the Ile de la Cité, that tiny island where Paris began its history as a Gallo-Roman village named Lutetia, is by the Pont Neuf, the oldest bridge, dating from 1604. At the statue of Henry IV, turn left into the charming Place Dauphine, walk around the massive Palais de Justice and into the court where stands that Gothic jewel known as the Sainte Chapelle. Built by St.-Louis to house the true crown of thorns and other holy relics, the chapel was consecrated in 1248. A marvel of stone lacework and ancient stained glass, this soaring chapel is one of the most impressive things in Paris.

A short walk from here will bring you to Paris' grand cathedral, Notre-Dame de Paris. Begun in 1163, completed in 1345, badly damaged during the revolution, restored by Viollet-le-Duc in the 19th century, Notre-Dame is one of the most beautifully proportioned of cathedrals, large enough to accommodate 9,000 persons. If your heart and legs are sturdy, climb to the top of the tower for a fuller appreciation of the architectural detail of the cathedral as well as for a view of the heart of Paris.

Don't miss a walk through the cathedral park and across the foot bridge to the Ile St.-Louis, whose historic houses and picturesque quais have hardly changed since the 17th century. From here, you have romantic views of the Seine and the apse of Notre-Dame, and from here it is just a step over to the Rive Gauche, the Left Bank, and the Latin Quarter, so called because the students of the Sorbonne spoke and heard lectures in Latin during the Middle Ages.

The Left Bank

St.-Germain-des-Prés, onetime citadel of Paris' intellectual life, is now invaded by foreigners and provincials who think they are rubbing shoulders with the intelligentsia on the terraces of the Café de Flore and the Deux-Magots. The area is still stuffed with expensive antique shops, avant-garde art galleries and bookstores, but the artists and writers who used to animate the cafés and bars have migrated to less expensive

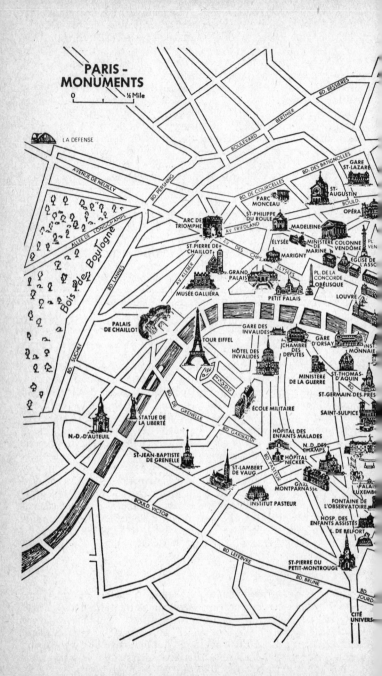

PARIS - MONUMENTS

0 ½ Mile

LA DEFENSE

AVENUE DE NEUILLY

BD. PERSHING

ALLÉE DE LONGCHAMPS

BD LANNES

Bois de Boulogne

BD SUCHET

BOULEVARD

BERTHIER

BD. BESSIÈRES

BD. DES BATIGNOLLES

GARE ST-LAZARE

BD. DE COURCELLES

PARC MONCEAU

ST-AUGUSTIN

BOULD.

ST-PHILIPPE DU ROULE

OPÉRA

ARC DE TRIOMPHE

AV. TRIFOLAND

MADELEINE

ST-PIERRE DE CHAILLOT

ÉLYSÉE

MINISTÈRE DE MARINE

COLONNE DE VENDÔME

PL. VEN

AV. DES CHPS.

MARIGNY

ÉGLISE DE L'ASSC

AV. KLEBER

GRAND PALAIS

ÉLYSÉES

PL. DE LA CONCORDE

OBÉLISQUE

MUSÉE GALLIÉRA

PETIT PALAIS

LOUVRE

PALAIS DE CHAILLOT

GARE DES INVALIDES

GARE D'ORSAY

INST. MONNAIE

TOUR EIFFEL

HÔTEL DES INVALIDES

CHAMBRE DES DÉPUTÉS

ST-THOMAS-D'AQUIN

MINISTÈRE DE LA GUERRE

BD.

ST-GERMAIN-DES-PRÉS

BD. DE GRENELLE

ÉCOLE MILITAIRE

SAINT-SULPICE

STATUE DE LA LIBERTÉ

N.-D.-D'AUTEUIL

BD GARIBALDI

HÔPITAL DES ENFANTS MALADES

N. D. DES CHAMPS

ST-JEAN-BAPTISTE DE GRENELLE

HÔPITAL NECKER

ST-LAMBERT DE VAUG.

BD. PASTEUR

GARE MONTPARNASSE

PALAIS LUXEMBO

BOULD. VICTOR

INSTITUT PASTEUR

FONTAINE DE L'OBSERVATOIRE

HOSP. DES ENFANTS ASSISTÉS

L. DE BELFORT

BD. LEFEBVRE

ST-PIERRE DU PETIT-MONTROUGE

BD. BRUNE

BD. JOURD.

CITÉ UNIVERS

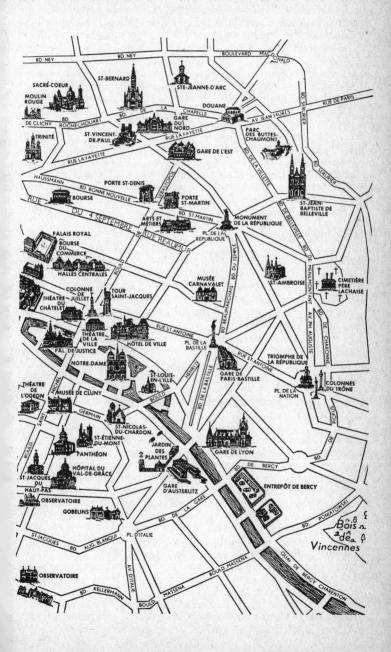

haunts. However, this old and romantic neighborhood has many permanent charms. Don't fail to notice the massive Romanesque bell tower of St.-Germain-des-Prés, dating from the beginning of the 11th century, one of the oldest *clochers* in France. The quiet streets in the immediate vicinity are worth a ramble, especially the enchanting little Place Fürstenberg, with its catalpa trees and old lamps, a stampsize remnant of the aristocratic glory of the Faubourg St.-Germain.

A short distance away is the busy Bvd. St.-Michel, heart of the student quarter. Deeper into the Left Bank you'll find the famous Rue Mouffetard market—visit either in the morning or after 4 P.M.—a riot of marvelously arranged foodstalls and the raucous cries of the vendors.

Even a short visit to Paris would be incomplete without a visit to Mansart's masterpiece of Jesuit architecture, the Church of the Invalides, with its golden dome, the most beautiful in Paris, under which, in a sarcophagus of red porphyry, lie the mortal remains of Napoleon Bonaparte. While you are in the neighborhood, you may want to take a look at one of the city's outstanding attractions in the way of modern architecture, the UNESCO buildings on Place de Fontenoy; multilingual guides will take you through during normal business hours (lunch time excepted) for a small fee.

The Right Bank

There are two places on the right bank that you must not miss. The first is the Palais-Royal, which Richelieu built opposite the Louvre. You can enter the palace garden from the Rue Montpensier or the Rue de Beaujolais, and you will be delighted by its arcaded shops and its oasislike tranquillity in the heart of bustling, modern Paris. The second place is the lovely Place des Vosges, all of whose homogeneous houses were built of rose-colored brick under the direction of Henry IV in the early 17th century. Once the center of fashion, royal tournaments and brilliant fêtes, this nobly-proportioned square keeps its Renaissance beauty today in the midst of the fascinating old quarter of the Marais. One of the outstanding annual attractions is the elaborate Festival du Marais, held in June-July, where you can combine enjoyment of the architectural beauty of this neighborhood with high-class modern and classical ballet, theater and music.

The nearby Les Halles quarter, once the home of the famous central market, is becoming something of a new St.-Germain-des-Prés/Montparnasse, full of kooky shops and far-out restaurants. This is mainly as a result of the amazing Centre National d'Art et de Culture Georges Pompidou (often referred to as the Centre Beaubourg), opened in early 1977 and a definite "must." Be prepared for a shock when you see the outside, with pipes and escalators visible in their naked glory. The Center, which attracted over six million visitors in its first year, is easily the most popular attraction in France at the moment, both because of its novelty and because it houses the National Museum of Modern Art (formerly in the Avenue Wilson), a very popular library, an acoustical research center, and all sorts of special exhibits. Don't miss the splendid view from the fifth floor.

Just as famous as the Invalides, though far less esthetic, is the Basilica of the Sacré Coeur, which dominates all of Paris from the heights of Montmartre. This and the nearby Place du Tertre are among the most popular tourist attractions of the city. The ascent into the dome of Sacré

Coeur will give you several vertiginous eyefuls of the huge interior of this church, and you will be rewarded for your dizzying climb by a 30-mile view over Paris and its environs from the top. As for the Place du Tertre and adjacent narrow streets, they're full of painters and pseudo-painters, all aching to paint or sketch your portrait.

The Opéra and the Eiffel Tower

You will probably not want to neglect two final symbols of Paris—the Opéra and the Eiffel Tower. M. Eiffel's celebrated *tour,* 1,000 feet high and still the fourth-tallest edifice in the world, was inaugurated on June 10, 1889, by Edward VII of England, then Prince of Wales. During the World War II occupation of Paris, the Germans thought of requisitioning its 12,000 sections of metal and 2,500,000 rivets, but they thought better of it, perhaps because so many Germans, like good tourists, enjoyed climbing it. It will cost you a few francs by elevator to the first *étage,* more if you go higher. The trip to the top is highly recommended on a clear day. Daily 10:30 to 5:30 (5 in winter). Allow ample time for your visit.

As for the Opéra, the only way to see the gilded, grandiose, marble interior of this immense baroque palace is by attending a performance of the opera or ballet. And it's worth it once: your reward will be Chagall's ceiling, offered by the aged master in 1964.

PRACTICAL INFORMATION FOR PARIS

 HOTELS. Several hundred hotels in Paris (and elsewhere in France), including many of the best, now charge *prix forfaitaire,* which includes room, breakfast, service charges, and taxes. If a hotel simply quotes the room rate alone, expect to pay at least an additional 30% for the "extras" that are otherwise covered by the *prix forfaitaire.* During the winter season (mid-Nov. to mid-Mar. as a rule), most Paris hotels reduce their rates by as much as 20%.

The *prix forfaitaire* for a double room with bath in a super deluxe hotel, in season, averages 300-500 francs. Luxury hotels, for the same accommodation, will charge about 250 francs. The first-class range is about 180 francs to 240 francs.

SUPER DELUXE

Meurice, 228 Rue de Rivoli, has 212 rooms, most with bath. It was once known as the hotel of kings, because so many of them stopped there. Small, *sympathique* bar.

Ritz, 15 Pl. Vendôme, has 209 large handsome rooms, most with bath, including 46 apartments. There are two tiny bars, the most elegant spots to meet before lunch or dinner as well as an excellent grill and restaurant. The number of staff here is greater than the number of guests, so service is supreme.

Crillon, 10 Pl. de la Concorde, has 220 rooms, most with bath; most of its good rooms, many with sitting rooms, face a side street. Along with the George V, it is the headquarters for visiting Americans.

Bristol, 112 Fbg. St.-Honoré. 220 rooms with bath; most elegant, studded with antiques and quite possibly the most expensive in Paris. Private parking. Favored by rich Germans and British (yes, there are some of the latter left).

George V, 31 Ave. George V, has 314 rooms some of them furnished with antiques. Fashionable, very handsome. Modern art exhibits in *Les Princes* restaurant, superb wine *cave.*

Prince de Galles, 33 Ave. George V, 203 rooms, most with bath. Restaurant, bar. On American Independence Day, U.S. patrons receive a free bottle of champagne.

Plaza-Athénée, 25 Ave. Montaigne; 250 rooms, most with bath. Very elegant. Its top-notch. *Régence* restaurant is where you'll see some of the prettiest girls in town at lunch; the *Relais-Plaza* is for an expensive after-theater supper, and in winter the downstairs *Bar Anglais* becomes an intimate discothèque.

Raphael, 17 Ave. Kléber; 87 rooms, most with bath. Old-fashioned, a favorite in spite of its rather out-of-the-way location near the Bois de Boulogne. Comfortable, very quiet.

LUXURIOUS

Opéra - Palais-Royal - Grands Boulevards. Largest in this area is the 600-room *Grand,* 12 Bd. des Capucines; on 4 July, U.S. visitors are invited to a cocktail party on the terrace of the world-famous Café de la Paix. Next in size are the *Ambassador,* 16 Bd. Haussmann, 300 rooms, and the 180-room *Commodore,* 12 Bd. Haussmann, with garage and restaurant, a bit friendlier than its big neighbor.

At 40 Fbg. St.-Honoré, the *Castiglione* has 107 rooms, almost all with bath; restaurant, bar.

Located between the Madeleine and Ave. de l'Opéra is the 130-room *Lotti.* In the Madeleine area are the *Bedford,* 17 Rue de l'Arcade, 142 rooms with bath; restaurant, bar; and the *Madeleine-Palace,* 8 Rue Cambon, 114 rooms, restaurant.

The *Inter-Continental,* 3 Rue de Castiglione; 500 rooms, superb comfort, has vast salons and a selection of restaurants, rôtisseries and bars.

On Pl. du Théâtre Français is the 228-room *Louvre-Concorde,* most rooms with bath, and the 140-room *Normandy,* 7 Rue de l'Echelle, comfortable, old-fashioned.

Champs-Elysées-Etoile. The *Lancaster,* 7 Rue de Berri, 67 rooms, has charmingly furnished suites overlooking a courtyard garden. The *Splendid-Etoile,* 1 bis Av. Carnot, is agreeably furnished, has reasonable prices for a hotel of this class. Bar and a good restaurant.

South of the Champs-Elysées, the *Trémoille,* 14 Rue de La Trémoille, has 106 pleasant rooms. The 130-room *Windsor,* 14 Rue Beaujon, has a pleasant restaurant.

Near the Etoile, are the *California,* 16 Rue de Berri, 200 rooms with bath, where U.S. newsmen congregate; the *Celtic,* 6 Rue Balzac, 80 rooms, most with bath; and the *Napoléon,* 40 Ave. de Friedland, 150 elegant rooms.

At 29 Rue Dumont d'Urville is the *Majestic,* 36 rooms. The *Résidence du Bois,* 16 Rue Chalgrin, has many rooms overlooking a quiet garden.

At the edge of this area—in fact, heading west towards the La Défense development, are two huge hotels: The *Concorde-Lafayette,* at Porte Maillot, and opposite, *Le Méridien,* on Bd. Gouvion-St.-Cyr. Each has 1000 rooms, restaurants for all tastes, coffee shops, bars, discothèques, etc. The 400-room *Club Méditerranée,* 58 Bd. Victor Hugo, in Neuilly is run rather differently from classic hotels, with a lot of do-it-yourself gadgets; agreeable, but seems rather overpriced.

Left Bank. *Paris Hilton,* 18 Ave. de Suffren, 489 rooms, has several restaurants, one atop the roof. Newest is the Japan-Air-Lines-owned *Nikko de Paris,* 61 Quai de Grenelle, overlooking the Seine in the new Front de Seine development. Japanese and French cuisine. The 112-room, air-conditioned, *Sofitel-Bourbon,* 32 Rue St.-Dominique, is not as luxurious, but is amiable and pleasantly staffed. *L'Hôtel,* 13 Rue des Beaux-Arts, 27 rooms, overpriced but chic. *Pont-Royal,* 7 Rue de Montalembert, 86 rooms, good restaurant, elegant bar. *Lutetia-Concorde,* 45 Bd. Raspail, 306 rooms, half with bath.

The *Paris Sheraton Hôtel,* 1000 rooms, is in renovated Montparnasse; the 650-room *Sofitel de Paris,* 2 Rue Grognet, is near the helicopter airport, convenient for businessmen; has excellent restaurant. The 812-room *PLM St.-Jacques,* 17 Bd. St.-Jacques. All include restaurants, coffee shops, nighclub, boutiques, etc.

FIRST CLASS

Opéra - Palais-Royal- Grands Boulevards. Near Pl. de l'Opéra are the 100-room *Edouard VII,* 39 Ave. de l'Opéra, and the *Etats-Unis-Opéra,* 16 Rue d'Antin. *London-Palace,* 32 Bd. des Italiens; no groups, reductions July-Aug. In the Bourse area is the 100-room *Ste.-Anne,* 10 Rue Ste.-Anne.

The fashionable Madeleine-Vendôme section is a favorite with many. Nearby is the *Métropole Opéra,* 2 Rue Gramont, 50 rooms, favored by respectable provincial businessmen who know a good thing when they find it. At Pl. des Pyramides, the 144-room *Régina.* At 218 Rue de Rivoli, above the arcades and overlooking the Tuileries, the 68-room *Brighton,* an old favorite.

On a quiet side street near the Madeleine is the charming, small *Queen Mary,* 9 Rue Greffulhe, all rooms with bath, no restaurant. *Concorde,* 1 Rue Rouget de Lisle. *Madeleine-Plaza,* 33 Pl. de la Madeleine, and *Burgundy,* 8 Rue Duphot, on a quiet street.

Champs-Elysées-Etoile. Just off the Champs-Elysées is the 63-room *Vernet,* 25 Rue Vernet. *Résidence Foch,* 10 Rue Marbeau, 15 rooms, with bath. The *Schweizerhof,* 11 Rue Balzac, is very small, calm and clean; *Royal Hôtel,* 33 Ave. de Friedland, warm, personalized service; *Etoile-Maillot,* 10 Rue du Bois-de-Boulogne, 23 rooms, all with bath, is so popular you must reserve at least a month ahead; *Princesse Caroline,* 1 bis Rue Troyon, little-known, quiet; *Victor-Hugo,* 19 Rue Copernic, 74 rooms, cheerful.

The elegant *Bellman,* 37 Rue François I, has 43 rooms with bath; nearby *Château Frontenac,* 54 Rue Pierre Charron, 100 rooms, bar and restaurant. At 6 Rue Belloy, the attractive *Sévigné.*

Left Bank. The *Bourgogne et Montana,* 3 Rue de Bourgogne, near the National Assembly, has 35 rooms. On the Seine at 19 Quai Voltaire is the select *Hotel du Quai Voltaire,* 32 rooms. The *Victoria-Palace,* 6 Rue Blaise Desgoffe, 120 rooms, restaurant, bar and garage, and the nearby 100-room *Littré,* 9 Rue Littré are extremely well-run. *La Bourdonnais,* 111 Ave. de la Bourdonnais, 60 rooms, cheerful bar, restaurant. At 4 Bd. Raspail is the 140-room *Cayré-Copatel.*

Montmartre. *Terrasse,* 12 Rue Joseph de Maistre, 108 rooms, most with bath; restaurant.

Near the Stations. For Riviera, Italy, Switzerland: *Paris-Lyon-Palace,* 11 Rue de Lyon and the *Modern Hôtel Lyon,* 3 Rue Parrot, no restaurant.

For Le Havre, Cherbourg, England: *Terminus-St.-Lazare,* 108 Rue St.-Lazare, big. Restaurant, bar.

COMFORTABLE

There are now many modest hotels where each room has a small bathroom, and décor is pleasant. The sign "NN" outside hotel means it has been recently modernized.

Opéra - Palais Royal - Grands Boulevards. *Hotel de la Cité Bergère,* 4 Cité Bergère, *Blanche Fontaine,* 34 Rue Fontaine, are in the Folies-Bergère area.

More central are the *Athénée,* 19 Rue Caumartin, *Etna,* 61 Rue Ste.-Anne, *Excelsior-Opéra,* 5 Rue La Fayette, *Métropole Opéra,* 2 Rue Gramont.

Near the Madeleine are *Newton,* 11 bis Rue de l'Arcade, *Fortuny,* 35 Rue de l'Arcade, *Havre-Tronchet,* 11 Rue Greffulhe.

All the above are small hotels.

Champs-Elysées-Etoile. *Mont-Blanc,* 51 Rue Lauriston, 46 rooms, most with bath; *Rochambeau-Copatel,* 4 Rue de la Boétie; *Farnese,* 32 Rue Hamelin, 35 rooms, near Etoile; *Copernic,* 20 Rue Copernie; *Regent's Garden,* 6 Rue Pierre Demours, 41 rooms, liké a country house; *Atala,* 10 Rue de Chateaubriand, 50 rooms, good food, garden; *Cecilia,* 11 Ave. MacMahon; *Bradford,* 10 Rue St.-Philippe-du-Roule, 50 rooms; *Kléber,* 7 Rue de Belloy, 22 rooms, combines charm with efficiency.

Left Bank. *Nice et des Beaux-Arts* 4 bis Rue des Beaux-Arts, 25 rooms furnished with antiques; *Colbert,* with 40 rooms, 5 Rue de l'Hôtel Colbert, is a true jewel; *Ferrandi,* 92 Rue du Cherche-Midi; *Scandinavié,* 27 Rue de Tournon, 22 attractive rooms; *Grand Hôtel des Gobelins,* 57 Bd. St.-Marcel, a useful address for visiting professors; *St.-Paul,* 43 Rue Monsieur-le-Prince, 28 rooms; *L'Abbaye-St. Germain,* 10 Rue Cassette, 45 rooms, in an old convent; *Angleterre,* 44 Rue Jacob, 32 rooms; *Lutèce,* 65 Rue St.-Louis-en-l'Ile, 23 rooms.

Montmartre. *Migny,* 13 Rue Victor Massé; 56 rooms, half with bath; *Central-Monty,* 5 Rue Montyon. At the new *Berthier La Tour,* 163 bis Ave. de Clichy, 324 rooms, you pay for rooms on arrival and additional services on the spot. Very impersonal and when we visited, we found the service indifferent.

Near the Stations. Gare St.-Lazare: *De Morny,* 4 Rue de Liège, very comfortable; *Flèche d'Or,* 29 Rue d'Amsterdam; at No. 20, same street, *Calvados; Rome,* 18 Rue de Constantinople, modernized; *Family,* at No. 11, late 30's atmosphere.

Gare du Nord—Gare de l'Est: *Diamond,* 73 Rue de Dunkerque; *Londres et Anvers,* 113 Bd. Magenta; *Europe,* 98 Bd. Magenta; *Métropol,* 98 Rue Maubeuge.

Gare de Lyon: *Le Foyer Moderne,* 45 Av. Gl.-Michel-Bizot, 104 rooms, no restaurant.

INEXPENSIVE

These are the cheapest hotels accustomed to receiving foreign clients. Rates will vary considerably, depending upon the hotel's location and amenities.

Opéra - Palais Royal - Grands Boulevards. The 44-room *Vivienne,* 40 Rue Vivienne, is near the Bourse; *Grand Hôtel de l'Oratoire,* 141 Rue St.-Honoré; *Londres et Stockholm,* at 13 Rue St.-Roch.

Champs-Elysées-Etoile. *Neva,* 14 Rue de Brey, near Arc de Triomphe; *Montaigne,* 6 Ave. Montaigne, 35 rooms, no restaurant, but popular café-restaurant next door; *Chambiges,* 8 Rue Chambiges, pleasant; *Wilson,* 10 Rue de Stockholm, young clientèle.

Montmartre. *Brochant La Tour,* 163 Ave. de Clichy, new. Walls seem to be made of paper, service indifferent, but baths are modern.

Left Bank. *Molière,* 14 Rue de Vaugirard; *Majory,* 20 Rue Monsieur le Prince; *Delavigne,* 1 Rue Casimir Delavigne; *Delambre,* 35 Rue Delambre; *Départ,* 19 Rue du Départ; *Ideal-Hôtel,* 108 Bd. Jourdan.

NEAR AIRPORTS

At **Orly,** the *Hilton-Orly,* 388 soundproof and air-conditioned rooms, opposite airport terminal. *Motel PLM Orly,* 200 rooms. *Air Hôtel,* 56 rooms. At **Rungis,** near Orly, the 206-room *Frantel,* and *Holiday Inn,* 180 rooms. At **Roissy,** the *Sofitel,* 1,352 rooms. All first class.

 RESTAURANTS. Paris has over 8,000 restaurants. If you ate out two meals a day, going to a different place each time, it would take you nearly 13 years to get through them! Almost all Paris restaurants have their bill of fare with prices plainly posted outside so you can study their offerings and calculate the price of the meal. You can be sure that any which do not post their menus thus are very expensive. Below are listed a number of tried and true restaurants. (Hotel restaurants are under Hotels, above.)

THE GASTRONOMIC TEMPLES. First of all, here are six of the top restaurants of Paris from the point of view of cuisine, atmosphere, and world renown; they're the places one "is glad to have been to". They are all extremely expensive, but the memory of a meal will linger on and on. Telephone for a table before going.

Tour d'Argent, 15–17 Quai de la Tournelle, elegant décor, gastronomic food. Wonderful view of Notre Dame. The Tour d'Argent is located on a roof, but its prices are higher. Closed Mon.

Maxim's, 3 rue Royale, is a sort of historical monument of gastronomy and elegance, one of the few places where you can really "dress up." Prices are horrifying but then, one only lives once! Closed Sun.

Le Grand Véfour, 17 Rue de Beaujolais, behind the lovely gardens of the Palais-Royal, tops in cuisine, historic atmosphere, and prices. Closed Sun.

Taillevent, 15 Rue Lamennais, near the Champs-Elysées, superb classical cuisine and extraordinary wines. Closed Sun.

Le Vivarois, 192 Ave. Victor Hugo, one of France's top restaurants under chef-owner Claude Peyrot. Unusual, subtle cooking. Reservations essential at least 24 hours ahead. Closed Sat. & Sun.

Lasserre, 17 Ave. Franklin-Roosevelt. Very elegant and priced to boot. Especially pleasant on hot summer evenings, for it has a sliding roof. Closed Sun.

EXPENSIVE RESTAURANTS

Drouant, 18 Place Gaillon, comfortable if not exciting, impeccable food and service. Closed Sat.

L'Archestrate, 84 Rue de Varenne, one of the best and most fashionable spots. Closed Sat. & Sun.

Prunier-Duphot, Rue Duphot, unrivaled for seafood, closed July, Aug. and Sun. The sister restaurant, *Prunier-Traktir,* 16 Av. Victor Hugo, is equally irreproachable.

Grande Cascade, Bois de Boulogne, authentic Napoleon III décor. Excellent service. Closed Mon.

Bessière, 97 Ave. des Ternes, rich food and superb wines in comfortable décor. Very non-touristy. Good service. Closed Sun.

Lucas-Carton, 9 Pl. de la Madeleine, a favorite of Parisian connoisseurs. Extremely expensive.

La Marée, 1 Rue Daru. Elegant, high-quality seafood cuisine in pleasant atmosphere.

Laurent, 41 Ave. Gabriel. Distinguished, with a charming view over the Champs-Elysées. Closed Sat. & Sun.

Ledoyen, Carré des Champs-Elysées, very elegant for outdoor lunch or dinner. Closed Sun.

Lous Landès, 9 Rue Georges Saché, in Montparnasse. Best Bordelais-Landes cooking in all of Paris. Closed Sun. & Mon.

Chez Denis, 10 Rue Gustave Flaubert, an unpretentious exterior and banal interior mask a delicious Bordelaise cuisine. Terrifyingly expensive.

Pré Catelan (open Mar.–Oct.), beautiful, in the Bois de Boulogne, dressy. Recently renovated. Superb cuisine. Closed Mon.

Le Duc, 243 Bd. Raspail, renowned for seafood, reservations essential. Closed Sun. & Mon.

La Barrière Poquelin, 17 rue Molière, "new French cuisine" light, delicious and unexpected in this unpretentious-looking bistro. Closed Sat. lunch & Sun.

Le Mercure Galant, 15 rue des Petits Champs, authentic Napoleon III decor, elegant and fashionable. Closed Sun.

Chez L' Ami Louis, 32 rue du Vertbois. A real bistro, where nothing seems to have changed since 1930. Prices are high . . . but one portion will feed two people.

Chez Allard, 41 Rue St.-André des Arts, one of the best bistro type restaurants in Paris, a favorite with writers and actors. Reserve ahead. Closed Sat. & Sun.

Relais Louis XIII, 8 Rue des Grands-Augustins, candlelight dinners with baroque music in a 17th-cent. house. Closed Sun.

Les Semailles, 3 Rue Steinlen (Montmartre). A sumptuous menu in a sophisticated "peasanty" décor. "New French Cuisine"; closed Sun. & Mon.

Bistrot d'Hubert, 36 Pl. du Marché St.-Honoré, very fashionable, small, reservations hard to get. Closed Sat. lunch & Sun.

L'Escargot Montorgueil, 38 Rue Montorgeuil. This famous old spot slid badly for several years, but is excellent once more. Closed Sat. lunch.

Lamazère, 23 Rue de Ponthieu, great. Elegant clientèle, both at lunch and dinner. Open until 1 A.M. Closed Sun.

Jamin, 32 Rue de Longchamp, very elegant, very "Parisian". Rich Bourdeaux dishes.

Le Pactole, 44 Bd. St. Germain, doesn't look like much, but rates as one of Paris' best. Closed Sat. & Sun.

Dodin-Bouffant, 25 Rue Frédéric-Sauton. Run by Jacques Manière, former *patron-chef* of *Le Pactole.* Inspired cuisine and superb, reasonably-priced wines. Closed Sat. & Sun.

Le Bernardin, 35 Quai de la Tournelle. One of the finest seafood restaurants in Paris. The *plateau de fruits de mer* is a specialty. Tiny premises, so be sure to book in advance. Closed Sun. & Mon.

Olympe, 54 Rue du Montparnasse. One of the newest and most fashionable restaurants in Paris. "New French cuisine" and turn-of-the-century décor. Small and always crowded, so book well in advance. Closed for lunch & Mon.

Faugeron, 52 Rue de Longchamp. One of the finest and most reliable "serious" restaurants in town, with marvellous food and wines, a large menu, comfortable surroundings, and excellent service. Closed Sat. lunch and Sun.

MODERATELY PRICED RESTAURANTS

Moderate can go from high moderate to very reasonable, so we'll start with some of the best, most fashionable, and therefore most expensive in this category. Very original is *Pantagruel,* 20 Rue de l'Exposition. Interesting and modish is *Le Barrière de Clichy,* 1 Rue de Paris (Clichy); the district is dismal, but the cooking is most certainly not; nor is the clientèle. Prices are rather high. *Le Relais de la Butte,* 12 Rue de Ravignan, possibly the best in Montmartre; pleasant décor; closed Thurs. & Fri. lunch. For seafood, *La Coquille,* 6 Rue du Débarcadère (closed Sun.), and *Marius,* 82 Bd. Murat (Closed Sun. & Mon.). *Les Belles Gourmandes,* 5 rue P.L. Courier has splendidly varied menu, reservations a must. Closed Sat. & Sun.

La Quetsch, 6 Rue des Capucines (closed Sat. & Sun.); *La Petite Auberge,* 38 Rue Laugier (Closed Sun. & Mon.); *Auberge de le Truite,* 30 Rue du Fbg. St.-

Honoré, in a quiet courtyard behind Lanvin, specializes in Normandy dishes (closed Sun.); *Chez Pauline,* 5 Rue Villedo (Closed Sat. & Sun.); *La Bourgogne,* 6 Av. Bosquet, rich Burgundy cooking. Closed Sat. & Sun.

A l'Ancien Gauclair, corner Rue de Richelieu and Rue St.-Marc, for wonderful grilled steaks (closed Sat. & Sun.); *Louis XIV,* 1 bis Pl. des Victoires, an unassuming *bistro* in a remarkable 17th-cent. circle of houses (closed Sat. & Sun.); *Le Mayfair,* 5 Chaussée d'Antin, a convenient—and satisfying—haven for tired shoppers; *Chez Max,* 19 Rue de Castellane, quiet atmosphere (closed Sat. & Sun.); *Auberge Médiévale,* 29 rue St. Lazare, excellent steaks, good beaujolais (closed Sat. & Sun.); *L'Auvergnat 1900,* 11 rue Jean-Mermoz, conveniently located right off the Champs-Elysées, open till 11 P.M. Closed Sun.

Lipp, 151 Bd. St.-Germain, an Alsatian *brasserie,* specializes in *choucroute* and in celebrities, both at lunch and dinner-time. (Closed Mon.) The *Renault Pub,* 53 Champs-Elysées at the back of the Champs-Elysées car showrooms, where you sit in reconstituted vintage cars, offers edible food, and you don't have to eat a whole menu. If you long for American cooking, drop in at *Joe Allen,* 30 Rue Pierre Lescot, very à la mode, but overpriced. *Leroy Haynes,* 3 Rue Clauzel, is more reasonable.

Chez Edgard, 4 Rue Marbeuf, comfortable and busy, with a most varied reasonable menu. Closed Sun.

Les Copains, 44 Rue de Verneuil, an amiable family bistro. Closed Sat. & Sun.

Try *Le Train Bleu* in the Gare de Lyon station: now classified a historical monument, it is deliriously Belle Epoque. The cooking is only fair, but wine list excellent.

Pierre-Traiteur, 10 Rue de Richelieu; the cooking is the way people think all French cuisine should be. Closed Sat., Sun. & August.

Nicolas, 12 Rue de la Fidélité, a step away from the Gare de l'Est. Excellent classical cooking. Closed Sat. & August.

La Coupole, 102 Bd. du Montparnasse. A brilliant and mixed clientèle, from elegant to hippy; fine wines, good frescos and adequate cooking makes Hemingway's old hangout very "in". Closed August.

Le Mange-Tout, 30 Rue Lacépède. A small restaurant specializing in cuisine from the Périgord-Quercy area. Some original dishes; modern décor. Often crowded, so preferable to book. Closed Sun. & Mon.

Moissonnier, 28 Rue des Fossés-St.-Bernard. A pleasant old bistro. Lyonnaise cuisine, excellent Beaujolais and Côtes-du-Rhône. Closed Sun. evening & Mon.

La Petite Cour, 8 Rue Mabillon. Run by a novelist's wife, this charming little restaurant gives on to a little courtyard where you can eat in the summer; offers good food and excellent service. Fashionable, youngish clientèle. Closed Sat. lunch and Sun.

INEXPENSIVE RESTAURANTS

L'Assiette au Boeuf, 123 Champs-Elysées; only one menu, very reasonable for this expensive avenue.

Bar des Théâtres, 6 Ave. Montaigne. Across from the Plaza-Athénée, its clientèle is heavily sprinkled with models, actresses, and their admirers. Simple food until late at night.

La Boutique à Sandwiches, 12 Rue du Colisée. Possibly the best sandwich joint in town. Open after midnight. Closed Sun.

Beaux-Arts, 11 Rue Bonaparte, a favorite old bistro, good cooking. Lots of students.

La Boulangerie St.-Philippe, 74 Ave. Franklin-Roosevelt, simple, savory cooking, very popular at lunchtime.

Brasserie du Pont Louis-Philippe, 66 Quai de l'Hôtel de Ville, a real bargain in an interesting area.

Chartier, 7 Rue du Fbg. Montmartre, copious and healthy food in a rather gloomy district.

Julien, 1 Rue du Pont Louis-Philippe. This former *boulangerie* on the embankment, not far from the Hôtel de Ville, offers excellent cuisine at a very reasonable price. Pleasant at lunchtime, too. Closed Sun.

Le Petit Saint-Benoît, 4 Rue St.-Benoît. A workman's bistro, always crowded, in the middle of St.-Germain-des-Prés. Good family-cooking and extremely reasonable prices.

 NIGHTLIFE. These are expensive by London standards, though not by those of New York. The topnotch clubs are apt to be full; better reserve a table. Your best bet for a big theatrical spectacle featuring nude dancers, *tableaux vivants,* fights under water, and everything else that modern stage machinery and production can devise, is the famous *Folies-Bergère.* The *Casino de Paris* is just about as good as, perhaps a little livelier, than the *Folies-Bergère.* In smaller clubs, striptease, *version raffinée,* is still the order of the day.

THE CHIC SPOTS

Maxim's, 3 Rue Royale. Already covered in our restaurant section, but Maxim's is much more than a restaurant. It is a favorite of international society—and of everyone who wants to watch international society.

Castel, 15 Rue Princesse. Its three dining floors include a restaurant decorated in the redplush style of 1900, serving up songs of the period along with very good and expensive food. Almost impossible for the average tourist to get into, unless accompanied by knowledgeable French friends, or one of the "beautiful people." A very young crowd these days.

Le Privé, 12 Rue de Ponthieu, just as snobby as Castel, but not as hard to enter. Crowded, but very "in".

François-Patrice-St.-Hilaire, 36 Rue de Ponthieu. Elegant, comfortable. Francois Patrice, one of Paris' charmers, has created the kind of place where clients stay on and on.

L'Aventure, 4 Av. Victor Hugo. One of fashionable Paris' hangouts. Dancing in the dark, whiskey and smoke. Difficult to get in.

Régine's, 49 Rue de Ponthieu. Second in Régine's empire, extremely luxurious and expensive, difficult to enter. Excellent orchestra, good food.

THE SHOW'S THE THING

Lido, 78 Champs-Elysées. The best show in Europe, a large lavish production; many American acts; dancing between shows; champagne theoretically obligatory, but you can always ask for their overpriced whiskey. You can also dine fairly expensively.

Don Camilo, 10 Rue des Sts.-Pères. Not too expensive, dining, floorshow.

Moulin-Rouge, Pl. Blanche. On the edge of Montmartre. Presently, the accent is on the old-time can-can.

Alcazar, 62 Rue Mazarine. Dinner and a witty floorshow in the roaring twenties style. For the moment, prices are reasonable, clientèle well-known. Must reserve. Closed Sun. & August.

L'Ange Bleu, 12 Rue de Marignan. One of the brightest of the big nightclubs, specializing in takeoffs of popular entertainers. Transvestites. A slightly ambiguously erotic show. Closed Sun. and August.

Chez Michou, 80 Rue des Martyrs. This spot, where you dine until showtime at midnight, is making all Paris, as well as the provinces, climb up again to Montmartre. Another boy-girl show.

Paradis Latin, 28 Rue du Cardinal Lemoine. The newest, most crowded show in town. Floorshow at 11 P.M. You can also dine, expensively.

LES GIRLS

Crazy Horse Saloon, 12 Ave. George V. The oldest, and best, striptease establishment in town.

Pussy Cat, 22 Rue Quentin-Bauchard. Open from 10:30 on. Dancing to a good, small orchestra.

Poppy, 4 Rue Auguste-Vacquerie. One of the more attractive striptease shows. A cozy, intimate room, pretty hostesses, a good orchestra, singers, dancers—and the girls.

La Villa, Carrefour Raspail-Montparnasse. Girls on the half shell, dancing, floorshow.

Topless, 2 Rue Coustou. Up-and-coming, with pretty girls and some acts as funny as rival Crazy Horse.

La Nouvelle Eve, 25 Rue Fontaine. A highly polished show where the girls are undressed with a lavish hand.

REEKING WITH ATMOSPHERE

Lapin Agile, 22 Rue des Saules. On top of the Butte Montmartre, famous former hangout of artists; hard wooden benches; old French songs.

Chez ma Cousine, 12 Rue Norvins. The ideal place to combine dinner and a show with a night visit to the Butte Montmartre, closed Thurs.

Le Monocle, 60 Bd. Edgar-Quinet. Not all the girls here look like men, but those who don't are dancing with girls who do. Males tolerated, provided they keep quiet.

Madame Arthur, 75 bis Rue des Martyrs. Exactly the opposite situation: here the women are men, and often very pretty. Good show.

Peanuts, 51 Rue Lucien-Sampais, an old-fashioned *ginguette,* overlooking the picturesque Canal St.-Martin. Awful food, but excellent songs and sketches in French and English.

Caveau des Oubliettes, 52 Rue Galande. An underground refuge, appropriately and tastefully decorated with chastity belts, instruments of torture, etc. Old French songs, sung in costume, in adjacent dungeons.

Le Balajo, 9 Rue de Lappe. One of the kitschiest places in town. Huge barn-like dancing hall interesting for those who want a glimpse of Parisian punks and the "little people".

El Djazair, 27 Rue de la Huchette. Arab. *Couscous* to eat, Oriental dancing to interfere with your digestion. Some of the belly-dancers are American!

La Canne à Sucre, 4 Rue Ste.-Beuve. Martinique is a French possession, which accounts for this West Indian place in Paris. Entertainment is excellent, food exotic and prices reasonable. Closed Sun. & Mon.

Pavillon Russe (Chez Ludmila), 4 Rue Lauriston. Vodka, balalaika and Russian emotion combine to make this a very romantic joint. Closed Sun. & Mon.

La Grange au Bouc, 42 Rue Chevalier de la Barre. On the top of the Montmartre hill, this small, but long-popular cabaret goes merrily on and on. Reasonable.

DINE AND DANCE

Samantha, Pavillon Royal, Bois de Boulogne, is presently very chic.

L'Ecume des Nuits, 81 Bd. Gouvion-St.-Cyr (in the Méridien Hotel). A voluptuous nightblue *boîte,* full of pretty girls who like to dance to sweet music. Hard to enter if you are not a client of the hotel or a member.

Tagada-Club. 107 Rue de l'Université. Gaby has been around for at least twenty years, but is still going strong. Cheerful and noisy; lots of provincial French visitors.

Navy Club, 58 Bd. de l'Hôpital. One of the few discothèques where you eat really well at bistro prices. Always something going on in this truly Parisian hangout. No sloppy dress.

Villa d'Este, 4 Rue Arsène-Houssaye. Dining and dancing at this long-time favorite accompanied by top drawer singers. Closed July and Aug.

IF YOU KNOW FRENCH. You may have fun at these places even if you aren't versed in French, but a lot of the jokes are going to sail right over your head.

Belle Epoque, 38 Rue des Petits Champs. A fast and witty show, the spot always crowded. Authentic turn-of-the-century décor.

Au Port du Salut, 163 bis Rue St.-Jacques. Also goes on and on with its young and witty imitators and funnymen. Happily moderately priced, very popular. Closed Mon.

A DRINK-A SONG

L'Abbaye de St.-Germain-des-Prés, 6 bis Rue de l'Abbaye. Gordon Heath and Lee Payant, singing French, English and American folk songs, are still going strong after these many years. Starts at 21:30 hrs., come early otherwise you won't get in.

Le Lapin Rouge, 4 Rue du Rocher. For lovers of true jazz, run by the energetic Moustache. His drinks raise the dead; but the cooking leaves something to be desired.

La Calavados, 40 Ave. Pierre Ier de Serbie. Popular spot for smart-set drinking, particularly late drinking. Entertainment until the sun comes up.

Rôtisserie de l'Abbaye, 22 Rue Jacob, St.-Germain-des-Près. Under 13th-cent. vaults and in a medieval ambience. Troubadours and minstrels.

Club des Sts.-Pères, 10 Rue des Sts.-Pères, a rustic, comfortable *cave.* But unlike other chic clubs, tourists are welcomed with a smile.

Piano-Club, 12 Rue Ste.-Anne. Excellent discothèque, run by an ebullient Cuban.

L'Hôtel, 13 Rue des Beaux-Arts, very cozy bar downstairs.

Via Veneto, 13 Rue Quentin-Bauchart (near Ave. Marceau). Scampi and guitars, pollo and tenors, this medium-priced spot is a favorite among the younger set.

Sherwood, 3 Rue Daunou. A charming English-type pub where you can simply drink, or eat at modest prices. Agreeable youngish clientèle.

CAFES-THEATRES. Though originally an import from the United States, the phenomenon of cafés-théâtres has been thoroughly absorbed into the cultural life of Paris. They are usually crowded and uncomfortable, but the show's the thing. A good understanding of French is essential.

Le Fanal, 85–87 Rue St.-Honoré. One of the oldest, most "intellectual" cafés-théâtres in Paris, set in a medieval cellar. Shows at 6:30 and 8:30 P.M.

Le Coupe-Chou Beaubourg, 94 Rue St.-Martin. The most elegant and comfortable of the Paris cafés-théâtres. Avant-garde shows at 8:30, 10, and 11:30 P.M. A good restaurant on the ground-floor.

Le Sélénite, 18 Rue Dauphine. Two adjacent locals offering about 6 shows each (some of them erotic). From 8:45 onwards.

SHOPPING. For an orientation tour and revelation of how the French live and shop, take a walk through one of the department stores: *Galeries Lafayette* and *Au Printemps,* behind the Opéra; *Aux Trois Quartiers,* near the Madeleine, and *Au Bon Marché* on the Left Bank. The *Prisunic* and *Monoprix* stores on the Champs-Elysées and the Opéra area, are inexpensive, as are the various *Drugstores* (for gifts and gadgets as well as clothes male and female). There are luxurious shopping centers in the Palais des Congrès at Porte Maillot, the Tour Montparnasse, and, of course, Orly and Roissy airports.

Specialized Shopping Service Houses will send your purchases direct to plane, boat or home (main specialties are perfumes, scarves, ties, gloves, pocket-books). Best-known are: *Michel Swiss,* 16 Rue de la Paix; *Freddy,* 10 Rue Auber (one flight up); *Obéron,* 9 Rue Scribe; *J. W. Chunn,* 43 Rue Richer and *Grillot,* 10 Rue Cambon.

Markets: The *Marché aux Puces,* Paris's famous Flea Market (Métro: Porte de Clignancourt), is open Sat., Sun., and Mon. The *Biron* and *Vernaison* sections are as expensive as in-town shops: in fact, many Paris antique dealers have stands there. At *Paul Bert* and *Jules Vallès* sections you can still find bargains, but beware of all that so-called Louis XVI and ancient African art.

The *Montreuil Puces* (Metro: Porte de Montreuil), also open weekends, is for the shopper with a sharp eye for bargains. As at the more expensive *Puces,* it's quite proper to make an offer below the stated prices.

The *Village Suisse,* on Avenue Suffren, is popular; clientèle and merchandise are a cut above the flea markets, but there are also a lot of fakes and copies of antiques. Closed Tues. & Wed.

There are other *Puces* at the Porte de Vannes, Bicêtre, and Place d'Aligre.

BOUTIQUES. Many of the famous couturiers now have boutiques where prices are less astronomical than for their *haute couture* creations.

On the Right Bank are: *Yves St.-Laurent* at 46 Ave. Victor Hugo and 38 Fbg.St.-Honoré; *Givenchy* at 66 Av. Victor Hugo; *Patou* at 7 Rue St.-Florentin; *Scherrer* at 51 Ave. Montaigne; *Laroche* at 30 Fbg. St.-Honoré; *Courrèges* at No. 46, same street; *Ungaro* at No. 25; *Balmain* 44 Rue François-Ier; *Cardin* at 118 Fbg. St.-Honoré.

On the Left Bank are: *Yves St.-Laurent* at 21 Rue de Tournon; *Scherrer* at No. 31, same street; *Courrèges* at 49 Rue de Rennes.

At the end of every season many couturiers dispose of their model dresses at reduced prices, selling them to resale houses. The best known of these are *La Solderie,* at No. 85 Rue la Boétie; *Anna Lowe,* 35 Ave. Matignon, and *Jean Pierre,* 59 Rue St.-Lazare. *La Nippérie,* 88 Rue de la Pompe.

If you have *haute couture* tastes but prefer to spend less, visit *Torrente* at 11 Fbg. St.-Honoré, *Réty* at No. 54, *Daniel Hechter* at No. 12, *Lapidus* at No. 23. *Sweater's Bazaar* at No. 83, *Knap* at No. 34. *Vicky Tiel,* has a boutique in the courtyard of 21 Rue Bonaparte.

There are many smart shops on Ave. Victor Hugo. Avant-garde boutiques are sprinkled around the Bd. St.-Germain and Rue de Sèvres. If you are looking for kooky clothes, you might try the area around Rue St. Denis, Rue Bergère etc.: everything ranging from stylish boutiques to antiques. The handsome Place des Victoires boasts several of the most interesting fashion shops in Paris: *Victoire, Françoise Andrevie, Jungle Jap* (Kenzo). The latter two are rather far-out, not particularly expensive, directed towards a young clientèle.

CRYSTAL AND PORCELAIN. *Lalique,* 11 Rue Royale and 31 Av. George-V, and *Au Vase Etrusque,* 11 Pl. de la Madeleine, are two notable houses for glass and tableware. The beautiful *Baccarat* crystal, one of the prides of France, can be seen at 30bis, Rue de Paradis. On the same street, at No. 31 is *Daum,* and at No. 30, *Saint-Louis,* who also has a shop in New York (useful for replacements). The big department stores also have a wide selection.

FABRICS are beautiful, though not in the bargain class. *Corot, Max,* and *Rodin,* all on the Champs-Elysées, have excellent choice and service. If you like to rummage for bargains, go to *Dreyfus* at 2 Rue Charles-Nodier at the foot of Montmartre.

GIFTS. *Lancel* has two shops, one at the corner of the Place de l'Opéra and the Bd. des Italiens, the other at the Rond-Point des Champs-Elysées; these can solve most gift problems with a superior selection of Paris souvenir articles, leather goods, luggage, perfumes, and many items whose styling and craftsmanship are typically Parisian. Other very attractive gift shops are *Françoise Thibault,* 1 Rue Jacob, *Janie Pradier,* 78 Rue de Seine, *Dona Carlotta,* 22 Rue François 1, *Céralène,* 16 Ave. Montaigne, and *Nicolas,* 27 Rue Marbeuf.

GLOVES couldn't be more beautiful than the ones made in this country. The greatest glovemaker in Paris is *Hermès,* 24 Fbg. St.-Honoré; his gloves are very expensive but worth it. Other addresses for gloves: *Anne Chanay,* 10 Rue de Castiglione and *Schilz,* 30 Rue Caumartin. Most *Grands Magasins* carry Dior gloves. For men's gloves, try *Peau de Porc,* 67 Fbg. St.-Honoré; *Knize,* 10 Ave. Matignon, and *Nicolet,* 18 Rue Duphot. A special mention to *Gant Perrin,* 45 Ave. de l'Opéra and 22 Rue Royale.

HANDBAGS. If you can afford a custom-made bag, the most beautiful and most expensive are at *Morabito,* 1 Pl. Vendôme, and for evening bags, *Germaine Guérin,* 243 Rue St.-Honoré. For expensive ready-mades *Hermès, Lucienne Offenthal,* 24 Rue de la Paix, *Gucci,* 25 Fbg. St. Honoré. *La Bagagerie,* 41 Rue du Four, 10 Rue de Passy, and 13 Rue Tronchet, carries inexpensive "in" items.

JEWELRY. The great jewelers are in the Place Vendôme *(Boucheron, Cartier, Chaumet, Van Cleef and Arpels, Mauboussin)* and along the fabulous Rue de la Paix where you can find original creations at *Mellerio* and *Tecla.* For highly original, hand-crafted, modern one-of-a-kind pieces, look at *Jean Vendôme,* 350 Rue St.-Honoré. *Ilias Lalaounis,* at No. 364, same street, also has unique pieces. For an original souvenir of Paris, such as a gold sparrow or a Pierre Cardin ring, go to 7 Rue Royale, chez *Worms. Bijou Box,* in the Lido Arcade, *Niort,* 420 rue St.-Honoré, carry attractive costume jewelry.

LINGERIE. Undoubtedly for tops in quality and price, go to *Pache,* 6 Rue de Castiglione. Other fine spots: *Roger et Gallet,* at 62 Fbg.-St.-Honoré, and *Christian Dior's* lingerie department. *Les Nuits d'Elodie,* 1 bis Ave. Mac Mahon and *Candide,* 4 Rue de Miromesnil, make more informal lingerie. *Gribiche,* 49 Rue de Rennes, has exquisite nightgowns.

ANTIQUES, PAINTING, PRINTS. Stroll down the Rue Bonaparte, de l'Université, de Seine, de Beaune, de Grenelle, de Lille, du Cherche-Midi or the Rue Jacob and you're in the heart of the Left Bank antique shop district. Antiques are not bargains but there are some mouth-watering items all the same along the quais and picturesque streets around St. Germain-des-Près.

If you're looking for religious objects, the neighborhood around St.-Sulpice or Notre Dame des Victoires has shops which specialize in them.

Our favorite spot for the graphic arts is the *Galerie R. G. Michel,* 17 the Quai St. Michel. *Paul Prouté,* 74 Rue de Seine, is a specialist in engravings and lithographs. Other top-notch shops for prints and lithographs are *Vision Nouvelle,* 6 Pl. des Etats-Unis; *La Hune,* 14 Rue de L'Abbaye; *Cailleux,* 136 Fbg. St.-Honoré; *Berggruen,* 70 Rue de l'Université.

If you are looking for extraordinary reproductions of great modern paintings, ask the *Galerie de France* 3 Fbg. St.-Honoré about the Aeply process.

FRENCH PERFUMES. Finally, there's the heady experience of buying perfume in Paris. Any of the department stores, shops and any *parfumerie* on the Champs-Elysées and around the Opéra will squirt you with almost any available flavor, and there are so many good ones that you'll be faced with an *embarras de choix. Sephora,* 50 Rue de Passy, claims to be the largest perfumery in the world, and may be right: at any rate, you can find everything in the way of perfumes and beauty aids (as well as diet juices) in this well-laid-out store and at lower prices. Of course, don't forget the airports for last-minute shopping.

MUSEUMS. There are over 90 museums in the Paris area. The ones most likely to interest you are listed here in order of their importance; the nearest Métro station is given in parentheses. Unless otherwise stated, these museums are closed Tuesdays and holidays, but not Sundays. Sundays are free or half-price days, but crowded. Many close an hour or so earlier, October to Easter.

Musée du Louvre (Louvre), 9:45 to 8. The world's largest museum in the world's largest palace, home of the Mona Lisa, the Winged Victory of Samothrace, the Venus de Milo. Don't miss the museum shop on the ground floor where you can buy reproductions of many of the paintings, statues and other *objets d'art* on exhibit. The Louvre is divided into six sections: Greek and Roman; Oriental; Egyptian; sculpture of the Middle Ages, Renaissance and modern times; paintings and drawings; art objects. Lecture visits in English and French start daily from the Porte Denon at 10:30 and 3, Fri. evenings at 9 from the door of whichever gallery is listed on the posters.

Centre National d'Art et de Culture Georges Pompidou, Plateau Beaubourg, Rue St.-Martin (Rambuteau, Hôtel de Ville). Gigantic museum housing an eclectic collection including the National Museum of Modern Art (formerly in the Ave. du Président Wilson), industrial and decorative art. Large library, video and music section.

Cluny, 6 Pl. Paul-Painleve (St.-Michel), 9:45-12:45, 2-5:15. Medieval museum in a delightful 15th-cent. abbey, with remnants of the Roman baths that once occupied the site still visible. Fascinating medieval accoutrements. Don't miss *La Dame à la Licorne* tapestry or the recently discovered fragments of sculptures from Notre-Dame.

Musée de l'Armée, Esplanade des Invalides (Invalides), 10-6 (5 in winter). Napoleon's Tomb, weapons, armor, battle flags.

Conciergerie, 1 Quai de l'Horloge, in the Palais de Justice (Cité), 10-12, 1:30-5. Relics of the French Revolution: Marie Antoinette's cell, fragments from the palace of the early kings of France.

Jeu de Paume, Tuileries Garden, Pl. de la Concorde (Concorde), 9:45-5:15, houses famous collection of Impressionists.

Orangerie, Tuileries Garden, Place de la Concorde (Concorde), 10-5, Monet's *Nymphéas* and important temporary exhibits.

Musée de l'Homme, Palais de Chaillot, Pl. du Trocadéro (Trocadéro), 10-5 or 6. One of the world's finest anthropological museums. Documentary films are shown daily.

Panthéon, Pl. du Panthéon (Luxembourg), 10-5. Formerly the Church of Ste.-Geneviève, now the burial place for great men—Voltaire, Rousseau, Victor Hugo, etc.

Archives Nationales, 60 Rue des Francs-Bourgeois (Rambuteau, Hôtel-de-Ville), 2-5. History of France. Documents dating back to Charlemagne.

Arts Décoratifs, 107-109 Rue de Rivoli (Palais-Royal), 10-12, 2-5. In the opposite wing of the Louvre Palace from the Louvre Museum proper; interior decoration and furniture, both French and foreign.

Nissim de Camondo, 63 Rue de Monceau, 10-12, 2-5. Closed Mon., Tues. Magnificent 18th-cent. furniture in former private home of a banker.

Carnavalet, 23 Rue de Sévigné (St. Paul), 10-5:40. Closed Mon., Tues. Costumes through the ages, furniture, china, history of Paris. Souvenirs of Mme. de Sévigné.

Gumet, 6 Pl. d'Iéna (Iéna), 9:45-12, 1:30-5:15. Indo-Chinese and other Far Eastern art.

Histoire Naturelle, Jardin des Plantes, 57 rue Cuvier (Jussieu), 1-5. Contains Duc d'Orléans collection of hunting trophies; zoological, mineralogical, and paleontological exhibits. Botanical gardens and zoo in park.

Palais de la Découverte, 1 Ave. Franklin-Roosevelt (Champs-Elysées–Clemenceau), 10-6. Closed Mon. Scientific, mechanical, and technical exhibits, working models, planetarium.

Popular Arts, 6 Route du Mahatma Gandhi, Bois de Boulogne (Sablons). Objects relating to rural activities in pre-industrial environments. Children enjoy the costumes and ancient circus figures.

Delacroix' Studio, 6 Place Fürstenberg (St.-Germain-des-Prés), 9:45-5:15. In a charming old square, the studio of the painter has been preserved as he left it.

Victor Hugo's House, 6 Pl. des Vosges (Chemin-Vert, Saint-Paul), 10-5:40. Closed Mon., Tues. Souvenirs of the writer. The harmonious old Place des Vosges is worth a visit in itself.

Rodin, 77 Rue de Varenne (Invalides, Varenne), 10-5 or 6; located in an old house set in a garden, both filled with the sculpture of Auguste Rodin.

Petit Palais, Ave. Winston Churchill (Champs-Elysées–Clemenceau), 10-5:40. Closed Mon., Tues. The permanent collection of French painting and medieval art occupying one wing is regularly supplemented by important temporary shows.

Grand Palais. Av. Winston Churchill. Occasional important temporary exhibits.

Palais de Tokyo, (formerly Musée d'Art Moderne), 13 Ave. du Président Wilson (Iéna), 9:45-5:15. Now that the Museum of Modern Art is housed in the Georges Pompidou Center, its old home is given over to Post-Impressionism.

Art Moderne de la Ville de Paris, opposite the above; 20th-cent. French and foreign painters, far-out exhibitions and experimental art. Also an active children's museum. 10-5:40. Closed Mon., Tues.

Jacquemart-André. 158 Bd. Haussmann (Saint-Philippe-du-Roule, Miromesnil), 1:30-5:30. Closed Mon., Tues. Italian and French art, temporary exhibits, often revolving around an interesting personality (Proust, St.-Jean Perse etc.).

Postal, 34 Bld. de Vaugirard (Montparnasse-Bienvenüe), 10-5. Closed Thurs. Stamps, rare and historic.

Vieux-Montmartre, 17 Rue St.-Vincent (Lamarck), 2:30–5:30. Exhibits associated with famous Montmartre figures, such as Toulouse-Lautrec, plus some of their works.

Among notable museums easily reached from Paris are these:

Céramique de Sèvres (Pont-de-Sèvres), 9:30-12, 1:30-5:15. Devoted to the famous Sèvres porcelain.

Versailles. Château and Revolutionary Museum, 9:45-5:30. Closed Mon. Grand Trianon and Petit Trianon museums, 10-5 between Oct. 1 and April 1, one hour later in summer.

Fontainebleau, 10-12:30, 2-5 or 6. There is a Chinese museum in one wing of the château.

St.-Germain-en-Laye, National Antiquities Museum. Best museum in the world for paleolithic objects, very well displayed. 9:45-12, 1:30-5:15.

Malmaison, Museum of the Château, 10-12, 1:30-4:30, Oct. through Mar., in summer 10-12, 1:30-5:30.

Stop press! Paris's very latest museum, the Poster Museum, is just opening as we write. The *Musée de l'Affiche* is at 18 Rue de Paradis, 10e, in what used to be the premises of a beautiful old china shop. It's open 12-6, closed Sat.

 BEST PARKS AND GARDENS. The parks and gardens of Paris are varied and beautiful, whether they are the large rambling wooded variety or the formally laid-out open spaces in the center of the city. Most are enclosed and are shut at dusk. These are the most important:

Bois de Boulogne (Métro: Porte d'Auteuil, Porte Dauphine, Sablons or Porte Maillot). Not enclosed, it is always open. It contains 7 lakes, the Cascade, the Longchamp and Auteuil racetracks, the Roland-Garros tennis stadium, a polo field, a children's zoo (the Jardin d'Acclimatation), camping grounds, Bagatelle Park (Métro: Pont de Neuilly), which exhibits roses (June) and water lilies, and a Shakespeare Garden. (Unaccompanied women should avoid the *Bois* after dark.)

Jardin des Plantes, 57 Rue Cuvier, near the Austerlitz rail station (Métro: Gare d'Austerlitz). Botanical gardens with special exhibits of pharmaceutical plants, an Alpine garden, green-houses, another zoo, and the natural history museum.

Bois de Vincennes (Métro: Porte Dorée). At the eastern edge of Paris. Contains a racetrack, three lakes (boats for hire on the Lac Daumesnil), and the Vincennes Zoo, largest in Paris.

Parc Monceau, on Bd. de Courcelles (Métro: Monceau), is quiet, charming, frequented mostly by the residents of the well-to-do-quarter about it and their children; genuine *Parisien* atmosphere.

Luxembourg Garden, famous throughout the world. On the Left Bank, off Bd. St.-Michel (Métro: Luxembourg), it encloses the Palais du Luxembourg and the now disused Petit Luxembourg.

Jardin des Tuileries, in the heart of Paris (Métro: Concorde, Tuileries). Designed by Le Nôtre, it is particularly notable for its trees and pools, its formal gradens embellished with statues, its continuation between the two wings of the Louvre, and above all for the magnificent vista that sweeps all the way from the Louvre through the Tuileries to the Arc de Triomphe.

Moorish Garden, in Paris Mosque, 1 Place de Puits de l'Ermite (Métro: Pl. Monge or Censier-Daubenton). Can be visited between 2 and 4. Don't go Friday, the Moslem holy day.

CEMETERIES. The cemeteries of Paris are remarkable for their statues and finely designed tombs of famous people. Opening times vary considerably, particularly at different seasons; best time to go is midmorning or afternoon. The most visited are:

Montmartre, 20 Ave. Rachel (Métro: Pl. Blanche or Pl. Clichy).

Montparnasse, 3 Bd. Edgar-Quinet (Métro: Edgar Quinet).

Passy, 2 Rue du Cdt.-Schloesing (Métro: Trocadéro).

Père-Lachaise, 16 Rue du Repos (Métro: Père-Lachaise). The most famous.

American Cemetery, 190 Bd. Washington, Suresnes, just outside of Paris, contains the graves of American soldiers who died in World War I. A memorial ceremony is held there on Decoration Day. Open 8-5.

OTHER SIGHTS. The famous Paris sightseeing boats, *Bateaux-Mouches,* have trips on the Seine every half hour in season (Palm Sunday to 12 November) between 10 and 12 A.M., 2 to 6:30 (or 7 if weather is fine) and 8:30–10 P.M. (11 if fine). The "cruise" lasts about 1¼ hours and costs 10 francs (half-price for children). Out-of-season trips start at 11, 2:30, and 4 (more frequently in good weather). You can have lunch on board for 80 francs (children under 12, 60 francs) inclusive (1–2:45 P.M., daily except Monday in season, weekends only out of season) or dinner for 175 francs (children 150 francs) inclusive (8–11 P.M. approximately; daily in season, weekends only out of season).Starting point is the Right Bank end of the Pont de l'Alma. The "Vedettes Paris–Tour Eiffel," using smaller (82-seat) boats of the kind so popular in Amsterdam, sail from the Pont d'Iéna (near the Eiffel Tower) and from Quai Montebello every 30 mins., from 10 A.M. to 6 P.M., with evening cruises between Easter and 1 October starting at 9 P.M. and continuing every 30 minutes to 11 or 11:30, depending on the weather. There's a taped commentary in French, English, and German. Fare 10 francs for a one-hour ride (half-price for children under 10). The "Vedettes Pont-Neuf" leave from Square du Vert Galant, near Notre Dame, at 10:30, 11:15 and 12 A.M., then every half-hour between 1:30 and 6:30 P.M. (5 P.M. in winter). From May to

September there are evening trips at 9, 9:30 and 10 P.M. Same fares as for the other *vedettes;* taped commentary in five languages.

The Ile de la Cité flower market, open daily except Sun. (when it becomes a bird market), from 8 A.M. to 7:30 P.M., is lovely to look at. The nearby Right Bank quais abound with amusing objects.

The floodlighting of *Paris buildings* is well worth seeing—especially the Arc de Triomphe, Madeleine, Notre-Dame, the Invalides, and Sacré Coeur. The schedule is somewhat erratic, but you can usually count on it in the summer, 9:30 to 11 on weekdays, 9:30 to 12 on Sun. and holidays.

If you're in Paris on *14 July,* you won't miss the dancing in the streets, but perhaps you will want to know where to go to see the most authentic popular dancing (Pl. de la République), the young student-artist-writer groups (Carrefour Montparnasse), or the Bretons dancing in local costumes to bagpipe music (behind the Gare Montparnasse, generally in the Rue du Départ). Firework displays from the Pont-Neuf, Auteuil aqueduct, Sacré Coeur, the Montsouris park and the Buttes Chaumont.

To visit the famous *sewers* of Paris, be at the Pl. de la Résistance, corner of the Rive Gauche and the Pont de l'Alma (Quai d'Orsay), Mon., Wed., and last Sat. in the month (except public holidays, and the day before and after them), between 2-5 P.M.

Another unusual excursion is to the *Gallo-Roman Catacombs* under the Left Bank. Meet at 2 Pl. Denfert-Rochereau on the first or third Sat. of the month at 2 between Oct. 16 and July 1, or on any Sat., same hour, between July 1 and Oct. 15. Bring your own torch.

 TRANSPORTATION. Buy a *Plan de Paris* at any newsstand; it is one of the best city guides in existence with alphabetical street directory and clear maps of all 20 *arrondissements,* Métro (subway) and bus lines. The quickest way to get about in Paris is by Métro. Every station has a big map showing all the lines and stations, and you can make as many transfers *(correspondances)* as you want to on a single ticket. Most economical way of travelling is to buy a *carnet* (10 tickets) for 11 francs (second-class). If you ride first class, hold onto your ticket; an inspector may ask to see it. The labyrinth of Paris bus lines also touches nearly every point of interest in the city, and there are obvious advantages to staying above ground and watching Paris go by. Your *carnet* of Métro tickets is also valid on the buses, though they work out to be more expensive this way, because for longer trips you'll need two tickets.

The RER (regional express subway) is now (since December 1977) linked with the Métro. The much-publicized official opening of the vital final stretch between the Opéra, Les Halles, and Luxembourg (with President Giscard, no less, at the controls of the first train!) means that the express lines to Boissy-Saint-Léger in the southeast and Saint-Germain-en-Laye in the northwest, and the old Ligne de Sceaux to the south, are now linked in one gigantic network. This has cut traveling time dramatically for people living in the suburbs and working in Paris, and is also a great help to tourists. There are clear maps in all Métro and RER stations. You can buy combined RER and metro tickets.

A special bargain is the "tourist ticket" *(billet de tourisme)* issued by the Paris Public Transportation System (R.A.T.P.). Valid for either four or seven consecutive days, it entitles you to unlimited travel on the Métro (first class) or RER, as well as all R.A.T.P. buslines in Paris and environs. Upon presentation of your passport, you may buy the tourist ticket from the R.A.T.P. Tourist Service, 53 bis Quai des Grands Augustins, or at their excursion bureau at 20 Pl. de la Madeleine (on the right side of the church), in any of more than 50 Métro or R.E.R. stations (look for the list posted up on Métro platforms), at the six main rail stations and at the rail terminal at the Roissy-Charles-de-Gaulle airport; at the Banque Nationale de Paris, 6 Bd. des Italiens, 9e, or the Crédit Commercial de France, 103 Ave. des Champs-Elysées, 8e.

Also economical are special weekend reduced-price rail tickets covering a radius of 100 kilometers round Paris (available from main rail stations).

DISABLED VISITORS. There is an excellent booklet, *Access In Paris,* available from 68B Castlebar Road, Ealing, London W5, England, price 50p. brimful of useful advice.

GUIDES. *Bureau Officiel de Placement des Courriers et Guides,* 237 rue de Belleville, tel. 203–17–16, closed Sat. Guides are busiest weekends. Rates are 160 frs. for 3 hours, 180 frs. for 4 hrs., 300 francs for a whole day. Same price for any language. *Meet the French,* 9 Bd. des Italiens, tel. 742–6602 run by two well-connected young Frenchmen, arranges really personal service. They will even take your children to places such as the Eiffel Tower, the Grévin Waxworks Museum, or the Zoo, leaving you a whole morning or afternoon free to visit Paris at your leisure. *Le Temps de l'Amitié,* B.P.26, 75622 Paris CEDEX 13, tel. 589-18-14 (for someone who speaks English) or 331-1610, puts visitors in touch with French families in Paris and the provinces. Apply at least a month in advance if possible, especially for major holiday periods.

USEFUL ADDRESSES. *Embassies:* U.S.A., 2 Ave. Gabriel; British, 35 Fbg. St.-Honoré. *American Express,* 11 Rue Scribe. *Wagons-Lits/Cook,* 2 Pl. de la Madeleine.

Information Office, French official tourist office, 127 Ave. des Champs Elysées, tel. 720-0496, open daily from 9-6:30, closed Sun. and holidays, gives information about other parts of France, as well as Paris, makes reservations in Paris hotels. The hostesses, smartly dressed with badges, are ready to help you. Branch offices at the airports.

American Hospital, 63 Bd. Victor-Hugo, 92200 Neuilly-sur-Seine (tel: 747-53-00); *British Hospital,* 48 Rue de Villiers, 92300 Levallois-Perret (tel: 757-24-10).

Ile de France

As the Ile de la Cité is the heart of Paris, so the Ile de France is the ancient heartland of France. It is a beautiful province of grey stone villages, silver poplars and great castles, all caught in a luminous haze which fascinated Renoir, Monet, Pissaro, Sisley and other great painters who captured this landscape on canvas. The average tourist takes in the Ile de France on one or more day-long excursions from Paris. There are excellent guided tours in luxury buses to Versailles, Chantilly, Compiègne, Fontainebleau and Chartres. Or you can rent a small car in Paris for a day and be the master of your own fate on the road.

Versailles

You can reach Versailles by the *autoroute de l'ouest* (A13) via St.-Cloud or on highway N 10 via Sèvres. However you go, don't try to do all of this vast royal domain in a single day. The main château, with its fabulous gardens, created over a period of 50 years by Louis XIV, is the secular climax of French architecture. Regular tours of the palace include the huge gilded reception rooms, the royal chapel (designed by Mansart) and the celebrated Galerie des Glaces (Hall of Mirrors), where the Treaty of Versailles ending World War I was signed in 1919. Ask to visit the *petits appartements* where the king and queen actually lived and the sumptuously decorated little opera house, built by Gabriel for Louis

XV and restored in 1957. In recent years, many of the once empty rooms have been furnished with items painstakingly collected or donated from all over France and other countries, particularly the United States. The palace gardens, created by Le Nôtre, cover some 250 acres. With their lawns, flowerbeds, fountains, and ornamental canal, they are the final word in formal French gardening. As a rule, the fountains play on the first and third Sundays of the months May through September. While at Versailles you will also want to see the Grand Trianon, now completely restored. Built by Mansart for Louis XIV in 1687, it is a national museum, completely furnished in the most elegant Empire (Napoleon I) style. The Petit Trianon was ordered by Louis XV and was built by Gabriel, designer of the Place de la Concorde in Paris. This little palace was a favorite of the ill-starred Marie-Antoinette, who preferred it to the overwhelming and overcrowded atmosphere of the main château. Nearby is her model village, *le petit hameau,* where she and her companions played at being shepherdesses among flocks of perfumed sheep.

Rambouillet and Chartres

Rambouillet, the 14th-century château of Catherine de Médicis and Henry IV, an official residence for the President of France, can be visited from 10 to 12 and 2 to 6 (5 in winter) when he is away (call 483-02-49 to check, especially during the shooting season). The beautiful park is open to the public except when the flag flying from the château turret indicates that the president is in residence.

Chartres should be approached by the Ablis road across the Beauce, whence you see the cathedral spires rising from a distance of 11 miles. As Versailles is the climax of French secular architecture, so Chartres is the religious apogee. All the descriptive prose and poetry which have been lavished on this supreme cathedral can only begin to suggest the glory of its sculpture and stained glass and the strange sense of the luminous which the whole imparts even to non-believers. Recently, some of the famous stained glass windows have been restored, and some people—including the painters Bazaine and Manessier—claim they have lost their imprecise glow and become flat and "colored." Notre Dame de Chartres, built after a fire in 1194 had destroyed most of the former church (except the lying-in shirt of the Virgin, whose preservation from the flames was considered miraculous), is an extraordinary fusion of Romanesque and Gothic elements brought together at a moment when the flame of medieval faith burned brightest.

Maintenon and Malmaison

Route D.6 on the way from Chartres back to Paris will take you to Maintenon. The Château of Maintenon, with its Renaissance façade and gardens designed by Le Nôtre, is one of the most delightful small castles in France. You can visit the interior, still furnished as it was in the days of Madame de Maintenon, that amazing woman who started out as the governess of Louis XIV's children by Madame de Montespan, replaced the latter as the favorite of the king, and finally became his morganatic wife.

Other Ile de France attractions west of Paris are Mansart's masterful Château of Maisons at Maisons-Laffitte; the little river town of Bougival on the Seine, a great favorite of the Impressionist painters, and Malmaison, the authentically-furnished small château where Napoleon spent his happiest years with Josephine, and where Josephine spent her remaining years after their divorce. This is the most moving of all the Napoleonic museums.

Fontainebleau

The principal excursion south of Paris is to the Forest and Château of Fontainebleau. On the way, you pass through the village of Barbizon, immortalized in the paintings of Corot, Millet and Daumier. The famous forest of Fontainebleau is typically and delightfully French, wild and romantic, yet thoroughly mapped and classified so that every path is recorded on Touring Club maps.

The Château of Fontainebleau was begun by Louis VII in the 12th century, then was transformed into a magnificent Renaissance palace by François I, who imported Primaticcio and Rosso from Italy to direct the army of decorators employed to make the place suitable for his mistress, the Duchesse d'Étampes. The king installed Benvenuto Cellini here and bought the famous *Mona Lisa* of Leonardo to hang in one of the rooms. François' successor, Henri II, ornamented the palace with his initial interlaced with D for Diane de Poitiers, his mistress. The gardens were designed by Le Nôtre under Louis XIV, who did some remodeling of the palace according to his own classic tastes. After that, Fontainebleau declined to the status of a royal hunting lodge. Napoleon rehabilitated the place, used it as a prison for Pope Pius VII, lived here himself for a while, first with Josephine and then with his second wife, Marie Louise of Austria.

North of Fontainebleau, just outside of Melun, is the fabulous château of Vaux-le-Vicomte, built for the young Louis XIV's minister of finance, Fouquet. When the château was finished in 1661, Fouquet gave a banquet for his king which was so sumptuous that Louis XIV, wild with rage at being outshone, imprisoned Fouquet, commandeered his artists, confiscated his wealth and proceeded to build Versailles. Vaux-le-Vicomte is open to the public March 20 to October 31, 10–12 A.M., 2–6 P.M., every day.

Near Fontainebleau, on the shores of the Loing River, you'll enjoy the charming village of Moret, immortalized by Impressionist painter Alfred Sisley, who lived here for 20 years.

A short distance southeast of Fontainebleau by way of Montigny will bring you to the ancient walled town of Provins. Famous for the growing of roses since the time of the Crusades, it introduced the red rose of Provins into the arms of the House of Lancaster in the 13th century. The old ramparts still enclose orchards and winding streets as they did in the Middle Ages, and there are one or two houses still standing from the 11th century along with the magnificent 12th-century keep known as Caesar's Tower, and the 12th-century abbey church of St.-Ayoul.

Battlefields and Champagne

East of Paris, a big round trip swing of about 200 miles will take you to the World War I battlefields of the Marne, to Meaux with its 13th-century cathedral, to Château-Thierry with its ancient castle built by Charles Martel in 720 and the 16th-century mansion (open to visitors) where La Fontaine was born, and to Reims, capital of Champagne.

The cathedral of Reims, begun in 1211, is one of the triumphs of Gothic architecture and sculpture. Here, in 1429, Joan of Arc arranged the consecration of Charles VII, one of many French kings who were crowned in this splended church. Reims' other famous contribution to civilization dates from 1665, when Dom Pérignon, a monk from nearby Epernay, conceived the brilliant idea of adding sugar, and consequently effervescence, to the excellent white wine produced on the chalky slopes of Champagne. The secret formula was standardized in 1836, since which time Reims has been the capital of Champagne in every sense of the word. A visit to one of the great wine cellars will show you the process involved in producing these sparkling wines and allow you to sample some, too. Contact the town Syndicat d'Initiative for a tour of the wine cellars.

Four Great Châteaux

Completing the eastern swing, you can return to Paris by way of four notable châteaux. The first is Jossigny, inhabited by the same family since 1577; its lived-in atmosphere gives the visitor an insight into a traditional way of life that still continues in old France. The next is Guermantes, with its lovely park and charming 17th-century interior; this was the château that supplied Marcel Proust with one of his favorite place and family names. The third is Champs, used by the French president or premier as a summer residence, and built in the early 18th-century. Its most celebrated tenant was the Marquise de Pompadour, whose bedroom and sitting room you may see, decorated with *chinoiseries* by Huet. The entire château is sumptuously furnished, and the gardens of Champs are among the most attractive in Ile de France. Finally, at the eastern gates of Paris, are the woods and Château of Vincennes. In striking contrast to the luxuries of Jossigny and Champs, the 14th-century *donjon* of Vincennes sums up all the military aspects of the *château fort*. A guided tour is recommended.

North of Paris: Senlis, Compiègne, Beauvais, Chantilly

Excursions north and northeast of Paris include the delightfully unspoiled town of Senlis, only 31 miles from the capital. Its Gothic cathedral is older than Notre-Dame and Chartres. Fragments of the Gallo-Roman walls are still standing, and the ancient streets and alleys invite exploration. Continuing by way of Pierrefonds, with its heavily reconstructed, but still stunning, castle and half excavated Roman ruins, you can take the drive along the Route Eugénie through the majestic oak and beech forests that lead to historic Compiègne, where the Armistice that ended World War I was signed (you can visit the famous railway car in which this historic event took place, in a clearing in the forest). Here you should see Louis XV's impressive château; the famous Vehicle Museum; the 16th-century Hôtel de Ville built by Louis XII; the Musée des Figurines Historiques, with its 85,000 lead, tin and wooden soldiers from Vercingetorix to De Gaulle; the 12th-century tower where Joan of Arc was imprisoned before she went to the stake. Compiègne's *son et lumière* spectacles are among the best.

At the northern edge of Paris, and reachable by metro is St.-Denis, whose basilica is the necropolis of the kings of France. Outside the city are: Enghien, with its casino and thermal springs; l'Isle-Adam, a wonderful weekend spot on the Oise; and the two tourist "musts" of this area—Beauvais and Chantilly. In the unfinished cathedral of Beauvais, Gothic architecture reached its most audacious heights. The vaulted roof soars to a height of 141 feet, and the whole history of the cathedral was one of soaring ambition. In 1573, the lofty tower built over the transept in 1569 collapsed because of inadequate buttressing in the naveless church. There is still no nave, just a choir and a transept with great pillars swooping skyward.

Chantilly is famous for lace, cream, horseraces, a forest and a romantic château, built on two islands in the midst of a small lake. The château houses the Musée Condé, whose treasures include a collection of miniatures by Fouquet and the fabulous 15th-century illuminated manuscript, the *Très Riches Heures du Duc de Berri*. In the park, designed by the ubiquitous Le Nôtre, visit the charming Maison de Sylvie, and don't fail to see the magnificent 18th-century stables, built to house 240 horses. The nearby heavily restored but still evocative Gothic Royaumont Abbey will give you an idea of monastic life in the late Middle Ages.

PRACTICAL INFORMATION FOR ILE DE FRANCE

The average tourist takes in the Ile de France on one or more day-long excursions from Paris. The Paris-Metz autoroute takes you to Rheims in no time. There are quite a few good restaurants in the area, as well as pleasant country hotels and inns. Restaurants are listed E, M or I, for expensive, moderate or inexpensive. Distances are given from Paris:

BARBIZON (36 miles). Hotels: *Les Pléiades* (M) and *Bas-Bréau* (Deluxe) have attractive gardens, excellent food. *Grand Veneur* is handsome, on road to Fontainebleau, crowded on Sundays. All (E). *Les Alouettes* (M).

BEAUVAIS (45 miles). Best hotel is *Mercure*. Restaurants: *Côtelette, Marignan,* and *Crémaillière,* all (M).

BOUGIVAL (11 miles). Two famous and expensive restaurants overlooking Seine: *Le Coq Hardy* and *Camélia.*

CHANTILLY (30 miles). Hotel: *Etoile,* small (I). Restaurant *Tipperary* and *Relais Condé* are both (E). In Lys-Chantilly try the *Hostellerie du Lys,* peaceful, with restaurant (M).

CHARTRES (55 miles). Hotels: *Grand Monarque,* rather expensive with good restaurant. The *Boeuf Couronné* has a good restaurant, and the *Vieille Maison* is cozy. Both (M).

COMPIÈGNE (51 miles). Best hotels are *Résidence de la Forêt* and *Harlay* (M); *Hôtel de France et Rôtisserie du Chat qui tourne,* has good restaurant.

DAMPIERRE (23 miles). In the lovely Chevreuse valley. Hotel: *Auberge du Château,* with good restaurant. Restaurant: *La Puszta* (M), outside town. Excellent Hungarian cooking, large garden.

DAMPMART (22 miles, near Lagny). A delightful lunch or overnight place on the banks of the Marne is the *Auberge de Quincangrogne,* fairly expensive.

DREUX (51 miles). Restaurant (4½ miles away): *Le Gué des Grues,* superb (E), a few lovely rooms overlooking fields and river.

FONTAINEBLEAU (41 miles). Hotels: *Aigle Noir,* first class; *Legris et Parc, Napóléon,* moderate. Restaurants: *Filet de Sole, Chez Arrighi, Franchard* (in the forest), all (M).

GOUVIEUX (31 miles). *Restaurant Pavillon St.-Hubert* (M), on D. 162, attractively situated on the banks of the Oise River.

L'ISLE-ADAM (24 miles). *Le Cabouillet* (E), comfortable and has excellent cuisine; restaurant is (M).

IVRY-LA-BATAILLE (50 miles). The *Moulin d'Ivry* (M), long a favorite with Parisians, is a tranquil hotel-restaurant built in an old mill on the banks of the Eure river.

LAON (86 miles). Hotel: *La Bannière de France* with restaurant (M), and 4 miles S on N2 at Etouvelles, *Au Bon Accueil* inn, inexpensive.

MARLY-LE-ROI (16 miles). *Au Roy Soleil* (M), excellent. Reserve ahead.

MARNES-LA-COQUETTE (9 miles). *Hostellerie Tête Noire* (M), good restaurant.

ORGEVAL (23 miles). Hotel: *Novotel.* President Georges Pompidou is buried here.

PROVINS (52 miles). Hotel: *Fontaine,* inexpensive. Restaurant: *Chalet* (I).

RAMBOUILLET (32 miles). *Saint Charles, Relays du Chasteau,* both (I).

REIMS (89 miles). Hotels: Deluxe: *Frantel;* first-class: *Novotel* (outside town); *Bristol* (without restaurant). Restaurants: *Boyer* (E), *La Chaumière, Le Florence,* both (M); *Colbert,* with rooms (I).

ST.-GERMAIN-EN-LAYE (14 miles). *Pavillon Henri IV,* attractive, good food (M), view over Paris; golf and river beach. *Cazaudehore* (E), best restaurant in town.

SENLIS (31 miles). Hotel: *Saint-Eloi,* a typical French provincial hotel, no restaurant, moderate. Nearby *Hostellerie Farmanoir,* in one of Senlis's oldest buildings, is a delightful place to eat (M); the unpretentious little *Chatel,* on the same street, is an amazing value (I).

VERSAILLES (14 miles). Hotel *Trianon Palace* compares in luxury and outstanding food with the best in Paris. *Home Saint-Louis,* modest, charming, in historic St. Louis quarter; modern little *Angleterre. Les Trois Marches* (E), is best restaurant proper. Near château is *de la Reine. Boule d'Or* boasts of being "the oldest inn in Versailles" and dates from 1696; both (M).

VILLE D'AVRAY (10 miles). *Cabassud* (E) restaurant, by Corot's pond.

Normandy and Mont-St.-Michel

Spending just one night away from Paris, you can easily see the Invasion Coast of Normandy, the famous Bayeux Tapestries depicting the Norman invasion of England in 1066, and that marvel of French architecture, Mont-St.-Michel. This sea-surrounded mass of granite, rising 400 feet, was begun in 709. The "Marvel", or great monastery that crowns it, was built during the 13th century, and the fortifications added 200 years later to withstand attacks from the English. You approach this tiny island by a *digue* or causeway, and enter a medieval village of 250 inhabitants by three massive stone gates. If possible, time your visit so you will be there a couple of days after the full moon, when the sunsets over the Atlantic are incredibly beautiful. The guided tours during the summer are apt to be too large. Try to arrange to have a private English-speaking guide, provided by the official guide service. It is worth every extra franc for the intimate, detailed and leisurely tour. *Be careful, however:* Don't wander around on the acres of inviting-looking sand that surround Mont-St.-Michel at low tide. There are many quicksands, and also the tide rushes in at the fantastic rate of 210 feet a minute.

The Norman coast has also been swept by the great tides of history, most recently in the D-Day invasion of 1944. In the coastal town of Arromanches, you can see the landings and history of the invasion recapitulated in a diorama. The remains of Le Mulberry, the great artificial port built by the British, and the American landing beaches of Omaha and Utah are moving reminders of World War II battles. In the impressive American cemetery at St.-Laurent, the columns of white crosses will stir silent memories.

Bayeux and Caen

Nearby is Bayeux, miraculously undamaged, with its fine Norman Gothic cathedral affording a splendid view from its high central tower. The museum here houses the world-famous embroidered scroll, 235 feet long and 20 inches wide, which Queen Mathilde made in 1077, to depict, in 58 colorful scenes, the conquest of England by her husband William in 1066.

At beautiful old Caen, "city of spires", visit the 11th-century Abbaye aux Hommes and the Abbaye aux Dames, built respectively by William the Conqueror and Queen Mathilde, and see the new university and the fine new city museum.

Rouen

Even the briefest tour of Normandy should include a visit to its charming and ancient, but increasingly chic and sophisticated capital, Rouen, packed with lovely churches, chapels, towers, fountains and old cross-beamed houses, as well as poignant reminders of Joan of Arc, who was burned alive here on May 30, 1431. The restored Tour de Jeanne d'Arc and the rooms where she was kept prisoner and interrogated may be visited. Of Rouen's many architectural masterpieces, the most important are the reconstructed Cathedral of Notre Dame and the Eglise St.-Maclou. The 525-foot spire of Notre Dame, weakened by war bombing, has been restored with the rest of the cathedral.

The picturesque Rue de l'Epicerie is a war casualty, but the curious Rue Eau-de-Robec still exists, with its stream over which little bridges lead to the old houses that line it. And, before leaving town, don't fail to ride up to the 540-foot summit of Bonsecours Hill, from which the panorama over the city and the twining Seine is impressive.

Beach Resorts

Normandy's beaches are extremely popular in summer, despite the rather frigid waters of the Channel, and Deauville, the queen of them all, is still one of Europe's fashionable spots in August. The Channel resorts to the west are now fairly extensively developed, and tend to be crowded all summer, with numerous camp sites and cheap *pensions*. North of the Seine estuary, picturesque Etretat and Trouville are popular family-style vacation favorites. For more information, consult *Fodor's France*.

PRACTICAL INFORMATION FOR NORMANDY

HOW TO GET THERE. There are many fast trains from Paris to the Norman cities of Rouen, Dieppe, Le Havre, Caen etc., and autoroute A13 now takes the motorist to Deauville in 2 hrs. For something new, try the Paris-Cherbourg turbo-train. Motorcoach tours from one to three days are offered by the various travel agencies. Ferry from Southampton to Le Havre.

AVRANCHES. Hotels: *Auberge St.-Michel,* good food. *Croix d'Or,* also with restaurant.

BAGNOLES-DE-L'ORNE. Largest hotel is the top-class *Thermes.* Good restaurant: *Bois Joli* (M), also a fairly expensive hotel.

BAYEUX. The restaurant of the *Lion d'Or* hotel is not at all expensive. Reserve ahead.

CAEN. Hotels: *Novotel; Relais des Gourmets* (first class). Restaurants: *Rabelais, Joignant.*

CAUDEBEC-EN-CAUX. *Manoir de Rétival* is a pleasant quiet hotel but has no restaurant. Both are first-class moderate. *Marine* is a fine hotel-restaurant.

CHERBOURG. *Sofitel,* handsome, comfortable, first class. *Moderna,* inexpensive. Restaurants: *La Toque Blanche* (I), *Vauban* (M).

DEAUVILLE. Hotels: *Normandy* and *Royal,* both deluxe although rather old-fashioned, as is the *Golf,* 2 miles south overlooking golf course. *Fresnaye, Océan* are modest. Restaurants: *Casino Grill Room, Ambassadeurs, Ciro's* (lunch only), all (E); *Augusto* (M); *La Joyeuse, Le Nid d'Eté* (I).

DIEPPE. Hotels: *La Présidence* is best; *Univers, Windsor, du Rhin et Newhaven* are all comfortable. Restaurants: Grill in *Présidence* (M), *Horizon* in casino (E), *Armorique* (I).

ETRETAT. Best hotel is *Golf-Dormy-House,* with view of the sea and cliffs. Restaurant: *Aiguille Creuse* (M).

FECAMP. Hotel: *Poste,* comfortable, simple. First-rate regional cuisine at the *Auberge de la Rouge,* a mile south of town on N25 (M–I).

LE HAVRE. Hotels: *Bordeaux, Normandie,* both first-class moderate, without restaurant, *Monaco* (I).

HONFLEUR. Hotel: *Lechat,* moderate. Hotel-restaurant: *Ferme St.-Siméon,* rich Norman food. (E).

MONT-ST.-MICHEL. Hotel-restaurants: famous *Mère Poulard* and the less expensive *Du Guesclin.*

PONT-AUDEMER. Restaurants: The colorful and famous *Auberge du Vieux Puits* (E). Nearby at Campigny, the delightful but expensive *Petit Coq aux Champs.* Both have a few rooms.

ROUEN. Hotels: Recent are the *Mercure* (on outskirts) and *Frantel. Dieppe, Poste,* first class. The *Cathédrale* has great charm, small prices. Restaurants: *La Couronne, Le Relais Fleuri* (in Poste hotel), *Le Beffroy* are tops, (M).

LE TOUQUET. Not really Normandy, but close. Hotels: *Westminster,* luxury; *Bristol,* first class; *La Chaumière* and *White Star,* have agreeable cooking. Restaurant: smart *Flavio Club de la Forêt* (M).

TROUVILLE. Hotels: *Bellevue* and *La Résidence,* first class; *Le Flaubert, St. James, Plage,* moderate; *Reynita,* inexpensive. Restaurants: *La Régence, A La Sole Normande* (E); *L'Excelsior, Chez Marinette, Chez Max, Pergola* (M); *Carmen,* also a hotel (I).

WIMEREUX. Not quite in Normandy, but very close. Hotel: *Atlantique,* a favorite with discerning Britishers. Fine cuisine (M). Modest: *Centre.*

Brittany, Province of Contrasts

When you have gone as far west as Mont-St.-Michel, you are at the border of one of France's most unusual provinces, Brittany. A short drive from Mont-St.-Michel and you are in the marvelous walled town of the corsairs, St.-Malo, jutting out into the English Channel. Just west of it, by ferry across the estuary of the Rance, is Dinard, a delightful resort town beloved by the English since 1826, full of imposing 19th-century Gothic villas rising from the rocky shore.

Brittany is a region of infinite variety and particular charm. The Bretons are of Celtic, rather than Latin, stock, and in many places, particularly the remote villages of lower Brittany, they speak Breton, a language related to Welsh and Cornish. For the tourist, eager to discover new places and customs, Brittany offers a living tradition of folklore expressed in the costumes of the women and in the great religious festivals known as Pardons. There are colorful fishing villages, remains of a pre-Christian Druidic religion such as the megaliths of Carnac and the dolmens of Locmariaquer; superb châteaux, and churches having that particular expression of Breton art, carved stone calvaries, in the church-yards.

The holiday-seeker will be delighted with the fine sandy beaches and the gaiety of social life at such resorts as La Baule, Dinard, Concarneau and Perros-Guirec. Smaller and more modestly-priced resorts are Benodet, Pornichet, Roscoff, Carnac-Plage, and Ile de Bréhat. The tidal estuaries of the Emerald Coast are excellent havens for yachtsmen. In contrast are wild and spectacular Cap Frebel, and stormy Pointe du Raz.

PRACTICAL INFORMATION FOR BRITTANY

LA BAULE. Hotels: Deluxe: *Hermitage.* First class: *Castel Marie-Louise, Royal; Alexandra, Bellevue Plage, Christina.* Moderate: *Welcome.* Restaurants: *Castel Marie-Louise* is probably best, closely followed by *Hermitage* restaurant (both E). Also *Espadon, Chez Henri,* both (M).

BÉNODET. Hotel: Comfortable *Gwell-Kaër.* Restaurant: *Jeanne d'Arc,* 3½ miles away outside town at Sainte-Marine; pleasant *Ferme du Lerty* no longer has rooms.

CARNAC. Best hotels are the *Diana* and *Britannia* at Carnac-Plage. Restaurants: *Lann Roz* (M) and *La Grande Métairie* (I).

CONCARNEAU. Hotels: *Ty Chupen-Gwenn* (M) and *Sables Blancs* (I) in town. At Concarneau-Sud, *La Belle Etoile,* hotel and bungalows. Restaurants: *Duquesne,* on the port; *La Douane,* a typical family restaurant. Both (M).

DINARD. Hotels: *Grand* and *Roche-Corneille.* Four miles southeast at Jouvente is the restful little *Hostellerie de Jouvente.* Restaurant: *La Coquille.*

NANTES. Hotels: *Duchesse Anne* (I), *Central* (M) and *Terminus* (I) new *Sofitel Jacques Borel,* and outside town, motel-types: recent *Frantel* and *Novotel.* Restaurants: *Les Maraîchers* (E), *Delphin* (M–E), *La Rôtisserie* (M)

PERROS-GUIREC. Hotels: *Grand Hôtel de Trestraou; Printania,* first class; *France,* moderate. Restaurants: *Les Rochers* (also hotel), *Le Homard Bleu,* both (E). *Crémaillère* (I).

PONT-AVEN. Best restaurant in Brittany, and, in fact, one of the best in France, is the *Moulin Rosmadec.* Essential to reserve ahead (M–E).

QUIBERON. Hotels: *Sofitel,* newest, handsome. *Beau-Rivage* and *Hoche,* both moderate. Restaurant: *Ker-Noyal* (also hotel) (M).

RENNES. Hotels: *Novotel, Frantel, Président.* Restaurants: *Le Corsaire, Ti-Koz, Auberge St.-Sauveur* all (M).

ROSCOFF. Hotels: *Régina* and *Talabardon.* Restaurant: *Goûter Breton* (M).

ST. MALO. Hotels: *Central, Duguesclin* (outside the walls), comfortable; *Hostellerie Grotte aux Fées* less expensive. Restaurants: *Chez Chuche,* chic; *Duchesse Anne,* both (M). Popular *crêperies: Corps de Garde* and *Chantal* (I).

Burgundy and its Vineyards

An easy day's drive southeast of Paris will lead you through the famous vineyards, the undulating countryside and the stone villages of Burgundy, one of the gastronomic centers of Europe's most gastronomic country.

Burgundy has more than a hundred well-preserved châteaux, many still family-inhabited, which have now opened their doors to the public.

Dijon and Area

At Dijon, capital of the province, wine quite literally flows in the Barenzai fountain during the September wine festival, and during the annual November Gastronomic Fair, gourmets can sniff, taste, sip and sample all sorts of French regional foods, as well as exotic foreign fare. Dijon, the ancient capital of the dukes of Burgundy, is considered to be one of the most complete cities in France from an artistic and intellectual point of view; the Ducal Palace, the first-rate Museum of Fine Arts, with a new and excitingly arranged modern section, and the 14th-century Chartreuse of Champmol are among the outstanding sights here.

Even if you aren't lucky enough to be in Burgundy during a wine festival, don't miss the fascinating wine district, a wonderful treat for both palate and eye. At Gevrey-Chambertin you may taste the famous Chambertin wine, prized above all wines by Napoleon. Clos-Vougeot's 16th-century Renaissance château rises in the midst of the vineyards planted by the monks of the Abbey of Cîteaux, whose ruins may be visited on this wine tour.

Beaune

Nuits-St.-Georges has been producing superb wines since Roman times. Stop here for a look and a sip before proceeding south to Beaune, capital of the great region known as the Côte de Beaune (including the famous vineyards of Pommard and Volnay) and chief wine center of Burgundy. Here in the skillfully restored 15th-century Hôtel des Ducs de Bourgogne is a Wine Museum, tracing the entire history of winemaking and the step-by-step process by which the sunshine of France is captured in bottles. There is one other "must" in Beaune: the celebrated Hôtel-Dieu or Hospice de Beaune, a hospital which has been receiving patients since it was first built in 1450. In its museum there is medieval and surgical equipment that will cure any romantic historical notions. But the chief attraction of the Hospice is the priceless polyptych of *The Last Judgment* by Roger Van der Weyden.

Burgundy's Art Towns

Even if there were not a drop of wine in Burgundy, this province, rich in history, art, and tradition, would be worth an extended visit. The remarkable Treasure of Vix, in the museum of Châtillon-sur-Seine, includes objects that decorated the tomb of a Celtic princess buried more than 2,500 years ago. At Vézelay, Autun, and Cluny you will find magnificent examples of the Romanesque architecture and art that flourished here with amazing vigor in the 12th century. A visit to the hill town of Vézelay and its splendid church of the Madeleine is especially recommended, also medieval Tournus, where the rose-colored stone Abbey of St.-Philibert heralded the dawn of Romanesque architecture.

PRACTICAL INFORMATION FOR BURGUNDY

HOW TO GET THERE. *American Express, Cook's,* the *SNCF* and the *Compagnie Française de Tourisme* offer two- and three-day motorcoach tours of this region from Paris, including "Gastronomic Weekends". There are fast trains from Paris to Dijon (about 2½ hrs.). A small airline called Air Alsace has a direct flight daily, except Saturday, London (Gatwick)–Dijon (1hr. 10min.).

HOTELS AND RESTAURANTS

AUTUN. Hotel: *St.-Louis et Poste,* famous with gourmets and those who love fine living, expensive. Garden for summer dining.

AUXERRE. Hotels: *Maxime* (first-class moderate); *Fontaine,* good cuisine, moderate.

AVALLON. Hotel: *Poste* has one of the best restaurants in the country. Expensive.

In the Vallée du Cousin, 2 miles west on D.427, is the *Hostellerie du Moulin des Ruats.* (E).

BEAUNE. Hotels: *Poste,* excellent comfort, pleasant restaurant (E); *Le Cep,* small, charming, with pool, in old Burgundy house, moderate. New *Bourgogne* (E), with pool, terrace, attractive restaurant. On the Chalons road, the comfortable *Motel Relais de Bourgogne. Motel Relais P.L.M.* on city outskirts. Restaurants: *Poste* (E), *Calèche* (in *Bourgogne* hotel), *Cloche* (M), *Central Hotel* restaurant (M).

CHAGNY. Hotel-restaurant: *Lameloise,* absolutely perfect (E), some lovely rooms.

DIJON. *Central, Chapeau Rouge,* with good restaurant, *Europe,* all first-class. *Pressoir,* moderate. Heading south is the *Novotel-Dijon* (M). Restaurants: *Grill* in the Central Hotel (M), *Chapeau Rouge* (M). *Pré aux clercs et Trois Faisans* (M–E); *Rallye, Chouette* (in attractive old street), both (M).

GEVREY-CHAMBERTIN. Restaurant, *La Rôtisserie du Chambertin* (M), high quality.

MÂCON. Hotels: *Frantel* (first-class). On A6: *Novotel* and *Jacques Borel.* Restaurant: Mme. Duret continues to uphold the reputation of her *Auberge Bressane* (M-E).

MONTBARD. Tucked away in the inauspicious little *Hôtel de la Gare* is a fine restaurant (M).

SAULIEU. Hotels: *Côte d'Or* with famous restaurant (E), *Poste* (M).

TOURNUS. Restaurant: *Greuze* (M), a "must". A few rooms available.

VÉZELAY. Hotels: *Poste et Lion d'Or,* very comfortable; *Cheval Blanc,* inexpensive.

Lyon and the Rhône Area

Busy bustling Lyon, France's second-biggest town after Paris, is surprisingly little known to foreign tourists, who tend to pass through on their way down south, maybe stopping off for a gastronomic meal (at astronomic prices, more than likely, but undoubtedly worth it) in the heartland of French *haute cuisine.* Because of its very size, Lyon doesn't perhaps have the immediate appeal of many of France's fine towns, but it's certainly worth visiting the fascinating Vieux Lyon, the "old city", which contains one of the most beautiful groups of medieval and Renaissance buildings in France. Try to visit the medieval city of Pérouges, unchanged through the centuries.

Valence is attractively situated on the Rhône (the Maison des Têtes and the Cathedral are certainly worth a visit), while Montélimar (world-famous for its nougat) is a good starting-point for many delightful excursions in the lavender-filled region stretching towards the Alps: Grignan has an interesting *château* where Madame de Sévigné used to stay; Nyons is a particularly pleasant small town. On the other side of the Rhône (and the *autoroute*) the Ardèche has much to offer for those who like exploring places off the beaten tourist track.

Alas! we have no space here to do justice to this little-known region of France, but we hope that we've whetted your appetite and that the few hotels and restaurants we give below will enable you to branch out on your own.

PRACTICAL INFORMATION FOR LYON AND THE RHÔNE REGION

HOW TO GET THERE. Frequent fast trains from Paris to Lyon (all the trains heading for the Riviera and Italy stop there). British Airways and Air France fly London–Lyon direct, daily. Lyon's newish Satolas Airport has direct flights to the U.S., and there are many internal flights to Paris, Nice, Marseille, and so on.

HOTELS AND RESTAURANTS

BOURG–EN–BRESSE. Just outside the town limits at Brou, opposite the magnificent flamboyant Gothic cathedral, is the superb restaurant *Auberge Bressane* (E), not to be missed if you're a true gourmet.

GRIGNAN. Small, modest *Sévigné* (no restaurant).

LYON. Hotels: Deluxe: *Sofitel,* recent, overlooking Rhône river, with superb terrace restaurant. *P.L.M. Terminus* is first-class superior; *Carlton, Beaux Arts, Bordeaux et Parc* and the *Frantel* are all first class moderate; *Verdun* is still three-star, but a little cheaper; *Angleterre, Russie,* moderate, *Moderne,* inexpensive.

At Lyon-Satolas Airport, the first-class *Méridien-Constellation;* at the smaller Bron Airport, the recent *Novotel.* Another *Novotel* at the northern exit of city. Also on northern outskirts, at the "Porte de Lyon" complex at Dardilly, junction of the Autoroute du Sud and the N6, *Holiday Inn,* and *Mercure.*

Restaurants: In this, France's capital of gastronomy, we can only provide the briefest selection. *Mère Guy* (E), located west of the Saône river; central are *Mère Brazier, Nandron, Vettard, Léon de Lyon, La Bonne Auberge, Chez Juliette,* all (M).

Outside town: at Charbonnières-les-Bains, 5 miles west on N.7, *La Sangria* (M); at Collonges, ¾ mile north on N.433 and D.51, *Paul Bocuse, au Pont de Collonges,* one of France's top restaurants. Twelve miles away at Mionnay is yet another not-to-be missed *Alain Chapel* (formerly called *La Mère Charles*). The latter two, of course, are both (E).

MONTELIMAR. Hotels: *Relais de l'Empereur,* fairly expensive, with garden and good restaurant; *Parc Chabaud,* quiet, attractive, with garden, a bit cheaper; *Auberge de la Crémaillière,* moderate; *Dauphiné-Provence* (I). Good restaurant at L'Homme d'Armes, 2½ miles away: *La Bastide* (M). Motel: *National 7.*

NYONS. Hotels: *Alizés, Caravelle,* both first-class moderate, without restaurant. At Aubres, 2½ miles away, is the small and peaceful *Auberge du Vieux Village,* with a nice view (M).

PÉROUGES. Hotel: *Ostellerie Vieux Pérouges,* an enchanting old hostelry. The setting alone makes it worth a visit. Moderately expensive.

PONT-DE-VAUX. This tiny town, about 4 miles north of Mâcon on N.433, has three small but good-value hotel-restaurants: *Commerce, Raisin* and *Reconnaissance.*

VALENCE. *Hôtel 2000* (no restaurant) and *Novotel* (just outside town) are best; *Négociants,* modest. Restaurant: *Pic* is one of the best-known restaurants in France, and also has 10 rooms.

VONNAS. *Chez la Mère Blanc,* a famous restaurant (E), with rooms, between Mâcon and Bourg.

VIENNE. *Résidence de la Pyramide,* a comfortable small hotel adjoining the world-famous restaurant. *Nord,* inexpensive.

Restaurants: *Pyramide* (E) (closed Tues. and Nov. 1 to Dec. 15), is one of the world's most famous restaurants, in a charming garden. Somewhat cheaper is the *Le Petit Ruinais,* 5 miles on N502.

The Châteaux of the Loire

The valley watered by the broad and shallow Loire is one of the most beautiful areas of France. It was here in the 15th and 16th century that the kings of France chose to build their fabulous *châteaux d'agrément,* or pleasure castles, and these are the chief attractions of a region rich in history. The best known of the châteaux, Amboise, Azay-le-Rideau, Blois, Chambord and Chenonceaux, date from the Renaissance and reflect the luxury and elegance of that epoch. But many were built as defensive fortresses in the Middle Ages, and you will see the stern necessities of feudal life in the massive walls of Châteaudun, Chinon, Langeais and Loches. To round out the picture, you should visit one of the later "classical" châteaux of the 17th or 18th century—Cheverny, for example, or Valençay. Before scheduling your visit to the château country, inquire about the dates of its *son et lumière* (sound and light) spectacles.

"The Five Ch's"

If your time is very limited, you can get an excellent idea of the château country from the "five Ch's"—Chambord, royal palace built by François I in the midst of a hunting preserve as big as the whole city of Paris; Chenonceaux, the lovely castle built across the Cher River and given by Henri II to his mistress, Diane de Poitiers; Chaumont, the rather forbidding-looking castle to which Henri II's widow sent Diane when the king died; Chinon, the fortified château where Joan of Arc performed her first miracle in 1429 by recognizing the Dauphin in disguise among 300 of his courtiers; and Cheverny, sumptuously furnished 17th-century château, still inhabited by a descendant of the original owners, but open to the public. Chinon, by the way, was one of the few towns of the Loire to escape excessive damage during World War II. Few other towns in France have more medieval atmosphere than the ancient center.

Abbeys and a Cathedral

Aside from the châteaux, there are three other major architectural attractions of this region. They are the Abbey of St.-Benoît-sur-Loire, dating from the year 1,000, one of the great achievements of Romanesque art; the Gothic cathedral of Bourges, one of the most beautiful in

France, with its five sculptured portals, its high vaulted roof and magnificent stained glass windows; and the Abbey of Fontevrault, which once housed a community of 5,000 monks and nuns.

In the latter, you may have the experience of being temporarily in prison, since part of the abbey is used as a government house of correction. But don't let that detail keep you from visting the curious, domed octagonal tower, one of the few remaining medieval kitchens in Europe, and above all, the abbey church. Here, in a pure Romanesque nave of white stone, unmarred by Gothic or Baroque additions, is the necropolis of the Angevin sovereigns—Eleanor of Aquitaine and her second husband, Henry II of England; their famous son, Richard Coeur de Lion, and their daughter-in-law, Isabelle of Angoulême, wife of England's King John. Their tombs lie side by side in the empty nave, surmounted by their polychrome statues.

PRACTICAL INFORMATION FOR THE LOIRE VALLEY

HOW TO GET THERE. The *SNCF* (French National Railroads), *Compagnie Française de Tourisme, American Express,* and *Thomas Cook* all run motorcoach tours of the château country from Paris during the summer months, usually of 2 to 3 days duration. If you are driving yourself, the most direct way from Paris is by the Autoroute to Orléans. If you have more time, take the more scenic Route des Pyrénées (N.10) from Paris to Tours via Versailles, Rambouillet, Chartres and Châteaudun. If pressed for time, *Air Inter* will fly you there in 2½ hours. The four principal excursion centers in the château country are Orléans, Blois, Tours and Angers. From Tours you can tour the Loire valley on board the British Hovercraft SRN 6: all information from the Syndicat d'Initiative in Tours.

DISABLED VISITORS. An excellent new booklet, *Access in the Loire,* full of helpful information obtained by on-the-spot surveying by a mixed group of handicapped and able-bodied people, is available from 68B Castlebar Road, Ealing, London W5, England (free of charge, though a contribution to cover postage would be appreciated).

HOTELS AND RESTAURANTS

While you are in the château country, don't forget to sample the wines produced from the vineyards that line the banks of the Loire. They are predominantly white. The dry ones are *Pouilly-sur-Loire, Quincy, Sancerre* and *Muscadet.* Sweeter and more full-bodied are the splendid *Vouvray, Saumur, Coteaux du Layon* and *Rosé d'Anjou.* The locally-produced red wines you should try are *Chinon* and *Bourgueil.*

AMBOISE. Highest recommendation to *Le Choiseul,* Louis XV décor. Excellent restaurant (E). Across the river is the *St.-Vincent,* inexpensive, with restaurant. At Chargé, a mile from Amboise, is the *Château de Pray,* a converted 12th-cent. castle with formal gardens, moderate.

ANGERS. Hotels: first-class *Concorde; Anjou,* central, garage. Also near château and cathedral are the moderate *Royal,* and the *Croix de Guerre.* A little farther out is the *Boule d'Or,* with garage. Restaurants: *Boule d'Or* (hotel). *Vert d'Eau,* near Hôtel Anjou. *Croix de Guerre* (hotel).

BEAUGENCY. Hotels: *Abbaye,* a pleasant place to stop, moderate, good cuisine. *Ecu de Bretagne,* comfortable. *Cuisine* (I) best in town.

LES BEZARDS. The *Auberge des Templiers* (E) is a supremely elegant rustic retreat and a favorite among Parisians.

BLOIS. Hotels: *Château,* and *Gare et Terminus,* with garage and restaurant, are situated behind the château. More atmospheric is the little *Hostellerie Loire,* on the Paris-Tours road below the castle, with river view, with good restaurant. *Grand-Cerf,* across from château. Small, excellent. *Novotel* (outside town).
At Les Grouëts, 3 miles from Blois, is the moderate *Relais Fleuri,* formerly a château, in delightful park setting.
Restaurants: *Loire* (hotel) (M). In town, *Tour d'Argent,* a small hotel restaurant, cheaper.

BOURGES. Hotels: *Angleterre,* first class. *Le Berry* and *Olympia* are moderate.
Restaurant: *Jacques Coeur* (M) (closed weekends and mid-July to mid-August). Very good.

CHAMBORD. The *St.-Michel* is comfortable and moderate.

CHAUMONT. Hotel: *Hostellerie du Château,* quiet, pool, excellent classical cooking.

CHENONCEAUX. Hotels: *Bon Laboureur et Château,* moderate and *Ottoni,* first class, both small, on main Tours road, not far from château.
Restaurants: *Bon Laboureur* (M), *Gâteau Breton* (I).

CHINON. Hotels: *Gargantua,* central, near château. Housed in 15th-cent. former residence of Baillis, its rooms are reasonably priced. *Boule d'Or,* river view, restaurant.
Restaurants: *Gargantua* (hotel); *Auberge St.-Jean,* with a few rooms. Both (M).

COUR-CHEVERNY. Hotels: *Trois Marchands,* best. Good restaurant. Also *Saint-Hubert.* Both (M).

MARÇAY. *Château de Marçay,* medieval, now a hotel, a few miles south of Chinon. Excellent cuisine (E).

MONTBAZON. Hotels: super-deluxe *Château d'Artigny,* superb restaurant, rooms furnished with period pieces, very expensive, a bit stuffy, and *Domaine de la Tortinière,* more intimate, quite reasonable.

ORLÉANS. Hotels: Newest: *Sofitel* (deluxe); *Les Arcades,* best with river view. More central, *Moderne.* At Orléans-La Source, the recent *Novotel.*
One mile from town, on the Blois-Orléans road, is the attractive *Auberge de la Montespan,* with garden restaurant of James Bond fame. *Motel des Bruyères,* south on N. 20.
Restaurants: *Jeanne d'Arc* (I), in center of town. Good food. *Auberge St.-Jacques,* excellent. *Auberge de la Montespan* (M), hotel terrace overlooking river.

ROANNE. Restaurant: *Troisgros* (M), run by father and sons, is one of France's best; makes a stopover in this uninteresting industrial town a true gourmet experience.

TOURS. Hotels: first class *Métropole* and *Bordeaux,* all with good restaurants. *Méridien* (formerly *Trois Rivières*), newest, has pool, bar, discothèque. Recent *Châteaux de la Loire,* is charming, moderate; *Italia* is inexpensive.

Restaurants: *Barrier* (E) (at nearby St. Symphorien) is another of France's very top restaurants. Also owned by Charles Barrier, and run by a young son and daughter-in-law, is *La Petite Marmite,* right next door, simple delicious food at minimum prices. *Le Lyonnais* (M) is another good choice, as are *Buré* and *Le Turone,* both (M), and *Le Trou Normand* (M–I).

Provence

The southern sector of the Rhône Valley, known as Provence (from *Provincia Romana),* will offer you some of the most perfect monuments of classical and medieval heritage under the Mediterranean sun. Although that sun can be awfully hot in summer, July is the month for the great music and drama festivals, staged amidst such magnificent surroundings as the amphitheater at Nîmes, the Palace of the Popes at Avignon, and the great Roman theater at Orange. The most famous of these summer offerings are the music festival at Aix-en-Provence and the Avignon drama festival. Reserve places long in advance if you want to attend (through your travel agent or the French National Tourist Office).

The outstanding antiquities of Provence include Orange's splendidly preserved Roman theater (seating 10,000) and its Triumphal Arch of Tiberius (49 B.C.); the Gallo-Roman city of Vienne with its perfectly-preserved Temple of Augustus and Livia; and Nîmes, a treasure house of Roman antiquities with its harmonious Maison Carrée, its vast arena and Roman baths. Nearby is the superb, three-tiered Roman aqueduct, the famous Pont du Gard, a miracle of engineering, still intact after 2,000 years.

Arles, "the little Rome of the Gauls", is one of the most fascinating of Provençal towns. You can see bullfights in its arena, capable of accommodating 25,000 spectators, and stroll down the Alyscamps, a pagan burial ground lined with Roman sarcophagi, transformed during the Middle Ages into a Christian cemetery. At St.-Rémy-de-Provence are some of the most interesting excavations in the Mediterranean area. So far, two ancient cities have been unearthed—a Gallo-Greek city dating from the second century B.C. and, at Les Antiques, the Gallo-Roman city of Glanum. The Roman remains at Vaison-la-Romaine are almost as complete as those of Pompeii, though less extensive.

Among the masterpieces of post-classical times, you should not miss the superb Romanesque Church of St.-Trophime in Arles with its 12th-century cloister, filled with remarkable statuary; the machicolated battlements of Avignon and the huge Palace of the Popes, dominating the town with its massive splendor. East of Avignon is the famous Fontaine de Vaucluse, an idyllic oasis where Petrarch retired at the age of 33. See also the impressive Carthusian monastery of Villeneuve-les-Avignon across the river, and St.-Bernard's Abbey of Sénanque, one of the finest Cistercian abbeys in France.

Aix-en-Provence

Finally, before swinging down to Marseille and the Riviera, you should not miss Aix-en-Provence, a lovely city which manages to keep its classical calm despite the growth of its suburbs. The famous Cours Mirabeau, a magnificent avenue lined with shady plane trees, is the

Champs-Elysées of Aix. Visit the Fine Arts Museum, in Rue du Quatre Septembre near the 17th-century Fountain of the Dolphins. Nearby is the studio of painter Paul Cézanne, one of Aix's greatest citizens. Lovingly restored by American admirers of the artist, the *atelier* is exactly as it was when Cézanne worked there. See also the Cathedral of St.-Sauveur, with its wealth of architectural styles, dating from the fifth to the 16th centuries, and the famous collection of Beauvais tapestries in the adjacent museum.

PRACTICAL INFORMATION FOR PROVENCE

HOW TO GET THERE. The *rail* route from Paris to Provence is via Dijon and Lyon, thence down the Rhône Valley. The overnight *Blue Train* and the daytime *Mistral* (TEE, supplementary fare) will take you from Paris' Gare de Lyon to Avignon in 6 hrs. The fastest *car* route from Paris to Provence is by the Nord-Sud Autoroute to Avignon or Aix-en-Provence (tolls all the way). A suggested alternative is to drive down by way of Nevers, Moulins, Vichy, Le Puy, Aubenas and Pont-St.-Esprit, joining N. 7 at Bollène; or, from Lyon you can head for Grenoble and the Route Napoléon (N. 85) via Gap, Sisteron and Digne.

Four direct flights weekly London–Marseille.

HOTELS

AIX-EN-PROVENCE. The *Roy René,* and *P.L.M. Le Pigeonnet* are both first class, with good restaurants. Moderate are the *Relais St.-Christophe,* with restaurant, and the *Europe.* About a mile out, motel *Relais du Soleil* (M), on N. 7. There are two *Novotels* outside town.

ARLES. *Jules César,* comfortable; *D'Arlatan,* 15th-cent. Provençal-style; *Calendal,* quiet; *Cloître,* in an old cloister; central *Nord-Pinus* and *Forum.* All moderate.

AVIGNON. *Holiday Inn,* newest. *Europe,* outstanding restaurant, fine cellar, first class. On outskirts, *Novotel, Sofitel J. Borel.* Comfortable hotels in city center: *Bristol-Terminus,* new *Cité des Papes* (M); *Louvre, Midi, Régina* (I).

At Noves, 8 miles S.E., an extraordinary but fairly expensive inn: *L'Auberge de Noves.*

LES BAUX. In village, *Hostellerie de la Reine Jeanne* (M); elegant *Oustaù Baumanière* and *Cabro d'Or; Mas d'Aigret,* new, lovely view from terrace.

MEYRARGUES. *Château de Meyrargues,* perched on a hill; top-notch restaurant, a few rooms.

NÎMES. *Mapotel Impérator,* deluxe, attractive location. Also deluxe, *Luxe Hôtel J. Borel. Midi, Carrière,* moderate. *Majestic, Univers,* inexpensive. *Novotel,* on outskirts, unattractive location, but comfortable. All except Majestic, Univers have restaurants.

PONT-DU-GARD. *Vieux Moulin* has a magnificent view of the aqueduct, illuminated at night. *Pont du Gard,* on the opposite bank, faces same sight. Both moderate. Small *Auberge Blanche,* inexpensive.

ST.-RÉMY-DE-PROVENCE. *Hostellerie du Vallon de Valrugues,* beautiful, not too expensive; *Arts,* small, comfortable, fine meals at modest prices. *Château de Roussan,* attractive, moderate.

VILLENEUVE-LES-AVIGNON. An exceptionally pleasant and attractive place to stay is *Le Prieuré* first class, wonderful food. The *Hostellerie Provençale du Vieux Moulin,* and *La Magnanerie* with pool, are both good.

RESTAURANTS

AIX-EN-PROVENCE Best food in the hotel-restaurants *Roy René* and *Riviera.* Then *Charvet* (E), *La Rotonde* (I).

ARLES. *Vaccarès,* low-cost menus. *Brasserie Provençale, Hostellerie des Arènes, La Grappe,* all (I). *Criquet, Le Galoubet,* budget.

AVIGNON. The *Hiely* (M), is extraordinarily good (usually closed Tues.). At nearby Angles is the marvellous *Ermitage-Meissonnier.*

BAUX, LES *Oustau de la Baumanière* (E): here you will be served one of the best meals in France, though there are occasional lapses; flowered terrace, pool. A few rooms are available, reserve ahead. *Cabro d'Or* (E), under same management. *La Riboto de Taven* (M), with a lovely terrace at the foot of the dramatic rocks.

VILLENEUVE-LES-AVIGNON. *Le Prieuré* (hotel), expensive but delightful, and easily worth a detour. For less expensive wining and dining, try the *Hostellerie Provençale du Vieux Moulin* (hotel), with sundrenched terrace overlooking the Rhône.

The Riviera—Pleasure Coast

From Marseille, east to Menton and the Italian border, stretches one of the most famous coastlines in the world, the French Riviera. From St.-Raphaël to the frontier, this coast is protected by the Alpes Maritimes, and the countryside breaks out in a riot of exotic vegetation—orange, eucalyptus, lemon, olive and pink laurel fill the air with their perfume, while palms and cactus lend a tropical atmosphere to the scenery. This is the sun-kissed Côte d'Azur, along which are strung the famous resorts of St.-Tropez, Port Grimaud, Cannes, Antibes, Nice and Menton. Here, it is worth while to visit out-of-season, since July, and most particularly August, are horribly crowded. There is always something going on on the Côte d'Azur: horseracing, automobile rallies, fashion shows, concerts, ballets and folk festivals. The most famous event of the year is the fabulous 10-day Carnival of Nice.

Unfortunately, the natural beauties of this coastline are becoming more difficult to find every year as gigantic marinas and building developments cover the sea-fronts with a wall of cement and sea and beaches grow more polluted. However, one can still discover patches of extraordinary beauty and secluded coves, often reached only by foot or boat.

In busy, animated Marseille, one of the world's most colorful big ports, you should see the celebrated Canebière, the main drag, bordered with luxury shops and enormous cafés; the Museum of Fine Arts; Le Corbusier's stunning La Cité Radieuse, and the Château d'If, from which Dumas' Count of Monte Cristo made his famous escape. See the *calanques,* cobalt blue miniature fiords of Cassis and take one of the fascinating guided tours through a perfume factory at Grasse.

Aside from the Mediterranean beaches, you should plan several drives to the nearby hill villages, ancient towns fortified against the Saracens— Vence, St.-Paul-de-Vence, Ramatuelle, Grimaud, Eze, Cagnes and Gourdon, all of which offer magnificent views.

The "Modern Art Road"

If you want to take the "Modern Art Road", start from Cannes and follow N. 7 to Vallauris, the charming pottery town to which Picasso brought world fame. Your next trip should be to delightful Antibes and its seafront Grimaldi Museum, a wonderful old castle in which are paintings and ceramics by Picasso. Go inland to Biot for the museum dedicated to the work of Fernand Léger; visit Renoir's home in Cagnes, and go to Vence for the celebrated Chapelle du Rosaire, decorated by Matisse (open only Tuesdays and Thursdays). Nearby, at St.-Paul-de-Vence, is the Maeght Foundation of Modern Art, where you can see works by Giacometti, Matisse, Miró, Bonnard and other lesser-known experimental painters and sculptors. In Nice, do not miss a visit to the Musée Matisse in the Cimiez quarter and the Chagall Museum; in Cannes, the stimulating Galerie des Ponchettes and the Riviera Villa Museum, home of painter Jean-Gabriel Domergue. At St.-Tropez, you'll enjoy the Museum of the Annonciade. The wedding ceremony room in the City Hall of Menton and the little fishermen's chapel at Villefranche were beautiful decorated by Jean Cocteau.

PRACTICAL INFORMATION FOR THE RIVIERA

 HOW TO GET THERE. There are daily flights between Nice and London (under 2 hrs.), Marseille, Lyon (summer only); several flights a day from Paris to Nice and Marseille, and daily New York-Nice flights. By car, the fastest route from Paris is via the Autoroute du Sud. Car-sleeper overnight trains to St.-Raphaël and Avignon save time and nerves, if not money. The *Compagnie Française de Tourisme* and *Europabus* have weekly motor coach tours to the Riviera and *Europabus* has a straight two-day trip Paris-Nice. By train from Paris, the daytime *Mistral* takes 7 hrs. to Nice, the *Train Bleu,* overnight, about 12 hrs. The TEE *Rhodanien* reaches Marseille in 6½ hrs. The most convenient train from the Channel is the *Flandre-Riviera Express* from Calais to San Remo.

TRANSPORTATION. There are frequent local bus services along the coast. The roads are very good. If you have your own car, the coast road from St.-Raphaël as far as Nice covers the high points of this section. From Nice to Menton you have choice of three *corniches:* the *Shoreline Corniche,* through Beaulieu and Monaco, often curving around high rocky promontories but with the Mediterranean always at your side; the *Middle* or *Moyenne Corniche,* darting inland to Eze and thence down to Monaco; and the *Grande Corniche,* with its splendid mountain panorama and hairpin bends amid the heights of the Alpes Maritimes. The Naviplane service connects Nice, Cannes, St.-Tropez, San Remo.

BEACHES. You might expect to find the best beaches near the popular resorts of Cannes, Nice, Monte Carlo and Menton. Actually, except for Cannes, these beaches are rather poor. At Cannes, the once-narrow sandy beach is being widened yearly with sand brought from Fréjus, and it is now quite a respectable size. Nice is also growing a sandy beach. From Nice to the Italian border, the beaches are of gravel or shingle. Between Cannes and St.-Raphaël is the magnificent Corniche, which, although breathtaking in beauty, provides little in the way of swim spots.

The best beaches are located along the more than 60 miles of coast from Ste.-Maxime to Hyères—at Cavalaire, Le Lavandou, St.-Clair, Cavalière, Pampelone; these range from tiny jewel-like crescent beaches to dazzling ones that sweep for over 3 miles along the sea. Off-season, they are all clean, fine, white-sand beaches that slope gently into the sea. From July 15-Aug. 31 when hordes sweep down, they become dirty and disagreeable.

Some beaches are "public", and crowded; but on most you pay for a spot of your own, with umbrella and chair. Prices vary from about 10 to 30 frcs. per day.

MONEY-SAVING TIP. The city of Nice has introduced a new scheme which could save you a lot of money. The Tourist Offices at the station or airport and the City Transport Office near Place Masséna will issue you with a *carte touristique* which entitles you to free entry to the city's museums *plus* free bus travel for 7 days. What's more, they'll give you a folder containing maps and bus routes, *and* their new "Love Nice" card which will entitle you to all sorts of reductions (at the opera, theaters and cinemas, and 5–10% at a long list of the city's finest shops and stores). Your travel agent may be able to give you a card if you book your stay within France.

CASINOS. This is the fastest place in the world to lose a buck while attempting to break the bank. Nice has four casinos, Cannes two, one at Juan-les-Pins, and three at Monte Carlo (see Monaco chapter). The French casino is more than an elegant gambling den. It's usually the center of social life, scene of concerts, movies, gala dinners and cabarets.

NIGHTCLUBS. The main nightclub centers are St.-Tropez, Cannes, Juan-les-Pins, Nice and Monte Carlo. St.-Tropez caters to a young and frivolous set, as well as to the wealthy but equally frivolous yacht-owners. Juan-les-Pins has a febrile, honkey-tonk night life that goes on into the wee hours. In Cannes, the accent is on international café society. Nice is nice for nudes.

ANTIBES. *La Siesta,* nightclub, restaurant. Karting, bowling, dancing—all fun, all day and night.

CANNES. *Aux Ambassadeurs* is the dinner-dance department of the Municipal Casino. Also at the Casino: *New-Brummel,* elegant.

Palm Beach Casino is even more stylish and exclusive. You really belong if you can manage an invitation, although dinners are not exactly given away. Open only in summer.

Whisky à Gogo, 115 Ave. de Lérins. At present one of the most popular late spots.

Play Girl Club—La Chimère, Ave. de Lérins, and *Roxy,* 10 Rue Tesseire, specialize in entertainment for the "third sex".

At Valbonne, 7½ miles from Cannes, in the mountains, you'll find the two most fashionable nightclubs of the area: the *Val de Cuberte,* with its pool where all sorts of people swim fully clothed; and the exotically decorated, but comfortable discothèque, *Akou-Akou,* which also has a pool.

NICE. *Casino Ruhl* (in Hotel Méridien) is very smart and has everything—floor-show, discothèque, gambling rooms etc.

A local favorite is *La Pignata,* 242 Chemin de Fabron: dinner and comic show (best to know French), Mini-*corrida* (yes, really!) in summer.

Au Pizzaiolo, 4bis Rue du Pont-Vieux, has a crazy madcap show.

JUAN-LES-PINS. Nightlife in Juan these days is very much for the young crowd; try *Cha in Cha* or *La Maison des Pêcheurs* if you're still close to twenty and like a lot of noise—otherwise we recommend you stick to the *Siesta* at the Pont de la Brague (see Antibes entry).

STE.-MAXIME. The Riviera's most attractive nightspot, *St.-Hilaire-de-la-Mer,* run by François Patrice, looks out over a calm sea.

ST.-TROPEZ. The 'in' spot is the *Papagayo,* noisy, smoky and crowded, as are *Voom Voom* and *L'Esquinade. Krak du Chevalier* in the Byblos hotel is quieter.

HOTELS AND RESTAURANTS. Marseille-Toulon sector: The unpretentious little resorts along this strip of coast attract a predominantly French clientele drawn in large part from the two largest centers, Marseille and Toulon. Restaurants listed (E), (M), or (I) denote expensive, moderate or inexpensive.

BANDOL. Hotels: *Ile Rousse,* deluxe; *Beau Rivage,* first class; *Reserve,* fine restaurant; charming *Goëland,* on the beach, inexpensive. A mile away on the Engraviers peninsula, is the deluxe *Athena,* with pool, yacht basin. On Bendor Island: *Delos,* expensive; *Palais,* first class.

Restaurants: *Auberge du Port* (E), *La Réserve* (M), *La Grotte Provençale* (I).

CARRY-LE-ROUET, 19 miles west of Marseille, restaurant *l'Escale* (E), famed for bouillabaise.

CASSIS. Hotel: *Roches Blanches,* has own beach, lovely site, quiet; small *Lieutaud.* Restaurants: *Chez Gilbert* (M), *El Sol* (I), both on port.

LA CIOTAT-PLAGE. Hotels: the *Rose Thé* and the *Chantemer,* comfortable, fairly reasonable.

LECQUES, LES. Hotels: *Grand Hôtel, Chanteplage* and *Terrasses.* All offer bathing, seclusion.

MARSEILLE. Hotels: Deluxe: *Concorde-Prado, Grand et Noailles, L'Arbois, Beauvau* and *Splendide,* all in town, plus the recent *Sofitel* and the very pleasant *Résidence le Petit Nice et Marina Maldormé* and *Concorde Palm-Beach* on the *Corniche* overlooking the sea. *Royal St.-Georges, Novotel* (6 miles east), *Grand Hôtel de Genève, Frantel,* first class. Moderate: *Dieudé, Deux Mondes* and *Lutétia.* Inexpensive: *Belle-Vue,* on the harbor, and *Esterel.* At Marignane airport, the *Sofitel* and *Novotel* hotel-motel. At nearby Fos, *Frantel* and *Novotel,* each with pool.

Restaurants: *Chez Maurice Brun* (E), overlooking old port. *Michel-Brasserie des Catalans* (M), famous for bouillabaisse. *New York Vieux-Part* (E), elegant. *Le*

Rosbif, Le Phocéen ABC, all (M). *Miramar; Chez Arnould; Au Pescadou, Auberge de la Rascasse,* all (M). *Le Petit Caveau* and *Le Rallye,* both (I).

Petit Nice (hotel), elegant, with a view; *Ombrelles* (I) open-air dining; *Chez Fonfon,* on the Corniche.

SANARY. Hotels: *La Tour,* moderate. *Primavera,* inexpensive and comfortable.

TOULON. Hotels: *Frantel Tour Blanche,* with bungalows and pool; *Grand* with top-floor restaurant and view over bay. Both first-class.

HYERES-CANNES

Prices here in the smaller and quieter towns are often less expensive than hotels around Cannes and Nice, but don't think you're going to get away for nothing. Several of the big hotels are definitely in the luxury class, and, with the growing popularity of the St.-Tropez area, the smaller ones are upping their prices too.

AGAY. Hotel: *Baumette,* superior cuisine, deluxe but reasonably priced.

CAVALAIRE. Hotels: *Bains,* on the beach; *Lido; Régina;* all moderately priced.

CAVALIÈRE. Hotels: *Le Club,* on the beach, first class, excellent cuisine, expensive. *Surplage,* comfortable, medium priced. *Moriaz,* good, moderate.
Restaurant: *Le Club* (hotel).

FRÉJUS. Hotels: *Les Résidences du Colombier* is first class. The *Oasis* is less expensive.

GASSIN, lovely hill town. Restaurants: *Micocoulier* (M), *Bello Visto* (I).

GRIMAUD. Hotel: *Kilal,* deluxe, new. Restaurant: *Les Santons* (E), one of the Riviera's best.

HYÈRES. Hotels: *Castel Ste.-Claire,* deluxe; *Suisse,* reasonable; 8 miles south, *Le Provençal* on Presqu'Ile de Giens. Charming atmosphere, excellent food; pool.
Restaurants: *Tison d'Or* (M), *Marius* (I).

ILE DE PORQUEROLLES. Hotels: *Alycastre* and *Mas du Langoustier,* moderate. *Miramar,* lovely site, inexpensive. *Ste.-Anne,* inexpensive.
Restaurant: *Auberge de l'Arche de Noé* (I), fine cooking, with a few rooms.

LAVANDOU, LE. Hotels: *Résidence Beach,* first class; *Beau Rivage,* nice view, and *Auberge la Calanque,* good food, pretty spot, both moderate.
Restaurants: *Au Vieux Port* (M); *La Bouée* (M).

NAPOULE, LA. Hotels: *Ermitage du Riou,* deluxe. *Résidence du Golf,* good restaurant, first class, lovely situation; *Beau Rivage,* less expensive and modern. *Le Rocamare,* inexpensive.
Restaurants: *L'Oasis* (E), and five minutes away, at Mandelieu, *Le Pavillon des Sports* (M).

PORT GRIMAUD. Hotel: *Giraglia,* with private beach and port (E). Restaurants: *Marine, Baronnet,* both (M).

RAMATUELLE. Hotel: *Le Baou,* ultramodern. Hotel restaurant: *Chez Tony* (M).

STE.-MAXIME. Hotels: *Club Maxima 2000,* newest: bungalows set in woods, pool, tennis. *Chardon Bleu* has fine restaurant. *Résidence Brutus* (M), *Riviera,* inexpensive. At Plan-de-la-Tour, about 6 miles up in the hills, is a charming, tiny, quiet hotel, *Ponte Romano,* good food.

Restaurants: *Hostellerie de la Belle Aurore* (E), terrace overlooks sea, elegant. *La Réserve* (I).

ST.-RAPHAEL. Hotels: *Beau Rivage,* first class with a pleasant view; *Continental, Les Algues* and *Beau Séjour,* moderate. At Valescure about 1 mile north on D.37, *Golf,* quiet, view, moderate. Near to 18-hole golf course.

Restaurant: *La Voile d'Or,* not too expensive.

ST.-TROPEZ. Hotels: *Byblos,* luxurious, exotic. *Résidence de la Pinéde* on the beach, expensive. The *Résidence des Lices* with pool and quiet garden is comfortable but pricey. *La Citadelle, La Ponche,* relatively moderate; *Yaca,* very pretty. *Le Ponant,* tiny, moderate, closed in winter.

Nearby, on the Route des Salins, is the pleasant, comfortable *Lou Troupelen.*

Restaurants: Leï Mouscardins and *Auberge des Maures,* seafood; *Yaca,* charming, excellent varied menu; *La Romana,* rather limited menu. All (E). *L'Escale,* on the port; *Café des Arts; Lou Pinet,* all (M). *La Frégate* and *La Goutade,* both (I). For people-watching, drinks, *Senèquier,* facing port.

CANNES-MENTON

ANTIBES. Hotels: *Royal,* quiet, first class, private beach. The *Djoliba* (M). Two miles out, the *Euromotel Côte d'Azur,* with snackbar, pool. *Château de la Brague,* 4 km. east on the Biot road, has pool.

Restaurants: *La Bonne Auberge* (E), one of Riviera's top eating spots. Lovely Provençal dining room and terrace, 3 miles north on N.7 at La Brague. *Vieux Murs,* chic and (E). *Oursin, Caméo* (I). On the road to Grasse, and rather hard to find, is one of the latest in the Novotel chain, *Novotel Sophia-Antipolis,* very secluded in the middle of a pine forest.

BEAULIEU-SUR-MER. Hotels: *La Réserve,* extremely luxurious interior, wonderful view, and famous table, very expensive. *Métropole,* vast terrace over sea, pool, also expensive. *Bedford,* on the Cap Ferrat side. *Le Havre Bleu* and *Flora* are less expensive.

Restaurant: *La Réserve,* excellent, *Metropole,* both (E).

CAGNES. Hotels: Le *Cagnard,* Provençal atmosphere.

Restaurants: At Haut-de-Cagnes, *Josyjo,* a cheerful bistro with very easy-on-the-pocket prices. *Auberge du Moulin* (M), on N.7, cozy atmosphere, better-than-home cooking.

CANNES. Hotels: *Grand, Carlton, Majestic, Sofitel-Mediterranée,* all magnificently situated along the beach, are deluxe, as is the *Mont-Fleury,* above the town, with its own pool. First-class superior: the elegant little *Victoria,* with pool, *Suisse, Canberra.* First class: *Mapotel-Embassy, Palma* (on Croisette). Moderate: *France, Ruc, Wagram.* Inexpensive: *Amirauté, des Voyageurs.*

Restaurants: *Reine Pedauque, Voile au Vent, Carlton Grill,* the famous and always modish *Félix* and *Blue Bar,* all (E). *La Mere Besson, Le Chapon, Toque Blanche, Le Pompon Rouge,* friendly, *Coquille,* all (M). *Au Mal Assis, Le Pacific,* (I).

CAP D'ANTIBES. Hotels: *Du Cap,* admirably situated; *Résidence du Cap,* both deluxe. *La Garoupe,* comfortable, moderate.
Restaurant: *Eden Roc,* famous, exclusive. (E).

EZE-BORD-DE-MER. Hotels: *Cap Estel,* on peninsula, private beach and pool, very expensive. *Cap Roux* and *La Bananeraie* are moderate.

EZE-VILLAGE. Famous restaurant *Chèvre d'Or* (E), also has 6 rooms.

GRASSE. Hotels: *Beau-Soleil* and *Régent,* both first class; *Bellevue,* moderate. Restaurants: *Chez Pierre* and *Houlotte* are both (M). At Magagnosc, 3 miles east on N. 85, the *Relais du Vieux Moulin,* with rooms (M).

JUAN-LES-PINS. Hotels: *Provençal,* beautifully situated, deluxe. Ditto for *Hélios, Belles Rives* and *Juana,* slightly less expensive. Comfortable, first class, *Astoria. Savoy, Alexandra, La Régence,* all modestly priced. *Paprika, Saint-Charles, Saint-Gilles, Charmettes,* inexpensive.
Restaurants: *Le Perroquet,* good and moderate in price, *Bijou-Plage,* more expensive. *Lou Capitol* is good and very reasonably priced.
La Maison des Pêcheurs (E), just outside town, super site and cuisine. Private port and water sports facilities.

MENTION. Hotels: Newest is *Europe,* first-class. Recent *Napoleon* and *Viking,* first class, with pool. Also first-class, *Princess et Richmond, Dauphin, Chambord, Parc. Carlton,* Comfortable, (*en pension* only), *Saint-Georges,* pleasant but not right by sea, both (M); *Beau Rivage,* old-fashioned but charming *Windsor-Trianon,* inexpensive; *France* and *Toulonnais* are both very inexpensive.
Restaurants: *Francine* (E). *L'Hacienda,* on road to Gorbio. *Le Pavillon Impérial,* both (M); *Le Bec Fin, Les Santons* (I).

MOUGINS. Hotels: *Le Vaste Horizon, Les Liserons,* both (M). At N.D. de Vie, 2 miles south, *Moulins de Mougins,* with marvelous restaurant (E), and *Clos des Boyères* (detached cottages). Restaurants: *La Fenière, Fournil, Trois Etages* (attractive decor) and *Le Bistro* (I).

NICE. Hotels: Deluxe are the *Méridien,* on the site of the long-known elegant old Ruhl; long-established *Negresco* and *Plaza.* First-class luxurious are *Park* and *Sofitel-Splendid,* with pool, solarium, and *Frantel.* Old-established in the same class are the *Royal* and *Westminster-Concorde.*
First class: *Europa, La-Pérouse,* chic, and *La Résidence,* older *Windsor* and *Victoria.*
Comfortable, moderate, are the *Magnan* and *Savoie,* the older *Vendôme, Busby.*
Inexpensive: *Helvétique, Flots d'Azur,* near the sea; *Azur-Etats-Unis,* with studio rooms.
Very inexpensive: *Magali.*
Near the airport, the *Novotel.*
Restaurants: Best by far is *Petit Brouant* (E), 4bis Rue Deloye (closed June and Mon.), followed by *La Poularde chez Lucullus* (M), across the street (closed July and Weds.). *L'Esquinade* (E), on port, very a la mode. Also on or near port, *Garac, La Cassine* (M).
In the old town, charming and fashionable spots include: *La Merenda,* 4 Rue de la Terrasse; *La Taca d'Oli, La Taverne du Château;* (all M); and the fairly expensive but very friendly *César-l'Univers,* just at the entrance to the Old Town. *Saetone, Vieille Auberge,* and *Jardin Fleuri* will not damage the budget too severely.

L'Estragon and *Florian* (Alsatian specialties) are both (M). If you're tired of seafood, try *Le Nissada* (I), 17 Rue Gubernatis.

ROQUEBRUNE-CAP MARTIN. Hotels: *Vistaëro,* first class, stunning view of coast, on Grande Corniche about 2 miles southwest. Attractively located *Alexandra* and *Victoria* are less expensive, as are the *Princessios* and *Westminster.*
Restaurant: *Chez la Mère Jeanine.*

ST.-JEAN-CAP-FERRAT. Hotels: *Grand Hôtel du Cap Ferrat,* isolated, exclusive, expensive, very good view. *Della Robbia,* lovely garden, moderate. *Panoramic,* moderate, *Voile d'Or,* expensive. *Brise Marine, Frégate,* modest.
Restaurants: *Cappa* (closed mid Oct.–Dec.), *Voile d'Or* (E), with a magnificent view; *Au Petit Trianon,* highly recommended, fairly expensive. *Les Hirondelles* (M), overlooks port.

ST.-PAUL-DE-VENCE. A few miles inland, fashionable. Overlooking the village is the elegant *Mas d'Artigny,* super-deluxe, bungalows each have mini-pool, superb views. *Colombe d'Or,* expensive, gorgeous setting, good food. *Les Remparts,* moderate.
Restaurants: *L'Aubergo dou Souleu* (M). One mile away is the picturesque *Mas de Serres,* with a few rooms. One mile by D.7 is *Les Oliviers,* good cuisine, moderate.

TOURTOUR, a growing artists' and artisans' village colony. Hotel: *La Bastide de Tourtour,* in pinewood, with pool. Less expensive *Auberge de St.-Pierre* has pool, good restaurant.

VENCE. Hotels: *Château du Domaine St.-Martin,* with pool under olive trees, fine restaurant. *Coq Hardi,* inexpensive.
Restaurants: *La Farigoule* and *Les Portiques,* both (I).

VILLEFRANCHE-SUR-MER. Hotels: *Versailles,* very comfortable, expensive. *Provençal, Welcome,* at the port, both moderate. *De la Darse,* (restaurant serves dinner only) (I).
Restaurants: On the Grande Corniche is the very smart and amusing *Ferme Saint-Michel,* where even your *apéritif* is served from a milk churn (E). *La Mère Germaine, La Frégate,* both (M); less expensive is *Nautic.*

VILLENEUVE-LOUBET. Hotels: *Motel Méditerranée, Palerme, Pesage,* all moderate. Restaurant: *Logis du Loup* (E), excellent.

The French Alps

Along the southeastern border of France rises a mighty barrier of mountains that provides some of the most spectacular scenery in Europe —the French Alps, soaring to their climax in Europe's highest peak, Mont Blanc, stabbing 15,781 snowy feet into the air. Its chief divisions, north to south, are—the Mont Blanc country; the Savoie, lying along the Italian border; the Dauphiné, of which Grenoble is the capital; the Hautes Alpes, centered about Briançon; and the Alpes-de-Haute-Provence-Alpes Maritimes, that slope down to the palms and bougainvillea of the Côte d'Azur. The region is equally attractive in summer and winter. Chamonix, for example, oldest and biggest of French winter resorts, is a summer mountain climbing center for alpinists who come to scale Mont Blanc.

Mont Blanc and Other Peaks

Every visitor to the region will want to set foot on Mont Blanc, so take a trip on the cogwheel railway up to the Mer de Glace. There are numerous other scenic attractions—the beautiful lakes of Geneva, Annecy and Bourget; Mont Pourri (12,409 ft.) and the curious Mont Aiguille (Needle Rock), whose 6,562-foot heights were first scaled in 1492, the first recorded ascent in mountaineering annals; the Col de la Croix-Haute and Col d'Izoard, where one passes from green Alpine pastures to Mediterranean vegetation; the mountain plateau of the Vercors, gallantly defended by a handful of Resistance fighters during 1944; the Col de l'Iseran (9,085 ft.), a high pass accessible to automobiles only in full summer; the Col du Galibier (8,386 ft.) and the Col du Lautaret, from which there is a superb view of the wild Pelvoux region dominated by the glaciers of La Meije (13,068 ft.) and Barre des Ecrins (13,454 ft.); the Vannois National Park with rare mountain animals in their natural habitat. In contrast to these heights are the spectacular gorges of Verdon, Cians and Romanche.

Alpine Highlights

In addition to scenery and resort centers, there are many other points of interest—the Abbey of Hautecombe, burial place of the princes of the House of Savoie, and remains of Roman baths at Aix-les-Bains; the castle of the dukes of Savoie at Chambéry, and nearby Les Charmettes, country residence of philosopher Jean-Jacques Rousseau and his patron, Madame de Warens; the secluded monastery of the Grande Chartreuse, original home of the world-famed liqueur; the 17th-century Château of Vizille, a residence of the president of the French Republic; the Lake of Laffrey, where Napoleon, returning from exile in Elba in 1814, was joined by the royal troops sent to arrest him; Grenoble, "capital of the Alps", with its 16th-century Palace of Justice, outstanding art museum, and museum devoted to novelist Stendhal; the 13th-16th-century Château of Menthon-St.-Bernard; the city of Briançon, with its ramparts by Vauban and statue of France by famed sculptor Antoine Bourdelle, and nearby Château-Queyras, with its medieval watchtower and fortifications; the modern (1950) church at Assy, designed by Novarina and decorated with paintings and sculptures by Matisse, Léger, Bonnard, Rouault, Braque and others; the Romanesque cathedral at Embrun; picturesque villages, such as Pont-en-Royans, Queyras, Bourget, Colmars, Tout, Flumet and Conflans; the 13th-15th-century Château Bayard, near Pontcharra, birthplace of Chevalier Bayard, the knight "without fear and without reproach"; the impressive Cathedral of St.-Pierre at Moutiers, with its rich treasure of medieval ivories and enameled ware; the medieval watchtower of Crest, dominating the Drôme Valley (may be visited weekday afternoons and Sunday, apply to Café du Tonneau, Place de Gaulle); the curious and fortified little stronghold of Mont-Dauphin.

Rivaling the other Alpine wonders are such engineering achievements as the 287-mile Route Napoléon-Route des Alpes, that transports the motorist from Cannes via Grenoble to St.-Julien, and the 416-mile Route des Grandes Alpes from Nice to Evian; the dam of La Girotte, built under the glacier; the 7½ mile long Mont Blanc tunnel connecting France and Italy; the dam of Tignes, highest in Europe; the *téléphérique* (cablecar) of l'Aiguille de Midi—still the highest in the world (12,600 ft.), although a higher one is now under construction nearby—and of Serre-Chevalier, the longest in Europe (almost two miles).

 WINTER SPORTS. All the resorts listed have excellent equipment. French ski schools are probably the best in Europe, with standardized instruction. Ski school tickets are valid in all stations, and from one year to another. New resorts are constantly being developed, and old ones improved, to meet the rapidly growing demand from both French and foreign skiers. Rates are lowest in Jan., and before Easter, in early March. Many resorts offer *forfait-skieur tout compris* arrangements in winter: a special all-inclusive 7-day hotel rate, and a Ski Pass for unlimited usage on 140 ski lifts, ski classes, local transport, etc.

There are good rail connections to major ski centers, as well as motorcoach liaisons from Geneva airport (many Paris-Geneva and New York-Geneva flights). *Air-Alpes* has small ski-planes which shuttle from Geneva to the largest and newest ski stations (Chamonix, Courchevel, Megève, Tignes, Val d'Isère, Avoriaz, Flaine, La Plagne, Alpe d'Huez etc.), and also has direct flights from Paris to Courchevel, Val d'Isère, Megève.

The skiing season for most resorts runs from 15 Dec. to 15 Mar., some until May, but in high altitudes it is a year-round sport.

MONT BLANC REGION

AVORIAZ. Railway station: Thonon. Airport: Geneva.
Hotels: *Dromonts,* expensive, *Les Hauts Forts,* moderate.

CHAMONIX. Railway station: Chamonix station. Airport: Geneva, bus connections.
Hotels: *Auberge du Bois Prin,* small, very pleasant. *Carlton, Mont-Blanc, Croix-Blanche, Albert I et Milan,* best, all first class. *Novotel, La Sapinière,* moderate.

LA CLUSAZ. Railway station: Annecy (20 miles). Airport: Geneva.
Hotels: *Beauregard,* (first-class). Moderate *Beaulieu* has nice view.

LES CONTAMINES-MONTJOIE. Railway station: Le Fayet (bus connections, 45 minutes). Airport: Geneva.
Hotels: *Le Chamois* (M); *Le Miage, Les Dômes, La Cordée* (I).

LES HOUCHES. Railway station: Les Houches, via Vallorcine. Airport: Geneva.
Hotels: *Motel Delta* is best; *Piste Bleue, Chris-Tal,* moderate; *Roches* (I).

MEGÈVE. Railway station: Sallanches (8 miles, bus). Main airport: Geneva; also direct from Paris.
Hotels: *Mont d'Arbois,* super-deluxe Rothschild-owned; *Mont-Blanc,* first-class, is *the* smart place to be seen, and its attractive airy restaurant *Les Enfants Terribles* (M–E) is very chic; *Mont-Joly,* first class with excellent restaurant; inexpensive *Rond Point d'Arbois* and many others.

ST.-GERVAIS. Railway station: Le Fayet (3 miles, bus service). Airport: Geneva.
Hotels: Best is *Alpenrose* (E); *Splendid, France,* both (M).

SAVOIE

LES ARCS. Railway station: Bourg St.-Maurice.

Hotels: *Cachette, Cascade* (first class); *Résidence des Trois Arcs,* moderate. *Winston,* English-owned, English personnel, very reasonable, full- or half-board only.

LE CORBIER. Railway station: Saint-Jean de-Maurienne (9 miles).
Hotels: *La Galaxie,* first class (no restaurant).

COURCHEVEL. Railway station: Moutiers (13 miles, bus). Air-Alpes air shuttle from Geneva serves Courchevel and Meribel (25 minutes). Also direct Paris-Courchevel with Air-Alpes.
Hotels: Deluxe *Carlina;* elegant *Rond Point des Pistes;* first class *Bellecôte; Célebataires* (for singles, as name implies); fairly expensive *Albaron,* also *New Solarium;* moderate *Pomme de Pin.* Restaurant: *Yaca* (M-E).

FLAINE. Railway station: Cluses (17 miles).
Hotels: *Sofitel Le Flaine,* first-class. *Totem, Gradins Gris,* more reasonable; *Aujon,* moderate. All new and comfortable.

MÉRIBEL-LES-ALLUES. Railway station: Moûtiers (1 hour by bus).
Hotels: *L'Ermitage, Vallon* (M); *Grand Coeur* (E).

LA PLAGNE. Recent resort complex. Railway station: Aime. (11 miles).
Hotels: *Christina, France* (first class).

TIGNES. Railway station: Bourg St.-Maurice (1 hour by bus). Airport: Geneva.
Hotels: *Hauts de Tovière, Ski d'Or,* all first class; *Curling,* fairly expensive, *Campanules, Pramecou, Aiguille Percée,* moderate; *Terrachu* (I).

VAL D'ISERE. Railway station: Bourg St.-Maurice (by bus, about 1 hour; by helicopter, 10 minutes). Main airport: Geneva; also direct from Paris.
Hotels: best are *Sofitel, Solaise* (deluxe); *Christiania,* first-class; *Edelweiss* (moderate).

VALLOIRE. Railway station: St.-Michel de Maurienne (45 minutes by bus).
Hotels: *Rapin* (first-class); *La Sétaz, Grand,* moderate; *Les Carrettes, Centre,* (I).

VAL THORENS, 6,600 ft. Newest high altitude resort. Railway station: Moûtiers (21 miles).
Hotel: *Novotel* (first-class).

DAUPHINÉ

L'ALPE D'HUEZ. Railway station: Grenoble (2 hours by bus; 15 minutes by helicopter).
Hotels: *La Menandière, Les Grandes Rousses, Ours Blanc, Christina,* all fairly expensive.

HAUTES ALPES – ALPES-DE-HAUTE-PROVENCE

BRIANÇON. Hotels: *Vauban,* (first class).

FOURS. On the road to the Col de la Cayolle, the modest *Auberge Arnaud.*

MONTGENÈVRE. Railway station: Briançon (40 minutes).
Hotels: *Les Rois Mages,* moderate; *Valérie,* inexpensive.

PRA-LOUP. Hotels: *La Patinoire, l'Estelan, Clos du Loup,* moderate; *Prieuré,* inexpensive but good.

LE SAUZE-SUR-BARCELONNETTE. Railway station: Prunieres is about 1 hour by bus. Direct bus from Marseille and Barcelonnette.
Hotels: *Séolanes, Alp,* both (I).

SERRE-CHEVALIER. Group of villages (St.-Chaffrey, Chantemerle, Villard-Laté, Les Panaches, Villeneuve, Le Bez). A favorite with many Americans. Railway station: Briançon (30 minutes by bus).
Hotels: at Chantemerle, *Chanteneige* (first-class); *Boule de Neige, Le Clos,* (I); at Villeneuve, *Lièvre Blanc* (M).

VARS. Centers are St.-Marcellin, Ste.-Catherine, Ste.-Marie, Vars-les-Claux. Railway station: Guillestre. Airport: les Claux.
Hotels: *Hostellerie Ste.-Marie* at Ste.-Marie-des-Vars, moderate; at Vars-les-Claux, *Caribou,* first class; at St.-Marcellin, inexpensive *Le Paneyron.*

ALPES MARITIMES

AURON. Railway station: Nice (3 hours by bus). Airport: Nice.
Hotels: *Pilon, Savoie,* (first-class).

ISOLA 2000, 57 miles from Nice.
Hotels: *Chastillon, St.-Pierre,* first class; *Pas du Loup,* more moderate.

VALBERG. Hotels: Best is *Adrech de Lagas;* then *Grand, Les Flocons,* with fine restaurant.

PRACTICAL INFORMATION FOR THE ALPINE CENTERS

 TRANSPORTATION. There are rapid trains from Paris (Gare de Lyon) to the principal Alpine centers, as well as to Aix-les-Bains, Grenoble, Briançon etc. *Air Inter* connects the major cities (Chambéry, Grenoble, Aix etc.) with Paris, and, of course, there are several flights each day to Lyon, Nice and Marseille.

HOTELS AND RESTAURANTS

AIX-LES-BAINS, France's top lake resort.
Hotels: Deluxe, *Albion.* In park, beautiful views of lake. Excellent cuisine. Also *Astoria.*
First class: *International Rivollier,* excellent cuisine. *Iles Britanniques,* nice location, quiet; *Cloche.*
Moderate: *Métropole.*
Inexpensive: *Soleil Couchant.*
Restaurants: *Nivolet; Lille,* at Grand Port, 2 miles north.

ANNECY. Hotels: First class: *Carlton, Splendid, Touring.* None has restaurant.
Moderate: *Crystal; Allobroges, La Régence,* about one mile east on the Rte. de Semnoz.
Inexpensive is *Coin Fleuri.*
On the lake shore, about one mile out on N. 508, you will find the fairly expensive *Robinson.*
At La Puya is the charming *Trésoms et Fôret,* first class, wonderful view.

At Albigny, 1 mile east on N. 509 are the inexpensive *Petit Port* and *Faisan Doré* (M).

On road to Aix-les-Bains: first-class *Mercure,* with pool.

Restaurants: best, *Auberge de Savoie, Le Nemours* (Casino), *Chez Yan,* at Albigany, all (M).

Pavillon Ermitage, at Chavoire, about 3 miles east on N. 509. Food good, flower gardens on lake.

CHAMBÉRY. Hotels: *Grand,* first class. *Touring,* moderate.

Restaurants: *Roubatcheff* (E). *Aux Ducs de Savoie* (M), in Grand hotel.

EVIAN-LES-BAINS, spa season: May–Sept. Hotels: *La Verniaz et ses Chalets* (E), at Verniaz, exclusive, isolated, excellent cuisine; *Casino Royal* (deluxe), near funicular.

First class: *Lumina.*

Moderate: *Plage,* near lake beach.

Inexpensive: *Cygnes,* 1 mile west on lake; nearby, *Panorama* very inexpensive.

Restaurants: *La Verniaz* (M), *Lumina* (I), both a little outside town.

GRENOBLE. Hotels: *Sofitel, Park,* pleasing yet functional, deluxe.

First Class: *Savoie;* recent *Alpotel, P.L.M.; Novotel,* on Lyon *autoroute,* 9 miles away.

Moderate: *Trois-Roses* (outside town), new; *Gallia.*

Inexpensive: *Stendhal; Globe,* small, good restaurant.

Restaurants: *Poularde Bressane,* outstanding, closely followed by *Les Trois Dauphins,* outside town at La Tronche. At Sassenage, 4 miles west, *Rostang,* outstanding. All (E). *Auberge Bressane* and *Grill Parisien* in town, both (M).

TALLOIRES. Hotels: The deluxe *Abbaye,* terrace, lake view, excellent cuisine.

Restaurants: The *Auberge du Père Bise* is one of the country's best, charmingly situated on Lake Annecy. It is closely followed by the *Cottage* (hotel) and the *Abbaye* (hotel).

Highlights of the Crossroads

France, as the traditional crossroads of Europe, has for centuries played host to travelers who are on their way to some other country. The same condition prevails today. But today's tourist, even the inveterate traveler who knows France very well, is always in despair at the riches he has to bypass or leave behind at almost every turn. We here suggest two routes, with their principal attractions.

From Paris to Germany

This is a very direct road from Paris via the new autoroute to Nancy, Metz and the Rhine. A short detour from the autoroute will take you to Strasbourg.

Nancy, capital of Lorraine, is one of the most charming cities of France, owing its harmonious beauty to Stanislas Leczinsky, the ex-king of Poland, father-in-law of Louis XV. The Place Stanislas, with its wrought-iron gates and railings and its fountains, is one of the loveliest and most perfectly-proportioned squares in the world. The Place de la Carrière, reached through Stanislas's Arc de Triomphe, is its close rival with its trees and elegant 18th-century houses.

A delightful detour along D. 64 between Contrexéville (a Vosges spa) and Void will take you through the Joan of Arc country, almost unchanged since the Maid of Orléans was born here in Domrémy in 1411. You may visit her birthplace and the garden where she first heard the voices at the age of 13.

Strasbourg, with its carved, timbered houses and its glorious red stone cathedral is worth more than a casual stop. It is now the home of the European Parliament. Take a drive along the Wine Road at the foot of the Vosges Mountains. Its vineyards produce the delectable Alsatian wines.

Don't miss Ribeauville, with its ruined castles and storks nesting on the roofs, and stop at Riquewihr so that you can explore on foot the medieval walls, ancient houses and old courtyards of this tiny village in the center of vineyards. Not much farther south is Colmar, with its old painted and sculptured houses and its "Venetian Quarter" traversed by the Lauch River. One of the loveliest towns in Alsace, Colmar is famous for its Unterlinden Museum, with its priceless *Descent from the Cross* by Grünewald and its collection of other painting, sculpture and Alsatian earthenware.

PRACTICAL INFORMATION, PARIS-GERMANY ROUTE

HOW TO GET THERE. Air Alsace has planes six times weekly, London (Gatwick) to Colmar and Nancy direct. Fast *autoroute* to Metz, Nancy, Strasbourg. Air France has two flights daily (except weekends), London (Heathrow)–Strasbourg direct; Air-Inter has many flights Paris–Strasbourg. Fast trains from Paris to main towns.

AMMERSCHWIHR. Excellent restaurant *Aux Armes de France* (E).

COLMAR. Hotels: *Terminus-Bristol, Champ de Mars* (first-class), *Novotel* (M) at the airport.
Restaurant: *Maison des Têtes,* in 17th-cent. house. Excellent and very reasonable prices. Also: *Meistermann,* classical brasserie, *Schillinger, Le Fer Rouge, Unterlinden,* all very honorable, all (M); *Unterlinden* (I).

ILLHAEUSERN. Restaurant: *Auberge de l'Ill,* one of France's greatest, beautifully situated on the banks of the river Ill.

METZ. Hotels: Newest: *Sofitel, Concorde,* first-class, as are *Novotel* (out of town), *Frantel.* Restaurants: best is the *Auberge de la Gare* (M), at nearby Ars-sur-Moselle.

NANCY. Hotels: Recent *Sofitel, Novotel* (outside town) and *Frantel; Grand Hôtel–Concorde,* in Pl. Stanislas; all first-class; *La Cigogne,* modest.
Restaurants: *Le Capucin Gourmand* (E); *La Gentilhommière* (M).

STRASBOURG. Hotels: Top-class are *Sofitel,* older *Terminus-Gruber, Holiday Inn;* first-class: *Maison Rouge, Mercure* (out of town); *Lutétia,* modest.
Restaurants: *Crocodile, Maison Kammerzell,* a 16th-cent. beamed house; *Zimmer, Au Gourmet Sans Chiqué* (M).

South to Spain

Go by way of Orléans, Poitiers, Périgueux, Cahors, Albi and Carcassonne. After following N. 10 from Tours to Poitiers and Angoulême, stopping, though hardly long enough, to see the Romanesque church of Notre-Dame-la-Grande in Poitiers and the domed cathedral of Angoulême, branch off via the charming town of Brantôme on the Dronne River, with its dance festival and sound-and-light spectacle, to Périgueux. From there on, take highways N. 710 and D. 6 to Rouffignac, where some very interesting prehistoric cave paintings were found in 1956, and thence via D. 31 to Les Eyzies, lying at the bottom of a 600-foot cliff, where there are probably more relics of our early ancestors than in any spot in Western Europe; they include the Cro-Magnon skeleton found in 1868, and numerous caves and grottos. Halfway up the cliff is the 16th-century château that houses the National Prehistoric Museum.

From Les Eyzies, journey south to Cahors, with its beautiful medieval bridge, swing southeast to Albi for a look at its splendid fortified cathedral and at the Toulouse-Lautrec Museum in the old Episcopal Palace, then south to Carcassonne.

The sight of Carcassonne, a walled and towered medieval city rising against a background of the snow-capped Pyrenees, is worth a long journey. At Carcassonne, you are near Toulouse, where dancers, musicians and Camargue cowboys gather in June for the unique Grand Fenetra folk festival. Or you can go down to the rapidly developing tourist region of the Languedoc-Roussillon coast, spend a while in the atmospheric city of Perpignan, take a detour to Prades in the eastern Pyrenees—where Casals' music festival has been revived—and then on to Spain via the northeast border.

If you want to cut southwest to Spain from Cahors, you should go by Moissac, with its splendid Church of St.-Peter and 12th-century cloister; by way of Auch, Tarbes and the great pilgrimage miracle city of Lourdes, and thence through the picturesque Basque country to Biarritz, St.-Jean-de-Luz and the Spanish border at Hendaye on the Bay of Biscay. *Note:* The annual "National Pilgrimage" from August 18 to 25 puts a great strain on the hotel accommodations of Lourdes. Better reserve early if you want to stay here then.

Biarritz has been the smartest of France's Atlantic beach resorts since the Empress Eugénie gave it its "coming out party". Her villa is now the Hôtel du Palais. You can sleep there too, but at a price and only with an advance reservation.

PRACTICAL INFORMATION, SOUTH TO SPAIN ROUTE

BIARRITZ. Hotels: The *Palais* is a true palace in the grand old style. *Miramar* and *Regina,* first class, rather chi-chi. Less expensive but elegant are the *Eurotel Biarritz* and *Le Président. Windsor* and *Edouard VII,* modest. *Océanic,* at nearby Bidart, is comfortable. Restaurants: *Café de Paris,* very grand and old-world, but recently some people have been disappointed by the food. (E); *Le Gant Biarrot* (M); *L'Alambic* (I), *Le Beau-Lieu* (I), *Français* (M).

BORDEAUX. Hotels: Deluxe *Frantel* and *P.L.M. Aquitania.* First class *Normandie* and *Novotel Bordeaux Le Lac.* Moderate *Continental.* Restaurants: *Dubern, St.-James,* both excellent and (M–E)., *Les Allées, Clavel,* (M).

CAHORS. Hotel: *Château de Le Mercuès,* overlooking Lot River Valley, luxurious.

Restaurants: *La Taverne* (M); *Les Templiers* (I), four miles south.

LES EYZIES. Hotels: First-class: *Cro-Magnon,* with excellent restaurant, *Centenaire; Les Glycines* (M).

LOURDES. Hotels: *Gallia et Londres, Grand Hôtel de la Grotte, Impérial, Chapelle et Parc, Moderne,* in descending order of price.

ST.-JEAN-DE-LUZ. Hotels: elegant *Chantaco* and *Miramar,* moderate *Guernica,* and at nearby Ciboure, a real bargain, the *Hostellerie Ciboure.* Restaurants: *Vieille Auberge* (M); *Le Petit Grill Basque* and *Chez Pablo,* both (I). *Arrantzaleak* in Ciboure has delicious fresh fish served in huge quantities, Basque songs, cheerful atmosphere (I).

Corsica, Napoleon's Homeland

The Mediterranean island of Corsica has been a department of metropolitan France for over two centuries. The Corsicans, a handsome, olive-skinned, hot-blooded people, have been famous throughout a long history for brigandage, vendettas, and taking to the brush or *maquis* as outlaws whenever the laws of the land displeased them. Today, the Corsicans can be friendly to the visitor, but are often cautious with foreigners and as insular as the inhabitants of most islands.

In the capital, Ajaccio, you can visit Napoleon's birthplace and the Napoleonic room in the Hôtel de Ville, among other Napoleona. Corte, high in the center of the island, is the ancient capital and lies on the main road between Ajaccio and Bastia, second largest port and town. Sartène —the "most Corsican of Corsican cities"—is ancient, perched in the mountains on the Ajaccio-Bonifacio road, and should be explored. Bonifacio, on the extreme southern tip of the island, is a fascinating medieval fortress town. The beaches of Corsica vary from long wide bays to tiny crescents, but most have fine sand. Ajaccio has both varieties; Ile Rousse, Calvi, Cargèse, Sagone, Propriano and Porto Vecchio have excellent beaches, while the smaller coves are at Porto, San Florent and around Cap Corse.

PRACTICAL INFORMATION FOR CORSICA

HOW TO GET THERE. *Air France* and *Air Inter* have daily flights from Paris (under 2 hrs.), Marseille (50 minutes) and Nice (40 minutes), to Ajaccio, Bastia or Calvi. *BA* and *Air France* fly regularly from London. *Air Transport* runs car-ferry services from Nîmes. *Compagnie Transméditerranéenne* has frequent sea services from Marseille, Nice and Toulon. *Corsica Line* has a car ferry service between Genoa and Bastia. Book well ahead if you are travelling in July or August, or at Easter.

HOTELS AND RESTAURANTS. Hotels, villa rental services, and other tourist facilities are steadily expanding. Prices are about the same as on the Riviera, which means high, for a quality which is usually not as refined. Meals are good and copious. Seafood and fruits are marvelously fresh; the regional wines are almost all excellent. Many interesting cheeses, too.

AJACCIO. Hotels. For pleasant atmosphere and lovely gardens, top rating goes to *Les Etrangers*. Try for a room in the delightful *villa* annex; *Continental,* formal garden; Rte. des Sanguinaires: modern *La Dolce Vita, Eden Roc, Cala di Sole.* All moderately expensive. Recent are the first class *Sun Beach,* and moderate *San Carlu. Stella di Mare,* on beach. At the airport, *Campo dell'Oro,* first class.

On the nearby Bay of Liscia is *Transat Hôtel de San Bastiano*—private beach, nursery, water sports, fairly expensive.

Restaurants: Best is *Aria Marina* (E), on Rte. des Sanguinaires; *La Reine Margot, Les Palmiers,* (M); *D'Mamma, D'Pardi* (I).

BASTIA. Hotels: Best are the modern *Bonaparte* (M) and *Ile de Beauté,* near the station, moderately expensive. Some people prefer to stay a little way out: *L'Alivi,* at Pietranera, 2 miles north. Small, pleasant. Comfortable *Pietracap.* Neither has restaurant.

Les Sablettes, at Miomo, 3½ miles north, small, well situated and good cuisine. Has motel annexe. *Transat Hôtel Club,* pool, tennis.

Restaurants: *Le Dauphin,* one of Corsica's best; *O'Stella* (M); *La Taverne* (I).

BONIFACIO. Hotels: *Solemare,* own pool, *La Caravelle,* pleasant dining room and cuisine, small. *Les Voyageurs.* Both on port or beach, moderately expensive.

CALVI. Hotels: *Grand,* deluxe, terrace restaurant. *Aloës,* modern; *Kalliste,* quiet, both fairly expensive.

Restaurants: *Ile de Beauté,* good.

ILE-ROUSSE, L'. *La Pietra,* first class, moderately expensive. *Splendid,* simple, inexpensive.

Restaurants: *La Bergerie, L'Auberge Chevalier,* (E), excellent. *California, Le Relais,* and *Grillon* (also hotel), all (M).

PORTICCIO, near Ajaccio. Hotels: *Sofitel-Thalassa,* deluxe, beautifully sited, pool, water sports. The attractive *Caribou,* with pool. *Maquis,* small bungalows, decorated in rustic style. All have private beaches. Newest: *Paradisu.*

PORTO. Hotels: *Kallisté, Marina, Vaïta,* near port, are comfortable but ugly. Nearby is the pleasant *Aiglon.*

Restaurants: *Le Robinson* and *Soleil Couchant* (also hotel), overlooking harbor and sea.

PORTO-VECCHIO. *Le Goéland* has its own beach, but no restaurant. On the port, the small *Roches Blanches.* Three miles away towards the Palombaggia beach is the hotel *Ziglione,* where you can eat one of the best meals on the island (E).

PROPRIANO. The *Marinca* is quiet, fairly expensive. *Arena Bianca, Miramar* and *Roc e Mare* are modern. All have private beaches or are within walking distance from the beach.

Restaurant: *Le Rescator,* overlooking port.

Corsica also has a fair number of "holiday villages" (including a couple for naturists), some of them pretty luxurious. Contact your travel agent or the French Tourist Office for information.

TOURS. You can take a variety of motorcoach tours from Ajaccio, Bastia, Calvi and Ile Rousse both winter and summer. Unless you are staying for a long time, it's cheaper to hire a car in Corsica than to bring your own. Small cars rent for about 57 francs a day (plus 60 centimes per kilometre); top price is for an automatic Mercedes: 254 francs a day (plus 2.05 francs per kilometre).

WEST GERMANY

Richly endowed with natural assets and a people capable of hard work, sacrifice and endurance, Germany has, since the end of World War II, achieved the seemingly impossible and has emerged as one of the wealthiest and technologically most advanced nations in Europe. Politically, the fact that the German word "Wirtschaftswunder" is understood all over the world sufficiently explains the phenomenon of Germany.

Having said this, however, it must be noted that Germany today is beginning to experience the sicknesses of too much success, witnessed by growing disenchantment with over-optimistic government and a hardening of prejudices against the huge colony of foreign workers who helped bring about the country's current affluence. As a member of the European Common Market, Germany wields enormous political influence through sheer economic capability, financial contributions and aid to retarded and underdeveloped countries.

There are still two Germanys, a fact which disturbs some and causes intense relief to others. "West Germany", officially entitled the Federal Republic of Germany, has made a kind of peace with "East Germany", also known as the German Democratic Republic, still ruled by a Communist one-party government. While it is doubtful that reunification will take place for many years, it is now an affirmation of faith on both sides that an increasingly close working relationship will come about between the two parts of what was once the major part of the Third Reich.

The West Germans, in many ways the most technologically adept people of Europe, have rebuilt their country from the rubble of war, and you will find them—at least in the Federal Republic—still in a state of constructive euphoria which is absolutely contagious. The cities—Munich, Düsseldorf, Hamburg, Frankfurt, Stuttgart, Cologne, Bremen, West Berlin—are literally throbbing with economic power, and a visit to any of them, especially the last, is recommended as one of the most stimulating experiences of modern European travel.

German hotels and restaurants stress comfort and efficient service. A large number of reconstructed and newly-built hostelries offer everything from moderately priced to super-deluxe accommodation. A special attraction, much sought after by foreign visitors, is the castle or manor hotel, once the haunt of medieval knights and seat of nobility or minor royalty, where the romantically-inclined guest may dream himself back into ages long past. You can obtain a brochure, "Castle Hotels in Germany", from the German Tourist Information Office or write directly to Vereinigung Gast im Schloss e.V., D-3524 Trendelburg 1.

In addition, the German countryside remains as beguiling as it has always been. This is a storybook landscape with an indefinable mystic beauty, serenely indifferent to politics, revolutions, wars and social change. Along the Rhine where the horn of Siegfried echoes in the memory; in the depths of the Black Forest with its fairy tale houses; in the crystal snow-bound silence of a Bavarian Alpine village—it is here that you will come the closest to the mysterious heart of Germany.

FOOD AND DRINK.

Germans love sausages, pork, veal and game. They cook with butter and go for starch in a big way—potatoes in the north, dumplings in the south. In the smaller Bavarian inns, anything that *can* be served with dumplings *is* served with dumplings. The food is delicious and very plentiful, a bit on the heavy side. We've listed some regional specialties for you later in this chapter. If you adopt the southern German habit of *Brotzeit* (a between meals snack of bread, sausage and beer) this is the time to sample those regional sausages: Frankfurters, for example, of which the American version is only a facsimile; Regensburger, a heavily-spiced pork sausage; Weisswurst, a white sausage made of veal, calves' brains and splean; Bratwurst, the pork sausage of Nürnberg, so famous that it inspired those special restaurants called Bratwurststube all over Germany.

Other outstanding German specialties are *Hase im Topf,* a sublime rabbit *paté; Renken,* salmon trout from the Alpine lakes; Schwetzingen asparagus, and a gamut of mouth-watering sweets including *Käsekuchen,* delicious cheesecake, *Schwarzwälder Kirschtorte,* a Black Forest cherry cake, *Lebkuchen* (gingerbread) and *Spekulatius* (cookies). You can always diet when you get home.

The beer is good. Say *helles* if you want light, *dunkles* if you want dark beer. Try the beer brewed from wheat, *Weissbier.*

Germany produces a lot of wine, some of it of superlative quality. Generally speaking, you will probably be happy with the wines of the house which most restaurants serve in glasses or with one of those earthenware pitchers of cold Mosel that are usually available. These are refreshing and cheap: from about three marks up for a ¼ of a liter. The southernmost end of the Rhine wine region is the Palatinate on the west bank of the upper Rhine, running all the way to the border of Alsace. The richest wines of this region come from *Forst, Deidesheim, Wachenheim* and *Ruppertsberge,* all white. Try also *Schwarzer Herrgott* from Herxheim, very good but not exported.

The Rhine Hesse region, beginning at Worms, produces the world-famous *Liebfraumilch,* but this will probably disappoint you, since the Milk of Our Lady is not a place name, and no guarantee of quality or precise vineyard. But a little farther north you will get two very fine wines indeed, the best of this region:

Niersteiner and *Oppenheimer,* from the villages of Nierstein and Oppenheim respectively. Other top wines in this region are *Nackenheimer* from Nackenheim and *Bodenheimer* from Bodenheim. The valley of the Nahe, which runs into the Rhine at Bingen, gives us the smooth white *Monzinger, Kreuznacher,* and *Hüffelsheimer.*

The Rheingau extends along the Rhine's right bank from Hochheim to Lorchhausen and produces some of the top wines. *Schloss Johannisberger* means Rhine wine at its summit. *Hochheimer* or Hock, a name indiscriminately applied in English to all Rhine wines, comes from this region, so does *Rüdesheimer* and *Rauenthaler,* one of the most expensive of the Rheingau wines.

The Mosel Valley grows grapes which make delicious, subtle wines, lighter and more delicate than those of the Rhine. *Piesporter Goldtröpfchen* is famous, but the experts prize *Wehlener Sonnenuhr* more highly. We suggest you also sample the Franconian wines, *Iphöfer* and *Würzburger Stein* in their specially-shaped flasks or *Boxbeutel.*

Shopping

Shops all over Germany are bursting with the products for which this nation of skilled craftsmen and technicians has always been noted. Prices, temptingly low compared with America's, are standardized on all items of current manufacture. So don't bargain except in antique shops. What to buy? Those incomparable German cameras are available in every major city at about one third less than the cost in America or Britain.

Other items to look for: antiques; Bavarian music boxes, handwoven Bavarian textiles, especially tablecloths; regional peasant dolls (some double as tea cosies and some as *Ei-Wärmer* (egg warmers); anything in that wonderful waterproof wool, Loden cloth; beer mugs of clay, pewter, copper and porcelain; beautiful Bavarian wax-art candles for Christmas and birthdays; Black Forest cuckoo clocks and the latest rage in Victorian revivals, those 400-day clocks, which you wind but once a year, are about half the normal British and American price; the famous Käthe Kruse and Hummel dolls and *all German toys* including the Steiff animals and those matchless Märklin trains; figurines; *Dresden, Rosenthal, Meissen* and *Nymphenburg* porcelain (Rosenthal china, though you can spend a fortune on it, starts as low as five marks a piece); silver; and last but certainly not least, steel carving sets, knives, tools and anything else in this line stamped *Solingen,* your guarantee of top quality and workmanship. See our selected list of shops under specific towns.

PRACTICAL INFORMATION FOR WEST GERMANY

WHAT WILL IT COST. Germany has one of the world's lowest (about 4%) inflation rates and it is not expected to rise in 1979. Even though prices have risen during the past years, the pinch felt by American and British tourists is mostly a result of the devalued dollar and floating pound, which simply don't buy as much in Germany as they once did. Nevertheless, a vacation in Germany still can be cheaper than one in either the US or Britain. You can save even more if you visit lesser-known cities and resorts, for instance skiing resorts in the Harz and Eiffel mountains, in Schwaben/Allgäu, Kleinwalsertal, the Black Forest, and especially in East Bavaria (Oberpfalz and Bayerischer Wald—Upper Palatinate and Bavarian Forest), which offers excellent quality at truly bargain rates. In all of these areas there are many new and comfortable vacation apartments and bungalows, 2–4-room flats accommodating up to six persons. Prices vary according to location, season and facilities offered, but run roughly from 115 marks per week for a small studio apartment for two, to 700 marks for a deluxe chalet accommodating at least 5 people.

Special all-inclusive rates are offered almost everywhere, but the many small towns along Lake Constance are a typical example: off-season, or better "edge-of-high-season" reductions range from a three-day weekend in a private room at 27 DM per person to 60 marks and up for a first-class hotel. Weekly rates 10-20% less. Special weekend rates are becoming a popular feature throughout Germany, including many large cities, such as Munich: a Munich Weekend offers special rates in three price categories, all with about 20% reduction and including city and countryside tours, museum, restaurant and theater ticket reductions, plus a 50% train reduction if you make the return trip from another major German city (Cologne or Hamburg, for instance).

Even exclusive Baden-Baden offers special out-of-season bargains, often including such extras as reductions in Casino admission. Several hotels in the Black Forest have joined forces to relieve the usual monotony of full-board terms: a guest staying in any one of these hostelries is free to alternate his meals at any of the other member-hotels. For a full list of all such special offers, write or visit the nearest branch of the German Tourist Department.

TYPICAL DAY

	(DM)
Moderate hotel, double room, with bath, breakfast and all charges included	30.00*
Lunch at moderately priced restaurant, *table d'hôte*	10.00
Dinner at moderately priced restaurant, soup plus main course	15.00
Coffee, in a good café	2.40
Pastry	2.00
Beer, ½ liter glass	2.00
¼ liter wine	3.50
Transportation: 1 tram	1.10
1 taxi	8.00
Theater ticket, middle price range	25.00
Miscellaneous (10% for contingencies)	9.00
	108.00

* It should be noted that this is a 60-DM double room, simply split in half to arrive at a per-person daily cost.

Special tips: considerable savings can be made if you eat as the Germans do: take the *table d'hôte* (daily special) lunch, offered *only* at noon, which consists of soup, main course, and (sometimes) a simple dessert. This will cost anywhere from 6 marks in an inexpensive restaurant to 9–12 marks in a moderate establishment. If your digestion and habits then require coffee and/or dessert, go to a café. The coffee served in most German restaurants is pretty bad. Germans eat a light meal in the evening: sauerkraut and sausages, or an omelette and perhaps cheese afterwards (5–10 marks, depending on the restaurant). Some, but not all, expensive restaurants also offer *table d'hôte* lunches. If you eat à la carte, there is virtually no difference between lunch and dinner prices.

Restaurant prices: from 25 marks for *table d'hôte* or lighter lunch in expensive restaurant; 35 on up for dinner. In a moderate restaurant, 9–12 marks for *table d'hôte* lunch, 12–20 for dinner. Inexpensive: 6–10 for *table d'hôte* lunch, 8–15 for dinner.

Miscellaneous prices: A ¼ liter of open wine costs 2.90–4.90 DM; Schnaps, about 1.70; whisky, 2.40 on up depending on the restaurant, bar or café; ½ liter glass of beer, 2.00 (this is the usual light beer; dark beer and special beers are more); coffee in a good café, 2–3 marks; dry cleaning costs from 4-8 marks for a dress, 8-12 for a man's suit; a haircut for the male is about 12 marks, for his spouse 12–20.

German cigarette brands cost about 2.85 DM per pack of 20. Several American brands (among them *Kent, Marlboro* and *Camel*) are produced in Germany on license and the price is about the same. British types are *Peer, Astor* and *Players.* Cigars cost 20 pf. to 1 mark.

HOTEL COSTS (in DM)

	Major cities & top resorts*	Smaller towns	Cheaper resorts*& countryside
Deluxe and luxurious			
Single	75–150	70–100	
Double	120–220	98–140	
First class superior			
Single	65–85	55–65	40–50
Double	86–160	85–100	60–80
First class reasonable			
Single	38–80	36–60	25–43
Double	50–107	45–88	40–70
Moderate			
Single	23–45	22–45	20–33
Double	45–83	40–60	35–57
Inexpensive			
Single	20–30	15–28	10–23
Double	25–50	29–46	20–40

*   These are top seasonal rates for resorts

CAPITAL. Bonn is the capital of the Federal Republic of Germany.

LANGUAGE. German. English spoken and understood in major cities.

CLIMATE. Moderate, cold in winter.
Average maximum daily temperatures in degrees Fahrenheit and centigrade:

Berlin	Jan.	Feb.	Mar.	Apr.	May	June	July	Aug.	Sept.	Oct.	Nov.	Dec.
F°	36	37	46	55	66	72	75	73	68	55	45	37
C°	2	3	8	13	19	22	24	23	20	13	7	3

Frankfurt												
F°	37	41	52	61	68	73	77	75	70	57	46	39
C°	3	5	11	16	20	23	25	24	21	14	8	4

SEASONS. May to end Sept. For winter sports in Bavarian Alps: Dec. through Mar.

SPECIAL EVENTS. From Dec. 31 through Ash Wednesday is Carnival (*Fasching* in German), particularly celebrated in Munich, Cologne, Düsseldorf, Mainz, Augsburg and Aachen. Int'l ski events at Garmisch-Partenkirchen, Jan. Leaders in the long list of annual musical and theatrical events are the *Wiesbaden International Festival* in May, the *Munich Opera Festival,* mid-July to mid-Aug., and the *Wagner Festival* in Bayreuth, late July through late Aug. *Munich Oktoberfest* (beer festival over two weeks beginning the third Sat. in Sept.) is world-known. Christkindl Markt, toy fairs all over Germany, especially Nuremburg, Dec. There are numerous folklore events and trade fairs throughout the year. For full details enquire at any German Tourist Office.

CLOSING TIMES. In general, shops are open from 8:30 or 9 A.M. to 6 or 6:30 P.M. and close Sat. afternoons, except for the first Sat. in each month. Hairdressers close Mon. Banks: 8:30–12:30 and 1:45–3:45, Mon.–Fri.; Thurs. until 5:30.

 SPORTS. The most popular spectator sport is *soccer* football, closely followed by *ice-hockey* and *athletics.* Horseback *riding* is available in many parts of the country; *racing* tracks abound. The fine Nürburgring in the Eifel mountains near Aachen is the scene of important *car races.* The top place in Germany for *gliding* is on Wasserkuppe in Rhön; also near Hornberg in the Swabian Mountains and Unterwössen in Bavaria (school). The chief *skiing* areas are the Bavarian Alps, Allgäu, the Black Forest, the Harz and Eiffel mountains, and the Bavarian Forest, the last three particularly for economy skiers. *Golf* courses throughout the country, but especially good at Wiesbaden and Frankfurt. *Sailing* on North Sea and Bavarian lakes.

MONEY. The German monetary unit is the mark (DM), which is divided into 100 pfennigs. Exchange rate at time of writing is about 2.10 DM to the US dollar, 4.09 to the pound sterling.

 TIPPING. The service charges on hotel bills suffice, but if for any reason you wish to tip (the porter who brings in your bags might be one example), quite small amounts are acceptable. Whether you tip the hotel concierge depends on whether he has given you any special service. Although restaurant bills include 10% for service, it is customary, as is also the case with taxi drivers, to round up the price to the next half-mark or full mark, but not more than 5%. Station porters (available only in resorts and small towns), get 2 marks for one bag, 1 mark for each additional bag; add 40–50 pfennigs as a tip. No need to tip doormen, theater ushers, or barmen.

 HOW TO REACH WEST GERMANY. By Air: daily direct flights from New York to Munich, Frankfurt, Stuttgart and Hamburg and several flights weekly from Chicago, Los Angeles, Anchorage, Philadelphia, Boston and Montreal to Frankfurt, all by *Lufthansa;* also daily flights from New York to Frankfurt, Munich, Stuttgart and several times weekly to Berlin by *PAA;* daily *TWA* flights to Frankfurt from Los Angeles, San Francisco, Chicago and New York. All principal German cities are connected by daily flights from London and all west European capitals.

By Sea: from Harwich (England) to Bremerhaven or Hamburg by *Prins Ferries.*

By Rail: From London (Victoria) to Dover-Ostend, thence to Aachen. From London (Liverpool St.) via Harwich and Hook of Holland.

CUSTOMS. You may bring in duty free all objects intended for personal use including 400 cigarettes, 100 cigars or 500 grams of tobacco if you're from a non-European country, half that amount if you are from Europe, except Common Market countries, whose allowance is 300 cigarettes, 75 cigars, and 400 grams of tobacco. You may bring into or take out of Germany any amount of German and foreign currency, without declaration or any other formality.

MAIL. Postcards, domestic and Common Market countries, 40 pfennigs, other foreign countries 50 pfennigs; letters up to 20 grams, domestic and Common Market countries 50 pfennigs, other foreign countries 70 pfennigs, including Great Britain; no extra charge for airmail within Europe. Airmail overseas for 5 grams (one airmail sheet of paper and envelope): 90 pfennigs to the United States, Canada and South Africa, 1 mark to Australia and New Zealand. Airmail postcards to US and Canada, 70 pfennigs. Telegrams within Europe are 48 pfennigs a word; to U.S. 1.44 marks per word. Postal rates are expected to rise slightly in 1979.

ELECTRICITY. Is 220 volts AC, 50 cycles, almost everywhere.

DRINKING WATER. Excellent.

TRAVEL IN GERMANY. By Air: From Hamburg to Munich, Germany's major cities are linked to each other by the frequent services of *Lufthansa,* many featuring wide body Airbuses. The airline is not, however, permitted to fly into West Berlin. *Pan American, British Airways* and *Air France* provide frequent and inexpensive flights, partly subsidized by the Government, to all major West German cities from Berlin to Tegel Airport. *DLT* (Deutsche Regional Luftverkehrsgesellschaft) flies to Helgoland and other islands in the north of Germany from major cities.

By Car. Transversing the country and still being extended, the German super-highways *(Autobahnen)* are the most important road network in Europe, where there are more than a hundred inns and numerous motels: other roads first class, with a 100-kph speed limit. Presently no speed limit on autobahns. Seat belts are compulsory. Autobahn Service, a folder with maps of entire network, is available at all autobahn gas stations and inns (English editions from Lufthansa and National Tourist Offices). Entrance formalities simple. International insurance card no longer required. Gasoline (petrol) prices are competitive in Germany and at time of writing vary from 90 pfennigs to 1 DM a liter. The Automobile Club of Germany has introduced a system of patrol cars (yellow) to help motorists on autobahns: telephones are situated at frequent intervals; emergency calls by foreign tourists are taken by Radio Hessen—dial 0611/1551. Children under 12 must sit in the back of any car in which they are riding. *Lufthansa* airline connects all major German cities with the exception of Berlin, and offers American-style weekend reductions within Germany. *Europabus* has several routes within Germany.

CAR HIRE. Self-drive cars may be ordered at the ticket windows of 130 major railroad stations and on TEE and Inter-City trains. Another railroad service is the *Autoreisezug* system by which a passenger's car is transported on the same train—usually overnight. All the larger Western German towns have drive-your-self car hire service such as *Autourist, Selbstfahrer Union* or *Metro Rent-a-Car. Hertz* and *Avis* have offices in major cities, *Auto Sixt* in Munich, Frankfurt and Hamburg.

Average car rental costs: from 28 marks (for a simple type of Volkswagen) to 112 marks (Mercedes 280) per day, plus, respectively, 28 pfennig to 1.12 Marks extra for each kilometer, this includes the third-party insurance, oil and engine servicing (if necessary), but not the gasoline; weekly, 4-weekly and longer rates are lower.

RIVER CRUISING. The best way to see the romantic Rhine Valley is by boat. There are several fast services daily between Düsseldorf, Cologne and Mainz. Luxury German hotel-boats cruise the entire length of the Rhine between Basel and Rotterdam, as well as the Mosel River. Other German cruising ships operate on the Main, the Neckar and the Weser rivers. Lake Constance has a boat service all year round. Heidelberg to Neckarsteinach on the Neckar.

BY TRAIN. The Federal Railroads, famous for comfort and service, have stewardesses on some trains, telephones as well as multilingual secretaries. The 100-m.p.h. *Rheingold* and *Rheinpfeil* trains are fitted with panoramic vista-dome cars. TEE (first-class only) and Inter-City (some with 2 classes) are the best.

GUIDES. Inquire at the nearest tourist office, or from your hotel porter.

CAMPING. The camping sites in Germany are numerous. The German National Tourist Office publishes a folder on camping sites, and the *German Camping Club,* Mandelsstr. 28, Munich 23, a complete guide which costs 12.80 DM for non-members, free for members. If you plan an extensive German and/or European camping tour, membership entitles you, among other privileges, to 20-30% reduction in all European camping sites.

Frankfurt

Frankfurt on the Main, Germany's traffic center, is the city most tourists reach first. It is a pleasant—not too attractive—city, and it has always been a center of trade and of German liberalism. Famous for trade fairs since the Middle Ages, the city continues this tradition with an annual international fair in March, a second one in September, and the greatest book fair in the world in September/October.

Charlemagne took up residence in this city in 794, and Frankfurt became the place of election and coronation of the Holy Roman emperors. Johann Gutenberg, inventor of printing, set up shop here in 1454; 100 years later, Frankfurt was Europe's most important printing center. Goethe was born here in 1749, and this great liberal city, to its everlasting honor, opposed the Nazis, so it has come into its own with the establishment of a liberal republic.

The chief tourist attractions of the Altstadt (Old Town) are Goethe's house, carefully and lovingly restored after its destruction in World War II; what is left of the 13th- 16th-century Karmeliterkloster; the 13th-century Romanesque Leonhardskirche (don't miss the wonderful old doors inside), the Steinernes Haus (now reserved for art exhibitions), and the Saalhof, once the palace of Frederick Barbarossa.

On no account should you miss the Römerberg, a marvelous medieval square, which was a scene of gay rejoicing during the coronations of the Holy Roman emperors of the German nation. Its name derives from the Römer, a group of three Gothic buildings located here. This structure, for centuries the symbol of Frankfurt (and also housing the Town Hall for 550 years), was remarkably well rebuilt after the last war. The emperors' coronation hall is among the rooms which can be visited. Also preserved are the Gothic church of St. Nicholas (with modern clock-orchestra) and the 15th-century Cathedral of St. Bartholomew, with its beautiful carved pews and murals. Across from the cathedral (Dom) is the restored Cloth Hall, built in 1399.

PRACTICAL INFORMATION FOR FRANKFURT

HOTELS. The *Frankfurt Intercontinental,* on Untermain-kai, by the river, is the largest with 814 rooms, and in top deluxe class; it has private suites, penthouse supper club with panoramic view, the *Dell'Arte* restaurant and a café-brasserie on the ground floor, ballroom and banquet hall for conventions. Also in the deluxe class are the old established and famous *Steigenberger Frankfurter Hof,* vast and glittering; *Parkhotel,* rooms in old section noisy; and *Frankfurt Savoy;* all near main station. *Sheraton,* 3 restaurants, several bars, discothèque, indoor pool, is at the airport.

First class superior: *Hessischer Hof,* near fair grounds. *Savigny* and a new *Holiday Inn,* to open in 1979, are near center; *Monopol* and *National,* both near the main station; *Crest Hotel,* 312 airconditioned rooms, and the smaller *Holiday Inn,* indoor pool, are both midway between airport and town; *Steigenberger Airport Hotel,* rooftop swimming, near airport. *Gravenbruch Kempenski,* in Neu Isenburg, south of the city, with fine restaurant, indoor pool. *Arabella,* in Nieder-rad suburb; *Ramada Caravelle,* in west suburb of Griesham, 3 restaurants, indoor pool; *Holiday Inn City Tower,* 190 rooms, new in 1978, in Sachsenhausen.

First class reasonable: *Admiral,* Hölderlinstr. 25, near Zoo; and *Moselhof,* Moselstr. 46, near main station.

Moderate: *Westfälinger Hof,* Düsseldorferstr. 10; *Wiesbaden,* Baseler Str. 52 and *Ebel* (garni), Taunusstr. 11, are near main station. *Schwille,* Grosse Bockenheimerstr. 50; *Rex,* Berlinerstr. 31, and the smaller *Zentrum,* Rossmarkt 7, are in center.

Inexpensive: *Württemberger Hof,* Karlstr. 14, and *Montana,* Speyer Str. 11, are near main station. *Maingau,* Schifferstr. 38, Sachsenhausen, is quiet.

RESTAURANTS. The best known specialties of Frank-furt are the *Frankfurter* and a liver sausage known as *Zeppelinwurst.* The city's culinary specialty is *Rippchen mit Sauerkraut* which consists of pickled ribs of pork, nested in Germany's best known vegetable dish.

Frankfurt's Apfelwein taverns, once a specialty of Alt-Sachsenhausen, have all but disappeared, as has also Alt-Sachsenhausen. But a few old places still remain, such as *Zum gemalte Haus* and *Zum grauen Bock;* both serve *Handkäs mit Musik,* a local symphony of cheese, vinegar, oil, onions and spices.

You will find very good restaurants, all expensive, in such top hotels as *Frankfurter Hof, Hessischer Hof, Parkhotel* and *Frankfurt Savoy.*

Restaurants are listed E, M or I, for expensive, moderate or inexpensive.

Brückenkeller (E), Schützenstr. 6, in an old cellar reeking of medieval atmosphere and excelling in vintage wines and culinary delights.

Frankfurter Stubb (M), in the cellar of Hotel Frankfurter Hof but with separate entrance; local specialties amidst mid-19th-cent. décor served by waitresses in the dress of the same period.

Taverne Royale (E), Junghofstr. 3, with ye-old-age décor in an elegant manner; Alsatian and French specialties, good wines.

Steinernes Haus (M), Braubachstr. 35, near city hall, specializes in game. *Alt Nürnberg* (I), Gr. Bockenheimer Str. 19; Nürnberg sausages and other Franconi-an dishes.

Altdeutsche Bierstube (I-M), Goetheplatz 4; good German food and beer.

American steaks and hamburgers at *Lum's,* Goethestr. 9, and at *Steakhouse,* Hanauer Landstr. 41 (near Zoo). Both (M).

Chinese food at *Tai-Tung,* Fürstenbergerstr. 179, and at *Asia,* Gallusanlage 2. Spanish: *Stadt Malaga,* Töngesgasse 11. Swiss: *Schwyzer Hüsli,* Mendelsohnstr. 56. All (M).

Alt-Frankfurt (M), Berliner Str. 10, romantic old-style locale, and *Haferkasten* (I), Grosse Friedberger Str. 3; both have beer fountains.

Heyland's Weinstuben, Kaiserhofstr. 7, fish specialties, and *Rheinpfalz Weinstuben,* Theaterplatz, have good wines.

Outdoor restaurants (also indoors, of course): At the Palmengarten and the Zoo, and several in the City Forest. Near Neu Isenburg, south of the city: *Hofgut Neuhof,* with antique furnishings, and *Gravenbruch* (see *Hotels*), rustic style (both E). Near the airport, but in green surroundings, is *Unterschweinstiege* (M), large terrace, children's nurse and playrooms.

An interesting sight is the *Henninger Turm* in Sachsenhausen district across the river, with two rotating restaurants at the top (400 ft.): *Panorama* and *Turntable* one floor above, revolving in opposite directions (good cuisine, but even better view). Both (M).

NIGHTCLUBS. There are a number of nice dancing spots, among them: on the top floor (21st) of *Hotel Intercontinental; Le Tourbillon* in Hotel Frankfurt Savoy; *Jimmy's Bar* in Hotel Hessischer Hof; *Park-Café Odeon* at Friedberger Anlage; *Paradieshof,* Paradiesgasse 23, in the colorful suburb of Sachsenhausen. Disc dancing at *Papillon,* Kaiserhofstr. 6, and *St. John's Inn,* Grosse Hirschgraben 20. One of the newest nightclubs is *Caesars Inn,* Junghofstr. 14. Jazz at *Jazz Kneipe,* Berliner Str. 70. In Kaiserstrasse, in Moselstrasse, and other streets in the vicinity of the main station there are many hot night spots, showing uninhibited striptease and crowded with dance hostesses; their mortality is high and they frequently change names; and beware of clip joint practices.

MUSEUMS. *Städel Art Institute* (10-4 daily, 10-1 Sun.), important collection of paintings by Botticelli, Tintoretto, Cranach, Dürer, Holbein, Rembrandt, Rubens, Vermeer, Goya, Velazquez, Degas, Renoir, Cezanne and many others.

Liebieghaus (Tues. and Thurs. through Sun. 10-4, Wed. 10-8, Mon. closed), fine sculpture collection—Egyptian, Greek, Roman, German and French medieval, Italian Renaissance, and baroque.

Museum of Artisan Art (Tues. through Sat. 10-4, Sun. 10-1, Mon. closed). Furniture, procelain, glass, silver, textiles and old books and handwritten scrolls.

Senckenberg Natural History Museum (9-4 daily).

Goethe's House & Museum (9-6 daily, 10-4 Sun.).

SHOPPING. Main shopping streets are the Rossmarkt, Goetheplatz, Rathenauplatz, three large squares in one; along the Zeil, Hauptwache and Kaiserstrasse. The Berlinerstrasse has many new stores.

Beer steins and mugs, *Roeslen,* Taunusstr. 45 and *Theissinger,* Schillerstr. 3.

Binoculars sell here for about one half the American or British price. Best are Leitz, Hensoldt and Zeiss. *Carl Zeiss,* Flinschstr. 67, and *Photo-Rahn,* Kaiserstr. 55 carry a full selection.

Cameras and lenses are the best buy of all. For all the top cameras, go to *Photo-Rahn* (above), *Foto-Koch,* Kaiserstr. 26, *Neithold,* Hauptwache 7, or *Arnold,* Weserstr. 11.

Bavarian Wax-Art candles, beautifully-designed Christmas and birthday fantasies, at *Theissinger,* Schillerstr. 3.

For the famous Black Forest cuckoo-clocks try *August Grüttert,* Kaiserstr. 46.

Dolls, *Käthe Kruse* variety and the equally famous Hummel family, are sold at *Spielwaren Behle,* Kaiserstr. 28; *Spielzeug Onkel,* Goethestr. 26, and for Hummel, *R. Roeslen,* Taunusstr. 45. They also carry big stocks of the renowned Märklin trains and accessories.

Famous Rosenthal Porcelain at *Rosenthal am Kaiserplatz,* Friedenstr. 10. For Hummel, Meissen and Rosenthal figurines, it's *Nikolaus Franz,* Steinweg 5, *Lorey,* Schillerstr. 16, and *H. Stern,* Liebfrauenberg 26 and Intercontinental Hotel.

USEFUL ADDRESSES. *Consulates:* U.S.A., Siesmayerstr. 21; British, Bockenheimer Landstr. 51. *American Express,* Neue Mainzerstr. 25. *Wagons-Lits/Cook,* Kaiserstr. 27.

Hesse—Spa Country

This is a land of storied castles and healing springs. Bad Homburg, only 12 miles from Frankfurt, has 11 therapeutic springs already famous in Roman times. More recently, Dwight D. Eisenhower declared his affection for Bad Homburg; the place has never lost its vogue. The state apartments of Bad Homburg's schloss can be visited on conducted tours. Other sights are the 13th-century Weisser Turm, the castle gate, the lower bridge and the Church of the Redeemer, with its rich marble and mosaic interior.

But the most famous attraction of Bad Homburg is four and a half miles away at Saalburg, where you will see the best preserved Roman fort in Europe. Bad Homburg is but one stop in Hesse's "international promenade of spas" stretching from Wiesbaden to Bad Wildungen. One of the best is Bad Nauheim, with its naturally warm carbonic acid springs.

From Marburg to Kassel

A visit to the castle and university town of Marburg is fascinating for the lover of folklore. Old customs and traditions have survived here. If you're in this area in summertime, see the folk plays and festivals in the park of the castle. Also not to be missed: St. Elizabeth's Gothic Cathedral, one of the oldest in Germany. Among the interesting old towns en route from Marburg to Kassel are Winterberg, a well-known health resort; Korbach, with its ancient church of St. Kilian and its medieval buildings; Waldeck, whose castle overlooks the Edersee; the cathedral town of Fritzlar; and Schotten, equally notable for its mountain road races and its gems of Baroque architecture. The country around here looks like a setting for Grimm's fairy tales, as indeed it was.

Kassel, industrial capital of Hesse-Nassau, has a museum which houses one of Germany's finest collections, the Landesmuseum und Gemäldegalerie.

PRACTICAL INFORMATION FOR HESSE

Hotels are listed D, 1, 2, 3, or 4, for deluxe, first class superior, reasonable, moderate, or inexpensive.

BAD HOMBURG. Hotels: *Steigenberger Ritters Parkhotel* (D), with excellent restaurant. *Kurhaus Hotel,* (2). The quiet *Hardtwald-Hotel* (3); *Taunus* (4).

Restaurants: *Zum Silbernen Bein* (M), in the castle, with terrace; *Zum Löwen* (I), Oberg. 14.

BAD NAUHEIM. Hotels: *Hilberts Parkhotel* (1). *Hessenland am Kurhaus* (2), all rooms with bath. The small *Grünewald* (3).

FULDA. Hotels: *Kurfürst, Hessischer Hof* and *Lenz.* All (3).
Restaurants: *Orangerie-Diana-Keller* in the Orangerie; *Hauptwache,* Bonifatiusplatz 2; *Stiftskeller,* Borgiasplatz 1. All (M).

KASSEL. Hotels: *Schlosshotel Wilhelmshöhe* (1); *Parkhotel Hessenland* and *Reiss* are (2); *Excelsior* and the quiet *Am Rathaus* are (3); *Holiday Inn* (2), 10 miles out, offers indoors pool, color TV.
Restaurants: *Weinstuben St. Elisabeth, Alt-Cassel* in Hotel Reiss, *Henkel, Ratskeller.*

KRONBERG. Motorists with well padded wallets should not miss the *Schlosshotel,* a converted baronial mansion reeking with atmosphere.

LIMBURG. Hotels: *Dom-Hotel* and *Huss* (3). *Waldecker Hof,* about 6 miles southwest, an annex of Schaumburg Castle above it, with pool and good restaurant, is also (3).

MARBURG. Hotels: *Kurhotel Ortenberg, Europäischer Hof* and *Waldecker Hof* (3).
Restaurants: Colorful is *Gasthaus zur Sonne* in half-timbered house from 1600, also a few inexpensive rooms.

SABABURG. Hotel: *Burghotel Sababurg* (3), the legendary castle of Sleeping Beauty, about 10 miles from Hofgeismar north of Kassel.

TRENDELBURG. Also near Hofgeismar, the 13th-cent. *Burghotel Trendelburg* (2), with dining indoors by candlelight and outdoors on the ramparts.

Westphalia
This province between the Weser and the Rhine is synonymous throughout the civilized world with ham. It is full of oak forests, and these have provided Westphalia's pigs with luscious acorns, which they have converted into even more luscious ham and bacon.

But this country's attractions are not limited to the table. It has a wide variety of appeal to all travelers, from the Youth Hostels center of castled Altena and the stalactite cave of Attendorn to the Stone, Bronze and Iron Age relics of the Lippisches Landmuseum of Detmold.

Osnabrück, Munster and Dortmund
Among the major cities of this area is Osnabrück, a lively town with a thousand-year-old cathedral. It was here in 1660 that George I of England was born, German founder of the dynasty which still rules Britain. The regional capital of Münster, seat of Westphalia University, is interesting for its many old buildings and as a center for excursions to such places as Freckenhorst, with its Romanesque church; Burgsteinfurt, with its important moated castle; Coesfeld, a Hanseatic city with its old walls and gates still standing; and Nordkirchen, with its impressive ensemble of baroque castles.

Dortmund, on the other hand, takes pride in modern achievements rather than in those of the past. Here is a booming city, typical of the resurgent industrial Ruhr, the empire of coal and steel which is "the forge of Germany". Take a look here at the ultramodern Westfalenhalle, largest sports arena in Western Europe, an ovaloid building made mostly of glass. Dortmund is the greatest brewing center of northern Germany, producing a product that goes perfectly with Westphalian ham.

PRACTICAL INFORMATION FOR WESTPHALIA

 HOTELS AND RESTAURANTS. Ach, those hams! If you want a man-sized breakfast, you'll find a huge slice of it served with rich pumpernickel bread. Hotels are listed D, 1, 2, 3 or 4, for deluxe, first class superior, reasonable, moderate or inexpensive. Restaurants, E, M or I, for expensive, moderate or inexpensive.

DORTMUND. Hotels: *Römischer Kaiser* (1), with fine restaurant and cafe; *Esplanade* and *Westfalenhof* are (2).

Restaurants: *Zum Ritter* (E), *Krone* (E), *Zum Alten Bergamt* (M), with terrace. *Am Alten Markt* (I), cold dishes only, is colorful. The rotating *Turmrestaurant* (M), on top of the TV Tower, has a fine view.

MÜNSTER. Hotels: *Kaiserhof,* (2); *Conti* (3), at the main station; *Horstmann* and *Überwasserhof* are (4). Just out of town are two castle hotels: *Schloss Wilkinghege* (2), good restaurant, and, a bit further, *Schloss Hohenfeld* (3).

Restaurants: *Rietkötter Schinkenstübchen, Stuhlmacher* all (M), *Altes Gasthaus Leve,* over 350 years old, is (I).

OSNABRÜCK. Hotels: *Hohenzollern,* at the main station, with good restaurant, and *Kulmbacher Hof,* both (2); *Central* and *Klute* (3).

A few miles west is the *Parkhotel* (1), with swimming pool.

Restaurants: *Deele* (E), Hasestr. 24. *Gambrinus* (M), Domhof 9. *Ellerbracke* (I), Neuer Graben 7.

The Northern Rhineland

The A, B, C and D of Northern Rhineland cities are Aachen, Bonn, Cologne and Düsseldorf. We could add a capital E for Essen, the largest city of the region. But despite its ninth-century Münster Church and other treasures, industrial Essen is not recommended for tourists.

Aachen

Aachen is another stein of beer. This spa (among the hottest springs in northwest Europe) is steeped in history. It was Charlemagne's capital, and 32 of the Holy Roman emperors were crowned here, either in the emperor's cathedral, begun in the ninth century, or in the Coronation Hall of the Rathaus. In the cathedral, you will see the marble chair of Charlemagne, and what remains of his body lies near the main altar. The cathedral's other great treasure is the Shrine of Mary, an intricately sculptured gold and silver reliquary, finished in 1237, possibly the finest medieval reliquary in Germany. The ninth-century octagonal Palatine Chapel (whence the French name for Aachen, Aix-la-Chapelle) has a unique interest, and the lofty Gothic choir, whose walls are virtually all glass, is a masterpiece of 14th-century architecture.

Bonn

Bonn, gateway to the romantic Rhine Valley, is more than 2,000 years old. Beethoven was born in this city in 1770, at Bonngasse 20, now a museum. The Beethoven-Halle is an important center of musical life. Among Bonn's other attractions are the Baroque Jesu Church, the 13th-century Remigius Church, and the Alte Zoll, a mighty bastion overlooking the Rhine, with a magnificent view of the Siebengebirge. The Drachenfels, with its romantic castle ruins celebrated by Lord Byron, is one of Europe's most frequently visited mountains. From the Alte Zoll, follow the attractive promenade along the Rhine to the Bundeshaus, the German equivalent of the Capitol or Houses of Parliament, for Bonn is presently the West German capital.

Cologne

Cologne, first city of the Rhineland, was almost wiped out by aerial bombardment in the war. But the great cathedral still stands, and much else remains of cultural interest.

The cathedral, nearly 500 feet long, is one of the largest Gothic churches in the world and one of the most beautiful. Don't miss the reliquary of the Three Magi, a masterpiece of medieval goldsmith's art, nor the altar's center panel, painted by Stefan Lochner, greatest native artist of Cologne. If you're feeling strong, the 500-plus-step climb to the top of the towers will be rewarded with a splendid view.

The Romanesque basilica of St. Pantaleon also survived the bombing, and in the rebuilt church of St. Ursula is the famous Golden Room, full of relics and treasures which are quite literally fabulous. Still another Romanesque monument is the extraordinary church of St. Gereon, with its ten-sided nave. The 15th-century Gürzenich, built for dancing and feasting in the Middle Ages, still serves the same purpose today, especially at carnival time.

But Cologne does not live on the glory of past monuments. The vitality of this city can be measured by the tremendous modern buildings that are replacing the lost medieval ones—the ultramodern Opera House, the Chamber of Commerce building, the Gerling skyscraper, the most modern radio building in Europe, and block after block of new structures. There is also a zoo, a botanical garden and a city forest with deer, and for wet days, several museums.

Düsseldorf

Düsseldorf, administrative center of the most industrialized area of Germany, is called "the desk of the Ruhr district". It is also an important cultural center, Heine. Brahms, Schumann and Goethe all lived here. The last is honored by the Goethe Museum, containing more than 20,000 manuscripts, drawings, first editions and other memorabilia. In the Municipal Art Museum you will find outstanding collections of painting, sculpture, medieval arts and crafts, including 2000 years of ceramics.

PRACTICAL INFORMATION FOR NORTHERN RHINELAND

 HOTELS AND RESTAURANTS. Don't leave without sampling *Hase im Topf*, a pâté of rabbit, pork, Madeira, brandy and red wine, highly flavored and baked for hours in an earthenware pot.

Hotels are listed D, 1, 2, 3, or 4, for deluxe, first class superior, reasonable, moderate or inexpensive: restaurants are E, M, or I, for expensive, moderate or inexpensive.

AACHEN (Aix). Hotels: *Kurhotel Quellenhof* (D); *Trawigo-Hotel* and *Berliner Hof* are (2).

Restaurants: The historic *Ratskeller* (E); *Elisenbrunnen* (M); *Gut Schwarzenbruch* (E), about 8 miles east. Roulette, Baccarat and Black Jack in the Casino.

BAD GODESBERG. The small, modern *Godesburg* (D), is attached to the medieval Godesburg castle. *Park Hotel,* modern, *Rheinhotel Dreesen,* with indoor seawater pool, and *Zum Adler,* with excellent restaurant are (1). *Rheinland* (3), quiet, is moderate; a bit less is *Drachenfels,* in Mehlem. On the other bank of the Rhine, at Königswinter, are the *Düsseldorfer Hof* and *Rheingold,* both (2).

Restaurants: *Wirtshaus Sankt Michael, Schaarschmidt,* and *Haus Maternus,* all (E).

BONN. Hotels: *Köningshof* (D), modern, excellent cuisine and wine cellar. *Steigenberger Bonn* (1), ultramodern, top five floors of the Bonn Center building. In the same price category are the *Bristol,* near the main station, indoor pool, and *Schlosspark-Hotel.* The *Sternhotel, Bergischer Hof,* and *Beethoven,* near the Rhine landing stage are all (2). *Eden, Savoy.* Both (3).

Restaurants: *Bundeshaus* (E), in Parliament Building, meeting spot of politicians; colorful *Weinhaus Jacobs* (M), Friedrichstr. 23; *Hansa-Keller* (M), Kaiserplatz. *Im Stiefel* (M), Bonng. 30; *Im Bären* (M), Acherstr. 1. Several restaurants in the Bonn Center.

COLOGNE (Köln). Hotels: The *Intercontinental,* with rooftop dining and dancing, bar, indoor pool, and the palatial *Excelsior Hotel Ernst,* on cathedral square, with fine French restaurant and grill-room, are super de luxe.

Dom Hotel, near cathedral, also with fine restaurant, and *Bremer,* in Lindenthal suburb, are both (D).

First class superior: *Senats-Hotel,* Unter Goldschmied 9, and *Consul,* Belfortstr. 9, indoor pool, both with good restaurants. *Eden,* all rooms with radio and TV, and *Europa am Dom* are near the cathedral. *Crest,* in Lindenthal suburb, two good restaurants, and *Holiday Inn,* near airport, are of recent vintage.

First class reasonable: *Haus Lyskirchen,* Filzengraben 30, pool; *Atlantic* (garni), Alter Markt 55; *Berlin,* Domstr. 10, near cathedral.

Moderate: *Kunibert der Fiese,* Am Bollwerk 1; *Regent,* Melatengurtel 15 in west suburbs, fine rooftop restaurant.

Inexpensive: *Lenz,* Ursulaplatz 9; *Stapelhäuschen,* Fischmarkt 1, small, old inn with good wine tavern.

Restaurants: *Wolff,* Komödienstr. 50; *Bastei,* on Rhine bank; *Goldener Pflug,* in Merheim section; all (E). *Im Walfisch* (M), Salzg. 13; *Haus Töller* (M–I), Weyerstr. 96; *Stapelhäuschen,* Fischmarkt 1, and *Em Kruzche,* Frankenturm, are old taverns and (M). *Alt Köln* (M), Trankg; *Brauhaus Sion* (I), Unter Taschenmacher 5; *Altstadt-Päffgen* (M-I), Am Heumarkt.

DÜSSELDORF. As befits the richest city in the Federal Republic, Düsseldorf has outstandingly good hotels. *Breidenbacher Hof,* one of Germany's best, Hein-

clean, comfortable ships between Cologne and Mainz, the most interesting stretch of the river. Upstream, count on from 13 to 16 hours for this trip, depending on whether or not you take an express steamer. Downstream, it will take 8½ or 9. You can buy a combined train-steamer ticket, enabling you to switch one to the other. You can also arrange to have your car driven up or downstream while you relax aboard one of the boats.

A shorter trip, one in which most of the attractions of the Rhine are concentrated, is the voyage from Koblenz to Mainz. Koblenz, in the shadow of the famous Ehrenbreitstein Fortress (you can reach it by chairlift), is the gateway to the most romantic section of the Rhine and the Mosel, at whose confluence the city stands. It is studded with such Romanesque churches as St. Castor's (ninth century), the Liebfrauenkirche (12th century) and St. Florin's (12th century with Gothic additions).

East of Koblenz

Just east of Koblenz is the internationally-known spa of Bad Ems, pleasantly laid out along the both banks of the Lahn River, and having a beautiful golf course; for 20 years (1867-1887), it was the spot Kaiser Wilhelm chose for his yearly cure. If you're in this neighborhood on the last Sunday in August, don't miss the Bartholomäusmarkt folklore festival.

From Koblenz onward, all the settlements are jewels, and if you want a quiet vacation, you can choose almost any of the riverside towns at random. One such town is Rüdesheim, center of Rhine wine production. The wine museum, the many wine cellars, the beautifully-designed old houses with their half-timbered walls and quaint gables and turrets, give this town a very special charm and this is the place for wine drinking in the operetta tradition.

Bingen, on the other side of the Rhine, is another tourist center, an important pilgrimage goal at the end of August when the town's deliverance from the Black Plague is celebrated annually in the Festival of St. Rochus. From Bingen, one enters the Palatinate at the "town of roses and nightingales", Bad Kreuznach, with picturesque 15th-century houses built on its bridge.

Wiesbaden

The Taunus is outdoor country, a region of pine forests, wooded hills and valleys, bounded on the west by the Rhine and on the south by the Main. One of the loveliest regions of Germany, it is a paradise for nature lovers, and has many spas, including Wiesbaden.

One of the leading watering places of the world, Wiesbaden has long been internationally renowned, a favorite with everybody from royalty to the US Air Force, whose European headquarters is here. The international May Festival presents opera companies, ballet groups and theatrical groups from all over Europe. This brilliant activity is centered about the famous Brunnenkolonnade (Spring Colonnade). Golf and tennis tournaments and horse racing are the order of the day at the height of this Wiesbaden season, and the roulette wheels never stop turning in the casino. If you want the gay worldly life of a leading spa, this is for you. If not, the surrounding countryside could not be more attractive.

OBERWESEL, between Bingen and Boppard. *Auf Schönburg,* a 1,000-year-old castle-fortress above Rhine, offers 10 period-furnished rooms at moderate prices, open March–Nov. *Römerkrug* (3), in old half-timbered house, 500-year-old wine cellar, good food, only 7 rooms.

RÜDESHEIM. Hotels: *Parkhotel Deutsches Hof* and *Rüdesheimer Hof,* both (2); *Aumüller* and *Rheinstein* (3); *Felsenkeller, Lindenwirt,* and *Krancher,* quiet location, are (4). *Jagdschloss Niederwald* (2), a castle-hotel in the forested national park, Rheingau-Untertaunus, above town, with terrace restaurant-café, is reached by cable car.

Restaurants: *Bauernstube Rüdesheim, Bergkeller, Aussichtsrestaurant* at the Niederwald Monument.

One of Germany's top attractions is the unbelievable double row of Weinhäuser in the Drosselgasse. This is *the place* for merry wine drinking in the musical comedy tradition. The *Lindenwirt, Drosselhof, Bei Hannelore* and *Zum Engel* are the chief attractions. Wine-tasting can be arranged for at the famous *Schloss Johannisburg* vineyards nearby.

SPEYER. Hotels are: *Goldener Engel, Wittelsbacher Hof.* Both (3). Across Rhine, near bridge, is the *Luxhof* (3-4), small inn, with delicious cuisine, fishing and hunting.

TRIER. Hotels: *Porta Nigra* (D), with several restaurants, 350-car underground garage. *Europäischer Hof* (1), modern, good restaurant. *Bürgerverein,* with good restaurant and the smaller *Römischer Kaiser* are (2). The colorful *Domhotel* and *Christophel* are (3). *Deutscher Hof* is (4).

Restaurants: *Schiefferkeller* (M), Simeonstr. 47; *Weinstube zum Domstein* (M), Hauptmarkt; *Simeonstor,* in an old house with cellar dating from 1200; and *Krokodil* (I), Böhmerstr. 10. *Schenk-Oster,* in nearby Waldrach, has good Ruwer wines.

WORMS. Hotels: *Domhotel* (2); *Europäischer Hof* (3); *Central* (4). Restaurants: *Kriemhilde,* at cathedral; *Domschänke,* nearby.

ZELL. *Schloss Zell* (2), dating from 1220, is a period-furnished castle-hotel whose vineyards produce the famous Mosel wine "Zeller Schwarze Katz".

PRACTICAL INFORMATION FOR MAINZ AND TAUNUS

MAINZ. Hotels: The deluxe *Hilton* (D), all the usual amenities, is situated on the Rhine. Nearby is the modern, *Mainzer Hof* (1), with fine view from roof-garden restaurant. In the same range is *Europa,* very modern, grill specialties in *La Poularde,* and the *Ramada Inn. Hammer* and *Am* Romerwall, both garni, are (3).

Restaurants: *Haus des Deutschen Weines* (M), wines from all parts of Germany; *Wilhelm's Weinstube* (M), small wine tavern.

WIESBADEN. Hotels: *Forum,* new, with café, rotisserie and pool, the even newer *Am Kochbrunnen,* in historic house, the *Schwarzer Bock, Nassauer Hof* and *Aukamm* are all (D). *Rose* and *Blum,* (1). *Hotel de France* is (2). *Oranien, Bären, Central* and *Klee,* all (3). Largest among the inexpensive is *Weisses Ross.*

Restaurants: Best are in hotels *de France* and *Schwarzer Bock, Mutter Engel* and *Kurhaus* (all E). *Siechenklause* is (M).

The best night bars are in hotels *Nassauer Hof, Schwarzer Bock* and *Rose.* Roulette and baccara in *Kurhaus Casino.*

Southwestern Germany

South of the Main, east of the Rhine, sharing a frontier with France and Switzerland, lies a region that looks as though it had come out of a story book. It includes the valley of the Neckar, the Swabian Mountains, the Black Forest, Lake Constance and the Allgäu, and that perfectly-named section, *Die Romantische Strasse,* the Romantic Road.

The Neckar River, flowing northward between the heights of the Black Forest and the Swabian Mountains, waters a fascinating land that includes the Odenwald, where you may see the very well from which Siegfried was drinking when he was killed by Hagen's spear, and the *Bergstrasse,* the Mountain Road, where fruit trees bloom in March and tobacco is grown, thanks to a freakishly warm climate.

Heidelberg

But the jewel of the Neckar is Heidelberg, with town, castle and wooded hills rising above the river. The ideal time for a visit is June through August, when the castle, one of Europe's most flourishing ruins, provides a superb backdrop for the Heidelberg Drama Festival and the open-air concerts. The castle is best reached by a cable railway, which will also take you to Königstuhl, 2,000 feet high, with a splendid panorama of the Neckar Valley.

A close runner up to the castle is Germany's oldest university, forever immortalized (or embalmed in sugar, perhaps) in *The Student Prince.* It is as delightful as any operetta, with its student inns, student prison (the university did its own disciplining, and no joking about it), and the narrow streets of the old town. This is an enchanting city to walk around in. Don't forget the old bridge, the Church of the Holy Ghost, the Jesuit Church, and the matchless Altar of the Twelve Apostles, an extraordinary example of 16th-century wood carving in the Kurpfälzisches Museum.

If you have the time you can go by boat from Heidelberg to Heilbronn and Stuttgart, a ten-hour trip on one of the loveliest stretches of the Neckar, lined with little wine towns and commanding castles.

PRACTICAL INFORMATION FOR HEIDELBERG AND HEILBRONN

HEIDELBERG. Hotels: The choice is wide. *Europäischer Hof* and *Crest,* in suburbs, are both (D). *Schrieder, Atlantic* (garni), and *Stiftsmühle,* the last in a remodeled mill just outside town, all (1). *Zum Ritter,* a 16th-cent. inn, is (2); *Hackteufel* and *Monpti* (3).

For motorists: *Holiday Inn* (D) and *Vorfelder* (1) are 10 miles south at Walldorf; *Neckarschlössl* and another *Zum Ritter* are both (3) and a few miles east on the river.

HEILBRONN. Hotels: *Insel* (2); *Kronprinz* (3); *Central* (4).
Restaurants: *Ratskellar* and *Harmonie,* both (M); *Schwabenbräu* (I).

CASTLE HOTELS: *Götzenburg* (3) at Jagtshausen in Jagst Valley; *Burg Hornberg* (2), *Schloss Hochhausen* (3) and *Burg Hirschhorn* (4) are all in the Neckar Valley.

The Swabian Mountains

If you are looking for something away from it all and almost literally out of this world, the Swabian Mountains are an answer to your prayer. Here, you will find marvelous caves, rocks, castles, endless woods and 7,000 miles of well-marked hiking trails. The farmers, shut up in their mountain villages, dress in somber black. This is Protestant country, and the people are less gay than the Catholics (to the south on Lake Constance) and the easy-going Rhinelanders. Nevertheless, you can be sure of a welcome, a comfortable bed and a good heavy meal in any mountain Gasthof.

Stuttgart

In contrast to the primitive charms of this countryside is the great city of Stuttgart, the largest in southwestern Germany. Home of Zeiss-Ikon, Bosch, Mercedes-Benz and Porsche products, it is a Mecca for architects. See the city hall and the concert hall, and dine in the panoramic restaurant 558 feet up in the television tower. A lesson for city planners, Stuttgart is actually a garden city with only 25 per cent of its area built over. The rest is woods, vineyards, market gardens, fields and parks.

Nearby Ludwigsburg boasts the largest Baroque castle in Germany, with a children's fairytale garden in its grounds. To the north, Schwäbisch Hall is the most romantic town in the Swabian Mountains.

Ulm

Another important city of the southwest is Ulm, with its 14th-century Gothic cathedral, described as having the highest church tower in the world. This Dom is one of the most beautiful in Germany; its 15th-century carved choir stalls by Jörg Syrlin are outstanding. The old city walls of Ulm are still standing, with their gates and towers.

Other interesting places in this area are: Donaueschingen, at the source of the Danube River, with the Duke Fürstenberg Palace housing an important art museum with major works of Grünewald, Holbein and Cranach; Beuron, with the famous Baroque Benedictine abbey, which has fostered arts and choral singing since 1077; Sigmaringen and its impressive castle of the princes of Hohenzollern, with a fine museum and painting gallery; Hohenzollern Castle, the original seat of this great German aristocratic family which, among others, produced Kaiser Wilhelm, on a high elevation commanding the surrounding area near the town of Hechingen; Reutlingen, a former imperial town with some very fine Gothic architecture; the area around Erpfingen, a speleologist's paradise, with its fantastic stalactite caverns (there were 70 at the last count), and finally Tübingen. This famous university town on the Neckar possesses many fine buildings—the Gothic Collegiate Church, the massive Pfalzgrafen Castle, and the 15th-century Rathaus, one of many well-preserved structures on the fascinating old market place.

PRACTICAL INFORMATION FOR THE SWABIAN MOUNTAINS

STUTTGART. Hotels: The *Graf Zeppelin,* with two fine restaurants, and *Am Schlossgarten,* also good restaurant and tavern, head the list. Both (D). *Parkhotel, Royal; Intercity* and *Bahnhof-Turmhotel* (both in the main station); all are (1). *Unger* and *Riecker* (2); *Kronen, Herzog Christoph* (3). The *Erika,* good location, is (4).

In the suburbs and outskirts are the very modern *Stuttgart International,* (D), near Autobahn exit south; *Flughafen-Hotel Stuttgart* at the airport; and *Holiday Inn* at Sindelfingen are (1). *Schlosshotel Solitude* in a wing of the baroque castle of the same name located on the wooded heights near the city, is (2).

Restaurants: *Exquisit* (E) is, as the name implies, exquisite. Atmospheric and tradition-filled are *Alte Post, Eberhard,* and *Alte Kanzlei,* all (E). Good Swabian food and wines in *Zeppelinstüble* (E) of Hotel Graf Zeppelin.

Schwobastub, opposite main station, *Ratskeller, Börse, Hirschbräu,* and *Bäckerschmiede* are all (M). *Killesberg* (M), in park of same name, with view, has music in the evening.

You might enjoy the "crow's nest" restaurant in the *Fernsehturm* (TV tower) on Bopser hill, more for the scenic panorama than the cooking.

Nightlife: Dancing in *Marquardt, Scotch Club* (Hotel Graf Zeppelin), *London Club* (Stuttgart International). Striptease: *Four Roses, Balzac, Imperial.*

USEFUL ADDRESSES. *Consulates:* U.S.A., Urbanstr. 7; British, Königstr. 45. *American Express,* Lautenschlagerstr. 3. All Stuttgart.

TÜBINGEN. Hotels: *Krone* (2), with good restaurant. *Am Herbstenhof,* in suburbs, all rooms with shower, roof garden, *Hospiz* and *Barbarina* are (3).

Restaurants: *Museumsgaststätte, Haug zum Hirsch* and *Schlosskeller* are all (M). Wine taverns: *Rebstock, Forelle, Deutsche Weinstube.*

ULM. Hotels: *Neutor-Hospiz* (2). *Stern, Am Rathaus, Ulmer Spatz* are (3). The quiet *Bäumle* is (4).

Restaurants: *Forelle, Kornhauskeller,* and *Weinstube Pflugmerzler,* all (M).

USEFUL ADDRESSES. *Consulates:* U.S.A., Urbanstr. 7; British, Kreigsbergstr. 28, both Stuttgart. *American Express,* Lautenschlagerstr. 3, Stuttgart.

The Black Forest

The Black Forest (Schwarzwald) is one of those magic names that evoke a feeling of romance. Its dark evergreens, which give it that "black" look, rise from a forest floor so free of underbrush that it looks as though it had been swept. These conifers clothe the hills and mountains east of the Rhine, starting at the Swiss frontier and extending north to Karlsruhe. It is not an unbroken forest. There are green valleys, open meadows, postcard towns, and farmhouses with steep thatched roofs. In this region, old traditions still live, and you may see colorful local dress on festive occasions and on Sundays; this pageant of folklore is what gives the Schwarzwald its special charm.

Baden-Baden

If the Black Forest conjures up an image of picturesque peasant life, its chief spa, Baden-Baden, evokes all the worldly luxury of a bygone day. But Baden-Baden, for all its memories of 19th-century glory, is very up to date. Among the ailments it undertakes to treat with its healing springs are "diseases due to the strain of modern civilization". This delightful spa has owed its fame since Roman times to radioactive chloride hot springs. You may drink their waters, recline in them, take mud baths made of them, or even inhale them in vapor form. Then, when you feel a little stronger, you can play roulette and baccara at the casino or participate, actively or as spectator, in the countless activities arranged here for your pleasure.

Walks and drives, either by car or carriage and pair, through the charming little resorts of the Black Forest are most rewarding. Typical is Freudenstadt, which claims to have more hours of sunshine during the year than any other German resort. It lies in beautiful country, surrounded by 100 miles of well-tended paths designed for the pleasures of walking in the Black Forest. Another recommended resort is Triberg, with its waterfalls and delightful swimming pool in the midst of the evergreen hills. If you are cuckoo on the subject of clocks, you are in the right country here; don't miss the remarkable clock museum at Furtwangen.

Freiburg im Breisgau, capital and largest city of the Black Forest, is an old university and cathedral town. The cathedral, begun about 1200, has a 370-foot steeple of open stone lacework which has been called the most beautiful tower of Christianity's finest period. It is a remarkable treasure house of painting, wood carving and 13th- to 16th-century stained glass windows. A colorful open-air market carries on its busy trade on the cathedral square in front of the Kaufhaus, a beautiful example of a medieval merchants' hall. Do not miss the two other fascinating squares in this attractive city—the Rathaus Square, with its old and new city halls (one medieval, the other Renaissance), and the Oberlinden, surrounded by medieval burgher houses, and the towering 13th-century Swabian Gate.

American visitors should stop to pay their respects to Martin Waldseemüller, the University of Freiburg geographer who first put the word "America" on a map.

PRACTICAL INFORMATION FOR THE BLACK FOREST

BADEN-BADEN. Hotels: *Brenner's Parkhotel,* near casino, internationally famous, super deluxe. *Bellevue, Europäischer Hof,* opposite pump-room and Kurhaus and *Badischer Hof,* all (D).

The *Golfhotel* and *Waldhotel Der Selighof,* in outskirts, both (1), have indoor and heated outdoor pools; *Zum Hirsch* (1), thermal baths in hotel.

Tannenhof, excellent restaurant, *Atlantic,* and *Holland* are (2). *Haus Tanneck, Haus Reichert* and *Müller* are (3). The attractive *Am Markt,* with good restaurant, is (4).

Restaurants: *Stahlbad* (E). *Kurhaus* (E), with wine tavern and dance-bar. *Sinner Eck* (M). *Krokodil* (I).

FREIBURG. Hotels: *Colombi; Stadt Freiburg;* and *Jägerhäusle* in Hadern suburb, mostly for reducing cures, indoor pool; all (1). *Victoria,* near station, and *Crest* in suburbs (2). *Rappen, City, Schlossbergblick,* quiet location, and *Zum Roten Bären,* are (3).

Restaurants: *Oberkirch* (E), own wines. *Falken* (E), near Rathaus, old furnishings, excellent cuisine and wines. *Eichhalde* (M); *Zum Storchen* (M); *Ratskeller* (E) in restored Kornhaus on Münsterplatz; *Weinkrüger* (M), wine tavern; *Alte Burse* (M); *Zum Roten Eber* (M). Magnificent views from *Dattler* (M) and *Greifenegg-Schlössle* (M) on Schlossberg.

Lake Constance (Bodensee)

Lake Constance (or the Bodensee, as the Germans call it) is shared by three countries. Most of its northeast shoreline is German; most of its southwest bank is Swiss; Austria has a toehold at its eastern end. However, the inhabitants of all its shores speak the same German dialects, and blood relations frequently link them across the borders. Konstanz

(Constance), its chief resort city, is a frontier anomaly, a German town on the Swiss side of the lake, completely surrounded by Swiss territory except where it fronts on the water, across which is the land to which it belongs. Konstanz is a delightful summer vacation spot, blessed with a fine cathedral, a 14th-century Council Hall, a Renaissance Rathaus, good hotels, facilities for all water sports and even a branch of the Baden-Baden Casino.

Among the jewels that line the German shore of the Bodensee, Meersburg is outstanding, a marvelous old town with a seventh-century castle, charming houses, and a number of colorful taverns appropriate to this ancient center of wine growing. Ferry boats ply between here and Konstanz, directly across the lake. Lindau, built on an island in the lake, is another gem of the Bodensee, a stage set of narrow streets and old buildings admiring itself in the tranquil mirror of Lake Constance. Try a moonlight sail from here; the steamers ply every Saturday night, and there's dining and dancing on board.

PRACTICAL INFORMATION FOR LAKE CONSTANCE

KONSTANZ (Constance). Hotels: *Insel* (D), former monastery on small island. *See-Hotel Hecht* and *Seeblick,* both (2). *Krone* and historic *Barbarossa* are (3). *Dom-Hotel St. Johann,* built in 10th century, noted restaurant, is (4).

Restaurants: *Casino* (E). *Stefanskeller* (M), historic wine tavern. *Konzil* (M), in old Council Hall. *Graf Zeppelin* (M-I). *Chalet Suisse Coralle* (M), French food and historic wine tavern. On Mainau Island: *Torkelkeller* (M), with huge wine barrel.

LINDAU. Hotels: *Bad Schachen* (at the nearby spa), is (D). *Bayerischer Hof* (1), closed in winter; *Reutemann* (2); *Lindauerhof* and *Seegarten* are (3) and closed winters. *Zum Stift* and *Alte Post* are (4).

Restaurants: *Spielbank* (E), in casino building; *Zum Lieben Augustin* (E), on Seepromenade (in hotel Seegarten), both have evening dancing. *Weinstube Frey* (M), Hauptstr. 15 (dates from 1560). *Gothenstuben* (M), in der Grub 32.

MEERSBURG. Hotels: *Strandhotel Wilder Mann,* café with music and dancing, and *Rothmund am See,* both (2). *Zum Schiff* and *Drei Stuben,* fine restaurants, are both (3). Atmospheric old inns include *Löwen* and *Zum Bären,* both (4).

On the hill above the lake, with marvelous views, are the modern *Villa Bellevue* and *Terrassen-Hotel Weisshaar,* both (2).

Restaurants (which in Meersburg means mostly wine taverns): *Zum Becher* (M), outstanding food. *Ratskeller* (I), vaulted town hall cellar. *Winzertrinkstube* (I), wines of the local wine growers' cooperative. *Burgkeller* (M), with garden and music.

The Romantic Road

The Romantic Road *(Die Romantische Strasse)* is much more than just a road from Füssen to Würzburg. Special buses travel up and down the road, and by all means use them. It's cheap, it's convenient, and it provides the concentrated essence of picture-book Germany, a progression through a continuous unbroken pageant of marvels. Starting at Füssen in Bavaria on the Austrian border, you proceed through the Allgäu Alps. Your only problem is going to be how long you would like to stay where; we warn you that each town on this route is more enchanting than the one before it.

Neuschwanstein

Just a few miles from Füssen, you will find lofty Neuschwanstein, facing Hohenschwangau on a nearby hill, another royal castle. Neuschwanstein has to be seen to be believed, and even then you may wonder if this pinnacled castle perched on a mountain peak is real or a dream. It was a dream of mad King Ludwig II of Bavaria, and yet it is quite real. If you have a chance to hear one of the summer Wagner concerts in this setting, don't pass it up.

Augsburg

Following the Lech River, you will pass through Schongau, Landsberg, one of the finest medieval cities in southern Bavaria with its matchless Gothic gate, then right through the Rote Tor (Red Gate) into the spectacular metropolis of the Romantic Road, Augsburg. The tower, bridge, ramparts, and moat of this castled city, against whose massive background Germany's finest open-air opera season takes place in July and August, will give you a foretaste of its architectural riches. Don't miss the cathedral, begun in 995, which has the oldest stained glass in the world (11th-century), altar paintings by Holbein (who was born here), and an early 11th-century bronze door. See St. Ulrich's Church, the only church with two towers and two religions, Catholic *and* Protestant, embodying in stone the spirit of the Religious Peace of Augsburg, achieved in 1555. And take a stroll down the Maximilianstrasse, the finest Renaissance street in all Germany.

North to Mergentheim

Continuing north through Bavarian Swabia, the Romantic Road follows a chain of medieval cities—Donauwörth, on the Danube; Harburg, with its castle and its splendid Gobelin tapestries; Nördlingen, "the living medieval city", where the night watch's call still echoes through the narrow streets as it has for centuries, and Dinkelsbühl, its walls still standing, complete with bastions, gates, towers, and a moat. In July, however, it celebrates its escape from destruction during the Thirty Years' War with the Kinderzeche (Children's Tribute), a festival of sword dances, guild dances and historic pageants. Rothenburg, a walled city on the Tauber, is another must stop on the Romantic Road. Its towers and gates are intact, its ancient fountains brilliant with scarlet geraniums. It holds *its* festival of salvation at Whitsuntide, commemorating its salvation with a play in the Rathaus called *Der Meistertrunk,* "The Master Drink", in honor of a burgomaster who saved the city by a prodigious feat of quaffing. Still another link in the golden chain is Bad Mergentheim, with its great castle of the Teutonic Knights and its healing springs, which, used in the early Bronze and late Iron Age, were rediscovered in 1826.

Würzburg

Würzburg is the terminus of the Romantic Road, an old university town which was the site of a bishopric as early as 741. Here you are in the center of the Franconian wine growing region, scene of a gay wine festival each September. Its chief ornament is the baroque residence castle of the prince-bishops, built by the master architect Balthasar Neumann. Here, with a background of Tiepolo frescos, an annual Mozart Festival is held in June, July or August. Open-air concerts are given in the castle garden, and the Marienberg, mighty fortress of the prince-bishops, is illuminated during the Main Festival of August. The great wood carver, Riemenschneider, who was mayor of this town, left his mark on it. We recommend a visit to the nearby Schlosspark Veitshöchheim. This is the most remarkable rococo garden in Germany.

PRACTICAL INFORMATION FOR THE ROMANTIC ROAD

AUGSBURG. Hotels: *Palasthotel Drei Mohren* (D), opened in 1723, is one of Germany's historic hotels; Russian Czars and German Emperors have been guests, as well as Mozart and Goethe. *Holiday Inn* (D), next to the Kongresshalle. *Alpenhof* and *Weisses Lamm* are (2).

Riegele and *Blaues Krügle,* with atmospheric tavern, are *(3); Viktoria,* at main station, is (4).

Restaurants: *Berteles Weinstube* (E); *Welser-Küche* (E), in old patrician Stiermann House, original medieval recipes in 16th-cent. atmosphere; *Ratskeller* (M); *Sieben-Schwaben-Stuben* (I); *Fuggerkeller* (M), in historic Fuggerhaus.

BAD MERGENTHEIM. Hotels: *Victoria,* (1), most rooms with bath, rooftop pool; *Kurhaus* (2), with indoor pool; *Stefanie* and *Garni* (3); *Zum Straussen,* in old (1557) half-timbered house (4).

DINKELSBÜHL. Hotels: Best is the half-timbered 15th-cent. *Deutsches Haus;* its *Altdeutsches Restaurant* with frescos, coats-of-arms, serves delightful local specialties and Franconian wines. *Goldene Rose,* nearby, with *Ratskeller* tavern, has been completely renovated. A few steps away is *Goldener Hirsch,* an unpretentious small hostelry with good food.

NÖRDLINGEN. Hotels: *Sonne,* established 1477, *Hotel am Ring,* at station, and *Schützenhof,* with good local specialties in restaurant, are (3). Historic inns are *Alte Post* and *Goldenes Lamm,* both (4).

ROTHENBURG. Hotels: *Eisenhut* (D), two historic buildings in perfect antique style, excellent cuisine and cellar. *Goldener Hirsch* (1), outstanding view, dining room on the *Blue Terrace; Zum Bären,* indoor pool, *Burg,* with view over valley, and the 700-year-old *Gotisches Haus* are a bit less.

The small *Adam,* the colorful *Markustrum* and *Roter Hahn* are (3).

Restaurant: The *Baumeisterhaus* (M), 16th-cent., good food and wines.

WÜRZBURG. *Rebstock* (1), in neo-Baroque building, wine tavern; *Schloss Steinberg,* on famous vineyard hill, outdoor pool; *Walfisch,* on river, and *Am Franziskanerplatz,* are all (2). *Russ,* with good food, garage, is (3).

Restaurants and taverns: *Burgrestaurant* and *Schiffbäuerin,* both (M). *Juliusspital* and *Hofkellerei* serve wines from their own vineyards and light snacks only.

Bavaria, Holiday Land

This extensive territory, holiday land for Germany and all of Europe, was for centuries an important nation in its own right. Upper Bavaria is in the south, Lower Bavaria is in the middle and towards the east, and Franconia is in the north. Upper Bavaria is called "Upper" because it is a mountain region, and Lower Bavaria is called "Lower" because it consists of undulating small hills interspersed by plains.

Franconia takes up most of northern Bavaria. It is dotted with medieval cities like Bamberg and Coburg and with old fortress towns like Kronach, but its chief attractions for the tourist, in addition to Würzburg (described above under the section on the Romantic Road), are Bayreuth and Nuremberg (Nürnberg).

Bayreuth

Bayreuth is world-famous for its Richard Wagner Festival in July and August, so popular now that it is advisable to book accommodations and buy tickets through your travel agent many months in advance. If you should arrive without reservations, however, the local tourist office can arrange for you to be put up in private homes. The Wagner productions still under the direction of the great man's family are the last word in modern stage technique, so different from the traditional productions that they scandalize the old guard, forgetful perhaps of the scandals Wagner himself caused with his bold innovations. If you are one of those who find Wagner a little on the long-winded side, go to Bayreuth in June for the Franconian Baroque Festival—ballets and concerts of the 18th century, given in the perfect setting of the Margraves' Opera House, which was built in 1745.

Nürnberg

Nürnberg (Nuremberg in English), pop. 510,000, was the home of Mastersinger Hans Sachs, of Tannhäuser and Albrecht Dürer. Renowned for its industry, its intellect, its high-roofed, half-timbered medieval dwellings and imposing public buildings, Nürnberg became a kind of prototype of German glory. Hitler's exploitation of this glory to exacerbate the nationalism he represented brought tragedy to this great city. But Nürnberg has survived both Hitler and his war. It's amazing how painstakingly the old buildings of the city have been reconstructed after the devastating air raids during World War II. If you're here in the summer, try to plan it for a weekend, when the old buildings are floodlighted. It's as though the Middle Ages had waited for electricity to reveal their mystery. And wander through "Alt Nürnberg" in the Waffenhof, where you can watch basketmakers, blacksmiths, bakers and other craftsmen at work—and buy their wares if you so desire.

Here are the other things you shouldn't miss: the riverside view from the Maxbrücke; the Kaiserburg (Imperial Castle), restored to its prewar state, with apartments open to the public; St. Sebald's Church (13th century) with the *Sebaldusgrab,* a masterpiece of bronze and silverwork by Peter Vischer and his sons; the Altstadt Museum (Fembohaus), the only surviving medieval patrician house; the restored 14th-century Gothic Frauenkirche, with its fine porch and statuary by Adam Kraft; the Albrecht Dürer House, an effective restoration of the destroyed original; St. Lawrence's Church, largest and most beautiful in the city (Gothic), with famous rose window, wood carving (the *Angelic Salutation* by Veit Stoss) and stone Tabernacle, with statues by Adam Kraft.

Finally, pay a visit to the Germanic National Museum. One of the finest in the nation, it presents a complete view of all German art up to the 18th century, including the applied arts. It has a fascinating collection of toys and dolls' houses, a link with the present, for Nürnberg today, as it has been for centuries, is the toy capital of Germany. The annual national Toy Trade Fair is held here in March, and if you really want to indulge in an orgy of top shopping, come here for the Christ Kindl Markt in December.

PRACTICAL INFORMATION FOR BAVARIA AND FRANCONIA

BAMBERG. Hotels: *Bamberger Hof* (1); *National, Straub* and *Alte Post* are (2); the quiet *Evangelisches Hospiz* is (3); *Roter Ochse* (4).

Restaurants: *Messerschmidt* (M), game and fish; *Schlenkerla* (I), old-style tavern (smoked beer); *Steineres Haus* (M), local fish dishes.

BAYREUTH. Hotels: *Bayerischer Hof, Am Hofgarten, Reichsadler* (garni) and *Goldener Hirsch* are (3). *Zum Edlen Hirschen* is (4).

About 4 miles south is *Schlosshotel Thiergarten* (2), period-furnished and excellent restaurant. About 16 miles south in Pegnitz is *Pflaums Posthotel* (1), with noted restaurant, in same family since 1787.

Restaurants: *Eule* (M), artists' tavern; *Lukullus-Keller* (M); *Wolffenzacher* (M); local color at *Mohrenstube* wine tavern.

NÜRNBERG (Nuremberg). Hotels: *Grand-Hotel,* top restaurant, and *Carlton* are (D). A bit less is *Crest,* in suburbs. *Merkur, Am Sterntor, Kaiserhof* and the colorful *Pfälzer Fass* are (2).

Am Hauptmarkt and *Am Heideloffplatz* are (3). A bit less are *Blaue Traube* and *Lorenz.*

Restaurants: For atmosphere, fine food, wine and music: *Nassauer Keller,* deep 13th-cent. cellar of Nassau House (M-E). *Goldenes Posthorn* (E), once frequented by Dürer and Hans Sachs. *Marientorzwinger* (M). *Ratsstuben* (M). *Heilig-Geist-Spital* (M), more than 100 wines from all over Germany. *Kronfleischküche,* with windows on Regnitz river.

Nürnberg sausages and local color: *Bratwurst-Herzle, Bratwurst-Häusle, Bratwurst-Röslein* and, to break the pattern, *Zunftstube.*

Worth the excursion is *Zur Grünen Weintraube* (M), in suburb of Grossreuth, in old half-timbered house; closed Aug.

 SHOPPING. Nürnberg has two excellent shopping streets: Karolinenstrasse and Königstrasse, with its extensions, Pfannenschmiedsgasse and Vordere Sterngasse. As the toy-making capital of Germany, if not the world, you can expect a rich assortment of toy stores, such as *Theinert,* Königstr. 2, and *Spielwarenhaus Virnich,* Luitpoldstr. 6. For those wonderful Bavarian folk art candles try *Kerzen Elsässer,* Augustinerstr.; craftmanship galore in Waffenhof *"Alt Nürnberg",* open in summer.

Munich, Capital of Bavaria

Munich (or München), capital of Bavaria, is a city with a great past, an exciting present and a promising future. Three-quarters of the old city was destroyed during the war; one-third of the inhabitants lost their homes. Yet you can walk through Munich today without being conscious of the damage, unless you are looking for it.

Dating from 1158, Munich is an old city, an industrial city (beer capital of the world), an intellectual city, and a gay city. The place is jumping all the time. The lid is really off at carnival time; Fasching, the Bavarians call it, and they celebrate it from New Year's Eve until Mardi

Gras. As Mardi Gras approaches, you will meet more and more costumed refugees from masquerade balls in the city streets, and on the day itself—*Faschingsdienstag* in German—shops close early and revelry reigns. Make reservations well in advance if you want to see Munich at Fasching time.

July and August, the height of the tourist season, are the months for the festivals of the Bavarian State Opera and Theater. The last two weeks in September are devoted to the famed Oktoberfest, a country fair in the big city. The big breweries put up tremendous beer halls on the fair grounds; Bavarian brass bands are everywhere; you drink beer from 1-liter (just over a quart) mugs which is the only measure allowed on the grounds and appropriately called *Mass* ("measure"), and the humor is fast and earthy (and sometimes furious and rowdy).

Munich has four major museums, each one tops in its field. The Alte Pinakothek is bursting at the seams with paintings by the old masters. The Haus der Kunst continues where the Alte Pinakothek leaves off, presenting works of Courbet, Cézanne, Renoir, Gauguin etc., along with paintings and sculpture by prominent contemporary artists. The Bavarian National Museum has one of the most complete displays of crafts in the world, including the best tapestries and wood carvings in Germany, and the unique Krippenschau Collection of Christmas Cribs (Nativity Scenes). The famous Deutsches Museum, replete with planetarium and hundreds of fascinating exhibits from alchemy to zymurgy, is the most impressive scientific museum you can hope to visit.

A visit to any one of the four superb collections should be punctuated by refreshment in one of Munich's many beer halls or beer gardens, where you will be surrounded by the spirit of Gemütlichkeit which is the soul of this gay Bavarian capital. After that, unless you've tarried too long, you may be in a mood to continue sightseeing.

Whether you are or not, here are the sights to see: the Residenz, now largely restored with the original furniture; the Hofgarten, palace park north of the Residenz, famous for its flowerbeds; the famed beer palace, the Hofbräuhaus, where you can have just one more liter of fabulous Munich beer; the Peterskirche, reconstructed (climb the tower if a white disk is posted on the north side of the platform; it means the view is clear all the way to the Alps; a red disk means visibility limited to Munich); the famous Frauenkirche, Munich's much-photographed cathedral; the Asamkirche, a little rococo gem.

One final attraction: Schloss Nymphenburg, far out in the northwest part of the city. Summer residence of the kings of Bavaria, Schloss Nymphenburg is an exceptionally harmonious baroque palace. Its showpiece is the great Festsaal, where concerts are given in the summer. Ludwig I's "Gallery of Beauties" is worth a passing glance, too, with its portraits of 24 ladies who took the king's eye, including the notorious Lola Montez. If you like porcelain, don't overlook the Residenzmuseum in the northern wing of the Schloss, or the showrooms of the famous Nymphenburger Porzellan Manufaktur, which are also here. The park around Schloss Nymphenburg is even more beautiful than the palace. In May and June its rhododendrons are in full bloom, but this excursion is worthwhile any time.

HOTELS. Several large supermodern luxury hotels were constructed for the 1972 Olympics, so a large number of top quality hotel rooms is now available. However, because of many seasonal events, such as Fasching, Oktoberfest, various trade fairs, and many conventions, it is still advisable to reserve rooms in advance in any type of hotel at any time.

Super deluxe: *Vier Jahreszeiten,* Maximilianstr. 17, palatial. *Bayerischer Hof,* Promenadeplatz 6, with old tradition, heated rooftop swimming pool, and special elegance in the Montgelas Palais annex. The *Continental,* Max-Joseph-Strasse 1, also in center, is modern. *Munich Hilton,* between English Garden and Isar near Tivoli Bridge, rooftop restaurant and bar, pool.

Luxurious: *Sheraton,* in Bogenhausen section, marvelous view. *Königshof,* Karlsplatz 25, terrace restaurant; *Residence,* Artur-Kutscher-Platz 4 in Schwabing.

First class superior: *Excelsior,* Schützenstr. 11, near main station. Two *Holiday Inns* at Leopoldstr. 200 on far edge of Schwabing and at Schleissheimer Str. 188 near Olympic Grounds. *Penta,* near Deutsches Museum, also has rooms in reasonable price range, rooftop swimming.

First class reasonable: *Reinbold,* Adolf-Kolping-Str. 11; *Schweizerhof,* Goethestr. 26; and *Metropol,* Bayerstr. 43, are all near main station; *Leopold,* Leopoldstr. 117 in Schwabing; *Apartment Hotel Mitterer* on quiet Nikolaiplatz in Schwabing, with cooking facilities.

Moderate: *Bosch,* Amalienstr. 25; *Dachs,* Amalienstr. 12; *Drei Mohren,* Schubertstr. 4; *Senefelder,* Senefelderstr. 4; *Schwabing,* Fendstr. 2 in Schwabing; *Stachus,* Bayerstr. 7. Inexpensive: *Kreuzbräu,* Brunnstr. 3; *Tannenbaum,* Kreuzstr. 18 near Theresienwiese; *Hungaria,* Briennerstr. 42; *Berta* (garni), Landwehrstr. 18 near main station, *Pension Beck,* Thierschstr. 36, near center.

RESTAURANTS

Restaurants below are listed E, M, or I, for expensive, moderate or inexpensive.

Die Kanne, (E), Maximilianstr. 30, intimate, candlelit rooms, theatrical mementos, frequented by theater people, late suppers.

Torggelstuben (E–M), on Platzl. Wine restaurant on 3 floors: antique-style upstairs, rustic ground-floor and cellar wine-tavern.

Haxnbauer (M), Münzstr. 5, pork and veal shank roasted over open fire, other Bavarian specialties.

Boettner, Theatinerstr. 8, and *Dallmayr,* Dienerstr. 14, both offer delicious delicatessen-type and expensive lunches.

La Cave, Maximilianstr. 25, exclusive, French-style cuisine; and *Maximilian Stube,* similar atmosphere and on same street, at No. 27, but the specialties are Italian; both are after-theater favorites and (E).

Neuner (M), Herzogspitalstr. 8, old wine-tavern, music in the evening. *Spöckmeier* (M), Rosenstr., old tradition. *Nürnberger Bratwurstglöckl,* at the Frauenkirche is (M).

Hofbräuhaus, Platzl, probably the most famous beer restaurant in Munich, beer hall on the ground floor (the *Schwemme*), restaurant one flight up (I–M).

Among the numerous restaurants specializing in foreign food are *Tantris,* Johann Fichte-Str. 7; *Aquitaine,* Amalienstr. 39; and *Le Gourmet,* next to fairgrounds at Ligsalzstr. 46; all French and (E). *Piroschka* (E), in Haus der Kunst, for Hungarian food and gypsy music. *Walliser Stuben,* Leopoldstr. 33, and *Chesa Rüegg,* Winzerstr. 18, both (E), for Swiss fare. *Don Quijote,* Biedersteinerstr. 6, Spanish and (E). *Fontana di Trevi* (E), Sonnenstr. 26, and *La Fattoria* (M–

E),Pündter Platz in Schwabing (Italian). *Datscha* (E), Kaiserstr. 3, and *Kasak* (M), Friedrichstr. 1, for food from Caucasus, Turkistan, and Russia.

Beer cellars, all (I), operated under the control of Munich's famous breweries: *Augustinerkeller*, Arnulfstr. 52; *Hackerkeller* and *Pschorr Keller* on Theresienhöhe; *Salvatorkeller*, Nockherberg; *Löwenbräukeller*, Stiglmaierplatz; *Thomasbräukeller*, Kapuzinerplatz 5.

 NIGHTLIFE. Folklore variety shows are headed by *Platzl* on the tiny square of the same name. Yodeling and *Schuhplattler* dances are regular features of these shows. Variety shows filled with striptease: *Maxim*, Färbergraben 33. Primarily striptease: *Intermezzo*, Maximilianstr. 34; *Fernandel*, Hans-Sachs-Str. 2 near Sendlinger Tor; *Lola Montez*, Am Platzl 1, and scores more.

Yellow Submarine in the Holiday Inn at Leopoldstr. 200 is an underwater nightclub built into a steel tank where the guests, protected by thick glass, are surrounded by swimming sharks from Florida; plan to pay at least twice as much for a drink here as you might elsewhere. *Nightclub* in Hotel Bayerischer Hof; *St. James Club*, Wittelsbacher Platz 1; *P.1* in Haus der Kunst. If you wish to dance, are past school-age and not looking for pro-company: *Ball der einsamen Herzen* (Ball of Lonely Hearts), Klenzestr. 71; *Philoma*, Schleissheimer Strasse 12, for merry widows and mature bachelors. For *intime* drinking: *Bei Heinz*, Herzog-Wilhelm-Strasse 7; *King's Corner Club* in Hotel Königshof.

In Schwabing, the artists' and students' area, there are many additional night spots, some of considerable originality in atmosphere and décor, others just routine, modern dance joints. You may try *Gaslight Club*, Ainmillerstr. 10; *Capt'n Cook*, Occamstr. 8; *Der brave Schwejk*, Neureutherstr. 15; *Ba-Ba-Lu*, Ainmillerstr. 1.

 SHOPPING. Munich is generally considered Germany's most varied shopping town. It is also its art center. Schwabing, the artists' quarter, has many art galleries where you are advised to browse. *Antiques:* About a dozen antique shops in the *Kunst-Block* at Ottostr. 6; also at *Bierstorfer* and *Wimmer*, both in Briennerstrasse as well as at *Kunstring*, Briennerstr. 4, which is tops for antique porcelain. *Bavarian* handicrafts at *Dirndl-Ecke* on Platzl near Hofbräuhaus and *Wallach*, Residenzstr. 3. *Beer steins: Mory*, in the Rathaus, is tops.

Cameras: Photo Schaja, Maximilianstr. 32. *Photo Pini*, Schützenstr. 1a, *Rodenstock*, Bayerstr. 7. *Wax Art Candles: Koron* on Frauenplatz, and *Seitz*, Pacellistr. 2 are both top quality shops. *Clocks: Hauser*, Neuhauserstr. 19, and *Andreas Huber*, Weinstr. 8.

Figurines, Porcelain, China: Rosenthal, Weinstr. 8; *Kuchenreuther*, Sonnenstr. 22 specializes in Hutschenreuther porcelain. For Meissen, Hummel and a wide selection of other figurines, it's *Haertle*, Neuhauserstr. 9. The main distributor of Nymphenburg Porcelain is here in Munich: *Staatliche Porzellan Manufaktur*, Odeonsplatz 1. For *Solingen* carving sets and other bargains in this famous German steel, you can't beat *Franz Widmann*, Karlsplatz 10. *Lederhosen and Loden Cloth: Loden-Frey*, Maffeistr. 7-9.

CAR HIRE: *Avis*, Nymphenburgerstr. 59; *Hertz*, same street, at No. 1; *Seubert*, Schiessstattstr. 10; *Auto Sixt*, Seitzstr. 11 (also chauffeurs); all also at airport.

USEFUL ADDRESSES. *American Express*, Promenadeplatz 3; *Cook's*, Lenbachplatz 3; local tourist information in the central front-section of main station, and at airport. *U.S. Consulate*, Königinstr. 5; *British Consulate*, Akademiestr. 7.

The Bavarian Alps

South of Munich lie the Bavarian Alps, those beautiful snow-clad mountains separating Germany from Austria, and providing one of the world's great winter playgrounds. This is a skier's paradise. Winter, spring, summer, fall—one of the loveliest parts of Europe.

Oberammergau

You certainly shouldn't skip Oberammergau, even if it is not the time of the famous Passion Play, given in fulfilment of a 300-year-old vow to present it every decade (years ending in zero) if the Black Plague were ended. You can still see the remarkable theater where it is given and the principal actors carrying on their daily occupations in this woodcarving center of Bavaria. The town itself is a rewarding place to visit, with its attractive old houses and church, peaceful against the background of the towering Alps.

You can take the bus trip from here to visit Schloss Linderhof, one of King Ludwig II's most extravagant palaces, a veritable eruption of crystal, gilt and lapis lazuli, a great tourist attraction for Germans and foreigners alike. Here is where his friend Wagner composed the *Lohengrin* Wedding March.

Winter Sports Centers

Garmisch-Partenkirchen, the number one winter sports center of Germany, has registered facilities for more than 5,000 visitors. Here you can depend on an unbeatable combination of snow and sun from the end of November to the middle of May. All the man-made facilities are here too—the stadia, the jumps, bobsled run, rinks, the ski lifts.

The number one excursion from Garmisch is by mountain railway and aerial cable cars to the summit of the Zugspitze, 9,722 feet high. Choose a very clear bright day for this, and you will see all the way to the central Alps of Switzerland. Otherwise, you may very well find yourself enveloped in a cold wet cloud.

Other Bavarian centers less popular than Garmisch are equally attractive. Try Mittenwald, famous for its manufacture of violins and for the supermodern aerial cable car, which takes you straight up over the vertical mountain walls to an elevation of 7,350 feet on the ridge of the Karwendel Range. Mittenwald prides itself on its slopes, easy ones for novices, and hard ones to challenge the skill of the experts. For an inexpensive skiing vacation, since it is better known to Germans than to foreigners, try Reit im Winkl, close to the Austrian border. It's a tiny place, reputed to receive the heaviest snowfalls in Bavaria. Recommended for beginners, since it has lots of wide snow fields happily free of obstacles.

Bad Reichenhall, on the Austrian frontier, is equally desirable in winter and summer, an important spa with luxurious hotels, a casino, and all the comforts of a smart watering place. South of this spa is the chief tourist attraction of the eastern Bavarian Alps—Berchtesgaden. However cracked he may have been on other subjects, Hitler had a good eye for scenery. One look at the grandiose landscape here is enough to make you understand why he chose to establish his eagle's nest here. Berchtesgaden has 14 ski and mountain huts, ski schools, skating and curling rinks, everything except a bobsled run. If that detail is essential to your happiness, you can always go back to Garmisch.

Regensburg on the Danube

Regensburg, which you may recognize more easily by its English name of Ratisbon, is an old city on the Danube, founded by the Celts about 30 B.C. It is the best center for exploring that unspoiled region of forested mountains along the border of Bohemia—the Bavarian Forest. In Regensburg, see the 12th-century Steinerne Brücke (Stone Bridge); the cathedral, "the finest Gothic church in Bavaria"; the Porta Praetoria, third-century gate of Celto-Roman Radasbona (whence Ratisbon); the 12th-century Romanesque Schottenkirche St. Jakob, famous for its north portal, on which Christian and pagan sculpture are curiously intermixed, and the Old Chapel, parts of which date from the year 1,000.

Other sights are the Residence of the Princes of Thurn and Taxis, originally an abbey and the adjoining St. Emmeram's Church, dating from the eighth century. The Municipal Museum of Regensburg houses a notable collection of prehistoric and medieval arts and crafts, including the unusual Medallion Carpet, depicting more than 50 amorous scenes of the 14th century. There are open-air operas and operettas in summer, presented in Dörnberg Park by Regensburg's excellent municipal theater, and you should try to hear the Boys' choir of the cathedral, famous throughout Germany.

PRACTICAL INFORMATION FOR THE BAVARIAN ALPS

BAD REICHENHALL. Hotels: *Axelmannstein* (D). *Luisenbad, Elite* (1). *Bayerischer Hof, Salzburger Hof* and *Tiroler Hof* are (2). *Deutsches Haus* is (4). *Berghotel Predigtstuhl,* at top of cable car station (4,320 feet), is (3).

BERCHTESGADEN. Hotels: *Geiger,* borders on luxurious; *Königliche Villa* and *Frauenbühlerhof* are (2); *Post-Leithaus* and the quiet *Krone* (garni) are (3). *Alpenhotel Hochkalter* in nearby Ramsau, indoor pool, is (2).

GARMISCH-PARTENKIRCHEN. Hotels: *Alpina* (D). *Golf-Hotel Sonnenbichl,* splendid view; *Partenkirchner Hof; Königshof,* with rooftop swimming, both near station; *Clausings Posthotel,* baroque chalet, outstanding cuisine, are all (1). *Obermühle,* (garni), in same family since 1634; *Posthotel Partenkirchen;* and *Wittelsbach,* indoor pool. All (2). The old (1611) *Husar, Garmischer Hof,* and *Roter Hahn,* indoor pool, are (3).

On nearby Eibsee, the famous *Hotel Eibsee* (1) has re-opened as a Holiday Inn. *Schneefernhaus* (2) on Zugspitze is Germany's highest hotel (about 8,700 ft.).

MITTENWALD. Hotels: *Wetterstein* and *Rieger,* both with indoor pools and cure facilities, are (1). *Post,* pleasant restaurant, and *Alpenrose,* in 13th-century house, are (2). *Jagdhaus Drachenburg,* above town, is (3).

OBERAMMERGAU. Hotels: *Alois Lang* (1); *Wolf* and *Alte Post,* both very Bavarian, are (3). *Wittelsbach* and *Ambronia* (4).

REIT IM WINKL. Hotels: *Steinbacher Hof* and *Unterwirt,* both with indoor pools, are (2). *Post* is (3). At Winklmoosalm (3,800 ft.), about 7 miles southeast, are the *Alpengasthof Winklmoosalm* and *Alpengasthof Augustiner,* both (4).

About 10 miles north in Grassau is *Sporthotel Achental* (2), in charming Bavarian style, indoor pool and numerous riding facilities.

REGENSBURG. Hotels: *Avia,* across the river, fine dining, *Karmeliten* and the newly renovated *Park Hotel Maximilian* are (2). *Bischofshof am Dom,* with cozy restaurant, and *Weidenhof,* are (3).

Restaurants: For a good atmospheric lunch, go to the *Historische Wurstküche* (I) near the Stone Bridge. There's open air dining at *Kaiserhof* (M), and all the good food and medieval atmosphere you could ask for in the 13th-cent. *Historisches Eck* (E) and the *Ratskeller* (M).

Hamburg, Northern City

Hamburg is a great city, and was once the leading port of Europe; it is penetrated by the River Elbe and threaded with canals, and hence, inevitably, is called The Venice of the North. If you see any real resemblance to Venice here, you've had one too many steins of beer. But this is not to disparage this ancient bastion of the Hanseatic League. She has charms of her own, and her size and vitality make Venice look like a tranquil toy city by comparison.

Hamburg's long cohabitation with the water is responsible for one of its outstanding characteristics. Where there's sailors, there's girls, to put it crudely, and Hamburg has the most roaring night life in Germany. It is concentrated in the St. Pauli Reeperbahn quarter, the Ankerplatz der Freude. That phrase means "The Anchorage of Joy". We guarantee you've never seen such a concentration of night clubs, neon lights, dance bands, jingling telephones and accessible ladies. Gentlemen, too—these Germans think of everything! You may have heard that the St. Pauli quarter is dangerous to visit. Not at all. It is blazing with light, most unpropitious to crime.

The energy that's concentrated on stripping at night is devoted to shipping by day. Every half hour in summer, and twice daily in winter, a boat leaves the St. Pauli wharf for a tour of Hamburg's bustling harbor. Don't miss this exciting trip, nor the famous Altona Fish Market, if you are an early riser (Sundays from 6–10 a.m.).

Sightseeing tours by bus are also recommended. Of course, you will see more and be freer to wander if you use choose walking. Here is a special suggestion: stroll to the Deichstrassenfleet on one of those days when the typical luminous fog of the city is hovering above the high and narrow old houses, whose reflections in the water are shrouded in the mist. There you will have a glimpse of old Hamburg as it was in Hanseatic days.

By contrast, study some of the modern office buildings, handsome massive structures, the last word in up-to-date building construction, yet carrying on the tradition and the spirit of the medieval builders.

Here are some of the other sights of Hamburg: the Kunsthalle, (16th- to 20th-century art); the view in both directions from the Lombardsbrücke; the Stadtpark (Municipal Park), one of the finest in Europe; the celebrated Planten un Blomen, a world-famous permanent display of the gardeners' craft at its best; the Musikhalle, number one concert hall, continuing the tradition of one of the city's most famous native sons, Johannes Brahms; Staatsoper (State Opera), founded as a theater in 1678, and boasting such notable premieres as "Lohengrin" and "Rigoletto;" the Hamburg Historical Museum (old ship models); and the Altonaer Museum (historical folkdress, toy collection, and other historical items of the area).

There's the 110-foot Bismarck Monument, and just east of it, St. Michael's Church, whose greenish cupola is accessible by an elevator. Try it for a good view over the town. Hard by St. Michael's, in little streets that haven't changed since the Middle Ages, you will find the Krameramtswohnungen, built for the widows of municipal officials in medieval times. Go east along the Michaelstrasse and explore the Fleete, a fascinating labyrinth of narrow canals and quaint streets. Grand climax of any tour in this area is the Renaissance Rathaus, with its tall clock tower. If you visit only one building in Hamburg, this should be it—for its fine festival hall, vaulted ceilings, elaborate doorways and other remarkable decorative features. The whole building is supported by 4,000 piles driven deep into the marshy ground, indicating that the Hamburgers have always been formidable engineers.

PRACTICAL INFORMATION FOR HAMBURG

 HOTELS. Hamburg is abundantly supplied with hotels. The city tourist office maintains a hotel reservation office, called *Hotelnachweis,* in the main railroad station near the exit on the Kirchenallee side and centralizes information on available hotel rooms. Hamburg's topnotch hotels rival the best of Europe's palaces. Prices are somewhat higher here than in other cities.

There are two super deluxe hotels: *Atlantic,* An der Alster 73-79, on lakeshore but central; *Vier Jahreszeiten,* Neuer Jungfernstieg 9-14, also on lakeshore.

Luxurious are *Intercontinental,* Fontenay 10 on Aussen Alster, large, several restaurants, pool; and the *Hamburg-Plaza,* Marseiller Str. 2, all rooms with color TV, heated pool, 2 excellent restaurants and bars.

First class superior: *Europäischer Hof,* Kirchenallee 45; *Reichshof,* next door; *Prem,* An der Alster 9; *Crest,* on edge of City Park at Überseering, all rooms with bath or shower, two restaurants and bar; *Ambassador,* Heidenkempsweg 34, modern, with pool and grill restaurant; and *Berlin,* Borgfelderstr. 1, with excellent restaurant.

First class reasonable: *Panorama,* in Billstadt suburb, indoor pool, also apartments; *St. Raphael,* Adenauerallee 41, near station.

Moderate: *Eden* (garni), Ellmenreichstr. 20; *Baseler Hospiz,* Esplanade 11; *Graf Moltke,* near station; *Wedina,* Gurlittstr. 23, pleasant.

Inexpensive: *Aachener-Hof,* St. Georg-Str. 10; *Monopol,* Reeperbahn 48.

To obviate your parking difficulties, you might try *Parkhochhaus* (2), Drehbahn 15, near the opera, all rooms with bath or shower, 600-car garage; or *Motel Hamburg International,* Hammer Landstr. 200, moderate.

RESTAURANTS

Restaurants below are listed E, M, or I, for expensive, moderate and inexpensive.

Leading are the restaurants in hotels *Vier Jahreszeiten* and *Atlantic* (both E), among the top in Germany.

Schümanns Austernkeller (E), Jungfernstieg 34, for seafood.

Die Schaffergilde im Alten Rathaus (E), Börsenbrücke 10, atmospheric, music in cellar tavern *Fleetenkieker.*

Cölln (E), Brodschrangen 1–5, old Hamburg atmosphere and tops for fish.

Fischereihafen Restaurant Carl Voss (E), Gr. Elbstr. 143, with view over Elbe and harbor; fish, of course, the specialty.

Landhaus Scherer (E), Elbchaussee 130, French cuisine.

Ratsweinkeller (M–E), the beautifully vaulted restaurant in the Rathaus cellar, sailing ship motifs.

Mühlenkämper Fährhaus (E), in northeastern suburbs, at Osterbeckstr. 1; lobster and breast of duck are the specialties.

For more fish: *Schiffer-Börse* (M), opposite main station; *Fischkajüte,* at St. Pauli Landungsbrucke; *Fischerhaus* and *Zur Hafentreppe,* both at St. Pauli Fish Market; all (M–I).

Peter Lembcke (E), Holzdamm 49, not far from main station, North German dishes.

For a view of the port: *Überseebrücke* (M), at overseas passengers' pier; *Landungsbrücken* (M), at St. Pauli pier; *Bavaria-Blick,* Bernhard-Nocht-Str. 99 (M). Wine Taverns: *Brahmskeller,* Ludolfstr. 43; *Weinkrüger,* Milchstr. 3.

In winter, the ship *Wappen von Hamburg* becomes a "swimming hotel" at the St. Pauli pier, with several restaurants, bars, discothèques, and dancing. Cabin rooms range from (3) to (1).

CASINOS. Roulette and baccara in the new (1978) Casino on the 9th floor of Hotel Intercontinental, and in nearby Hittfeld (direct bus service).

NIGHTLIFE. Nightclubs being subject to high mortality and swift changes of pace, it is pretty impractical to give individual recommendations, but in Hamburg it isn't necessary to try. All you have to do is to go to St. Pauli, say a little before 10 p.m., find the Reeperbahn (get off at the St. Pauli station on the underground, or take a taxi) and look around.

The neon lights will tell you what's going on where, sandwichmen will be performing the same feat, and if you seem to be at a loss it is not impossible that someone will volunteer to help you decide what to do with your evening. There are plenty of places that go in for girls wearing as little clothing as the law allows (the law in Hamburg is liberal) and most of them are located in the street properly and remarkably named Grosse Freiheit (Great Freedom).

Elegant dancing in *Die Insel,* Alsterufer 35, and in hotels *Vier Jahreszeiten, Intercontinental* and *Atlantic.* Less elegant, but more typical of Hamburg: *Bocaccio,* near main station; *Ball Carré,* also at station, where ladies must invite men to dance when the light is red and it's the men's turn when the light is yellow.

Variety programs of high international quality are offered at the *Hansa-Theater,* Steindamm 17.

There are a vast number of jazz, dixieland, and other "live music" locales, as well as discothèques, mostly in the Eppendorf, Eimsbüttel, and Karolinen districts, and near the University.

SHOPPING. The shops along the Jungfernstieg, Grosse Bleichen, Neuer Wall and Dammtorstrasse are gorgeous. So are the picturesque bordering streets like Arkaden and Colonnaden. Mönckebergstrasse and its side streets are crowded with less expensive stores.

For binoculars, cameras, anything in the optic line, we recommend *W. Campbell,* Neuer Wall 30. *Foto Hiby.* Neuer Jungfernstieg 17 and opposite the main rail station is also good. For porcelain go to *Weitz,* Neuer Wall 26, excellent selection of Meissen. Steelware: the *Henckels* local outlet is at Colonnaden 36. As for toys, *Kinderparadies* at Neuer Wall 7 is just that: a kids' paradise.

USEFUL ADDRESSES *Consulates:* U.S.A., Alsterufer 28; British, Harvestehuder Weg 8A. *American Express,* Glockengiesserwall 14, *Wagons-Lits/Cook,* Ballindamm 39.

Bremen, Germany's Oldest Port

Forty miles up the Weser is Bremen, Germany's oldest, and today her second, port (Hamburg is the first), a great center of world trade since the days when, with Hamburg and Lübeck, it was one of the Big Three of the Hanseatic League. Since World War II, the port of Bremen has surpassed its highest prewar traffic volume by 75 per cent, with some 13,000 ships docking here yearly.

Servicemen who remember Bremen as a staging area are familiar with St. Peter's Cathedral, with its lead-crusted crypt and mummies in open coffins; with the famous Rathaus, a colorful building with its Renaissance façade of rose-colored brick and its sidewalk arcade, and with the Schütting Guild House of the merchants, to say nothing of Bremen's trademark, the Roland Monument, whose huge medieval knights has been in the marketplace since 1404.

Hannover

Hannover is a big industrial city with a long cultural tradition. Badly damaged during the war, its monuments are now almost restored. The 17th-century Leine castle looks as good as it ever did now, and the classic Opera House, considered the most beautiful in Germany, has been completely repaired. Even more interesting, however, are the modern buildings like the Funkhaus am Maschsee, the 15-story Continental-Verwaltungsgebäude, and the Anzeiger "skyscraper", designed by the architect of Hamburg's famous Chile Haus: there's a fine view of the city from its ninth-floor restaurant. More impressive than anything in Hannover is the Guelph Herrenhausen Castle outside of it, celebrated for its beautiful baroque garden.

Among Hannover's special attractions are two zoos (one supplies animals to zoos all over the world); the Landesmuseum (Rembrandt, Rubens, Van Dyck and modern paintings); the Kestner Museum, showing arts and crafts of all times and countries (wonderful Egyptian collection) and the Maschsee, city lake for swimming, sculling, canoeing and motorboat regattas. Each spring, Hannover is host to the famed International Industries Fair.

West of Hannover is the town of Hamelin (Hameln), worth a visit for its wonderful examples of Weser Renaissance houses. Among the palatial timbered homes, you will see the residence of the famous Pied Piper.

Lübeck

"Queen of the Hansa", Lübeck is one of Germany's most exciting old cities, a short drive by autobahn north from Hamburg into Schleswig-Holstein. It owed its dominant position in the Hanseatic League to its favorable location on the Trave River, where it empties into the Baltic. The old harbor buildings and docks still indicate the ancient prosperity of this former Imperial Free City, and so do the handsome buildings in the center of town. Most spectacular of these is the City Hall, a masterpiece of Lübeck brickwork, retaining the black glazed tiles characteristic of this region. See also the impressive Marienkirche (St. Mary's church), the cathedral, dating from 1173, with its Romanesque interior and Gothic façade; the striking Holstentor, fortified gateway of the medieval city; the 700-year-old Holy Ghost Hospital, oldest almshouse in Germany; and Buddenbrooks House, in the Mengstrasse.

Travemünde

Fourteen miles from Lübeck is Travemünde, most popular of all Baltic beach resorts, and very lively the whole year round, thanks to its luxurious gambling casino overlooking the beach. In addition to roulette and baccara, the casino provides a restaurant, café, dancing and nightclub. This is the first of a whole string of sandy dune beaches backed by thick pine woods, characteristic of the Baltic coast. Your bathing hut will probably be one of those enormous wicker chairs, set in the middle of its individual crater scooped into the sand to keep it from rocking in the Baltic breeze. For detailed information on other Baltic beach resorts and the delightful North Frisian islands, see the latest edition of Fodor's *Germany*.

BREMEN HOTELS AND RESTAURANTS

Park, in beautiful, landscaped Bürger Park is (D); *Columbus* (1), opposite station; *Crest,* in suburbs, and *Zur Post,* on main station square, indoor pool and sauna, are (2). *Überseehotel,* near Rathaus, and *Konsul-Hackfeld-Haus,* quiet location facing the park, are (3).

Restaurants: *Ratskeller* (E), since 1408, is long on wine, atmosphere and tradition. *Deutsches Haus* (M), good food and view from upstairs *Ratstuben.* In Haus St. Petrus the eating is best in *Flett* (M) and more expensive in *Robinson. Schnoor 2* (E) is long on wine, atmosphere *and* food. *Alt-Bremer Brauhaus* (M) has decorated its 24 rooms with different motifs from 18-19th century Bremen. *Alte Gilde* (M), in deep vaulted cellar of Gewerbehaus.

Lots of nightclubs and bars here, among them *Karens Tabatierre* and *Red Horse.* Dancing in *Halali Bar* of Park Hotel and *Hillmann.*

HANNOVER. Hotels: *Hannover Intercontinental* (D), with roulette in its casino, *Kastens, Hotel am Stadtpark* next to Stadthalle, *Crest,* near Autobahn exit, and *Holiday Inn,* near airport, are all (1). Somewhat less are *Grand-Hotel Mussmann,* near main station, and *Georgenhof,* in the outskirts at Herrenhauser Kirchweg. *Am Stadtpark* (2), next to Stadthalle, indoor pool; *Europäischer Hof* (3).

Restaurants: In addition to the excellent restaurants in hotels *Intercontinental, Crest, Kastens* and *Europäischer Hof,* there are *Wichmann, Ratskeller* and *Zum Alten Borgentrick;* all (E). Inexpensive to moderate wine taverns include *Fey's Weinstuben* and *Wein-Wolf.*

LÜBECK. Hotels: *Lysia* is superior; *Parkhotel, International, Jensen, Schwarzbunte* and *Autel,* near Lohmühle autobahn exit, indoor and outdoor pools, are (2).

Good restaurants: *Schabbelhaus,* with garden dining and the medieval *Haus der Schiffergesellschaft,* Breitestrasse, renowned for cuisine and atmosphere.

TRAVEMÜNDE. Hotels: *Maritim* (D), large, with thermal baths. The quiet *Golf-Hotel* is (1); *Deutscher Kaiser* (3). In addition to roulette, the *Casino* also has a restaurant, nightclub and beautiful terrace.

Berlin, City of Contrast

For an exciting sense of history in the making and a striking contrast between two systems of life, you should include Berlin in your German itinerary. The best and easiest way to approach Berlin is by air, landing at Tempelhof airport. You can fly in regularly by Pan American, British Airways or Air France from Hamburg, Frankfurt, Munich, Düsseldorf, Hannover, Cologne or Nuremberg. If you prefer to drive or go by train, you will need a transit visa from the German Democratic Republic, otherwise known as East Germany, obtained at an interzonal border checkpoint. The so-called "People's Police" of East Germany have been known to cause great difficulties and complications for the pettiest—or even nonexistent—reasons and extricating oneself from these complications can easily turn out to be extremely difficult, which is why most tourists fly.

Transit visas are issued at the following border crossing points: Helmstedt-Marienborn (rail/road); Töpen-Hirschberg (road); Ludwigsstadt-Probstzella (rail); Büchen-Schwanheide (rail); Bebra-Wartha (road); Warnemünde and Sassnitz ferry landings. These, incidentally, are only some routes permitted to American and British tourists. Each traveler is charged a very high fee. See that your exit point is indicated correctly —if you don't say anything, your return transit visa is issued for the same border check point as your entry.

High points of the Western Sector of Berlin are: the Kurfürstendamm, a great shopping and entertainment street; the Berlin Zoo in the Tiergarten, one of the best in Europe; the Siegesäule or Victory Column (commemorates Franco-Prussian War), from the 210-foot top of which you will have a sweeping view of Berlin; the English Garden, dedicated by Anthony Eden and hence known to Berliners as The Garden of Eden; the Hansa Viertel, a district of gaily painted and fancifully balconied apartment houses including the work of leading architects from a dozen nations; and the Soviet Victory Monument, a semi-circular colonnade surmounted by a massive statue of a Russian soldier, a perfect marvel of socialist realism. This Russian enclave is flanked by World War II tanks and guns. It was once guarded by a single Soviet sentry who defected to the West. Now there are two, armed with sub-machine guns, so that one can check up on the other.

Historical Milestones

Under Prince Frederick-William, the "Great Elector", Berlin, the obscure little capital of Brandenburg, began to prosper. He encouraged merchants and tradesmen, as well as many French Huguenot refugees, to settle in Berlin, and by the time of his death the city had a population of over 20,000. By the end of the reign of Frederick II (the Great), Prussia was a major power and Berlin an important city. Capital of the German Empire since 1871, her fortunes were tied to those of Germany as a whole.

The Reichstag building on Strasse des 17 Juni, burned by the Nazis on the night of February 28, 1933, has now been reconstructed; here also is the repaired Brandenburger Tor, once the Arch of Triumph of the German capital. Here is the infamous Wall of Shame, built of concrete and running for 28 miles across the city, barring all but official communication between the sectors. For a peep over the wall, you can mount one of the small "observation" platforms along the western perimeter to stare across at the desolation on the other side, with its Volkspolizei guards. A further 65 miles of barbed wire divide the rest of Berlin.

Two symbols that cannot fail to impress American and British visitors are the replica of the Liberty Bell, which rings out at noon every day from the tower of the new Rathaus, and the soaring three-pronged monument at the Platz der Luftbrücke (Place of the Air Bridge), in front of Tempelhof Airport. This salutes the 31 American and 39 British airmen who lost their lives flying in food, medicine and other necessities of life during the grim year of the Russian blockade. It is a striking reminder of that great air lift from June 24, 1948 to October 6, 1949, which reached the astounding tempo of a thousand planes a day.

PRACTICAL INFORMATION FOR BERLIN

 HOTELS. Berlin has many small hotels, rooming houses, and pensions so it's always possible to get in somewhere even without a reservation. For the hotels listed below, it is advisable to wire or write for reservations in advance.

LUXURIOUS

Berlin Hilton, Budapesterstrasse; super deluxe. Its 350 rooms all have bath and color TV; restaurant, bar, café and dancing on the roof garden; own bus service to and from the airport. Located five minutes' walk away from the Kurfürstendamm.

Kempinski, Kurfürstendamm 27; famous and luxurious; meeting place for international travelers. All 350 rooms with bath. Good restaurant; indoor pool in Spanish patio style with bar.

Ambassador, Bayreutherstr. 42; 120 rooms with bath; pool and sauna.

FIRST CLASS SUPERIOR

Palace, in Europa-Center, Budapester Strasse; 200 rooms with bath, two elegant restaurants and a well-stocked bar.

President, An der Urania 16; smaller, all rooms with bath or shower, roof garden.

Seehof, Lietzensee Ufer 11, overlooking the Lietzensee; 120 beds, suites; restaurant and lakeside café terrace; indoor pool.

Crest, near Kürfurstendamm, with 200 beds, is scheduled to open in 1979.

Savoy, Fasanenstr. 9, near the Kurfürstendamm. Modern and efficient with the best service in town. All rooms with bath.

Parkhotel Zellermayer, Meinekestr. 15, near Kurfürstendamm. All rooms have bath.

Schweizer Hof, Budapesterstr.; 370 air-conditioned rooms with bath or shower. Grill restaurant. Pool and fitness center.

Hotel Gerhus, Brahmsstr. 4-10, Grunewald. For those who like an exclusive, quiet location, try this former private residence converted to a small luxury hotel. In the park district of Grunewald, it has 40 rooms plus apartments, surprisingly good value.

Arosa, Lietzenburgerstr. 79; good facilities, including open-air pool.

Berlin, Kurfürstenstr. 62, large and modern, noted *Berlin Grill* restaurant.

FIRST CLASS REASONABLE

Hamburg, Landgrafenstr. 4; 240 soundproof rooms on 11 floors, all with bath; restaurant and bar.

Sylter Hof, Kurfürstenstr. 114-116; 130 rooms with bath, restaurant in Empire style, bar in baroque style.

Alster Hof, Würzburgerstr. 1-3; 120 beds.

Europäischer Hof, Messedamm 10; all rooms with bath or shower. Roof garden café-restaurant *Bellevue* with dancing in the evening.

Lichtburg am Kurfürstendamm, Paderborner Strasse 10, corner Brandenburgische Strasse. A modern 80-bed hotel.

Plaza, Knesebeckstr. 63 (near Kurfürstendamm); 250 beds. Modern and attractive.

Bremen, Bleibtreustr. 25, just off Kurfürstendamm, small and comfortable.

Börse, Kurfürstendamm 34, with *Black Angus* grill restaurant.

Moderate: *Frühling am Zoo,* Kurfürstendamm 17; *Ariane,* Keithstr. 45, *Askanischer Hof,* Kurfürstendamm 171 and *Astoria,* Fasanenstr. 2, are all garni.

RESTAURANTS.

Restaurants below are listed E, M, or I, for expensive, moderate or inexpensive.

Ritz (E), Rankestr. 26, just off Kurfürstendamm, where you can take your pick of Arabian, Chinese, Japanese, Korean, Indian, or Russian food. Celebrities are steady customers. Excellent service.

Waldhaus (M-E), on Lake Havel, for poultry and game.

Ratskeller Schmargendorf (M), Barkaer Platz 1. Berlin specialties.

Kopenhagen (E), Kurfürstendamm 203. Danish food and beer on the terrace.

Hardtke (M), Meinekestr. 27, just off Kudamm. Typical Berlin atmosphere, huge portions.

Steglitzer Turm, Schlossstr. 17 in west suburbs, on each of the top 3 floors a different establishment, all with view: café on top, barbecue restaurant (M-E) and wine and beer tavern (M-I).

Le Paris (E), Kurfürstendamm 211. French cuisine and wines in the upstairs, sophisticated location with windows overlooking the Kudamm. Dancing.

I-Punkt Berlin, on the 20th floor in Europa-Center, several sections, dancing and fine view (E-M, depending on section).

Maître (E), Mainekestr. 10. French cuisine, bouillabaisse on Tues. and Fri., superior food.

Heckers Deele (M), Grolmannstr. 35; Westphalian décor and specialties.

Kardell (M-I), Sybelstr. 33, good German cooking, usually crowded, service requires time and patience.

Ratskeller Schmargendorf (M), Berkaer Platz 1. Still another typical Berlin restaurant, popular.

Funkturm-Restaurant (E), Messedamm 11. In the high radio tower at the fair grounds; excellent food along with a panorama of the city.

Lilo Ruschin (M), Alt Pichelsdorf 32, in Spandau, large selection of German wines.

Blockhaus Nikolskoe (M), Wannsee. In a charming sylvan location at the southern end of the Wannsee and a long, long taxi ride from downtown. In your own car, turn off Königsstrasse on Nikolskoer Weg.

Wannsee Terrassen (M), Wannsee. Terraces that overlook the Wannsee and not quite as far out. Worth it on the right kind of day. Near the Strandbad Wannsee, where you can swim (dressing rooms) before adjourning for a meal. Dancing, but not every night.

For a treat more typical of Berlin, drop in at one of the excellent *Konditoreien* for delightful cakes and pastries accompanied by coffee or tea. Three on Kurfürstendamm, *Schilling* at 234, *Kranzler* at 19, *Carousell* at 27, are calculated to tempt, as is *Hillbrich,* Rankestr. 35.

Tea dances are held almost daily from 4 to 6 P.M. at *Petit Palais,* Kurfürstendamm 68; *Palais am Funkturm* in Charlottenburg; *Stadion Terrassen,* Stadion Allee; *Janika Dachgarten,* Hohenzollerndamm 174. Ladies galore without escorts.

 ENTERTAINMENT. Berlin is a music center. The *Berlin Philharmonic,* under Herbert von Karajan, is the focus of musical activity. There is also the *Radio Symphony Orchestra.* Among the pleasantest musical events are the summer outdoor concerts in the courtyard of the Jagdschloss Grunewald. There are three principal concert halls, the *Konzertsaal am Steinplatz* (Hardenberg-strasse, in the Charlottenburg quarter), the *Philharmonic Concert Hall* (home of the Berlin Philharmonic), and the *Caeciliensaal* (Nikolsburger Platz Wilmers-dorf).

The Deutsche Oper Berlin is in Bismarckstrasse, Charlottenburg, on the site of the prewar Opera House. There are daily performances of the standard operatic repertoire. Light opera can be heard at the *Berliner Operettentheater,* Schlosstr. 5 (Steglitz quarter) and musicals at *Theater des Westens,* Kantstr. 12. The ticket office is open daily from 10 to 2 and one hour before the beginning of perfor-mances.

NIGHTCLUBS. Berlin's nightlife has always been fa-mous, not to say notorious. There are a number of small places of no particular distinction, almost indistinguish-able from one another—small smoke-filled rooms, minute bars, barmaids with plunging necklines, three-piece bands—but the specialty of Berlin is huge entertainment places, with shows of varying elaborateness. Here are some of the best:

Ballhaus Resi, Hasenheide 32, corner of Gräfestrasse. A big place (accommo-dates 800), whose specialty is telephones and message chutes on each table. This makes it possible for you to look over the field, pick the member of the opposite sex of your choice, and invite the lucky nominee for a dance, a drink, or what have you. No one will be offended by an invitation, even when accompanied by an escort—that's what they come for. It's customary for groups of men or girls to come separately, and find partners after. Another moderately priced telephone-exchange is *Toff-Toff,* Residenzstr. 2.

Separé Centrum, Kantstr. 162 (upstairs), at Joachimstalestrasse. Striptease, German style; very expensive.

New Eden Saloon, Kurfürstendamm 71, two dance bands and midnight show; its sister establishments are *Big Eden* and *Old Eden Saloon.*

Chez Nous, Marburgerstr. 14, Empire-style plush and show beginning at 10:30 P.M.

Chesa Veglia, Lietzenburgerstr. 79, in Hotel Arosa. Small dance-bar with Swiss rustic décor.

Mazurka, same street at No. 74, Russian songs and food.

Olé, Droyenstr. 10, in Charlottenburg section; dancing in Spanish atmosphere; also restaurant.

Rififi, Fuggerstr. 34, one of the spiciest stripteases in Berlin.

Scotch Club 13, Augsburger Strasse 30, with a good striptease program and reasonably priced drinks at the bar.

Small favored bars in the Kurfürstendamm district include *Le baronet,* Ku-damm 192; *Bei Wilma,* Joachim-Friedrich-Strasse 30; *CD, Cretins dangereux,* Damaschkestr. 20; *Inge und ich,* Lietzenburger Strasse 41.

French roulette, American roulette, Black Jack and baccara in the *Casino* in the Europa-Center.

MUSEUMS. Most outstanding of Berlin's museums is the *Dahlem Gemäldegalerie,* Arnimallee 23, open daily except Mon., 9–5. The painting collection ranges from 13th to the 18th centuries, and includes no less than 26 Rembrandts (*Man with Gold Helmet, Vision of Daniel, Samson and Delilah,* etc.), 14 by Rubens, and other topnotch masters from Giotto to the Impressionists. These are from the former Kaiser-Friedrich collection and the Berlin National Gallery.

Museum für Völkerkunde (Ethnology), Arnimallee 23, open same hours as the above, whose building it shares. Especially noted for its Aztec collection and for artifacts from Asia.

Egyptian Museum, opposite Schloss Charlottenburg, houses many exciting objects, most particularly the celebrated bust of Queen Nefertete (1377-1358 B.C.), discovered in 1912 during excavations at Tel el-Amarna in Egypt.

Musical Instrument Collection, at Bundesallee 1-12.

Neue Nationalgalerie (New National Gallery), in a new building designed by Mies van der Rohe. It includes collections from the old Nationalgalerie (19th-20th cent. art) and the previous Galerie des 20. Jahrhunderts (20th-cent. art, including Picasso, Braque, Chagall, Munch and their German counterparts).

The *Automobil-Museum,* near Schloss Charlottenburg, has a good collection of old automobiles.

 SHOPPING. The shops of West Berlin are glittering with merchandise; the Berliners have made their beloved *Kudamm* (Kurfürstendamm) a sparkling show-window of the West. (Many shops open to 11 P.M.)

A dozen or so antique dealers have settled in the block of Keithstrasse located between Kurfürsten and Kleist Strasse. The *Meissen* porcelain shop (selling also Dresden) is at No. 10. *Altkunst* at No. 8 specializes in porcelain, crystal, pewter, silver and objets d'art; *Dürlich,* at No. 5, in furniture. *Krause* at No. 12 and *Gutmann* at No. 8 have a bit of everything.

EXCURSION INTO EASTERN ZONE: see East Germany chapter.

USEFUL ADDRESSES: *Consulates:* U.S.A., Clay-Allee 170, Dahlem; Gt. Britain, Uhlandstr. 7-8. *Tourist information:* Berlin Tourist Information Office, Fasanenstr. 7-8; Pavillon am Zoo, Hardenbergstr. 20; Pavillon in Tempelhof Airport. *American Express,* Kurfürstendam 11. *Wagons-Lits/Cook,* Kurfürstendam 42.

EAST GERMANY

East Germany (or, in local terminology: German Democratic Republic or G.D.R.), is slowly gaining ground as a tourist objective. It has many attractions to make it one; fine art, fine scenery and the theater. When you have finished with the magnificent museums of Berlin and Dresden and tasted the thrills of excellent drama and music, you can add the scenery for decoration.

The authorities have been working hard to present the country to visitors and have, to a large extent, succeeded in offering some very attractive packages. Too, relations with the West are easier than they were and this has inevitably affected the tourist picture. Travelers to East Germany may still encounter red tape, formalities and a pervasive atmosphere of state control. But even if it takes an immigration official several minutes to scrutinize a traveler's face and compare it with the passport photograph, it is not necessary to become uneasy. This and many other cultural and social differences are attributable to a mixture of Teutonic, particularly Prussian, thoroughness and a lingering Soviet influence, blurring somewhat the emergence of a national identity.

East Germany covers some 67,000 square miles. Apart from picturesque "Saxon Switzerland" *(Saechsische Schweiz)* in the upper Elbe Valley, the Erzgebirge, the Forest of Thuringia and the legendary Harz Mountains the country is flat—it is an extension of the immense Baltic Plain whose sandy soil has been partly won back from the marshlands.

The Harz Mountains, rich in historic places and medieval legend are—like an unintentional symbol of unity—shared by the two Zones. In Berlin, the tradition of independence has always been alive, sometimes in a spectacular way, as shown by the revolts of 1848 and 1953—against vastly different masters—and Mayor Goerdeler's almost lone fight against Hitler before and during the war should not be forgotten. Over 4,000,000 East Germans decided not to remain in their own land; most left via Berlin and without official blessing. Today emigration seems a less attractive, and much more difficult proposition. Yet, paradoxically, the Berlin Wall has been responsible for much of the easing of tension along the border between the two Germanys. East Germany has become the fifth-strongest country in Europe, economically speaking, and 10th in the world, with a long tradition of devotion to theater and music (its 86 theaters and opera houses perform to some 13 million people a year).

PRACTICAL INFORMATION FOR EAST GERMANY (D.D.R.)

WHAT WILL IT COST. Hotel rates vary according to class, from about $10.06 (£5.50) to $41.17 (£22.50) a day per person, covering bed and breakfast. The additional daily charge for full board is $9.15 (£5). Food and drink vouchers are obtainable from travel agents (value 5, 10, and 20 marks) and are accepted at all Interhotels and official government hotels. They are exchangeable at any hour in bars, restaurants, and night-clubs. Youth hostels (western style) cost $5.95 (£3.50) a day for bed, breakfast and one main meal (but official travel agencies abroad have given up promoting them). (See YOUTH HOSTELS.) Campsite vouchers cost $9.51 (£5.20) plus $3.66 (£2) plus VAT, and part of the money, MDN20, can be used for food, camping fees, parking charges and other expenses.

CAPITAL. East Berlin.

CLIMATE. Summer, same as in W. Germany. Winter colder.

LANGUAGE. German. English spoken by members of the travel industry.

SPECIAL EVENTS. The Leipzig Trade Fair is held usually the first week of March and September; Weimar holds a Shakespeare Festival in April; in July the Hanseatic cities of Rostock and Stralsund stage a week of festivities, the *Ostseewoche;* Sept./Oct. sees the Berlin Music and Drama Festival. These months are liable to be altered occasionally however and dates must be checked when booking.

CLOSING TIMES. Variable. Stores are mostly open from 9-6 outside Berlin, 10-7 (8 on Thurs.) in Berlin. Only departmental and larger stores open Sat. morning. Banks open from 8 to midday, Mon.-Fri., and from 2:30 P.M. to 5:30 P.M., Tues. and Thurs., closed Sat.

MONEY. The monetary unit is the Mark (Mark der Deutschen Notenbank, or MDN), divided into 100 pfennigs. There are banknotes of 100, 50, 20, 10 and 5 marks; coins of 20, 10, 5, 2, and 1 mark; 50, 20, 10, 5 and 1 pfennig. Present official exchange rate: about MDN 2.38 to the dollar, about MDN 4.01 to the pound sterling.

TIPPING. Officially abolished, but generally accepted in hotels and restaurants.

HOW TO GO. Visa requirements have been very much simplified. Advance accommodation booking through your travel agent is advisable and in acknowledgement of this a voucher and confirmation are sent to you. These, and your passport are all you need to obtain a visa. Apply either to the Embassy of the German Democratic Republic (Consular Section) 34, Belgrave Square, London SW1 or 1717 Massachusetts Avenue NW, Washington DC 20036 or at the frontier crossing point. Visas cost 15 marks ($6.96, £3.80). If you intend staying with friends or relations, the Embassy also has application forms and full details; in this case it is advisable to apply at least six weeks in advance. Visas are issued only for the number of days you pay for.

Transit visas for a stay of up to 72 hours are issued at certain entry points, where accommodation must be booked and paid for at the same time. Direct transit visas for road travel (without an overnight stop) can be obtained at stated frontier points against payment of visa fee, road tolls. (Check frontier points with your travel agent.)

Hotel booking: can be effected in Berlin at the Reisebüro D.D.R., Alexander-platz 5; at Berlin-Schönefeld airport, or at official agencies abroad, such as:

Maupintours, 900 Massachusetts St., Lawrence, Kansas 66044, and other cities.

Berolina Travel Ltd., 19 Dover St., London W.1. is the representative in Britain for the DDR Reisebüro, and also makes bookings. Lists of British travel agents dealing with East Germany can also be obtained here. For a fee they will handle the whole operation.

Koch Travel Bureau, 208 E. 86 St., New York, N.Y. 10028 is a specialist with experience in travel to East Germany; and *Travelworld,* 6922 Hollywood Blvd., Los Angeles, CA, runs East German along with other East European trips.

HOW TO REACH EAST GERMANY. By Air: *Pan American, British Airways* and *Air France* are the only airlines authorized to fly into West Berlin's two airports, from whence you can cross into East Berlin. Direct flights to East Berlin's Schönefeld Airport on LOT Polish Airlines from London, Paris, Brussels and Amsterdam. The airport is about 15 miles from Berlin center, 40 mins. by bus. For transit travelers hourly coach service goes from Schönefeld Airport to the Helios travel agency and the Radio Tower Bus Station in West Berlin and vice versa. Fare: DM (West) 5.00.

Duty-free airport shop is good, but duty-free shops in Interhotels are more convenient.

By Train: there are through-coaches to East Berlin from Paris, Ostend, Hook of Holland, Basel, and from all large West German cities. Trains are frequent, fast, and comfortable. Western rail frontier points are at Herrnburg, Schwanheide, Oebisfelde, Marienborn, Gerstungen, Probstzella, and Gutenfuerst, and at Sassnitz (from Trelleborg, Sweden) and Warnemünde (from Gedser, Denmark). There are several road and rail crossing-points from Poland and Czechoslavakia. At all of these, entry and transit visas can be obtained. Alternatively, you may be given a pass and instructed to collect your visa at your first destination point. The Reisebüro will fix this for you.

By Car: Crossing into E. Germany at Hirschberg (Munich-Hof-Berlin Auto-bahn); at Marienborn (Hanover-Berlin); at Wartha (Frankfurt/Main-Eisenach); at Horst bei Boizenburg (Hamburg-Berlin, no. 5 highway); Selmsdorf (from Lübeck to Schwerin). You may also enter or transit coming from Denmark (Gedser-Warnemünde car-ferry) or Sweden (Trelleborg-Sassnitz ferry). An auto-route is now open for Scandinavia-bound transit motorists from Lübeck to these two ports. There is a road toll.

CUSTOMS. Customs officials are courteous. Generally you can take in anything for personal use. On leaving the country gifts and articles purchased up to the value of MDN 100 can be taken out duty free. There is no limit to the amount of foreign currency tourists may bring into East Germany but they must declare it on a special form which has to be shown on leaving the country. Change your foreign currency at Deutsche Notenbank branches or official tourist agencies. Do *not* under any circumstances try to change foreign money on the black market, as penalties are severe. No East German marks may be taken in or out.

ELECTRICITY. 220 volts A.C.

TRAVELING IN EAST GERMANY. By Air: Berlin (Schönefeld) is connected with Dresden, Leipzig, Erfurt, and the two Baltic resorts of Barth and Heringsdorf by the national airline Interflug.

By Car: There are nearly 1000 miles of motorway and nearly 7000 miles of trunk roads; generally roads are in a good state of repair. Gasoline (petrol) and oil may be had at reduced prices against coupons (value MDN 5, 10 and 20), which you can purchase at Berolina Travel, frontier crossing points and some Reisebüro (travel agency) city branches. A liter of gasoline (petrol) up to 96 octane costs about MDN 0.74, with petrol coupons. Without, it costs MDN 1.50–1.65. You must carry an international driving license. Speed limit: Autobahn 63 m.p.h., other roads outside towns 55 m.p.h. Built-up areas 30 m.p.h. Foreign cars pay a tongue-twisting *Strassenbenutzungsgebühr,* (Road Users' Tax or road toll) MDN 5.00, 15.00, 20.00, or 25.00 for up to 200 km, 300km, 400km, or 500km, respectively. Tolls are to be paid in foreign currency. *Minol* denotes motorway filling stations and *Mitropa* service stations, sometimes with motels.

Drink and drive is strictly forbidden.

Car Hire: Cars are Lada 1200 (Fiat 128) or Miafiori 1600 (Fiat 131), and bookable through the official tourist agencies or your local travel agent, or the Rent-a-Car service at any Interhotel. They can be collected at one place and left at another and can be used for excursions into Czechoslovakia and Poland. They cost £6.60 ($12.07) daily, £39 ($71.37) weekly, plus 6p (9¢) per km, petrol not included, for the Fiat 128; and £10.80 ($19.77) daily, £60 ($109.80) weekly, plus 12p (18¢) per km, petrol excluded, for the Fiat 131.

By Train: Trains are frequent, cheap and fairly comfortable.

TOURS. The Reisebüro D.D.R. organizes several group tours, including special interests such as railway tours, health spas, farming, riding, etc., lasting from 3 to 12 days. Book through your travel agency.

There are also inclusive holidays in various towns and resorts; like the Baltic coast towns, the Thuringian forest, all the major cities and Potsdam. Inclusive holidays based on twin-bedded accommodation and full board start at about £45 ($82.35) excluding travel for 8 days.

Starting From West Berlin. Autobus excursions are offered on a per-person basis: afternoon and full-day trips to East Berlin and Potsdam; full-day excursions to Karl Marx Stadt and, so long as there is a minimum of 15 persons, to Dresden. Groups of 25 or more can go any time by mutual agreement. Bookings are accepted by the *Deutsches Reisebüro,* Berlin W.30, Kurfürstendamm 17, and by the principal hotels. Visitors from West to East Berlin get passes at the road crossing point (Friedrichstrasse-Zimmerstrasse) or at the Friedrichstr. station if you come by underground or suburban railway. You must change DM 6.50 into East German marks (about £1.70, $3.10).

CAMPING. There are over 30 camp sites with electricity, water and sanitation, as well as many other useful facilities. Full details from Berolina or Maupintours. For costs see WHAT WILL IT COST.

YOUTH HOSTELS. See WHAT WILL IT COST. Official agencies claim that both replies and accommodation are hard to obtain but they concede that if you are adamant and press them, and allow ample time, they will get results. There are youth hostels in Berlin, Dresden, Potsdam, Weimar, Erfurt, Halle, Leipzig, Kühlungsborn, Binz, Stralsund, Saalfeld and Bad Schandau. You can also apply direct to Jugendtourist, 1026 Berlin, Alexanderplatz 5.

NOTE: The address of the American Embassy in East Berlin is Neustadtische Kirschstr. 4–5. The British Embassy is located at 108 Berlin, Unter den Linden 32/34.

East Berlin and Potsdam

The Brandenburger Tor, landmark of the former German capital and later the East-West crossing point, has been restored to its former state, complete with gilded quadriga. It dominates the well-known Unter den Linden which leads down to Marx Engels Platz and Karl Marx Allee, with its many post-war buildings. This 300 ft. wide and 2 miles long avenue certainly is *kolossal,* even when dominated by the monstrous TV tower (viewing platform and restaurant at top). The once elegant Unter den Linden has arisen from its ashes and the colossal Soviet Embassy there is of significant importance. St. Hedwig's Cathedral and the National Gallery have been fully restored. The famous Pergamon Altar and the Market Gate of Miletus are on display at the Pergamon Museum, whose collection of ancient cultural monuments of the Near East is only surpassed by those of the Louvre and the British Museum, while the Bode Museum has important Egyptian works.

Berlin is a theater town *par excellence.* The reconstructed State Opera is famous, as are the productions by Dr. Felsenstein at the Comic Opera, which opened its present doors in 1966. Among the theater companies is the *Berliner Ensemble.*

Potsdam, a smallish settlement, became a flourishing town in 1660 when the Prince Elector Friedrich Wilhelm decided to build his castle there. His successors, kings of Prussia, of whom Frederic the Great is the best known, embellished Potsdam in the Versailles manner, and left many a gem of baroque architecture. Of the many palaces in Potsdam the finest is *Sans souci,* built by Knobelsdorff in 1745. Its Concert Room is the best, but also see the room where Voltaire lived. A sidetrip to the Cecilienhof, the 20th-century palace where the Potsdam Agreement was signed by Truman, Stalin and Attlee in 1945 is worth while, not least for the ingenuity with which the Potsdam Agreement is interpreted.

Leipzig, Trade Center

As a center of the printing and book trade as well as of European fur trade, Leipzig acquired world renown soon after the Napoleonic wars. Richard Wagner was born here and was moulded by a long-established musical tradition which boasts such names as the Gewandhaus Orchestra, founded in 1781. Astride great trade routes, Leipzig became an important market town in the early Middle Ages. Thus the scene was set for the twice yearly Trade Fair (March and September) which has brought together exhibitors and buyers from all over the world for more than half a century. Little is left of old Leipzig: the Renaissance Town Hall, some baroque buildings in the inner city, and in Gohlis, the poet Schiller's house and a charming rococo palace, the Gohliser Schlösschen, can be visited. Of recent vintage are the Opera House in Karl Marx Platz, and the enormous sports stadium. Leipzig has an International Bach festival every year, and the University in Schillerstrasse has the largest Egyptian collection of its kind in Europe.

Halle, birthplace of Handel, is only 22 miles from Leipzig. There is an annual Handel Festival here. Visit his monument and museum, the Luther University and the church where Luther preached.

Dresden and Saxon Switzerland

Splendidly situated on the banks of the Elbe, Dresden can be visited in one day by sightseeing bus leaving Berlin once a week. Though the city was the capital of Saxony as early as the 15th century, its architectural masterpieces date from the 18th century. The most outstanding baroque buildings are the Zwinger Palace, the Opera House, the Hofkirche and the National Gallery, which houses a fine collection of paintings. The Picture Gallery in the Semper Building of the Zwinger Palace complex houses, in addition to its most famous masterpiece, Raphael's *Sistine Madonna,* 12 Rembrandts, 16 Rubens and 5 Tintorettos, to mention only a few of the masters. For a pleasant respite after the museum, you can combine the cable-car trip to Weisser Hirsch, a hill overlooking the city, where you can dine at the *Luisenhof* restaurant.

A short trip down-river brings us to the city of Meissen, famed for its porcelain. Its castle and late-Gothic cathedral (an excellent Cranach in the latter) are vivid reminders of the town's ancient history. A few miles inland, the baroque Moritzburg Castle houses a fine museum. Upstream by river boat, you can enjoy the mountains rising steeply from both banks of the meandering Elbe. The most impressive of all hills is the Lilienstein, opposite the fortress-town of Königstein.

The Baltic (Ostsee)

Crossing the northern lakeland district we soon reach that part of the coast known as Ostsee (German name of the Baltic). Old Hanseatic cities alternate with well-known beach resorts. Largest of East German ports, Rostock lies almost in the geographical center of the coastline. The train-and car-ferry (about the cheapest in Europe and thoroughly comfortable) for Denmark leaves the coast at Warnemünde, one of the best known seaside resorts. To the west, Wismar, for nearly two centuries a Swedish possession (1648-1803), gives evidence of old Hanseatic traditions, but architecturally the most enchanting place is Stralsund with its fine examples of northern Gothic. Further inland, Schwerin is typical of the old German provincial capitals, with its stately castle and opera house.

The woodlands of the Darss Peninsula represent perhaps the last example of primeval forest formations in Europe and were declared a national park some decades ago. To the east, the narrow island of Hiddensee was always a favorite summer haunt of artists and bohemians. The highlight of the coast is Rügen, Germany's largest and most beautiful island, dented by hundreds of bays and creeks. Of the many fishing villages and beach resorts, Binz is the best known and has some good hotels. Southwest of Rügen is the island of Usedom, with a string of seaside resorts.

Other Places of Interest

At the two extremities of the Thüringer Wald lie two historic cities: Eisenach and Saalfeld. The former is dominated by the Wartburg, mentioned in many a German legend. It served as a refuge to Martin Luther during the stormy days of the Reformation, and Bach was born in this city in 1685. Further east, Erfurt, untouched by events, remains one of the finest German cities with its Cathedral and the church of St. Severin, its matchless Gothic and German Renaissance houses, and its bridge, with 33 houses built on it. Only a few miles away, Weimar retains the atmosphere of the old residential town of German princes. Lucas Cranach lived and worked here. Its greatest period came at the turn of the 18th century when it became the capital of humanist literature and philosophy.

Situated on the Elbe, Wittenberg recalls the life and work of Luther. At the gates of the Palace Church, cast in bronze, are his 95 Articles posted there in 1517 challenging the spiritual leadership of Rome. The church itself houses a unique altarpiece with paintings by Cranach. Also on the Elbe, Dessau, with its Bauhaus, became between the two world wars the cornerstone of modern art and architecture.

The Harz is the best known of mountain districts in central Germany. Delightful surroundings help to enhance the medieval character of Wernigerode, dominated by a feudal castle. The thousand-year-old Quedlinburg is now a dreamy little town, with its half-timbered houses, winding lanes and its outsize cathedral.

PRACTICAL INFORMATION FOR THE REGIONS

BERLIN (EAST). Hotels: *Stadt Berlin,* 40 stories, several restaurants, parking; *Berolina, Unter den Linden; Newa,* and the brand new *Metropol* on Friedrichstrasse, with every possible facility.

Restaurants: *Ganymed,* Friedrichstrasse, international cuisine. On Karl-Marx-Allee are *Moskau, Haus Budapest* and *Café Warschau,* most with bar and dancing. *Telecafé* restaurant 600 ft. up in the new television tower.

COTTBUS. *Lausitz,* very adequate, middle-range hotel, all rooms with private facilities.

DRESDEN. Hotels: *Interhotel Newa,* very modern. *Pragerstrasse Interhotel, Bastei, Koenigstein* and *Lilienstein* are all recent. Self-service restaurants. *Interhotel Astoria. Motel Dresden,* on the outskirts, first class, restaurant, Interhotel shop, car park, filling station.

Restaurants: Try the *Luisenhof, Szeged* (Hungarian), *Altmarkt, Café Prag* (at TV tower), or *Radeberger Bierkeller.*

ERFURT. *Erfurter Hof Interhotel,* restaurant, café, nightclub. *Tourist hotel,* simple.

EISENACH. *Stadt Eisenach; Parkhotel.*

FRANKFURT/ODER. *Stadt Frankfurt,* good quality, middle range hotel, all rooms with private facilities.

GERA. *Stadt Gera,* smart 4-star.

KARL-MARX STADT. Both the *Kongress* and the *Moskau* are business-type hotels, all rooms with private facilities.

HALLE. *Interhotel Stadt Halle,* good restaurant, pleasant terrace and café; *Thüringer Hof,* simple.

JENA. *International* Interhotel, fairly modest, some private facilities.

LEIPZIG. *Astoria Interhotel,* elegant, all comforts, *Am Ring, Stadt Leipzig, International, Zum Löwen,* all Interhotels, all comfortable, very modern; *Parkhotel,* simple.
Restaurants: *Auerbach's Keller,* 16th-cent. locale of a scene in Goethe's *Faust. Zum Kaffeebaum,* also historic. *Falstaff.*

LUTHERSTADT-WITTENBERG. At the *Goldener Adler,* a little of the past is evoked; no private facilities though.

MAGDEBURG. *International Interhotel,* several restaurants; busy but pleasant.

POTSDAM. *Potsdam Interhotel,* sophisticated, on the water. Many restaurants, grill room, café. Water and other sports facilities.

ROSTOCK. *Warnow Interhotel,* all modern comforts.

SASSNITZ. Hotel: *Rügen,* restaurants and cafés, sauna, roof garden, pool.

SCHWERIN. *Stadt Schwerin* is inexpensive for its quality; all rooms are with private facilities; *Hotel Polonia* is simpler, with some private facilities.

SUHL. *Thüringen Tourist Interhotel,* 184 beds, very modern, comfortable, and with restaurants, cafés, bars and nightclubs.

WARNEMUNDE. Hotel: *Neptun;* pool, restaurants, bars, all sports.

WEIMAR. *Elephant Interhotel,* modernized, vastly traditional hotel (Goethe, Wagner, Liszt were guests) dating from 1696.
Restaurant: *Zum Weissen Schwan,* historic.

GIBRALTAR

The outline of the great Rock of Gibraltar is known to millions all over the world, even if they have never seen it. This tiny British Crown Colony, usually called simply "Gib," is just under 2 square miles in area. Much of that is sheer rock. Although a well-known landmark in classical times, it acquired its present name (more or less) in the eighth century, when it was captured by a Moorish chief called Tariq, giving it the title "Jib al Tariq" - the rock of Tariq. Captured by Spain (basically the Castilians) in 1492 (the year Columbus discovered America), it was held by them until 1704. But the Spanish have always claimed it as their territory.

In spite of the change of government in Spain in the last few years, the land frontier between the Rock and Spain remains closed; the ferry service to Algeciras is likewise suspended. It could be that either or both of these will re-open soon, although neither the Gibraltarians nor the Spaniards are prepared to comment on this. For the present, you enter Gib by car-ferry that operates between Tangier and the Colony, or by the hydrofoil service on the same route. The quickest way, however, is to fly in by British Airways from London. The services are operated in conjunction with Gibraltar Airways. One flight per week also stops at Madrid en route; and many cruise liners call for several hours at Gib.

The Rock is a tourist destination in its own right. An intriguing mixture of British, Spanish, and Moorish, you hear English (spoken by almost everybody), Spanish, and some Arabic (there are several hundred Moroccan workers) in the streets. Part naval base, part air force base, part commercial port, part resort, it is steeped in history and always seems to be busy. The town itself climbs steeply up from the harbor. The terrace roads on the rock face provide spectacular views. If you get lost, ask a policeman the way. (He would look perfectly at home in London with his "Bobbie's" hat.) If you want to escape from the town, go round to the east side of the Rock and Catalan Bay, which, in spite of its name, was founded by Italian settlers. Today it is a small fishing village with a beach.

PRACTICAL INFORMATION FOR GIBRALTAR

WHAT WILL IT COST. Costs in Gibraltar need not be prohibitive—running at about 15% less than their equivalents in Britain. Hotels run from £12 with full first class board per person to £4 or £5 for good, inexpensive bed and breakfast. Tax is minimal, so shopping costs are among the lowest in Europe, and there are excellent shops full of luxury merchandise. Taxis run on fixed tariffs.

LANGUAGE. English and Spanish.

CLIMATE. Same as for Southern Spain.

MONEY. Gibraltar bank notes issued in same denomination as British money. British pounds sterling can be used.

WHAT TO SEE. Don't miss the famous Barbary apes, the only wild apes in Europe. St. Michael's Cave, with marvellous stalagmites and stalactites is perhaps the most extraordinary natural amphitheater in the world. The top of the Rock is reached by cable car, sells souvenirs, and gives a panoramic view of the African coast and the Spanish mainland. Changing of the Guard takes place every Monday in front of the Governor's residence in town. A couple of minutes walk from here is the Gibraltar Museum, which, although small, is packed with interest and staffed by friendly, knowledgeable caretakers. Also visit the Trafalgar Graveyard at the southern gateway of the old fortifications. Many of the victims of the famous naval battle are buried here.

WATER SPORTS. Good swimming and yachting facilities. There is excellent deepsea angling (shark, bream, groupers), with a shark-fishing contest in April, while bass and grey mullet can be caught from the harbor wall. All beaches in Gibraltar are being improved with the building of chalets and swimming pools.

HOW TO REACH GIBRALTAR. British Airways in conjunction with Gibraltar Airways, operate jet service between London (Heathrow) and the Colony. These run five or six times a week, with one service-stop en route, at Madrid. Non-stop flights take about 2½ hours. There are also occasional charter flights from London (Gatwick) in conjunction with inclusive holidays operated by tour companies to Gibraltar, full details of which can be got from travel agents.

TRAVELS FARTHER AFIELD. Gibraltar Airways also operate a twice-daily flight to and from Tangier, Sundays excepted. The flight by prop-jet Viscount takes approximately 20 minutes. Royal Air Inter (a subsidiary of Royal Air Maroc) also operate on this route, with two or three flights weekly, according to season.

By sea, Bland Line operate the drive-on, drive-off car ferry "Mons Calpe" (the Roman name for Gibraltar) to Tangier. The crossing takes about 2½ hours, and services are either daily or on certain dates twice a day, in summer, and four times a week in winter. There is also a hydrofoil service linking both places, taking about an hour for the crossing. Daily or several days weekly services, according to season, but subject to cancellation in adverse weather. Can allow up to six hours in Tangier or, in the opposite direction, eight in Gib.

CAR HIRE. *M. H. Bland* are agents for Avis and Herz. Cars hired in Gibraltar can be taken across to Morocco but not back to Spain. Car hiring is cheaper in Gibraltar than in Morocco.

HOTELS AND RESTAURANTS. The *Rock,* Europa Road overlooks the bay. Most of its rooms have balconies, private bath and telephone, pool, restaurant, disco, and garage; quite expensive and not in the prime of life. The *Holiday Inn,* first class, expensive, has 123 rooms with bath, TV, pool, nightclub, sauna. The *Caleta Palace* is on the cliff overhanging the picturesque village of Catalan Bay; 200 rooms, all with bath or shower (most have a balcony), telephone. Pool, disco, boutique, restaurant and bars. *Both Worlds* on Sandy Bay has 122 apartments; central restaurant or supermarket for do-it-yourself families; baby sitting. *Bristol,* Cathedral Square, 56 rooms, many with bath or shower, sauna, restaurant, pool, worth the relatively high prices; *Montarik,* central, 71 rooms with bath or shower and telephone, bar, sun terrace with superb view of sea and sunsets. Good, and less expensive: the *Victoria* on Main Street.

Restaurants: *La Bayuca,* Turnbull's Lane, good menu, Spanish specialties; *Winston's,* Cornwall's Parade, English fare.

At Catalan Bay, *The Mermaid* specializes in seafood.

At Sandy Bay, the terrace restaurant of *Both Worlds* is excellent.

Reader recommended: *Copper Kettle* for lunch or a sandwich; *Lotus House* for Oriental; and the *English Eating House.*

ENTERTAINMENT. *Casino:* Open 24 hours a day for gambling; also nightclub, dance hall, restaurant and shops.

Summer concerts, Sound and Light spectacles and ballets are held in St. Michael's Cave, a perfect natural auditorium.

There are also four cinemas in Gib usually showing English-language films. The local TV station transmits nightly in English and in colour. Spanish TV can also be received.

Addresses: Gibraltar Tourist Office, Cathedral Square, Gibraltar. Gibraltar Tourist Office, 2 Grand Buildings, Trafalgar Square, London, W.C.2.

SHOPPING. Because Gibraltar is considered a developing country, many of the things you buy there may be exempt from U.S. customs duties under the G.S.P. plan, as explained in the section on Customs in *Facts at Your Fingertips,* at the beginning of this volume.

GREAT BRITAIN

If people who don't actually despise them could use only one adjective to describe the British, it's likely that the word "civilized" would crop up. Perhaps they are too civilized: laissez-faire, for some, is an unpleasant side-effect of the Englishman's easy-going character.

So is envy. It's nearly 1000 years since William the Conqueror landed, but the British are stuck with a legacy that at times has made them the object of scorn among other industrial nations—the feudal system. It is not just a matter of history. Not as long as the factory worker believes in his heart that all managers, despite plenty of evidence to the contrary, drive Rolls Royces and wear pinstripe trousers. Nor as long as the middle classes believe that all workers are secretly communists.

Not that life is unpleasant. Indeed, the more feudal life is, the more agreeable it may seem to be, especially for the tourist. Those exquisite country estates, village greens and thatched roofs are fairly safe now from the developer, but fifteen or twenty years ago it was only the supposedly wicked landowner who stood between them and the concrete mixer. Because the Englishman's home is his castle, and he is very conscious of his heritage, visitors can now take their pick of literally hundreds of fine houses to wander about in, more or less at will, many of them (although in daily use as family homes) containing more art treasures than some metropolitan museums.

Trade unionists may writhe and curse the aristocracy, but the system of primogeniture, which ensures that great estates are not sub-divided as in most European countries, has helped the English countryside to become the most beautiful and varied in the world.

It would be nice to think that the country's natural charms and generally tolerant and hospitable people are responsible for the great tourist boom going on at the moment. But it is probably the exchange rate. Busloads of Belgians, Germans and Scandinavians come to London and the Channel ports to buy clothing, and such items as china and glassware, for a fraction of what they would pay at home. And not only are prices low to begin with, as a foreign visitor you can buy goods free of Value Added Tax, which is a further saving.

Understandably, most people begin their visit in London. And there is enough to see in the capital to occupy one for a month. But it is very easy indeed to get outside London on a weekend or even a day trip to the elegant seaside resort of Brighton, or Oxford or Cambridge, or by the new high-speed train, to Bath or York, or any of a hundred other destinations.

There is, nevertheless, a kind of revolution, though a *civilised* one. Britain is going metric, so that some road signs express distances in kilometers as well as miles, but beer is still and will, even after metrication, be sold by the pint. Sex equality is the accepted ideal, but it is still expected that gentlemen will give up their seats on a crowded bus or underground train at least to an elderly woman.

Britain is a mass of contradictions. She sees the world leaving her behind, one hopes temporarily, and she is full of doubt. If that makes her less arrogant, and there are signs that it will, then people will probably begin to feel more well disposed towards her.

This is a fascinating country to visit, and the people are comparatively easy to get to know. If you don't actually get invited to a private home, which is probably the best thing of all, at least you'll be welcome in the pubs. And that is the next best thing!

Food and Drink

The appalling reports you've heard about British cooking apply mostly to the provinces and the 10,000 London restaurants that cater to a clientele which spends more money on cigarettes, football pools and drinks than it does on food. There are still about 3,000 London cafés and restaurants designed for people who like to eat, and a couple of hundred can meet the most exacting standards.

Out in the country, about the same ratio applies, but armed with our selected list, and perhaps the *Good Food Guide,* or the latest of *Egon Ronay's* excellent hotel and restaurant guides, you should be able to eat well anywhere in the United Kingdom, and that is beginning to be true of Scotland and Wales. There are all sorts of specialties, from game soup and potted shrimps through Yorkshire pudding and steak-and-kidney pie to syllabub and trifle. They're often hard to find, and never better than when served in a friend's home.

Drink in Britain generally means beer, thanks to unbelievably high taxes on spirits. There's bitter, brown ale, light ale and stout, but when in doubt we recommend lager, which is closer to the German idea of a beer. You'll find it's a bit colder than it used to be, but be prepared for tepid beer outside the fancier places, though do remember that it's not tepid by accident. The flavor comes over better if it is less than icy.

Shopping

The "Made in England" trademark connotes today, as it has for generations, the highest standards of craftsmanship. In the London shops you will find a wealth of British goods outstanding for their quality, variety, and design. Visitors from abroad can be exempt from VAT, (Value Added Tax), which represents a great saving on many items, especially in the luxury class. If you enquire, especially in large stores, at time of purchase, they will advise you about the latest way to export goods, tax-free. In the smarter shopping districts, you'll see many small but distinguished shops displaying "By Appointment" signs, along with elaborate Coats of Arms. This means that the shop has supplied a royal household with goods. This is the highest honor a British shopkeeper can achieve and is a sure guarantee of quality.

You can find almost anything you want in London, from original *haute couture* creations and copies of Parisian models to fine antiques, excellent leather goods and beautiful handcrafted guns and saddles. We have a rule of thumb about what to buy here for North Americans—buy handmade things here, and save the mass-produced items for back home. Generally speaking, good mass-produced items (especially in the electrical and textile fields) are cheaper back home. But almost anything handmade or requiring skilled labor will be cheaper in Britain (except tailored shirts).

So buy your tweeds here, and boutique items, custom-made suits, silverware, etc. And for antiques and "junk", especially glass, and furniture if you can carry it, you'll still do better here in many categories than you will at home.

PRACTICAL INFORMATION FOR GREAT BRITAIN

WHAT WILL IT COST. Americans and Canadians find some British costs reasonable although costs have soared recently, especially in London. Hotel rates range from a rock-bottom £5 per person for bed and breakfast in the inexpensive category to £13–14, which would be about average in London. First-class in London, allow £20–25 min. for single. Boarding or guest house charges for a single room with meals on a weekly basis (though not easy to find in London) would come to about £30–40.

Breakfast is usually available from 75p-£1.50. In a top restaurant you'll pay (with wine) from £5 up for lunch, from £7 up for dinner; in a less lavish place, from £2 up for lunch, £3 up for dinner. Popular chain cafés are somewhat cheaper, and frequently awful.

RESTAURANTS

Eating well in London *can* be as expensive as in most cities in Europe, with the possible exception of Switzerland and Norway. But you can rest assured that for about £10–20 a head you have the pick of some of the most interesting and reliable restaurants in the world (like the *Connaught,* for example or *Le Gavroche,* in Sloane Street). For good and comparatively inexpensive meals in London, use Italian restaurants, or if you are a little bit adventurous, Indian (expect to pay about £3 a head). If you're traveling by road, don't use motels for meals, but rather country pubs for snacks in the bar—you'll pay about £1.75 for chicken with "chips", beer and cheese and crackers—or the 2- and 3-star inns in country towns. Britain is not at all well served by roadside restaurants, though the *Little Chef* chain is adequate (except that service can be painfully slow. If the car park is full, drive on!). One word of warning: in our opinion, cheap chain restaurants, such as pancake houses, most "hamburger" grills, self-service cafés and, *especially,* motorway restaurants, should always be avoided. If you are desperately homesick, you will be glad to know that McDonald's, who are always reliable, are now well established here.

CAPITAL. London.

LANGUAGE. The Queen's English plus assorted regional dialects.

CLIMATE. Rarely too hot; cooler air in the north. Often showery. (Always take warm and thoroughly waterproof clothes to Scotland, especially.)

Average maximum daily temperatures in degrees Fahrenheit and centigrade:

Edin-burgh	Jan.	Feb.	Mar.	Apr.	May	June	July	Aug.	Sept.	Oct.	Nov.	Dec.
F°	43	43	46	52	57	63	64	64	61	54	48	45
C°	6	6	8	11	14	17	18	18	16	12	9	7
London												
F°	45	45	50	55	63	68	70	70	66	61	50	45
C°	7	7	10	13	17	20	21	21	19	16	10	7

SEASONS. Main tourist season runs from mid-April to mid-October, though it seems to get longer year by year. April through June is the time to see the countryside at its fresh, green best. September and October see the Scottish Highlands at their colorful best. The winter season in London is brilliant with the Covent Garden opera, Royal Ballet, English National Opera and theater among the main attractions, though unlike several countries theater is an all-year-round thing.

SPECIAL EVENTS. *February,* Cruft's Dog Show, London; *March,* Ideal Home Exhibition; Oxford and Cambridge Boat Race; Grand National Steeplechase (sometimes early April) at Liverpool. *April,* beginning of the season at the Royal Shakespeare Theatre, Stratford-upon-Avon (through Nov.); Pitlochry Festival (through Oct), Scotland. *May,* Royal Horse Show at Windsor; Chelsea

	Category	Major City	**HOTEL** Major Resort
*	Deluxe:		
	Single	£20.00-35.00	15.00-20.00
	Double	35.00-60.00	25.00-45.00
**	1st Class:		
	Single	£15.00-20.00	10.00-15.00
	Double	20.00-35.00	15.00-25.00
	2nd Class:		
	Single	£ 7.00- 9.00	6.00- 8.00
	Double	12.00-14.00	11.00-13.00
***	Demi-Pension:		
	Single	£ 7.00- 9.00	6.00- 8.00
	Double	12.00-14.00	11.00-13.00

Flower Show; International Festival of Music, Bath; Chichester Drama Festival (through Sept.). *June,* Glyndebourne Opera Season (through Aug.); The Oaks and The Derby horse races at Epsom; Trooping the Colour, celebrating the Queen's birthday; Royal Horse Shows at Richmond, Windsor and Ascot; Royal Ascot Race Meeting (third week in June); Open Tennis Championships at Wimbledon; Antique Dealers' Fair, London; Aldeburgh Festival. *July,* Royal Regatta at Henley-on-Thames, Festival of Contemporary Music in Cheltenham; International Eisteddfod, Wales; British Open Golf Championship; Chester Music and Drama Festival; Albert Hall Promenade Concerts (through Sept.). *August,* Edinburgh Festival (late Aug. and mid-September); Cowes Week, Isle of Wight. *September,* Highland gathering in Braemar, Scotland, and similar events at about the same time in many of the towns and villages. Three Choirs Festival (Hereford, Gloucester or Worcester). *November,* The Lord Mayor's Show, London; London to Brighton Antique Car Rally.

NATIONAL HOLIDAYS. Jan. 1; Good Friday, Easter Monday; Spring Holiday last Mon. in May; Summer Holiday last Mon. in Aug.; Christmas Day, Boxing Day.

CLOSING TIMES. Shops do not usually close for lunch, except in small country towns or villages, and are open from 9 to 17:30 hrs. They close at 13:00 hrs. on one weekday which is variable according to district, but most shops in central London remain open all day, 6 days a week, and until around 19:30 hours or 20:00 hours on Thursdays. Banks are generally open 9:30 to 15:30 hrs. Mon.-Fri., closed Saturdays and Sundays, with slight variations in Scotland.

SPORTS. Englishmen, originators of most outdoor games, are said to be more interested in sports than in women. Their sporting activities are so vast and complex that we advise you to contact one of the British Tourist Authority's offices in the U.S.A. and in Canada or see the *Sports* chapter in Fodor's *Great Britain.*

PRICES

Provincial Capital	Quiet Resort	Small Town
13.00–15.00	13.00–15.00	13.00–15.00
15.00–35.00	15.00–35.00	15.00–35.00
12.00-15.00	12.00-15.00	12.00-15.00
15.00-20.00	15.00-20.00	15.00-20.00
5.00- 7.00	5.00- 7.00	5.00- 7.00
10.00-12.00	10.00-12.00	10.00-12.00
5.00- 7.00	5.00- 7.00	5.00- 7.00
10.00-12.00	10.00-12.00	10.00-12.00

*	All rooms with bath
**	Most rooms with bath
***	Breakfast *and* evening meal available on an all-inclusive basis in last two categories only.

MONEY. The monetary unit is the pound sterling, approximately $2 at the current rate of exchange. Britain has had a full decimal system since 1971.

There are banknotes of £20, £10, £5 and £1. The £ is divided into 100 New Pence and there are cupro-nickel coins value 50p, 10p, and 5p; bronze coins value 2, 1 and ½p. All are clearly marked "New Pence" and the 50p one is seven-sided, otherwise hardly distinguishable from the 10p coin. The old "florin", or two shilling piece, is the equivalent of 10p.

Here is a table of comparative values (approx. at press time):

New pence	100	75	50	25	10	5
US$	2	1.50	1	.50	.20	.10

Curiosities: Irish and the new Isle of Man currencies are not legal tender in England, though vice versa is operable (for some subtle reason). Scottish banknotes are acceptable in most large shops and all banks, though more readily in the north of Britain than the south.

TIPPING. Some restaurants and most hotels add a service charge to the bill, usually 10 to 15%. If hotels do not add a service charge, divide this proportion among those giving you service. Bellboys and doormen calling you a cab are tipped separately. Tip taxi drivers about 15% with a 10p minimum, barbers about 20p, cloakroom attendant 5p–10p. Railroad porters get about 10p per bag, though they may not be available. Be prepared to help yourself to a baggage trolley and "do it yourself".

HOW TO REACH BRITAIN. See **Practical Planning** section for details.

CUSTOMS. You may bring in, i.e. from the U.S., 400 cigarettes or one pound of tobacco in any other form duty free (half of this if arriving from Europe); one bottle of spirits, 4 liters of wine and a pint of perfume or toilet water. In general all articles you are carrying with you for your personal use may be brought in free of duty. You may import any amount in British notes but you may only take out £25 in that form. You may bring in any amount of foreign currency, and take it out again, but be certain on entering the country to have the amounts entered and stamped in your passport. The amount of foreign currency notes brought in by the traveler may be taken out, or the equivalent of £300, whichever is the larger. These restrictions do not apply if you are traveling to the Irish Republic, the Channel Isles or the Isle of Man.

MAIL. The postage rates at time of going to press: these will certainly be increased by 1978: *Inland:* letters and postcards up to 2 oz., 6½p (slow), 8½p. *To Europe:* letters up to 1 oz., 10p; postcards 7p. Letters and postcards go by air at these rates so there is no need to use airmail stickers, though lightweight paper will make for minimum postal rates. *To the United States* (airmail): letters up to ½ oz., 10½p; postcards 9p (airmail stickers should be used). These rates apply also to South and Central America, Canada, Rhodesia and South Africa. *To Australia and New Zealand:* letters up to ½ oz., 13p; postcards 10p.

ELECTRICITY. Generally 220-240 volts A.C., 50 cycles.

WATER. Perfectly safe in all areas.

TRAVEL IN BRITAIN. By Air: The major airlines flying within the United Kingdom are British Airways, British Caledonian and British Midlands. In spite of the relatively high cost of rail travel in Britain now, high speed trains have made internal flying fairly impractical except between London and Scotland, Northern Ireland and the Channel Islands. BA has a no reservations Shuttle Service between London Heathrow at Glasgow, Edinburgh and Belfast which is modelled on the shuttle between Boston, New York and Washington.

By Car: You drive on the *left*. Your local license is valid. Speed limit in cities and outskirts is 30-50 m.p.h., clearly designated. Maximum speed is 70 m.p.h. All the continental road signs apply in Britain, though in country areas some old-fashioned ones appear still. Gasoline averages 85p-90p an Imperial gallon. The Imperial gallon is larger than the American: five of the former equal six of the latter. Prices vary slightly according to regions and firms.

Car Hire. There are many London car hire firms, among them *Avis,* 35 Headfort Place, S.W.1. *Kennings,* 84 Holland Park, W.11. *Hertz,* 243 Knightsbridge, S.W.7. *Godfrey Davis,* Wilton Rd., S.W.1. Godfrey Davis will arrange to have a self-drive car waiting for you at a railway station, and both or either of the others will do the same at airports. All you do is order it when you buy your railroad ticket at a major terminus. Similar arrangements can be made through most firms to have cars waiting at ports or airfield of entry.

For a personalized tour, contact American Express or the London Tourist Board, 4 Grosvenor Gardens, S.W.1, for a list of firms offering chauffeur-driven transportation or detailed tour planning.

By Rail: A network of diesel and electric express trains operates throughout the country. Many inexpensive full-day and half-day excursions are offered (ask at the mainline termini for these), and the *Britrail Pass* permits up to one month's unlimited travel by rail in England, Wales, and Scotland. The latter must be bought at home, before you leave for Britain.

By Bus: Numerous services link London with remote country districts and main towns (for economy travel). For information, contact Victoria Coach Station, Buckingham Palace Rd., London S.W.1.

By Air: Main centers are connected by frequent services by British Airways, British Caledonian, Northeast Airlines, Cambrian and other domestic companies. Fares are little more than first-class rail fares.

By Boat: Information about organized all-inclusive cruises can be obtained from the *Inland Waterway Holiday Cruises Ltd.,* (Preston Brook, Runcorn, Cheshire), and the *Association of Pleasure Cruise Operators* (The Wharf, Braunston, Northamptonshire).

HISTORIC HOUSES. Many historic houses, both publicly and privately owned, are open to the public for anything between 50p and £1.50. Times of opening vary from season to season, especially when the houses are still owner-occupied. We list some of the 'not-to-be-missed' houses under each section. For an almost complete listing of the more than 500 that can be visited get *Historic Houses, Castles and Gardens,* an ABC publication, price about 75p.

USEFUL ADDRESSES. *American Embassy,* 1 Grosvenor Sq., W.1. *British Tourist Authority's Tourist Information Centre,* 64 St. James's St., S.W.1. The *London Tourist Board,* 4 Grosvenor Gardens, S.W.1., has information offices at the Arrivals Hall at British Airways (Overseas) Terminal, Buckingham Palace Rd., and at Victoria Station, opposite platform 9.

American Express has offices in London (Haymarket) and at 25 Smallbrook Ringway, Birmingham; India Buildings, Water Street, Liverpool; Queens Way, Southampton; 139 Princes Street, in Edinburgh; 115 Hope Street, Glasgow.

Thomas Cook has offices in London and all major cities. *Robert Fisher Ltd.,* 32 Lexington Street, London W.1., will take care of shipping home your overweight luggage, purchases, or even a car. Especially good handling antiques and art objects.

American Automobile Association, Grosvenor Square, London W.1.

Royal Automobile Club, Pall Mall, London S.W.1.

For *emergency calls* throughout the country (fire, ambulance, police) dial 999.

London

London is one of the most fascinating cities in the world, a conglomeration of villages that have brought nearly 11 million souls together in a vast metropolis, more than you could explore in several lifetimes, much less in a few days. Discovering London for the first time (or the tenth) is an exciting business, and a pleasant one. The London policeman or "bobby" is famed for his courtesy and patience, even under the stress and strain of London traffic. People in the street, however busy, will usually go out of their way to help you if you lose your way.

Let's get a few orientation spots and neighborhoods identified before proceeding. For the British, Piccadilly Circus is the hub of the universe, the place where you're bound to see *everybody* if you wait long enough. Ablaze with lights and featuring Eros in bronze, it's the Times Square of London. Eastward, along Coventry Street, you'll come to another center of conviviality, Leicester Square. You'd never think that it was once a residential place, housing such eminent Englishmen as Hogarth, Swift and Reynolds, to say nothing of French aristocrats fleeing the terrors of revolution. In the center of the square sits William Shakespeare, unperturbed by the welter of cinemas, restaurants, and pubs that have sprung up since Londoners crossed the Thames to see his plays at the Globe almost four centuries ago.

Now, back to Piccadilly. *Old* Bond Street, created from a muddy country lane by Sir Thomas Bond in 1686, leads out of Piccadilly to join *New* Bond Street, built in 1700. Here the upper class built country houses to escape the smoke and noise of Westminster and the City. Tailors, milliners and glovers followed. The aristocrats eventually moved farther west, but the tradesmen remained in what is, consequently, one of the most famous shopping streets in the world.

You'll also want to explore the Burlington Arcade, a fascinating rank of luxury shops that runs down from Burlington Gardens to Piccadilly, and, running out of Piccadilly, St. James's Street, a special world of men's clubs and shops. Don't miss the William IV street lamps in Little

St. James's Street and the great houses bordering the Green Park, a perfect place for strolling on a spring or summer day.

To the north of Piccadilly a bit are two famous squares, Berkeley and Grosvenor. Berkeley Square, once a distinguished residential center (the Walpoles lived here and so did Clive of India), has been taken over by business firms, but it is still beautiful with its fine trees and gardens. Grosvenor Square, the site of the American Embassy, the Roosevelt memorial, and many memories, has been called "Little America". John Adams, first American ambassador to Britain and second president of the United States, lived in the house at the corner of Brook and Duke streets here. The statue of Franklin D. Roosevelt in the center of the square was largely paid for by the ordinary people of London.

The West End also includes crescent-shaped Regent Street, one of London's handsomest shopping streets, and Knightsbridge, west of Hyde Park Corner, where lived William Penn, "founder" of Pennsylvania. But the heart of the fashionable West End is Mayfair, the district bounded by Park Lane on the west, Bond Street on the east, Piccadilly on the south, and Oxford Street on the north. You will probably succumb to the special charm of this neighborhood as you wander through its streets lined with fine old Georgian houses and expensive antique shops.

Hyde Park

Hyde Park, with its great trees, quiet walks and flowers, will help you relax, as it has done for Londoners for generations. You can ride along Rotten Row, swim or row in the Serpentine, have a meal in the café among the trees. Best time to see the famous soapbox orators in action is Sunday morning. They hold forth just inside the gates at Marble Arch. Virtually no subject is sacrosanct here. Only treason and obscenity are illegal. You'll hear everything from incendiary appeals to revolution to earnest pleas for vegetarianism.

Houses of Parliament and Westminster Abbey

Westminster was the first important settlement to appear beyond the walls of ancient London. It encompasses not only the Abbey but also Whitehall, administrative center of the Commonwealth, whose most famous address is No. 10 Downing Street, home and office of the prime minister.

Westminster Abbey, founded in 1050 on an earlier church site, is where all but two of England's kings and queens have been crowned since Saxon Harold in 1066. The core of the Abbey as we know it today is Edward the Confessor's Chapel, around which, in the 13th century, Henry III built a series of chapels. Many kings and queens of England are buried here. In addition there are buried in the Abbey poets from Chaucer to Kipling; statesmen like Disraeli, Palmerston, Gladstone and Robert Peel; scientists like Newton and Darwin—in short, so many famous Englishmen that William Morris described the Abbey as "a registration office for notorieties". Don't miss the Henry VII Chapel, a gem of Tudor architecture, and the Coronation Chair of Edward I, enclosing the celebrated Stone of Scone. Outside the Abbey, the old atmosphere has been preserved in the cloisters, which date from the 14th century, and from which you have the best views of the Abbey itself. See also the adjoining Church of St. Margaret with its east window, the oldest in London, a gift from Ferdinand and Isabella of Spain.

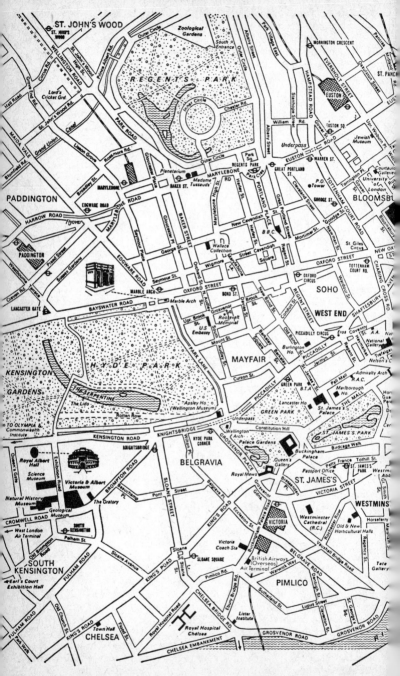

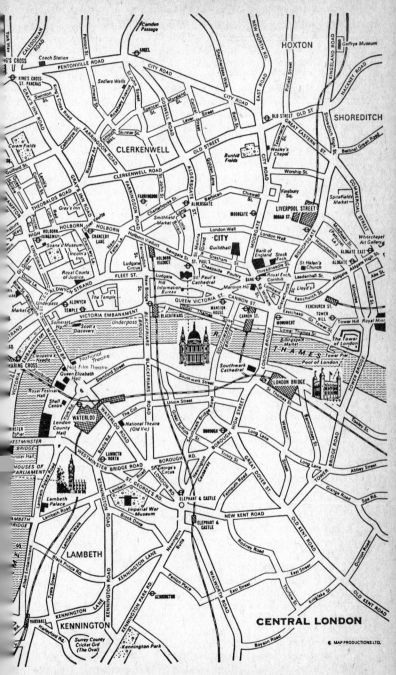

CENTRAL LONDON

Across the Parliament Square from the Abbey are the imposing Houses of Parliament, built between 1840 and 1860 in the late Gothic-Tudor style. Practically all that remains of the medieval palace of Westminster is Westminster Hall, which dates from 1097. The magnificent hammerbeam roof was added in Richard II's reign. The House of Commons, destroyed by German bombs in 1941, was restored and reopened in 1950. The 320-foot-high Clock Tower of Westminster Palace incorporates the most popular landmark of London, Big Ben, named after the portly Sir Benjamin Hall, Commissioner of Works when the tower was erected. For millions of citizens of the Commonwealth, the sound of Big Ben's leaden chimes is a mystic link with the heart of the empire. For millions of democratic people all over the world, the majestic Palace of Westminster is a symbol of the triumph of popular government after a protracted struggle with divine-right autocracy. For an amusing and instructive insight into the workings of the British parliamentary system, you are recommended to visit the Strangers' Gallery in the Commons (or the House of Lords). In busy times, tickets can be had from the American Embassy—though you will need to give several days' notice. The Lords is easier to get into than the Commons.

Trafalgar Square and the Strand

Trafalgar Square, commemorating Nelson's defeat of the French fleet at the Battle of Trafalgar in 1805, is dominated by a statue of that naval hero, three times life-size, atop a column of 185 feet high. There are as many pigeons here as there are in St. Mark's Square in Venice, and they're just as photogenic and even more dirty. They roost along the cornices of the National Gallery, St. Martin's in the Fields and South Africa House. Trafalgar Square is a great place for political meetings.

The Strand, once a thin line of houses linking the City and royal Westminster, later a center of London nightlife, is now one of the famous thoroughfares of the world. Every visitor to London goes down this great street, which links such varied locales as Covent Garden Opera House, Drury Lane Theatre and the *My Fair Lady* church of St. Paul's to the north with the lovely Adelphi houses to the south.

Drop in at Somerset House, home of the Inland Revenue and the Probate Registry, where, for a modest fee, you see the last will and testament of such well-known Englishmen as Shakespeare and Milton. You can't miss the Law Courts, at the Fleet Street end of the Strand, an overpowering edifice in latter-day Gothic style, but you'll find more of human interest at the Magistrates' Court in Bow Street, whose doors are immediately opposite the entrance to the Royal Opera House in Covent Garden.

"The City"

The City, underneath which lies the original Roman London, can be entered from the west at Temple Bar in the Strand. A little further along you enter Fleet Street, headquarters of many of Britain's newspapers. Journalists are a thirsty lot, and you'll find the taverns of Fleet Street are worth a visit. Try *El Vino's* for sherry; *The Cock,* if you want to hobnob with lawyers from the nearby Inns of Court; above all, *Ye Olde Cheshire Cheese,* rebuilt in 1667 after the Great Fire, and as much a part of the London scene today as it was then. Nearby, in Wine Office Court, you'll find the house in which Oliver Goldsmith lived and wrote *The Vicar of*

Wakefield and, in Gough Square, where Johnson lived and prepared his celebrated Dictionary. Up Ludgate Hill is St. Paul's Cathedral, surrounded by modern office blocks that have risen from the ashes of the most bomb-devastated area in the City. The narrow streets and Cheapside, Cornhill, and Leadenhall Street, are somber with great banking houses, insurance companies, shipping offices, the Stock Exchange, the Bank of England, the Royal Exchange and Lloyds.

St. Paul's Cathedral

St. Paul's Cathedral was completed in 1711 when its architect, Christopher Wren, was nearly 90. This ambitious Baroque structure (365 feet high, 515 feet long, with a nave 125 feet wide) is crowded with memorials. See the effigy of the great John Donne, once Dean of the cathedral, in the south choir aisle. The huge funeral car of the Duke of Wellington is in the crypt, along with the tombs of the Iron Duke, Nelson and Christopher Wren, the latter's adorned with a proud and laconic epitaph: *Lector, si monumentum requiris, circumspice* (Reader, if you seek his monument, look about you).

The East End and the Tower of London

The East End, home of the still recognizable Cockney, is full of districts seldom visited by tourists—Limehouse, Wapping and the Isle of Dogs, the center of what used to be one of the world's biggest dock complexes. It's easy to get lost here, and it's easier for the average tourist to see the East End of London aboard boats that in summer ply between Westminster, the Tower of London and Greenwich. But we recommend the veranda of *The Prospect of Whitby,* a fascinating pub in Wapping High Street, if you really want to absorb the atmosphere of London's waterfront, or the *Mayflower,* near Rotherhithe Underground Station, or the *Waterman's Arms,* Glengarnock Avenue, E.14. Greenwich is the home of the National Maritime Museum, the Royal Naval College, the Old Royal Observatory, the *Cutty Sark,* last of England's great clipper ships, and *Gipsy Moth IV,* in which Sir Francis Chichester sailed solo around the world in 1967.

Started about 1078 under William the Conqueror, the White Tower, or central keep of the Tower of London, is one of the oldest buildings in the capital. Once used as a palace, this fortress-like Norman building became a prison, its history one of imprisonment, execution and murder. Among the scores of famous people who were beheaded in the Tower were Sir Thomas More, two of Henry VIII's wives (Anne Boleyn and Catherine Howard) and that versatile favorite of Queen Elizabeth, the Earl of Essex. Elizabeth herself was imprisoned here in the Bell Tower by Bloody Mary, and Sir Walter Raleigh spent 13 years in the Tower of London, working on his *History of the World.* The axe which severed so many distinguished heads from their bodies can still be seen but you will probably prefer the dazzling splendor of the Crown Jewels (see *Museums*) and the Yeomen Warders of the Tower, (the "Beefeaters"), resplendent in their Tudor-style uniforms.

Bloomsbury and Soho

Bloomsbury is London's student quarter, dominated by the white pile of the University of London Building on Malet Street. It is a district of neat squares—Russell, Bedford, Woburn and Bloomsbury, the last and oldest having been planned by the Earl of Southampton. Disraeli lived in Bloomsbury as a youth; Virginia Woolf reigned here in the 'twenties. The focal point is the British Museum. The district's busiest thoroughfare is Tottenham Court Road, one of London's main north-south arteries. It must have been more interesting in the 17th century when it was a country lane, notorious for gaming, prizefighting and general hellraising.

The areas to the west, north, and east of Bloomsbury provide a rich counterpoint to its academic theme. They have two historic Inns of Court, Gray's and Lincoln's; the famous though often overcrowded waxworks of Madame Tussaud; the impressive Wallace Collection in the imposing town house of the Marquis of Hertford in Manchester Square; Oxford Street, one of the world's greatest for medium-priced shops; Baker Street, made famous by Sherlock Holmes, who "lived" here; Harley Street, in whose calm and expensive precincts many of Britain's most distinguished doctors have their consulting rooms; and Regent's Park, with its stupendous variety of flowers, the delights of its open-air theater, and its 34-acre zoo, one of the best in the world.

Soho, London's oldest cosmopolitan quarter, is full of foreign restaurants, French, Italian, Spanish, Chinese, Hungarian, etc., mostly concentrated in Frith, Dean, Greek, Gerrard, and Old Compton streets. Soho is Bohemian, slightly raffish, a bit on the "wicked" side and a lot less interesting than it used to be. The district has long attracted men with missions and ideas. Karl Marx lived in Dean Street—film companies have their offices in Wardour Street.

Fashionable Kensington and Chelsea
Kensington, officially known as the Royal Borough, is one of the capital's most distinguished residential districts, site of Kensington Palace, a royal residence occupied by Princess Margaret and her family. Don't miss delightful Edwardes Square, one of London's loveliest, developed around 1802 by a Frenchman named Changier; not surprisingly, it has an outdoor pub. You'll enjoy strolling along the quiet streets and terraces on either side of High Street and prowling among the antique shops, some of the best in the country, on Church Street.

Chelsea is the most central of the riverside suburbs and the traditional artists' quarter of London. The scene along Chelsea Embankment is no longer as tranquil as it was when painted by Turner, but there are pleasant little streets throughout the area which appear not to have changed for decades. Cheyne Row and Walk constitute one of the most attractive groups of houses in London. Carlyle, Leigh Hunt, George Eliot and Dante Gabriel Rossetti were among the distinguished residents of Cheyne Row. See the Chelsea Hospital, a fine example of Sir Christopher Wren's secular style, for old or disabled warriors. (The famous Chelsea Flower Show is held in the grounds in May.) Look for antique shops and boutiques along King's Road, the principal thoroughfare. The best time to be there is on Saturdays, about lunchtime.

Not to be Missed
The colorful changing of the guard in two ceremonies—Queen's Life Guard, daily at 11 a.m. (10 on Sun.), (20 min.), Horse Guards, Whitehall and Queen's Guards, on alternate days at app. 11:30 a.m. (30 min.) except in bad weather or in times of military alerts, at Buckingham

Palace. The Guildhall, 15th-century council hall of the City, restored after the Great Fire of 1666, and again after German bombs ruined it in 1940; the legal enclave called the Temple at the entrance to Fleet Street, comprising the Inns of Court or Courts of Law. The whole area from the Law Courts across the Middle Temple and down to the Thames is worth your careful contemplation on a tranquil afternoon, for this is Old London at its most charming. Finally, you will not want to neglect imposing Buckingham Palace. With St. James's Park and the wide sweep of the square in front of it (dominated by a statue of and an elaborate memorial to Queen Victoria) this symbol of the continuing tradition of British monarchy is a notable exception to the rule that Londoners do not know how to set their monuments and public buildings off to the maximum advantage.

PRACTICAL INFORMATION FOR LONDON

HOTELS. London no longer suffers from a lack of hotel accommodation. Many new hotels have been built in recent years. Most of the latter are in the luxury and first class category, well up to American standards, and each seems to be beating the next for height. Service is good, though often impersonal. In fact, most hotels employ Continental waiters and chefs in a supervisory capacity. But at smaller hotels the service has a habit of fading away into thin air well before midnight.

If you have difficulty finding a vacant room, there are several commercial hotel booking agents who will make reservations. Try *Hotel Booking Service Ltd.*, 137 Regent St., W.1. or *Hotac Accommodation Service Ltd.*, 180 Wigmore Street, W.1. Lists of hotels can be obtained from the British Tourist Authority in New York, in Chicago, in Los Angeles, in Dallas, and in Toronto.

The general custom in London is for rates to be quoted including "bed and breakfast". What Americans call "European Plan" is rare in Europe and rarer still in Britain. A few London hotels have begun to quote rates for room only and we, among others, regret the widespread substitution of the "Continental breakfast" for the good old English breakfast. Rates charged in June, July, and August may be up to 30 percent higher.

Among the newcomers are the 611-room **Kensington Hilton,** on Holland Park Avenue; the 575-room **Gloucester,** just around the corner from West London Air Terminal; the **Penta** near West London Air Terminal; **Skyline Park Tower,** opp. Albert Gate entrance to Hyde Park, 300 rooms; **Tower,** near the Tower of London in the City, 826 rooms, theater, cinema; one of the best modern hotels, and not over-priced. **Holiday Inn** at Marble Arch, 250 rooms; **Inter-Continental,** over 500 rooms, right by busy Hyde Park corner; **Holiday Inn** at Swiss Cottage (a bit far out but worth it if you want to be near pleasant Hampstead), 300 rooms.

VERY EXCLUSIVE

Berkeley, Knightsbridge, S.W.1, a Savoy Group hotel with 152 rooms (all with bath). Arguably one of the best hotels in the world. *Le Perrequet* restaurant is just right for that extra-special evening out.

Claridge's, Brook St., W.1. Haunt of visiting royalty. Acme of expensive comfort.

Connaught, Carlos Pl., W.1. Quietly luxurious, county clientele. All rooms with bath. Consistently reckoned to serve the best food in Britain.

Ritz, Piccadilly, W.1. Fabulous rendezvous, with chandelier-hung elegance, excellent dining. Short of funds? Then go for afternoon tea.

Savoy, Strand, W.C.2. Increasingly popular with foreign potentates and celebrities, impeccable service. Social rendezvous.

LUXURIOUS

Carlton Tower, Cadogan Pl., S.W.1. International atmosphere, 60 suites, fine décor. 250 rooms with bath. Try Chelsea Room for Regency elegance up-to-date.

Churchill, Portman Sq., W.1. 489 rooms with bath. Conveniently situated a couple of blocks north of Oxford Street.

Dorchester, Park Lane, W.1. A fine building of elegance and "with-it" modernity. 285 rooms with bath.

Grosvenor House, Park Lane, W.1. A long established favorite with society and wealthier visitors. 500 rooms with 50 suites.

Hilton, Park Lane, W.1. A tower of a building overlooking Hyde Park. Good restaurant. 510 rooms.

Inn on the Park, Hamilton Pl., Park Lane, W.1. Modern neighbor for the London Hilton. 230 rooms with bath.

Inter-Continental, Hyde Park Corner, W.1. Up-to-the-minute comfort, overlooking Green Park. 546 rooms and all established services expected of the chain. Restaurant and coffee shop. Often busy with conventions and trade fairs.

May Fair, Berkeley St., W.1. A popular rendezvous for society, charity events, dinner dances, and with a super restaurant. 385 rooms.

Royal Lancaster, Lancaster Tce., W.2. Has 392 rooms, six well-stocked bars, 24-hr. grill. Overlooking Hyde Park.

Westbury, New Bond St., W.1. Known for comfort, good service and cuisine, a well-established attractive hotel in the heart of Mayfair. 255 rooms with bath; 24 suites.

FIRST CLASS

Bloomsbury Centre, near British Museum, has 247 rooms.

Britannia, under same management as *Europa* (but superior), is in Grosvenor Square; 460 rooms.

Brown's, Dover St., W.1. 165 rooms, 101 with bath. Charmingly old-fashioned. Loved by discriminating Americans. Good for afternoon tea.

Capital, Knightsbridge, behind Harrods Store. All rooms with bath.

Cavendish, Jermyn St., S.W.1. Offers a 24-hr. restaurant. 252 rooms in heart of London.

Charing Cross, Strand, W.C.2. Although above a rail station, 200 rooms (all with bath) are quiet. Sauna. Close to London's center. Good and interesting restaurant.

Cumberland, Marble Arch, W.1. 897 rooms with bath. A beehive, but comfortable.

Europa, Grosvenor Sq., W.1. 300 bedrooms, 18 suites, all with bath, and iced water dispenser.

Goring, Grosvenor Gardens, S.W.1. 100 rooms with bath. Comfortable, historic, family-run hotel.

Great Eastern, Liverpool Street Station, E.C.2. 167 rooms, 47 with baths.

Hampstead Post House, Haverstock Hill, Hampstead, N.W.3. 140 rooms with bath. A bit far from the West End, but arty Hampstead has its own rewards.

Holiday Inn, Edgware Rd., W.1. 245 rooms with bath.

Hyde Park, Knightsbridge, S.W.1. 193 rooms with bath; has considerable elegance. Near Oxford St.

Imperial, a 450-room structure replacing old one of same name, opened in Russell Square on the same site.

Kensington Palace, De Vere Gdns., W.8. 300 rooms with bath.

London International, Cromwell Rd., S.W.5. 430 rooms with bath.

London Metropole, Edgware Rd., Marble Arch, W.2. 555 rooms, all with either bath or shower. A bit far out.

The Londoner, Welbeck St., W.1. Near shopping center. 120 rooms with bath.

Montcalm, Cumberland Place, W.1. 112 rooms with bath.

Mount Royal, Marble Arch, W.1. 700 rooms with bath.

Park Lane, Piccadilly, W.1. 400 rooms with bath, 40 suites.

Piccadilly, Piccadilly, W.1. 222 bedrooms with bath.

Portman, Portman Sq., W.1, 290 rooms with bath.

Regent Centre, Carburton St., W.1. 350 rooms with bath.

Royal Garden, Kensington High St., overlooking Kensington Palace and gardens. 500 rooms with bath. Excellent restaurants and grills.

Royal Kensington, 380 Kensington High St., W.14, 400 rooms with bath.

Royal Trafalgar, St. Martin's St., W.C.2. 108 rooms with bath.

Sherlock Holmes, 108 Baker St., W.1. 150 rooms with bath.

St. Georges, Langham Pl., W.1. Atop a tall building. 85 beautifully decorated rooms with bath.

St. James's, Buckingham Gate, S.W.1. 500 rooms, 150 with bath, 120 suites. (St. James's Court, adjoining, for apartments.)

Stafford, St. James's Pl., S.W.1. 47 rooms with bath. Has lots of atmosphere. The bar is a chic rendezvous.

Washington, Curzon St., W.1. 154 rooms with bath, 6 suites.

White's, 90/92 Lancaster Gate, W.2. 60 rooms with bath.

REASONABLE

Bedford, Southampton Row, W.C.1. Good location near British Museum. Commercial hotel atmosphere, 181 rooms, all with bath. Stereo and TV.

Belgravia Royal, Chesham Pl., S.W.1. 120 rooms with bath, air-conditioning, color TV.

Clifton-Ford, Welbeck St., W.C.2. 282 rooms, 126 with bath. Quiet and home-like atmosphere.

Grosvenor Victoria, Buckingham Palace Rd., S.W.1. 240 rooms, 50 with bath.

Kensington Close, Wright's Lane, W.8. 503 rooms with bath. Pool and most other facilities.

Lowndes, Lowndes Square, Knightsbridge. 80 rooms with bath. Elegant.

Mandeville, Mandeville Pl., W.1. 90 of its 165 rooms have bath. Close to Oxford Street shops. Rear rooms look over pleasant gardens.

President, Russell Sq., W.C.1. 447 rooms with bath. Restaurant, bar, quick grill.

Queensway, Princes Sq., W.2. 122 rooms, 5 with bath.

Regent Palace, Piccadilly Circus, W.1. 1144 rooms, none with bath. Functional, but very central.

Rembrandt, Thurloe Pl., S.W.7. 168 rooms, 152 with bath.

Royal Horseguards, Whitehall Court, S.W.1. 286 rooms with bath.

Royal Scot, Kings Cross Rd., W.C.1. Handy for Kings Cross Station and the north. 349 rooms with bath.

Royal Westminster, Buckingham Palace Rd., S.W.1. 134 rooms with bath.

Russell, Russell Sq., W.C.1. 300 rooms with bath.

Rubens, Buckingham Palace Rd., S.W.1. 137 rooms, 87 with bath.

Strand Palace, Strand, W.C.2. 776 rooms with bath.

Tara, Wright's Lane, Kensington W.8. Jumbo-sized Aer Lingus-owned with 850 rooms with bath.

Tavistock, Tavistock Sq., W.C.1. 301 rooms with bath.

Waldorf, Aldwych, W.C.2. Located in theaterland. 300 rooms, 250 with bath.

INEXPENSIVE

If really inexpensive accommodation in and around London is required, consult the list published by the British Tourist Authority and check personally before booking. There are any number of inexpensive, clean, unlicensed hotels and pensions, *but it is not wise to book without personal inspection as conditions vary so much.*

AT OR NEAR LONDON AIRPORT (HEATHROW)

Sheraton-Heathrow, West Drayton, 5 minutes from the airport. Reasonably priced, considering the many facilities.

Holiday Inn, all usual amenities expected of this chain.

Heathrow, London Airport. The only hotel actually on airport property. A luxury hotel at lower-than-luxury prices, with frequent courtesy buses into London and to the terminals. 725 rooms with bath.

Skyline, near London Airport in Harlington, has 360 rooms with bath.

Skyway, London Airport, Hounslow. 260 rooms with bath. Also near the airport, *Ariel,* 190 rooms, soundproofed, all with bath. Ditto for the 360-room *Forte's Excelsior,* London Airport. *Post House,* 600 rooms with bath.

Gatwick Piccadilly, 100 rooms, first class superior services and prices. Gatwick Airport.

All above are first class.

 RESTAURANTS. In London there are about 600 fine restaurants that cater to the standards of British and international gourmets, offering fine fare from the traditional roast sirloin or steak and kidney pudding, to exotic oriental dishes. Of these, which include several of the finest restaurants in the world apart from the Paris temples of gastronomy, we have selected the following list for your eating pleasure.

The price is generally right. This is a solid advantage that London restaurants have over equivalent establishments in Paris or New York. At the most expensive restaurants, lunch or dinner with wine will cost from £8–10 up, for moderate establishments £3 up. You can still get a good meal in London for £2, especially if you have a taste for Indian or Chinese food.

In the classified list below, we have omitted grill rooms and restaurants of deluxe hotels like the *Savoy, Connaught, Claridge's,* etc., which are always fairly reliable for fashionable lunching and dining whether you're staying there or not. If you're going to one of the better places, it's wise to ring up ahead and book a table, especially between May and September. Restaurants are often *closed* on Sunday. The following centrally-located hotels have restaurants open 24 hours a day: *Cavendish,* Jermyn St., S.W.1; *Charing Cross,* Strand, W.C.2; *Hilton,* Park La., W.1; *Portman,* Portman Sq., W.1.

Insider's tip: some of the very best food in Britain is served at the more expensive gambling casinos. Visitor's membership is available at most of these, effective after 48 hours' notice.

TOPS IN ELEGANCE AND/OR CUISINE

Au Fin Bec. 100 Draycott Avenue, S.W.3. Intimate, unobtrusive little French restaurant with small but splendid menu.

Carrier's. Camden Passage, N.1. Well out of central London, in Islington, and surrounded by antique shops. Recommended for lunch, but a bit cramped.

Le Carrosse. 19 Elystan St., S.W.3. Large and faithful following here ensures continuing with standard of cuisine and presentation. Rather suave atmosphere.

Empress. 15 Berkeley St., W.1. Large, opulent room with a superb table of cold food at entrance. Wide menu with unusual selection. Useful for lunch when shopping around Piccadilly. Open Sun.

L'Ecu de France. Jermyn St., S.W.1. At lunchtime it is difficult to get a table: you can't see the *boeuf bourguignon* for the businessmen (expense account variety). Excellent cuisine; good after-theater stop.

Le Gavroche. 61 Lower Sloane St., S.W. 1. Very fashionable. *Haute cuisine* and even more *haute* prices. Reckon on about £45 for dinner for two.

Keats. 3–4 Downshire Hill, N.W.3. Another memorable restaurant in Hampstead; expensive, high-quality food well presented. Décor mostly concerned with the poet, who lived near here.

Mirabelle. 56 Curzon St., W.1. Highly fashionable Mayfair lunch and dinner rendezvous. Dinner served in the garden on warm evenings. Luxury cuisine and wines with high prices.

Parkes. Beauchamp Pl., S.W.3. Excellent and unusual dishes, well served. Fine wines. Expensive.

Rule's. Maiden Lane, W.C.2. An 18th-century eating place with an Edwardian atmosphere—all red plush and paneled walls. Good English fare, copious.

EXPENSIVE

Au Père de Nico. 10 Lincoln St., S.W.3. One of London's few chances for outdoor summer dining. Food almost lives up to surroundings. Must book.

Au Savarin. 8 Charlotte St., W.1. Attractive French atmosphere, continental cuisine, with *steak Diane* as a specialty. But other dishes well worth trying.

Brompton Grill. 243 Brompton Rd., S.W.3. French decor, mainly English and French menu. Really excellent wine list. Moderate to expensive.

Café Royal (Grill Room). 68 Regent St., W.1. Home of Edwardian *literati*, its grillroom is excellent and all that remains of the old aura. Food good to excellent.

Le Cellier du Midi. Church Row, Hampstead N.W.3. Excellent French cuisine. Atmosphere of provincial France.

Chez Solange. 35 Cranbourn St., W.C.2. This French-owned, French-run restaurant makes an ideal before or after-the-show stop-off. Bourgeois cooking, unpretentious but good.

Didier's. Warwick Pl., W.9. Good French cuisine in a small, charming street in Little Venice.

L'Etoile. 30 Charlotte St., W.1. Excellent French cuisine in almost provincial (but elegantly so) surroundings.

Gay Hussar. 2 Greek St., W.1. Considered to serve the best Hungarian food in town. Atmosphere and service pleasant. Can be surprisingly moderate.

Genevieve. 13 Thayer St., W.1. The best *steak flambé* and *crêpes Suzette* in London, according to many. Not spacious.

Hungarian Csarda. 77 Dean St., W.1. Small dining spot with authentic Hungarian cuisine and wines. High standards. Magyar décor.

Kettner's. Romilly St., Soho, W.1. Tops. The perfect after-theater restaurant. Very good food, reasonable wine list. Owned by the de Vere Hotel company which also runs Verrey's (see below).

La Bussola. 42 St. Martin's Lane, WC2. Pre-theatre dinner and late-night opening. Dancing. A consistently good reputation.

La Napoule. 8 N. Audley St., W.1. Lino and Giulio, formerly of White House, Mirabelle and the Savoy, in a modern and elegant setting, provide good food and service here. Handy for an after-shopping treat.

Leith's. 92 Kensington Park Road, W.11. Superb food by one of Britain's leading experts, Prudence Leith. Reservations essential.

Nick's Diner. Ifield Rd., S.W.10. Fashionable cellar restaurant. Imaginative menu. The *crême brulée* is a must.

L'Opera. Gt. Queen St., W.C.2. Near Royal Opera House and Drury Lane. Opulent in plush and gilt. Fine French cuisine, attractive wine list and attentive service.

Le Poulbot. 45 Cheapside, E.C.2. Saves the City from becoming a gastronomic desert. A sophisticated French cellar restaurant.

Provans, 306b Fulham Road, S.W.10. Relaxed atmosphere; the chef takes worthwhile risks. Moderate.

Quo Vadis. 26–29 Dean St., W.1. Italian, heart-of-Soho, old-fashioned, reliable and good cooking. Karl Marx lived upstairs. Open Sunday (dinner).

Simpsons in the Strand. W.C.2. Old English cooking at its best. A large restaurant with several rooms, one for men only. Joints carved at your table (give the carver a tip).

Snooty Fox. 52 Hertford St., W.1. This Shepherd Market spot offers French cuisine. Dark interior, spacious, smart.

La Speranza. 179 Brompton Rd., S.W.3. Another gastronomic oasis in Knightsbridge, this one Italian.

Stone's Chop House. Panton St., S.W.1. Good English food; theater dinners a specialty. Unbelievable décor.

La Terrazza. 19 Romilly St., Soho, W.1. An excellent Italian restaurant in Soho and formerly one of the best in London. Air-conditioned.

Verrey's. 233 Regent St., W.1. Old-established, good restaurant with good international menu, attentive service. Many prefer the downstairs room. Good luncheon or dinner spot.

REASONABLE TO CHEAP

Armenian. 20 Kensington Church Street, specializes in Middle Eastern cooking and regional wines (including Moldavian, Lebanese and Georgian). Very good.

Bianchi's. 21a Frith St., Soho, W.1. Don't let the unpretentious entrance deter you. Climb to the second floor, and you'll be rewarded by courtesy, and good simple Italian cooking.

Bistingo Bistro has branches at 117 Queensway, W.2., 45 Kensington High Street, Fleet Street, and 57 Old Compton Street, in Soho. Consistently reliable, given the moderate prices.

Bloom's. 90 Whitechapel High St., E.1. "The most famous kosher restaurant in Britain", it says across the front, and quite right, too. Noisy, crowded, friendly, huge servings of excellent food. Open Sunday (of course!).

Casserole. 331 King's Rd., S.W.3. Very good value for money. Young and arty crowd.

Chanticleer Taverna. Roebuck House, S.W.1. Delicious Greek food, with Greek music and dancing. Open to 3 A.M. "A little bit of Athens", well worth the trip. (Near Victoria Station.)

Chez Victor. 45 Wardour St., W.1. Another old Soho favorite that goes on and on. French décor and cuisine.

Cordon Bleu. 31 Marylebone Lane, W.1. Food cooked by young lady Cordon Bleu graduates. Very popular spot.

Le Chef, Connaught St. W.1. Inexpensive, set lunches vary, but can be excellent.

Mon Plaisir. 21 Monmouth St., W.1. A favorite French bistro, whose motto reads: *on y mange bien, on y revient* (one eats well here and one comes back). Try the *paté maison* and the *tournedos,* both truly superb. The service is pretty harassed.

San Frediano, 62 Fulham Rd., SW3. Trendy Italian restaurant, but it doesn't take its success for granted. Can be crowded and noisy. Good food, good fun.

Trattoria Santa Lucia. 20 Rupert St., W.1. Food invariably excellent—chicken and veal specialties, tempting wine list, but house wine delicious. Open Sunday.

SEAFOOD

Bentley's. 11 Swallow St., W.1. One of London's finest seafood restaurants. The accent here is on oysters. Expensive.

Golden Carp. 8a Mount St., W.1., just off Berkeley Square. Has an Oyster Bar as well as dining room and specializes in *bouillabaisse* and fried carp; chicken and steak dishes also.

Overton's (opposite Victoria Station), S.W.1. A seafood favorite. Unpretentious, friendly and very English service. Try a glass of stout (dark ale) with your crab salad or oysters.

Scott's. 20 Mount St., W.1, has over a century-old tradition for fine seafood, and still retains some of the old *ambience.* Expensive.

Vendôme. 20 Dover St., W.1. Another member of the Wheeler's group. Fish is the basis of the menu, but there is a range of French dishes, too. Rather opulent, can be expensive. Open Sundays.

Wheeler's. 19 Old Compton St., Soho, W.1. Also at 12a Duke of York St., W.1. and 17 Kensington High Street, W.8. *(The Alcove.)* Sea-food chain. Quality variable, but worth trying.

Wilton's. 27 Bury St., St. James's, S.W.1. The seafood and wines are tops—so are the prices.

ORIENTAL

Bali. 101 Edgware Road, W.2. Authentic Indonesian dishes. Huge helpings. Good value for money.

Chuen Cheng Ku. 17 Wardour St. W.1 (also 22 Lisle St., W1). Vast, usually crowded, but authentic Chinese.

Gallery Rendezvous. 53 Beak St., W.1. Peking dishes, including the duck, cold appetizers and fried dumplings, are favorites here, but everything is good.

Good Friends and **New Friends,** Salmon Lane, Stepney, E.14. Both small, unpretentious, but offering delectable Chinese cooking which makes it worth the long ride into dockland. Equally good is a third member of the chain, the *City Friends,* 11 Creed Lane, E.C.4. Open Sundays. Reasonable.

Hiroko. 6 St. Christopher's Pl., W.1. London's first Japanese restaurant. Style and atmosphere suggest the real thing. Expensive, but certainly very good.

Hokkai, 59 Brewer St., W1. One of the simplest and least expensive of London's Japanese restaurants. Authentic, with easily understood menus, helpful waiters, and kimono'd waitresses.

Manchurian. Baker Street, W.1. Expensive in the evening and chic. But there's a worthwhile businessman's lunch at this spacious Chinese restaurant.

Shezan. Cheval Pl., S.W.7. Regarded by many Indians and Pakistanis as the best Indian restaurant in London.

Tandoori. 153 Fulham Road, S.W.3. A taste of Northern India in a dark and exotic downstairs Chelsea hideout. Book early.

Trader Vic's in the London Hilton, Park Lane, W.1. Polynesian décor and food, plus Indian, Hawaiian and other specialties. Open for lunch and dinner; expensive.

Veeraswamy's. 91 Regent St., W.1. Quite a production, with curious plush décor and turbaned waiters. Possibly the best-known Indian restaurant in town (echoes of the British Raj), not necessarily the best.

Woodlands, Meard St., W1. Pleasant waiters, some tasty South Indian specialties (most of those being vegetarian).

LUNCH

Brasserie du Coin, 54 Lamb's Conduit St., W.C.1. Parisian decor. French food can be excellent. Moderate.

Causerie. (Claridge's Hotel.) Brook St., W.1. Smörgasbord vies with chic chapeaux in this citadel of class as the prime attraction. The perfect luncheon spot. Reservations essential.

Danish Food Centre. Conduit St., W.1. Tiny restaurant just off Regent Street featuring, quite naturally, delicious open-faced smørrebrød sandwiches. Be careful—the center shuts some days at 2 P.M.

Floris. 24 Brewer St., Soho, W.1. Best-known patisserie in London—they make Royal wedding cakes and all that. The little restaurant upstairs caters for typically feminine tastes.

Gloriette. 128 Brompton Rd., S.W.3. Our favorite London pastry shop. Vienna brought to Knightsbridge.

The Vine. 3 Piccadilly Pl., W.1. Over a delightful little pub standing mid-way between Piccadilly and Regent Street. Much frequented by discerning businessmen. Reservations a must. Moderately expensive. (Under same management as Bentley's fish restaurant.)

Ye Olde Cock Tavern. 22 Fleet St., E.C.4. Excellent lunches in the tavern favored by Dickens—so they say!

For shoppers, many **department stores** have restaurants where you can gather strength for even more shopping with anything from a snack to a three-course meal . . . and, of course, the always welcome cup of tea. Among the best are— **Fortnum and Mason,** Piccadilly, W.1. Also has excellent *Fountain Restaurant* for lunch and late snacks. **Simpson's,** Piccadilly, W.1. Not to be confused with Simpsons in the Strand. **Harrods,** Knightsbridge, S.W.1. **Selfridge's,** Oxford Street, W.1.

Pubs. London has no less than 5,000 "pubs", usually open from 11 A.M. to 3 P.M. and 6 P.M. to 11 P.M. The atmosphere is informal and convivial. You can usually get very good lunches at the better pubs and their sandwiches are often excellent. Beer, spirits, wine and soft drinks are served in that order of popularity. Aside from drinking and talking (the most loquacious Englishmen are those who frequent pubs), the public bar usually features games of darts, and billiards or pool.

 NIGHTCLUBS AND DANCING. In London, nightclubs usually put more emphasis on cuisine than elsewhere. They are really clubs, and most people join them for the exclusive atmosphere, for the floor shows, and for an opportunity to dance way into the small hours. To join a nightclub, telephone the secretary, then take your passport along to be shown at the door. Most Americans will be made temporary members for a nominal subscription fee right on the spot. Commonwealth or foreign visitors resident in London will have to join normally, and annual subscriptions vary from one to ten pounds. Establishments requiring membership are indicated by "sub" after the name.

Nightclubs come—and they go—so we list only the well-established ones, together with some good dinner-dance spots. Evening dress is optional in most, desirable in a few (see list). The average expenditure for parties of four is £50–70. At some clubs there's a special low-price dinner-dance arrangement available before midnight. Since the recent licensing law amendments came into force, clubs have far more freedom in serving hours—but the law is still complicated so you'll have to check as you go.

Hotel Dining & Dancing is a popular pastime in London. Among the very best are the restaurants at the *Berkeley, Dorchester* and *May Fair.* The *Hilton* has its Rooftop and the *007.* The *Savoy* still leads them all, with elegant dancing and cabaret in its restaurant.

CLUBS AND NIGHTSPOTS

Annabel's. (Sub.) 44 Berkeley Sq., W.1. Very elegant *boîte* below the *Clermont Club,* London's most posh gambling den. Hard to get in. Discothèque.

Astor. (Sub.) Fitzmaurice Pl., Berkeley Sq., W.1. Intimate; French cuisine; dancing to two bands from 10:30 P.M. to 4 A.M. Vaudeville-style floorshow at 1 A.M.

Blue Angel, 14 Berkeley Sq., Quite sophisticated, expensive.

Churchills. 160 New Bond St., W.1. Cozy spot with dim lights. Star-studded floorshows. Open 6 P.M. to dawn, with free breakfast. Most people dress here.

Latin Quarter. 13 Wardour St. W.1. Good floorshows, not too expensive.

L'Hirondelle, Swallow St., W.1. Two bands, floorshow. Three-course menu about £5.

Omar Khayyam, 50 Cannon St., E.C.4. Claims to be the only Persian restaurant in London. Two floorshows. Serves lunches, too.

Penthouse Club. (Sub.) 11 Whitehorse St., W.1. The British answer to Hugh Hefner's place. Excellent food (inc. good buffet).

Pigalle. 190 Piccadilly, W.1. Bright spot for dinner. Two bands and lavish cabarets help it into the top category rather than the food and drink, which are just good.

Playboy Club. (Sub.) 45 Park Lane, W.1; usual ambience. Prices high.

Quaglino's. 16–17 Bury St., S.W.1. Mainly for the cabaret, which can be very good.

Raymond's Revuebar. Brewer St., W.1. Two shows nightly of super-sexy striptease; the only one we can list as good value for money.

Talk of the Town. Hippodrome Theatre Restaurant, off Leicester Sq., W.C.2. Two glittering shows nightly, excellent bands and a fixed price menu. You get your money's worth.

Tramps. Jermyn St., S.W.1. Has survived the course and is a pleasant place with mature clientele.

GAMING CLUBS. Although gambling is legal, you must go to the club of your choice 48 hours before you can play there, filling in application form for temporary membership, so be forewarned! The ultimate in gambling clubs is *Crockfords,* most famous establishment in the world, now restored to its former elegance by the Curzon House Group at a cost of £1,000,000. Excellent food, quiet and swift service, famous clientele, and a warm welcome for foreign visitors. You can dine well and gamble at the *International Sporting Club,* Berkeley Square; the *Palm Beach,* 30 Berkeley St.; and perhaps best of all, *Curzon House,* 21 Curzon St. All in Mayfair save Crockfords, which is off Pall Mall.

ENTERTAINMENT. Theaters. London has about 50 theaters staging plays and musicals all the year round. West End productions maintain a high standard, and many Broadway shows are put on with top casts from Britain and America. Most theaters have a matinee twice a week, and an evening performance beginning between 7:30 and 8:30 P.M. Prices for seats vary widely; unreserved gallery and "pit" seats *can* be had for about £1, but you have to queue for hours. The reserved seat list usually starts with upper circle at £1.50–1.75, then dress circle (reminiscent of the days when theater-goers all wore tuxedos for the better seats) at £2.00 up and stalls (center to front) at £2.50 to £4.50. Boxes cost around £10, depending on their size.

Of the experimental theaters, the *Royal Court,* in Sloane Square, puts on the best productions. And the productions at the *Mermaid Theatre,* at the remarkable address of Puddle Dock, Blackfriars, E.C.4., are usually worth seeing (also excellent restaurant for non-theatergoers, with view of the river). But if you're interested in off-beat theater, which can be fun and is cheap, as well as a whole range of entertainment, including pub shows, get the magazine *Time Out,* weekly. Most theaters have at least one bar. In some theatres you can reserve your intermission drink before the performance starts.

OPERA, BALLET. May be seen at: *Royal Festival Hall,* South Bank, S.E.1. *Royal Opera House,* Covent Garden, W.C.2. *Sadlers Wells Theatre,* Rosebery Ave., E.C.1. *The Coliseum Theatre,* where the *English National Opera* and visiting companies perform.

CONCERT HALLS. *Royal Albert Hall,* Kensington, S.W.7. *Royal Festival Hall, Queen Elizabeth Hall* and *Purcell Room,* South Bank, S.E.1. *Wigmore Hall,* Wigmore Str., W.1.

Best place to find out the programs at the various theaters is in the weekly magazine *What's On In London,* or see the Sunday or daily newspapers.

 MUSEUMS AND ART GALLERIES. London is one of the two or three most important centers of western civilization, and many of its museums are incomparable in their scope, variety, and imaginative presentation. Museums are open daily including Bank Holidays, except where otherwise stated. The best times to visit are between 10 A.M. and 4 P.M., or Sunday afternoon. Opening times given are for weekdays. Unless otherwise stated, museums are open Sunday afternoons but, be warned, some museums are liable to close in full or part one day a week to save costs. At press time, for example, the Victoria and Albert Museum is closed on Fridays. In most, entry is free; in some, there is a small charge.

British Museum, Great Russell St., W.C.1. (10–5). The most important institution of its kind in the world. Among the various departments are prints and drawings; coins and medals; Egyptian and Assyrian antiquities; Greek, Roman, British, and Medieval antiquities; Oriental antiquities. Don't miss some of the stunning new displays—e.g. the Elgin Marbles. Lecture tours begin at 11:30 A.M. and 3 P.M. weekdays from the main entrance hall. The excellent ethnography collection is now excitingly displayed at the Museum's *Burlington House* extension in Burlington Gardens, off Old Bond St.

Courtauld Institute Galleries, Woburn Sq., W.C.1. Italian paintings of 14–16th century, French Impressionists, also varying modern collection. Private collection of the Courtauld family. (10–5)

Dickens' House, 48 Doughty St., W.C.1. (Weekdays 10–12:30, 2–5, closed Sundays.) Occupied by the author from 1837 to 1839. On display are portraits, letters, first editions, furniture and autographs.

Guildhall Museum, the Royal Exchange, Bank, E.C.3. (Closed Sundays.) Portrays the history of the City of London from Roman times to the present. Also an outstanding collection of clocks.

Imperial War Museum, Lambeth Rd., S.E.1. Comprehensive collection of the Empire during two world wars, including an art collection and a library of films and photographs. Open 10–5.

Dr. Johnson's House, 17 Gough Square, Fleet St., E.C.4. (Open weekdays 10:30–5 in summer, otherwise 10:30–4:30, closed Sundays.) The home of the great wit, writer and lexicographer.

London Planetarium, Marylebone Rd., NW1. Take a vicarious trip through the galaxy.

Madame Tussaud's, Marylebone Rd, N.W.1. The world's most famous wax-works.

National Army Museum, Royal Hospital Road, Chelsea, S.W.3. The story of the British Army.

National Gallery, Trafalgar Sq., W.C.2. One of the world's great collections. Open till 9 P.M. on Tuesdays and Thursdays during the summer.

National Maritime Museum, Romney Rd., Greenwich, S.E.10. Superlative collection of marine memorabilia.

National Portrait Gallery, St. Martin's Place, Trafalgar Sq., W.C.2. British men and women over the last 450 years.

National Postal Museum, King Edward St., E.1. British stamps dating from 1840. Closed Sunday.

Natural History Museum, Cromwell Rd., S.W.7. A branch of the British Museum containing collections of animals, plants, minerals, fossils, and insects.

Public Records Office Museum, Chancery Lane, W.C.2. Historical documents include Domesday Book, two exemplars of Magna Carta, many rare items of Americana. Open 1–4 Monday-Friday. Closed Sunday.

Queen's Gallery, adjoining Buckingham Palace. Selection of paintings and other masterpieces from the Royal Collection. Weekdays (exc. Mon.) 11–6, Sunday 2–5.

Science Museum, Exhibition Rd., S.W.7. Every branch of science marvellously displayed. A must for children.

Tate Gallery, Millbank, S.W.1. Modern foreign painting and sculpture, but primarily dedicated to British painters such as Turner, Blake, pre-Raphaelites.

Tower of London, Tower Hill, E.C.3. (Closes at 4 P.M. from October.) Unrivalled collection of armor, relics and especially the Crown Jewels. Get there early—or queue for hours.

Victoria and Albert Museum, Cromwell Rd., S.W.7. Illustrates fine and applied arts from all over the world. The free lectures are especially valuable. Closed Fridays.

Wallace Collection, Hertford House, Manchester Sq., W.1. Fine art collection, with china, gold etc.

Wellington Museum, Apsley House, Hyde Park Corner, W.1. The London home of the famous duke containing relics and art.

PARKS AND PLEASURE GARDENS. London's great parks (*Hyde, Kensington, Regent's, Green, St. James's* in the center, *Battersea* and *Hampstead Heath* further out) are more than just wide green oases in the middle of a concrete desert. They are places where you can go boating, picnicking, riding, play tennis, listen to a military band, and more.

Other parks well worth a visit are *Greenwich* (where the world's central time is taken from the former Royal Observatory), *Holland Park* (Kensington), with remains of an Elizabethan mansion, now a youth hostel, and open air concerts, *Blackheath* and *Hampstead Heath, Kew Gardens* (botanical), with magnificent, extensive grounds, and Richmond. Richmond is easily accessible by bus or underground, and it still has the atmosphere of a medieval forest or heath—with real deer.

STREET MARKETS. Traditional home of the "barrow-boy", the true Cockney accent, good humor, bargains (and "spiv" swindles), and old London color are the open-air markets held in various parts of the capital. They are always good fun. Always watch your pockets in case the odd pickpockets are on the prowl. One word of advice: it's always worth bargaining, especially on a Friday in wet weather—the stall holders may have had a bad week and be glad to get what they can!

Portobello Market, Portobello Rd., W.11. (Take bus or tube to Notting Hill Gate.) Best day is Saturday, from 9 A.M. to 6 P.M. for all kinds of curios, silverware, antiques, etc. *No bargains!*

Camden Passage, Islington. (Tube or buses 19, 30, 73 to "The Angel".) Open air antique market, Saturdays.

Church Street, N.W.8. Nearest underground Edgware Road. (Bakerloo Line). Lots of junk, small and large items of furniture, some silver, porcelain and interesting bric-a-brac.

Petticoat Lane, in Middlesex St., E.1. Open on Sunday mornings only for pets, clothes, fabrics and curios of all descriptions. Rather on the decline.

Billingsgate, Lower Thames St., E.C.3. This is the world's most colorful fish market and it has been thriving since the 17th century. Open daily, 4 A.M. and 7 A.M. Officially wholesale only, so if you go as a sightseer, don't get in the way.

Smithfield, E.C.1. London's main meat market and one of the biggest in the world. Best days are Mondays and Thursdays. Observe same sightseer role as at Billingsgate.

 SHOPPING. For orientation on the finest of British products you can hardly do better than visit the *Design Centre,* in the Haymarket, just off Piccadilly Circus. You cannot buy goods at this permanent exhibition, but you *can* see the best and latest designs in everything for the home and then ask for them in the stores. For fine British craftmanship, visit the *Crafts Centre of Great Britain,* 43 Earlham St., W.C.2.

Department Stores. The most famous is *Harrods,* now in its second century in Knightsbridge, a vast emporium noted for the high quality of its goods. They have a special information department for guests from abroad, and so does *Fortnum and Mason* in Piccadilly, a smaller store, renowned for its food department, but equally good for fashions, accessories and luxurious gift items.

Selfridges, in Oxford Street, is another London landmark, one of the largest and most popular stores. *Peter Jones* in Sloane Square has every possible requirement for the home and home decoration; *Heal's* in Tottenham Court Road has a wonderful selection of things for the home, as well as gift items.

Liberty's of Regent Street has an international reputation for their beautiful silks, Liberty prints and fashions; this is a happy hunting ground if you're in search of the exceptional.

Quality Fashion. The quality and design of readymade clothes have made tremendous strides since the war, and the big stores have excellent dress departments. *Liberty* and *Harrods* (Paris names) have our personal recommendations. For the classically sporty type of British clothes, *Jaeger* have their famous coats as well as an array of jersey dresses.

Burberry and *Aquascutum* keep their longstanding reputation for waterproofs, raincoats and superlative overcoats for both men and women, and *Simpsons* in Piccadilly, though catering especially for men, has excellent clothes for women too. Sportswear specialists with original and unconservative ideas are *Lillywhites* and *Wetheralls.*

By the Yard. All the big stores, especially *John Lewis* in Oxford St., have a wide selection of fabrics at varying prices. The usual quest of the visitor is for traditional British tweeds and suitings, and in this matter the showrooms of *John G. Hardy* in New Burlington Street cannot be beaten for their display of the best woolens and worsteds obtainable. If you're looking for tartan, *Scott Adie* in Clifford Street or the *Scotch House* in Knightsbridge will supply all the truly authentic Scottish patterns of every clan.

The Shopping Mecca For Males is world-famous Savile Row, synonymous with all that is best in tailoring. Not perhaps in the Row itself, but in the immediate neighborhood, are the aristocrats of tailoring—catering for aristocrats, publicity-shy, and immensely civilized. *Henry Poole & Co.,* (10 Cork Street); *H. Huntsman & Sons* (11 Savile Row) are undoubtedly the most expensive tailors in London; *Hawes & Curtis* (43 Dover Street) number the Duke of Edinburgh among their customers; *Gieves and Hawkes* (1 Savile Row) first opened in 1771, dresses many public figures, as does *Kilgour, French & Stanbury* (33a Dover Street).

Here's a tip for the male traveler who left his dinner jacket at home to help conform with the baggage allowance: Moss Bros of London will rent you at reasonable cost anything from a complete outfit for the Ascot Races to immaculate evening dress for a society ball. Everything correct to the last detail. A godsend in case of an unexpected invitation to a formal affair.

Sportsmen. The most renowned maker of all requirements for the fisherman is *Hardys;* the most illustrious of British gunsmiths is *Purdey,* and the outstanding firm for sports equipment and accessories is *Lillywhites,* Lower Regent Street.

Grand Luxe. *Bradley, The National Fur Company, Molho* or *Woolf* will show you the latest in fur fashions, and if you want jewelry to go with them, you'll find *Cartier, Boucheron, Benson and Drayson, Kutchinsky,* all in that garden of temptation known as Bond Street. Do a little window-gazing here in any event, and don't miss the equally fascinating collection of genuine antique jewelry at the *Collector's Curio Corner* in Dover Street. As for the windows of the Burlington Arcade, you might see everything there from a golden toothpick to a reproduction of a gem from the Russian Crown Jewels.

China, Glass and Pottery. *Thomas Goode & Sons* in South Audley Street has a fascinating display. Two popular places with Americans are *Lawley's* of Regent Street and *Chinacraft* in Oxford Street, near Marble Arch. Both have their own potteries in Staffordshire and specialize in fine bone china. We have long been partial to the exotic wares of the *General Trading Co.,* located at 144 Sloane Street, S.W.1.

Best Shops for Silver, both antique and modern, are concentrated in the region of St. James's or Regent Street. You can't go wrong at either of the famous establishments of *Garrard & Co.,* and *Mappin and Webb.*

In Chancery Lane, at Nos. 53–63 (entry 53), is the *Chancery Lane Safe Deposit;* in the cellars you will find the Silver Vaults where some 50 dealers offer probably the largest collection in the world of antique and modern silverware. It's worth just looking at this glittering display.

Antiques. Streets with the densest number of antique shops are: Kensington Church Street, Brompton Road, King's Road in Chelsea, Crawford Street, off Baker Street. Try also the markets (see Street Markets).

Day Trips from London

Rural calm and places of historic interest are within easy reach of London. If you are not driving yourself, check the schedule of the Green Line, and also the "London Country Buses", whose excellent bus service extends to about a 30-mile radius from London. London's electric suburban train services are also top flight.

Especially recommended in the western environs of London are the following—Richmond, with its famous view of the Thames from Richmond Hill, and the enchanting 2,350-acre Richmond Park, full of flowering shrubs and freely-wandering deer.

Hampton Court, red brick Tudor palace residence of rumbustious English monarch Henry VIII, reputedly haunted (of course!), and surrounded by courtyards, gardens, fountains and deerpark. As an additional attraction you can puzzle your way through the celebrated Maze.

Windsor Castle, the base of whose Round Tower was built in the 12th century by Henry II, has long been one of the chief residences of English sovereigns. Don't miss its beautiful St. George's Chapel. Begun by Edward IV and finished in 1516, it ranks next to Westminster Abbey as a royal mausoleum (Henry VIII and George VI, among others, are buried here). See also the adjoining reception rooms with their Gobelin tapestries, the Rubens room, the Van Dyck room, and the royal library, whose collection includes drawings by Leonardo da Vinci and 87 portraits by Holbein. In the town of Windsor itself, you can see houses formerly inhabited by Jane Seymour, third wife of Henry VIII and mother of Edward VI, and Nell Gwynne, the Restoration actress who became the mistress of Charles II. A short walk from Windsor Castle is worldrenowned Eton College, most exclusive of English public schools.

Guildford, 40 minutes south by rail from Waterloo station, has a Norman castle, modern cathedral, and a steep cobbled main street plunging down between 17th-century shops and inns to the winding River Wey and the excellent Yvonne Arnaud Theatre.

Epsom also lies to the south, and should not be missed, especially if you can come at the beginning of June, when the Derby is run. This famous affair is one of England's noisiest and most boisterous picnics, guaranteed to change your ideas about the quiet and reserved English. Yes, this is also the birthplace of Epsom Salts, discovered here in 1618 in the mineral springs that made Epsom a fashionable 18th-century spa.

Visit Sevenoaks in Kent and nearby Knole Park for a clear, indelible impression of old England. Another must in Kent, Winston Churchill's former home, Chartwell, is open to the public. A Green Line bus takes you all the way, via the interesting town of Westerham.

Harrow, to the north of London, was founded in 1572 and granted a charter by Queen Elizabeth I. It is one of England's most famous schools, numbering Byron, Robert Peel and Winston Churchill among its alumni.

St. Albans, the ancient Roman city of Verulamium, 20 miles north of London, offers unusually interesting Roman remains and many ancient buildings. See the Verulamium Museum, the handsome Norman cathedral (which claims to have the longest nave in the world, after Winchester Cathedral), and the 15th-century clock tower. Also in St. Albans—a lot of good antique shops.

PRACTICAL INFORMATION FOR THE ENVIRONS OF LONDON AND THE SOUTH EAST

HOTELS AND RESTAURANTS. Here are some selected hotels and restaurants in the most attractive towns within easy reach of London by rail, bus, or car, which may appeal to those who prefer a quieter atmosphere and prefer to visit the metropolis on a day basis. Mileage from London is indicated in parentheses. Hotel categories are moderate to first class reasonable, and all have sufficient bathrooms available where there are no rooms with bath. (*Note:* In April

1974, many of Britain's counties changed their names and their boundaries. The British, typically, will take years to accept the new designations; so in the following pages we have used new names only where we think they are likely to be in fairly quick common use.)

ASCOT (Berkshire). (25). Packed during Royal Ascot Week (mid-June) otherwise delightful. On edge of Windsor Great Park. *Berystede,* 106 rooms. *Royal Berkshire,* 52 rooms, all with bath. The latter, especially, is expensive.

CHIGWELL (Essex). (14). *King's Head,* old world and full of atmosphere, for good beer and food. Non-residential.

DORKING (Surrey). (25). Good walking center. *White Horse,* 69 rooms, all with bath. Top drawer. An ancient coaching inn. *Burford Bridge,* 30 rooms with bath.

EGHAM (Surrey). (20). Thames-side town with Runnymede meadow nearby; also John Kennedy and Commonwealth Air Forces Memorials. *Great Fosters,* a 16th-cent. manor, once the home of Anne Boleyn. 25 rooms, 9 with bath.

EPSOM (Surrey). (16). During Derby week, early June, you'll not get in anywhere. *Drift Bridge,* 19 rooms. *White House,* 9 rooms, 4 with bath.

GUILDFORD (Surrey). (30). The *Angel,* coaching inn. Good food. 24 rooms, all with bath. The *Mad Hatter* is a good restaurant.

HAMPTON COURT (Surrey). (12). *Greyhound,* 30 rooms, half with baths. Good accommodations. *Bastions* is a good French restaurant. And there are at least ten pubs.

OXTED (Surrey). (22). The *Old Bell,* richly timbered old country pub and restaurant.

PENSHURST (Kent). (3). The *Leicester Arms,* cozy old country inn with good Kentish beer. Also has 8 rooms.

REIGATE (Surrey). (22). At the foot of the North Downs. *Bridge House,* 30 rooms with bath, excellent restaurant.

RICHMOND (Surrey). (10). Beauty spot on the Thames, *Gate,* 52 rooms with bath. Spectacular views from some rooms.

ST. ALBANS (Herts.). (20). *St. Michael's Manor* (23 rooms), and *Sopwell House Hotel* (17 rooms), both in lovely grounds, good restaurants, both expensive. *White Hart* (10 rooms), ancient hostelry, with lots of oak beams.

SHEPPERTON (16) (Surrey) *Warren Lodge,* 40 rooms with bath, overlooking the River Thames.

WESTERHAM (Kent). (23). Churchill's former home at Chartwell nearby. *King's Arms,* 16 rooms. For good food, *Le Marquis de Montcalm.*

WEYBRIDGE (20) (Surrey) *Oatlands Park.*

WINDSOR (Berks.). (22). Home of English royalty for 850 years. *Old House,* 40 rooms, 16 with bath. *Castle,* 63 rooms with bath. *Royal Adelaide,* 39 rooms, some with bath.

HISTORIC HOUSES OPEN TO THE PUBLIC
(For further information see note under *Historic Houses* earlier.)

BEDFORDSHIRE. *Woburn Abbey.* Owned by the Duke of Bedford. 18th-century house and "Wild Animal Kingdom" safari park. Open daily in afternoons, every day of the year.

BERKSHIRE. *Windsor Castle.* Royal residence. Open daily except when the Royal Family is in residence and never during Ascot week, in July.

BUCKINGHAMSHIRE. *Hughenden Manor.* Former home of Disraeli. Open February to December, afternoons only.

ESSEX. *Audley End House,* open April through September.

HERTFORDSHIRE. *Hatfield House.* Home of the Marquess of Salisbury. Queen Elizabeth I lived here. Open April to September. *Knebworth House.* Tudor mansion with Victorian gothic additions. Open April - early Oct.

SURREY. *Hampton Court Palace.* Former royal residence. Open all year. *Syon House* (Brentford). Home of the Duke of Northumberland. Open April through September, Mon. through Fri. *Kew Palace.* Built in Dutch style, 1631. Open April through September, weekdays and Sun. afternoons.

The Thames Country
The Thames (on which Windsor is situated) rises in the lovely Cotswold Hills and pursues its historic 209-mile course through Gloucestershire, Berkshire, Oxfordshire, Buckinghamshire and Surrey to the sea. Cirencester, near the head of the Thames, is locally pronounced "Sisister", almost, but not quite, enough to make us supporters of Bernard Shaw's campaign to reform English spelling!

Highlights of the Thames Country include the enchanting villages of the Cotswolds, a rural world of golden stone cottages and meticulous gardens—Old England, apparently untouched by the necessary horrors of the industrial revolution.

Gloucester is a historically-important town with some quaint streets and gabled and timbered houses among modern development. Its chief glory, and one of the glories of England, is Gloucester Cathedral, erected in the 11th century on the foundations of a seventh-century abbey, and with a beautiful Gothic tower added in the 15th century. Don't miss the crypt and the splendid fan vaulting in the cloister.

Oxford
Oxford, whose earliest colleges, University, Balliol and Merton, were founded in 1249, 1263 and 1264 respectively, is probably the most famous university in the English-speaking world. You can spend a delightful day here, wandering down the splendid High Street, flanked by the façades of a score of colleges, then among the buildings, quadrangles, spires and bridges of this ancient university. The most rewarding colleges from the tourist point of view are St. John's, All Souls and Magdalen.

The last, pronounced "Maudlin", has the most beautiful gardens of all. See also the handsome garden of New College, surrounded by part of the old city wall, and its chapel with 14th-century stained glass windows; the superb 13th-century chapel of Merton College; the famous Bodleian Library, where you can browse among a fascinating collection of curious and old manuscripts; the Ashmolean Museum, oldest in the country.

PRACTICAL INFORMATION FOR THE THAMES COUNTRY AND THE COTSWOLDS

Many hotels in the area are small, often ancient hostelries full of atmosphere. Comfort scales from the cozy to the semi-luxe. Majority of those listed have a few rooms with bath.

ABINGDON (Thames Valley). Many old buildings. Abbey. *Upper Reaches,* 20 rooms with bath: incorporates remains of a medieval corn mill.

BROADWAY (Cotswolds). Elizabethan houses. *Lygon Arms,* extremely popular, so book well ahead. *Dormy House* also first class reasonable.

BURFORD (Cotswolds). Delightful old country town. Renowned ancient *Bull* and *Bay Tree,* first class.

CHELTENHAM. Not strictly in this area, but an excellent center for the Cotswolds. *Moor End* and *Queens,* both first class reasonable. *Golden Valley,* a 100-room motel. Good cabaret.

CHIPPING CAMPDEN (Cotswolds). Medieval town, picturesque. *Noel Arms, Cotswold House,* moderate.

CHIPPING NORTON. Highest town in Oxfordshire, beautiful old houses. *White Hart,* moderate.

CIRENCESTER (Cotswolds). Near source of Thames. *King's Head,* first class.

GLOUCESTER. On the Severn river, not the Thames, but a good center for the Cotswolds, and an ancient town. *Fleece* and *New County,* moderate. Restaurant: *Don Pasquale.*

HENLEY (Thames Valley). During the Royal Regatta (late June-July), accommodation is impossible unless booked about six months ahead. The *Sydney House,* 9 rooms, is comfortable.

MAIDENHEAD (Thames Valley). Popular riverside resort. *The Beal* is ancient, the *Maidenhead ESSO* motel is modern. Both, in their own way, are good.

MARLOW (Thames Valley). Yet another popular resort, good for angling. *The Compleat Angler* is well-known, has excellent restaurant, garden. First class.

MORETON-IN-MARSH (Cotswolds). Market town with stonebuilt houses. *Manor House, Redesdale Arms,* both first class. Nearby, at Blockley, the *Lower Brook House* has superb food and acceptable accommodations.

OXFORD (Thames Valley). Best hotel is the *Randolph,* but book ahead. *Oxford,* good restaurant, moderate. *Lodge,* motel.

Restaurant: *Elizabeth,* 84 St. Aldgates, has good French cuisine, wines; *La Sorbonne* is good.

THORNBURY (Gloucestershire). Just one reason for coming here, *Thornbury Castle,* genuine 16th-century, and one of Britain's top restaurants.

WESTON-ON-THE-GREEN. *Weston Manor,* very comfortable and of great historical interest. Some rooms have four posters.

WOODSTOCK (Oxfordshire). Ancient village next Blenheim Palace. *Bear, Dorchester, Marlborough Arms,* (all expensive).

GETTING THERE BY RIVER BOAT. Steamers serve the upper and lower Thames throughout the summer. *Salters Steamers,* of Folly Bridge, Oxford, run services from mid-May to mid-September. Their vessels leave Walton, Windsor, Marlow, Reading, Henley and Abingdon daily with return journeys starting at Oxford. Combined railway and steamer tickets are issued from many British Rail stations.

Every day from mid-May to mid-September *British Rail* run a combined rail and steamer trip to Henley and Reading. Ring Paddington Station (tel. 262 6767) for details.

Daily river trips from Easter until the end of September are operated from Windsor by *Arthur Jacobs Ltd.,* Thames House, Barry Avenue, Windsor, Berks, tel. Windsor 62933. Trips take in, principally, stretch of river between Windsor and Reading. Alternatively, if you would rather be your own skipper, you can hire a cozy 4-berth U-drive cabin cruiser, fully equipped, from *Bushnell's of Maidenhead,* Ray Mead Road, Maidenhead. Berks, tel. Maidenhead 24061; while *Hoseasons Boat-Hire Holidays* of Sunway House, Lowestoft, Suffolk, tel. Lowestoft 64991, can book you with 20 Thames-side boatyards through their centralized agency service. For information of the river write to the *Thames and Chilterns Tourist Board,* P.O. Box 10, Abingdon, Berkshire.

HISTORIC HOUSES OPEN TO THE PUBLIC
(For further information see notes under *Historic Houses,* earlier.)

MORETON-IN-MARSH. *Chastleton House,* built 1603. Box garden said to be the oldest in England. Open all year daily except Wednesdays.

WINCHCOMBE. *Sudeley Castle.* Historic home dating from 15th century. Open April to September.

WOODSTOCK. *Blenheim Palace,* home of the Duke of Marlborough. Open April to October, weekday afternoons; also weekends, Aug. and Sept.

Southern England
All around the coasts of Kent, Sussex and Hampshire, resort towns stretch along beaches and bays, their hotels and guest houses cheek-by-jowl. Only a sprinkling of the hotels in each town remain open all year; most of them do seasonal business from Easter to the end of September.

Exploring Kent and Sussex
The gentle, orderly landscape of southeast England is packed from end to end with castles, country houses, cathedrals and historic highspots by the score. And none of them are more than a couple of hours from London.

Down in the apple-blossom county of Kent, the chief tourist magnet is Canterbury, with its historic religious associations and magnificent Gothic cathedral. It was here that the Archbishop of Canterbury, Thomas à Becket, was murdered on orders of King Henry II in the 12th century, and here that the Canterbury Pilgrims came to seek the holy blissful martyr. Not far from Canterbury is the first English Christian Church, St. Martin's, where the Christian wife of the Saxon King Ethelbert worshipped in the sixth century. See also Chiddingstone and Chilham, "the prettiest villages in Kent". And remember to book hotel reservations way in advance for Canterbury—in July and August every good inn is full to the rafters.

In East and West Sussex are Rye, of the cobbled streets, timbered dwellings and oak-paneled *Mermaid Inn;* historic Hastings and nearby Battle (the Normans called it Senlac), where William the Conqueror defeated Harold in 1066 and changed the whole course of English history. Hastings Castle, and Bodiam, not far away, are both ruined, but Bodiam nevertheless provides you with a moated, curtain-walled fortress without equal in England. Popular summer coastal spots are Bexhill-on-Sea, Eastbourne and the dizzy chalk cliffs of Beachy Head, where begin the South Downs and the charming villages of Sussex like Alfriston and West Dean. In the ancient and romantic town of Lewes, see the handsome Elizabethan residence, the so-called "Anne of Cleves House", and Bull House, home of Thomas Paine, author of *The Rights of Man.*

Brighton is the brightest and most sophisticated of the south coast resorts. Try also to include Chichester on your itinerary. Its cathedral is a "sermon in stone"; its ancient market cross one of the most impressive things in Sussex. In summer the Festival Theater provides some excellent drama. A couple of miles out of town is Fishbourne Palace, the excavated remains of the Romano-British palace. Well worth a visit. Try dining by candlelight amidst the tapestried walls and copper pans of Midhurst's *Spread Eagle,* one of England's most attractive old inns. *Chequers,* at Pulborough, 12 miles east, is another.

Hampshire and Wiltshire

Highlights of Hampshire include Winchester, the ancient capital of Alfred the Great. The steep and narrow High Street is flanked by some of the oldest houses in England, and the Great Hall, all that remains of the castle, has in it what is traditionally supposed to be King Arthur's Round Table. Winchester's huge cathedral, where Alfred and other English kings were crowned, has a handsome baptismal font (Norman) and some interesting Gothic tombs of the 15th-century bishops. See also Winchester's public school, the oldest in England, opened in 1382. Don't miss its chapel and the ancient cloisters.

Along the county's coastline are the naval base of Portsmouth, Southampton and fascinating old Lymington (from which ferries run to the Isle of Wight). Bournemouth, in Dorset, is one of England's best seaside resorts and an ideal base from which to explore the New Forest, once the hunting preserve of the Norman kings and still roamed by wild deer and ponies.

The rounded hills of Wiltshire form a breezy plateau called Salisbury Plain, south of which lies Salisbury, the county town, dominated by the 404-foot stone spire of its Cathedral, frequently painted by Constable, who was not alone in thinking it the most glorious spire in Christendom.

Inside the cathedral, see the lancet windows, the 14th-century wrought iron clock, and the tombs of Englishmen who died in the crusades and at the great victory of Agincourt in 1415. And don't miss the octagonal chapter house. Close to Salisbury is Wilton House, splendid home of the Earls of Pembroke, with an incomparable art collection including 16 Van Dycks in the double-cube room, where Eisenhower and staff planned the invasion of Normandy. On Salisbury Plain stands Britain's most famous prehistoric circle, Stonehenge, whose impressive monoliths may date as far back as 2,000 years before Christ. Closer to our own times are the 18th-century landscape gardens of Stourhead, owned by the National Trust and considered to be among the finest in the world.

PRACTICAL INFORMATION FOR THE SOUTHERN COUNTIES

 HOTELS AND RESTAURANTS. Holiday hotels often quote all-inclusive rates for a week's stay, a plan that works out a good deal cheaper than taking a room and meals by day. But the overseas visitor probably hasn't time or doesn't care to spend more than a day or so in each part of the country, so we've listed a selection of hotels at popular centers where you can put up for the night pretty comfortably. And if you are not stopping overnight, most of the larger hotels and all inns serve meals.

COASTAL RESORTS

BOGNOR REGIS (Sussex). An elegant resort, year round temperate climate. *Royal Norfolk Hotel* is good, first class.

BOURNEMOUTH (Dorset). An all-year resort, famous for its pines and clear air. Best hotels are: *Carlton, Palace Court, Highcliff, Royal Bath* and the *Round House.* All have about 100 rooms, some with bath. All first class superior.
　　Restaurants: *El Pozo, Topo Cigio, La Cappa;* 10 miles north, on A35, the *Cat and Fiddle* at Hinton Admiral.

BRIGHTON AND HOVE (Sussex). Popular with day-trip Londoners and commuters. See here the Regency *Brighton Pavilion,* a "pocket palace." Hotels include the large *Grand* and *Metropole,* first class.
　　For dining, try *Le Français, The French Connection, The Starlit Room* at the *Metropole. The Pump House* and *Au Pied du Cochon* are good.

DOVER (Kent). *White Cliffs,* 92 rooms, 16 with shower. *Dover Stage,* designed for ferry passengers and motorists, has 42 rooms (a Holiday Inn).

EASTBOURNE (Sussex). Retains a good deal of elegance. Best are the *Burlington,* and *Grand,* both large, having rooms with bath; first class.
　　Good Italian food at the *Court House.*

FOLKESTONE (Kent). The *Burlington, Garden House,* and *Clifton,* all first class reasonable, can offer rooms with bath.

HASTINGS AND ST. LEONARDS (Sussex). Best and largest are the *Queens* (Hastings) and *Royal Victoria* (St. Leonards), both first class superior, both having some rooms with bath. North of Hastings is *Beauport Park,* a country house hotel.

SOUTHAMPTON (Hampshire). *Royal,* 100 rooms, and *Dolphin,* 76 rooms. All first class superior. Motels: *New Forest Motel,* Ower; *Skyways,* Southampton Water, 126 rooms.

ROMNEY MARSH. Between Hythe and the Sussex border lies desolate yet fascinating Romney Marsh, with its ancient history of smuggling and trade with France. Visiting French yachtsmen like the Rye inns for Kentish cider, and the Marsh folk are just as at home with wine. The best place to stay in Rye is at the ancient and beautiful *Mermaid,* or the *George,* both small, first class reasonable.

INLAND

AMESBURY (Wiltshire). A center for tours of Salisbury Plain and Stonehenge. *Antrobus Arms,* 19 rooms, most with bath.

CANTERBURY (Kent). Ancient cathedral city. *Abbots Barton,* 36 rooms, 9 with bath. *County,* 74 rooms, over half with bath. *Chaucer,* 50 rooms, 30 with baths. *Slatters,* 30 rooms, many with bath.
For dinner, try the *Trattoria Roma Antica.*

CASTLE COMBE (Wiltshire). "Britain's prettiest village". Over-publicized but still beautiful. The *Manor House,* 36 rooms, almost all with bath, extensive grounds, has excellent restaurant. *Castle,* small country inn.

CHICHESTER (Sussex). Worth a visit for its Festival Theatre, *Chichester Lodge,* 34 rooms with bath, reasonable food. On A27 at Westhampnett round-about *Ship,* 30 rooms, 9 with bath.

CHRISTCHURCH (Dorset). *King's Arms Inn,* a pretty half-timbered hostelry with Elizabethan furnishings.

HASLEMERE (Surrey). A mile outside this little country town is *Lythe Hill Hotel,* 38 rooms, most with bath, one with 4-poster bed. Fine cuisine.

LACOCK (Wiltshire). Charming National Trust village. Stay (or dine) at the *Sign of the Angel.* Small, cozy.

LYNDHURST (Hampshire). In the heart of the New Forest. *Lyndhurst Park,* 66 rooms, over half with bath. *David Bell's Forest Lodge,* 12 rooms, 6 with baths.

MAIDSTONE (Kent.). At Hollingbourne, near Maidstone, on the M20 London-Dover-Channel route, is Rank Hotel's *Great Danes,* a luxurious establishment with 78 rooms and very extensive facilities. Also: *Boxley,* at Boxley, 10 rooms (all with bath) and *Royal Star,* 40 rooms (10 with bath). At nearby Burham, the small *Toastmaster's Inn,* excellent for food and, especially, wine.

MIDHURST (Sussex). Pleasant country town; golf, fishing. The *Spread Eagle,* an ancient showplace inn, 30 rooms, fine food.

SALISBURY (Wiltshire). Cathedral city, touring center. *King's Arms,* 16 rooms; lovely old inn, modern amenities. *White Hart,* 73 rooms, 45 with bath. Restaurants: *Crane's* is our choice for dining. *LeProvençal* runs it a close second.

WINCHESTER (Hampshire). Ancient city, once the capital of England. The modern *Wessex,* opposite the cathedral, is first class; 91 rooms with bath.

GLYNDEBOURNE FESTIVAL OPERA is held during summer in a fine, but small, auditorium set in beautiful grounds of a private estate near Lewes, Sussex. During the long interval, the audience picnics, or dines in the excellent restaurants. For tickets to Glyndebourne's Opera, apply well in advance to any ticket agency (Keith Prowse, for example) or through your travel agent. Wear evening dress—tuxedoes for men (you should change before you arrive). Take a train from Victoria (most opera-goers ride down to Lewes Station on the 3:45 P.M.) and a special bus meets you. An expensive outing. Reckon on about £60–75 for two.

HISTORIC HOUSES OPEN TO THE PUBLIC

(For further information see notes under *Historic Houses,* earlier.)

SUSSEX. *Arundel Castle.* Home of the Duke of Norfolk. Open from mid-May to mid-September. *Great Dixter,* near Rye, 15th-century manor house with lovely gardens. Open Easter to September.

HAMPSHIRE. *Beaulieu Abbey,* New Forest. Home of Lord Montagu of Beaulieu. Remarkable National Car Museum. Abbey open daily except winter, when Sundays only, by Memorial Trust.

WILTSHIRE. *Longleat,* near Warminster. Home of the Marquess of Bath, built 1566. Open daily all year. *Wilton House,* Salisbury. Home of the Earl of Pembroke. Noted for ancient lawns, Cedars of Lebanon and sumptuous Double Cube Room. Open April through September.

KENT. *Ightham Mote,* near Ightham. *Chartwell,* Sir Winston Churchill's beautiful former home. *Knole,* home of Lord Sackville. Built 1456. Open March through December.

The Southwest (Dorset, Somerset, Devon, Cornwall and Avon)

Dorset remains one of the last truly unspoiled corners of the old rural England of popular imagination, full of mellow stone manor houses, thatched cottages, cider apple orchards and winding country lanes, leading from one steep little valley to the next. This is the "Wessex" of Thomas Hardy's pastoral novels. In Dorchester, the county town, there is a special room of Hardy relics in the museum, along with other relics of the town's Roman origins, and Hardy's birthplace at Higher Bockhampton, only three miles away, is open to visitors. Dorchester is an excellent center for visiting Dorset's sightseeing highspots, which include the giant Iron Age ramparts of Maiden Castle; the unique Swannery at Abbotsbury; Sherborne, with its ancient Abbey Church and two castles (one formerly the home of Sir Walter Raleigh); the dramatic Purbeck Coast around Lulworth Cove, and, guarding a gap in the Purbeck Hills, the ruins of Corfe Castle.

Somerset offers the spectacular natural attractions of Cheddar Gorge and Wookey Hole Cave, the windswept Exmoor Hills piled against the Devon border, and the man-made charms of Bath, Glastonbury, Wells and Dunster.

In the newly designated county of Avon is Bath, full of handsome buildings, streets, squares and crescents in the classic style of the 18th century. But Bath's special glory are the famous Roman Baths themselves, which rank among the most striking Roman relics in Europe. And underlining the classical appeal of Bath is a summer festival with a strong emphasis on 18th-century music and drama. In nearby Claverton Manor is the American Museum, complete with Conestoga wagon and a replica of George Washington's herb garden.

Back in Camelot-haunted Somerset, Glastonbury is one of the most ancient places in Britain, a cradle of early Christian faith and the traditional burial-place of King Arthur. Wells is a charming old cathedral city with a village atmosphere. At its heart stands the West Country's loveliest cathedral. Dunster is an old market town with a 17th-century Yarn Market, a wide main street lined with old shops and houses, and a magnificent castle, lived in by the Luttrell family since 1376.

Devon has not one, but two, holiday coasts, both completely different in character. The rugged north coast faces the Atlantic, with surfing beaches around Woolacombe, towering cliffs at Ilfracombe, the leading North Devon seaside town, and thickly-wooded hills plunging into the sea around picturesque Lynton and Lynmouth. One of the most-visited spots on this coast is Clovelly, whose cobbled main street is so steep that it can be explored only on foot. The South Devon coast is more gentle, almost Mediterranean in appearance, with rich red sandstone cliffs framing the intensely blue waters of Torbay. Torquay is perhaps the best of all the West Country resorts, and together with the neighboring seaside towns of Paignton and Brixham, is comprehensively promoting itself as a three-in-one resort under the name of Torbay. Farther west is the little port of Dartmouth, which figures in the story of the voyage of the *Mayflower*, and from which today you can cruise for 12 miles by steamer up the River Dart to Totnes. Highly recommended. Another and much larger port with *Mayflower* associations is the proud city of Plymouth, also famed for its links with Sir Francis Drake. Between the north and south coasts lie the high and empty hills of Dartmoor, crowned by gaunt granite outcrops known as "tors", and roamed by shaggy wild ponies. And to the east of Dartmoor, at the head of the Exe estuary, is the historic city of Exeter, complete with Elizabethan guildhall and great medieval cathedral.

Cornwall is the sharp end of the rocky wedge that is the West Country peninsula. The principal center on the Atlantic coast is Newquay, England's surfing capital, while Falmouth, its gardens bristling with palm trees, is the main resort on the Channel coast. From either one, you can visit all the regular Cornish haunts—St. Michael's Mount; the ruins of King Arthur's clifftop castle at Tintagel; the shark-angling port of Looe; St. Ives, part fishing port, part holiday resort and artist colony; and of course, the tumbled granite cliffs of Land's End, westernmost point of mainland England.

PRACTICAL INFORMATION FOR THE SOUTHWEST

COASTAL RESORTS. (Many hotels close in winter.)

CLOVELLY (Devon). Picturesque, one steep cobbled street. No cars allowed. *New Inn,* 20 rooms.

DARTMOUTH (Devon). Castle, Royal Naval College. *Royal Castle,* moderate. Restaurant: Try the *Carved Angel Restaurant.*

FALMOUTH (Cornwall). Try the *Green Lawns,* for luxurious living, or the *Green Bank* or *Palm Beach.* All have rooms with bath.

ILFRACOMBE (Devon). Popular, scenic resort. Largest is the *Cliffe Hydro,* but the *Carlton* and the *Dilkhusa Grand* are also good.

LOOE (Cornwall). Cobbled streets and gabled houses. *Hannafore Point,* 42 rooms, most with bath.

LYME REGIS (Dorset). An old Georgian town. *Mariners,* 12 rooms. *Alexandra,* 25 rooms.

LYNTON & LYNMOUTH (Devon). Twin towns, at top and bottom of a lovely cleft. *Tors* (Lynmouth), 43 rooms, 12 with bath. *Combe Park* (Lynton), 10 rooms, 6 with bath.

MINEHEAD (Somerset). On a wide bay, pebble and sand beach. Best is the *Beach,* 39 rooms, some with bath. Also recommended, the *Benares* and the *York.*

NEWQUAY (Cornwall). A popular modern resort with nine spacious surf beaches. *Headland,* 120 rooms, 45 with bath. *Atlantic,* 62 rooms, 24 with bath. *Glendorgal,* 33 rooms, 11 with bath.

PENZANCE (Cornwall). *Queen's,* first class, most rooms with bath.

PLYMOUTH. The *Mayflower Post House,* 104 rooms with bath, and *Holiday Inn,* 225 rooms with bath. Both first class.

SALCOMBE (South Devon). Rather smart sailing center. *Marine, St. Elmo, Tides Reach.* All have many rooms with bath. *Grafton Towers.*

ST. IVES (Cornwall). Another picture resort. *Tregenna Castle,* 90 rooms, 50 with bath, *Porthminster,* 50 rooms, 20 with bath.

ST. MAWES (Cornwall). Yachting socialites' rendezvous. *Tresanton,* luxurious, excellent cuisine. *Rising Sun,* on the harbor, noted for good food, and *Green Lantern,* both first class.

TORQUAY (South Devon). *Imperial,* 150 rooms and suites (all with bath), is one of the finest resort hotels in Britain, with nearly half a mile of private cliffs and beaches. Also recommended: *Palace,* 150 rooms. *Osborne.* Most rooms with bath at both.

WESTON-SUPER-MARE (Somerset). Popular resort on the Bristol Channel with excellent beach. *Grand Atlantic,* first class, not too large, some rooms with bath.

IN THE COUNTRY. (Hotels are mainly open all year.)

BATH (Avon). Best book ahead, especially in June for the Festival. *Francis,* 86 rooms, 26 with bath. *Lansdown Grove,* 50 rooms, 12 with bath. *Pratt's,* 55 rooms, 17 with bath. *Beaufort,* 100 rooms with bath.

Restaurants: Delightful cellar-like *Hole in the Wall.* If you can't get in, try the *Priory Hotel* in Weston Road.

BRISTOL (Avon). Old port, 7 miles up the Avon river. Best are the ultramodern *Unicorn,* with unique garage facilities, 200 rooms with bath, *Holiday Inn,* in city center, 300 rooms with bath, *Dragonara,* 210 rooms with bath, and *Grand,* 206 rooms, half with bath. At Clifton, *Grand Spa,* 67 rooms, half with bath. On M4, south of city, *Esso Motor Hotel,* 156 rooms.

DORCHESTER (Dorset). Ancient town, connected with Thomas Hardy. *Antelope,* 23 rooms. *King's Arms,* 28 rooms.

EXETER (Devon). County town and touring center. *Buckerell Lodge,* 15 rooms, 6 with baths; *Countess Weir Lodge* (motel), 43 rooms with bath.

GLASTONBURY (Somerset). Old pilgrimage town, good touring center. *George & Pilgrim Inn,* 13 rooms; famous 15th-century inn for pilgrims. Book ahead. *Beckets* is a very good restaurant.

TRURO (Cornwall). Cathedral city. *Brookdale,* 54 rooms, some with bath. Eat at *Roundhouse.*

WELLS (Somerset). Beautiful cathedral city. *Crown,* 10 rooms, 4 with bath. *Swan,* 25 rooms.

Restaurants: At nearby Priddy, the nationally-known *Miners' Arms* features superb food, as does the *Bowlish House,* also nearby, at Shepton Mallet.

HISTORIC HOUSES OPEN TO THE PUBLIC

(For further information see notes under *Historic Houses,* earlier.)

SOMERSET. *Montacute House,* Yeovil. Elizabethan house open some days all year.

DORSET. *Athelhampton,* Puddletown. Great medieval stone house. Open April through Sept.

DEVON and **CORNWALL.** *Buckland Abbey,* Tavistock. 13th-century Cistercian monastery with relics of Sir Francis Drake. Open all year, daily in summer. *St. Michael's Mount,* Penzance. Fairytale castle-capped islet. Open all year.

AVON. *Claverton Manor,* near Bath, contains the only *American Museum* in Britain. Open daily (ex. Mon.) Easter to mid-October.

East Anglia

This was the name of the ninth-century Saxon kingdom on the east coast of England. Today it refers to the counties of Essex, Suffolk, Norfolk, Cambridgeshire and Lincolnshire, all within the area bounded by the Thames, the Wash and the North Sea, and east of the railroad line from London to Doncaster. Time is said to have had less effect upon Norfolk than anywhere else in the British Isles, and though Suffolk is already becoming an overspill for London, the area is still largely agricultural. The Norfolk Broads (over a hundred miles of rivers and lakes) are a unique sailing and cabin-cruising holiday playground which is unfortunately currently ruined by serious water pollution problems. The translucent light is ideal for painters—East Anglia produced Gainsborough and Constable. If you are not traveling by car, a good network of buses covers the area, taking you through delightful villages on the way.

Exploring East Anglia

Dominating the flat, far-spreading East Anglian farms and fenlands are four ancient cathedral cities—Ely, Norwich, Lincoln and Bury St. Edmunds. Ely was the last stronghold of the Saxons under Hereward the Wake, who defied the Normans until 1072. Norwich not only has a fine Norman cathedral, but also 30 other medieval churches and an outstanding collection of paintings in the city's old Castle Keep, mainly of the Norwich School. Lincoln's triple-towered cathedral is one of the supreme architectural glories of Britain; it also contains one of the original drafts of *Magna Carta.*

Other historic East Anglian towns are Colchester, renowned for its oysters, roses and Roman treasures; Bury St. Edmunds, which has an interesting cathedral, market square and abbey ruins; and Ipswich, county town of Suffolk, where you should seek out the *Ancient House,* oldest and most picturesque bookshop in Britain, and Christchurch Mansion, a museum of folk art and antiques.

But in between the big cities, lying like tight little islands in a sea of cornfields and elm-bordered meadows, are the small towns and villages in which you will capture the true feel of East Anglia. Places like Lavenham and Long Melford, with their timbered inns and handsome churches; Kersey, where you drive through a watersplash in the main street; the Essex village of Finchingfield, dreaming around its duckpond and village green; and the little coastal town of Aldeburgh, which stages a famous music festival each year in summer, though there are spring and autumn programs, too.

Cambridge

Seventeen miles south of Ely is Cambridge, seat of the great university. Most tourists find it more charming than Oxford, which, as they say, "is a university in a town" whereas "Cambridge is a town in a university". You can't miss King's College Chapel, one of the greatest examples of ecclesiastical architecture in existence. See Trinity College gateway and Great Court, and stroll along the "Backs", the lawns and gardens which extend behind the colleges to the River Cam. See also St. John's College (1511), one of the most beautiful; Magdalene, with its 17th-century library given by Samuel Pepys; Jesus College, in the 12th-century Benedictine abbey of St. Radegund, and Christ's College (1436), with its beautiful gardens and associations with John Milton.

PRACTICAL INFORMATION FOR EAST ANGLIA

ESSEX

COLCHESTER. Center for the Constable country and oysters. *George,* 40 rooms, 12 with bath. *Red Lion,* 40 rooms, 12 with bath, a 15th-century hostelry, excellent cuisine. *Rose and Crown,* 18 rooms, some with bath.

DEDHAM. On the river Stour and often painted by Constable. *Dedham Vale,* 12 rooms, 4 with bath. *La Talbooth,* 10 rooms with bath. (very chic).

HARWICH and PARKESTON QUAY. Continental harbor and ancient seaport (traces of Nelson). *Samuel Pepys,* 7 rooms. *Cliff* (Dovercourt), 40 rooms, some with bath.

SUFFOLK

ALDEBURGH. Home of the Britten music festival. *Brudenell,* 45 rooms, 27 with bath. About 15 miles away, at Orford, the *King's Head* has a reputation for good food. (Limited accommodation.)

BURY ST. EDMUNDS. Georgian town with medieval remains. *Angel,* 50 rooms, 14 with bath. *Suffolk,* 32 rooms, half with bath.

FELIXSTOWE. Popular seaside resort, golf, yachting. *Orwell,* 60 rooms, most with bath, luxurious.

IPSWICH. County town and inland port. *Belstead Brook Hotel,* 24 rooms with bath; good food, comfortable. *Post House,* 120 rooms with bath.

LAVENHAM. A preserved medieval "showplace" of East Anglia. *Swan,* 14th-century inn, 42 rooms with bath.

LOWESTOFT. Large seaside resort, good sands; golf, sea and river fishing; large fishing industry and harbor. *Victoria,* 50 rooms, a third with bath.

NEWMARKET. Famous racing center; all accommodation booked solid during big race meetings. *White Hart,* 23 rooms, 10 with bath. *Rutland Arms,* 34 rooms, 4 with bath.

WOODBRIDGE. Lovely old town and yachting center. On river Deben. *Crown,* 13 rooms. *Seckford Hall,* 18 rooms, several with bath.

NORFOLK

CROMER. Popular center for Norfolk Coast; good sands, sports facilities. *Hotel de Paris,* 60 rooms, 22 with bath. *Cliftonville,* 50 rooms, a few with bath.

KING'S LYNN. Ancient town and seaport on river Ouse. *Duke's Head,* recently restored; 75 rooms, all with bath. Excellent restaurant.

NORWICH. Historic county city, now with a university. *Maid's Head,* oldest hostelry, has genuine Elizabethan bedroom, 95 rooms, some renovated, good cuisine. *Royal, Castle. Hotel Norwich,* 84 rooms with bath. *Post House Hotel,* 120 rooms with bath. *Nelson,* 43 rooms, all with bath.

THETFORD. Old market town; good golf. *Bell,* 42 rooms with bath.

CAMBRIDGESHIRE

CAMBRIDGE. University city, ancient buildings. *University Arms,* 126 rooms, 90 with bath. *Blue Boar,* 47 rooms, 7 with bath. *Royal Cambridge,* 77 rooms, a third with bath. *Garden House,* luxurious, 54 rooms, all with bath.

ELY. Cathedral city on the Isle of Ely. Good center for fishing and boating. The *Old Fire Engine House* serves good traditional English food. Not expensive.

LINCOLNSHIRE

BOSTON. Ancient port and fresh water angling center. *New England,* 11 rooms, 5 with bath.

LINCOLN. Old cathedral city; racing, golf, fishing. *White Hart,* 68 rooms, most with bath. *Eastgate,* 61 rooms, all with bath.

HISTORIC HOUSES OPEN TO THE PUBLIC
(For further information see notes under *Historic Houses,* earlier.)

ESSEX. *Audley End House,* Saffron Walden. Jacobean mansion. Open daily April through September.

SUFFOLK. *Ickworth House,* near Bury St. Edmunds, late Regency. Open mid-April to October.

NORFOLK. *Holkham Hall,* Wells. Palladian mansion. Open June to September. *Sandringham House*—including interior—property of H.M. the Queen.

CAMBRIDGESHIRE. *Anglesey Abbey,* near Cambridge. Elizabethan manor. Open Easter to October. *Sawston Hall,* near Cambridge. Said to be haunted. Open at limited times.

LINCOLNSHIRE. *Fydell House,* Boston. Houses Pilgrim College. Open weekdays, all year. Admission free. *Belton House,* Grantham. Open April to October.

The Midlands (Shakespeare Country)
The tourist center for any exploration of the English Midland shires is Stratford-upon-Avon in Warwickshire, the very heart of England. The town is a shrine, and you will feel very close to Shakespeare when you see his alleged birthplace in Henley Street, his baptismal record in Holy Trinity Church, Anne Hathaway's Cottage at Shottery (partly destroyed by fire in late 1969, but rebuilt), and the poet's grave with its mysterious epitaph which has stimulated such flights of speculation. But even without these Shakespearian links, the town of Stratford would attract visitors with the charm of its half-timbered houses and its strong connections with America—Harvard House in High Street, built in 1596 by the grandfather of John Harvard (who bequeathed half his estate and a library to the college that bears his name) and the *Red Horse Inn,* where Washington Irving worked on his *Sketch Book.*

Exploring The Midlands
In addition to these historic houses, here are some of the places to watch for in your exploration of the Midlands—Kenilworth, the romantic, ruined castle immortalized by Walter Scott, not far from Warwick; Leamington Spa, a pleasant watering place on a tributary of the Avon, famous for its mineral springs since the Middle Ages; Sherwood Forest, north of Nottingham, heart of the Robin Hood country; Nottingham Castle, built on a rock honeycombed by caves; Derbyshire's idyllic wooded limestone dales and historic houses, notably medieval Haddon Hall, Elizabethan Hardwick Hall and 18th-century Chatsworth, the "Palace of the Peak".

Also: Lichfield, with its cathedral, whose three spires are called the "Ladies of the Vale", and the house, now the Johnson Museum, where the celebrated Dr. Johnson was born in 1709. Shrewsbury, with its great wealth of magpie-colored houses, dominated by its red sandstone castle. For fans of A. E. Housman, there is the Shropshire town of Ludlow, with its black-and-white houses and great castle, and "Clunton, Clunbury, Clungunford and Clun, the quietest places under the sun".

The city of Worcester, with its ancient buildings and cathedral, still embracing part of the monastery founded in the seventh century by monks from the Yorkshire Abbey of Whitby. Malvern, renowned for its 11th-century Norman priory church.

Hereford, a lovely town still sleeping beside the River Wye. Its magnificent cathedral contains the *Mappa Mundi*, one of the oldest maps of the world in existence. Hereford is the heart of that beautiful area between the Malvern Hills and the uplands of the Welsh Border, with its rich farmlands and matchless black-and-white villages.

PRACTICAL INFORMATION FOR THE MIDLANDS

The Shakespeare Birthplace Trust Properties, Stratford-Upon-Avon. Inclusive ticket admitting you to all five properties costs about £1.50. Each of these can be visited for 25p-50p. *Anne Hathaway's Cottage: Hall's Croft: Mary Arden's House; New Place; Shakespeare's Birthplace,* Henley Street. Most of these are open every day of the year except Christmas Eve, Christmas Day and Boxing Day.

Seats for performances at *Royal Shakespeare Theatre* on the banks of the Avon can be reserved in advance at any office of *Keith Prowse,* London, or by writing to the box office at Stratford. Balcony and reservable seats cost around 50p-£4. You have to book weeks ahead for Saturdays in popular months.

HOTELS AND RESTAURANTS

STRATFORD-UPON-AVON (Warwicks). Over a dozen hotels, but among the most atmospheric: *Shakespeare,* older than the man himself, 70 rooms, most with bath. *Falcon,* 69 rooms, all with bath. *Welcombe,* 89 rooms, almost all with bath. There's also a 260-room *Hilton* on the banks of the Bard's Avon.

Alveston Manor, 129 rooms, most with bath, and *Red Horse,* 60 rooms, 21 with bath, are also of historical interest.

Good restaurants are surprisingly scarce. But try *Buccaneer,* Warwick Rd., or drive out to nearby Wilmcote for Sunday lunch at the *Swan House Hotel* (4 miles).

BIRMINGHAM (Warwicks). The *Albany* on Ringway, central, has 254 rooms with bath. *Holiday Inn,* 320 rooms with bath. *Centre,* (very central!), 200 rooms with bath.

COVENTRY (Warwicks). Magnificent modern cathedral. *Leofric,* 100 rooms, 72 with bath. *De Vere,* 215 rooms with bath. *Post House,* 200 rooms with bath.

DERBY (Derby). Home of Rolls-Royce and Crown Derby; fine cathedral. *Midland,* 64 rooms, 27 with bath. *Pennine,* 104 rooms with bath, recent.

Restaurants: the *Ristorante San Remo.* A nice "canal pub" is the *Green Dragon* at Willington, near Derby.

GREAT MALVERN (Hereford & Worcester). A strange hillside town. *Abbey,* 112 rooms, half with bath. *Cottage in the Wood,* 12 rooms, half with bath. Excellent.

HEREFORD (Hereford & Worcester). On the River Wye. *Green Dragon,* 94 rooms, over half with bath.

LEICESTER (Leicester). The county town, famous for hosiery. *Abbey Motor Hotel,* 72 rooms with bath, *Europa Lodge Hotel,* 31 rooms, *Holiday Inn,* 190 rooms, all with bath. Motel *Leicester Post House,* 183 rooms with bath.

LICHFIELD (Staffordshire). *Angel Croft, George, Little Barrow,* all moderate.

LUDLOW (Salop). *The Feathers,* Elizabethan, excellent.

MARKET HARBOROUGH (Leicester). Heart of the hunting country. *Peacock,* 7 rooms. *Three Swans,* 11 rooms, half with bath.

NOTTINGHAM (Nottingham). The county town, famous for lace and Robin Hood. *Albany,* a 14-story member of Strand chain, first-class. *Bridgford,* Trent Bridge, 90 rooms with bath or shower, recent, has nightclub.

SHREWSBURY (Salop). County town, delightfully situated, with many timbered houses. *Lion,* 60 rooms, 43 with bath. *Beauchamp,* 25 rooms, all with bath. Try the *Penny Farthing* restaurant.

WARWICK (Warwicks). Historic town with castle and ancient buildings. *Lord Leycester,* 47 rooms, 8 with bath. *Woolpack,* 28 rooms, 2 with bath. Good food at the *Westgate Arms.*

WORCESTER (Hereford & Worcester). Cathedral city of great interest. Glovemaking and porcelain manufacturies. *Giffard,* 99 rooms with bath. *Diglis* (quietly situated), 13 rooms, 2 with bath.

HISTORIC HOUSES OPEN TO THE PUBLIC
(For further information see notes under *Historic Houses,* earlier.)

The entire Midland plain, especially the "hunting shires" country and the "Dukeries," is liberally dotted with magnificent mansions, some still lived in, some derelict. Here are a few, according to the name of the nearest town:

GRANTHAM (Lincoln). *Belvoir Castle,* home of the Duke of Rutland. *Belton House.* Both open April through September.

BANBURY. *Sulgrave Manor.* Home of ancestors of George Washington. Open daily, except Weds., all year.

NOTTINGHAM. *Newstead Abbey.* Houses Byron relics. Good gardens. April-September.

WARWICK. *Warwick Castle,* former home of the Earls of Warwick. Open weekdays, all year. Sundays, May-October.

MELTON MOWBRAY (Leicester). *Stapleford Park,* home of Lord Gretton. Lion reserve. Open May to September.

The North, Scenic and Historic
The long ridge of hills running through northern England from the Scottish border to the Midlands shires is known as the Pennine Chain. English schoolchildren learn to speak of it as "the backbone of England". Here you will find a varied countryside, ranging in interest from the wild Yorkshire moorlands immortalized in *Wuthering Heights* to the medieval walled cities of York and Chester, the bustling industrial hives of Manchester and Liverpool, and the romantic ruins of Fountains Abbey, near Ripon.

Don't miss Richmond, whose castle, with its perfect Norman keep, is one of the noblest specimens of medieval fortification in the land; York

Minster, the biggest medieval cathedral in England, with magnificent stained glass windows; Durham cathedral; Whitby, one of the glories of the Yorkshire coast, with the gaunt ruins of Whitby Abbey lowering over the North Sea, and the grand headlands of the Northumberland coast, crowned with ancient castles like Dunstanburgh and Bamburgh. The latter overlooks some of the finest sandy beaches in Britain.

A mecca for American visitors lies between Durham and Newcastle. It is the little village of Washington, with the ancestral home of George Washington, Washington Old Hall, a 17th-century manor house (parts of which go back to 1183).

If you could visit only one city of the north, medieval Chester, 15 miles from Liverpool, would be a good choice. Founded in 70 A.D., when the Romans built a military camp (*castra,* which became Chester) here, Chester was the last of the Saxon towns to surrender to William the Conqueror. It is completely encircled by its medieval walls, and a walk around those walls will bring you closer to the Middle Ages than anything we can think of unless it's a shopping expedition in the city's medieval Rows, arcaded, timber-framed two-story shops, unique in England. But avoid office-hours if you just want to sightsee, as the place is seriously crowded with traffic.

PRACTICAL INFORMATION FOR THE NORTH

 HOTELS. In the vast area of the North of England, with its wealthy industrial centers, accommodation is plentiful and runs from the luxurious to the tucked-away ancient inn, small but comfortable. Food is usually good and plentiful—the northcountryman is a hearty eater. But you are more likely to find regional dishes such as Lancashire hotpot, Yorkshire pudding and Bakewell pudding in the country than in the towns.

BERWICK-ON-TWEED (Northumberland). The Anglo-Scots fortified border town. *King's Arms,* 30 rooms, *Castle,* 16 rooms.

CHESTER (Cheshire). Britain's most complete medieval city. *Grosvenor,* 100 rooms with bath, tops in luxury. *Blossoms,* 75 rooms, most with bath.

DURHAM (Co. Durham). The county town, Norman cathedral and castle. *Royal County,* 122 rooms, most with bath.

HARROGATE (Yorkshire). Attractive spa resort on Yorkshire moors. *Old Swan,* 150 rooms. *Majestic,* 160 rooms. *Cairn,* 161 rooms. Both top category, all have most rooms with bath. *Prospect,* a little smaller, some rooms with bath.

HEXHAM (Northumberland). Historic market town, near Hadrian's Roman Wall. Magnificent scenery. *Beaumont,* 21 rooms, 2 with bath.

Blanchland, 11 miles away, is a unique tiny village hidden in the moors; *Lord Crewe Arms,* converted from the Prior's House of the 12th-cent. abbey. A few rooms, attractive restaurant, expensive.

Near **MATLOCK** (Derbyshire). An inland resort with fine mountain scenery. The *Peacock* at Rowsley (Matlock-Buxton road) (15 rooms, a few with bath) is excellent, also for dining. Book well ahead.

RIPON (Yorkshire). Cathedral city on the River Skell; center for Fountains Abbey. *Spa,* 45 rooms, 23 with bath.

YORK (Yorkshire). One of the greatest centers in Europe for medieval architecture. *Post House,* 104 rooms with bath. *Royal Station,* 124 rooms, 64 with bath, excellent; *Viking,* 99 rooms with bath; *Chase,* 80 rooms, 40 with bath. *Dean Court,* close to the Minster, 25 rooms, cozy.

INDUSTRIAL CITIES OF THE NORTH
(All good centers for exploring the surrounding areas.)
BRADFORD (Yorkshire). The Brontë country. *Norfolk Gardens,* 125 rooms with bath. *Victoria,* 57 rooms, most with bath.

LEEDS (Yorkshire). *Queen's,* 200 rooms, most with bath. *Metropole,* 116 rooms, 65 with bath. *Merrion,* 120 rooms with bath.

LIVERPOOL (Lancashire). *Adelphi, St. George's, Atlantic Tower, Holiday* and *Liverpool Centre,* all with 100-plus rooms and baths, all first class superior.

MANCHESTER (Lancashire). *Midland,* 295 rooms, 194 with bath. *Forte's Excelsior Airport Hotel,* 150 rooms with bath, restaurant. *Piccadilly,* central, ultra-modern 14-story complex, 260 rooms with bath. The 201-room *Post House,* 5 miles from center, all rooms with bath.
Restaurants: *Midland Hotel, Mario and Franco's Terrazza.*

NEWCASTLE - UPON - TYNE (Northumberland). Old shipbuilding and mining center; Roman remains. *Swallow,* 83 rooms with bath. *Gosforth Park* (3 miles out) (expensive) has over 100 rooms, all with bath. *Royal Station,* 143 rooms. *Royal Turk's Head,* 107 rooms; both have plenty of rooms with bath.

SHEFFIELD (Yorkshire). *Royal Victoria,* 65 rooms. *Hallam Tower, Grosvenor House,* both ultra-modern, first class. Both have 100-plus rooms, all with bath.

SEASIDE RESORTS
Lancashire flocks to Blackpool, Southport, and Morecambe. Scotland, Yorkshire and Northumberland use Scarborough and Whitley Bay. These places are also the venue for great conferences and conventions.

BLACKPOOL (Lancashire). The Coney Island of the North. *Imperial,* 154 rooms, 125 with bath. *Clifton,* 125 rooms, some with bath. Do as the holidaymakers do, and eat fish and chips!

SCARBOROUGH (Yorkshire). Beautiful resort with two bays. *Crown,* 74 rooms, all with bath. *Holbeck Hall,* 30 rooms, 18 with bath. Eat at the *Lanterna Ristorante.*

SOUTHPORT (Lancashire). Extensive sands, famous golf center. *Prince of Wales,* 96 rooms. *Palace,* 130 rooms both offering many rooms with bath.

HISTORIC HOUSES OPEN TO THE PUBLIC
(For further information see notes under *Historic Houses,* earlier.)

DERBYSHIRE. *Chatsworth,* near Bakewell. Home of the Duke of Devonshire. One of the greatest private houses in the world. Open April to October. *Hardwick Hall,* near Chesterfield. Home of the Dowager Duchess of Devonshire. Open April through September.

YORKSHIRE (including Humberside). *Burton Agnes Hall,* Bridlington. Open May to October. *Harewood House,* Leeds. Home of the Lord Harewood. Open from May to October. *Castle Howard,* near York. Vanbrugh's masterpiece. Beautiful gardens. Open Easter to October. *Sledmere,* near Driffield. Open from May to October. Exquisite interior.

NORTHUMBERLAND. *Alnwick Castle.* Home of the Duke of Northumberland. May to October. Varying days. *Seaton Delaval Hall,* near Newcastle. Home of Lord Hastings. Regular medieval banquets. Open May to September.

The Lake District

The famous English Lake District, in the county of Cumbria, has the peace which brought Wordsworth here as to a spiritual home, although some roads are now heavily congested on summer weekends. The entire area, with its hills and calm lakes, is preserved as a National Park, and it has been consecrated in the dreams of the poets. Wordsworth spent 60 years here. Gray found the region enchanting, and so did Coleridge, De Quincey, Shelley, Keats, Scott, Carlyle and Tennyson. So if you are looking for a few days or weeks of Wordsworthian wandering among hills, vales and somnolent villages, you can count on enough tranquillity in which to recollect a whole lifetime of emotion. If you are carless and don't especially hanker to go about on foot as Wordsworth did, the National Bus Company (National Travel) obligingly services the main towns and outlying villages of the Lake District, and steamers run on Lake Windermere and Ullswater during the summer months. *Mountain Goat Ltd.,* based in Windermere (Telephone W.5161) run special tours into the hills.

PRACTICAL INFORMATION FOR THE LAKE DISTRICT

AMBLESIDE. *Rothay Manor,* 90 rooms, good food; *Waterhead,* 26 rooms, some with bath.

COCKERMOUTH. Birthplace of Wordsworth. Lake, and center for climbing, hill walking. *Trout,* 18 rooms, *Globe,* 38 rooms.

CONISTON. *Sun,* 13 rooms. Beautifully situated.

GRASMERE. *Prince of Wales Hotel,* 78 rooms, *Gold Rill,* 23 rooms, *Swan,* 25 rooms.

KENDAL. *Shenstone Country. Woolpack,* 53 rooms. *County,* 31 rooms, 25 with bath.

KESWICK. *Royal Oak,* 67 rooms, 30 with bath. *Red House,* 23 rooms, a few with baths. Eat at *The Cumbrian.*

POOLEY BRIDGE. *Sharrow Bay,* 26 rooms, many with bath. Excellent food, lakeside views.

WINDERMERE. *Langdale Chase,* 38 rooms, nearly half with bath. *Belsfield,* 85 rooms, all with bath. *Miller Howe,* 14 rooms, 8 with bath, has our vote. A glorious spot with superb food.

HISTORIC HOUSES OPEN TO THE PUBLIC

(For further information see notes under *Historic Houses,* earlier.)

Levens Hall, (superb topiary), June through September, and *Sizergh Castle,* home of the Strickland family for 700 years. Open April to September. Both are located near Kendal, Westmorland.

Wales, Land of Poets and Singers

Wales is the most romantic and mystic section of Great Britain, the place in whose mountain fastnesses the Britons sought refuge from conquering Romans, Saxons and Normans. Here they preserve their poetic legends of King Arthur, their sense of Celtic individuality and their own language. There is a flourishing 'Home Rule' faction, the effect of which enhances the Principality's tourist appeal: an intriguing language, used more than ever, a pride in Welsh food, less resentment about central government. The Prince of Wales, Prince Charles, carries on a link with the royal family forged nearly 700 years ago.

Except for the capital, Cardiff, a cosmopolitan seaport and university town with a splendid collection of Welsh handicrafts in the National Museum of Wales, and the ruins of Tintern Abbey, we suggest you concentrate on the west coast and North Wales. High points, in addition to stunning Caernarfon Castle, are Conwy (Conway) Castle, Harlech Castle high above Tremadog Bay, the woods and waterfalls of Betwys-y-Coed in the mountainous Snowdonia National Park, Bodnant Gardens, one of the great gardens of the world, and Llandudno, most popular of Welsh seaside resorts.

If you have time, try and save a day or two to visit southwest Wales, whose attractions include St. David's Cathedral; the rugged Pembrokeshire Coast National Park; Tenby, one of the prettiest little coast resorts in Britain; and the area around Laugharne, immortalised by Dylan Thomas in *Under Milk Wood.* There's also a week of coracle races (coracles are primitive basket-shaped one-man boats) in Cilgerran every August.

Llanrwst is often host to the National Eisteddfod, a poetry and music festival presided over by white-robed Druids. It is a kind of tournament of song, with the best poets and singers of Wales participating. But the sites vary, so consult your travel agent or write to the Wales Tourist Board, High Street, Llandaff, Cardiff, for detailed information about these festivals.

PRACTICAL INFORMATION FOR WALES

HOTELS. The places mentioned below are all in or near some of the loveliest parts of Wales. You may find hotels in the small spots simple, but you'll be compensated by the scenery. In July and August there are *Eisteddfodau* song, dance, and poetry festivals). Wales is a great outdoor country, with ample opportunity for mountaineering, angling, golf and pony trekking. Drinking laws differ from those in England and not all public houses are open on Sundays. If you plan to visit Wales during either Eisteddfod period, best book well ahead.

ABERYSTWYTH (Dyfed). Fairly large resort on Cardigan Bay. *Conrah,* 13 rooms with bath. Fishing, extensive grounds.

BANGOR (Gwynedd). Cathedral and university city. *British,* 50 rooms, 30 with bath.

BEAUMARIS (Isle of Anglesey). Small quiet watering place overlooking Menai Straits. Popular yachting headquarters. *Bulkeley Arms,* 40 rooms. First class reasonable. *Henllys Hall,* 16 rooms. Moderate.

BETWYS-Y-COED (Gwynedd). Lovely Welsh village in majestic surroundings. Popular Snowdon area. *Royal Oak,* 38 rooms, half with bath. *Glan Abel,* 22 rooms, 6 with baths. Both moderate.

CAERNARFON (Caernarvonshire). Castle-crowned gateway to Snowdonia. *Royal,* 68 rooms, all with bath, moderate.

CARDIFF (South Glamorgan). Capital of Wales, *Cardiff Centre,* 160 rooms with bath. *Post House,* 150 rooms with bath. *Angel,* 110 rooms. *Royal,* 72 rooms. All have a number of rooms with bath.

CONWY (Gwynedd). Fortified medieval town, picturesque aspect. *Castle,* 27 rooms, most with bath. Eat at *Alfredo's,* a former inn.

DEVIL'S BRIDGE (Gwynedd). Ancient inn among exceptional natural beauty. *Hafod Arms,* 25 rooms.

HARLECH (Gwynedd). Castle, and golf resort, good sands. *St. David's,* 83 rooms, 16 with bath. Eat at *Rum Hole.*

LLANBERIS (Gwynedd). Mountaineering center at foot of Snowdon (rack railway to summit). *Royal Victoria,* 90 rooms, 10 with bath. *Dolbadarn,* 15 rooms.

LLANDRINDOD WELLS (Powys). Most important spa in Wales, situated over 1000 feet. *Commodore,* modern, 43 rooms. *Glen Usk,* 83 rooms. Both good, both have rooms with bath.

LLANDUDNO (Gwynedd). Popular coast resort. *Gogarth Abbey, Imperial, St. George's, Hydro.*

LLANGOLLEN (Clwyd). Beautiful old town in a hollow. *Bryn Howel,* 38 rooms, 20 with bath. Good views. *Hand,* 59 rooms, 25 with bath.

NEWPORT (Gwent). Famous castle and cathedral. *Westgate,* 70 rooms, 18 with bath.

PORTMEIRION (Gwent). Deluxe up-market holiday village on a peninsula. The *Portmeirion* has 80 rooms, 22 with bath. Delicious food.

RUTHIN (Clwyd). *Ruthin Castle,* converted medieval stronghold, has 62 rooms, stages nightly banquets in 16th-century style.

SWANSEA (West Glamorgan). The *Dragon,* a modern hotel, 117 rooms, all with bath or shower, also private suites. *Dolphin,* 67 rooms with bath. Both modern, first class superior. Eat at the *Apollo.*

TALYLLYN (Gwynedd). Lovely village, terminus of narrow-gauge railway run by enthusiasts. *Tynycornel,* 19 rooms, 11 with bath.

TENBY (Dyfed). Ancient town and Atlantic resort. *Royal Gate House,* 90 rooms, many with bath. *Atlantic,* 47 rooms, 21 with bath.

TINTERN (Gwent). Beautiful Abbey ruins. *Beaufort,* 27 rooms, 15 with bath. *Royal George,* 19 rooms, most with bath. Pleasant atmosphere.

WREXHAM (Clwyd). Yale's burial place, and birthplace. Important North Wales town. *Wrexham Crest,* 80 rooms.

HISTORIC HOUSES OPEN TO THE PUBLIC
(For further information see notes under *Historic Houses,* earlier.)

CAERNARFON (Gwynedd). *Caernarfon Castle.* Open all year, 9:30 A.M. to dusk; Sundays, 2 P.M. to dusk.

CARDIFF (South Glamorgan). *Cardiff Castle.* Open daily and Sunday afternoons. Closed Nov.-Feb.

WREXHAM (Clwyd). *Chirk Castle.* Built 1310. Open May to end of September.

PLAS NEWYDD (Anglesey). Superb views. July to October, afternoons.

HARLECH (Gwynedd). *Harlech Castle,* famous in song ("The Men of Harlech") and history. Open daily all year.

WELSHPOOL (Powys). *Powis Castle.* Open June to September, daily in afternoons, except Mondays and Tuesdays.

Scotland
The Scots have a personality and a national tradition which is very much their own and, in places, vastly different from those of England. You will sense it the moment you cross the Tweed, even before you see your first Scotsman in a kilt or hear the first stirring sound of the pipes. It's in the language and in the very special welcome which Scotsmen accord to Americans (or anybody else who's had a brush or two with the English in the past). The important fact is that the Scots, politically united for three centuries now with the English, have not lost any of their individuality and national character. And Scottish Nationalism has become an important political force. Although there are no border formalities and no basic change in language, when you have crossed the Tweed, you have entered a different country.

Edinburgh
Edinburgh is one of Europe's great and beautiful cities, "the Athens of the North". Only the most stolid visitor to Scotland's capital could fail to respond to the broad, handsome sweep of Princes Street and its gardens, beyond which is the thrilling vista of Castle Rock, dominated by the ramparts of historic Edinburgh Castle.

Of Edinburgh's many monuments, two are worth the special attention of even the hurried tourist—Edinburgh Castle and Palace of Holyroodhouse. The first, commanding a splendid view of the city and the Firth of Forth, is steeped in Scottish history. In the heart of the castle, there is a magnificent display of the ancient regalia of Scotland—crown, scepter, sword of state and other treasures of the Scottish people. Holyrood Palace is rich in memories of the turbulent life of Mary Queen of Scots, not least the room in which Lord Darnley, husband of Mary, murdered her favorite, Rizzio. The Palace is still occasionally used as a residence by members of the royal family when they visit Scotland.

Among recommended excursions by car or bus are the following: Abbotsford, the elaborate medieval-style home built by Sir Walter Scott; Dryburgh Abbey, where Scott is buried; Dirleton and Tantallon castles; the romantic ruins of Melrose Abbey, where lies the heart of Robert the Bruce; ten-centuries-old Traquair House; Linlithgow Palace, birthplace of Mary Queen of Scots; and historic Stirling Castle.

PRACTICAL INFORMATION FOR EDINBURGH

HOTELS. There are so many hotels and in Edinburgh that it is impossible to give more than a representation. The figure in parentheses indicates the number of rooms available with bath. For approximate hotel rates in the various categories, consult *Planning Your Trip*. Book well in advance if you are going to Edinburgh during the Festival. At several hotels you will be able to eat the dishes of haggis, (made of sheep's offal and oatmeal, and traditionally accompanied by whisky), porridge and Scotch pancakes. There is a hotel reservation service near Waverley Station, at the Tourist Information Centre.

Motels: *Forth Bridges Lodge,* S. Queensferry, 9 miles out, expensive. Also the *Derry Motel* at Dalkeith, on the A68 route, and *Esso Motor Hotel* in Queensferry Road, both first class.

First Class. *Caledonian* located at Princes Street Station, 224 rooms (198). Several suites.

North British located at Waverley Station, 200 rooms (130). At the opposite end of Princes Street from the Caledonian. Fairly expensive.

Prestonfield House has very few rooms, is completely *unmodern,* yet a luxury spot, dating from 1687. Peacock-patroled grounds. Superb and famous food.

Roxburghe, in Charlotte Square, 73 rooms, 60 with bath. Food and service very good. Expensive.

Mount Royal, 154 rooms, most with bath. Central, no frills.

King James, 146 rooms, all with bath. Somewhat impersonal, but convenient.

RESTAURANTS. Edinburgh is splendidly served by a wide variety of restaurants, including internationally famous names like the *Prestonfield House Hotel Restaurant.* Other hotel restaurants worth a visit are the *North British,* and *Dalhousie Castle,* 8 miles out, for Jacobean banquets. Among the general favorites, the following offer a great deal in the way of normal full-scale meals with wine and all that goes with it. Most restaurants are closed Sunday.

Prestonfield House (see above) tops for atmosphere and food.

Denzler's, Lower Hanover Street. Authentic Swiss/German fare.

Café Royal, 17 West Register St. Licensed. Another top restaurant. Seafood a specialty.

Vito's, 109 Fountainbridge. Elegant Italian restaurant.

Edinburgh Rendezvous, 10a Queensferry St. Better-than-average Peking food. Moderate.

Henderson's Salad Table, 94 Hanover St. A famous vegetarian restaurant.

THE EDINBURGH FESTIVAL

Just after World War II, Edinburgh inaugurated a three-week season that has become world-famous as the Edinburgh International Festival of Music, Drama, and Art. The title gives only a slight idea of the immense range of attractions—exhibitions of painting and handcrafts, ballet, instrumental recitals, opera, a festival of documentary and other films—these are only a few of the items on the varied program.

The Festival Fringe, an offshoot of the Festival itself, has a wide-ranging schedule of theater, music, poetry, dance and exhibitions. Programs from Festival Fringe Society, Royal Mile Centre, Edinburgh.

Scottish orchestras, choirs, composers, instrumentalists, dramatists, and actors participate, too. Certainly the Edinburgh Festival has done more to awaken Scottish artistic energies than anything since the great days of Walter Scott and the Edinburgh School. This is an event that no visitor interested in the intellectual life of Europe should miss, especially as tickets are among the cheapest of any European festival.

Running concurrently is the Film Festival and, one of the most spectacular of all displays, the Tattoo.

The Festival takes place each year during the last two weeks in August and the first week in September. For a detailed program or other information, write to the Festival Office, 21 Market Street, Edinburgh 1.

ENTERTAINMENT. The straight theaters in Edinburgh include the *King's,* Leven Street, the *Royal Lyceum,* Grindlay Street, *Lyceum Little Theatre,* Cambridge Street. Most experimental these days is the *Traverse.* During the winter concert season the Scottish National Orchestra, the BBC Scottish orchestra, and internationally known singers and musicians on tour appear in the *Usher Hall,* off Lothian Road. There are weekly band performances and daily (including Sunday) concerts in West Princes Street Gardens, where displays of Highland dancing, variety, Scottish country dancing, oldtime dancing and open-air dancing are also presented in summer.

Late night entertainment includes *Jamie's Cabaret* in the King James Hotel, an affair of Scottish one-up-manship; dinner and dancing in the *Baron Suite,* Chesser Ave., with cabaret; and, for atmosphere, the *Waverley Bar* on St. Mary's St., and the *World's End,* High St.

 GOLF was an invention of the Scots, and they were playing the game before the *Mayflower* set sail for America. From May on, Edinburgh is the golfer's promised land. Besides the Open and Amateur Championships held in Scotland every second or third year, there is a wide variety of amateur and professional tournaments for spectators and competitors. Most visitors, however, come to play over one or more of the great Scottish courses—St. Andrews, Carnoustie, Turnberry, Muirfield, Troon, Gleneagles, and a score of others. Golf is cheap in Scotland and there are hundreds of courses that offer challenges to cunning and skill.

 MUSEUMS, GALLERIES, GARDENS. (A highlight or two of each is given. But remember that opening hours are often extended during the Festival.) *Royal Botanic Garden,* Inverleith Row, open 9 A.M. till sunset, Sunday 11 A.M. to sunset. *Scottish National Zoological Park,* Corstorphine. Daily in summer, 9 till 7, in winter 9 till sundown.

Scottish Craft Centre, Acheson House, Canongate. Daily, 10 to 12:30 and 2 to 5:30. Saturdays, 10 to 12:30. Closed Sundays.

Canongate Tolbooth, Canongate. Highland dress, tartans. Weekdays, 10 to 5.

Huntly House (City Museum), Canongate. Weekdays, June to Sept. 10–6, rest of year 10–5. Old-fashioned Scots kitchen.

National Gallery of Scotland, The Mound. Weekdays, 10 to 5, Sundays, 2 to 5. Scottish art to 1900.

National Museum of Antiquities, Queen St. (east end). Weekdays, 10 to 5, Sunday, 2 to 5. Relics of Celtic Church, Roman finds.

Royal Scottish Academy, foot of Mound. Open weekdays, 10 to 9, Sundays, 2 to 5.

Royal Scottish Museum, Chambers St. Monday to Saturday, 10 to 6, Saturdays, 10 to 5, Sundays, 2 to 5. Largest overall collection in the United Kingdom. Outstanding scale models in Technology Department.

Scottish National Gallery of Modern Art, Inverleith House. 20th-century paintings. Weekdays, 10 to 6, Sundays, 2 to 6. Opens one hour later in winter.

Scottish National Portrait Gallery, Queen St. (east end). Weekdays, 10 to 5, Sundays, 2 to 5. Famous Scots.

Lady Stair's House, Lawnmarket. Weekdays (June to Sept.) 10–6, rest of year 10–5. Relics of Burns, Scott and R. L. Stevenson.

John Knox's House, High St. Daily, 10 to 5. Memorabilia of the fiery 16th-century preacher.

Georgian House, No. 7 Charlotte Square: owned by the National Trust for Scotland. Easter to mid Oct, 10.00–17.00, Sun 14.00–17.00—rest of year Sat. and Sun. only. 18th-cent. square, one of the most outstanding of its period in Europe. The lower floors of No. 7 have been furnished to reflect the domestic surroundings and social conditions of that age.

Wax Museum: High Street. Wax models of prominent figures in Scottish history & Never Never Land & Chamber of Horrors.

TOURS. Forty day and afternoon tours are operated from Edinburgh throughout Scotland to the Highlands, the Borders and Abbey country, the east coast, the Trossachs, and Loch Lomond. There are also 15 holiday tours of from three to 15 days. Particulars may be obtained from *Scottish Omnibuses Ltd.,* Clyde Street, Edinburgh.

For detailed information contact: *Scottish Tourist Board,* 23 Ravelston Terrace, Edinburgh EH4 3EU.

Glasgow, Industrial Giant

Glasgow boasts that it is the friendliest city in Scotland, but even that formidable reputation will probably not be enough to lure the average tourist to this bustling industrial city. Nevertheless, it has its moments—a fine cathedral; one of the best art museums (Rembrandt, Rubens, Corot, Turner, Whistler); the trip down the Clyde Estuary to the place where the Atlantic rolls in to die, some impressive Victorian domestic architecture, a famous Necropolis and the Botanical Gardens.

GLASGOW HOTELS

FIRST CLASS

Central, at Central Station, 240 rooms, more than half with bath, old-established hotel of great character. Its Malmaison restaurant is excellent. Expensive.

Royal Stuart, Clyde St., recent, is almost deluxe. 110 rooms, most with bath. Expensive.

North British, 140 rooms, 90 with bath.

Excelsior Glasgow Airport Hotel, at Paisley (Abbotsinch airport). Has 360 rooms with bath, air-conditioned and sound-proofed. Expensive.

Airport Hotel, near Glasgow Airport, Renfrew, 121 rooms with bath, has fine restaurant. On the A8 route, a mile from the airport, is the 142-room *Normandy,* both expensive.

Albany, central, 250 rooms with bath, and the *Esso Motor Hotel,* 180 rooms, 2 miles from Abbotsinch Airport.

MODERATE

Gresham, 7 rooms, is a pleasant if small hotel in quiet street (West End).

Bath, 152 Bath St., 34 rooms, *Ivanhoe,* 185 Buchanan St., 70 rooms, a few with bath.

Lorne, 86 rooms, many with bath.

RESTAURANTS

Epicure's, 46 West Nile St. Licensed. Exciting eastern European dishes here, nice atmosphere. Moderately priced.

Fountain, 2 Woodside Cres. Good French food in attractive house. Pricey but usually worth it.

Grant Arms Grill, 186 Argyle St. Licensed. Good food in interesting surroundings. Expensive.

Malmaison, in the Central Hotel. Licensed. Terrific cooking and top-class atmosphere. Expensive.

Exploring Scotland

Most visitors prefer to avoid industrial Glasgow and concentrate on the wild, romantic beauty of the Scottish Highlands and the historic houses and castles of Scotland. The following are selected lists of the outstanding resorts and towns, together with best hotel possibilities in all parts of Scotland. This includes the Inner and Outer Hebrides, the Orkneys and the Shetlands, remote islands of unspoiled beauty. In the hotels listed here, the figure in parentheses indicates the number of rooms available with private bath. *Note:* in this edition, the names of newly-designated Scottish regions are not given. As yet, they are seldom used except by officialdom.

PRACTICAL INFORMATION FOR THE REGIONS

Car Ferries to the Isles: Drive-on-and-off, stabilized ferries connect, among other places: Mallaig-Armadale (Skye); Uig (Skye)-Tarbert (Harris) and Lochmaddy (N. Uist); Oban-Craignure (Mull); Lochaline (Morven); Fishnish (Mull). For details of other services write: Caledonian MacBrayne, Ltd., The Pier, Gourock, Renfrewshire, and Western Ferries Ltd., White House, Tarbert, Argyll.

The *Highlands & Islands Development Board, Bridge House,* 27 Bank St., Inverness, produces excellent summer and winter brochures featuring Highland activity holidays, including golf, skiing and pony-trekking.

ABERDEEN (Aberdeenshire). Now oil boom center. Three theaters. *Station,* 62 rooms (13). *Caledonian,* 70 rooms (11). *Marcliffe,* 30 rooms with bath. *Gloucester,* 87 rooms (5). Eat at *Luigi's* pizzeria.

ABERFOYLE (Perthshire), good fishing. *Bailie Nicol Jarvie,* 30 rooms (2). *Covenanters' Inn,* 46 rooms (28). *Inverard,* 24 rooms, half with bath.

ARRAN (Bute). Mountainous holiday island in the Firth of Clyde. Served by steamers to Ardrossan or (summer only) Claonaig. Magnificent scenery; fishing.

Douglas (Brodick), *Kinloch* (Blackwater Foot), *Kildonan.* Recent *Corrie* hotel (Corrie), 22 rooms.

AUCHTERARDER (Perthshire). Magnificent golfing center. *Gleneagles Hotel.* 200 rooms, all with bath, a self-contained luxury resort with its own railway station. Closed Oct.-Apr.

AVIEMORE (Inverness-shire), winter sports resort, with good facilities in summer. *Strathspey,* 90 double rooms, deluxe, as is *Coylumbridge,* 133 double rooms. *Post House,* 103 rooms with bath. Several moderate hotels.

BRAEMAR (Aberdeenshire). Center for Braemar hills and Balmoral Castle. *Invercauld Arms,* 57 rooms.

BRORA (Sutherland). Quiet sea and golf resort; salmon fishing. *Links,* 31 rooms (3). *Royal Marine,* 24 rooms.

DUMFRIES (Dumfriesshire). *Station,* 28 rooms (10). *Cairndale,* 40 rooms. *County,* 50 rooms (2).

DUNOON (Argyll). Beautiful holiday resort; center for day cruises around the Firth. *Selbourne,* 91 rooms.

FORT WILLIAM (Inverness-shire). Popular resort on the "Road to the Isles". *Inverlochy Castle,* 12 rooms with bath, fine cuisine. Very expensive. *Mercury Motor Inn,* 95 rooms.

GRANTOWN-ON-SPEY (Moray). Magnificently situated fishing and golfing resort, also key point of Scotland's winter sports season. Many ski runs nearby. *Grant Arms,* 46 rooms (23). *Craiglynne,* 56 rooms (3). *Palace,* 45 rooms (1).

INVERNESS (Inverness-shire). *Station,* 75 rooms (33), *Caledonian,* 120 rooms with bath. *Mercury Motor Inn,* 84 rooms with bath.

JOHN O'GROATS (Caithness). Most northerly inhabited place on Scottish mainland; sandy beaches. *John O'Groats House,* 24 rooms.

KIRKCUDBRIGHT (Kirkcudbrightshire). *Royal,* 25 rooms. *Selkirk Arms,* 16 rooms, an 18th-cent. inn, fine restaurant, shooting and fishing on estate.

LEWIS & HARRIS. Largest islands of the Outer Hebrides. Most accommodation is on Lewis: *Acres* (Stornoway) 52 rooms. *County* (Stornoway), 16 rooms. *Royal* (Stornoway), 23 rooms.

LOCH TORRIDON (Ross-shire). Luxury 24-room hotel, the *Loch Torridon.* Angling, stalking, fishing and sailing opportunities.

MALLAIG (Inverness-shire). Fishing village and port of call for ferries to Skye, the smaller Hebridean islands, and Outer Hebrides. *West Highland,* 30 rooms, most with bath.

MONTROSE (Angus). Old town with excellent beaches; fishing, golf. *Park,* 40 rooms (23).

NAIRN (Nairnshire). Fishing, mountaineering and ski center. *Golf View,* 54 rooms (31). *Newton,* 30 rooms.

NEWTONMORE (Inverness-shire). Spey Valley resort, center for pony trekking, fishing, skiing. *Main's,* 34 rooms. Moderate.

OBAN (Argyllshire). Chief resort in west Highlands; center for touring the Western Isles; golf, fishing, yachting. *Great Western,* 80 rooms (50). *Park,* 62 rooms (18). *Marine,* 44 rooms (11). *Caledonian,* 70 rooms (31).

ORKNEY. Group of some 70 islands lying north of the Scottish mainland. *Stromness* (Stromness), 40 rooms. *Kirkwall* (Kirkwall), 31 rooms. *Royal* (Kirkwall), 41 rooms.

PEEBLES (Peeblesshire). *Peebles Hydro,* 135 rooms (110). *Tontine,* 43 rooms (all). Center for the Border Country.

PERTH (Perthshire). Elegant old town, once Scotland's capital. *Station,* 53 rooms (42). *Royal George,* 43 rooms with bath.

PITLOCHRY (Perthshire). Famous Festival Theatre. *Hydro,* 71 rooms (33). *Fishers,* 79 rooms (40), good restaurant. *Dundarach,* 23 rooms. *Green Park,* 36 rooms (17).

ST. ANDREWS (Fife). Historic home of golf. *Scores,* 34 rooms (12), with new *Old Course,* 80 rooms with bath, and *St. Andrew's,* 27 rooms (18) are tops, expensive.

SHETLAND. Distinctive and self-sufficient group of about 100 islands, 17 of which are inhabited. Remarkable seascapes. In Lerwick there is the *Grand,* 23 rooms, all with bath. In Sumburgh, the *Sumburgh,* 17 rooms, a few with bath.

SKYE (Inverness-shire). Largest of Inner Hebridean islands. Car-ferry from Kyle of Lochalsh; steamer from mainland to Portree, Armadale and Uig. *Skeabost House* (Skeabostbridge), 20 rooms (10). *Sligachan* (Sligachan), 29 rooms (3).

STIRLING (Stirlingshire). County town, 16th-cent. palace built by James V. *Golden Lion,* 58 rooms (17).

TOBERMORY (Argyll). On Isle of Mull, where the treasure galleon lies buried in the bay. *Western Isles,* 50 rooms (15); private fishing, golf, tennis.

TROSSACHS (Perthshire). Famous tourist district for scenery; *Loch Achray,* 44 rooms.

TURNBERRY (Ayrshire). Famous golf course. Culzean Castle (pronounced Cullane) nearby. *Turnberry,* 120 rooms, most with bath. Indoor swimming pool, cinema. Luxurious.

UIST. North and South Uist, islands of the Outer Hebrides. Noted for ancient stone circles, crofting and fishing. Air and sea links to mainland. *Lochmaddy* (North Uist), 16 rooms. *Lochboisdale* (South Uist), 20 rooms, 6 with bath.

ULLAPOOL (Ross & Cromarty). Unusually mild resort on Loch Broom in Wester Ross, featuring palm trees and swimming. *Caledonian,* 43 rooms. Well situated by the side of a loch. *Royal,* 61 rooms. *Mercury Motor Inn,* 60 rooms, all with bath. There is a car ferry to Stornaway and the Outer Hebrides.

HISTORIC HOUSES OPEN TO THE PUBLIC
(For further information see notes under *Historic Houses,* earlier.)

ALLOWAY (Ayrshire). *Burns' Cottage.* Open all year daily. Sunday afternoons in summer only.

ARRAN (Buteshire). *Brodick Castle,* owned by trustees of the 12th Duke of Hamilton. A 14th-century castle. Open daily during summer afternoons. Gardens open all year.

BALLATER (Aberdeenshire). *Balmoral Castle,* 8 miles from town. Residence of H.M. the Queen. Gardens only open most weekdays, May through July, except when members of the royal family are in residence.

BLAIR ATHOLL (Perthshire). *Blair Castle,* residence of the Duke of Atholl. Open May through September.

CULROSS (Fife). *Culross Palace,* 7½ miles west of Dunfermline. Vernacular architecture. Owned by Department of the Environment. Open weekdays and Sun. afternoons all year.

ECCLEFECHAN (Dumfriesshire). *Carlyle's House,* owned by National Trust for Scotland. Thomas Carlyle born here in 1795. Open all year daily (except Sundays).

FALKLAND (Fife). *Royal Palace of Falkland.* National Trust for Scotland property and home of Major Crichton-Stuart. Open weekdays and Sun. afternoons, April through September.

GLAMIS (Angus). *Glamis Castle,* pronounced "Glarms". Home of the Earl of Strathmore and Kinghorne; the family of Queen Elizabeth, the Queen Mother. Open Wed. and Thurs. afternoons, May to September, also Sun. afternoons from July.

INNERLEITHEN (Peeblesshire). *Traquair.* Said to be Scotland's oldest inhabited house. Old brew-house on grounds. Open June-September.

INVERARAY (Argyllshire). *Inveraray Castle.* Ancestral home of the Dukes of Argyll. Easter, and May to October.

LINLITHGOW (West Lothian). *Linlithgow Palace,* property of Department of the Environment. Birthplace of Mary, Queen of Scots. Open weekdays and Sunday afternoons all year.

MAYBOLE (Ayrshire). *Culzean Castle,* (pronounced Cullane) in country park; owned by National Trust for Scotland. Contains President Eisenhower's former apartment. Open daily March through October, weekdays and Sunday afternoons.

MELROSE (Roxburghshire). *Abbotsford House.* The home of Sir Walter Scott. Open from late March through October.

ISLE OF SKYE. *Dunvegan Castle,* was home of the late Dame Fiona MacLeod of MacLeod. Continuously inhabited by the chieftains of Clan MacLeod for centuries. Open Easter to mid-October.

STIRLING (Stirlingshire). *Stirling Castle,* property of the Dept. of the Environment. Open weekdays and Sunday afternoons all year.

SCOTLAND'S GARDENS SCHEME. In recent years a Scottish Gardens Committee has been formed which helps to preserve the most notable of Scotland's gardens. Several hundreds of these are now on view to the public, and full details may be had from the General Organiser, Scotland's Gardens Scheme, 26 Castle Terrace, Edinburgh 1.

The Holiday Islands

The Channel Islands of Jersey and Guernsey are the warmest places in Britain. From April to October, day temperatures usually exceed 60 degrees; sharp frosts are rare, though the islands can be windy. The archipelago of which Jersey and Guernsey are the chief islands is an admirable blend of France and Britain. It lies closer to the French than the British coast. St. Helier, capital of Jersey, and St. Peter Port, the Guernsey capital, are full of quaint streets and good hotels. The food here is better cooked than in most English resorts; you'll delighted with this touch of France on British soil. And don't miss a boat trip to the tiny, traffic-free islands of Sark, Herm and Alderney.

The Isle of Wight, opposite Southampton Harbour, has a stretch of coast known as the Undercliff, facing south along the channel. Here, there are palm trees and subtropical vegetation, accounting for the popularity of such resorts as Ventnor, Sandown and Shanklin. At the mouth of the Medina River lies Cowes, scene during the first week in August of the annual Cowes Regatta, one of the greatest yachting events in the world.

The Isle of Man is in the Irish Sea. Though interesting for its Norse relics (it was once a Viking colony), Man is apt to be overcrowded in summer by hordes of tourists from the great English Midland cities. But despite the noise (including international motorcycle races) and overcrowding on the main beaches, there are still some secluded coves and solitary glens within access of the main centers. One form of amusement for which the Isle of Man has long been famous is the casinos, where anyone can enjoy the classic games for low stakes.

PRACTICAL INFORMATION FOR THE HOLIDAY ISLANDS

CHANNEL ISLANDS

HOW TO REACH THE ISLANDS. *British Airways* operate daily services from London and Gatwick airports to Jersey and Guernsey, with several flights daily during holiday months. Flying time is 55 minutes. *Caledonian-BUA* and *Northeast Airlines* operate from Gatwick to Jersey, Guernsey and Alderney. They have regular flights from main provincial centers. There is a good inter-island air service. *British Rail* operates a one-class steamer service from Weymouth to Guernsey and Jersey on weekdays, April through August (4 hours to Guernsey, 6½ to Jersey). Additionally there are some Sunday services, including overnight sailings, during the height of the season. A fast boat train from London (Waterloo) connects with all sailings. Winter services are overnight, with two or three sailings a week. There are steamer services between the islands. A daily (summer) hydrofoil service operates between St. Peter Port (Guernsey) and St. Helier (Jersey), continuing to St. Malo (France).

CAR FERRIES. Cars may be shipped from Weymouth: apply Continental Car Ferry Centre, 52 Grosvenor Gdns, London, S.W.1.; or to the Divisional Shipping Manager, Weymouth Quay, Dorset.

HOTELS AND RESTAURANTS

ST. HELIER (Jersey). Capital of the island. Recommended is the luxury-class *Bonne Nuit,* right near the sea front at Bonne Nuit Bay. 99 rooms, all with bath, balconies. Also in the top class is the modern *Ambassadeur* at St. Clement's Bay, just outside of St. Helier proper. The *Revere,* in town, has 40 rooms, 25 with bath; dancing and the excellent Candlelight Grill room. Restaurants: *The Shakespeare, La Capannina, Bistro Borsalino.*

ST. BRELADE'S BAY (Jersey). Small resort with good sands. Recent is the *Atlantic,* 42 rooms. Expensive. *L'Horizon,* 106 rooms, over half with bath. *La Place,* 42 rooms, most with bath.

LA CORBIERE (Jersey). *Le Chalet,* 28 rooms, 20 with bath.

ROZEL (Jersey). *Le Couperon de Rozel,* on the beach. Luxurious. *La Chaire,* small, excellent.

ST. PETER PORT (Guernsey). *Old Government House,* 74 rooms, all with bath. *Royal,* 80 rooms, 60 with bath. Restaurant: *La Frégate.*

PETIT BOT (Guernsey). Small resort with good sands. *Manor,* 56 rooms, several with bath.

ST. MARTINS (Guernsey). *La Villette,* 26 rooms.

ALDERNEY. *Grand,* 33 rooms; *Chez Andre,* 20 rooms, 13 with bath.

SARK. Privately owned, picturesque islands. Great and Little Sark are connected by a causeway. *L'Aval du Creux,* 10 rooms, all with bath. *Hotel Petit Champ,* 18 rooms, 8 with bath.

HERM. *White House,* 50 rooms, 12 with bath.

HIGHLIGHTS OF JERSEY: The *"Battle of Flowers"* on the Thursday before the August Bank holiday at St. Helier. *Golf courses:* one 9-hole and two 18-hole. *Motor* racing and hill-climbs. *Ancient castles and monuments:* Grosnez Castle (St. Ouen); Mont Orgueil Castle (Gorey); St. Aubin's Castle (St. Brelade); Elizabeth Castle (St. Helier); The Hermitage (Elizabeth Castle). *Megalithic remains:* St. Saviour, Samares, Gorey, Rozel, Trinity, St. Ouen, St. Brelade.

ISLE OF WIGHT

HOW TO GET THERE. By British Rail ferry boats from Portsmouth Harbour to Ryde (passengers only) or Fishbourne (car ferry); from Lymington to Yarmouth (cars carried). Frequent services on all routes, but accommodation should be booked in advance on car ferries. Rail services from London, Waterloo Station, connect with the ferries. Crossing time is from 30 to 45 minutes according to route.

By Hovercraft: Numerous summer roundtrip services operate from Southsea and Portsmouth to Ryde (about 10 minutes), also Portsmouth to Cowes.

HOTELS (most are open April through October only)

BEMBRIDGE. *Royal Spithead,* 30 rooms, half with bath.

COWES. Famous yachting center. *Gloster,* 20 rooms. *Grantham,* 21 rooms.

FRESHWATER. *Farringford,* 40 rooms, all with bath.

RYDE. *Yelf's,* 31 rooms, several with bath.

SANDOWN. *Ocean,* 100 rooms, most with bath. *Royal Cliff,* 30 rooms. *Sandown,* 46 rooms. *Sandringham,* 84 rooms.

SHANKLIN. *Cliff Tops,* 100 rooms, most with bath. First class superior. A little smaller are *Keats Green,* 34 rooms, a few with bath; and *Shanklin.*

VENTNOR. *Metropole,* 40 rooms. *Royal,* 57 rooms, 36 with bath. *Ventnor Towers,* 33 rooms, 16 with bath. Also *Peacock Vane,* 16 rooms, 7 with bath, at nearby Bonchurch. Good food.

YARMOUTH. *Royal,* 57 rooms, most with baths.

HISTORIC HOUSES OPEN TO THE PUBLIC
(For further information see notes under *Historic Houses,* earlier.)

Carisbrooke Castle, near Newport. Fine medieval castle where Charles I was imprisoned. Open daily all year.

Osborne House, near East Cowes. Where Queen Victoria died. Open weekdays, late April to Sept. "Osborne weather" is when it rains. So go when the sun shines and see Osborne at its best.

ISLE OF MAN

HOW TO GET THERE. By car ferry from Liverpool to Douglas in 3½ hours, daily in winter, twice daily in summer; car ferries operate seasonally from Belfast, Ardrossan (Scotland), and Dublin to Douglas. Also in the summer there are services from Llandudno, North Wales.

Cambrian Airways have excellent summer services to Ronaldsway Airport, 8 miles from Douglas, from Liverpool, Manchester, London, and Belfast. Services from London to the island take 55 minutes' flying time. In winter there are daily flights from Liverpool and Manchester; twice weekly from London and Belfast. Aer Lingus maintains a seasonal link with Dublin.

HOTELS. The Island's tourist season operates from Easter to mid-October, but the larger hotels in Douglas are open throughout the year catering for conference and business traffic. Accommodation charges are reasonable in the private hotels and guest houses. The only hotel of top international standard is the *Palace Hotel* in Douglas, which also adjoins Britain's only public casino. The *Castletown Golf Links Hotel* at Derbyhaven near Castletown is also of first-class standard.

CASTLETOWN. *Golf Links,* 75 rooms with bath or shower.

DOUGLAS. *Hydro,* 73 rooms. *Castle Mona,* 110 rooms, all with bath.

PORT ERIN. *Belle Vue,* 81 rooms. *Eagle,* 30 rooms. *Ocean Castle,* 93 rooms.

PORT ST. MARY. *Bayqueen Hotel,* 146 rooms.

RAMSEY. *Grand Island,* 61 rooms, 28 with bath.

Northern Ireland—The Six Counties

Editors' note: As we feel that we can no longer recommend our readers to visit Northern Ireland, we have dropped all information concerning the Six Counties from this edition.

GREECE

Breathtaking natural beauty, archeological treasure and reasonable prices have combined to make Greece one of the most appealing areas of contemporary tourism. The birthplace of Western civilization is catching up with its modern adverse effects, particularly those felt so acutely during the height of the travel season, but persistent efforts are being made to improve the comfort and convenience of travelers. Greece has always drawn lovers of art, history or mythology and she will continue to do so. But Greece has also become one of Europe's leading centers for sailing and yachting as well as remaining ideal for skin-diving and spear-fishing.

The turmoil prevailing in the Eastern Mediterranean has highlighted Greece's political stability due to a government reelected with a comfortable majority in November 1977. Prices compare favorably with other Mediterranean countries, but food is often undistinguished.

The nearly nine million present-day Greeks call themselves Hellenes, their country *Demokratia Tis Ellados,* the Republic of Hellas. Dotted with cypress groves, oleander and olive trees, the nation's 51,123 square miles (about the size of New York State) are cut by rugged mountain chains, often plunging sheer into the sea. The Pindus Range, running from north to south, touches on the fabled peaks of Mount Olympus, home of the Gods, and Mount Parnassus, favorite haunt of Apollo and the Muses. From the quarries of Mount Pentelicon came the gleaming marble of the Parthenon.

About 30 percent of these vigorous people are peasants, raising olives, grapes, figs, currants (whose name derives from Corinth) and the best tobacco in Europe, the only crop that approaches tourism in economic importance. They also make cheese from sheep and goat milk, and beautiful rugs and other handwoven textiles from the wool of their flocks. But gone are the days of colorful regional costumes, which are now only to be seen at folkloric events organized by the National Tourist Organization.

Food and Drink

A great specialty of the Greek cuisine is stuffed vine leaves, piquantly seasoned rice, meat and onions. The Greeks call it *dolmades,* and it's very good. More familiar to Anglo-Saxon palates is *moussaka,* a delicious meat and eggplant combination. Try *kalamarakia,* morsels of hot fried squid; they'll remind you of fried shrimps. *Youvetsi* is lamb with noodles. *Souvlakia* is Greek for shishkebab. Also recommended: *youvarlakia,* tiny meat balls sautéed in butter and served with a lemon sauce; octopus cooked in a wine and onion sauce; *barbounia,* grilled mullet, and *kedonia,* little Greek clams on the half shell. A Greek favorite is *tyropitta,* cheesecake, and there's the whole gamut of *baclava, kadaif* and other sweet pastries.

The best table wine is Porto Carras, white rosé (*kokineli*) and red, followed by the three varieties of *Cellar.* Also drinkable are the white *Amalia, Elisar* and *Santa Helena. Castel Danielis,* as well as the red *Mirabello, Petit Chateau* and the rougher *Naoussa;* sweet dessert wines are *Mavrodaphni* and *Samos.* Since ancient times, the Greeks have been adding resin to their wines, and the resulting mixture is called *retsina.* Try it if you must, though more likely than not, you'll return to *aretsinoto,* meaning no resin. The best-known of Greek contributions to tippling is *ouzo,* the national aperitif. It has a faint overtone of licorice while its country cousin is *tsipouro,* stronger and cruder. Greek beers are refreshing light lagers, but soft drinks are often too sweet, as are the prettily colored liqueurs.

PRACTICAL INFORMATION FOR GREECE

WHAT WILL IT COST. Inflation is still high, but a favorable exchange rate has kept hotel and meal prices comparatively low. With the exception of the beach resorts near Athens, there are no regional price differences, variations within the categories depending on the location and the frills: swimming pool, sauna, conference facilities, etc. Bungalows are priced 5 to 10% higher. Off-season rates are 10 to 30% lower from November 1 through April, excluding Christmas and Easter holidays. All prices in the table below include 15% service charges, taxes, airconditioning, in the top categories, and heating. Meal prices, without beverages, are for hotels or equivalent restaurants or taverns. A word of warning: seaside taverns, despite their deceptively simple appearances, are often classified A or B, charging accordingly. Check the category, always prominently indicated, and follow the Greek habit of choosing your fish in the kitchen, having it weighed and priced.

An *ouzo* costs from 10 to 25 dr., a bottle of beer 25 to 40 dr., a bottle of local wine from 55 to 200 dr., half a liter of *retsina* 20 to 40 dr., Turkish coffee 10 to 15 dr.

Hotel prices (drachmas)

Category	L	A	B	C	D
Single	900–2000	550–800	350–550	300–400	190–240
Double	1100–2500	650–900	450–700	350–450	250–350
Breakfast	80–150	60–90	50–75	45–65	40–50
Lunch/Dinner	450–700	250–450	200–300	150–220	90–150

CAPITAL. Athens, population 3,000,000 (est.).

LANGUAGE. Greek. English is widely spoken and understood in Athens and large towns.

CLIMATE. Greece is radiant with sunshine from April to November. There is almost no rain except in winter, which is mild. June, July and August are hot but not humid; the air is crystal-clear and dry, the sky and sea a brilliant dazzling blue.

Average maximum daily temperatures in degrees Fahrenheit and centigrade:

Athens	Jan.	Feb.	Mar.	Apr.	May	June	July	Aug.	Sept.	Oct.	Nov.	Dec.
F°	55	57	61	68	77	86	92	92	84	75	66	59
C°	13	14	16	20	25	30	33	33	29	24	19	15

SPECIAL EVENTS. Performances by renowned foreign orchestras and theater groups in late June are the curtain raiser to Greece's main cultural manifestation, the *International Athens Festival,* which lasts well into September, alternating nightly concerts, opera and ballets with classical Greek tragedies and comedies in the ancient Herodes Atticus open-air theater on the slopes of the Acropolis. The *Epidaurus Festival* presents ancient drama every weekend from mid-July through August, while a week or two of the same classical fare is the norm through the summer in antique theaters all over the country.

Greek Folkdances from May to September on the Philopappou Hill opposite the Acropolis, where the pageant of the *Sound and Light* spectacle is presented from April through October as well as on the islands of Corfu and Rhodes.

The *International Fair of Thessaloniki* is held in the first fortnight of September in the capital of northern Greece. This event is accompanied by a *Song Festival* and followed first by a *Greek Film Festival* and in October by the *Dimitria,* a *Byzantine Art Festival* dating back to the 13th century.

From July to mid-September a *Wine Festival* is held in the park of the Byzantine monastery of Daphni, just outside Athens. Similar *Wine Festivals* at Alexandroupolis (Northern Greece) and Rhodes.

In February, *Carnival* is celebrated everywhere, culminating in a parade with floats on the last carnival Sunday (usually early March) in Patras.

Most famous of many Holy Day celebrations is that of the *Epitaph* on Good Friday with impressive Greek Orthodox processions.

SPORTS. Enthusiasts of *spear fishing* and *skin-diving* will find the waters of the Aegean ideal. Be sure to bring your full equipment. *Angling* is free and its principal catch is the mountain trout.

Sailing and *yachting* are an important activity in Greece; sub-marine fishing is becoming increasingly popular. There are excellent *golf courses* near Athens, in Corfu and in Rhodes.

MONEY. Monetary unit is the *drachme,* divided into 100 *lepta.* Rate of exchange at presstime: app. 36 drachmes to the dollar; 64 to the pound sterling. **Subject to change.** There are coins of 10, 20 and 50 lepta, as well as 1, 2, 5, 10 and 20 dr. coins.

You may bring in unlimited amounts of foreign currency, but sums in excess of $500 must be declared for reexport. Only 1,500 dr. may be imported or exported.

HOTELS. Greek hotels are officially categorized as L (deluxe), A (first class), B (moderate), C (inexpensive), and D (rock-bottom). All L, most A's and many B's are airconditioned. Even the D's in main tourist centers are adequate, all with private showers. Few C and D hotels have their own restaurant.

TIPPING. Hotels add 15% service charge, but a little extra is expected. Restaurants and nightclubs also add 15%, rising to 20% round Christmas and Easter. Service is included on the taxi meter, but you pay 5 dr. extra per bag for luggage. Porters charge according to a fixed scale, usually 10 dr. a bag; hatcheck girls, theater and cinema ushers, and washroom attendants receive 3 to 10 dr.

HOW TO REACH GREECE. By Air: *TWA* and *Olympic Airways* from New York and Montreal to Athens; *BA* from London also to Rhodes, Corfu and Crete; and from all European capitals.

By Sea: from Southampton by *Chandris Line;* from Genoa, Venice and especially Brindisi, numerous regular car ferries to Corfu and Patras (Peloponnese).

By Car: Ostend-Athens, the fastest route via Cologne-Munich-Vienna-Budapest-Belgrade is about 1,850 miles. Same from Paris via Basel-Innsbruck-Ljubljana.

Car-Sleeper Expresses: Useful services for motorists en route for Greece: London-Ljubljana (Yugoslavia); or London-Paris-Milan; Milan-Brindisi, connecting with the car ferry. Only summer services, 2 or more times weekly.

CUSTOMS. Two hundred cigarettes or 50 cigars or one quarter lb. smoking tobacco and one bottle of liquor duty free. No duty on articles for personal use. Your car, camping and sport equipment, typewriter, etc. are registered in your passport upon entry to prevent sale within the country.

MAIL. Airmail letter within Europe, 7 dr. for 20 grams; postcards 3.50 dr. To U.S.A. and Canada: 10 grams, 11 dr.; postcards 5 dr.

ELECTRICITY. 220 volts, 50-cycle. 110 volts on some of the islands.

DRINKING WATER. Safe in all towns and resorts. Take bottled mineral water *(Sáriza, Loutràki)* or try the wine elsewhere.

TRAVEL IN GREECE. Greece is a country of small distances, but chopped up by mountains and separated by the sea. Air travel is the most practical means for those in a hurry. *Olympic Airways* serves the country's principal cities and tourist centers. Its passenger rates are among the lowest in Europe. On the sparse railroad lines, keep to the somewhat faster diesel trains *(automotrice)*. They are, however, efficiently complemented by a dense network of cheap motor coaches. A variety of steamers ply the Aegean; check on everchanging schedules and travel first class only. Among the treats are the cruises in the Aegean and Ionian Seas, visiting Rhodes, Mykonos, Corfu, Crete, etc.

PLACE AND STREET NAMES are given in Greek and Latin characters, according to the modern Greek pronunciation, so that Piraeus becomes Pireéfs. *Odós* (street) is omitted, but not necessarily *Leofóros* (avenue) or *Platia* (square), while the name is in the possessive case; thus Stadium Street becomes simply Stadiou.

 MOTORING. You drive on the right side of the road. International driving license and green card required. Frontier points are Gevgelija (Yugoslavia) to Evzonoi Bitola (Yug.) to Niki Kulata (Bulgaria) to Promahon, Kastanea and Kipi-Ipsala Bridge (from Turkey). Major points are open night and day. Daily connection by car-ferry boats between Brindisi (Italy) and Corfu, Igoumenitsa and Patras from April to October. The Automobile & Touring Club of Greece (ELPA), Athens Tower, 2 Mesogion, Athens, is most helpful to foreign tourists. The AAA is at Syntagma Square, Athens.

Price of gasoline (petrol) with tourist coupons for cars with foreign license plates is 11 dr. per liter for regular (86 octane), 13 dr. for super (94 octane); without coupons 18 dr. and 21 dr.

Car Hire: *Byron Car Hire,* 71 Vassilissis Sofias Ave., *Hellascars,* 7 Stadiou, *Hertz,* 12 Syngrou Ave., and *Avis,* 48 Amalias Ave., Athens; all have branches in the bigger towns.

USEFUL ADDRESSES. *American Embassy,* 91 Vasilissis Sophias; *British Embassy,* 1 Plutarchou; *Canadian Embassy,* 4 Ioannou Genadiou. *Tourist police* 15 Ermou; *Emergency first aid* tel. 52-55-55. *American Express,* 2 Syntagma Square; *Nat'l. Tourist Info. Office* and *Wagons Lits/Cook,* 2 Karageorgi Servias, *B. Koutsoukellis,* 7 Syngrou Ave. (yacht hire). All in Athens.

Athens

Athens is a growing city of about 3 million inhabitants, including the harbor of Piraeus and the outlying suburbs. The Old City clusters at the foot of the famous, flat-topped hill known as the Acropolis. The new city sprawls over the Attic plain from the sea to the mountains. It is intersected by wide boulevards and squares, lined with high new buildings constructed of the same Pentelic marble as the ancient Parthenon.

But the chief point of interest in Athens is the Acropolis. You will want to spend at least a morning seeing the 2,400-year-old Parthenon, the Erechtheion with its famous Porch of Maidens or Caryatids (plaster casts—the originals are in the museum), the Temple of the Wingless Victory, and the fascinating Acropolis Museum. Having withstood 2,500 years of wars and occupations, the sacred rock is today threatened by a more insidious enemy, air pollution. The director general of UNESCO launched in front of the scaffolded Parthenon in 1977 a 15 million dollar campaign to preserve what remains of the "shrine to the moment when European art was born".

The Acropolis is open from 7:30 A.M. to sunset, from 9 P.M. to midnight on full moon nights. Admission 50 dr.

Other highlights which even a one-day visitor to Athens should not miss are the Monument of Lysicrates, the Arch of Hadrian, the Temple of Olympian Zeus, the Olympic Stadium, the Theater of Dionysus, the Odeon of Herodes Atticus and the Theseion, best-preserved of all the temples dominating the Agora, focal point of ancient Athenian community life, a kind of combination market place and civic center. Here you will find the impressive Stoa of Attalos, reconstructed through the contributions of the Rockefeller Foundation by the American School of Classical Studies in Athens. This impressive building will give you an excellent idea of what life was like in the ancient city-state of Athens. It also houses the Museum of the Agora Excavations, conducted by the American School.

If you have time for only one museum, it should be the National Archaeological Museum. Its collections are the most important in Greece. Do not overlook the Byzantine Museum and the Benaki Museum, the former for its unique collection of icons, the latter for an equally rich variety of Greek regional costumes, Byzantine and Moslem *objets d'art* and weapons. The most interesting Byzantine churches in Athens are St. Theodore, Kapnikarea and Aghios Eleftherios.

Excursions from Athens

These may be taken in one of the many comfortable coaches that operate regularly from Athens. Largest of the companies are *American Express,* Syntagma Sq., *Chat,* and *Hellas,* 4 and 7 Stadiou. Their English-speaking guides all sound as though they had gone to graduate school in archeology, and we recommend seeing the sights with them.

Among the shorter excursions well worth taking are: Mount Parnis, 19 miles, altitude 3,281 feet, with lovely alpine scenery; Marathon Lake, 19 miles Marathon Mound, 24 miles, with collective tomb of the Athenian soldiers killed in the great victory over the Persians in 490 B.C.; and Sounion, 44 miles, with the Temple of Poseidon on a hill overlooking the Aegean Sea.

PRACTICAL INFORMATION FOR ATHENS

HOTELS. The large deluxe *Athens Hilton* on Vassilissis Sofias Avenue is resplendent with a swimming pool, restaurants and nightclub on the roof terrace; the slightly cheaper *Caravel* is across Vas. Alexandrou Ave. On Syntagma Square are the *King George* and the distinguished *Grande Bretagne.* The *King's Palace* opposite has a roof garden and nightclub. Round the corner in Stadiou is the *Athenée Palace.* The *St. George Lycabettus* commands a splendid view from the slopes of the Lycabettus hill. The *Amalia* on Amalia Blvd., overlooks the Royal Gardens, while the *Royal Olympic,* Diakou St., featuring a small swimming pool, faces the temple of Zeus. The *Park* is farther out on Alexandras Ave. On the highest mountain encircling Athens, reached by cable car, is the *Mount Parnis,* with casino, nightclub, swimming pool.

First Class

The *Acropole Palace* is opposite the Archaeological Museum. *King Minos* is on noisy Omonia Square. The *Ambassadeurs,* in the same district insists on half-board; *Ariane* and *Embassy,* furnished apartments, are behind the U.S. embassy; *Delice* and *Golden Age* are near the Hilton. The others are around Syntagma Square: *Astor, Attica Palace, Electra, Esperia Palace,* and *Olympic Palace.*

Moderate

Near Omonia Square, *Achillion, Alfa* (half-board), *Athens Center, Atlantic, Candia, Dorian Inn, El Greco, Eretria, Grand, Marmara, Titania;* beyond the square, *Anastasia, Plaza, Stanley,* with rooftop pool, and *Xenophon.*

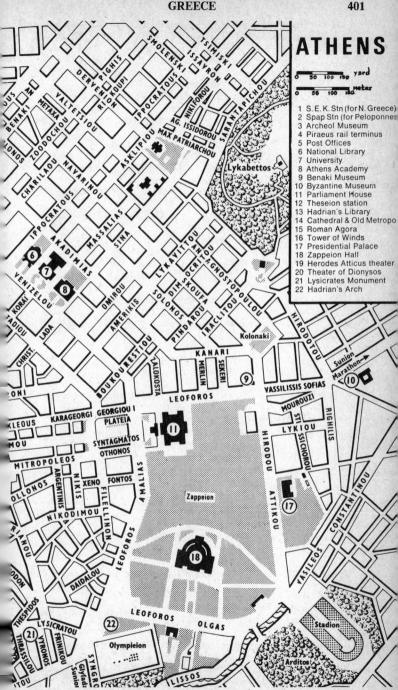

ATHENS

yard
0 50 100 190

meter
0 50 100 180

1 S.E.K. Stn (for N. Greece)
2 Spap Stn (for Peloponnes
3 Archeol Museum
4 Piraeus rail terminus
5 Post Offices
6 National Library
7 University
8 Athens Academy
9 Benaki Museum
10 Byzantine Museum
11 Parliament House
12 Theseion station
13 Hadrian's Library
14 Cathedral & Old Metropo
15 Roman Agora
16 Tower of Winds
17 Presidential Palace
18 Zappeion Hall
19 Herodes Atticus theater
20 Theater of Dionysos
21 Lysicrates Monument
22 Hadrian's Arch

Closer to Syntagma Square are: the airconditioned *Aphroditi, Arethusa, Pan, Omiros, Akadimos Galaxy Athens Gate* (half-board), *Lykabette, Minerva.*

Behind the U.S. embassy, *Alexandros, Athinais,* behind the Hilton, *Ilissia.* Beyond Syntagma are *Damon, Dimitrios, Christina,* and *Sirene.*

Inexpensive

Albion, Alcestis, Alma, Amaryllis, Apollo, Ares, Aristides, Aristoteles, Asty, Attalos, Capitol, Diros, Elite, Epidavros, Evripides, Jason, Kosmos, Nestor, Odeon, Omega, Omonia, Paradise Rock, Parnon, Solomos, Tegea, Theoxenia, Zinon, all near Omonia.

At Piraeus

Cavo D'Oro (B); *Arion* and *Kastella* (C) overlook the Saronic Gulf from Vassileos Pavlou Ave. Near the main harbor, the *Argo, Atlantis, Capitol, Cavo, Delphini, Diogenes, Glaros, Noufara, Omiridion, Serifos* and *Triton* are modern C's.

BEACH RESORTS. The southeast coast of Attica, from Faliron to Sounion, is studded with hotels authorized to charge an extra 20%, mostly half board. Distances from Athens are shown in parentheses.

Anavissos (31). *Pelasgia Beach* (A); *Apollo Beach, Kalypso Motel* (B); *Silver Beach* (C).

Glifada (11). *Astir Beach* (L), bungalows and nightclub. *Atrium, Palace, Palmyra* (A); *Antonopoulos, Delfini, Fenix, Florida, Four Seasons, Gripsholm, Kreoli, London, Niki, Riviera, Sea View, Triton* (B); *Adonis, Avra, Beau Rivage, Glyfada, Oceanis, Perla, Rial, Themis* (C).

Kalamaki (8). Near noisy airport. *Albatros, Saronis, Tropical, Venus* (B); *Attica, Blue Sea, Galaxy, Hellenikon* (C).

Kavouri (14). *Apollo Palace* (L); *Kavouri* (A); *Pine Hill* (B).

Lagonissi (25). *Lagonissi Beach* (A), hotel and bungalows on private beach, nightclub. 3 miles farther on, *Eden Beach* (B).

Paleon Faliron (5). *Coral, Poseidon* (B). *Aura, Ephi* (C).

Saronis (27). *Saronic Gate* (A).

Sounion (44). *Belvedere Park* and *Sounion Beach* (A), bungalows; *Aegeon* on beach and *Sun,* (B), bungalows.

Varkiza (19). *Sun Palace* (L), bungalows and villas; *Glaros* (A); *Varkiza* (B); *Holiday* (C).

Voula (13). *Voula Beach* (A); *Castello Beach* (B); *Noufara, Orion, Palma, Rondo* (C).

Vouliagmeni (16). *Astir Palace* (L), hotel and bungalows, pool, private beach. *Greek Coast, Margi House* (A); *Blue Spell, Strand* (B).

RESTAURANTS. Beside the dining rooms of the (L) hotels, among which the King George's *Tudor Hall* and St. George Lycabettus' *Grand Salon* command outstanding views, you might try the very reasonable roof garden of the *Astor,* the *Athinean* at the Esperia Palace, the *Kastalia* at the Lykabette.

Expensive

Dionysos enhances its excellent food by the sight of the Acropolis opposite.

The *in* place for diners, with dancing and floorshow, on the 24th floor of Athens' first highrise is the very expensive *Tower Suite,* but the *Tower Village* cafeteria on the first floor is quite reasonable. Simpler but even more panoramic is *Lykabettus* atop the mountain reached by cog rail from the town center.

Floca's and *Zonar's,* both 9 Venizelos Ave., are the leading café restaurants.

International cuisine at *Maxim,* 4 Milioni, off Kolonaki Sq.; *Riva,* 114 Michalakopoulou; and *Papakia* 5 Iradanou, behind the Hilton. *Flame Steak House 9,* Chatziyanni Mexi and *Steak Room,* 6 Aeginitou, specialize in grills.

In the cool Kifissia suburb you can select trout from the pond at the *Belle Hélène; Blue Pine Farm* also recommended.

Constantinopolitan cuisine at the *Gerofinikas,* 10 Pindarou; American at the *Stage Coach,* 4 Loukianou; French at the *Bagatelle,* 9 Ventiri, *L'Abreuvoir, Je Reviens,* 49 and 51 Xenokratous; Italian at *Al Convento,* 4 Anapiron Polemou; Chinese at *Mr. Yung,* 3 Lamachou and *Pagoda,* off Alexandra Ave.

For seafood you have a wide choice all along the coast from Piraeus to Vouliagmeni. The *Papakia aux Falaises,* next to the Yacht Club, also serve duckling like the branch in town; below, in the picturesque boat harbor of Mikro Limani, a string of excellent fish restaurants line the waterfront. Further along *Marides* and *Soupies* at Kalamaki, *Antonopoulos* and *Psaropoulos* at Glifada, *Leönidas* at Vouliagmeni, are the pick of the bunch.

Moderate

Corfu, behind the Kings' Palace hotel; *Delphi, Meteora,* and *Syntrivani,* are all off Syntagma Square; *Vassilis,* 14 Boukourestiou.

Among the bewildering variety of *tavernas* in the maze of the old Plaka district at the foot of the Acropolis the *Epta Adelfia, Kastro, Mostrou. Old Rock* and especially *Palaia Athena* are really nightclubs with Greek food and floorshows. Opening earlier and content with orchestras are the *Arias, Attalos, Bacchus, Erotokritos* and *Kalokerinos.* More genuinely Greek, with only the traditional three guitarists are *Fandis, Geros tou Morea, Ton Theon, Vlachou, Xynou.*

 NIGHTLIFE. Almost as varied as the indigenous tavernas are the western-style nightclubs, from the Hilton's *Galaxy,* the Caravel's *Horizon,* the King's Palace *Coronet* and the *Acropole Palace* to the Piraeus harbor dives.

"Bouzoukia" music and dancing made popular by several films can be sampled in numerous tavernas, *Architektoniki, Marinella* and *Stork* in the center, *Archontissa, Napoleon* (rather surprisingly) and *Perikles* in the Plaka, *Athena* and *Diogenes,* Syngrou Ave., *Delta,* on the sea opposite the race course.

NEWSPAPERS. The two English dailies, *Athens Post* and *Athens News* (10 dr.), contain useful local information. *International Herald Tribune* and English papers available same day at most central news stands.

MUSEUMS. Opening hours: Winter (Oct. 15–March 15) 9 A.M.–4 P.M.; Summer, 8 A.M.–1 P.M., 3–6 P.M. Most closed on Tuesdays. Free admission Thursdays and Sundays.

Delphi

Less than 100 miles northwest of Athens is one of the most impressive sights in Greece—Delphi—where the famous Delphic Oracle once foretold the destiny of men. When you see these extensive ruins 2,000 feet above the Bay of Itea, you will realize why it was regarded with religious awe by the ancient Greeks. In the lee of windswept Mount Parnassus, this is one of the most beautiful spots in Europe, the silver-green Sea of Olives extending to the blue gulf. See the Temple of Apollo, the Treasuries along the Sacred Way, the Theater, the Stadium, the Temples of Athena, the masterpieces of sculpture in the museum, especially the famous bronze charioteer, and the sacred Castalian spring from whose pure waters you may drink as pilgrims to the Delphic Oracle did thousands of years ago.

En route between Athens and Delphi, your tour guide will point out the fateful crossroads where Oedipus fulfilled the dreadful prophecy of the Sphinx by killing his own father.

Olympia

200 miles southwest of Athens, by the motorway via Patras, capital of the Peleponnese, the first Olympic Games were held in 776 B.C. Among olive groves and pine trees is the first Olympic stadium, the imposing ruins of the temples of Zeus and Hera and the superb Olympia Museum, among whose many treasures is one of the most perfect pieces of sculpture in existence—the *Hermes of Praxiteles*.

Daphni and Corinth

En route from Athens to Mycenae, stop at Daphni to inspect the noted Cistercian convent and Byzantine church with its celebrated mosaics. Old Corinth, 58 miles by the motorway and across the spectacular Corinth canal, was a Roman town founded by Julius Caesar on the site of the destroyed Greek city, of which only the sixth-century B.C. temple of Apollo remains. You can drive up to the huge Crusader castle of Acro-Corinth, once crowned by a sanctuary to Aphrodite.

Mycenae

Mycenae, 80 miles from Athens, was a fortified town, destroyed in 468 B.C. and totally forgotten until 1874, when the German archaeologist Schliemann unearthed this fabulous stronghold of the 13th-century B.C. Achaean kings. This was the seat of the doomed house of Atreus, of Agamemnon and his wife, the vengeful Clytemnestra, sister of Helen of Troy. When Schliemann uncovered the six shaft graves of the royal circle he felt sure that among these were the tombs of Agamemnon and Clytemnestra. The gold masks and crowns, the daggers, jewelry and other treasures found in the tombs of Mycenae are now in the National Archaeological Museum in Athens. The astounding beehive tombs cut into the hills outside the reconstructed walls, the Lion Gate and castle ruins crowning their barren hill are the shell of a civilization as rich as that of Egypt or Babylon. Further south, beyond Argos, Europe's oldest continuously inhabited town, and the cyclopean ramparts of Tiryns, Nafplion is a beautifully situated, picturesque little town protected by huge Venetian fortifications.

Epidaurus

Even if you are not in Greece for the Epidaurus Festival, you should visit Epidaurus, only 18 miles from Nafplion, another shrine of ancient Greece, the sanctuary of Aesculapius, God of Healing. See the foundations of the temples and hospitals, but especially the incomparable open-air theater, whose acoustics you can test yourself. You can actually hear a stage whisper from the top row of this theater which still seats 14,000 spectators at the summer festival.

Thessaloniki and Mount Athos

Thessaloniki, Greece's second city, is a large modern town containing some outstanding Byzantine churches, most famous being St. George's, originally the mausoleum of the Roman Emperor Galerius, whose Triumphal Arch (303 A.D.) still stands.

The lovely beaches along the three prongs of the mountainous Halkidiki peninsula to the east have become the playground of northern Greece, with a large choice of modern hotels. On Mount Athos, the eastern prong, about three hundred Orthodox monks still live the secluded life of the Middle Ages in 30 imposing monasteries, the oldest dating back to 963.. Women are not permitted to visit this living vestige of medieval piety and seclusion; men only during the day.

Meteora

On the western confines of the Thessalian plain, Greece's granary, rises a forest of gigantic rock needles to 1,820 ft., crowned by improbable 14th-century monasteries. Visitors used to be hauled up in nets, but in the 1920s, stairs were hollowed out of the sheer cliff face. One of Europe's unique sites, Meteora is easily accessible by road from Kalambaka, two miles away.

The Isles of Greece

Rhodes, less than an hour by air from Athens, is like a splendid outdoor museum of ancient Greek, Roman and Byzantine history. Among the chief sights is the medieval city of the Knights Hospitalers of St. John of Jerusalem, still girdled by impressive walls. See also the acropolis of the ancient town of Lindos, with its temple of Athena overlooking the blue Aegean. Rhodes has taken first place as a tourist resort and a large choice of excellent modern hotels is available.

Corfu is just as beautiful. It lies in the Ionian Sea, less than an hour by air from Athens. The civilized formality of Venetian life still lingers on, despite the intensive tourist development.

Mykonos is a perfect place for swimming and exploring in the Aegean Sea. Marked by the quaintest windmills you've ever seen, and gleaming white houses in stunning contrast to the blue sea, it is a great favorite with artists.

Crete is a paradise for the amateur of archaeology who does not consider it infra dig. to relax on fine sandy beaches. Forty-five minutes south of Athens by air, this large island was the seat of the great Minoan civilization, whose fascinating remains, including the stupendous Palace of Knossos, are one of the most impressive sights in the entire Mediterranean area. The more beautifully sited Palace of Festos near the south coast is 36 miles from the largest town, Iraklion, which is still surrounded by the Venetian ramparts that withstood a 24-year Turkish siege. The less imposing ruins of Malia dominate the loveliest north coast beach.

Hios, Kos, Lemnos, Lesbos and *Samos* are becoming increasingly popular. Kos, the birthplace of Hippocrates, Father of Medicine, rivals neighboring Rhodes in variety of sites. Wooded Lesbos, where burning Sappho loved and wrote, and mountainous Samos close to Turkey abound in antiquities and scenic beauties.

The islands of the Saronic Gulf, off the mainland shores, are more easily visited than any others. In summer the frequent daily ferryboats to *Egina, Poros, Idra* and *Spetse* are supplemented by one-day cruises.

PRACTICAL INFORMATION FOR THE REGIONS

HOTELS

CORFU. The *Corfu Palace* (L); *Cavalieri* (A); *Arion, Astron, King Alkinoos,* (B); *Arkadion, Marina, Olympiakon, Bretagne, Ionion* (C) in the lovely town. The *Atlantis,* outstanding *Corfu Hilton,* the former royal residence *Castello, Eva Palace, Marbella Beach, Miramare Beach, Poseidon Beach* (L); *Aventura, Chandris, Corcyra Beach, Corfu Kanoni, Delfinia, Ermones, Faeax, Grand Glifada, Kerkira Golf, Kontokali Palace, Nissaki, Steyia* (A); *Aeolos Beach, Akti, Ipsos Beach, Messonghi, Oceanis, Paleokastritsa, Potamaki, Roda Beach* (B) to name but the best on or near beaches on this dreamy island.

The *Achilleion,* once the palace of the Empress Elizabeth of Austria, later of William II of Germany, was converted into a casino.

DELPHI. *Amalia, Delphi, Vouzas* (A); *Castalia, Europe* (B); *Hermes, Leto, Parnassos, Phaeton, Pythia, Stadion* (C).

Meals on the hotel terraces overlooking the olive groves in the gorge below are more memorable for the setting than the food.

CRETE. Agios Nikolaos. *Minos Beach* (L); *Hermes, Mirabello* (A); *Ariadne Beach, Coral* (B); *Akratos, Creta, Cronos, Du Lac, Rea* (C). 4 miles out of town, *Elounda Beach* (L) **Hania.** *Kydon, Xenia* (A); *Doma, Lissos, Porto Veneziano, Samaria* (B); *Canea, Creta, Diktyna, Lucia* and the bungalows of *Aptera Beach* (C). **Iraklion.** *Astir, Astoria, Atlantis, Xenia* (A); *Castron, Esperia, Mediterranean* (B); *Daedalos, Domenico, El Greco, Galini, Heraklion, Olympic, Park,* comfortable (C's). Nearby bungalows: *Creta Beach, Knossos Beach* (A), *Amnissos, Motel Xenia* (B). **Limin Hersonissou.** *Belvedere, Candia Beach, Creta Maris* (A); *Nora* (B); *Avra, Glaros* (C). **Maleme.** *Maleme Beach* (B). **Malia.** *Ikaros Village, Kernos Beach, Sirens' Beach* (A); *Malia Beach* (B); *Grammatikaki* (C). *Rethymnon. El Greco, Rithymna* (A); *Ideon, Xenia* (B).

EGINA. *Nafsika* (B); *Brown, Danae, Klonos, Pharos* (C); 4 miles from town *Moondy Bay* (B). On the beach of **Agia Marina:** *Marisa* (A); *Apollo* (B); *Aphaea, Argo, Galini, Marina* (C).

HALKIDIKI. Quite outstanding the huge selfcontained resort complex of *Porto Carras,* villas, bungalows, (L) and (A) hotel, golf course, yacht marina, opened 1977. *Athos Palace, Eagle's Palace, Kassandra Sani, Mendi, Pallini Beach,* (A); *Ammon Zeus, Gerakina Beach, Mount Athos, Sermili, Vassos, Xenia Ouranopolis* and *Xenia Paliouri* (B); *Kallithea, Strand* (C).

IDRA. *Hydroussa, Miramare, Miranda* (B); *Hydra Beach* (A) bungalows are on the mainland opposite.

KALAMBAKA. *Motel Divani, Xenia* (A); *Aeolian Star, Odission* (C).

KOS. *Atlantis, Continental Palace* (A); *Alexandra, Dimitra Beach, Kos, Theoxenia* (B); *Christina, Elizabeth, Elli, Koulias, Milva, Oscar, Veroniki* (C).

MYCENAE, *Agammemnon, Petite Planète,* small modern C's.

MYKONOS. *Lito* (A); *Kouneni, Rhenia, Theoxenia* (B); *Manto* (C). *Aphrodite, Alkystis,* (B); *Mykonos Beach, Paralos Beach* (C) bungalows on private beach.

MYTILENE (Lesbos). *Xenia* (B); *Blue Sea, Lesvion, Sappho* (C).

NAFPLION. *Amphitryon, Agamemnon, Xenia* (A); *Xenia Palace Bungalows* (L) above the town with a splendid view. *Alkyoni, Dioskouri, Galini, Nafplia, Park* and *Rex* are comfortable C's.

OLYMPIA. Best is the *Spap* (A) overlooking the ruins. *Apollo, Neda, Neon Olympia, Xenia* and *Xenios Zeus Motel* (B); *Ilis, Kronion* (C); *Miramare Olympia Beach* is a first-class hotel, bungalow and villa complex with swimming pool, sports facilities, on a sandy beach 18 miles from Olympia.

PATRAS. *Astir, Moreas* (A); *Galaxy, Majestic* (B); *Delfini, Esperia, Mediterranee* (C). On neighboring beaches *Achaia Beach, Alexander Beach, Florida* (B); *Rion Beach* (C).

POROS. *Poros, Sirene* (B); *Aegli, Angyra, Latsi, Saron* (C). At **GALATAS** on the mainland opposite, *Stela Maris* (B); *Galatia* (C).

RHODES. Quality and quantity of accommodation is as high as anywhere in the Mediterranean. Out of town the *Rodos Palace* (L) groups chalets round a hotel, but only the *Miramare Beach* (L) bungalows, *Electra Palace* and *Golden Beach* (A) are directly on the sea; just across the road to the airport along the west coast are *Avra Beach, Bel Air, Dionyssos,* the huge *Metropolitan, Oceanis, Rhodos Bay* (A); *Leto, Solemar* (B); on the east coast, *Eden Roc, Faliraki Beach* (A). In town the leader is the *Grand Hotel* (L) which houses the casino; attractive A's are the *Belvedere, Blue Sky, Cairo Palace, Chevaliers Palace, Ibiscus, Imperial, Kamiros, Mediterranean, Park, Regina, Riviera, Siravast, Sunwing.*

Anywhere else the following B's would be in a higher category: *Acandia, Alexia, Amphitryon, Angela, Athina, Delfini, Despo, Europa, Konstantinos, Lito, Phoenix, Plaza. Achillion, Africa, Aglaia, Als, Aphrodite, Esperia, Manoussos, Semiramis* are the larger C's.

SAMOS. *Meropi, Xenia* (B); *Samos* (C).

SPETSE. *Kastelli, Spetsae* (A); *Possidonion, Roumanis* (B); *Ilios, Mirtoon, Star* (C). At Costa on the mainland opposite, *Cap D'Or* and *Lido* (B).

THESSALONIKI. *Macedonia Palace* (L) with pool; and *Mediterranean* (L), on the seafront. *Capitol, Electra Palace, Mediterranean* (A); large *Capsis, Aegeon, Astor, City, Egnatia, El Greco, Metropolitan, Palace, Queen Olga, Rotonda, Victoria* (B); and the equally modern *A.B.C, Amalia, Delta, Esperia, Olympia, Park, Pella, Telioni* (C) are all in Thessaloniki's rather noisy center. The *Asteria, Nefeli* and *Panorama* (A) in the hills of Panorama command an enchanting view over the town and the Thermaïc Gulf.

The *Olympus Naoussa* restaurant on the seafront is famed for its *media tiganita* (fried mussels). Delicious seafood in the fish restaurants of the Aretsou suburb.

HOLLAND

"God made the world," say the citizens of Holland, "but the Dutch made the Netherlands." Nearly half of this democratic monarchy's 15,-450 square miles has been reclaimed from the sea, and the doughty inhabitants have been working for generations to keep it from slipping back. Hence the special look of the Dutch landscape. Dikes are every-where, holding out the waters, and picturesque windmills, along with a far more important network of ingenious pumps, are ceaselessly engaged in keeping the land dry or carefully irrigating it. In addition to the encroaching flood, the Dutch have had bouts with the Romans, the Franks, the Burgundians, the Spanish, the English, the French and the Germans. Their national life has thus been an endless struggle, so you will not be surprised to find the Hollanders a serious, determined, hard-working people, by tradition open, above board and absolutely trust-worthy, their officials untouched by scandal until the shock waves of international bribery revelations in early 1976 reached even up to the Dutch royal family.

Now a nation numbering over 14 million, and shorn of her former Indonesian colonies, Holland is preoccupied today with the problems of providing a living for her rapidly expanding population. (Her resettle-ment of thousands of Indonesians, who chose to remain Dutch when the colonies became independent, is a rare instance of intelligent and com-passionate handling of a potentially dangerous problem, that of immigra-tion by non-whites into a European country, and remains a good example for others faced with the same problem, such as Britain, Belgium or France). But since 1976, the settlement of well over 100,000 from Surinam and the Dutch Antilles, after those last Dutch "colonies" were given independence, has been more difficult. The reclamation of land proceeds apace, and a large number of the surplus population are encouraged to emigrate to Australia, Canada and the United States.

The Dutch have one of the highest birth rates in Europe, and the greatest density of population; they love children and are very keen on a close-knit family life; but the "pill," their increasing awareness of world overpopulation and their attitude toward abortion are gradually changing this. During 1976 and into 1977, there were heated debates on abortion, with deep moral disagreements between the upper and lower houses of parliament preventing a change in the law to bring it into line with the recent more liberal practice. But you certainly won't be conscious of any overpopulation problem as you travel through the green countryside, spacious and flat, laced with blue canals and tree-bordered roads. The biggest slopes are those leading up to the canal bridges; the tallest objects are the church spires (visible for miles) and many multi-storied modern apartment blocks, offices and factories. You will find cozy villages tucked away behind streamlined motorways, and noisy, overcrowded cities. The Dutch, though not outwardly humorous, are far from dour. Their ideal of social behavior is to be at one and the same time *deftig* (dignified, respectable and decorous) and *gezellig* (cozy, comfortable, and enjoying oneself).

Food and Drink

Of the many earthly pleasures the Hollander enjoys, eating probably heads the list, with the appetite sharpened by the national institution of the *borreltje,* a little nip of gin at five o'clock. You'd better take something to stimulate your appetite in this hearty land. Your breakfast, replete with several varieties of bread, cheese, cooked ham or meat, possibly a boiled egg, butter, jam and steaming coffee or tea, is a far and welcome cry from the usual continental *petit déjeuner.* It will hold you until the Dutch ritual of eleven o'clock coffee, just as the *Koffietafel,* a "light" lunch of bread, cold cuts and cheese, or particularly an *uitsmijter,* slices of bread topped with cold meat or ham and fried eggs, will fend off starvation until dinner, usually around 6 P.M.

Typical Dutch dishes appear in season (mostly in winter). Indonesian and Chinese foods are always available. Some of the best Dutch specialties are: *Erwtensoep,* a rich and delicious thick pea soup with bits of sausage or pig's knuckles, a meal in itself, but served only from October to March as is *Hutspot,* a meat, carrot and potato stew. *Haring,* especially the "new herring" caught between May and September and served brined, garnished with onions; *Rodekool met Rolpens,* red cabbage and rolled spiced meat with sliced apple; *Pannekoeken* and *Flensjes,* pancakes, in various varieties, shapes and sizes, all of them delectable and often eaten in special pancake restaurants. *Koeken* and *Koekjes,* cakes and cookies, usually on the sweet and rich side.

As for cheeses, the two famous classifications are *Gouda* and *Edam,* both mild in comparison with French and Italian cheeses. Try the spicier *Leidse* cheese with cumin or *Friese* cheese with cloves for a change. Seafood is abundant and well-prepared; most shellfish is rather expensive, except for the delicious mussels from the province of Zeeland.

If run-of-the-mill Dutch fare begins to pall, try an Indonesian restaurant (the best are in Amsterdam and The Hague) where the specialties of Holland's former colony are served. The chief dish here is *rijsttafel,* a heaping bowl of perfectly steamed rice together with 20 or more side dishes like *saté babi,* bite-size morsels of pork skewered on a wooden spit and cooked in a mouth-watering sauce. The best beverage to accompany an Indonesian *rijsttafel* is beer, of which there are several excellent varieties, both Dutch and foreign.

The indigenous Dutch short drink is *jenever* (gin), a potent and warming spirit. It comes in many varieties depending on the spices used, but most popular are the *jonge* (young) and the *oude* (old). Neither has the remotest similarity to dry gin, being both sweeter and oilier. Jenever is drunk neat and chilled (it's not a good mixer). Dutch liqueurs are good, and follow the French originals at infinitely less cost.

Over 700 Dutch restaurants offer a tourist menu of three courses at fl 13 all-in. They may be identified by special emblems carrying the words: "Tourist Menu", and a full list is obtainable from all VVVs.

PRACTICAL INFORMATION FOR HOLLAND

WHAT WILL IT COST. On a *deluxe* level, staying in the best rooms of the best hotels, patronizing top restaurants, using taxis, and spending the evening at theaters and nightclubs, you will spend not less than fl.295 or fl.325 per person per day. *Comfortable* travel—rooms with bath at good hotels, ample meals at good restaurants, sightseeing by rented car, an occasional evening out—will average fl.240 to fl.290 per person per day. *Economical* travel—comfortable rooms but without bath, at good hotels, table d'hôte meals at average restaurants, careful sightseeing, modest evening amusements—about fl.130. At a country pension with three meals a day it is possible to cut the last figure by one-third.

CAPITAL. Amsterdam.

LANGUAGE. Dutch. English is widely spoken and understood.

CLIMATE. Moderate, inclined to sudden showers and strong winds. Average maximum daily temperatures in degrees Fahrenheit and centigrade:

Amster-dam	Jan.	Feb.	Mar.	Apr.	May	June	July	Aug.	Sept.	Oct.	Nov.	Dec.
F°	41	41	48	54	61	66	70	70	66	57	48	43
C°	5	5	9	12	16	19	21	21	19	14	9	6

SEASONS. Main tourist season is May through September. Famous bulbfields normally in bloom from early April to mid-May.

SPECIAL EVENTS. *Late March,* opening of annual Keukenhof Flower Exhibition in gardens of a great country estate, Lisse (to mid-May). *April,* Cheese markets, on Thursday at Gouda, Fridays at Alkmaar (through Sept.). *May,* International Tulip Rally. *June,* Annual Holland Festival of concerts, opera and ballet in all major Dutch cities. *July,* About 15 windmills in action every Saturday afternoon at Kinderdijk, near Rotterdam (through Aug.). *September,* opening of Dutch Parliament by the Queen, in golden coach and royal procession in The Hague (3rd Tuesday).

CLOSING TIMES. Shops are open in general from 8:30 or 9 to 17:30 or 18:00 hours weekdays, but close at midday once a week; days vary locally. Do not plan to shop on *Mondays:* department stores and most shops, especially in shopping precincts (Hague, Amsterdam, Rotterdam) do not open till 13:30 hours and many others close on Wednesday afternoons. Late night shopping is usually Thursday, but varies locally.

Banks open from 9 to 16.00 hours, close Saturdays. Only central post offices in the large cities are open on Saturday until noon.

 SPORTS. Holland offers splendid facilities for all forms of water sports. The principal *yachting* centers are the lakes of West Holland, Friesland; the deltas of South Holland, Zeeland. Kagerplassen, Braassemermeer, Westeinder Plas and other lakes are at a convenient distance from Amsterdam. The VVV Offices everywhere can give you useful hints and waterways charts. For renting of cabin cruisers write to National Tourist Office (N.T.B.), Bezuidenhoutseweg 2, The Hague. There are seven 18-hole golf courses in Holland; and try exploring the country on a rented *bicycle;* available at most railway stations (about 4 guilders a day). Special cycle paths make this sport a pleasant experience.

 MONEY. Monetary unit is the guilder. There are about 2.19 guilders to the U.S. dollar, 4.17 to the pound sterling. **Subject to change.** There are 100 cents to the guilder. Guilder is written, "fl.", or "f", standing for florin, which is another name for guilder. But be careful not to mix up the fl.2.50 coin with the fl.1 coin, as the former is only a little bit larger.

You can bring in unlimited amounts of foreign currency and of guilders and take out unlimited quantities of any currency you can (legally) get hold of.

 TIPPING. Hotel prices now include a 15% service charge and the VAT, as do most restaurant checks, and nightclub charges. Tip porters or bellhops fl. 1 per bag or per service, especially if it is personal, while the doorman expects a similar sum for calling a cab. Taxi fares generally include 15% service charge (when indicated on meter), but it is usual to give the driver any small change. Tip for hairdressers and barbers is included in the price. Rail and airport porters get fl. 1 per package. Hatcheck girls expect 25 cents to fl. 1, depending on the type of place and the number in your party. Washroom attendants receive from 25 to 50 cents.

 HOW TO REACH HOLLAND. By KLM and PanAm jet flights from New York or Montreal. By KLM or BA from London to Amsterdam, and by KLM and British Caledonian from London and Southend to Rotterdam; by drive-on/off car ferries from Harwich to Hook of Holland (day and night boats), from Hull to Rotterdam, Immingham to Amsterdam, Sheerness to Vlissingen by the more recent *Olau* Line; Felixstowe to Rotterdam; from Gt. Yarmouth (Norfolk) and Middlesborough to Scheveningen.

By TEE deluxe train from Paris or by train from London (Liverpool St.) via Harwich and Hook of Holland or from London (Victoria) via Dover-Ostend. In addition there are 29 separate TEE (Trans Europe Express) routes to European cities including Milan, Zürich, Nice, Frankfurt and Copenhagen.

CUSTOMS. You probably won't even be asked to open a suitcase. Visitors from overseas are limited to 400 cigarettes or a pound of pipe tobacco or 50 cigars or 100 cigarillos (or a combination of same), and one liter of liquor. Visitors arriving from EEC lands can bring in slightly less than these quantities.

MAIL. A letter to most countries in Europe or seamail to America costs 75 ct for up to 20 grams, from 20–50 grams it costs fl. 1.30, and thereafter on a graded scale. It goes by air within Europe at no extra charge, but airmail letters to countries outside Holland are priced on a complicated zoning system, so it is better to ask at a post office. In the main, letters to the United States and Canada cost fl. 1 for the first 10 grams, and thereafter on a rather complicated scale. Aerograms (folding airletters) obtainable at post offices cost 75 ct. to all countries. Letters within Holland and to some of the Common Market countries cost 55 ct, postcards in Holland and some of the EEC lands 40 ct; elsewhere 50 ct, but these rates are increased periodically, usually every summer, so check. All rates given in Dutch cents.

ELECTRICITY. The standard is 220 volt, 50 cycle, alternating current but a few areas still have 110, so check before plugging in.

DRINKING WATER. Excellent everywhere.

TRAVEL IN HOLLAND. By car: Drive on the right. Cars coming from the right have right of way. When turning left at a crossing, leave the pylon or policemen pedestal to your *right.* Green card showing proof of third party insurance is required. Gasoline (petrol) or, in Dutch, *benzine* costs at least fl.1.06 per liter. Prices are continually being raised but are fixed by the Government. Experienced uniformed mechanics of the *Wegenwacht* patrol the highways in yellow cars to give help in case of emergency.

Car Hire. Renting a self-drive car in Holland is relatively inexpensive. One of the small European or mini cars will cost at least fl. 30 a day in season, no free mileage and fl. 0.25 per kilometer with the renter paying for the fuel. The rates will be proportionately higher for bigger cars. You will be asked to show your domestic driver's license at the time the car is delivered to you and to pay the full rental in advance and additionally fl. 7.50 per day to waive your liability (the first 600 guilders) in case of accident. And the "drop charge" of around fl. 106 will apply, although this charge is sometimes not made if the car is hired for 14 days or longer. All charges are subject to a 16% Government tax, but for foreigners using the car largely outside the Netherlands, only 1.6% Government tax applies.

Avis-Holland (operates in conjunction with KLM), 485 Keizersgracht, Amsterdam. *Tromp Garage N.V.,* Trompstraat 276, The Hague. *Hertz,* Prinsengracht 737, Amsterdam, Schiphol and Rotterdam airports. Godfrey Davis, 51-53 Overtoom, Amsterdam and at Schiphol and Rotterdam airports.

You may arrange when purchasing your KLM plane ticket to have a self-drive or chauffeur-driven car awaiting you at the airport.

By Train. Regular services are operated to all parts of the country with electric and diesel-electric engines. Services are swift, comfortable, and dependable, running at fixed times past the hour from early morning until late at night. Also many inter-city non-stop trains.

Eight-day unlimited travel tickets are sold in Holland or at authorized travel agents and rail offices abroad. A passport photo is necessary for tickets bought in Holland. There are also numerous one-day excursions. Evening return fares are the single fare plus 25 ct. Ask about cheaper family travel by rail.

USEFUL ADDRESSES. *American Embassy* and *U.S. Information Service,* Lange Voorhout 102; *British Embassy,* Lange Voorhout 10; *Canadian Embassy,* Sophialaan 7, all The Hague. *American Consulates,* Museumplein 19, Amsterdam; Vlasmarkt 1, Rotterdam.

American Express, Amsterdam, Damrak; Enschede, Blvd 1945 (nr 7); The Hague, Plaats 14; Rotterdam, Meent 92. *Wagon Lits/Cook,* Amsterdam, Dam 19; The Hague, Buitenhof 46; Rotterdam, Schiedamsevest 56. *Lissone-Lindeman,* in all major cities, is the most efficient and helpful of the Dutch travel agencies, with excellent worldwide connections.

National Tourist Office (N.T.B.), The Hague, Bezuidenhoutseweg 2 (head office). Local information offices (V.V.V.) in all major cities and tourist centers. Their Get in Touch with the Dutch program enables tourists to meet local people of similar interest.

NRC Holland (National Reservation Centre) P.O. Box 3387 Amsterdam. Telephone 020–211211. Telex 15754. Cables RESCENTER AMSTERDAM. This is an organization set up by the Dutch hotel trade, through which you can make bookings in a large number of hotels all over Holland, covering every price range. The reservation service is free.

Amsterdam, Cosmopolitan City

Built on a latticework of concentric canals, Amsterdam is a delightful city, the largest and most cosmopolitan center of the Netherlands. May through September is the best time to come; the peak season, July and August, is apt to be crowded. If you arrive by plane, you'll land at Schiphol Airport, adjacent to the old one, now a freight airport—the two cover over 4,000 acres and lie 13 feet below sea level on land reclaimed from the old Haarlem Lake.

Arriving by train, you'll discover that the Central Station, which stands on an artificial island in the IJ river, is right in the middle of everything.

Once you get settled, your first excursion should be a sight-seeing tour in a glass-roofed canal boat. Several companies run them from piers in front of the Central Station, and alongside the Damrak, along the Rokin and the Stadhouderskade (near the Rijksmuseum). The trip lasts about an hour, during which time a multilingual guide points out and describes the principal sights.

After this introduction to the City of Canals, we suggest you explore on foot—the stately Royal Palace on the Dam Square; the Tower of Tears from which Hendrik Hudson set sail in the *Half Moon* in 1609 to discover New York and the river that bears his name; Rembrandt's house; the fascinating attic church of the Amstelkring Museum; the Begijnhof Almshouse with its memories of the Pilgrim Fathers; and the Mint Tower. Not far away are three other "musts": the Rijksmuseum, the Stedelijk Museum and the Van Gogh Museum, a magnificent trio of art galleries containing many of the world's finest masterpieces.

Those with more time will be rewarded by visits to the Amsterdam Historical and Jewish Historical Museum in a wonderful 15th-century building which was once a town gate and then a guild hall, the Scheepvaartmuseum (Maritime Museum), and the Six Collection, home of Jan Six, who was a friend and patron of Rembrandt. Still in the Six family, the house may be visited by applying to the Rijksmuseum at Stadhouderskade 42, as can the house at Prinsengracht 263, where Anne Frank and her family hid from the Nazis.

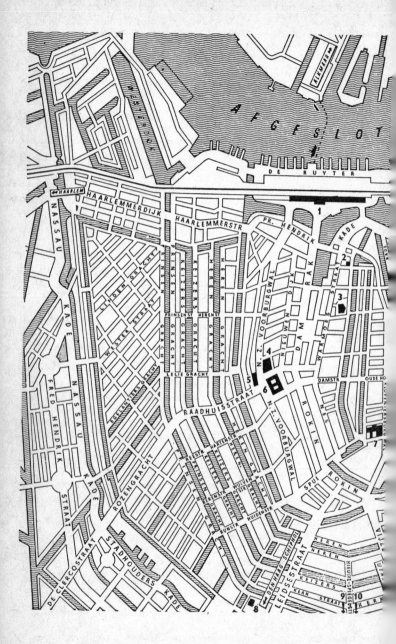

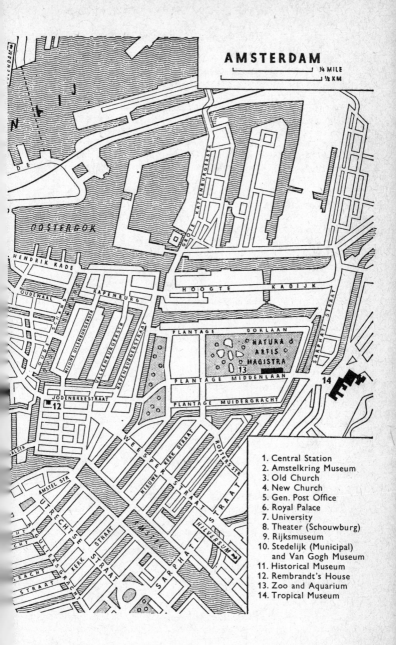

AMSTERDAM

¼ MILE
½ KM

1. Central Station
2. Amstelkring Museum
3. Old Church
4. New Church
5. Gen. Post Office
6. Royal Palace
7. University
8. Theater (Schouwburg)
9. Rijksmuseum
10. Stedelijk (Municipal)
   and Van Gogh Museum
11. Historical Museum
12. Rembrandt's House
13. Zoo and Aquarium
14. Tropical Museum

PRACTICAL INFORMATION FOR AMSTERDAM

 HOTELS. Amsterdam's important hotels lie mainly in the city center, though some of the best are more outlying. During the peak months they fill to bursting point. Thus, if you arrive around Easter or between June and September without a reservation you run the risk of finding all the better hotels fully booked. In an emergency, invoke the aid of the official VVV office, Rokin 5 and near the Central Station. If traveling by tram and bus, buy books of tickets from the GVB ticket office near the Central Station VVV. For a single journey, buy a fl. 1 ticket from the slot machine at the back of the tram, near the yellow machine with which you have to stamp your own ticket. This records the time, as it is possible to use the ticket within three-quarters of an hour on another tram to complete your journey. There are also special day, two-day and three-day tickets.

DELUXE

Amsterdam Hilton, 138 Apollolaan. This is Amsterdam's most luxurious hotel in the modern tradition. 276 rooms with bath or shower. Attractions are the glassed-in floral garden, heated in winter, *The Diamond* restaurant for sophisticated dining, the *Half Moon Bar* and *New Amsterdam Grill.* Not always worth the high charges.

Schiphol Airport Hilton, Schiphol Centrum. 414 beds. 204 rooms with bath or shower.

Amstel, Prof. Tulpplein 1, 105 rooms with bath or shower. Situated on the Amstel River, reputation for solid comfort.

Apollo, Apollolaan 2 (main entrance on Stadionweg). at the junction of five canals, 230 rooms with bath. Fine restaurant, private landing stage.

Okura, 175 Ferd. Bolstraat. 768 beds. All rooms with bath or shower. 22 suites including some Japanese-style rooms, but the Japanese flavor is noticeable in all parts of the hotel. French roof-top restaurant: *Ciel Bleu.*

Pulitzer, Prinsengracht 315-31, in a row of restored medieval houses. 320 beds, each of the 176 rooms in a different style. American-style food.

de l'Europe, Nieuwe Doelenstraat 2–4. 85 rooms with bath. Just opposite the Muntplein with a view of the Amstel.

Amsterdam Marriott, Stadhouderskade 21, 400 rooms, two restaurants, outdoor dining café, series of suites. Within walking distance of city center.

Memphis, 87 de Lairessestraat. 90 rooms with bath or shower; furnished in French style.

FIRST CLASS SUPERIOR

Doelen, Nieuwe Doelenstraat 24, 77 rooms, all with bath. Pleasantly situated, with canal view, but rather old-fashioned.

Ibis Amsterdam (ex-Frommer), 181 Schipholweg. 709 beds, all rooms with bath or shower. Regular shuttle service to the airport. Good conference facilities.

Grand Hotel Krasnapolsky, Dam. 548 beds. 205 double and 49 single rooms with bath, generally attractive. Very central.

Adda-Parkhotel, 25 Stadhouderskade. 350 beds. Most rooms with bath. Close to the Rijksmuseum.

Amsterdam Sonesta, 1 Kattengat, near Central Station. 720 beds, all rooms with bath or shower. Beautifully restored old building.

Alpha, on Europa Blvd., opposite RAI Center. 600 double rooms, especially planned for large tourist groups. Has *Grenadier Pub* and *Falstaff* restaurant.

Amster Center, Herengracht 255, 110 rooms with bath; reconstructed row of patrician houses.

Amsterdam Crest Hotel, de Boelelaan 2, has 260 rooms with bath or shower on 16 floors, also penthouse suites. *Bourgogne* restaurant coffee shop, bar.

Victoria, Damrak. 240 beds, 150 rooms with bath. Opposite Central Station.

American, Leidsekade 97, 184 rooms, all with bath. Next door to the City Theater, a few minutes from the center of town. Nice art nouveau interior.

FIRST CLASS REASONABLE

Caransa, Rembrandtplein 19, 132 beds, 66 rooms with bath or shower.

Sheraton Schiphol Inn, 495 Kruisweg. 252 beds, most rooms with bath or shower. Easy access to the airport.

Centraal, 7 Stadhouderskade, south of Leidsestraat. 120 rooms, 104 with bath.

Die Port van Cleve, Nieuwe Zijds Voorburgwal 178. Already well known as a restaurant (see restaurants), it also has 110 rooms with bath and shower.

Euromotel Amsterdam, Oude Haagseweg 20, on main highway to the Hague and Rotterdam; 210 beds, 80 rooms with shower.

Euromotel E9, Joan Muyskenweg 10, on main highway to Utrecht, 140 rooms, all with shower. On the River Amstel, it has a landing stage and yacht basin.

 RESTAURANTS. Service tends to be formal—be prepared for the spectacle of your waiter in white tie and tails at noon in the most expensive establishments—and unhurried; the Dutch don't believe in rushing at mealtime. If all you want is a light lunch and an opportunity to sit down, try one of the sidewalk cafés, snack bars or "broodjeswinkels," which sell soft buns stuffed with anything you like: smoked eel, eggs, ham, crab, cheese, and other tempting fillers.

Vijf Vlieghen (Five Flies), Spuistraat 294. This is a tourist mecca: you come for the décor, not the food or service, although it has the best of Dutch food. It's located in a steep-gabled building which is classified as a national monument. Expensive.

Dikker en Thijs, Prinsengracht 444. Elegant and formal dining. French cuisine. Its *Café du Centre,* ground floor, is for lunch, snacks or tea. Expensive.

Excelsior, Nieuwe Doelenstraat 2. Located in Hotel de l'Europe, shares its view of the Amstel river. Expensive.

De Boerderij, Korte Leidsedwarsstraat 69. Converted farmhouse. The atmospheric interior and good cooking make this a favorite. Moderately expensive.

Club Gaslight. Beulingstraat 5–9. Something new even in Amsterdam. First-class dining, a choice of bars, and many hide-away corners. Not cheap.

De Prinsenkelder, Prinsengracht 438; old Amsterdam atmosphere.

De Gravenmolen, Lijnbaanssteeg 5. In the capital's old center. Closed Sundays.

Adrian, old Dutch house at Reguliersdwarsstraat 21. French cuisine, good wines. Expensive but worth it.

Het Begijntje, Begijnensteeg 6. A real find off the famous Kalverstraat where the food is as good as the service.

Chalet Suisse, Leidseplein 10a. Noted for its generous helpings of Swiss-Italian fare. Bursting with people. Reasonable.

Flambow Bar and Grill, Keizersgracht 464; small, modern, extremely friendly, excellent for after-theater dining.

Sluizer, Steaks and chops at Utrechtsestraat 45 and sea food, reasonable and excellent value.

Finch's, Amstel 100. Good steaks and chops, but limited menu otherwise.

De Gouden Eeuw, Keizersgracht 402. Lively, with waiters who sometimes sing; an amusing bar.

Dorrius, Nieuwe Zijds Voorburgwal 342. Another businessmen's haunt, where the emphasis is on serious eating. Reasonable and possibly best real Dutch cooking in town. Large. Closed on Sundays.

Molen de Dikkert, Amstelveen. Moderately expensive dinner in old windmill.

Toga, Weteringschans 128. First Japanese establishment of this type in Holland. Attractive, exciting, excellent sukiyaki and tempura menus. Closed on Mondays.

Yamazato Oriental Restaurant, Ferdinand Bolstraat 175. Part of Okura Hotel; possibly the best Japanese restaurant in town; Japanese waitresses in kimono. Also Chinese food.

De Groene Lanteerne (The Green Lantern), Haarlemmerstraat 43. Three floors high but only five feet wide, this is the narrowest restaurant in all Holland and probably in all Europe. Old-Dutch interior. Inexpensive. Waiters in traditional Dutch dress. Closed on Tuesdays.

INDONESIAN AND CHINESE FOOD

Bali, Leidsestraat 95. Fast for a day before you come here! The *saté* is delicious, and so is everything else. Decidedly expensive.

Fong Lie, P. C. Hooftstraat 80. Probably the best Chinese food in the city at attractive prices. Prawn, fish and chicken specialities.

De Orient, Van Baerlestraat 21. Well worth trying for something different. Reasonable. Closed on Wednesdays.

Indonesia, Singel 550, probably the best Indonesian restaurant in town.

Peking, Vijzelsgracht 28, Authentic Chinese rijsttafel.

China, Rokin 20. Good for shark-fin soup and similar unusual Oriental fare. Moderate.

Lotus, Binnenbantammerstraat 5–7. Good quality Chinese and Indonesian menu within walking distance of the central station.

NIGHTLIFE. Amsterdam has a wide variety of nightclubs, bars and cabarets, and now has places even surpassing the "hot spots" of cities like Hamburg, although none have the elegance of Paris. The most bizarre sexy haunts are not over-publicized, but any hotel porter or good barman will supply the information. Apart from these special (and very expensive) "live" shows in the areas around Rembrandtplein, Leidseplein and Thorbeckeplein, there is plenty of respectable though earthy entertainment and near-honkytonk spots, some open until 2 or 4 A.M.; though names or locations, or both, change from year to year.

Except at weekends, very few of the nightclubs make an admission charge, although the more lively ones sometimes ask for a "club membership" fee of 10 guilders or more. Moreover, drinks are normally not exorbitant in price. The following are worth a try:

CASINO, Leidseplein 31. The show starts at midnight and the customers stay until dawn. The most cosmopolitan place in town. Operates on private club basis, bring your passport.

MOULIN ROUGE, Thorbeckeplein 5. Not quite up to Paris standard, but attractive.

LEMAXIM, Leidsekruisstraat 35. Dancing with reasonably good floorshow. Good orchestra.

KING'S CLUB, Korte Leidsedwarsstraat. Cozy, plus discothèque.

BLUE NOTE, Korte Leidsedwarsstraat 71, open till 4 A.M. Popular with both Dutch and tourists—tends to be crowded on most nights. Has a topless girls' band.

FEMINA, Rembrandtplein 44. Brassy, bright and noisy.

LA PORTE d'OR, Rembrandtplein 24. Dancing and floorshow.

BIRD'S CLUB, Rembrandtplein 11. Private, but will admit foreign guests. Lively turns.

SHOPPING. The main department store is the *Bijenkorf,* on Damrak; more elegant is *La Maison de Bonneterie,* at Kalverstraat 183 and Rokin 142. Good shopping areas for all types of goods are Kalverstraat, a long, narrow street (now for pedestrians only) running from beside the Royal Palace south to Spui; Rokin, with several antique shops, and the Leidsestraat.

Diamonds. *Asscher,* Tolstraat 127; *A. van Moppes,* Albert Cuypstraat 2; *Diamant Firma Streep,* Amstel 208. At all, you can visit the workrooms and need not buy. **Jewelry.** *Bonebakker & Zoon,* Rokin 88; *Begeer van Kempen en Vos,* Leidsestraat 79; *Willem J. J. van Pampus,* Kalverstraat 117.

Excursions from Amsterdam

You would miss much of interest if you saw no other part of Holland than the Amsterdam area, but there is no other district which so well merits several days' stay. Within the span of a single day, you can roll the centuries back from Dudok's modern city hall at Hilversum to a 14th-century castle at Muiden, from the cosmopolitan glamour of Zandvoort's North Sea beaches to the dreamy lassitude of Hoorn on the Ijselmeer. If you have money to spend, you would love a visit to the newly opened casino in Zandvoort. You can feast the eye with field after field of flowers, marvel at the wonder of a dike that stretches across open water for 20 miles, or motor across a three-mile-long bridge over a North Sea estuary.

Touring Through the Tulips

Above all, this is the Holland of tulips, hyacinths and daffodils, ablaze with the colors of Easter in the spring. Alas, the time is unpredictable because of the usual unreliability of the weather. In normal years, the first week of May is the best moment to see the famous bulbfields, but an early spring will bring the flowers to their peak as early as April 15. The fabulous Keukenhof Garden, the number one floral attraction of this flower-minded country, opens in late March and can be visited until approximately mid-May. The Linnaeushof Garden at Bennebroek, with flowers of every variety, is open from April to October.

Cheese and Market Towns

If you're looking for local color and folk costumes, you will find Volendam and Marken as colorful and quaint as they've been advertised. In fact, the atmosphere at these famous places is a bit on the self-conscious side at this point. But the popular Friday-morning cheese market at Alkmaar (between April and October), though crowded, is genuine. On your way there, pause at Zaandam, where Russia's Peter the Great studied shipbuilding in disguise. Edam is also a cheese town, but you come here to hear Holland's oldest carillon (1561) and to visit the fascinating captain's house with its floating cellar. From mid-June to the end of August, on Thursday mornings, Gouda has a colorful cheese market with handicraft demonstrations.

Historical Towns

For history, Hoorn and Enkhuizen are musts. Hoorn is an archetypal Dutch renaissance town, unchanged for over 300 years, and as lovely as ever. It is perhaps better than Delft in this respect. And if you like vintage trains (steam engines), you can travel with these to Medemblik, another renaissance town (daily from July to September). Also sleeping for three centuries is Enkhuizen, whose Zuiderzee Museum will fascinate anyone interested in boats, fishing, peasant furniture or regional costumes. The castle of Muiden, east of Amsterdam instead of north, has survived as a national monument and museum.

Land from under Sea

For polders and land reclamation, the 20-mile-long *Afsluitdijk* (enclosing dike) that stretches across what was previously the Zuiderzee is a marvel of imagination, courage, perseverance and skill. To see the kind of dikes built centuries ago, drive along the shore (instead of the highway) between, say, Volendam and Edam or Edam and Hoorn. On the southeast outskirts of Heemstede is a fascinating museum of land reclamation in the Cruquius pumping station, which helped pump out the Haarlemmermeer and form a new polder on which Schiphol Airport was later built. A room-size relief map of the Netherlands is flooded and drained before your eyes in a vivid demonstration of the sea's threat to Holland.

Don't neglect the charming village of Spaarndam (two miles northeast of Haarlem), where a statue has been raised in honor of the legendary lad who plugged the leak in the dike with his finger. Or Haarlem, the city of Frans Hals, with its gallery of his portraits housed in one of the old courtyard houses of his time, some delightful architecture of the Golden Age, the St. Bavo church with its famous organ, and the flower market. Also in Haarlem is one of the oldest "official" museums of Europe: Teylers Museum. It has kept its 18th-century interior and has a fascinating atmosphere.

A fine day's outing is to Flevohof near Harderwijk in the North East Polder. This is a huge Dutch farm showing every facet of agriculture and horticulture in a way specially devised for visitors, supplemented by many surprises and attractions.

A circuit of the IJsselmeer is one of the most interesting trips you can make. Amsterdam, with its car rental and many coach facilities, is a logical starting point for this tour. It's possible to drive around the IJsselmeer in a single day, but we recommend taking two days to do the journey with a little more leisure to enjoy it fully.

AMSTERDAM AREA

 HOTELS AND RESTAURANTS. Because the towns and villages in the above area are easily visited on day excursions, most tourists choose Amsterdam as their base, and hotels in the area tend to be relatively simple, though spotlessly clean. Really good restaurants are also scarce.

ALKMAAR, *Victory* (2), 18 rooms, 10 with bath. *Motel Alkmaar,* Arcadialaan 2, 92 rooms. Restaurant: *Het Wapen van Heemskerk.*

BAARN, In beautiful setting, also not far from the Lage Vuursche woods, pancake house restaurants and tourist attractions. *Kasteel De Hooge Vuursche* (L), 27 rooms, castle hotel. Restaurant: *De Prom.*

BUSSUM, *Jan Tabak,* 31 rooms, tennis and pool nearby.

HILVERSUM, *Het Hof van Holland* (L), 30 rooms; *Hilfertsom* (1), 50 rooms.

HOORN, *Petit Nord* (2), 55 rooms, 13 with bath.

LAREN, *Herberg 't Langenbaergh,* 1 Deventerweg, 10 rooms, 3 with bath.

VREELAND, *Nederlanden* (2), only 9 rooms but is renowned for its *Rôtisserie Napoleon* restaurant.

The Hague and Scheveningen

Contrary to general belief, The Hague is *not* Holland's capital, but it *is* that of South Holland Province. It used to be the royal residence and that is why foreign diplomatic missions, the parliament and government offices are still located here. This also explains your confusion. But The Hague, which the Dutch call Den Haag and write 's-Gravenhage, is always regarded as the seat of government, and retains all the pomp and decorum of a capital city on the third Tuesday in September, when you will see Queen Juliana driven in a golden coach to the 13th-century Ridderzaal or Knights' Hall to open the new session of parliament. Her cortege passes through part of the city, coming and going, in a display of color and ceremony that has no equal on the continent.

This is a good place to be in spring too; the bulbfields are practically around the corner. In June begins The Holland Festival, traditionally filled with concerts, ballet and opera.

Scheveningen used to be a fairly lively year-round suburb of The Hague. But the traditional amenities of the town are undergoing major reconstruction. A casino, new hotels and many recreational facilities are being built. The pier, Holland's only one, remains. The best beaches are at Scheveningen, but mid-summer they do get crowded. The former music season has moved to the Hague.

Sightseeing in The Hague

Top of the list is the Mauritshuis, a collection of Dutch masters in an authentic 17th-century mansion. Vastly smaller than Amsterdam's Rijksmuseum, it is also more intimate. The canvases on display are so uniformly excellent that you can see more beauty in a single hour here than probably anywhere else in Europe. In a different category is the Gemeente Museum, where the emphasis is on modern art, including Piet Mondriaan, not to mention an unusual collection of musical instruments. The Mesdag Museum has some French Impressionists plus a great many Dutch artists of the same period whose names are not generally known abroad.

The Hague's most popular attraction is doubtless the miniature city of Madurodam, open from the end of March to the middle of October, in which have been gathered models of typical buildings, industry and transport from all over Holland on a scale of 1-25th life size, with everything moving that will move.

As for historical buildings, the Ridderzaal or Knights' Hall is easily the oldest. Around it are grouped various government and parliamentary chambers. Nearby is an old town gate, used today to house a torture museum that is guaranteed to send chills down anyone's back. In Paviljoensgracht is the entrance to a charming almshouse, now an old peoples' home, and a statue to the philosopher Spinoza opposite the privately owned house in which he once lived. You can take the opportunity to see The Hague and Delft in one day on the Royal Tour by coach. (Ask local VVV for information.)

HOTELS IN THE HAGUE AND SCHEVENINGEN

DELUXE

Promenade, van Stolkweg 1, The town's top hotel. 210 beds.

Hotel Bel Air, 30 Johan de Wittlaan, adjacent to international Congress Center in Churchilllaan. 700 beds. Specially geared for Congress delegates. Heated swimming pool.

Des Indes, Lange Voorhout 56, 75 rooms, all with bath. Its location makes this the first choice of diplomats. Recently renovated.

Grand Hotel Central, Lange Poten 6, 137 rooms, all with bath. Located in the middle of The Hague near to everything of touristic interest.

Parkhotel de Zalm, Molenstraat 53, 109 rooms, all with bath. In a quiet, narrow street around the corner from Noordeinde antique shops.

Atlantic, 200 Deltaplein. Modern, central, 300 beds, all rooms with bath or shower. Sauna, swimming pool.

FIRST CLASS SUPERIOR

Europa, Zwolsestraat, 300 rooms, most with bath. Close to beach. Moderate restaurant, and underground garage for 60 cars.

Eurotel Scheveningen, Gevers Deynootweg 63, Wide range of rooms, also apartments with kitchenette for 2-5 persons.

Hotel Babylon, Bezuidenhoutseweg, next to the Central Station. 144 rooms, 250 beds, very central.

FIRST CLASS REASONABLE

Badhotel, Gevers Deynootweg 15, 96 rooms with bath or shower. Near Scheveningen beach.

Hoornwijck Motel, on the right side of the highway just before you reach The Hague, coming north from Delft and Rotterdam, 82 rooms with bath or shower. Breakfast not included. Snackbar and restaurant make this a popular call point.

MODERATE

Zeehotel, Harteveltstraat 6, 12 rooms with bath. Reasonable.

Corona, Buitenhof 41, recently renovated. Overlooks The Hague's central square. Old Dutch café downstairs.

Bianca, Gravestraat 1, Wassenaar, 13 rooms, 10 with bath, reasonable.

Alba, Gevers Deynootplein. 23 rooms. Close to sea.

Bali, Badhuisweg 1, 34 rooms, joined to the famous Indonesian restaurant.

Harrison's, Spuistraat 16, 65 rooms, 13 with bath, central.

RESTAURANTS

Royal, Lange Voorhout 44. On embassy row, therefore very formal. The best French cooking in town. Very expensive if you lose your head over the à la carte.

House of Lords, Hofstraat 4. Same building as Grand Hotel Central. Also formal, also tops, also expensive, but the gypsy fiddlers will help console you when the bill is presented.

Saur, Lange Voorhout 51. Seafood is the specialty here, though the steaks are excellent, too. Edwardian, formal and expensive.

De Kieviet, in Wassenaar, favorite meeting place of resident Americans. Very good food, served in the garden in summer. Member of the Alliance Gastronomique Néerlandaise. Really expensive.

1001 Nachten, Begijnestraat 24. Middle Eastern specialties to gypsy music.

Meer en Bosch, Heliotrooplaan 5 (top end of Laan van Meerdervoort), converted old farmhouse in wooded surroundings. Cozy bar, good food. Closed Monday and Tuesday.

Seinpost, Zeekant 14, overlooking Scheveningen Promenade. Most attractive for lunch or dinner. Reserve in advance for a window seat. Has a good snack bar, grill and pub around the corner.

Ducdalf, Dr. Lelykade 5, Scheveningen. Fish-restaurant, first-class for really fine fish delectably cooked and served.

Chalet Suisse, Noordeinde 123. One of the few places in town where there are waitresses instead of waiters. Reasonable. A branch in this small chain has opened in Pander Passage shopping center.

Table du Roi: in den kleynen Leckerbeck, Prinsestraat 130. Tiny, intimate. Generous portions, expensive. Lots of local atmosphere.

't Goude Hooft, Groenmarkt 13. Large edifice near Grote Kerk. Old Dutch atmosphere. Reasonable.

Bistroquet, Lange Voorhout 98. Exclusive, expensive, very good.

The Copper Kettle under Hotel Des Indes, Lange Voorhout 54. Attractive food in unusual atmosphere, moderately priced.

Onder 't Oude Raedthuys, Groenmarkt, in the cellars of the centuries-old Town Hall. This has its own atmosphere.

Boerderij de Hoogwerf, Zijdelaan 20. A converted 17th-century farmhouse, on the border of The Hague and Wassenaar. Dutch food. Reasonable.

Pier, Scheveningen. Unusual circular restaurant right over the sea. Reasonable.

INDONESIAN AND CHINESE CUISINE

Kota Radja, Plaats 16a. The best place in town for *rijsttafel* or *nasi goreng*. Upstairs, practically next door to American Express.

Garoeda, Kneuterdijk 18a. Also central and a favorite, thus popular with tourists and businessmen, and also for morning coffee.

Verre Oosten, Badhuisweg 2, Scheveningen. Real Oriental food, and even a Japanese meal on order.

Bali, Badhuisweg 1. At Scheveningen; take your time here to enjoy a memorable and gigantic Indonesian meal. Expensive.

SHOPPING. The main department stores are *La Maison de Bonneterie,* the *Bijenkorf* and *Vroom & Dreesmann.* The Hoogstraat-Plaats-Noordeinde complex is now an attractive shopping precinct without traffic, as is the Spuistraat area. Within these areas there is a comprehensive selection of goods, with antique shops concentrated on Noordeinde and the Denneweg.

Highlights of South Holland

Rotterdam, 14 miles from The Hague, all but wiped off the map in a savage Nazi saturation air raid on May 14, 1940, has risen again as a new city of steel and gleaming glass. Taking full advantage of its strategic position on the delta of the Rijn (Rhine) and the Maas (Meuse), its rapid growth has made it the chief seaport of Europe and it is now the largest in the world. Take one of the regular sightseeing tours of the city, a harbor tour from the Spido Pontoon, or visit the 600-foot Euromast with spacetower, restaurant and ship's bridge.

PRACTICAL INFORMATION FOR ROTTERDAM

HOTELS. Several of Rotterdam's best hotels are conveniently located near the railway station and the shopping center. Most are of recent vintage, as is the city itself. All have restaurants open to the public.

Rotterdam Hilton (L), 10 Weena, 487 beds, all rooms with bath, convertible into two or three-unit suites, several restaurants (*Moby Dick* is best), discothèque.

All (1) are: *Atlanta,* Aertvan Nesstraat 4, 175 rooms with bath or shower; *Parkhotel,* Westersingel 68–70, 96 rooms with bath, prewar but comfortable, pleasant terraces; *Central,* Kruiskade 12, 70 rooms with bath, moderate prices; *Rijnhotel Rotterdam,* Schouwburgplein 1, 140 rooms with bath or shower, good restaurant, snackbar, sauna; *Savoy,* Hoogstraat 81, 100 rooms with bath or shower, reasonable rates; *Euromotel Rotterdam,* Vliegveldweg 61, 100 sound-proofed rooms with bath.

At Vlaardingen, 8 miles from Rotterdam, the unique *Delta Hotel* overhangs the river Maas, its restaurant with fine river view, 24 rooms with bath.

RESTAURANTS. Best are the *Old Dutch,* Rochussenstraat 20, a member of the Alliance Gastronomique Néerlandaise, and *Coq d'Or,* Vollenhovenstraat 25, which has snacks on the ground floor, candlelight dining upstairs. Both expensive. *Chalet Suisse,* Kievitslaan, is also good. Also, *In Den Rust Wat,* Honingerdijk 96, a charming old-style cottage, *Moby Dick,* Meent 81, for seafood, *Falstaff,* Schouwburgplein 1, and the *Van Creveld Steakhouse,* at No. 27.

The *Euromast's* snackbar near the top is fair, the grill excellent though expensive.

Kota Radja, Mathenesserplein 31, is the place for Indonesian dishes. Reasonable.

NIGHTCLUBS. There are four reasonable nightclubs: *The Embassy,* Schiedamsesingel, *Casino de Paris,* Het Park, *La Bonanza,* van Speyckstraat, and *El-Amra,* Hartmanstraat. All have a large dance floor, good music, and cabaret.

 MUSEUMS. *Boymans-Van Beuningen,* Mathenesserlaan 18, Dutch painters, also modern section. Sculptures. *Historisch Museum,* Korte Hoogstraat 31, exhibits pertaining to the development of Rotterdam. *Maritiem Museum,* Burgemeester's Jacobplein 8, fine collection of ship models, atlases, globes, etc.

SHOPPING. You will enjoy shopping in the ultra-modern Lijnbaan, a shopping center from which all traffic is excluded. Many of the names will be old acquaintances from Amsterdam and The Hague. For new names around this area: *Het Huis van St. Eloy,* Lijnbaan 69, displays superb gold bracelets and twisted pins. *Jungerhans,* Binnenweg 3-5, offers a wide range of Dutch and imported porcelain and crystal.

Delft, Ancient Royal Seat

Delft, world famous for its china, is a lovely old town whose tree-lined canals and step-gabled houses preserve the atmosphere of the 16th and 17th centuries as well as any other city in the country. See the New Church, dating from 1383, housing the burial vaults of the Dutch royal family and the monument to William the Silent, the national hero who defied the Spanish and began the unification of the Netherlands under the aegis of the House of Orange. Visit the venerable Prinsenhof (now a museum), where he lived and was assassinated. The Tetar van Elven Museum preserves an artist's studio from the time of two great painters of Delft, Vermeer and Pieter de Hoogh.

DELFT HOTELS. Best is the *Wilhelmina* (2), 28 rooms, 25 with bath, comfortable. Good restaurant. *Juliana,* 21 rooms, 16 with bath or shower, moderate.

SHOPPING. A highly instructive visit is the one to the showrooms of the *Porceleyne Fles,* where you will see exquisite museum pieces as well as demonstrations with the potter's wheel, the oven, and the brush. Look out for phoney Delftware. The genuine article always has a triple signature: a plump vase topped by a straight line, the stylized letter F below it, and the word Delft.

Delft has some fine curio shops, all clustered around the charming Prinsenhof.

If you are a real antique lover, try to plan your excursion to Delft to coincide with the annual Antique Dealers' Fair, a summer date which should be checked with any Dutch Tourist Office.

Leiden and Gouda

Leiden, site of one of Europe's greatest universities, founded by William the Silent in 1575, was also the birthplace of Rembrandt. New Englanders are fond of making a pilgrimage here to the Pieterskerk, church of the Pilgrim Fathers, who lived and worshipped here for 10 years before setting sail for America in 1620.

From Leiden, it's only a few miles' drive to the smart seaside resort of Noordwijk. This is comparatively quiet, even in high season, and you can swim in a heated seawater pool or play a game of golf on the dunes.

Gouda is justly famous for its Thursday cheese market and should be more so because of its superb 15th-century Town Hall and the wonderful stained glass in the Sint Janskerk. Nearby on the Lek River is the quiet village of Schoonhoven, a silver center, and Kinderdijk, which has a greater concentration of windmills than any other town in the world. At Oudewater you can be weighed to discover whether you are a witch, and be presented with a certificate, if found innocent.

HOTELS AND RESTAURANTS

GOUDA. *De Zalm,* (2) 34 Markt, has 52 beds, 12 rooms with bath.

LEIDEN. In town, the *Nieuw Minerva,* 77 rooms with bath. On the Amsterdam-Hague highway, *Holiday Inn,* 185 rooms with bath; restaurant, bar, pool. Both(1).
Restaurants: *Oudt Leyden,* Steenstraat 51, member of the Alliance Gastronomique Néerlandaise. Expensive. *'t Karrewiel,* Steenstraat 55, reasonable.

NOORDWIJK. Despite closings, there are still many good hotels. Among the best are: the huge *Grand Hotel Huis ter Duin,* 5–6 Koningin Astrid Boulevard with 166 beds, all rooms with bath or shower, recently reopened, more comfortable than ever; the *Palace, De Baak,* and *Noordzee,* all (1). The *Belvedere, Zeeleeuw, Zee en Duin, Clarenwyck* and *Zinger,* are all (2).

OEGSTGEEST, just outside Leiden. The gastronomic restaurant *De Beukenhof,* a handsome inn.

SASSENHEIM, in the heart of the bulb area, now has a fine motel, 85 beds.

Utrecht

Utrecht, capital of the province bearing its name, is noted for its great variety of industrial fairs, important throughout Europe. Climb the 465 steps to the top of the Dom Tower, which stands apart from the church, part of which was destroyed by a great storm in 1674. The view over the countryside is superb, especially in April and May when the apple, cherry and pear trees are at their peak. Best place to hear the seven chiming bells of 1506 and the famous 48-bell carillon of 1663 is in the cloister between the new cathedral and university. Utrecht has enough curiosities and antiquities to warrant an overnight stop. There are the Dutch Gold, Silver and Clock Museum, a very interesting University Museum and the Netherlands Railway Museum with a superb collection of original engines and carriages. The little town of Amersfoort is worth a visit (10 miles from Utrecht) as it has kept most of its medieval houses and town-walls. The important castles of De Haar and Zuilen are nearby.

Zeeland and North Brabant

Vlissingen, which we call Flushing, is the largest city in Zeeland, that southwestern province of Holland that looks like three fingers pointing westward toward the North Sea. It is an attractive seaside resort. But the showplace of Zeeland is Middelburg, a few miles north of Flushing; also the ancient seaport of Veere. The Roosevelt's family roots are at Oud-Vossemeer on Tholen, one of the smaller islands of Zeeland.

Don't miss the Delta project which is linking all the islands with the mainland by dams and bridges. There is already a faster connection from the north over the two new road toll bridges—the Haringvliet Bridge and the Oosterschelde Bridge, the latter being more than three miles in length and the longest in Europe. Ask at any VVV for details of interesting road and boat trips to the Delta Works, with a guide to explain all about it.

's Hertogenbosch (Bois-le-Duc), the capital of North Brabant, 49 miles southeast of Rotterdam, is distinguished for its magnificent Gothic cathedral of St. John, a masterpiece of 15th-century flamboyant style. Buy the souvenir booklet with detailed reproductions of the extraordinary carvings. Hieronymus Bosch, that fantastic painter of medieval nightmares, was born here in 1450, took his name from the town, and is honored by having his statue in the market square. In the neighborhood of 's-Hertogenbosch lies the little village of Drunen, where you will find Lips Autotron, home of 400 vintage cars and motorcycles. In Oisterwijk, near Tilburg, you can meet Snow White and the Seven Dwarfs or peep into Sleeping Beauty's castle in the large fairy-tale park De Efteling.

At Eindhoven, you must see the Evoluon, a permanent exhibition showing what science has done and can do for man. Ultramodern building, with many surprises and do-it-yourself ideas.

HOTELS AND RESTAURANTS

EINDHOVEN, *Holiday Inn,* 215 rooms. *Grand Hotel de Cocagne,* 47 Vestdijk, 300 beds, all rooms with bath or shower, both (L). *Eindhoven Motel,* 300 beds, 100 rooms with shower.

's-HERTOGENBOSCH. *Eurohotel* (2), new, 27 rooms with bath. Restaurant: *Chalet Royal,* provides some of the finest cooking in Holland. Expensive.

MIDDELBURG. *De Nieuwe Doelen* (2), 3–7 Loskade, 55 beds, 17 rooms with bath or shower.

UTRECHT. *Des Pays-Bas,* 10 Janskerkhof, 75 beds, some rooms with bath. *Smits* (2), 36 rooms with bath. On the Utrecht-Arnhem highway, *Motel Bunnik* and *Motel Maarsbergen. Holiday Inn* (1), adjacent to Industries Fair complex, 20 stories, 430 beds, ultramodern. *Hes,* 2–4 Maliestraat, (1) 40 beds, all rooms with bath or shower.

VEERE. *De Campveerse Toren* (2), in medieval powder magazine at entrance to harbor. Only 8 rooms, good restaurant.

VLISSINGEN. *Grand Hotel Brittannia* (1), 105 rooms with bath, modern.

Gelderland—Ancient and Modern

Arnhem, provincial capital of Gelderland, has a wonderful 75-acre open-air museum, with farms, windmills, thatched cottages, medieval crafts, costumes, etc. Nearby in the Hoge Veluwe National Park is the Kröller-Müller Museum at Otterlo, one of the major art collections of the Netherlands. There are many paintings by Van Gogh making it one of the most important collections of his works anywhere.

Nijmegen, second city of Gelderland, was an imperial city of the Hanseatic Empire and a favorite residence of Charlemagne. See the 18-sided chapel in the Valkhof or Falcon's Court, all that remains of his palace. Take the bus to Berg en Dal, from whose 350-foot summit (high for Holland) you'll have a splendid view over the Waal into Germany.

Apeldoorn is another "must" because it is now a lovely garden city, so beautiful that the late Queen Wilhelmina, upon her abdication in 1948, chose its 17th-century Palace of Het Loo in which to retire. Part of the palace has now been turned into a unique historic vehicles museum.

Wageningen, 11 miles west of Arnhem, is the seat of Holland's great agricultural university and arboretum.

Overijsel, Groningen and Friesland

Giethoorn, 24 miles north of Zwolle in the northeastern province of Overijsel, is the quaintest village in Holland. It has no streets, only canals. Every house is like a tiny hermitage set amidst trees, reached only by its own high-arched bridge or along its own off-shooting stream. A motorboat or punt will take you on a tour of the village from the main canal.

Groningen, capital of Groningen province and seat of a famous university, is considered one of the finest cities of the Netherlands from the architectural point of view. The shrine of St. Martin, patron saint of all tourists, is the 15th-century St. Martin's church. Friesland, "the water province", is next door. Stay at the quiet capital, Leeuwarden, and from there fan out to the maze of lakes which make it a water sports paradise. The area is also full of quaint old farms and villages. At Hindelopen you can watch skilled art craftsmen painting traditional designs on wooden furniture and household articles.

Limburg Province

Maastricht (known from Roman times) and, eight miles east, medieval Valkenburg, in the southern "tongue" of Limburg Province, offer a historic galaxy of romantic castle ruins, ancient buildings, Gothic churches, catacombs and caves of unknown antiquity. There is also a unique underground coal-mine which can be visited. If you stay at Hotel Prinses Juliana in Valkenburg, in the heart of the 1,000-foot-high Dutch Alps, you'll eat some of the finest food in the whole of Holland, as well as being able to make a trip touching France, Germany, Belgium and Luxembourg—thus having visited five countries in a single day!

HOTELS AND RESTAURANTS

APELDOORN. *De Keizerskroon* 7 Koningstraat, (1), 24 rooms, half with bath. Belongs to the royal family. *Motel Apeldoorn* (3), 32 units with bath. Restaurant: *De Echoput,* a gastronomic establishment.

ARNHEM. *Rijnhotel* (1) on the river, 26 rooms, all with bath. The large *Haarhuis,* facing the rail station, and *Groot Warnsborn* are (1). All have good restaurants. *The Postiljon Motel,* Europaweg 25, 38 beds, recommended.

BORN. *Crest Hotel Born* (1), Julianaweg 6, 49 rooms with bath or shower.

ENSCHEDE. *Parkhotel,* 18 rooms, 6 with bath.

GIETHOORN. *Prinsen-Beulakerwiede* (3), 16 rooms.

GRONINGEN. *Helvetia* (2), 30 rooms with bath, cozy and comfortable; *De Doelen* (1), 39 rooms; *Clingendael Motel* (2), on E43 highway, 114 beds.

HAREN. near Groningen. *Postiljon Motel,* 57 rooms, all with bath.

HEERLEN. Limburg. *Grand Hotel* (2), 80 beds, very comfortable.

LEEUWARDEN. *Oranje* (1), 86 rooms, 34 with bath. *De Kroon,* 21 rooms, 8 with bath, is noted for good food and service, while the *Euro-Hotel* has 62 rooms. Both (2).

MAASTRICHT. *Du Casque* (1), 46 rooms, most with bath. *Hotel Maastricht* (1) on the Meuse Bank, 112 rooms with bath, fine view of river Meuse.

NIJMEGEN. *Esplanade* (2), 30 rooms, 9 with bath; own Indonesian restaurant. Three miles southeast, at Berg en Dal, *Parkhotel Val Monte* (L), with sports facilities in a real country atmosphere. *Schaeferhotel* (1), 39 Grote Markt, 33 beds, all rooms with bath or shower.

VALKENBURG. *Prinses Juliana* (1), 45 rooms, 35 with bath or shower, one of the best restaurants in Holland.

HUNGARY

The Hungarian People's Republic is a small mostly flat land almost entirely surrounded by mountains. One of the country's most striking features is the Great Plain (Nagyalföld) stretching east from the Danube to the foothills of the Carpathians in the Soviet Union, to the mountains of Transylvania in Romania, and south to the Fruska Gora range in Yugoslavia. Traversed by the River Tisza, it is a vast granary and the historic habitat of Hungary's great horsemen, still visible cracking their long whips and driving their herds across the landscape of the Hortobágy, a corner of the Great Plain equally famous for the mirages that develop over its horizons on hot summer days.

Lake Balaton, the largest unbroken stretch of inland water in Europe, offers splendid summertime facilities, while the beauty of the Danube near Esztergom, the gaiety of the capital Budapest, superb cuisine and good wines, and the hospitality of the people can be enjoyed the year round. Roughly the size of Ireland or Indiana (35,919 square miles), Hungary's yearly visitors almost equal its population of 10.5 million.

Budapest is the largest and brightest of all Communist capitals with smart (and sometimes privately owned) shops and a way of life that is the envy of neighboring nations. Restaurants and cafés stay open late into the night serving excellent pastries and strong coffee to a clientele that loves gossip, political satire and style in all things.

A Bit of History

A thousand years ago, a fiery nomad chieftain named Árpád led his warlike Magyar tribes from the region of the river Dnieper into the flat fertile Danube plain. The Magyars, unlike their Slav neighbors, were fighters, not farmers, and sent out raiding parties into Germany, Italy and as far as southern France. All Europe trembled before these "Asiatic hordes". A later chieftain, Stephen (who became Hungary's patron saint) was converted to Christianity and the reformed ogres became stout sentinels of Christian Europe. From the 17th century Hungary was a Hapsburg vassal state, despite all efforts by the national hero Prince Rákóczy, until World War I.

After a brief communist regime under Béla Kún in 1919 the country was governed for twenty-five years by Nicolas Horthy as a kingdom without a king. In 1947 the communists took over, but with a regime unswervingly loyal to Moscow, Hungary has nevertheless developed the most liberal atmosphere within the Soviet orbit.

The October 1956 revolt taught the leadership the limits of oppression which the traditionally volatile Magyars will tolerate, and János Kádár, imposed as party leader by the Russians, began in a few years a policy of national reconciliation that has lasted ever since. It has included giving culture and the media a quite unusual degree of freedom to discuss touchy topics or provide sheer entertainment. The country's economic reforms have been the most comprehensive and most successful in Eastern Europe in doing away with over-centralization, freeing initiative and providing the goods which consumers want.

Food and Drink

One of the few original cuisines in Europe, Hungarian cooking is too often identified with paprika only. True, dishes flavored with this piquant spice are ubiquitous. But roasts, vegetables and desserts are often superb, too.

Paprika dishes come in a great variety—from mild to burning hot. Incidentally, the six "basic" dishes are called *gulyás* (a soup with cubed beef or pork and diced potatoes, spiced with sweet red paprika). The *pörkölt* (outside Hungary called goulash) can be made from veal, pork, beef or chicken; it's a stew in which onions play a bigger role; *paprikás* (sauce of onions, sour cream and red pepper) used for fish and poultry dishes; *tokány* (stew with black pepper flavoring); *rostélyos* (round steak potted in paprika sauce), and *halászlé* (fish soup—Hungary's answer to *bouillabaisse*).

In the dessert department, Hungary's classic is *rétes* (strudel to you). Crisp and flaky it comes filled with cherries, apple, nuts, almonds, poppy-seed or cottage cheese and, believe it or not, peppered cabbage (eaten as a savory).

Wine-tasting is a prime tourist activity. Vintners and wine co-operatives welcome visitors to their cellars for sampling and discussion. Budafok, on the southern outskirts of Budapest, is a town of wine-cellars with miles of passages tunneling into the hillside. One of its casks, built in 1850, held nearly 26,500 gallons.

Tokay wine comes from the hillside of Tokaj, in northeastern Hungary. The most famous variety is the *Tokaj Aszu,* a sweet syrupy nectar. *Szamorodni* is a much drier wine of the same vintage.

Fine wines also come from the volcanic slopes on the northern shore of Lake Balaton and the hillsides near Pécs. Don't leave Hungary without tasting "bull's blood" *(bikavér)* from the sunny region of Eger. Apricot brandy, *barack,* (pronounced "borotsk") has been distilled for centuries on the great plain between the Danube and Tisza rivers, particularly in the city of Kecskemét. Other fruit brandies are plum brandy *(szilvapálinka)* and cherry brandy *(cseresznyepálinka).*

PRACTICAL INFORMATION FOR HUNGARY

13.06
5.34
24.00
42.30

WHAT WILL IT COST. Traveling as an individual, your stay in Hungary will cost between $12.50 and $80 (£7 and £35) per day for hotel accommodation and breakfast, without main meals. These will add another $15 (£8) per day, on average. As a member of a group, budget for about $10 (£6) up, for bed and breakfast only.

Hotel accommodation is classified as deluxe (L), A-1 first class superior (1), A-2 first class reasonable (2), B moderate (3), C inexpensive (4). Motels or touring hotels are (4). Accommodation in private houses is available in Budapest and major resorts and is inexpensive. There are 60 campsites, two in Budapest, others near cities and resorts. Wooden chalets can be rented at Lake Balaton for reasonable rates.

Meals in restaurants range in price from less than 60 forints to as much, at the more famous establishments, as 400 forints.

A bottle of wine costs 30 to 50 forints; a carafe, 14 forints; best theater or concert tickets 80 forints.

A typical moderate day
(A-2 hotel and moderate restaurant)

	forints
hotel (room with bath)	350
lunch	60
dinner	90
transport by taxi	40
" by bus	6
theater ticket	50
one coffee	10
one beer	20
miscellaneous	60
total	686

For a room *without* bath reckon at least 100 forints *less*

CLIMATE. The four seasons, but very hot in July and August.
Average maximum daily temperatures in degrees Fahrenheit and centigrade:

Budapest	Jan.	Feb.	Mar.	Apr.	May	June	July	Aug.	Sept.	Oct.	Nov.	Dec.
F°	34	39	50	63	72	79	82	81	73	61	46	39
C°	1	4	10	17	22	26	28	27	23	16	8	4

SPECIAL EVENTS. *February,* Budapest: Gypsy Festival. *March,* Budapest: Spring Festival Week. *May,* Budapest: Int'l. Trade Fair. *May-June,* Miskolc: Film Festival. *July,* Debrecen: Bartok Choral Festival; Veszprém: Chamber Music Festival; Szeged: Open-air Drama Festival; Siofok: Film Week. *August,* Keszthely: Ethnic Folk Festival; Debrecen: National Flower Festival; Bekescaba: Summer Music Festival; Kiskunság region: Horse Show. *September,* Budapest: Art Weeks, including Liszt and Bartok International Piano Competition, and Autumn Trade Fair. *October,* Aggtelek: Limestone Cave Concerts.

$P£ **MONEY.** You may bring in any amount and kind of foreign currency including travelers checks, and freely exchange it at all Ibusz offices, rail and air terminals, banks and railway dining cars. The import and export of Hungarian currency is *not* permitted beyond the sum of 400 forints.

Monetary unit is the *forint,* divided into 100 *fillér.* There are coins of 5, 10, 20 and 50 fillérs and 1, 2, 5 and 10 forints; bank notes circulate in denominations of 20, 50, 100 and 500 forints. The exchange rate is about 20 forints to the US $, 36 forints to the pound sterling, but **check before changing.**

Hotel prices (in forints)			
Category	*Budapest*	*Balaton*	*Provinces*
Deluxe			
double	1400*		
First-class (A-1)			
double with bath	700–1000	600**	450
Second-class			
double without bath	400–500	550–700**	400
Moderate			
double without bath	300	450–500**	250

*Breakfast and service charge *not* included
**Full board

Private accommodations can be obtained at from 150 forints per person per night; breakfast is not included.

TIPPING. Tips are generally expected, in addition to any service charge. Hotel porters, waiters and barber shops should be given around 10 percent. Taxi drivers receive 15 to 20 percent of the fare.

HOW TO REACH HUNGARY. By Air: From New York by *Pan Am* twice weekly, from London by *BA* and *Malev, Hungarian Airlines,* and from European capitals by most airlines.

By Train: Budapest can be reached directly from Paris and Munich by the *Orient Express* and from Zurich by the *Wiener Walzer.* Passengers from London and Brussels by the *Ostend-Vienna Express* change at Vienna West; the Budapest train awaits them on the other side of the platform.

By Car: Budapest is on routes E5 from Germany and Austria to Yugoslavia, E15 from Czechoslovakia to Romania and the Black Sea, and E96 to Yugoslavia and the Adriatic. Motorists require an international driving license and green international insurance card. Visas are issued at border crossings.

By Bus: Scheduled services on comfortable coaches from many European cities. Contact *Europabus* offices.

By the Danube: A hydrofoil service runs from May 1-August 30 daily except Sunday, Vienna-Budapest and return. Travel time about 4 hours one way. Danube cruises from Vienna to the Black Sea call at Budapest.

HOW TO GO. Foreign tourist travel to Hungary is handled by *Ibusz,* the national tourist bureau, 5 Felszabadulás tér, Budapest V. *Ibusz* represents the best hotels in Hungary, runs everything for tourists and has branch offices in major hotels and the more important cities throughout Hungary. In most Western countries, Ibusz is represented by accredited travel agents who take care of all arrangements, including visa, hotel accommodation and payment. Below is a partial list.

The *Hungarian Equestrian Federation* in conjunction with Ibusz offers riding tours. A 10-day tour for skilled riders starts at £315; horseback holidays at studfarms and riding clubs start at £6.70 per day, with accommodation and tuition.

In the United States:

American Express Co., 65 Broadway, New York, N.Y. 10006.
American Travel Abroad, 250 W. 57th St., New York 10019.
General Tours, 49 West 57th St., New York, N.Y. 10019
Maupintour, 900 Massachusetts St., Lawrence, Kansas 66044
Travelworld, 6922 Hollywood Blvd., Los Angeles, Calif. 90028.
March Shipping Services, 1 World Trade Center, Suite 5257, New York, N.Y. 10047 (Multi-country Danube cruises).

In Great Britain:

Danube Travel Ltd. 6 Conduit Street, London WIR 9TG.
Thos Cook Ltd., 45 Berkeley St., London W1.
Hungarian Travel Service, 10 Vigo Street, London W1.
Peltours, 72 Wigmore St., London W1H 0DD.
Wakefield Fortune, 176 Tottenham Court Road., London W1P 0DE (spa holidays).

TRAVEL DOCUMENTS. A valid passport and visa are required. Visas are issued at airports and road border points but not on trains. To save time, it's advisable to get a visa beforehand from a Hungarian embassy or Ibusz representative; three photographs and application forms are necessary for visits up to 30 days. Visa fees are $6.00, or £3.

Campers must have an int'l. membership carnet before arrival to qualify for reduced rate vouchers. There are also special rates for visiting relatives; check with a travel agent.

CUSTOMS. Personal belongings and 250 cigarettes, one liter of spirits and two liters of wine may be brought in duty-free. Items to a total value of 1,000 forints may be taken out of Hungary without a license, though this excludes certain antiques and precious metal objects, other than art objects purchased at Inter-Tourist shops. Keep receipts for any purchases you may have made.

DRINKING WATER. Safe in all main towns.

PHOTOGRAPHY. Do not photograph military installations or railways.

TRAVEL IN HUNGARY. Train, Bus and River transport are well developed throughout the country. Interlocal buses run by *Volán* mark the bus stops with this name. **By Car:** Cars drive on the right; Continental rules of the road observed, plus right turn permitted in front of red light. City transport has priority. Speed limits are 60 kph in town, 100 kph on main roads and 120 kph on highways. The state roads are identified by a one-digit number: thus Highway No. 1 runs from Budapest toward Vienna; highways 2-7 radiate out from Budapest, in a clockwise direction. An excellent road map showing camp sites is available through Ibusz.

Gasoline (petrol) is obtainable in three grades. Extra (98 oct.) costs about 9 fts. per liter, super (92 oct.) 7.20 fts., and normal (86 oct.) 5.40 fts. per liter; these prices are subject to increase.

Car Hire. Cars can be hired through Ibusz offices and hotels with prepaid vouchers, otherwise a deposit of about $100 is required. *Avis* is at the airport and Martinelli Ter 8, Budapest.

Budapest

The city is divided by the Danube into two sections: Buda and Pest. Buda dominates the scene with its many rounded hills and bluffs rising from the curved arms of the Danube. Pest is east of the river, flat, commercial and almost entirely rebuilt since the forties. The lovely Margaret Island (Margitsziget) is a 112-acre park. Budapest has 526 parks and green spots, totalling some 1500 acres. It has a wonderful zoo, 123 mineral hot springs, Roman ruins, a 100,000-fan sports stadium, and the second subway (Metro) in the world (after London), in 1897.

For a first, wonderful look at Budapest, go to the Buda side, climb the Gellérthegy from Gellért Square, and see the panorama of all the Danube bridges, Parliament and Pest to the south, Buda Castle and the blue mountains to the north.

Gellért Hill is crowned by a stone fort built in 1851, and topped by a towering memorial to the liberation of Budapest by Soviet troops in 1944-45. During the 14-week winter siege, 33,000 buildings were totally destroyed, and every bridge between Buda and Pest demolished. Restoration work was not completed until the late sixties.

Two other hillocks rise up from the Danube on the Buda side—Castle Hill (Várhegy) and the Hill of Roses (Rózsadomb). Behind these scenic summits curves a range of higher hills, of which the loftiest is the conical Jánoshegy, 1,435 feet in height, and topped by a lookout tower. The hills are easily reached from Buda by a cogwheel railway (terminus at Városmajor). In summer the chair lift runs to János Hill from the Zugligeti Ut.

Before leaving the Buda side, ramble around Castle Hill (Várhegy) with its many Gothic landmarks. This oldest section of the city suffered the most damage during the Second World War. Bombardments destroyed a great deal of Renaissance and baroque architecture, revealing many older walls and arches, some medieval. The postwar governments rebuilt much of the district following its original town plan. The rebuilt former Royal Palace, now a museum and cultural center, covers the southern end of Castle Hill; it is here that the Holy Crown of St. Stephen and the other historic Hungarian regalia, recently returned to Hungary by the United States Government, are on display. Farther north is the

Fisherman's Bastion, a round Romanesque lookout tower and wall built in the last century. Close to the Bastion stands the 13th-century Coronation Church.

By the time your stroll has brought you to No. 7 Szentháromság Utca you'll feel like walking right in. This address belongs to Ruszwurm Café, Hungary's oldest pastry and tea shop. The building was already ancient by 1500 when it became a bakery, and is still very much in business.

Leaving the Várhegy, stroll or drive north along Buda's main street, Föutca, lined with unusual buildings of varied architecture.

A few hundred yards away is one of the city's beauty spots, the tomb of Gül-Baba, a 16th-century Turkish poet.

Margaret Island and Pest

Back on the embankment, a few steps beyond Bem József Tér, you come to the Margit Híd (Margaret Bridge) which connects Buda and Pest with lovely boat-shaped Margaret Island, or Margitsziget. Seven centuries have passed since a young princess named Margaret retired to a nunnery here, but it is only recently that she was canonized by the Church, and is revered as Budapest's patron saint. The island is also notable for its roses, sports facilities and a Japanese rock garden.

When the Budapest Opera House and theaters close for the summer, their companies stage operas, operettas, plays and ballets in the open air theater on Margaret Island. Just beyond are the ruins of Saint Margaret's cloister and a Gothic chapel.

Across the handsome chain bridge (Lánchid)—built nearly 150 years ago by a British engineer, Adam Clark—lies flat, bustling Pest. This modern part of the city has no hills to slow down its development. Nucleus of old Pest is the Belváros, or Inner City, included within the irregular semicircle of the Inner Körút (Boulevard). The stretch of riverside running south is known as the Corso, whose outdoor terraces and gay cafés are crowded in fine weather. The south end of the Corso broadens out into Március 15 Tér, on which stands the 12th-century Belvárosi Templom, the oldest church in Pest. Just off the square stands a slightly sunken building, the Száz Eves (Hundred Year Old) restaurant. A wide arched passage leads under the nearby Central University to Váci Utca, one of the main shopping streets. Many good cafés and restaurants, such as the Mátyás Pince, made this section the heart of old Budapest.

Beyond the Inner City, Pest's main thoroughfare curves down from the Margaret Bridge all the way to the Petöfi Bridge. Within its sweep lie most of the city's main buildings, including the neo-gothic Parliament House. Budapest's grandest boulevard, the Nepköztársaság útja, runs for 1½ miles out from the Inner City to the Hösök Tere, at the entrance to the city park, following the original Metro line.

Városliget Park has a lake used for boating in summer, skating in winter. On an islet are replicas of several medieval buildings. In the north corner of the park is the only zoo in Europe where hippopotami give birth to calves in captivity, due, it seems, to the natural hot mineral spring which feeds their pool.

Adjoining the city park is the Vidám Park, Budapest's Coney Island, complete with scenic railway, dodgems, and rollercoaster.

PRACTICAL INFORMATION FOR BUDAPEST

USEFUL ADDRESSES. *United States Embassy,* 12 Szabadság Tér (near the Houses of Parliament). *British Embassy,* 6 Harmincad Utca, Budapest V (near Vörösmarty Square). *IBUSZ,* 3/c Tanács Körút, Budapest VII (in Pest).

TRANSPORTATION. Bus, trolleybus and tramlines cover the city efficiently, and very cheaply and make sightseeing painless. Tickets from tobacconists and vending machines cost 1.50 fts. each for any distance. A short subway (underground) line, built as early as 1896 (and the first such line on the European continent), runs straight from Vörösmarty Square, in the heart of the business section, to the City Park. New and very up-to-date subway lines, whose stations are marked with the capital letter "M" are now in operation and the system is being extended. One line (the so-called "East-West Line") connects the Eastern Railway Station with the Inner City, dives under the Danube and terminates at the Southern Railway Station. The so-called "North-South Line" is already partly open; it crosses both the previously mentioned lines at Deak Square Station, in the inner city. The celebrated cog-wheel railroad offers escape in the opposite direction up to the Buda Hills, reached in less than half an hour. Taxis are identified by a "Taxi" sign on their roof. Many small boats criss-cross the Danube in the central area.

HOTELS. Very crowded during the summer season and it's advisable to have confirmed bookings from Ibusz. There's a good transit hotel at Ferihegy Airport.

DELUXE

Duna Intercontinental on the Danube quay has 360 rooms, all with bath; garage, conference rooms. Excellent Czárda restaurant serving traditional Hungarian cuisine. A center of the city's social life.

Budapest Hilton, The most recent. Situated next to Fishermen's Bastion on the Buda Hills with spectacular view over the Danube towards Pest. 323 rooms with all amenities; several restaurants.

FIRST CLASS SUPERIOR

Gellért. Old established hotel with 234 rooms, outdoor terrace restaurant, two swimming pools. Overlooks Danube and is also self-contained spa.

Grand Hotel Margitsziget. Park location on island, 161 rooms with bath, hot thermal spring water, garden terrace. Elegant.

Thermal, due to open shortly on Margitsziget Island. Quiet location, swimming pool and medicinal baths.

Royal, centrally located, 370 rooms most with bath; garden terrace, cinema and nightclub. Good restaurant.

FIRST CLASS REASONABLE

Budapest, circular building, 280 rooms with bath, all doubles; popular wine cellar.

Szabadság, large, near East Rail Station, 400 rooms, many with bath; good restaurant, beer hall.

Astoria. 200 rooms, 94 with bath; fine restaurant, nightclub with floorshow. In the heart of the Inner City, so ask for quiet room.

Béke, 140 rooms; cellar bar has Hungarian cuisine and gypsy music.

Europa, situated on outskirts of Buda in wooded area, 160 rooms with bath, restaurant, new.

Vörös Csillag in alpine style on top of Mt. Széchenyi, good connections by tram from city. 40 rooms, fine restaurant, garage, mini-golf.

Volga, away from town center; favorable family-type accommodation, 316 rooms with bath, good restaurant.

Sport, in Buda near park, 176 rooms with bath, good terrace restaurant.

MODERATE

Aero, near the airport, 138 rooms with bath, good restaurant.
Emke, central location, 71 rooms, most with bath.
Metropol, centrally situated, 103 rooms, some with bath.
Olympia, picturesquely located on Szabadsag Hill. 180 rooms, many with bath, swimming pool, sauna, restaurant and nightclub.
Wien, situated in suburbs near Routes 1 and 7. 110 double rooms, some with bath; car repair shop and filling station.

 RESTAURANTS. Atmosphere is the prime ingredient; music (and paprika) the main seasoning. Remember real goulash (gulyás) is a soup, not a main course. Breakfast is served from 7 to 10; lunch from 12 to 3; dinner from 7 to 10. Restaurants listed below are all moderately expensive unless otherwise stated.

ON THE PEST SIDE

Budagyongye, Vöröshadsereg utja 36. Renaissance interior, dishes and music.
Kárpátia, Egyetem út 4. Pleasantly decorated. Gypsy music. Bar, dancing.
Mátyás Pince, Március 15, tér 7. Renowned for its gypsy orchestra and Hungarian food, especially fish. Not cheap; book your table.
Százéves Étterem, Pesti Barnabás utca 2. Fairly small, excellent food and no music played during meals. It means "100 years."
Berlin, Szt. István Körút 16. Latest and most modern. Restaurant, coffeehouse; bar open to 5 A.M. Excellent.
Apostolok, Kigyó Utca 5, in the heart of the city, good food and beer hall; atmospheric, reservations a must.
Havana, Jósef körut 46. Restaurant, nightclub Cuban style; interesting atmosphere.
Hungaria Café Restaurant, Lenin Boulevard 9. A beautiful *art nouveau* coffee house, it is a meeting place for writers and journalists; good coffee, excellent food.
Moszkva, Gorki fasor 35/b; nice situation, garden in summer; dancing at its bar.
Two typically Hungarian inns (csárda) with gypsy music; *Kis Kakuk,* Pozsonyi út 12, and *Megyeri csárda,* Váci út 20.

ON THE BUDA SIDE

Budagyönge, recently renovated, Renaissance atmosphere with menus to match.

Halászbástya, in Fisherman's Bastion, overlooking city and river; excellent food.

Fortuna, Hesz András tér. Blend of ancient and modern. Fashionable, excellent cuisine.

Kis Royal. Márvány utca 19. Intimate, gypsy band, both food and price moderate.

Alabárdos, Országhaz 12, one of the poshest and best. *Régi Országház* in the same street at No. 17, is less sophisticated, has Hungarian décor, atmosphere, as do many other delightful little places in this area. Often crowded, a reservation helps.

Postakocsi, on main square; restaurant and wine cellar. Rustic décor, traditional food. Expensive.

Rózsadomb, Keleti Károly utca 8. A modern, inexpensive restaurant.

Kis Rabló, Zenta utca 3. Genuine Hungarian food and gypsy music.

Citadel Restaurant, Gellért Hill; fine view of the Danube and the Castle at Buda. There is also a nightclub.

Vasmacska, Laktanya 3 near main square; fishy surroundings and specialties, sramli music.

Aranyhordó, Tárnok utca 16, cheery and reasonable, Hungarian and international food.

Pastry and Coffee Shops

Vörösmarty, Vörösmarty tér 7. Long-famous, has marble tables, crystal chandeliers; often quite crowded.

Pilvax, Városház utca 10. Historic haunt of 19th-century patriots. Good restaurant, too.

Ruszwurm, Szentháromság ter 7, close to Buda castle. Oldest pastry shop, a bakery since 1500.

Mackó, Kigyó utca. Cold buffet.

Jégbüffé, Petöfi Sándor út 2. Ice cream specialities.

ENTERTAINMENT. Budapest has two opera houses, two concert halls and twelve theaters. One of the best shows in town is Bartok's "Miraculous Mandarin" at the opera house. In summer, open-air performances on Margaret Island and other outdoor theaters.

Nightlife. Take in the floorshow at the *Moulin Rouge* nightclub, Nagymezö utca 17, which is also a fancy restaurant, known as the haunt of Hungarian café society. For dancing, the charming *Old Firenze,* in Buda, Táncsis Mihály utca 25, or the *Casino* on Margaret Island (only in summer). *Pipacs,* Aranykéz utca and *Berlin* coffeehouse, Szent István körút. In old baroque house in Buda: *Casanova,* Fö utca 4. *Maxim* is a popular nightclub in the Hotel Emke. There is dinner dancing on board cruise boats down the Danube (departures near the Corso). Lively discos include *Funko Disco* at Eden Bar, 7 Széna ter, Buda. There is plenty of student activity if you can get an introduction.

 MUSEUMS. To the visitor, Budapest's two dozen main museums (open every day but Monday) offer the sweep of history from pre-Roman times to the present day and the panorama of world art from Italian and Flemish masters to modern Hungarian painting and sculpture. Fittingly enough, there is also the world's first gastronomic museum.

National Museum, Múzeum krt 14-16. Itself a museum-piece of flawless classic architecture. Its collections include Beethoven's piano and the Monomachos gold crown from 1042. The Hungarian crown, returned by the U.S. in 1978, also now has its rightful place here.

Roman ruins and relics are displayed in four museums built on the sites of ancient Roman camps and towns. *Aquincum* Museum, Szentendrei ut 139. *Roman Museum,* Korvin Ottó út 63; *Herculean Villa* at Meggyfa Utca (Óbuda) and *Archeological Park* (near the Elizabeth Bridge).

Fine Arts Museum (Szépmüvészeti Múzeum). Hösök tere. Egyptian exhibits and European painters.

National Gallery, Buda Royal Palace. Superb exhibition of 14th-century Gothic sculpture, also modern Hungarian painters.

Danube Exhibition on Gellert Hill, includes interesting objects retrieved from the river. Restaurant and panoramic lookout.

Gastronomy Museum, Fortuna utca 4, illustrates aspects of Hungarian cookery with many original menus and utensils.

Underground Railway Museum, Deák Square. Original old vehicles, relics, atmosphere of the world's second underground railway.

Golden Eagle Pharmacy Museum, Tarnok utca 18; 15th- to 18th-century developments in appropriate setting.

SHOPPING. Main shopping street is Vaci Utca, where the famous *Herend* porcelain factory outlet is located. Prices are fixed, no bargaining. Fine *Matyó* embroidery and needlework from *Mezökövesd,* spiderweb laces from *Kiskunhalas,* pottery, porcelain and majolica, bone, horn and woodcarvings, regional homespun cloth, many-hued *Torontál* peasant carpets, and wonderful wooden toys may be purchased at Kossuth Lajos utca 2 and Váci utca 14; souvenir shops at Vörösmarty tér 2, and Kossuth Lajos utca 6. In the *Konsumtourist* and *Intertourist* shops only foreign currency is accepted. Other good buys include an enormous selection of classical music records. Browse around Hungary's largest department store, the new *Skála* in south Budapest, just off the Balaton road. In the city center, the big central indoor food market on Dimitrov Square is well worth a visit. This is where the Budapest housewife comes for quality and value.

LAUNDROMAT. Patyolat, Városháza utca, Budapest V.

THERMAL SPRINGS. In the area around Budapest there are over 100 mineral springs, many naturally hot. Try *Palatinus Bath* on Margitsziget Island or the *Gellert Medicinal Bath;* prices are reasonable. *Széchényi Medicinal Bath* at City Park offers very hot (163-169 deg. F) baths, various treatments, nude sunbaths.

MAIL AND TELEPHONE. English is spoken at the main post office, Városház útca, and at the post offices of the East Railway Station, Baross tér, and West Railway Station, Marx tér.

Public telephones are operated with tokens, sold by post offices, tobacconists and certain shops and restaurants; or with a 1-Ft. coin. For long-distance calls, dial 01, for telegrams, 02, in case of accident 04. Be sure to check the price of a long-distance call from your hotel as many hotels add exorbitant service charges to the basic cost of the call.

Exploring the Danube Bend

An all-day excursion steamer trip up the Danube from Budapest to Szentendre, Visegrád, and Esztergom voyages through a thousand years of history. Two hours upstream is the photogenic town of Szentendre, which has hardly changed in the last 150 years. Its old streets lined with baroque and rococo houses have attracted many Hungarian artists. Two hours farther north is Visegrád, where the medieval kings of Hungary held court.

Still farther upstream the boat comes to Esztergom. This ancient town was once Charlemagne's eastern border fortress. Later it was the birthplace of Saint Stephen, and for over seven centuries has been the seat of Hungary's Roman Catholic primate. Its massive domed basilica is visible for many miles across the country. The primate's palace is the Christian museum, rich in early Hungarian and Italian paintings and Gobelin tapestries.

Balaton, the Landlocked Riviera

Two hours or less from Budapest, by car or train, lies a family-style paradise named Lake Balaton. Here the sun shines an average of 2,000 hours per year, the beaches are sandy, the water tempers the summer heat, the bass bite on any bait, and children can wade out for hundreds of feet in the shallow water, which sparkles with bracing carbonic gas as well as sunlight. Both shores of the 48-mile-long "Hungarian Sea" (slightly larger than Lake Geneva) form one continuous summer resort; winegrowing, fishing and running the attractive hotels keep the local inhabitants busy.

A storybook thumb of land, the Tihany Peninsula, all but cuts Lake Balaton in two. Its two or three-mile area is a national park, riddled with extinct geyser craters surrounding a tiny lakelet. Aromatic lavender fields clothe its volcanic hills, rare birds nest by the lake, and nature lovers can count 800 different kinds of butterfly. Tihany is also the site of Hungary's oldest piece of architecture—an 11th-century monastery crypt. Just north lies Balatonfüred, oldest watering place on the lake. Here the mineral hot springs, prototype of the legendary "fountain of youth" in literature, are particularly reputed for cardiac sufferers, and the Balatonfüred State Hospital for Heart Diseases is world-famous.

Among indoor sports, along the Balton's north shore winetasting is an odds-on favorite, best practiced in the cool cellars of Badacsony, a hillside village on volcanic soil, famed for its bottled grape. At Tapolca, a flight of steps on Kisfaludy street (looking for all the world like a subway train entrance) leads to an underground lake system, explorable by boat. At Héviz, near the far end of Lake Balaton, is a large lake of water whose mineral springs run warm even in winter.

Kis-Balaton is a large marshland area, like the Florida Everglades. Here, 3,700 acres were set aside as a nature preserve, where many kinds of wild fowl are being saved from extinction.

Lake Valance, only 30 miles from south-west of Budapest, lies on the route to Balaton and offers a mini-version of the latter's aquatic and natural attractions; of special appeal to anglers and bird watchers.

PRACTICAL INFORMATION FOR BUDAPEST ENVIRONS AND LAKE BALATON

BALATONALMÁDI. *Aurora,* (2), 240 rooms, all with bath, restaurant in building next door. Private beach and tennis nearby. Large camping site.

Restaurants: *Kek Balaton, Halászcsárda.*

BALATONFÖLDVAR, formerly the most chic resort. *Motel* with restaurant. *Kukorica Csárda,* reed-thatched inn, regional food, *Neptun,* all (3).
Keringö Bar, nightclub popular with tourists.

BALATONFÜRED. *Annabella* (2), very picturesque; 384 double rooms with bath and balcony. Private beach and tennis nearby. *Marina* (2), efficiently run, lakeside location, 400 double rooms, large restaurant, private beach. *Arany Csillag* (3) in town center, 120 rooms. *Motel* on lake shore. Two excellent camping sites.
Restaurants: *Molo Inn, Baricska Inn, Tölgyfa* hewn into the mountainside. *Koloska Inn,* 3 miles distant in picturesque old monastery.

DOBOGÓKÖ. *Nimrod* (3), situated behind Buda Hills; 82 rooms with bath.

ESZTERGOM. *Fürdo* (3), spa hotel, 92 rooms, many with bath, garden restaurant.

HÉVIZ, famous spa for diseases of the locomotive system. New *Thermal* (2) *Beke* and *Zsófia* (4).

KESZTHELY. *Helikon,* (1), 240 rooms with bath; *Amazon* and *Motel,* both (4). *Motel* in park; large campsite near lake.
Restaurants: *Halászcsárda.* Nearby *Gyöngyösi Csárda.*

RÁCKEVE, on Csepel Island 40 kms south of Budapest. New resort complex including motel, camping, outdoor sauna. Good sports facilities and angler's paradise.

SIÓFOK. *Europa,* modern, 138 rooms with shower; *Balaton, Lido* and *Hungaria* are identical hotels on lakeside; 136 rooms in each, central restaurant nearby. *Napfeny,* small, near lakeside, double rooms with bath and balcony. All (2). *Venus,* 57 rooms with bath (3).
Restaurants: *Fogas* and *Matróz,* both with garden. *Borharapó* for local wines.

TIHANY. *Tihany,* (2), next to yacht marina, 135 rooms with shower; mini-golf, tennis. *Kis Tihany* (2), 20 rooms with bath and balcony. Campsite. There is a holiday village at Kopaszhegy with self-contained chalets.
Restaurants: *Fogas csárda* and *Halásztanya.* At Szántód opposite, *Révcsárda.*

VISEGRAD. *Sylvanus* (3), attractively located in wooded region of Danube Bend; 75 rooms with bath, restaurant.

The Northeast

If at all possible time should be found for a visit to the vast beech forests of the Bük and Mátra mountains, home to big and small game. Time seems to have forgotten this remote corner, with its endless limestone caverns rich in traces of prehistoric man. The Aggtelek Caverns to the north of Bük, near the Czechoslovak border, is a 14-mile chain of weirdly beautiful vaults and chambers and Europe's largest stalactite cave system. Orchestral concerts are held in one called "Concert Hall" with unique acoustics.

Mezökövesd, main town of Matyó Land, is a living museum; the population walks around in folk costumes on Sundays. Matyó House in the middle of town is a cooperative workshop where the local folk art is preserved and developed on a cottage industry basis.

Eger and Tokaj are two of Hungary's chief wine-producing centers. Eger is a historic and artistic treasure, the loveliest baroque town in Hungary. Lillafüred is a famous resort and rest area; Miskolc, Hungary's second city, is a center of heavy industry.

Eastern Far West

Longhorn cattle, fast range ponies, cowboys in broadbrimmed hats—Hungary's Far West lies 100 miles due east of Budapest. Its quarter million acres of tree-less rangeland is called the Hortobágy Puszta. Actually, the puszta is more of a marsh (like the French camargue) than a prairie, and is the country's first national park. There are various historical inns where you can eat or stay over and the horse shows are very entertaining.

Debrecen is the main town in this area and is famous for its August Flower Festival.

Another fascinating and less-known puszta region is Bugac, part of the Kinskunság National Park 80 miles south-east of Budapest, where sand dunes alternate with marshes and various types of forest, and a chain of small lakes yields rich bird life.

The town of Sopron in the far west, near the Austrian border, has a well-preserved quarter and an interesting bakery museum among other monuments. There are many attractive old towns in this area and, 35 minutes' drive away off Highway 84, is the new thermal resort of Bük.

PRACTICAL INFORMATION FOR THE REGIONS

BÜK. *Kastely* (3) in 18th-century castle; motel, weekend cottages and campsite.

DEBRECEN. *Arany Bika* (2/3), historic and one of Hungary's best hotels. Recently reconstructed with new wing, 280 rooms, many with bath. *Fonix* (4). Campsite at Nagyerdö.
Restaurants: *Hungária, Szölöskeri, Kisdiófa.*

EGER. *Eger* and *Park,* both (2/3) with swimming pools and thermal baths. Restaurants: *Vörös Rák* and *Mecset.*

GYÖNGYÖS. *Matra* (3), folkloric decoration.
Restaurants: *Kékes, Szabadság.* Eight kms away is the resort village **Má-trafüred.** *Avar* (2), 115 rooms many with bath, restaurant, pool, sauna.

GYÖR. *Rába* (2), 200 renovated rooms, most with bath.
Restaurants: *Vigadó* and *Vaskakas.*

HORTOBÁGY. In the center of the national park is the country's oldest roadside inn, the *Nagycsárda* (1). Primarily a restaurant but 10 rooms, garden, also.

KAPOSVÁR. *Kapos* (2/3), 79 rooms, many with bath, restaurant. *Dorottya* (2), renovated 44 rooms, some with bath.

KECSKEMÉT. *Aranyhomok* (2/3) about 100 rooms, many with bath, restaurant, garage.
Restaurants: *Hirös Étterem, Toronyház, Halászcsárda.*

MISKOLC. *Avas* (4), 60 rooms with bathroom on each floor; *Pannonia* (4), smaller.

Restaurants: *Polonia, Belvárosi, Béke.*

At nearby spa **Tapolca,** *Juno* (2), new, near famous thermal baths in underground cave; restaurant, terrace-bar.

PÉCS. *Nádor* and *Pannonia,* both (2/3), some rooms with bath, restaurant. *Tourist* (4). Campsite.

Restaurants: *Elefánt, Rózsakert* and *Százéves Borozó.*

SÁROSPATAK. *Motel Borostyán* (4), next to ancient castle; 13 simple double rooms, restaurant in castle cellar.

SIKLÓS, beautiful 13th-century castle hotel, 30 kilometers from Pécs. *Tenkes,* 17 rooms, restaurant (2).

SOPRON. *Fenyves* and *Pannonia,* the former situated out of town in hills, both (2/3), many rooms with bath. Lakeside campsite.

Restaurants: *Gambrinus, Kékfrankos.*

SOSTO. Small holiday village on lovely lakeshore; peasant-style 3-bedded cottages with all mod. cons.

SZEGED. *Royal* (2), centrally located, 110 rooms some with bath; grill but no restaurant. *Tisza* (2/3), 83 rooms, some with bath, restaurant. Camping site along the river.

Restaurants: *Alabárdos, Szeged.* Nearby, *Postakocsi Vendeglo,* an atmospheric inn; and *Feherto Csárda* on lakeside of bird sanctuary specializes in fish dishes.

SZÉKESFEHÉRVÁR. *Alba Regia* (2), central, close to historic old town; 110 rooms with bath. *Velence* (3), renovated, 60 rooms.

Restaurants: *Ösfehérvár* and *Kulacs. Stop Espresso* on main square.

SZEKSZÁRD. *Gemenc* (3), new, near game preserve; 92 rooms with shower, large restaurant, nightclub, popular.

SZENTENDRE. *Danubius* (3), attractive 130-bed hotel on Highway 11.

SZEREŃCS in northern Tokaj wine growing region. *Huszárvár* (3) castle hotel which once belonged to the Rákóczi family. About 20 rooms, more in the tourist category section.

SZOLNOK, *Pelikán* (2), new, 100 rooms. *Tisza* (2/3), thermal bath, restaurant, garden terrace.

SZOMBATHELY. *Claudius* (1), pleasant, modern, on lakeshore; 110 rooms, thermal baths, sauna, restaurant and nightclub. *Isis* (2), modern, 72 rooms, many with bath, restaurant.

Restaurants: *Tóvendéglö, Gyöngyös.*

TATA. *Diana* (1), in converted castle 6 kms. from town; 20 rooms, restaurant; recommended for motorists.

TOKAJ. At present only bungalow accommodation, but several good restaurants: *Tiszavirág, Halászcsárda* and *Rákóczi* cellar wineshop.

VESZPRÉM. *Veszprém,* (2/3), modern, 88 rooms, many with bath, restaurant.

ICELAND

Iceland remains comparatively undiscovered as a tourist destination, despite all the publicity from the mini-war with Britain over cod fishing rights. Some travelers on their way across the Atlantic stop off for an hour or two in the capital Reykjavik and that suffices for most people. But if you're not so much interested in sun, sand and cheap wine as the wonders of completely unspoilt Nature, this is the country for you. You may even want to qualify for the new snobbism by being able to say: "What, you went to Reykjavik? We went round Iceland and stayed in Akureyri." That's Iceland's second city, with a population of 10,000, which makes it fully eight times as exclusive as Reykjavik, which has an absolutely teeming population of 80,000!

In keeping with its status as an off-beat tourist destination, Iceland has three negative advantages. It doesn't have trees, it doesn't have railroads, and it doesn't have snakes. It shares this last advantage with another island, Hawaii. Iceland, like Hawaii, also has active volcanoes, but there the resemblance ends.

PRACTICAL INFORMATION FOR ICELAND

WHAT WILL IT COST. Prices are very high in Iceland, mainly because almost everything has to be imported, and with the present inflation rate of over 30% per annum, they may well rise further. Devaluation has been talked of for several years and this could help, but at the time of writing a room in a first class superior hotel will cost from Kr. 3,500, and between Kr. 2,500 and 4,500 for a room in a moderate one (double room 60% more). Restaurants charge from Kr. 1,750 for lunch and from Kr. 2,200 for dinner. Always check if 20–25% service charge is included in hotel and restaurant prices. "Stopover" hotel prices for periods of 24, 48 and 72 hours through Loftleidir/Icelandair are from Kr. 2,250, including certain extras, but all prices are subject to change without notice. Hotel classifications are first class superior (1), first class (2), and moderate (3). Airport Taxes: international, £4.50; domestic, .60 p.

CAPITAL. Reykjavik.

LANGUAGE. Icelandic, which bears about the same relationship to other Scandinavian languages as Anglo-Saxon does to English. English is widely spoken.

CLIMATE. Surprisingly mild in winter, thanks to the Gulf Stream.
Average maximum daily temperatures in degrees Fahrenheit and centigrade:

Reykjavik	Jan.	Feb.	Mar.	Apr.	May	June	July	Aug.	Sept.	Oct.	Nov.	Dec.
F°	36	37	39	43	50	54	57	57	52	45	39	36
C°	2	3	4	6	10	12	14	14	11	7	4	2

SEASONS. Mid-June to the beginning of September is the best time to visit. In June and July there is perpetual daylight and at the end of August the colorful Northern Lights (Aurora Borealis) being to appear.

MONEY. The Icelandic *krona* (crown) consists of 100 *aurar.* Present exchange rate is approx. 256 Kr. to the US $ and approx. 494 Kr. to the pound sterling (at press time). **Subject to change.**

TIPPING. Except for the service charges on your bill, there is no tipping.

HOW TO REACH ICELAND. *Icelandic Airlines* (Loftleidir) from New York; they also arrange GIT tours to Scandinavia with a 48-hr. stopover in Reykjavik. From London or Glasgow by *Icelandair/Loftleidir Icelandic.* *Icelandair* is currently serving some 13 domestic points, and runs summer excursions to Greenland.
By boat: Summer sailings from Scrobster (Scotland) and Bergen.

CUSTOMS. Officially you may bring in 200 cigarettes and a bottle of "ardent spirits". In transit or leaving you can stock up original Icelandic sweaters, local liquor, handicrafts, etc. at the duty-free Keflavik Airport store.

TOURS. Conducted tours from Reykjavik or Akureyri are organized by Iceland Tourist Bureau (*Ferdaskrikstofa Rikisins)* during the summer months. These include such things as a visit to the Whale Station (whale permitting), day tours by plane and bus to northern Iceland from Reykjavik, and aerial views of volcanos and glaciers (weather permitting). Individual tours can be arranged to suit personal tastes on inclusive tour fare bases. Other guided trips include fishing expeditions, geologist and naturalist tours and excellent coach/air/boat tours of varying lengths. You can go round Iceland by sea or by bus—which is still a novelty even to Icelanders since the final completion of the road across the glacier rivers of the southeast. Costs are high: upwards of Kr. 15,000 for two days and proportionately higher thereafter. *Pennworld* offers two weeks camping and mountainbus from £258 (London to London). *Scantours* offers eight days on a traditional itinerary

WEST ICELAND

Akranes: *Akranes* (3). Borganes: *Borganes* (3). Stykkisholmur: *Summerhotel* (3).

IRELAND

Ireland is a traveler's delight, despite the erroneous impression given by the media that the island is engulfed in strife . . . the "troubles" are in Northern Ireland, the six counties belonging to the United Kingdom, and the overwhelming majority of people in the whole country want nothing more than for an end to the madness in the north. In the tranquil south, you'll be enchanted with the sound of the Irish accent, the musical cadences of the Irish voice, and the striking imagery employed in the everyday speech of this nation of natural poets. The Irish are a hospitable and loquacious people, in love with words and never at a loss for them.

The beauty of the country itself, and the fact that there are no language problems and that the Irish really do welcome Americans are reasons why American readers might consider making Ireland the first stop on a tour of Europe, or a base for further exploration of the continent. Furthermore, being small and homogeneous, Ireland is easy to cover in a limited time, convenient to get about in, and very well organized and equipped for tourists of all ages and tastes. And, what is more, the prices are right. A recent survey showed that Dublin was the least expensive destination in Europe. Even allowing for a touch of financial blarney, it is clear that a single good hotel room or a three-course dinner for four were as cheap in Dublin as anywhere else in Europe. There is plenty to see and do, and if you've come with relaxation in mind, there's no better place to unwind. We recommend fishing, watching the horses (or riding them), cruising down the River Shannon, lolling around on lawns of castle hotels, golfing on almost-empty courses, ambling along in a horse-drawn caravan, or larking around the lakes of Killarney in a pony-drawn trap. Ireland is one of the European countries that's virtually pollution-free on the beaches and in the air. The castle entertainments are great fun, and there are short tours of excellent quality offered from Shannon Airport should you have time only for a brief stopover in the country.

Food and Drink

The food is familiar to British and American visitors, with heavy reliance in menus on beef, mutton, and plenty of fresh fish from stream and sea. Dublin Bay prawns are fine, especially with a spicy sauce; and the mussels from the Wexford coast are superb—try *moules mariniere* when you see them on the menu, and oysters with Guinness is a combination no mere mortal could surpass. Typical Irish dishes include corned beef and carrots, boiled bacon and cabbage, Irish stew, crubeens (pig's feet), colcannon (potatoes and cabbage cooked together in a mix), soufflé flavored with seaweed, and soda bread.

Ireland has been distilling a well-known spirit for about eight hundred years, calling it *Uisge Beatha* and pronouncing it, more or less, as "whisgeh" (water) "baha" (life). The Irish whiskey of today has a distinctive smoothness and a flavor totally different from that of Scotch whisky—note the difference in spelling, too. Another favorite Irish drink is Guinness stout, available on tap or in bottles in every pub in Ireland, but if you like a lighter brew there is Harp Lager brewed in Dundalk. And of course, Irish coffee—i.e. a jigger of whiskey added to hot black coffee with sugar and topped with thick cream.

PRACTICAL INFORMATION FOR IRELAND

(Irish Republic)

WHAT WILL IT COST. Prices are modest; based on predictions for 1979, you should live very well for £18 a day, and much better by buying one of the packages offered by U.S. and British tour operators. (For current offers contact Irish Tourist Board in New York, Chicago, London or Dublin.) Good buy: 15-day coach tour starting and finishing at Shannon, embracing all the highspots, at around $870, including air fare. If you want freedom of choice buy an air fare/car hire package and go-as-you-please, staying in farmhouses, hotels or guesthouses. £10 for bed and breakfast in a good Dublin hotel, about half that in a guesthouse; around £6.50 in hotels in rural areas, and £3.50 in farmhouses or guesthouses. There is usually a reduced rate if you are making a three-night stop. A two-week package with open hotel vouchers good at any of 18 hotels around the country can be had for about $400.

Check with your travel agent for a wide range of special fares such as Super Apex and Apex, which can cut travel costs sharply. The agent will also have details of advanced booking charters and other "specials," which can leave you extra spending money if you don't want a group deal.

Because it's the best known, Killarney, like Dublin, is more expensive, but even here accommodation in a hotel can be had from £7 to around £15 for bed and breakfast at the season's peak (June–Sept.); about one-third less at other times.

"Discover Ireland" packages, designed for the home market, can be bought on the spot. Sample: summer week in Ballina, Co. Mayo, £98 covers first class superior hotel, all meals, indoor swimming pool, squash court, dancing; golf, riding and fishing are available locally. A demipension deal in a farmhouse in the same area would cost only about £40.

If you plan to take the family, rent a cottage, either from Rent-an-Irish-Cottage at Shannon Airport or through the regional tourism offices—prices range from

£80 a week up, but most accommodate a family of four or six so it's economic buying if you want a based holiday. Each region has a list of approved accommodation—get it through the Irish Tourist Board offices in the U.S. or Britain; also get the current *Official Guide to Hotels* and *Guide to Approved Town and Country Homes and Farmhouses* from the same source. These list maximum prices and it's a useful check against your budget. Both are free.

Hotels are classified deluxe (L), first class superior (1), first class reasonable (2), moderate (3) and inexpensive (4).

CAPITAL. Dublin.

LANGUAGE. English with a lilting accent. Also Gaelic, but everyone speaks English.

CLIMATE. Moderate.

Average maximum daily temperatures in degrees Fahrenheit and centigrade:

Dublin	Jan.	Feb.	Mar.	Apr.	May	June	July	Aug.	Sept.	Oct.	Nov.	Dec.
F°	45	46	50	54	57	64	66	66	63	57	50	46
C°	7	8	10	12	14	18	19	19	17	14	10	8

SEASONS. May through September. 12 to 14 hours a day of sunlight in summer. You can play golf as late as 11 P.M. in the west.

SPECIAL EVENTS. *January,* International Rugby Football match against France. *March,* Arts Festival, Dublin; Saint Patrick's Day, celebrated with Gaelic football, horse racing and dog shows all over the country. *April,* Irish Grand National at Fairyhouse, Co. Meath. *May,* Dublin Spring Show and Sale of country's finest cattle; Maytime Festival, Dundalk. *June,* Irish Derby, Curragh; Cork Film International; Writers' Week, Listowel, Co. Kerry; International Sea Angling Festival, Westport, Co. Mayo. *July,* Dublin Flower Show; Strawberry Fair, Enniscorthy, Co. Wexford. *August,* Dublin Horse Show Week; Antique Dealer's Fair, Dublin; Puck Fair, Killorglin, County Kerry. *September,* International Folk Dance Festival; Oyster Festival, Galway. *October,* Wexford Festival Opera; Gaelic Festival, Dublin; Great October Fair, Ballinasloe, Co. Galway, reputedly the world's oldest horse fair.

Hours. Shops and stores 9 A.M. to 5:30 P.M. daily. (Early closing days Wednesday or Saturday depending on locality.) Banks: 10–12.30 and 1.30–3 (1.30–5 on Thursdays). Closed Saturdays and Sundays. Best time to fix a business interview is between 10 A.M. and 4 P.M. Business lunches can be long.

LICENSING HOURS. On weekdays in summer, from 10.30 A.M. to 11.30 P.M., closing at 11 P.M. the rest of the year; there's an hour shutdown from 2.30 to 3.30 P.M. Drinking on Sunday becomes a little more complicated depending on where you are. Usually Sunday hours are 12.30 to 2 P.M., and again from 5 to 9 P.M. (one hour earlier in winter). Of course, if you are staying in a licensed hotel you can have a drink there any time.

SPORTS. *Horse racing* is the most important feature in the sporting life of the country. Several leading tracks are within easy reach of Dublin. The Irish Derby, The Guineas and other classic events are held at The Curragh, County Kildare. The Irish Sweeps Hurdle is the big Christmas event at Leopardstown eight miles from Dublin. In addition, horseback riding and equestrian tours (8-day) are available. *Hunting* ranks next; visitors are welcomed by hunts. Where *shooting* is not entirely free (hotels), it can be had at a moderate fee from landowners. Some of the best West of Ireland grounds are vested in the Irish Land Commission, Merrion St., Dublin, from whom particulars can be obtained. Most good hotels offer free *fishing* to visitors; salmon and trout are good. Outstanding *deep-sea fishing* is from Kinsale, Ballycotton and Cobh, Co. Cork; at Kilmore, Co. Wexford and Westport, Co. Mayo. There is scarcely a district in Ireland without a *golf* course. Visitor's tickets are issued for a day or a week without formality. Write to the Irish Tourist Board for their list, with details, of 170 courses: *Guide to Irish Golf Courses.* Ireland, with 2,000 miles of indented coastline, is heaven for the visting *yachtsman.* Dun Laoghaire and Cork are the main centers. Inland waterway cruising on the River Shannon and canals. Among the spectator sports *greyhound racing* and the national games of *hurling* and *Gaelic football* are very popular.

MONEY. Irish currency is in the same denominations as British and negotiable at the same rates of exchange (approx. $1.90 to the pound, **subject to change**), but you will find it marked with harps and other Gaelic motifs. British money is also legal tender.

TIPPING. The standard tip in Ireland is 12½%. Most hotels include this service charge on the bill: guesthouses don't. In more elegant establishments, an extra tip is expected. It's common practice to tip porters, car-park attendants, taxi drivers, barbers, and waiters or waitresses.

HOW TO REACH IRELAND. By Air: Several airlines have direct flights from New York and European cities to Shannon. Shannon, Dublin and Cork have duty-free shops. From England: there are direct flights to Dublin, Cork and Shannon airports from London, Liverpool, Bristol and other cities.

By Sea: There are week-day Sealink ferries with drive-on/off car facilities between Fishguard and Rosslare, Holyhead and Dun Laoghaire, with connecting boat trains from non-motorized passengers from London (5 hours) and in Ireland to Dublin, Waterford, Mallow (change for Killarney) and Cork; twice daily car ferry Liverpool-Dublin. A direct Swansea—Cork car ferry daily. Some trips take 6½ hrs, some overnight. The Irish Continental Line operates a year-round car ferry service between Le Havre (France) and Rosslare (20 hours) and another between Cherbourg (France) and Rosslare. Brittany Ferries operates a summer service from Roscoff (France) to Cork.

CUSTOMS. Only verbal declaration necessary. Coming from overseas, you may bring in 1,000 cigarettes or 2½ pounds of tobacco, 2 bottles of spirits, a pint of perfume, and 2 bottles of wine duty free. No limit on importation of Irish pounds, U.S. or other foreign currencies. You may not take out British or Irish currency in excess of £25, except direct to Great Britain. You will be given a certificate indicating how much you bring in in dollars and foreign currency; you may take out up to £250 worth of dollars or other foreign currency in excess of that amount.

MAIL. Airmail rates overseas to Canada, United States and Commonwealth are 17p for the first 20 grams plus 10p for each additional 20 grams; airletters 10p. Postcards 10p. All first class mail to Great Britain or the Continent goes automatically by air: 10p for letters, 8p for postcards; to the continent 12p for letters, 9p for postcards.

ELECTRICITY. 220 volts, 50 cycles, A.C.

DRINKING WATER. All right, but Guinness is good for you.

TRAVEL IN IRELAND. By Car: One of the most rewarding ways to explore this country. Keep to the left is the rule in Ireland. Petrol costs about 93p for extra grade per Imperial or Irish gallon (5 of which equal 6 U.S. gallons). Third party insurance compulsory. Maximum speed is 60 mph.

Car Hire. Among the many agencies in Dublin are *Hertz,* 19-20 Pearse St.; *Cahill's,* 36 Annesley Pl.; *Dan Ryan,* 42 Parkgate Street; *Avis,* 1 Hanover Street East; *Murrays-Pal,* Baggot St. Bridge. Some have offices in other towns. Cars for hire at both Shannon and Dublin Airports, and most operate one-way rental program, pick up at Shannon or Dublin and leave at point of departure, usually without extra charge. Many Irish car rental companies have offices in the U.S. For example: *Murray's Rent-a-Car,* 15 E. 48th St., New York, N.Y. 10017; *Auto Europe,* 770 Lexington Avenue, New York, N.Y. 10021; *Boland's,* 161 Pinewood St., Stamford, Connecticut 06903; *Hughes International Travel,* 420 Lexington Ave., New York, N.Y. 10017.

By Train or Bus. All of Ireland can be reached by either train or bus, the latter running between cities and into remote areas. C.I.E. (*Coras Iompair Eireann*) run luxury bus tours in summer to all the major points of interest from Dublin and from many other centers as well. There are one-day tours at reasonable prices or extended bus tours from several days to two weeks' duration in which the price includes hotels, meals, tips, etc. A six-day tour of the south costs about £95. C.I.E. also provides a 15-day "rambler" ticket for unlimited use on rail services for about £22, and a rail/road "rambler" for about £27. Tickets for Irish train and bus travel may be bought in the United States.

USEFUL ADDRESSES. *United States Embassy,* 42 Elgin Road. *Canadian Embassy,* 65 St. Stephen's Green. *British Embassy,* Merrion Road. *Irish Tourist Office,* 14 Upper O'Connell Street. *American Express,* 116 Grafton Street. *Thomas Cook,* 118 Grafton Street. *C.I.E.,* 35 Lower Abbey Street. *Automobile Association,* 23 Suffolk Street. All in Dublin.

Dublin

"Dublin's fair city—where girls are so pretty" is the capital of Ireland and one of the most charming cities of Europe, still redolent in parts of the dignity of the 18th century. It is a shopper's and sportsman's paradise (there are 27 golf courses in the immediate vicinity), and if you can schedule your trip to include the world-famous Dublin Horse Show in August, you will be seeing the capital at its gayest. Dublin doesn't suffer extremes of climate, so low-priced fall-through-spring special interest vacations and tours are a good buy.

Statue-filled O'Connell Street makes a good beginning for a walking tour around town. We recommend visiting Trinity College with its John Henry Foley statues of alumni Edmund Burke and Oliver Goldsmith, and don't miss Trinity College Library with its fabulous collection of manuscripts including the world-famous Book of Kells, dating from the eighth century, perhaps the most beautiful illuminated manuscript in existence. Dublin's noblest public buildings are the 18th-century Parliament House (now the Bank of Ireland) and the Custom House, located on the north bank of the River Liffey, and designed by the great architect, James Gandon, in 1791. Another Gandon masterpiece is the restored Four Courts on the northern quays. Dublin Castle, dating from 1208, has magnificent state apartments and a famous heraldic museum, the only one of its kind in the world; for a modest fee its trained staff will trace your family tree for noble ancestors.

St. Patrick's Cathedral was founded in 1130. Jonathan Swift was dean here for 32 years, and you can see the pulpit from which he preached (1713 to 1745) and the great satirist's tomb with the bitter epitaph he composed himself. Another church you should not miss is Christ Church, begun by King Sitric the Dane in 1038. Its nave is considered the finest example of Gothic architecture in Ireland. For an experience on the macabre side, the vaults of Saint Michan's church have on display a number of bodies that have been there in a perfect state of preservation for centuries. For a glimpse of some of Dublin's most beautiful 18th-century mansions, go to Merrion Square where Oscar Wilde, Daniel O'Connell, the Duke of Wellington and the writer George Moore once lived. In the same area, visit the National Gallery where a fine collection of paintings and sculpture is well displayed. Leinster House, once the home of the Dukes of Leinster and now the seat of the Dail and Senate (Congress/Parliament) is close by.

Horse enthusiasts will also want to visit the farms of Ireland's National Stud, nursery of some of racing's most famous horses, in Tully, County Kildare. For a complete list of all racing events and information about such great Gaelic games as hurling and Gaelic football, write to the Irish Tourist Board. (For addresses, see *Practical Planning* section.) They can also supply information on hunting, golfing and fishing holidays in a land which has few rivals in them.

PRACTICAL INFORMATION FOR DUBLIN

HOTELS. It's well to make your reservations in advance if you're coming to Dublin during the season. If you can't find accommodation, the Tourist Information Office will be able to help.

DELUXE

Shelbourne, St. Stephen's Green. 172 rooms, most with bath. Has a quiet dignity that is very much in accord with its century-old tradition. *Saddle Room* for good beef and fish, a popular grill and a snackery cater for anybody's appetite.

Berkeley Court, in Ballsbridge, near American Embassy, is new. 200 rooms with bath, indoor swimming pool.

Jury's, also in Ballsbridge, 314 rooms with bath. New complex includes indoor/outdoor heated pool, *Dubliner Bar,* elegant restaurant and a coffee shop.

Gresham, downtown, on O'Connell St. Updated and now owned by Swan Ryan group. 175 rooms (153 with bath). Good restaurant and a grill bar.

Royal Hibernian, Dawson Street, has 117 rooms (94 with bath), puts the stress on elegance. Several luxury penthouse suites. Its fine dining room ranks along with its *Buttery* among the most popular places of Dublin and there is a quick grill bar.

FIRST CLASS SUPERIOR

International, Dublin Airport, 150 rooms with bath.

Burlington, Burlington Rd. 435 rooms with bath. Conference center. Indoor pool. Restaurants, bars.

FIRST CLASS REASONABLE

Royal Dublin on O'Connell Street has 120 rooms with bath.

Montrose, on the edge of the city, 190 rooms with bath. Grill bar, restaurant, parking space.

Clarence, Wellington Quay, overlooks the Liffey. Has 70 rooms, some with bath.

Other hotels in this category are *Skylon,* 88 rooms with bath; *Green Isle* (on city perimeter), 56 rooms with bath; *Tara Tower,* 84 rooms with bath, at Merrion on South city boundary; *Ashling,* Parkgate St., near rail terminal (Heuston Station) for south and west, 50 rooms, 26 with bath; *Crofton Airport,* 91 rooms with bath. *Buswell's,* opposite Leinster House, 53 rooms with bath.

MODERATE

Wynn's, on mid-city Abbey Street, which has 62 rooms; *Ormond,* on the Liffey at Ormond Quay, with 80 rooms, modernized.

INEXPENSIVE

The family-type atmosphere is an attraction in this price range: *Powers Royal; North Star* near rail terminus to the north; *Montclare* near Merrion Square.

GUEST HOUSES

The *Mount Herbert,* Ballsbridge, has 88 rooms, 77 with bath; others are smaller but comfortable, among them the *Ariel,* 52 Lansdowne Road; *Embassy,* 35 Pembroke Road, *Montrose House,* 16 Pembroke Park.

 RESTAURANTS. Irish food is good, inexpensive, and served in ample portions. Fine grills and thick steaks are famous. Game is plentiful in this sportsman's heaven. Menus will feature all the fish—salmon, trout, lobster— you can eat plus game birds such as wild duck, snipe, plover, pheasant and partridge in season. Dublin's top hotels have excellent dining rooms that rate high in cuisine, wine cellars, décor, and service (see hotels, above). Recommended restaurants below are listed E, M, or I, for expensive, moderate or inexpensive.

Soup Bowl, (M), 2 Molesworth St., first class food. Small, best book in advance.

Snaffles (E), Leeson St., is another small spot with outstanding food.

Celtic Mews (E), 109A Lower Baggot Street, is small, attractive and its food is superb.

Lord Edward (M), Christchurch Place, is fine for fish: best book a table.

Golden Orient and *Tandoori Rooms* (E), Leeson St., for authentic Indian dishes.

National Gallery Restaurant (I), Merrion Square, is attractive and quick.

Berni Inn has a group of restaurants in one building in Nassau Street, beside Trinity College, and attracts bright patrons. *McDonald's,* a name familiar to Americans, has opened (1977) its first Irish spot in Grafton Street. Just like home.

Restaurant na Mara (Restaurant of the Sea) at Dun Laoghaire (6 miles out) is in the top bracket for fish.

Mirabeau (E), also at Dun Laoghaire is popular spot with top show-biz people.

Murph's (I), 99 Lr Baggot St., 18 Suffolk St. for salads.

King Sitric (M) at Howth (north side of Dublin Bay) is another top spot for fish dishes.

BEST BARS. *Bowes Bar,* Fleet Street, meeting place for journalists and the literati, which also goes for *Scotch House,* Burgh Quay. *Mulligan's,* Townsend St., *Bailey* and *Davy Byrne's,* Duke Street, typically Irish and very popular. *Shelbourne's Horseshoe Bar,* St. Stephen's Green, where the VIPs of business and industry meet. *Mooney's* and *Flowing Tide* are both in Abbey Street. *Madigan's* in Earl St. (another in Moore St.) are both spots for meeting Dubliners. *The Buttery* in the Royal Hibernian Hotel is a fashionable meeting place, and so is the *Dubliner Bar* of the Jurys Hotel, and the *Malt* at the Gresham.

SINGING PUBS. Best known are *Slattery's* in Capel St., and Terenure, *Grace's,* 26 Wexford St., *The Embankment* at Tallaght on the edge of town, *Old Shieling* at Raheny and the *Abbey Tavern* in the northern suburb of Howth. For folk music fans there's the *Pipers' Club,* 14 Thomas St. (Saturdays) and the *Coffee Kitchen,* Molesworth St. Best check with hotel porter for the current top spot.

ENTERTAINMENT. The famous *Abbey Theatre* is in a new building on Abbey Street with an experimental outfit, the *Peacock,* in a miniature theater in the same building. *Gaiety,* South King Street, grand opera, musical comedy, drama. *Olympia,* Dame Street, offers similar fare and sometimes vaudeville. *Gate,* Parnell Square, for modern drama and Irish plays (usually in English). There's a pocket theater, the *Eblana,* in the basement of Busarus (bus station) where satirical revue can often be caught. The *Project* in Essex St. is another pocket theater with strong off-beat interest; and if you're staying on the south side, there is the *Oscar* at Ballsbridge, and the *Pavilion* at Dun Laoghaire. Several hotels offer theater presentations and *Jury's* Irish cabaret is famous. Dublin isn't a nightclub city and those advertised are mainly disco spots. Check for current offerings with Tourist Information Office or the hotel porter.

MUSEUMS. *The National Museum of Irish Antiquities,* between Kildare and Merrion Street. Open from 11 A.M. to 5 P.M. on weekdays and from 2 to 5 P.M. Sunday. *National Gallery,* Merrion Square, 10 A.M. to 6 P.M. Monday to Saturday and 2 to 5 P.M. on Sunday. *Municipal Gallery of Modern Art,* Parnell Square, open 10:30 A.M. to 6 P.M. daily except 1 to 2:15 and Mondays. But Sunday 11 to 2; Tuesday to 9 P.M. (September through May). *Hugh Lane Municipal Gallery,* Charlemont House, Parnell Square for modern paintings. *National Portrait Gallery* is at Malahide Castle on the north side of the city. Check for opening time.

Marsh's Library, adjoining St. Patrick's Cathedral, 25,000 volumes include some annotated by Dean Swift, original carved bookcases and cages into which readers were locked to prevent stealing; open Monday 2 to 4, Wednesday–Friday 10.30 to 4 except 12.30 to 2. *Trinity College Library,* College Green, open from 10 to 4 between February and October and from 10 to 3 from November to January. Closed two weeks in July.

National Library in Ireland, Kildare Street, open weekdays from 10 A.M. to 10 P.M., and 10 A.M. to 1 P.M. on Saturday.

The fine *Civic Museum,* South William Street, open from 11 to 1 and 2:30 to 6 weekdays except Thursday (11 to 1) and Sundays (2 to 5 P.M.), is full of interesting sidelights on old Dublin. *Kilmainham Jail Museum,* open Sunday afternoons, has many relics of the Irish fight for freedom. There's an *Aviation Museum* in the Terminal Building at Dublin Airport. New *Maritime* Museum in one-time Mariner's Church at Dun Laoghaire should be open this year.

SHOPPING. Among the bargains are Irish handwoven tweeds, including the white tweeds known as *bawneen.* The price is remarkably standard and very reasonable.

Switzer's on Grafton Street, *Kevin & Howlin* in Suffolk Street, and the *Irish Cottage Industries* in Dawson Street all have extensive stocks. For a man who wants to have a sports jacket made up right away, *O'Beirne & Fitzgibbon,* 14 Upper O'Connell Street, specialize in this department.

If you really want to explore the tweed possibilities, you should visit Connemara and Donegal where the wool is washed, dyed and teazed. If you are in the West try *Mairtin Standun* at Spiddal, near Galway, for a wide choice of excellent tweeds at reasonable prices. The *Avoca Handweavers* at Avoca, Co. Wicklow, and the *Crock of Gold,* nearer to Dublin at Blackrock, and *Weaver's Shed,* Duke Lane, Dublin, are also good for tweeds.

Sybil Connolly at 71 Merrion Square has an international reputation with her imaginative use of tweeds for every occasion. Also worth visiting are *Raymond Kenna,* 56 Merrion Sq., *Ib Jorgensen,* 24 Fitzwilliam Sq. and *Mary O'Donnell,* 43 Dawson St.; also *Thomas Wolfangel,* 99 Lower Baggot St., and *Rufina,* 10 Lr Leeson St.

And don't miss the smart tweed bags and other accessories at the *Cottage Industries Ltd.* Nearby at Duke Street there's *Creation Boutique* filled with the magnificent traditional sweaters knitted by the women of the West.

Irish linens? Try *Arnott's* on Henry Street, *Brown Thomas* on Grafton Street, and *Switzer's,* all of whom feature wonderful selections at low prices.

Other excellent buys in Ireland are Waterford glass, Belleek china and Peterson pipes—and, to go with the pipe, a blackthorn walking stick, perhaps from *Johnston Ltd.,* Wicklow St. For a gun or a rod, try *Garnetts & Keegan's,* 31 Parliament St.

Irish jewelry is unusual and attractive; see *Rionore,* 38 Molesworth St., and *Market Ireland,* 75 Grafton St. Old Irish silver is a good buy at auctions or antique shops in the Grafton Street area. The *Kilkenny Shop* has a fine display of jewelry and other Irish crafts in the Setanta Center on Nassau St., beside Trinity College.

TOURS FROM DUBLIN. C.I.E. (Coras Iompair Eireann) operates rail and bus tours in and around Dublin at reasonable prices. In summer they also offer tours to some of the most lovely parts of the country.

Environs of Dublin

Not to be missed are: Howth Castle, a 16th-century baronial mansion in a setting of azaleas and rhododendrons; Malahide Castle, where a sensational discovery of important Boswell manuscripts was made in 1950; a trip from Drogheda along the Boyne Valley, where Irish history goes back 5,000 years to the days when all roads led to Tara; Slane, where St. Patrick, celebrating the Christian rites of Easter, kindled, in defiance of the Druid religion, the fire "that would burn forever and consume Tara"; Brugh na Bóinne, the pre-Christian burying ground of Tara's kings, and the fascinating primitive cairns and tombs near Dowth, Newgrange, and Knowth; the impressive church, abbey, and castle ruins, like an outdoor museum, at Meath; Kells, in whose eighth century abbey the Book of Kells was written—see also the perfect round tower, St. Columbcille's House, and the Kells collection of high crosses. The beautifully-sculptured high crosses at Monasterboice are worth a special trip. Sportsmen will be interested in Navan, a fox-hunting center, and the National Stud in Tully, County Kildare. South of Dublin, visitors can see Torca Cottage on Dalkey Hill, where Bernard Shaw lived for many years, and may be admitted for a small fee to Powerscourt Demesne to see the formal gardens and the 3,400-acre park. Finally, there are the great religious ruins of Glendalough, 30 miles south of Dublin by way of picturesque Sally Gap. The round tower and tiny barrel-vaulted Church of St. Kevin still survive.

Practically on Dublin's doorstep there's a vast playground of fine beaches, quiet country retreats, resorts, hunting and fishing centers and historic villages. Dun Laoghaire with its mile-long harbor piers and Marine Parade is Dublin's most popular seaside spot. To the city's north, Howth and Malahide are not far behind in unsophisticated appeal.

PRACTICAL INFORMATION FOR THE ENVIRONS

TOURS FROM DUN LAOGHAIRE. These include: (1) Moore's famed *Meeting of the Waters.* Via Bray, Greystones, Wicklow, Avoca. Return via Little Bray and Stillorgan (81 miles). (2) *Glendalough.* Via Foxrock, The Scalp, Enniskerry. Come back via Wicklow Gap, Blessington, Brittas, Rathfarnham, Dundrum, and Stillorgan (72 miles). (3) *Enniskerry.* Via Bray, Powerscourt Desmesne. Return via Scalp, Foxrock (40 miles). (4) *Drogheda.* Via Dublin, Howth, Malahide, Swords, Skerries, and Balbriggan. Return via Ashbourne and Dublin (100 miles).

COUNTY DUBLIN

DALKEY, a seaside suburb that contrives to maintain much of the atmosphere of the little fishing township around which it developed. Hotels: *Dalkey Heights* (2), 11 rooms with bath, overlooks Killiney Bay. *Dalkey Island,* (2), has 15 rooms with bath. Updated and extended in 1978.

DUN LAOGHAIRE. Hotels: *Royal Marine* (2), fashionable and gay, 115 rooms, 90 with bath, and the standard of cuisine is high. Modern *Pierre* overlooks harbor (2).

HOWTH, a fishing port and sailing center across Dublin Bay from Dalkey and Dun Laoghaire. Hotels: *St. Lawrence* (2), 24 rooms. *Deerpark* (3) with its own golf course, 27 rooms, 15 with bath.

KILLINEY overlooks attractive sandy bay. *Fitzpatrick's Castle,* remodeled with about 50 rooms, has setting and style, heated swimming pool; and *The Court,* also recently remodeled, both (1).

KILTERNAN. *Dublin Sport* (2) located on attractive estate with grand views of countryside and sea; facilities include golf course, artificial ski run, 48 rooms with bath.

MALAHIDE. Coastal village 9 miles north of Dublin. Hotel: *Grand* (2), in extensive grounds. 61 rooms, 20 with bath, golf, fishing, horseback riding, bathing.

SUTTON, on north arm of Dublin Bay. Hotels: *Sutton House* (1), 22 rooms, 17 with bath, is converted mansion on a hill overlooking the sea. *Marine* (2), inside Dublin boundary, 27 rooms, 6 with bath; heated indoor pool overlooked by dining room.

COUNTY WICKLOW

BRAY, a seaside resort, 13 miles south of Dublin. Hotels: *Royal Starlight* (2), main street, 104 rooms, most with bath; rooftop restaurant. *Strand* and *Lacy's,* both (3).

Bray is a good center for touring the "Garden of Ireland" and hotels with a rural setting are the *Delgany Inn* (1), *Royal* at Glendalough and *Glen View* at Glen o'the Downs; *Roundwood Inn,* at Roundwood (near Glendalough); *Downshire House,* farther inland at Blessington; all (2).

Across Bray Head at Greystones, good sea angling spot, *La Touche* (2), 50 rooms, overlooks the sea. *Woodlands,* (2) 16 rooms, 7 with bath, also at Greystones, is on an estate beside the sea.

Southeast Vacationland

Southeast of Dublin is the beguiling scenery of the Vale of Avoca and Tom Moore's country. Near the "Meeting of the Waters" you can sit under the same tree in whose shade the poet dreamed lyrics while looking over his beloved countryside. The town of Avoca itself is the place to see and buy the Avoca handwoven tweeds.

Wexford was a Danish settlement for two centuries, subsequently a walled stronghold of the Anglo-Norman conquerors. See the Westgate Tower, part of the old fortifications, the ruins of 12th-century Selskar Abbey, the Bull Ring where the Normans baited bulls, and Johnstown Castle, now an agricultural college. Wexford County was John F. Kennedy's ancestral home. To commemorate this, the Kennedy Memorial Park has been opened nearby. The Wexford Festival of Opera (late October) is a major cultural event. For information and bookings, write well in advance to Wexford Festival Office at the Theatre Royal, Wexford.

Waterford brings to mind the dazzling cut glass that has carried this city's name to the homes and banquet halls of the world. Nearly ruined by a 19th-century British excise tax, the glass industry has been revived and Waterford glass is again available. The factory may be visited to see craftsmen at work. Phone (051) 3371 for time of tour, or check with your hotel porter. See the great fortress, Reginald's Tower, erected in 1003, now a museum, the city walls dating back to the Danish invasion, and the 18th-century City Hall. Eight miles from Waterford is Tramore, a popular beach resort with swimming, fishing, golf, and, as the high point of interest, horse racing, especially in August.

PRACTICAL INFORMATION FOR THE SOUTHEAST

ARKLOW. *Arklow Bay* (2), modern motel, 29 rooms, 19 with bath.

ROSSLARE, point of arrival for ferry services from Fishguard (Wales) and Le Havre (France). Hotels: *Strand* (2), 91 rooms, 55 with bath, lively; sauna, heated indoor pool. The 100-room *Great Southern,* same category, also has indoor pool and sauna. *Harbour View,* recently modernized and noted for food, 26 rooms, 5 with bath, and *Golf,* 25 rooms, 13 with bath, are both (2).

TRAMORE, 8 miles south of Waterford City, one of the most popular seaside resorts in Ireland, caters for a busy seasonal trade. Hotels: *Grand, Majestic* (indoor pool) and *Shalloe's Cliff* (2). *Atlantic, Seaview* and *Tramore* (3). *Majestic Holiday Apartments* (new) have an indoor heated pool; *Tramore Failte* offers holiday chalets.

WATERFORD, a busy port and industrial center. Hotels: *Ardree,* 100 rooms with bath is recent and overlooks the port from a height. *Tower* (1), 100 rooms with bath or shower, is modern and with excellent cuisine. The *Bridge,* on the quays, and the *Metropole* (3).

WEXFORD. Hotels: *Talbot* (1), both quiet elegance and comfort. Excellent cuisine. *White's* (1), is based on old family inn with modern bedroom block and public rooms. *Bargy Castle* (2), Tomhaggard, 10 miles south of Wexford, is a 12th-century castle with modern comforts on 170-acre estate.

While hereabouts join the *Galley* at New Ross for an excellent lunch or dinner cruising on the rivers Barrow, Nore and Suir (April through October).

Cork, City and County

Cork, on the River Lee, is Ireland's second city, and has a long history of rebellion against oppression. In the 19th century the city spearheaded the Fenian Movement, and "Rebel Cork" supplied a number of patriots for Irish independence including two lord mayors, Thomas MacCurtain and Terence MacSwiney, who died for the cause, the latter starving himself to death in jail after a hunger strike of 74 days, the longest fast in medical history. Cork people are reputed to be the most talkative in Ireland—which is saying a lot. This may have something to do with nearby Blarney Castle, with its stone which reputedly imparts the gift of eloquence to all who kiss it. Nearby is the seaport of Cobh, with its lofty St. Colman's Cathedral.

PRACTICAL INFORMATION FOR CORK AND ENVIRONS

HOTELS

CORK. *Cork Jury's,* on Muskerry Island, 96 rooms with bath, all modern amenities. *Metropole,* remodeled (1978) to provide baths for all 130 rooms, and new restaurants. The *Imperial* has been updated and all its 83 rooms have baths; excellent cuisine. All (1).

Silver Springs, (2), 72 rooms with bath or shower.

Arbutus Lodge (outstanding for food), *Ashbourne, Glengariffe* and *Moore's* are all (3).

BALLYLICKEY. Free fishing for both salmon and trout is a bonus attraction at *Ballylickey House* (2), 26 rooms with bath. Food is memorable.

BLARNEY. *Blarney* (2), 76 rooms with bath, located beside the famous Blarney Castle.

COBH. The *Commodore* (2), 50 rooms, most with bath. *Rinn Ronain* and *European* are (4).

GLENGARRIFF. *Casey's* (2), *Eccles* (3), *Golf Links, Mountain View* and *O'-Sheas,* all (4).

INISHANNON. The *Inishannon* (2) has 10 rooms, 8 with bath, and is well worth going off the beaten track to visit; excellent food.

KINSALE. Well known as an international big game fishing spot. *Trident* has 40 rooms with bath, boat hire, etc. *Acton's,* 63 rooms, 37 with bath, modernized, swimming pool. *Monastry,* 10 rooms with bath. *Blue Haven,* 11 rooms, all (2). Several outstanding restaurants: try *Man Friday* and *The Spinnaker.*

YOUGHAL. *Hilltop,* 50 rooms with bath and *Monatrea House,* both (3).

 RESTAURANTS. The top hotels feature good food. *Blackrock Castle,* located on the edge of the River Lee, is a must. *The Tivoli Restaurant and Grill,* Patrick St., is another top spot for top Corkonians. Both moderate. *The Mall Tavern,* Marlboro' St., and *Halpin's Delicatessen,* Cook St., are good places for inexpensive snacks. Out of town is the famous *Yeats Room,* Shanagarry, and Myrtle Allen's equally renowned *Ballymaloe House Restaurant,* for country house cooking. Book ahead.

 WHAT TO SEE. In *Cork City:* Shandon Church with its famous bells; modern Christ the King Church designed by an American architect; the University College with its Hiberno-Romanesque Honan Chapel; French Gothic style St. Finbarr's Cathedral. In *Cork County:* Blarney Castle (five miles from Cork City); with its famed Blarney Stone, Youghal, popular seaside resort (pronounced "Yawl"), villa where Sir Walter Raleigh lived; Ballycotton, noted sea angling spot on Ballycotton Bay; Kinsale, first class center for deep-sea fishermen; Bantry and Glengariff, both on Bantry Bay, seaside spots with a fine rural setting. Visit Garnish Island from Glengariff; beautiful gardens.

The Lakes of Killarney

Killarney deserves all of its fame in song and story, and so does the whole Kingdom of Kerry, with its romantic glens, towering peaks, majestic seacoast and constantly-changing colors. It's been said more than once that Kerry is the best that Ireland has to offer, and when you see it, you won't be surprised that visitors flock from all over the world to see this magnificent southwestern tip of Ireland. Since you can't do Killarney's famous lakes by car we recommend slowing down here and seeing them from one of the slow-moving horse-drawn jaunting cars, a trademark of Killarney. Don't miss the Muckross Estate and Muckross Abbey, under whose spell Tennyson wrote, "The splendor falls on castle walls . . . " and travel the famous Ring of Kerry, the complete circuit around the peninsula between the Kenmare River and Dingle Bay, one of Europe's greatest scenic drives. "Irish Nights", an entertainment of ballads, dancing and old tales, are regular events: ask at your hotel for the location. Accommodation is tight in summer, so contact your travel agent early. (Fall and spring are good times to visit, too.) Best headquarters for seeing Killarney's lakes and the spectacular coastline of Kerry are Killarney, Kenmare, Parknasilla, Glenbeigh.

PRACTICAL INFORMATION FOR KERRY

Cottages. You can rent a thatched Irish cottage (newly built with all modern conveniences) at Ballyvaughan or Corofin (Shannon Airport, 48 miles) at basic weekly rental charges from approximately £50 in April to £150 in July/August. Contact *Rent-an-Irish-Cottage* (Shannon Airport, Co. Clare).

DINGLE. *Sceilig* (2), 80 rooms with bath, is deep in the heart of Kerry's dramatic scenery, right by the Atlantic edge.

KILLARNEY. Hotels: In town are the *Great Southern* (L), 165 rooms with bath, *International* and *Three Lakes* (2). *Aghadoe Heights* (1), overlooking the Middle Lake, has 25 rooms with bath, excellent grill bar.

Pleasantly situated just outside are *Europe,* 168 rooms with bath, overlooking the lakes, and *Dunloe Castle,* 140 rooms with bath, same management, both (1). All equally pleasantly situated are: *Lake Hotel,* 72 rooms, *Muckross,* 42 rooms, *Cathernane,* 40 rooms, half with bath, and *International,* 130 rooms, 66 with bath, all (2). *Killarney Ryan,* 168 rooms with bath, and *Torc Great Southern,* 96 rooms with bath, are (2) motor hotels.

KENMARE. *Riversdale House,* 40 rooms, 30 with bath, and *Kenmare Bay,* 50 rooms with bath, are (2).

PARKNASILLA. Hotel: In an exotic setting is C.I.E.'s *Great Southern* (1), 76 rooms, 57 with bath; has food and service to please the discriminating guest. Heated pool.

TRALEE. Hotels: *Mount Brandon,* 164 rooms with bath; *Earl of Desmond,* 52 rooms with bath, and *Ballyseede Castle,* 13 rooms most with bath, all are (2). Last-named is updated 15th-century castle in 300-acre estate; medieval banquets in summer.

WATERVILLE. An angler's paradise, whether for sea or river fishing. Hotels: *Waterville Lake* (L), 102 rooms with bath, is recent, has it own golf course. *Butler Arms,* 49 rooms, 10 with bath; *Bayview* (2), 29 rooms, some with bath. *Ostlann Rinn Rua,* (2) 45 rooms with bath.

VALENTIA ISLAND, tiny and reached by bridge from the mainland. Hotel: *Royal* (2), 47 rooms, 25 with bath, offers excellent sea fishing, shooting, swimming and boating. For the young there is sub-aqua exploration in the waters hereabouts.

Limerick City

Limerick is the gateway to Ireland, only an hour's bus ride away from Shannon Airport. It is a good place from which to explore the Shannon Estuary, the magnificent Cliffs of Moher (one of Ireland's top sightseeing attractions), and the Lough Gur excavations of dolmens, megalithic tombs and other relics from neolithic to medieval times. In the city itself, see the Treaty Stone (Limerick's trademark), King John's Castle (13th century) and St. Mary's Cathedral, dating from the ninth century—its tower once housed the legendary "Bells of St. Mary's". Also visit Adare Manor (small fee), home of the earls of Dunraven since the 17th century. If you're touring and want to miss the city there is a useful car ferry downriver across the Shannon from Tarbert in Kerry to Killimer on the northern shore, on the way to Connemara. Trip takes 14 minutes and cuts out a lot of mileage.

PRACTICAL INFORMATION FOR LIMERICK AND SHANNON

LIMERICK. *Limerick Jury's* is top of the list; 96 rooms with bath. *Cruise's,* O'Connell St., 80 rooms, most with bath. *Royal George,* 36 rooms with bath. *Limerick Inn,* 133 rooms with bath; all are (2). There are several motor hotels: *Limerick Ryan,* 184 rooms with bath) and the *Parkway,* 103 rooms with bath, both (3).

SHANNON. *Shannon International* (1), at the airport, 126 rooms with bath. Eight miles away at Newmarket-on-Fergus, 16th-century *Dromoland Castle* has been converted into one of Ireland's most luxurious hotels, 67 rooms with bath. The *Clare Inn* (1), located on the same estate, has 121 rooms with bath. *Shannon Shamrock Inn* (2), 85 rooms with bath, at Bunratty. Pleasant setting, convenient for Shannon Airport.

Shannon Airport has a number of stopover tours. Medieval Banquet at restored *Bunratty Castle* is a lively night out in the 15th-century manner. There's more entertainment at *Knappogue Castle* which offers nightly pageants. There's an Irish folk village beside Bunratty Castle that is certainly worth a visit.

An internal air service links Shannon with Waterville in Kerry; Cong, Co. Mayo; Galway and the offshore Aran Islands. Check with Aer Lingus for schedules at Shannon.

Castle Matrix at Rathkeale, Co. Limerick, features medieval banquets in summer.

Tipperary

The Golden Vale of Tipperary is the heart of Ireland's dairyland and fine sporting country. It's only 112 miles from Dublin and worth making the trip to see The Rock of Cashel, thousand-year-old buildings topping a rocky hill. From the road they look as sound as the day they were built. In County Tipperary see also Holycross Abbey, a 15th-century church restored for present-day use. Longfield House, at Goold's Cross (near Cashel).

Galway and the Islands

Galway, main city of western Ireland, is an ancient seaport whose waterfront promenade was frequented by Spanish grandees and traders of more prosperous times. Little of old Galway remains today, but there is still a hint of the Iberian influence in some of the buildings. The salmon fishing in the River Corrib is unsurpassed. In early summer you can stand at the Weir Bridge and watch thousands of these fish in the clear water as they leap and teem through the narrow access to the inland lakes. Lynch's "Castle" in Shop Street, now a bank, is an example of a 16th-century fortified house. In Kennedy (formerly Eyre) Square, stands the statue of Padraic O'Conaire, greatest of Irish storytellers.

Galway is also the center from which one visits the fascinating Aran Islands—Inishmore, Inishmaan and Inisheere. The mode of life on these islands, 30 miles off the coast, epitomizes man's unremitting struggle against nature in the most dramatic and primitive terms. The strikingly handsome men of Aran wear knitted tams, fanciful woolen sweaters, heel-less rawhide slippers called *pampootie,* white *bawneen coats,* and a really colorful woolen *crios* (waistband). During summer, boats leave Galway at least three times a week for the islands, and it's possible to visit the main island for several hours and pick up the boat on its return trip. An air ferry operates to Inishmore and Inishmaan; check locally for schedules. There are no hotels on the isles, but there are three guesthouses.

Early in September there is an Oyster Festival at Galway to inaugurate the new season. This is a lively festival, with oysters from Clarenbridge and stout.

Many people have found relaxation at places like Achill in County Mayo, an island reached by bridge, and Cong, between Lough Mask, and Lough Corrib, where the lonely, lovely countryside has a soothing effect. While in the vicinity, see Westport House (Westport), a well-preserved and still lived-in Georgian mansion by a lake, now a museum of antiques and paintings; it's the family home of the Marquess of Sligo.

Sligo, Donegal and Leitrim

Sligo is the gateway to Ireland's scenic northwest. Hereabouts are the places and lakes immortalized by William Butler Yeats, who is buried, where he chose, in lonely Drumcliff churchyard, in the shadow "of Ben Bulben's head". Sligo Town, with its seaside resorts and championship golf courses, is the main center. See Sligo Abbey founded in 1252; St. John's Church, dating from 1635; Glencar Lough, a lake with waterfalls, rivaling Killarney for beauty; the ancient Celtic Cross by the roadside at Drumcliff near the grave of Yeats, whose work is studied at annual Yeats International Summer School sessions in Sligo.

Tucked up in the northwestern corner of Ireland is mountainringed Donegal, Ultima Thule, "the world's end". Now that highways span the windswept moors and highlands, it is easy to reach this land, and see the handloomed Donegal tweeds, gems of craftsmanship produced by village weavers. A good on-the-spot place to buy them is at *McNutt's* in Downings, where the selection of patterns is wide.

Leitrim is a county neglected by visitors, but it's the place where the River Shannon starts to attract inland waterway holidaymakers and fishermen. The principal town, Carrick-on-Shannon, is the base for river-cruise boat operators.

The Inland Counties

Although the inland counties of Ireland may lack the inspiring scenery of Kerry, the West and Donegal, the motoring tourist will find plenty of interest. For the angler in search of the coarser varieties of fish, Cavan and Monaghan have hundreds of lakes and all you need is a rod and a license that costs £2. Robert Trent Jones designed the golf course in the grounds of Glaslough House in County Monaghan.

Westmeath is noted mainly for its hunting country, but Tullynally Castle near Mullingar is a must. It's the family home of the Earls of Longford and is open to visitors in summer, when there's usually a member of the family around to talk entertainingly about the wonderful collection of antiques gathered by their ancestors. To the south, in Offaly, Cloghan Castle at Banagher (built in 1120) is one of the oldest inhabited buildings in Ireland; it may be visited, and so may the gardens of the Earl of Ross's estate at Birr Castle—the gardens are famous, and so were the giant telescopes of his forebears, parts of which can still be seen.

PRACTICAL INFORMATION FOR THE REGIONS

ACHILL ISLAND. The island is reached by a bridge and provides both conviviality in its hotels and plenty of uncrowded beaches. Hotels: *Ostan Gob a'Choire* (2) has 36 rooms, most with bath; *Achill Head, Atlantic, Corrymore House* (noted for its restaurant), *Slievemore* and *Wavecrest* are all (3).

BALLYNAHINCH (Co. Galway). The historic castle of the Martyn family has been converted into the *Ballynahinch Castle Hotel* (L), which provides country club accommodation in the midst of superb scenery and fine fishing water.

BUNDORAN. Gateway to the Donegal highlands. Hotels: *Great Northern* (1), 105 rooms, half with bath, right on the golf links, with a fine view of sea and cliffs. *Hamilton,* with swimming pool, *Central, Holyrood, Imperial* all (2).

CARRIGART. Another open space spot in Donegal and one of the places where you'll hear great talk, particularly at the *Carrigart* (2), 56 rooms most with bath.

CASHEL. Hotels: *Cashel Palace,* once an archbishop's palace, has been converted to a luxury hotel with pleasant character. *Derby Grill* in the old cellars. *Cashel Kings* (3), 40 rooms with bath, located close to famous Rock of Cashel. *Longfield House* (2), not far away at Goold's Cross, is an historic house converted to a 10 room hotel, most rooms with bath.
Restaurant: *Chez Hans,* (M) for outstanding meals.

CASTLEBAR. Hotels: *Breaffy House* (1), based on an old mansion, 43 rooms, all with bath. *Traveller's Friend* and *Welcome Inn* are (4).

CLONMEL. Hotels: *Clonmel Arms,* (2) 41 rooms, 20 with bath, on bank of river Suir. *Minella,* 40 rooms most with bath and *Hearn's,* 31 rooms, half with bath, both (3).

CONG. Hotel: *Ashford Castle* (L), a former castle in the Ashford Demesne. Acres of green lawns, lakes teeming with fish. 77 rooms with bath.

DUNFANAGHY. On Rosguil peninsula. Hotel: The proverbially hospitable *Port-na-Blagh* (1), has 60 rooms, some with bath.

DUNGLOE. The heart of Donegal's famous Rosses. Hotel: *Ostan na Rossan* (2), 50 rooms with bath.

GALWAY. Hotels: In the heart of the city, *Great Southern* (L), one of the larger hotels in the C.I.E. chain; 128 rooms with bath, rooftop restaurant, swimming pool. *Ardilaun House* (1), 65 rooms, 43 with bath. *Galway Ryan,* a motor hotel, has 96 rooms with bath. Other motor hotels are *Flannery's,* 72 rooms with bath, and *Corrib Great Southern,* 117 rooms with bath.

MALRANNY (Mulrany). Hotel: on the way to Achill Island. A fine scenic setting. *Great Western* (1), 71 rooms most with bath; swimming pool, big game fishing.

NENAGH. Hotels: *O'Meara's* and *Ormond* are modern and (2). *Nenagh Motor Inn,* Dublin side of town, 20 rooms with bath.

RENVYLE. *Renvyle House* (2), beside the Twelve Pins Mountains in Connemara, 78 rooms with bath. Excellent food.

ROSAPENNA. On the Rosguil peninsula. Hotel: *Rosapenna Golf Hotel* (L), 40 rooms with bath, close by one of the finest golf courses in the country.

ROSSES POINT. Hotel: *Yeats Country Ryan* (2), 100 rooms, most with bath, has splendid view to the sea and mountains over the greens of the celebrated golf course.

ROSSNOWLAGH. Hotel: *Sand House,* (2) 40 rooms, half with bath, overlooks Donegal Bay.

SLIGO. Hotels: *Innisfree,* 54 rooms, 39 with bath, *Sligo Park,* 60 rooms with bath, *Silver Swan,* 24 rooms, 16 with bath, all (2).

THURLES. *Hayes,* 37 rooms, 15 with bath. Good center for County Tipperary.

WESTPORT. Hotels: *Westport Woods,* 56 rooms with bath; *Westport,* 49 rooms with bath; *Cavanaugh's,* 18 rooms most with bath; *Clew Bay,* 37 rooms, some with bath. All are (2) and located in top sea angling and touring center.

Northern Ireland
As the situation in the Six Counties, the northeastern corner, has been changing at press time, we have felt it wise to omit this section. Consult your travel agent on current conditions.

ITALY

For the past 2,000 years, more foreigners have been exploring Italy than any other European country. Why? Not just because she is a pace setter in the field of fashion, design and the cinema, not to mention being the birth place of *la dolce vita*. Those are only recent manifestations. The reason for her age-old fascination lies more in the fact that she has been at the very basis of our Western way of life, creating incredible works of art, century after century, producing some of the greatest thinkers, writers, politicians and saints. And the traces of their lives and works still exist in the great buildings and lovely countryside.

The whole of Italy is one vast attraction, but since we must select a target area, we'd advise the triangle of her most-visited cities—Rome, Florence and Venice—for first-time visitors, with side trips, time permitting, to Naples and Milan. Art lovers can see most of their highlights in these cities. Lovers of natural beauty should make for the Naples area, with Amalfi, Sorrento, Capri, Ischia and Positano, or the lake region, or, for wild mountain scenery, the Dolomites. For water sports, Sardinia, the area around Rimini, or the Western Italian Riviera. For winter sports in an elegant setting, try Cortina d'Ampezzo.

For the religious faithful, a trip to Italy can concentrate on visits to the Vatican, to Assisi, Loreto and Turin, among other sites of pilgrimage. For a combination of art, history, religion and vibrant humanity, it's Rome!

The natural splendor of this sunflooded peninsula, flanked by the Mediterranean and the Adriatic, and stretching 700 miles from the Alps and flowerbordered lakes of the north to the cobalt seas and golden beaches of Sicily, is good enough reason to come. But that is just a happy accident of geography. More important is the fact that this varied landscape is almost everywhere punctuated by the works of men, and the men on this promontory seem always to have had the instincts and skills of creative artisans.

The People

The Italian people, inheritors of all the beauty that surrounds them in such profusion, have that old, conservative respect for technical competence which comes to them from a long background in which artisans were artists and artists remained artisans. And their reactions, both negative and positive, are apt to be vocal, violent, as direct as a child's. They do not bottle up their resentment; they just explode.

You will always know where you stand with the Italians. Their approach to you as a tourist will be refreshingly direct. They will be curious about you in a simple friendly way because their chief interest is in human personality. Less intellectual, less closed, more accessible and far more sentimental than the French, they will put themselves out for you in all sorts of ways.

Do not expect any uniformity of physical type among the Italians. Remember that 1,400 years of almost continual invasions have added Greek, Saracen, Norman, Spanish and German blood to that of the original Roman stock, which in itself was far from homogeneous. In general you will find the South Italians swarthy, stocky, dark-eyed and black-haired, although blondes are always showing up in Sicily to remind you that the ubiquitous Normans were there. The North Italian is usually lighter of skin and eye than his compatriot of the Mezzogiorno, and his hair is often brown rather than black.

Food and Drink

Italian food, one of the world's truly great cuisines, is so complex and colorful that we have had to describe it separately in the regional sections of this chapter. Just a hint of its exciting variety should remind you what you're in for, however: white truffles from Piedmont, *osso buco* from Milan, *minestrone* from Lombardy, *scampi* from Venice, sausages from the Dolomites, *calamaretti* from Trieste, *fritti misti* from Liguria, *tagliatelle* from Bologna, dried codfish with tomato sauce from Florence, *cacciucco* from Viareggio, black truffles from Umbria, *brodetto* from the Marches, *fettuccine* from Rome, pizza from Naples, fish soup in Sardinia, roast kid in Calabria and eggplant in Sicily!

And most regions have their own wines and cheeses. The virtues of *Chianti, Soave Bolla, Bardolino* and *Valpolicella,* are well-known throughout the world. The cheeses are less popular outside Italy, but if you haven't tried Gorgonzola or Bel Paese elsewhere this is the place to get them.

Shopping

Today, shopping in Italy means fashion accessories, textiles, and anything else you can hang on your body, cover it with, or use for decoration or practical purpose. For both men and women, the fashion houses and boutiques of Rome, Florence, Venice and Milan, are the places to go. In addition, good buys include leather goods, ceramics, straw goods and other handicrafts, and then all the regional specialties such as Venetian glass and cameos from Naples, which are outlined in the regional sections of this chapter, following.

PRACTICAL INFORMATION FOR ITALY

WHAT WILL IT COST. Just to give you an idea, here are some prices for various items and services in Italy: Hotels —in a deluxe hotel in Rome, Milan or Venice you will pay 35,000 to 55,000 lire for a single with private bath; 45,000 to 80,000 for a double with bath, considerably less in the provinces. The charges in a first-class hotel will be 15,000 for a single without bath up to 30,000 for a single with, or 23,000 and 50,000 respectively for double accommodations. Second-class tariffs are about 9,000 lire for a single without bath up to 16,000 for a single with, or 15,000 and 20,000 respectively for a double. Third-class hotels charge about 6,000 without, 8,000 with bath for a single; 8,000 without, 12,000 with for a double. **Note:** *It's probable that by 1979 these rates will be increased by about 10 percent.*

Outside large cities and major resorts, you will be able to do somewhat better. Don't forget, however, that service charges and taxes can increase the above as much as 20%, not to mention supplements for heating in winter (or for air conditioning in summer!).

Meals are an equally elastic quantity. Breakfast in a bar falls into the 800-1,500 lire range but for lunch and dinner you can spend anywhere from 6,000 lire per person in a modest restaurant up to 20,000 in a first-class one, including wine and service. Deluxe hotels and chic dinner clubs cost much more. Bottled wine ups the tab by 4–6,000 lire. Fixed-price meals (including service charge) are offered in most restaurants; the price varies according to the restaurant's category. Ask for the menu turistico.

A man's haircut runs to about 5,500 lire with tip. A woman's shampoo and set comes to at least 6,000. A few other items: 500 lire for a pack of Italian cigarettes, 750 for American; 250 for a Havana cigar; opera seats from 2,000 to 8,000; movie, from 1,500 to 2,500; 10,000 and up for a nightclub.

Beach charges can add to your expenses at coast resorts unless your hotel has a private beach. Entrance charges at bathing establishments run from 1,000-5,000 lire and include cabin, umbrella and deckchair. Public beaches are free but are scarce in built-up areas such as the Ligurian and Adriatic rivieras and are uncomfortably crowded on summer Sundays.

Cost-trimming Tips: If you're staying at a big-city hotel, forego their usually skimpy breakfasts (cost, up to 2,500 lire) in favor of the nearest bar, where the coffee will be hotter and the brioches crispier at half the price.

Bottled wine in restaurants may be better than the local carafe wine, but it can be very expensive: and the carafe wine is usually pleasant, so order it now and again as a pocket-saver.

Don't make long-distance calls from your hotel. Go to the Post or "Telefoni" Office.

Give a thought to varying the usual tourist itinerary. Of course you'll want to see Rome, Venice and Florence, but how about all those lesser-known (and cheaper) places in between? Try the smaller resort towns on the big Italian lakes, the quieter ski resorts in Alto Adige (South Tyrol) and the Valle d'Aosta. Entire regions that have for too long been ignored offer unspoiled beauty at bargain prices: Umbria (Perugia, Assisi, Spoleto); Abruzzi (L'Aquila, Pescara); Calabria, Apulia, and most of Sardinia *except* the Costa Smeralda.

CAPITAL. Rome.

LANGUAGE. Italian, English spoken in most hotels and shops.

CLIMATE. July and August temperatures can soar into the 90's in Rome, Venice, Florence and Naples.

Average maximum daily temperatures in degrees Fahrenheit and centigrade:

Milan	Jan.	Feb.	Mar.	Apr.	May	June	July	Aug.	Sept.	Oct.	Nov.	Dec.
F°	41	46	55	64	73	81	84	82	75	63	50	43
C°	5	8	13	18	23	27	29	28	24	17	10	6
Naples												
F°	54	55	59	64	72	79	84	84	79	72	63	57
C°	12	13	15	18	22	26	29	29	26	22	17	14

SEASONS. Main tourist season is from beginning of May to end of September. Secondary seasons: December to March for winter sports in the Dolomites; February to March in sunny Sicily. Seasoned travelers prefer Florence in May, Venice in September, Rome at Easter or in October.

 SPECIAL EVENTS. *January,* Greek Catholic Epiphany rites at Piana degli Albanesi, near Palermo. *February,* pre-Lenten carnivals particularly the Viareggio Carnival before Shrove Tuesday (sometimes in March); Almond Blossom Festival at Agrigento; the Saint Agatha Festival at Catania; the Flower Show at San Remo. *March,* nationwide mid-Lent festivals, and popular feasts, usually on St. Joseph's Day, the 19th; Florence's Scoppio del Carro (sometimes in April). *April,* International Handicrafts Fair, Florence; "Spring in Merano" automobile rally; International Horse Competition, Rome. *May,* Feast of S. Efisio in Cagliari; Festa dei Ceri, Gubbio; Sardinian Costume Cavalcade at Sassari; Maggio Musicale, Florence; Italian haute couture week, Florence. *June,* Tournament of the Bridge, Pisa; Festival of the Two Worlds, Spoleto; Terni (near Rome) Water Festival; International festival of Drama, Venice. *July,* the Palio, Siena (repeated in August); the Feast of the Redeemer, Venice; International Ballet Festival, Nervi; Palio della Contrade, medieval horse races, Siena. *August,* Tournament of the Quintana, Ascoli Piceno; opening of the International Film Festival, Venice; Feast of the Redeemer, Nuoro (Sardinia). *September,* The Joust of the Saracen, Arezzo; Historic Regatta, Venice; Feast of the Peidigrotta, Naples; Italian Grand Prix racing, Monza. *October,* celebrations in honor of Columbus, Genoa; Biennale, International Art Exhibition, Venice. *November,* Feast of the Madonna della Salute, Venice; International Automobile Show, Turin. *December,* traditional Christmas celebrations throughout the country; opera season opens at La Scala, Milan and other major opera houses (through April).

 CLOSING TIMES. In Rome, Naples and the south, shops are usually open from 9 to 1, closed from 1 to 4:30, then open again from 4:30 to 8. In the northern cities, this siesta is either not observed or considerably abbreviated. At all events, there will be individual variations in this individualistic land of *dolce far niente.* Banking hours are very short: from 8:30 to 1:30, closed afternoons. Banks are closed on Saturdays. Exchange (*cambio*) offices, however, have store hours. Museum hours vary greatly, and it's best to check locally. All are open at least in the morning; some close Monday. Vatican Museums close Sundays and religious holidays. Rome shops close Saturday afternoons in July and August.

National Holidays: January 1, Easter Sunday and Monday, May Day, June 2, August 15, November 1, November 4, Christmas, December 26.

SPORTS. *Football* (season runs September-June), *cycling, motor racing* (Grand Prix at Monza in September), and *tennis* are popular. The Dolomites and the Italian Alps offer the *skier* a vast selection of outstanding resorts that are also the scene of some daring *mountain climbing* expeditions in summer. The Aeolian Islands, Ustica, Sardinia and Elba are ideal ground for *underwater* and *deepsea fishing*.

MONEY. The monetary unit is the lira. There are about 909 lire to the dollar, 1727 to the pound *at presstime*. **Subject to change.** It may be advantageous for Americans to buy lire in New York. Another opportunity for buying at best rates is afforded to the tourist coming by way of Switzerland. In Italy you'll find a chronic shortage of small change.

 TIPPING. Charges for service are included in all hotel bills and restaurant checks. In general, give chambermaids an additional 300 lire per day (1500 per week), bellboys 200 lire per bag. Figure on 15 percent for the concierge if he has provided extra services. Checkroom attendants expect about 100 lire, as do washroom attendants. Theater ushers expect 200 lire. A service charge of 10-18 percent is included on restaurant bills, but add another 10 percent for the waiter. Taxi drivers expect about 10 percent, slightly more on short rides. Railway porters are entitled to charge 300 lire for each piece of luggage. If your suitcases are unusually heavy, or if you keep your porter waiting for longer than normal, an additional 200 lire will be appreciated. Service station attendants are tipped about 200 lire if they do more than fill the tank of your car.

HOTELS. In our listing of hotels, unless otherwise described, the indications L, 1, 2, 3, or 4 appearing in parentheses after the hotel name stand for deluxe, first, second, third or fourth-class ratings. The letter P preceding the number means it is a pension; a first-class pension is equal to a second-class hotel, etc. These ratings, which reflect the official government classifications, can be misleading: often hotels prefer to retain second- or third-class status for tax purposes even though their service and facilities would merit a higher rating from the traveler.

RESTAURANTS. One of Italy's boasts is that in almost all its restaurants, from the ultra-chic to the most unpretentious, you'll find food that is good, often excellent. A *ristorante* can be anything from deluxe to just another *trattoria*. And a *trattoria* is generally a rather simple, family-run place where the emphasis is on wholesome, appetizing food. At *rosticcerie* or the *tavola calda* you can get snacks or dinners at the counter. The very efficient restaurants along the *Autostrada del Sole* offer a variety of menus and every comfort imaginable for the traveler. Where we list restaurants (E), (M) or (I), this indicates expensive, moderate or inexpensive.

 HOW TO REACH ITALY. All roads and most airways lead to Rome. *Alitalia, TWA, JAL, El Al, Pan Am* and *Air India* have regular jet flights from New York and other cities. Numerous services from London and most Continental capitals. Leisurely Mediterranean sea routes by *Greek Line*.

Motorists can save time and energy by using the car-sleeper summer services: Boulogne-Milan; Ostend-Milan; Amsterdam-Milan; Paris-Milan; Düsseldorf-Milan. Also the Italian trains: Milan-Brindisi; Milan-Rome; Bolzano-Rome; Genoa-Rome.

The St. Bernard tunnel and the Mont Blanc tunnel are open, facilitating entry from Switzerland and France. All-year traffic. Toll.

CUSTOMS. Travelers arriving in Italy from an EEC country are allowed, duty-free, a total of 300 cigarettes (*or* 150 cigarillos *or* 75 cigars), 1½ liters of alcoholic spirits *or* 3 liters of sparkling wine, *plus* 3 liters of still wine — if duty and taxes have already been paid on them at the time of purchase. Travelers carrying goods from outside the EEC or goods that were purchased in duty-free shops or on aircraft are allowed 200 cigarettes (or 100 cigarillos or 50 cigars), 1 liter of spirits, 2 liters of still wine. Officially 10 rolls of still camera film and 10 reels of movie film may be brought in duty-free. Not more than 35,000 lire in Italian banknotes may be taken into or out of Italy.

 MAIL. Letters to England are 180 lire up to 20 grams (half an ounce; add 20 lire per 5 gr.) airmail, postcards about 150 lire; check with post office. Airmail to U.S. and Canada is 350 lire for one thin sheet and envelope; postcards about 250 lire air mail. Cables to the U.S. cost about 275 lire per word, to Britain less than half this rate. Post office hours: 8:30–midnight, Monday-Sat. Central post offices open until 9 P.M.; telegraph office, 24-hour service.

ELECTRICITY. Italian voltage is generally 125 or 220 AC.

DRINKING WATER. Safe in all larger towns. Off the beaten track, sample the regional wines. Bottled mineral waters available everywhere. Best known are *San Pellegrino* and *Fiuggi*. Sterilized pasteurized milk in sealed cartons and canned milk are sold everywhere.

 TRAVEL IN ITALY. By Train: Service is almost completely electrified. There are excellent services between major centers and *Rapido* trains are the fastest.

By Air: Italian cities on the mainland are linked to each other by air and to those on Sicily and Sardinia by the services of *Alitalia, Aerolinee Itavia* and *Aero Transporti Italiani,* all of which operate modern jet aircraft. Bookings for all domestic flights can be made at any travel agency.

By Ferry: Overnight boats connect Naples-Palermo. Sardinia is connected by daily boat to Civitavecchia, 6 times a week to Genoa, twice weekly to Naples, and by new car ferry between Genoa and Cagliari and on to Palermo (Sicily). There is an airferry service for cars between Naples and Catania (Sicily). Fast hydrofoil services operate between the mainland and various offshore islands, to Sicily and between San Remo and Nice (France); other new car ferries between Toulon (France) and Porto Torres, Sardinia, from Corsica to Genoa and Barcelona to Genoa.

By Bus: CIAT operate excursion coaches and offer a vast choice of sightseeing tours.

 MOTORING. Drive on the right side of the road; that's the rule, even if the Italians show a proclivity for preferring the middle. And that's why automobile insurance is now compulsory in Italy. Gasoline (petrol) costs about 500 lire per liter for super, 480 for regular. Tourists driving their own cars can buy gasoline discount coupons for up to 400 liters at Italian government tourist offices *abroad.* A second gasoline assignment is permitted within the same calendar year.

It is compulsory to exhibit a red warning triangle at a reasonable distance from your stationary car—a useful precaution on narrow and winding roads. The triangle will be lent you at Italian frontier posts against a small deposit which will be refunded when leaving the country. ACI offers emergency breakdown service.

Throughout Italy, dial 116 for quick towing and/or repairs, charge-controlled by ACI.

The Italian Automobile Club has built a chain of wayside motels or *autostelli,* in effect, small second-class hotels for motorists. Beginning in central Italy, they are strategically located along highways south along both coasts to Sicily. For a complete list, write to Motels, Via Marsala 8, Rome. Rates vary from about 4,000 to 12,000 lire for a double room with bath. Members of the Italian Automobile Club enjoy a discount of 10% at these motels and other discounts on tolls, car rentals, etc. Apply at frontier or local ACI offices. The AGIP oil co. also owns a chain of good motels; consistently clean, comfortable and reasonable.

There are several motorways crossing Italy, most scenic of which is the *Autostrada del Sole* joining Milan and Reggio Calabria; others link Turin-Venice, Rome-Civitavecchia, Milan-Genoa, Florence-Pisa, Naples-Bari, Milan-Como— still growing. These are all toll roads so your ticket must be kept and given up when quitting the autostrada. The speed limit throughout Italy, unless otherwise posted, is 100 kilometers per hour on state highways, 130 kilometers per hour on autostrada.

CAR HIRE. There are numerous firms from which automobiles can be rented. Members of the American Auto Assn. can obtain information through their Rome office at Via Vittoria Veneto 84. The club maintains a list of all car-hire firms in Italy and travelers are advised to get in touch with it. In most big cities there is a branch of the *Avis, Hertz,* and the *Fiat Sadem* organization, which also rents chauffeur-driven and self-driven cars; (reservations through travel agencies or directly). Cars may also be rented at several railroad stations (Rome, Milan, Naples, Genoa, Florence, Venice, etc.) and at major airports; arrange reservation in advance at the stations or at travel agencies. Alitalia and Avis offer a Jet-Drive combination: car included in ticket price; seven-day, two-adult minimum.

OFFBEAT TOURS: For a really unusual tour, join a riding party, especially organized for equestrian tourists. For information: *Associazione Nazionale per il Turismo Equestre,* Via Toscana 10, Rome. Or rent a farmhouse in Tuscany; information from *Azienda Autonoma Soggiorno,* Via Banchi di Sotto, Siena. If you prefer the lazy life, rent a yacht (small or large) and see Italy from the sea. Inquire *Moncada Yachts,* Via Paieselle 26, Rome. Local EPT tourist offices in Florence and Asti sponsor unusual villa and vineyard special-interest tours. A free-wheeling camping tour departing from London can be arranged through *Frontier Travel,* 4 The Boulevard, Crawley, Sussex.

CAMPING. There are about 800 campsites well-distributed throughout Italy, many with bungalows, many open all year. Apply to the *Federazione Italiano del Campeggio* Casella postale 255, 50100 Florence) for an international camping carnet and for the *Guida Camping Italia,* with multilingual text.

 USEFUL ADDRESSES. *American Embassy,* Via Vittorio Veneto 119; *British Embassy,* Via XX Settembre 80a; *Canadian Embassy,* Via G. B. de Rossi 27; *Irish Embassy,* Via Circo Massimo 9; *South African Embassy,* Piazza Monte Grappa 4; *Australian Embassy,* Via Sallustiana 26. All in Rome.

AAA Port Agents: Automobile Club d'Italia, Viale Brigate Partigiane 1, Genoa; Piazzale Tecchio 49d, Naples; Viale N. Turrisi 30, Palermo; Piazzale Roma 518a, Venice.

American Express, Via Tornabuoni 12-14r, Florence; Via San Vincenzo 22r, Genoa; Via Vittor Pisani 19, Milan; Via Santa Lucia 146, Naples; Piazza di Spagna 38, Rome; San Marco, Bocca di Piazza 1261, Venice. *Thomas Cook,* Via Vittorio Veneto 9-11, Rome. *Wagons-Lits/Cook,* Via Buoncompagni 25, Rome;

Piazza Strozzi 14, Florence; Piazza San Carlo 132, Turin; Via Porta degli Archi 12, Genoa; Piazzetta dei Leoncini, Piazza San Marco 289–305, Venice, Via Depretis 126, Naples; Via Vittor Pisani 27, Milan; Corso Nuvoloni 19, San Remo; Via Generale Magliocco 29, Palermo; Via Amendola 10, Bologna; Viale Venti Settembre 45, Catania; Corso Vittorio Emanuele 137, Bari.

C.I.T. (*Compagnia Italiana Turismo*), offices in every large town.

Rome: Tourist Information (*EPT*): 11 Via Parigi, Fiumicino Airport and Termini Station.

The nationwide emergency telephone number is 113, for police, ambulance, fire, or highway accident.

Rome, the Eternal

Popes, Vandals, the Borgias and Napoleon, Garibaldi, Michaelangelo and Mussolini, all these have left their physical and spiritual mark on Rome, but though she keeps the glory of an ancient day about her, she remains a wellspring of creative energy; in short, she really *is* the Eternal City.

You might as well begin your search for Rome in the Piazza Venezia. You can't avoid the huge white Victor Emmanuel Monument, known to the Italians as the "Altare della Patria" (the Country's Altar). The unknown soldier is buried here, and all official ceremonies take place in this square. The view from the top is wonderful. Behind, Michelangelo's stairs lead you to the Campidoglio, Rome's City Hall. Behind the Campidoglio lie Rome's greatest archaeological treasures, the ruins of the Imperial Fora and the Roman Forum.

Highly recommended from here is the half mile walk down the Via dei Fori Imperiali to the most stupendous monument of ancient Rome— the Colosseum. See it at dawn, at sunset, and at night with the spotlights illuminating the old stone. And walk to the top for an impression of the real size of this stadium, which used to seat 50,000 persons.

Outside the Colosseum, you will pass under the Arch of Constantine on your way to the Baths of Caracalla, the grandest of Rome's ruined public baths. See a summer opera in this great stone bathing place—it's a magnificent experience.

The Highlights

Here are some other sights of Rome you should try to fit in even if your time is limited: The Palazzo Venezia, with Mussolini's office and balcony, now a museum; the Piazza del Quirinale, with the Quirinale Palace, residence of the Italian president—see the changing of the guard every day at 6 P.M.; the Porta Pia, huge arch designed by Michelangelo; Piazza Navona, much as it was in the 17th century, and Bernini's great Fountain of the Rivers; the Church of Sant'Agnese fuori le Mura, with its maze of third-century catacombs, a refuge of the early Christians; the Fountain of Trevi, where a coin tossed into the huge basin guarantees your return to toss another one; the bustling Piazza Barberini, with its Fountain of the Triton, designed by Bernini in 1640; the macabre Church of the Capuchin Monks (Santa Maria della Concezione), with its subterranean chapels full of skeletons, after which sobering experience you may look with a jaded eye on the nearby Via Veneto. Once a great cosmopolitan boulevard, it has lost a lot of its luster in recent years, but its sidewalk cafés still come to life on pleasant evenings. As a tonic antidote to this, we recommend a stroll through the Trastevere region, where you will find "the Romans of Rome", blunt, uninhibited, sharp-eyed, hawk-nosed, friendly, sincere, often beautiful and seldom varnished. They mix with American and English bohemian types in the atmospheric Piazza di Santa Maria.

You will, of course, want to explore the Piazza di Spagna, with its lovely Bernini fountain and the famous Spanish steps which ascend past Babington's tea room and the house in which Keats died to the Church of Trinita dei Monti. Nearby is the Pincio, Rome's original Public Gardens and the fabulous Villa Borghese garden, with its fountains, glades, statues and museums. Of the last, the best is the Casino Borghese, where the second floor art gallery houses numerous Titians, Tintorettos and El Grecos. The ground floor is devoted to sculpture, and here you should not miss Canova's nude of Pauline Borghese, Napoleon's sister, reclining so realistically on her couch.

Three major antiquities demand your attention before proceeding to St. Peter's and the Vatican. They are the Castel Sant'Angelo, built by the Emperor Hadrian in 135, a most impressive castle from whose terrace you will have all Rome at your feet; the Pantheon, rebuilt by Hadrian as a pagan temple, the best-preserved monument of Roman antiquity; and the Piazza Colonna, with its fountain and huge column erected about 193 in honor of Emperor Marcus Aurelius.

Vatican City

Since the Lateran Accord of 1929 the Vatican City has been an independent and sovereign state. When you step into the great square before St. Peter's, you are on Vatican territory. You can enter the basilica, the Borgia apartments, the Sistine Chapel, and the museums without showing any papers. To enter the Vatican City proper, or to visit the Apostolic Palaces, however, special permission is required. Apply well in advance to the information office on the left of the staircase to St. Peter's for entrance to a papal audience or for a bus tour of Vatican City and its exquisite 16th-century gardens.

San Pietro in Vaticano, better known as St. Peter's (it is not a cathedral), is the largest church in the world and a fitting climax to Rome, no matter what your religion. The enormous Piazza San Pietro, which took Bernini 10 years to build, has held as many as 400,000 people within the confines of its quadruple colonnade; it is one of the world's most beautiful squares. The church had its beginnings about 326, when the Emperor Constantine built a basilica here over the tomb of St. Peter, but it was not until 1626 that St. Peter's stood as we know it today, a masterpiece of Renaissance architecture and art. Bramante, Raphael, Michelangelo, Peruzzi and Antonio Sangallo were all busy beautifying this church at the time of their deaths. Note the mosaic by Giotto in the portico, Michelangelo's *Pieta* in the first chapel, the reliquary of St. Peter's Chair by Bernini and the Confessional Altar marking the burial place of St. Peter. Visit the Treasury and the Vatican Grottos. Save the dome for last (highly recommended *unless you have vertigo or a weak heart*). An elevator will take you to the roof of the basilica, above which the incomparable dome of St. Peter's soars for another 308 feet. You proceed by a narrow stairway to the first gallery and the second, which at 235 feet provides the best view of the dome's interior.

PRACTICAL INFORMATION FOR ROME

 WHEN TO GO. More tourists crowd into Rome during the blistering hot July-through-September period than any other three months of the year. Yet late April, May, June and early October are far and away the best months to see the city. December, January, early February run to rain and cold.

Opera season in Rome opens just before Christmas and continues through May at the city's world-famous Opera House. And in July, open-air performances begin, with the Opera House staging its magnificent productions in the ancient Baths of Caracalla and the Academy of St. Cecilia organizing a series of concerts at the Basilica of Maxentius, using the entire Roman Forum as an age-old backdrop. On Palm Sunday, the Pope blesses palms sent to him by the Breschi family under a privilege granted four centuries ago, and the Holy Week follows, with its processions, sacred rites in the Colosseum and Catacombs. One of Rome's oldest quarters, Trastevere, celebrates the Feast of *Madonna del Carmine,* July 16-31, with its own peculiar *Festa de Noantri* (Festival of We Others), a roaring rousing mixture of worship and carnival. The Christmas fair at Piazza Navona is fun, too.

 HOTELS. Rome is an an all-year-round city, well provided with hotels, but it's always a good idea to make a reservation in advance. You can't go wrong if you book with one of the Italhotel group or Bettoja chain establishments. To get a clear picture of your total costs, ask for quotations of the inclusive rate that takes in all extras. As for the top-level hotels in the Italian capital, they are all excellent. All better hotels are air-conditioned.

A hotel information service operates at Termini railroad station and at Fiumicino airport.

SUPER DELUXE

Cavalieri Hilton, splendid panoramic views and *La Pergola* restaurant-nightclub on the roof terrace. 400 rooms and suites on 11 floors, two more restaurants, pool, tennis in 7-acre park.

Parco Dei Principi, at Villa Borghese, big, modern, all rooms with balconies, baths, some suites. Grill room, two restaurants, pool.

Excelsior, Via Vittorio Veneto 125, big, bustling and overflowing with service, is a favorite. Garage.

Grand, Via Vittorio Emanuele Orlando 3, is a big place, like the Excelsior, catering in general to a more conservative, solid clientele. It's Rome's most elegant and expensive. Grill room; *Rallye* restaurant.

Hassler, Piazza Trinità de Monti 6, an Italhotel, combines all the advantages of modernity with an ancient location of remarkable picturesqueness—at the top of the spectacular Spanish Steps.

DELUXE

Ambasciatori, Via Vittorio Veneto 70, quieter, smaller and elegant. An Italhotel; bright, spacious rooms, some facing Via Veneto and U.S. Embassy.

Bernini, Piazza Barberini 23, ultra-modern hotel in one of the busiest squares of Rome, with the famous Triton fountain. Attractively furnished, spotless rooms.

Flora, Via Vittorio Veneto 191, has rather dated atmosphere but is popular with Americans. Good-sized rooms, some overlooking Villa Borghese. Subdued furnishings, personalized service.

Mediterraneo, Via Cavour 15, near station. Finest of the family-run Bettoja chain. A new 450-room wing with roof terrace and underground garage. Lowest rates in category.

Eden, Via Ludovisi 49, near Via Veneto, also very fine (and a little more expensive), rooftop bar, restaurant; member of Italhotels group. Central but quiet.

FIRST CLASS

It is not necessary to pay the deluxe scales to be very well housed indeed in Rome, and in attractive locations.

Atop Via Veneto is the strikingly modern *Jolly,* highest rates in this category: 200 rooms with bath, TV, refrigerator-bar; 200-car garage.

On Via Veneto, the *Regina Carlton* has cheerful, soundproofed rooms, spacious lounges.

Visconti Palace, Via Cesi, in Prati section, is large, efficient, tastefully modern.

The *Royal Santina,* Via Marsala 22, is near station, and *Hôtel de la Ville,* Via Sistina 69, has a pleasant garden.

Lord Byron, Via de Notaris 5, handsomely renovated villa near Borghese park, is fine for quiet comfort.

The *Savoia,* Via Ludovisi 15, is just off Vittorio Veneto, as are *Boston,* Via Lombardia, and elegantly modern *Londra Cargill,* Piazza Sallustio.

On the outskirts, *Holiday Inn,* new, 350 rooms, large pool, vast park. Free bus service into town, all creature comforts, as at recent *Parco dei Medici Holiday Inn,* free bus service to town or airport, 15 minutes away; ideal for stopovers.

On the Via del Corso, in the heart of the shopping area, is the rather ornate but comfortable *Plaza,* at no. 126.

And on the Via Cavour *Massimo d'Azeglio,* all rooms with bath, the *Palatino,* ultra-modern, and the *Atlantico,* the last two first class moderate. On nearby Via Torino, the *Commodore* is modern, soundproofed.

Overlooking the old Imperial Forum is the quiet, posh *Forum,* Via Tor de' Conti 25. Elegantly furnished rooms, all with bath. Attractive dining terrace on roof with view of ruins.

Marini Strand, Via del Tritone, closest to shopping; soundproofed and modern. *Cardinal,* Via Giulia in Old Rome; handsome newcomer, historic palazzo, beautifully and comfortably furnished.

Near Piazza Navona is the attractive *Raphael,* on Largo Febo. 100 rooms with bath, roof garden.

Also very central, *Minerva,* Piazza Minerva, has lots of old-fashioned charm, reasonable rates; many private baths, no restaurant.

SECOND CLASS

In the favored Vittorio Veneto quarter is *Alexandra,* Via Veneto 18. Near the railroad station, *Nord,* Via G. Amendola 3, first class in quality, a Bettoja hotel. *Bologna,* Via Santa Chiara, near Pantheon, is reliable. On the important Via Nazionale, you might try the *Esperia* at No. 22. *Oxford,* Via Buoncompagni, near Via Veneto, is recent, comfortable.

Highly recommended is the popular *Inghilterra,* Via Bocca di Leone 14; attractive, old-fashioned, near the Spanish steps.

Very near St. Peter's, the *Columbus,* Via della Conciliazione 33, is good, as are *Quattro Fontane,* Via Quattro Fontane 149, the *Caprice,* Via Liguria, and recent 25-room *Carriage,* Via delle Carrozze, near Piazza del Popolo, recommended.

Britannia, Via Napoli, is central and quite modern.

La Residenza, Via Emilia, is pleasant renovated villa, just off Via Veneto.

THIRD CLASS

Best are *Aventino* and *Villa San Pio,* Via Sant' Anselmo, in quiet Aventine section, under same genial management. In same area, *Santa Prisca,* Largo Gelsomini 25. *Ivanhoe,* Via Ciancaleoni, near S. Maria Maggiore, is another good buy. *Astoria Garden,* Via Varese 8, near station but quiet.

Motels. All outside city: Standardized but efficient with pool, *Agip* is on the Via Aurelia, about 5 miles from center. Actually a first-class hotel, the *Americana,* 10 miles out on Via Aurelia, is modern, has pool, as does *Autostello ACI* on Via Cristoforo Colombo. Also bright, modern, with pool; *American Palace* (2) on Via Laurentina, at EUR.

RESTAURANTS. There are scads of deluxe, international al restaurants in Rome where they can serve any specialty of Italy or the world at large with a fine flourish of silver and linen and a whopping *conto* (check) at the end. But if it's true Roman cuisine you want, then move along the back streets, into the older quarters of the city, among the palaces and churches and musty old buildings of another age. Here you find the ten-to-twelve-table *trattorie* (from the Latin word, *tractare,* meaning "to treat"), with their wandering musicians, ordinary silverware, cloth-covered tables—*and* good food. These neat little establishments present a bill averaging 5,000–6,000 lire for a full menu with carafe wine. Many Rome restaurants, from deluxe down, now have a fixed price menu (service included); all now close one day a week, many close for mid-August vacation.

Expensive. *Hostaria dell'Orso,* Via Monte Brianzo 93, in medieval palace, elegant. Dancing, piano bar. *Da Pancrazio,* Piazza del Biscione 93, two vaulted subterranean dining rooms, fine food.

Ulpia, Piazza del Foro Traiano, excellent restaurant upstairs. *Il Passetto,* just off Piazza Navona, a Rome classic for pleasant service and memorable food.

Favored by celebrities and lovers of haute cuisine, *Eau Vive,* Via Monterone, is delightfully run by French missionary sisters. More worldly atmosphere but equally heavenly French food at *Charly's Saucière,* Via S. Giovanni in Laterano 268. *Al Vicario,* Via Uffici del Vicario 31, where Rome's VIP's dine.

George, behind the Excelsior. Definitely for gourmets. Cool summer garden. *Angelino,* Tor Margana 37, favorite of self-styled intelligentsia. Outside tables, stunning view.

Antica Pesa, Via Garibaldi 18. The clientèle: artists, jet set, crème of Roman crème. *Taverna Flavia,* known as Selvaggino, Via Flavia 9. Delicious food. Reserve.

El Toulà, Via della Lupa 29, Rome's smartest luxury restaurant. Vaulted ceilings, impeccable service, and excellent food; jacket and tie a must.

Ranieri, Via Mario dei Fiori 26, founded by Queen Victoria's chef; faded elegance, top-notch food. *Al Fogher,* Via Tevere 13, rustic decor, outstanding Venetian cuisine.

Moderate to Expensive. *Grappolo d'Oro,* Piazza della Cancelleria 80, serves excellent Roman specialties at reasonable prices. *Barroccio,* Via dei Pastini, near Pantheon, Tuscan accent, moderate. Near Trevi Fountain, popular *Al Moro,* Vicolo delle Bollette, slightly more expensive, reserve. For hamburgers, snacks: *Piccadilly* or *Wimpy* on Via Barberini, *California* on Via Bissolati.

Ippocampo, Passeggiata Ripetta 10, near Piazza del Popolo, is pleasant, moderately expensive. Nearby *La Buca,* on Via Ripetta, popular with cinema, international set, but tiny.

The Bolognese, on Piazza del Popolo, is a favorite for hearty pastas; sidewalk summer terrace is pleasant but noisy.

ROME

500   800 Metres
500   700 Yards

1. VATICAN CITY
2. FARNESE PALACE
3. AUGUSTEUM
4. MAIN POST OFFICE
5. TREVI FOUNTAIN
6. EXHIBITION HALL
7. OPERA HOUSE
8. to TERMINI STN.
9. NATIONAL MUSEUM
10. Sta. M. MAGGIORE
11. to LATERAN MUSEUM
12. OSTIA STATION

N

The *Giovanni,* Via Marche 19, two blocks behind the Excelsior hotel is excellent. Another *Giovanni,* this one at Via Salandra 1, is outstanding for typical dishes.

At *Cesarina,* Via Sicilia 209, Cesarina herself oversees the best of Bolognese cooking.

Outdoor Dining. Every trattoria that can cadge a bit of sidewalk or courtyard will set up bright tables for good-weather dining. Some are particularly attractive: *Piperno,* on Piazza Cenci in the old Ghetto, famous for artichokes *alla giudia; Mastrostefano,* on Piazza Navona, with Bernini's fountains as a backdrop; *Galeassi,* on Piazza S. Maria in Trastevere, with the excellent *Sabatini* around the corner. *Donus Aurea,* Viale Monte Oppio, overlooking the Colosseum. All (M-E). *La Norcina del Prestidigiatore,* Via del Moro 43, for pleasant meals in the garden.

Taverns. *Toscano de Mario,* Via Forli 41, excellent; *Otello alla Concordia,* Via delle Croce 81, dining in courtyard. *Taverna Zi Gaetana,* Via Cola di Rienzo 263, serves pizza and other specialties. On the Via Appia Antica, *Cecilia Metella* and the charming *Hostaria dell'Archeologia,* both (M.)

Picturesque. *Da Meo Patacca,* at the old river port in Trastevere, is an old tavern with ancient Roman wine cellars, good Roman food. Heavy on atmosphere but can be fun.

Also in Trastevere: *Corsetti-Il Galeone,* Piazza San Cosimato, sailing-ship motifs and good food; *Tana di Noiantri,* Via della Paglia, Roman specialties; *La Cisterna,* Via della Cisterna, touristy, goes in for music, jollity and native costumes, outdoor dining in summer.

Then *Ambasciata d'Abruzzo,* Via Tacchini 26, a bit out of the way in Parioli area, incredible quantities of wholesome country food; *prix fixe* includes all the wine you can drink.

The *Pizzeria Sant'Ignazio,* in the square of the same name, is a pleasant place to dine, with the imposing façade of the 17th-century Church of Sant'Ignazio, across the square, for a backdrop. A nearby restaurant, *Il Buco,* Via Sant'Ignazio 8, has excellent steaks.

Fashionable restaurants, popular with movie folk: *Piccolo Mondo,* Via Aurora 39, *Chianti,* Via Ancona 17, *Alla Carbonara,* Piazza Campo dei Fiori, or *Nino's,* Via Borgognona 11, the latter perhaps the best.

For Pleasant Loafing. *Doney,* Via Vittorio Veneto, whose tables spill all over the sidewalk in fine weather, is famous.

Café de Paris, Via Vittorio Veneto 90, has snack counter, cocktail lounge, and excellent restaurant. Rather overpriced.

Other favorites are *Rosati,* Piazza del Popolo, and *Tre Scalini,* Piazza Navona.

 ENTERTAINMENT. The top place to go in the evening, and the most expensive, is the *Cabala,* which is above the *Hostaria dell'Orso* restaurant mentioned above. It is small, the entertainment is discreet and intimate, and there is dancing upstairs, a piano bar downstairs (closed in summer). *Jackie-O,* Via Buoncompagni, very much *in* with celebrities and such. The cellar of the *Ulpia* (again, see above) is usually thronged with a lively after-dinner crowd, which takes its coffee and liqueur between the old Roman brick walls which have stood there for centuries. *Scacco Matto,* Via Ferdinando di Savoia 6, and *Scarabocchio,* Piazza dei Ponziani, are the latest *in* places. In the summer the action is on the shore, at *Corsetti* in Torvaianica and the *Oasi* at Fregene.

Popular, reliable are *Piper Club,* Via Tagliamento, which offers a full-scale floor show along with late suppers, dancing, and *Gattopardo,* Via Mario dei Fiori 95, for pizza and champagne suppers. *Astoria,* Via S. Nicolò di Tolentino, features strippers. Usually the last to close for the night, *Club 84,* Via Emilia 84, is always lively. As nightclubs everywhere are ephemeral and many close during the summer, for the latest information it is best to *ask your hotel porter.*

Organized Rome-By-Night tours are dreary, expensive affairs. Better to arrange with a taxi driver to show you some of the illuminated piazzas and monuments and drop you off at a good nightclub or disco for a drink.

Opera fans will find the opera house at Via Viminale; performances in the winter only. In summer, there are open-air performances in the Baths of Caracalla, concerts in Basilica of Maxentius, and outdoor ballet performances at Villa Giulia.

SHOPPING. Start from the American Express on Piazza di Spagna, roam around the square, then head down the famous Via Condotti, exploring irresistible Via Borgognona, Via Frattina, Via della Vite and Via del Corso. You'll be fascinated by the sumptuous array of fine leather goods, china, fashions, silver and gift items all the way down the street. You'll enjoy the *Rinascente* department stores on Piazza Colonna and Piazza Fiume.

For good little silver gifts for men and women, stop in at the *Alberto Fornari* store on Via del Gambero: wide selection from a few thousand lire to the stratosphere. Good values in silver (look for the mark "800" which means it's sterling) at *Vespasiani Tito,* Via Frattina 88.

Terrific Italian handicrafts at *Myricae,* Via Frattina 36, a sort of glorified general store, crammed with fabrics, glassware, ceramics, carved angels, in short, the ideal gift shop. Also excellent *Bella Copia,* Via dei Coronari 8. Antique fanciers will find gallery after gallery of tempting stuff on the Via del Babuino, leading from the Piazza di Spagna to the Piazza del Popolo.

Women's gloves are a good buy in Rome. Try our favorite shops *Manco* and *Perrone.*

Rosaries, medals and other religious mementos abound in the shops around the Vatican. Try also the Piazza Minerva and these specialists: *Al Pellegrino Cattolico,* Via Porta Angelica 83; *Savelli,* Piazza San Pietro. *Garey,* Piazza Farnese.

For small gifts, look for charming old prints at *Alinari* on Via Due Macelli, or in little shops around the Piazza di Spagna or behind the Pantheon.

Città del Sole, Via Dogana Vecchia, and *Rinascente* at Piazza Fiume have enchanting gift items for kids.

The Environs of Rome

All major tourist agencies in Rome feature bus tours through both environs and the Lazio area. Recommended itineraries: the Appian Way, ancient Rome's "Queen of Roads", built over 2,000 years ago by Appius Claudius and literally walled with ancient monuments and Roman tombs; the Castelli Romani (Roman Castles), a day's trip to Albano, Frascati, Castel Gandolfo, Rocca di Papa and other fascinating towns of the Alban Hills.

Also suggested: Ostia, port of ancient Rome (Roman ruins), Coney Island or Brighton of the modern capital (but it's too crowded for comfort on hot weekends); Tivoli, with its ruins of Hadrian's sumptuous villa, and the fabulous Villa d'Este, with its indescribably lovely gardens, its beautiful fountains floodlit in summer; Anzio and Cassino, both completely rebuilt after the ravages of war; medieval Viterbo, and Tarquinia, famous for its medieval monuments, museum and the Etruscan Necropolis.

The shoreline of Lazio is a broad stretch of fine sand beach, dotted with resorts, some chic, some just crowded. Newly popular with those trying to get away from the packed beaches nearest Rome are the resorts of Terracina, San Felice Circeo, Sperlonga, Gaeta and Formia, to the south; and Santa Marinella and Santa Severa to the north. A 40-mile superhighway speeds motorists to the northern beaches and the Etruscan treasures of Cerveteri and Tarquinia. The island of Ponza, 30 miles off the coast, overflows in summer but is pleasant off-season (hydrofoil from Anzio April-September; car ferry from Formia year-round).

PRACTICAL INFORMATION FOR LAZIO

 HOTELS. In the Lazio region, it is essential to make reservations in advance during the full season, particularly important for the beach resorts.

ANZIO, beach, resort, former battle city. *Dei Cesari* (2), bright, functional resort-type with pool, beach. *Esperia e Parco* and *Parco,* both (2), are older, more modest.

BAIA DOMIZIA, new resort. *Domizia Palace* (2), excellent. *Park* and *Baia,* both (2), good. *Motel Agip* (2). *Giulivo* (2), a big, modern beach hotel.

CIVITAVECCHIA, port of Rome. *Mediterraneo* (2), nearly all of its 67 rooms with bath, plain but comfortable. At Baia del Sole, *Sunbay Park* (1), smart; beach, tennis, pools, nightclub, marina.

FIUGGI, important spa. *Palazzo della Fonte* (L), most rooms with bath. Swimming pool. *Villa Igea,* many rooms with bath; park. *Vallombrosa e Majestic,* very good. Both (1).

FORMIA, beach resort. *Miramare* (1), tennis court, garage. Private beach. *Ariston,* friendly atmosphere, *Fagiano,* elegant villa on beach. *Romantic,* balconied rooms; beach is across busy road. All (2).

FREGENE, Chic beach resort. *Golden Beach* (2), most rooms with showers. *Villa dei Pini* (P1), largest. *Conchiglia* (P1), smartest. Also: *Fiorita* (P1), *Corallo* (P2), good, beach facilities.

GAETA, beach resort. At Località Serapo, *Serapo* on beach-front and *Mirasole,* both (2). *Le Rocce* (2) and *Argonauta* (P2), both at San Vito, private beaches.

NETTUNO, beach resort. Site of U.S. war cemetery. *Scacciapensieri* (2), on private beach; pool.

PONZA, island resort. *Chiaia di Luna* (1), bungalows overlooking island's best beach; pool. *Torre dei Borboni, Bellavista,* both (2), comfortable, sea views, beaches. All except *Bellavista* seasonal.

SABAUDIA. Site of popular Baia d'Argento resort colony. *Le Dune* (1) is smart, modern; pool, beach, tennis. *L'Aragosta* (P1), on beach.

SAN FELICE CIRCEO. Elegant beach resort. *Carillon* (2). All rooms with bath. Tennis. *Maga Circe* (1), tennis, swimming pool. *Punta Rossa* (2), white-washed bungalows in park; pool and beach.

SANTA MARINELLA. Popular beach resort. Best are *Cavalluccio Marino,* with tennis, pool; *Le Naiadi,* all rooms with bath, pool. *Majorca,* recent, pool. All (2). At Frazione Santa Severa, *Maremonti* (2), with pool.

SPERLONGA, old town, fine beaches. *Parkhotel Fiorelle* (2), on beach. *Aurora* (3), 51 rooms with shower in modest beach hotel below town.

SUBIACO, ancient abbey. *Belvedere* (3). At nearby Monte Livata ski area, *Europa* and *Livata* (2), both recent, pleasant.

TARQUINIA, Etruscan treasures. *Tarconte* (2), excellent in category, recommended for location, good service, fine restaurant.

TERRACINA. Medieval town; beach resort. *L'Approdo* (1), new; 40 rooms overlooking sea, private beach. *Palace* (2), just off beach drive, traditional décor. *Riva Gaia* (2), recent resort hotel, pool, beach.

VITERBO, art town. Best hotels are on outskirts: *Mini Palace* (2), quiet, with modern, balconied rooms; *Tuculca* (2), new (1976) motel-type with pool, tennis, on Via Cassia at Ponte de Cetti. In center, *Tuscia* (3) is clean, unpretentious.

RESTAURANTS

ANZIO: *Caprera, Gambero, Garda,* all at port and all moderate, specialize in seafood.

CASTEL GANDOLFO: Best are *Mirador,* with terrace and garden, *Pagnanelli,* with panoramic view, both (M–E). *Cacciatori* (M), modest place with lakeview veranda.

CIVITAVECCHIA: *Villa dei Principi* (E), overlooking sea, and *Taverna della Rocca* (M–E), at port, are famous for fish dishes.

FRASCATI: *Spartaco, Cacciani, Buongusto* are good, all (M).

GROTTAFERRATA: *Castagneto* is good for regional dishes. *Al Fico* has wonderful view.

MARINO: *Quattro Mori* (M), hearty local specialties and heady wines.

OSTIA: *La Capricciosa* (E) for fine seafood. *Trattoria del Pescatore* and *Guerrino,* fish specialties; at Ostia Antica, *Monumento.* All moderate.

TIVOLI: Don't miss the *Sibilla,* an open-air restaurant built in a setting more than 2,000 years old. *Villa Gregoriana,* (E), and *Eden Sirene* (M), have same beautiful view.

VITERBO: The best restaurants here are *Antico Angelo* and *Scaletta. Aquilante* (E), at La Quercia, is best in area.

Piedmont and the Valle d'Aosta

Piedmont—the region of Turin and the Valle d'Aosta in the northwest corner of Italy—is a land of spectacular natural beauty with medieval villages in close proximity to Europe's highest mountains—Mont Blanc, Monte Rosa, the Gran Paradiso, and the Cervino, which last is Italian for the Matterhorn. The mountain valleys of Piedmont provide some of the finest skiing in the world. Your best bets as far as winter resorts are concerned are Sestriere, Courmayer, Breuil-Cervina, Gressoney, Bardonecchia, Limone Piemonte, and Saint Vincent, where there is also a year-round casino. But remember that all these towns double as summer resorts for tourists in search of cool restful holidays as well as for those more ambitious characters who want to climb mountains.

Turin, Capital of Piedmont

Turin is an Italian city with a French accent. The Piedmontese are very proud of its beauty, calling it *La Parigi d'Italia,* the Paris of Italy. It is situated on the left bank of the Po on level ground, dramatically encircled by the Alps. The city is characterized by its wide streets, its many beautiful squares, its fine buildings, and its modern spirit. Via Roma, a handsome shopping street, connects three striking squares, the Piazza Carlo Felice, the Piazza San Carlo and the Piazza Castello. The Piazza San Carlo, with its two churches of Santa Cristina and San Carlo, is considered by some to be the best square in Italy after St. Mark's in Venice.

Things to see in Turin—the Castello or Palazzo Madama, housing the civic museum of ancient art; the Royal Palace with its sumptuously-furnished interiors and Royal Armory, one of the most important collections of armor in Europe; the Palazzo Carignano, a masterpiece of baroque architecture containing several museums; the Egyptian collection in the Palazzo Carignano; and the bizarre Mole Antonelliana, built as a synagogue in 1863. From the top of its spire, you will have a wonderful view of the city and the Alps.

Along the left bank of the river Po, you'll see the Parco del Valentino and the 17th-century Castello del Valentino, thoroughly French in style. Farther along, close to the river's edge, is the medieval village and castle built in connection with the Turin Exposition of 1884. A visit to this village with its furnished houses, stores and shops is fascinating.

Automobile-conscious Turin (the big Fiat works are nearby) holds an international auto show in November and has the fascinating Biscaretti antique auto museum, on Corso Unità d'Italia.

Finally, don't miss Turin's unique relic of the Holy Shroud in the 15th-century white marble cathedral in the Piazza San Giovanni. In the monumental chapel is the urn containing one of the most precious relics of Christendom, the shroud in which Jesus Christ is said to have been wrapped when he was taken from the cross and which still retains the imprint of his body.

PRACTICAL INFORMATION FOR PIEDMONT

HOTELS. Reserve well in advance, especially if you want to stay in Turin during the International Automobile Salon (November), which attracts thousands of visitors and taxes the city's hotel resources to the limit. Hotels in the Piedmont winter and summer resorts are generally open between December 20-March 31, and from June 15 to September 30. Some also reopen for the Easter holidays. Be sure to check on these dates. Valle d'Aosta area hotels offer special bargains off season, mid-January–mid-April, September–late December.

AOSTA. All ski facilities at nearby Conca di Pila. Best is *Valle d'Aosta* (1), a Rank hotel. 103 rooms with bath. *Norden* (2), all rooms with bath. *Ambassador* (2). *Corona e Posta* (2), central, comfortable older hotel.

BARDONECCHIA, resort town. *Riki* (1), modern, 76 rooms with bath; pool, minigolf. *De Geneys-Splendid* (2), half of rooms with bath.

BREUIL-CERVINIA, resort of Valle d'Aosta. *Cristallo* (1), *Cervinia* (1), both sunny, comfortable, good service. *Gran Baita* (2), half of rooms with bath. *Breuil* and *Planet,* all rooms with bath, comfortable. *Lo Stambecco,* on ski slopes, isolated at night when lift stops. *Petit Palais,* modern Alpine look, near lifts. All (2). *Bucaneve* and *Valdotain,* both (3), pleasant.

CLAVIERE, a resort. *Bes* (2) is good. Garage. *Passero Pellegrino* is recent, most rooms with bath. *Miramonti,* small. Both (2).

COURMAYEUR, most important winter sports and summer resort of the Valle d'Aosta, below Mont Blanc. *Royal* (1), best, all rooms with bath. Modern and friendly. *Palace Bron* (1), also good; all rooms with bath. *Pavillon* (1), lively, modern, heated indoor pool. *Moderno* (1), central; large rooms, all with bath. Seasonal: *Croux,* attractive *Cristallo,* all (2), good.
Crest Hotel (1) at exit to Mt. Blanc tunnel, open all year; 48 rooms with bath.

GRESSONEY, important winter sports and summer resort in Valle d'Aosta, with more fashionable Gressoney La Trinité about 800 feet higher than Gressoney St. Jean. At La Trinité: *Busca-Thedy* (2), biggest, most rooms with bath; tennis; garage. *Residence* (2), alpine modern décor, fine views.
At. St. Jean: *Stadel* (3), lots of atmosphere and comfort; cozy *Rododendro* (3), has only 15 rooms, all with bath; garden. Just above St. Jean, at Chemonal, tiny *Villa Tedaldi* (P2) is comfortable, friendly.

LIMONE PIEMONTE, principal winter sports and summer resort of southern Piedmont. *Limone* (1), modern, all rooms with bath or shower. *Principe* (2), comfortable. At Colle di Tenda, *Tre Amis* (2), large, newish; pool.

SESTRIERE, top winter sports and summer resort. *Principi di Piemonte* (L), all rooms with bath. Tennis court, garage. Swimming pool; one of Italy's best known hotels. *Duchi d'Aosta* (1), yet another famous establishment. Most rooms with bath. Garage. Second-class annex, half of rooms with bath. *Cristallo* (1), central, bright alpine modern furnishings, comfortable rooms; lively bar for *après-ski.*
Savoy Edelweiss (3), about half of rooms with bath; good value at *Miramonti* and *Olympic,* both (3), pleasant, friendly atmosphere.

SAINT VINCENT, popular spa resort. *Billia* (L), all rooms with bath. Tennis, swimming pool. *Parc* and *Elena,* both (2). *Posta* (3), good value.

TURIN. *Principe di Piemonte* (L), at Via P. Gobetti 15. One of Italy's leading hotels, all rooms with bath. Air-conditioned elegance.
In category (1) are: *Ligure,* Piazza Carlo Felice 85, recommended; *Ambasciatori,* Corso Vittorio Emanuele, recent, air-conditioned; *Palace Hôtel Turin,* Via Sacchi 8, another fine hotel. Garage. *Swizzera Terminus,* Via Sacchi 4, handy to station, older hotel. *City,* Via Juvarra, is elegant, modern. *Villa Sassi,* sumptuous villa in park just across Po.

In category (2) are: *Fiorina,* Via Pietro Micca 22; *Roma e Rocca Cavour,* Piazza Carlo Felice 60. Garage. *Patria,* Via Cernaia 42. Garage. *Victoria,* Via Nino Costa 4; *Luxor* (2), recent.

The above hotels, in both categories, have at least half their rooms with bath. *Eden,* Via Donizetti, and *San Silvestro,* Corso Francia, are adequate, both (3).

RESTAURANTS

TURIN. It may very well be true that the best restaurant in Turin is the *Cambio,* Piazza Carignano, with its belle époque décor, attentive service and excellent *fonduta.* Expensive. Most unusual—and among the most expensive—is the *San Giorgio,* in a replica of a medieval castle in the Parco del Valentino, on the shore of the Po. The setting and the food justify the prices. Also in the top rank are the *Gran Giardino, Gatto Nero,* and elegant *Ferrero.*

Villa Sassi, on hillside two miles from center, is enchanting antique-furnished villa restaurant with gardens; very expensive. Also first-class are *Rendezvous, Taverna, Dantesca* and chic *Poster Lancia. Vecchia Lanterna* has good atmosphere, local and Venetian dishes, pianist in evening. All (E).

Just below these leaders are half a dozen others which are very good, but about a third cheaper: *Alpi Cozie,* Via Guarini 1; *Cervo,* Corso U.R.S.S. 242, *Due Lampioni,* Via C. Alberto 45; *Italia,* Colle di Superga; and *Pigna d'Oro,* Pino Torinese. In a lower price class, but still of excellent quality, are the *Cenacolo,* Galleria Subalpina 11; *Gli Orsi,* Via G. Amendola; *Pescatori,* Lungo Po Machiavelli 29; *Taverna Citrone,* Via M. Pieta; and *Fiaschetteria,* Via XX Settembre 1. Atmosphere, authentic local cuisine at tiny, family-run *Da Giuseppe,* Via S. Massimo 34; leave choice to host and enjoy the exceptional antipastos and desserts.

SHOPPING. The "Balon" flea market (at Porta Palazzo on Saturdays) is fun but junky; at the Crocetta open-air market (at the Church of the Crocetta, Tuesday, Saturday), you'll find first-quality goods at one-third off.

If you like lace, you'll find an incredible variety (9,000 types, they claim) at the *Fabbrica Pizzi* (lace factory), Cascine Vica at Rivoli. Factory prices; open to the public on Tuesday, Thursday, Saturday.

Mimma Grandi, Via Cavour 3, creates original costume jewelry; for the real thing in gold or silver, *Ostorero,* Via Battisti 17, or *Guido Audero,* Via Mercanti.

SPORTS. The principal sport is skiing, at the resorts named in the text. Most Piedmont resorts offer "ski-week" rates all inclusive of hotels, meals, ski lessons and lifts. Summer ski schools at Cervinia and Courmayeur.

Lombardy and its Capital

The fabulous Lombardy area of Italy stretches south from the Alps to the river Po. It takes its name from the Lombards who pounced on the lush fields of the Po in the sixth century and were eventually defeated by Charlemagne, who was crowned with their famous iron crown. The region's recorded history dates back 3,000 years to the Etruscans and includes domination by Rome, the Huns, the Goths, the Spanish, the Austrians—and Mussolini, which last the Milanesi strung up by his heels.

Milan

Milan, capital of Lombardy, is a great industrial city and a great art city, the commercial capital of Italy. Its center is the Piazza del Duomo, with its great cathedral, second largest church in the world and the biggest Gothic building in Italy. As elaborate as a wedding cake, the exterior of this edifice is decorated with 2,245 marble statues and 135 marble spires. The stained-glass windows of the 15th and 16th centuries illuminate the five great aisles and huge pillars of the church with a dim religious light. The effect is magnificent and should not be missed. Walk or take the elevator to the terraces of the cathedral. These constitue a wonderful promenade, with views of Milan, the Lombardy Plain and the distant Alps seen through a filigree of spires and statues.

From the Piazza del Duomo you can enter the celebrated Galleria Vittorio Emanuele, with its roof of glass, cafés, restaurants, bars, bookstores, souvenir shops and everything necessary to make it the traditional smart gathering place that it is. A stroll through this fabulous gallery will bring you into the Piazza della Scala, with its world-famous Teatro della Scala. The opera season runs from December to June here, the concert season from October to December. Tickets are a problem, especially for the opera performances, which are invariably sold out well in advance. Ask your travel agent's advice about getting them. Most of the big hotels in Milan will assign a porter to stand in what passes for a line at La Scala in order to procure tickets. Don't attempt to do this yourself. It's an exhausting, frustrating, time-consuming experience. There's too much else to see in Milan.

For example—the Palazzo di Brera with its superb collection, one of the greatest in Italy; the Castello Sforzesco, designed in 1450 by Filarete and decorated by Bramante and Leonardo da Vinci; the 17th-century Palazzo dell' Ambrosiana, with its gallery including works of Botticelli, Titian, Raphael and 1,750 notes and drawings by Leonardo da Vinci; San Satiro church, rebuilt by Bramante in 1480, a masterpiece of Renaissance design and optical perspective which makes the rather small interior seem vast; San Lorenzo Maggiore with its fourth-century mosaics and Roman columns; Sant' Ambrogio, Milan's greatest medieval monument (and founded even earlier, in 386).

Finally, a pilgrimage to one of the most famous paintings in the world—Leonardo da Vinci's *Last Supper,* still glowing faintly with glory, after centuries of abuse from damp weather and war, from the wall of the refectory of Santa Maria delle Grazie on the Corso Magenta.

Modern Milan thrusts upward in some of Italy's largest, most striking skyscrapers (*grattacieli*), and burrows underground with the city's ultramodern subway, which connects both ends of the city along a 25-station route.

Environs of Milan

Suggested excursions by car or bus from Milan include visits to the Certosa di Pavia, one of the world's greatest monasteries, a complete masterpiece of Lombard Renaissance architecture; to Cremona, famous for its Stradivarius and Guarnerius violins and for its splendid Piazza del Comune, which, with its 12th-century Duomo, is one of the most impressive squares in Italy; to Mantua, the birthplace of Vergil, with the Gonzaga castle, containing Mantegna's stupendous frescos; and to Brescia, whose marble Renaissance *Loggia* palace and whose 11th-century Rotonda cathedral are worth a visit, to say nothing of its Roman Age and Christian Age Museum. Bergamo Alta, the older, upper part of Bergamo, is steeped in authentic medieval atmosphere. Its fine monuments include the Colleoni Chapel, tomb of the great *condottiere* whose statue is in Venice.

PRACTICAL INFORMATION FOR MILAN

 HOTELS. Booming business trade in this thriving commercial city has resulted in large hotel development, but best book well ahead, especially for April 12-27, when the International Trade Fair crowds city hotels to bursting point. New second-class hotels tend to have pint-sized rooms but do have shower or bath, and serve breakfast only. Mainly concentrated around the cathedral square or the railroad station, hotels tend to be noisy: ask for a room at the back if possible.

DELUXE

MILAN HILTON, with 338 rooms, on top of Alitalia air terminal, near main station. Each room with bath, air-conditioning and TV.

EXCELSIOR GALLIA, a comfortable Italhotel, is handy to the railway station. Fully air conditioned, classic décor, good service.

PALACE is Milan's most modern, quiet but centrally located; roof garden; smart Casanova grill room.

CONTINENTALE GRAND is an Italhotel and one of the leading hotels in town.

PRINCIPE E SAVOIA is near Duomo and very popular; 300 rooms, many furnished with fine period pieces.

GRAND HOTEL ET DE MILAN is central, traditional style.

DIANA MAJESTIC retains sumptuous art nouveau style. A quality hotel.

FIRST CLASS. *Aerhotel Executive* lives up to its name; big, impersonal, highly efficient, near air terminal and station. The modern *Manin* and the *Touring e Gran Turismo,* top favorites.

Cavalieri, noted for its modern décor, roof restaurant; central.

Duomo has duplex suites, and is air-conditioned.

The *Francia Europa,* 111 rooms with bath, is air-conditioned.

The *Marino alla Scala* is conveniently located, as are the *Plaza,* and modern *Michelangelo.*

The *Cavour, De la Ville,* near the Scala, *Lloyd,* are fairly new and air-conditioned.

The *Amedei* is central, yet quiet.

Jolly President, Largo Augusto 10. 196 rooms with bath, modern.

Splendido, Via Andrea Doria 4, and *Select,* Via Baracchini 12, are both large, modern, efficient.

The *Carlton Senato* is superior first-class; *Rosa* and *Auriga* are reasonable.

Leonardo da Vinci, one of Milan's most recent, is big, modern, efficient, with swimming pool, but it's out-of-the-way on Via Senigallia.

Windsor, near luxury hotels, is modern, reasonable.

SECOND CLASS. Best include the *American,* 182 rooms with shower; the *Andreola* and *Mediolanum,* recent, most rooms with bath or shower; the *Capitol,* 103 rooms with bath, also has swimming pool; *Biscione,* near post office; small, elegant.

Monopole, Via Filzi 43, *New York,* Via Pirelli 5, and *Lord Internazionale,* all good.

The popular *Manzoni* has 56 rooms, most with bath or shower.

The *Centro* has 54 rooms, is near La Scala; *San Carlo,* 62 rooms with bath. Others are the *Ambasciatori, Bristol Schmid, Zurigo.*

D'Este, Viale Bligny 23, is modern, comfortable, but ask for room off street, where trams roar by.

THIRD CLASS. Numerous, but at this level you'll be lucky to get a private bath. Try the *Eden,* the *Torino* or the *Losanna.*

The two best pensions are: *Montenapoleone* (P1), Largo Santa Babila 5, and *Del Corso* (P2), in the very central Galleria.

RESTAURANTS

The most famous restaurant in Milan—and one of Italy's best—is *Giannino's,* Via A. Sciesa 8, where you can watch the chefs at work. Garden court atmosphere. Delicious food but *very* expensive.

The luxuriously-decorated *Barca d'Oro,* Via Borgospesso 18, is possibly even more expensive. *Crispi* is also good, also a strain on the budget. *Da Massimo,* specializes in Tuscan cooking. *Gourmet,* Via Torino 2, for deluxe dining.

The restaurants in the Galleria provide some excellent food. Best-known and most expensive is *Savini,* superb steaks and exquisite ice-cream. *Biffi, Pam-Pam and Penny* are now highly Americanized. Alfredo, renowned ex-chef of Biffi-Scala holds forth at his *Gran San Bernardo.* Reserve. Popular with newspapermen, actors, *Rigolo* is lively, ideal for a (costly) snack if you're out late.

Cavallini, on Via Mauro Macchi, boasts an attractive garden as does *Brasera Meneghina,* Via Circo. Both (E). *Boeucc* (E), Piazza Belgioioso, with summer garden, specializes in crepes and excellent meats.

Collina Pistoiese (E), Via Amedei, mother-house of famed Gori dynasty of restaurateurs. Tuscan-style pastas and meats.

El Toulà (E), Piazza Ferrari, is famed for pleasant atmosphere, excellent versions of Venetian dishes; *Girrarosto* (E), Corso Venezia, offers succulent steaks, spit-roasted meats and reliable Chiantis.

On the less expensive side, there are many fine restaurants in Milan. To mention just a few: *Osteria del Vecchio Canneto,* with fixed menu emphasizing fish; *Bagutta,* Via Bagutta 14, summer garden; the *Boccaccio,* Piazza Virgilio; *Abetone,* Via Quintino Sella, always a safe bet; *Tantalo* off Piazza Duomo, another good bet; *Veneziano,* Via Agnello, for seafood. Classics; *Vecchia Milano,* Via Gian Galeazzo, and *Trattoria della Pesa,* Viale Pasubiolo.

In the Brera district choose among *Soldato d'Italia* or *Franco,* both on Via Fiori Chiari, and *Ciovassino,* Via Ciovassino.

There are several ways to eat cheaply in Milan. At the confectionery shops run by the *Motta* and *Alemagna* chains and similar establishments you can grab a stand-up snack. When you see a sign reading *tavola calda,* that's a lunch counter, where the food is always cheap and often surprisingly good. Several of these are located in and around the Galleria.

SHOPPING. This is the center of the silk area so you will find the best selections of Italian fabrics: lavish brocades; upholstery materials, lovely dress fabrics. In contrast, a vast assortment of just plain junk is on view at Milan's flea market on Via Calatafimi every Saturday.

By all means take a look around the most modern department store in Italy, *Rinascente* on the Piazza del Duomo, full of fashion merchandise, utilitarian articles, and an inviting assortment of gifts.

For antiques: *Ars Antiqua*, 9 Via Mozart. A splendid shop full of china and glass ware is *Richard Ginori*. For ceramics, *Arte e Folclore*, 29 Via Montenapoleone; next best to a Sardinia trip is the *Isola* handicraft store.

Walk down Via Montenapoleone, one of the world's most elegant shopping streets; you'll see the ultra-chic boutiques of *Mila Schön, Valentino* and *Roberta di Camerino* interspersed with those of top French designers. The *Vergottini,* lively family of famous hairdressers, are here too. *Fiorucci's* big shop on Via Torino is an exhilarating experience.

SPORTS. *Automobile racing* is a favorite sport of this region. Italy's auto and motorcycle Grand Prix are both held in Monza, eight miles from Milan, during September.

If you have a hankering to watch the nags, this can be satisfied by a visit to the San Siro Hippodrome, where some of Italy's most important *races* are held. Greyhound racing is also offered in Milan.

If you want to spend part of your stay on the green, the beautifully kept 18-hole *golf* course at nearby Monza Park is one of Italy's finest.

The Lakes

The lake region of Lombardy—famed throughout the world for the beauties of Como, Garda, Maggiore and Lugano—lies at the foot of the Alps. Lake Garda, ten miles wide, stretches for 32 miles through groves of olive, lemon and orange trees at the foot of mountains often covered with snow. A complete tour of it by private car is recommended. Failing that, the bus is fine. If you have more leisure, by all means take a lake steamer for a restful, tranquil cruise through this lovely scenery.

Lake Como, bordered by delightful towns like Como, Bellagio and Colico, lies placidly in a setting of lush green foliage, brilliant flowers and beautiful villas. Take the lake steamer and get off anywhere your fancy dictates—there'll be another one along in an hour or so—and proceed by foot along the roads and lanes that wind through the gardens on the banks. The mountain air is perfumed with a thousand flowers here, as it is at Lake Lugano.

Perhaps the most brilliant gem in this crown of Northern Italy is Lake Maggiore, a two-mile-wide ribbon connecting the plain of Lombardy with the Alps of Switzerland 40 miles away. The loveliest of the many cruise possibilities here is from Stresa to Arona and Baveno. The climax of the cruise is Isola Bella, ten terraces of gardens forming a setting for the 17th-century Palazzo Borromeo. The view from here is one of the scenic wonders of the world.

PRACTICAL INFORMATION FOR THE LAKE REGION

LAKE REGION HOTELS. The lake resort hotels of Lombardy are open only from spring to late autumn while hotels in towns like Bergamo and Mantua are open the year round, of course. It is advisable to check before making your plans and be sure to reserve early. If you take full pension at a lake hotel, you can often have a picnic lunch packed for you. Today's moneyed jet-setters tend to shun the grand old palace hotels on the lakes, so you can get the grandeur at more attractive rates, particularly April, May, late September-end October.

BAVENO (Piedmont). Resort on Lake Maggiore. *Splendido Nuovo Italia* (1), has heated pool, tennis courts, and extensive lakeside grounds, private beach. *Beau*

Rivage, has small garden, but is on main road. *Simplon,* private beach, pool, park and tennis. All (2).

BELLAGIO, Lake Como resort. *Grand Hotel Villa Serbelloni* (L), a magnificent establishment; elegant furnishings, tennis, pool.

Du Lac, opposite steamer landing, is comfortable, has restaurant with panoramic view. *Metropole* has lakeside terraces. *Excelsior Splendido,* swimming pool. All (2). *Belvedere* (3), terrace restaurant, pool.

BERGAMO, *Excelsior San Marco,* air conditioned, classic; most rooms with bath. *Moderno* is central; attractive rooms, sidewalk café. Both (1). *Touring* (2), pleasant, with view. Recent *Arli* (2), near station, comfortable, well-equipped, no restaurant. But nearby is the *Moro* (2), with excellent restaurant. *Agnello d'Oro* (3), in the heart of picturesque Bergamo Alta.

BRESCIA, important art city near Lake Garda. *Vittoria* (1), central and modernized. *Gambero* (1), central, 16th-century building; comfortable, modernized interiors. *Ascot* (2), just outside center, pleasant rooms, cool garden. *Europa* (3), superior in category.

On Viale Bornate, *Crest Hotel* (2) and *Motel AGIP* (3).

CERNOBBIO, Lake Como resort, *Villa d'Este* (L), one of Italy's, or for that matter, the world's, most luxurious hotels. Very expensive. Its 171 rooms, most with bath, are arranged in beautiful Renaissance villa. Floating swimming pool. Tennis court, international golf tournaments on private course, horse show (May-June). Also lakeside, *Regina Olga* (1), only slightly less palatial at one-third the price; pool.

COMO, summer resort on lake. *Barchetta-Excelsior,* recent, comfortable, fine food; *Metropole e Suisse,* best in Como proper; *Villa Flori,* on Cernobbio Road, recommended. All (1). *San Gottardo,* traditional; *Como,* modern; both (2).

CREMONA, violin city, art town. *San Giorgio,* largest, best; *Continental,* fairly new, small rooms, expensive for what it is. *Este* (2), all rooms with bath.

DESENZANO DEL GARDA, summer resort on Lake Garda. *Miralago,* most rooms with bath; *Park,* comfortable, pleasant; *Barchetta,* overlooks lake. All (2). *Vela* and *Vittorio,* both (3), basic, in attractive lakeside locations.

GARDONE RIVIERA, on Lake Garda. *Eurotel,* all rooms with bath; tennis, pool. *Grand, Fasano,* classic lakeshore hotels, good service, private beaches. All (1). *Monte Baldo, Villa del Sogno,* both fine (2).

MANTUA (MANTOVA), art town. *San Lorenzo* (1), Piazza Concordia, is smallish, elegantly furnished, splendid views from terrace. Recent *Rechigi* (1), very modern, bustling. *Dante, Apollo,* recently renovated *Italia;* all (2).

MENAGGIO, popular Lake Como resort. *Victoria,* largest. Tennis court, garage. Open April 1-October 31. *Grand Hotel e Menaggio,* very good, both (1). *Bellavista* (2), on lakeside, modern.

PAVIA. Art town. *Palace* (2), some bad reports, but no other choice here.

SIRMIONE. Popular Lake Garda resort. *Grande Terme, Sirmione,* and *Continental,* all lakeside and very comfortable, with fine views, are all (1). *Olivi* (2), *Du Lac* (3).

STRESA (Piedmont). Principal summer resort on Lake Maggiore. *Grand Hôtel et des Iles Borromées* (L), most famous of Stresa's many fine hotels, situated on lakeside. Tennis, golf, private beach.

Regina Palace (1). Member of the Italhotels group. On lakeside. Tennis court, garage, traditional décor.

Bristol (1). Most rooms with bath. Tastefully furnished. Private beach.

Milano (2). Lakeside situation, pleasant terrace restaurant, excellent food and service. Half of rooms have baths.

Speranza Hôtel du Lac (2). Lakeside situation. Half of rooms with bath.

La Palma (1), 66 rooms with bath; private beach. *Astoria* (2) overlooks park and lake; heated swimming pool.

TREMEZZO. Lake Como resort, *Grand Hotel Tremezzo* (1), 91 rooms, 59 with bath. All front rooms with balcony and panoramic view; lido, bar, dancing. Has second-class annex. *Bazzoni* (2), 128 rooms, half with bath or shower. Modern, attractive décor. Restaurant with panoramic view of lake.

VERBANIA-PALLANZA (Piedmont), Lake Maggiore summer resort, quiet, noted for its mild climate. *Majestic* (1). Fine, lakeside. *Metropole* and *Belvedere* (2). *Tre Ponti* (3). Rates here in all categories much lower than in nearby Stresa.

RESTAURANTS

BAVENO (Piedmont): The *Bellevue* is, with one possible exception, the best place to eat in the Lake Maggiore region. A little expensive, but worth it. A fairly close second is the *Suisse;* both (E).

BELLAGIO: Tops here is the restaurant of Hotel *Villa Serbelloni,* expensive. *Ferrario* and the *Barchetta* are good, lower-priced.

BERGAMO: The dining room of the hotel *Moderno;* also in the upper price bracket, excellent, are the *Montanina,* Colle San Vigilio; *Taverna Pianone,* Via Castagneta; *Cristallo,* Foppolo; *Marianna,* Upper Bergamo, with terrace. *Del Sole* is noted for game in season and regional dishes. Try also the *Taverna dei Colleoni.*

BRESCIA: The dining room of the *Vittoria,* small, and not too expensive, heads the list. If you want to stuff yourself, try the *Archimede,* Via Mazzini, where portions are copious. *Gottardino* is another good bet. Recommended are *La Sosta* and *Augustus.* Bargains are *Agnello,* Corso Garibaldi 20, and *Da Peppino,* Viale Venezia.

COMO: You can do pretty well on the top level either at *Lario,* Piazzo Cavour, or at the *Barchetta* restaurant in the Excelsior hotel, in same square. But make it a point to eat at least one meal at *Cassè,* on the Piazza Funicolare.

Moderately priced restaurants include the *Pizzi,* Viale Geno 12, *Il Faro,* Via Luini 44, and *Da Pietro,* across from the cathedral, which also has a snack bar.

GARDONE RIVIERA: Of the two best eating places here, both in hotels, one, the *Grand,* is in Gardone Riviera proper, while the other, the *Fasano,* is in the outlying quarter of the same name. There are two excellent restaurants, a little less expensive than the hotels, *Barbarano,* and *Birreria Wuehrer,* which specializes in beer.

ISOLA DEI PESCATORI (Piedmont). This little island, reached by boat from Stresa, is graced with one remarkably good restaurant, the *Verbano,* where you may lunch in peaceful and picturesque surroundings. Moderate.

MANTUA: *Cigno,* 13th-century inn; lots of paintings, excellent local dishes. *Gastone* and *Due Albini* also fine for regional specialties. *Romani, Garibaldini* are good trattorias. Just three miles from center, *Da Baffo,* a must; rustic fare, homemade bread. All (M).

MENAGGIO: The restaurants of the *Grand e Menaggio, Principe* and *Victoria* hotels are good. *Pesce,* Piazza Garibaldi, is more moderately priced.

SIRMIONE: *Terme, Sirmione* hotel restaurants are fine; *Vecchia Lugana* and *Nuova Lugana* on road to Peschiera beat them for romantic atmosphere. Very good, *Vittoria da Marina, Grifone,* moderate.

STRESA (Piedmont): The restaurant of the *Grand et Iles Borromees* challenges the Bellevue at Baveno for tops in the region. Other good hotel restaurants: *Milano* and reader-recommended *Moderno.*

TREMEZZO. The Hotel *Tremezzo* (E) is best here and the view from the dining terrace is unbeatable. The *Azalea* (E) cooks up a classic *osso buco.*

Hydrofoil Service. Operates four times daily, round trip Como-Bellagio-Menaggio-Como. On Lake Maggiore: Arona-Stresa-Locarno. Service also on Lake Garda.

Venice and Venetia

Venice is eternally preoccupied with the comtemplation of its own beauty. Founded on the marshes it rose to dominate the Adriatic and hold the gorgeous East in fee. At the height of her power in the 16th century, Venice was a wealthy city-republic glorying in fêtes and pageants, reveling in the splendor of her painting, sculpture and architecture. Those days of glory are gone, but art survives, and the grace and refinement of Venice remain in all the cities of the Venetian area—Verona, Vicenza, Padua, Treviso and Belluno. A visit to any of these is enough to fill the soul, but if your time is limited, let it be to Venice alone.

Best time to come is April, May, September and the first weeks of October. The summer months can be hot and humid, but better Venice in the 80's than no Venice at all. Throughout the year, the famous International Biennial Exhibition sponsors events in all arts. In August, there's a night fête on the Grand Canal and the opening of the International Cinema Festival. Venice's "Musical Autumn" begins in September with a regatta on the Grand Canal, and the illustrious La Fenice theater, where *Rigoletto* and *Traviata* were first performed, is the scene of distinguished musical events. (The regular opera season here is from December to March.) On the third Sunday in July, the Feast of the Redeemer is celebrated, and Venetians and visitors flock across the Giudecca Canal to the Church of the Redeemer, built to commemorate the end of a devastating plague, for a day of worship, feasting and carnival, followed by a regatta.

Arrival in Venice is a thrill. If you come by train, you walk down the station steps right to the Grand Canal. If you fly, you land at Marco Polo airport, and the motorboat that takes you to Venice gives you a view from the lagoon of its pink and gilded palaces. If you drive, you park your car in the huge 2,000-car garage at Piazzale Roma or on the 5,000-car Tronchetto parking island, directly connected to the bridge from the mainland, and then proceed by vaporetto to your hotel.

Exploring Venice

You could spend a year exploring this city and its environs. For a short term visit (two or three days) concentrate on the Piazza San Marco, the Grand Canal and environs, and the lagoon islands of Murano, Burano and Torcello.

A gondola (or vaporetto) picked up at the San Marco station will take you on the leisurely two-mile tour of Venice's 'main street', the S-shaped Grand Canal, which winds through four centuries of Gothic-Renaissance palaces. There are at least 200 of them, and your gondolier will point out the outstanding ones.

On foot you will explore the Piazza San Marco, the heart and soul of Venice, a regal square bordered on three sides by arcades, on the fourth by the great Basilica of St. Mark, one of the world's most magnificent churches. The interior, faced with marble and gold mosaic, is incredibly rich. Qualified English-speaking guides are available to point out the plethora of treasures in detail. If you prefer to do it alone, don't miss the Vault of Paradise with Titian's *Last Judgment* or the *Pala d'Oro,* a 10th-century altarpiece of gold and enamel, studded with precious gems. Take the stairway to the outer terrace for a view of the replicas of the four magnificent horses of gilded copper, a third-century (B.C.) Greek work, which once adorned the Hippodrome of Constantinople, they were installed here in 1207.

The Palazzo Ducale, the Doges' Palace, next to the Basilica, a fantasy of pink and white marble with its immense rooms and Scala dei Giganti (Stairway of the Giants) is one of the treasure houses of the world. Visits with English-speaking guides are recommended. The tour ends on a somber note with a visit to the gloomy cells of the Piombi Prison, which you reach from the palace by the celebrated Bridge of Sighs, from which convicted prisoners caught their last glimpse of freedom.

Other Highlights

Before going to the Lido or the outer islands, here are a few other highlights of Venice proper which require a lot of footwork but are decidely worth the effort: The Academy of Fine Arts (Accademia), the world's finest collection of Venetian paintings, crammed with Titians, Tintorettos, Giorgiones and the whole Venetian school; the octagonal Church of Santa Maria della Salute, with paintings by Titian and Tintoretto; Santa Maria Formosa, built in 1492; 18th-century Palazzo Querini-Stampalia, with 18 rooms of paintings (Bellini, Tiepolo, etc.) open to the public; Santa Maria dei Miracoli, a 15th-century Renaissance masterpiece; Verrocchio's statue of Colleoni on horseback in the Campo San Zanipolo; Church of San Zaccaria with its 13th-century Romanesque belfry and paintings by Bellini, Tintoretto and Titian; and the magnificent Church of San Giovanni in Bragora, with art of Cima and Vivarini.

We almost forgot Santa Maria Gloriosa dei Frari (Titian and Bellini), the Church of San Rocco, with 6 Tintorettos, and the School of San Rocco, with its 56 Tintorettos!

The Lido and Islands

By this time, you should be ready for a long rest. Every 20 minutes, steamers leave from Riva degli Schiavoni for the 15-minute trip across the Venetian Lagoon to the Lido, with its very smart beach hotels and not much else to recommend it as an excursion; it's very lazy and *very* expensive. The water, so shallow that you have to wade about half a mile before you swim, is as tepid as pea soup. The Municipal Casino is open at the Lido in summer (and from October 1-March 31 at Vendramin-Calergi Palace on the Grand Canal), and there are plenty of tennis courts, an 18-hole golf course, a riding school and everything else you could want if you can work up the energy. If you want more reasonable prices and less effete surroundings, try the beaches at Sabbione or Sottomarina, beach suburb of picturesque Chioggia.

The lagoon trips to Murano, Burano and Torcello, departing from the Fondamenta Nuova, are highly recommended. Murano, ancient center of the glass-blowing craft, is rather commercial. Visit the Museo Vetrario (Museum of Glass) here, and walk into any of the glass-blowing establishments on the Fondamenta dei Vetrai to watch this interesting procedure. Generally, you'll do better to buy glassware in Venice and, if possible, take it with you. Some tourists have been disappointed, to put it mildly, when the goods they received back home were inferior to what they ordered. Burano, more colorful and picturesque, is a small island fishing village, the center of the Venetian lace industry. Here, too, visitors are welcome to watch lacemakers at work. Torcello, a mile from Burano, was the first colony of the Venetian lagoon, established by the Venetians when they fled the barbarian hordes. It's a romantic, restful place with a cathedral dating from the seventh century, recommended for an hour, or a week, of complete repose. Take the regular public-service steamers, not organized boat tours, on which you're pressured to buy at each stop.

PRACTICAL INFORMATION FOR VENICE

HOTELS are no problem in Venice. A city which seems sometimes to contain no buildings other than palaces, it has converted many of them into hotels. When you go to a palace hotel in Venice, you can take the term literally. However, make sure you have an understanding as to prices, including service charges, taxes, and whether or not you are expected to take one or more meals per day at your hotel. Venice is Italy's most expensive city for a tourist, so be prepared! Complaints about overcharging should be taken to the official tourist office, Piazza San Marco.

DELUXE

Danieli Royal Excelsior. Of the five deluxe hotels, the favorite among Anglo-Saxon tourists seems to be this hotel and with good reason. It has a superb location, serves gourmet food on a terrace commanding a wonderful view, and the service is swift.

The *Gritti Palace* is preferred by those who like a smaller, quieter hotel. It is distinctive, beautifully funished, superbly run. Hosts week-long art history, gourmet cooking courses. The *Bauer* is one of the finest in Italy; its style is elegant and contemporary. There's a terrace restaurant and roof garden for summer dancing.

The *Europa-Britannia,* same management as the Gritti and Excelsior Lido whose beach is at patrons' disposal.

The *Cipriani,* on the tip of Giudecca island, overlooks the lagoon, is quiet, smart and expensive. All rooms with bath, air-conditioned. Gardens, pool, terrace restaurant. Five minutes from St. Mark's Square by boat provided by the hotel.

FIRST CLASS

Monaco e Grand Canale is comfortable, bright. The *Londra* on Riva Schiavoni, renovated, front rooms overlook lagoon.

Regina e di Roma, superior, dining terrace on Grand Canal.

Gabrielli and renovated *Saturnia Internazionale* both in elegant historical palaces, all comforts.

Metropole, on Riva Schiavoni, elegant, well-furnished; back rooms quieter.

Palazzo del Giglio apartment hotel, central, well-appointed; minimum 7-day stay at attractive rates.

SECOND CLASS hotels are still good in Venice—most rooms have private bath or shower. In the San Marco area, top choices are:

Concordia, overlooking basilica, friendly, attractively furnished, comfortable.

Cavaletto e Doge Orseolo, pleasant, on side canal.

Bonvecchiati, vine-covered dining terrace.

Savoia e Jolanda, Riva Schiavoni. *Do Pozzi,* smallish rooms but delightful.

La Fenice, charming, with garden court.

Flora and *Bisanzio* are smaller, comfortable and pleasant. All above have private baths or showers; no restaurants.

Near the station, *Principe,* Lista di Spagna, is good.

THIRD CLASS hotels do not appeal to Anglo-Saxon tourists in many Italian cities, but since Venice is a tourist-minded town, budget travelers may be willing to make an exception here.

Among the most comfortable are the *Rialto,* San Marco 5147, the *Antico Panada,* San Marco 656, and *Giorgione,* Santi Apostoli 4587, which is off to the far side of Venice. The 17-room *Leonardo,* San Leonardo 1385.

Paganelli, Riva Schiavoni, basic furnishings but fine location, pleasant restaurant. *Città di Milano* on charming square just off Piazza San Marco.

Bel Sito, overlooks S. Maria del Giglio; ample, simply furnished rooms.

There is just one first-class pension: the *Locanda Cipriani,* Isola di Torcello 17, expensive.

A good second-class pension is *Seguso,* Zattere 779. Almost all rooms with bath.

Among the third-class pensions, the *Wildner* is on the Riva degli Schiavoni; across the lagoon on the Guidecca, *Casa Frollo,* 17th-century villa, is recommended.

THE LIDO is more expensive than Venice proper. The beach is on the far side of this famous strip of land, 15 minutes by steamer from Venice, and the hotels here are most favored, open only in summer.

The only deluxe hotel, the *Excelsior Palace,* stands on the beach itself; has 257 rooms, most with bath. Large rooms and suites, many with balconies. Private beach; cabanas. Nightclub, several restaurants, garage.

Just back of the beach is the older first-class hotel, the *Grand Hôtel des Bains e Palazzo al Mare,* 300 rooms, most with bath. Park and gardens. Pagoda Restaurant on shore. Large, well furnished rooms. Private beach, cabanas, tennis, swimming pool.

Recent, first-class, is *Eurotel,* tennis and swimming pool.

There are a number of second-class hotels; best and most expensive is the *Quattro Fontane,* where all rooms have baths, and there are tennis courts. Also expensive is the *Petit Palais,* comfortable, with private beach.

Villa Eva Quisisana is fine, but expensive in category. *Helvetia* (2) has most rooms with bath. *Villa Mapaba* is attractive, has pleasant garden.

Slightly less expensive are *Bortoli, Riviera,* and two charming villa-hotels, *Adria Urania* and *Villa Nora,* quiet, 5 minutes from beach.

Of the many third-class hotels, *Villa Ada* and *Atlanta* might be mentioned. The first has both singles and doubles with bath, the other has bath only with doubles.

Golfers might like to try the *Vianello,* Via Ca' Rossa 10, hard by the links.

Pensions on the Lido begin with the second category, of which *La Meridiana, Albertina, Buon Peace* and *Villa Laguna* may be cited.

RESTAURANTS

Restaurant prices here are about 15% higher than elsewhere.

Among restaurants, the luxuriously furnished *Quadri* (E), in Piazza S. Marco, widely known for its exquisite food and wine list.

The *Taverna La Fenice* is one of Venice's truly outstanding eating places.

Another standout is *La Colomba,* Frezzeria 1665, whose seven dining rooms are hung with modern paintings. Efficient service and excellent seafood.

Another excellent restaurant is the famous *Antico Martini,* Campo San Fantin, 1981, which is also a nightclub with dancing from 10 P.M. In summer you may dine and dance in courtyard. Reserve.

Those in the know go to *Veccia Cavana* (M) for local cuisine.

Caravella (E) of Hotel Saturnia Internazionale has exceptional cuisine and intimate atmosphere.

La Madonna (M) is tops in Venice for seafood.

All' Angelo, also in San Marco (not the piazza), is highly regarded for both food and atmosphere.

Others of first rank include *Al Gambero, Da Noemi* (also a hotel), and *All' Antica Carbonera.* Also good: *Peoceto Risorto, Gala d'Oro, Marco Polo, Bonvecchiati.*

Hotel restaurants are seldom exciting. Exceptions must be made in Venice for the terrace restaurants of the *Danieli* (with dancing) and *Gritti Palace,* which overlooks the Grand Canal, and particularly of the *Cipriani* with its terrace overlooking St. Mark's Square.

Americans will like *Harry's Bar* for its atmosphere; pricey. At San Marco 1665. *Café Florian,* Piazza S. Marco; popular meeting place; old world charm. Coffee and pastries (L. 1,500), with music, at *Florian's* or *Quadri.*

A pair which specialize in traditional Venetian cooking, *Nono Risorto,* San Cassiano 2337, and *Simionato Mario,* Calle delle Rasse 4533. For unique pasta (*bigoli*) and tasty quail, *Alla Quaglia,* at Cannaregio 4518, right behind Santi Apostoli. *Al Campanile,* off Campo San Polo, pleasant. All (M).

La Vida (M), Campo San Giacomo dall'Orio, unobtrusive facade, local favorite for exquisitely simple fish cook cooking.

Da Mondo, Calle Racchetta, is good. Art students gather at *Montin,* Fondazione Eremite 1147, for Venice's best *pasta e fagioli.*

On the Lido, *Gino* or *Belvedere,* both on Piazzale Santa Maria Elisabetta; *Tavernetta Gransevola* at Alberoni.

Three islands in the lagoons, close to Venice, are well worth visiting for a good meal.

TORCELLO. Delightful boat excursion. *Locando Cipriani,* to crown your memorable outing; try their fish specialties. This is also an excellent small pension. Information at *Harry's Bar.*

BURANO: *Da Romano,* one cut below luxury, good for fish dishes and located to give you a lunch stop if you visit the lacemakers.

MURANO: *Da Mazzega.* This restaurant caters for those who take in the glass blowing establishments.

SHOPPING. When you first see the displays of glassware around St. Mark's Square you may think that the Venetian glassmakers have had their day. Be patient. There's still some exquisite glass available; you just have to be discriminating enough to pick it out from the mass of mediocre' stuff that the makers think will appeal to tourists.

If you have time to go to Murano, shop at *Societa Veneziana Conterie e Cristallerie* at Fondamenta Navagero 34, a well-known and reliable firm. In Venice, *Salviati* at San Gregorio 195 and Piazza San Marco 79B and 110, has a huge collection including museum pieces, worth a visit even if you don't buy.

Venetian lace is as expensive as it is beautiful. If you want to buy or merely look, you can see how lace is made without going to Burano by visiting *Jesurum & Co.* behind St. Mark's cathedral. At 1091 Campo San Gallo is *Lorenzo Rubelli & Figlio's* luscious display of velvets and velvet brocades.

For stunning handbags go to *Roberta da Camerino,* Piazza S. Marco 127 and 5864 Campo S. Maria Formosa.

For souvenirs and gifts try the following on the Piazza San Marco: *C. Giubelli,* 91 and *G. Nardi,* 69 and 143. For ceramics: *Richard Ginori,* Calle Larga San Marco 416. Leather goods: *Luce,* 258 Mercerie Orologio, and *Marforio,* San Salvatore 5033.

You'll have a wonderful time on that Rialto Bridge, which is lined with shops, and don't disdain the little portable stalls along the lagoon. Amid all the junk there are some nice novelty chokers of pastel-colored blown glass beads and some good toy gondolas and other amusing souvenirs.

PORTERAGE AND BOATS. *Porters'* charges are fixed according to a rather involved schedule, depending on the distance, number of bags, etc. For example, between any two points within the center of town (bounded by the railway station and Piazzale Roma), you must pay 2,000 lire for the first bag, 750 for each additional one. From the railway station piazza to the nearby hotel area, 500 lire per bag.

Gondolas can be expensive; inquire at your hotel or at local tourist office for current rates, and come to terms with gondolier before you set out. Figure on about 10,000 lire for one to five persons for a half-hour. *Water taxis* (motorboats) cost about 8,000 lire for up to five persons for a short ride. *Vaporetto* fare is about 100 lire; Line One takes you the length of the Grand Canal.

After 10 P.M. a supplement of 25-30% is applied to all public transportation, including gondolas.

To and from airport, take bus or *Cooperativo San Marco* motorboat (6,000 lire per person).

VENICE'S CANALS. A word about the city itself. Venice is unique in that it's sliced by about 150 canals into more than 115 little islands intricately bound together with the 400 arched bridges that link one to another across the canals. "Main Street" is the Grand Canal; other principal "boulevards" are smaller canals some 15 feet wide, known locally as *rii.* Streets, as the term is commonly understood, do exist on the individual islands, but only as narrow, tortuous byways more closely associated with alleys and answering to the names of *Calle* (*Calletta, Calleselia*) this or *Ruga* and *Stretto* that, instead of the *Via* generally used elsewhere in Italy. Only one square (*Piazza*) remains as such in Venice—that of San Marco—while the few other open spaces that might be called squares become the *campo, campello* or *campazzo.* Adding to this general confusion is the fact that all names of streets and canals appear on signs in pure Venetian dialect.

The Tourist Office under the arcades of Piazza San Marco distributes a useful map of the city (free), and you can buy a very clearly illustrated guide of the Grand Canal (Canal Grande, Raccanelli).

Art Cities near Venice

Padua, about 20 miles west of Venice, has a famous university, founded in 1222; the 650-year-old Scrovegni Chapel, with frescos by Giotto; and the 13th-century Basilica of Sant' Antonio, built over the tomb of Saint Anthony of Padua, scene of an important pilgrimage every June 13. See the Donatello bronzes in this church and his celebrated statue of Gattamelata on the square nearby.

Vicenza, badly hit during the war, is still a treasure trove of Palladian architecture. Palladio's first major work, the Basilica Palladiana, dominates the Piazza dei Signori; the Corso Palladio is lined with palaces, and the beautiful Teatro Olimpico, Palladio's last work, is still intact.

Verona, the city of Romeo and Juliet: Juliet Capulet is said to have lived in the 13th-century building at 17-25 Via Cappello, and her alleged tomb can be visited near the Campo della Fiera. An unforgettable experience in this unforgettable town is an open-air opera performance given in the Roman Arena. It seats 25,000 spectators and is so acoustically perfect that you can hear clearly from the last row. The performances begin in July.

For an unusual sidetrip, a comfortable excursion boat glides along the Brenta Canal between Padua and Venice, past the stately villas of 17th- and 18th-century Venetian nobles. The trip takes seven hours, includes a luncheon stop at Oriago and a visit at Villa Nazionale, Stra, most magnificent of them all. (Excursion starts alternately at Venice or Padua, with return trip by bus.) Off the beaten track, well worth a leisurely excursion by car through lovely countryside, are the villas around Treviso, notably Palladio's villas. CIT offers two all-day villa tours weekly from June 15-September 15.

PRACTICAL INFORMATION FOR VENETIA

LIDO DI JESOLO, popular beach resort. Newest, ultra-modern and improbably named *Las Vegas,* the only (1) here; right on beach; all rooms with balcony, seaview; pool. *Bellevue* on Pineta beach, all rooms with bath or shower, *Elite,* quiet, with pool, on beach, as is *Cambridge,* modern, are all (2). Recent in this class are *Ambasciatori, Cesare Augustus* and *Soleil,* all on beach, pools, gardens, good decor.

PADUA (PADOVA), art and university city. *Padovanelle,* new, just outside town, pool, and *Storione,* 100 rooms with bath, air-conditioned, both (1).

Europa, recent, 57 rooms with bath. *Milano,* well-appointed rooms. *Biri* and *Grande Italia,* most rooms with bath, all (2).

Donatello (3) near center, recent, all rooms with bath.

TREVISO. Medieval art town. *Continental* and *Carlton* are best. Both (2). *Al Foghèr* (2), in outskirts, is comfortable.

VERONA, important art center. *Due Torri* (L). Rebuilt on a centuries-old hostelry site, this is delightful. Central, soundproofed; authentic period furnishings. Recent member of prestigious Italhotels chain.

Colomba d'Oro, half of rooms with bath, has attractive glass-roofed restaurant. *Grand,* Corso Porta Nuova, traditional but comfortable. Both (1).

Good (2) is *San Luca,* handy to Arena but quiet, off street; modern, all rooms with bath. *Europa* (2) is fine but on noisy Via Roma.

Accademia and *Giulietta Romeo,* both (2), central, comfortable.

VICENZA, notable architecture and art works. *Jolly (1),* most rooms with bath or shower. *Stazione,* attractive, *Continental* and *Cristina,* both comfortable. All (2).

In category (3) are *Basilica,* good; *Vicenza,* some rooms with bath, and *Adele.*

RESTAURANTS

ASOLO: *Cipriani* (E), this romantic and elegant first-class hotel has outstanding restaurants.

MONTECCHIO MAGGIORE: *Romeo and Juliet Medieval Tavern.* Eight mile drive from Vicenza towards Verona. Attractive restaurant in ascribed Montague/ Capulet fortress ruins. Expensive.

PADUA (PADOVA): Best is probably the *Storione* hotel dining room. The *Isola di Caprera,* Via Marsilio da Padova, follows close behind, along with *Leon Bianco, Zaramella, Da Dotto* and *Biri.* All (M-E).

Stop in center of town for lunch or aperitif at *Pedrocchi Café.*

VERONA: Undisputed leader is the *Dodici Apostoli* (Twelve Apostles) (E), Corticella San Marco, gourmet's delight in 14th-century locale; their masterpiece: salmon baked in a bread crust. Reserve. Moderate: *Re Teodorico,* Castel S. Pietro; *Pedavana,* Arena square. *La Greppia* and *Torcolotti* less expensive. *La Serra di Mamma Sinico* (M-E), Via Leoncino, recommended for attractive atmosphere, fine pastas and roasts.

VICENZA: The leading restaurant here is *Da Pasquale,* Corso San Felice, though it is closely followed by *Tre Visi,* Contrá Porti and the *Righetti,* Via San Antonio. *Trattoria all' Olmo* (I) is in the locality of the same name.

Al Pozzo, Via San Antonio, also serves pizza.

The Dolomites

Few Americans or Englishmen find their way into the Alpine paradise of the Dolomites, a year-round mountain playground of unspoiled villages and unsurpassed scenery. An easy way to catch a glimpse of this country from Venice is to take the CIT bus trip that starts daily from the Piazzale Roma between June 1 and September 30, leaving at 8 A.M., passing through Treviso, Vittorio Veneto, Pieve di Cadore and Cortina d'Ampezzo, and returning at 6:30 P.M.

Cortina d'Ampezzo, scene of the 1956 Winter Olympics, is the jewel of the Dolomites. It has everything from the gentlest beginner slopes to spectacular jumps, a bobsled run, numerous cableways and chair lifts, the complete works to make it one of Italy's outstanding ski centers. If you've ever dreamed of a place where you could ski the year round, the Dolomites can make that dream come true—believe it or not, a giant slalom contest takes place every year at Solda, in the middle of July!

Among the highlights of this attractive region—Trent (Trento), its southern bastion with a thousand years of history and art concentrated in its Piazza del Duomo; Bolzano, the heart of the Alto Adige, which to many Austrians is their lost province of South Tyrol; the famous Brenner Pass to Austria; Belluno, dating from pre-Roman days, surrounded by castles and towers of medieval times; and Merano, with its combination of skiing and sun bathing in mild winter temperatures and its world famous "grape cure". Although the city has a calming effect, Merano offers many activities typical of the whole Dolomite region—

tennis, polo, horse racing, swimming, trout fishing, canoe races, shooting the rapids, mountain climbing, golf.

PRACTICAL INFORMATION FOR THE DOLOMITES

 HOTELS. This list contains a mixed lot of winter and summer resorts as well as city hotels. Peaks of season in the first category are December 20-January 6; January 20 through February; July 25-August 31, when prices are highest and early reservations essential. Ask about ski-week terms.

BELLUNO, important town, fine architecture. *Astor* (2), all rooms with bath. *Europa* (3), is excellent in category. *Dolomiti,* all rooms with bath, is a recent (3).

BOLZANO, lively mountain city. *Park Laurin* (1), best. Tennis court, pool. *Alpi,* newish, central location. *Grifone,* central, pool, gardens; recommended. *Scala,* pool. (All 2).
Herzog (3), budget value. *Motel AGIP* and *Motel Kampill,* both (3), modern.

BRESSANONE, medieval town. Category (2) are: *Elefante,* 16th-century villa, pool; memorable restaurant, expensive. *Gasser, Albero Verde,* in quiet, attractive locations; *Jarolim,* at station, with pool in garden; all (3).

CORTINA D'AMPEZZO, Number One winter sports and summer resort of the Dolomites. *Miramonti-Majestic* (L.). A luxurious hotel, comparatively expensive, but good value for your money. Nearly half the rooms have baths. Tennis, golf, pool.
In category (1) are *Savoia.* Also a fine hotel, somewhat less expensive than the preceding, tennis, pool. *Cristallo Palace.* Same rates as preceding. Quiet location; large, pleasant rooms. Heated pool, sauna. *Bellevue* is a trifle cheaper. *Corona,* a quiet, comfortable place, with lots of good modern art works. Has second-class annex. *De La Poste,* center of town; large rooms, most with bath. Gay, lively public rooms, *the* place to be seen. Fully renovated after 1976 fire.
All (2) are: *Cortina,* central, friendly; comfortable, modern rooms. *Europa,* smallish rooms, all with bath. *Ancora,* close to cableway; attractive rooms, efficient service. *Park Hotel Vittoria,* central position, elegant but friendly, most large-size rooms with bath.
Umbria, nearly half the rooms with bath, is a first-class pension. Garage.
Menardi, on outskirts, comfortable; *Montana,* central, basic, bustling; both (3). At Pocol, *Argentina, Tofana* (2), are good.

MADONNA DI CAMPIGLIO, summer-winter resort. Recent (1), *Grand des Alpes,* well-furnished rooms with bath, handsome public rooms; tennis. On a par with *Golf,* with 9-hole golf course. Slightly less expensive is newly refurbished *Savoia Palace,* both (1). Category (2) are *Caminetto,* small, cozy, all rooms with bath; *Spinale,* comfortable rooms, all with bath; dancing in tavern.

MERANO, important spa resort. *Bristol* (L), an Italhotel member, modern, has 150 outside rooms with bath or shower, spacious balconies. Rooftop pool, open-air dance floor. Garage.
In category (1) are: *Palace,* about the same size as the above, and even larger *Emma,* with pool on grounds. *Eurotel,* modern, all rooms with baths; pool. Traditional *Meranerhof,* comfortable; all rooms with bath; pool. *Savoy,* fine Swiss-type hotel.

All (2) are *Schloss Labers,* with pool, tennis; *Juliane,* attractive, pool; *Anatol,* thermal pool.

At nearby Marlengo, *Castello Forst* (2), modern comforts in a renovated castle. At Fragsburg, *Castel Frieberg* (1), beautifully adapted castle.

TRENTO, historic regional capital. *Trento* (1), all rooms with bath, some with balconies; terraces overlooking park. *Vittoria* (2), recent; contemporary décor, well-equipped. *Everest* (3), good value. *Villa Madruzzo* (P2), 12 miles from Trento, attractive; first-class comforts.

Motel Agip (3), on Via Brennero, 45 rooms with shower, is reasonable. At Sardagna, *Autostello ACI* (2).

RESTAURANTS

BELLUNO: Regional dishes at *K 2,* Via Cipro; *Al Sasso,* Via Consiglio. *Zumelle,* romantic restaurant in castle out of town. All (E).

BOLZANO: *Grifone* hotel restaurant (E) is excellent for regional specialties. Try *Frederic* (M), Via Diaz, *Caterpillar* (M-E), or rustic *Cavallino Bianco* (M).

CORTINA D'AMPEZZO. Best: *Toula,* elegant and expensive; *Fogher,* almost as good; *Ra Stua,* trattoria. *Capannina,* Via Sopiasez.

MERANO has a wide range from the modern *Turri Bar* to the *Municipio,* which is completely Italian and furnished like a country *osteria.* The *Palace* is a good hotel restaurant, not too expensive. Don't miss the *Ca de' Bezzi* (E), Via Portici, where the food is wonderful, Tyrolean setting. *Andrea,* Via Galilei, small and excellent. Better reserve. *Forsterbräu* also is good.

STELVIO PASS. The *Albergo Passo del Stelvio* enjoys a remarkable location on the very summit of the pass. The food is good, the prices reasonable and the service excellent.

TRENTO: *Chiesa,* Via San Marco, handsome old dining room, prize-winning cuisine; *Trento's* best. *Nino,* Via Travai, noted for game; *Tino,* wine cellar, simple, hearty food. All (M). *Cantinota* (E), another wine cellar, for sophisticated suppers.

The Trieste Area

Varied and off the beaten track, Italy's easternmost provinces of Udine, Gorizia and Trieste are worth exploring. The area, long part of the Austro-Hungarian Empire, has a strong slavic flavor. An almost continuous border of sand sloping gently to the sea between Venice and Trieste provides splendid beaches like Lignano Sabbiadoro.

Udine has a 13th-century cathedral standing on the Piazza della Libertà, an arcaded square, one of the loveliest in Europe. If you like Tiepolo, you should make an excursion to this town—his paintings are everywhere, especially in the splendid Bishop's Palace.

Aquileia has an impressive basilica, built in 1061, and many relics of Roman times, including a recently-discovered forum. Grado is an unusual island port with an attractive beach, a gridiron of quays and canals, a harbor full of fishing boats and pleasure craft and a gem of a sixth-century Byzantine cathedral.

Bustling Trieste, with its impressive Piazza della Libertà right on the sea, is a center for yachting, horseracing and water sports. Its international samples fair each June is a big event, and the open-air opera given each July in the 17th-century Castello di San Giusto rivals that of Verona. The June-September 'Sound and Light' spectacle at romantic Miramare Castle is a must. Tarvisio, which stages various racing and ski jumping competitions in January, is the chief resort for sportsmen in this region, providing excellent hunting and fishing, too.

PRACTICAL INFORMATION FOR THE TRIESTE AREA

WHEN TO GO. The summer resorts located in the hill and mountain areas of the region are their busiest from late June through August, while the seaside resorts are filled up from the middle of June through August. The winter sports season is at its height during December and January, and some resorts continue to be active through February.

HOTELS

BIBIONE, beach resort. *Palace,* bright, modern, with pool, beach. *Park,* similar resort-type on beach. *Bembo, Principe.* All (2). *Italy* (3), on beach.

GRADO, important spa and beach resort. *Astoria,* (1) 190 rooms with bath or shower, is on busy square; *Tiziano Palace,* all rooms with shower, refurbished. *Savoy,* with pool and garden, *Isola d'Oro,* modern, functional. *Al Bosco* is on beach at La Rotta. All (2).

LIGNANO SABBIADORO, beach resort. *Atlantic, American, Columbus,* all (2). At smart Lignano Riviera, *Eurotel* and *President,* both (1), elegant, modern.
At Lignano Pineta, *Delle Palme,* on beach, *Greif,* with pool. *Continental,* near beach, 43 rooms. *Medusa Splendid,* 56 rooms with bath. All (2). *Duna Fiorita* (3), all rooms with shower; tennis.

TARVISIO, summer and winter sports resort on the Austrian border. *Nevada* (2) is recent, good.

TRIESTE, art center. Best, *Duchi d'Aosta* (1), on main piazza, modern, well-appointed. *Jolly Cavour* (1), near station, air-conditioned; pleasant lounges. *Milano, Columbia,* both (2), in station area, comfortable.
At Miramare, *Maximilian's Residence* (1) and *Al Castello* (2) overlook sea.
At Grignano, chic yachting port, *Adriatico Palace* (1) and *Riviera* (2) are modern, private beaches.

UDINE, art center. *Ambassador Palace,* most rooms with bath; recent *Astoria,* well-equipped. Both (1), *Cristallo* (2), all rooms with bath. *Motel Agip* (3).

RESTAURANTS

TRIESTE AND SUBURBS. Best fish restaurants are: *Nastro Azurro,* Riva Sauro 12; *Al Granzo,* Piazza Venezia, a classic; and *Piccolo,* Via Santa Caterina, all (M-E). *Camillo* (M), Via S. Lazzaro, is a favorite.
Antica Bonavia, Piazza Unita 2 and *Da Dante,* Via Carducci 12, offer from fish to fowl as does *Istria,* Via Milano 14, all (E).
Suban, Via Comic 2, Slovenian cooking. For Austrian atmosphere: *Birreria Forst Europa,* Via Galatti 10 or *Birreria Dreher,* Via Giulia 77, a proper beer cellar. Popular *Benedetto* (1), really good food in two small dining rooms beyond delicatessen front.
Bottega del Vino, at Castle San Giusto, dine and dance out of doors in summer.

Liguria's Two Rivieras

Liguria is a strip of coastline stretching 217 twisting miles from the French border to Tuscany. Its seaside towns have been compared to a string of precious stones, the central pearl of which is Genoa. East of Genoa, the region is known as the Riviera di Levante; the western string is the Riviera di Ponente.

These twin rivieras are a popular year-round tourist area. It's carnival time here from January on. The spring opera season in Genoa, La Spezia and San Remo gets underway in February. Easter celebrations, flower parades, water games, regattas, motor races (Genoa's Sea and Mountains Cup in March), tennis, golf, swimming and skin diving—these are the diversions of Liguria. Safe, gently sloping fine sand beaches of the Riviera di Ponente are perfect for children and non-experts. The best are San Remo, Imperia, Diano Marina, Laigueglia, Alassio, Finale Ligure, Spotorno, Savona, Albisola Marina and Celle Ligure.

After Genoa, the aspect of the coast changes, and the bathing here is generally for expert swimmers who prefer to dive from the rocks into deep water. The warm, limpid quality of the water along this coast makes it ideal for underwater fishing. Portofino, Nervi and the area betwen Sestri Levante and La Spezia are ideal for this sport. Chief rendezvous for yachtsmen are Portofino, Pegli, San Remo, Santa Margherita Ligure and Genoa.

Resorts, East and West

West of Genoa, the top resort is San Remo, which has a casino and a lively social and sports life. Bordighera, with its April parade of flowers and exhibition of *haute couture,* runs it a close second. Alassio, an international watering place, is a particular favorite of the English; it boasts a fine 18-hole golf course.

On the Riviera di Levante, Rapallo, also beloved by the English, is queen, followed closely by two beautiful small resorts, Santa Margherita Ligure and Portofino. The latter has become one of the most *chi-chi* spots on the Riviera in recent years.

La Spezia is a good excursion center for trips to such quaint towns as Portovenere, a recently "undiscovered" fishing village on the site of an ancient Roman fortress. The Cinque Terre, five fishing towns with good beaches and magnificent scenery, are recent resort finds.

Genoa

Genoa is a handsome maritime city, set in a great semicircle around its busy port. The *Genovesi,* although they have the reputation in Italy of being *avari* (misers), have known how to spend money to beautify their city. The Via Garibaldi is typical, with its princely mansions and sumptuous villas and its two important museums, the Palazzo Bianco and Palazzo Rosso, facing each other across it. The Piazza de Ferrari is the setting for the Municipal Opera house (season from December until the end of May) and the church of Sant' Ambrogio, reconstructed in 1527 from a tiny fourth-century chapel.

This is one of 400 churches in Genoa, among the most interesting of which are the Cathedral of San Lorenzo, started in the third century and rebuilt in its present romanesque style in 1100, and Santo Stefano, where one of Genoa's most famous seafaring men, Christopher Columbus, was baptized. You can visit his home, and also the house of the great violinist Paganini, another famous native son.

To get the flavor of medieval Genoa, go to the Piazza San Matteo, where a group of ancient houses, belonging to the celebrated Doria family, date from the 12th century. The exploits of the Dorias are recounted on the black and white marble façade of the San Matteo chapel, built in 1125, while all the flavor of Genoa's mighty days of empire is summed up in the great palaces of the city—Palazzo Doria, Palazzo Ducale, Palazzo Reale and Palazzo San Giorgio.

Recommended: a drive along the spectacular Circonvallazione la Monte, overlooking the city. The view changes at every turn, and sometimes includes the entire sweep of the Riviera from La Spezia to Imperia.

PRACTICAL INFORMATION FOR LIGURIA

SEASONS. The bathing beaches of the Riviera di Levante (Ligurian coast *east* of Genoa) are apt to be most crowded in July and August. June and September are the best months in our opinion. The season on Riviera di Ponente (*west* of Genoa) is more staggered, but it is always best to reserve ahead. *Beach charges* are made generally (except by hotels with private beach): from 1,000 lire up for entry to beach, chair, changing facilities, umbrella. Off season (May, end September-end October) hotel rates are attractive.

N.B. The waters of both Rivieras are polluted; swimming in the immediate area of Genoa is highly risky, *when* permitted.

HOTELS

ALASSIO, beach resort. *Mediterraneo,* best, most rooms with bath; private beach. *Diana,* good, modern, has beach, pool. *Spiaggia,* all rooms with bath or shower, at beach. All (1). *Majestic, Beau Sejour, Regina,* all (2), overlooking beach. *Eden, Beau Rivage,* both (3), pleasant, beach facilities.

Laigueglia, about 10 mins. away by bus, has broad sandy beach, is lively and less expensive. *Laigueglia, Splendid,* both (1). *Windsor, Bristol,* are on beach, both (2).

ARENZANO, beach resort. *Punta San Martino* (1), best, 16 rooms, with bath; promontory with beautiful view of sea, outdoor dining terrace, pool, tennis, very comfortable; highly recommended but expensive. *Grand* (1), also good.

BORDIGHERA, second most important resort of the Riviera di Ponente. *Del Mare,* with pool, beach, is tops for comfort, but expensive. *Cap Ampelio,* recent, has pool in garden. Both (1).

Belvedere (2), half of rooms with bath, lovely grounds. *Astoria* (2), modern, terrace. *Brittannique et Jolie* (3). *Villa Elisa* (3), most rooms with bath, garden.

CAMOGLI, beach resort. *Cenobio dei Dogi* (1), best, attentive service, beautiful location, pool, tennis.

CELLE LIGURE, beach resort. In category (2) are: *San Michele,* most rooms with bath; *Riviera,* pleasant; *Piccolo,* with garden. A good (3): *Ancora.*

GENOA, capital of Liguria, important port, art city. *Colombia-Excelsior* (L), opposite railroad station; marble floors, linen sheets, truly "grand."

In category (1) are: *Savoia Majestic,* at railroad station, faded elegance, is one of the top-ranking Fioroni hotels, a Genoa group, and also a member of Italhotels.

Bristol e Palazzo. Recent, nearly all rooms with bath. Also a Fioroni Hotel and a member of Italhotels. *Plaza,* many rooms with bath or shower.

Category (2) hotels include: *City,* very central, but quiet; *Elisee,* central, comfortable, well-furnished. *Metropoli,* central, breakfast only. In category (3): *Simoncini Garden, Torinese. Orti Sauli* (P2), near Brignole Station, is pleasant, air-conditioned.

IMPERIA, beach resort, chief town of its district. *Corallo,* best. Most rooms have baths. *Croce di Malta,* on tiny beach. *Kristina,* small on quay. All (2).

LA SPEZIA. *Jolly* (1), recent, very comfortable. *Palazzo San Giorgio* (2). At Sarzana, *Motel Agip* (2). At Portovenere, *Royal* (1), fine.

LERICI, beach resort. *Byron, Shelley,* comfortable, but can be noisy. *Nido,* at Fiascherino, private beach. All (2). *Panoramic* (3), good value.

OSPEDALETTI, beach resort. *Rocce del Capo* (1), has pool; expensive. *Petit Royal* (2).

PORTOFINO, very fashionable seaside resort and yachtsmen's rendezvous. *Splendido* (L), an outstanding hotel. Majority of rooms have baths. Tennis court, garage. Smart clientele. *Nazionale,* most rooms with bath or shower; *Piccolo,* most rooms with bath. Both (2), and rooms without bath inexpensive at both. *Eden* (4), small. All are booked years ahead in season.

RAPALLO, Elegant seaside resort, favored for its sandy beach.

Category (1): *Grand Hôtel et Europa,* pleasantly located across small square from water, in own gardens; half of rooms with bath. *Bristol,* pool, balconied rooms, most with bath. *Eurotel,* on hillside overlooking sea; air-conditioned rooms; pool in pleasant garden.

Category (2): *Riviera,* modern. All rooms with bath; good value. *Moderno e Reale,* unpretentious family hotel overlooking port. *Splendor Solarium,* all rooms with shower. *Miramare,* almost on the seafront, most rooms with bath. *Sorriso* (3), in quiet park.

SAN REMO. Number One resort of the Riviera di Ponente. *Royal* (L), in park near casino, most rooms with bath. Elegant and comfortable, pool, tennis court, garage. *Grand des Anglais* (1), palace-type; old-world comfort.

Londra, Corso Matuzia, facing sea, traditional elegance. *Residence Hotel Principe,* all rooms with bath or shower. *Miramare Continental Palace,* 67 rooms, most with bath, near beach, delightful restaurant. All (1).

Category (2) include: *Villa King,* small, and *Europa e della Pace,* both good; *Nazionale,* next to casino, half of rooms with bath, some with shower.

About a mile to the east, the attractive *Montecarlo* (2), 43 rooms, pool and private terraces. Two miles east, at Arma di Taggia, are the *Vittoria* (1), with beach and pool, and *Miramare* (2), all rooms with bath or shower, overlooking the sea.

SANTA MARGHERITA LIGURE, select seaside resort. *Imperial Palace* (L), largest, most expensive, pool. Almost in the luxury class: *Miramare,* private beach, water-ski club, two nightclubs. Nearly as good, *Park Hotel Suisse* (1), quiet location, pool, terraces. *Regina Elena, Vela, Continentale,* are (2). *Conte Verde* (3).

SESTRI LEVANTE, beach resort. *Villa Balbi* (1), largest. Majority of rooms have baths. *Dei Castelli* (1), most expensive. Most rooms have baths; pool, tennis, garage. *Miramare e Europa,* small, most rooms with bath; garage; *Grande Albergo,* some rooms with bath; *Mimosa,* new, good. All (2). *Helvetia,* beach; *Villa Segesta,* recommended. Both (3).

VARIGOTTI, ancient seaside town. *La Giara* (1), all rooms with bath; private beach. *Al Saraceno,* private beach, bar, sun terrace, garage. *Plaza,* most rooms with shower. Both (2).

VENTIMIGLIA, frontier town and seaside resort. *Francia* (2), most rooms with bath or shower, and *Eden La Mortola* (2), just outside town, are best. *Suisse Terminus* (3), friendly atmosphere. *Sea Gull* (3), modern, with beach, good value.

ZOAGLI, near Rapallo. *Terrazze* (2), modest, splendidly situated, most rooms with bath.

RESTAURANTS

ALASSIO: Some of our readers suggest the *Roma Roof Garden,* with cabaret and good food inexpensively. *Stella Marina,* with dining terrace on seafront, is good. Exceptional menu, authentic local cuisine, jovial host Silvio at *La Palma* (E).

BORDIGHERA: *Pinin,* on San Remo road is best. *Gino,* on Dolceacqua road, fish specialties. Snacks at *Chez Louis,* Corso Italia. All (M).

GENOA: *Vittorio al Mare* at Boccadasse, for genuine Genovese food (M-E). *Stella,* also good.

Other fine restaurants: *Cucciolo,* Viale Suali 33, Tuscan cuisine; *Marinetta,* Corso Italia 19, seafood; *Pichin,* Vico Parmigiani 6. For more fish: *Da Mario,* Via Conservatori del Mare 33, *Caravella d'Oro,* Corso Italia 15, *Punta Vagno,* Corso Italia 3, both overlooking the sea.

At Boccadasse, *Santa Chiara,* with a sea view, or *Le Gheise,* both (M), are good and, of course, the emphasis is on fish. A group of moderately priced restaurants includes *Olivo,* Piazza Raibetta 15, *Perelli,* Vico Falamonica 41; and the *Pesce d'Oro,* Piazza Caricamento 63, which makes a specialty of fish dishes. If you want to eat cheaply, but still well, try *Cavanna,* Via Fieschi 37; *Due Colonne,* Piazza Matteotti 31; or *La Lanterna,* Via Fieschi 78. *Osvaldo,* at Boccadasse, for fish soup.

PORTOFINO: Splendid setting at the *Splendido* hotel, followed by *Delfino* and the *Nazionale. Pitosforo* is excellent: good menu and guitar music on attractive dining patio. *Da u Bati,* a picturesque *osteria. La Terrazza,* Via Gramsci; Via Maragliano; *Basilico,* Via Monte Carlo, all (M).

RAPALLO: At the top of the eating places of this popular resort—*Da Fausto,* the one gastronomic must here. However, the *Taverna Azzurra* and *Rosa Bianca* are good, and for fish, *Porticciolo* and *Tigullio.*

SAN REMO: One of the best places to eat in San Remo is the *Casino,* while two hotels are also topnotch—the *Reale* and the *Savoia. Pesce d'Oro* (E), misleadingly modest décor, excellent cuisine, with *Nostromu* (M) a good second choice. After these come a group of others all good, and less expensive than the leaders— *Castel Doria, Daetwyler, La Lanterna* and *Pastorino. Da Nico* (M), a classic.

SANTA MARGHERITA LIGURE. A top restaurant on the Riviera di Levante coast is the *Trattoria dei Pescatori,* which is not too expensive. The smarter

Taverna del Brigantino costs more. *Saltincielo,* high above town, recommended. *La Terrazza* (M), on Via Gramsci.

VENTIMIGLIA. *Mortola* is one of the finest restaurants in Italy. It's very expensive, but worth every lire of it. Also good, *Europa* (M).

SHOPPING. Seasoned travelers tell us that you'll find better buys in angora in Genoa than you will in Rome. Try the shops along the Via Luccoli and Via XX Settembre.

There are a number of towns in Liguria which have handicrafts of outstanding interest to the tourist. Albisola is noted for its ceramics; Rapallo is known for its handmade lace, which comes mostly from nearby Portofino and San Fruttuoso; Zoagli is a silk center; Chiavari has two specialties: those wonderful towels with the long fringe, and rush bottom chairs. San Remo has many good shops.

The Emilian Way

The region of Emilia is laid out for the most part along the famous old Roman road, the Emilian Way, which runs from Milan through Piacenza in the northwest to Rimini on the Adriatic. Among its chief tourist attractions are Bologna, one of the chief art and gastronomic cities of Italy; Parma, another place that combines these two pleasures; Ravenna, once the capital of the Byzantine Empire; Piacenza, a city of Gothic treasures; the art towns of Rimini, Reggio Emilia and Ferrara, and a string of beaches, from the quieter, pollution-afflicted ones among the pine woods to the north, Marina di Ravenna, Marina Romea, Lido degli Estensi, and Lido delle Nazioni, to noisier, smart, but crowded Rimini, Cervia, Cesenatico, Bellaria, Riccione and Cattolica. Last-named beaches can be recommended for their fine sand, gentle slope and safe swimming. Salsomaggiore, the leading spa of Italy (except for Tuscany's Montecatini) is celebrated for its summer entertainment season and its battle of flowers in June.

Things to see: in Piacenza, the 16th-century Palazzo Farnese, the 12th-century Lombardian-Romanesque cathedral; the 13th-century Palazzo del Comune, and the Lombard Church of Sant' Antonino.

In Parma: the 12th-century Romanesque cathedral with Correggio's fresco of the Assumption decorating the dome, a masterpiece of Renaissance art; the churches of San Giovanni Evangelista and the Madonna della Steccata; the Palazzo della Pilotta, containing one of Italy's greatest collections of art, superbly lighted in air-conditioned setting of luxurious comfort. In this same palazzo, don't miss the National Museum of Former Ages, with its valuable Etruscan and Roman antiquities.

Reggio Emilia is worth a brief stop for its 16th-century cathedral and Parmeggiani Gallery of paintings (Veronese, El Greco and Van Dyck among them).

Modena has a world-famed collection of illuminated manuscripts in its Biblioteca Estense, and the city itself, once capital of the Duchy of Este, is charming, with its fountains and 12th-century bell tower, a rather incongruous background for the Communist posters all over the place.

Bologna

If you love art, architecture and good food, you will be in heaven wandering through the porticoed streets among the Renaissance palaces and fountains of Bologna. If you go to *Pappagallo's* on the Piazza Mercanzia for lunch, just ask for *un pranzo alla Bolognese,* "a Bolognese luncheon" and leave the rest up to the waiter. When you stagger forth from that epic meal, visit the great Church of San Petronio, one of the most beautiful Gothic structures in Italy. Climb the 11th-century Torre degli Asinelli (350 feet high) for a fine vista of Bologna's grandeur. Spend some time in the Piazza del Nettuno, one of this city's major attractions for its marvelous Fountain of Neptune by Giambologna.

A walk down the Strada Maggiore, lined with medieval houses, will lead you to the 15th-century church of Santa Maria dei Servi, with its Cimabue Madonna. Other noteworthy churches—fourth- to 16th-century Santo Stefano, Santa Maria della Vita, and San Domenico, with sculpture by Michelangelo. The most beautiful private palaces in Bologna are on the Via Zamboni, and a fine collection of the Bologna School is on view in the city's Art Gallery, along with such outstanding examples of other work as Raphael's *Ecstasy of St. Cecilia* and Titan's *Crucifixion.*

Ravenna

Ravenna means mosaics, specifically the wonderful Byzantine mosaics in the sixth-century Church of San Vitale and in the Basilica of Sant' Apollinare at Classe. These two things alone would warrant a long, long voyage, but you may want to make an excursion past the once-splendid pine forest along the shores to picturesque Comocchio and the nearby Abbey of Pomposa.

PRACTICAL INFORMATION FOR EMILIA

 HOTELS. Emilia is well-provided with hotels, especially in the leading towns and resorts. Distances between the most rewarding places are short, so that you're sure to find a good place to stay the night. Reserve early for Parma in May and September, and for the coast resorts in peak season of July-August. At beach resorts here pension plan rates are very low, and include beach facilities. These resorts are especially favored by German and Scandinavian tourists.

BOLOGNA, art city. *Royal Carlton* (L), ultra-modern elegance. Air-conditioning, car park.
Internazionale, central, attractive, efficient. *Garden,* central, renovated monastery, pleasant garden. *Elite,* on outskirts, sleek, functional. All (1).
Europa (2), is small and good; air-conditioned rooms. *Roma,* an inconspicuous little hotel, air-conditioned; *Alexander,* near station, first-class comforts; *Nettuno, San Donato,* all (2), central, comfortable. *Motel Agip* (2), on Via Emilia, a good value.
Tre Vecchi (3), comfortable, with good restaurant.

CATTOLICA, beach resort. *Caravelle* (1), 45 rooms with balcony, bath. Private beach. *Victoria Palace* (1), is comfortable. Class (2) are: *Beau Rivage,* most rooms with bath or shower. Private beach. *Doge·Mare,* fine, modern; quiet location. *Cormoran,* 157 rooms with bath, all recent. All a few steps from beach. *Diplomat,* good; right on beach.

FERRARA, art city. *Astra* and recent *De La Ville* are best; both (2), with air conditioning. *Europa* (2), simpler but reliable.

LIDO DELLE NAZIONI, new well-planned beach resort. *Hotel delle Nazioni* (2) has spacious family-size apartments, pool, tennis, beach. *Club Spiaggia* (3), excellent value.

MODENA, art city. Best are *Fini* (1), an excellent motor hotel, and recent *Canal Grande* (1) modern, comfortable rooms, attractive décor. *Donatello* (1), on outskirts. *Motel AGIP* (2), on Via Emilia.

PARMA, important art city. *Palace* (1), recent, best. *Park Stendhal* (1), all rooms with shower, and *Park Toscanini,* older but comfortable. *Daniel* (2), recent.

PIACENZA, art city. *Roma* (1), most rooms with bath or shower, air-conditioned. *Cappello* (2), traditional. Garage. *Florida* (2), all rooms with bath.

RAVENNA, important art city, famed for its mosaics. *Jolly,* is best; garage. *Bisanzio,* very good. Both (1), rooms with bath or shower. *Argentario, Trieste, Romea Motel,* 3 miles outside town. All (2).
Classensis Touristhotel (3), small, comfortable.
Motel Adriatico and *Motel San Vitale,* both (3).
At Marina Romea beach resort, *Corallo, Meridiana,* both (2).
At Marina di Ravenna resort, *Park* (1), has pool, tennis, private beach.

REGGIO EMILIA, art town. Hotel accommodations scarce. Best: *Astoria* (1), followed by *Posta* (2).

RICCIONE. *Atlantic* (1), all rooms with bath or shower. On the beach. *Beau Rivage,* on private beach, tennis, all rooms with bath or shower, covered terrace facing sea. *Grand Hôtel Riccione,* tennis, garage. *Lido Mediterraneo,* pool, kosher cuisine. *Savioli Spiaggia,* recent, 70 rooms overlooking beach and harbor. Recent *Zanarini* and *Abner's,* all private baths, both overlooking beach. All (1). *Club,* cheerful, recommended; *Carlton,* facing tennis, playground; *Baltic,* ultra-modern; *Bel Air, Tiffany, Carignano,* are near beach. All (2). *Plaza Rizz* (3) is good. *Grattacielo* (3), shares Grand Hotel's beach, pool; good value.

RIMINI. *Grand* (L), topnotch, palace-type; balconies, terraces facing sea. Beach club, pool, tennis, kosher cuisine on request.
Savoia-Excelsior, near the sea, tennis, garage. *Ambasciatori. Imperiale.* All (1).
Biancamano, Aristeo, Admiral, all (2), near beach. *Milton, Eurogarden, Ciotti,* all (3), pleasant.
Villa Argia (P3), beach and park.

SALSOMAGGIORE, second most important spa in Italy. *Milano* (L), big, elegant; pool, spa. *Perro, Centrale Bagni,* both (1), have spa treatments at the hotel. *Daniel,* modern, quiet; *Valentini;* both (2). *Suisse* (3).

RESTAURANTS

BOLOGNA: This is in some opinions the top gastronomic city in Italy, and in all opinions one of the first three. The *Pappagallo,* Piazza Mercanzia 3, is one of Italy's top restaurants.

The *Tre Vecchi,* another of Bologna's best restaurants, at 47 Via Independenza, is across the street from the good and expensive *Diana. Don Chisciotte-Sancio Panza,* ViaDegli Alberghi 2, excellent and not wildly expensive. *Guido,* Via Andrea Costa 34. *Rosteria da Luciano,* Via Nazario Sauro, chicken is the word. *Guiseppe,* Piazza Maggiore, *Nerina,* Piazza Galileo, and the *Sampierí,* Via Sampierí, for atmosphere. *Al Cantunzein,* Piazza Verdi, is excellent. All (M-E). A find: *All' Abbadia.*

There are plenty of good places in the moderately priced group. Try *Brunetti,* Via Caduti Cefalonia 5; *Cesarina,* Via San Stefano 19; *Ciuffo,* San Vitale 10; *Tura,* Via Marchesana 6, or *Donatello,* Via Righi. Others in this category are *Gambrinus,* Via Zamboni 11, where the beer is good; *Mela,* Via Fusari 5; and *Pepoli,* Via Pepoli 4. *Palmirani,* Via Calcavinazzi 2, recommended.

MODENA: *Fini* ranks with the finest restaurants of Italy. The *Oreste* restaurant is also very good. Both (M-E).

PARMA: Highly recommended are *Aurora, S. Ambrogio,* and *Filoma,* or *Angiol d'Or,* all (M). Try *Dsevod* (M).

RAVENNA: *Bella Venezia, Scai, Torre* and *Teodora,* all good and not expensive. For a bargain, try the *Aggio.*

RIMINI: *Vecchia Rimini,* Via Gambalunga 33, excellent. On harbor, *Taverna del Marinaio. Elio,* Viale Vespucci, is unpretentious but good. All (M).

Tuscany

The region is a happy blend of high mountains, fertile valleys and long stretches of sandy beaches curving along the west coast into the pine woods of La Maremma. But the magnet which has drawn educated people to this region for centuries is not the fabled green valleys of Tuscany, but the cities and towns, living symbols of the centuries-old Tuscan culture that brought forth the Renaissance and masters like Michelangelo, Dante, Leonardo da Vinci, Boccaccio and Petrarch. Florence, "the Athens of Italy", Siena, Arezzo, Pisa—it is cities like these, with their atmosphere of antiquity almost intact, that have made Tuscany the leader in the field of Italian tourism.

Florence

It's a tribute to the people and spirit of Florence that signs of the extensive and severe damage to the city, caused by the 1967 flood, have been practically erased; buildings have been cleaned, works of art are being restored, and fine handicrafts are being produced as before. The face of the city, especially along the Arno, has changed slightly, as some businessmen yielded to the temptation to rebuild their charming old shops in glittering modern style.

Best place to begin a survey of the staggering riches of Florence is in the Piazza del Duomo. The lofty cathedral (Santa Maria del Fiore) is the largest church in the world after St. Peter's in Rome. Its exterior, faced with white, green and red marble, may take some getting used to, but inside, the church is a stupendous example of Tuscan Gothic architecture. The giant dome, designed by Brunelleschi, is decorated by an immense fresco, *Universal Judgment,* by Vasari and Zuccari. Over the entrance to the Sacrestia Vecchia is a terracotta by Luca della Robbia. The mosaic over the Porta della Mandorla along the north wall is by Ghirlandaio, and in the first chapel of the left apse is an unfinished group by Michelangelo.

Next to the cathedral, Giotto's 14th-century Campanile rises to a height of 292 feet. It has been called the most beautiful bell tower in the world. Luca della Robbia did the first row of exterior bas reliefs with Andrea Pisano. Climb 414 steps for a superb view of Florence.

Across the square from the cathedral, you will find the famous Baptistery of San Giovanni, with Ghiberti's greatest work, the East Door or "Gate of Paradise" to use Michelangelo's phrase. It took the artist 27 years—from 1425 to 1452—to complete this matchless work in bronze. The North Door, representing the Life of Christ and the Evangelists, is also Ghiberti's work. Andrea Pisano is the sculptor of the South Door, completed in 1336.

Behind the cathedral is the Museo dell'Opera del Duomo, with a wealth of treasures including the charming *Cantoria di Luca della Robbia* and *Cantoria di Donatello.*

Take the Via Calzaioli from the Piazza del Duomo to the Church of Orsanmichele. Its exterior niches hold statues by Nanni di Banco, Donatello and Verrochio, wonderful examples of Renaissance sculpture. Inside, see the 14th-century tabernacle by Andrea Orcagna.

Resuming your walk along the Via Calzaioli, you will come to the Piazza della Signoria, in whose center Savonarola was burned alive. The square is dominated by the Palazzo della Signoria, better known as the Palazzo Vecchio (The Old Palace). Built between 1298 and 1314, it is now the city hall. That Michelangelo David on your right is a copy; the original is in the Academy Gallery, safe from the ravages of weather.

Next to the Palazzo Vecchio is the 14th-century Loggia della Signoria, with famous sculptures by Giambologna, Benvenuto Cellini and others. Nearby is the Piazza degli Uffizi, with the Palazzo degli Uffizi almost entirely surrounding it. This is the Uffizi Palace, which houses what may be the most important collection of paintings in the world. Don't try to do it in less than half a day.

Other Highlights

Here are other selected highlights of Florence—the Mercato Nuovo (New Market), covered by an arcade; the Ponte Vecchio (Old Bridge) across the Arno, spared by the Germans but hit hard by the 1967 flood, lined on both sides with shops of goldsmiths, silversmiths and Florence's best jewelers; the Palazzo Pitti (Pitti Palace), a massive 15th-century building full of vast halls and salons, which in turn are full of tapestries, portraits, sculpture and an important collection of 16th- and 17th-century paintings which occupy 28 rooms of the palace; the finely planned Palazzo Strozzi, outstanding Renaissance palace and courtyard; Brunelleschi's Church of San Lorenzo, with the adjoining New Sacristy by Michelangelo with its famous tombs of Giuliano and Lorenzo, Duke of Urbino; the Church of San Marco, with its museum containing the most important works of Fra Angelico: his *Annunciation* is here, and we recommend this particular visit even if it means giving up something else.

Incidentally, no car parking is allowed in the center of the city from 8:30-10 A.M. or 3-4:30 P.M., so you'll be doing some walking. For a rest, try a horse-carriage ride right through the Cascine, Florence's beautiful public park stretching for two miles along the Arno, or pedal off on the free bicycles the city provides there.

And what more? The Bargello Museum, with its fabulous collection of sculpture by Michelangelo, Verrocchio, Donatello and others; the Church of Santa Croce, largest and most beautiful of all Italy's Franciscan churches, burial place of Michelangelo, Galileo, Machiavelli and other illustrious Italians, and repository of priceless works of art, many of which were almost irreparably damaged in the floods. A "museum pass" for 21 of these art-filled buildings costs only $1 (40p) and is issued through the AAA, AA or RAC outside Italy and only at ENIT Frontier Offices in Italy.

By foot, car or bus, you should explore the lovely four mile promenade along the Viale dei Colli. The road winds outside and above Florence to a height of 340 feet at the Piazzale Michelangelo. The view here is superbly Tuscan—Florence, the plain beyond, Pistoia, and, in the far distance, the highest peaks of the Apennines. We almost hesitate to tell you while you're enjoying the view, but behind you at the top of the hill, there's the Romanesque church of San Miniato al Monte, built in 1013, one of the most beautiful and famous in Florence, and you really ought to climb that extra hundred feet and see it.

Environs of Florence

The "villa towns" just outside Florence are easily accessible by street-car and bus. Many of the great Tuscan villas and their beautiful gardens are open to the public. Fiesole, with its 11th-century cathedral, Roman ruins and magnificent views, is 20 minutes by municipal bus from Florence.

The route down Tuscany's coast will take you to famed Carrara, where you can visit the marble quarries; Forte dei Marmi, with its pine-bordered beach of fine white sand, and Viareggio, largest bathing resort on the Tyrrhenian coast and one of Europe's best.

West of Florence, the road out to Pisa passes through three remarkable cities—Prato, Pistoia and Lucca. Prato's 12th-century Romanesque cathedral contains works by almost all the major artists of Tuscany. If you're here on September 8, 9, 10 or 11, you'll be in the midst of an exciting fair combining plenty of entertainment with opportunities to get bargains in wool and cotton goods, two famous Prato products. Eight miles beyond the art city of Pistoia is Montecatini, Italy's leading spa for afflictions of the stomach and liver. It's a charming hill town with enough hotels and swank restaurants to send you back to the waters. Season is from April to November. Don't miss Lucca, one of Tuscany's most picturesque towns. Its 16th-century ramparts are delightful, treeplanted promenades; its cathedral, same epoch, is pronounced by many experts the most spectacular monument in Tuscany. Check the Della Robbias in the Church of San Michele.

PRACTICAL INFORMATION FOR FLORENCE

HOTELS. As an important tourist center, Florence naturally has many good hotels, but best to reserve well ahead in summer. Also, try to avoid Florence during fashion shows in October and March/April when hotels and restaurants are uncomfortably crowded. To encourage more off-season trade, a large convention center, with all modern equipment, has opened near the central railroad station. Top of the deluxe hotels is the *Excelsior-Italia,* Piazza Ognissanti 3, on the Arno. It's big, posh, beautifully appointed. More centrally located, hardly a stone's throw from the cathedral, is the *Savoy,* Piazza della Republica 7. In the heart of old Florence, the *Villa Medici,* Via del Prato, has roof-restaurant and pool.

FIRST CLASS hotels are headed by the excellent *Majestic,* near the station, recently rebuilt, furnished in period décor. Just off the station square is recent *Aerhotel Baglioni,* 220 rooms, garage; roof-garden restaurant.

The *Jolly Carlton,* near the Cascine Park, is air-conditioned, has roof garden and pool.

One of a few first-class hotels with its own garage is the *Minerva,* Piazza Santa Maria Novella 16, also not far from the station. Good are the *Astoria,* again the railway station neighborhood: the *Kraft,* a smaller quieter place located well out of the center; and the *Lucchesi,* on the river. *Crest* has 92 rooms with bath, two pools. *Principe,* on river, warm atmosphere, bright rooms.

Park Palace, has 30 rooms with bath; tennis, pool on hillside above Boboli gardens. Well-served by taxis.

Croce di Malta, Via della Scala; recently renovated, pool.

SECOND CLASS hotels. *Continental,* at Ponte Vecchio, small but comfortable rooms, much street noise. Nearby *Berchielli,* lots of charm. *Helvetia e Bristol,* Via Pescioni 2, near the cathedral. *Umbria,* Piazza d'Azeglio, comfortable. *Della Signoria,* Via Terme, all rooms with bath or shower. Conveniently located near a number of the principal sights. *Rivoli,* on central Via della Scala, smallish but pleasant rooms, garden court. *Jennings-Riccioli,* Lungarno delle Grazie, facing Arno, friendly service, all private baths.

Villa Belvedere, behind Boboli Gardens, splendid view of Florence; pool, excellent cuisine, easy parking.

Recent are: *Lungarno,* Borgo San Jacopo 12, highly recommended, a gem; *Villa Domenico,* Via della Piazzola 55, in lovely setting; bath; *Leonardo da Vinci,* Via Guido Monaco, most rooms with bath; *Laurus,* central, excellent.

THIRD CLASS hotels are not beyond the pale in Florence, and in this category you might try the centrally located *Paris,* Via dei Banchi; nearby *Gioconda,* Via Panzani; or *Columbia Parlamento,* Piazza San Firenze. *Rapallo,* Via S. Caterina, is 10-min. walk from cathedral; many private baths.

ON OUTSKIRTS: At Candeli, three miles out, *Villa la Massa* (1), almost deluxe, 40 rooms with bath, in two villas, pool. Same distance in the opposite direction at Sesto Fiorentino: *Villa Villoresi* (P1), lovely rooms all with bath or shower, in 12th-century villa; pool. *Villa le Rondine* (2), near Fiesole, reader-recommended; pool.

Motel: *AGIP* motel at Autostrada del Sole.

RESTAURANTS

Top choices: *Lume di Candela,* on Via delle Terme, excellent cuisine, expensive, warm atmosphere, *Natale,* Lungarno Acciaioli; *Alfredo sull' Arno,* near Ponte Vecchio, Via dei Bardi 46; and *Sabatini,* Via Panzani, one of Italy's best, traditional atmosphere; recently reported to be slipping.

Other first-class restaurants are *Oliviero,* Via delle Terme, excellent; *Villa San Domenico,* Via della Piazzola, all rooms with and *Otello,* Via Orti Oricellari 28.

Beppino, Via Pellicceria 28, reader-recommended for fine food, friendly host. The *in* place is *Le Cantine,* Via di Pucci 4. *Harry's Bar,* Via del Parione, is expensive. Recommended by residents are *Le Rampe,* Viale Poggi 1, menu with French accent; *Mamma Gina,* Borgo San Jacopo 37.

Buca Lapi, Via del Trebbio 1, is a big favorite with American tourists. *Paoli,* is attractive, central. *Cammillo,* very good. *Giovacchino,* Via Tosinghi 2, is also a good restaurant in this class, but even better is *Osteria Natalino,* Borgo degli Albizzi. Also good, *Giannino's Self-Service,* near cathedral. All (M).

At Fiesole, overlooking the valley and—farther away—Florence, is the open-air terrace of *Albergo Aurora,* a favorite with excursionists, as is the *Zocchi* in Pratolino and *Trattoria le Cave* at Mariano, all (M). Other favorites for good basic Florentine food: *La Sostanza* or *13 Gobbi,* both on Via Porcellana; *Buca Mario,* at end of Via della Spada; *Buca dell'Orafo,* near Ponte Vecchio; *Federigo,* Piazza dell'Olio. Delightful light luncheons (and great wine) at *Cantinetta Antinori,* in Palazzo Antinori. All (M).

Inexpensive and good, too, are *Frizzi,* Borgo degli Albizzi, *Buca Nicolini,* on Via Ricasoli, and *Antico Fattore,* Via Lambertesca, behind Palazzo Vecchio.

NIGHTLIFE: Florence quiets down noticeably in the late evening, but there are a few spots for night owls. At *Oliviero* and the *Baglioni* you can dine and dance, and *Harry's Bar* remains a popular rendezvous. *George and the Dragon,* at Borso Apostoli, is a nice British-style pub; the *Red Garter,* Via Benci, offers beer and banjo music.

SHOPPING. Most fashionable street is the Via Tornabuoni which runs from the Arno to the Piazza Antinori.

Don't miss that marvelous jumble of shops on the Ponte Vecchio. Look especially for the famous *Settepassi,* the shops of *Gambacciani* and *Del Bono,* and the tortoise shell and cameos of *V. Gherardi.* Across the bridge in Borgo Jacopo is the silversmith *Peruzzi;* more silver (and decorated woodware) at the *Lily Silver Shop,* Piazza S. Croce. Ceramics, glassware and china: *Menegatti,* Via Tornbuoni 77; *Botto,* Via Strozzi; *Fantoni,* Via Vigna Nuova 53.

Leather goods are the specialty of *Gherardini,* Via Vigna Nuova 57, and *Spulcioni,* Via Calimala 10. *Manco,* Via Tornabuoni, for gloves. For moderately priced leather goods and regional handicrafts, we recommend *S.E.L.A.N.* at 107 Via Porta Rossa. Straw and raffia goods are outstanding buys in Florence. *Emilio Paoli,* Via della Vigna Nuova 26R, has a grand array of smart designs and gift items. So does *Piero Mecatti* at 62R Via Guicciardini.

But by all means go to the outdoor straw market near the Ponte Vecchio. There you'll see everything in straw: skirts, table settings, hats, and hat boxes that make wonderful carryalls. Haggling is a fine art here; don't hesitate to practice it.

Pisa

Pisa's four major monuments are conveniently located in the Piazza del Duomo—the 900-year-old cathedral with its 69 antique columns; the 12th-century Baptistery, where you can admire the early Renaissance pulpit and the echo of your own voice; the extraordinary Camposanto (cemetery), and the Campanile, which is the famous Leaning Tower of Pisa. Begun in 1173, the Leaning Tower sags about 14 feet off center because of a slight slip in the land during its construction. Some 294 steps spiral up to a terrace at the top, where the view of Pisa is worth the hike. Don't leave this beautiful Tuscan town without casting at least a brief glance at the Piazza dei Cavalieri, one of the finest squares in the region.

Elba

You won't miss too much if you skip the important commercial port of Leghorn (Livorno), but we heartily recommend a visit to Elba if you can fit it in. Aside from its Napoleonic connections, this little island has wonderful camping sites in the pines, lovely beaches you can call your own, a splendid round-the-island drive by car or bus through tremendous scenery, and tiny coastal towns where the sweet white wine of Elba comes cold and sparkling at roadside inns and restaurants. Be careful after the second glass or *you'll* be saying "Able was I ere I saw Elba". This delightful island, 18 miles long by 12 wide, is reached by steamer from Piombino several times a day. It's a 15-mile trip to Elba's biggest town, Portoferraio. There's also a hydrofoil service from Piombino.

Siena and Arezzo

If you have time for only one town in Tuscany outside of Florence, make that town Siena. It is the best-preserved Italian vestige of the look and spirit of the Middle Ages. The perfect time to visit Siena would be on July 2 or August 16, when the Corsa del Palio (Parade of the Banner) has the whole town parading and competing in horse races in the beautiful Piazza del Campo in medieval costume. Highly recommended, but make your hotel reservations in advance and pull all strings to get grandstand seats for the race.

Off the beaten track between Florence and Siena is San Gimignano, medieval town of the towers, a charming place that is just being discovered by tourists. One other storehouse of Tuscan art treasures which should not be skipped is Arezzo, birthplace of Petrarch and home of the famous Guido of Arezzo, who invented the musical scale. Don't miss Piero della Francesca's series of frescos, *The Story of the Cross,* in the 14th-century Church of San Francesco. They are a high point in the whole history of painting. The 12th-century Romanesque Santa Maria Church should also be visited here. To enjoy the full flavor of this wonderful town, just sit at one of the numerous outdoor cafés on the medieval Piazza Grande and drink the Tuscan atmosphere with your Chianti. And if you're here on the first Sunday of September, you'll see the medieval Saracen's Joust, which rivals Siena's Palio in pageantry and thrills.

Porto Santo Stefano and Porto Ercole, on the Argentario Peninsula near Grosseto, are "in" resorts with the international set but are "out" in August, unless you have your own yacht to escape the crowds.

PRACTICAL INFORMATION FOR REST OF TUSCANY

 HOTELS. Avoid the central part of Tuscany in midsummer. The best month is May. The beach resorts are usually full-up from June through September and some beach hotels close November-April. Reserve well in advance if you want to stay overnight during such folklore festivals as Siena's *Palio* (July 2 and August 16), Arezzo's Joust of the Saracen (in September) and Viareggio's Carnival (February). Hotels are booked way ahead by out-of-towners coming to see these spectacular events.

AREZZO, art city. *Continentale,* best. Half of rooms have baths or showers. *Europa* (2), on station square, comfortable, no restaurant. Both (2). *Graverini* (2) and *Etruria* (3), both near station, are basic. *Minerva* (2), on outskirts; modern, pleasant.

CASTIGLIONE DELLA PESCAIA, smart beach resort. *Park Hotel Zibellino* and *Riva del Sole,* (1), with tennis, beaches, all amenities. *David-Poggiodoro* (2), pool. At Roccamare holiday village, *Roccamare* (1), expensive.

CHIANCIANO, smart spa. *Grand e Royal* (L), traditional, elegant. *Excelsior* and *Michelangelo,* both (1), all comforts. *Fortuna, Capitol,* both (2), modern, good.

ELBA. At Magazzini, *Fabricia* (2), modern, near beach; balconied rooms; pool. At La Biodola: *Hermitage* (1), pool, on beach. At Marciano Marina: *La Primula* (1), beach and pool. At Marina di Campo: *Iselba* (1), cottage-style. At Cavoli: *Bahia* (2), cottages overlooking beach. At Procchio: *Del Golfo* (1), on beach. At Porto Azzurro: *Cala di Mola* (2). At Capoliveri: *International* (2), modern, impersonal; pool, lift to beach. *Acacie* (3), friendlier, attractive, on beach.

FIESOLE, art town. Florence suburb. *Villa San Michele* (L), centuries-old villa, once outstanding, reported to be slipping badly. Only alternative on this level are Florence's top hotels. See also *Villa Villoresi, Villa La Massa* (Florence, Outskirts).

FORTE DEI MARMI, important, very smart beach resort. *Augustus* (L), all comforts, outstanding; beach club, disco. *Hermitage* (1), in quiet park, pool; mini-bus service to beach (2 km.). *Park* (1), all resort facilities.
Private beaches at *Astoria* and *Villa Angela,* both (2). *Goya* (2) is modern. *Adam's Villa Maria* (3), garage. Has annex. *Florida* (2), comfortable; *Bertelli* (P1), beach.

GIGLIO, island hideaway. At Giglio Porto, *Castello Monticello* with pool, tennis; *Demo's* (P1) with swimming area, and *Saraceno,* modest. All (2). At Campese, where there's a lovely beach, *Campese* (2), noisy in season.

LUCCA, picturesque art city. *Universo* and *Napoleon,* good, both (2), *Villa Principessa* (1), at Massa Pisana, elegant villa-style, pool.

MONTECATINI TERME, most important spa in Italy. *Grand Hôtel & La Pace* (L), palace type. Most rooms have baths. *Nizza e Suisse* (1), most rooms have baths. *Croce di Malta* (1). Most rooms have baths. Garage. Has second-class annex, *Aquila d'Oro e Dei Cavalieri,* all rooms with bath. *Ariston* (2), most rooms with bath or shower. *Tamerici e Principe* and *Cristallo,* both recent (1), are pleasant. *Reale* (3), all doubles with bath; nice garden.

ORBETELLO-MONTE ARGENTARIO, an elegant beach area. *Corte dei Butteri* (1), at Fonteblanda, two pools, on beach, own chapel. *Il Pellicano* (1), at Port-Ercole, pool, located in villa colony. *Don Pedro* (2), on hillside, is modern, good buy. *Motel AGIP* (3), south of Grosseto.
At **Porto Santo Stefano,** picturesque fishing port: *Torre di Cala Piccola,* clifftop hotel on secluded coast five miles from town, 40 rooms, pool, private beach. *Filippo II,* also smart, expensive. Both (1).

PIOMBINO, jumping off point for Elba. *Centrale* (2). *Collodi, Aurora,* both (3), modest overnight halts.

PISA, famous art town. *Dei Cavalieri* (L), all rooms with bath or shower. *Duomo* (1) is central and quiet; comfortable rooms, all with bath. *La Pace,* half of rooms with bath and *Villa Kinzica* are (2).
California Park Motel (2), at kilometer 338 of Aurelia Highway. All rooms with shower. Pool.

PRATO, art city. *Flora* (2), half of rooms with baths, good restaurant. *Palace* (2), on outskirts, modern, very good.

PUNTA ALA, elegant beach resort in bowl of low hills, villa colony, 18-hole golf course. *Gallia Palace* (1), elegant, all rooms with bath or shower, private beach. *Golf* (2), 84 rooms, most with bath or shower, near beach. *Cala di Porto* (1), recent, posh; pool, park.

SAN GIMIGNANO. Medieval art town. *La Cisterna* (2), fine view, good restaurant; modest decor. Scheduled to open: modern 250-room hotel, three kilometers out on Volterra road.

SIENA, Italy's best preserved medieval city. In town, *Excelsior's* total renovation may be complete by '78, promises to be outstanding (1). *Continentale* (2), very central; older hotel, only pedestrian traffic in vicinity. On outskirts: *Park Hotel* (1), handsome 15th-century palace, delightful grounds with pool; excellent food. Rooms are spacious, with fine views, but *not* soundproofed. *Villa Scacciapensieri* (1), also outside town; large country house with pool, small cottages in garden; comfort rather than chic. *Garden* (2), same type as last two but more modest.

VIAREGGIO, important beach resort. *Grand Royal* and *Palace,* both imposing, central, front rooms noisy; *Principe di Piemonte,* also fine, seaside. *Astor,* very modern, overlooking beach. All (1). *American,* well-furnished; *Maestoso,* with pool; *Garden,* attractive small hotel, all (2).

VOLTERRA. Fascinating fortified town. *Nazionale* (2), modern.

RESTAURANTS

AREZZO: *Buca di San Francesco,* atmospheric old place; *Graverini. Tonino,* is outstanding. Also good: *Arlecchino, Spiedo d'Oro.* All (M).

CERTALDO: Boccacio's birthplace. The *Osteria del Vicario,* a small hotel, has the best restaurant in town. On top of steep hill, fine view. Also good, *Castello.*

CERTOSA DEL GALLUZZO: two good restaurants, the *Bianca* and the *Calamandrei.*

FLORENCE: See previous pages.

FORTE DEI MARMI: One of the best restaurants along this whole stretch of beach resorts is here, *Hosteria il Pozzetto* (E). *Maitò* (E) is justly famous, very "in." *Bruno* (M).

LUCCA: The most luxurious food in town is served in the dining room of the *Universo* hotel. Rival for best is *Buca di Sant' Antonio.* Excellent, four miles outside town, *Villa Mansi* (E), in lovely manor. Moderate, fine, *Sergio.* In the same class is *Perduca.* A bargain is the cheaper *Garfagnana.*

PISA: The most expensive and highest rated restaurant is that of the hotel *Cavalieri,* but the *Nettuno* is another hotel which serves excellent food, and at lower prices. Near the Leaning Tower are *Nando* (M),and *Buzzino* (E), garden dining, fish specialties. *Centrale* (M), on station square, is good. *Rosticceria Fiorentina,* is outstanding for Tuscan steaks.

PISTOIA: The best place to eat here is the *Cucciolo della Montagna,* (M-E).

SIENA: The top restaurants are *Il Mangia, Tullio-Tre Cristi,* and the dining room of the hotel *Villa Scacciapensieri,* all (E). Good are *Le Campane, La Speranza,* and *Da Guido, Mugolone,* a find. All (M).

VIAREGGIO: Here we have one of the leading restaurants—that of the Hotel *Astor,* where you dine pleasantly on the terrace. *Tito del Molo,* excellent, fairly expensive, as is *Buonamigo. Belmare, Fagiano,* all good.

Umbria, the Mystic Province

Roughly half way between Florence and Rome is the mystic province of Umbria, wrapped in a strange bluish haze that gives an ethereal, painted look. Its three principal tourist centers—Assisi, Orvieto and Perugia—are all more than a thousand feet high, which helps in the hot months of July and August, though May, June and September are more comfortable months to visit here. To the three cities just mentioned, a fourth can now be added—Spoleto, where Gian-Carlo Menotti's annual Festival of Two Worlds draws cosmopolitan crowds in June-July (information from the Festival Office, Via Margutta 17, Rome).

Assisi, Orvieto and Perugia

Assisi seems to be actually redolent of the sweet personality of St. Francis, who is buried here in the huge 13th-century basilica on the Hill of Paradise. The Master of St. Francis, Cimabue, Giottino, Giotto and Pietro Cavallini are just a few of the great artists whose work glorifies this church. Take a flashlight with you to see the frescos in the dim lower level of the Basilica; two flights below is the crypt where you can see the tomb of St. Francis himself. To the left of the marvelous 14th-century Sienese altar, you will see a number of relics of the saint, including his patched gray cassock and crude sandals said to have been worn when he received the Stigmata in 1224.

Orvieto stands dramatically atop an island of volcanic rock in the middle of the Tiber Valley. Its chief attraction is the cathedral, a magnificent 13th-century church with marble sides in alternating stripes of black and white. Seen in that special net of Umbrian light, it is most impressive. Before exploring the rest of this atmospheric town, try a *fiasco* of Orvieto wine, at its best here at the source since it doesn't travel well.

Perugia's contributions to the happiness of this world include Perugina chocolates, Luisa Spagnoli's angora sweaters, and the 15th-century Umbrian master, Perugino. He and his pupil, Raphael, decorated the Stock exchange, which, with a chapel and art gallery are all included in Perugia's 13th-century Municipal Palace. If it's lunch time, you can get a good medium-priced meal in the trattoria across from the Duomo, after which we recommend a brief meander through Perugia's medieval streets, especially the Via delle Volte, a favorite photographic subject.

PRACTICAL INFORMATION FOR UMBRIA

HOTELS

ASSISI, town of St. Francis. *Subasio,* with garden restaurant, near basilica; *Umbra; Giotto;* all (2) and have rooms with bath. *S. Francesco* (2), opposite the basilica. *Roma* (3), small, nearly all rooms with bath or shower. *Fontebella* (2), recent, attractive.

GUBBIO, art center and medieval city. *Cappuccini* (1), recent, below town. Attractive, spacious rooms, tranquil atmosphere, so-so service. *San Marco* (3), simple accommodations, excellent restaurant (M). *Bosone* (2), is central, modern, well-equipped.

ORVIETO, art city. *Maitani* (1), elegant, best. *Italia* (2), most rooms with bath or shower. *Reale* (2), most rooms with bath. *Virgilio* (2) recent, is small, delightful.

PERUGIA, art city, principal town of Umbria. *Brufani Palace* (1), once elegant, but slipping. Better service at *Excelsior Lilli* (1), large, good. *La Rosetta* (2), has fine reputation, is central, comfortable, cheerful.

SPOLETO, art and festival center. *Manni* (3), comfortable. *Dei Duchi* (2), modern, all rooms with bath, view, good restaurant.
Motel AGIP (3), Via Flaminia.

RESTAURANTS

ASSISI. There are few pleasanter places to eat here than on the vine-covered terrace of the Hotel *Subasio.* Medieval atmosphere at *Taverna dell' Arco. Giardino Paradiso* pleasant. *La Stalla,* in outskirts.

ORVIETO. *Morino,* Via Garibaldi, is one of Italy's best. Tops for atmosphere is *La Badia,* in a restored medieval monastery just below the town. Grilled meats at *Cocco* (M), Via Garibaldi 6.

PERUGIA. This is the best city for gourmets in Umbria. Leaders are the dining rooms of the hotels *Brufani Palace* and *La Rosetta,* which has plesant garden terrace. *Trasimeno* and *Ricciotto* are fine. Good, less expensive are: *Altro Mondo, Pavone, Ricciotti, Taverna della Streghe, Falchetto,* and *Lanterna.*

SPOLETO. *Pentagramma* (E), chic. *Tartufo, Pennello, Del Teatro,* and downhill from center, very good *Sciattinau,* Via Martiri Resistenza 51. All (M).

MUSEUMS. Many of Umbria's museum pieces are still in its churches, but some have been removed to small, attiguous museums. At Orvieto, the *Museo dell'Opera del Duomo,* to the side of the cathedral, has a noteworthy early Renaissance collection. There's a delightful Etruscan museum opposite the cathedral, and the Etruscan necropolis just below the city is fascinating. The *Galleria Nazionale dell'Umbria* at Perugia houses many Renaissance masterpieces.

The Marches Region

The Marches constitute an unusual region for unusual travelers: those who have seen the showplaces—Rome, Tuscany, Venice—and want to get to know the unselfconscious heart of Italy. The country, bounded by the Apennines and the Adriatic, is full of isolated towns, rushing torrents, and mountains from 3,000 to 8,000 feet high.

The jewel of the Marches is Urbino, a living monument to the Renaissance. The great Ducal Palace of Frederick of Montefeltro, dominating the city from its rocky eminence, is worth a pilgrimage. Its library includes some of the finest illuminated manuscripts in existence; its art gallery, major works of Paolo Uccello, Piero della Francesca, Signorelli and Titian. The whole castle will tell you more of the bursting wealth and energy of the Italian Renaissance than any history book. Raphael's birthplace, is another attraction of an exceptionally attractive town.

Loreto and Ancona

Special trains bring sick pilgrims from all over Italy to the Holy House of Loreto, reputedly the Virgin's home at the time of the Annunciation, and transported by Angels to Loreto in the 13th century, when the Holy

Land was overrun by Mohammedans. Special pilgrimage days are March 25, August 15, September 8, December 8 and December 10. On the last date, which celebrates the miraculous transference of the Holy House, bonfires are lit all over the region.

Pesaro, one of whose sons was Rossini, is a pleasant seaside town, perfect if you want to combine swimming with art.

Ancona, also on the sea, is a wonderful place for wandering, especially in the old town between cathedral and port, where you walk on ancient stone ramps under Gothic arches. The Romanesque cathedral has a commanding position with an excellent view of the town and its colorful harbor. The marble Arch of Trajan, just 300 yards as the crow flies from the cathedral's lovely white and rose stone door, remains intact. It is just about the finest Roman arch in Italy. Don't miss the toy-like church of Santa Maria della Piazza, the lacy arches of the Loggia dei Mercanti, or the powerful *Crucifixion* by Titian in the San Domenico Church.

PRACTICAL INFORMATION FOR THE MARCHES

HOTELS

ANCONA, art town, seaside resort. *Jolly* and *Passetto* are first-class, as is the *Grand Palace,* recent, all rooms with bath, and perhaps the best.

In category (2) are the *Moderno,* most rooms with bath; and *Fortuna. Motel AGIP* (3) on Adriatic highway. At Portonovo beach, *Fortino* and *Emilia,* both (2), resort hotels with good restaurants.

FANO, beach resort. *Elisabeth* (1); *Continental* and *Lanterna Azzurra,* both (2), good. *Motel Bellanotte* (3), outside town on Via Adriatica, has private beach.

LORETO, pilgrimage center. *Marchigiano* (2), largest, best, has some rooms with baths. Garage. *Giardinetto* (2), modernized.

PESARO, art city, seaside resort. *Caravelle* (2) and *Cruiser* (2), are both bright, modern, comfortable. All rooms with bath or shower. Others in category (2) are: *Spiaggia,* on beach, all rooms with bath; *Sporting,* 50 rooms, all with shower, private beach; *Caravan,* 35 rooms; *Excelsior,* pool, near beach; *Garden. Victoria* (1), recent, comfortable.

SAN BENEDETTO & PORTO D'ASCOLI. Twin beach resorts. *Roxy* (1), is good. *Excelsior Grand,* on sea, first-class comforts, ideal for families; *Villa Sorge,* modern, as is *Arlecchino.* All (2). At Porto d'Ascoli, *Pierrot* (2).

URBINO, important Renaissance art city. *Montefeltro* (2), modest, most rooms with shower. *Italia* (3), some private baths. *Piero della Francesca* (2), 88 rooms with bath.

MUSEUMS. Ancona: *Museo Nazionale,* Via Pizzicolli, impressive collection of archaeological finds. Pesaro: *Musei Civici,* Via Toschi-Mosca 29, has one of Italy's most important collections of antique ceramics, including some from the Renaissance. Urbino: the Palazzo Ducale houses the *Galleria Nazionale's* extraordinary art works.

Scenic Campania

The Campania section of Italy stretches south from Capua and Caserta through a region of evocative names. Vesuvius, the destroyer of Pompeii and Herculaneum; the Cave of the Sibyls, near Lake Averno, one of the gates to hell; Capri, sybaritic playground of the emperors. The view of Naples from the Sorrento Peninsula is breathtaking—as, in a different way, are the hairpin bends of the Amalfi Drive.

The high season in the Campania is April, when the weather is ideal. The next best months are May, June, September and October. July and August are hot, but Capri, Ischia and the seaside resorts have their obvious consolations during these big vacation months, and they are apt to be crowded.

Naples

The greatest attraction of Naples is its extraordinary National Museum, chock full of beautiful Greek and Roman art, especially from Pompeii. Unless you can give a whole day at least to these collections, you should engage a guide to show you the highlights. There are literally *no* signs in this museum to assist visitors, and none of the exhibits are identified, a situation that has driven almost as many tourists to distraction as does the ubiquitous cameo salesman of Naples. The famed collection of Roman and Hellenic erotic art (from Pompeii and Herculaneum) is now open to the adult public.

By way of contrast, the Capodimonte Royal Palace, atop the hill of the same name, is one of the most sumptuous museums in Europe, its armor, china and picture collections arranged with great taste.

Best view of the city and its marvelous bay is from the Carthusian Monastery (Certosa di San Martino), on the slopes of the Vomero. A fine example of Neapolitan baroque architecture, it contains the National Museum of San Martino, with priceless works of art and relics from the Kingdom of Naples. Step out on the balcony for a view you'll never forget. Another great view from terrace atop Capodimonte Palace.

Attractions of the city proper include the Umberto Gallery; Via Santa Lucia, best shopping street for gifts, cameos, tortoise shell, coral and other Neapolitan specialities; the San Carlo Opera House, one of the most famous in the world; the massive Castel Nuovo, begun in 1282, with its Arch of Triumph. The Piazza del Mercato and the harbor are both worth a visit, for here you will be rubbing elbows with one of the chief attractions of this city, the gay, animated, spontaneous, effervescent, arm-waving Neapolitans, who, when they aren't hawking their dubious wares, are as charming as any casual acquaintances you could want to meet.

Excursions from Naples

On the western outskirts, near the Mergellina Station, the Tomb of Virgil begins one's explorations to the west. Solfatara, with its churning crater of boiling mud, can be visited. Don't miss the Roman amphitheater at Pozzuoli, smaller but far better preserved than the Colosseum at Rome; the ancient Temple of Serapis should be seen here, too.

Branching right from Pozzuoli along the Via Domiziana, you pass Lake Averno (Lago di Averno), an entrance to the underworld, through which Aeneas went to visit his dead father, Anchises, and less than a mile beyond is the ancient Greek colony of Cuma, where you should visit the Antro della Sibilla, celebrated grotto of the Cubaean Sibyl. Cuma overlooks the coast of Campania, so you won't be continuing west from here unless you're in an amphibious jeep. Instead, turn south to Baia, the luxury-loving Roman Baiae, whose hot springs made it the largest (and most dissolute) spa of the empire.

North of Naples (18 miles) is Caserta, whose greatest attraction is the royal palace, built in 1752 for the Bourbon kings of Naples and Sicily and intended to be more grand and beautiful than Versailles. It isn't, but then again, it isn't exactly a slum.

Herculaneum and Vesuvius

East and south of Naples the first point of interest is Herculaneum (Ercolano). If your time is short, choose this even in preference to Pompeii. Like Pompeii, Herculaneum was buried by the eruption of Vesuvius in 79 A.D., but it was destroyed by a mass of volcanic mud that sealed and preserved wood and other materials which were consumed by red hot cinders at Pompeii. Smaller than its more famous neighbor, Herculaneum was wealthier, more select, and more has been left in place. Here there is more of a sense of a living community than Pompeii can communicate. *Highly recommended.* Also recommended: the 128-page guide book, *Herculaneum,* published in English, with 81 illustrations, by the Libreria dello Stato. You can buy it on the spot.

The summit of Vesuvius can be reached by car from the Ercolane or Torre Annunziata exits of the Naples-Salerno Highway, and the view of the Bay and the Campania countryside is splendid. The crater itself may be explored only in the company of a local guide; for details inquire at EPT tourist offices at Via Partenope 10 and at central station or at Azienda Autonoma tourist office in the Royal Palace.

Pompeii

Pompeii is the most famous system of excavations anywhere, and one of the largest. Absolute minimum for a visit is two hours, and a guide is necessary if you want to avoid a lot of aimless wandering about this city that once housed 20,000 people. The best is to take a whole day, buy the excellent 182-page guide, *Pompeii,* published by the Libreria dello Stato, available at the gate, and do it on your own. This book, a map of the excavations, and a little patience will give you a real impression of how a Roman provincial city lived.

All this fascinating re-creation of the past is not without its frustrations, however. The excavation administrators have shown little imagination in either assisting tourists or guarding their treasures. Guards are importunate, doors locked (and not always to conceal over-rated pornography). Worth the exasperation, however—Pompeii under the floodlights at night.

The Amalfi Drive

One of the highlights of the entire Campania is the trip along the Amalfi Drive as it twists and turns along the contours of the beautiful southern coast of the Sorrento Peninsula. Our advice is to leave your car behind, take this trip from west to east (Positano, Amalfi, Maiori) by bus, sitting on the right-hand side, where you will have an unobstructed view of the water and the precipitous cliffs. This scenery is also superb from the steamer that runs from Naples to Amalfi and back, with stops at Sorrento and Capri. Personally, we rate Positano, Amalfi and Ravello way ahead of Sorrento, which has become very touristy in the bad sense of the word.

Capri

Capri continues to be one of the greatest playgrounds of Campania, as it was when the Emperor Tiberius reputedly diverted himself by flinging his former favorites off the cliffs. This pint-sized paradise is an island four miles long, two miles wide and in spots more than 1,900 feet high. It's as old as the Phoenicians; in fact they are supposed to have cut a rock stairway that connects Marina Grande with the upper town of Anacapri.

The town of Capri itself is afflicted with more than its quota of perpetual tourists and weird characters. But the beauties of the island more than compensate for this. See the famed Gardens of Augustus at Marina Piccola, near the best sea bathing on the island, or the Tiberius villa (on donkeyback); also the impressive medieval survivals: the 11th-century Byzantine Church of San Costanzo; the 14th-century Carthusian monastery; the ruins of the Castle of Castiglione, high up on the heights of San Michele; and the fabulous Castello di Barbarossa, 800 steps up (worth every one of them). Axel Munthe's house is a delightful spot to visit, also.

But Capri's most celebrated wonders are natural. The famed Blue Grotto is as beautiful as they say. Boats visit only in calm weather and the entrance is so small that everybody must duck his head; if there's a queue of boats, the visit is brief. Less famous, but known since the days of antiquity, are the Green Grotto, the Yellow Grotto, the Pink and White Grotto, their colors in each case resulting from the refraction of light from the walls and waters through the entrance of the grotto.

Ischia

If the long-established charms of Capri have been slightly staled by custom, those of the Island of Ischia across the Bay of Naples are still enjoying the springtime of recent discovery. More than twice the size of Capri, Ischia is reached in 40 minutes by hydrofoil from Naples. Porto d'Ischia, the point of debarkation, is the chief settlement and a spa, site of many new luxury hotels. If you want something quieter, try Casamicciola, with its delightful beaches, Lacco Ameno, and Sant' Angelo, a charming fishing town. Forio is quite unspoiled and has fine beaches. A bus makes an 18-mile circular tour of the island, but it's better to go by private car.

Paestum

One final excursion in the southerly direction from Naples is to the old Greek colony of Paestum which has some of the best-preserved Greek architectural monuments in the world, not excepting Greece itself. The Temple of Poseidon, a perfect example of Doric architecture, is one of many sights which more than warrant the 60-mile trip from Naples; see the recently excavated Greek frescoes in the museum.

Incidentally, the CIT agency offers a full round day trip from Naples to Paestum in addition to trips to Pompeii, Amalfi, Capri and other points of interest. CIAT services will take you on excursions from Naples to Pompeii, Amalfi, Positano and Sorrento.

PRACTICAL INFORMATION FOR CAMPANIA

HOTELS. The Campania region, except for Naples, Capri, the Amalfi Drive, and a few other leading tourist centers, is rather sparsely provided with good hotels. The Jolly Chain has helped to open up some of this region by putting up modern hotels at Caserta, Salerno and other places. Your best bet is to use Naples or these other places as centers for your explorations, unless you are staying at one of the beach resorts. Reserve in good time! A cluster of seaside resorts have recently developed south of Paestum near the site of ancient Velia. Best-equipped resorts are delightful Acciaroli (*La Plaja* (2); *Il Faro* (2), both on beach, recommended), bustling Agropoli (*Hotel Mare* (2), picturesque Palinuro (*Conchiglia* (2), *Saline* (2). Santa Maria di Castellabate (*Castelsandra* (1), on beach), and Sapri (*Tirreno* (3). At Marina di Camerota, *Baia delle Sirene* (2).

AMALFI, lovely old town, important seaside resort. *Cappucini-Convento,* picturesque hotel converted from old convent, whose cloisters still remain. Garage. *Santa Caterina,* lift to pool and private beach. *Excelsior,* modern, high above Amalfi on mountainside, pool, garage. *Luna,* also a remodeled convent, complete with cloisters; pool. Superior hotel. All (1). *Miramalfi* (2), outside town, private beach. *La Bussola* (2).

ANACAPRI, upper town on island of Capri *Europa Palace* and *Caesar Augustus.* Both beautifully situated but make sure of room away from nearby road. *Europa Palace* has pool, is grander. Both are (1). *San Michele* (2), villa with view. *Bellavista* (3), small; good value. (*Note:* Capri now connected by helicopter to Naples airport.)

CAPRI, fabulous island resort. *Quisisana e Grand* (L), very luxurious. *Morgano e Tiberio Palazzo, Luna,* 48 rooms with bath, excellent, *Regina Cristina,* 49 rooms, ultra modern. All (1). In category (2) are *Flora,* a villa and honeymooners' dream; *La Floridiana,* well-situated; *Semiramis,* rooms with bath or shower. *Villa Pina* (3), pleasant, stairs. *La Pergola* (2). Newcomers are *Vega* (2), and *Villa Sanfelice* (2), quiet but central.

ISCHIA, island in Bay of Naples. At Ischia: The best are are *Excelsior-Belvedere; Terme Jolly; Bristol Palace,* recent; *Aragona Palace,* attractive, beach; nice position, *Parco Aurora.* All (1). *Regina Palace* and *Ischia,* family-type, both (2).
At Punta Molino: *Moresco,* hacienda style; *Grand Hotel Punta Molino,* recent; air-conditioned, beach and pool. Both (1), quiet, chic.
At Lacco Ameno: *Regina Isabella* (L), 120 rooms with bath, beach, pool, tennis, spa; very elegant and expensive. *La Reginella* (1), also good. Tennis, pool. *San Montano* (1), recent, modern, tranquil.
At Casamicciola, *Cristallo Palace,* on hill. *Madonnina,* on beach. *Manzi,* recent. All (1).
At Sant'Angelo, *Vulcano* (1), pleasant, with pool, spa; at nearby Maronti beach, *Parco Smeraldo,* all resort amenities.

NAPLES, capital of the Campania. Many of its best hotels are closing down; check this list locally. Finest is the deluxe *Excelsior,* on the waterfront. Air-conditioned. The other deluxe hotel, the *Vesuvio,* of Italhotels group, is next door. Both are elegant, palace-type, with attentive service.
There are several first class hotels. Try *Parker's,* garage; *Royal,* largest, newest, air-conditioned, rooftop pool; *Majestic, De Londres.* Also good is the *Mediterraneo* (splendid view).

Second-class hotels include: *Britannique,* garage; *Cavour, Commodore, Santelmo, Universo, Grilli,* garage.

PAESTUM. All (2) category are *Autostello ACI,* near the ancient city ruins; *Poseidon,* private beach; *MEC* and *Calypso,* both on beach.

POMPEII, famous Roman ruins. *Bristol,* most rooms with bath. *Rosario,* comfortable. Garage. Both (2). Better to stay at Naples hotels.

POSITANO, delightful but touristy, where anything can happen and usually does. *Le Sirenuse,* probably quaintest, the modern comfort enlivened by period pieces; all rooms with bath as has *Miramare. Royal,* recent, good, boasts a pool (beach is minute). All (1). *Buca di Bacco,* with gay terrace restaurant and *Covo dei Saraceni,* newish, are (2). Recent *Palazzo Murat* (2) is villa style, in tranquil garden but near beach, shops. Recent, elegant *San Pietro* (1), has lift to beach.

RAVELLO, noted for its gardens. *Palumbo* (1), excellent, has garage; *Caruso Belvedere,* smaller, but also very good, garage; *Rufolo,* rooms with bath. All (2). *Convento* (3) has rooms with bath. *La Panoramica* (P2).

SALERNO, beach resort. *Jolly,* on waterfront, car park, is best (1), but is beginning to show its age. *Grand Hotel Diana,* which refers to itself as the *grattacielo* (skyscraper), is the largest; *Montestella.* Both (2).

SORRENTO, important beach resort. *Excelsior Grand Hôtel Vittoria,* fine hotel with excellent service, cooking, and accommodations, if old fashioned. *Europa Palace* is more modern, has same standout view and pleasant terrace to enjoy it from. *Royal,* also a good view. *Parco dei Principi,* modern, attractive; lift to private beach. *Cesare Augusto,* modern, on hillside, has pool. All (1). *Aminta* (1), stupendous location high above town; pool.

VICO EQUENSE, upcoming seaside resort. *Capo La Gala* (1), deluxe atmosphere; pool, beach. *Le Axidie* (1), delightful, attractively furnished, terraces, pool.

VIETRI. Spectacularly situated, *Lloyd's Baia* (1) has lift to take you to its private beach.

RESTAURANTS

AMALFI. Best is *Caravella* (M), fish specialties, and dining rooms of hotels *Luna* and *Santa Caterina.* Somewhat cheaper are the restaurants, the *Sirena,* a very fine little place, and *La Marinella,* on the waterfront.

Along the Amalfi coast road, at Praiano, is *Luca's* and a very special nightclub in a cave, the *Africana:* truly marine, reached by a gangway from the sea, waves lap under the dance floor; also reached by boat from Capri.

CAPRI. Top-price deluxe are *Pigna,* Via Roma, and *Canzone del Mare,* run by the famous Gracie Fields. Expensive. A considerable cut below this in price are the dining rooms of three of Capri's luxurious hotels, the *Quisisana,* the *Morgano e Tiberio Palazzo* and the *Europa Palace,* the last at Anacapri.

Good and moderately priced places, the *Grottino, Da Pietro* at Marina Piccola, and *Michele. Faraglioni, Casina della Rose* (E). Special mention goes to the *Pizza Maria* for its Caprese version of this famous Bay of Naples dish. Expensive.

For lunch with a view, go by ski-lift to Monte Solaro and enjoy eating at the *Canzone del Cielo;* dancing nightly during summer.

ISCHIA. At the port, *Nannina* and *Di Massa* are good, as is *San Montano,* on the beach at Lacco Ameno, but last is very expensive.

NAPLES. Aside from the leading hotel dining rooms—the *Excelsior,* or equally expensive *Vesuvio* (which contains a good nightclub, the *Vesuvietta*),—most visitors will be attracted towards the Santa Lucia waterfront and its pleasant establishments. Best of these is *Transatlantico* (E), gourmet-class dishes, mostly seafood. At the *Bersagliera* (E), tables spill out along a wharf lined with luxury sailboats. Next door is *Da Ciro.*

For food with a view, you have to travel farther. On the *Posillipo* hill to the west is the elegant *Galeone* (E).

At Marechiaro, *Fenestrella* and *Da Mimi* are fine for seafood, with a spectacular view of the bay.

In a slightly different part of town, halfway up the Vomero hill, are *Le Arcate* and *D'Angelo,* both on Via Aniello Falcone and both with a view, as also *Sbrescia* (M), off Via Orazio.

Centrally located, reasonably priced are *Giacomino,* Via San Carlo; *Ciro,* Via Santa Brigida 71; *Al Pappagallo,* Via Carlo de Cesare 14; *Rugantino,* Via Diaz.

Dante e Beatrice (M), Piazza Dante, modest ambiance, exceptional cooking (*pasta e fagioli,* roast kid).

RAVELLO. Best here, dining room of *Caruso Belvedere.*

SORRENTO. The plushest place in town (and most expensive) is the *Parco dei Principi* dining room. *Bottaro,* Via Correale, is gayer, *Minervetta,* Via del Capo, better known. *Tonnarella* (M), a gem.

The Deep South

Off the beaten tourist track—but not for long—are the three southern provinces of the Italian boot—Apulia, the heel; Lucania, the instep; Calabria, the toe. Good new roads and the beginnings of a new modern, well-equipped resorts are attracting tourists to the region's extraordinarily beautiful shores and mountain valleys. Apulia (except for the Gargano) and Lucania have extremes of summer and winter climate that make it advisable to visit them between seasons. Calabria has more welcoming weather. You'll find majestic forests and splendid mountain scenery at Gambarie d'Aspromonte or San Giovanni in Fiore, two places you never heard of before. The ski runs on Mount Aspromonte can be reached easily from Reggio Calabria.

This is an old land, with literary and historical associations going back as far as Homer. Scilla in Calabria, for instance, is the famous Scylla facing the whirlpool of Charybdis, which menaced the ship of Ulysses. Lecce, one of the most strikingly beautiful cities of Italy, has recently been "discovered", with its charming baroque palaces and churches, and this fact suggests one of the appeals of the south—these regions offer a fascinating experience to the traveler who enjoys visiting places seldom seen by the average tourist.

The beaches along this coast are among the most beautiful in Italy. Names to remember among the newly popular resorts—off the beaten track, but with all the amenities of better-known, higher-priced places—are, in Basilicata-Lucania—Maratea; in Calabria—Praia, Tropea, Squillace, Stalleti, Copanello; in Apulia—Molfetta, Polignano, Castrignano, Vieste on the Gargano Peninsula, and San Domino in the Tremiti Islands.

PRACTICAL INFORMATION FOR THE DEEP SOUTH

 HOTELS. Accommodations in the south were not too good until the Jolly hotel chain got to work; it has done wonders in opening up a region hitherto poorly prepared to receive visitors. Many of the smaller places named below could hardly have expected tourists to remain overnight before the Jolly hotels in them were built. Now you can look forward to clean, comfortable, and modern lodgings. Reserve in advance for Bari in September, month of the Levant Fair. March, April, October are good months here.

APULIA

ALBEROBELLO. Two scores of cottages in the ancient local style form the *Trulli* (1), all rooms with bath; pool. *Astoria* (2).

BARI, capital, important seaport. *Jolly,* opened 1974, attractive comfortable; *Palace,* all rooms with bath or shower, air-conditioned; *Delle Nazioni,* on seafront. All (1). *Moderno, Boston, Motel Agip* at Torre a Mare, all (2).

BRINDISI, port. *Jolly* (1), best. *Mediterraneo* (2), modern, functional. *Barsotti* (2), budget value.

FOGGIA, regional capital. *Palace Hotel Sarti* (1), best. *Cicolella* (2), largest. Air-conditioned rooms, all with shower. *President* (2), modern, on airport road.

GALLIPOLI, pretty seaside town. Two big beach resort hotels, *Costa Brada,* (1), best, on sandy beach; and recent *Le Sirenuse* (2), all doubles with balcony, view of sandy beach, sea; large pool; tennis.

GARGANO, beautiful peninsula. *Del Faro* (2), all rooms with bath, pool, beach, good resort hotel. At Vieste, *Pizzomunno,* pool; *Gargano,* both (2), beach across road. *Gattarella* (2), resort village. At Mattinata, *Baia delle Zagare* (2), on beautiful inlet; cottage-style, lift to beach. At Peschici, *Gusmay* (1), modern; long walk to private beach.

LECCE, noted for baroque architecture. *President* (1), recent, modern and efficient. *Astor* (1), air-conditioned, comfortable rooms. *Delle Palme* (2), good.
At nearby Castrignano, *L'Approdo* (1), all rooms with bath or shower; beach. *Terminal* (2), 22 rooms with bath; beach, tennis.

TARANTO, naval base. *Jolly,* best, pool. *Delfino,* good; pool, beach. Both (1). *Bologna, Plaza* both (2).
At Lido Azzurro, *Tritone* (2), tennis, pool, beach.

LUCANIA

MARATEA. Splendidly situated beach hotel: *Santavenere* (L), quiet location, all resort facilities, including lift to beach. Also peaceful, *Villa Cheta, Villa del Mare,* both (2), nicely furnished, share lift to pebbly beach on pretty cove.

POTENZA, regional capital. *Grand* (1), *Turistico* (2), *Park* (2), outside town, is modern.

CALABRIA

CATANZARO, provincial capital. *President Joli* (1), comfortable, air-conditioned. *Motel Agip* (2), modern. Few miles away at beach, *Palace* (2).

CETRARO, on sea. *San Michele* (1), recent; all rooms with bath; tennis, pool, lift to private pebbly beach. Palatial, isolated.

COPANELLO, new resort. *Villaggio Guglielmo, Club Vitale,* are big tourist villages on beach.

COSENZA, provincial capital. Category (1): *Jolly,* best, has garage, *Imperial,* largest, also garage. *Mondial* is (2).

GAMBARIE D'ASPROMONTE, summer and winter sports resort. *Gambarie* (2). Garage.

PRAIA A MARE, seaside resort. *Jolly* (1), best. *Astor* (2), on beach. At Fiuzzi, *I Normanni* (2), 9 rooms with bath; beach.

REGGIO CALABRIA, largest city and capital. *Excelsior* (1), best, most rooms with bath or shower, beach. *Miramare* (2), largest. Garage. *Lido* (2). 40 rooms, 30 baths. *Continental* (2), modern, all rooms with shower. At Villa San Giovanni, *Piccolo* (1), at station. At Cannitello, *Castello* (2), converted castle hotel; pool, beach, nightclub.

TROPEA, picturesque resort. On outskirts, *Rocca Nettuno* (2), handsome holiday complex; balconied rooms, all amenities. In town, *Vigilio* (2). On sandy beach below town, *Pineta* (2), modest. Nearby, at Parghelia, two large vacation villages: *Baia Parahelios* and *Sabbie Bianche,* both (2).

RESTAURANTS. Among the restaurants worth mentioning, at Crotone, on the Ionian Sea, *Girrarosto* for *quadaro* (fish soup); near Reggio Calabria, at Gallico Marina, *Fata Morgana* for stuffed mussels, and at Scilla, *Matteo* for swordfish steaks and *tonno alla marinara.* At Maratea, *Settebello,* mussels and shrimp specialties. In Potenza, *Taverna Oraziana* offers *capretto alla paesana* (kid) and the classic *strascinati* pasta. In Taranto, *Al Gambero,* for magnificent *calamari* and spaghetti. In Bari, *Pignata* (E). At Alberobello, *Cucina dei Trulli* (M).

Sicily, Southernmost Island

Sicily, tinged with the color and subtlety of the East, is quite unlike Italy. It is itself a unique land in which it is possible to ski on a snowy slope, stroll among palms and orange groves, and swim in the sea in sight of flowering almond trees—*all in the same day.* Spring is the best time to come, when the countryside is at its best, but Taormina is popular year round; its mild winters are renowned. Summers are hot, and the *scirocco,* that hot wind from Africa, can make things pretty miserable and listless for periods of three days and more.

If you have the time, we recommend CIAT's two excellent five-day circuits of the island, the Golden Ribbon and the Sunshine Ribbon. Here are the high points of tourist interest as we see them, however: Palermo, an unforgettable city with its almost Oriental languour and its monuments of all the civilizations that have enriched it; Monreale, with its cathedral's perfectly preserved mosaics, 6,000 dazzling square yards of them; Selinunte, with its colossal Temple of Apollo and other reminders of the glory that was Greece; Agrigento, at once a modern city and the site of some of the most stupendous Greek ruins in existence (many of them better preserved than the ones in Greece); Syracuse, with its fine Greek theater; Catania, handsome city, built on lava, and center of excursions to the craters of 10,000-foot-high Mt. Etna; Cefalù, whose 12th-century Norman cathedral has mosaics that almost approach those of Monreale; and finally, Taormina, "so beautiful that it is unreal". Here the water is as clear as crystal at the lovely beaches below the town, and the town itself seems suspended in the air between the cobalt sea and snowy Etna.

You will enjoy walking down the Corso, the main street of Taormina, and shopping for Taormina embroidery and lace. But here's a practical hint—the best place for it is at the School of the Franciscans on Via Pirandello. By all means go to the Greek Theater, if not for one of the splendid performances of Greek plays by the Italian Institute for Classical Drama, at least for the view, which will remain with you always, a memory of the beauty of Sicily which is perhaps best epitomized by "the Circe-like enchantment of this magic town". But if you can, turn inland to Enna, Ragusa or Caltagirone for a clearer view of genuine Sicilian life and landscape.

PRACTICAL INFORMATION FOR SICILY

HOTELS. There are two hotel chains in Sicily which deserve special attention. The Società Grandi Alberghi Siciliani is a group of top-notch hotels in Sicily only. The Jolly hotels, which have done so much to open up under-exploited areas throughout Italy to tourists, have also provided a number of fine modern establishments in this area. In addition, well-equipped tourist villages are springing up in some of the island's best beach locations.

AEOLIAN ISLANDS. Some of Europe's best deep-sea and underwater fishing. Hotel situation is improving with *Carasco, Rocce Azzurre,* both (2), on Lipari; *Arcipelago, Garden, Sables Noirs,* all (2), on Vulcano. Simpler accommodations on Stromboli, Panarea, and Santa Maria Salina.

AGRIGENTO, famous for its temples. *Villa Athena* (1), best for beautiful location at temples and for handsome ambiance. In town, *Jolly* (1). Near temples, *Jolly dei Templi* (1), and *Akrabelle* (2), both air-conditioned, modern, pool.

CALTANISSETTA, provincial capital, with Greek and Roman remains. *Concordia Villa Mazzoni, Diprima,* both (2).

CATANIA, beautiful city. *Grand Hotel Excelsior* (1), newest, air-conditioned, all rooms with shower or bath. Garage. *Jolly* (1). In category (2) are: *Bristol, Costa,* on main shopping street. *Motel Agip,* (3), on Highway SS. 11, at Ognina.

CEFALU, delightful old town. Sandy beaches. *Baia del Capitano, Kalura, Calette* are all (2), comfortable beach hotels. At Santa Lucia, *Sabbie d'Oro* (2) is big tourist village with pool, beach.

EGADI ISLANDS, off southwest shore. At present one major hotel, *Approdo di Ulisse* (2), on Calagrand beach. More tourist development on the way. Good fishing.

ENNA, town with Greek and Roman remains. *Belvedere, Grande Sicilia,* on noisy central square; 60 rooms with bath. At lovely Pergusa lake, six miles away, recent *La Giara,* swimming pool. All (2).

GELA, archaeological center. *Motel Agip,* all rooms with shower. *Autostello ACI.* Both (2), adequate overnight halts in this grim town.

MESSINA, important city, provincial capital. In category (1) are: *Jolly,* best. Air-conditioned, pool, garage. *Riviera Grand,* 140 rooms with bath; beach.

Belvedere and *Venezia,* both (2). At Lido Mortelle, *Lido* (1), modern beach hotel, pool.

PALERMO, capital and most interesting city of Sicily. *Villa Igiea* (L), member of Grandi Alberghi Siciliani. Luxurious and picturesque. Tennis court, pool. *Mondello Palace* (L), member of Italhotels. Located at beach outside Palermo, as is *La Torre* (2), with pool. *Jolly* (1), central, an old favorite, recently modernized; pool.

Pleasant second-class hotels, many rooms with private bath: *Mediterraneo, Centrale, Sole. Motel AGIP* (2), Via della Regione, almost all rooms with bath.

PIAZZA ARMERINA, interesting archaeological center. *Jolly* (1), has good restaurant.

SYRACUSE (Siracusa), important city with famous Greek Theater. Best in town is *Jolly* (1). Recent *Park; Bellavista; Panorama,* in archaeological zone, are all pleasant (2), with gardens. *Motel AGIP* (2), modern, reliable.

TAORMINA, important tourist city. *San Domenico* (L). Dominican monastery, complete with Renaissance cloister, now converted into a modern hotel; aloof staff.

In category (1) are: excellent *Timeo,* near Greek Theater, quiet, handsome; *Excelsior,* attractive, traditional; *Jolly Diodoro,* villa-type, with pool; *Bristol Park,* well-furnished, with pool. All these dominate bay, have most rooms with balconies, view; all have bus service to beach facilities in summer. *Velo d'Oro,* in heart of town; garish but comfortable.

Sirius (2), attractive villa-type, terraces. Same price category are excellent *Villa Fiorita, Villa Paradiso, Villa Riis, San Pancrazio,* all (P1), pleasant, well-furnished.

At Mazzaro, the beach resort of Taormina: *Sea Palace* (L), attractive; pool, beach. *Atlantis Bay,* attractive; pool, swimming in pretty cove. *Villa St. Andrea,* tasteful traditional furnishings, friendly atmosphere; garden terraces directly on beach. Both (1). *Lido Mediteranée,* modern beach hotel; *Stockholm,* on good, sandy beach. Both (2).

At Naxos, *Holiday Inn,* big modern complex. Quieter, more elegant *Arathena Rocks* (2), *Assinos* (2), recent, pool, beach.

TRAPANI, provincial capital, fishing town, *Nuovo Russo* (2).

At Erice, picturesque town high above Trapani: *Jolly* (1), modern; *Pineta* (2), cottages in pine grove. On the beach below Erice, *Nuovo Tirreno* (2), modern.

RESTAURANTS

CATANIA. *Giardini, Lido dei Ciclopi,* at Acitrezza, and *Costa Azzurra* (E) at Ognina are tops. *Finocchiaro, Gennarino.*

MESSINA. *Borgia* is good. *Lisi* and *Da Pippo* (M).

PALERMO. *Charleston* (E), chic and tops. *Pappagallo* (M), *Giannettino* (I). Reader recommended: *Ristorante 59, Catena d'Oro* (M), down street from Mediterraneo hotel. *Ficodindia* (M), colorful, local specialties. *Olimpia, Conca d'Oro, Castelnuovo* (all M), fine.

TAORMINA. *Pescatore,* overlooking sea, is best. *Ciclope* and *Myosotis.* At the beach, *Delfino* and *Mazzarò.* Back in town, *Naumachie* (M).

MUSEUMS, Palermo's *Museo Archeologico,* on Piazza Olivella, is Sicily's most important and contains one of Italy's richest collections of ancient sculpture. The *Museo Nazionale* in Messina offers a variety of styles and periods, notably some Renaissance masterpieces. Agrigento's *Museo Archeologico,* Piazza Municipio 361, contains pieces found in its famous Greek temples. The *Museo Archeologico* in Syracuse, on Piazza del Duomo, rivals Palermo's in importance, contains prehistoric, Greek, and Roman remains.

COACH TOUR. A one-week tour of the island operates out of Palermo at least three times weekly. "Sicilrama" offers a good insight to Sicily, plus time off for swimming at various beaches.

Sardinia—Fascinating Island

Sardinia, the largest island in the Mediterranean after Sicily, is still a land of short, dark, goodlooking people, dwarf donkeys, colorful folk costumes and festivals, and unspoiled natural and human charm. However, the island's sleepy air is being stirred by investors (the Aga Khan among them), who are developing parts of its coast as lush rivieras and building new hotels in the towns.

You can reach Sardinia by air or sea. The best way to see Sardinia is by car, since bus and train service is unsatisfactory for touring. You can take your car to Sardinia without worry, since recent development has improved the road system considerably.

Take a look at changing Sardinia—small fishing villages and inland towns where the women wear black and cover their faces with shawls at the approach of a stranger; the terribly expensive, terribly chic resorts where yachts and the nude look are "in". And between the two extremes, such bustling cities as Cagliari and Sassari. Cagliari has a good museum of antiquities, Sassari an excellent museum of regional art. Ghilarza has some fine medieval buildings. Bosa is photogenic, with its narrow streets untouched since the 12th century. A fascinating town is Castel Sardo, perched on a cliff which drops to the sea; its streets are steep narrow staircases. Best bets for seeing local costumes are Quartu St. Elena, Dorgali, and Marmoiada. The curious prehistoric monuments called *nuraghi* are unique; best are at Barumini and St. Antine.

The spectacular scenery of the Costa Smeralda near Olbia, Porto Conte and the Costa Argentiera near Alghero, and the Capo Carbonara coast near Cagliari are not to be missed, if you're a folklore enthusiast or someone who is looking for distinctive atmosphere off the beaten track.

PRACTICAL INFORMATION FOR SARDINIA

HOW TO GET THERE. You can reach it by air or sea. There are daily flights to Cagliari, Olbia and Alghero from Rome, Milan and Genoa. There's also a daily boat service from Civitavecchia to Cagliari and Olbia, a bi-weekly service from Naples and a weekly one from Palermo; and a daily Genoa-Porto Torres service. Canguro Rosso ferries operate three times weekly between Genoa and Cagliari and twice weekly between Genoa and Olbia. Another ferry links Santa Teresa di Gallura with Bonifacio in Corsica. Advance round-trip booking is essential.

HOTELS. Many resort hotels are open only from April/May through September/October. Reservations are a must.

ALGHERO, port and health resort. *Calabona,* (2), and *Villa Las Tronas* (1). Both have most rooms with bath, rocky beaches. *Coral,* 46 rooms with shower and balcony. *Catalunya,* modern, central, own bus to beach. Both (2). *Majorca* (3), attractive.

At nearby Porto Conte: *El Faro,* natural pool. *Capo Caccia,* pool and beach. Both (2). At Fertilia, *Dei Pini* (2), on sandy beach.

CAGLIARI, capital and largest city. *Jolly* (1), air-conditioned. Swimming pool. *Mediterraneo* (2), and *Motel AGIP* (3), both comfortable, good values. At Calamosca, *Capo Sant' Elia* (2) has beach.

At Santa Margherita di Pula, upcoming resort, *Is Morus* (1), quiet, pool and beach. *Forte Village, Abamara* and *Flamingo,* all (2), on beach.

COSTA SMERALDA, splendidly planned and equipped resort area, expensive. At Arzachena, *Cala di Volpe* (L), proprietor, the Aga Khan. In form, a picturesque village; in taste, princely. Pool, motor boats, beaches. *Pitrizza* (L), club atmosphere; suites in villas on flowered terraces; *Romazzino* (L), 100 large, well-appointed rooms with bath and seafront balcony; private beach. *Cervo* (1), 62 rooms with bath in custom-built village of Porto Cervo; private beach is livelier, jazzier. *Liscia di Vacca* and *Luci de la Montagna,* both (2).

All, except the Cervo, are seasonal hotels with rather spotty service. First three are officially category (1) but strictly deluxe prices.

LA MADDALENA. Picturesque island off the north coast. At Porto Massimo, *Cala Lunga* (1), modern resort complex.

NUORO, regional capital. *Jolly* (1); *Motel AGIP* (2). High above town on Mount Ortobene, *ESIT* (2), large rooms in fine hotel with view of sea and plains.

OLBIA, port. *Jolly* (1), *Caprile* (2) on sea at Lido del Sole. On the gulf of Marinella: the recent *Abi d'Oru* (1), air-conditioned suites; tennis, golf, water skiing.

At smart resort of Porto Rotondo, *San Marco* (2) is pleasant, *Sporting* (1), elegantly "in," expensive. At Baia Sardinia, excellent sandy beaches. *Bisaccia, Club, Cormorano,* all good (2). At San Teodoro, 15 miles south, big *San Teodoro* (2) bungalow resort.

ORISTANO, historic town. *I.S.A.* (2), air-conditioned. At Torre Grande, *Del Sole* (2), 54 rooms with shower; pool. At Arborea *Ala Birdi* (2), pine-shaded cottages on beach.

SANTA TERESA GALLURA, tiny port at the northernmost tip of island. *Moresco* (1) and *Gallo di Gallura* (2), in both, all rooms with bath or shower; five minute walk to rock bathing. *La Conchiglia* (2), on beach. *Capo Testa* (2), recent; pool, beach. *Shardana* (2), recent; bungalows overlooking sandy beach; pool, dancing. At Costa Paradiso, *Rosi Marini* (2), modern resort complex.

At nearby Palau, *Excelsior Vanna* (2), beach and pool. *La Roccia* (2), *Porto Pollo* (3), both on beach.

SASSARI, provincial capital, second largest city. *Jolly Grazia Deledda* (1), 140 rooms with bath; pool. *Jolly* (2). *Motel AGIP* (2).

At Platamonta Lido, *Pineta Beach* (2), all rooms with bath or shower; pool, beach. *Del Golfo* (2), same resort-village type.

At Stintino, *Grand Hotel Rocca Ruja* (2), beach, pool, tennis.

SINISCOLA, *La Caletta* (2), all rooms with bath or shower and balcony. Terrace restaurant, beach.

VILLASIMIUS, 40 miles east of Cagliari by good road. *Grand Hotel Capo Boi* (1), magnificent beach, pool, air-conditioned. Good value. *Timi-Ama* (2), 64 apartment-type rooms with bath; beach.

RESTAURANTS. In Sardinia, you eat at the hotels, which have more or less a monopoly on feeding tourists. But if you want to branch out, here are a few alternatives: in Alghero: *Lepanto, Las Tronas, Corsaro, Pesce d'Oro.* At Arzachena: *Papagallo.* At Cagliari: *Il Corsaro* (M-E). At Golfo Aranci: *L'Asino que ride.* At Palau: *Franco.* At Sassari: *Da Michi.* At Nuoro, *Trattoria Sacchi.* At Porto Cervo: *La Tartaruga, Pizzeria,* both (M-E).

LIECHTENSTEIN

On the eastern side of the Rhine, between Lake Constance and the Swiss canton of the Grisons, is the pocket-sized Principality of Liechtenstein. Last remnant of the Holy Roman Empire, it is a prosperous, independent, hereditary monarchy of 62 square miles and about 24,000 loyal subjects. The current ruler is His Highness Franz Joseph II, Maria Alois Alfred Karl Johann Heinrich Michael Georg Ignatius Benediktus Gerhardus Majella, Prince von und zu Liechtenstein and Duke of Troppau and Jaegerndorf. The heir apparent is Prince Johann Adam Pius. His mother is Princess Gina, and Liechtensteiners fondly remember her during the war-time gas rationing, careening down from the castle on a bicycle to do her shopping. The whole family is charming, good-looking and unpretentious.

Liechtenstein, which is united with Switzerland in a customs union and represented by Switzerland abroad, got its start as an independent nation when a wealthy Austrian prince, Johann Adam von Liechtenstein, bought up two bankrupt counts in the Rhine Valley, united their lands, and in 1719 obtained an imperial deed, creating the Principality of Liechtenstein.

Like most Alpine resorts, Liechtenstein has two main seasons, from June to September, and (for skiing) from December to March. In early May the country is especially attractive, for then the orchards of the Rhine Valley are in blossom. Art connoisseurs will find a side trip to Liechtenstein rewarding at any time of the year. On exhibition every day in the Prince's Gallery above the National Tourist Office in the mini-capital of Vaduz are works selected from the Prince's famous private art collection—at present, priceless paintings by Flemish and Dutch masters and a fabulous Rubens grouping. On the floor below (the entrance price covers both) is the Liechtenstein National Gallery which stages important loan exhibitions—at present, Italian 14th-16th century art. There's an interesting Historical Museum, and philatelists shouldn't miss the Stamp Museum.

PRACTICAL INFORMATION FOR LIECHTENSTEIN

CAPITAL. Vaduz, reached by Postal bus from Buchs (SG) or Sargans (Switzerland) or Feldkirch (Austria) railroad stations.

LANGUAGE. Mostly German.

CLIMATE. Bracing; similar to Switzerland.

CUSTOMS. There are no formalities for entering Liechtenstein from Switzerland; all travel documents valid for Switzerland are also valid here. If you come from Austria, frontier formalities are the same as if you were entering Switzerland. Swiss customs officials and border police do the checking.

MONEY. Swiss currency regulations and rates of exchange apply, the Swiss franc being Liechtenstein's legal tender (see *Switzerland* chapter).

WHAT WILL IT COST. Liechtenstein prices (including postage) are roughly on a par with Switzerland. In Vaduz, hotel prices are about those of a Swiss budget resort. Full pension (bed, private bath or shower, all meals, tips and taxes) will cost about 42 to 115 francs a day depending on the room and class of establishment. But in mountain villages hotel prices are appreciably less (except during the winter sports high season), sometimes almost touching rock bottom.

 HOTELS. In the past, with a few notable exceptions the best hotels (although none were deluxe) have been in or near Vaduz. But new ones are now springing up along the Rhine valley and in the mountains. A Liechtenstein specialty is its mountain inns, all at least 4,000 feet up but easily accessible by car. Ideal for those seeking quiet—and clean air. Some of these inns have recently been enlarged and modernized.

BALZERS. Best are *Post* (17 beds; all rooms with bath) and *Römerhof* (32 beds); both economy.

SCHAAN. *Sylva* (24 beds), all rooms with bath and *Schaanerhof* (43 beds), indoor pool, are top medium grade.

VADUZ. Outstanding at first class rates is enlarged *Sonnenhof* (55 beds), near Vaduz castle. Lavish, tasteful decor; indoor pool, sauna; fine gardens. Also first class *Schlössle* (50 beds), sauna; and *Real* (16 beds). Medium grade: *Landhaus Vaduzerhof* (44 beds), indoor pool, sauna, breakfast only. *Hotel Vaduzerhof, Engel, Adler* and *Lowen* are economy.

RESTAURANTS. The cuisine is Swiss with Austrian overtones. Except in hotels there are few restaurants. Best food is at the *Real,* but the *Engel* is good, and the *Adler* noted for game. For a nice, reasonably priced meal the *Linde's* the spot. The *Torkel* restaurant, owned by the Prince and surrounded by his vineyards barely 5 minutes walk from Vaduz center, is a good place to sample Vaduzer, the potent local red wine. A good lunch or dinner ranges from about 8 francs in an unsophisticated spot to around 35 in the best.

ENTERTAINMENT. There are movie houses at Vaduz, Schaan, Bendern and Balzers. There is dancing at the *Vaduzerhof* and *Engel* hotels in Vaduz, and at the *Post* at Schaan, the *Motel Waldeck,* and Malbun's *Gorfion, Galina* and *Turna,* among other places.

SPORTS. Several hotels have *indoor swimming pools,* these being mentioned above. But the Rhine is for first class swimmers only, and hardy ones at that; the water's mighty cold. Although relatively unknown, Malbun is ideal for *winter sports* with a near certainty of good snow. An excellent network of reasonably priced chairlifts and ski lifts, rarely congested except at high season weekends, serves a wide variety of slopes. The beginners' slopes are unusually good. There are *ski schools,* and guides are available for longer excursions.

USEFUL ADDRESS. National Tourist Office, Engländerbau, Vaduz.

Sightseeing in Liechtenstein

This begins in Vaduz, the attractive, 4,500-citizen capital to which low taxes lure the fortunate few who are not confined to a certain spot by their jobs. The little town is dominated by Vaduz castle, a princely looking edifice if ever there was one. Normally, the interior is out of bounds for tourists, but although you can't enter the castle, go see it. Originally built in the 13th century, it was frequently rebuilt over the years until the complete 20th-century overhaul which gave it its present form. Vaduz has another outstanding medieval building, the Rotes Haus, once a fortress for the bailiffs of a Swiss Benedictine monastery. If you're feeling energetic, a 40-minute climb northeast of Vaduz will take you to the romantic ruins of the Wildschloss.

From Vaduz, we strongly recommend a tour along the twisty, climbing road past Vaduz castle and a succession of splendid views of the Rhine Valley, to the little town of Triesenberg. About a mile beyond the town, a turn-off on the left leads to the mountain hotels of Masescha and Gaflei. The latter, at 4,920 feet, is the starting point for the Furstensteig, a path along the high ridge dividing the Rhine and Samina valleys. It does not involve any dangerous climbing. Masescha, Gaflei, nearby Silum and Triesenberg, are unpretentious, do-it-yourself skiing centers in winter and lovely spots for walking in summer.

But our road continues upwards and then plunges into a tunnel to emerge near the hamlet of Steg (4,200 ft.) in a high Alpine valley; wild, impressive and with rushing mountain streams. In summer, Steg is an excellent starting point for a wide choice of not over-strenuous mountain hikes, such as that up the Samina valley to the Bettlerjoch pass (6,400 ft.). When the snow arrives in winter the hamlet becomes a simple, no-frills skiing center.

If you now take the excellent new road which continues beyond Steg you will find that, after a couple of miles, it ends abruptly at Malbun

(5,200 ft.), a small higgledy-piggledy village nestling on the floor of a huge mountain bowl. Malbun is gaining in popularity on the international ski scene for its varied facilities. It is particularly good for beginners. There's regular bus service between Vaduz and Malbun but, if possible, go by car. The return journey will take well under two hours including brief viewing stops en route, but leave more time if you can.

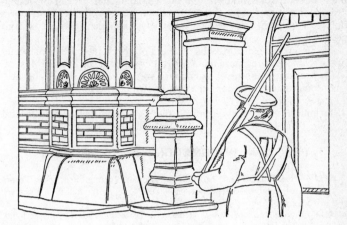

LUXEMBOURG

While the old idea of Luxembourg as a toyland monarchy still lives on, this little grand duchy is now a major center for tourism from North America, thanks to Icelandic Airlines, whose cheaper fares from North America make this the starting point for many young people and other budget-minded visitors to Europe.

Squeezed in between Belgium, Germany and France, the Grand Duchy of Luxembourg is a thriving, Rhode-Island sized land whose 360,000 contented inhabitants offer the traveler one of the tourist bargains of Europe. Prices are 10 to 15% lower than in neighboring Belgium, whose currency is valid in Luxembourg. Typical of the country's tourist amenities are 50% weekend reductions on the National Railways. There are loads of villages with simple clean hotels and excellent country restaurants. If trout fishing is your idea of paradise, you need go no farther than this little duchy, where the trout outnumber the people. This is a country of parades and processions, good cheer, and a hearty capacity for beer and Moselle wine.

Food and Drink

Luxembourg cooking combines German heartiness with Franco-Belgian finesse. Smoked pork and broad beans or sauerkraut *(carré de porc fumé)* is of Teutonic origin, but *cochon de lait en gelée* (jellied suckling pig) is a more authentic local dish. The preparation of trout, pike and crayfish is excellent. You can get the famous smoked Ardennes ham *(jambon d'Ardennes)* all year round.

Pastry and cakes are excellent. Ask for *tarte aux quetsches.* Outstanding desserts are prepared with the aid of local liqueurs: the better restaurants will make to order the delicious *omelette soufflée au kirsch;* or a dollop of quetsch, mirabelle or kirsch may be added to babas or fruit cups.

Luxembourg's white Moselle wine is a dry hock resembling the wines of the Rhine perhaps more than the fruitier wines of the French Moselle.

Brewing beer, another Luxembourg specialty, is an old established, traditional industry. Among the best known brands are *Funck, Mousel, Clausen, Diekirch* and *B B B Bofferding.*

To round out a satisfying meal, there's nothing better than a local liqueur. When at Beaufort, try the blackcurrant wine *(cassis).*

PRACTICAL INFORMATION FOR LUXEMBOURG

WHAT WILL IT COST. As Luxembourg is small, it can limit rising costs more easily than its neighbors, and will probably keep to its prediction of an 8 percent rise in the cost-of-living during 1979.

Hotel costs range from *Deluxe* at between 850-1,750 francs, single; through *First class,* 700-1000 francs in Luxembourg, 500-600 francs in budget towns; to *Third class,* 400-600 francs for Luxembourg, 300-400 in budget towns. *Pensions,* with single room and meals for at least three days, work out at 500-550 francs in Luxembourg and about 50 francs less in smaller places.

Restaurant prices begin at 200 francs for a moderately priced meal in a small town, up to 750 for a super one in the capital.

Local cigarettes cost 28 francs, imported ones 36 francs; a bottle of wine 150 francs; a woman's shampoo and set 250 francs; a man's haircut 125 francs—or 200 francs if it is razor styled; a cinema seat 75 francs and one for the opera 275 francs.

Ask the *Office National de Tourisme* for their mini-vacation and weekend brochure, "Pouponné au Grand-Duché," which offers package bargains.

CAPITAL. Luxembourg City.

LANGUAGE. Letzeburgesch, but don't let that stop you. French and German are spoken throughout the Grand Duchy, and English is spoken and understood in the tourist centers.

CLIMATE. Moderate.

Average maximum daily temperatures in Fahrenheit and centigrade:

Luxem-bourg	Jan.	Feb.	Mar.	Apr.	May	June	July	Aug.	Sept.	Oct.	Nov.	Dec.
F°	37	39	50	57	64	70	73	72	66	55	45	39
C°	3	4	10	14	18	21	23	22	19	13	7	4

SEASONS. Easter to mid-September, and summer is best. But there are many off-season attractions and price reductions.

SPECIAL EVENTS. Early May: great pilgrimage procession to Our Lady of Luxembourg; Whit-Tuesday, the famous dancing procession of Echternach, the Springprozession in honor of St. Willibrord. July, open-air theater and music festival at Wiltz; third weekend in September, Wine Festival and Folklore Parade at Grevenmacher. Many wine festivals and tasting days along the Moselle from May on.

CLOSING TIMES. Shops are open from 8:00 A.M. to noon; 14:00 to 18:00 hours, except Mondays, when they open at 14:00 hours. Banks, 8:00 to 12:00, 13:00 to 17:00 Monday to Friday. On holidays both are closed.

 MONEY. Monetary unit is the franc, divided into 100 centimes. Belgian money is legal tender in Luxembourg, but Luxembourg francs can be used only within the confines of the Grand Duchy. Therefore, change all remaining Luxembourg banknotes before leaving. At presstime there were about 31 Luxembourg or Belgian francs to the U.S. dollar, 58 to the pound sterling. Check the bank or exchange office announcement boards upon arrival.

TIPPING. Service and taxes are included in the bill, but for especially good service you might give an extra 5 percent. Taxi drivers expect a tip, whether they merit it or not.

HOW TO REACH LUXEMBOURG. *By air:* From New York and Chicago by *Loftleidir Icelandic Airlines;* from S. America and Miami by *International Air Bahama* via Nassau; from London by *British Airways;* from London, Paris, Rome, Amsterdam, Nice, Palma, Athens, Johannesburg and Frankfurt by *Luxair. By train:* Frequent service from Brussels (3 hrs.); on *TEE Edelsweiss* route Amsterdam-Zurich, or Paris-Koblenz as well as the *Iris* and *Schumann.*

CUSTOMS. Same as for Belgium (see chapter).

MAIL. Airmail to U.S. and Canada 14.00 francs for first 5 grams (one airmail sheet and envelope), 2.00 for each additional 5 grams. To England (automatically by airmail): 12 francs for first 20 grams. Postcards: 8 francs.

ELECTRICITY. 220 volts mostly, but some areas in Luxembourg City still use 110.

 LAUNDRY. Laundromats are to be found near the station at the Place de Strasbourg and 6 Rue Bender, Luxembourg City, as well as in the suburbs. Ask at the National Tourist Office, Place de la Gare, for a free map and help in locating them.

DRINKING WATER. Safe. Much of it from deep underground springs.

 TRAVEL IN LUXEMBOURG. By Car. Premium fuel costs about 65 francs (value added tax included) per Imp. gal. Speed limit is 60 km. (37 mph.) in towns. Open road speeds outside towns limited to 90 km. (56 mph.). Safety belts must be used unless a medical certificate exempts one. Blue zone parking in Luxembourg City and other centers is supplemented by parking meters and a system of ticket dispensers allowing motorists to buy any time period desired for parking at 1 franc for each 6 minutes. Green card must be good for the EEC countries, but English and other EEC-member travelers need not show it at the frontier. Police may impose on-the-spot fines up to 1000 francs. Try the *Circuits Auto-Pedestre* guides for combined motoring-hiking.

Car Hire. Cost: about 750 francs per day, plus 8 francs per km. Refundable deposit from 6000 to 11,000 francs required. *Avis,* 13 Rue Duchscher; *Colux,* 24

Dernier Sol; *Inter Rent,* 88 Route de Thionville; *Hertz,* 25 Ave. de la Liberté. All in Luxembourg City and most with representation at the airport. Campers can await you by pre-arrangement with the Kemwel (Europak) Group, Inc., 247 W. 12th St., New York City, serviced in Luxembourg by *Prestige International, Auto Europa* and *Colux.*

By Train. Weekend return tickets, 1 and 5-day network tickets (which include buses) and party tickets offer savings. Tourists over 65 can have 50% reductions upon showing their passport or ID card. Free *Circuits Trains-Pedestres* guides show how best to reach areas for beautiful walks. Services to most points in the country run nearly hourly all day.

By Bus. System operated by Luxembourg Rail, plus some private lines, well cover the Grand Duchy. Even most remote spots have three or four buses daily.

By Boat. During the tourist season a regular boat service runs between Schengen and Wasserbillig.

GUIDES AND TOURS. These can be arranged through the *Syndicat d'Initiative,* P.O. Box 181, Place d'Armes, Luxembourg City, or at any of the major tourist centers. A guide's services cost (for 1-10 persons), 500 francs for 1 to 2 hours, 800 for a half day and of not more than four hours, and 1,000 francs (plus guide's lunch) for a full day. Transportation is not included.

CAMPING. Campsites are numerous for tents or caravans.

USEFUL ADDRESSES. (Luxembourg City). *American Embassy,* 22 Blvd. Emmanuel Servais; *British Embassy,* 28/IV Blvd. Royal; *Office National de Tourisme,* Air Terminal, Place de la Gare, and at Airport; *Automobile Club of Luxembourg,* 13 Route de Longwy; *Mathieu-Wagons Lits/Cook,* 80 Ave. de la Gare and 103 Grand'Rue.

Exploring the Capital

Luxembourg City will not disappoint you. The old town looks exactly like a setting for the operetta *The Count of Luxembourg,* and you would never suspect that the city is the judiciary and banking center of the European Economic Community, and the meeting place of its Council of Ministers for three months of the year. The visitor will not be conscious of the mighty steel foundries and model farms of this progressive duchy, but only of a pleasant world of castles, turrets and moats, especially on summer nights when the bridges, spires and ramparts reassert themselves in the stunning illumination of the floodlights.

The city itself is small (about 90,000 inhabitants), a perfect place to explore on foot. With a little imagination, a walk outside over the ramparts will recreate the past when this was one of the impregnable bastions of Europe. Visit the splendid late Gothic cathedral of Our Lady of Luxembourg, and don't miss the guided tour through the nearby casemates of the citadel (summer only). This is a veritable voyage into the past, when Luxembourg's three rings of defense included 53 forts linked by 16 miles of tunnels and casemates hewn into solid rock.

Don't miss the area around the Marché aux Poissons (Fish Market), site of the capital's oldest buildings, and the National Museum, which contains priceless works of art and a model of the citadel in its heyday. Walk along the beautiful Promenade de la Corniche, with its magnificent view over the deep valley below. Especially recommended is a walk to the head of the Old Bridge, the Passerelle, and a descent into the valley by the Montée de la Petrusse. At the foot of the hill, partially cut into the rock, is the Chapel of Saint Quirinus, one of the oldest shrines in the country.

Of special interest to Americans is the United States Military Cemetery, three miles east from Luxembourg City. More than half of the 10,000 American soldiers who fell in Luxembourg during the Rundstedt offensive of World War II lie buried here. Among the thousands of graves is that of General George S. Patton, Jr., commander of the 3rd U.S. Army. A mile down the road is the German Military Cemetery.

The Countryside

There are many excursions out of Luxembourg City. One, by Route 7, will take you into the romantic winding valleys of the Ardennes, cut by swift streams that are ideal for angling. For hiking, there are well-marked trails through lovely forests.

Take route E 42 northeast from Luxembourg to Echternach and a lovely region which the Luxembourgers call their Switzerland. Junglinster is the site of one of the most powerful transmitting stations in Europe, Radio Luxembourg.

The Moselle Valley is best reached by way of Route 1 out of Luxembourg City. It joins Route 10 at Grevenmacher, where you may visit the Cooperative of Vinegrowers' cellars or the celebrated caves of Bernard-Massard. At Remich, the Caves St. Martin, hewn from rock, may also be seen and their champagne sampled. Route 10 follows the Moselle south past Remich, a wine center of Roman origin, then leaves the river and brings you to Mondorf-les-Bains, a noted spa which, along with physical re-education and cures for the liver, features concerts and fireworks on the occasions of the Luxembourg, French, British and American national holidays.

A two-day tour of the Grand Duchy of Luxembourg which will touch all the major points of interest is as follows:

Depart Luxembourg City—Mondorf-les-Bains—Moselle Valley (Remich-Grevenmacher-Wasserbillig)—Echternach—Little Switzerland (Beaufort—Müllerthal-Larochette)—Diekirch. Approximately 75 miles.

Diekirch-Vianden Castle-Stolzembourg-Clervaux Castle-Wiltz-Bavigne-Esch sur Sûre—the Upper Sûre dam and lake (approximately 50 miles).

Upper Sûre Valley—Bourscheid Castle—Erpeldange—Ettelbruck—Berg—Mersch—Castles Hollenfels and Ansembourg-Septfontaines-Koerich-Steinfort-return to Luxembourg City (approximately 65 miles). Total about 190 miles.

PRACTICAL INFORMATION FOR CAPITAL AND REGIONS

HOTELS. Luxembourg has both luxury and economy. Everywhere you can find a clean establishment with excellent and plentiful food. Most hotels have rooms with bath, and all have bathrooms available on each floor. Many hotels encourage tourism by granting special off-season terms for a three-day stay.

Youth hostels are plentiful, at Clervaux, Echternach, Hollenfels, Luxembourg City, Vianden and a number of other places.

LUXEMBOURG CITY. The *Aerogulf-Sheraton* offers 150 rooms near the airport in delightful surroundings. The *Holiday Inn,* 260 rooms, fully air-conditioned, has pool and sauna. The *Alfa,* 100 rooms, is an old stand-by. The *Kons,* nearby, is in a higher category, as are the *Cheminée de Paris* and *Des Ducs.* The *Cravat,* 60 rooms, overlooks the valley and Pont Adolphe. The *Eldorado* offers TV and stocked refrigerators in each room, and telex service for businessmen.

Among the (2) category: *Central-Molitor,* 28 Ave. de la Liberté, *Continental,* 86 Grand' Rue, the *Dauphin,* Ave. de la Gare, *International,* Place de la Gare, *Italia,* 15 Rue d'Anvers, *Terminus* and *Empire,* on the station square and *Um Bock* in the old town.

Of the more moderately priced hotels, the best are: *Français,* Place d'Armes, *Théâtre,* Rue des Capucins; *Graas,* Ave. de la Liberté, *Schintgen,* Rue Notre Dame, *Carlton* and *City,* Rue de Strasbourg, and the tiny *Airfield Hotel* at Findel Airport.

Des Ardennes, 59 Ave. de la Liberté, and *Weber,* Pl. de Paris, are inexpensive. Just outside town, at Dommeldange on the Echternach road, are the new *Novotel* and the moderately expensive *Euro Parc.*

BEAUFORT. *St. Jean* and *Cigrang* are the best known, but the top hotel here is the *Meyer* with 45 rooms.

BERDORF. Tourist oriented, many hotels. *L'Ermitage* is in the forest. *Parc* and *Bisdorff* have private swimming pools.

CLERVAUX. Has 12th-century castle housing the "Family of Man" photographs by Edward Steichen, models of ancient castles, and a WW II museum. The Abbey shows dioramas of medieval monasticism. Hotels: *du Commerce* (swimming pool), *de l'Abbaye, Claravallis, Central, Koener* and *des Nations* are among many good establishments.

DIEKIRCH. Good for an overnight stop. Best rooms and cuisine: *Hiertz,* followed by *de l'Europe,* and *Kremer,* with *Beau Séjour* and *de la Paix* (rooms only) next.

ECHTERNACH. Over 30 hotels. The *Bel Air* is best, followed by *du Parc* with its indoor pool. *Grand Hôtel, Universel* and *de la Sûre.* Also good: *du Commerce, St. Hubert, Petite Marquise* and the more modest *de Luxembourg* and *Petite Suisse.*

ESCH-SUR-ALZETTE. Biggest industrial city. Best are *Astro, Auberge Royale, Mercure, de la Poste.*

ESCH-SUR-SURE. A 1000-year-old haven for tourists. *Hôtel des Ardennes,* and *Beau-Site* are good, but *Du Moulin* has the best situation, close to the riverbank.

ETTELBRUCK. Excursion center and good overnight stop. The best hotels are the *Cames, Central, Solis, Herckmans,* in that order.

GAICHEL (EISCHEN). Good excursion center. *La Bonne Auberge,* 15 rooms; *La Gaichel,* 14 rooms. Fishing. Cuisine in both is superb.

GREVENMACHER. Great wine center. Try the *Govers,* or *de la Poste.*

LAROCHETTE. The three best hotels: *de la Poste, du Château* and *Résidence.*

MONDORF-LES-BAINS. The *Grand Chef* (1), has an excellent restaurant. Try the crayfish. Another reasonable hotel is the *Windsor,* followed by *Bristol* and *Beau-Séjour.* Many hotels close for the winter.

MÜLLERTHAL. In lovely valley of the Ernz Noire. *Central* is a fine stopover. Try the *Réserve du Müllerthal.*

REMICH. Viticultural center on the Moselle. Choose among *Beau-Séjour, Belle-Vue, Châlet Beau-Lieu, Esplanade, Parc* or *des Ardennes.*

VIANDEN. Best is the *Heintz.* Other good hotels: *Oranienburg, Victor Hugo* and *Hof van Holland. L'Esperance* and *Réunion* are (4).

WILTZ. Center of cultural activities in tourist season. *Du Vieux Château,* tops in cuisine, comfort, is followed by *du Commerce, Belle-Vue* and *Beau-Séjour.*

RESTAURANTS. Most hotels have restaurants, so finding an eating place is no problem. For food that is out of the ordinary, here is a list of the best restaurants in the Grand Duchy.

LUXEMBOURG CITY. *Des Empereurs,* 11 Ave. de la Porte Neuve, is costly but good, as are the *Cordial,* 1 Place de Paris and *Au Gourmet,* 8 Rue Chimay. Reservations are a good idea.

Um Bock, 6-8 Rue de la Loge, near the National Museum, is characteristic of Luxembourg.

The *Commerce,* 13 Place d'Armes, has a wide range of prices. *Rôtisserie Ardennaise,* 1 Ave. du 10 Septembre, is moderate. The *Buffet de la Gare* has restaurants in four categories.

Italia, 15-17 Rue d'Anvers (for those fancy Italian dishes), *Ancre d'Or,* 21 Rue du Fossé, *San Remo,* Pl. Guillaume, and *Marmite, Rendez-vous* and *Le Cellier,* 6-15 Place d'Armes, and *l'Académie,* Place d'Armes, are interesting.

BOUR. The restaurant *Janin (Beau-Site)* is well worth the trip.

DIEKIRCH. *Hiertz* prepares an unusual kidney dish (rognon de veau sur canapé).

ECHTERNACH. *Bel-Air* hotel's restaurant offers the best meal in town. At nearby Berdorf, *Bisdorff* is excellent. At Grundhof, *Charles Brimer* sets a splendid table. Expensive.

EHNEN. Picturesque, good lunch halt. *Simmer* has fish specialties (pike). Fine view. Expensive.

ESCH-SUR-ALZETTE. *Auberge Royal* hotel's restaurant and *Au Bec Fin,* 15 Place Norbert Metz. Both expensive.

GAICHEL (EISCHEN). *La Bonne Auberge* specializes in young wild boar in wine sauce (marcassin au Chablis). *Gaichel's* strong point is the preparation of crustaceans. Both have guest rooms. Expensive.

GREVENMACHER. The *de la Piscine* overlooks the Moselle. Moderate.

LEESBACH. The *Vieux Moulin* in the valley of the Seven Castles, is worth a visit. Nearby, Tuntange has the excellent *Le Coq d'Alsace* and Saeul, the *Maison Rouge.*

MONDORF-LES-BAINS. You'll eat well at the *Grand Chef* hotel. Specialty: grills. Also good, the *Astoria.* Both moderate.

VIANDEN. The *Hostellerie Trinitaires* at Hotel Heintz is an atmospheric restaurant of the first order. Expensive.

 ENTERTAINMENT. (Luxembourg City.) The leading nightclub is the *Splendide,* 18 Rue Dicks. The floorshows are fair and the prices are not excessive. Clubs must close at 03:00 hours. All nightlife rolls along quietly in Luxembourg, except the discothèques, which are numerous and vibrant.

 MUSEUMS. *The National Museum,* Marché-aux-Poissons, in Luxembourg City, houses priceless works of art and archaeology. Open 10:00 to 12:00 hours and 14:00 to 18:00 hours daily, except Mon. Entrance free. In the park, the *J. P. Pescatore Museum* has exhibits from the 17th to 19th centuries, chiefly Dutch and French. Open in season 14:30 to 18:30 hours weekdays, 10:30 to 12:30 hours Sunday. Admission 10 francs. Regional museums at Bech-Kleinmacher, Clervaux, Diekirch, Schwebsingen, Vianden, and Wiltz are of interest. Rumelange has installed a mining museum, authentically enough, in a mine. Children's parks and small zoos dot the country and an "oldtimer" train runs, in season, from Rodange.

 HISTORIC BUILDINGS AND SITES. Luxembourg City: Ruins of the *Castle of Sigefroi,* founder of Luxembourg, always open. *Casemates* (open summer only), some 16 miles of underground passages and fortifications. Cathedral of *Notre Dame* (1613-1629). Ask about the recently discovered Rubens painting.

Castles at Ansembourg, Beaufort, Bourscheid, Brandenbourg, Clervaux, Esch-sur-Sûre, Hollenfels, Larochette, Mersch, Schuttbourg, Wiltz and Vianden, the cradle of the Orange-Nassau dynasty. Mersch has a *Roman villa; Roman mosaics* there and at Diekirch. Diekirch also has *Celtic* and prehistoric relics. At Echternach is the *Benedictine Abbey* founded in the 7th century by St. Willibrord, whose tomb is in the crypt.

BUSINESS IN LUXEMBOURG. Luxembourg, banking center for the EEC and host to innumerable international meetings, is accustomed to the demands of traveling business people. The larger hotels can provide an office with typewriter and make photocopies, and they have telex facilities. The post office can arrange to send either telex or cable; check the service number in the telephone book under Postes et Télécommunications, as it differs from town to town.

On weekdays secretarial service can be arranged through Aide Temporaire, 19 Rue Glesener, Luxembourg City, tel: 48.23.23, or by courtesy of a business friend who may know a willing extra-hours worker. On weekends it is next to impossible to find office help.

Photocopies can be made at Repro or Linster, both in Rue Glesener near the station. More extensive duplication is possible through Rank-Xerox, 12, Rue Heine, or one of the many printing houses in town.

The pace of business is more leisurely than in Paris or New York. Appointments can be scheduled for as early as 9 A.M., but it is prudent to let the office get the day organized, so 9:30 might be better. Business may be done in a neighboring café during a break, and business lunches and dinners frequently accomplish the work which offices then formalize.

The Office National de Tourisme, Place de la Gare, tel: 48.11.99, can orient business people to other available services.

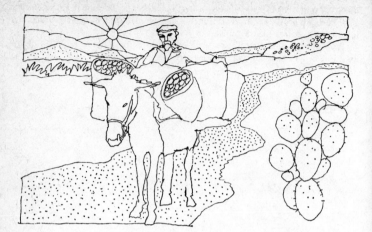

MALTA

Malta, so fortunately situated in the middle of the Mediterranean, with its mild, sunny climate, is a perfect place for a holiday. Although a small island—including Gozo and Comino it covers only 122 square miles—its strategic position has always brought it fame. It tempted maritime nations since the Phoenicians sailed the seas. Indeed, they colonized it. It was later seized by the Carthaginians. Rome took the islands in 218 BC.

From early days Malta has been a protagonist of Christianity. St. Paul was shipwrecked on the island and converted the inhabitants. In 1565 the Knights of Jerusalem held the island with a handful of men as a Christian stronghold against the Turks in one of the most spectacular sieges in history.

The Maltese are charming, religious and hard working. Without in any way detracting from the pride they have in their island home, the comings and goings of other nations have bequeathed an international veneer that makes them naturally gregarious and hospitable. They have climbed on the bandwagon of tourism with zeal.

There are religious festivals, richly decorated churches and plenty of fascinating places for the sightseer and archaeologist to visit. The Blue Grotto is reminiscent of the one in Capri. There are Crusader remains, Neolithic temples and an underground temple called the Hypogeum, cut deep into the rock—the only one of its kind in the world.

Gozo is connected to Malta by ferry. It is a charming island studded with farms and fishing coves. It has more vegetation than Malta, but there are many flat topped hills and craggy cliffs. Comino, the island between Gozo and Malta, is one of the world's best underwater hunting grounds, the aquamarine water being clear and unpolluted. Even Byron could not resist visiting Malta's sister islands—"not in silence pass Calypso's isles . . . "

PRACTICAL INFORMATION FOR MALTA

CAPITAL. Valletta, inhabited by about one-fifteenth of the total population of 320,000.

LANGUAGE. Maltese and English are the official languages.

CLIMATE. Hot in summer, tempered by sea breezes. The archipelago is delightful year round, but May to October is the high season. April-May for spring freshness.

 SPECIAL EVENTS. On Good Friday, solemn but colorful processions are held in several towns and villages. Carnival is held in the Capital, Valletta, and starts on the second Sunday in May. The "Mnarja" (folk festival) is held on the nearest weekend to the 28th of June and is an all night traditional festa with folk music, dancing and singing. Some 30 festi are held throughout the island between May and October. On September 8th, a water carnival, boat races and band marches commemorate the Great Siege of 1565 and the lifting of the more recent one of 1940-43. Malta's National Day is December 13th—Republic Day.

 SPORTS. The sporting life on this sun-blessed island is very varied. There are excellent facilities for sailing, water-polo, surfboard riding, waterskiing, etc. Specially favored for underwater fishing. Equipment including aqua-lungs is on hire locally. You may go out fishing in a fisherman's *dghajsa* and bring back a variety of catch, from the large tunny to the succulent little rosette. Polo, golf and tennis tournaments follow each other in close succession. Wednesday and Saturday afternoons throughout the summer sailing regattas take place at various points around the island. Horse trotting and racing are popular pastimes.

 MONEY. Malta adopted decimal currency in 1972 in which 10 mils equal 1 cent and 100 cents 1 Maltese pound (£M1). Gold and silver coins are legal tender (£M1 = $US 2.54 & £1.33.) **Subject to change.** At this writing you can take in any amount in travelers checks and other currency. Visitors may take out of Malta foreign currencies up to the amount imported or £250, whichever is higher. Maltese currency up to £M25 may be taken out.

WHAT WILL IT COST. With Malta's rapid tourist development, prices are inevitably rising, though less than most. The deluxe hotels charge from about £M10 upward for bed and breakfast. First class A £M6.50; first class B £M5.50; second class A £M4.80; second class B £M4.30; simple establishments down to as little as £M2.80. Self-catering prices are very reasonable. Fresh vegetables, fruit and fish are cheap. Even imported gin and whiskey cost less than in the rest of Europe.

HOW TO REACH MALTA. *By air:* Malta is linked to various capitals by regular air services throughout the year. Tourists from North and South America and Japan, holding a "Eurail Pass," can travel to Malta on a reduction of 20% on tourist tickets. Consult your travel agent for the latest schedules and how to get there by air or sea, rail or road.

The following airlines run scheduled services to Malta: *Air Malta* (which can also offer a weekly link from the island to Cairo enabling the visitor to have a two center holiday), *Alitalia, British Airways, Libyan Arab Airlines* and *Union de Transports Aériens* (UTA). Companies in Great Britain offering package and villa holidays include *Medallion Holidays* 182/184 Edgware Road, London W,2, *Cadogan Travel,* 159 Sloane St., London, SW1, *Exchange Travel Holidays Ltd.,* Parker Road, Hastings, E. Sussex, England.

SHOPPING. Remember that because Malta is considered a developing country, many of the things you buy there may be exempt from U.S. Customs duties under the G.S.P. plan, as explained in the section on customs in Facts at Your Fingertips, at the beginning of this volume.

CUSTOMS REGULATIONS. Malta adheres to international agreements: 200 cigarettes, one bottle of liquor and one of wine, ½ pint of perfume are free of duty.

USEFUL ADDRESSES (in Valletta): *Malta Government Tourist Office,* Freedom Square. *Thomas Cook,* 20 Republic Street. Sightseeing tours: A list of agents organizing tours is featured in fortnightly booklet obtained at hotels and travel agencies called "What's On".

HOTELS

VALLETTA TOWN. *Phoenicia Hotel,* deluxe, 112 air-conditioned rooms with bath, heated pool, gardens. *Grand Hotel Excelsior,* 196 rooms, 2 restaurants, pool. At *Sliema, Sliema,* 210 rooms with bath, nightclub, restaurants, pool. *Fortina,* 52 air-conditioned rooms with bath, pool. *Metropole,* 76 air-conditioned rooms with bath, sunroof. At the yacht marina, *Marina,* air-conditioned, 66 rooms with bath. *Plevna,* 50 rooms with bath, private lido and bar on the sea. In old Sliema, *Imperial,* 75 air-conditioned rooms, pool.

GOLDEN BAY, 15 miles from the airport, *Golden Sands,* overlooking bay, 118 rooms with bath, pool.

MELLIEHA BAY, *the* place for underwater sports and fishing. The *Mellieha Bay,* 214 rooms with bath.

PARADISE BAY. About 14 miles from Sliema. *Paradise Bay,* on the sea, 180 air-conditioned rooms with bath, pool.

RABAT. *Grand Hotel Verdala* with 164 luxury rooms, two pools, sauna baths, and fantastic views over the island.

SALINA BAY. About 6 miles from Sliema. *Salina Bay,* air-conditioned, facing sea, 100 rooms with bath, pool.

ST. ANTON, in the center of the island. *Corinthia Palace,* air-conditioned, 160 rooms with bath, balcony, pool.

ST. GEORGE'S BAY. *Villa Rosa,* 154 rooms with bath, two pools, garden. Boating, water skiing, skin diving facilities.

ST. JULIAN'S BAY. *Malta Hilton,* 200 luxurious rooms, all amenities, recent, on the bay. The *Dragonara Hotel,* with 200 air conditioned bedrooms, is within the 15-acre grounds of Malta's only casino of the same name.

ST. PAUL'S BAY. *Dolmen,* 121 rooms with bath and balcony or patio, pool, private beach.

OUTER ISLANDS

COMINO ISLAND, only 20 minutes by launch from Malta, is a tranquil spot with an ancient fortress. *Comino,* on the sea, 100 rooms with bath, two pools.

GOZO ISLAND. Can be reached by ferry from Malta in about 20 minutes. Cars £M1.25 return; passengers 30 cents. Glorious beaches. *Ta' Cenc,* 46 rooms, several bungalow suites, open-air restaurant, pools, lounge, bar.

MONACO

Between Nice and Menton, in the very heart of the French Riviera, lies the glittering principality of Monaco. An independent state, its frontiers controlled by France, Monaco consists of 11 square miles of expensive apartment buildings and beach clubs, cliffs, flowers and coastline. The Monegasques are gay and friendly, not without reason: they pay almost no taxes, have no military service, and live in an atmosphere of perpetual summer holiday. This happy state of affairs is now destined to continue since Princess Grace and her husband, Prince Rainier, 30th descendant of the Grimaldi dynasty (which has ruled Monaco since the Middle Ages), have produced three heirs.

The principality consists of four towns: the ancient community of Monaco, high on a rock, with the prince's postcard palace, a modern cathedral in Romanesque style, and a world famous aquarium; La Condamine, where business thrives and the Monegasques live; Monte Carlo, where another sort of business thrives; and Fontvieille, rapidly coming up as an industrial center. The world-famous casino of Monte Carlo is the center of social life, scene of gala dinners, elegant parties and spectacular shows. The casino also houses the delightful Salle Garnier, a gilded theater which looks like a chocolate box version of the Paris Opera. This theater, made famous by Diaghilev and the Ballets Russes, offers a glittering winter season of ballet, opera and drama. The famous Harkness Ballet of New York continues the tradition, making Monte Carlo its winter headquarters. The old casino now has a rather gaudy rival in the gaming rooms in the Loew's Monte-Carlo hotel, which old-timers refer to as Las-Vegas-on-the-Mediterranean, and in the new Monte Carlo Sporting Club.

Gambling is still the main activity of this pleasure palace, and the casino and its popularity account for a fair percentage of the income of the principality, although Prince Rainier has embarked on a vast program of reclaiming land. In fact, during the last 20 years, Monaco has beaten all world records for peaceful territorial expansion, increasing the country's area by 20% through land reclamation. Beaches and hotels have been built with the purpose of attracting a wider range of visitors, middle and lower-income groups as well as the more affluent. This process of attracting more money is called "Americanizing", with all the overtones, good *and* bad, which follow.

Exploring Monaco

First and foremost, visit the Casino. Try your luck if you think it wise; otherwise, reserve in advance for dinner, take in a floorshow, have a drink, or just watch the suckers trying to break the bank.

There are other things to do, places to go, and people to meet in Monaco, believe it or not. The Mt. Agel Golf Club provides a magnificent mountainous course, but watch your step, or you'll end up in the Mediterranean several hundred feet below. There are golf and tennis tournaments all the year round and galas at the Sporting Club (December-April) and the Sporting d'Eté at Larvotto, during the summer season. The famous Automobile Rally, the Monaco Grand Prix, is in May, and an international bridge tournament each June. The summer calendar of events features a dazzling ball each Friday night at the Sporting d'Eté. There are the aquatic distractions of swimming, skin-diving, water skiing, and yachting.

You will want to make short excursions to Beausoleil, popular residential district just north of Monte Carlo (and less expensive); to the hilltop village of Eze; to the fortified village of Roquebrune, with its curious tangle of narrow stepped lanes, and the equally ancient village of La Turbie, with its magnificent view from the Grande Corniche.

PRACTICAL INFORMATION FOR MONACO

CAPITAL. Monaco.

LANGUAGE. French. English spoken in major hotels.

CLIMATE. Southern California.
Average maximum daily temperatures in degrees Fahrenheit and centigrade:

Monaco	Jan.	Feb.	Mar.	Apr.	May	June	July	Aug.	Sept.	Oct.	Nov.	Dec.
F°	54	55	57	61	66	73	79	79	75	68	61	57
C°	12	13	14	16	19	23	26	26	24	20	16	14

SEASONS. All year round, but the winter season, marked by ballet, opera-music festival, fancy dress balls, yachting regattas and the Monte Carlo Rally, is still the smart one. The summer season also has a diversity of water and other sports events, concerts, etc.

SPECIAL EVENTS. *April,* Battle of Flowers; sailing regattas. *August,* International Yacht Races.

CUSTOMS. None.

MONEY. The French franc.

MAIL. Same rates as France.

WHAT WILL IT COST. Same as the expensive parts of France.

WHAT TO SEE. Each day at noon, changing of the Guard, Palace Square; Palace apartments (open 10-noon, and 2-6 in summer, except when the royal family is in residence); *Jardin Exotique; Musée Océanographique,* the *Centre d'Acclimatation Zoologique, Museum of Prehistoric Anthropology,* and *Villa Ispahan,* former mansion of a Persian prince.

SPORTS. *Tennis* and *badminton* at Monte Carlo Country Club; *golf* (18 holes) at 2,500 foot above sea level at Mt. Agel Golf Club; *deep-sea fishing, underwater exploration and fishing, water-ski school* at Yacht Club; *swimming* at pebbly but ultra-exclusive and expensive Monte Carlo Beach or at the luxurious artificial beach and pool at Old Beach; at sandy, popular reasonable Larvotto Beach, or the enormous Olympic pool overlooking the port, or the fashionable Terrasses pool. Beach charges vary considerably, from about 3 francs at Larvotto to at least 40 francs at the fashionable places.

HOTELS AND RESTAURANTS. The top hotels of Monte Carlo are the last word in luxury, and less expensive than you might imagine. You can get a single room and bath at the fabulous *Hôtel de Paris* for about 230 francs, off-season, but you can pay all you have for a suite in which the management will obligingly change the furniture to suit your taste. This, the most famous of Monte Carlo's hotels, is diagonally across from the Casino. It has a swimming pool, heated in winter. Its restaurant is first rate and its *cave* of vintage wines probably unequalled on the Côte d'Azur. All hotels are in town, except the two deluxe ones at Monte Carlo Beach.

Vying with the Hôtel de Paris in deluxe apartments are the *Hermitage* and the *Métropole,* the latter with heated pool.

Newest in this category is *Loew's Monte-Carlo,* part of the giant Spéluges project of residential apartments, convention center, etc., built on a concrete platform jutting into the sea below the Belle Epoque Casino. The hotel has every amenity, so the lazy guest need never leave the premises.

The elegant little *Mirabeau* is also deluxe, with the usual amenities and gambling rooms.

Le Siècle, near rail station, is inexpensive.

At Monte Carlo Beach, the *Old Beach,* with pool, is expensive and therefore exclusive.

Next in category come the *Splendid,* and *Balmoral,* (a bit more expensive), whose restaurant is air-conditioned. Less expensive, *Alexandra,* without restaurant. *Des Palmiers,* inexpensive, central; *de la Poste,* very expensive.

Restaurants: *Le Grill* and *La Salle Empire,* both (E), in the Hôtel de Paris are by far the best, with elegant, refined dishes, sumptuous wines. *Le Bec Rouge, La Calanque, Rampoldi* are all excellent, if rather overpriced. *Belli* (M) has the best *pasta* (Italian dishes). More reasonable are: *Bambi, Café de Paris* (open all night), *Vesuvio, L'Avenir,* all (M) and family places with "honest" cooking.

For snacks: *The Restaurant,* at the beach near the pool, serves bathers with Hôtel de Paris menus. *Costa-Rica,* for a bite, on Bd. des Moulins.

Nightlife. The place to be seen, if you can afford it, is the elegant *Monte-Carlo Sporting Club d'Eté,* a restaurant and nightclub complex by the sea which includes a gaming room; the *Maona* restaurant; *Jimmy's,* nightclub queen Régine's spot, pool, and the *Salle des Etoiles* for dancing and big shows. The *Sporting Club d'Hiver* is open in winter.

Other good nightspots are the glittery, noisy *Parady's; Tiffany's; Black Jack,* in the Casino; the quieter *St.-Louis,* and Loew's *Folie Russe.*

MONACO. Hotels: *du Siècle,* moderate. *Cosmopolite* and *de France,* both handy to rail station, inexpensive.

Restaurants: *Bar-Restaurant International, Aurore* (I).

LA CONDAMINE has a number of good eating places, best among them: *La Chaumière,* fairly expensive. For a reasonable meal go to *Quicksilver,* Quai Kennedy.

USEFUL ADDRESSES. *Tourist Information:* 2a, Bd. des Moulins at Monte Carlo. *Travel Agents: Havas-Exprinter,* Bd. des Moulins; *Wagons Lits-Cook,* Ave. des Spélugues.

Car Rental: Hertz, 43 Ave. de Grande-Bretagne (30–20–88); *Avis,* 9 Ave. d'Ostende (30–17–53).

NORWAY

Most northerly and most beautiful of the Scandinavian countries is Norway. The country, about 1,100 miles long and about the size of New Mexico, is literally laced by the sea, which penetrates its western side with a series of *fjords* or inlets. These fjords have given the nation a coastline of more than 12,000 miles and some of the most magnificent scenery in the world. You should certainly try to get to the North Cape, extreme northern point of Europe, where, from May 15 until August 1, the sun stays above the horizon all night, for this is the luminous land of the Midnight Sun. Conversely, there is a period in midwinter with no daylight above the Arctic Circle when there appears the unforgettable and eerie brilliance of the aurora borealis (the Northern Lights).

Norway has made great strides to cope with the tourist trade, which now ranks among the most important of the nation's industries. However, if you are planning to visit by the water route, that is to say, either by the year-round express steamers or by the many summer cruises, better make reservations through your travel agent several months in advance.

There is a certain moral justice in the fact that Norway's scenic splendor is now attracting so much tourist business, for all this natural beauty has been of little economic value in the past; seven-tenths of Norway is bare rock, glaciers, and wild romantic mountains rising to heights of more than 8,000 feet. Less than four percent of the land is tilled and mineral resources are comparatively small. But more fish are brought ashore than in any other European country and its merchant fleet is the fourth largest in the world. Royalties have begun to flow in from North Sea oil and Norway's economic prospects are brighter than most countries' in western Europe (despite its non-membership in the Common Market).

Known as the land of Vikings, Ibsen and Grieg, Norway is not the enigmatic, introverted place of popular preconception; the Norwegians are full of good humor, friendly to foreigners and glad to exchange ideas—in English fortunately.

Food and Drink

Hearty is the word for Norwegian meals. Breakfasts are often enormous with a variety of fish, cheese, and fine bread served from the cold buffet along with coffee and cooked eggs. A national institution is the *Koldtbord* (cold table) which will often be in evidence at lunch time, featuring smoked salmon, fresh lobster, shrimp and other products of the sea. The sandwiches are a meal in their own right, single-decker meat, cheese, fish or salad concoctions as open and friendly as the Norwegians themselves. They are called *smörbröd.* Equally appreciated by Norwegians and their visitors are the roast venison, ptarmigan in cream sauce, wild raspberries and a special berry called *multer* with a flavor all its own. If you have a strong palate and really want to go Norwegian, try *lutefisk,* a highly flavored codfish that tastes as though it had been preserved in a potash lye. After that even the fiery Norwegian schnaps, *aquavit,* seems cool by comparison.

Liquor and wine are sold only by the State through special monopoly and licensing laws are rather severe. You can't drink at a bar before 3 P.M. and they are closed on Sunday, but if you can afford it, you can buy more than enough at the *Vinmonopolet* stores to tide you over those arid spells. Alcohol is scarce in most provinces, except at the top *høyfjells* and *turist* (mountain and tourist) hotels, and costs are high. However, most hotels and restaurants are licensed to sell beer and wine at any time.

Shopping

First and foremost, the world-famous enamel on silver work and silver in traditional designs. Then, any of the wonderful hand-crafted items: textiles, ceramics, and carved wood. Furs are a good buy and so is hand-knitted sportswear.

PRACTICAL INFORMATION FOR NORWAY

WHAT WILL IT COST. A single room in a first-class hotel in Oslo will cost from N.Kr. 300 up, second-class from N.Kr. 200, and moderate from N.Kr. 150. Deluxe meals are for the expense-account brigade only. Average meal costs upward of N.Kr. 70 excluding wine. Rates in the provinces are somewhat lower.

Modestly typical day with second-class hotel accommodations, meals, taxis, theater or other entertainment, will cost upwards of N.Kr. 400, but with steadily rising costs, rates can only be approximate and vary considerably with individual requirements.

CAPITAL. Oslo.

LANGUAGE. Norwegian. Nearly everyone speaks English.

CLIMATE. Offshore Gulf Stream currents prevent extremes; the north averages 20° colder.

Average maximum daily temperatures in Fahrenheit and centigrade:

Oslo	Jan.	Feb.	Mar.	Apr.	May	June	July	Aug.	Sept.	Oct.	Nov.	Dec.
F°	28	30	39	50	61	68	72	70	61	48	37	32
C°	-2	-1	4	10	16	20	22	21	16	9	3	0

 SPECIAL EVENTS. *January,* Bergen Music Festival (through June); ski festivals in Lillehammer, Geilo. *March,* Winter Festival, Narvik; Winter Sports week, Lillehammer; Holmenkollen week, world-famous international ski competitions in Oslo. *April,* Reindeer herding, Finnmark. *May,* Constitution Day celebrations (17th). *June,* Jazz Festival, Kongsberg. *July,* Fishing Festival, Harstad; Fishing Festival, Stavanger (through August). *August,* Jazz Festival, Molde. *September,* Nomadic Lapps leave coasts for moors (also October). *December,* Bosekop Market, Lapp fair, Alta.

CLOSING TIMES. Shops from 8:30 to 17:00 hours (16:00 hours in summer). On Saturdays they may close as early as 14:00 hours, especially in summer. Banking hours are 9:30-15:30 hours, Monday through Friday, but closed on Saturdays. Shop early, then sightsee. Museums, etc., are usually open until 1900 hours in high season (June, July, August). Other times consult Tourist Offices or OSLO GUIDE (printed weekly).

 SPORTS. *Skiing* (see section earlier in book). "Nordic Ski Touring" packages from the US to winter resorts such as Lillehammer, Voss, Geilo, Beito and Tyin. The Norwegian Mountain Touring Association has chalets for those on long excursions, and organizes dogsled tours with guides. Glacier skiing can be practiced far into June in the mountains of the Fjord Country (Stryn, Andalsnes, Geiranger). *Hunting* starts in autumn and June-August is the season for salmon *fishing,* one of the best in the world. You can play *golf* at midnight at Trondheim and at Oslo, Bergen and Stavanger in daytime. *Pony trekking* with hardy mountain breeds *(fjording),* organized every summer by the Norwegian Mountain Touring Association, 28 Stortingsgaten, Oslo.

Salmon and seatrout fishing as well as other *big game hunting* tours are operated by Mytravel International A/S, N. Vollgate 19, Oslo, who have American and United Kingdom correspondents. Bennett Tours, 270 Madison Ave., N.Y. or 35 Karl Johansgate, Oslo, will arrange photography expeditions on request.

MONEY. The Norwegian crown or *krone* is the unit of currency, divided into 100 *öre.* There are about 5.32 kr. to the American dollar, 10.10 to the £ sterling. **Subject to change.**

 TIPPING. Norway is not accustomed to much tipping, particularly outside the main centers. Service charge of 12 percent is always added to the bill in hotels, restaurants and bars. Round out this bill in the latter if you wish, and of course tip for special service. Porters are usually tipped 2 N.Kr. per bag. Beauty parlors do not expect tips. Taxi drivers don't expect tip either, but if in doubt add small amount.

 HOW TO REACH NORWAY. By Air: *SAS* (Scandinavian Airlines) and *Pan Am* fly direct, or via Copenhagen, from New York, Chicago, Los Angeles, Seattle, Montreal (Canada), and Anchorage to Bergen and Oslo. *Icelandic Airlines* (Loftleidir) fly from New York to Oslo via Iceland at less cost than other airlines. *British Airways* excursion fares offer considerable savings. *Dan-Air* year round to Kristiansand from Gatwick. Other flights from Newcastle.

By Sea: Newcastle (train connections from London) to Stavanger, Oslo, Kristiansand, Bergen. Harwich to Kristiansand. All by Fred Olsen/Bergen Line. All have drive/on/off car facilities. Inclusive cruises from five days upward are organised almost year round, but particularly prolific in summer. Companies include Royal Viking Line, Norwegian American Line, P&O, etc. For full list consult your travel agent.

By Car: drive to Kiel or Cuxhaven (Germany), Amsterdam (Holland), or Aarhus, Copenhagen, Frederikshavn and Hirtshals in Denmark then take a car ferry to Oslo, Fredrikstad, Larvik, Arendal, Kristiansand, Stavanger or Bergen.

For the Disabled An extremely useful booklet is called Access in Norway. Available from the Central Council for the Disabled, 34, Eccleston Square, London, S.W.1. It gives valuable information for handicapped or otherwise less mobile travelers.

 CUSTOMS. One liter of spirits, one liter of wine and up to 200 cigarettes may be brought in duty free (overseas visitors: 400). You may bring in foreign currency in unlimited amounts, also Norwegian currency, but not notes of higher than 100 kr. You may be asked to declare this when you enter, and you cannot take out more than 800 kroner.

MAIL. Air mail rates Kr. 1.80 first 20 grams. Postcards U.S. and Canada, Kr. 1.30; to U.K. Kr. 1.00. No extra for air mail within Europe.

ELECTRICITY. 220 volts A.C. throughout Norway except at Stavanger where it's still 110 in the smaller hotels.

DRINKING WATER. 100 percent safe and pure.

 TRAVEL IN NORWAY. By Air: Air travel is well developed in this vast and relatively empty country. All main centers even in the far, far north are linked to Oslo by jet services of *SAS* and Norway's domestic carrier, *Braathens SAFE.* And apart from regular flights, there are special aerial trips in summer to see the Midnight Sun. Any travel agent will give you full details. **By Car.** Keep to the right. Mountain routes are narrow; don't expect to burn them up and survive. The official speed limit on the open road is 50 mph. You can drive to the North Cape, using the ferry service from Repvag to Honningsvaag. Gasoline currently costs 2.50 krone per liter, subject to fluctuation.

CAR HIRE. *Scandinavian Car Rental,* Fredensborgveien 33; *Bislett Car Rental,* Pilestredet 70; *Avis,* Munkedamsveien 27, also Fornebu, Bergen, Stavanger and other towns; *Center Car,* Drammensveien 126B. *Kjøles* (Hertz), General Birchsgt 16. All in Oslo.

GUIDES. Apply to *Oslo Guide Service,* Munkedamsveien 15. Rates are 100 kr. for the first hour; 45 kr. each consecutive hour thereafter; tipping not required.

KNOW THE NORWEGIANS. Norway has a special program *Know the Norwegians* through which you are introduced to Norwegians whose professions or interests are similar to yours. Visits arranged by *Oslo Tourist Information* (see below).

USEFUL ADDRESSES. Embassies: *American,* Drammensveien 18; *British,* Drammensveien 79; *Canadian,* Oskarsgate 20. *Norway Travel Association,* H. Heyerdahlsgate 1. *Oslo Tourist Information Office,* Munkedamsveien 15. *Norwegian Mountain Touring Assn.,* Stortingsgate 28. *Royal Norwegian Automobile Club* (KNA), Parkveien 68. All in Oslo.

Oslo, Norway's Capital

The bright, breezy and outdoorsy capital of Norway is a hospitable city of almost 470,000 people at the head of the Oslofjord. You may be surprised to know that in area it is one of the largest metropolises in the world (it was enlarged by 27 times its size in 1948, to include huge areas of surrounding country). Here is a world capital with Nature at its very doorstep, a perfect place to adjust from a frenetic, over-sophisticated existence to the simpler and more wholesome values of Norwegian life.

This usually begins on the main street, Karl Johansgate, which leads from the East Station to the Royal Palace. Half of this street is now a pedestrian precinct, but the trams still traverse it, so watch out. Below the Palace is a small green park, on the harbor side of which is the Stortingsgate and the National Theater, with its entrance flanked by statues of Norway's two great dramatists, Henrik Ibsen and Bjørnsterne Bjørnson. Despite the recent building of a splendid new concert house, this is still the focal point of Oslo's cultural life. A stairway behind the theater leads to the underground trolley station, departure point for excursions to the outlying sections of Oslo.

Visit the twin-towered red brick Radhus or Town Hall, the interior of which contains 2,000 square yards of bold-figured murals by Henrik Sørensen, Alf Rolfsen and other leading Norwegian artists, depicting all phases of life and work in Norway. Just beyond the Town Hall, and in striking contrast to it, are the romantic spires and ramparts of Akershus Fortress, which dates from about 1300. This fascinating place is redolent of medieval and modern history. The occupying Nazis used it from 1940 to 1945, and, close beside the stone monument which honors the memory of the Norwegian patriots who were executed within these walls, is a very interesting and completely unembittered Resistance Museum. A military museum was also opened in 1978. Frogner Park is the scene of 150 groups of bronze and granite sculpture by Gustav Vigeland. Opinions vary as to the esthetic and plastic value of this huge lava flow of sculpture. See it for yourself—you can hardly avoid it—and if you like it, go to the artist's studio at Nobelsgate 32, now the Vigeland Museum. For one of the few reminders of medieval Oslo visit St. Halvard's Square; and for the best view of the city take the trolley to Sjømannsskolen, the Merchant Marine Academy. From the front terrace there you can see the harbor, the two fjords, and the old and new towns.

The most rewarding of Oslo's many excursions is to Bygdøy. You take the boat marked "til Bygdønes og Dronningen" from the Pipervika or wharves behind the Town Hall and dock in front of a wedge-shaped building that houses the famous polar ship, *Fram,* the vessel on which Fridtjof Nansen and Roald Amundsen traveled farther north and farther south than any other ship has ever been before or since. Rigging and all equipment are still intact. A harpoon's throw away is the museum, built in 1957, which contains another symbol of modern Viking courage, the famous *Kon Tiki* balsa raft, which carried Thor Heyerdahl, four of his countrymen, one Swede and one parrot (international type!) 4,800 miles from Peru to Polynesia, and "Ra II," in which he drifted across the Atlantic in 1970. Apex of a seafaring triangle is the Maritime Museum, which presents the whole story of Norway's success on the seven seas. Farther inland is the greatest memorial of all to Norway's seafaring prowess, three original Viking vessels—the Tune ship, the Oseberg ship, and the Gokstad ship. Also at Bygdøy is the Folklore Museum, one of the most impressive in the world. In addition to over 80,000 exhibits there are 150 original houses, barns, *stabburs,* etc., brought from every part of Norway, painting a vivid picture of Norwegian life and culture through the ages. Don't miss the Gol stave church, built around 900 A.D. of wood, in an extraordinary mixture of pagan and Christian symbolism.

At Høvikodden, you can visit the magnificent collection of 20th-century art given to Norway, together with its museums, by the late Sonja Henie and her husband Niels Onstad. Another excursion is by No. 36 bus from Groenlands Torg to Sundvollen, passing through the magnificent scenery of Tyri Fjord. On arrival, you can take a lift up to Kongens Utsikt for a superb view (but this involves some walking). The same bus goes to Hadeland Glass Works, where one can see the traditional glassblowing arts which have been in continuous operation for 200 years. One can buy souvenirs in the shop.

The organized tours of Oslo are well worth taking, especially the "grand tour" and the evening "folklore tour"; information from hotels or the Oslo Tourist office.

PRACTICAL INFORMATION FOR OSLO

 HOTELS. Hotels are graded according to price, location and size, and standards are high, but none can be considered inexpensive with the possible exception of the "summer hotels." The term *turisthotell* denotes a first-class resort establishment near some scenic attraction.

DELUXE

SCANDINAVIA, facing the Royal Palace, 21 stories, several restaurants, night-club, indoor pool.

GRAND, traditional but renovated, top floor bar, pool, restaurant with dancing.

BRISTOL, centrally located on a quiet side street; grill room.

CONTINENTAL, across the street from National Theater, restaurant and popular theater café.

FIRST CLASS

Carlton, near main downtown area, every room with bath; restaurant.
KNA, near town center, run by the Royal Automobile Club; every room with bath.
Norum, in residential section near Frogner Park; restaurant.
Ambassadeur, near Royal Palace, recently refurbished; sauna and pool.
Viking, near the East Station, rather small rooms but superb view from 13th floor restaurant.

Globetrotter, at Fornebu Airport; all rooms with bath or shower.

Helsfyr, Stromsveien. New hotel should be opened in 1979 (260 beds).

Esso Motor Hotel, Baerumsveien 305. Opening 1979, all rooms with bath or shower. Suitable for disabled visitors.

Stefan. Rosenkrantzgt Unlicensed. Comfortable. 200 beds.

Mullerhotel Grefsen, Grefsenkollveien 12. Modern, comfortable. 41 rooms, all with shower. Ten minutes by car; 20 minutes by tram.

Astoria, in quiet district; restaurant.

Nobel, in town center; bistro and bar.

West, just behind Royal Palace, charmingly small with excellent cuisine.

MODERATE

Garden, near the palace, cosily old-fashioned, some rooms with bath; *Bondeheimen,* central, some rooms with bath, pleasant; *Filadelfia,* central, some rooms with bath; *Forbundshotellet* is near the palace, comfortable, some rooms with bath; *Norrøna,* central, some rooms with bath.

Ansgar Misjonshotel, a block from the flower market; and *Indremisjonshotellet,* central, some rooms with bath, are unlicensed.

RESTAURANTS. All the major hotels have dining rooms where both cuisine and service are generally very good. Oslo's restaurants have plenty to offer in quality and variety, but there are certain liquor licensing restrictions, particularly on weekends. Restaurants are rated expensive (E), moderate (M), but these are comparative terms applicable to Norway only.

EXPENSIVE

BLOM'S in courtyard of Karl Johansgate 41. Bohemian décor, chic, piano music; price reflects quality. Many original works of art, and coats of arms of well-known people. Closed Sundays.

FROGNERSETEREM, with marvelous view at Holmenkollen. Norwegian specialties.

WESSELS KRO, Stortingsgrata 6. Distinctive interior. Fish and traditional food.

REGNBUEN, Klingenberggate 4, is Oslo's largest dinner-dancing place; floor-show.

TRE KOKKER, Drammensveien 30, serves fine meals and is expertly run.

FRASCATI'S, Stortingsgate 20, is a relaxing spot just across from the National Theater.

NAJADEN, in the Maritime Museum at Bygdøynes, very smart.

CARAVELLE, at Fornebu Airport, has excellent food, dinner dancing, and an adjoining cafeteria.

DRONNINGEN, at Bygdøy, is open summer only; dinner dancing overlooking the fjord, intimate upstairs bar.

CHRISTIANIA GLASSMAGASIN, Stortorvet. Cafeteria and restaurant. Good value. Closed Sundays.

THE SCOTSMAN, Karl Johansgt 17. Pizza, pub and steakhouse. Good value.

SORIA MORIA, Vogtsgt 64. Old district restaurant. Good cuisine.

VILLA SANDVIGEN, by Lake Gjersjøen on Gamle Mossevei, 20 minutes by car from Oslo. 100-year-old posting inn. First-class restaurant. Not far from Roald Amundsen's home Svartskog. (Bus 77, Drobak to Sandvigen.)

MODERATE

Two charming old inns serving typical Norwegian fare are *Stortorvets Gjaest-giveri,* Grensen 1, and *Engebrets Kafe,* Bankplassen 1.

Telle, Fr. Nansens Plass 4, is small, quite exclusive.

Theater Grill, around the corner from the Continental Hotel, very good value for food and décor.

Bagatelle, Bygdøy Alle 3, for French cuisine.

Gallagher's, Karl Johansgate 10, serves steaks and pancakes American-style.

Kongen, in Bygdøy at the end of the pier, is a lively place with dancing and floorshow; summer only.

Al Capone, Olavsgate, modern bodega bar with dancing.

Munkedammen, opposite the concert hall, is a good place for lunch.

 MUSEUMS. Oslo's museums include the National Gallery (Scandinavian and continental painting and sculpture); the Historical Museum (celebrating its 150-year Jubilee from December 1979.); Artists' House (changing exhibitions of fine and applied arts); the Applied Art Museum (Kunstindrustrimuset) whose collection includes the Baldishol tapestry from 1180; the Munch Museum; Monastery ruins at Hovedøya (ferry from Vippetangen) built by English monks who arrived in 1147; Teknisk Museum (moved in 1978 to Frysja district; the world's oldest ski museum at Holmenkollen; and many art galleries (see Oslo Guide from Tourist Office).

 ENTERTAINMENT. In Oslo the drama has been elevated to a position of unusual importance. Foremost is the *National Theater,* rich in classic and modern drama. Other theaters are the *New* and the *Norwegian,* which specializes in ultra-native versions of Holberg and Ibsen, and contemporary works. There is a philharmonic orchestra and national opera (with ballet). Several restaurants have cabaret and floorshows; there are many nightclubs, and restaurants with dancing to 2 A.M. Spirits are not served after 11 P.M., and there are no hostesses. Typical floorshows at *Rosekjellern* and *Regnbuen.*

 SHOPPING. Permanent sales exhibitions at Arts and Crafts Center (in the arcades behind the Cathedral), Karl Johans gate 11 *Forum,* Rosenkrantzgate 7, *Husfliden,* Mollergata 4, *Norway Designs* A/S, Stortingsgate 28 (with special facilities for export, and efficient English-speaking personnel).

FURS. Seal and fox are the specialties. *Pels Backer,* Kongensgate 31; *Walker,* Prinsengate 18; *Thorkildsen,* N. Slottsgate 9.

KNITWEAR. *Heimen,* Kristian 4desgate 4 (and regional costumes to order); *William Schmidt & Co.,* Karl Johansgate 41.

SILVER. *David Andersen's,* Karl Johansgate 20, manufacturer of the famous "David Andersen Enamel"; *J. Tostrup's,* Karl Johansgate 25.

Skiing in Norway
The valley of Morgedal in the mountains of Telemark is the cradle of modern skiing, but the best known resorts are those situated along the railway lines that run across south Norway from Oslo to Bergen, and northward from Oslo to Trondheim, as well as along the approaches to the Jotunheim Mountains. The ski season generally lasts from December to the end of April with spring the best time for sun and snow though all resorts are then jammed packed and you have to book months in advance. There is summer skiing at Stryn in the Jotunheims and many other places. Oslo itself has some excellent ski runs with lifts and floodlit for nighttime skiing. Economy is a major attraction with most resorts geared to a family-type atmosphere.

PRACTICAL INFORMATION FOR SKIING AREAS

BERGEN-OSLO RAIL RESORTS

FINSE. *Hotel Finse.* Comfortable, 35 rooms with shower.

GEILO. *Holms,* renowned, has nightclub. *Bardøla,* modern and popular. *Highland,* special appeal to English skiers; *Geilo Sportel,* log-style with excellent cabins. *Ustedalen Hoyfjellshotell,* indoor pool, 50 rooms with shower.

GOL. *Pers,* indoor pool, chalets for hire. *Thorstens Motel.* Several inexpensive hotels.

USTAOSET. *Ustaoset. Ustaoset Motel.*

VOSS. *Park Hotel Liland. Fleischer,* traditional. *Voss Youth Hostel.*

TELEMARK RESORTS

BOLKESJÖ. *Bolkesjö,* charming. *Uppigard,* superior pension.

MORGEDAL. *Morgedal,* well equipped.

RAULAND. *Rauland.*

OSLO DISTRICT

KONGSBERG. *Grand. Gyldenlöve.*

NOREFJELL. *Sole,* by the lake. *Fjellhvil* and *Norefjellstua* (Ski Association's lodge) on mountainside.

GUDBRANDSDAL

LILLEHAMMER. *Victoria, Smestad Summerhotell,* and *Kronen* are pleasant. Nearby, Nordseter and Sjusjøen: try the *Halla Fjellstue* (mountain inn) at the former, the *Rustad* at the latter.

North of Lillehammer is Tretten and in the mountains above the *Gausdal* and *Skeikampen* hotels, both of them top-raters.

Running north from Lillehammer, up the Gudbrandsdalen is Vinstra, with the spacious and attractive log-style *Fefor Mountain Hotel.*

VALDRES-JOTUNHEIMEN

BEITOSTÖLEN. *Beito Höyfjellshotel* and *Beitostølen Høyfjellshotel.* Several pensions and mountain inns.

FAGERNES. Best is the recent *Fagernes.*

TYINKRYSSET-NYSTOVA. *Nystuen,* pleasant; several inexpensive mountain pensions.

Bergen and Stavanger

Bergen, an important port on Norway's west coast, is strung out from north to south between the fjord and spectacular mountain slopes. Birthplace of Edvard Grieg and Ole Bull, this ancient Hanseatic city has much to offer. The animated Torget fish market is fascinating, and so are the surviving 17th-century warehouses, and the Bergenhus Fortress with the Haakon's Hall, a restored example of Bergen's 13th-century architecture. The Hanseatic Museum is rich in ancient equipment and furniture. See the 12th-century Mariakirken (St. Mary's Church) and Gamle Bergen (Old Bergen), a collection of pleasant early 19th-century houses with a period restaurant, and the modern aquarium.

Stavanger, founded in the eighth century, is an interesting town with old streets and houses side by side with modern buildings. Norway's fourth city (after Oslo, Bergen and Trondheim), it is the fish canning capital of Europe, and the heart of Norway's North Sea oil hopes. The town has expanded considerably in recent years but still retains its charm; its marketplace, at the head of Vagen, is a riot of color with fish, flowers, vegetables and fruit, and attracts the country people from miles around. The city's pride is its Anglo-Norman cathedral of the late 11th century.

Some of Stavanger's sights are outside the city precincts. Said to be the oldest homestead in Northern Europe, Viste Cave is several thousand years old. But when it comes to excursions, there is nothing to beat the dramatic Lysefjord. This, and the deep-sea fishing jaunts, run on the principle "no catch—no cash" on board the *Sea Queen,* are Stavanger musts.

From Stavanger, Norway's southernmost resort area stretches down along the island-dotted coast and almost back to Oslo. Increasingly popular with ferry passengers from England.

Trondheim

Trondheim, a good starting point for cruises to the Land of the Midnight Sun, is a delightful city with a "colonial" air about it. Its famous Nidaros Cathedral, in the English Gothic style, is one of the prides of Norway. Also impressive is the Stiftsgarden, or royal residence, a magnificent rococo structure dating from 1775, the second largest domestic wooden building in Scandinavia (the largest is a students' hostel, also in Trondheim). The Bishop's Palace is a fine relic of Trondheim's medieval glory, and the whole town has an atmosphere worthy of its historic position as the coronation place of Norway's kings.

The surrounding countryside, immortalized by Sigrid Undset in *Kristin Lavransdatter,* is beautiful. The Bymarka region, 20 minutes from the center of town by bus or train, is an inexpensive must for winter sports fans.

PRACTICAL INFORMATION FOR THE CITIES

BERGEN. Hotels: Top is the *Norge* (L), 238 rooms with bath, central, over-looking the park. Excellent *Norge Grill* with dinner-dancing (expensive), *Karjolen* bar, and popular *Hjørnet* café.

Bristol, central, fully licensed bar, restaurant, dancing; *Orion,* modern, most rooms with bath, fine position overlooking harbor, both (1).

Slottsgarden, modern, overlooking harbor, half of rooms with bath; *Grand Hotel Terminus,* opposite rail station, 115 rooms, 60 with bath; *Toms,* recent, most rooms with bath; *Neptun,* most of its rooms with bath, good restaurant.

Students' hostels converted to summer hotels (mid-June to end August): *Hatleberg, Fantoft* and *Alrek* (best), on the outskirts.

Lower-priced hotels include the *Rosenkrantz* and the *Hordaheimen. Augustin, Bergen, Turistheim, Skandia.*

Pensions: Fagerheim in Kalvedalsveien, and the equally well-managed *Park* in Parkveien.

Montana Youth Hostel commands a wonderful view and is undoubtedly the finest in Europe. Situated near the aerial cableway to Mount Ulriken. 200 beds, open May through September.

Restaurant: *Bellevue* is a vista-rich period-style spot.

KRISTIANSAND. Hotels: *Caledonian* (1), 130 rooms with bath; *Ernst,* traditional, some rooms with bath, and *Fregatten,* modern, both (2). *Metropole* and *Norge* (3). *Bondeheimen.*

STAVANGER. Hotels: *SAS Royal Atlantic,* 116 rooms, most with bath. Facing a park, this is an excellent hotel with atmospheric *Mortepumpen* restaurant (expensive), also folk dancing as a weekly event.

KNA Ocean, 70 rooms with bath or shower, bar-grill and rooftop restaurant. *Victoria,* 55 rooms, 14 with bath. Has the popular *Place Pigalle,* French cooking, dancing.

St. Svithun Hotel, mission hotel.

Esso Motel, on outskirts, is recent.

Two miles south of town, at Tjensvoll 4, the *Alstor* has 45 rooms half with bath; dinner-dancing.

Money-savers are *Gjesteheimen, Kristelig, Sjøfartsheim, Melands Hospits, Øglands Hospits.*

TRONDHEIM. Hotels: *Prinsen,* 100 rooms, most with bath, *Britannia,* most rooms with bath. The *Astoria,* most rooms with bath.

Phoenix and *Sentrum,* both have some rooms with bath.

Studentbyen (best), rooms with bath or shower; *Trøndelag Misjonshotell.*

Restaurants: Palmen (E), excellent; *Nausloftet* (M) for seafood and gay décor; *Tavern Inn* (I), at the Folk Museum.

The Fjords

Norway's two principal tourist attractions are spread quite widely over this elongated country, and they require a good deal of traveling, but they are worth every minute and mile of it—first, the incomparable fjords, and, second, that much-advertised, much-described terrain within the Arctic Circle, the fabulous Land of the Midnight Sun.

The most comfortable way to see the magnificent scenery of Norway's fjords is by steamer, but you can get a good impression by taking the trip by car and ferry, and they can also be seen by bus and train. A number of excellent package tours by bus and fjord steamer are available.

The Sognefjord (110 miles) is the longest of these narrow inlets, and at Balholm you will realize the full magnitude of this scenery, with towering snow-capped mountains dropping 4,000 feet to a fjord no wider than a city street and dwarfing the steamer to the proportions of a toy. Here the normal grandeur of the surroundings is further embellished at the end of May by hundreds of apple and cherry trees in full blossom at the base of the snow-capped mountains. (Daily 13-hour fast boat trips leave Bergen at 8 A.M.)

Near here, a slim finger of the Sognefjord, the Fjaerlandsfjord, probes toward Jostedalsbreen, Norway's biggest glacier. Near the head of the fjord, the Suphelle Glacier, like a massive avalanche, pushes its glittering ice over the precipice. Many visitors consider the Hardanger Fjord even more beautiful than the Sognefjord. This is an ideal vacation spot, especially in May and in September, when the orchards are heavy with ripe fruit. Access to Ulvik is easy: by rail from Bergen or Oslo on the Oslo-Bergen line, with a transfer at Voss. Even better is to take the autocar from Bergen to Norheimsund, then board the fjord steamer that goes direct to Ulvik. About 45 miles north of Ulvik, at the top of impressive Stalheim Gorge, is the superior Stalheim Hotel, with a marvelous view of the valley below and its waterfalls. There is trout and salmon fishing in the River Nerøy.

The Land of the Midnight Sun

You can drive the 1,200 miles from Oslo to Kirkenes on a good to indifferent road, but that isn't exactly restful. The best bet, if you have the time, is to go by local steamer from Bergen or Trondheim. Once you have crossed the invisible parallel of 66° 33', you are north of the Arctic Circle, in the Land of the Midnight Sun. The effect is that of a combined sunset and sunrise. After three days of cruising through stupendous scenery, you reach Hammerfest, the northernmost city in the world. On leaving Hammerfest, you have 24 hours sailing past that famous chunk of rock known as the North Cape. If you want to explore this Ultima Thule of Europe at close quarters, get off the boat in the fishing village, Skarsvag, and board the bus which will take you to North Cape. Relax in the welcoming restaurant 1,007 foot above the Arctic Ocean, then cover the 22 miles to Honningsvaag, also by bus, and reboard your ship. The road is narrow, winding and dramatic, and it passes a colorful Lapp encampment at Nordmannset. If you get off the boat at Honningsvaag instead, you can park yourself at the Grand Hotel and take the midnight bus to North Cape. Here, if the weather is kind, you can face the glowing Midnight Sun across the Arctic waters.

But the rest of the trip is not at all an anticlimax. When you rejoin the boat it will be steering a southeast course along the coast of East Finnmark until you reach the end station of this historic route of northern Norway—the important shipping and mining town of Kirkenes. From Kirkenes, you have two ways of returning to Trondheim: by plane, with landings at Lakselv, Alta, Bardufoss, Bodø and Trondheim, or by bus or car, specifically three days to either Tromsø or Narvik, with two overnight stops, or from Bodø you can go South by train. The plane trip offers a wonderful bird's-eye view of the top of Norway, but the slower route overland is more rewarding, more intimately connected with the arctic glories of Finnmark. If you have time, do it this way; this is the heart of Norway.

Tromsø has a cable car which will take you 2,400 feet up to the top of the Fløy Mountain, where you can have a meal overlooking the town and surrounding countryside. Its modern mile-long bridge connects the island downtown district with the new suburbs on the mainland. At the mainland approach to the bridge is one of northern Europe's most stupendous modern churches.

PRACTICAL INFORMATION FOR FJORDS AND NORTHERN NORWAY

FJORDS

ANDALSNES. *Grand Hotel Bellevue,* very comfortable.

BALESTRAND. *Kvikne,* long-standing high reputation. *Kringsja.*

FØRDE. *Sunnfjord,* modern.

GEIRANGER. *Union,* comfortable, excellent cold table. *Geiranger* and *Meroks.*

LOEN. *Alexandra,* large, excellent cold table (family run). *Richards Motel.*

OLDEN. *Yris, Olden Fjord,* comfortable, rebuilt. Should reopen in 1979.

SKEI. (Lake Jölster) *Skei,* comfortable, excellent trout.

SOGNDAL. *Sogndal,* modern, comfortable, pretty position. *Hofslund* and *Park Minitell.*

STALHEIM. *Stalheim,* stupendous view overlooking valley. Open summer only.

STRANDEBARM. *Strandebarm Fjord Hotell,* comfortable, modern.

ULVIK. *Brakanes,* wonderful view. *Ulvik Turist* and *Strand.*

NORTHERN NORWAY

ALTA. *Alta New Hotel. Alta Hotel.*

BODO. *SAS Royal,* modern. *Grand.*

HAMMERFEST. *Grand Nordic,* modern. *Finnmarksbo,* summer hotels.

HARSTAD. *Viking Nordic. Grand.*

KARASJOK. *Karasjok Gjestgiveri,* good.

KAUTOKEINO. *Kautokeino,* good food.

LOFOTEN ISLANDS. (Svolvaer) *Lofoten Nordic,* new. *Havly.*

MO-I-RANA. *Meyergarden. Holmen.*

NARVIK. *Grand,* recently renovated. *Den sovende Dronning,* comfortable; *Wivel.*

TROMSO. *SAS Royal; Grand Nordic; Polar Nordic;* all expensive. *Saga,* comfortable.

POLAND

Poland is a squarish country lying between Eastern Germany and the U.S.S.R., in a geographic position that has made its history one of almost continuous warfare. It is about the size (121,000 square miles) of New Mexico or the British Isles, and its population has, since the territorial changes and human losses of World War II, consisted predominantly of Polish-speaking Roman Catholics. Due to the loss of some six million people (half of them Jews) during the war, followed by an extended baby boom, over half of the present population of 35 million is under thirty—making Poland one of the most youthful countries in Europe. Every one of its major cities with the exception of medieval Krakow is recently built (or restored) after the wholesale destruction of the war. Particularly splendid restoration work has been done on Warsaw's Old Town and in Gdansk on the Baltic coast.

Poland, a late-comer to the international tourist boom, has now thrown itself into the business of entertaining foreign visitors with zest. Impressive new hotels, some built by western construction companies and now run with western know-how, have gone up in Warsaw and provincial centers in the past few years, including eastern Europe's first Holiday Inn, in Krakow.

Moderately expensive as a tourist destination, Poland offers a wide variety of outdoor holiday activities: unexcelled hunting and fishing in the lush lake and forest regions, first-class skiing in the dramatic Tatra and Karkonosze Mountains; swimming and sailing in the innumerable lakes or at the splendid Baltic beaches, where the sea may be a bit coolish for western tastes. Whatever your reason for going—to look up relatives, take in the annual Poznan Fair or merely stop over on your way else-where—the Poles will be glad to see you.

Poland Today

Under communist rule since 1947-48, Poland is now seeing a consumer boom, combined with a vast modernization program based on new machinery and up-to-date know-how bought from the West. The policy of rapidly increasing real wages (by about 40 percent in five years) has kept the population happy, the new purchasing power itself leading to some fresh shortages. But the regime is loyalty itself towards the Soviet Union, a loyalty seen as the price of being able to get away with a good many unorthodox things on the home front.

Despite all that they have been through, most Poles these days are not interested in taking the path of westward emigration, followed by so many millions among Poland's pre-war generations. Living are are, lower than in America, and people often have to take second jobs to provide for other than basic necessities. But Poles eat well, drink a great deal—and mostly in cafés and restaurants where you will have little difficulty in joining them—and fashions in everything from pop music to clothes freely follow the West. Political satire as well as sheer entertainment draw well over capacity crowds at nightclubs, and indeed if you want to get in, you had better get there early to join the queue, unless you can get tickets specially reserved through friends (the extent to which everybody seems to know everybody in Warsaw's cultural life will amaze you.)

Urban life is, however, by no means the whole story, as anyone traveling through Poland in a car or by train will soon realize. The Polish peasantry, religious and conservative and now largely uncollectivized with 75 percent of the land in private hands, has done especially well out of the new policies since 1970. Rural life is nevertheless centered on the home and work in the fields and the raising of animals in fairly traditional, not to say hidebound, ways. Horses abound as a means of transportation to an extent now unknown in much of the rest of eastern Europe.

Food and Drink

Polish food is basically Slavic with Baltic overtones, meaning an interesting variety of soups and meats (with emphasis on pork) as well as fresh water fish. Pastries are rich, delectable.

Some of the best typically Polish meals are to be found in the villages and market towns where delicious *barszcz* (beetroot) soup is served in large helpings along with sausage, cabbage, potatoes, sour cream, *czarny chleb* (coarse rye bread) and beer. *Chlodnik* is a cold, rich cream soup with crayfish. Other dishes are: *Flaki,* a very select dish of tripe, served boiled or fried; *Bigos,* sauerkraut with smoked meats; *Kolduny,* small lamb meat turnovers. Bottled *Zywiec* (beer) is delicious. Western drinks (whisky, gin, brandy) can be had at most bars, but are extremely expensive. *Wodka,* of course, is a Polish specialty; some brands are flavored with forest herbs *(Zubrowka).* And by all means try Polish mead, a honey wine.

PRACTICAL INFORMATION FOR POLAND

13.06
5.34
24.00
42.30

WHAT WILL IT COST? A 21-month price freeze is keeping costs at a stable level until well into 1979. Poland's **hotel** prices are about the same throughout its major cities, mountain and seaside resorts (low season prices from October 1 to April 1. Can be up to 50% less). Approximate prices quoted here are for room with bath and breakfast: deluxe single: $35-$45, double: $50-$70; first-class single: $25, double: $35; moderate single: $15-$22, double: $25-$30. Rooms without bath available at lower cost; prices outside Warsaw are generally less. In the countryside, there are plenty of colorful roadside inns, providing inexpensive lodging and home cooking.

Restaurants: Expensive (E) around 250-400 zl., moderate (M) 200-250 zl., inexpensive from around 100 zl.

Other costs: guide-interpreter for 1-9 persons for 4 hours about 430 zl.; opera tickets from 100 zl.; theater and concert tickets from 50 zl.; movies from 15 zl.; hairdresser about 80 zl. for women, 30 for men; museums from 5 zl. or free; foreign cigarettes between 35-45 zl. A short coach tour with guide costs about 200 zl.

CAPITAL. Warsaw.

LANGUAGE. Polish. But English, German and French spoken in hotels and understood in the larger cities.

CLIMATE. Quite varied. Tatra mountains have alpine weather, with warm air current *(halny)* in winter: springtime can be windy, autumn long and sunny.

Average maximum daily temperatures in Fahrenheit and centigrade:

Warsaw	Jan.	Feb.	Mar.	Apr.	May	June	July	Aug.	Sept.	Oct.	Nov.	Dec.
F°	34	36	46	55	66	72	75	73	68	57	45	39
C°	1	2	8	13	19	22	24	23	20	14	7	4

SPECIAL EVENTS. *March:* Jazz on the Odra and Students' Art Festival at Wroclaw. *May:* Polish and International chamber music festival, Lancut; Festival of Polish Contemporary Plays, Wroclaw; Festival of 15 mm. International Films, Krakow; International Book Fair, Warsaw. *May-December:* Symphonic and chamber music concerts in courtyard of Royal Castle, Krakow. *June:* Festival of Polish Song, Opole; Folklore festivals, Plock. *June 23:* Midsummer night (wianki) celebrations everywhere. *June-September:* Recitals of Chopin's music at composer's birthplace, Zelazowa Wola. *July-August: August:* International Festival of Music, Sopot; *September:* Oratorio and Cantata Festival, Wroclaw; International Festival of Song and Dance Ensembles, Zielona Gora; International Festival of Contemporary Music, "The Warsaw Autumn", Warsaw. *October:* International Jazz Festival, Warsaw. *November-December:* Presentation of year's most outstanding dramas, Warsaw. *December:* Exhibition of best Christmas creches, Krakow.

WHEN TO GO. December-March for winter sports, spring-summer for pleasant sightseeing, in autumn to get the most out of the cities' cultural life.

HOW TO GO. Foreign travel to Poland is handled by the Polish travel office *Orbis,* Intraco Building, 2 Stawki and 16 Bracka, both in Warsaw, 500 Fifth Ave., New York, N.Y. 10036, 333 N. Michigan Ave., Chicago, Ill. 60601, and 313 Regent St., London W1. There are branch offices in the main cities and towns. Orbis operates the best hotels and pensions in Poland. Through its representatives abroad, it arranges group and individual tours to Poland, shooting parties, and is responsible for everything connected with your trip. Examples of tour prices ex-UK, including return flight, are: from £95 for a weekend in Warsaw or from £125 for a week in Krakow (room and breakfast); from £220 for two weeks visiting four main centers (mainly half board); or from £315 for a two-week grand tour of Poland (full board). You can also join an Orbis tour once you're in Poland (a 9-14 days all inclusive tour costs from $200-$400).

Commercial traveling is handled primarily by Orbis' subsidiary, *Polorbis,* 82 Mortimer St., London W1; student trips by *Almatour,* 9 Ordynacka, 00-953 Warsaw, who put young people up in hostels for about $6 (£3.25) per day full board.

Orbis is represented in most Western countries by accredited travel agents, who will handle all arrangements for your trip, including visa, hotel accommodation and prepayment. Plan your trip as far ahead as possible, allow one month for your travel agent to arrange details. In Poland, look out for "it" stands or kiosks from which information of all kinds is available in airports, railway stations, hotels, big stores, etc.

For the last few years American Travel Abroad, Inc., 250 W. 57th St., New York, N.Y. 10019, and some of their associates, Wegiel Travel Service, Inc., 1985 Main St., Springfield, Mass. 01103, and also agencies associated with SPATA— Society of Polish American Travel Agents—are the most prominent promoters and organizers of charters to Poland. They handle bookings of groups and individuals.

In the United States

Thomas Cook, 587 Fifth Ave., New York 10017
General Tours, 49 West 57th St., New York 10019
Maupintour, 900 Massachusetts St., Lawrence, Kansas 66044
Travelworld, 6922 Hollywood Blvd., Los Angeles, Calif. 90028
American Travel Abroad, 250 W. 57th St., New York, N.Y. 10019.

In Great Britain

Polorbis Travel, 82 Mortimer St., Regent St., London WIN 7DE.
Magic of Poland, 100 Dean St., Oxford St., London W1V 6AQ.
Peltours, 72 Wigmore St., London W1H 0DD.
Balkan Holidays, 130 Regent St., London W1

TRAVEL DOCUMENTS. In order to obtain a visa you must have: a) signed valid passport, valid no less than three months from expected date of departure for Poland; b) duly executed application form with two signed photos. Persons under 16 years and included in family passport, no application required. Applications should be submitted at least 14 days before intended departure to any Polish consulate personally, by post, or through a travel agency; in New York: 233 Madison Ave., New York 10016; in London: 19 Weymouth St., W1. or 26 Buckingham Terrace, Great Western Road, Glasgow G12.

A visa costs $10 or £5.50, a transit visa valid for two days, $6 or £3.

All visitors must register within 24 hours at a hotel, campsite, or local administration authority.

CURRENCY EXCHANGE REQUIREMENTS: All visitors have to exchange the following amount of foreign currency per person per day: $12 or equivalent in pounds sterling. Exceptions are: people under 26 years of age and students, regardless of age, who pay $5 or sterling equivalent; campers who obtain camping coupons (from Orbis, valid only May 1 to September 30) who pay $5 or sterling equivalent; and foreign passport holders and their families whose Polish descent has been recognized by the Polish consulate, who pay $2.50 or sterling equivalent.

Exempt altogether from this obligatory daily currency exchange are: children under 16, transit visitors to neighboring countries, and visitors who have already prepaid for their stay either through vouchers or through package bookings.

The rate of exchange is currently about 33 zloty to the dollar, 63 to the £. **Subject to change.**

MONEY. You may bring in any amount of foreign currencies, including travelers checks, and exchange it at border points, air, sea and road, in most hotels, and at any Orbis exchange counter. Exchange of foreign currency outside of these permitted exchange offices is strictly forbidden and subject to penalties. The import and export of Polish currency is *not* permitted. Foreign currency thus imported must be declared upon arrival and recorded in a special certificate. When departing, you may take with you in foreign currency the balance of the declared amount, less sums exchanged for Polish money.

The major credit cards are accepted as are personal checks on the Euro-card scheme.

Poland's monetary unit, the *zloty,* is divided into 100 *groszy.* Banknotes are issued in 50, 100, 500 and 1,000 zlotys; coins in 1, 2, 5, 10, and 20 zloty, 1, 2, 5, 20, 50 groszy.

HOTELS. Hotel accommodation in Poland is available in six categories, but only Deluxe (L), 1A, and 1B are recommended to foreign visitors. In Category L you have a single or double room with bath in a deluxe hotel in Warsaw, Krakow or Poznan, the only cities with this grade of accommodation. Category 1 represents a good international standard and provides a single or double room with bath; Category B means a single or double room with or without bath in a similar hotel. You can take just bed and breakfast, demi-pension or full pension. Room reservations are from 2 P.M. to 2 P.M. next day at Orbis hotels; to 4 P.M. at others. Many hotels have more than one-class rooms.

You can also let a room en pension in a private dwelling through Orbis. Students and young people under 26 can be housed in hostels.

Motels. Orbis has built several *Novotels* along major routes, about 1B standard with restaurants serving regional specialties.

CAMPING. Camping coupons covering 120 sites throughout the country are available at a cost of £.295 per person per day. In addition to one-night stays, parking and registration fees, these entitle visitors to £.175 cash spending money. Campsite facilities include washroooms, canteens and nearby restaurants, food kiosks, and power sockets for touring caravans. These arrangements apply between May 1 and September 30.

TIPPING: Service charge is usually added to restaurant bills; if not, add 10 percent. Tipping not obligatory, but readily accepted; 5-10 zlotys is ample. Cab drivers get 10 percent.

HOW TO REACH POLAND. From New York and Montreal, *LOT* the Polish airline and *Pan Am* fly regularly to Warsaw. From London, *LOT* and *BA* have almost daily flights to Warsaw. Most major airlines also fly there from European capitals.

By Sea. From New York, occasional freighter service to Gdynia. Contact *Gdynia-America Line* or *Polish Ocean Lines,* both at 1 World Trade Center, New York 10048. From the UK, *Polish Ocean Lines* operate 11- to 12-day round trips to Poland on their monthly transatlantic service from Gdynia via Rotterdam and London to Montreal. Details from Stelp & Leighton, 238 City Road, London EC1V 2PR.

By train. From London to Warsaw via Hook of Holland about 32 hours. Second-class return fare is approximately £95. From Vienna, the Chopin Express takes 13 hours. Both have sleeping cars. During the peak season, several UK tour firms offer special deals on train services from London's Liverpool Street Station.

By car. Best route from England is via Harwich to Hook of Holland by night. An early start next morning from the Hook will bring you to the Polish frontier soon after 7 P.M. Or put your car on the Poland Auto-Couchette Express at the Hook. *Prins Ferries* have a car service from Harwich to Hamburg, Germany. Car ferries cross from Copenhagen (Denmark) and Ystad (Sweden) to Swinoujscie; from Helsinki (Finland) to Gdansk.

International drivers' license required. Visa a *must.* Third party insurance (green card) is required and can be purchased at the border.

By bus. From London to Poznan by *Europabus* and *Anglo-Polish Enterprises.* *Note:* Visas are not issued at border points.

CUSTOMS. Personal belongings may be brought in duty-free, including sports equipment (but guns and ammunition require Polish permit), musical instruments, typewriter, radio, two cameras with 24 films or 10 rolls film for each as well as 10 rolls film for one movie camera (16 mm.), one liter each of wine and spirits, and 250 cigarettes or 50 cigars or 250 grams tobacco.

Articles not exceeding 1,000 zl can be taken out of Poland, duty free. Also articles purchased at special shops for foreign currency or its equivalent in Polish currency, on presentation of sales receipts.

MAIL. An airmail letter to the US costs 9 zl., a postcard 7 zl. A letter to Great Britain costs 4.90 zl., a postcard 3.60 zl.

Telephones: Public telephones take a 1 zl coin. If you place a long-distance call from your hotel be sure to check the service charge; some hotels almost double the basic price of the call.

SPORTS. For *winter sports,* the most popular resorts are *Zakopane* in the Tatra mountains and Karpacz in the Karkonosze, where you'll find some Orbis hotels and facilities.

Swimming pools are found in most cities; sandy beaches along the Baltic coast and Mazury Lakes. Avoid swimming in the rivers.

Poland is definitely a *hunting* country, but fairly expensive. In a number of preserves stags, red-deer stags, roe bucks, lynx, wild boar, and Euro-bison are found, and you get a run for your money. Prices for accommodation, food and guide obtainable on request from Orbis.

Other sporting opportunities available are very varied. *Horse-riding* is popular. Bialy Bor stud farm has an excellent program, $15 a day plus $3.50 per hour per horse but other horse farms charge less. *Angling* in some of Europe's finest waters. License costs $12 a fortnight to $23 per week in the better rivers. *Sea yachting* (contact Polish Sailing Union, ul. Cholimska 14, Warsaw), or *ice boating.* Arrange details through your travel agency or directly with Orbis. *Cycling* is popular and well organized; bicycles can be rented and tours are arranged. *Gliding* and *canoeing* attract a lot of participants.

SPAS. *Ciechocinek* in central Poland is the country's largest and cures primarily circulatory disorders; *Krynica* in the Beskid mountains is famous for diabetic cures; *Kudowa* and *Polanica* both located in the Sudety mountains, the latter in an attractive wooded setting, specialize in the heart and circulatory system; *Kolobrzeg* in western Pomerania has physiotherapy for respiratory, circulatory and occupational diseases, as well as diabetes.

Rates are about $15-$25 per person per day in double room with bath, according to spa and season, including full board and out-patient treatment.

 TRAVEL IN POLAND. By air: *LOT,* operates daily flights linking all larger cities. Air fares are roughly double the train fares.

BY TRAIN: Internal train travel in Poland is quite cheap, but it is advisable to travel first class. For example, the 200-mile run from Warsaw to Krakow would cost about 300 zl. by first-class electric express; about 200 zl. by second-class. The excellent Polrailpass entitles bearer to unlimited travel for various periods: for 15 days, the cost is $45 first-class, $30 second-class. You can buy this in your own country.

BY BUS: Buses service areas not covered by rail routes. Can be enlightening for the adventurous.

BY TAXI: Taxies are metered and cost about 5 zl. per km.

BY CAR: Cars drive on right; usual Continental rules of the road prevail. Motor traffic is sparse, but roads tend to be narrow and cluttered with horse-driven carts on country roads. Main highways are adequate; the trunk road across Poland from East Germany via Poznan and Warsaw to Brest-Litovsk on the U.S.S.R. frontier is an excellent concrete or tarmacadam highway with occasional patches of uneven cobbles. Speed limit on the open road is 100 kilometers per hour, in built-up areas, 50 kilometers per hour. Blowing of horns is forbidden in developed areas, under penalty by law.

Motor fuel and lubricants may be purchased freely at all service stations. These are found in main towns and are usually open between 6 A.M. and 10 P.M., but many stations are open 24 hours For repairs consult the Polish Motor Union *(Polski Zwiazek Motorowy)* or its branches, 6-14 Krucza Street, Warsaw. Bring a spare-part kit with you.

Gasoline coupons, giving about 15 percent reduction on local prices, (not reimbursable) can be bought through a travel agent, at Orbis hotels and offices and at the Polish motoring office (see above). Coupon booklets come in sets of ten and cost about £7.10 for 40 liters (about 8½ gallons) for 94 octane fuel, a bit less for 78 octane. For one coupon you can obtain 4 liters super, or 5 liters normal grade gasoline, or 1 liter lubricating oil.

Car Hire. *Avis* at the airport and at Krakowskie Przedmiescie 13, Warsaw. Cars may be rented from Orbis offices in several towns, at Warsaw airport and a number of hotels. Fly/drive arrangements are also available: from £105 ex-UK for a week in Warsaw with unlimited mileage. Rates are about $10 per day plus insurance and mileage at 11¢ per kilometer. Also available are chauffeur-driven Fiat 132 cars.

Hitchhiking. Poland is one of the few countries that does not frown on this method of travel. Hitchhikers can buy special books of coupons at border points, tourist information centers, etc., and, on obtaining a lift, give drivers the appropriate coupons covering the distance they plan to ride. Drivers who collect the largest number of coupons during the year actually receive prizes. A system of inexpensive accommodation for hitchhikers has also been evolved. Directing this unusual aspect of travel is the Hitchhiking Committee (Komitet Autostopu), ul. Narbutta 27a, Warsaw.

MISCELLANEOUS. *Photography:* not allowed to take photographs from the air, nor of industrial and transport installations.
Electricity: 220 volts AC.
Newspapers: Klub Miedzynarodowej Prasy i Ksiazki, Al. Jerozolimskie, Warsaw, has numerous foreign publications.

Warsaw

In January, 1945, Warsaw—Poland's capital since the 17th century—was a heart-breaking desert of ruin and rubble, a prostrate victim of systematic Nazi destruction. In that same year, only a third of its pre-war population remained; of its half-million Jews, some 200 were still alive. But Warsaw's survivors, determined to rebuild their ancient city, set about the task so energetically that today a new Warsaw of a million-plus inhabitants amazes its visitors. This phoenix even includes painstakingly accurate replicas of Warsaw's historic old quarters.

With ironic humor, Warsaw citizens will tell you that the best vantage-point from which to admire the view of their rebuilt city is atop the 37-story Palace of Culture and Science. Why? Because it's the only spot from which you can avoid looking at the Palace of Culture and Science—a wedding-cake skyscraper, personal gift from Stalin. From this pinnacle you can see the river Vistula to the east, with two of its bridges, the Slasko-Dabrowski and the Poniatowskiego, crossing to the Praga side of the city. To the north, on the bluff above the river, lies the faithfully reconstructed Old Town of Warsaw, with its ancient market place, Pod Blacha Palace, Sigismund Column, the rebuilt and refurnished Royal Palace, and Barbican Wall. Here you will find outdoor exhibitions of modern paintings by local artists. The busy main thoroughfares, Krakowskie Przedmiescie and Nowy Swiat, lead to the parks and palaces of Belvedere and Lazienki, fine examples of neo-Classic Polish architecture, and the 18th-century Theater on the Isle. You can visit the living replica of the town's old marketplace, the cobble-stoned Rynek Starego Miasta with its pastel house fronts, charmingly uneven roofs and wrought-iron grillwork. All over the Old Town, churches, palaces, and lovely burghers' houses have been restored just as they were before the war on the basis of plans and documents which miraculously survived the devastation.

If you cross the bridge near Rynek Starego Miasta, you come to the Zoological Gardens. Cross by the Poniatowskiego bridge to get to the giant Zieleniecka stadium. Along the river opposite the Stadium are many foreign embassies.

Warsaw's Hinterland

North: Seven miles north of Warsaw is Mlociny with its Ethnographic Museum, situated in a beautiful old park on the banks of the Vistula.

West: Zelazowa Wola (35 miles from Warsaw) is the place where Chopin was born. The charming little country house with its lovely garden is now a museum. Each Sunday, from June to Sept. Chopin's music is played by Poland's most famous pianists or guest artists from abroad. On your way back, drive through the primeval forest, an elk reserve near Kampinos, and visit Palmiry Cemetery, scene of mass executions of Polish hostages by the Nazis.

South: At Wilanow southeast of Warsaw, visit the old palace of King Jan Sobieski, one of Poland's loveliest residences, now a museum with a rich collection of paintings and antiques. Here, too, is a Poster Museum. At Czersk, 30 miles south of Warsaw on the same road, is the lovely medieval castle of the Mazowiecki princes since 732. Kazimierz-Dolny, an hour out along the Vistula, is a picturesque village with relics of Polish Renaissance architecture. A favorite with artists. Lowicz, 50 miles from Warsaw, a folklore center, has a fascinating museum in a 17th-century Baroque Palace. The Palace of the Radziwill family, with original 17th-century furniture, is at Nieborow, 55 miles out. Arkadia, 57 miles away, has a lovely 17th-century park with many statues and monuments. About 100 miles southeast of Warsaw is Lublin, one of the oldest cities in Poland. At the entrance to the old part of town is the curious Gothic Krakowski Gate and the castle which towers over the city. Old Lublin harbors magnificent churches, delightful houses, secretive nooks, vaulted archways and romantic courtyards. Nearby Pulawy is the site of the Czartoryski's palace. Zamosc is the best preserved Renaissance architectural complex in Poland.

PRACTICAL INFORMATION FOR WARSAW

WHEN TO GO. Warsaw is best visited from May to mid-October. Winters are likely to be severe or dreary; summers warm and dry.

TRANSPORTATION. City transport is now good and cheap. Fares are 1 zl. for trams and 1.50 zl for buses (3 zl. for express buses). Tickets can be bought from 'Ruch' newsstands but not on the vehicles. Fares are doubled after 11 P.M. Taxis are cheap (5 zl. per kilometer in the inner-city zone) but scarce. Some horse cabs remain, the fare is agreed with the driver—around 200 zl. per hour. Inexpensive sightseeing tours by mini Melex cars are also arranged by the Warsaw Tourist Services Office Syrena, 16 Krucza St.

Orbis runs a "Warsaw by Night" bus tour daily except Monday, mid-June to mid-September; includes dinner and wine at a nightclub for $30 each. In season Orbis also has bus tours of Warsaw and environs, as well as throughout the country.

HOTELS

Victoria Inter-Continental (L), 11 Krolewska, in ideal location, modern, 370 rooms with bath and air conditioning, several restaurants, nightclub, indoor pool, sauna, and garage. New in 1977.

Inter-Continental Forum (L), Nowogrodzka 24. Completely air-conditioned, 750 rooms. Cocktail lounge, informal gourmet meals.

Orbis-Europejski (L), Krakowskie Przedmiescie 13, best for food and service. 278 spacious rooms, suites, most with bath; restaurant with dinner-dancing, nightclub.

Orbis-Grand (1A), Krucza 28. 430 rooms and 21 suites with bath, radio, telephone. The rooftop café-restaurant, with its glass-enclosed terrace (and heliport) offers jazz bands, dancing, variety shows and a city view.

Orbis-Bristol (1A), Krakowskie Przedmiescie 42. This 50-year-old Victorian hotel with distinctive Polish atmosphere, centrally located and convenient. 224 rooms, half with bath, 8 suites. Its restaurant is one of Warsaw's best.

Orbis-Solec (1A), Zagorna 1; 150 rooms with bath; restaurant, dancing.

Orbis-Novotel, 1 Sierpnia 1, 150 rooms with bath, restaurant, outdoor pool.

Others in the 1A to 1B category, though not all Orbis hotels are: *Metropol*, Marszalkowska 99a; *Dom Chlopa*, P1, Powstancow Warszawy 2; *MDM*, P1, Konstytucji 1; *Nowa Praga*, Bertolda Brechta 7; *Saski*, P1. Dzierzynskiego 1.; *Dom Turysty*, Krakowskie Przedmiescie 4/6.

Warsaw Environs. Lublin: *Orbis-Unia, Lublinianka* and *Victoria;* Pulawy: *Izabella.* Plock: *Orbis-Petropol.* (All 1A).

RESTAURANTS. The best hotel restaurants are in the new *Victoria's Canaletto* which serves Polish specialties, and the restaurant in the *Forum,* both (E).

There are several very nice atmospheric places on Rynek Starego Miasta: *Kamienne Schodki,* has candlelight and duck and wine specialty, *Fukier* is a popular wine cellar cum coffeehouse, *Starapolska* is small, informal and famous for its fish, all (M). *Hortex,* Old Town Market, *Kameralna,* Foksal 16, *Ambassador,* on Piekna opposite the US embassy, *Rarytas,* Marshalkowska 15, with floorshow, *Kaukazka,* Georgian specialties, floorshow and dancing, and *Lowicka,* are other good (M)s.

Inexpensive student favorites are *Hybrydy, Stodola* and *Medyk.*

At Wilanow try: *Kuznia Krolewska,* (M), Wiertnicza 2.

CAFES. Warsaw teems with cafés which move outdoors in summer. It is a way of life with the Poles. Coffee, tea and those luscious cakes can be found at: *Krokodyl,* Rynek Starego Miasta 21. *Gong,* Al. Jerozolimskie 42, has a marvelous selection of imported tea. *Alhambra,* A1. Jerozolimskie 32, Turkish coffee. *Teatralna,* Corazziego 12. *Telimena,* Krak. Przedmiescie. *Trou Madame,* Lazienki Park, in a beautiful setting.

 ENTERTAINMENT. The *National Philharmonic Theater,* Jasna 5, puts on excellent concerts. Poland's 13 opera companies stage frequent operas and operettas. The famous folk dance troupes, *Mazowsze* and *Slask,* perform to full houses. Each Sun. from June-September there are concerts at Zelazowa Wola, Chopin's birthplace, 40 miles from Warsaw.

There are some 17 theaters in Warsaw, many with bold and original stage sets and excellent acting. Those which visitors might enjoy are: *Teatr Wielki* (Grand Theater, Opera & Ballet), superb operatic stage; *Syrena,* Litewska 3 (revues); *Teatr Narodowy,* Plac Teatralny; *Teatr Dramatyczny,* Palac Kultury; *Teatr Studio* (contemporary); *Ateneum* (traditional and contemporary), Jaracza; *Wspolczesny* (contemporary), Mokotowska 13. Concerts in summer at open-air theater at *Lazienki Park.*

For a different slant on the city, try *Wanda Warska's Modern Music Club,* a very popular, candle-lit jazz club. Must reserve. Or *Amfora,* on the East Wall, an intimate redecorated club with music and good food; romantic.

MUSEUMS. Open daily except Monday. Of Warsaw's many museums these perhaps are of most interest to out-of-town tourists: *Muzeum Narodowe* (National), Al. Jerozolimskie 3. Poland's main collection of ancient, classical and modern Polish art and handicraft, as well as other masters; *Muzeum*

Sztuki Ludowej (Folk Art), Al. Na Skarpie 8; *Muzeum Historyczne m.st. Wars-zawy* (Warsaw Historical Museum), Rynek Starego Miasta. Don't miss the historical movie "Warsaw Prevails"; *Muzeum Towarzystwa im. Fryderyka Chopina* (Frederic Chopin Museum), Ostrogski Palace.

Zacheta (The Art Gallery), Pl. Malachowskiego 3; *Sculpture Museum* and *Fine Art Gallery of the Union of Polish Painters & Sculptors,* Marszalkowska; *Modern Art Gallery,* Rynek Starego Miasta 2.

Outside Warsaw: *Lazienki Park Palace,* once summer residence of King Stanislaw Poniatowski, museum of palace interiors; *Wilanow Palace,* former royal summer residence now housing exhibition of contemporary posters (10 kms); *Lowicz Ethnographic Museum,* collection of folk costumes, also gallery of Polish 19th-century paintings (50 kms).

 SHOPPING. Opening hours tend to be long. Some food shops open at 7 A.M., others stay open until 8 P.M. Beautiful handicraft things and specialties are plentiful. Shop along Rynek Starego Miasta, Nowy Swiat, Krucza and Marszalkowska for all sorts of attractive local craftwork. Don't forget to take home some Polish *bison* or *Wyborowa*-brand vodka. Try the *Cepelia* stores for a wide range of Polish folkcraft, such as glass and enamelware, amber and lovely hand-woven woolen rugs; *Orno* shops for silverware and hand-made jewelry; and *Desa* stores for works of art, ornaments and objets d'art. These accept local and foreign currency. *Pewex* hard currency shops sell local and imported items. A visit to the *Flea Market* is highly recommended. Open Sundays in Mariensztat, atmospheric and full of bargains.

USEFUL ADDRESSES. Embassies: *American:* Al. Ujazdowskie 29; *British:* Al. Roz 1; *Canadian:* Katowicka 31. Polish Travel Office (Orbis), Stawki 2 and Bracka 16. Polish Motoring Ass'n., Krucza 14. LOT, Al. Jerozolimskie 44, Warynskiego 9, Grojecka 27. Nationwide emergency telephone: 999; police: 997.

Exploring Krakow

Medieval Krakow, ancient seat of Polish kings and Poland's oldest academic institution, the Jagiellonian University, is the only major city in the country that escaped devastation during the war. Today, its fine ramparts, towers, dungeons, and churches, summing up seven centuries of Polish architecture, as well as its lively theatrical and musical life, make Krakow once again a major attraction for tourists.

Krakow's main showpiece is its well-preserved 16th-century castle called Wawel, "Poland's Acropolis". A pre-Romanesque 10th-century rotunda, discovered within the walls of Wawel castle, is one of the city's oldest monuments. Pearls of Renaissance architecture are: the arcaded castle courtyard and Sigismund's chapel. The castle has an exotic collection of Oriental art and 16th-century Gobelins tapestries. Wawel cathedral, close by, shelters the delicately carved sarcophagi of many kings. Below Wawel hill in the heart of the city, you can wander through Krakow's medieval Town Square with its famous Cloth Hall. Scattered throughout the town are 67 Romanesque, Gothic and Baroque churches. Don't miss 12th-century Mariacki (St. Mary's) church with its 15th-century triptych by Wit Stwosz, a masterpiece of Gothic woodcarving. If you take a guided tour, you won't be allowed to miss Krakow's model industrial suburb of Nowa Huta. Puszcza Niepolomicka is a fine zoo in a forest game preserve.

Krakow's Hinterland

South of Krakow about 10 miles is the ancient salt mine of Wieliczka, renowned for its sculptures and underground chapel hewn in crystal rocksalt. A recent addition is the "Jubilee Chamber" with performances open to the public. Between Krakow and Czetochowa (100 miles to the north) is an unusual group of 125 medieval castles, mostly in ruins, with a few restored. Visit the one at Pieskowa Skala, with a museum and café. Forty miles due west of Krakow is the former Nazi concentration camp of Oswiecim (Auschwitz), where some four million Nazi victims were put to death. Today a grim museum tells the story.

PRACTICAL INFORMATION FOR KRAKOW

HOTELS. (L) *Inter-Continental,* new in 1978. (1A) *Holiday Inn,* the first in eastern Europe, Koniewa 7, 308 rooms, all the usual amenities. (L) *Orbis-Cracovia,* A1. Puszkina 1, 420 rooms, 10 2-room suites, restaurant, cocktail bar. (1A) or (1B) are: *Orbis-Francuski,* Pijarska 13, modernized 59 rooms and 12 apartments, *Monopol, Europejski,* Lubicz 5; *Polski,* Pijarska 17; (2) *Pod Zlotq Kotwicq,* Szpitalna 30. Restaurants and cafés in all.

RESTAURANTS. The best in town are at the hotels: *Holiday Inn* and *Francuski,* also *Kaprys,* Florianska 32. All (E). Others recommended are: *Balaton,* Grodzka 37 (Polish and Hungarian food); *U Wentzla,* Rynek Glowny 18, quite elegant; *Ermitage,* Karmelicka 3, cozy, pleasant, inexpensive; *Hawelka,* Rynek Glowny 34; *Maurici,* Rynek Glowny; all (M). With dancing: *Kaprys,* Florianska 32; *Feniks,* Sw. Jana 2 and *Warszawianka,* 1 Maja 4. Also *Baszta.*

CAFES. *Literacka,* Pijarska 7; *Antyczna,* Rynek Glowny 38; *Florianska,* Florianska 24; *Kopciuszek,* Karmelicka 13; *Pod Jaszczurami,* Rynek Glowny 8, student club; good jazz. *Sukiennice,* Rynek Glowny; *Sniezka,* ul. Sw. Jana 2; *Pod Ratuszem,* Rynek Glowny.

CABARETS. Two of Poland's best literary cabarets are found here: *Piwnica pod Baranami* (Ram's Cellar), a vault of an ancient palace, presents shows based on nonsensical humor; *Jama Michalikowa* (Michalik Cave) Florianska 45, has 19th-and 20th-century wall paintings.

 MUSEUMS. Open 10 A.M. to 2 P.M. *National Gallery of Polish Painting* (Cloth Hall), Rynek Glowny. Historical collection of Polish canvases; *Czartoryski Museum* (Collection of the Princes Czartoryski), Pijarska 9. Canvases of old European masters, including some works of Rembrandt and the only Da Vinci in eastern Europe; *History Museum,* Sw. Jana; *Ethnographical Museum,* Pl. Wolnica, an excellent folk museum; *Wawel Castle Museum;* 71 rooms of treasures.

THEATERS. *Teatr Slowackiego,* best in Poland, opera and drama; *Philharmonic,* Zwierzyniecka 1. *"Stary" im. H. Modrzejewskiej,* Jagiellonska 1; *Groteska-Lalki* (Puppets), Sw. Jana 6; *Operetkowy* (light opera), Lubicz 48.

USEFUL ADDRESSES. *Orbis,* Puszkina 1; *Polish Motoring Assoc.,* Slawkowska 4; *LOT,* Basztowa 15.

Zakopane, Mountain Paradise

Zakopane, 3,000 feet high in the dramatic Tatra mountains, along the Czechoslovak frontier, is Poland's most popular health and holiday resort. Native and foreign visitors flock to this mountain valley outpost for winter and summer sports and to witness ski-jumping and ice-skating competitions. Take the teleferic to snowbound Gubalowka or Kasprowy peaks. A 6,522-foot-long chairlift (be prepared for a long wait in the season) runs to Kasprowy peak where there is a mountain-top restaurant. Well worth a visit is Morskie Oko, a craterlike lake nestled among snowy, soaring peaks. A horse-drawn sleigh for local excursions is a thrilling experience. Zakopane has many hotels, a museum, theater, cafés, dance spots and restaurants. Krynica, in the nearby Beskid mountains, is also a winter sports center as well as a famous spa. Accommodations are inexpensive but satisfactory. Not far beyond the Tatras lie the picturesque Pieniny Mts., with 1000-foot deep canyons. For a different type of thrill, take the nerve-twisting half day raft ride down the sinuous turbulent Dunajec river from Czorsztyn to Szczawnica.

Wroclaw, the Young-Old City

Situated midway between Krakow and Poznan on the Odra River in Lower Silesia, this city dates back to the 10th century. The restored medieval Town Hall, in the Market Square, is regarded as a magnificent example of burgher architecture. Of equal interest are the cathedral and university. A new, modern section has sprung up, with additional construction planned. And here you'll find Jerzy Grotowski's Experimental Theater and the Tomaszewski Mime Theater.

Poznan, the Fair City

Poznan, halfway between Warsaw and Berlin, has been an East-West market place for a thousand years. The important International Trade Fair, held here since 1922, has become in recent years a major trading center between the communist and capitalist worlds. It regularly attracts American and British participation.

A look around the town is rewarding: Visit the Old Market Square with its decorated, Italian-style Town Hall and richly façaded burghers' houses. Poznan has numerous historical churches and palaces. Of particular interest are: Dzialynski Castle, with neo-Classic sculptures; Przemyslaw Castle, former seat of the Great Dukes of Poland; Franciscan Church, with an interior richly decorated with baroque stuccos; Raczynski Library, built in the 19th century with Paris' Louvre as its model; Gorki Palace, unique Renaissance structure, with roof-garden-cum-fishpond; State Ballet school with a beautiful baroque arcaded courtyard; baroque Parish Church, with 17th-century stuccos and polychromy; gothic cathedral, with 18th-century baroque spires and 10th- and 11th-century relics in special crypt.

The new town of Poznan houses the Mickiewicz University, Opera House, Academy of Medicine, Post Office buildings and many fine parks.

Poznan is the center for some interesting excursions, which include Kornik, with its medieval castle library; Biskupin, a resurrected prehistoric fort, the 'Polish Pompeii'; and Gniezno, with its magnificent Romanesque art.

PRACTICAL INFORMATION FOR THE REGIONS

CZESTOCHOWA. Hotels: *Orbis-Patria* (1A), 107 rooms, restaurant. *Centralny* (2), 62 rooms, restaurant with dancing.

GDANSK. New in 1978, *Orbis Hevelius* (1A), 250 rooms, 10 suites. *Orbis-Monopol* (1B), 126 rooms, many with bath.

KARPACZ, ski resort. *Skalny* (1A), 154 rooms with bath; restaurant.

NOWY SACZ. Hotel: *Orbis-Beskid* (1A), 145 rooms, some with bath or shower.

POZNAN. Hotels: (heavily booked during the Fair). New in 1978, *Orbis Poznan* (1A), 425 rooms, 20 suites. (L) is *Orbis-Merkury,* 351 rooms, every comfort. Other (1As) are: *Polonez,* 408 rooms with bath, *Novotel,* 154 rooms with bath, and *Wielkopolski,* 110 rooms, some with bath. *Poznanski* is (1B) and *Bazar* (2). *Motel Poznan-Strzeszynek* is 12 kilometers out of town and there are a campsite and bungalows as well.

 RESTAURANTS. Apart from the hotel restaurants, you can dance at: *Magnolia,* Glogowska 40; *Adria,* Glogowska 14; *Astoria,* 23 Lutego 29; *Rarytas,* Mielzynskiego 21; *Pod Koziolkami,* Stary Rynek 65. *Moulin Rouge,* Kantaka 8/9. *Smakosz,* 27 Grudnia 9, *Arkadia,* Pl. Wolnosci 11, have a good reputation for top quality food.

USEFUL ADDRESSES: *Poznan Fair Info.,* Stary Rynek 77; *US Consulate,* Chopina 4; *Orbis,* Swierczewskiego 14; *LOT,* Czerwonej Armii 69.

SOPOT, main Baltic beach resort. *Orbis-Grand,* 154 rooms, many with bath.

WROCLAW. Hotels: *Novotel,* 150 rooms, outdoor pool, *Panorama, Monopol* with good restaurant, and *Grand,* all (1A). *Europejski* (2).
Restaurants: *Stylowa,* Kosciuszki, *Lotos,* Grabiszynska 9, both (E). *Bieriozka* (Russian food) and *Ratuszowa* (traditional Polish dishes), both (M). *Herbowa,* Rynek 19, is a moderate tearoom, café.

ZAKOPANE, famous ski resort 65 miles south of Krakow. Hotels: *Orbis-Kasprowy* (L), 300 double rooms with bath, restaurant, nightclub, indoor pool, sauna, ice rink and minigolf. *Giewont* (1A) has an excellent restaurant. *Morskie Oko* (2). Also several guest houses.
Restaurants: with dancing, *Jedrus, Harnas, U Wnuka* (regional dress), *Gubalowka, Watra,* and *Wierchy,* all (M-E). *Kmicic* is a nice café.
Local sights include the *Tatra Museum* (folk) and the *Kenar School of Carving.*

HINTS FOR BUSINESSMEN. The Orbis Congress Office can organize most requests, from a secretary-typist ($20-$30 daily) and arranging a picnic (50-100 persons for $1,300-$2,000) to providing exhibition space and laying on technical equipment, interpreters, etc. The main conference halls are in Warsaw, including the Hotel Victoria-Inter-Continental, specially designed for the organization of congresses; and Poznan. The individual rental of equipment, such as typewriters, calculators, tape recorders, dictaphones, telex and special telephone connections, is also available. Contact Congress Services Section "Orbis," P.O. Box 146, 00-050 Warsaw.

PORTUGAL

A land of mystery to most outsiders, Portugal some time ago learned to live with a great lack of understanding on the part of other countries for one basic reason: it chose not to join the mainstream of Europe for almost four decades, decades in which profound changes were taking place elsewhere. This opting-out prevailed in political ideas and ideals, in economic development and in ways of life. Under António de Oliveira Salazar, the prime minister from 1932 to 1968, Portugal turned its back on the world as much as it could, and time slowed down. Things were so slow that thousands of Portuguese chose to leave the country to work elsewhere, especially after the Second World War.

With the end of Salazar's regime and the subsequent deposing of his successor by a democratically inspired military junta in the spring of 1974, Portugal opened up to outside influences and a deluge of new ideas. Changes came swiftly, bringing massive new problems. For a time it seemed that armed revolution was imminent; then in 1975 a measure of stability was achieved. But with the voluntary loss of the African colonies came a tremendous new problem: over half a million refugees flooded into Portugal, and they had to be accommodated. The government's policy was to house them in hotels—all the country's hotels, indiscriminately. Many observers would say that it was one proof that a viable democratic ideal was at work; in any case it was a compassionate short-term solution. Now the greater part of these *retoruados* have started businesses and found work. The few who are not yet settled, have been moved out of the hotels and pensions to other institutions.

But despite its many problems, Portugal can offer much for the tourist with a keen open mind and a taste for something changing and developing. Outside the cosmopolitan environs of Lisbon and Estoril, this land possesses a deeply individual national character. Every province has its own traditions and folklore, as colorful and picturesque as any in Europe. Hospitality here is endemic, and beauty is appreciated in the Latin sense—with color everywhere, and a fine disdain for plate glass and aluminum. The Salazar government had started many years ago to exploit all this in a highly intelligent way, attracting tourists with a network of new roads, filling stations and *pousadas,* state-run inns which offer comfort at rigorously controlled prices. But now the country has an uphill task to reorganize itself for visitors. However, the authorities are—optimistically—hopeful that soon many of their more serious problems will have been resolved. Certainly, the favorable exchange rate will draw many visitors who will find the basic attractions of Portugal unchanged by the recent traumatic upheavals.

Food and Drink

Fish is one of the staples of Portugal, and you will find none finer, nor more of it. The Portuguese never tire of *bacalhau* (salt cod). According to legend there are 365 ways of preparing it, one for every day of the year. The whole gamut of shellfish is available: so try the jugged lobster, stuffed crab *(santola),* and the big clams with bacon. *Mexilhaes* means mussels; *ameijoas* are small clams; both are excellent. If you're a real gourmet, try *polvo* (octopus), grilled, stewed or with rice. Then tackle *lulas* and *chocos,* squid and cuttlefish with white wine en casserole.

In the north, a great specialty is *caldo verde,* a delicious soup of potatoes, shredded cabbage and olive oil. River fish—salmon, lamprey, trout—are fine. Portuguese beef is not famous, but *bife na frigideira,* steak with mustard sauce, can be very good. If you see cuts of beef or a suckling pig, or more often sardines, being roasted barbecue style at a country fair, that should be your meat.

Caldeirada, a fish soup similar to *bouillabaisse,* can be found all along the coast from Aveiro to Algarve, prepared with slight variations according to the region and the fish.

Sample all the cheeses, *rabaçal* (goat) and especially those made of ewe's milk, *queijo da Serra* and *queijo de Azeitao.* They have a highly distinctive flavor.

There are many pleasant wines apart from Mateus, which is ubiquitous outside the country but less regarded at home. For an apéritif Sercial (Madeira) is excellent, the white Colares and the earthy, red Dao are well worth trying. As is Vinho Verde, 'green wine', exquisite and lightly sparkling. The regional wines, both red and white, are usually delicious and still comparatively unknown: Vidigueira, Evel and Borba from the Alentejo; Lagoa from Algarve; Mabantino from Tomar; and best of all Buçaco from Coimbra. But the greatest of Portuguese wines are port, and the greatest of all ports is vintage port, unblended and matured in the bottle; vintage port is not at its best until it is 15 to 20 years old, and reaches its prime at 30, though a few do not "fade" until they are even older.

Ruby port is a blend of different vintages bottled before it loses its red color, while tawny port usually has matured in the cask; white port, amber-colored and drier, can successfully compete with sherry as an elegant apéritif. Only vintage port is dated, since the rest are all blends of different years.

Madeira is the other great Portuguese wine, from vines on the island of Madeira. It is produced in four main types: Sercial, dry and usually drunk as an apéritif or with soup; Verdelho, a medium wine; Bual, rich with a bouquet of its own; and Malmsey, a sweet dessert wine.

Shopping

Good buys in Portugal include copper, pewter (caution: not the leaded), cork, glazed tiles and pottery, Christmas crêche figures, textiles (linen, cotton, woven carpets), women's leather gloves, beautifully designed and decorated lace, embroidery, and hand-wrought jewelry in silver and gold.

PRACTICAL INFORMATION FOR PORTUGAL

WHAT WILL IT COST. Although prices have risen during the last few years, Portugal is still almost Europe's cheapest country for tourists. In Lisbon, deluxe and first-class superior hotels do not offer pension terms. Elsewhere, in first-class establishments count on paying 500-750 escudos, in moderate, 300-500 escudos a day with continental breakfast. The *pousadas* around the country are government-owned: accommodation and service are normally first class and rates very reasonable; there are never many rooms, and in high season a stay is limited to five days. *Estalagems* and *Pensions* all over the country are usually excellent and offer very reasonable full pension rates. Service charge in hotels is 15 percent, tourist tax 3 percent, which is included in the bill; to this add 10 to 20 escudos for any special personal service.

CAPITAL. Lisbon.

LANGUAGE. Portuguese. Portugal is Britain's oldest ally, and you will find English widely understood, especially in Lisbon and Oporto.

CLIMATE. Sunny and almost no rain, except in spring and fall, but a permanent breeze—in summer.

Average maximum daily temperatures in degrees Fahrenheit and centigrade:

Lisbon	Jan.	Feb.	Mar.	Apr.	May	June	July	Aug.	Sept.	Oct.	Nov.	Dec.
F°	57	59	63	68	70	77	81	82	79	72	63	59
C°	14	15	17	20	21	25	27	28	26	22	17	15
Algarve												
F°	59	59	61	64	66	70	72	72	72	70	64	61
C°	15	15	16	18	19	21	22	22	22	21	18	16

SPECIAL EVENTS. The most outstanding folklore festivals are: June 13-20, St. Anthony, in Lisbon; June 23-24, S. Joao in Oporto and almost all over the country; Gulbenkian Festival of Music in Lisbon and principal cities, winter and spring, July, *Colete Encarnado* (bullfights), Vila Francade Xira, usually second week; August 17-19, *Nossa Senhora da Agonia,* at Viana do Castelo; *Festa dos Tabuleiros,* Tomar, every second year in July; September, festivities at Nazaré, with folklore groups and bullfights; Nov. 11, *São Martinho* at Golega (lively horse fair); and the great religious pilgrimages to Fatima from May through October on the 13th of each month.

CLOSING TIMES. Shops open at 9, close at 7, with a usual lunch closure from 1-3. Banks: weekdays 9:30-12 and 2-3:30.

SPORTS. Main spectator sports are bullfights on horseback and football. Riding and sailing are popular and facilities available in most districts. Several good golf courses, particularly at Estoril, and in Algarve, Penina, Vilamoura of Vale do Lobo, Palmares and Quinta do Lago.

HOW TO REACH PORTUGAL. By air: From New York and Boston there are direct daily flights by *TWA*, *PanAm* and *TAP* to Lisbon. From London, direct daily flights by *TAP* and *British Airways* to Lisbon, frequently to Faro (Algarve), and in Lisbon via Oporto. **By sea:** From Plymouth, Brittany *Ferries* will take you and your car to Santander (Spain) twice a week, from April to October, where it is an easy drive into Portugal.

CUSTOMS. You are limited to 200 cigarettes duty free, or to 50 cigars or 250 grams (about ½ pound) of tobacco in other forms. Everything else for personal use during your trip is duty free.

MONEY. The Portuguese monetary unit is the escudo. There are 100 centavos in an escudo. The current rate of exchange is about 40$00 to the U.S. dollar, 76$00 to the pound sterling, but the escudo is "floating," so this is leading to steady though gradual devaluation, an advantage to tourists.

The maximum amount of Portuguese currency that may be taken into the country is 1,000 escudos per person. Any amount up to 5,000 escudos per person, or the equivalent in foreign currency, may be taken out of Portugal. Amounts over 5,000 escudos or equivalent in foreign currency may be taken out only if it can be proved that a larger amount was brought in. For this reason it is advisable that, when entering Portugal, all currency carried should be declared.

Note: The symbol for the escudo is a $ sign, written between the escudo and the centavo unit. It takes a few hours to get used to it. When you see $37 in Portugal, that means 37 centavos.

HOTELS. In our listings, hotels are indicated L, 1, 2, 3, 4 equating to deluxe, first class superior, first class reasonable, moderate or inexpensive. In first-class hotels, all rooms are with bath. However, some of the two-star hotels can turn out to be more pleasant than certain of the newer 3-star ones in which space has been too carefully calculated. In the family pensions the atmosphere is friendly and rates are moderate.

RESTAURANTS are listed E, M, or I, for expensive, moderate or inexpensive.

TIPPING. Hotels and restaurants charge 10% service and 3.1% tourist tax usually included in the price list. Waiters will expect extra tips. Taxis expect 15-20%. Minimum tip for small services: 5 escudos.

ELECTRICITY. 210-220 volts A.C., 50 cycles.

DRINKING WATER. Generally safe everywhere in Portugal from the tap, but avoid drinking from wells or springs.

TRAVEL IN PORTUGAL. By Air: Domestic routes link Lisbon with Faro and Oporto, Funchal, Madeira and the Azores, all flown by *TAP* jets. There are also services, often only once a week, to out-of-the-way towns such as Braganza. These may be dependent on weather and other factors, so check. **By car:** Roads are generally good but occasionally narrow. Attention: local drivers are notably rash and careless. There is no lack of fuel stations all over the country. You can hire self-drive cars from *Contauto* (Carop) in Lisbon or 5 other cities, *Sarmentauto* in Lisbon, *Avis* with office at the airport. In Oporto, Estoril, Cascais, Faro and other major towns there are agencies.

So-called "super" fuel is 90 octane, price 26$00 escudos the liter, 23$00 the so-called "normal", about 80 octane. Oil, depending on quality, about 53 escudos the liter.

BY TRAIN: The Lisbon-Oporto (one train a day each way, takes cars), and Lisbon-Algarve services are excellent. Trains are clean and usually run on time. Passengers over 65 years of age can get a 50% reduction on rail and internal air fares in Portugal (when the trip is more than 50 kilometers) by showing passport or identity card. Frequent local electric trains from Lisbon to Estoril, Cascais and Sintra.

BY BUS: Excellent bus service connects the main points of interest, such as Fátima, Tomar, etc., and the Algarve coast. The Tourist Offices give all information on schedules, price and time.

CAMPING. Excellent camping sites (50) all over the country. *Clube do Campismo,* Rua Misericordia 137, Lisbon, furnishes all information.

USEFUL ADDRESSES. *American Embassy and Consulate,* Av. Duque de Loulé 39. *British Embassy and Consulate,* Rua S. Domingos à Lapa 37. *Canadian Embassy and Consulate,* Rua Rosa Araujo 2, 6°. *Portuguese Tourist Office,* Palácio Foz, Praça dos Restauradores and Ave. Antonio Augusto de Aguiar 86. *American Express,* main office at Star, Av. Sidonio Pais 4, also at Praça dos Restauradores 14. *Cook's,* Av. da Liberdade 91/103. *Guides' Syndicate,* Rua do Telhal 74 *British Hospital,* Rua Saraiva Carvalho 49. Guided tours, *Claras Turismo,* Ave. Casal Ribeiro 18. All in Lisbon.

Lisbon, Cosmopolitan City

Luminous, pastel-colored Lisbon is the capital, chief seaport and nerve center of Portugal. Few sights are more arresting than that of Lisbon seen at dusk from the left bank of the Tagus. The suspension bridge across the river is the longest in Europe. Built by an American consortium, it offers a fine view as you cross it.

A cosmopolitan city of over one million inhabitants, Lisbon rose like a phoenix from the ashes of a terrible earthquake in 1755, and is a fascinating combination of the new and the old, of internationalism and colorful provincialism.

Driving in from the airport, you will see the capital in its most modern aspect with new apartments and vast avenues, speckled with rapid autobuses, the city's finest gesture toward urbanism. The Avenida de Liberdade is the Champs Elysées of Lisbon, and Lisboans will be quick to tell you that it's longer than its Paris counterpart. However, many a link with the past delights the eye in the old parts of the city, where colored tiles adorn ancient buildings, cobblestoned streets wind their way uphill and centuries-old grey walls tower high above the river. The delicate greens, yellows and pinks of the houses account for Lisbon's pastel freshness.

The famous Praça do Rossio is the very heart of Lisbon, a fascinating, animated forum, in perpetual motion over the stylish black-and-white inlaid pavement. The entire Baixa, or Lower Town, was planned by the great Marquis of Pombal after the earthquake of 1755. The architectural gem of this reconstruction, known to foreigners as Black Horse Square, is the Praça do Comercio (or Terreiro do Paço), which opens onto the river, the other three sides flanked by handsome, arcaded buildings.

If you want a change from geometry and modernity, put on your most sensible walking shoes and climb the ancient cobbled streets of the Alfama quarter toward the Castelo. You don't need a guide. There are only two basic directions here—up and down, and you can wander into the darkest alley with no fear of molestation. We promise you will be fascinated by the whole quarter which is teeming with life.

From the Castelo S. Jorge, a former stronghold of the Moors, the view over Lisbon and the Tagus is magnificent, as it is also from the terrace of the *miradouro* of Santa Luzia, which you pass on your way up. There are several *miradouros* or belvederes in Lisbon, all at strategic vantage points.

Cafés abound in this city, and so does good wine. The interiors of the select cafés of the Rossio and Chiado are as gloomy as caves. The male Lisboans, gossips and gourmands by nature, are never happier than when ensconced in one of these dens, devouring cakes *(pasteis)* and coffee.

Far removed is the surging animation of the so-called *bairros populares,* the oldest parts of the city around St. George's Castle or the fishwives quarter of Madragoa. Between Lisbon's patron saint's (St. Anthony) day on June 13, St. John's on the 24th, and St. Peter and Paul's on the 29th, there are nightly parades, and the people sing and dance in the streets of the old town. If you want to see the people of Lisbon at their liveliest, this is your chance.

Amusing food markets are all over Lisbon. The *Feira da Ladra* (Thieves Market) for junk and some antiques in the Camfrode Sta. Clara is open on Tuesdays and Saturdays.

You will hear about the "Manueline style". This is one of Portugal's contributions to architecture. Inspired by the sea and the 16th-century passion for discovery, sculptors added richly carved motifs of rope, seaweed, palms, exotic flora and other evocative material to their Gothic models. The result was an exuberant new style. You will see examples all over northern Portugal. The Jerónimos Church in Lisbon is one of its most beautiful monuments, along with the famous Tower of Belém (Bethlehem) nearby. At once graceful and robust, delicate and vigorous, this early-16th-century fortress stands on the Tagus today as it has for centuries, the watchtower and symbol of a nation.

PRACTICAL INFORMATION FOR LISBON

 HOTELS. *Note:* The hotel situation in Portugal is rapidly settling down, but be sure to check with an experienced travel agent before you leave.

In **deluxe** category, and all with restaurants, bar, etc., are the *Sheraton,* 388 rooms, pool, ballroom, centrally located; *Ritz,* 290 rooms, magnificent view, nightclub; *Tivoli,* 354 rooms, view and nightclub; *Altis,* 176 rooms with bath; *Avenida Palace,* 95 rooms, convenient, plush furnishings.

First Class Superior

Tivoli Jardim, Rua Julio Cesar Machado; 119 rooms with bath, good restaurant and snack bar. Large free parking area.

Lutécia, Av. Frei Miguel Contreiras; 151 air-conditioned rooms with TV, 17 suites, top-floor restaurant with panoramic view; parking for 200 cars.

Fenix, Marques Pombal Square; 116 very pleasant rooms with bath. Choice Spanish dishes in the grill room.

Diplomático, Rua Castilho, near Pombal Square; 90 super-modern rooms, 17 suites, terrace with fine view, bar, private parking.

Embaixador, Av. Duque de Loulé, near the American Embassy; 96 rooms with bath. Rooms rather small.

Lisboa-Plaza, Travessa do Salitre; 90 rooms with bath; but near a rather noisy amusement park.

Flórida, Rua Duque de Palmela. 208 rooms with bath or shower. Very popular with Americans.

Penta, Av. dos Combatentes, 336 rooms, some way from center. Very modern.

Mundial, Rua Dom Duarte; 146 rooms with bath, splendid panoramic restaurant. But the location is on a very noisy thoroughfare.

First Class Reasonable

Jorge V, Rua Mousinho Silveira; 49 air-conditioned rooms with bath.

Eduardo VII, Av. Fontes Pereira Melo 3; 95 rooms with bath. Attractive rooftop-restaurant terrace.

Senhora Do Monte, on Calçada do Monte in the oldest part of town. All 27 rooms with bath, balcony. Bar terrace has fine view.

Rex, on Rua Castilho 169, past the Ritz; 40 rooms with bath and radio. Stunning view from top-floor terrace. Easy parking.

Flamingo, Rua Castilho near Pombal Square; 35 rooms with bath.

Impala, 47 Rua Filipe Folque; 25 apartments with bath and kitchenette.

Reno, next to *Príncipe,* Av. Duque d'Avila; 46 rooms with bath. German management and cooking.

Capitol, Rua Eça Queiroz; 50 rooms with bath or shower. Quiet.

Moderate

Príncipe, Av. Duque d'Avila; 52 rooms with bath.

Borges, on Rua Garrett; 94 rooms, most with bath. Old-fashioned, good food. On main shopping street.

Miraparque, Av. Sidónio Pais, but not all the rooms have bath. Quiet.

Among the countless pensions *York House* (Pensao Residencia Inglesa), Rua das Janelas Verdes, is charming. Former private mansion in quaint garden up long flight of steps. Book well in advance. *Pensao Residência América,* Rua Tomas Ribeiro 47. Deluxe. *Pensao Nazareth,* Av. A. Augusto Aguiar 25.

 RESTAURANTS. Lisbon's biggest restaurants are of the international type and, since they depend largely on the unpredictable tourist trade, the smaller places are apt to change in quality, or even go out of existence, overnight. However, those given below are considered quite stable. Expect to pay 400-550 esc. in an expensive restaurant, 300-400 in moderate, 150-300 in inexpensive spots.

Restaurant Aviz (E), Rua Serpa Pinto 12b. Has the right atmosphere and the right food, excellent.

Tavares (E), Rua Misericórdia 37. In a turn-of-the-century setting the much praised cuisine is taken very seriously.

Góndola (M), Av. Berne 64. Serves rich Italian food, and in fine weather you can eat in the garden.

Michel (E), Largo de Santa Cruz do Castelo 5. On small, elegant square inside castle walls. Serves classic French food.

Cota d'Armas (E), in old part of city. Perhaps a shade heavy on atmosphere, but good food. No language problems. Run by owners of old family mansion.

O Peixe (M), in Belém near the waterfront, for seafood, truly excellent.

Quinta (M), at the top of the elevator (corner of Rua do Ouro and Rua Santa Justa). If you secure a table by the window you have the city at your feet, but the food served tastes like that on an airplane.

Vera Cruz (M), Av. Joao Almada 17b. Their specialty is steak flambé prepared at your table with due ceremony.

Gambrinus (M), Rua Portas S. Antao 25, specializes in seafood.

Solmar (M), a vast seafood restaurant, is at 108 of the same street.

Tábuas (E), Barros Queirós 49, with 17th-century décor and costumed waiters.

Hong Kong, Rua Camilo Castelo Branco, and *Xangai,* Av. Duque Loulé are pleasant (M) Chinese restaurants.

Paco (M), opposite the Gulbenkian Museum, has amusing décor, literary clientèle, regional dishes.

Floresta do Ginjal (M), across the river at Cacilhas. Immense dining rooms on the first and second floors, each with a narrow terrace and a captivating sight of Lisbon across the Tagus.

Bonjardim (I), Travessa Santo Antao, very simple, very crowded, good food. Chicken and suckling pig, spit-roasted.

ADEGA TIPICA. These are the restaurants where you listen to *fado* singers and eat Portuguese specialties. Meals are not obligatory; you can spend your time from after dinner until the wee hours on local red or white wine or whatever other drink you may favor. Guitars accompany the *fadistas* and when the mood calls for it, one or the other waitress joins in and a musical dialogue ensues made up entirely on the spur of the moment. Most genuine *fado* places are situated in the oldest parts of the town, Alfama or Bairro Alto. *Parreirinha de Alfama* and *Nau Catrineta* are by far the most picturesque, situated near the waterfront.

Tourists are generally directed to *Machado,* a rather over-done place; *Mesquita* and *Toca* somewhat less for show. *A Severa,* Rua das Jáneas 55, always has very good singers. Perhaps the most unspoilt is *Lisboa à Noite* (ancient wishing well on the premises). *Viela* was started by a sister of famed Amália Rodrigues. *Cesária* and *O Faia* are favored by locals. All these are in the Bairro Alto.

 MUSEUMS. All museums are closed Mon. and holidays. *Ancient Art,* Rua das Janelas Verdes; 10 A.M. to midnight, 3 to 5 P.M. One of Europe's great collections of paintings, ceramics, jewelry, tapestries, etc. Fine Portuguese primitives (the famous 15th-cent. polyptych by Nuno Gonçalves, *Triumph of St. Vincent*) and works by Hieronymus Bosch, Frans Hals, Holbein, Dürer, and many others. *Folk Art,* Av. Marginal, Belém; 12-4.

Religious Art, Largo Trinidade Coelho; closed for reorganization.

Contemporary Art, Rua Serpa Pinto.

Royal Coaches, Praça Afonso de Albuquerque, Belém; Closed for reorganization. The richest collection of royal coaches in the world.

Military Museum, Largo do Museu de Artilharia; 10-5. Armor, weapons from 15th cent.

Ethnological Museum, Praça do Império, Belém; 10-5. Prehistoric, Greek, and Roman relics. Also *Marine Museum* nearby.

Costume Museum, Lumiar; Lisbon's latest museum in lonely old Palmela Palace. 10-5.

Fundaçao Ricardo Espírito Santo, in the old palace at Rua de Sao Tomé. Museum-school of decorative arts. Workshops for the reproduction of antiques, for gold beating and gilding, tapestry work, bookbinding.

Botanical Gardens, Rua de Escola Politécnica; and a remarkable greenhouse collection, *Estufa Fria,* and hothouse, *Estufa quente,* open 10-5, Parque Eduardo VII.

The Gulbenkian Foundation Museum, Av. Berne. Collection includes 3,000 items, most from Leningrad's Hermitage Museum. Among them, 4,000-year-old Persian prayer mats; Turkish textiles and tile work; silver plate; 18th-cent. French sculpture and cabinetwork; Italian primitives; French Impressionists; Art Nouveau jewelry.

CHURCHES. These and other ecclesiastical edifices provide Lisbon's most notable buildings. First and foremost is the only important building that survived the Lisbon earthquake, the Portuguese Renaissance monastery and church of *Jerónimos,* Praça do Império, Belém, whose cloister is the greatest existing example of the Manueline style. The *Cathedral,* Largo da Sé, is a rebuilt 13th-cent. structure. *Madre de Deus,* Rua da Madre de Deus, is a masterpiece of Portuguese Baroque; note its fine tiles and gilded woodwork.

Also important: the ruins of the *Carmelite Convent,* Largo de Carmo, for the Gothic apse and portal; *S. Vicente,* the royal Pantheon, an impressive building with exquisite wall tiles; *Basílica da Estrela,* Praça da Estrela, from whose dome there is a splendid view. Huge 18th-century Christmas crib with hundreds of figures in a room off the sacristy.

TRANSPORTATION. During rush hours cabs are hard to find. Once you have one, the fare starts at 7$00, increasing 1$20 per 230 meters. If more than four passengers get into a small cab (more than five in a large), the police will stop the driver for overloading. The cab's rated capacity is printed over the meter. There is a 50 percent increase for baggage weighing over 66 pounds; no increase in fares at night. Rates for hiring by the hour or kilometer are posted in the cabs.

From the airport costs to at least 65$00. To and from Estoril or Cascais to Lisbon you are obliged to pay for both ways whether you return or not. The fare currently is 250$00 to 300$00. Tip about 15%. Taxis are recognizable: black cars with light green tops.

The cheapest way to get around is by tram or bus, though beware of the rush hours. There are a couple of subway lines (Metropolitano) and more under construction. Fare 5$00, cheaper weekly season tickets. Your hotel porter will explain which transportation to take.

In the heart of the city, off the Rua d'Ouro, is the Eiffel-built lift which whisks you up to the ruins of the Carmelite Convent. Cable cars solve the problem of ascending the steepest streets.

Frequent (and excellent) electric trains leave from Cais do Sodré for all the riverside suburbs, terminating at Cascais.

Passenger ferry boats to the south side of the Tagus leave every 10 to 15 minutes from Praça de Comércio.The large ferry boats carrying cars leave for Cacilhas from the Estaçao Fluvial do and from Cais do Sodré, for Trafaria and Porto Brandao from the Estaçao Fluvial de Belém every 15-20 minutes.

Panoramic view and time gained is ample reward for the 20$00 one way to cross the suspension bridge.

SHOPPING. Lisbon offers the tourist a number of local products as well as a wide assortment of goods from all over Europe. You'll have a grand time window shopping in the Rua Garrett, commonly called the Chiado, in the Rua do Ouro, Rua Augusta and Rua da Prata. But don't be afraid to wander from these beaten paths; there are many fine shops in all of Lisbon's residential districts. Almost all stores shut from 1 to 3. To make up for this Latin lunch hour, they stay open until 7 in the evening, as they do in nearby Cascais. Shops close at 1 P.M. on Saturdays.

Remember that because Portugal is considered a developing country, many of the things you buy there may be exempt from U.S. Customs duties under the G.S.P. plan, as explained in the section on Customs in Facts at Your Fingertips, at the beginning of this volume.

ANTIQUES. Most shops are concentrated in the Rua de S. Beato, Rua de S. José, Rua do Aleirum and the Rua Escola Politécnica.

CORK. *Casa das Cortiças,* Rua Escola Politécnica 4. Cork boxes, buckets, wine bottle holders, coasters, dolls; almost every item you can imagine in cork. *José Alexandre,* Rua Garrett 8.

GIFTS. *Matens & Leitao,* Rua Castillio 61. This firm also ships goods abroad, including those bought elsewhere. Very large selection of Portuguese goods.

HANDICRAFTS. *Grandela* department store: *Madeira House,* Rua Augusta 135 for embroideries, and *Quinto,* Rua Ivens 30, for hand-embroidered carpets. *Lavores,* Rua Aurea 179, for typical embroidery. Also *Madeira Supérbia,* Av. Duque de Loulé 75; at the Ritz Hotel, *Supérbia* boutique, for hand-embroidered blouses, cloths, etc.

JEWELRY. *Sarmento,* Rua do Ouro 251, has the largest choice of gold and silver Portuguese filigree work as well as stylish copies of antique jewelry and silverware.

LIQUOR. *Solar do Velho Porto,* Rua S. Pedro de Alcântara 45, is an amazing place run by the port wine trade: you can sample any of the 200-300 varieties prepared, by reinforcement with vinic alcohol, for export. *Martins e Costa,* Rua do Carmo 41, Rua Garrett 17, for wine and exotic food. For liquor, *José Luis Simoes,* Largo do Chiado 16-17.

PORCELAIN. Tableware and artistic statuettes at showrooms of the manufacturers: *Vista Alegre,* Largo do Chiado 18.

POTTERY. Brilliantly colored glazed earthenware, a Portuguese specialty, and the shiny square tiles called *azuléjos* are available at the *Fábrica de Sant' Ana* at Rua do Alecrim 91 and *Viúva Lamego,* Largo do Intendente 25. The regional department of *Grandela,* Rua do Ouro, stocks Caldas da Rainha ware, some very attractive. *Festival,* Rua do Ouro 263, has a large selection of copies of the lovely antique glazed earthenware dishes and bowls made in Coimbra since the 13th century.

Estoril and Cascais

Westward from Lisbon, along the Tagus, it's a half-hour ride by way of Algés, Caxias and attractive Carcavelos to the elegant resort of Estoril, with its triumphal palm-lined esplanade descending to a fine sand beach. The new casino, with its restaurant, orchestra, nightclub, cinema and, of course, its gambling rooms, is the center of the area's social life.

The sea road west from Estoril leads almost at once into the fishing village of Cascais, with its sunny harbor thronged with boats and festooned with reddish-brown nets. More bohemian, less old-fashioned than Estoril, this hospitable village with its ancient citadel and sun-baked ramparts has a strong appeal. Beyond the fortress, the country has the barren beauty of scrubby pines and sun-bleached dunes extending to the rocky spine of the Serra de Sintra, above the westernmost point of Europe—Cabo da Roca.

Queluz and Sintra

The inland road from Lisbon to Sintra passes the gardens of Queluz, a rosy royal 18th-century palace, as romantic as the castle of the Sleeping Beauty. It is a good curtain raiser for enchanting Sintra, one of the gems of Portugal. In the center of an open plain, a volcanic eruption thrust the spine of Sintra into being, with its mass of rocks from which burst thousands of springs. Around Sintra the vegetation combines jasmine, arbutus, bamboo, camellias, mimosa, tree ferns and 90 species of exotic flowering plants that are found nowhere else in Europe.

Don't miss the old Palácio de Sintra, with its small Moorish garden and many mosaics. Linked with every king of Portugal since John of Aviz, this palace is a lecture in stone on Portuguese architecture, combining Gothic, Moorish, Manueline and Victorian elements in a surprisingly harmonious way. Take a *fiacre* in the square to within reach of the ruined Moorish castle with its ramparts and dungeons and its sweeping panoramic view to the sea. This is the oldest castle in Sintra. The newest, Pena, was built in 1840 for a German prince consort, Ferdinand of Saxe-Coburg. It is an architectural fantasy, ranging from genuine medieval to equally genuine Victorian, copied from Balmoral. From the terraces and grounds there are superb views of the surrounding countryside and right back to Lisbon. The road to both castles is steep and tortuous. Palace and castles closed on Tuesdays, as is Queluz.

North of Lisbon

This is a delightful area, full of the unexpected details that make the charm of Portugal. The farms are cultivated by hoe and irrigated by hand, the wells worked by rope and pulley or by little donkeys turning water wheels. In the midst of such a pastoral setting, the monumental convent of Mafra rises up, the "Escorial" of King Joao V, built with the wealth of Brazil and the labor of 50,000 men.

Time has been kind to Obidos, snug within its encircling ramparts. The narrow, winding main street is rather misleadingly called Rua Direita (straight), but it does lead straight to the restored 15th-century castle now functioning as a tiny but inviting *pousada*.

A bronze statue of Queen Leonor stands at the entrance to Caldas da Rainha (literally, the Queen's Thermal Baths), a town which she made famous by promoting the ill-smelling springs which cured her rheumatism. Caldas is also a noted ceramic center, specializing in glazed earthenware figures in human, animal and vegetable form.

Alcobaça and Batalha

In the midst of peach and apricot orchards at the confluence of the Alcoa and Baça streams is the town of Alcobaça. The chief attraction is the famous Monastery of Santa Maria, built by the Cistercians in 1152. The abbey church, with its breath-taking interior, is the largest in Portugal. See the Gothic tombs of Dom Pedro I and his murdered secret wife, Inès de Castro. They are splendid examples of Portuguese sculpture, despite their profanation by Napoleon's soldiers.

Another "must" to the north of Alcobaça is Batalha, with its celebrated monastery of Our Lady of Victory, built in the 14th and 15th centuries. The finest example of flamboyant Gothic in Portugal, it contains the impressive sarcophagus of Joao I and his English queen, and the tomb of Portugal's two unknown soldiers, one for Europe and one for Africa.

Fátima

About 10 miles east of Batalha is one of the famous shrines of Christendom, Fátima, where, on May 13, 1917 the Virgin is said to have appeared to three little shepherds. On the 13th of each month from May until October, huge crowds of pilgrims make their way to the shrine at Fátima. On these occasions, it is impossible to get a room and the pilgrims pray all night in the open.

Nazaré

Northwest on the coast is the fishing town of Nazaré. Here the ocean hurls itself in fury on a dangerous beach, bounded by a 300-foot cliff on top of which stands the Chapel of Our Lady of Nazaré, a shrine for fishermen. The fishing boats here are rounded and turned up at bow and stern to enable them to cut through the huge breakers. When the catch is good, the whole village harnesses itself to the dripping nets, sometimes so heavy that tractors are used to help pull them in, although oxen are still used now and then. This scene has been painted hundreds of times—the fishermen in their brilliant plaid shirts and breeches of coarse wool, like strangely sophisticated harlequin costumes. If you want to understand the primitive strength and dignity of Portugal, watch the fishing ships come in at Nazaré (not during July or August).

Southward from Lisbon

The promontory that juts out between the estuaries of the Tagus and the Sado is a delightful area, easily explored from Lisbon in a day. You can take a ferry to Cacilhas or drive across the impressive suspension bridge to Almada. A charming shady road takes you to Azeitao. At the summit of a long ascent, you will have a magnificent panorama of Lisbon and the Sea of Straw in the characteristic opalescent light. Ahead is an unobstructed view of the Sado, with its languid waters and rice paddies.

A 15-mile round-trip detour will take you to the beach of Portinho da Arrábida, a reasonable place to have lunch before returning to the main road at Azeitao.

The very name of Vila Fresca d'Azeitao is an indication of the coolness of the spot. It was here that King Manuel built for his mother the first summer residence of Portugal, the manor of Bacalhoa, the gardens of which may be visited on application.

South of Azeitao, along one of the loveliest roads in Portugal, lies Sesimbra, probably the most romantic seaside resort in Portugal, with matchless bathing. A magnificent old convent and a 16th-century Spanish castle are nearby. Many wealthy Portuguese have built houses here. From Setúbal (fine Manueline church of Jesus) you return to Lisbon by the same route or via the great Templar's Castle of Palmela. The whole trip covers less than 100 miles.

PRACTICAL INFORMATION FOR ENVIRONS OF LISBON

For descriptions of hotel categories here and in subsequent sections, see paragraph on *Hotels* at the beginning of the chapter.

ESTORIL. *Hotel Palácio* (L), 172 rooms, a combination of modern comfort and old-fashioned elegance; pleasant bar looking on to heated pool. *Sintra-Estoril* (L), 186 rooms, indoor pool (located at Alcabideche, on the road to Sintra).

Cibra (1), 89 rooms, splendid view from top-floor dining room. *Lido,* 65 rooms, very quiet, pleasant situation; *Alvorada,* 29 rooms, service flatlets, faces the casino, both (2). *Londres* (3), 71 rooms, pool. *Paris* (3), 87 rooms, pool, noisy; *Inglaterra* (2), 49 rooms, pool, good family hotel.

At Monte Estoril: *Grande Hotel* (1), 72 rooms, a short walk from the sea.

Atlántico (2), 175 rooms, overlooks sea, but disadvantage is the train running between hotel and sea. *Miramar* (3), 39 rooms, quiet, in small park, with pool, English-owned. *Zenith,* 60 rooms, top-floor restaurant.

Estalagems: *Belvedere,* 14 rooms, charming atmosphere plus great comfort. *The Founder's Inn,* English-owned, 14 rooms, grill room, English bar. *Lennox Country Club,* 17 rooms, small pool; patronized by golfers. *Claridade,* 10 rooms, near golf course.

The above establishments have all rooms with bath.

Restaurants: *Choupana* (E) is right on the sea just before you drive into Estoril. It's the smartest place along the coast. The three-man band plays practically non-stop, food is good, and they also serve lunch. The *English Bar,* near the Atlántico hotel. At the *Ronda* nearby there is dinner-dancing. *Borsalino* is the latest "in" bar-lounge.

The *Casino* is the center of Estoril's social life. Roulette, baccarat, and chemin de fer are played (you need your passport to get in). Both the restaurant and the nightclub have good floorshows.

Estoril has a beautifully-located 18-hole golf course, and a 9-hole one.

CASCAIS. The towering *Estoril-Sol* has 400 rooms; the *Albatroz,* right on the sea, has improved, 16 rooms, with attractive bar; restaurant. Both (L).

Cidadela (1), also has several self-contained flatlets, supermarket, pool.

Baía (2), 80 rooms with balcony, view over the bay.

Restaurants: *Fim do Mundo* (E), with a cuisine of long-standing fame. *Pescador* (M), folksy and crowded, but good seafood and atmosphere. *Beira Mar* (M), where turbot with curry is the specialty. *O Pipas,* excellent seafood. *Boca do Inferno* for sidewalk snacks and coffee.

GUINCHO. Fascinating rugged coast, sea for strong swimmers only. *Hotel de Guincho* (L), 36 rooms, in old fortress. *Estalagem Mar do Guincho* (1) and *Estalagem do Muchaxo* (L), both with excellent, mainly seafood restaurants, the latter somewhat overrated, and (E).

QUELUZ. *Cozinha Velha* (E), is the most romantic restaurant in the Lisbon region. The original kitchen of the Queluz palace, it has retained its old fittings, gleaming copper pots and pans and even the spits on which oxen used to be roasted whole.

SINTRA. *Hotel Palácio de Seteais* (L), 18 rooms. Formerly the property of the counts of Marialva, well worth at least a lunch visit. *Central* (2), in the main square; *Estalagem da Raposa* (4). Excellent restaurant, *Galeria Real.*

NORTH OF LISBON

ALJUBARROTA. The *Estalagem do Cruzeiro* (1), 13 rooms, 6 with bath.

BATALHA. On road to Fátima, *Motel Sao Jorge* (2), 10 rooms. The 28-room *Estalagem do Mestre Domingues* (L), recommended.

FÁTIMA. *Santa Maria* (2), 59 rooms; *Fátima* (3), 39 rooms; *Estalagem Três Pastorinhos* (1), 92 rooms, all with bath; *Pax* 51 rooms. Most of the religious houses take guests. Reserve if going 12-13th of any summer month.

FOZ DO ARELHO. *Hotel do Facho* (3), facing sea, pleasant and comfortable. Inexpensive.

NAZARÉ. *Nazaré,* 53 rooms and *Praia,* 40 rooms, both (2); all rooms with bath. *Dom Fuas* (3), 36 rooms.

OBIDOS. The place to eat here, and to stay, is the small *Pousada do Castelo,* right in the castle; *Estalagem do Convento,* pleasant, is just outside city walls; *Mansao da Torre,* 6 rooms. All (1).

SOUTH OF LISBON

AZEITAO. *Estalagem Quinta das Torres,* charming former residence. Lakeside dining in summer. Renowned cuisine.

PORTINHO D'ARRÁBIDA. The *Estalagem de Santa Maria* (2), few rooms. Restaurant in pepperpot fortress overlooking bay.

SESIMBRA. The *Hotel do Mar* (1), 120 rooms, pool. *Espadarte,* 80 rooms, on the sea.

SETÚBAL. *Pousada S. Felipe,* 16 rooms, atmospheric, great view.

Ribatejo and Bullfighting

If you follow the west bank of the Tagus north from Lisbon, you will enter the green pastures of Ribatejo. This is the country of the horses, bulls and *toureiros,* whom you will see in the highly expert spectacle of Portuguese bullfighting. The long-horned herds are led by *campinos,* or cowboys, armed with long, javelin-like staves, and wearing their striking costumes—short blue breeches, white hose, bolero, red waistcoat and green and red cap. The best time to visit the Ribatejo is during the bullfights at Vila Franca or Salvaterra, and certainly at the time of local *fêtes,* the "Colete Encarnado", at Vila Franca de Xira, the second Sunday of July, or the "Barrete Verde", at Alcochete, the second Sunday in August. In all major towns, *feiras* are held on a certain day of the year (check locally whether any are in the offing while you are there). Sometimes, as at Golega, it is a horse fair; at others, it is a fair for the fair's sake, with livestock, pottery, country produce abounding.

Those travelers startled by the strong flavor of Ribatejan celebrations will be moved by the charm of Almourol. This was originally a strategic feudal castle, built in the middle of the Tagus by the grand master of the Order of Knights Templar. In striking contrast to this medieval ruin is the great dam of Castelo de Bode, on the River Zêzere. Completed in 1950 by British engineers, it is one of the more impressive accomplishments of modern Europe.

Tomar

But the treasure of Ribatejo is Tomar, built in a region of ravishing beauty, where subtle colors and lines are reminiscent of Tuscany. Churches are numerous, each one more lovely than the last. But one visits Tomar chiefly in order to see the celebrated Convent of Christ. The

Templars were installed there in the year 1160, and one can still see their original sanctuary, the Charola, with seven cloisters in the vast complex.

Out of gratitude, King Manuel gave to the Convent of Tomar a church of exquisite beauty. One sees first a marvelous portal by Joao de Castilho, and, above all, the famous window of the Chapter House, finest work of Manueline art.

PRACTICAL INFORMATION FOR RIBATEJO

TOMAR. *Dos Templarios,* sumptuous, 84 rooms, pool; *Estalagem Santa Iria,* delightfully located on a small island, 10 rooms, 7 with bath; both (1). In town, *Pensao Muno Alvares* (4), 28 rooms, 3 with bath.

Beira Rio, pleasant little restaurant, or *Bela Vista* ditto.

VILA FRANCA DE XIRA. *Estalagem do Gado Bravo,* 18 rooms, and *da Leziria,* 77 rooms, both (1).

The Beiras and Estremadura

Watered by the Mondego River, Beira, with its population of peasants and fishermen, is a true synthesis of Portugal. Pride of the area is Portugal's third city and former capital, Coimbra. This town, perched on a promontory above the river, is famous for its university. Founded in 1290, it is one of Europe's oldest. Its alumni roster includes Camoes, Portugal's great epic poet; the novelist Eça de Queiroz; Saint Anthony of Padua; Antero de Quental, the philosopher, and António de Oliveira Salazar. Coimbra vibrates with life during the school year, and the *fado* is king of music here, more intellectual and sophisticated than Lisbon.

Take your children to Portugal dos Pequeninos, a vast park containing copies of many monuments and dwellings typical of the country and of the former overseas provinces, all built to scale for a child of five. The finest among the city's many churches is the Romanesque Sé Velha (Old Cathedral), with its evocative cloister, Machado de Castro Museum, notable early sculpture.

South of Coimbra are the splendid Roman remains at Coimbriga and the magnificent feudal castle of Queen Isabel and Dom Diniz at Leiria.

Aveiro and Buçaco

Aveiro, a provincial fishing town, is worth a visit, especially in March during the popular fair, when there is dancing on the brightly-painted, flower-garlanded fishing boats. Aveiro's great sport is night fishing in the lagoon, and its great dish is the result—a delicious fish soup called Caldeirada à Pescadora. At nearby Ilhavo, site of the 130-year old Vista Alegre porcelain factory, there is a fascinating small museum containing many unique early pieces.

Buçaco was the scene in 1810 of a ferocious battle in which Wellington defeated Napoleon's troops. On the eve of his victory, he slept in a cell of the Carmelite Monastery here. Take a walk through the mysteriously-lighted *mata,* the high cedar forest planted by the monks of Buçaco 300 years ago.

Once the hunting lodge of Portuguese royalty, the Buçaco Palace, situated within the forest, is a deservedly well-known luxury hotel. Luso and Curia, in the neighborhood, are both well-known and greatly-frequented spas, with hotels and pensions suited to all tastes. In the Serra da Estrela, the highest point of which rises to 6,500 feet, there is good skiing in winter under blue skies.

PRACTICAL INFORMATION FOR THE BEIRAS

AVEIRO. *Hotel Imperial* (2), 49 rooms, most with bath. *Arcada* (3), 52 rooms, most with bath.

BUÇACO. *Palace Hotel* (L), former royal hunting lodge in forest, 76 rooms, quiet and restful. Outstanding service.

COIMBRA. *Astoria,* 70 rooms, good food and Buçaco wine; *Oslo,* panoramic view; *Bragança,* not quite up to first class rating. *Mondego, Estalagem Santa Luzia,* both (3). Specialty restaurants: *Dom Pedro* and *Santa Cruz.*

CURIA. *Palace,* 132 rooms, 146, most with bath. *Das Termas,* 45 rooms, 28 with bath. Both (2). Curia is a famous spa resort.

FIGUEIRA DA FOZ. Splendid beach. *Grande Hotel* (1), 111 rooms; *Hotel da Praia* (2), 65 rooms; *Estalagem da Piscina* (1), 20 rooms; all with bath. Casino.

GUARDA. First large town on the main road from Spain. *Hotel de Turismo* (2), 76 rooms with bath, pool. *Pensao Residência Filipe* (1), some rooms with bath.

LUSO. Thermal baths. *Grande Hotel das Termas* (2), 156 rooms with bath, pool.

SERRA DA ESTRELA. *Pousada de Sao Lourenço,* two miles from Penhas Douradas, between Manteigas and Gouveia, altitude 4,500 feet, picturesque, comfortable; 12 rooms, 6 with bath. Sometimes closed, so check.

VISEU. *Hotel Grao Vasco* is attractive, 57 rooms; *Estalagem Viriato,* 11 rooms; both (1), have rooms with bath.

Douro

Douro's capital is Oporto, and Oporto's capital is port. The whole province owes its wealth to that wonderful wine, made from the grapes that ripen all along the scorching, terraced slopes of the Douro River; Henry of Burgundy, a Duke of Portucale (hence the name), brought in the vines in the 11th century.

Try to visit this province of Portugal in late September, because this is the way you've always imagined a wine harvest. Watch the "must" poured into enormous casks and loaded on the trains or, more rarely, on the *rabelos,* strange, Phoenician-looking boats.

Oporto

Oporto, so old that it claims to have been founded by Noah, is a thriving bourgeois city, grown rich on the grape and its natural harbor. For many years, a royal edict forbade nobles to build within the city walls, hence the ascendancy of commerce and artisanship. The chief ornaments of Oporto are its gardens, filled with roses and camellias, and the river Douro itself, with its golden green water speckled with white sails and spanned by three splendid bridges. Of these, the most interesting is the two-level Dom Luis Bridge. The Dona Maria Bridge, a filigree of steel, was built by Eiffel; the impressive Ponte da Arrabida was inaugurated in 1964. The granite quays along the river hum with activity, for Oporto is a great center of foreign trade.

See here the Romanesque chapel of Sao Martinho de Cedofeita, the oldest in Portugal, and the church of the Clerigos, which dominates the city with its 10-story tower. Sao Francisco's gilded woodcarvings are worth seeing as are those in Santa Clara.

There is a large colony of Portugal's oldest allies here, the British, many of whose families have been here for generations in connection with the British cloth and Portuguese wine trades.

Popular beach resorts in the environs of Oporto include Foz do Douro, Póvoa de Varzim, an exceedingly picturesque fishing community, and Miramar, a pleasant little family beach with very few hotels and a golf course.

PRACTICAL INFORMATION FOR DOURO

ESPINHO. *Hotel Praiagolfe* (1), 119 rooms, is on a scale seen nowhere in Portugal except Algarve. Two superb golf courses, pool, conference rooms, banquet halls, casino.

MATOSINHOS. Colorful fishing village near Oporto. *Porto Mar* (3), 24 rooms, 8 with bath.

OFIR. *Hotel do Ofir,* 222 rooms; *Pinhal,* 89 rooms; *Estalagem Parque do Rio,* 30 rooms; all (1), all rooms with bath, and on or near beach.

OPORTO. *Infante de Sagres* (L), 82 rooms; *Dom Henrique,* 102 rooms, panoramic 15th-floor roof restaurant; *Castor,* 61 rooms. Both (1). *Grande Hotel do Porto,* 100 rooms; *Batalha,* 147 rooms; *Imperio,* 85 rooms. Both (2), and all rooms with bath.

Best pension: *Albergaria Corcel* (1), 30 rooms with bath.

The countrywide famous restaurant is *Escondidinho,* unpretentious outside, tip-top cuisine. *Chinês* serves lobster Chinese-way; *Acquario Marisqueiro,* mainly seafood; *Portucale,* the rooftop restaurant of Albergaria Miradouro, deluxe. *Neptuno,* for good cheap seafood.

PÓVOA DE VARZIM. *Vermar* (1), 208 rooms, many facilities. The *Grande Hotel* (2), 117 rooms, 106 with bath, on the sea. Casino.

Minho

For the tourist with the taste and leisure to explore out-of-the-way places, the lesser-known provinces of Portugal can be richly rewarding. Minho, bounded by Spain, the Atlantic and the Douro River, has the most colorful folk costumes, the loveliest landscapes, and the liveliest peasants of all. Their rapid, whirling folk dances, the *vira* and the *caninha verde,* are dazzling and dizzying.

Renaissance Viana, Baroque Braga and medieval Guimaraes all preserve their epochal charm intact, and all are worth a visit by the tourist in search of the unspoiled.

The Alentejo

Alentejo, the largest province, is the granary of Portugal. Her vast forests furnish the country's most important export product, cork. The country fairs in this wealthy, hospitable region are especially animated. You might try the one at Estremoz, held every Saturday in the main square, Rossio.

At Évora, you can trace the cycles of history in stone. The graceful colonnades and marble capitals of the temple of Diana will remind you that the Romans were firmly established in the peninsula. But Évora has in addition a fine Romanesque cathedral, a fortified Gothic chapel, and the ruins of the palace where Manuel the Fortunate received Vasco da Gama. If you have a taste for the macabre, the Church of Sao Francisco boasts a chapel of bones, whose walls and columns are made of human skulls.

PRACTICAL INFORMATION FOR OTHER PROVINCES

BRAGA (Minho Province). *Turismo,* 132 rooms; *Joao XXI* (3), 28 rooms; at Bom Jesus do Monte, *do Elevador* (1), 25 rooms; *Pousada de Sao Bento,* on Braga-Gerês highway, 10 rooms, pool. All rooms with bath.

BRAGANÇA (Trás-os-Montes Province). *Pousada de S. Bartolomeu,* charming, 10 rooms; a few miles from Spanish border.

ELVAS (Alentejo Province). *Pousada de Santa Luzia,* just outside city walls and 4 miles from Spanish border, 11 rooms, 9 with bath. *Estalagem D. Sancho II* (1), 24 rooms with bath, pool.

ESTREMOZ (Alentejo Province). *Pousada Rainha Santa Isabel* (L), in old castle, 23 air-conditioned rooms with bath.

ÉVORA (Alentejo Province). The ancient convent is the romantic *Pousada dos Lóios* (L), by the ruins of the Temple of Diana; 28 rooms with bath. *Planicie* (2), 33 rooms with bath.

MIRANDA DO DOURO (Trás-os-Montes Province). *Pousada de S. Catarina,* 12 rooms with bath.

POVÓA DAS QUARTAS (Beira Province). *Pousada de Santa Barbara,* 16 rooms with bath. On Coimbra-Guarda highway.

VALENÇA DO MINHO (Minho Province). *Pousada Sao Teotónio,* a mile from Spanish border, 16 rooms with bath.

VIANA DO CASTELO (Minho Province). *Hotel Santa Luzia,* 36 rooms with bath; *Afonso III,* 89 rooms with bath. Both (1). *Parque,* 140 rooms with bath, pool.

The Algarve

Brilliantly tinted, aromatic Algarve is the exotic southernmost province, indelibly marked by centuries of Arab occupation. Sun worshippers love it in the almost tropical heat of summer. But the best time to come is at the beginning of February, when the whole place is a sea of white almond blossoms. The flat-roofed white houses, the fig and palm trees, will remind you of Morocco.

The port of Olhao, where sardine-canning is big business, is easy on the eye, though a bit hard on the olfactory senses. The entire Barlavento coast is highly picturesque, ranging from golden, peaceful beaches to the jagged cliffs and roaring waves at Sagres.

If the Algarve coast is too hot, you have only to mount to the cool heights of the Monchique Range a few miles inland, where there are quiet footpaths among waterfalls and an amazing variety of trees, both tropical and northern. May is a good month here; the rhododendron and azalea are in full bloom then.

Algarve, Portugal's most developed tourist area, sprouts hotels and residential villas all along its coast. Many visitors find rental of villas, complete with maids and pools, more satisfactory than hotels. (For fuller information, see *Fodor's Portugal.*)

PRACTICAL INFORMATION FOR ALGARVE

Hotels listed have all, or majority of rooms with bath, often with balcony. Hotels and restaurants are so plentiful around here that our selection is only representative of the best at going to press.

ALBUFEIRA. *Sol e Mar* (1), 74 rooms, two bars, nightclub, rather noisy, but overlooks beach; *Boa Vista,* on hillside, has rooms and apartments, restaurant, glorious view; *Baltum,* 26 rooms, near beach, with annex. Both (3).

Estalagem do Cerro, 50 rooms, in town but with fine view; *Estalagem Mar a Vista,* 29 rooms, on hillside; both (1). *Pensao Albufeirense* (2), 18 rooms.

Three miles east, on clifftop, *Hotel Balaia Penta* (L), 150 rooms, air-conditioned, bar, pool, nightclub, tennis, shops; furnished bungalows.

Restaurants: *Alfredo* (E), elegant. *Fernando,* on main square, low-priced tourist menus. *Sir Harry's Bar,* sort of English pub. *O Cabaz da Praia,* on clifftop, for picnic baskets, serves meals, too.

FARO. *Eva* (1), 149 air-conditioned rooms, rooftop terrace. *Faro,* 52 rooms, on main square; *Casa Lumena,* 12 rooms; both (2). *Estalagem Aeromar,* right on beach.

Al-faghar (M), restaurant in old house. *Porto Fino,* fun décor, good food.

LAGOS. *Meia Praia,* 66 rooms, only hotel on the sea; *Sao Cristovao,* 76 rooms, modern, well-recommended. All (2).

Hotel de Lagos (L), 273 rooms, 12 suites, 3 bars and water pumped specially from Monchique spa.

At Praia Dona Ana, *Hotel Golfinho* (1), 157 rooms.

MONTE GORDO. The *Vasco da Gama* (1), 186 rooms, nightclub, pool, tennis. In pinewood *Das Caravelas* (2), 87 rooms.

MONTES DE ALVOR. *Penina Golf Hotel* (L), 214 rooms, casino, pool, 18-hole golf course (on Eurogolf Circuit). Located between Portimao and Lagos.

PORTIMÁO. *Globo* (2), 68 rooms. *Estalagem Miradouro* (1), 30 rooms. *Alfredo's, Porto de Abrigo, A Feitoria* are all good spots for food.

PRAIA DA ROCHA. *Algarve* (L), 200 air-conditioned rooms. *Jupiter,* 144 rooms, pool, nightclub; *Estalagem Alcalà,* 20 rooms; both (1).

Nearby, at **Praia de Alvor,** *Alvor Praia* (L), 215 air-conditioned rooms, casino, floorshow, seawater pool, golf and riding facilities. Also the imposing *Torralta Holiday Club* (1), has 250 self-contained apartments, shopping center, nightclub, several pools. *Hotel D Joao II,* 220 rooms, 18 suites.

SAGRES. *Pousada do Infante,* high above the sea, combines great comfort with fine view, 15 rooms. *Hotel da Baleeira* (2), 108 rooms, perches over a small sandy bay.

SAO BRÁS D'ALPORTEL. *Pousada de Sao Brás,* three miles outside the village, 17 rooms, panoramic view.

At Vale do Lobo-Almansil, *Dona Filipa* (L), 125 rooms, 18-hole golf course, pool. On the Henry Longhurst Eurogolf Holiday Circuit.

MADEIRA AND THE AZORES: for information on these outlying Portuguese areas, see Fodor's *Portugal* guide.

ROMANIA

The first nation to publicize a monster to attract tourists, Romania is unique in many other ways, not the least of which is her zesty independence from the U.S.S.R. while remaining within the Soviet bloc. It may seem odd to organize "Dracula Tours" to Transylvania, but with the ever-growing popularity of special interest tours, Romania may be on to a good thing. In fact, the tour aims at separating Bram Stoker's fictional main character from the real 15-century King of Walachia, Vlad III Dracula, and delivering the vampire firmly back to his storybook world. A romantic country, Romania should be seen through the eyes of a lover, even if only a temporary one, and it takes time to get into the right mood, even in this Latinized land. We should point out that while we have in years past had many complaints about the difficulty of traveling in Romania as an independent tourist, this has now improved considerably. Tremendous strides have been made in devising means by which independent travelers can go where they like, see what they wish, meet the local people, and still enjoy inexpensive group-travel rates. Package tours continue to be well-organized and are a good way of getting the most out of visiting Romania.

Romania Today

The formidable achievements of the Romanian Socialist Republic in geriatrics, in social welfare, in the war against such age-old evils as illiteracy and child mortality, are everywhere evident. These and other aspects of social change add to the fascination of contemporary Romania. You will see a society in the course of transformation. The

Romanians have now survived two millennia of incursions by both enemies and "disinterested friends", and until recently the process of determining their own national destiny has been a slow one.

For well over a decade, Romania has pursued a freewheeling foreign policy, carefully combined with strict adherence to Communist orthodoxy at home. This includes strongly centralized planning and an economic strategy that combines the highest annual increases in industrial output in Eastern Europe with the slowest rise in living standards; but now they are reaping the benefits, as evidenced by an annual average income per person of the equivalent of $1,000 in 1975 compared with $80 in 1946, and a forecast of $2,500 in 1985. It is the only member of the Eastern bloc to have relations with Israel; it was the first country in the Soviet sphere of influence to entertain an American President, and the first to recognize West Germany. But this free approach does not extend to travel abroad by Romanians as a whole, nor has it meant much loosening up of everyday life. All the same, Western visitors will encounter great friendliness and more freedom of movement than would have been the case a few years ago. The fascination of Romania, a fascination which suggests the Middle East rather than Europe, has not been undermined by the recent upsurge in the sophistication of Bucharest, nor by the huge increase in visiting tourists, especially to the Black Sea resorts (numbering several million). The pace of change may have been slower than elsewhere, but Romania, once a Balkan peasant nation, is showing all the symptoms of a developing economy.

The Country and the People

To find the uninhibited expression of the national spirit, you must go to the villages of Romania. The impulse of individual expression has invested them with a peculiar beauty which reflects a long tradition of craftsmanship. The houses, built in differing traditional styles, have a clean-cut, almost classic simplicity, punctuated by the rich ornamentation of handcarved wooden doors, pillars, balustrades, usually in a contrasting color, a striking blue, a strong vermilion. The love of bright colors and good design runs like a *leitmotif* through Romanian embroidery, hand-woven rugs, beautiful pottery and wooden sculpture, which are the delight of connoisseurs. It is most fully expressed in the magnificently-embroidered folk costumes, red, green, white, gold and blue, combined with instinctive good taste. Save some color film for Romania, for you won't find subject matter like this anywhere else east of Portugal.

The same color sense, combined with a love of strongly marked rhythm, has produced one of the richest bodies of folk music in existence, music whose vigorous accelerando cadences have quickened the blood of concert-goers the world over in the Romanian Rhapsodies of George Enesco. If you have the good fortune to be on hand when a village or a regional festival is in process, prepare for a lengthy session of the liveliest and most colorful dancing you've ever seen. The most beautiful costumes are produced and the whole village joins in the fun.

You will be welcome at these festivities, treated as an honored guest. Your hosts will offer you fruits, their strong *tzuica* brandy distilled from plums, and yoghurt, key to longevity in their eyes. It will make you live beyond a hundred years, the peasants will tell you.

The handsome and temperamental Romanian satisfies his desire for gregarious strolling, for chance meetings with friends, for gossip and the free exchange of ideas in the "corso", a symbol of the Romanians' conscious loyalty to their Latin descent, a concept kept alive and handed down from generation to generation. In Bucharest, Paris of the Balkans, you will be aware, as in no other eastern capital, of that Latin flavor.

Food and Drink

Although there are some regional differences between the provinces, there is none-the-less a pronounced national culinary tradition, highlighted by such dishes as *ciorba de perisoare,* a soup with meatballs, *ciorba taraneasca* with meat and lots of vegetables, lamb *bors* flavored with lovage, giblet soup, and richly varied fish soups. Sour cream or eggs are often added to soups.

The Romanians' all-purpose staple is *mamaliga,* a highly versatile cornmeal mush or *kassa,* which can be served in countless different ways. *Tocana* is a stew made with pork, beef or mutton, seasoned abundantly with onions, and served with mamaliga. *Ghiveci,* also called "monastic hodge-podge" when it has no meat, is a preparation of over twenty vegetables cooked in oil and served cold. Another typical dish is Moldavian *parjoale*—flat meat patties, highly spiced, served with a wide variety of garnishes.

One great specialty of Romania is charcoal-grilled meat, often in the form of sausages. Among the countless varieties are *mititei,* highly seasoned mincemeat grilled to order in cafés and restaurants, and *patricieni,* resembling frankfurters.

Romania is rich in game and fish of all kinds, prepared in innumerable ways. Most famous are the fish soup and barbecued carp as cooked by the Danube delta fishermen.

Fruit is plentiful, delicious and inexpensive. Among the Romanian desserts you will enjoy trying are *placinte cu poale in briu,* rolled cheese pies, and Moldavian *cozonac* (brioche) or *pasca,* a sweet cream cheesecake similar to the Russian *paskha. Baclava, cataiff* and other cakes of Oriental origin are now definitely part of Romanian cuisine.

Entrées are traditionally accompanied by a small glass of *tzuica,* the usually powerful plum brandy whose strength, dryness and aroma all vary according to region and locality. Romanian wines are famous: the *Feteasca* or *Grasa* of Cotnari, the *Riesling, Muscat, Pinot* and *Chardona* of Murfatlar, the *Babeasca* of Niculitel, and many others.

PRACTICAL INFORMATION FOR ROMANIA

13.06,
524
2400
423 0

WHAT WILL IT COST. Prices are generally government controlled and standardized throughout. Daily **hotel** rates per person, including full board, are approximately deluxe: from 500 lei; first class: 400 lei; tourist: 200 lei. Prices are 20 percent lower off season.

Restaurants: in most hotels and other expensive places a good three-course meal will cost about 80 lei. Moderate restaurants charge about 70 lei, inexpensive ones around 50 lei.

Other costs: taxis charge about 3 lei per km., plus 3 lei on starting; opera ticket, 5–20 lei, theater, 6–15 lei, movie, 2–5 lei; museums, 3 lei. American cigarettes are from 18–22 lei per pack.

CAPITAL. Bucharest.

LANGUAGE. Romanian. French especially, German and English are spoken by the educated; most hotel employees speak foreign languages.

CLIMATE. Moderate on coast, hot inland in summer. Winters are variable.

Average maximum daily temperatures in Fahrenheit and centigrade:

Bucha-rest	Jan.	Feb.	Mar.	Apr.	May	June	July	Aug.	Sept.	Oct.	Nov.	Dec.
F°	34	39	50	64	73	81	86	86	77	64	50	39
C°	1	4	10	18	23	27	30	30	25	18	10	4

SEASONS. Spring or summer (mid-April to mid-October) for sightseeing, but try to avoid inland towns in July and August, when the thermometer often reaches 90°F. January to March for winter sports, June–September for Black Sea bathing.

SPECIAL EVENTS. *July,* Young Girl's Fair, Mount Gaina. *September,* Folklore Festival, Bucharest.

$P£ **MONEY.** You may bring in any amount or kind of foreign currency, including travelers checks, and freely exchange it at State Bank branches, and at some hotels. The import and export of Romanian currency is not permitted.

Tourists with prepaid services and children under 14 years are exempt from compulsory currency exchange. Otherwise, they must exchange $10 or its equivalent per day per person for the number of days for which they have requested a visa. Romania's monetary unit is the *leu* (plural *lei*), divided into 100 *bani.* At the present tourist rate of exchange there are 12 lei to the dollar, 23 to the pound sterling. **Subject to change.** You may also cash additional hard, freely convertible currency or travelers checks at this rate inside Romania. If you intend to do some shopping, try the "dollar shops" where you are allowed to pay only in hard currency or travelers checks and where prices of traditional Romanian items are cheaper.

TIPPING. For specially good service, tip waiters 5–12%, though tipping is by no means obligatory. Porters and taxi drivers get 5–10 lei.

 HOW TO GO. All foreign travel to Romania is handled by the national tourist offices, among them *ONT Carpati-Bucuresti,* Magheru Blvd. 7, Bucharest and *Litoral,* Hotel Bucharest, Mamaia. The tourist office address in New York is: 573 Third Ave., New York, N.Y. 10016; in London, 98 Jermyn St., W1, where they will provide you with information but do not make arrangements. For this you must go to an accredited travel agent who will handle all the bookings including hotel accommodation.

The Romanian tourist office is represented, among others, by:

In the United States:
American Express Company, all U.S. offices.
General Tours, 49 W. 57 St., New York, N.Y. 10019.
Maupintour Associates, 900 Massachusetts St., Lawrence, Kansas 66044.
Travcoa, Hancock Center, 875 N. Michigan Ave., Chicago, Ill. 60611.
Unitours, Unitours Building, 1671 Wilshire Blvd., Los Angeles, Calif. 90017.
American Travel Abroad, 250 W. 57th St., New York, N.Y. 10019.

In Great Britain:
Sunquest Holidays, 43/4 New Bond St., London W1
Balkan Holidays, 126-30 Regent St., London W1
Thomson, Greater London Hse., Hampstead Rd., London NW1
Peltours, 72 Wigmore St., London W1
Black Sea Holidays, 8 Belmont Crescent, Glasgow G12 8EU.

Sovereign Holidays, P.O. Box 410, West London Air Terminal, London SW7 4ED.

TRAVEL DOCUMENTS. American and British passports are valid for travel in Romania. Visas are required, but are provided free on arrival to Americans, at a nominal fee to Britons (free if they have prepaid services). No photos or application forms required. Business visitors should enquire about visa requirements from a travel agent or a Romanian consulate.

HOW TO REACH ROMANIA. By Air: *TAROM,* the Romanian national airline, has a weekly flight from New York to Bucharest, stopping in Amsterdam. *Pan Am* has a twice-weekly service.

From London, *BA* flies twice weekly to Bucharest, as does Tarom. Charters fly direct to Mamaia. Connections from most European capitals.

There is a bus service from Bucharest airport to the town terminal costing 8 lei, and a public bus costing 2 lei.

By Ship: You can take a boat from Vienna down the Danube, or pick up a Black Sea cruise ship to Constanza.

By Train: Bucharest can be reached via the *Balt-Orient Express* from Stockholm and Malmö via East Germany, Czechoslovakia and Hungary, or the *Wiener Walzer* from Paris, Basel, Zurich or Vienna. From London, second-class fare is approximately £150 return.

By Car: Romania may be entered by car from the USSR, Hungary, Yugoslavia and Bulgaria. The following are convenient border points and distances to Bucharest: (from Hungary) Bors, 400 miles on DN 1 - E 15, or Nadlac, 392 miles on DN 7; (from Yugoslavia) Moravita, 389 miles; or the even shorter route over the new Iron Gates Dam bridge; (from Bulgaria) Giurgiu, 40 miles, or Negru Voda, 197 miles, or Vama Veche, 194 miles; (from USSR) Albita, 261 miles or Siret, 296 miles, or (from Czechoslovakia via USSR) Halmeu, 423 miles.

No customs documents are required. Green Card insurance is recognized. So are international or national drivers licenses.

The government has devised an extremely ingenious way of allowing individual car travelers to remain completely independent and still benefit from very low group rates; you buy a week's or two weeks' half board which you can use at listed hotels throughout the country without even making advance reservations, provided you turn up at each night's chosen stopping-place by 6 P.M. Five liters of fuel per day are provided free with this plan, available to both personal or rented cars. Fly/drive arrangements from London, using this flexibly packaged motoring tour with a hire car, including the accommodation vouchers with half board and the free fuel allowance, cost from £120–£190 for a week, according to the number in the party.

By Bus: From London. Contact *Europabus* Victoria Station, London, or a travel agent.

CUSTOMS. Personal belongings may be brought in duty-free, including such items as two cameras with black and white or color films, a small movie camera, portable radio, portable typewriter, etc., as well as 300 cigarettes, 2 liters of liquor and 5 liters of wine. Gifts may be imported duty-free to a value of 2,000 lei. Have your valuables (gold watch, etc.) registered on entry.

MAIL. Airmail rate to the U.S. is 10.50 lei for a letter, 4.80 for a postcard. To Britain: 5.65 lei for a letter, 4.80 for a postcard, but check before mailing.

If you place a long-distance call from your hotel be sure to check the hotel's service charge which can sometimes double the basic cost of the call.

ELECTRICITY. Most establishments have 220 volts; only older ones have 110 or 115 volts, 50 cycles A.C.

TRAVEL IN ROMANIA By Air. *Tarom* connects all major cities and resorts on its domestic routes. **By train.** There are fairly good services connecting major cities; first and second class, dining cars. **By car.** The motor highways are in good condition. Secondary roads are mostly unsurfaced, badly signposted, and best avoided, unless you have a well-developed sense of adventure when they can be very rewarding. A thoroughly serviceable map showing roads and surfaces is available free from the tourist offices. Fuel costs 4.50 lei per liter for super, subject to increase. Emergency number when touring is 12345 (in Bucharest 123456).

Car Hire. *Avis* has offices at the airport and Str. Cihoski 2. The tourist offices can also arrange a rental car; charges are about 125 lei a day and up, plus mileage. See also Fly/drive arrangements already mentioned.

CAMPING at Oradea, Sibiu, Dimbu Morii near Brasov, Baneasa Forest and Lake Snagov near Bucharest, Mamaia or any of 46 other sites. There is also accommodation in private and guest houses.

TOURS. First choice is to Romania's unique painted churches of Moldavia. There are flights to Suceava, the regional capital, where you can arrange for a car and driver, or you can take a special tourist bus that makes the circuit of the monasteries.

Operating regularly now is the "Dracula" tour: 8 days spent visiting Bucharest, Brasov, Piatra Neamt and Bistrita—all places associated with either the real, or the novel's, Dracula.

Special interest tours including skiing in the Carpathians near Poiana Brasov and Sinaia, riding, and senior citizens' outings are also good value.

SPAS. An expanding number of spa resorts, for foreigners wishing to take advantage of Romania's thousands of mineral springs, are being opened. Of the 160 spas, 15 are of international standard including Otopeni near Bucharest, Herculane, Felix and Eforie.

USEFUL ADDRESSES. *Embassies:* United States, Dionisie Lupu St. 9; British, Jules Michelet St. 27. *National Tourist Office,* Blvd. Magheru 7. All in Bucharest.

Exploring Bucharest

With a population of over 1,800,000, Bucharest can boast of being one of Europe's larger cities. Its buildings surrounded by spacious courtyards, gardens and centuries-old trees, it is also one of the most gracious European capitals. Although it was inhabited more than 1,000 years ago, the hamlet of Bucharest in the vast Danube plain only began to take shape in the 14th century. From that time on, it grew rapidly. Today its 19th-century houses share the metropolis along with great modern blocks of apartment buildings, ten or more stories high. From beside the cathedral on the city's one low hill you have a fine view of the city and of the Dimbovita River, which divides the town. A blue-green chain of park-rimmed lakes dotted with tiny islands borders the city on the northeast.

NOTE

The tragic earthquake which destroyed many buildings in Bucharest in the spring of 1977 caused many casualties and disrupted the economy. As a result of remarkable efforts, all industrial production has been resumed and the loss of tourist beds compensated by the opening of new hotels.

Busiest part of town is the area around the Calea Victoriei, with its big government buildings, museums, shopping centers and modern apartments, liberally landscaped with gardens and courtyards. In this heart of Bucharest, the older houses are interspersed with modern blocks. Stroll up this main thoroughfare toward the Piata Victoriei and the Herastrau Park, where you will come to the House of the Army, with its monumental French neoclassical façade, the huge modern Telephone Palace and the S.R.R. Palace (former Royal Palace, built in 1933), today housing the National Art Museum. Bd. Magheru is mostly modernized. On Bd. Gheorghiu-Dej are the lovely Cismigiu Gardens with lakes, twisting walks, springs, grottos and fountains. Bucharest's most beautiful concert hall is the Romanian Athenaeum, halfway up the Calea Victoriei, noted for its elaborate interior decoration. An example of ultramodern Romanian architecture is the S.R.R. Academy on your left.

Kiseleff Avenue leads on out of the Piata Victoriei to the Herastrau Park, or the Park of Culture and Rest. This municipal paradise on the shores of Lake Herastrau displays an open-air theater and library (where you can read beneath the trees), and an amusement park. You can go boating, swimming, fishing, or watch the world go by from pleasant lakeside restaurants. Here, too, is one of the oldest and most charming of Europe's "village" museums.

For nature-lovers, other Bucharest parks to see are Liberty park (Parcul Libertatii), with its lakes, mosques, fountain and Zoo; and the August 23 Park, the home of the gigantic 80,000-spectator stadium and Romanesque open-air summer theater.

PRACTICAL INFORMATION FOR BUCHAREST

HOTELS
Deluxe

Intercontinental. Recent, 423 rooms, all facilities.
Athénée Palace. 297 rooms, garden bar, good restaurant, old world charm.
Continental, all facilities.
Dorobanti. 304 rooms, modern.

First Class
Bulevard and *Parc* are of good standard.

Moderate
Muntenia, Cismigiu, Grivita, Tranzit, Oltenia are adequate.

RESTAURANTS. Restaurants with good cuisine in most major hotels. There are several elegant restaurants on the shores of Lake Herastrau, including the *Pescarus* at Herastrau.
Bucuresti, on Calea Victoriei, is the best in town.
Berlin, Str. Mille. Nice garden.
Bumbesti, 90 Calea Rahovei. Romanian décor and cuisine.

Carul cu Bere, traditional beer restaurant, Strada Stavropoleos 3.
Pescarul, 7–9 Bd. Balcescu. Fish specialties.
Gambrinus, 22 Bd. Gheorghe Gheorghiu-Dej.
Bucur and the *Doina* offer an intimate décor, atmosphere, and excellent meals.
For typical Romanian dishes try: *Odobesti* and *Doi Cocosi,* wine cellars. Romantic dining at *Hanul lui* Manuc, converted 18th-century inn with Oriental atmosphere, which also rents out a few rooms. In Baneasa Park, just outside of town, *Padurea Baneasa* is a delightful open-air restaurant with rustic atmosphere serving Romanian specialties. Regional folk dancers.

CAFÉ-BARS. On the Boulevard Gheorghe Gheorghiu-Dej are the *Tosca,* the *Ciresica,* the *Tic-Tac* and the *Tomis.* The *Turist* is on Boulevard Magheru, the *Unic* on Boulevard Balcescu.

TRANSPORTATION. Taxis (stands at main intersections). Start at 3 lei, plus 3 lei for each kilometer. Buses cost 1 lei, trams 30 bani, some are self-service. The tourist office arranges sightseeing tours by bus—"Historic Bucharest", "Bucharest at Night", etc.

ENTERTAINMENT. Pre-war Bucharest was the gayest, wickedest capital in the Balkans. Today, the communist regime has channeled most of its exotic excitement into *opera, ballet, theater, concerts,* and other more "cultural" outlets. But try the *Athénée Palace* nightclub, elegant night spot with sophisticated floorshow; *Bucuresti,* also sophisticated; *Continental* or *Melody.* Bucharest still has a healthy quota of cafés with cheerful orchestras and dancing, bars with jazz bands and variety shows, and a good many taverns. Restaurants in the larger hotels double as nightclubs, with dance orchestras and variety acts. Take in the circus, a permanent feature housed in a marble and glass building in traditional circus-tent shape, or a puppet show at the *Teatrul de Marionete.* Two major symphony orchestras give concerts in the splendid *Athenaeum* concert hall. In summer, theatrical productions are staged in the vast Roman-style open-air theater in 23 August Park.

PARKS. Cismigiu Garden; Libertatii Park, with lake and fountains; 23 August Park, with stadium and open-air theater; amusement park, boating, bathing, fishing at Herastrau Park; fine 9-hole golf course.

MUSEUMS. Bucharest has 20 museums, of which the following are of greatest interest to foreign visitors: *Muzeul de Arta S.R.R.* (Art Museum), in former Royal Palace, national, oriental and west European art; El Greco, Titian, Rembrandt; modern French and Romanian painting. *Muzeul de Istorie de România* (Museum of Romanian History), now in the former Central Post Office building, items from regional and local collections, beautifully displayed but labeled only in Romanian; crown jewels and other treasures. *Muzeul de Arta Populara* (Folk Art Museum). All located on Calea Victoriei. *Minovici Museum,* a villa furnished in traditional Romanian style, and the *Village Museum,* with genuine peasant houses, fully furnished, from all parts of the country, are on Kisselef Ave.

SHOPPING. For souvenir or simply window shopping, stroll down Bucharest's main thoroughfares, Calea Victoriei and Bd. Magheru. Romania's superbly rich folk art includes rugs; embroidered sheepskin coats, blouses and scarves, and skirts; ceramics, pottery and carved wooden objects. The traditional shopping area of Lipscani boasts picturesque, varied and old-style shops within walking distance of central hotels.

Some addresses: the folk-art shop at no. 1 Strada Pictor Verona; the *Bucuresti* department store, 2 Str. Baratiei; *Romarta,* 66–68 Calea Victoriei, for readymade clothes, accessories, knitwear. *Melodia,* 16 Bd. Magheru, sells records, wines and the famous *tzuica* liquor.

Remember that because Romania is considered a developing country, many of the things you buy there may be exempt from U.S. Customs duties under the G.S.P. plan, as explained in the section on Customs in Facts at Your Fingertips, at the beginning of this volume.

Exploring the Interior

Only 22 miles from Bucharest on the road to ancient Brasov is Lake Snagov, in the middle of an immense oak forest. It has fine sandy beaches, water sports, sailing and open-air theatricals. Visit the 14th-century monastery on the island. Further along is Breaza, a delightful Romanian village and health resort. Sinaia, 2,600 feet above sea level, is one of the loveliest spots in the southern Carpathians. It offers a wonderful view of the Prahova Valley, and facilities for mountaineering and winter sports. Economically important Brasov, with its many medieval reminders, is one of Romania's best known tourist centers and is still the capital of the ancient province of Transylvania. Visit its Black Church built in 1385. Several hours drive east of Brasov is 13th-century Sibiu in the shadow of snow-capped Fagaras mountain peaks. In the center of town, you will find monumental 18th-century Brukenthal Palace, which contains a striking collection of European art (fine Van Dycks), Romanian folklore, books and documents.

The Black Sea Beaches

Romanians can be justly proud of their splendid beaches, with their gentle surf and fine sands. Most popular seaside resort is Mamaia, three hours from Bucharest. Its nine-mile stretch of shore is lined with villas and hotels, well-equipped with sports facilities. As it caters mainly to group tours, you can get extremely good value here, at low cost. Constanza is a busy Black Sea port (second only to Odessa in shipping) built on the ruins of the old Greek colony, Tomi, where Ovid spent his last years. Today, its narrow streets and one mosque add Oriental charm and color to an otherwise modern town. Eforie, 14 km. from Constanza, has hotels of all categories, minigolf, tennis and other sports, with motorboat trips on Lake Techirghiol. It is a famous year-round health spa with well-equipped bathing pavilions, treating rheumatic ailments and skin diseases. Neptun, close to Comorova Forest, has a wide beach with dozens of modern hotels, good water skiing, tennis, etc., and is quieter than other seaside resorts. Mangalia (called Callatis in ancient times) is a town, port and resort at the same time. Two thousand-year-old Greek and Roman remains, and old houses with wooden balconies stand next to streamlined hotels built in concrete, glass and ceramics. In Jupiter there are several new high-rise hotels standing right on the beach. The newest resort is Venus, 43 kilometers from Constanza, with very daring architecture. In most hotels, each room has a balcony.

The Moldavian Monasteries

The famed Bucovina painted monasteries are located in the northeast near the Russian border, and are most easily reached from Suceava, the regional capital. Built in the 15th and 16th centuries, the monasteries, painted with frescos inside and outside are: Voronet, Humor, Arbore, Sucevita and Moldovita. They are each different and all enchanting, but the most exquisite is the Voronet church, with an outside wall entirely dedicated to the depiction of *The Last Judgment*. Wind and rain have slightly eroded some of the frescos, but the majority retain their vivid colors.

At Moldovita, and also at other abbeys, you can rent traditional-style wooden houses and rooms from the nuns. At Agapia, near Piatra Neamt, there is also a small motel. Putna, another famous abbey, has a small hotel in the village below.

Transylvania

Thanks to the barrier of its natural mountain citadel, this region of vast pine forests, deep gorges and fertile valleys was much less affected by invading Tartar or Turk. It thus preserves its medieval architecture (and folkways) to an extent rare in any comparable area of Europe. The Hungarian minority, about a third of the population, has kept alive its folklore in both music and folk art from ceramics to embroidery, much more strongly than its kinsmen in Hungary proper. One of the most charming areas is Maramures in the northwest where beautiful peasant dress and traditional crafts survive in a way of life that make this one of the least spoiled corners of Europe. Here you will find a whole string of delightful villages, each with its lovely old wooden church, carved gateways and a wonderful friendliness. Capital of this area is Baia Mare, which has developed into a modern town but is a good launching point for exploration.

The historic city of Cluj in the west is an important university and cultural center, replete with historic and architectural monuments. Lacul Rosu (Red Lake) is a fittingly named scenic resort in the high mountains northeast of Tirgul Mures. Sighisoara is a veritable museum town, with an enchanting 14-15th-century citadel where the house in which the historical Dracula was born still stands.

Southward from Cluj to the Yugoslav border you will pass a number of resorts and historic cities which flourished twenty centuries ago as Roman colonies in the outpost province of Dacia. Alba Iulia, Hunedoara (with the ruins of Sarmisegetusa) and Herculane are worthwhile stops; the last is Romania's best-known thermal spring resort. Another area little known to tourists is the mountainous Apuseni where old traditions survive amid grand karst scenery. This is a good area for walkers, but the road network is also improving.

Transylvania has not yet been much discovered by Western tourists. Little publicized, it is one of Europe's last—but most rewarding—places for an away-from-it-all adventurous vacation.

PRACTICAL INFORMATION FOR THE REGIONS

ARAD, Transylvania. Hotel: *Astoria, Muresul, Parc,* all first class. Restaurant: *Zarand,* good local cuisine.

BAIA MARE, main center for Maramures. *Carpati,* first class.

BRASOV, interior tourist center, Hotels: The *Carpati,* deluxe; *Capitol,* first class.

CLUJ, Transylvania. Hotels: *Napoca* and *Belvedere,* both first class.

CONSTANZA, Black Sea port. *Continental, Palace,* both first class with restaurants.

EFORIE NORD, Black Sea resort. Hotels: *Europa,* deluxe, restaurant; *Carmen,* deluxe, small.

HERCULANE, Transylvania. Hotels: *Roman, Hercules,* first class.

JASSY (IASI), near Soviet border. Hotel: *Unirea,* very modern, and *Traian,* both first class. Restaurants: *Bolta Rece, Vinatorului.*

MAMAIA, top Black Sea resort. Hotels: Best and oldest is the *International,* deluxe; then *Dorna; Riviera; Flora,* all first class, with restaurants, dancing, etc.

MANGALIA. *Mangalia,* first class.

NEPTUN, recent Black Sea resort, lovely beach, quiet. *Neptun,* deluxe. *Dacia* and *Delta,* first class, pleasant. Both serve meals in adjacent restaurant.

ORADEA, Transylvania. Hotel: *Dacia,* first class, on river bank.

PIATRA NEAMT, Moldavia. Hotels: *Ceahlaul,* deluxe; *Central,* first class.

POIANA BRASOV, winter sports resort, ski lifts, sleigh drives, tobogganing, après-ski amenities. Hotels: *Teleferic, Alpin, Bradul, Poiana,* all first class.

PREDEAL, in the Prahova valley, 3,000 feet, ski facilities. Hotels: *Orizont, Cioplea,* first class. Also others combining first and second class.

SIBIU, interior resort. Hotels: *Continental* and *Boulevard,* first class.

SIGHISOARA, Transylvania. Hotel: *Steaua,* first class.

SINAIA, mountain resort, ski facilities. Hotels: *Palas,* lovely situation, restaurant, dancing. *Alpin,* 4,500 ft., has a fine view over the Prahova valley; *Sinaia, Montana,* all first class.

SUCEAVA, Bucovina. Hotels: New *Bucovina,* first class, *Arcasul,* first class and modern, all rooms with showers; older *Suceava,* better known for its restaurant.

TIMISOARA, Transylvania. Hotels: *Continental,* recent, comfortable. *Banatul, Central.* All first class.

TULCEA, Danube Delta. Hotel: *Delta,* recent, first class.

TURNU SEVERIN, on Danube, near Iron Gates. Hotel: *Parc,* recent, first class.

 SPORTS. Romania has wonderful *swimming* on the Black Sea coast; rich and varied *fishing* (best bring your own tackle), and excellent *sailing* on Lake Siutghiol at Mamaia, a freshwater lake with aquatic clubs along its shores. The long-established ski resorts of Sinaia, Predeal and Poiana Brasov have been lately further developed.

WILD LIFE SANCTUARY, in Danube Delta. A bird-watcher's and picture-hunter's paradise. You live on comfortable two-bunk houseboats or in tourist bungalows. Inquire through your travel agent. The Carpathian mountains are also rich in rare fauna; no hunting allowed.

EXCURSIONS. From Suceava to the painted monasteries by car or bus. From Constanza, Black Sea cruisers ply up and down the coast. Other excursions to Istanbul by ship, Odessa by plane, to Murfatlar for wine-tasting. (See tourist office, 48 Bd. Tomis, Constanza for information.) A cruise along the Danube on Romanian ships can be initiated at Vienna, entering Romania at Moldova, terminating at Hirsova in Delta region. From there, by bus to Constanza and plane to Bucharest.

Something quite out of the ordinary is the Danube delta excursion out of Tulcea.

The interior regions are all covered by comfortable day excursion buses.

MUSEUMS. The *Regional Museum* in Constanza contains mainly relics, bas-reliefs, fragments of ceramics and statues. *Brukenthal Museum* in Sibiu has paintings, furniture and superb folk costumes. Others of special interest are: *The Museum of Transylvania Ethnography* at Cluj; *Museum of Petrol,* Ploiesti; *The Navy Museum* and *Museum of Archaeology* at Constanza; *Museum of the Iron Gates,* Dorbeta-Turnu; *Museum of the Danube Delta* at Tulcea.

SAN MARINO

Not far from Rimini in northern Italy, on the eastern slopes of the Apennines overlooking the Adriatic, there is a small republic of 23 square miles and about 20,000 inhabitants which claims to be the oldest in the world. San Marino is the capital, and there are eight villages scattered around the surrounding hills, as well as the famous Castelli Sammarinesi.

The people of San Marino live on the income from postage stamps and tourists. Nearly a million of the latter come each year to admire San Marino's medieval fortresses, kept in a fine state of preservation and reconstruction. The effect is of time arrested.

The tourist trade is further encouraged by the complete absence of any border formalities. You don't need a visa to go there, not even a passport. If you want yours stamped for souvenir purposes, you'll have to request it. (For a really spectacular ride, take the helicopter service between San Marino and Rimini.)

PRACTICAL INFORMATION FOR SAN MARINO

WHAT WILL IT COST. As regional areas of Italy (see chapter).

CAPITAL. San Marino.

LANGUAGE. Italian.

SEASONS. Peak is July and August.

SPECIAL EVENTS. In summer, usually July–September, International Festival of Arts; and September, the *Palio dei Balestrieri*, dating from the 16th century, with colorful crossbowmen in traditional dress. Check for dates with the Tourist Department, Palazzo del Turismo, San Marino. A picturesque investiture ceremony of newly elected regents takes place on April 1 and October 1.

MONEY. Italian lire (see Italy chapter) and own coinage, which is primarily for collectors, just like the postage stamps.

MAIL. See rates under Italy.

HOTELS. The *Grand Hotel San Marino*, situated on top of Mount Titano is in the first-class superior category. The class (2) *Diamond* is small, comfortable and reasonable. The *Excelsior* is a good second-class hotel. We can also recommend the first class *Titano*, especially for the splendid view from its restaurant terrace. *Joli*, at Piazzale Stazione, first class, with a good restaurant. *Tre Penne* is reasonable and has a fine restaurant.

Among the restaurants, we recommend *La Taverna* and *Buca San Francesco*, both (M).

SOVIET UNION

The second greatest country in the world (measured in gross national product), the largest nation in size and the second (if not the first) in muscle power, the U.S.S.R. attracts its fair share of American and British tourists, among others, largely through the pull of curiosity. Everyone wants to know what makes Russia tick, and especially since the Great October Revolution of 1917, the whole world *has* to learn, one way or another, what goes on in this vast and frequently mysterious land.

The Highlights

Soviet citizens are proud of their country, which they refer to as "the land where the sun never sets". When you sit down to a seven o'clock supper in Moscow, it is already midnight on the shores of Siberia's Lake Baikal, and five A.M. milking time on the Chukotsk Peninsula, across the Bering Straits from Alaska. It's as far from Vladivostok to Moscow as from the Equator to the Pole, and takes more than one week by fast train. Statistics like this are as pleasing to a Soviet citizen as a new toy to a child.

When Caucasian roses bloom and dates ripen in the subtropical climate of the southern U.S.S.R., at Verkhoyansk, in Northern Siberia, the thermometer drops to 70 degrees below zero, and your breath turns instantly to ice crystals. Even at Moscow, the temperature varies between 20 degrees below zero in winter and the high 70's or 80's in summer.

In the north country, you can hunt polar bear, fox, partridge and snow owl by the ghostly light of the aurora borealis. Squirrel and sable swarm in the Siberian forest. Soviet Turkestan is tiger country, and farther south live camel, antelope and flamingoes. In the Askania Nova National Park of the Ukraine, ostriches imported from Australia roam free, and feel perfectly at home.

As conditions continue to improve and Intourist keeps expanding its facilities, more and more of the Soviet Union is opening up to foreign travel. You may now visit, for example, the village of Mikhailovskoye in the Pskov region, where Pushkin lived and is buried. New routes are open from Leningrad via Narva to the Estonian capital of Tallinn, or northward to the island of Kizhi with its ancient churches; and from Moscow via the artistic and religious historical cities of Vladimir and Suzdal to Bogolyubovo. Especially noteworthy: the 12th-century cathedrals at Vladimir, the 1165 Church of Pokrov at Bogolyubovo and the churches of Kideksha (1152), near Suzdal. Soon more fascinating itineraries may be available to foreigners: check with your travel agent, or directly with the official Soviet agency Intourist for latest information. Meanwhile, in the following pages, we have tried to give you an idea of the more widely beaten tracks through this endlessly fascinating country.

Three Facets of Russia

To see Russian life, approach Moscow across the Finnish frontier through Leningrad, Novgorod and Kalinin. Outwardly, Leningrad is an exception to the general rule of Soviet cities. It is a Western capital in every sense of the word. Broad, ruler-straight avenues, bordered with trees, are lined with comfortable cut-stone buildings, palaces designed by the finest architects of the 18th and 19th centuries, among them the famous Rastrelli. Petrodvorets, summer palace of the Czars, is a pleasing copy of Versailles. In June, you can read a book in bed at midnight by the pale enchanting light of Leningrad's polar "White Nights", in which you imagine you can see the ghosts of the city's past splendor. Leningrad citizens consider themselves the natural aristocrats of the country. For them, the true capital is still their city, built by Peter the Great as "a window on Europe".

Novgorod is different; "cradle of the Russian nation", it has changed little in a thousand years. A city of the past, it still feels as well as looks medieval. However, it is in Moscow that the impact of new on old throws off the most sparks. The U.S.S.R.'s capital city is a mirror image of the country as a whole. Moscow is Europe mixed with the Arabian nights come to life. As one literary tourist recently exclaimed. "East is East and West is West, and Moscow's where they meet!" Here the Kremlin and its high red-brick walls, its gold-domed edifices, its royal palaces carefully preserved as they were in Ivan the Terrible's day, rub shoulders with skyscrapers that would have done credit to Manhattan a few decades ago.

In Moscow, you will find Georgian, Armenian and Ukrainian shops, Uzbek and Turkmenian restaurants, Siberian specialties, exotic fruits, Caspian caviar and Pacific salmon. Western European cuisine, usually with a heavy Russian accent, is served in the large hotels.

New Tourist Regions

A number of localities in Central Asia and Siberia have recently been added to the list of places where Intourist accommodates foreigners. The Uzbek SSR is of particular interest. Here, tourists can visit the four fabulous cities of Tashkent, Bukhara, Samarkand and Khiva (the last only as a day trip). Tashkent, the capital of the republic, is the economic and cultural center of Central Asia. Numerous old monuments are still standing in the city, among them the 16th-century Kukeldash madrasah. The Uzbek SSR is of particular interest. The city of Bukhara, founded in 830, is even more famous for ancient architecture: here you will see mosques, palaces, and other monuments from the 9th to the 20th centuries. Located on the ancient routes of commerce from India and China, the old town still preserves much of its Oriental exoticism. It has a dry climate, with temperature extremes, like most of the Uzbek Republic.

Samarkand, one of the oldest cities in the Soviet Union, celebrated its 2,500th anniversary in 1961. Known as Maracanda in ancient times, it was taken by Alexander the Great in the 4th century B.C.; long a center of Arabic learning, it became part of Uzbekistan in 1924. Many architectural wonders still bear witness to the glories of Samarkand as the capital of Tamerlane's empire. The city boasts a Karakul Breeding Institute, unique of its kind: Uzbekistan is known the world over for its karakul lamb pelts.

Other Central Asian cities you may want to visit are Dyushabe (or Dushanbe, formerly Stalinabad), capital of the Tadzhik Soviet Socialist Republic, and Frunze, capital of the Kirghiz Republic.

Highlights of Siberian tourism are: legendary Lake Baikal, which contains almost as much water as all the Great Lakes of North America; Bratsk, whose hydraulic power station is a modern marvel of engineering; and Irkutsk, modern cultural center of East Siberia and fur provider to the world.

Note: as these areas are outside Europe, there is no practical information section in this book for them. For a comprehensive guide to the USSR, see *Fodor's Soviet Union*.

The Country

The Union of Soviet Socialist Republics covers, roughly, the territory of the former Russian empire—over eight million square miles. It is comprised of fifteen union republics, of which the largest by far is the Russian Soviet Federated Socialist Republic (RSFSR), with a number of so-called "autonomous" republics and regions, as well as "national districts". The Soviet Union is a multi-national state. The Russian people are the most numerous, and their language is the common denominator for the whole country, even though the other nationalities preserve their own languages as well.

Next in importance to the Russians are the Ukrainians, who make up over 16 percent of the population of the USSR. Many of them are descended from the famous Zaporozhye Cossacks who settled near the Dnieper river rapids (Zaporog means "across the rapids"), and became known in song and story as bitter enemies of the Turks. As for the other well-known Cossack groups, such as the Don and Kuban Cossacks and many others, they have no official identity in the USSR.

Then come the Byelorussians, a Slavic people closer in some respects to the Catholic Poles than to the Orthodox Russians. Then the peoples of the Baltic States—Latvians, Lithuanians, Estonians, who have stronger affinities with Western Europe and Scandinavia than with the Slavs. And so on—south to the Crimea, where Slavs, Tartars, Greeks and Caucasians mingle in a rich mosaic of religions and languages; the Caucasus itself, peopled by Armenians, Georgians, Circassians, Ossetians, Abkhazians, Daghestanis and others; the strongly Moslem republics of Central Asia—an area increasingly open to Western travelers and to which, for lack of space, we regret being unable to devote adequate attention in the present chapter; and, finally, Siberia and the Far East, where national and cultural diversity abound. Certain minority groups, especially in the Caucasus, are hardly larger than the population of a few villages. But each group guards its traditions, its customs, and its dialect, in spite of the homogenizing effect of Soviet Communism.

This vibrant variety of ethnic cultures has withstood centuries of Russification and innumerable foreign invasions.

Religion has an uncertain existence in this country, ranging from restricted tolerance to outright repression.

Food and Drink

Modern Russian meals are often (but not always) more a means of refueling than a pleasure to the palate. You'll find finer Russian cooking in Paris or New York than in most Moscow restaurants, although the *Moscow* and *Central* specialize in genuine Russian cuisine. Although starches account for 80 percent of the diet, there is an amazing variety of national dishes (translated into English on most Intourist menus).

Zakouski are salted spicy *hors d'oeuvres* of all kinds, which lead off the meal. The most typical of these, of course, is *caviar* although it is rapidly becoming an expensive rarity. *Red caviar,* a "poor man's" version, comes from the salmon rather than the sturgeon.

Siberian pelmeny is a ravioli-like combination of meat and dough; *borshch* (Russian cabbage and beet soup) is best served hot with cold sour cream; *bliny,* leavened pancakes, also taste best with sour cream, melted butter and caviar; *kasha* is coarse buckwheat prepared somewhat like rice. *Gurievskaya kasha* is a sweet farina porridge served with stewed fruit.

Ukrainian cooking, slightly more exotic than Russian, produces such taste-tempters as *kotlety po-kievsky* (Kiev-style cutlets) which are not cutlets at all, but hollow chicken croquettes stuffed with melted butter, which spurt when you stick them with a fork. Georgian food, on the other hand, is downright Oriental; its prize dish, *shashlik,* features lumps of spiced mutton skewered on a dagger.

Russians are a nation of year-round ice-cream lovers; you will find it in theaters, department stores, milk bars and on the street. Introducing American ice-cream was Mikoyan's gift to the USSR when he returned from his first trip to the U.S.A. Delicious expensive cream cakes are also sold at theaters.

Moscow has many restaurants featuring national dishes from Georgia, the Ukraine and Armenia, as well as Hungary and even China. Food specialties may be purchased at the high-priced, "exclusive" *Gastronom* shops. Moscow also has a number of special cheese stores, offering cheeses from all parts of the USSR.

Most fixed-price tours include a set menu. When face to face with a square breakfast or lunch, be sure to make the most of it; with your heavy itinerary, you can't always be sure when you will eat again. Breakfast at Intourist hotels may start with smoked salmon (caviar if you pay extra), and include three fried eggs, sliced tomatoes, fried potatoes, much bread, *kefir* (something like buttermilk) and coffee or tea. Tourist lunches and dinners usually lead off with borshch (caviar is extra), toughish meat (chicken, steak or veal cutlet), potatoes, peas and ice-cream or stewed fruit. Russian tea—very hot, in glasses with a metal holder—is served on trains by car attendants from samovars. Coffee is disappointing. Fresh fruits and vegetables are often missing from menus; it is well to take along vitamin pills.

A Word to the Wise: Restaurant service in the U.S.S.R. still tends to be *incredibly* slow—in some places reports of three hours to get your dinner are common. We can only advise you to eat where the crowds aren't if you are in a hurry or to avoid the mob by coming as early or as late as possible. Sitting at the same table for each meal and trying to use the Russian words when ordering also help speed things up. A copy of *War and Peace* will help pass the time.

Most restaurants in the large cities are open from 6 in the evening until 1 A.M. They usually include an orchestra for staid dinner dancing.

Vodka, which needs no introduction, flows freely in the Soviet Union, despite many recent moves to limit its promiscuous public sale. If each fierce gulp is accompanied with a black caviar sandwich, you'll come out all right! Russians drink it down by the tumblerful. Rivaling vodka as the national drink is *kvass,* a tasty fizzy brew (often home-made) of fermented black bread or apples. Kvass has a low alcohol content and a tremendous kick.

Soviet wines and brandies are many and choice, especially those from the sunny Georgian and Armenian slopes. Leningrad beer is excellent. Draught beer may be had at street kiosks. On certain holidays hot mulled wine is sold in the streets.

Shopping and Souvenirs

Handicraft and folk-art run deep in the Russian tradition, as you will see for yourself in the palaces and mansion-museums of Moscow, Leningrad and Kiev. The old serf artisans, artists and architects imbued their creations with a simple, almost mystical love of "Mother Russia", and of the wood, stone, bone, leather, metals and other materials given them.

There has been a deliberate revival of folk handicraft as an export industry. Wherever you go, you will find a great variety of more or less beautiful and useful souvenirs for sale in department stores, gift shops and in the lobbies of hotels. Prices are high and firmly fixed—no bargaining.

Carved and painted birchwood objects make the most typical Soviet souvenirs. Rarer woods, walrus ivory and many shades of Ural marble also lend themselves to carving. From the Urals too, come quartz, jasper, anhydrite and amber brooches, earrings, cuff-links, cigarette-holders and rings.

The famous *Palekh, Mstera* and *Fedoskino* miniatures, painted with egg pigment and gilt on boxes and other objects, portray classical folklore and fairytale themes, as well as modern *kolkhoz* (collective farm) country life, and they are really beautiful.

The wooden *matryoshka* or *babushka* doll, a nest of five to seven gaily painted wooden figures, one inside the other, makes a perfect children's gift. *Khokhloma* household woodenware glorifies ordinary dippers, spoons, salt-cellars and sugar bowls with a bright Russian fresco in lively colors. Unlike many souvenirs, these are surprisingly functional and inexpensive.

Furs are a good buy and there are special *Beriozka* shops selling magnificent wolf and lynx hats, fox coats and other items sure to be novelties at home. Don't, however, expect real bargain prices; they can be fairly expensive.

Ukrainian women are highly skilled in embroidering linens and panels for dresses and blouses, though these can be very expensive in souvenir shops.

From Georgia the perfect souvenir is a horn goblet with a silver handle. White felt skullcaps known as *svankyd,* worn in the high mountains of Georgia, may also be bought. Gorgeous embroidered silk and gold caps come from central Asia. Chess pieces, buttons and cigarette boxes are made from the amazingly hard, heavy wood of the Caucasian palm or "iron tree".

Vodka and caviar *(ikra),* of course, make welcome gifts. You may find it practical to purchase these at the last minute by handing over your unused Intourist coupons to the hotel staff, who will procure the items for you. But if you have foreign cash, go yourself to the *Beriozka* delicatessen shops. In Moscow, at hotels Metropol, Ukraine and Leningradskaya and at Vnukovo and Sheremetyevo airports; in Leningrad, at hotels Astoria and Evropeiskaya; in Sochi, at Hotel Intourist and in Muzeinaya Street, opposite the Primorskaya hotel.

PRACTICAL INFORMATION FOR THE SOVIET UNION

WHAT WILL IT COST. To balance perhaps the often formidable difficulties encountered in traveling in the USSR, price-wise it is quite uncomplicated. Not inexpensive but uncomplicated because prices are all government controlled and because all major expenses must be pre-paid in advance through the government tourist agency *Intourist,* which also arranges visas, itineraries, etc. Package tours are always the cheapest way to travel at whatever standard, first class or tourist, since the cost is inclusive. See *How to Go* and *Tour Categories* following for details. Individual travel is permitted but it must be planned through Intourist; the following approximate costs are indicative of basic expenses:

Hotel rates: *Deluxe* single room with bath, breakfast, £46 ($105) per day. This includes private car for three hours a day, guide-interpreter for six hours a day, transfer on arrival and departure by car, and porterage of two pieces of hand luggage. (At least three hours' notice required for the car.) *First-class* single room with bath, breakfast, £28 ($62); includes transfer on arrival and departure, porterage and one conducted tour of the city. *Tourist class* single room without bath, breakfast, £19 ($43); services as for first class. Full board costs between £3 and £4.50 ($7–$10) a day more. All rates high season. Less for double occupancy.

Restaurants charge from 4 to 8 rubles for lunch or dinner, depending on the category; drinks are extra (and in many hotels must be paid for in hard currency, not Intourist vouchers).

Private car tour rates are £25 ($58) for first class single room and breakfast, £17 ($38) for tourist. Car camping is from £4 ($9) per person, including parking space for car and space for your own tent/caravan. Hiring a tent or berth in a bungalow is extra.

Incidental expenses: hotel bath, 30 kopeks; doctor's services free, hospitalization charges 16 rubles per day; admission to museums, parks, etc. minimal.

CAPITAL. Moscow. Two hours later in time than London, eight hours later than New York.

LANGUAGE. Russian is the dominant language, understood and spoken everywhere. Each republic of the Union has its own second official language as well. English is often understood by personnel in hotels.

CLIMATE. In this vast country it is difficult to speak of mean temperatures. In the Baltic it resembles that of the Scandinavian countries. The Central part has a Continental climate: warm summers and cold winters. The Crimea and Georgia are the USSR's California. Siberia's winter is proverbial . . .

Average maximum daily temperatures in degrees Fahrenheit and centigrade:

Moscow	Jan.	Feb.	Mar.	Apr.	May	June	July	Aug.	Sept.	Oct.	Nov.	Dec.
F°	16	21	32	50	66	70	73	72	61	48	36	23
C°	-9	-6	0	10	19	21	23	22	16	9	2	-5

WHEN TO GO. The Soviet Union is a year-round country, with specific activities and tourist attractions geared to each of the seasons. *Springtime* has the advantage of moderate climate, off-season rates and a series of special musical events and festivities culminating in the famous two-day *May Day* celebrations. Best time for Ukraine area.

Summer however is quite bearable throughout European Russia. This is the high season on the Black Sea coast, where there is swimming from May to

October. Also the season for Riga. The major theatrical and musical companies close down in *June,* and their places are taken by provincial troupes. The summer season is marked by important sports events, of which the high point is the annual *Spartakiada* athletic meet in *August.* Avoid Tiflis in July and August, when it is too hot. In 1980 the big event will be the Olympic Games in Moscow.

Autumn in the Moscow and Leningrad regions lasts only a week or two and is abruptly followed late in September by *winter* weather. Theater, concert, opera and ballet begin their new season. November 7 and 8 are lavishly celebrated as the anniversary of the "Great October Revolution" and adoption of the Soviet Constitution (now replaced by the new "Brezhnev Constitution") on 5 December. Autumn is the best time to visit the subtropical Crimea and Caucasus. No tourist can really know Russia until he has spent a few weeks of winter in Moscow or Leningrad. Winter, with its heavy snow, heavy clouds, sparkling sunlight and extreme cold (sometimes 20 degrees below zero F.) lasts six months of the year, and the hardy Russians have learned to live with it—and like it. Hotels, homes, shops and transport are well and evenly heated; fur and felt clothing, copious tea and vodka provide inner warmth. Bring snow boots and thick coats for outdoors; restaurants provide huge coat racks. Intourist rates go down in winter (until April), and the tempo of cultural life goes up, including winter sports competitions and demonstrations. The height of a truly Russian trip is to sit around a gorgeously decorated *yolka* (fir tree) eating caviar, drinking vodka and listening to the Kremlin bells ring in the New Year.

Art Festivals: The best ballet, opera, drama and folk dancing can be seen at the annual festivals: "Moscow Stars", app. May 5–13; "Russian Winter", December 25-January 5; in Leningrad "White Nights", approximately June 21–29; "Kiev Spring", in Kiev, May 25-June 3; there is a fifth festival, held every year in a different republic.

HOW TO GO. Meet *Intourist:* All foreign tourist travel to the Union of Soviet Socialist Republics is the responsibility of *Intourist,* the national tourist bureau. *Intourist* runs hotels and restaurants throughout the Soviet Union, organizes group and individual travel itineraries, tours and excursions, provides transport, guides and interpreters, handles visa and currency formalities, obtains tickets and reservations for special events and entertainment, and in general caters to all tourist needs, from visiting a collective farm to buying souvenirs.

Intourist headquarters is at Prospekt Marxa 16, Moscow K-9. Also Intourist has information offices at:

45 East 49th Street, New York 10017.

292 Regent St., London W.1.

Special opportunities for youth and student visits are handled by *Sputnik,* tourist bureau of the *Committee of USSR Youth Organizations,* 4 Lebyazhi Pereulok, Moscow, to whom inquiries should be addressed.

Group tours are also operated by the *Central Trade Union,* in conjunction with foreign trade unions.

ACCREDITED TRAVEL AGENTS: *Intourist* is represented abroad by accredited travel agents, authorized to handle all practical arrangements for tourist travel to the Soviet Union, including visa applications, hotel reservations, tour itineraries and prepayment. Among these are:

Afton Tours, 1776 Broadway, New York 10019.

American Travel Abroad, 250 West 57th St., New York 10019.

American Express Company, American Express Plaza, New York, N.Y. 10004.

Caravel Tours, 8 West 40th Street, New York 10018.

Cosmos Travel Bureau, Inc., 488 Madison Ave, New York 10022.

Embassy Tours, 505 Fifth Ave., New York 10017.

General Tours Inc., 49 W. 57th St., New York 10019.
Harvard Travel, 1310 Mass. Ave., Cambridge, Mass. 01238.
Maupintour Associates, 900 Massachusetts St., Lawrence, Kansas 66044
Orbitair International, 20 East 46 Street, New York, N.Y. 10017.
Trafalgar Tour East, 30 Rockefeller Center, New York, N.Y. 10020
Travel Go Round, 516 Fifth Avenue, New York, N.Y. 10036.

In *Great Britain (2-week tours from £246–£399);* consult—
Thos. Cook & Sons Ltd., 45 Berkeley Street, London W.1.
Wayfarers Travel, Cranfield Ho. 97, Southampton Row, London W.C.1.
Progressive Tours Ltd., 12 Porchester Place, Marble Arch, London W.2.

WHERE TO GO. *Tourable Areas:* Most major cities and tourist areas in European Russia have been opened to Western tourists by inclusion in one of *Intourist's* 100 special tour itineraries. Besides Moscow, Leningrad, and Kiev, it is now possible to visit the Black Sea resorts of Odessa, Yalta, Sochi, Sukhumi and Batumi; Tbilisi (Tiflis) and Gori; nearby Ordzhonikidze and Pyatigorsk; the important industrial cities along the Volga, including Kazan, Volgograd and Rostov-on-Don; the Ukrainian centers of Kharkov, Zaporozhye and Simferopol on the highway from Moscow to Yalta; Minsk and Smolensk on the highway from Brest to Moscow; the Baltic port of Riga, as well as Tallinn and Vilnius and the Transcarpathian towns of Uzhgorod and Chernovtsy. Also special trips to Siberia if you wish! (*Intourist* also offers tours to Armenia and Central Asia and transits by rail, air and boat combined to India and Japan, which are beyond the scope of this Guide to Europe.) In Central Asia the ancient oasis cities of Tashkent, Samarkand, Bokhara and Khiva still evoke a totally different civilization.

Some typical itineraries: A 15 day, 4-center tour with 2½ days in Kiev, 4½ in Yalta, 2½ in Leningrad and 3 in Moscow, air transportation between cities, conducted sightseeing. A 15-day Central Asia tour takes in Moscow, Samarkand, Bukhara, Tashkent, back to Moscow, then on to Leningrad, by air travel. A 15-day Ukrainian tour includes Kiev, Odessa, Kishinev (in Moldavia), Lvov, ending up in Moscow; or Kiev, Poltava and Kharkov, going on to Leningrad and Moscow. The Baltic capitals of Tallin, Riga and Vilnius are often combined with Leningrad and a visit to the old cultural center of Novgorod.

River cruises can be taken on the Dnieper or the Volga, with ample time for sightseeing at all ports of call. The cruise lasts 15 days.

Special-interest tours include: a series of 12-day "Music and Theater" festivals, visiting Kiev, Leningrad and Moscow during the height of the concert and drama season (September–June); general tours are timed to bring you to Moscow for the big festivities on May Day, October Revolution Day or New Year's Day. Another tour is aimed at hunters: cost for the 10 days at the Crimean hunting reserve (based on all-inclusive service) is about 400 Rs. This includes transfers by car, deluxe hotel accommodation, four meals daily, three group excursions by bus with services of guide-interpreter and experienced huntsman. Check with Intourist for current trophy costs, which vary considerably. Siberian bear hunting is even more expensive.

Easter and Whitsun school cruises are organized by Royal Mail Lines in conjunction with Baltic Steamship Lines: about 12 days, starting from London and calling at Copenhagen, Helsinki, Riga or Leningrad. Also other cruises to Baltic seaports during summer.

There are camping tours lasting 10 to 15 days along the Leningrad-Kalinin-Moscow-Kursk-Kharkov-Kiev-Chernovtsy and the Brest-Minsk-Smolensk-Moscow roads. The motorist is provided with a tent, water supply, electricity, parking space etc., at the various camps. The tour, which does not include catering, can be prepaid but the motorist can get these facilities and meals for on-the-spot cash payment; the charges are reasonable.

Spas. There are several health and spa resorts where treatment is available to foreigners at inclusive rates. Treatment usually lasts about 26 days. Spas include: Sochi, Yalta, Kislovodsk, Pyatigorsk, Essentuki, Odessa, Sestroretsk and Zheleznovodsk.

TOUR CATEGORIES: There are two ways of visiting the Soviet Union: *Individually* or in organized *groups* of 7 persons or more. Individuals may wish to travel in *deluxe category,* which includes single hotel suite with private bath, three à la carte meals a day (high tea is no longer included), daily 3-hour excursions by private automobile with guide-interpreter, free entry to museums and exhibitions. Deluxe rail travel: berth in double compartment of deluxe sleeper where available: deluxe cabin on boats and ships. In deluxe category you may choose any tour from the list of *Intourist* itineraries, or make up your own itinerary. If your trip includes business dealings with any Soviet commercial enterprise, you may be booked into deluxe hotels at reduced rates upon recommendation of the Soviet commercial delegation in your country.

Organized *groups* of more than 7 people have a choice of two tour categories: *first class* and *tourist.* Various group tours are offered by American and British travel agents by arrangements with Intourist and you can combine the Soviet Union with other countries if you wish. These tours have fixed starting dates but may also be joined on arrival in Moscow. Cost varies with the category, itinerary and season (from October 1 through April 30 prices drop 15-25 percent). Tours generally comprise about 20 people, grouped by language, and vary from 8 to 23 days. There are also long weekend tours available from London. With the recent liberalizations of the rules governing them, charter flights to every destination have mushroomed, and the Soviet Union is no exception. A few examples: *Travel Go Round* (address above) offers a one-week tour of Moscow and Leningrad for $659 to $769; two weeks in Moscow, Leningrad and Kiev for $975 to $1140; three weeks in Armenia, the Caucasus and Georgia for $1275 to $1440. *General Tours* (address above) offers eight days in Moscow, Leningrad and Kalinin from $699; plus a wide variety of 1-, 2-, and 3-week itineraries to the main tourist areas of European Russia as well as Central Asia, Siberia and Mongolia. Prices for Russia range from $799 to $1299. *American Travel Abroad* (address above) has eight-day tours to various destinations from $599.

Air travel: all three categories travel tourist class and have 44 pound baggage allowance.

HOTELS. *Rule No. 1:* You can never be sure you will get the one you want. *Intourist* operates at least one hotel for foreign tourists in each Russian city on its itineraries. Unlike Western European capitals where hotels differ in quality of comfort and service provided, Intourist hotels all offer the same full range of accommodations, corresponding to the following Intourist tour categories: *Deluxe,* (suite with bath); *First Class,* (single or double room with bath); *Tourist Class,* (room with two or four beds, and bathroom on same floor). Some hotels are brand new, others date back to Czarist days, but most run more to heavy plush luxury than solid comfort. However all are fully equipped with modern facilities, (which may not always work) including hot and cold water, bathrooms, telephones, central heating. Elevators may be tiny and temperamental. Pick up your room key from the service desk on each floor. Most large hotels have a barber shop, "Scientific Medical Beauty Institute", and souvenir shop. Hotel bars demand payment in foreign currency. Hotel laundry service is good, cleaning and pressing so-so. Do not take items from your room as souvenirs.

Each Intourist hotel includes a *service bureau* with English-speaking staff equipped to order tickets for theaters, cinemas and other entertainment, as well as for rail, plane and other transport. The bureau also provides guide service and general information. Amiability and competence alternate with staggering inefficiency and boorishness.

Children: 50% discount on services for children ages 2 to 12 (over 12 pay full costs). Children must share parents' accommodations: extra cots provided. No travel documents needed for children under age 2.

Diners Club and American Express credit cards are now accepted in several Moscow and Leningrad hotels. At least 13 new Moscow hotels are to be completed in time for the 1980 Olympics.

WHAT TO TAKE. Besides the usual things you take with you for a long trip there are some items you might be glad to have in your baggage when in Soviet Russia. A good supply of cigarettes; soap and plenty of tissues; chewing gum for kids; toothpaste and cosmetics; extra pair of glasses and a supply of regular medicines; Tampax, etc. Small gift items, a dictionary and powdered coffee, (which at around $40 a pound jar would make a munificent present), and a flat rubber sink-stopper will also come in handy.

MONEY. You may bring in any amount and kind of foreign currency, travelers' checks, and freely exchange it at any border point, *Intourist* hotel or state bank. Foreign currency thus imported must be declared upon arrival and recorded in a special customs certificate, to be presented upon departure. In addition to drinks in hotel bars, foreign currency will be demanded in payment for items like watches, cameras, furs, etc., purchased in duty-free shops located in major cities. So buy rubles cautiously . . . and always ask for a chit when you do. Import and export of Soviet currency is *not* permitted. All unused rubles must be turned in. You may receive their equivalent in the original currency. Check before your trip on the current regulations. *All currency transactions except through Gosbank or Intourist are strictly illegal, and you may be prosecuted for black-market exchange of currency.*

The present rate is *about* 60 Kopeks to one US$ and 1.35 rubles to the pound sterling.

At the present time, coins are in 1, 2, 3, 5, 10, 15, 20 and 50 kopeks denominations. Their value is clearly marked. Ruble bills come in 1, 3, 5, 10, 25, 50 and 100 notes. There are 100 kopeks to the ruble.

TIPPING. Communist countries condemn tipping as a "relic of capitalism and an insult to labor". You can, in fact, tour the Soviet Union without leaving a single gratuity; in theory none is expected. However, the recent influx of Western tourists has revived the custom: tip 20 kopeks in the cloakroom, 5 to 10 percent to hairdressers, barbers, taxi drivers and in restaurants; baggage porters charge 30 kopeks a bag. Don't tip Intourist guides, but small neutral gifts are sometimes accepted. Only Moscow's Rossiya Hotel adds a 5 percent service charge to the bill.

HOW TO REACH THE SOVIET UNION. By air: Direct flights from New York to Moscow by *PanAm* or *Aeroflot;* from London by *Aeroflot, Air India, British Airways, PIA.* From Toronto by *BA* via London. From Perth, Australia, weekly flights via Bombay.

From London to Moscow is less than 4 hours by *British Airways* or *Aeroflot* jets. There are daily flights from most European capitals, including Amsterdam, Brussels and Paris.

By sea: Canadians who like a long sea trip (about 13 days) can go on *Baltic Steamship Line's* service from Montreal to Leningrad, calling at London on the way. The same company runs regular services between London and Leningrad via Helsinki. Starting from Mediterranean areas, Soviet ships from the Black Sea ports of Odessa, Yalta, etc., call at French, Italian, Greek and Yugoslav ports.

By train: There is a *sleeping car train* service from Hook of Holland (connecting with London-Harwich service) or from Victoria via Ostend to Moscow, daily. The journey takes 2 days and the single fare, including sleeper but no meals, is about £87 second class, £149 first class. A similar service operates from Paris. Direct sleeper from Oslo-East Germany-Poland.

By bus: *Viking Safaris,* 12A Archer St., London W.1, organize 6-week coach-camping trips London to Russia via Scandinavia for about £160. *Europabus:* London via Poland, 3½ days, weekly in summer.

For the adventurous, the whole of the USSR can be crossed on the Great Siberian Route by ship, train and air between Hong Kong and Moscow.

 TRAVEL DOCUMENTS. *Tourist visas* are issued through accredited travel agents for the length of time covered by prepaid hotel reservations. Fill in visa application forms provided by agent and supply three passport-size photographs. Visas come through fairly promptly, about 5–7 days. Transit visas are issued for a period not exceeding 48 hours. Visas can also be obtained from Soviet Consulates without charge within a week of application.

No visa, only valid passport, is required on the bi-weekly Helsinki-Leningrad mini-cruise of the *B.O.R.E.* Steamship Co., enabling tourists, who sleep on board during the stay, to visit the city, the Peterhof and the fabulous treasures of the Hermitage collection.

Prepayment Procedure. Itinerary and accommodation must be planned, reserved and paid for in advance in hard currency. Upon arrival in the USSR you will receive from *Intourist* a book with coupons valid for all hotels and Intourist restaurants. Before departing, you may request from the waiter vodka and caviar for the value of unused coupons. No refund can be made for them in the United States or in Britain.

If you wish to alter your travel itinerary after arrival, consult *Intourist.* Changes depend upon availability of hotel accommodation. If for some reason you must cut short your prearranged and prepaid trip, ask *Intourist* before leaving to certify the number of unused coupons left over. Reimbursement in hard currency, less 10 percent handling charge, will be made through your travel agent.

Visiting Relatives: Arrangements for foreigners of Russian origin to visit and stay with relatives in the Soviet Union are handled by USSR consular authorities rather than *Intourist.* It is necessary to submit a visa application in three copies, with three signed photos and a brief biographical sketch in triplicate. A formal invitation must be received from the relatives, signed by their local militia. With these papers, you go in person to the Soviet Consulate for an interview. Visas to visit relatives take a long time, but once secured they may make it possible to visit cities not on the *Intourist* list, and which are normally barred to Western tourists. *Don't* make surprise calls, it may cause your Russian relatives or friends embarrassment.

Health Certificates. Travelers to the USSR from South America, Asia and Africa are currently required to present certification of smallpox vaccination. Check beforehand for latest regulations.

CUSTOMS. Personal belongings may be brought in duty-free, including clothing, sports equipment, one still and one movie camera, typewriter, radio, record player and reasonable quantities of food, drink and tobacco for personal consumption. Stock up on cigarettes, 400–600, and bring along 3–4 bottles of your favorite drink if you don't like vodka or wine. Don't forget your rations if you are a chocolate addict; you won't like its taste and its price. (Soviet Customs are easy on these items.) Regulations prohibit the import of "army weapons and ammunition; pornographic pictures, printed matter, clichés, negatives, films, photographs and cinema films, manuscripts, drawings and similar articles which may be considered politically and economically harmful to the USSR". It is advisable to enter jewelry on the customs declaration form. Customs officers are courteous, inspection of luggage erratic. The export of *objets d'art* is permitted only by special authorization and heavy duties may be payable.

CLOSING TIMES. Small shops are open from about 11 to 19 hours. In the larger cities department and larger stores are open from 8–21 hours (19 hours on Monday). All stores close Sunday, with the exception of a few grocery shops.

HOLIDAYS. New Year's Day; Women's Day, March 8; May 1–2; Victory Day, May 9; Revolution Days, Nov. 7–8; Constitution Day, December 5.

VISITS TO SOVIET PLANTS. Visitors interested in the progress of Russian industry should make advance arrangements via their travel agents and Intourist. Impressive letter-headings and Chamber of Commerce recommendations help.

MAIL. Envelopes, stamps and postcards are sold by *Intourist* hotel service bureaus, which accept letters for mailing. Minimum postage: postcards, regular 4 kopeks, airmail 18 kopeks; letters, 20 grams (¾ ounce), regular 6, airmail 32 kopeks. Letters from London usually take two to four days, five to seven days from the States, sometimes longer. Safest address is c/o Intourist, Prospekt Marxa 16, Moscow, where your guide can pick it up for you. If your mail is sent c/o U.S., British or Canadian Embassy you must call there personally. If you want mail forwarded, leave precise instructions as you leave your hotel.

If you want to place a telephone call, it is best to ask your hotel service bureau to help.

DRINKING WATER. For external use only outside of Moscow. Bottled mineral water recommended, *Borzhom* or *Narzan*.

PHOTOGRAPHY. You may take pictures of most things, but there are exceptions and their application depends on the international climate of the moment. Your guide is your best counselor. Do not take pictures from airplanes or trains or close to the frontier area. Before you photograph a Soviet citizen, ask his or her permission. Photographing some non-sensitive (or non-military) public installations, collective farms, schools, bridges in tourist locations, etc., is usually allowed. Use common sense, and check if in doubt. In some cases advance permission may be needed. Authorization for commercial filming is granted only by Sovexportfilm, 7 Malyi Gnezdnikovsky Pereulok, Moscow. Your hotel service bureau will arrange for developing and printing if you wish, or you may take your exposed film out of the country with you. Agfa color printing can be processed in the USSR.

ELECTRICITY. 50-cycle, 127 or 220 volts. Pack regular shaving kit, there are outlets for electric razors. European plug required.

LAUNDRY: There are no centrally located launderettes in Moscow, let alone other cities. Those that do exist tend to be in new housing estates on the city fringes. The long travel time and inevitable queue make them impractical for the tourist—a waste of time. Use your hotel service, if necessary.

TRAVEL IN THE SOVIET UNION. By air: Aeroflot, the Soviet civil airline, operates an extensive and highly efficient network within the Soviet Union, as well as flying to some two dozen foreign capitals. Helicopter service connects resort towns in the Crimea and on the Black Sea coast. Rates are often competitive with rail and bus fares.

By train: Foreign tourists benefit by a "premium" on one-way fares between two cities of an itinerary which are less than 621 miles apart; this applies to deluxe, first class and tourist second class travelers only. Russian trains are very clean; sleepers are luxurious and (because of wide gauge tracks) smooth riding. Tea is served in every car. Trains leave without "all aboard" warning. For a new experience take the Moscow-Leningrad Red Arrow Express (sleeping cars only). First class is called "soft class", second class is "hard".

By sea: A number of cruises on the Black Sea, with stops at Odessa, Yalta, Sochi, Sukhumi and Batumi, are available in the summer months, with accommodation and prices ranging from third class to deluxe. Intourist also offers a Volga river cruise from Moscow several times between June and September. New stops include Zhiguli and Ilyevka.

MOTORING. *Intourist* issues motor maps listing services and rates at the many motels going up all over the country, and the routes open to independent motorists, as well as the gasoline (petrol) stations, camping sites, etc. Some routings, with the border point italicized: Warsaw-Slodice-*Brest*-Minsk-Moscow; Helsinki-*Vyborg*-Leningrad; Prague-*Uzhgorod;* Budapest-Cluj-Bucharest-*Parubnoe* (or *Leusheni*). Cracow-*Shaginia*-Lvov.

There is a full complex of services for motorists in Moscow, Leningrad, Kiev, Sochi and Yaroslavl; a filling station at Lubashevka.

Motorists require international driving license and car log book; insurance not compulsory but obtainable at the border. Traffic is on the right. Speed limit in towns is 60 kilometers, no limit on open road.

Traffic violations are treated severely, so be warned!

Europe-Assistance: With the cooperation of *Intourist,* Europe-Assistance, 6 Rue de Londres, Paris 9, has set up an organization within the Soviet Union to meet unforeseen emergencies, e.g.: although medical treatment is free in the USSR, except for hospitalization charges, you might prefer to be moved back home after an accident, or be incapable of driving your car back to Western Europe.

Motoring itineraries now open to foreign tourists: Vyborg-Leningrad-Moscow, 588 m.; Brest-Minsk-Moscow, 655 m.; Leningrad-Narva-Tallinn, 240 m.; Moscow-Yaroslavl, 161 m.; Moscow-Vladimir-Suzdal, 150 m.; Moscow-Kharkov-Yalta, 925 m.; Kharkov-Rostov/Don-Grand Caucasian Circuit, 1178 m.; Uzhgorod-Lvov-Rovno-Kiev-Kharkov, 789 m.; Chernovtsy-Vinnitsa-Kiev, 362 m.; Chernovtsy-Kishinev, 213 m.; Leusheny-Kishinev-Odessa, 168 m.; Odessa-Kiev, 293 m.; Tbilisi-Yerevan, 140 m.; Tbilisi-Pyatigorsk-Kharkov, 900 m. A large number of historically and touristically interesting localities are used as overnight stops on these routes: Novgorod on the Vyborg-Moscow route, Smolensk between Minsk and Moscow, Orel and Kursk on the way from Moscow to Kharkov, Poltava and Zaporozhye in the Ukraine, Simferopol in the Crimea, Pyatigorsk and Ordzhonikidze in the Caucasus, and many others. Motels are being built in many centers.

Car Hire. Self-drive Volga and Moskvich automobiles can be hired in the larger cities at rates from 5 rubles a day. Chauffeur-driven, from about 31.50 rubles for 10 hours, plus 12 kopeks per kilometer above 240 kilometers. *Hertz* and *Avis* now have offices in major cities.

Gasoline costs from £2.50/3.40 rubles per 10 litres (95 octane), £2.20/2.97 rubles per 10 liters (72 octane).

USEFUL ADDRESSES. *Embassies:* American, 19/21 Tchaikovsky St.; British, 14 Quai Maurice Thorez; Canadian, 23 Starokonyushenny Pereulok. *Intourist,* 16 Prospekt Marxa. *American Express,* in the Natsional hotel. *Emergencies:* for ambulance, dial 03; for fire, 01; for police, 02. All in Moscow.

Exploring Moscow

The capital of the world's largest country is rapidly becoming one of the world's major cities. In the last few years it has expanded considerably; several big new suburbs have sprung up and the whole city now covers over 500 square miles with a population of nearly eight million. Moscow is not among Europe's oldest cities; in 1947 it celebrated its 800th birthday, while Parisians were preparing for their city's 2,000th anniversary.

From the University skyscraper crowning the Lenin Hills south of the city (where Napoleon watched Moscow burn), you may see for yourself the contrast of Moscow's many-hued onion-domed church steeples sharing the skyline with a scattering of massive, strangely unmodern "multi-story buildings", as Muscovites call their skyscrapers. At night, the Moscow city lights are dominated by the most potent advertising "spectacular" this side of Times Square–five immense rotating red stars topping the Kremlin's highest towers and glowing a lurid ruby red.

Muscovites love their city and are proudly conscious of its historic importance, as well of its role as a double capital today: that of the USSR and of the RSFSR.

To Western visitors, Moscow may mean one (or more likely several) of many things:—a dense and dazzling concentration of ornate buildings, museums and art galleries; an endless offering of some of the world's best music, dance and drama; an opportunity to peek at the fascinating contrasts of modern Soviet life and participate in a small way in the expansion of East-West trade or cultural exchanges. Even the briefest Moscow visit should of course include the Kremlin, Red Square, Gorky Street, the Metro, the Agricultural and Industrial Exhibition, the new University campus and one or more parks.

You will almost certainly be invited to visit a "Palace of Culture", belonging to some factory, industry or profession. These are super civic centers, replete with reading rooms, game rooms, lecture halls, theaters and other facilities for distraction and self-improvement.

And of course, no one can leave the Soviet capital without an evening of theater, opera or ballet, a shopping trip to the GUM department store, and an afternoon at some park, stadium or racetrack. However, if you're looking for hilarious nightlife, floor shows or fast music, go to Paris—or even Budapest—but don't count on Moscow!

The Kremlin

Much of Russia's past, present and future is compactly summed up in a walled cluster of imposing buildings crowning the steep banks of the Moskva River. The word "Kremlin" (or Kreml) means "citadel" in the Tartar language. Today, Moscow's Kremlin is a triangle of stone and brick battlements broken by 19 towers and five gates enclosing an out-of-the-world area of 64 acres—a museum of past glories and the seat of present Soviet power. To appreciate the Kremlin's full beauty, look at it by night from across the river (in front of the British Embassy on Sofiskaya Quay), or from one of the bridges flanking its approaches. Before visiting the Kremlin buildings, stroll around the crenellated walls, nearly a mile and a half in circumference. Inside these walls, the Kremlin is a dreamlike "landscape in stone" which you must see to believe. The main square is graced by three cathedrals, which inside and out reflect the rich religious and artistic heritage of "Mother Russia". Largest and oldest is the five-domed Uspensky (Assumption) Cathedral which set the style for Moscow church architecture after its completion in 1479. Besides its famous frescos, icons and decorations, notice the intricately carved walnut throne of Ivan the Terrible, who came here often to repent his sins. Blagoveshchensky (Annunciation) Cathedral was built ten years later; beneath its nine domes are housed some of the most precious icons in Russia. Archangelsky Cathedral, finished in 1509, has five cupolas; most of the early Czars, including Ivan the Terrible and the son he murdered, are buried within its ornate confines.

The Armory Museum

A fabulous collection of weapons, costumes, carriages, gold and silver objects, jewelry and royal regalia is housed in the Oruzheinaya Palata (Armory Museum), opposite the three cathedrals. You will see the ancient Cap of Monomakh, with which Ivan III crowned his grandson Dmitri in 1498; Ivan the Terrible's coat of mail; Boris Godunov's throne, carriage, and jewel-encrusted ring; gold-brocaded church vestments, whose pearls alone weigh over 30 pounds. Special tickets are needed to see the fabulous "Room of Diamonds"; inquire first at Central Intourist Office.

In the center of the Kremlin's main square stands the 16th-century Bell Tower of Ivan the Great; its 266-foot height dominated the Moscow horizon until Joseph Stalin began building skyscrapers in the city. Its carillon contains 22 large bells and over 30 smaller chimes. The Kremlin's largest bell of all stands on a low pedestal alongside the bell tower. It is called Czar Kolokol, meaning "king of bells". In 1747, it fell from its scaffolding and a fragment weighing a mere 11½ tons, chipped off. Nearby on the ground you will see Czar Pushka (king of cannons), cast in 1586, and intended to discourage Tartar attacks. This medieval "intercontinental" ballistic missile was supposed to fire two-ton cannon balls half a mile or more. Just before the Russian Revolution, people used to say, "Czar Bell doesn't ring, Czar Cannon doesn't shoot, and Czar Nicholas doesn't reign!"

Granovitaya Palata's façade is finished in small faceted stones, from which it takes its name (Hall-of-many-facets). Built on the site of the Khan's palace, it contained the Czar's throne room and among its other marvels, boasted central heating. Just beyond is the Kremlin's greatest structure, the Bolshoi Kremlyovsky Dvorets (Grand Kremlin Palace) built in 1849, and housing the seat of Soviet government. Its huge green dome and red flag are visible from far beyond the Kremlin walls. Here the USSR's two-chamber "Supreme Soviet" holds its sessions, as does the Soviet Communist Party. On holidays, the Palace is the scene of gala balls for young people; New Year trees are lit for schoolchildren, who are invited 50,000 at a time. Lenin, and later Stalin, had their private apartments as well as their offices in this palace; the present Soviet chief of state works here but lives on the outskirts of Moscow.

Red Square

In Russian, the word *Krasnaya* means both "red" and "beautiful". Moscow's immense main square is both. Its western side is flanked by the crenellated red brick walls of the Kremlin and the black and red stone Lenin Mausoleum. Foreign tourists who wish to view the embalmed body of Lenin in his glass coffin are usually ushered into the mausoleum ahead of a long line of waiting Russian sightseers. Other Soviet leaders, including Stalin, are buried by the wall of the Kremlin facing Red Square. To the left of the mausoleum is the red and white Spassky (Savior) Tower, 221 feet high, whose belfry rings the famous Kremlin chimes. Opposite the tower is the GUM department store. The square's northern approach is covered by the multi-spired red façade of the Historical Museum, facing St. Basil's Cathedral. This exotic cathedral was built by Ivan the Terrible in 1560 to commemorate his victories over the Tartars. The group of eight pillar-like structures surrounds a ninth central pillar 150 feet high. The bulging domes capping each pillar are all different shapes and colors, giving a strangely gaudy but cheerful effect to the cathedral. Look in on its muraled walls and ceilings. Dominating the southeastern approach to the square is Moscow's largest modern luxury hotel, the *Rossiya*.

In past history, Red Square has known red of another color. It was long the site of public executions and the scene of bloody vengeance by the populace against the hated feudal boyars. It was also Moscow's main market place. In 1917 on Red Square, the Bolsheviks won their last battle for possession of the Kremlin itself, at a cost of 500 dead. Twice a year, on May 1 and November 7, huge military and civilian parades march through Red Square with music, banners and flowers; the spectacle is well worth seeing.

Behind the Historical Museum at the north end of Red Square is busy Manezhnaya Square, from which Gorki Street takes off in a northwest direction. This recently reconstructed two-mile thoroughfare bordered with linden trees is Moscow's main artery. Lined with theaters, museums, modern dwellings, cafés and stores, it traverses Pushkin Square, (whose statue is a favorite rendezvous spot for young Muscovites) and Mayakovsky Square on its way out of town, where it becomes Leningrad Highway. Another newly rebuilt central thoroughfare, Kalinin Prospekt, is a modern showcase of urban development containing some of the city's most attractive new stores.

The Moscow Metro

Unlike the Paris Metro, the London tube, or the New York subway system, Moscow's Metro is more than merely a way of getting to and from work. To Muscovites who use it every day, it is a source of pride and a spectacular symbol of Soviet know-how; to tourists, it is an object of admiration.

Moscow's Metro system is laid out much like a wheel, with six spokes, most of which project beyond the rim. The rim line encircles the city's downtown section just beyond the outer chain of belt-line boulevards, which trace the one-time ring of medieval fortifications. The spoke lines radiate from a central point just north of Red Square. The entire system, still expanding, is now served by 96 palatial stations, and carries over six million passengers daily. Each station is a monument of "modern" Soviet architecture. Take Komsomolskaya Station. Its theme is "historic Russian victories against foreign invaders". In its enormous barrel-vaulted ceiling are eight mosaics illustrating victories against the Teutonic knights, the Mongols, the Poles, the Prussians, Napoleon, and the Nazis. Equally florid use is made in the Metro's other stations of many-colored marbles from all over the Soviet Union, of stained glass, heroic statuary and other grandiose features. The system is vast and still growing. The first ten-station line was opened in 1935, and other lines have followed ever since; construction went ahead even during the war. The Agricultural and Industrial Exhibition grounds and the Moscow University campus are accessible by Metro. For the Exhibition, take train to station VDNKh (in Russian letters BДHX); for the University, go to station *Lenin Hills* (Leninskie Gory).

Exploring Moscow's Suburbs

To glimpse the Soviet Union as a whole, and get a hint of what makes it tick, take a trolley bus five miles due north of Moscow to the All-Union Agricultural and Industrial Exhibition.

Sokolniki Park is one of the favorite recreational areas for Muscovites. It was the site of the 1959 USA exhibition; many countries hold exhibits here. The park has countless attractions, including theater, summer and winter skating, cafés and restaurants.

Close to the Luzhniki sports center is the 16th-century Novodevichi Convent, containing the impressive Cathedral of Our Lady of Smolensk, a rich art and history museum, and a cemetery with the graves of many of Russia's most illustrious dead.

The village of Kolomenskoye, now within the city limits, is a must for the tourist interested in the culture of old Russia. Among other examples of Russian architecture, Kolomenskoye has the 210-foot-high Church of the Ascension, built in the 16th century in celebration of the birth of Ivan the Terrible.

Ostankino Palace-Museum

This exquisite edifice, in a park adjoining the V.D.N.Kh. exhibition to the west, is a work of art in wood, built in the late 18th century by the gifted artisan-serfs of a nobleman named Sheremetyev. Each floor, wall and ceiling of this magnificent country mansion is a masterpiece of woodworking. Halls are filled with precious paintings and sculptures by the great western masters of the 17th and 18th centuries. Its largest hall was a private theater where Count Sheremetyev invited his friends to drama, dance and music performances put on by his most gifted serfs, one of whom he later married.

Moscow University

On the hill where Napoleon once watched Moscow burning, stands the 32-story, 790-foot skyscraper of the Moscow University campus. Clustered around this main edifice are a complex of 37 separate structures forming an integral architectural ensemble in what has been unkindly called "Stalin Gothic" style. Just across the river is the Central Lenin Stadium, completed in 1956. The Lenin Hills are where you'll get the finest view over Moscow.

Moscow's Environs

Northeast of the capital is the region of Vladimir-Suzdal, currently being developed as a major Soviet tourist area for foreigners who want to form an idea of old Orthodox Russia at its most beautiful. Suzdal itself, once a mere day-trip, is now equipped for overnight stays: you will soon even be able to sleep in a cell of an ancient Russian monastery. The fabulous cities of Vladimir and Rostov the Great, with their kremlins, old churches and artistic wealth, are enduring monuments to the country's colorful past. The most perfect architectural gem in this region is the lonely church of Pokrov on the Nerl, between Vladimir and Bogolyubovo.

Fifty miles due north of Moscow at Zagorsk is one of Russia's most famous monasteries. This cluster of fortifications and church buildings with its pink steeples, red roofs and blue star-spangled domes, dates from the 14th to the 16th centuries. The original monastic retreat was founded in 1340; a contemporary monastery still functions on the site as well as an ecclesiastical seminary. You'll find the long-haired full-garbed monks humorous as well as hospitable. Zagorsk is also famous for its Museum of Applied Art (iconography, embroidery, pottery handicraft) and above all for its Museum of Toys, and has often been used as a location for historical movies.

The region round about Moscow contains many former great estates, now converted into museums. The most famous of these is Yasnaya Polyana, where Leo Tolstoi lived, died, and is buried. The museum includes original illustrations for many of his works, and much contemporary material of historical and literary interest.

PRACTICAL INFORMATION FOR MOSCOW

HOTELS. Freedom of choice hardly exists even for *individuals,* traveling in the "deluxe" Intourist tour category. Let the *service bureau* in your hotel solve your problems, make your theater and plane bookings, get your exit visa, etc. Our grading in this chapter is: (L) for deluxe, (1) for first-class superior, (2) for first class reasonable, (3) for moderate, (4) for inexpensive.

Deluxe

Natsional, 1/14 Gorki St. 208 rooms. Intourist hotel on Moscow's main thoroughfare. Dancing. Perhaps best.

Intourist, opened 1970, 3/5 Gorki St., next door. 466 rooms. Restaurants, cafés, shops.

First Class

Metropol, 1 Marx Prospect. Intourist hotel now renovated from its heavy Victorian décor; in heart of theater district; restaurant dance band plays jazz. 404 rooms.

Berlin, 3 Zhdanov St. Intourist hotel. Bedraped Victorian elegance. 90 rooms.

Rossiya, 6 Razin St., two blocks southeast of the Kremlin, is the tallest and largest, with 3,182 rooms. Ask for a room with Kremlin view. Take the "express breakfast" on first floor, or queue in the 10th-floor cafeteria. Prepare to wait in all Rossiya restaurants.

Ukraina, 2/1 Kutuzovsky Prospekt. 28-floor skyscraper, 1026 rooms, 20 minutes from center of town by car. Spacious interior, three restaurants.

Leningradskaya, 21/40 Kalanchovskaya St. Sumptuous 26-floor skyscraper, 505 rooms, palatial décor.

Aeroflot, 37 Leningradsky Prospekt on road to airport, if you're just in transit.

Minsk, 22 Gorky St., large, central, restaurants.

Belgrad, new, 5 Smolenskaya St., 21 floors, 918 rooms, good restaurant.

Also-rans

Armenia, 4 Neglinnaya St. Modest, agreeable, good service.

Balchug, 1/15 Sadovnicheskaya Embankment.

Budapest, 2/18 Petrovskiye Linii.

Bukharest, 1 Balchug St. Centrally located; no private baths.

Kievskaya, 2-i Bryanski Pereulok, located near Kiev rail station.

Mir, Prospekt Kalinina.

Pekin, 1/7 Bolshaya Sadovaya St., superior accommodations and service, three restaurants, one of them Chinese.

Tourist, 17/12 Selskokhozyaistvennaya St.

Warsaw, 2 Oktyabrskaya Square, superior accommodation and service, close to the Gorki park.

Yaroslavskaya, 8/1 Yaroslavskaya St.

Tsentralnaya, 10 Gorki St.

 RESTAURANTS. Most of Moscow's main restaurants are situated in the big hotels, which follow the "European plan". This means in theory that group tourists eat all meals at their hotel. In practise you can eat at other Intourist hotels and the better restaurants, but tell the waiter beforehand that you'll pay with Intourist vouchers. You pay in cash for extras. Hotel restaurants offer both western European and Russian cooking. Individuals unattached to a group tour are freer to sample Moscow's specialty restaurants. A number of these *regional* restaurants are well known; each specializes in the national cuisine of some Soviet Republic or neighboring country. Ask your hotel's *service bureau* to make your reservation; they tend to be crowded in the evening.

Aragvi, 6 Gorki St. Georgian cuisine, wines and musicians.

Ararat, 4 Neglinnaya St. Armeniani cooking and dry wines.

Baku, 24 Gorki St. Azerbaijan cuisine.

Ukraina, 2/1 Kutuzovsky Prospekt. Ukrainian cuisine.

Pekin, 1 Bolshaya Sadovaya, best Chinese food.

Praga, 2 Arbat St. Czech. Has a café on the roof in summer.

Uzbekistan, 29 Neglinnaya St. Uzbek cuisine, clients and music.

Airline Terminal Restaurant, at the terminal on Leningradsky Prospekt. Modern elegance, fine food.

Lastochka, good riverboat restaurant near the Krimsky Bridge.

Slavyansky Bazar. Jazz, traditional Russian food, expensive.

TV Tower restaurant, Ostankino, has so-so food, good view, but the view from Lenin Hills is much better—and free!

TRANSPORTATION. *On foot* is the best way to see downtown Moscow. Anti-jaywalking regulations are strictly enforced.

Your own car is quite practical. Traffic is lighter and parking easier than in many western European cities. Turn left on two green lights; one red and one green means straight ahead only. A lane between two white parallel lines is reserved for official cars only. A white line crossing an entire street means no right turn. Sounding your horn (klaxon) is prohibited.

The Moscow Metro is the quickest, pleasantest means of all-purpose city transport. Fare is 5 kopeks. Trains every 90 to 120 seconds during the day. Rush hours to be avoided, from 7 to 10 and 17 to 20 hours. Trolleybus, tramway and autobus service are also cheap (3-5 kopeks) and efficient. Stops tend to be much farther apart, especially in suburbs, than in many western cities. This applies to all forms of public transport.

Taxi-stands at all main hotels, squares and rail stations. Basic fare, registered on the meter, is 20 kopeks per kilometer and a 20 kopek service charge. Tipping is optional. *Chauffeur-driven limousines* for special trips are provided upon request by Intourist. For *trolleybus,* keep 2, 3 and 5 kopek change in your pocket, as some vehicles have no ticket-taker.

You can view Moscow from the *air* by helicopter taxi or travel to one of the airports: Sheremetyevo, Vnukovo, Bykovo and Domodedovo. The *Aeroflot* helicopter station is at 37a Leningradsky Prospekt.

ENTERTAINMENT. Moscow offers more than 30 theaters and half-a-dozen concert halls. Most famous of these of course is the *Bolshoi* theater on Sverdlovsk Square, not far north of Red Square. The Bolshoi specializes in opera and ballet. For best view of stage in upper balconies, avoid the center. For classic and modern Russian plays, go to the *Maly Teatr* (Little Theater), also on Sverdlovsk Square. It is the oldest dramatic theater in Moscow. Or—especially if Chekhov is on—the *MKhAT* (Moscow Art Theater), at 3 Proyezd Khudozhestvennogo Teatra.

Bolshoi tickets range from 2 to 5.50 rubles, seats in other theaters are cheaper. Guides do not accompany tourists to the theater, but you may invite them as your guests.

Musical centers are the *Tchaikovsky Concert Hall,* at 31 Gorki St., and the *Moscow State Conservatory* at 13 Herzen St. To see and hear some of the best Russia has to offer in the way of national, popular and folk dancing and choral work, watch for performances by the world-famous Moiseyev Folk Dance Ensemble, the Beryozka Dance Ensemble, or one of the two great Russian choirs: Aleksandrov and Pyatnitsky.

The *Kremlin* theater, inside the Kremlin near the Spassky gate, was designed to present opera, theater, or wide-screen movies. Each seat is equipped with earphones for foreign-language simultaneous translation.

A fairly recent and highly original addition to the Moscow theater scene is the *Teatr Mimiki i Zhesta,* specializing in dance and pantomime: the actors are deaf-mutes!

MOSCOW THEATERS

Affiliated Bolshoi Theater (opera and ballet), 6 Pushkinskaya St.
Affiliated Maly Theater, 69 Bolshaya Ordinka St.
Affiliated Mossoviet Drama Theater, 26 Pushkinskaya St.
Art Theater (Annexe), 3 Moskvina St.
Drama and Comedy Theater, 76 Chkalov St.
Dramatic Theater, 26 Spartakovskaya St.
Gogol Theater, 8a Kazakov St.

Green Theater, 9 Krimsky Val. Gorki Recreation Park.
Hermitage Summer Variety Theater, 3 Karetny Ryad.
Komsomol Theater, 6 Chekhov St.
Maly Theater, 1/6 Sverdlov Sq.
Mayakovsky Theater, 9 Herzen St.
Moscow Art Theater, 3 Proyezd Khudozhestvennogo Teatra. Annex at 3 Moskvina St.
Moscow Drama Theater, 2 Malaya Bronnaya St.
Moscow Music Hall, 2 Tretyakov Pereulok (Lane).
Mossoviet Drama Theater, 16 Bolshaya Sadovaya St. (in the "Akvarium" Garden).
"Obraztsov" Central Puppet Theater, 3 Sadovo-Samotechnaya.
Operetta Theater, 6 Pushkinskaya St.
Pushkin Drama Theater, 23 Tverskoi Boulevard.
Romany Gypsy Theater, 26 Pushkinskaya St.
Satire Theater, 18 Bolshaya Sadovaya St.
Soviet Army Theater, Commune Sq.
Sovremennik Theater, Chistiye Prudy.
Stanislavsky and Nemirovich-Danchenko Musical Theater, 17 Pushkinskaya St.
Stanislavsky Drama Theater, 23 Gorki St.
Vakhtangov Theater, 26 Arbat St.
Variety Theater, 20/2 Bersenevskaya Naberezhnaya (Quay).
Yermolova Theater, 5 Gorki St.
Young Spectator's Theater, 10 Pereulok Sadovskikh.

CONCERT HALLS

Concert Hall, Central House of Culture of Railwaymen, 1/131 Komsomolskaya Sq.
Concert Hall, House of Scientists, 16 Kropotkin St.
Hall of Columns of Dom Soyuzov (House of Trade Unions), 1 Pushkinskaya St.

NIGHTLIFE. Cabarets and nightclubs are unknown in Moscow, and dance bands uninspired. All the big hotel restaurants provide dinner-dancing usually until 1 in the morning; the *Hotel Metropol* has bright Friday and Saturday evenings. Dancing to cool jazz most nights at the café *Molodyezhnoye,* 41 Gorki St. and at the *Romantiki,* 40 Komsomolski Prospekt. Both places close towards 23 hours. Ruble bar at *Arbat* on Kalinin Prospekt is pleasant. Two late-night bars (hard currency only) are in hotels *Metropol* (ground floor) and *Intourist* (basement), open till 2 A.M.

 MUSEUMS, LIBRARIES, ART GALLERIES. Greatest hazard in Moscow is that dread tourist affliction, "museum feet". Over 150 museums and exhibitions are open daily. Of these, the most celebrated is the *Tretyakov Gallery* on Lavrushinsky Lane, just off the south bank of the Moskva River opposite the Kremlin. Here are housed the richest treasures of Russian fine art, some 50,000 works of painting and sculpture ranging from 11th-century icons to 20th-century masterpieces.

Russia's greatest medieval painter, *Andrei Rublyov,* (about 1360–1440) has a museum to himself, although his best single work, the *Trinity Icon,* is exhibited in the Tretyakov Gallery. The Rublyov Art Museum, near Ulyanovskaya Street in the eastern part of the city, was formerly the Andronikov Monastery where Rublyov lived as a monk, and created a new school of medieval icon painting.

In a class by itself is the *Lenin State Library,* the world's largest collection of books, located on Kalinin St., just west of the Kremlin. A gem of 18th-century

Russian architecture, the library houses 19 million books, manuscripts and periodicals, in some 160 languages.

FINE ARTS

Bakhrushin Theatrical Museum, 31/12 Bakhrushin St.
Gorki Academic Art Theater Museum, 3-a Proyezd Khudozhestvennogo Teatra.
Gorki Museum, 25a Vorovsky St.
Kremlin Museum, at the Kremlin.
Gogol Museum, Suvorov St., in the writer's former apartment.
Leo Tolstoi Museum, 11 Kropotkinskaya St.
Museum of Architecture, 5 Kalinin Prospekt. Its annex is at 1 Donskaya Square.
Museum of Folk Art, 7 Stanislavsky St.
Musical Culture Museum, 12 Herzen St.
Ostankino Estate-Museum of Serf Art, 5 Pervaya Ostankinskaya St., in Ostankino.
Pushkin Museum of Fine Arts, 4 Marshal Shaposhnikov St., (French Impressionists).

NATURAL SCIENCES

Anthropological Museum, 18 Prospekt Marxa.
Biological Museum, 15 Malaya Gruzinskaya St.
Darwin Museum, 1 Malaya Pirogovskaya St.
Durov Scientific, Cultural, and Educational Corner, 4 Durov St.
Mineralogical Museum, 14–16 Leninsky Prospekt.
Moscow Planetarium, 5 Sadovo-Kudrinskaya St.
Museum of Eastern Culture, 16 Obukh St.
Palaeontological Museum, 16 Leninsky Prospekt.
Polytechnical Museum, 3/4 Novaya Square.
Zoo, 1 Bolshaya Gruzinskaya St.
Zoological Museum, 6 Herzen St.

POLITICAL

Clandestine Bolshevik Printing Press, 55 Lesnaya St.
Museum of the Revolution, 21 Gorki St.
Kalinin Museum, 21 Prospekt Marxa.
Labor Protection Museum, 10 Bolshaya Kaluzhskaya St.
Lenin's Funeral Procession Museum, 1 Kozhevnichesky Square.
Lenin Central Museum, 4 Revolution Square.
Soviet Army Museum, 2 Commune Square.

HISTORICAL

Historical Museum, 1/2 Red Square.
Borodino Panorama Museum, 38 Kutuzovsky Prospekt. Close by, same address, is Kutuzov's cottage *(izba).*
Museum of Moscow's History and Reconstruction, 12 Novaya Square.

 SHOPPING. The Soviet Union's biggest department store, GUM *(Gosudarstvenny Universalny Magazin),* occupies a block on the northeast side of Red Square. The entrance is at October 25th Street. Among the countless thousands of items stocked by GUM are good wood carvings, furs, excellent long playing records, musical instruments, lacework, fine rugs and cloisonné inlay. Very good ice cream is sold on all floors, or you can sip a glass of champagne as you shop. Other Moscow emporia of tourist interest include the TSUM Department Store at 2 Petrovka St., the "Childrens' World" at 7 Prospekt Marxa and the following specialty shops. Another enormous State store, the *Moskva,* is located on Leninsky Prospekt, one of the longest and widest avenues in the Soviet capital.

ANTIQUES. 19 Arbat St.; 31 Sretenka St.

ART GALLERIES. 11 Kuznetski Most; 25 and 46b Gorki St., 24 Kutuzovsky Prospekt, 12 Petrovka St.

CERAMICS. 6/20 Stoleshnikov Pereulok (Lane); *Crystal and Glassware:* 15 Gorki St.

FOOD. *Gastronom* shops at: Prospekt Marxa; 14 Gorki St.; 12 Dzherzhinsky St.; 2/54 Smolenskaya Square. *Beriozka* shops at the leading hotels.

GIFTS AND SOUVENIRS. *Podarki* shops at: 4 Gorki St.; 10 Petrovka St.; 13/15 Stoleshnikov Pereulok.

JEWELRY. 8 Petrovka St.; 13 Stoleshnikov Pereulok. 9 Kutuzovsky Prospekt.

MUSIC. *Phonograph records:* 6/2 Arbat St.; 2/3 Dzherzhinsky Sq.; 17 Kirov St.

PHILATELY. 20 Kuznetski Most; 16 Dzerzhinsky St.

PHOTOGRAPHIC SUPPLIES. 25 and 41 Gorki St.; 12 and 15 Petrovka St.

RUGS. 9 Gorki St.; 10 Petrovka St.

TOYS. *Detsky Mir* (Children's World), a large store at 7 Prospekt Marxa near the Metropol hotel.

Leningrad

If, like many tourists, you arrive in the Soviet Union by the northern steamship route, you will probably land at the busy port of Leningrad. Second only in size to Moscow, Leningrad rates as one of the world's most impressive cities. Peter the Great had it built according to plan by the best architects of the epoch, at the beginning of the 18th century. This modern-minded Czar wanted a "window looking on Europe" as well as a fortress to fend off the Swedes. Hundreds of thousands of serf laborers gave their lives to turn the chill mud and marshland of the Neva River delta into a splendid stone panoply of palaces, churches and monuments overlooking the gulf of Finland. Czar Peter modestly named his new city St. Petersburg; in 1914 this was changed to Petrograd and after 1924 to Leningrad.

For two centuries, until the Russian revolution, Leningrad was Russia's capital—and a world capital of art, music, luxury and industrial growth. During World War II, Leningrad's three and one-half million citizens withstood a 900-day siege against Hitler's armies. From 1941 to 1945, the beleaguered city was under constant bombardment, and 600,-000 people died of starvation. The sole source of supply was a precarious ice highway across frozen Lake Ladoga.

Another "Venice of the North", Leningrad is built on 101 islands, with some 35 graceful arched bridges spanning more than 200 miles of waterway within the city. It is 400 miles from Moscow along a railroad which follows a perfectly straight line.

Leningrad is a city of splendid vistas and palaces. Among its most outstanding sights are the Hermitage, one of the world's greatest art museums, and the exquisite fountains, parks and palaces of suburban Petrodvorets.

Exploring Leningrad

Leningrad's most typical landmark is the slim gilt spire of the Admiralty Building, which stands at the end of Nevsky Prospekt and dominates the city skyline. To the right of the Admiralty, along Palace Quay, is the famous Winter Palace, a pompous 18th-century Russian baroque edifice. Here in 1917 was enacted one of the final scenes of the Bolshevik Revolution, when the mutinied cruiser *Aurora* steamed up the river and fired its cannons point-blank at the Winter Palace, where the Kerensky provisional government was in session.

Today, the Palace is the central structure in the group of buildings housing the Hermitage Museum. Its 400 rooms, filled with more than 2,300,000 exhibits, including 8,000 paintings, reflect the history of culture and art from the work of ancient Greece, Rome, Egypt, China and India through the Italian Renaissance, right down to the French moderns. Besides its artistic treasures, the Hermitage itself is an unequaled work of art, as your first glimpse of the splendor of the main staircase and the Malachite Hall will prove.

In the center of Palace Square stands the Alexandrovskaya Column, an impressive monolithic stone monument. On the other side of the Admiralty rises the 330-foot gilt cupola of St. Isaac's Cathedral. This grandiose century-old structure is decorated with 112 monolithic columns. To the left of the Admiralty, in Decembrist Square, stands the monument to Peter the Great, immortalized in Pushkin's poem, *The Bronze Horseman.* Along the Nevsky Prospekt, one of the most imposing buildings is the Kazan Cathedral, a semi-circular colonnade reminiscent of St. Peter's in Rome. It now houses a "Museum of the History of Religion and Atheism". Such museums, in the Soviet Union, are essentially centers for the display and dissemination of atheistic propaganda (as is the Soviet magazine called "Science and Religion"). Just over the Anichkov Bridge beyond is located one of Leningrad's attractions—the Pioneer Palace. This children's wonderland caters to over 600 separate hobby clubs, covering every subject from nature study to painting, music, singing and games.

Many stores, restaurants, cafés and cinemas line the Nevsky Prospekt which leads to the Moskva railroad station. To the left towers the Smolny Church and next to it, the historic Smolny Institute, once a girl's finishing school founded by Catherine the Great. It was taken over by Lenin as his headquarters in 1917; here was proclaimed the establishment of Bolshevik power.

Between the Liteiny and Kirov bridges are the delightful "Summer Gardens" in which you may visit the modest personal palace of Peter the Great. Strolling along the quays in this vicinity can be one of the nicest moments of your Leningrad sojourn. From the middle of Kirov bridge there is a good view of the massive Peter-Paul Fortress which Peter the Great erected against the Swedes; it is now a museum. Next to it rise the lovely outlines of Peter-Paul Cathedral, where Peter is buried. Nearby

on the Neva banks under a brick casing is the little wooden house Peter
had constructed when he first decided to build St. Petersburg. For a last
panoramic look at Leningrad, climb the monumental main staircase of
the Kirov Stadium. The view will remind you that Leningrad is more
than a symphony of stone palaces and museum pieces; it is a major center
of heavy industry and shipping.

Environs of Leningrad

Petrodvorets. Right on the gulf of Finland, 18 miles from Leningrad,
is a spread of imperial pleasure palaces originally conceived by Peter the
Great and perfected during the 18th and 19th centuries. It now numbers
seven parks and a score of palaces and pavilions. This luxurious riot of
architecture, art, sculpture, landscaping and spouting water was severely
damaged during the war and only the façades have been restored.

Twelve miles beyond is the town of Pushkin, formerly Tsarskoye Selo
(Village of the Tsars) which was, before the revolution, the permanent
residence of the last Czar of Russia, Nicolas II, and his family. It is also
the place where Catherine the Great ended her days; she contributed
widely to its arrangement, which has been strictly preserved. Wartime
damage has been carefully repaired, and the famous parks, pavilions, and
palaces have been restored and maintained exactly as they were. Five
miles from Pushkin is the magnificent park of Pavlovsk with its many
fine architectural monuments dating from the 18th century. The chief
attraction is the Grand Palace on·the bank of the Slavyanka River,
designed by Cameron and built in 1782–6. The throne room, the
Knights' Hall and the Greek Hall are magnificently decorated.

Petrodvorets can be reached from Leningrad by local train, bus or
hovercraft; Pushkin by train or bus; Pavlovsk by train and bus.

PRACTICAL INFORMATION FOR LENINGRAD

HOTELS. Well-known *Astoria* (1), faded but still the best
available; central location, 380 rooms, good restaurant.
Evropeiskaya (2), 1/7 Brodsky St. 257 old-fashioned
rooms. Recent *Leningrad*, 5/2 Pirogovskaya Naberezh-
naya, is modern with Finnish décor, 746 smallish rooms, and a less central
location across the Neva. Don't confuse with older *Leningradskaya*, 10/24 Mai-
orov Prospekt, a traditional tourist hotel. *Moskva* (2), 2 Alexander Nevsky
Square, 777 rooms, new. *Rossiya* (3), has 414 rooms. *Moskovskaya*, 43 Ligovsky
Prospekt and *Neva*, 17 Tchaikovsky St. At nearby Novgorod is *Sadko* (1), *Volkhov*
and *Intourist*.

RESTAURANTS. For a good meal outside your hotel go
to *Sadko*, Sadovaya St., *Baku*, Sadovaya St., a new Azer-
baijani place, or the *Del'fin*, a floating restaurant in front
of the Admiralty. *Okolites*, Primorsky Prospekt 15 is on
the road to Helsinki. Also *Kavkazsky*, near Kazan Cathedral or *Severny*, Nevsky
Prospekt. The *Dinamo* at the stadium has dancing. The *White Nights* nightclub
features jazz.

ENTERTAINMENT. Your choice of 18 theaters and five concert halls, many of them located on the aptly named Arts Square (Ploshchad Iskusstv). Most famous of course, is the *Kirov Theater* (formerly the *Marinsky*), cradle of Russian opera and ballet. On Arts Square are located the *Maly Opera,* the *Philharmonic,* the *Musical Comedy Theater,* and the *Dramatic Art Theater.* The *Alexandrinsky Theater* is on the Nevsky Prospekt.

 MUSEUMS. All told, Leningrad has 47 museums of which the best known are: *Hermitage,* on Palace Quay (see *Exploring Leningrad section*). *Kazan Cathedral Museum of Religion and Atheism,* Nevsky Prospekt. *Peter-Paul Fortress Museum.* The *Russian Museum,* on Arts Square Art Place, contains over 200,000 works by Russian artists and sculptors.

 SHOPPING. Leningrad's main street, the *Nevsky Prospekt,* is lined with stores and shops of all descriptions. The second floor of the DLT department store on Zhelyabov St. has a souvenir handicraft shop. Also the *Beriozka* shops in hotels, at corner of Herzen and Dzerzhinsky streets (another one next door). Also *Gastronom* for food if time.

 TRANSPORTATION. The Leningrad Metro system is still fairly new and its expansion continues. It connects the center of the city with outlying industrial suburbs and four main railway terminals; it is four times faster than tram or bus. As in Moscow, each Metro station is an underground palace, boldly revelling in marble, glass, plaster, steel and lighting to create varied effects of "socialist symbolism".

The Black Sea Coast

When visiting the Soviet Black Sea coast, you'll find yourself in the most idyllic, climatically hospitable part of the Soviet Union. Here you are in for lots of sunshine, subtropical trees, flowers and fruits, forested mountains, curative springs, and baskable bathing beaches. The stretch of littoral extending from Odessa through the Crimea, past Sochi and Sukhumi down to Batumi on the Turkish border, is somewhat reminiscent of the French and Italian Riviera. It is twice as long as those two combined.

Odessa and Batumi, which bracket the Soviet Black Sea coast from northwest to southeast, are important ports and manufacturing centers. In between, the sun-drenched land produces oranges, lemons, and tangerines, tea, olives, tobacco and other subtropical crops. Yet the main industry of the area is—health. The entire coast is one big resort area, stubbed with huge white palaces, formerly private residences, now sanatoria. Something like half a million visitors come to these "sanatoria" every year. However, most of them are not invalids or convalescents, but merely vacationers who wish to spend their holidays building up strength for the rigors of a northern Russian winter and the arduous pace of Soviet life.

Although relatively few foreign tourists "take the cure", the effect of a brief stay on the balmy Black Sea coast is strikingly tonic and restorative. Besides the area's natural beauties and kindly climate, each of its main resort centers has a lively theatrical season, as well as museums, botanical gardens, excursions—and of course, bathing in the Black Sea.

Georgia

Inland from Sukhumi and Batumi is the romantic Caucasian mountain republic of Georgia, and its strangely beautiful capital city of Tiflis (Tbilisi).

Two and a half hours by air from Moscow, a little more by train from Sukhumi, Tiflis, founded in the fifth century, is one of the oldest cities in the Soviet Union—and one of the newest. Nestled in a mountain valley, this thriving Caucasian metropolis of half a million people is the capital of the once-proud kingdom of Georgia, now a Soviet Republic. Georgia's history goes back to ancient Greek and Roman times. At its height, from the 12th to the 15th centuries, it extended over virtually the entire Caucasus area. Its most famous ruler was the legendary (but real) Queen Tamara (1184–1214), whose reign was graced by Georgia's national poet, Shota Rustaveli; his epic *Knight in the Tiger Skin* is known in many languages to this day.

The Georgians are a dark, handsome mountain people, who still sport their national costumes as everyday clothing. Georgian women wear brilliantly-hued flowing robes and do their hair in knee-length braids. Georgian songs, dances and national dishes all express the hot-blooded, spicy character of this exotic hospitable people.

Exploring Tiflis

Tiflis itself (the Georgian name means "place-of-hot-springs") is best seen as a whole from the funicular cablecar that lifts tourists some 800 feet above the city to a delightful restaurant on top of Mount David. This height is also called Mtatsminda (Holy Mountain); here you may visit an historic church and pantheon, burial place of great Georgians. Looking north you will see the main Caucasus Range, and to the southwest, the massive wall of the Trialetsky subrange.

Tiflis is built on the steep banks of the Kura River. On the left bank in Ordzhonikidze Park is a railroad run by children; its one-mile right-of-way includes bridges, switches and other real railroading refinements. Other beauty spots of Tiflis include the Botanical Garden, the Academy of Arts and the Conservatory. Georgia's history is told in displays in the State Museum. The Museum of Art shows off works of the region's modern artists. Round about Tiflis you may visit the Samgor Sea, a six-mile long freshwater lake resort; the old town of Mtskheta, Georgia's ancient capital; and, 50 miles away on the banks of the Kura, the brisk little town of Gori, home town of a shoemaker's son named Dzhugashvili, who "made good" under the alias of Stalin. His birthplace is now a museum.

Odessa

A Soviet seaport second only to Leningrad, Odessa is also a major manufacturing center. But for tourists it is above all a popular seaside resort. Odessa's Opera and Ballet Theater is reputed to be the most beautiful structure in the Soviet Union. From Primorsky Boulevard a broad flight of famous stairs descends 455 feet to the sea front. It is called the Potemkin Stairway in memory of the battleship *Potemkin,* whose crew mutinied in 1905 and invested Odessa.

The Crimea

This huge diamond-shaped peninsula of steppe and mountain has a romantic past. Once an important bread-basket for ancient Greece, it was later overrun by Huns, Khazars, Mongols, Russians, British and French (Crimean war of 1854–5) and finally the Germans, who occupied it in 1918 and again in 1942–4. The Soviet naval base of Sevastopol, on the Crimean peninsula's southern tip, is out of bounds to foreign and Russian tourists alike. However, a little to the south motorists may pass by the inlet of Balaklava, mentioned in Homer's Odyssey, and scene of the famous and futile "Charge of the Light Brigade".

Yalta, Popular Resort Center

A few miles farther east, in a natural amphitheater ringed with vineyards, lies the resort of Yalta, all but smothered in cypress, acacia, mimosa, mountain laurel, magnolia, palms and oleander. Roses frequently bloom here in December. In addition to its hotels, villas and holiday houses, Yalta has 112 sanatoria or rest homes, staffed by some 700 physicians. The climate is mild and sunny, shielded from the north wind by surrounding mountains. Yalta is a bright, lively vacation spot, with music in the park, dancing, cafés and restaurants, ice-cream parlors, souvenir shops—in fact, everything but a casino. One mile southwest of the town on the way to Alupka beach, you will pass an enormous white Italian Renaissance palace, which used to be the summer residence of Czar Nicholas II, and is now Livadia sanatorium. Pyjama-clad health-seekers today play ping-pong in the hall where Roosevelt, Churchill and Stalin foregathered at the famous Yalta Conference in February 1945, to settle the postwar world. Other excursions from Yalta include Massandra, a major wine-making center with a collection of 45,000 bottles of vintage wine, some dating from the 18th century. Here at the "Kuibyshev State Vineyard" you may sample the best wines in the Soviet Union. You can take a short trip, preferably by sea, to the Nikitsky Botanical Gardens; its oldest specimen is a wild pistachio tree planted some 1,000 years ago. Stone Age dwellings have recently been discovered in the vicinity of Yalta. The Crimea's southern tip is Cape Ai-Todor, almost 8 miles from Yalta. Remains of an ancient Roman naval base have been excavated here. For a lovely view of the coast, visit the handsome Gothic "Swallows-Nest" castle overhanging the cliff.

The Caucasian Riviera

Eastward from the Crimean peninsula, beyond Novorossiisk and Tuapse, lie the exotic Caucasian coastal towns of Sochi, Gagra, Sukhumi, Poti and Batumi, surrounded by citrus trees and olive plantations, bamboo groves (all collective farms, of course), subtropical forests, high mountains and hot mineral springs. The coast road connecting these points is, to quote a local Georgian saying, "as long and twisted as a mother-in-law's tongue".

Sochi

This increasingly popular resort with its parks and pebbly beach stretches for 12 miles along the sea. The nearby Matsesta health resort, with its hot sulphur springs, attracts some 30,000 vacationers yearly. Much of the bottled mineral water sold in the Soviet Union comes from this area. The Sochi Dendrarium is a collection of rare trees from all over the world. On its 30 acres there are 800 different species, from the Himalayan cedar to the Mexican agave and the Australian eucalyptus. Near Matsesta is the famous Agura waterfall, which you can reach by an easy mountain path. If you are feeling energetic, you can hike up to the 100-foot observation tower of the 2,172-foot Bolshoi Akhun mountain. Take in the incredibly beautiful panorama of sea and mountain; it's worth the effort. Five hours by bus from Gagra (near Sochi) bring you to the real high point of your Black Sea holiday—Lake Ritsa, a Caucasian mountain lake 3,116 feet above sea level, one and one-half miles long, half a mile across, and as deep as it is wide. There is a good hotel here, and a restaurant where Georgian *shashlik* (lumps of lamb broiled on a dagger) is served up by genuine Georgians. If you miss Lake Ritsa while in Sochi, you can still make this scenic side-trip from Sukhumi. Down the coast from Sochi on the way to Sukhumi, you pass the bathing beaches of Khosta, Adler, Gagra and Akhali-Afon.

Ancient Sukhumi

Capital of the Abkhaz Autonomous Soviet Socialist Republic, Sukhumi is a busy little city inhabited since ancient Greek times. In fact, the land of Colchis, where Jason came to find the Golden Fleece, lies just to the south of Sukhumi in the suburb of Poti. Today, Jason would have loaded his vessels with tea, tobacco, oranges and lemons, which grow luxuriously in the subtropical climate. However, Sukhumi's most photogenic spectacle is the 60-acre park on Trapetsiya hill, which teems with monkeys. At this famous monkey nursery of the Soviet Academy of Sciences' Medico-Biological Station, scientists observe these monkeys as part of their study of human behavior.

Batumi, Handsome Metropolis

For a major refining and shipping port, and industrial center, Batumi, capital of the Adzhar Autonomous Soviet Socialist Republic is a surprisingly handsome and impressive metropolis. Its pipelines connect it with the oilfields of Baku on the Caspian Sea, some 500 miles across the Caucasus. Batumi glows with a particular year-round green, a combination of the camphor laurel, palms, cacti and evergreen trees which line its streets and waterfront. Five miles out of town in the suburb of Zelyony Mysh is a 250-acre Botanical Garden where plants from all over the world recreate jungle, desert and alpine scenery. This area's tea plantations and citrus groves are considered the richest in the Soviet Union. The best and warmest beach in Georgia, six miles long and 350 feet wide, is at Kobuleti, 21 miles from Batumi.

PRACTICAL INFORMATION
FOR THE BLACK SEA COAST AND GEORGIA

HOTELS AND RESTAURANTS

BATUMI. *Intourist* (1), 124 rooms, garden setting. Restaurant: *Primorsky* in park of same name.

KHERSON. Recent *Intourist* on Svoboda Square is best. *Pervomaisky* has a good restaurant. Also *Kiev* on Ushakov Prospekt. Restaurants: *Dnieper,* at harbor; *Ogonyok* on Ushakov Prospekt.

ODESSA. *Odessa* (1), one of USSR's best, with view of sea. *Krasnaya* (2). *Chernoye More* (2), new. Also *Arkadya,* 150 rooms. Restaurants: *Ukraina,* Karl Marx St. and *Yuzhny,* Khalturin St.

ORDZHONIKIDZE. New *Intourist,* 19 Miv Prospekt. On the outskirts, spacious *Motel Daryal,* all facilities, pretty view. *Kavkaz* in town. Restaurant with a view is *Gorny Orel* atop Mt. Lysaga 7 miles out.

SIMFEROPOL. *Ukraina,* Rosa Luxemburg St., *Moskva,* Yaltinskaya St. *Airport* for intransit stays; *Yuzhnaya,* and *Vokzalnaya* at railway station. Restaurants: *Chaika,* by the reservoir or *Otdykh* in Kirov Gardens.

SOCHI. The *Camelia* is almost (L), 184 traditionally tasteful rooms, good restaurant, park location. *Magnolia* (also known as the *Sochi*) (1), modern, and has a view of the sea. *Intourist* (1), 110 rooms, own beach. The *Zhemchuzhina* overlooks beach, has 658 rooms. *Leningrad,* 503 rooms; *Primorskaya,* 434 rooms. Restaurants: *Cascade* has good food, terrace; *Izbaq* in outskirts has Georgian setting. *Akhun* on Mt. Akhun for atmosphere; *Morskoi* at passenger wharf. *Pazhka* (opened 1976), Armenian specialities, recommended, beautiful location on hill five minutes' drive from center of Sochi.

SUKHUMI. On Tbilisi highway, the *Sinop* with camping site, beach, restaurant, is best. *Abkhazia.* Third choice *Tbilisi.* Restaurants: Best 'food at *Aragvi* on Mir Prospekt but for atmosphere it's *Dioskuri* in the fortress; *Amza* on top of Sukhumi Hill or *Amra* on the seafront.

TIFLIS (TBILISI). Best is recent *Iveria* (1), 282 rooms, good restaurant, central location. Roof-top pool. The *Intourist* is ageing (2). *Tbilisi* (3), 113 rooms. Restaurants: Georgian cuisine is original and tasty. Best food (and service) at *Daryal,* 22 Rustaveli Prospekt; *Aragvi,* 29 Pushkin St. For atmosphere, *Mt. Mtatsminda.*

YALTA. Recommended *Oreanda* (1), in town center but only 30 yards from sea, restaurants, shops, Intourist office. *Yalta (1),* on hill overlooking sea, 100 steps! to beach, 10-15 minutes walk from harbour. *Tavrida,* (3), 53 rooms. *Motel* overlooks the river. Others are the *Yuzhnaya,* and *Crimea.* Restaurants: *Ukraina* at 34 The Promenade has a self-service counter. For atmosphere it's the *Otdykh* atop main harbor building; *Aquarium* on Moskovskaya St. straddles a stream; in Primorsky Park, the *Priboi* and *Leto.*

ENTERTAINMENT. The *Odessa* Philharmonic emphasizes Cossack folk music and dances. In *Tiflis* see Georgian folk dancing.

MUSEUMS. The Black Sea Coast has a variety of regional and national museums, some of which are: **Odessa.** *Archeological Museum, Museum of Western and Eastern Art, State Archeological Museum,* specializing in the past of the Black Sea Coast. *Odessa Regional Historical Museum.* **Sochi.** *Museum of Local History, Dendrarium* (Botanic Garden). **Tiflis.** *Georgian State Museum, Art Museum.* **Yalta.** *The Eastern Museum,* formerly palace of the Emir of Bokhara, displays oriental rugs, silks, ivories, embroideries and other handicrafts, illustrating the history and folklore of the Crimean Tartars. The *Chekhov Museum* is at the end of the Lenin Embankment. Reported closed for restoration and due to reopen by 1980, but check—it may be ahead of schedule.

The Ukraine and its Capital

Russia's third largest city is Kiev, capital of the Ukrainian Soviet Socialist Republic. The Ukraine, a Texas-sized territory of 231,000 square miles, extends from Poland to the Black Sea, has a population of more than 41 million, and occupies a seat in the United Nations. Always a granary area, the Ukraine has in recent years grown into a primary region of mining, shipping, manufacturing and mechanized agriculture.

Kiev itself is a modern city of almost two million inhabitants, situated on the right bank of the mighty Dnieper River. It was the harnessing of this 1420-mile stream in 1932, by the famous Dniepropetrovsk Dam and Hydroelectric Plant, that gave the Ukraine its start toward industrialization.

In the heyday of its might and splendor, medieval Kiev was one of Europe's most brilliant capitals, with a rich artistic and commercial life. In 1654, however, after centuries of pressure from Poles and Tartars, delegates of the Ukrainian people met and voted to merge with Russia; Kiev was thereafter governed from Moscow.

During World War II, Hitler's armies occupied Kiev for almost two disastrous years, from 1941 to 1943. Today, nearly all trace of this destruction has vanished, and modern Kiev is larger and handsomer than its pre-war predecessor.

Exploring Kiev

Wide, tree-lined Kreshchatik Street is Kiev's main thoroughfare. It runs inland from the high bank of the Dnieper, with residences on one side and public buildings on the other. The city's principal historic landmark is the church of St. Sophia (Sofiisky Sobor), built in 1037. In form, the church is inspired by the great Hagia Sofia (Holy Wisdom) in Constantinople, but its construction reflects the high skill of Kiev artisans in the 11th century. Its inner walls are adorned by mosaics of colored glass, icons, and painted frescos some of which depict the everyday life and amusements of the people of the period.

In the early days, Kiev was fortified against the Tartars by stone walls and towers. Huge oaken gates with brass-bound hinges barred access to the city. One of these has been preserved to this day—the famous "Golden Gates" (Zolotiye Vorota) of Kiev, at the corner of Vladimirskaya and Sverdlovskaya streets. They were called "golden" because of the brass hinges, and the gilded spire of a small church built above the gate.

Kiev's most intriguing 11th-century monument is the celebrated Pecherskaya Lavra, a 12th-century monastery named for the labyrinth of catacombs which the monks spent seven years in digging beneath the monastery buildings. The complex, with its caverns, churches, museums of historical treasures, manuscripts and craft exhibits, is well worth visiting. The city boasts some splendid monumental statues of saints, heroes and poets.

Kiev is a city of parks and gardens as well. The huge Central Recreation Park, with its open-air Green Theater, runs for several miles along the right bank of the Dnieper. Close to the opposite bank is Trukhanov Island, a favorite outdoor spot for Kievites and tourists alike. It has a splendid beach, and its 220-acre Hydro Park offers boating, swimming pools, playgrounds, libraries, cinemas and other entertainment. A recently built footbridge connects it with the city.

PRACTICAL INFORMATION FOR KIEV

HOTELS. *Dnieper,* Lenkomsomol Square, 200 rooms, good restaurant, and smaller *Intourist,* 26 Lenin St., both (1). *Moskva,* October Revolution St., 370 rooms, and *Ukraine,* Shevchenko Blvd., 319 rooms both (3). *Lybed,* 1 Pobeda Square, 280 rooms, 19 floors.

Restaurants: Most hotel restaurants serve Ukrainian dishes which are delicious. Others include the *Dynamo,* 3 Kirov St., and *Stolichny,* 5 Kreshchatik.

ENTERTAINMENT. Kiev has seven theaters; the largest is the *Shevchenko,* devoted to ballet and opera (sung in Ukrainian). The highlight of any tourist visit is a performance of one of the national Ukrainian song and dance ensembles.

MUSEUMS. To become acquainted with Ukrainian national art, visit the *Kiev Museum of Ukrainian Art* at 6 Kirov St. The collections date from the 16th century to the present. One of the city's two botanical gardens is located on Shevchenko Blvd.; the second on the sloping right bank of the Dnieper. There is also a *Museum of Western and Oriental Art,* at 15 Chudnovskaya. Everything from Greek sculpture to African totems—via Bellini and Van Eyck and the *Monastery of the Caves.* Gold, jewelry, vestments, religious treasure, manuscripts and illuminations.

SHOPPING. Ukrainian handicraft is proverbially imaginative and artistic in its use of color and design. You will find handicrafts shops at 23 Chervanoarmiiska and 93 Kirov Streets; a *Podarki* gift shop at 9 Karl Marx St., and the *Farfor Fayance* ceramic shop, 34 Kreshchatik St.

The Ukraine Hinterland

Besides Kiev, a mainline tourist goal, Intourist itineraries enable travelers to stop over briefly in the Ukrainian cities of Odessa and Simferopol (see *Black Sea Coast* section), Kharkov, Chernovtsy, Lvov, Uzhgorod, Kherson, Poltava, Vinnitsa and Zaporozhye. For a good look at everyday life and work in the Soviet Union, these waypoints offer a more intimate picture than do the overwhelming sights and sounds of Moscow or Leningrad.

The major industrial city of Kharkov, second largest in the Ukraine, lies exactly halfway (460 miles) along the 932-mile highway from Moscow to Yalta, and 297 miles east of Kiev. Founded by Cossacks in the 17th century, it was more than half destroyed during the last war, and has been rebuilt as a showpiece of modern Soviet city planning. Kharkov, with over one million inhabitants, is primarily an industrial city. Beyond its suburban green belt lie collective farms *(kolkhoz),* one of which usually figures, along with industrial plants, among sights shown to tourists. Ancient monument fanciers will find few objects for their attention in this brand new metropolis, beyond a handful of old churches. Among these is the 17th-century Pokrovsky Sobor and a surviving bell-tower of the Uspensky Sobor.

The legendary old Cossack stronghold of Zaporozhye lies 175 miles south of Kharkov on the road to Yalta. Today it is an enormous hydroelectric, transport and steel-making center on the Dnieper river, at the site of the great dam and power station, one of the largest in Europe. Old Zaporozhye (Aleksandrovsk before the Revolution) is situated on historic Khortitsa Island in the river. Here, from the middle of the 16th century, Ukrainian Cossacks—romantic mounted warrior-peasants—defended the southern reaches of Russia for hundreds of years. (In fact, the word Ukraine means "border".)

Transcarpathia

For bus or automobile travelers entering the Soviet Union from Romania, the town of Chernovtsy, 23 miles beyond the border station of Porubnoye, is an especially interesting stop-over possibility. When founded in the 12th century, Chernovtsy was an important medieval marketplace, and a Carpathian foothill fortress against the Tartars. Chernovtsy's tourist interest lies not so much in the Krayevoy Museum of local history, or in various old church buildings now part of the University, as in the opportunity to observe how newly settled Ukrainians live in a light industrial town.

Transcarpathia is a most picturesque and wild land of wooded mountains, rushing streams, vinecovered slopes, ruined castles and small white houses with red tiled roofs. For a view of Uzhgorod, climb the 13th-century castle at the end of tree-lined Kremlyovskaya street. You can take a ride on the Malaya Zakarpatskaya (children's railroad) from the city park to handsome Stalingrad Quay, flanking the Uzh river, and leading to Red Square. The ivy and vine-clad buildings that surround it were built just before the war.

Lvov

In the northern Carpathian foothills, 168 miles northwest of Chernovtsy on the road to Warsaw, is the important and historic city of Lvov. In medieval times, this was the famous market center of Lemberg on the Vienna-Kiev trade route. Among its historic monuments are two 14th-century cathedrals and a 16th-century palace of the Galician princes who founded the town in 1265. Lvov University dates from 1658. The city is an industrial center.

OTHER UKRAINIAN CENTERS

CHERNOVTSY. *Kiev* and *Bukovina,* both (1).

KHARKOV. *Intourist* (130 rooms) is central, but noisy, *Kharkov* both (1).

KHERSOM. *Kiev.*

KURSK. Good stopover on Moscow-Kharkov road; *Kursk, Oktyabrskaya,* and Motel *Solovinaya Roshcha* with Intourist facilities.

LVOV. *Lvov* (1), 226 rooms, and *Intourist* (3), in center. *Dnieper,* adequate. Restaurants: *Moskva, Leto* and *Pervomaisky.*

POLTAVA. *Kiev,* Motel *Poltava,* both (1).

UZHGOROD. *Kiev* (1); *Verkhovina* (2). *Uzhgorod* (3). Restaurant: *Konditerskaya Café* on Sholokov St.

VINNITSA. *Ukraina, Oktyabrskaya,* both (1).

ZAPOROZHYE. Best is *Zaporozhye,* 504 rooms; *Teatralnaya.*

Volgograd and the Volga

Most of Soviet Russia's great cities are a striking mixture of past and present—ancient churches and palaces alongside modern factories and skyscrapers. However, the major industrial metropolis of Volgograd (called Stalingrad before 1961 and Tsaritsyn before 1925) has no visible past—it was wiped off the map in the seven-month battle of 1942–3, which made the name of Stalingrad a worldwide watchword of heroism, and a turning point in World War II.

You can take in a view of the handsomely constructed new city from historic Mamai Mound on the western outskirts, where some of the fiercest battles against the Nazi besiegers were fought. The new Volgograd stretches for 40 miles along the Volga's right bank. Its vast expanse of housing, cultural and office buildings, parks and boulevards, are rimmed with factories (try to visit the Tractor Works), grain elevators, oil tanks and cranes.

Since July 1952, Volgograd, although hundreds of miles from the sea, has become one of the Soviet Union's main seaports. That year saw completion of the monumental Volga-Don Canal connecting the Volga and Don rivers by a 63-mile ditch containing 15 locks. The new combined waterway totals nearly 3,500 miles in length, and includes immense hydroelectric and irrigation installations. It links the Baltic and White Seas of the north with the Caspian, Azov and Black Seas to the south.

You may reach Volgograd by air from Moscow in less than two hours, but the most rewarding way to come is by steamer down the Volga. The river excursion, from Moscow via Volgograd and the Volga-Don canal to Rostov-on-Don, offers a dramatic introduction to the Soviet Union as a whole, rather than isolated tours of a few individual cities. The 2,000-mile cruise, one of best tourist opportunities, and highly recommended, passes such historic and industrial centers as Yaroslavl, Gorki (formerly Nizhni-Novgorod), Ulyanovsk (formerly Simbirsk), Kazan (capital of the Autonomous Tartar Republic), Kuibyshev (formerly Samara), Zhiguli, Ilyevka, Volgograd, and Rostov-on-Don.

PRACTICAL INFORMATION FOR THE VOLGA REGION

KAZAN. May be visited in daytime only. *Kazan, Soviet* and *Tartarstan* are best hotels.

ROSTOV. Hotels: Functional *Moskovskaya,* and *Intourist,* 524 rooms, both (1). *Don* or *Yuzhnaya* (2). Restaurants: *Tsentralny,* 76 Engels St. and *Volgadon,* 31 Beregovaya St.

VOLGOGRAD. Hotels: Provincial *Intourist* and *Volgograd,* both on Ploschad Pavshikh Bortsov (Square of the Fallen). Restaurants: *Leto* in city park, *Mayak* on embankment.

ULYANOVSK. Hotels: Best is *Volga; Venets* is in town center; *Rossiya.*

Minsk, Smolensk and Byelorussia

The Byelorussian (White Russian) Soviet Socialist Republic, of which Minsk is the capital, has an area of 80,000 square miles, a population of over ten million, and a vote in the United Nations. For tourists entering the U.S.S.R. by car, bus or train via Poland, the newly rebuilt city of Minsk is a likely stopover. As over 80 percent of the city was razed in the war there is little of antiquity left, but it is a thriving modern place, with attractive avenues. It is one-third of the way along the 660-mile highway from Brest-Litovsk to Moscow. Two-thirds of the way down the road is the second stopover city, Smolensk. This once-famous medieval trading center on the Dnieper river, built in the ninth century at the same time as Moscow, Kiev and Novgorod, was almost completely destroyed during the battles of World War II. A number of 12th-century churches and fragments of the old city wall escaped destruction, but the kremlin was demolished.

Try to fit in a visit to Talashkino, a 20-minute drive from Smolensk, where there is a real Russian *terem,* a typical gaily-colored and fairytale-like wooden house, with a display of linens, wood carvings and pottery.

PRACTICAL INFORMATION FOR BYELORUSSIA

MINSK. Best hotels are *Minsk,* 250 rooms, and *Yubileinaya,* 249 rooms, both (1); then the *Byelorus.* Restaurants: *Neman,* Lenin Prospekt and *Raduga,* Privok-zalnaya (Station) Square.

SMOLENSK. Hotels: the modern *Rossiya,* central, or the *Smolensk,* both (1). Restaurants: *Sputnik* on Nikolayev St., and *Otdykh* in Glinka Gardens.

 ENTERTAINMENT. At the *Bolshoi Theater,* Paris Commune Square, you can see Russian or western ballets and operatic performances. Lyrical Byelorussian folk songs can be heard at performances of the *Byelorussian Folk Chorus.* The *Yanko Kupala* theater puts on regionally inspired plays. A 40,000-spectator stadium in the *Dinamo Sports Park* is the kick-off place for many sports events.

Riga, Baltic Port

Opened to tourists a few years ago, the Baltic port of Riga is a stopover for travelers arriving in the U.S.S.R. by sea. If you time it right, you can join in the fun during the "Ligo", Holiday of Song Festivities, early August. Singing and dancing Latvians, fireworks, bonfires and beer encourage timid souls to participate. Coming from the West, you will be particularly welcome.

From the 12th century right up to World War II (when the U.S.S.R. annexed Latvia), Riga—once a proud port city of the Hanseatic League —was an object of rivalry and foreign invasion. Hints of its turbulent past can be seen in the old part of town. Medieval churches in narrow winding streets contrast with the wide postwar boulevards and parks, which in summer vibrate with outdoor concerts. The 14th-century Riga Castle (now Palace of Pioneers) is worth a visit, as is St. Peter's Church (today the Riga Museum). Another museum on the shores of Lake Juglas reproduces a whole ancient rural community to illustrate the former life of Latvian peasants. Its genuine cottages, barns and furnishings were collected from all parts of the country.

One of the biggest artistic attractions in the Latvian capital is the 13th-15th-century Dom Cathedral, whose former organ has an equally venerable history of renovation and restoration. Lately rebuilt after World War II damage, the instrument has recovered its 127 registers, and the cathedral concerts are a major event.

The Gulf of Riga freezes solid from December to February, but in summer a relatively mild climate (thanks to the considerably warm Gulf Stream) permits bathing at the pine-lined suburban beach resort of Rigas Jurmala.

PRACTICAL INFORMATION FOR RIGA

HOTELS. *Intourist,* 670 rooms; centrally located *Riga,* all 300 rooms with bath or shower, both (1). *Daugava,* Kugyu St., 265 rooms (2); *Jurmala,* out of town. There is a moderately good beach hotel at Bulduri, 15 miles from Riga: *Rizhkoye Vzmoriye.*

ENTERTAINMENT. Particularly recommended for tourists are: *Theater of Opera and Ballet* and State *Philharmonia.*

MUSEUMS. *Museum of Latvian Art. City Historical Museum. Museum of Fine Arts.*

Tallinn

On the southern shores of the Gulf of Finland, almost opposite Helsinki, lies Tallinn, capital of Estonia. The bilingual street signs are one reminder that this ancient Baltic city, with its narrow streets and gabled medieval guild-houses, is now not a Hanseatic but a Soviet city. Tallinn is noted for good service and for shopping advantages that are favorable by Soviet standards. The hotels are simple but clean. Five hours by rail from Leningrad.

PRACTICAL INFORMATION FOR TALLINN

HOTELS. *Hotel Viru,* (L) new, Scandinavian-style high-rise on edge of old city, 462 rooms. *Hotel Tallinn,* (1) good food and service. Others: *Palace, Europea.*

RESTAURANTS: Best is attractive cellar with good food, *Vanatoomis.*

ENTERTAINMENT: Russian Drama Theater, State Opera and Ballet Theater, Openair Musical Theater in Kadriorg Park.

MUSEUMS: State Museum of Fine Arts, Historical Museum of Estonian Academy of Sciences, City Museum.

SPAIN

Spain means crisp white beaches to many travelers, castles and knights-errant to others—to us it means both, and we heartily recommend a healthy dose of each to anyone planning a trip to this second-most popular tourist destination in Europe (after Italy). Long the number one target for British tourists, and increasingly popular with Americans, Spain has become a kind of paradise for holidaymakers, if one can believe the legend which has grown up in the past few years. She has done this with a fantastic hotel-building program, fairly stabilized prices (until recently), a goodly supply of cheap labor and a fine disdain for letting political problems get in the way of making money—Spain welcomes the British tourist while trying to wrest Gibraltar away from the United Kingdom, for example. Costs are up again, as everywhere else, with inflation 28% in 1977.

Hotels are, by and large, very good—Spain has managed nearly to achieve the impossible by building many hotels quickly yet giving some an air of Spanish elegance at the same time. They don't all look like egg cartons, faceless slabs or Bauhaus barracks, but are filled with Spanish artwork, wrought iron balustrades, frescos and murals, potted palms and imitations of patios . . . all done to remind you that you're still in Spain, despite the English language spoken all around you and the gin-and-tonic in the bar.

The beaches are there, complete with the grade of tourist you have paid to meet, and occasionally, a native or two. The air of puritanism has disappeared. Film and theater censorship was abolished in 1977, and an air of freedom is sweeping the land. There are passable attempts at nightlife in the smallest resort.

For beach resorts, there are Málaga in the south, where nearby Marbella and Torremolinos have become quite a rendezvous for international society. A similar role has always been played in the north by San Sebastián, in the Basque country, formerly the summer capital of Spain. Farther west are the resort city of Santander and, over on Spain's strip of the Atlantic, La Coruña, a long-standing favorite of British visitors, and the island of La Toja, near Pontevedra. In the east is the enormously popular Costa Brava, the northernmost stretch of the Catalan coast, from the borderline between Barcelona and Gerona provinces to the French frontier. To the south, from Valencia to Alicante, is the Costa Blanca, its most fashionable center Benidorm: south of Huelva the recently developed Costa de la Luz, with the beaches of Cadiz not far off.

When you tire of roasting in the sun, hire a car and head for one of the thousands of castles, ruins or bulging museums nearby. Our idea of the highlights of Spain is as follows:

Perhaps the number one tourist attraction of Spain is the Alhambra at Granada. Following close behind it in the same category of sights, that of architectural wonders in cities that are also gems, come the Mosque of Córdoba and the Alcazar and Cathedral of Seville. Santiago de Compostela is a museum city and Ávila a historic walled town. Madrid, the capital, contains some of the greatest art collections in the world, and the Escorial Monastery near it is another of Spain's great sights; the excursion can be combined with a visit to the Valley of the Fallen Memorial. Barcelona, the capital of Cataluña, has a charm and vitality quite its own. El Greco's home may be seen in Toledo, an interesting art city.

The Country and the People

There are immense variations in climate, topography and regional personality within Spain itself. You would never confuse the treeless Mancha tableland or the austere Castilian plateau with the rice swamps and orange groves of Valencia, for example, nor the pink and olive hills of Andalusia with the snow-capped Pyrenees. And if you travel widely in Spain you will begin to note the differences between the dark-haired, white-skinned Castilians, proud, elegant, conservative and reserved; the up-and-coming "progresista" Catalans, often with blonde or reddish hair, an inheritance from the Visigoths; the exuberant, easy-going, voluble Andalusians, whose dark and languorous eyes have that unmistakable Arabian Nights look, quite a contrast to the wiry, round-headed, light-eyed Basques.

But you will also be aware of characteristics that all the Spaniards seem to have in common, a unifying quality, in short, a national spirit. First of all there is the unity of religious sentiment. Despite certain exceptions, the majority of the Spanish people still maintain the religious enthusiasm that sustained them through seven centuries of Holy Wars against the Moorish Infidel, the Counter Reformation and the flesh-searing horrors of the Spanish Inquisition. There is something violent in this religious emotion. The thorns and the blood are real in Spain.

Secondly, you will find the Spanish are proud with a pride of race. They carry themselves like a proud people. España, they will remind you, was a great nation for centuries during which Italy and Germany were a mere conglomeration of squabbling little duchies. If it is true that Spanish character oscillates between idealism and materialism, it is usually idealism that triumphs in the end, or at least until the advent of industrialism over the past fifteen years.

Courage and the Bulls

The greatest of Spanish national virtues is courage. This explains the popularity of Spain's most typical spectacle, the bullfight. The bullfight is basically an ordeal of courage.

To see a *corrida,* literally a "running" of the bulls, is to understand the violent smouldering heart of Spain. The bullfight season in Spain runs from the end of March through October. Almost every major town has its Plaza de Toros with its bull ring. Madrid is the place where you will see the most famous *toreros* (they're only called *toreadors* in *Carmen*). The second most important place is Seville.

Before seeing a bullfight, read a brief explanation of this essentially Spanish drama. A good essay is "Bullfighting for Beginners" in *Fodor's Guide to Spain.* You'll certainly have a more exciting time if you know what's going on, and it will help you to understand the reactions of the *aficionados,* the colorful crowd who jam the arena. When you buy a ticket for a bullfight you will be asked if you prefer *sol* or *sombra,* the sunny side of the ring or the shady side. Take *sombra* even though it costs more. You'll know why we recommend this once you've become acquainted with the burning sun of Spain.

Spanish Folklore

If Spain is the home of the *siesta* (though in the big cities this is quickly disappearing), it is also, *par excellence,* the country of the *fiesta* which, except during Holy Week, are the reverse of solemn—and a local saint's day is apt to consist of a half-hour Mass in the church, followed by bullfights, dancing, music, fireworks and general rejoicing. There are countless *romerias* (picnic excursions to shrines), and these are extremely colorful with long cavalcades of beautifully caparisoned horses and carts. There are *verbenas,* night festivals on the eve of religious holidays, and there are *fallas,* which are celebrations of almost pagan revelry. *Ferias* are local fairs. We have listed the outstanding folkloric events in the *Practical Information* section of this chapter.

There are many extremely colorful folk dances in Spain, such as the *jota* of Aragon, the *fandango* of Andalusia, and the gay but subtle Catalan *sardana,* which last you will see danced in the streets of almost any Catalan town or village during its Fiesta Mayor. But the most famous of Spanish dances is the fiery, passionate Andalusian *flamenco,* strongly suggestive of Arab influence. When that rhythmic stamping and clapping starts and you hear the wail of the vocalist, you'll be close to the mystery of this Catholic-pagan country, so special and so different from any other.

Food and Drink

Olive oil is at the base of Spanish cooking and contrary to expectation, Spanish cooking is not generally fiery and peppery like the Mexican cuisine. Don't hesitate to order seafood anywhere, even inland at Madrid. A fast service brings the fresh catch daily to the market, and the crabs, shrimps, prawns, crayfish and other crustaceans are excellent.

Here are some special dishes to look for; *Gazpacho,* a cold soup of tomatoes, garlic, bread crumbs, cucumber and green pepper with croutons, which is delicious and refreshing at the end of a long hot day. *Paella* delights most visitors, and is now so widely known outside Spain as to be thought of as the country's national dish. Try *jamon serrano,* suncured mountain ham, dark red in color and served in thin, translucent slices. The Basques are great eaters, and some of their specialties are *Bacalao a la Vizcaina,* salt codfish cooked in a tomato sauce; *angulas,* tiny eels cooked whole in oive oil with garlic and red-hot peppers; *almejas marinera,* steamed clams with a sauce of garlic, chopped parsley and olive oil; *calamares,* squid or cuttlefish "in their ink" or cut up and fried crisp. In the Basque Country and Galicia, order *centollo,* a huge crab cooked in the shell with a spicy sauce. If all this sounds too exotic you can always have grilled meat by asking for *a la parrilla.*

Sherry is the most characteristic of Spanish drinks. There are the *finos,* pale, dry, and drunk widely as an aperitif; *amontillados,* medium dry, same purpose; *olorosos,* dark, sweet and heavy sherries, generally drunk as a dessert wine. *Manzanilla,* not technically a sherry, is popular in Spain; it has a higher alcoholic content than any sherry. The principal table wines are *Rioja* and *Valdepenas* named for the regions where they are produced. *Rioja* is something like a French Bordeaux, though nowhere near as delicate. Try the unbottled wine of the house *(vino de las casa):* it is usally good, and inexpensive. Spanish beer is also good.

Shopping in Spain

Some of the highlights of buying and bargaining in Spain are obvious, some not. Here are the items we recommend you look for: damascened Toledo ware (including daggers, swords and knives), ceramics (including blue and yellow Talavera pottery, green pottery from Puente del Arzobispo, and more), wrought ironwork, and leather goods of all kinds.

PRACTICAL INFORMATION FOR SPAIN

WHAT WILL IT COST. The Spanish State Tourist Department has fixed maximum and minimum hotel prices which are inclusive of service and taxes, but not meals. Within these limits, managements may charge what they think fit, but the charge must be posted up in the hotel bedroom.

In this chapter, hotels are listed L, 1, 2, 3, or 4, denoting deluxe, first-class superior, first-class reasonable, moderate or inexpensive. An (L) hotel may cost anything between 3,900 to 5,800 pesetas for a double room; category (1), 2,000 to 3,500 ptas.; (2), 1,000 to 1,600 ptas.; (3), 850 to 1,200 ptas., and (4), 500 to 1,000 ptas. Inexpensive hotels and pensions are authorized to charge an extra 20% if you don't take at least one meal.

Restaurants are listed L, E, M or I, for deluxe, expensive, moderate or inexpensive. Breakfast will cost 75 to 125 pesetas; lunch or dinner, 1,000 ptas. and more in an (L) restaurant; around 750 in (E) category; 575 in (M); about 350 in (I). Prices may be lower in provincial towns, other than top resorts, and all restaurants are compelled to offer a fixed-price table d'hôte meal (wines extra).

A typical day in Spain with first-class hotel accommodations, meals, transportation, theater or other entertainment, sightseeing, coffee, beer, a couple of taxi rides and other miscellaneous expenses should not exceed 3,500 ptas.

The Spanish State Tourist Department, Generalísimo 39, Madrid 16, has a string of hotels *(paradores)* and inns *(albergues)* where excellent accommodations and meals can be had at reasonable prices. Some are converted castles, and often they are the best accommodation in the area.

SEASONS. Tourist season is from April through October. Peak vacation months of July and August are apt to be too hot for comfort except at seaside resorts. Madrid should be visited in late spring or fall if possible. Seville is best in April and May.

CAPITAL. Madrid.

LANGUAGE. Spanish. Catalan, a mixture of Spanish and ancient French is spoken in Cataluña and the Balearics. Basque is spoken in the Basque Provinces, and Gallego in the northwestern province of Galicia.

CLIMATE. Hot and dry in summer; moderate in winter, except for bitter cold for some weeks on the central plateau.

Average maximum daily temperature in Fahrenheit and centigrade:

Madrid	Jan.	Feb.	Mar.	Apr.	May	June	July	Aug.	Sept.	Oct.	Nov.	Dec.
F°	48	52	59	64	70	81	88	86	77	66	55	48
C°	9	11	15	18	21	27	31	30	25	19	13	9
Málaga												
F°	63	63	64	70	73	81	84	86	81	73	68	63
C°	17	17	18	21	23	27	29	30	27	23	20	17

SPECIAL EVENTS. *January,* commemoration of Granada's liberation from the Moors in 1492 (2nd); parades on the 5th and 6th. *March,* the Fallas of San José in Valencia (19th); Holy Week processions at Seville, Málaga, Valladolid, Murcia, Granada and Lorca; Seville Fair with important bullfights. *April,* Feria of Jerez de la Frontera (through May); Burial of the Sardine, Murcia; Romeria (religious pilgrimage) of the Virgin del Rocio, Almonte, in Huelva, Whitsun; Corpus Christi processions at Seville, Toledo, Granada, and at Sitges where the streets are carpeted with flowers; bullfights and fireworks at the Seville Fair. *May,* Feast of St. Isidro, with top bullfighting in Madrid from the 20th; Fair of Ronda; National Festival of Spanish Dances, Granada (through June). *June,* Granada International Music Festival, in the 14th-century Moorish Alhambra (through July). *July,* fiesta of San Fermin in Pamplona with the running of the bulls. *August,* Bilbao fair; Assumption Mystery Play at Elche, near Alicante (14th and 15th); music festival, Santander; Málaga Festival (9th to 19th); Festival of Honor of St. Lawrence in the Escorial, Madrid (10th); La Semana Grande, Festival of the Assumption (15th) at San Sebastián Fiesta of St. Michael, Seville. *September,* fiesta of the Virgin de las Angustias, Granada; Vintage Festival, Jerez de la Frontera; film festival, San Sebastián. *October,* festival of the Virgin de El Pilar at Zaragoza. *December,* Christmas is celebrated throughout the country from the 24th to January 6. Gifts are given on the 6th.

Best check on the spot regarding all these events as dates are liable to change from year to year.

NATIONAL HOLIDAYS. Jan. 1; Jan. 6, Epiphany; March 19, St. Joseph's Day; Maundy Thursday and Good Friday; May 1, Labor Day; Ascension Day; in June, Corpus Christi; June 29, Sts. Peter and Paul; July 25, St. James's Day

(Patron Saint of Spain); Aug. 15, Assumption Day; Oct. 12, Race Festivities; Nov. 1, All Saints Day; Dec. 8, Feast of Immaculate Conception; Dec. 25, Christmas Day.

CLOSING TIMES. Shops in Spain open at 9 A.M., close at 2 P.M., reopen at 5 P.M., and close again at 8. Many now close on Saturday afternoons; in summer the afternoon closing times tend to be even longer. Department stores in Madrid and Barcelona may stay open through lunchtime. Banks open from 9 A.M. to 2 P.M., Saturday until noon. Best check with your hotel, since opening and closing hours are liable to change periodically.

SPORTS. *Soccer:* Spanish clubs are among Europe's best. Tickets through hotel porter (season Sept. to May). Ditto for *pelota,* a fast and spectacular ball-game. *Golf:* Puerta de Hierro Club in Madrid and all larger cities as well as at Torremolinos Beach, near Málaga. The Sotogrande course at La Linea is excellent. *Horse racing:* Spring and fall seasons at Madrid's Zarzuela track while San Sebastián holds its meets in summer. *Winter Sports* in the Eastern Pyrenees can be reached from Barcelona. Centers: La Molina, Camprodón, Puigcerda and Nuria. The Guadarrama mountains and the Sierra Nevada (Granada) have long sunny days in winter; Navacerrada, in the Guadarramas, is about 1 hour by car from Madrid.

MONEY. Monetary unit is the peseta, which contains 100 centimos. Legal exchange rates inside Spain are about 82 pesetas to the dollar, 164 to the pound, which is the rate obtained when cashing travelers' checks at any branch of the Bank of Spain (Banco de España). Private banks deduct a small commission.

TIPPING. In addition to the 15 percent service charge on hotel bills, give the hall porter and chambermaid 50 pesetas or more per week. Give about 10 ptas. a bag to whoever carries your luggage up. Same to bellboys for services rendered. Tip nightclub and restaurant waiters 5% in addition to the service charge on the bill. Twenty-five pesetas to the barber, 75 to beautician, 5 to theater or movie usher, 15 for hatcheck girls and washroom attendant, 10% to taxi drivers, 10 ptas. per bag to the railway porter, 25 to the doorman who gets you a cab, 25 to 50 ptas. to hall porter when you check out, depending on the service you've had.

HOW TO REACH SPAIN. By Air. From New York direct to Madrid, Barcelona, Málaga via *Iberia, TWA;* from London by *British Airways,* main European capitals via *Iberia.* **By Train.** Puerta del Sol from Paris to Madrid via Bordeaux and San Sebastián, the TEE Geneva to Barcelona (both requiring reservation and supplementary fare), or the Sud Express from Paris to Madrid.

CUSTOMS. You can bring in anything intended for personal use duty free, but be reasonable about it. Only 200 cigarettes duty free. You may bring in a maximum of 50,000 pesetas, but you may take out only 3,000 pesetas. Luggage is rarely checked.

MAIL. Current rates for airmail letters up to 5 grams, to the U.S.: 19 ptas.; to the U.K. and rest of Europe: 12 ptas. Postcards are 9.50 ptas.

ELECTRICITY. Mostly 110 volts AC, 50 cycles; newer buildings may have 220-volt supply.

TRAVEL IN SPAIN. By Air. All large cities and the Balearic and Canary islands are linked by an internal air net of the two national airlines: *Iberia,* Plaza Cánovas 4, and *Aviaco,* Alcalá 42, Madrid. **By Bus:** Long distance luxury buses cover all tourist itineraries. **Rail travel** is quite cheap, but it is advisable to travel first-class or on TAF Diesel trains serving all main lines. The Talgo train runs between Madrid and San Sebastian (French frontier), Madrid to Barcelona, Valencia, Seville. The Costa del Sol Express from Madrid has airconditioned sleeping cars and a special automobile platform (also on the Madrid-Vigo and Madrid-La Coruña lines). The Costa Brava Express (Madrid-Port Bou) saves the change at Barcelona. Also TAF train between Madrid and Gijón.

MOTORING. An expansive road-building program is in progress, and this means some of the main roads are blocked at spots that are impossible to predict at this writing. Always inquire as to what's ahead of you when driving. Gasoline (petrol) costs 31 ptas. per liter, normal (one US gallon equals 3¾ liters; one Imperial gallon equals 4½ liters), but we strongly advise you to use premium grade (super), which is 37 ptas. (may soon rise). If you use the ordinary gas in Spain, you'll think your car is going to fall apart.

Documents required: car registration papers, international driver's license and green international insurance card.

CAR HIRE. Rentals in Spain are among the cheapest in Europe. Prices run about 750 ptas. per day plus 8 ptas. per kilometer for a SEAT 127. There is no collection charge if the hire ends either at the place of acceptance or at any of ATESA's offices in Spain (main: Capitán Haya 7, Madrid and 46 Lauria, Barcelona. Branches all over the country).

Avis, José Antonio 60, Madrid, has offices around the country. *Hertz,* at No. 80, same street, is also well represented in the country.

TOURS (long-distance and local). Up-to-date package arrangements by reliable Spanish operators: *Atesa, Viajes Melia, Marsans* or *Conde. Renfe,* the national rail service, has several all-inclusive trips (National Ferrotours) with daily departure. The cost includes rail travel, hotels (full board and tips) and excursions.

Madrid, Capital and Tourist Mecca

Madrid, capital of Spain, is one of the boom towns of Europe. On the direct firing line during the Spanish Civil War, it was badly damaged, and entire districts were destroyed. Reconstruction was undertaken and now skyscrapers, ministries, plush hotels, restaurants and cinemas are seen everywhere; the population doubled in 20 years to over three million. Today it is a modern, 20th-century city built up around a 17th-century core.

The real life of Madrid can best be savored from the terrace of one of those numerous cafés on the Castellana where, in the dappled shade of aromatic acacia trees, you can watch the Madrileños pass—vivacious, handsome men and women, well-dressed, friendly and proud.

Aside from a view of the people's everyday life, the foremost tourist attraction of Madrid is the Prado Museum. Situated in a rose-colored palace, a stone's throw from the Ritz and Palace hotels, this is one of the world's greatest art museums. Even if your stay in Madrid is a short one, you should devote at least a morning or an afternoon to the incomparable El Grecos, Velázquez', Murillos and Goyas in this collection.

And don't forget that, thanks to the extraordinary taste and acquisitiveness of Charles V, Philip II, and Philip IV, the Prado is also rich in the works of Italian and Flemish masters—Titian, Raphael, Botticelli, Fra Angelico, Veronese, Tintoretto, Rubens, Van Dyck and Breughel, and a fine collection of Bosch paintings. After the dazzling and staggering experience of the Prado, we recommend a rest cure in nearby Park of El Retiro where you can sit in a shady corner or stroll at your leisure, perhaps from the rose garden along the tree-lined avenues to the lake.

You should not miss the Goya Pantheon in the Hermitage of San Antonio de la Florida. Here lies the great artist, headless, his head having inexplicably disappeared between his burial in Bordeaux in 1828 and the exhumation of his body for transfer to Spain in 1888. At all events, the irrepressible Goya is immortalized here in his frescos, depicting some of the more respectable court officials hobnobbing with some of the less respectable ladies of his considerably varied acquaintance. There are more works of Goya, more El Greco, Zurbarán and Velázquez at the Lazaro Galdeano Foundation, which has the best collection in Europe of ivory and enamel; and you will also enjoy the tapestries, paintings and lovely old porcelain in the Cerralbo Museum.

To recuperate from *this* bout of museum crawling, take an *aperitivo* at one of the softly-lighted pavement cafés in the Castellana, then an early Madrid dinner about 9:30 P.M., finishing just in time for the "evening" performance of a *flamenco* show at the theater, which begins at 10:30 P.M. and lasts until about 1 A.M. If these hours seem too outlandish, we remind you that there's an "afternoon" at 7 P.M.! Early or late, you should take in one of these exciting gypsy flamenco shows, which will bring you closer to the violent heart of Spain than anything else except a bullfight.

The Royal Palace—variously known as the National Palace and the Palace of the Oriente—is worth an entire morning. One immense side of the building looks from the crest of a hill to the snow-capped Guadarrama Mountains, 40 miles away. The 30 main salons face east across an open square to the Royal Theater and a formal 18th-century garden. In the center of the square is a striking equestrian statue of Philip IV, from a design by Velázquez. The palace was spared by mutual agreement of both sides during the civil war. Inside the palace you will see Tiepolo frescos, porcelain clocks, about 800 tapestries, portraits by Goya, Mengs and Ribera, and roughly five miles of the most beautiful carpets you have ever seen. Also impressive are the palace's royal chapel, the armory with a fine collection of weapons and armor from the 15th through the 18th centuries, and the royal pharmacy.

In addition to the Castellana, the Avenida de José Antonio and the Puerta del Sol, Madrid's Times Square or Piccadilly Circus, you will want to see a little bit of "old" Madrid. Cross the Puerta del Sol and turn sharp left to the Palacio de Santa Cruz, now the Ministry of Foreign Affairs, but once the headquarters of the dreaded Spanish Inquisition. From this point, you can trace the steps of its victims to the Plaza Mayor where they underwent the terrible ordeal of the *auto de fé*. Built in 1619, this beautiful, partially-arcaded square is the point at which old Madrid begins. On the corner farthest from the Ministry of Foreign Affairs, you will find a steep flight of stone steps cut into a section of the city's medieval walls. As you descend these stairs you will pass three notable eating places, El Pulpito (at the top), Botín, 50 yards from the foot, and Las Cuevas de Luis Candelas, at the bottom (see *Restaurant* listings). Beyond, and to the right, begins as quaint a cobbled rabbit warren as you will find in any European town. Always colorful, invariably fascinating, this is old Madrid. A city map is useless. Follow your fancy; eventually you'll find a cab to take you back to the unpicturesque comforts of the 20th century.

Here are two highly recommended visits, not usually on the conventional tourist list for Madrid. The first is a visit to the Royal Tapestry Factory where, for two centuries, some of the world's most beautiful tapestries and carpets have been made. The second visit is to the Archeological Museum, Calle Serrano 13, which features a magnificent all-round collection including Iberian vases and many porcelains. There is a huge assortment of Roman artifacts, medieval art and objects, Moorish rooms, Egyptian mummies, navigational instruments, jewelry, etc. Entrance fee includes the right to visit the excellent reproduction of the prehistoric Altamira Caves. The museum now houses the exquisite Iberian-carved bust *The Lady of Elche,* formerly in the Prado.

Excursions from Madrid

Nine miles from Madrid is El Pardo Palace, a former royal shooting box.

Thirty-one miles from Madrid, at the foot of the Guadarrama Mountains, is San Lorenzo de el Escorial, burial place of Spanish kings and queens. The monastery, built by that religious fanatic, Philip II, as a memorial to his father, Charles V, is a vast rectangular edifice, conceived and executed with a monotonous magnificence worthy of the Spanish royal necropolis. The church, in the shape of a Greek cross, contains a famous cross by Benvenuto Cellini, and paintings by Velázquez, Ribera and El Greco. The spartan private apartment of Philip II and the bare cell in which he chose to die are in striking contrast to the fabulously beautiful carpets, porcelain and tapestries with which his less austere successors decorated the rest of this immense monastery-palace.

It is possible to include in your trip to El Escorial a visit to the monumental Valle de los Caidos—Valley of the Fallen—a memorial to the million men who died on both sides in Spain's civil war. A crypt, cut through 853 feet of rock, is surmounted by a 492-foot cross of reinforced concrete faced with stone. An elevator will take you to the top of this sad and impressive monument, which is also now the last resting place of Franco.

Twenty-one miles from Madrid is Alcalá de Henares, birthplace of Catherine of Aragon, Cervantes and other famous Spaniards. You can visit the old university, the house where the author of *Don Quixote* was born, and the Church of Santa Maria la Mayor in which he was baptized. Try lunch at 16th-century Hosteria del Estudiante.

Thirty miles from Madrid, on a good road, is a lavishly-furnished copy of the Trianon at Versailles. The gardens, with their cascade falling into the Tagus River, are delightful, the last word in formal landscape designing. Visit Charles IV's Casa del Labrador (farm house), whose elegance may be suggested by the fact that its lavatory walls are done in platinum and gold. Have lunch at one of the outdoor restaurants that border the river.

PRACTICAL INFORMATION FOR MADRID

HOTELS. Madrid offers a wide range of hotels, all the way from the millionaire *Villa Magna* to modest little pensions where you can live, and eat remarkably well, for 600 pesetas a day.

Deluxe

VILLA MAGNA, Castellana 22, is now the best and most elegant; 200 sound-proofed rooms, impeccable service, superb food, faultless amenities.

PLAZA, Plaza de España, has pool. On its 25th floor is a roof garden restaurant with outstanding view. Mostly tours, so-so facilities, going downhill.

RITZ, Plaza de la Lealdad 5, is conservative, aristocratic, and very quiet, with beautiful rooms and fine suites. It is the choice of foreign diplomats and wealthy Spanish families.

LUZ PALACIO, Castellana 67, has tasteful décor, restaurants, cocktail lounge.

MINDANAO, San Francisco de Sales, every modern amenity. Its restaurant *El Candelabro* offers original Spanish dishes and French cuisine.

MELIÁ, Calle Princesa, conveniently near Plaza de España, has 250 rooms, numerous restaurants; very comfortable.

EUROBUILDING. Located in the Generalísimo area, Juan Ramón Jimenez 8, it has pool, restaurants, bar, lounge, boutiques. A favorite with Americans, show-biz clients, and businessmen.

MIGUEL ANGEL, on pleasant part of the Castellana; over 300 rooms, all amenities. With *Zacarias* restaurant-disco.

IFA, Avda. del Valle 13. Has 126 rooms and all amenities, plus pleasant garden and pool. On outskirts.

MONTE REAL, in the posh Puerta de Hierro section out of town, is elegant. Quiet and dignified, it has 79 rooms.

PALACE, Plaza de las Cortes, a busy, bustling place. Popular bar and restaurant. Good and central. Oldish.

BARAJAS. A mile away from the airport, with 250 rooms, pool, nightclub, etc.

WELLINGTON, Velázquez 8; competes with the Ritz for the leading role among hotels attracting a solid conservative clientele.

PRINCESA-PLAZA, Princesa 40; 406 rooms, all amenities, recent, well-located, pleasant.

First-Class Superior

EL WASHINGTON, Avda. José Antonio 72, near shopping area. Rooms with bath or shower, air-conditioned. Roof garden and solarium.

GRAN HOTEL COLON, Avda. Dr. Esquerdo 115. 400 rooms with bath; pool, garage. Modern and functional. A bit far removed.

VELÁZQUEZ, Velázquez 62, is smaller, quieter, and more select than the giants, but no less comfortable and spacious.

SANVY, Calle Goya 3, quiet, has roof garden restaurant and pool. Air-conditioned.

AITANA, Generalisimo, 42. 111 rooms, air-conditioning, cafeteria, functional.

RICHMOND, Plaza de la República Argentina 8, apartment hotel, with a garden restaurant, and popular in its own right.

MELIÁ CASTILLA. Over 2,000 beds, 15 floors, two restaurants, parking. Located on Calle Capitán Haya, near the Plaza de Castilla.

Others are: *El Coloso,* Leganitos 13, modern, near Plaza de España; *Gran Versalles,* Covarrubias 4, in pleasant central area; *Alcalá,* Calle Alcalá 66, modern, comfortable, near Retiro Park; *Bréton,* Bretón de los Herreros 29, small and pleasant; *Liabeny,* Salud 3, central; *Pintor,* Goya 79, quiet, elegant, in center of shopping area. *Sideral,* Casado del Alisal 14, *Suecia,* Marqués de Casa Riera 4, and *Don Quixote,* Federico Rubio y Gali 145, are all excellent. *Castellana,* formerly a Hilton, now mostly for tours. Has been downgraded to four stars.

The *Ecuestre,* Zurbano 79 is small and select as is the *Calatrava,* Tutor 1, near the Plaza de España. *Menfis,* José Antonio 74. *Mayorazgo,* Leganitos 16, central, clean and comfortable.

Los Galgos, Diego de Léon, off Serrano, rooms only, good location near American Embassy, most rooms with balconies.

First-Class Reasonable

Tried and approved by various Fodor editors or contributors include the *Capitol* and *Gran Via,* both on Avda. José Antonio.

Those who like quiet are apt to plump for the *Montesol,* Montera 25-27. The *Balboa,* Nuñez de Balboa 112, is mainly patronized by Americans. The *Príncipe Pio,* Paseo de Onésimo Redondo 16, and *Sace,* Gen. Sanjurjo 8, are pleasant, quiet, and recent.

Carlos V, Maestro Victoria 5, has a reputation for good and willing service.

Elegant and quiet is the *Zurbano,* Zurbano 81, situated in the most aristocratic district of the capital, just off Avda. Castellana.

Other good choices are the *Claridge,* Plaza del Conde de Casal 6; *Conde Duque,* Plaza Conde Valle de Suchil 5; *Tirol,* Marqués de Urquijo 4.

MODERATE hotels can be quite good in Madrid. Among the better ones are: *Alexandra,* San Bernardo 29, small, modern, in heart of town; *Internacional,* Arenal 19, ancient, in oldest part of city; *Londres,* Galdós 2; *Paris,* Alcalá 2, overlooking Puerta del Sol.

Several readers have warmly recommended the *Hotel Roma,* Travesia de Trujillos 10. *Francisco I,* Arenal 15, is modern, clean, in the heart of Old Madrid, excellent value, restaurant.

PENSIONS. Although there are plenty of inexpensive hotels, you will probably be more comfortable at a deluxe (price level of moderate hotel) or first-class pension. Among the deluxe are: *Hostal Alcazar Regis,* Avda. José Antonio 61 and *Pensión Mirentxu,* Zorrilla 7. First-class, *Alonso,* Espoz y Mina 17; *Don Juan,* Recoletos 18.

OUTSIDE MADRID

For motorists: *Motel los Olivos,* 12 km. (7½ miles) out of town on the road to Andalusia, and the *Motel Avión,* 14 km. (8¾ miles) out of town, with bar, restaurant, pool etc. on road to Barcelona.

ARANJUEZ, about 29 miles south of Madrid. Best is *Las Mercedes* (2), 37 rooms, on highway km. 46. *Delicias,* good pension. *Pastor* (4), simple, homey, but excellent.

EL ESCORIAL. *Victoria Palace* (1), with pool, very pleasant, recommended; *Miranda y Suizo* (3), is well spoken of.

RESTAURANTS. If Madrid is your first stop in Spain, you may feel ravenous before you see any signs of food on the way; normal meal hours in the capital are even later than in the rest of Spain, where they are already later than anywhere else in Europe. No one thinks of eating lunch in the capital before 2 P.M.; 3 P.M. is quite normal, 3:30 not at all unusual; and while most Spanish diners begin to eat at 10, 10:30 is about the earliest for *madrileños,* and 11 is normal. If you can't wait, go to any of the numerous cafeterias around town, where warm meals, sandwiches and "combination plates" are served at all hours.

If you want to be really economical, look for a *taberna*—a small café dispensing drinks in the front room, with a few tables tucked away in the back. At the bottom of the scale in price, but not in quality, many of them will give you a hearty meal for 180 pesetas, and there is no obligation to order a full-course dinner.

Many of the city's best known establishments close during the summer months, so check ahead.

SMART INTERNATIONAL RESTAURANT FAVORITES

At the top, for price certainly, is the exclusive *Jockey* (L), Amador de los Rios 6. Excellent French-international cooking. Closed August.

Second in line is *Horcher* (L), Alfonso XII 6. Limited seating, so reserve ahead of time.

The *Club Mayte* (L), Plaza de la Republica Argentina 8, has a cozy dining room and cocktail lounge.

Across the square is the *Commodore* (L), pleasant outdoor dining area.

Tres Encinas (E), Preciados 33, one of the best for seafood.

Alcalde (E), Jorge Juan 10, mansized portions in a cave setting.

El Bodegón (L), new location at Pinar 15, but equally good food, pleasant décor.

Zalacain (L), Alvarez de Baena, 6, exclusive, one of the city's best.

Bajamar (L), José Antonio 78, is unbeatable for seafood, top service.

Las Lanzas (L), Espalter 8 and 9; and *El Senado* (E), Torija 7, are recommended by Spanish and foreign gourments alike.

Bellman (L), in the Casa Suecia, Los Madrazo 19. Swedish and French specialties. Smorgasbord.

Korynto (E), Preciados 36, another top seafood spot, popular with politicians and executives.

Clara's (L), Arrieta 2, run by former manager of Maxim's in Paris and Madrid's Villa Magna.

Nicolasa (E), Velázquez 150, a branch of the famous one in San Sebastián.

Delightful garden dining at *Los Porches,* Pintor Rosales 1, adjoining the Parque del Oeste.

Club 31 (E), Alcalá 58, is under the same ownership as *Jockey.*

GOOD, MODERATE TO INEXPENSIVE

Chalet Suizo (M), Fernandez de la Hoz 80. Cozy setting, good food and service. Try their *fondue.*

La Bola (I), an old stand-by at Calle Bola 5 (near Teatro Real), plenty of charm and good, simple food.

Casa Paco (M), Puerta Cerrada 11, famous over 70 years for its huge steaks.

La Barraca (M), Reina 29. Meals from noon to midnight. English menu. Best *paella* in town.

Pagasarri (I), Calle del Barco 7, is an old-time favorite.

Spanish food and good service at the *Sixto,* Ortega y Gasset, 83, with pleasant sidewalk dining in the summer.

ATMOSPHERIC

Botín (M), Cuchilleros 17, is considered more or less of a must for tourists. Located in the picturesque quarter back of the Plaza Mayor, in a 17th-cent. building. Essential to reserve.

Tranquilino (E), Calle Jardines, excellent steaks. Another *Tranquilino* at Puerta de Hierro, outdoor dining.

Las Cuevas de Luis Candelas (M), Cuchilleros 1, is built inside a part of the old walls of Madrid, off the Plaza Mayor. Good roast lamb and suckling pig.

Also one of the best, at the top of the same flight of stairs is *El Púlpito* (M), Plaza Mayor 9, for seafood, steaks and roasts.

Mesón de San Isidro (M), Costanilla de San Andrés 16. Good food in Toledo setting, in old Madrid.

Valentín (M), San Alberto 3. Longtime favorite of business and art crowds, with bullfight devotees thrown in. Good, solid, Spanish food without frills. 4 branches around town.

Corral de la Moreria (M), Moreria 17, end of viaduct. Authentic flamenco music and dancing. Dinner from 10 to early hours.

Julián Rojo (I), Ventura de la Vega 5. Bullfight atmosphere. Lunch 1:30–5, dinner from 7:30. Simple Spanish fare.

La Gran Tasca (M), Garcia Morato 22, topnotch Spanish dishes in rustic setting. Good service, intimate.

FOREIGN COOKING

House of Ming (E), Castellana 74, for Chinese delicacies.

For Italian cuisine, *Alduccio* (E), Concha Espina 8, opposite the Bernabeu Stadium, is best.

Popular, recent, is the cozy *La Trattoria* (M), Plaza del Alamillo 8, in old Madrid.

Edelweiss (I), Jovellanos 7, serves magnificent German food, but is apt to be crowded.

About the best (M), Chinese restaurant is the *Pagoda,* Leganitos 22, and nearby *Shangri-La.* In Generalisimo area try the *Yangt-Ze,* Felix Boix 5. For Japanese food there is the *Mikado* (E), Huesca 71. Cozy, friendly and intimate, serving excellent Russian food, is *El Cosaco* (E), Alfonso VI 4, in old Madrid, though portions tend to be skimpy.

Specializing in French steaks and filet mignon is the *Bistroquet* (M), Conde 4, in old Madrid, small and intimate.

Indian food at *Vihara* (M), Plaza de S. Barbara 8.

The new deluxe *La Troïka,* General Sanjurjo corner Santísima Trinidad. Russian cooking, violins, caviar, free parking. Closed Sun.

AMERICAN STYLE CUISINE

Foster's Hollywood, Magallanes 1 and Apolonio Morales 3, best hamburgers in town, in comfy lounge setting. Faulty service, but okay food. Popular with foreigners and young set. Also well-known to Americans is *Kentucky Fried Chicken,* Juan Hurtado de Mendoza, 13, with take-out service.

Self service cafeterias are mushrooming up all over Madrid; best are: *Topics* at Princesa 5, Puerta del Sol 14, Orense 8, Fuencarral 126, plus 5 more, and *Sau-Sau* at Avda. del Brasil

Another chain of pleasant cafeterias, also open on Sun. and holidays, featuring newspaper stands and gift shops is called: *VIPS.*

The so-called *Drugstores* at Fuencarral 99 and Velázquez 24, are open now till 5 a.m., popular with teen-agers and late night revellers. *Burger King* duplicates its questionable food here too, at Princesa 3, Orense 4, Conde de Peñalver 96 and Arenal 4.

OUTSIDE MADRID.

On the La Coruña highway leading out of town are several pleasant outdoor restaurants including the *Parque Moroso* (E), 12 km.; *Rancho Criollo* (E), with dancing; *La Pérgola* (M), 9 km. and *El Churrasco* (M), the latter specializing in steaks and chops.

ALCALA DE HENARES. *Hostería del Estudiante* (M), Colegios 3 y 5, a government-operated establishment in a classic Castilian inn, specializing in basic regional cooking.

ARANJUEZ. Best is *El Castillo* (E), magnificently set in the royal gardens. *La Rana Verde* (M), on Puente Colgante.

EL ESCORIAL. Several restaurants in the Plaza Generalísimo: *Mont Blanc* (M), outdoor dining area. Also good is *La Cueva* (M), San Anton 4, small rustic dining rooms on several floors, plenty of atmosphere.

EL PARDO. In the village, many local restaurants specialize in rabbit and trout; most atmospheric is the *Mesón del Pardo,* Calle Eugenio Pérez.

NIGHTCLUBS. Over the past two years, the nightclub scene, just like cinema, theater and magazines have taken a wild swing towards liberalization. Not only is on-stage nudity allowed, but it is often flaunted and just about anything seems to go. Permissiveness is the by-word of the post-Franco era, and there's now little to differentiate Spanish clubs and shows from those in France or Germany.

For what is called a "music hall", which means dancing and a show, the tops are *Xairo,* Paz, 11, open till 4 A.M., *Top Less,* Padre Xifré, 3, plus other established nightclubs such as *Florida Park,* in the Retiro, with restaurant, local comedians and talent; *Biombo Chino,* Isabel la Católica, 6, with three shows every night; *Lido,* Alcalá 20, with sex shows; *Micheleta,* Constanilla de los Angeles, 20, in similar vein and *York Club,* José Antonio 70, more for the hoi polloi.

Best discos are the *Cerebro,* Magallanes 1 and *Cerebro-Boite,* Princesa 5. Also popular is *Cleofas,* Goya, 7; *Bocaccio,* Marqués de la Ensenada, 16, *New Sunset,* Tutor, 1. Dozens of others, for gay, drag, etc. Buy *Guia del Ocio* (15 ptas.) for complete listings.

Many of these places follow the standard nightclub pattern visible all over the world—they are noisy, smoky and glittery. The usual formula is an entrance fee,

300 to 500 ptas., which covers your first drink, and for this (and a tip to the waiter), you can theoretically stay put until they turn the lights out.

Good flamenco shows at *Torres Bermejas,* Mesonero Romanos 15. *Arco de Cuchilleros,* Cuchilleros 7, will show you the purest flamenco and has a continuous show from 10.30 to 3 A.M., but serves drinks only. Also topnotch is the *Corral de la Morería* (M), Calle Morería, and the *Café de Chinitas* (L), Torija 7.

CAFÉS. You can trust any of the cafés along the boulevards, but there are some worth special attention. The most popular, bona-fide café in town is the *Gijón,* Paseo de Calvo Sotelo 21, a popular hang-out for show people, artists, writers, etc. Somewhat similar is the *Comercial,* Glorieta de Bilbao.

SPORTS. Bullfighting (if it is a sport) comes first to mind in Spain. Madrid has two main rings. If you have a choice during your stay, don't miss the big Plaza de Toros, which seats 25,000, and is something to see when it's packed to overflowing with an enthusiastic crowd. The season is April–October, and there is almost always a fight on Sunday, and often on Thursday as well. Starting time may vary from 4:30 P.M. until 6. Bullfights and Mass are the only things in Spain that start on time. Tickets: Calle Victoria 9, the day before fight.

Pelota is definitely something you shouldn't miss. Played at night, on brightly illuminated cement courts, enclosed on three sides, with the spectators protected by netting, on the other, it is the hardest, fastest ball game in the world. It is also a betting game, in which you get fast action for your money. If you want to try your luck, put 50 or 100 pesetas on Red or Blue and trust to luck. The most popular *frontón* (pelota court) is the *Frontón Madrid* at Dr. Cortezo 10. Pelota matches are usually played twice a day, from about 5 P.M. to 8 P.M., and again from 11 P.M. to 1 A.M.

Soccer fans should not miss one of *Real Madrid's* games (September–May).

Tennis at *Club Puerta de Hierro* (with adjoining golf links), *Club Alameda, Club de Campo.*

Swimming during hot weather can be enjoyed at various hotel pools such as the *Plaza, Velázquez, Sanvy, etc.* Clean public pools are *El Lago,* Carretera del Pardo 37, and *Castilla,* Avenida Habana 187.

Bowling at the *Bolera Stadium,* Alcalá 106; but better is the mini-bowling at Princesa 5. *Greyhound racing* at the Canódromo, near Vista Alegre bullring, Friday, Saturday, Sunday, at 5:30 P.M. *Horse racing* at the *Zarzuela Race Track* (bus from Calle Princesa and Hilarion Eslava), on Sundays, except in summer when all races are held in San Sebastián. *Car racing* at the Jarama Track on the road to Burgos. *Ice skating* at the Ciudad Deportiva (on Generalísimo, past the Plaza de Castilla).

AMUSEMENT PARK, in the Casa de Campo Park (bus from Plaza de Isabel II). Admission 20 ptas. Well kept, clean, with many wonderful rides for adults and children and with a restaurant and snack bars. One way of getting to the Amusement Park is to take the cablecar that runs from the Paseo de Rosales to the Casa de Campo Park. You will still have a good distance to walk, though, from the cablecar station to the funfair, or you can take a bus linking the two. Nearby is the Madrid zoo, pleasantly cared for with most animals outdoors, and including a children's zoo and a good inexpensive outdoor restaurant, camel rides, etc.

TRANSPORTATION. Madrid is well supplied with taxis. The minimum fare is 25 ptas. and every 225 meters (about 700 feet) it rings up another peseta. Subway (Metro) tickets cost 8 ptas. (11 on Suns.), and buses 12 ptas. The more comfortable micro-buses cost 19 ptas.

Taxis to Barajas Airport charge a 75-peseta supplement. The driver can also charge 10 ptas. per suitcase, 8 ptas. more on Sunday, and 10 ptas. after midnight. However, if going to the airport, you can use one of the buses which leave from the Plaza Colón underground station. Fare 35 ptas.

 SHOPPING. Less expensive than other capitals and full of odds and ends you'd never find anywhere else in this world. Madrid is one of Europe's most exciting shopping cities. For the odds and ends go to the Rastro, Madrid's flea market, where a crowd of golden-toothed vendors will offer you anything from bullfighting outfits to medieval medical instruments. Much of it is good; there are some wonderful handmade antiques, old jewelry and Spanish knick-knacks.

The Official Handicraft Exhibition *Artespaña,* José Antonio 32, Hermosilla 14, and Don Ramón de la Cruz 33, has a permanent and representative display of Spanish handicrafts.

DEPARTMENT STORES. There are two department store chains in Madrid: *Galerías Preciados* at Goya, corner Hermanos Miralles, Plaza Callao and Calle Arapiles, and *El Corte Inglés* at Goya corner Narvaez, Puerta del Sol, Generalísimo and Princesa areas. They all have interpreters, are open until 8:30 P.M. and have cafeteria and snack bar service.

Sear's, located on Serrano, corner of Ortega y Gasset. This American-owned store features a wide variety of Spanish goods. Prices are a bit higher, but the store is less crowded than other department stores.

Woolworth, on Juan Hurtado de Mendoza, is fancier than its American counterparts and more expensive.

Celso García is a much more sophisticated department store. On Serrano near *Sear's.* Better quality and higher prices.

LEATHER, a great Spanish specialty since the Spaniards first learned leatherwork from the Arabs. *Loewe,* at Avda. José Antonio 8 and Serrano 26, has everything made of leather including magnificent lightweight luggage for air travel, handbags that are out of this world. *Nestares,* José Antonio 11. Down the street at No. 49, *Rustarazo* is a lot less expensive than the two just mentioned; look at the women's handbags here. *Elysardo,* Velázquez 49, wide variety of top leather designs and finest quality.

GLOVES. You can't go wrong on price or quality at *Guante Varade,* Avda. José Antonio 56, Serrano 54, or Montera 14; *Zurro,* Carmen 1; *Vargas,* Carretas 21, and Preciados 16; *Mario Herrero,* Calle Carretas 10, is good.

SHOES are one of the best buys in Spain. Prices have undoubtedly gone up; however the supple leather and beautifully hand crafting of Spanish shoes are still a bargain. A word of warning: half sizes and different widths are not available so if the shoe doesn't fit you comfortably, don't buy it! You'll find many shoe-shops along Goya, Serrano and Velázquez streets and on the Avda. José Antonio.

BEST GIFT AND SOUVENIR SHOPS. Three new mini-shopping centers, with lots of boutiques and stores in them are the *Unicentros.* They are located at Serrano, 88, another on Princesa, opposite the Plaza Princesa Hotel, and a third on the Calle Orense. *Rocamar,* José Antonio 15, tops in elegant souvenirs, handmade items, furniture, etc. *Kreisler,* Calle Serrano, American-run with wide range of tourist items of all descriptions. Downstairs a fine art gallery.

For a complete selection of elegant and flattering Spanish shawls see *Rafael García,* Bailen 7, and *Casa Jiménez,* Preciados 52. *Artesania Toledana,* Plaza

Canovas del Castillo; *El Washington*, José Antonio 72. Also try the department stores.

SPANISH POTTERY AND TILES are all over the place. Try *La Ceramica de Talavera*, Calle Lagasca 44, or *Antigua Casa Talavera*, Isabel la Catolica 2.

USEFUL ADDRESSES. *American Embassy*, Serrano 75. *British Embassy*, Fernando el Santo 16. *Thomas Cook & Son*, Calvo Sotelo 14 and Alcalá 23. *American Express*, Plaza de las Cortes. *Spanish Information Office*, Edificio de la Torre de Madrid; *British American Hospital*, University City.

Fascinating Toledo

Toledo, an hour and a half by bus southwest from Madrid, is like a living national monument, depicting all the elements of Spanish civilization in hand-carved, sun-mellowed stone. Set on a hill overlooking the Tagus River, this ancient city is a fascinating architectural blend of Christian and Moorish elements, especially rich in buildings of the late 15th and 16th centuries. The best time to visit Toledo is in the spring or fall, because in summer it is scorched by the sun and in winter it is swept by icy winds. But better to see this town and be uncomfortable than not to see it at all! The most important festivals take place during Easter Week and Corpus Christi with their stately religious processions; if you can schedule Toledo for either of those times, so much the better. Several travel agencies run daily tours to Toledo from Madrid by bus. Inquire of your hotel porter. *Do not go by train!*

There are three outstanding attractions. The house in which El Greco lived until his death in 1614 is the sort of place you would like to move into yourself. It couldn't be more charming, with its tiled kitchen and lovely garden which affords a panoramic view over the Tagus. The house contains many of El Greco's finest works. Of equal if not greater interest is the 13th-century cathedral, See of the Cardinal Primate of Spain. One of the most beautiful churches in the world, it is blazing with jeweled chalices, gorgeous ecclesiastical vestments, hundreds of historic tapestries, 750 stained-glass windows and pictures by Tintoretto, Titian, Murillo, El Greco, Velázquez and Goya. Finally, do not miss a visit to the Palace of the Duchess of Lerma, which gives a striking impression of actual living conditions in a 15th-century feudal mansion. It is now a museum open to the public. The beautiful Hospital de Santa Cruz, near the Alcazar, is also open as a museum.

The Synagogue del Transito reveals not only Christian and Moorish, but also Jewish, influences in its architecture and decoration. It is just one reason among others to spend the maximum time possible in this city with its Moorish houses, its exquisite iron work, and its tortuous network of cobbled alleys. Wear your most comfortable shoes. It is worth hiring a car for a drive around the city on the Carretera de Circunvalación, across the Tagus. This gives you views of Toledo's striking silhouette from all sides, especially impressive at dusk.

HOTELS. At the *Carlos V,* Plaza Magdalena 3, the accommodation is excellent but the food rather dull. The *Alfonso VI,* comfortable, with lots of atmosphere, is near the Alcazar. Both (2). *Los Cigarrales* (pension) is a delightful converted country house two miles outside town with outstanding views of Toledo and a garden. Also with fine view, the *Parador Conde de Orgaz* (1), on the river between two bridges.

Centrally located in town are *Maravilla,* and *3 Carabelas,* both very simple.

The *Residencia La Almazara* (2S) is in a converted monastery, Carretera Piedrabuena, just outside town, convenient for motorists. Excellent.

RESTAURANTS. Toledo has always had top eating places, and one of them rates with the best in Spain, the *Venta de Aires,* (L), Circo Romano 15, a little out of town. Its specialty is partridge, which is also a specialty of the city in general, and bears its name—*salmorejo de perdiz a la toledana.* You get not only good food, but a friendly homelike atmosphere. In the same class is *Hostal de Castilla,* Marqués de Mendigorria 4, beyond the ramparts.

You can eat outdoors at the *Jardin Maravilla* (M), Avda. Barber 8. Near El Greco's house try the *Placido,* Santo Tomé, 6. The *Mesón del Cazador* (I), atmospheric, is at 23 Circo Romano. The *Hostal del Cardenal* (M), managed by Botín of Madrid, has interesting food, pleasant service. The *Sinai,* Calle de los Reyes Catolicos 7, serves strictly kosher food.

SHOPPING. Toledo is renowned for its damascened steel and embossed leatherwork. Reliable is *Artesania Española,* Samuel Levi 4.

Castile and the Western Provinces

The provinces of Old Castile lie to the north and west of Madrid, and their three main centers, Ávila, Segovia and Burgos, can be reached easily from the capital, though Burgos is usually included as a stop en route from Madrid to France or vice versa. New Castile (which includes Madrid and Toledo), has Cuenca, Ciudad Real and Guadalajara as other interesting towns.

Ávila

Ávila, 4,000 feet above sea level, is the highest provincial capital in Spain. Alfonso VI rebuilt the town and walls in 1090, bringing it permanently under Christian control. It is these walls, the most complete military installations of the kind in Spain, that give Ávila its special medieval quality. Thick and solid, they entirely enclose the city and you should begin your visit to Ávila with a tour of these walls. The religious atmosphere of the city is as striking as the military. The personality of Saint Teresa, the Mystic to whom the city is dedicated, lives today as vividly as it did in the 16th century. Pilgrims to Ávila can visit the Convent of the Augustine Nuns where she was educated; the Encarnación, where she made her profession and became Prioress; the convent of St. Joseph, first establishment of the Carmelite reform; and finally the monument to Saint Teresa, which stands on the site of her birth. The Cathedral of Ávila, begun in the 12th and completed in the 15th century, is a fine example of Gothic Transition architecture. See the Church of San Pedro, a Romanesque gem with a beautiful rose window; it's in the center of the city. The Basilica of San Vicente, Romanesque and Gothic of the 12th to 14th centuries, stands outside the walls on the spot where the saint was martyred. More than a sightseeing experience, Ávila is a spiritual and historic adventure.

Segovia

Segovia is 60 miles from Madrid, over the 5,000-foot Navacerrada Pass of the Guadarrama Mountains, or more quickly through the Guadarrama Tunnel. It can also be reached in about an hour by car. The ATESA three day "Castles in Spain" tour from Madrid (highly recommended) includes the romantic Alcazar fortress palace of the great Queen Isabella in Segovia. Even more striking, however, is the undamaged Roman aqueduct, still in use, one of the best-preserved Roman remains in the world. The ancient, crooked streets of Segovia are picturesque beyond description. But the city's most subtle beauties are in its many Romanesque churches, untouched for six centuries. The finest examples are San Martin and San Millan, San Lorenzo and San Clemente. San Juan de los Caballeros is today a studio for ceramics, founded by the Spanish artist Zuloaga. Vera Cruz, just outside the town and affording a superb view of the Alcazar, is one of the most notable churches of the Knights Templar in Europe. It was consecrated in 1208. The 16th-century cathedral, one of the finest in Spain, rises in glory at the highest point in the town. It was the last Gothic building to be erected in Spain, and it's one of the newest buildings in Segovia!

Salamanca

Salamanca, 133 miles from Madrid, is an ancient and lovely city, and your first glimpse of it is bound to be unforgettable. Beside you flows the swift Tormes River and beyond it rise the old houses of the city, topped by the golden walls, turrets, domes and spires of the Plateresque cathedral. The name Plateresque comes from "plata" (silver) and implies that the soft stone is chiseled and engraved like that metal. Salamanca's cathedral and university buildings are among the finest examples of this style in existence. There are fine 15th- and 16th-century houses around the Plaza Mayor, and the famous House of Shells. If you plan to go for Salamanca's fiesta in September, book well ahead.

Valladolid

Valladolid is a province rich in castles and ancient buildings. The capital city (same name) is like an oasis in this arid landscape, thanks to its beautiful gardens, watered by the Pisuerga River. The *Ferias Mayores* or Great Fairs provide a gay time here in September. The Easter processions of the *Semana Santa* are unusually impressive. Tourists in Valladolid will want to see the house where Columbus died in 1506; the old home of Cervantes, now a museum; the Casa de los Viveros, where Ferdinand and Isabella were married in 1469; late Renaissance cathedral, where you should ask to see the magnificent monstrance by Juan de Arfe in the sacristy. What must not be missed in Valladolid is the National Museum of Sculpture, housed in the College of San Gregorio. It is the best in Spain. Here you will find that polychrome sculpture in wood to which Spanish artists brought a brilliant and original genius, a striking sense of realism and tragedy.

Burgos

One of those historic cities in Burgos, birthplace of El Cid, the national hero who embodies the Spanish idea of chivalry. You can visit El Solar del Cid, the house where he was born, and see his tomb in the transept of the cathedral. This Gothic cathedral, whose twin towers greet the visitor to Burgos from afar is of imposing grandeur and breathtaking richness. Don't miss the Condestable Chapel, the Escalera Dorada (Golden Stairway) and the superb ironwork. The 13th-century Gothic cloister contains many statues of interest; in fact, the whole cathedral is a treasure house of sculpture. The greatest treasures of all are locked up; engage a guide if you want to see them. Other highlights of Burgos are the churches of San Esteban, San Nicolas, and San Gil; the celebrated Casa del Cordon of the 15th century, where Columbus was received by Ferdinand and Isabella when he returned from his second voyage to America; the typical 16th-century manor houses, Casa de Miranda and Casa del Angulo; and the Monasteries of Las Huelgas and Cartuja.

Cuenca

Cuenca, 102 miles southeast of Madrid, is a charming city long neglected by tourists, but now coming into its own due largely to the breathtaking beauty of its "hanging houses", which are literally suspended over a precipice, and in one of which a modern art museum, one of the finest in Spain, has been opened. A stroll through the old part of the town, with its cathedral (famous for its grillework) is a perennial delight. Some 25 miles away is the unforgettable Ciudad Encantada, the so-called "city" being in reality vast prehistoric rock formations which have been eroded by millions of years of water and the elements into curious shapes.

León

León, almost 200 miles by road from Madrid, is the gateway to the northern and northwestern provinces of Asturias and Galicia. The León cathedral, with its magnificent stained-glass windows, is justly famous. Also noteworthy is the Collegiate Church of San Isidoro, begun in 1005.

Cáceres

In little-visited Extremadura province, the traveler comes to extraordinary feudal towns, rich in medieval palaces, fortified houses and twisted streets. This is the land of the *conquistadores,* and ample evidence of them remains in the escutcheoned palaces they built with profits from gold brought back from the New World. Cáceres, with its Plaza Mayor, its antique walls, clock tower of Bujaco and statue of Ceres, is among the most imposing towns of Extremadura. The church of San Mateo was originally a mosque, and Santa María La Mayor retains its Romanesque doorway. In the old part of the town is the famous Casa de Los Golfines, a fortified palace. Thirty miles east of Cáceres is the town of Trujillo, where Pizarro, conqueror of Peru, was born. His house still stands in the Plaza Mayor.

Mérida

Mérida is particularly famous for Roman ruins, which include a superb theater where classic dramas are still performed at night. Two aqueducts, Trajan's Arch, a Circus and an excellent Museum of Archeology are among the highlights of Mérida. A few miles away, at Medellín, Hernán Cortés was born in 1485.

Badajoz

Badajoz, a border town between Spain and Portugal, southwest of Madrid, is situated on the left bank of the Guadiana River and is one of the oldest towns in the peninsula. In appearance it resembles a huge fortress. The most important sight is the Alcazaba, or Moorish part of the town. There are also the cathedral, the Vauban fortifications, and an interesting bridge across the Guadiana.

PRACTICAL INFORMATION FOR CASTILE AND WESTERN PROVINCES

HOTELS. There are a number of government-operated establishments in this area, and they are always a good bet, often the best available. The **Paradores** are at: *Oropesa,* west of Talavera de la Reina, and *Ciudad Rodrigo,* both in old castles and on route to Portugal; *Gredos,* in the mountains, 35 miles southwest of Ávila; *Santillana del Mar,* near Santander; *Tordesillas,* 20 miles southwest of Valladolid; *Villafranca del Bierzo* and *Ribadeo,* on different roads to the Galician coast; *Alarcon; Ávila; Mérida; Soria; Zamora.*

The best **Albergues** are at: *Aranda de Duero,* a very necessary oasis on the road from Burgos to Madrid, otherwise poorly provided with hospitality, 50 miles south of Burgos, 100 miles north of Madrid. *Manzanares,* east of Ciudad Real, on the main road south from Madrid, 108 miles from the capital, 141 from Cordoba. *Villacastin,* roughly halfway between Avila and Segovia.

ALMURADIEL. On the Madrid-Cádiz road, just before Despeñaperros Pass, is the elegant, comfortable *Hostal Los Podencos* (2).

ARANDA DE DUERO, on the Madrid-Burgos route. *Hosteria Castilla* (1); *Los Bronces* and *Montehermoso,* both (2) at Kms. 161 and 163 of the Madrid-Irún road. *Tres Condes* (2), new.

AVILA. Recent, the *Palacio Valderrabanos* (1) is highly recommended, opposite the cathedral. *Cuatro Postes* (3) has splendid view. *Reina Isabel* (4), modern and comfortable.

BADAJOZ. *Gran Hotel Zurbaran* (1), garden, pool, air-conditioned. *Residencia Rio* (2). *Conde Duque* (3).

BURGOS. *Landa Palace* (L), south of town. *Almirante Bonifaz,* rather old-fashioned, and *Condestable,* both (1). A few miles on the road to Irún: *Santiago Apostol Hotel,* bar, restaurant; *Hostal el Cid,* also out of town; both (2).

CÁCERES. *Extremadura* and *Alcantara,* both (2).

CUENCA. *Torremangana* (1). *Alfonso VIII* (2). *Hostal Xucar* (3).

LEÓN. *Hostal San Marcos* (L), a converted 16th-century monastery; nightclub, bar. *Conde Luna* (1). *Oliden* (3).

LOGROÑO. Best, recent, is *Carlton Rioja* (1). *Gran* (2). *Murrieta* (3), a nice choice. *Cortijo* (4).

MÉRIDA. The *Emperatriz* (2), a medieval palace converted to a comfortable hotel. *Texas* and *Las Lomas,* both (3).

NAVACERRADA, a winter sports resort at 3,900 ft. *Arcipreste de Hita* (2). *Las Postas,* pension just out of town, with magnificent mountain views, cozy décor.

SALAMANCA. Best are the *Gran, Monterrey* and *Regio,* all (1) and fairly large. Close runner-up is the *Alfonso X* (2). *Clavero,* though (2) is modern, clean and comfortable. The new *El Zaguan* (2)

SEGOVIA. *Acueducto,* with splendid view of the aqueduct; *Las Sirenas;* both (2). *Los Linajes,* Doctor Velasco, 9. Recently opened. (2)

SORIA. Recent are *Alfonso VIII* and *Caballero;* also *Méson Leonor;* all (2).

VALDEPEÑAS. *Meliá el Hidalgo* (2), on the Madrid-Granada road. *Vista Alegre* (3), is at km. 200 out of town.

VALLADOLID. Biggest and best is the *Olid Meliá* (1), with all amenities. *Conde Ansúrez* (1) is a fine hotel. *Felipe IV* is (1); *Inglaterra* (3).

RESTAURANTS. Here is a list of some of the better restaurants of Old and New Castile. Not included are the hotels listed above, whose restaurants are always a good bet.

ARANDA DE DUERO. The *Frontón,* Carretera Madrid-Burgos and *Guijarro,* Avda. José Antonio are good (I).

ÁVILA. *Piquío* (M), Estrada 6; *Parador del Rastro* (I), Plaza del Rastro, rustic Castilian décor; *El Torreón,* Calle Tostada 1, near the cathedral, with typical *cave.*

BURGOS. *Arriaga* (M), Lain Calvo 3, has the best food in town. *Auto Estaciones* (M), Miranda 4, has a rather unattractive dining room, but is spotlessly clean and serves excellent food. Excellent is *Casa Ojeda* (M), Calle Vitoria 5, rustic setting, good food and service.

CUENCA. One of the most pleasant is the *Posada de San José* (M), in the "hanging houses". Also good is *Mesón de las Casas Colgadas* (M). Cheaper are *Las Torcas* and *Juanito,* in new part of town.

LOGROÑO. *Los Leones* (E), General Mola 64; *El Cantabrico* (M), General Mola 19.

SALAMANCA. *Regio* (E), Zamora 9, has good food; *El Mesón* (I), Plaza del Poeta Iglesias, is regional. *El Candíl* (M), Ruiz Aguilera 10, has reasonable meals. *Feudal* (E), in the Gran Hotel, superb meals in medieval setting.

SEGOVIA. *Casa Cándido* (E), Azoguejo 7, is one of the best-known restaurants in Spain, where you should reserve a table early to get one at the window, facing the famous aqueduct. In an old building of typical Segovian atmosphere.

Casa Duque (M), Cervantes 12, also dates from turn of century, typical Castilian décor. *La Oficina* (M), is still another delightful rustic spot with topnotch local food and cozy atmosphere. *Garrido* (I), Ruiz de Alda 2, despite its modest rating will feed you well.

VALDEPEÑAS. *Paris* (M), hotel dining.

VALLADOLID. *La Goya,* at Puente Colgante, both (E). *Mesón La Viña* (E), Ferrari 5, quaint. *Risko,* Santiago 6, is a pleasant cafeteria and snack bar. *El Cardenal* (E), Plaza Tenerías, good, nice view. *Machaquito* (I), Calixto de la Torre, 5, best budget restaurant in town. Top rate are *La Fragua* (L), Zorrilla 4, and *Oskar* (E), Ferrari 3. *Caballo de Troya,* Correo 1. Quaint mesón, good food, pleasant patio.

Pamplona, Magnet of Navarre

The regions of Navarre and Aragon are generally neglected by tourists except for Zaragoza (Saragossa), chief city of Aragon, which is on the Madrid-Barcelona route, and Pamplona, the famous Navarese city of the Running of the Bulls.

The Pamplona Fiesta de San Fermin, when the bulls are run, takes place annually between July 6 and 15. Hotel prices are doubled at this season, but even so it is very difficult to find accommodation unless you apply far in advance. The Spanish Tourist Bureau in Pamplona is at Duque de Ahumada 3. Don't expect to do much sleeping if you come to Pamplona for this vigorous affair. The climax is the running of the bulls. Ahead of them run the young men of Navarra—and an occasional misguided tourist—dodging the infuriating charges of the stampeding bulls for the edification of their girl friends. Very special mad fun only a little spoiled by too much publicity. Rooms along the streets along which the bulls run can be rented. *Remember to reserve early.*

HOTELS IN PAMPLONA. *Los Tres Reyes* (L); *Maisonnave* and *Ohri,* both (2); *Yoldi* (3); *La Perla* (4), and the recent *Hostal del Toro.*
Restaurants: *Hostal Rey Noble* (E), Paseo Sarasate 6; *Hostería Avala* (M), San Nicolas 12 and *Caballo Blanco* (M), at end of ramparts.

Zaragoza

Zaragoza, capital of Aragon, has always been a city of great strategic importance. Equidistant between Madrid and Barcelona, it is an obvious stopping place for travelers, either by road or rail. Of tourist sights, there is the cathedral and even more important, the Basilica del Pilar, set upon the banks of the Ebro River. With its cupolas and blue tiling, its baroque magnificence seems at first sight to belong to Baghdad rather than to Aragon. Bayeu and Goya both contributed to the frescos in the choir of the chapel. The other architectural highlight of Zaragoza is the Castle of the Aljaferia (11th century), which is situated on the outskirts. There is also a Museo de Pintura with some Goya paintings, and El Greco's *St. Francis.*

HOTELS AND RESTAURANTS IN ZARAGOZA

Zaragoza has plenty of hotels. *Corona de Aragon* (L), is large, air-conditioned, 3 restaurants, pool; the long-established *Gran* (1), a bit oldish, but recently renovated. *Goya, Ramiro I,* and *Alfonso I* are all (1).
Motel el Cisne, Madrid road at km. 309, *Europa Paris,* and *Don Yo* are all (2).
Restaurants: *Savoy* (E), Coso 42, is excellent. *Maravilla* (M), Independencia 1, no style but some of the best cooking in town. *Mesón del Carmen* (I), Hernán Cortés 4, good value. A few houses farther on, the *Taberna Aragonesa* (I); *Casério Vasco* (I), Estebanes 7, for fine Basque specialties.

The North Coast and Hinterland

The northern coast of Spain is a rectangle that looks in two directions across the Atlantic. It embraces the Basque country (the section closest to France), Santander, Asturias and Galicia. To explore this area by bus, ask the tourist bureau about the Gran Cornisa-Finisterre Circuits. It is possible to get in on the section of ATESA National Tours that runs through this region: San Sebastián, Bilbao, Santander, Oviedo, La Coruña, Santiago de Compostela, La Toja, Vigo, Orense and León.

Relatively unknown to the casual tourist to Spain, the northern provinces present a charm all their own, yet just as "Spanish" as the better-known attractions of Andalusia and the south. Along the coast of Asturias and Galicia the sea is often rough and cold, though the deep Galician *rías,* or estuaries, are sheltered and calm, and the landscape is as green and lush as southern Ireland. Here you will find the snowy mountains of the Picos de Europa, variable skies, and ancient, grey stone towns rich in Romanesque architecture, nestled among tall trees.

There are three top tourist attractions in this area: the fabulous medieval town of Santillana del Mar and the neighboring caves of Altamira with their world-famous prehistoric paintings; Santiago de Compostela; and San Sebastián, one of the leading international resorts.

San Sebastián

San Sebastián, with a population of 132,000, 12 miles from the French frontier, is the tourist capital of Spain and the official seat of the Spanish government from July 20 to October 1, when it's burning hot in Madrid. It has two of the best beaches in Europe—La Concha, first, Ondarreta, a close second. San Sebastián is provided with all the luxury hotels, shops, restaurants, bars and nightclubs a tourist could desire. The climate is lovely, the city attractive and never excessively hot, thanks to the fresh Biscay breezes. An added bonus is a quaint fishermen's section with picturesque streets and excellent restaurants in all price ranges.

In the Basque provinces, beside San Sebastián, there are numerous points of great interest to be visited. In the province of Guipúzcoa, there is an uninterrupted chain of superb beaches which goes right to the French border. At Deva there is a fine bathing beach. The charming little port of Zumaya, and the tiny port of Guetaria are each well worth a visit. Nearby Zarauz is a fashionable bathing resort. Inland, Tolosa houses the baroque monastery of Ignatius de Loyola, founder of the Jesuit order. The basilica of Aránzazu is a must for anyone interested in modern architecture.

HOTELS AND RESTAURANTS IN SAN SEBASTIÁN

There is a great shortage of hotel space here, recently made worse by the closure of several large hotels.

Londres e Inglaterra, on the boardwalk, is best, with top comfort, continental charm, excellent service and food. Newest on the scene is the *Costa Vasca* (4S), 203 rooms, on Avenida Pio Baroja.

Monte Igueldo (1), perched atop a mountain with magnificent panoramic views. In same category are *Orly* and the newer *San Sebastián,* a little out of town. *Avenida* (2), on road up to Igueldo, is good.

The *Hispano-Americano* commands a good view, is central, comfortable and pleasant. Excellent is the *Parma* (3); some of its rooms have oceanside views.

A *parador* at Fuenterrabia (airport) is in a 16th-century castle.

Restaurants: The best-known is *Nicolasa* (E), Aldamar 4, next to the market: food excellent. The *Chomin* (E), Infanta Beatriz 14, near Ondarreta Beach is pleasant.

For lunch with a view it's *Akelare,* in the village of Igueldo.

Juanito Kojua (M), Puerto 14, famous, small, crowded. Fabulous *platos combinados* at budget prices at the *Dover,* Avda. de España 21. *Arzac* (E), on outskirts, has excellent offbeat dishes in intimate cottage setting.

The Caves of Altamira

Santillana del Mar is a lovely old city that would still be slumbering in its 15th-century sleep if something far older had not been discovered in the vicinity. These are the fascinating caves of Altamira on whose walls are colored drawings that were made 13,000 years ago. The caves, which are 18 miles west of Santander and only two miles from Santillana del Mar, were discovered in 1875. They are floodlighted so that you can see the extraordinary shades of yellow, ochre, red and gray which these prehistoric artists achieved with their colored pigments. Admission is limited to 3,500 persons a day, so in the summer expect a fairly long wait.

At press time, it was expected that the Caves would be kept open only during the summer months, with only a limited number of daily visitors allowed. Check first.

In Asturias, the rugged coastline is specked with charming fishing villages such as San Vicente de la Barquera, Llanes, Ribadesella, Cudillero, Luarca, etc. Gijon, the major Asturian port, boasts a magnificent two-mile beach.

Santander

Santander has long been a cultural as well as a vacation center. Unfortunately most of the city was destroyed in a fire after the civil war, but Santander has come back into its own and in summer virtually every hotel (of which there are a great many), is jammed with Spanish and foreign tourists. El Sardinero beach and the Magdalena are justly famous for their fine sand. The promenade along the seashore in Santander is one of the prettiest in all Spain, and further to enhance the charms of the city, each August sees a music and art festival, with top international stars participating.

Vitoria

Vitoria, in the province of Alava, is an interesting little town set in beautiful country. There are Van Dyck and Rubens paintings side by side with the 12th-century Virgin in the Cathedral of Santa María, but of greater importance to the locals is the jasper White Virgin of Vitoria in the equally old Church of San Miguel.

Bilbao

Bilbao, with a population of just under a quarter of a million, is the largest city in the Basque country. It is an industrial center and port more than a tourist resort, but in the summer months it has quite a gay season when the luxurious villas of the residential suburbs of Santurce and Portugalete fill with guests from Madrid. Iron ore is extracted in the locality and the largest blast furnaces in Spain are found around Bilbao.

Santiago de Compostela

Since the Middle Ages Santiago de Compostela has been the holiest place in all Spain. In medieval times it was, with Rome and the Holy Land, one of the three great centers of pilgrimage in Christendom, and the Jacobean Route, which can still be followed today, is lined with a chain of magnificent Romanesque monasteries and churches. The great nave of the 12th-century cathedral, said to have been built over the grave of St James the Apostle, soberer in style than is common in Spain, is immensely impressive. The principal chapel, under whose altar St. James and two of his disciples are buried, is dazzlingly rich. The Archbishop's Palace is outstanding, even in this country of ancient palaces, and the entire town is ringed with historic monasteries, churches and pilgrims' hostels.

The feast day of St. James, July 25, is the great moment of Santiago de Compostela, but it is a protracted moment which actually begins on the night of the 24th and continues for a week. This is the time to come if you want to participate in the religious festivities, *but make sure you have your hotel accommodation first.* Other times are recommended if you want to move leisurely about the cathedral and along the arcaded streets of this ancient holy city.

North of Santiago de Compostela, La Coruña has become a popular seaside resort, especially for the English and Scandinavians, while further south, the beauty of La Toja Island draws vacationers from all over Spain and abroad.

PRACTICAL INFORMATION FOR THE NORTH

HOTELS

There are *paradores* at Bayon (near Vigo), Gijón, Pontevedra, Santillana del Mar (famous, in ancient palace), Verín.

BILBAO. Tops is recent *Villa del Bilbao* (L), followed by *Aranzazu, Avenida, Carlton* and *Ercilla,* all (1). *Almirante* and *Conde Duque* are (2).

COVADONGA. *Pelayo* (2), right next to the famous cave.

CORUÑA, LA. *Finisterre* (1), beautifully located on the bay; recent *Atlántico* (1); *Riazor* (2); *Marineda* (3).

GIJÓN. *Hernán Cortés* (1); *Robledo,* (2); *Miami* (3); *Pathos* (4), recent.

OVIEDO. Newest and best, *Reconquista* (L), *La Jirafa* and excellent *Ramiro I* are (1).

SANTANDER. The *Bahía* (1), has tended to outstrip the *Real* (L). Among (2) hotels, the *Rex* is modern; good, less expensive, are *Mexico* and *Roma,* on Sardinero beach. Recent *Residencia María Isabel* is (2).

SANTIAGO DE COMPOSTELA. The *Hostal de los Reyes Catolicos* (L) one of the most magnificent hotels in Spain, is housed in a converted hospital built by Ferdinand and Isabella at the close of the 15th century. *Compostela* (2), is old-fashioned, but clean and comfortable. Others are the recent, well-equipped *Hostal Universal* (4), *El Peregrino* (2), *España* and *Gelmirez,* both (3). *Mexico* (4).

SANTILLANA DEL MAR. If the parador is full, try the *Altamira* (4), but with some first-class facilities. Also tops is *Los Infantes* (2), rustic décor, comfy rooms, good location.

TOJA, LA. *Gran Hotel* (L), between the sea and pine woods, a magnificent spa hotel, with aristocratically-furnished rooms, impeccable service and lots of old-world charm and amenities. *Loujo* (1), recent. *Balneario* (4), modest.

VIGO. *Bahía de Vigo* and *Samil Playa* are (1); *Ensenada, Mexico* and *Niza* are (2), last in town center. *Almirante* and *America* (3). Newest is the *Ciudad de Vigo* (4S), with 101 rooms open all year.

VITORIA. *Canciller Ayala* (1); *General Alava* (2); *Paramo* (3).

ZARAUZ. *Gran* and *La Perla, Zarauz,* all are (2); recent *Paris* (3), on Bilbao-San Sebastián road.

Restaurants

BILBAO. The *Torróntegui* (E) hotel serves wonderful food in a glass-enclosed rooftop dining room with outstanding view. *Luciano* (M), Barrencalle 38, founded 1890, service friendly but slow and inefficient. Also good are *Victor* (M), Mártires 2, *Abra* (E), Hurtado de Amezaga 24, *Arenal* (C), Espalza 2. *Urkia* (M), Ronda 31, good.

CORUÑA, LA. Virtually all the restaurants are to be found on the calles of de los Olmos, de la Garlera and de la Estrella. Noted for seafood is *Fornos* (M), Olmos 25. Also good, *Lhardy* (E), Galera 45, *Petit Lar* (M), Galera 45.

GIJÓN. The best, *Mercedes,* Calle 14 de Agosto (M). *Rincón de Antonio* (I), near the Plaza Mayor.

OVIEDO. *Malani* and *Pelayo,* on Pelayo, and *Alaska,* Mendizabel 3, are all (I).

SANTANDER. Among the best are *Casa Valentín* (E), and *La Gloria* (M), Castelar. *Jauja* (C), Medio 3. *Posada del Mar* (I), Juan de la Cosa 3, excellent meals in simple setting. *Sexto Continente* (M), Pasaje del Arsillero, superb seafood. *Casa Albo* (I), Peña Herbosa, 15, cozy with good service.

SANTIAGO. Tops are the superb restaurants in the *Hostal de los Reyes Catolicos. Alameda* (M), Puerto Fagera, is a type of cafeteria. *El Caserío* and *Victoria,* both (I), are average. *Tacita de Oro* and *La Arzuana,* both (I) and on Gen. Franco.

VITORIA. Highly reputed are *La Antonia* (E), Alto de Armentia, and *Mesón Nacional* (M), Dato 35, wood-paneled walls, friendly waitresses and local dishes. Old-world charm at *El Portalón* (M), Correría 151. *Dos Hermanas* (E), Postas 27, good seafood.

Barcelona and the Costa Brava

Barcelona, capital of the province and ancient county of Catalonia, is a big city (1,900,000 inhabitants), a flourishing Mediterranean port, and a great tourist center. It commands a glorious position, similar to that of Naples, with a beautifully carved-out gulf and harbor. It enjoys a climate milder than that of Naples or Rome, and is only rarely oppressive in summer. A lively, sophisticated city it rather looks down its Catalonian nose at the parvenu capital of Madrid. Barcelona is not only the gateway to the Mediterranean, it is a center of tourist excursions to the Holy Grail Monastery of Montserrat, to La Molina, a top ski resort of the Spanish Pyrenees, to Tarragona and the castled towns of Catalonia, and to that 90-mile stretch of summer playland known as the Costa Brava.

Exploring Barcelona

To get the atmosphere of Barcelona, go to the Ramblas, those wide promenades which in 1860 replaced the city walls which once encircled the old town. The Ramblas are alive into the wee hours of the morning, humming with the incessant murmur of voices. The inhabitants of this Catalan capital never tire of strolling up and down here, enchanting themselves and the tourists with their irrepressible animation.

In the more conventional sightseeing department, the cathedral has the place of honor, dominating the old town, which stretches from the Plaza de Cataluña to the Puerta de la Paz. Known to the local citizens as La Seu, it is a splendid creation of Catalan Gothic, at once strong and exquisite. The cloisters are among the best in Spain. The buildings in the cathedral area share the church's noble character—the Episcopal Palace; Palacio de la Generalidad, the seat of the ancient parliament of Catalonia, with a magnificent patio and staircase, and the Archdeaconry. On the nearby Plaza del Rey and in the Calle del Rech, the 14th- and 15th-century palaces have a grace and elegance reminiscent of Florence. Their severity contrasts with the stalactite-stalagmite fantasy of Gaudi's Church of the Sagrada Familia, started in 1881, never finished, and now one of Spain's (if not the world's) most visited buildings.

If you are interested in Spain's regional architecture, visit the Spanish Village, where each province is represented and where craftsmen turn out in front of you handicrafts of their region, which, by the way, are the best souvenir buys in Barcelona. From the hill of Tibidabo on clear days you can see all the way to Montserrat and the Pyrenees. Some people have claimed to see the Balearic Islands from here.

A source of entertainment always popular is the aerial transporter from Miramar, on Montjuich hill, to La Barceloneta, a ride which affords a thrilling view of the harbor and city.

Excursions from Barcelona

The Number 1 excursion from Barcelona is to the world-famous monastery of Montserrat, where medieval legend placed the Holy Grail. The fantastic, mystic mountain, jutting abruptly up to a height of 3,725 feet above the valley of the River Llobregat, inspired Wagner's consecrational play of *Parsifal*. Founded in 880 A.D., the monastery is still occupied by 300 Benedictine monks. The sanctuary as you see it today dates from 1410. See the Grotto of the Virgin, the Mirador, the Chapel of San Miguel, and the Chapel of Santa Cecilia (Romanesque, dating from 872). A funicular will take you to the Grotto of San Juan Garin, and an aerial railway to the Hermitage of San Jeronimo and a sweeping panoramic view. Montserrat, with its man-made buildings dwarfed by nature's grandeur, will leave you with a profound impression.

South of Barcelona you will find Sitges, the seaside spot to which the people of Barcelona flock for bathing, fishing and golf. Thirty-four miles farther south, through vineyards and olive groves, is Tarragona, one of the most fascinating places in the whole of Europe. Regarded as one of

Rome's finest urban creations, it still keeps the stamp of Empire in the surviving Circus Maximus. The Middle Ages added wonderful city walls and citadels, and the town still exerts the evocative charm of living history.

PRACTICAL INFORMATION FOR BARCELONA

HOTELS. There are many deluxe and near-deluxe hotels in Barcelona. Newest are the *Gran Hotel Sarriá* and *Princesa Sofia.* Modern are the *Presidente,* and the *Diplomatic.* The *Avenida Palace* is good and there is the long-established favorite, the *Ritz.*

First-class superior hotels include: *Colón,* Avda. de la Catedral 7; *Residencia Derby,* Calle Loreto 21, modern, as is *Residencia Balmoral,* Via Augusta 5, with garage. All tops in their category. *Cristina,* Generalísimo 458, *Dante,* Mallorca 181, and *Cristal,* have all rooms with bath, fully air-conditioned; garages. *Barcelona,* Caspe 13, is so-so. Others are *Arenas,* Capitan Arenas 20; *Condor,* Via Augusta 127; *Europark,* Aragón 325; *Regente,* Rambla de Cataluña 76; *Nuñez Urgel,* Urgel 232. *Gala Placidia,* Via Augusta 112, is modern, offering only suites. *Royal,* Ramblas 117, modern, rooms only. The *Avenida Victoria* is an apartment hotel, Avenida Victoria 16 (near Generalisimo). New on the scene is the *Bellaterra* (4S) outside town on the by-pass near town of Cerdañola. *Expo Hotel,* Mallorca, I-35, is modern, 432 rooms, pool, cafeteria.

Best among the (2) hotels are *Oriente,* Ramblas 45; *Condado,* Aribau 201; *Astoria,* Paris 203; *Residencia Rallye,* Travesera de las Corts, 150 rooms with bath, pool. Aseptic but good is the *Gaudí,* Conde de Asalto 12. *Terminal,* occupying three top floors at corner of Calles Provenza and Infanta Carlota.

Among the (3) and (4) category hotels are such old favorites as the *España,* San Pablo 9-11; *Cataluña,* Santa Ana 24, *Principal,* Junta Comercio 8. Recent is the *Numancia* (2), Numancia 72-74. 150 rooms, all with air conditioning. *Majestic* (1), Paseo de Gracia 70-72, all amenities.

RESTAURANTS. Barcelona is rich in fine restaurants. Lunch is served from 1:30 to 3:30, and dinner, in theory, from 8:30 to 11 P.M., but if you're on the early side, you may have the dining room all to yourself. Better hold out until 9. At the other end of the scale, some hotels will let you start dining at midnight. In many of these late places, it is difficult to tell where restaurants with music and dancing shade off into nightclubs, where professionals may do some of the dancing—or, in the gypsy *bodegas,* even amateurs who dance like professionals. Barcelona restaurants charge about the same prices as in Madrid.

DELUXE DINING

Atalaya, Avda. Generalisimo Franco 523, splendid view from the 21st floor.

Reno, Tuset 27, just off the Diagonal, has the highest repute for elegance and *haute cuisine.*

El Ast, perched up on Montjuich, makes a specialty of roast chicken.

Also top-notch are the *Finisterre,* Generalísimo 469 for Catalan specialties; *Via Veneto,* Ganduxer 10, highly recommended. *Sandor,* Plaza Calvo Sotelo; *Hostal del Sol,* Infanta Carlota 138, good dining, Spanish specialties. *Guriá,* Basque décor and food. *Dom,* Carretera de Esplugas 79, gardens and music.

GOOD EATING

The following are all (E), well recommended:

Baviera, Rambla Canaletas 127; *Il Giardinetto,* Calle Granada, fashionable Italian restaurant, top food. *Oratava,* Consejo de Ciento 335. Good for game and seafood, plush setting. *El Pescador,* Mallorca 314, good for seafood.

FOR ATMOSPHERE

These include one special type, the waterfront restaurant (*restaurantes tipicos marineros* is the way they are described).

Siete Puertas (M), Paseo Isabel II 14, near waterfront, an old standby from the turn of the century.

Agut D'Avignon (E), Trinidad 3, good Catalan food and décor.

Caballito Blanco, Mallorca 196, unpretentious, but excellent food; an old Catalan standby.

Caracoles (M), at Escudillers 14. Small rustic rooms, lots of atmosphere.

Casa Sole (M), San Carlos 4, specializes in seafood.

Better in this category is *El Cantábrico* (E), Santa Ana 11.

Hostal San Antonio (M), Tamarit 115. (M), *Los Borrachos,* Via Layetana 122, famed for meats.

El Canario de la Garriga (E), Lauria 23, favorite spot for Catalans, magnificent food, simple setting. Also delightful is *Joanet* (E), Paseo Nacional, in Barceloneta area, with plenty of old-world charm and top seafood. Old firemen's museum downstairs.

Scala (E), Paseo de San Juan 47, has floorshow. Lido-like atmosphere. May now be reopened after gutting by fire in early 1978.

La Venta (M), delightful, turn-of-century place, at funicular station end of Dr. Andreu. Indoor and oudoor dining.

For Galician food, the best place is *Carballeira* (I), Reina Cristina 3.

Basque food will be found at the *Amaya* (M), Rambla Santa Mónica 24, and *Guría* (M), Casanova 97.

La Dida, Roger de Flor 230, charcoal-grilled meat good.

OUTDOOR DINING

La Font del Gat (E) in a large villa on Montjuich, dining on patio midst fountains and flowers.

Also good are *La Pergola* (L), Avda. Reina Cristina s/n; *La Masía* (L), at the end of the Generalísimo avenue; and *Tres Molinos* (L), in the same neighborhood.

NIGHTLIFE. About the best all-around club for dinner, dancing and show is *La Scala,* Paseo de San Juan 49, plush décor. Burnt down in 1978; check if now reopened.

The *Pub 240,* Aribau 240, is the latest rage in Barcelona; Spanish and South American folk singing in elegant surroundings. The *Pub 140,* corner of Viladomat and Corcega, is in a similar vein and cheaper.

Crazy Horse, Avda. Generalisimo Franco 490, dinner and show nightly (E).

Among places with a more Spanish, or Catalan flavor are *Barcelona de Noche,* Tapias 7; *Apolo,* Marques del Duero, 61 and *Buena Sombra,* Ginjol 3.

Flamenco shows at *Los Tarantos,* Plaza Real; *El Cordobés,* Ramblas 35; *La Macarena,* Nueva San Francisco 5, (Puerto); *El Patio Andaluz,* Nueva San Francisco 2.

Important discotheques are the *Bacarra,* Bori y Fontesta 21; *Equilibrio,* Plaza Pie Inferior del Funicular del Tibidabo; *Charly Max,* Beethoven 15; *Metamorfosis,* Beethoven 9; *Bocaccio,* Muntaner 505.

THEATER AND CONCERTS. Barcelona has one of the world's finest opera houses, with a seating capacity of 4,000, the *Gran Teatro del Liceo,* Ramblas 65, but no permanent opera company to use it. There is, however, a winter opera season, running from Nov. to Feb. It is also used for symphony concerts. Concerts are held twice a week in the Palau de la Música.

MUSEUMS Barcelona has a baker's dozen of museums. The one you should not miss is the *Museum of Catalan Art* in the Palacio Nacional de Montjuich. It's usually open from 10 to 2, but best check for this and all other museums as times vary from season to season. The greatest collection of Catalan art in existence can be found in this museum. Sacheverell Sitwell called it "the most astonishing collection of primitive paintings in the world". It houses some outstanding paintings by Rembrandt, also El Greco and Velázquez, in addition to a rich collection of Spanish ceramics and Roman antiquities. The *Archeological Museum* is in the old Palacio Real of the Bourbon kings in the Parque de Montjuich. Try the *Museum of Modern Art* too, in the Parque de la Ciudad, a reminder, not that it's necessary, that Barcelona is very much a city of the present, as proud of its 20th-century accomplishments as of its glorious Catalan past. You won't be able to spend too much time in the Modern Art Museum either; it's open from 9:30-1:30.

SPORTS. *Bullfights,* end of March to October; *Pelota,* several "frontons". *Soccer:* F.C. Barcelona, one of world's best teams. *Golf:* Real Club; Prat. El Terramar Club at Sitges (20 miles out); Club de Golf Vallromanas (near Alella, off Gerona Motorway); San Cugat Club (ten miles inland from the center, train from Plza Cataluña); Llavaneras Club (22 miles north near Mataro). For all these see your hotel porter.

OTHER ENTERTAINMENT. In the evenings you might visit the amusement park on top of Montjuich Park. Amusement booths also on top of the Tibidabo Mountain. During the daytime it is pleasant to take one of the excursion boats that leave from the Plaza de Colon for a sail around the harbor. Not to be missed is the local Catalan dance, the *sardana,* which is performed by young and old every Sunday morning on the steps of the Cathedral.

SHOPPING. One of the characteristics of Barcelona is elegance. Add that to its prosperity, and you have necessarily a fine city for shopping. The best shopping streets are the Paseo de Gracia, the Avenida José Antonio, the Ramblas, the *Barrio Gótico* between the Cathedral, Plza Cataluña and the Ramblas, and the Avenida Generalísimo Franco, between Paseo de Gracia and Calle Ganduxer.

If you are feeling adventurous you might wander over to the Mayor de Gracia area, just above and north of Paseo de Gracia. This is really a small, almost independent *pueblo* within a large city, a warren of small, narrow streets, changing name at every corner, and filled with tiny shops where you'll find everything from old-fashioned tin lanterns to real feather dusters. Don't worry if you get lost: just hail a taxi, and it will get you back out to your hotel.

For gifts a good bet is the *Pueblo Español,* with a selection of everything from embroidered linens, mantillas, fans, glassware, Majorica pearls, ceramics, sandals, rugs, etc.

Shoes. *Calzados Alvarez,* Mariano Cubi 3, *Calzados Durany,* Ronda San Pedro 14; *José Torrens,* Avda. José Antonio 630; *Christiane,* Moya 1, Corcega 307; and *Bravo Java,* Rambla Cataluña 16, Avda. José Antonio 632.

Barcelona, like Madrid, has its flea market—or, rather, markets, known as Els Encants. The Belle Caire market, Plaza de Las Glorias Catalanas, operates all day every day except Tues. and Thurs. The San Antonio market, in the Calles de Urgel, Borrell and Viladomat, is open all week, though on Sunday morning it deals mostly in second-hand books. The cloth market, between the Calle de Valencia and the Calle de Aragón, also open all week.

For antiques your best bet is to wander in the area around the cathedral in the Barrio Gótico. Calle de la Paja and Calle Baños Nuevos have one antique shop after another. There you'll find old books, maps and in a small shop at Calle de la Paja 33, a very friendly old couple still have genuine *pergaminos* (medieval parchments) at very reasonable prices.

The Costa Brava

This is an extraordinarily beautiful stretch of jagged shoreline that begins at Blanes, 40 miles northeast of Barcelona, and continues with 90 miles of sun-drenched coves and beaches to the Franco-Spanish frontier town of Port Bou. Every step of the way is a delight, and you needn't worry about this region's meteoric rise to popularity having spoiled too much of its natural beauty. There are two ways to explore the Costa Brava if you aren't driving yourself. First is by luxury coaches operated by the Costa Brava Express Company daily from Barcelona north along the coast. The old-fashioned *coche de linea* makes two trips daily, too, carrying mail, freight and passengers. Here your fellow travelers may occasionally include a couple of chickens or a goat.

When to visit the Costa Brava? This seems to be a matter of taste. The Mediterranean has usually warmed up enough for swimming by the middle of May and it stays warm until late November. If you're on the Costa Brava on July 24, don't miss the procession of garlanded fishermen's boats to the shrine of their patron saint at Santa Cristina. Each village has its own fiesta; you couldn't avoid them if you wanted to. The full beauty of the Costa Brava is most apparent from the sea, and there are boats which run in season from most resorts.

Just outside Cadaqués is Salvador Dali's house—you may have the opportunity to see his unique garden if not the artist himself, and inland, in Figueras, the Dali Museum.

PRACTICAL INFORMATION FOR THE COSTA BRAVA

HOTELS. Here is a list of principal resorts along the Costa Brava, with a cross section of hotels and pensions. Many have been opened so recently that we have only been able to visit them once and thus cannot be sure that our initial impressions are still correct. We urge our readers to inform us of their own experiences in finding hotels along this booming coast. We have not included second and third-class pensions. Although usually clean, they are apt to be too primitive for all but the young and enthusiastic.

BAGUR. Best is the *Cap Sa Sal* (L), with every amenity and magnificently sited. The setting of the *Aiguablava* (1), is perfect; its large terrace, shaded by pine trees, is one of the most satisfying places on the entire Costa Brava for an evening drink. *Dos Calas* (2) and *Parador Nacional* (1), are recent. For the less affluent, *Bonaigua* (2) is acceptable.

BLANES. The modern *Park* and *Hostal Pop Coronat* are the leaders. Also good, the *Horitzó* and *S'Auguer.* All (2). Attractive camping site, *El Pinar.*

CADAQUES. The *Rocamar* (2) stands on a cliff half a mile from the center of town and has little balconies on which you can breakfast while enjoying the sea view. The *Playa Sol* (2) has a good restaurant. *Port Lligat* (4), 2 miles out, opposite Salvador Dali's house, has fine location, restaurant, own pool. Better than official category. Houses Dali's guests. Also *Llane Petit* (2).

ESTARTIT. *Belle Aire* and *Hostal Club de Campo Torre Grau* are both modern (2).

LLAFRANCH. Best are the *Terramar* (1) and *Paraiso* (2). Next comes *Santa Rosa* (3).

LLORET DE MAR. The most-developed resort on the Costa Brava. Best are the *Roger de Flor,* the *Santa Mara, Rigat Park,* and *Gran Hotel Monterrey,* nicely sited amidst gardens and woods. All are (1). *Rosamar,* with terraces, pool, and smaller *Eugenia,* with some amenities, are the top (2) hotels: also *Carabela* (2). The *Reina Isabel* (4) is pleasant and comfortable.

MATARO. *Castel de Mata* (1), by the sea on main road to France, with garden, pool, car park. Enchanting atmosphere.

PALAMOS. The *Trias* is one of the very few Costa Brava old-timers; has an attractive garden. *San Luis.* Both (2). *San Juan* (3), good, with pool.

PINEDA. The *Taurus Park* (2) has a pool, tennis, sports.

PLAYA DE ARO. Two miles out of town is the *Costa Brava Golf Hotel* (1), with pool, restaurant and use of 18-hole golf course and tennis courts. The recent (2) hotels are *Aromar* and *S'Agoita.* One of the best is *Columbus,* with garden, tennis and pool. Then *Cosmopolita* (private beach, garden, bar and nightclub), *Rosamar* and *Claramar.* Among the (3) are *Els Pins,* rooms with bath and balcony, *Xaloc,* excellent bar and large garden, *Costa Brava* with annex, and *Acapulco. Roura* (4), owner-managed, is recommended. *Clipper* (4).
　Nearby, *Cala Gogo,* deluxe camping, bungalows, nightclub.
　Cabo Buena Esperanza, and *Hostal Jaspet* are best among pensions.

ROSAS. *Almadraba Park* (1), on Almadraba beach. *Coral Playa, Nautilius, Mariam Platja* and *Vista Bela,* all (2).

S'AGARO. The most luxurious hotel on the Costa Brava is the *Hostal de la Gavina,* with exquisitely decorated rooms. Besides being a social center, it sponsors excellent *sardana* dancing contests in August and is the headquarters for yacht regattas.

SAN ANTONIO DE CALONGE. Best is *Rosamar,* overlooking beach. Newest is *Rosa del Vents.* Both (2). *Aubi, Ferrer, Lys,* and *Reymar,* all (3).

SAN FELIU DE GUIXOLS. *Reina Elisenda,* modernized, and *Murlá Park,* with pool near beach, are both (1). *Montjoi,* on a cliff overlooking the harbor, *Rex*

TOSSA DE MAR
COSTA BRAVA (Gerona)

THE PRETTIEST AND MOST TYPICAL
TOWN ALONG THE COSTA BRAVA

Extensive beaches and marvellous natural landscapes. Most agreeable mild climate. Brilliant sunshine. "Vila Vella"— XII century town centre—artistic National Monument.

Hotels and Boarding Houses of all categories. Apartments and Villas for sale and letting. Camping. Watersports. Horse-racing. Tennis. Excursions by boat. Spanish Fiestas. Folklore. Grand entertainments.

Communication: All roads which lead to TOSSA offer an extraordinarily beautiful view.

Season: April to October.

Information: Oficina Municipal de Turismo, TOSSA DE MAR, COSTA BRAVA, Spain

I, Forcas, Piscina Port-Salvi, Roca, all (2). *Monte Carlo,* on a cliff with fine view; *Nautilus,* pleasant restaurant, and *Caleta Park* are (3).

Santa Cristina de Aro (3). 18 hole golf course.

SITGES. Popular coastal resort, so book well ahead. *Terramar* is right on the beach, excellent value, all amenities, nice rooms. Also *Calípolis,* which towers over most of the other hotels. Both (1). Also good are *Los Pinos* and *Galeón,* both (2).

Sitges Park (with annex), an excellent budget spot, with pool, garden, restaurant, is (3).

TOSSA DE MAR. Best is the *Reymar* (1), then the *Costa Brava,* the smaller *Florida, Delfin, Mar Menuda* and *Vora Mar,* all (2). The *Ancora* (3) has pleasant terraces facing the beach.

You'll be well taken care of at the *Avenida* (3). *Capri, Ramos, Rovira* and *Mare Nostrum. La Atlanta, Las Acacias, Don Pancho* and *Marbella* are all (4). The *Hostal Suizo* is a deluxe pension.

 RESTAURANTS. In general, you dine in your hotel or pension at most places along the Costa Brava. Indeed, only the larger and more fashionable resorts have restaurants of interest to visitors. Moreover, they tend to be much alike, so you might as well let the scenery be your guide and have your dinner or whatever outdoors on some pine-shaded bluff overlooking the Mediterranean. Spain's best known mineral water comes from this region—Vichy Catalan —a product of the little spa of Caldas de Malavella.

FIGUERAS. On main France-Barcelona route, inland from Rosas. *Durán* (M), one of the best in Catalonia; *Ampurdan,* highly recommended by readers.

LLAFRANCH. *Costa Brava* (M). *La Langosta* (L).

LLORET DE MAR. *Hotel Rosamar* restaurant (M); *Celler de la Masia* (I), rustic setting. *Restaurante Playa* (I) on the beach itself. Especially pleasant for seafood is the *Alhama,* right on the beach.

ROSAS. *El Cazador* (M); *Club Moli Blau* (Canyelles Petites) has a restaurant, too.

SANTA CRISTINA. The *Santa Cristina Hotel* (I) is noted for its crayfish, which you can enjoy outdoors, sitting under Europe's largest umbrella pine and enjoying the sea view.

TOSSA DE MAR. *Maria Angela* (M), behind Paseo del Mar, excellent seafood. The *Bahía* is famous for its Catalan dishes. Outdoor dining terrace. *Hotel Capri's* restaurant has prices somewhat lower than the other. Also *Las Acacias* (M), on the beach. For budget dining try *El Mano* (I), Calle Iglesia 18, clean and pleasant.

The Balearic Islands

Lying about 120 miles south of Barcelona, Majorca is as old as legend and just as fascinating. It was here that Hercules found the Golden Apples of the Hesperides in the mythical times of the Greek Argonauts. This island and 15 others are the fabled Islas Baleares. They have been occupied by Romans, Vandals, the Byzantine Empire under Belisarius, Moors and the English. The English are still there as tourists. So are the Americans. And they couldn't be happier.

Although prices are rising with the rapidly increasing popularity of the Balearics, they are still somewhat lower than those on the Costa Brava, with the exception of the luxury hotels. If you want a holiday that mixes rest with sociability, Palma is your best bet. Minorca and Ibiza are simpler and cheaper. The former is being vigorously developed, with numerous new hotels and tourist centers opening. Ibiza, on the other hand, has become the "hippy" center of Spain, with droves of long-haired youngsters seeking "happiness" and the simplicity of island life by settling there.

PRACTICAL INFORMATION FOR THE BALEARICS

WHEN TO GO. All year round. Majorca has an especially fine climate, mild in winter and saved by sea breezes from oppressive heat in summer. Generally speaking, Ibiza is hotter and Minorca colder than Majorca in all seasons, but these are relative differences. Winter can be chilly though in the Balearics, and many hotels close November–April.

HOW TO GET THERE? By Air. Many European capitals are connected by air to Palma. You can fly direct from Paris to Palma in two hours. *Caledonian-BUA* have scheduled flights during summer to Ibiza and Palma from Gatwick Airport (London). Non-scheduled flights to Palma operated from Bournemouth, Gatwick and Manchester. *Iberia* flies you from Madrid in less than one hour to Palma and maintains regular services between Andalusian cities and the Balearics.

Aviaco flies a *"car-ferry"* between Palma and Barcelona and Valencia from May 1 to October 31, and ordinary passenger services to Minorca and Ibiza from Barcelona.

By Sea. *Compañia Trasmediterránea* runs nightly services between Palma and Barcelona, thrice-weekly between Palma and Valencia, and weekly between Palma and Alicante. It also links Palma and Ibiza three days a week and runs twice-weekly services between Palma and Port Mahón and one a week to Ciudadela on Minorca. The *Ybarra Co.* also services the Barcelona-Palma route.

HOTELS. It is essential to book in advance. By the end of April all the best-known resorts are booked to capacity until mid-October. In the list below deluxe and first-class pensions are classified (PL), (P1). Our list is only representative: such is the hotel building boom that there are over a thousand hotels.

MAJORCA (MALLORCA)

BAÑALBUFAR, 16 miles northwest of Palma near the most beautiful coastal scenery in all Majorca. The *Mar y Vent* (PL) is a bargain for its category.

CALA BONA. Near Cala Millor. The German-managed *Gran Sol* is best, followed by *Levante* and *Levante Park;* all (3).

CALA D'OR. On the coast, about 40 miles southeast of Palma. Newest is the *Cala Esmeralda* (1), all amenities. The *Cala Gran, Rocador, Costa del Sur, Tucan, Corfu, María del Carmen, Skorpios Playa,* all modern, all (2). The *Cala d'Or* (4) is modern and set in a pine grove. Restaurant and bungalows *Playa D'Or* (1)

CALA FORNELLS, 16 miles from Palma. Recent, *Coronado* (1), pool, garden. *Cala Fornells* (3).

CALA MILLOR. Between the Caves of Drach and those of Arta, not far from Son Servera, some 40 miles east of Palma. The huge *Flamenco,* all amenities, *Hotel Playa Cala Millor,* with two pools, garden, terraces, the *Talayot,* modern, with fine beach, and the recent *Sumba* are all (2). *Biniamar* and *Temi,* both (3), and *La Niña* (4), with pool, are recent.

CALA RATJADA (Capdepera). For lovers of the simple life, 50 miles northeast of Palma. Best are the *Aguait, Bella Playa, Son Moll* and *Lago Playa,* all (2); then *Cala Gat, Capricho, Carolina,* all (3).

CALVIA. At Cala Fornells, the hotel of the same name (3) has a peaceful location among pines, with private sand beach; on the beach, Coronado (1). In Calviá, *Club Galatzo* (1), has bungalows, apartments. Newest is the swanky *Hotel Golf Santa Ponce* (5S), only 18 rooms, all amenities, next to golf course.

CAMP DE MAR, 16 miles from Palma. *Camp de Mar* (1) is perfectly situated above a first-rate beach. *Villa Real* and *Playa,* both (2), also on beach.

DEYA. About 20 miles north of Palma. *Esmoli* (1), all comfort. The *Costa d'Or* (4), at Lluch Alcari, is cheap but delightful.

EL ARENAL. About 7 miles west of Palma. Best is the ultramodern *Garonda Palace* (L). Next come *Cristina Palma* (1), and modern *Acapulco* (2), right on Maravilas beach. Next in line is the *Neptuno,* also on the beach. Also *Riviera, Flamingo, Amazonas, Aya, Ayrón, Venus,* all (2), as is *Copacabana,* set in a garden with pines, a little way from the sea. *Lido, Maritimo,* attractive *Los Angeles,* with sea view, all (3).

FORMENTOR (Pollensa). Almost at the northeast tip of Majorca, 42 miles from Palma. The *Formentor* (L) is set among exquisite gardens with magnificent views of sea and mountains plus attractive bathing beach.

ILLETAS. About 5 miles west of Palma, near Calviá. The *Hotel del Mar* is (L). The *Illetas* is built in a series of terraces in the rock directly above the sea; *Bon Sol* has a wonderful view over Palma Bay; *Albatros,* with mini-golf, private beach, heated pool. All (1). *Playa Marina* and *Villas Bon Sol,* both (2). *Bonanza Park* and *Gran Hotel Bonanza Playa* both (1)

MAGALUF, about 11 miles from Palma. *Meliá Magaluf, Atlantic, Coral Playa, Flamboyan, Barbados, Antillas* and *Forte Cala Viñas,* all (1). *El Caribe, Jamaica, Pax, Trinidad, Magaluf Park* and *Samos,* all (2).

PAGUERA. A huge beach beginning 15 miles west of Palma. *Sunna,* with pool and tennis; *Villamil,* set amid pines above the sea. Both (1). *Bahía* and *Gaya* (2).

PALMA. Chief city and tourist center of Majorca. The *Meliá Mallorca* (L), overlooking the sea near town, is sumptuous; its pool is magnificent.
The *Fenix* (L) is air-conditioned throughout. Lovely tropical gardens.
Apartotel Meliá Magaluf (L), has 320 furnished apartments, all amenities.
The *Victoria* (L) commands a magnificent view of Palma Bay, has a handsome pool, and is renowned for its cuisine. *Valparaiso Palace* (L), in Bonanova section, with garden and super view.
Nixe Palace (L), at Calamayor beach, has tennis, terrace garden, dancing.

La Bonanova (L), in residential area.

The *Son Vida* (L), about 3 miles out of Palma; some rooms have original period furniture of the old castle in which the hotel has been installed. Extensive grounds, panoramic open-air restaurant, pool, tennis, horseback riding and 9-hole golf.

The *Bellver,* in town and *Raquet Club* are (1).

A standout is the *Araxa,* with pool, pretty lawn and trees in front; *San Carlos,* air-conditioned; pool. Both (2). *Bellver,* in town.

Club Nautico is the yachtsmen's headquarters. The *Mirador* has a sea view though it is in town. *Jaime I,* comfortable, unpretentious, right in town; the vast *Majorica.* All (3S).

Borenco, Caballero, Jumbo Park, El Paso, with attractive garden, tennis, and *Bonanova,* excellent value, all (3).

PORTO CRISTO (Manacor). Charming fishing village with excellent bathing beach, near the Drach Caves and 40 miles due east of Palma. *Drach* (3). The *Felip* is famous for its *paella; Perello* is simple, also on the beach. Both (4).

PUERTO DE POLLENSA. A delightful fishing port near Formentor and 36 miles from Palma. Best is *Diana* (1), with every facility for water sports and relaxing. The *Uyal* has pleasant garden overlooking the sea. Also the *Eolo.* Older, quieter, and set in a grove of fine shady trees, the *Illa d'Or* has tennis. The delightfully furnished *Miramar* has outstanding food, a friendly atmosphere. All (2).

PUERTO DE SÓLLER. Small port 22 miles due north of Palma. *Eden* overlooks harbor. *Espléndido* is also right on the beach, has two terraces for dining. Both (2). *Mare Nostrum* and *Porto Soller* are (3). The ultramodern *Roma,* the *Costa Brava, Marbella,* and *Miramar,* all (3) and on the beach. Recently opened *Eden Park* (2).

MINORCA (MENORCA)

CIUDADELA. The *Cala Blanca,* has pool. *Eleycon,* with pool, lovely garden, is good. Both (2). *Cala Caldana, Cala'n Blanes, Los Delfines* and *Ses Voltes* are all (3).

At Cala Forcat, the *Almirante Farragut* is (2).

At Cala Galdana, the *Audax* (1). *Tamo* and *Laguna Playa* at Son Bon. At Arenal d'en Castell, biggest and best is the *Castell Playa* (2).

PORT MAHÓN. Best is *Port Mahón* (1), which stands on a cliff directly above the yacht club with a broad view of the harbor.

Down in the port itself are the older *Bustamente* and *El Paso,* both (3).

VILLACARLOS. *Agamenón* and *Rey Carlos III* are both (2). *Hamilton* (3).

IBIZA

IBIZA. No good hotels in town itself. At nearby Figueretas Beach are the *Ibiza Playa* (2); *Victoria, Don Quijote* and *Copacabana,* all (3). At Playa d'en Bossa, 3 miles away, are the *Torre del Mar* and the inland *Los Molinos,* both (1). *Algarb, Tres Carabelas, Don Toni, Goleta* and *Playa d'en Bossa* are (2).

SAN ANTONIO ABAD. A charming resort. Newest is the *Nautilus;* then *Palmyra.* Both (1). *Acor Arenal, Bahía, Bellamar, Cala Gracio,* and *Columbus,* all (2).

SANTA EULALIA DEL RIO. The *Fenica* is just across the river from town. The vast *S'Argamassa,* 6 miles north, has private beach. Newest is *Los Loros.* All (1). *Don Carlos, Ses Estanques, Panorama* and *Siesta,* are all (2). *La Cala* (4), *La Cala* (1S), sleepy, unpretentious, but with a matchless view. The *Buenavista* (PL), almost next door, is older and larger. Another pensión is the *Cas Catalá,* near the beach.

RESTAURANTS. Majorcan food is Catalan food, but richer and more highly seasoned. The best wines come from the Vinicola Binisalem. The island also has a particularly interesting apéritif called *palo,* a bitter-sweet concoction made from St. John's bread, which grows on the island. There is also a popular anise drink.

IBIZA. *El Olivo* (E), in Alt Vila, top service, international food, charming decor. *El Bistro* (M), next door, excellent French cuisine. *Ibiza Country Club* (E), breathtaking view of bay, impeccable food and service; *Vesuvio* (L), at Figueretas Beach has magnificent seafood. Curry, steaks and English meals at *Johnny Bull,* also at Figueretas. *Celler Balear* (M), simple setting, good, solid, Spanish food.

INCA. An excursion to this locality is a must for the picturesque *Cellar Ca'n Amer.*

PALMA. Center of Palma nightlife is around Plaza Gomila. *Samantha* (E), Plaza Mediterráneo, excellent food.

Tirol (E), Calle Apuntadores serves Austrian specialties in a delightful large patio setting. *El Siglo* (I), for curried chicken. *Gina's* (M), Plaza de la Lonja, top Italian and Spanish dishes in bistro setting. *Texas Jack's,* San Felio 26, for mansized chiliburgers; *Celler Sa Premsa* (I), Plaza Obispo de Palou, is set in an old wine cellar. Hearty local food. In Terreno, best are *La Casita* (I), on Calvo Sotelo, French-American cooking in simple setting and *La Pizzería,* Calle Bellver 31 (M), for topnotch Italian food, garden dining. *Casa Sophe* (M), Calle Apuntadores, good French cooking.

NIGHTCLUBS. Palma: *Tito's* is the top now. It has displaced *Jack el Negro,* which continues, however, to be picturesque and gay. Others are *Tiffany's, Barbarela* and *Crazy Daisy,* all near Plaza Gomila in Terreno. A "fun" place is *Baviera,* adjoining the Crazy Daisy, for German food and dancing. All the above keep open until 3 A.M. So do the *Patio Andaluz* and *El Chico,* both at the Bahía Palace Hotel, where there are authentic flamenco singing and dancing. Out of town are *Los Rombos,* at El Arenal, with good flamenco show; *Bolero Night Club* in Palma Nova; *Las Velas* in Santa Ponsa (no show, but wonderful surroundings and music).

Dancing only, up to midnight or 1:30, is offered in the Fenix Hotel's *Rontonda,* and the *Aquarium Bar* of the Hotel Victoria. Nightly guitar concerts at 10 P.M. in the *Guitar Center,* Montenegro 10, also good for drinks, chatting or even playing chess. *Riki's Place* is owned by an American disc-jockey and caters to an expatriate crowd. Great seaside view. *Formentor Bar,* Avda. José Antonio 1, is favorite café hangout for foreign locals.

There are nightclubs galore on Ibiza island. In Ibiza town, *Mar Blau,* Los Molinos, offers a good Spanish floorshow. *Pasha's,* at Talamanca Beach, is a farmhouse converted into a disco. In San Antonio Abad, the most attractive is the cellar of *El Refugio,* where guitar music is the thing (no dancing). Most of the dancing is done at the *Playboy, Capri,* and *Cocacabana.* Santa Eulalia del Rio has two nightclubs: *La Cala* and *Ses Parres.*

SHOPPING. Among Majorcan specialties are ceramics—tiles, cups, and plates, all brightly colored, with blue and red prevailing—embroidery, and wrought iron articles of all kinds, from lamps to flower bowls. Wrought iron work is done with great taste and skill here, and extremely cheaply. Sandals, men's hats, ladies' handbags, and shopping bags of raffia are also inexpensive. Majorcan pearls can be bought at *Perlas Islas,* Felanitx; *El Drach,* Santo Domingo. Exquisitely embroidered tablecloths and napkins can be found at the *Casa Bonet,* Calle de San Nicolas.

WHAT TO SEE. Cathedral; the Lonja, now a regional museum; fairy-tale Bellver castle, overlooking the bay. The monastery of Valldemosa where George Sand bossed Chopin in 1838; Drach Caverns with world's largest underground lake. Visit to Formentor and Selva, where you can see Mallorcan dancers on certain days. Well-organized excursions to all these places.

Southeastern Spain

The most interesting provinces of southeastern Spain are Valencia and Alicante. The first place of note after entering Valencia is Sagunto, with its Roman theater big enough to hold 8,000 people. In 219 B.C. Sagunto, resisting Hannibal during the Punic Wars, knew one of the most violent and heroic moments in Spain's heroic and violent history. Rather than surrender, the inhabitants became cannibals, living on their own dead. Finally, when defeat was inevitable, they set the town on fire and perished in mass suicide. Hannibal found no survivor in Sagunto.

Valencia

Only 14 miles away is Valencia, third city of Spain with a population of over half a million. Famous for its orange groves which perfume the night with the heady scent of their blossoms, Valencia is popular with tourists despite its heat and noise. The port is about two miles from the center of the city. There are two bathing beaches, the Arenas and the Nazaret. We recommend the less-crowded Pinedo y Saler and its pine grove, a little farther from town. The 13th-century cathedral of Valencia claims possession of the Holy Grail, the chalice used at the Last Supper (though this is also claimed by Montserrat, near Barcelona). See also the 15th-century bell, affectionately known as "Miguelito", and an extraordinary silver figure of the Virgin, dating from the fourth century. Two other highlights of Valencia are the 15th-century Lonja del Mercado with its Orange Court, more impressive architecturally than the cathedral, and the art gallery in the Convent of Pio V, one of the best in Spain. But Valencia's chief attraction for the tourist is its famous *fallas* on March 19, climaxing a festival with the burning of hundreds of papier-mâché figures of famous Spanish personalities, often embodying sharp satirical digs at the ruling powers. There are also tremendous fiestas here in Easter Week and the last week in July, with bullfights, battles of flowers, folk dancing, fireworks—in fact, the *whole* works!

The Costa Blanca

The stretch of coast between the Peñon de Ifach and Alicante is the Costa Blanca, or "white coast", with its heart at the extremely attractive and rapidly expanding beach resort of Benidorm. It is a sun-worshippers' paradise, far hotter than the Costa Brava.

Here you are in the land of the carnation, a flower so prevalent that it even faintly perfumes the local wine, and here, too, you come to one of those strange but lovely places with which the entire Costa Blanca is strewn—the Peñon of Ifach (or Ifach Rock). It is located three miles away to the left of the main road, past the not very attractive little town of Calpe. A mile farther on, the 1,000-foot monolith of the Peñon rises sheer from the sea. At the foot of the Peñon are two perfect bathing beaches.

Back on the main Levante road, which dives through tunnels in the rock, the next town is Benidorm, with its lovely sand beaches. Six miles farther is the happy-sounding little town of Villajoyosa, and then Alicante's summer resort of San Juan.

Alicante

Alicante, founded as a Carthaginian colony in the third century B.C., has that African look, with its superb avenue of date palms (the only ones in Europe upon which the fruit ripens), its vast Moorish castle dominating the city from a rocky peak, and its palm-lined harbor from which ships sail to the Balearic Islands and Algiers. This town is torrid in the summer. If you get tired of 90 in the shade temperatures, you can cool off at the little spot of Busot, 14 miles away and set among pine woods at a height of over 4,000 feet. Another excursion from Alicante is the 26-mile bus trip to Elche with its famed palm forest.

PRACTICAL INFORMATION FOR THE SOUTHEAST

HOTELS

ALICANTE. Recent is the *Meliá,* every conceivable amenity. The *Gran Sol* has magnificent views, panoramic snackbar. Then comes *Palas;* neither has restaurant. All (1). Recent *Maya,* fully air-conditioned, 3 pools, tennis, *Gran, Reycar, Covadonga, Cristal, Leuka* and on the Playa de San Juan the new *Castilla,* and *Bernia* are all (2). *Bahía, La Balseta* (3). New is the *ADOC* (4S), on Albufera Beach, 93 rooms, tennis, cafeteria. On the Alicante-Valencia road, KM. 108, is the new *El Montiboli* (4S), built in Moorish style, two private beaches, two pools, dancing.

BENIDORM. The *Delfin* (L), has a park setting, pool, private beach. All (1) are: *El Corregidor Real,* all amenities, pool, minigolf; *Glasor, Costa Blanca, Avenida, Celtibero* and *Don Pancho.* In (2) are: *Les Dunes,* perhaps best, then *Los Alamos, Alameda, Brisa, Bristol Park, Didac.* Newest additions are the *Cimbel* (4S) and the *Rosamar* (3S), both on Levante beach with all amenities.

ELCHE. Newest, best, is *Huerto del Cura* (1). *Los Arenales,* at Arenales beach, and *Cartagena* are (2). *Don Jaime* (3).

VALENCIA. The *Sidi Saler Palace* (L), on Saler beach, the *Dimar, Rey Don Jaime* and *Azafata* at Manises Airport, all (1), are all new. The *Astoria Palace* has all amenities, including nightclub. *Reina Victoria.* All (1). Then come *Excelsior,* air-conditioned, recommended by Fodor readers who enjoyed good food and service; *Llar,* air-conditioned; *Oltra,* with pool; *Inglés.* All (2). *Marcelina* (3). Eleven miles from Valencia is the *Monte Picayo* (L).

Restaurants: Best is *Viveros* (L), set in gardens, top international food. *Barra-chino* (M), Plaza del Caudillo, snack bar, bakery, delicatessen and restaurant; magnificent *paella*. *Méson del Conde* (M), Calle José Iturbi 18, is small, intimate, Italian. *Casa Cesareo* (I), Guillen de Castro 15, specializes in *paella*. Cozy décor.

Andalusia and its Capital, Seville

Andalusia is the heart of the mystery of Spain. The closest you can come to that heart is in Seville, 1½ hours from Madrid by air. This is the city of Don Juan and Carmen, the spiritual capital of Andalusia.

Seville's cathedral, begun in 1402 after St. Ferdinand delivered the city from the Moors, can only be described in superlatives. It is the largest in Spain (and the largest Gothic building in the world), the highest, and the richest in decoration and great works of art. This immense monument to Christianity enshrines the mortal vestiges of St. Ferdinand and Christopher Columbus. Every day, characteristically, the bell that summons the faithful to prayer rings out from a Moorish minaret, relic of the Arab mosque whose admirable tower of Abou Yakoub the Sevillians could not bring themselves to destroy. Now topped by a five-story bell tower, called the Giralda (weathercock), this splendid example of Arabic art is one of the marvels of Seville.

Other sights which you should not miss are the Tower of Gold and the Alcazar, fortress palace of the Arab kings; the fascinating quarter of Santa Cruz with its twisting byways, dignified old houses and flagstoned patios, splashed with the color of potted plants and the water of drowsy fountains; and the beautiful baroque Alms House of La Caridad. Here you may see the portrait and death mask of Miguel de Mañara, the original Don Juan, who died within these walls.

There is no more pious and no more boisterous festival in all of Europe than Holy Week in Seville. The first procession begins Palm Sunday afternoon, the last ends with the final streaks of sunset on Good Friday. In the meantime you have never seen such an incongruous spectacle of sacred and other rejoicing. There are mummers dressed up as Roman centurions, a parade of toreros, a procession of Spanish beauties in evening dress and flowing mantillas, gypsy songs and dances, firecrackers, barefoot penitents staggering under the weight of crosses, pious women actually bleeding under crowns of thorns, weeping at the sight of the Macarena, the Virgin of Hope; there are the improvised *saetas*, anguished songs inspired by the sufferings of Jesus, and there are extravagant, theatrical gestures—dramatic prostrations before the Madonna, the thrusting of fingers into the wounds of Christ. You can watch this extraordinary exhibition of agony and joy from rented seats, but we must warn you that Seville is jammed at this time and that all hotel accommodations are heavily booked well ahead of this date.

PRACTICAL INFORMATION FOR SEVILLE

HOTELS. *The Alfonso XIII* (L), was formerly the *Andalucia Palace,* and it is exactly that—a real Andalusian palace, sumptuously decorated, huge, and with fine gardens. It is air-conditioned, has restaurant and pool.

The *Cristina* (L), opposite Jardines Cristina park, is modern. Its rooms all have air-conditioning, but are smallish and noisy.

The *Luz Sevilla* (L) is fully air-conditioned.

Inglaterra (1), is magnificently situated. Excellent accommodations and service, some rooms with terraces. Also (1) are the *Colón* and newer *Macarena,* near Macarena Arch, in somewhat tawdry neighborhood, the *Nuevo Lar,* and the *Pasarela,* next to María Luisa Park. Newest is the *Lihsa Porta Coeli* (4S), with 250 exterior rooms on Avda. Eduardo Dato, 49. Cafeteria.

In (2) category: the recent *Doña María, Acuarium, Don Paco, Fernando III, Fleming, María Luisa Park, Bécquer.*

Montecarlo, Residencia Ducal (rooms only), *Niza,* and well recommended *Otte,* all (3).

Tucked away in the Barrio de Santa Cruz is the pleasant *Murillo* (3). *Hostal Sudan* is a good pension, highly recommended by readers.

 RESTAURANTS. One of the best is the restaurant of the *Alfonso XIII* (L), much favored by the smart set. The *Parrilla del Cristina* (L), at the Cristina hotel, with its flamenco floorshows (outside in summer) is another.

Among restaurants pure and simple, try: *El Burladero* (M), Canalejas 1, cozy; *Bodegón de Torre del Oro* (M), Santander 15, a huge tavern-like spot, popular for decades and serving topnotch food. *El Puerto* (I), Betis 59, commands a beautiful view of the river. Beside it, *Rio Grande,* has a huge outdoor terrace with splendid city view. For *tapas,* try *Los Duendes,* reader recommended.

NIGHTLIFE. Seville is at its best in the flamenco shows, which can be seen at *El Patio Andaluz,* Plaza del Duque 4, and *El Oasis,* Lido Sevillano. Try also *Parrilla del Cristina* (see under Restaurants). Out on the Cádiz road is *Marcelino,* rather nightclubbish, but also with flamenco.

 SHOPPING. The best part of town for shopping is the fascinating quarter around the Calle de las Sierpes, reserved for pedestrians only, since the streets are so narrow no cars can get through.

Most elegant shop for leather and suede is *Loewe,* Plaza Nueva. Also *Miguel Sanchez Garcia,* Calle Murillo 5 y 7; *Peribé,* Plaza del Pan 5. Try *Aleixandre,* Sierpes 33 (branch of Madrid store) for jewelry and evening bags.

Gloves can be bought at *Idigor,* Calle Sierpes, 53. Men's leather jackets and slippers, *Sobrino de Galan,* Sagasta 21. For shoes, go to *Varela,* José Antonio 14.

Spanish shawls are a specialty at *Antonio Vadillo Plata,* Calle Tetuán 34. Tiles and ceramics at *Manuel Montalban,* Alfareria 13, *Ceramica Santa Ana,* San Jorge 31, and *Bensaque, Rodriguez y Cia.,* Evangelista 47.

Cordoba

Corboda is worth a visit even in the unrelenting heat of summer for its incomparable eighth-century mosque. Abd el Rahman, an emir of the great caliphate of Cordoba, intended it to surpass all other Arab mosques in grandeur. When you cross the threshold, you are immediately overwhelmed by the evidence of the rich Moorish civilization which was and still is the glory of this Spanish city. Even after Saint Ferdinand had driven out the Moors, the citizens of Cordoba refused to disturb a single stone of their wonderful mosque. They simply blessed the building and consecrated it to the Virgin. When, three centuries later, a zealous clergy decided to erect an altar in the midst of the Moorish columns, the citizens were so outraged that they even threatened the lives of workers who undertook the demolition. Nevertheless, and at great expense, the *crucero* was built, with the approval of Charles V. It is an impressive baroque affair, but heavy and incongruous in this airy forest of columns.

Granada

Granada is another monument of Moorish Spain, perhaps the most impressive of all. When Boabdil, the last Moorish king, surrendered the city to Ferdinand and Isabella, his heartbroken sob found a lasting echo in Arab hearts. As for the Catholic Monarchs, they wept with joy, kneeling among their monks and soldiers on that January day in 1492 to thank God for victory as their flag was raised on the tower of the Alhambra. They lie side by side, Ferdinand and Isabella, in the Royal Chapel of the cathedral of Granada, immortalized in bas reliefs and glorified by paintings of El Greco and Ribera—but even this glory is dimmed by Granada's most famous monument, the dazzling Arabian Nights palace of the Alhambra.

It needs a poet to describe the subtleties and complexities of this fortress pleasure-dome, still redolent of the intrigues of the seraglio, the pomp, voluptuousness and violence of the Arab court. In spite of the relentless droning of the guide (you cannot visit the interior unescorted), you will retain a series of indelible images—the marble baths, perforated like incense burners, the turquoise green and black of the Pool of Myrtles, the Fountain of Lions into which once flowed the blood of 36 beheaded princes. The rose-red Alhambra and the nearby Generalife, summer residence of the caliphs, are sure to be among your most vivid memories of Spain.

PRACTICAL INFORMATION FOR MOORISH SPAIN

HOTELS AND RESTAURANTS

There are excellent *paradores* at Jaén, near Córdoba, at Granada, and in the Sierra Nevada mountains.

CORDOBA. Hotels: Tops is the vast, air-conditioned *Meliá Córdoba,* then *Gran Capitán,* both (1). *Los Gallos,* with pool, and *Maimonides,* opposite the Mosque, good, clean, are both (2). *El Brillante* (3), out of town, near the *parador,* is modern, clean.

Restaurants: *Los Califas* (M), Deanes 9, near the cathedral. *Caballo Rojo* (E), Calle Deanes, quaint and pleasant. Budget restaurants on Calle Victoriano Rivera, off Plaza José Antonio.

GRANADA. Hotels: Best and most luxurious is the *Meliá Granada* in elegant colonnaded side street in center. *Alhambra Palace* is beautifully set in Alhambra gardens. *Luz Granada,* noisy and rather impersonal, geared for group tours. Both (1). *Guadalupe* (2), has best view in city, overlooking Alhambra and Generalife; modern, air-conditioned, good service, food. *Los Angeles,* balconies to each room, pool. *Residencia Kenia* is old but good, has garden. *Victoria,* good service.

Excellent, centrally located, are the *Montecarlo* (3), and the *Suizo* (4). Best budget bet is the *Macia* (4), clean, but no restaurant.

A good, cheap pension is *Royal,* San Matias 18, highly recommended.

In the Sierra Nevada mountains, 34 kilometers (21 miles) out of Granada, is the *Sol y Nieve* (2), with all conceivable facilities for winter and summer sports. Also the *Olympia Sport* (1), with nightclub, pool, restaurant, etc.

Restaurants: *Los Mariscos* (E), Escudo Carmen 25, excellent seafood. *Torres Bermejas* (E), good international and Spanish fare. *Sevilla* (M), Oficios 14, fine food, but in cramped area. *Los Manueles* (M), Zaragoza 4, okay food. *Alcaicería* (M), Oficios 8, touristy, but lots of charm and atmosphere.

JAEN. Hotels: *Zauen* (2); *Rey Fernando* (3).

The Costa Del Sol

One of Europe's newer resort areas, the Costa Del Sol stretches along 106 miles of coast between Motril and Estepona. This is a coastal region well worth exploring and with a number of uncrowded beaches despite its growing popularity. The chief centers include Almuñecar, a fishing village since Phoenician times 3,000 years ago; Nerja, with its fantastic lookout known as the Balcony of Europe high above the sea, and equally fantastic Neolithic caves discovered in 1959; Málaga, a thriving city of 300,000 inhabitants, famous for its grapes, its cathedral, and a winter climate equalled in hours of sunshine only by Sicily.

Málaga and West

Málaga is the unquestioned capital of the Spanish Riviera, rivaling San Sebastián and Palma de Majorca as one of the great tourist towns of Spain. Eight miles west of Málaga is Torremolinos, the magnet for a heterogeneous assortment of bohemians, jetsetters, charterflight groups and vacationing sunseekers from all over Europe and America. Its streets are lined with a seemingly endless array of restaurants, cafés and boutiques. The construction of gigantic high-rise buildings has long since transformed what was once a poor fishing village into a concrete metropolis. Its five-mile-long beach is one of the Mediterranean's finest. Continuing west, you come to Fuengirola, Marbella, the poshest of the Costa del Sol's resorts, with an excellent beach, Estepona, delightfully "untouristy", and finally San Roque, a romantic-looking town built by the Spaniards when the British captured Gibraltar in 1704 and devoted until recently to the pursuit of smuggling.

From San Roque, it is only eight miles along a road winding through eucalyptus trees to the busy town of Algeciras. From this port and rail terminus, connected to Madrid by a crack, ultramodern boat train, there is daily ferry service to Tangier in North Africa. The drive from Algeciras to historic Cadiz by way of Tarifa takes you 75 miles along one of the most beautiful stretches of road in the world with views of the straits of Gibraltar, the coast of Africa and the Atlas Mountains of that dark continent looming black against the sky.

Cadiz, Sherry Country and Ronda

Cadiz, the brawling southern port destroyed by Drake in revenge for its contribution to the "Invincible Armada", is African in appearance, with palm trees, white houses, cupolas and street stalls piled with oranges. North of here are the orderly vineyards that signal your approach to a famous little town, Jerez de la Frontera, home of one of the world's great wines. Visit the *bodegas* of Gonzalez Byass or Pedro Domecq for a taste of some of the rarer vintages of sherry and for a look at the casks signed by royalty, bullfighters, writers, musicians and other distinguished admirers of this heady wine.

From Jerez to Seville is only 60 miles by a good highway, but if you are driving, don't mind a bumpy road, and haven't imbibed too much of that golden *Jerez,* we recommend the inland road cutting from Jerez to Málaga, the rough route leading through Ronda. One of the oldest towns in Spain, Ronda is perched above a rocky cleft, 1,000 feet deep, spanned by a Roman bridge. Practically untouched since the 18th century, this romantic kingdom of mountaineers and smugglers has long exerted a magnetic attraction for artists, Goya and Hemingway among them.

PRACTICAL INFORMATION FOR THE COSTA DEL SOL AND SOUTHWESTERN SPAIN

There are *paradores* at Nerja, Málaga, and off the Málaga-Torremolinos road.

ALGECIRAS. *Reina Cristina,* an outstanding, justly famous hotel, lovely garden and a terrace with a view of Gibraltar; *Meliá Guadacorte,* air-conditioned, pool, tennis; both (1). *Alarde* (2), modern, clean, impersonal, in town center. *Colonia Solimar,* with bungalows and villas among pines. *Termino* (3).

ALMERIA. Best in town is the *Gran* (1), modern, terraces, pool, used by film people. But 12 kilometers out of town is the swank *Aguadulce* (1), with all facilities. In town, the *Costasol, Indalico,* both (2), and *Embajador* (3).

Costacabana, all amenities, near the airport; *Satelit Park,* on the Málaga road, with apartments, pool, tennis, restaurants, etc. The new *Torreluz II,* Plaza Flores and the recently opened *Playasol* on Roquetas de Mar, are all (2). On Dalias, *Golf Hotel Almerimar* (1), new.

ALMUÑÉCAR. The suggestively named *Sexi* (4) has a private beach, a charming setting, and excellent service. The *Caribe* and *Portamar* (2) are newer.

ANTEQUERA. Best is *La Vega* (2), cozy, comfortable, in parador-like setting. Good stop-off between Cordoba and Málaga, on main road. Also *Albergue* (4).

BENALMÁDENA, near Torremolinos. *Triton,* with two pools, (L). *Alay,* recommended, also with two pools, and *Park* (1). *Delfin* and *Siroco,* with pool, are (2).

CADIZ. In town center, *Francia y Paris* (3); on the beach, *Playa Victoria* (2), but run-down and impersonal. *Atlántico* (3), excellent old hotel.

Andalucia Aparthotel (1) at Zahara de los Atunes. *Pensión Bahía,* good budget bet, superb views.

ESTEPONA. *Atalaya Park* is the leader. *Santa Marta* 31 rooms, most attractive. Newest is the *Golf El Paraiso,* disco, tennis, private beach, revolving restaurant, 18-hole golf course.

FUENGIROLA. The *Mare Nostrum* has attractive curved layout enabling each room to get the sun, private beach, air-conditioned, two pools, tennis, bowls, a self-contained complex with nightclub, shops, car hire; *Las Pirámides,* recent, 160 rooms; both (1). *Florida, Torreblanca* (2).

MÁLAGA. *Málaga Palacio* (L), all amenities. *Luz Málaga* (1), pool, tropical gardens, *Casa Curro,* in city center, modern and comfortable; *Las Vegas,* in residential area, has panoramic dining room. Both (2).

Others are: *Lis* (3), rooms only; *California; Olletas; Niza* (4).

MARBELLA. In the (L) category are: *Loews Marbella Beach, Loews Marbella Golf, Meliá Don Pepe* and *Los Monteros,* the latter being one of the best on the coast. The *Hotel Marbella Hilton,* now called *Hotel Don Carlos.* Two new additions are the *Hotel Atalaya Park* (L), golf and Country Club and the *Marbella Inn,* part of the *Holiday Inn* chain.

Hacienda de la Carolina, garden, pool; *Marbella Club Hotel,* operated by Prince Max von Hohenlohe-Langenberg, very select, lovely gardens, pool; *Las Chapas,* features a ring for teaching bullfighting with hornless calves; all are (1).

The *Rancho Wellington,* with 12 bungalows for 4-6 persons, pool; *Estrella del Mar,* apartment accommodations; *Skol,* on beach, apartments, and *Guadalpin,* bungalow-style, at km. 186 between Málaga and Marbella, are all (2).

At the Andalucia Nueva complex, *Aloha Marbella,* apartments and small *Golf Hotel Nueva Andalucia,* are both (L). *Andalucia Tower* (2).

The *Don Miguel* is within walking distance of town.

Golf Hotel Guadalmina (1), at San Pedro de Alcántara, 6 miles from Marbella, has golf course. *Motel Artola* (2) is 3 miles east.

Near Marbella, the *Andalucia Plaza* (1), is a resort complex with private beach, two 18-hole golf courses and riding stable. *Cortijo Blanco* (2).

NERJA. *Balcon de Europa* (3), own beach.

SAN ROQUE. *Rio Grande* (3). *Motel San Roque* (4) at km. 124.

TORREMOLINOS. All (L) with top facilities are: *Pez Espada; Castillo de Santa Clara* (L), open last August; *Apartotel Meliá Torremar,* apartments and hotel; *Nautilus; Al-Andalus.* The *Holiday Inn* is 3 kilometers from airport, with pool, golf, tennis; *Duquesa de España,* gardens, pool, underwater club, restaurant, etc.; *Aloha Puerto,* suites, pool, tennis, nightclub; *Meliá Costa del Sol;* all are (1).

Las Palomas and *Sidi-Sol* are apartments; *El Pinar,* villas in landscaped grounds; *Los Nidos; Amaragua; Alta Vista,* central; all are (2).

Lloyd's, English-owned, delightful but rather far from beach; *El Panorama,* recent; *Las Mercedes* (at Cerril del Tajo); *El Motel* (at Montemar). All (3).

Hungria and *Auto Hotel,* both (4), are on *Carretera de Cadiz.*

SWEDEN

Larger than California, nearly twice the size of the British Isles, Sweden is the biggest and richest of the Scandinavian nations. Its 173,000 square miles stretch from the sunny, fertile plains of the south to the frozen tundra of the Arctic Circle. It is a land of stunning contrasts. From the cobbled streets of Stockholm's old town you can look across the water to modern apartments equipped with individual yacht basins; not far from the medieval Riddarholm's Church where Sweden's kings are buried, there is a modern hospital with a heliport on its roof. And in the far north, where Lapps still herd their reindeer as they have done for a thousand years, the iron ore city of Lulea has a civic center whose sidewalks are centrally heated.

The main sights to see are: the beautiful capital Stockholm; the medieval cities of Visby, Uppsala and Sigtuna; the chateau country of Scania; folkloric Dalarna province; the resort town Bastad; Gripsholm and Skokloster castles near Stockholm. If you have more time, "midnight sun" excursions to the far north, and along the Gota Canal which runs the breadth of the country are also worthwhile.

There are 8,000,000 Swedes, descendants of those roving Vikings who conquered Russia in the ninth century, penetrated as far south as Constantinople, saved the Protestant Reformation with their intervention in the Thirty Years' War, and had all Europe in turmoil with the military exploits of their brilliant young warrior king, Charles XII, in the 18th century. After that the Swedes had had enough and for the last century and a half have pursued a policy of neutrality. Then, Sweden was struggling with crop failures and near famine that sent more than a million

Swedes to the United States where they settled predominantly in Minnesota. Now, Sweden ranks as a leading industrial country. Politically, it is a parliamentary monarchy, following a middle course between capitalism and socialism.

Food and Drink

The Swedish *smörgasbord,* someone once said, is often abused in spelling, pronunciation, and preparation. Smörgasbord is a large table which is usually placed in the middle of the dining room and is easily accessible to all guests. On it are placed a large variety of hors d'oeuvre type dishes and you help yourself—often several times—and take what you like of them. Traditionally, the order goes something like this: pickled herring (possibly more than one kind) with a boiled potato; a couple more fish courses, probably cold smoked salmon, fried Baltic Sea herring, and sardines in oil; the meats, liver paste, boiled ham, sliced beef, not uncommonly smoked reindeer; a salad, fruit and or vegetable; and finally the cheeses. Order *snaps* (the collective name for *aquavit* or *brannvin* liquors) with the meal, drink it neat and chase it with water or beer.

Other national dishes are: crayfish, pea soup and pork followed by pancakes, and goose.

Liquor is served in two, four and six centiliter quantities; best specify the size you want or you may be served a stiff 6 cl. drink with an equally stiff check. Before noon (1 P.M. on Sundays) it's soft drinks only unless you buy your own bottle at one of the state-owned liquor shops which open at 9 A.M. At midnight everything is usually put away except wine and beer.

Shopping

Look for excellent Swedish design in crystal, silver, stainless steel, ceramics, candles, textiles and furniture, to mention only a few items to which the sober and elegant Swedish sense of taste has been applied. Handicraft items are always a good buy, but there are also furs, interesting modern art, superb sporting goods, and accessories for the home, all designed with that flair and feeling for the materials used which is the Swedish hallmark.

PRACTICAL INFORMATION FOR SWEDEN

WHAT WILL IT COST. Be prepared for the fact that Sweden ranks as one of the world's most expensive countries, but then the standard of living is comparably high too. *Hotel rates:* single room with running hot and cold water without bath or shower 55–80 kr., single room with bath or shower 60–100 kr., single room in hotel of high standard throughout from 105 kr. upwards; doubles cost from 160–260 kr. Full board in a holiday resort might come to 125 kr. in a better hotel and to about 100 kr. in a moderate place. There is no official hotel rating in Sweden yet. For the benefit of the reader they are rated here first-class superior (1), first-class reasonable (2), moderate (3), and inexpensive (4).

Take advantage of *hotel checks,* which are valid May-September at 370 hotels. The Swedish Quality Hotel check costs approximately 100 kr. and the Swedish Budgetprice Hotel check 60 kr. The prices cover bed and breakfast in double rooms. Contact the Swedish National Tourist Office in New York or London for information about where these checks can be bought.

Restaurants are rated expensive (E) from 50 kr. up; moderate (M) 25-50 kr; and inexpensive (I) around 18 kr. In self-service cafeterias you can get a meal for 13–18 kr.

CAPITAL. Stockholm.

LANGUAGE. Swedish. Many Swedes speak English well.

CLIMATE. The four seasons, with bitter winters and cool summers; an average June day in Stockholm has 19 hours of daylight. Beyond the Arctic Circle the Midnight Sun reigns: from mid-May to mid-July the sun never sets.

Average maximum daily temperatures in Fahrenheit and centigrade:

Stock-holm	Jan.	Feb.	Mar.	Apr.	May	June	July	Aug.	Sept.	Oct.	Nov.	Dec.
F°	30	30	37	46	57	66	72	68	59	48	41	36
C°	-1	-1	3	8	14	19	22	20	15	9	5	2

 SPECIAL EVENTS. *February:* Great Lapp Winter Fair in Jokkmokk; *March:* Vasa Ski Race, 55 miles cross-country Sälen to Mora; *April* 30: Walpurgis Night Festival all over Sweden; *June:* Ballet Festival at the Royal Opera in Stockholm; international tennis matches at Bastad; *July:* Visby Festival in medieval cathedral ruin; Swedish Derby at Jägersro, Malmö; *August:* Swedish-American Day in Skansen Park, Stockholm; Minnesota Day in Vaxjo southern Sweden; *December:* Nobel Festivities in Stockholm (by invitation only); St. Lucia Day (13th) celebrated throughout.

NATIONAL HOLIDAYS. January 1, 6 (Epiphany), Good Friday, Easter Monday, May 1 (Labor Day), Whit Monday, Midsummer Day (Saturday nearest to June 24), All Saints' Day, December 25 and 26.

 CLOSING TIMES. *Shops* usually open from 9 A.M.—6 P.M. Monday-Friday. On Saturdays and the day before a holiday closing time varies between 1 P.M. and 4 P.M. Department stores and many other shops in the larger cities keep open until 8 P.M. one evening in the week (usually Monday or Friday) but *not* in June–July. *Banks* are open from 9:30 A.M.–3 P.M. Monday, Friday. Many banks also open in the evening between 4:30 P.M. to 6 P.M. In many larger cities the banks are open for business continually from 9:30 A.M.–6 P.M.

 SPORTS. *Golf.* Sweden has more golf courses than any other European country; visitors are welcome; green fees about 15–25 kr.

Fishing. Great along the Baltic and West coasts, for salmon in Mörrum and Ätran rivers in southern Sweden. Licenses cost about 15 kr. per day, 25–35 kr. per week, obtainable from tourist offices, sport shops and resort hotels.

There is *moose hunting* in September–October; about 50 kr. for license and insurance.

Sailing on vast Vänern, Vättern and Mälaren inland lakes and in the archipelagos outside Stockholm and Gothenburg. Annual big regattas in Sandham (Stockholm), beginning July and beginning August and at Marstrand (West coast) mid-July.

Skiing all over central and northern Sweden from January through April. Slalom slopes and skilifts are plentiful, also marked trails for cross-country skiing.

Sweden is working very hard to become the host country for the Olympic Winter Games 1984.

MONEY. The Swedish *krona* (plural *kronor*) is divided into 100 *öre*. There are banknotes for 5, 10, 50, 100, 1,000 and 10,000 kronor. The current rate of exchange is about 4.70 kr. to the US dollar, 8 to the pound sterling, but check before changing.

TIPPING. Hotel prices include a 15% service charge. Bigger hotels also charge extra for the porter service, in which case porters do not have to be tipped. Inquire whether the porter service will be charged or not when you arrive at the hotel. A porter should be paid 3 kr. per bag. The service charge in restaurants is 12½%, automatically added to the bill. Late at night the service charge is higher. Hatcheck girls and washroom attendants get 2 or 3 kr. Cab drivers are always tipped at least 10% of the fare on the meter; 10 to 15% is paid in barber shops and beauty salons.

HOW TO REACH SWEDEN. By air to Stockholm from New York by *SAS (Scandinavian Airline)* direct. All flights have connections with Gothenburg, Malmö and the entire Swedish domestic network by air. Daily flights from London to Stockholm, Gothenburg and Malmö. **By sea** from Britain by *United Steamship Co.* (DFDS) Harwich-Stockholm, and by *Torline* from Immingham and Felixstowe to Gothenburg. From the U.S. there are now only passenger-carrying freighter sailings, no more liners. For details contact your travel agent.

CUSTOMS. Visitors who reside outside Europe may bring in 400 American cigarettes, two bottles of spirits or wine containing a maximum of one liter each. Other travelers may bring in 200 cigarettes, 1 bottle of spirits and 1 bottle of wine. All are allowed to bring into and take out of Sweden a maximum of 6,000 Swedish kronor in banknotes. 1,000 kronor banknotes cannot be imported. Foreign currency unlimited.

MAIL. Ordinary, 1.70 kr. (weight up to 20 grams) airmail within Europe, no extra charge. Airmail to US 2.20 kr. up to 10 grams; air letters below 5 grams cost 1.70 kr. Airmail postcards to US and Europe are 1.30 kr.

ELECTRICITY. 220 volts A.C. All Swedish plugs are made to a single (safety) standard, and American and British plugs cannot be used.

DRINKING WATER. Drinking water is excellent and safe everywhere.

TRAVEL IN SWEDEN. By air: SAS and LIN (Swedish Domestic Airlines) operate several daily flights linking all larger cities, the Arctic region (Kiruna) and the lake district with the capital. Stockholm has two airports: *Arlanda,* 25 miles north of the city for international and SAS domestic flights; and *Bromma,* 6 miles west for LIN domestic flights. Buses leave from Vasagatan 6-14 next to the Sheraton Hotel (fares 15 kr. and 8 kr. respectively).

By boat: In summer services ply from Stockholm and Gothenburg to the islands of the archipelagos; to the islands of Gotland and Öland (also inter-island services) and to Ven in Öresund. There are cruises on the famous Göta Canal, on the Dalslands and Kinda Canals, and on several inland waterways.

By car. Sweden drives on the right. Speed limits are: 50 km/hr (30 mph) in built-up areas, 110 km/hr (70 mph) on motorways and 90 km/hr (56 mph) on all other roads except extremely good ones where the speed limit is 110 km/hr (70 mph). Third party insurance is compulsory.

Gasoline (bensin) varies in price from one part of Sweden to another; it is roughly about 7 kr. per US gallon.

Try to park your car in the parking lots or special places in the streets where there are meters. Wrongly parked cars are towed away in the larger cities. To get your car, you have to pay a penalty of about $150.

Never drive after drinking. This is absolutely forbidden, and the penalties are severe.

Car hire. *Avis,* Sveavägen 61; *Hertz,* Birger Jarlsgatan 43; *Intercar,* Surbrunns-gatan 49; *Scandinavian Car Rental,* Mäster Samuelsgatan 1, all in Stockholm and at the airport. *Esso* rents cars at 70 service stations in 35 cities.

By train. Daily express between Stockholm-Malmö and v.v. (383 miles, 6 hours), and between Stockholm-Gothenburg and v.v. (282 miles, 4 hours 10 minutes). Stockholm-Lulea-Riksgränsen (933 miles) takes 25 hours. The rolling stock on all main lines was replaced during the sixties and a high standard of comfort and cleanliness is to be found throughout; second class is comparable to first in many other countries. Over about 62 miles (100 km) a return ticket is cheaper than two single tickets. Children aged 6 but under 12 travel half price. Tickets are valid for two months. There are a number of special reduced fares, among them family tickets, weekend fares, pensioners' tickets, party tickets.

By bus. *The Swedish State Railways* (SJ) operate a network of buses all over Sweden. In addition to this regular traffic, there is a summer service of express coaches over longer distances. The *Dala-bus* runs daily Gothenburg-Karlstad-Falun-Rättvik-Mora and v.v., 12 hours.

GUIDES. Apply to the local tourist information office. In Stockholm: Tourist Center, Sweden House, Hamngatan 27, 160 kr. basic charge for less than 2-½ hours and 70 kr. per additional hour.

CAMPING. About 530 camping sites approved by the *Swedish Tourist Board.* There are about 164 3-star sites (highest standard). Some sites also have cottages for over-night accommodation (2-4 beds) equipped with heating and electricity. There are about 2,000 cottages of that type. Sites are generally open from June 1 to September 1. A camping card is required at most of the larger sites which can be obtained at the site for 5 kr.

SUMMER CHALET HOLIDAYS. About 15,000 chalets and similar accommo-dation available for this sort of holiday, in every part of Sweden. Chalets are usually rented out by the week. Contact *Inter-Holiday,* Lilla Kungsgatan, 211 08 Gothenburg; *Jämtland-Härjedalen Resor,* Box 74, 831 01 Östersund; RESO Byg-desemester, 105 24 Stockholm; *Swedish Touring Club,* Fack, 103 80 Stockholm 7; *Svensk Stuguthyrning,* Svartbäcksgatan 21, 753 32 Uppsala.

USEFUL ADDRESSES. *American Embassy,* Strandvä-gen 101. *British Embassy,* Skarpögatan 6. *Canadian Embassy,* Tegelbacken 4. *Swedish Tourist Board,* Sweden House, Hamngatan 27. *American Express,* Birger Jarlsga-tan 32, *Wagons Lits/Cooks,* Vasagatan 22; all in Stockholm.

In case of emergency telephone 90 000. For tourist information in English call (08) 221840.

Stockholm and Environs

Stockholm has been called one of the world's most beautiful cities and few will deny that it is a handsome and civilized capital with a natural setting. Founded as a fortress on a little island in Lake Mälar, over the centuries the town spread to nearby islands, and then to the mainland. Today, the "Venice of the North" delights the visitor with its vistas over water, its parks, tree-lined squares and boulevards. Nature and city planning have combined to create a pleasing metropolis, and it is hard to realize as you gaze out over the water from a table on the Strömparterren terrace that you are in the heart of a bustling metropolis, a town that has grown from less than 100,000 inhabitants to nearly a million in the space of a century.

Since World War II increasing urbanization and traffic demands have caused extensive replanning and rebuilding. First came the two huge satellite city centers of Vällingby to the west and Farsta to the south, connected by a subway (T-banan). Next came the wholesale rebuilding of a vast area in the heart of the city (from the Hötorget market place to the "Sergels Torg") constituting an enormous yet compact trade and commerce center. The newest shopping area is the Arcade Gallerian near NK and the Sweden House.

June, July and August are the best months to visit here. Then you have the best weather and the greatest variety of sightseeing facilities. Bring reasonably warm clothing along. What most people would call a mild summer day is apt to be announced in the Stockholm papers as a heat wave. But don't be afraid to come as early as May, or as late as September or October.

For purposes of exploration, the city's island geography divides Stockholm into neat parcels. First, there's the city between the bridges, or the Old Town, site of the Royal Palace and its adjoining islands, Riddarholmen (Isle of Knights) and Helgeandsholmen (Island of the Holy Spirit). This is essentially the heart of the capital and the nation. Södermalm is the southern section, across the bridge leading from the Old Town. Norrmalm, north of the Old Town, is the business and financial district of Stockholm. Kungsholmen, a large island west of Norrmalm, is the site of the famous Town Hall and offices of the municipal government, Östermalm, east of Norrmalm, is mostly residential, full of embassies and consulates. Finally there is Djurgarden, a huge island, projecting east toward the Baltic in the channels between Östermalm and Södermalm, with the marvelous park of Skansen, the open-air museum, the Royal Flagship *Wasa* and her museum, the amusement parks and summer restaurants.

The Royal Palace is huge, and like so many royal properties in the democratic monarchies of Scandinavia, easy of public access; you can stroll into the inner courtyard any time during the day. Interior parts which may be visited are the Hall of State, containing the king's silver throne; the Chapel Royal with its historic and artistic treasures, the Festival and Bernadotte suites, and Gustav III's collection of classical sculpture, the palace museum and the Treasury with the crown jewels. The changing of the guard takes place Wednesdays and Saturdays at noon and on Sundays at 1 P.M. (during July and August every day; on weekdays at noon and on Sundays at 1 P.M.).

Diagonally across from the south side of the palace is the Stockholm Cathedral, the national church of Sweden, dating from 1250. Also known as The Great Church, its chief treasure is a 15th-century statue of St. George and the Dragon, set up to commemorate a Swedish victory over the Danes in 1471. When you come out of the Great Church, turn right and walk down the Storkyrkobrinken, following a medieval route as do most of the lanes in the Old Town. Passing between centuries-old buildings you emerge in a little square called the Riddarhustorget. Here is the Riddarhuset, House of the Nobility, containing the crests of Swedish noble families. The bridge across the canal and railroad tracks will lead you to the famous Riddarholm Church, once part of a Franciscan monastery, the weathered red brick and open spire of which are symbolic of Sweden's ancient glory. Here lie Gustavus Adolphus, hero of the Thirty Years' War, and the brilliant, dashing Carolus Rex whose victories over the Russians and Continental Armies stunned the world until he fell in Norway in 1718. The last king to be buried in this ancient church, was Gustav V in 1950.

Before leaving the Old Town, visit Stortorget, the oldest square in Stockholm with its tall old houses and the Stock Exchange, containing on its second floor the headquarters of the Swedish Academy which awards the Nobel Prize for literature. And don't miss the Marten Trotzigs Gränd, a tiny lane no more than three feet wide, and half of it a staircase. It connects the Prästgatan with Västerlanggatan, the latter something of a shopping street for over 200 years and still retaining its bazaar atmosphere.

By all means go to Skansen, Stockholm's unique outdoor playground. To say that it has a museum, a zoo, a fascinating lookout tower is merely to give a dull enumeration of its facilities. To say that it is the scene of concerts, popular celebrations and folk dancing is merely to suggest its gaiety. It's full of open air dance floors, coffee shops and workshops (handicrafts and various peasant skills are demonstrated in the old buildings). It is the perfect place to get a real idea of the culture and traditions of Sweden. Whole estates, churches and farm houses have been moved here bodily from all over Sweden. You can even get married in the 18th-century church. When still at Djurgarden, you should not miss the *Wasa*. This royal flagship sunk on her maiden voyage in 1628, was recovered from the Stockholm harbor and painstakingly preserved by a complex humidifying method. It is housed in a special museum.

Still another highlight is the Stockholm Town Hall, which has been called "the most beautiful building of this century in Europe". Built by Ragnar Östberg, dedicated in 1923, it has become a symbol of modern, progressive Stockholm. You should visit the Golden Hall with the ancient technique of mosaic work used to cover the high walls with boldly-designed modern pictures; the Blue Hall, the Prince's Gallery with its large murals by Prince Eugen; the Terrace, a formal garden which seems to be floating on the water of Lake Mälar and which affords beautiful views of the Old Town and a chance to study the loggia and massive architecture of the Town Hall itself, and finally the Tower, partly accessible by elevator and providing a splendid view of Stockholm and the archipelago. You will get a still better view of Stockholm and surroundings from the outlook terraces of the Kaknäs Television Tower.

If you're interested in more modern architecture and the model housing developments with which Stockholm has earned its reputation for city planning, we recommend the following areas, apart from the new city center of Nedre Norrmalm, which you can hardly miss: Danviksklippan, skyscraper apartments overlooking the city from the south; the "star-type" apartment houses at Torsvikplatan, by subway, change to bus at end of line (Ropsten); for suburban planning, Vällingby, Farsta Skärholmen and Kista.

Short Excursions from Stockholm

Lidingö, an island suburb of Stockholm, was the permanent home of famed Swedish sculptor Carl Milles, whose house, full of his own work and outstanding pieces which he collected, is now a museum. Sited on a bluff, overlooking the water, a trip out here on a fine day is a wonderful experience. Take the subway to Ropsten, whence buses (No. 3) leave for the Milles house (Millesgarden) twice an hour.

Drottningholm Palace (50 minutes by steamer from the Town Hall quay; 20 minutes by blue bus 2 or 3 from subway station, Brommaplan) is one of the most charming royal residences in Europe. Inspired by Versailles, it is open to the public when the royal family is not in residence. The Court Theater, with its 18th-century scenery intact, is unique. Performances are given two to four times a week, late May until mid-September. The repertoire consists almost entirely of 18th-century operas and ballets, in other words, of works written for that kind of stage. There are beautiful gardens, as well as the charming little China Pavilion.

Saltsjöbaden (literally, Salt Sea Baths) is the principal winter and summer resort of the archipelago, 18 minutes by train from Stockholm (Slussen). In summer this is a rendezvous for yachtsmen and motorboat buffs. Among other amenities is an excellent harbor, 9-hole golf course, tennis courts, riding stables, and nude swimming in summer (but not mixed; a wooden wall separates the sexes). Skating, skate-sailing, ice-boating and cross-country skiing are the winter sports.

The Haga Pavilion, located in the vast park surrounding the Haga Palace (at present uninhabited), is just a few minutes by bus no. 515 from Norra Bantorget. It is an exquisitely furnished miniature 18th-century summer palace from the time of Gustav III.

Another interesting excursion, 35 minutes by bus from Slussen, is Gustavsberg, where the noted ceramics works may be visited by groups on arrangement.

Longer Excursions from Stockholm

The Swedes call the great archipelago east of their capital, Skärgarden or Garden of Skerres. There are thousands of these islands, forming a unique summer playground for the Swedes who have summer cottages scattered all over the region or rent rooms from the inhabitants. It's easy to visit this watery paradise. If you want to go first class, call the Stockholm Tourist Association and ask about chartering a motor cruiser with pilot. Otherwise, you can use the comprehensive network of scheduled passenger steamer services. There are no resorts, only a few villages, among them Sandhamn (yachting center, sandy beaches, hotel and restaurants), three hours from Stockholm by boat from Grand Hotel quay, and Vaxholm (small town with fortress, tennis courts, hotel, restaurants), one hour from Stockholm.

West of Stockholm is the valley of Lake Mälar, the cradle of Swedish history. The following excursions can be completed in a day or less from Stockholm: Uppsala, ancient pagan and Christian capital of Sweden and site of Scandinavia's oldest university (celebrated its 500th anniversary in 1977), and largest cathedral. Visit the 16th century castle where Queen Christina abdicated; Hammarby House, and some pagan burial mounds, the latter two both some miles from town.

Sigtuna is an idyllic little town with an 11th-century fortified church ruin and other monuments of Sweden's history.

Gripsholm, a 16th-century castle three and a half hours by steamer through the lovely scenery of Lake Mälar, has the largest collection of historical portraits in the world. Don't miss the little theater in the castle, better in some ways than the more famous one at Drottningholm.

Skokloster is another impressive castle, about 45 miles by road from Stockholm; built in the 17th century it still has its original rich furnishings. There is also a veteran car museum.

PRACTICAL INFORMATION FOR STOCKHOLM

HOTELS. It's recommended to reserve rooms in advance during the summer months. If you arrive without a reservation, consult the Hotellcentralen in the underground level of the Central Station. This room booking service is open in summer, weekdays from 8 A.M. to 11:30 P.M., (Sundays from 5 P.M.); shorter opening times in winter. A charge is made for each room reserved. There are several chain hotels and restaurants such as SARA, RESO and ICA offering a dependable, generally moderate standard.

The *Swedish Touring Club* operates some 200 hostels and touring lodges throughout the country, some located in scenic spots or old, interesting houses. Open to all, charges are about 10 kr. per person per night. For further information contact: Swedish Touring Club, Birgir Jarlsgatan 18, Stockholm 7.

First Class Superior

AMARANTEN, Kungsholmsgatan 31; 380 rooms with bath or shower. Restaurants, cocktail lounge, conference rooms. Sauna, sunbathing terrace and exercise facilities. Bank and shops on the ground floor. Subway station in hotel. Garage. *(SARA.)*

ANGLAIS, Humlegardsgatan 23 (Stureplan); 165 rooms with bath. Restaurant, garage.

DIPLOMAT, Strandvägen 7C; 107 rooms with bath. Central, wonderful view of harbor.

GRAND, S. Blasieholmshamn 8; 348 rooms with bath or shower. Central. Terrace restaurants overlook the water.

GRAND HOTEL SALTSJÖBADEN, a castle-like place on the waterfront in the surburban resort of Saltsjöbaden; 101 rooms with bath. Restaurants.

STAR HOTEL, near St. Eriks Fair, 105 rooms with large double beds; sauna, pool.

PARK, Karlavägen 43; 215 rooms with bath. Solarium and sauna. Restaurant.

REISEN, Skeppsbron 12-14; 128 rooms with bath. The hotel is built inside the setting of three 17th-century houses, facing the sea in center of Stockholm. Sauna and pool in basement. *(SARA.)*

SHERATON—STOCKHOLM, Tegelbacken 6; 476 rooms with bath. Fine restaurant, popular cocktail lounge, and sauna. Garage, SAS office and shops; air terminal nearby.

First Class Reasonable

BIRGER JARL, Tulegatan 8, 259 rooms with bath or shower. Coffee shop. Garage.

CARLTON, Kungsgatan 57; 141 rooms, 110 baths. Situated near the Concert Hall and shopping district. Restaurant.

CONTINENTAL, Klara Vattugränd 4; 250 rooms with bath. Convenient, opposite the central station. Main restaurant elegant, the café popular for lunch and quick meals. *(RESO.)*

MALMEN, Götgatan 49; 270 rooms with bath, on the southern heights, a few minutes from downtown by subway. Restaurant. *(RESO).*

MORNINGTON, Nybrogatan 53; 82 rooms with bath or shower. Central, quiet. Restaurant.

PALACE, St. Eriksgatan 115; 230 rooms, 175 baths; garage in the basement. Restaurant.

SJÖFARTSHOTELLET, Katarinavägen 26; 184 rooms with bath or shower. Restaurant. *(RESO).*

STOCKHOLM, Norrmalmstorg 1; 107 rooms, 50 baths. Situated on top floors of downtown office building. Only breakfast served.

STRAND, Nybrokajen 9; 95 rooms most with bath. Central. Three first class restaurants.

Moderate

Alexandra, Magnus Ladulasgatan 4; 100 rooms with bath or shower.

Bromma, Brommaplan; 196 rooms with bath. Restaurant. 15 minutes by subway from downtown shopping area. *(RESO.)*

Excelsior, Birger Jarlsgatan 35; 77 rooms, 33 baths. Central. Only breakfast served.

Flamingo, Centralvägen 20, Solna; 125 rooms, most with bath. Located 10 mins. outside Stockholm proper. Restaurant, bar, grill.

Flyghotellet, Brommaplan, near Bromma airport, 54 rooms with bath. Only breakfast served.

Frälsningsarméns Hotel City, Drottninggatan 66; 147 rooms, 18 baths. Central. Operated by the Salvation Army.

Tegnérlunden, Tegnérlunden 8; 73 rooms most with bath. Quiet. Only breakfast served.

Terminus, Vasagatan 20; 94 rooms, 40 with bath. Restaurant, cocktail bar. Near central station and air terminal.

Summer Hotels: *Jerum,* Student-backen 21; 136 rooms with shower and *Frescati,* Professorsslingan 13-15; 115 rooms with shower are open from June 1 to Sept. 1; during the rest of the year they are blocks of comfortable one-room flats for undergraduates. Restaurants, bars, lounges and reading rooms. Members of student or youth hostel organizations are charged about 23 kr. per night, 8 kr. for bed linen.

Inexpensive

Kristineberg, Hj. Söderbergs väg 10; 143 rooms, 12 public baths. 10 minutes by subway from downtown shopping area. Pleasant restaurant *Krillans Krog.* *(RESO).*

Savoy, Bryggargatan 12B; 54 rooms. Only breakfast served.

af Chapman, a unique hostel, formerly a sailing ship now moored at Skeppsholmen; open March 15–November 1. Clean, adequate and very popular so stays are limited to five nights. 20–25 kr. per night.

MOTELS

ESSO, on Highway 4 south. 274 rooms with bath or shower; sauna, gym, pool, restaurant.

GYLLENE RATTEN, 4 miles southwest. 109 rooms most with bath, cafeteria.

ESSO, Highway 18, 4 miles north. 154 rooms with bath or shower, sauna, pool, two restaurants.

OK MOTOR, at Arsta. 104 rooms, adequate facilities.

RESTAURANTS. Although atmosphere varies greatly in Stockholm restaurants, the food is fairly standardized, making the distinction one of quality. The following is a representative selection.

Expensive

AURORA, Munkbron 15, sited in a beautiful 300-year-old building in the Old Town with pleasant small rooms in cellar vaults. Excellent food. Closed Sunday *(SARA.)*

BERNS SALONGER, Näckströmsgatan 8. Carries on its 100-year-old tradition with the orginal décor; enormous. Dancing nightly. International floorshow. Casino. Closed June–August.

DJURGARDSBRUNNS WÄRDSHUS, few minutes from downtown by taxi or bus. A 17th-cent. inn overlooking a meadow and canal.

FEM SMA HUS, Nygränd 10; charming spot located in the Old Town. Very good food. Its name means "five small houses". (ICA)

OPERAKÄLLAREN, famous restaurant in the opera house, overlooking harbor and the palace; under same management as the Riche, thus excellent. Main dining room has a summer terrace, the *Opera Grill* retains its cozy atmosphere and the *Bakfickan* snack bar is recommended for quick meals.

RICHE and *Teatergrillen,* Birger Jarlsgatan 4. The Riche is a plush institution with cocktail lounge, good food, good drinks, and music. The Teatergrillen, or Theater Grill, is more intimate. Steaks among the best in town. The former is open all year, but the latter closes July.

STALLMÄSTAREGARDEN, Norrtull near Haga, old inn on outskirts with historical traditions, modern management. Coffee in the court, a lovely garden, after a good meal of a summer evening can be a delightful experience. Same management as Riche, thus good food, including *smörgasbord.* Music, dancing.

STRANDS TERASS (open May–Sept.) and **Maritim,** both in Strand Hotel. The first has an excellent view, the second has good food and nice setting.

Moderate

Brända Tomten, Stureplan 13, has delightful dining rooms with antique furnishings. *Bäckahästen,* Hamngatan 2, has modern décor. Both have open air summer service and are popular for good food at reasonable prices. Wines and beer.

Cattelin, Storkyrkobrinken 9, one of the best restaurants in the Old Town.

Cosmopolite in Sweden House, Hamngatan 27. Good food. During summer months a small smorgasbord is served.

Den Gyldene Freden, Österlanggatan 51. Medieval cellars, historic traditions, atmosphere, lute singers some evenings.

Gondolen, Slussen. Suspended high in the air at the top of the Katarina elevator. Magnificent view.

Konstnärshuset, Smalandsgatan 7. Good food and drinks in intimate surroundings in the heart of town. Murals by Swedish painters. Service in the grill is better than average.

Östermalmskällaren, Storgatan 3, with modern décor, quiet atmosphere. *(SARA).*

Solliden, Skansen. On the heights of Stockholm's favorite pleasure grounds, ten minutes from the center of town, this modern establishment overlooks city and harbor. Vast enough for 600 guests. The *smörgasbord* is outstanding. *(SARA).*

Stortorgskällaren, Stortorget 7, in a medieval cellar.

Sturehov, Stureplan 2. An unpretentious restaurant, comparatively large, which makes good fish its business. Located in the heart of town.

Victoria, friendly place conveniently open till 3 A.M.

ENTERTAINMENT. The *Royal Opera* and the *Stockholm Concert Hall* have their season from September to mid-June; tickets range from 10–40 kr. The theater at *Drottningholm Palace* has several performances a week, end-May to mid-Sept.; buses run from the Grand Hotel and from Vasagatan opposite the Central Station 45 mins. before the performance. Tickets from 25–50 kr.

NIGHTLIFE. For addresses, opening times, etc. check with *This Week in Stockholm* published by the Tourist Association. Most places are open from 9 P.M. to 3 A.M. and charge an entrance fee of about 10 kr. if there is a floorshow. Restaurant-nightclubs: *Sheraton* heads the list with its popular casino; *Berns, Ambassadeur, Bolaget,* and *Nya Bacchi* among many others. Discos: *Bobbadillo, Gardsmygen* and *Muggen* (with ballad singing). There is open-air dancing in summer at the Skansen and Gröna Lund amusement parks.

MUSEUMS. *Museum of Modern Art,* Skeppsholmen Isle, state collection of 20th-century paintings and sculpture; daily 12–10 P.M. *Wasavarvet,* Djurgarden, for the 17th-century ship incredibly preserved; daily 10–8 P.M. *Millesgarden,* Lidingo, former home of sculptor Carl Milles; open daily 11–5 P.M. *Skansen,* Djurgarden, collection of authentic Swedish farms, villages, portraying lifestyle. Small admission fees.

TOURS. Sightseeing tours by bus, starting from Karl XII's torg (near the Grand Hotel), and from Gustav Adolfs torg (in front of the Opera House). Sightseeing tours by boat: departures from Strömkajen (in front of Grand Hotel), Stadshusbron (below the City Hall), Nybroviken (near the Dramatic Theater), and Munkbron (Old Town).

SHOPPING. Very expensive but you can be sure of quality and workmanship. Visit the *Konsthantverkarnas* exhibition rooms at Mäster Samuelsgatan 2-8 where a great number of handcraft items (enamel work, textiles, ceramics, woodwork, etc.) are displayed.

Furs. Swedish furs are of the highest quality; alas, so are the prices: *Lindners,* Birger Jarlsgatan 18: *Rune Landert,* Nybrogatan 29; *Ivan Petersson AB,* Birger Jarlsgatan 6; *Wasa Päls,* Vasagatan 11.

Glass and Ceramics. *Aveny,* Kungsgatan 47; *Nordiska Kristallmagasinet,* Kungsgatan 9; *Svenskt Glas,* Birger Jarlsgatan 8; *AB Gustavsbergs Fabriker,* Birger Jarlsgatan 16. The gift shop at Sweden House.

Handcrafts. *De Fyras Bod,* Birger Jarlsgatan 12; *Svensk Hemslöjd,* Sveavägen 44; *Klockargardens Hemslöjd,* Kungsgatan 64; *Märta Maaaas-Fjetterström AB,* Myntgatan 5; *Stockholms läns och stads hemslöjdsförening,* Drottning-18; *Svenskt Tenn,* Strandvägen 5a.

Jewelry and Silver. These are renowned for fine design. Among best shops are: *Atelier Borgila,* Sturegatan 24; *Claës Gierta,* Drottninggatan 77; *Torndahl,* Biblioteksgatan 9; *Rey Urban,* Sibyllegatan 49.

Stainless steel. *Rostfria Bodarna,* Götgatan 21, Tegelbacken 6 (Hotel Sheraton).

SPORTS. *Horseracing* at Täby Galopp track, 6 miles north of Stockholm, reachable by train from Östra Station or by bus from Brommaplan. Usually Saturday or Sunday April–October. *Trotting* at Solvalla track, 5 miles west of Stockholm, reachable by bus from Abrahamsberg subway station. Racing once or twice a week. *Fishing:* Most of the waters around Stockholm teem with fish, fishing license needed (5 kr. per day). Available at the Tourist Center, Hamngatan 27. *Golf* courses at Lidingö, Kevinge, Drottningholm, Ingarö, Saltsjöbaden, and Hammarby, all 18 holes; Djursholm, 27 holes; green fees from 15-30 kr. Season: May-Oct. Green fees: 10-30 kr. *Swimming:* Indoor pools: Centralbadet, Drottninggatan 88; Eriksdalsbadet, Eriksdalslunden; Forsgrénska Badet, Medborgarplatsen; Sturebadet, Sturegatan 4; Aakeshovsbadet, Bergslagsvägen 60, Bromma.

Gothenburg

Gothenburg, first port and second city of Sweden, may very well be your first port of call. It is a pleasing city with its leafy avenues, great sprawling harbor, network of canals, and combination of Dutch Renaissance and modern architecture. Its Liseberg amusement park is one of the most delightful in the world, more modern than Copenhagen's Tivoli Gardens, and a pleasant place to dine outdoors. See the magnificent City Theater and Concert House with fountain by Carl Milles; the performances in both are exceptionally good. The Stora Theater presents first-rate opera and musical comedy. A trip to the Elfsborg Fortress (1670) in the harbor is a must: there is a museum, church, and cafeteria. The city also has a supermodern airport.

Bohuslän, north from Gothenburg, is an archipelago with rocky islands, skerries and deep fjords. Among numerous resorts are popular Marstrand (1½ hours by bus from Gothenburg, hotels, restaurants, yachting center), Lysekil and Fiskebäckskil further north, and near the Norwegian border, Strömstad. They are invaded by Swedish vacationers in July, but June and August offer a splendid season and catering possibilities are easier.

The Göta Canal

If you want to enjoy a completely relaxed three-day travel experience, the Göta Canal trip from Gothenburg to Stockholm or vice versa comes highly recommended. The steamer ties up at some of the principal points of interest for brief guided tours (for a small extra cost) which you can take or leave, and you can always get off and stroll for awhile, while the boat is going through the little locks. Starting from Gothenburg, here are some of the highlights of this unique journey:

Bohus Fortress. As you steam up the majestic Göta River, you see the town of Kungälv, with medieval Bohus Fortress above it. It was built by the Norwegians in 1308 and was once one of the most important strongholds in Scandinavia.

Trollhättan Falls. These falls power one of the country's major hydroelectric stations but, although much of the power is harnessed, the water still hurtles wildly over the cliffs.

Läckö Castle. Shortly after entering Lake Vänern from the southeast, you arrive at this monument to Sweden's imperialistic 17th century. Across the bay is Kinnekulle, one of the unique "table mountains".

Vadstena. The steamer ties up almost in the shadow of the huge Vasa Castle. You have time to inspect it, as well as the medieval church and nunnery founded by St. Birgitta, mother of the Birgittine Order.

Vreta. On the days when the steamer is moving through the many sets of locks between Vadstena and Berg you can stop off to visit Vreta cloister, Sweden's first nunnery (1162).

The Baltic Coast. You come out on the island-strewn Baltic Sea south of Norrköping, and follow the coast north before turning into the Södertälje Canal. A lovely archipelago.

Lake Mälar. The Södertälje Canal carries you into Lake Mälar, which brings you, via the beautiful channel from the west, right to the heart of Stockholm. You tie up almost in the shadow of the characteristic profile of the Stockholm Town Hall. You can make the same trip in the opposite direction, from Stockholm to Gothenburg as there are two or three sailings a week in each direction from late May until the beginning of September.

PRACTICAL INFORMATION FOR GOTHENBURG

HOTELS. Advance reservations are advisable here. *Park Avenue* (1), 320 rooms with bath, three top restaurants, nightclub; best in town. *Windsor, Opalen* and *Rubinen* are all modern (2)s.

Europa, 400 rooms and *Scandinavia,* 309 rooms are good (3)s. Short on bathrooms but clean are *Kung Karl, Eggers* and *Royal,* all (4).

RESTAURANTS. Seafood is the specialty of this town which has many good eating places.

Valand (E), Vasagatan 41, has casino. *Langedrag* (E) is a charming place overlooking the yacht harbor.

Lisebergs Rondo in the Amusement Park has dancing; *White Corner,* Vasagatan 43b is a steakhouse and pub.

Fiskekrogen (I), Lilla Torget 1, is a restaurant but for other inexpensive places you'll have to try some of the self-service spots: *Baretten,* NK-Baren, and *Rubinetten.*

Dalarna Province

Four or five hours by train northwest of Stockholm, Dalarna province is one of Sweden's major tourist attractions, a favorite holiday region, rich in history, local color, folk costumes, popular art and handicrafts. You can visit an old summer farm—called *fäbod*—up in the mountain and forest region where, in olden times, the cattle were driven on the arrival of summer. Industry also has an old tradition in Dalarna. The Stora Kopparberg Company is the world's oldest business company, with charters dating from 1288. The most interesting parts of the copper mine at Falun are open to visitors. The weekend celebration of Midsummer Eve is particularly vigorous and colorful here in the Lake Siljan area. The lakeshore resorts hold miniature Viking ship races, open-air plays and many other folklore events. Best introduction to the marvelous arts and crafts of Dalarna is at Tällberg or at Rättvik, both with good rustic art museums, handicraft exhibits and tourist hotels. One of the most interesting provincial towns is Mora, with a superb collection of 40 timber buildings, some of them 600 years old, which constitute Zorn's Gammelgard, an outdoor museum. This is also the gateway to skiing country. The first Sunday in March attracts·tens of thousands of spectators to Mora to see a great cross country ski race commemorating the 55-mile trip that two Dalecarlian skiers took in 1521 to inform Gustavus Vasa that the men of Dalarna would fight for his war of liberation against the Danes.

Recommended skiing centers in northern Dalarna: Sälen and Grövelsjön. In southern Dalarna: Leksand, Rättvik and Tällberg.

Visby and the Isle of Gotland

This historic island in the Baltic with its capital, Visby, is less than an hour by air from Stockholm. It's a five-hour trip from Nynäshamn to Visby by comfortable boats, which carry cars, and you can drive or take a bus directly to the Nynäshamn pier in an hour or so from Stockholm. Or take your car on a four-hour ferry trip from Oskarshamn to Visby, or Västervik to Klinthamn. No matter how you go, you'll be glad you did. The walled city of Visby is one of the medieval jewels of Europe, full of reminders of the Golden Age of the 12th and 13th centuries when this town was commercial queen of the Baltic. You'll have a wonderful time prowling around here, climbing the 700-year-old stairways to the watchtowers and battlements, admiring its medieval merchant palaces and churches. Visby is an excursion center too. There are 92 beautiful churches on Gotland, all but one dating from the Middle Ages, innumerable prehistoric remains such as Viking "ship-burials" and prehistoric camps, well-preserved medieval farms and picturesque fishing villages. Interesting sights are also the stalactite caves at Lummelunda, the bird islands of Stora and Lilla Karlsö and the small "russ" horses, of which one species is half-wild and lives in the deep woods near Lojsta. All along Gotland's wonderful coasts you will find sandy beaches and excellent opportunities for swimming. The climate is mild, and, incidentally, the reddest roses you ever saw are still blooming in "the city of ruins and roses" in November.

Skane, the Breadbasket of Sweden

Southernmost province of Sweden, Skane is the breadbasket of the country with its fertile agricultural plains. It also has many tourist attractions and if you are in Denmark without time for an extended visit to Sweden it's a good idea to make a day excursion here by hydrofoil to Malmö, returning by boat and train, or car via Hälsingborg (Helsingborg)-Helsingör.

This is a prosperous area, and there are many chateaux and castles open to visitors. One-day excursions by bus into the "Château Country" operate daily during summer from Malmö and Hälsingborg. The north-western corner of Skane is a popular resort area with Bastad the most fashionable of the summer resorts here.

Northward from Bastad is Halmstad, capital of the province of Halland, and nearby is Tylösand, a big popular seaside resort (plenty of hotels, golf, tennis). Afterwards come Falkenberg and Varberg, with its imposing old cliff fortress; both have good beaches.

In Smaland, the neighboring province, the city of Kalmar has a twin fascination for tourists. First, there is the magnificent Kalmar Castle with a highly recommended tour, which evokes the building's romantic past. Secondly, from Kalmar there are train and bus connections to some of the finest glass works of Europe: *Orrefors, Kosta, Boda, Lindshammar,* and *Strömbergshyttan.* The region is not at all industrial looking; the plants are scattered through the wooded wilderness of Smaland in a series of isolated villages. Watching the skilled craftsmen blowing and shaping the red-hot glass is a fascinating experience. Bus tours to the glass works, where you can often buy "seconds" at a good price, operate from Växjö and Kalmar (the works usually close for three weeks in July).

PRACTICAL INFORMATION FOR THE REGIONS

DALARNA

AVESTA. *Star* (2).

FALUN. *Grand* (1) and *Esso Motor* (2).

GRANGÄRDE. *Turisthotellet* (3).

HEDEMORA. *Stadshotellet* (3).

LUDVIKA. *Star Elektra* (2).

MORA. *Siljan* and *Mora,* both (2).

RÄTTVIK. *Persborg* and *Lerdalshöjden* (2); *Tre Hästar* motel.

SÄLEN. *Högfjällshotellet* (3), open Dec.-April only.

TÄLLBERG. *Laangbersgaarden, Klockargaarden, Dalecarlia* and *Green's,* all (2).

GOTLAND

VISBY. *Visby* (2), 94 rooms, half with bath. Just north of Visby on a magnifi-cent coastal site is *Snäckgärdsbaden* (1), 92 rooms, 10 cottages, pool casino.

HALLAND

FALKENBERG. *Grand* and *Strandbaden,* both (2), some rooms with bath.

HALMSTAD. *Hallandia,* 92 rooms with bath; and *Stenwinkeln,* 70 rooms with bath, are both (2).

VARBERG. Modern *Stadshotellet* (3) has 48 rooms.

SKANE

BASTAD. *Malens Havsbad* (1), 160 rooms, pool, tennis; beautiful location by the sea. *Hemmeslövs Herrgaardspensionat* (2), 120 rooms is situated in a forest. Skanegarden (2) has 25 rooms and a lovely location.

HÄLSINGBORG. *Grand, Hogvakten* and *Mollberg,* all (2). Nearby motels *Fleninge* and *Tre Hästar.*
Restaurant: *Parapeten* (M).

MALMÖ. *Kramer* and *Savoy,* traditional (1)s; modern *Scandinavia,* 181 rooms, *Garden Hotel,* 170 rooms, and *St. Jörgen,* 304 rooms, are (2). *Esso Motor* (2), 60 rooms. At Jägersro race course just outside town is the *Motel Jägersro* (2). *Hotel Winn,* 99 rooms with shower, near central railway station ferries and airport buses.

Southwest of Malmö is the fashionable *Falsterbohus* (1), a complete resort in itself with beach, golf course, and all amenities.

Restaurants: *Kronprinsen* and *Ambassador* both (E) with dancing and floor-shows.

SIMRISHAMN. *Svea* (3).

YSTAD. *Continental du Sud* (1) on the Baltic; golf, tennis.

Värmland and the Highlands

Sweden's most celebrated region in song and legend is Värmland. Karlstad, the provincial capital, can be reached from four to six hours by train from Stockholm, Gothenburg or Oslo, also by plane from Stockholm in one hour, and by motor coach from Gothenburg in 4½ hours. From here in summer there are numerous guided bus tours that will take you through the lovely countryside around Selma Lagerlöf's home. The house, Marbacka, is now a museum, maintained as she left it at the time of her death in 1940. Just a few miles below nearby Sunne, you can wander freely through the grounds of Rottneros, a splendid example of an estate of the landed Swedish gentry. Make a stop at Jössefors Manor, near Arvika, to see a full-scale replica of the Gokstad Viking ship, visit the handcraft shops, and have coffee at the *Kaffestuga.* Open June-August.

The Swedish highlands, ranging from central Sweden up beyond the Arctic Circle for a distance of 500 miles, offer you holidays unlike any others. Jämtland is skiing country—slalom and cross country—but this region is equally recommended in summer for hiking. Trails are well-marked for both skiing and mountaineering. Many come for the fishing, with rainbow trout, grayling and char as the leading attractions. It is only a short flight from Östersund to any of the hundreds of mountain lakes where the angler can test his skill.

There are plenty of good, reasonable mountain resorts, all served by the railroad that goes west to the Norwegian border from Östersund. Östersund can also be reached by air (two hours from Stockholm), with further connection by bus or car to the different mountain resorts. Motorists reach them by following the Europe highway 75 which runs from Sundsvall, on the east coast, across middle Sweden via Östersund to Trondheim in Norway. Motorists are also urged to visit the mountain region of Härjedalen Province which lies south of Jämtland, a little off the beaten track. One of the country's most scenic roads is over the Flatruet mountain plateau (975m above sea level).

North to Lapland

If you are looking for the sensation of being out of this world, the region north of the Arctic Circle will give it to you. The sun never sets from the end of May until the middle of July in this strange, unreal world, peopled by the Laplanders in their costumes of red, blue, green and yellow, still pursuing their ancient way of life as they follow their reindeer from one grazing region to another. You can fly from Stockholm to Kiruna in 2½ hours or there's the Stockholm-Narvik express train which leaves Stockholm in the late afternoon. From Kiruna there are a number of fascinating excursions to make. An hour or so further on the main railway line north of Kiruna is Abisko, one of the most popular resorts of Lapland. An aerial ropeway, one and a half miles long, takes you up to Mount Nuolja. The very last resort before crossing into Norway is Riksgränsen; it's above the timberline, and there are ski instructors and guides. The skiing season runs to June, and it is here that you can enjoy the sensation of skiing in the light of the Midnight Sun. Near the Tarnafjallen mountain area in southern Lapland is the Vindel-Lais nature reserve, Hemavan and Tärnaby being tour centers: both have hotels, ski lifts and other amenities.

If you are short of time you could join a "Midnight Sun Adventure" tour, operated twice a week from the beginning of June through mid-July. You take the regular SAS flight Stockholm-Lulea-Kiruna, leaving Arlanda airport in the evening. You will fly over wild wooded country dotted with lakes and etched with rivers and over snow-covered peaks to Kiruna, where your stay includes a midnight supper by the light of the Midnight Sun, sightseeing tour of Kiruna City, including the Town Hall, a visit to a Lapp museum and an excursion underground to Kiruna's famous iron mines. You arrive at Stockholm again in broad daylight. You've missed a night's sleep, but it's one you'll never regret. Take an overcoat or a warm sweater; even though the sun is up all night long, you're still north of the Arctic Circle. This trip could be a fine excuse for buying one of those handknitted Bohus sweaters. And, don't forget your camera; you can take pictures at midnight here without a flash.

You can also go on the Arctic Circle Day Tour, run by SAS, flying from Stockholm to Lulea, then rented car (including fuel) to Jokkmokk, and return the same way. In Lulea you stop at the Handicraft Center and the museum, and after lunch drive to Storforsen, the biggest waterfall in Sweden. Then you head north for an hour and cross the Arctic Circle south of Jokkmokk, capital of Lapland. You then drive southwards to the Edefors Tourist Hotel for an excellent dinner (reindeer specialties): or you can continue to the Stadshotell at Lulea for dinner; before the return flight to Stockholm at 9.30 P.M. SAS will present you with a certificate showing that you've crossed the Arctic Circle, on either of the above trips.

PRACTICAL INFORMATION FOR THE HIGHLANDS

AARE, located in the beautiful Aare valley at the foot of Mount Aareskutan, is popular both winter and summer. Hotels: *Aaregaarden, Grand, Sporthotellet,*

124 rooms, *Fjällgaarden,* 42 rooms, *Granen,* 53 rooms, *Tott,* 58 rooms, *Aarevidden,* 61 rooms. Cablecar.

EDSAASDALEN is a mountain village and tourist center both summer and winter. Hotels: *Köja Fjällhotel* and *Nilsgaarden.*

KALL is beautifully situated on Lake Kallsjön on the northern side of the Aareskutan mountain. Hotels: *Kallgaarden, Edhsgaarden* and *Permings.*

KIRUNA, 90 miles north of Polar Circle. Hotels: *Ferrum* (3), 112 rooms with bath, recent; *Centralens* and *Motel Pallia* (4).

ÖSTERSUND, Main center in Jämtland. *Hotel Winn,* 138 rooms. New in 1978.

STORLIEN, the last point in Sweden on this rail line, is actually a border and customs station. Hotels: *Storliens Högfjäll,* 290 rooms, 57 with bath; *Storvallen, Storlien* and *Järnvägshotellet,* (4).

VALADALEN is located a few miles south of Aare in a region of impressive mountains. Hotel: *Vaalaadalens Turiststation* (3), 63 rooms.

SWITZERLAND

Switzerland is such a peculiar kind of country that people either have no feelings about it whatsoever, or they are at the opposite end of the pole—madly in love or badly hating it.

"The Swiss—there is no getting away from it—are outrageous people and the rest of humanity feels deep resentment towards them. They have not been involved in wars for over a century; they have no outlet to the sea, founded no empires, and still are prosperous and rich; the Swiss franc has the arrogance of being a much better currency than the pound sterling, or indeed the dollar; then, to add insult to injury, the Swiss have helped their neighbors and the rest of humanity in all possible ways. That is why they are called dull, unintelligent, uninteresting, a nation of waiters, etc. The truth is that they have behaved like civilized people in a lunatic world and that cannot be easily forgiven."

Thus the Hungarian-born British humorist, George Mikes, summed up some of the specific virtues of the Swiss and the general perversity of the human race. He might have added—and probably did—that the Swiss have four different racial backgrounds and folk traditions, four different languages (German, French, Italian and Romansch, their German being an outlandish spoken dialect called Schwitzerdütsch) and yet function with perfect success in a political confederation of 22 sovereign states, or Cantons, three of which are each divided into two sub-cantons.

The Highlights

If any one were to be put at the head of the list, it would probably be the ascent of the Jungfrau by Europe's highest railway. Other ascents to which tourists flock (mountaineering skill is required for none of them) are up the Bürgenstock elevator, or up Rigi or Mount Pilatus by cableway or cogwheel railway, all in the Lucerne region; up the Zermatt-Gornergrat cogwheel railway and lofty Stockhorn aerial cableway; or in the cablecars from Engelberg to the top of Kleintitlis, and from Stechelberg to the top of Schilthorn. Probably the top scenic excursions are those to the falls of the Rhine and the glacier of the Rhône. Then there are the automobile or bus rides over some of the famous passes—the Susten, the Furka, the Julier, the Simplon, the Gotthard (even the scenery from the train, which seems to spend much of its time in tunnels, is spectacular in this region). Of other spectacular train journeys, that on the Glacier Express from Zermatt and Brig, past the Rhône glacier to Chur and the Grisons, is among the finest. The lake boats provide wonderful trips almost everywhere, but perhaps the best is that from Lucerne to Flüelen, which you can make on your train ticket as part of your journey southward if you are going that way. Finally, the single most visited building in Switzerland is probably the Château of Chillon, near Montreux on Lake Geneva, and scene of Byron's famous poem *The Prisoner of Chillon.*

Skiing in Switzerland

Almost year-round skiing is possible in the high Alpine regions of the Valais, Grisons and the Bernese Oberland. The normal season around the well known resorts is from December to April, sometimes even into May. The best time of all is March and April when the days are longer, the *Sulz* (spring snow) fast, and the sun bright and warm, although February is a popular month. If you are wondering about resorts and ski schools, your only problem will be one of elimination. If you want up-to-the-minute information on all aspects, from hotel availability to snow conditions, the Swiss National Tourist Office in New York, San Francisco, Chicago, London or Zürich will supply it.

Beginners should think first perhaps, of Saas Fee as well as Lenk, Adelboden, Leysin and Wengen. For moderate skiers top choices would include Gstaad, Klosters, and Lenzerheide, while Davos, Pontresina, St. Moritz, Verbier and Zermatt would be high on the list of both moderate skiers and experts. Ski-bobbing, skijöring, acrobatic skiing (Leysin has an acro ski school) are some of the extra-curriculars available, after which the charms of a toboggan may seem a little tame. We remind you only that the St. Moritz Cresta Run is 1,327 yards long, that the record time from the top is barely 55 seconds, that speeds often exceed 80 m.p.h., and that the eight hairpin turns of the Cresta are guaranteed to keep you from worrying about your income tax, though the thought of inheritance taxes may flit through your mind from time to time.

The Country and the People

It will be obvious to any traveler that there are important and delightful differences between the gay, colorful, almost Mediterranean people of the Italian Ticino; the serious, purposive, sentimental, kindly German Swiss of the eastern cantons; the friendly, almost shy Baslers with their rustic joviality and wit; the lively, spirited, higher-keyed French-speaking denizens of Geneva and Lausanne. Yet they all are first and foremost Swiss.

Given such diversity, it is astonishing that anything so unified as a Swiss Way of Life should have emerged. The national character of the Swiss is composed of many elements, each one tempered by the complexities of history. Above all is their proverbial thoroughness. The spirit of William Tell proudly refusing to bow before an Austrian bailiff's hat lives on among the Swiss too. This is a nation of equals without an aristocracy. Every Swiss shares the passionate love of independence of a people who won their freedom after many centuries of foreign oppression, bloody contention, civil and religious conflict. As for other aspects of the Swiss character, a general love of quality is sure to strike you on all levels from the humblest hut to the most deluxe hotel. Poor workmanship is considered a disgrace. This national trait is reflected in the Jungfrau-high standards of Swiss craftsmanship and the country's world-wide reputation for the manufacture of high quality goods. It is perhaps best symbolized in the meticulously-controlled production methods of Switzerland's most famous industry: the making of fine watches. Within the confines of this tiny nation (16,000 square miles, about twice the size of Massachusetts or New Jersey, and containing 6,400,000 people) you will find almost every kind of landscape, except an ocean coast, that a traveler's heart could desire, from valleys of Mediterranean warmth to 12,000-foot-high glaciers, all rendered accessible by the skill of Swiss engineers, and supremely habitable by "a nation of hotel keepers", the world's best.

Food and Drink

Swiss cuisine (*Kochkunst* or *cucina,* if you prefer the German or Italian-speaking cantons) is varied, if not especially subtle. The great specialty is *fondue,* the yummy concoction of Gruyère or Emmental cheese melted and skillfully mixed with white wine, flour, kirsch and a soupçon of garlic. There are lots of other cheeses and cheese specialties in this dairyland. Two you ought to try are *Emmentaler* and *Tête de Moine.* If you like pig's feet, don't leave Geneva without ordering *pieds de porc au madère,* a great specialty of this town. A Valais specialty is *viande séchée* (dried beef or pork). The meat is not cured, but dried in airy barns in Alpine valleys. Cut wafer-thin, with pickled spring onions and gherkins, it makes a delectable, although somewhat expensive, *hors d'oeuvre.*

Pork meat in sausage form has a variety of names, each locality having a special recipe for their making: *Knackerli* and *Pantli* (Appenzell), *Mostmöckli,* and *Kalbsleberwurst* (the latter made of calf's liver). The Grisons boasts of its *Salsiz* (small salami), *Landjäger, Beinwurst, Engadiner Wurst,* and *Leberwurst.*

Cakes and sweetmeats are equally varied in this part of the world. *Leckerli* are Basel specialties: spiced honey cake, flat and oblong in shape, with a thin coating of sugar icing on top. In Bern, they are sold with a white sugar bear for decoration. *Fastnachtküchli* are sugar-dusted pastries, eaten everywhere during Mardi Gras. *Gugelhopf* are large, high, bunlike cakes with a hollowed center, useful for stuffing with whipped cream. *Schaffhauserzungen,* which as the name implies are made in Schaffhausen, are cream-filled cakes.

The Swiss, especially those of the west and the south, are great drinkers of wine. White wine is appreciated as an appetizer in preference to spirits or vermouth and—if only for the sake of your budget—you should at least give it a try: start with the fuller, softer Valais whites (*Johannisberg* or *Fendant*), as some Swiss wines are too dry for non-Swiss palates.

Shopping

According to some statisticians it is a ten to one chance that you will leave Switzerland with a new watch chosen from a bewildering selection. All the best makes will be familiar to you, for you will have seen them well advertised at home, but if you buy here, you'll almost certainly save on the purchase price at home, will get the same one-year guarantee, and have absolute confidence that parts will be available locally should your watch ever need repair. The Swiss Institute for Official Chronometers Tests has taken care of this by promoting standardization of parts, organizing a worldwide parts distribution system, and sponsoring an extensive repair education program. One thing to remember is that you can't go wrong buying a Swiss watch. Some are better than others, but for as little as 130 francs you'll get a respectable watch with a deservedly famous name.

Swiss watches fall into price and quality categories by trade names, much the same as automobiles. Absolutely supreme in class are *Patek-Philippe, Vacheron-Constantin, Audemars-Piguet,* and *Piaget* (manufacturers of the world's thinnest watch). Some *Gübelin* and *Corum* watches are in the same class, but they also make medium-priced timepieces. *Ulysse-Nardin,* too, is among the top-ranking names. These are luxury watches—usually not waterproof or shockproof—delicate and exquisite timepieces.

Fine high precision watches may be identified by the following trade names: *Baume & Mercier, Bucherer, Bulova, Eterna, Girard-Perregaux, International, Jaeger-Le Coultre, Longines, Mido, Movado, Omega, Rolex, Universal, Zenith, Zodiac.* The following firms offer equal quality but also make highly serviceable watches in a lower price range: *Ernest Borel, Büren, Certina, Consul, Cortebert, Cyma, Doxa, Ebel, Enicar, Eska, Favre-Leuba, Fortis, Gruen, Juvenia, Nivada, Paul Buhré, Roamer, Rodania, Sandoz, Solvil, Tissot, Titus,* and a large number of smaller firms, like *Clarenzia, Rado* or *Heno.*

Many make unusual watches. The *Marvin* company, for example, has a tiny timepiece to be attached to the ignition key of your car. *Vulcain* has a wristwatch with a built-in-alarm. *Gübelin* manufactures a clock that indicates the hour by means of a turtle floating in a basin of water. *Breitling* is the specialist for complex chronographs for engineering and aviation. *Heuer* is another specialist. And *Bulova* makes the Accutron electronic timepiece with a tiny tuning fork instead of a balance wheel.

Of the many *Rolex* specialist watches, the waterproof, self-winding GMT-Master tells clearly and simultaneously the time in any two time zones—invaluable for all world travelers as well as pilots, navigators and ship captains. *Rolex* are the inventors of waterproof watches with their Oyster chronometers.

The Swiss claim their chocolate is the world's best and you'll have plenty of opportunities of testing this in the countless candy shops. For a different but uniquely Swiss flavor, go to one of the *Heimatwerk* shops; they specialize in Swiss handicrafts, textiles, ceramics and metalwork, and there's usually a branch in big cities and tourist centers. Swiss wood carving is world-famous, and is a particularly good buy in Brienz, where the craft originated. And Swiss clothing and leather goods are not only well styled (for basic, durable good taste, that is, rather than flashy fads), but they are practically indestructible, hence genuine bargains over the long haul.

PRACTICAL INFORMATION FOR SWITZERLAND

WHAT WILL IT COST. A few years ago all Switzerland's financial wizardry and gnomish know-how failed to keep the inflationary wolf from her door. Inflation reached 10%—frightening enough to the Swiss, but the envy of many another nation. Now it is almost negligible, and for Americans the problem is rather that while the franc holds fairly steady the dollar declines relentlessly. In March, 1977 you could buy a Swiss franc for $0.39; in March, 1978 you could buy a Swiss franc for $0.52, a one-third decline in the U.S. dollar.

If you were coming to Switzerland tomorrow you'd buy a Rolex

Officially approved jewelers

Geneva: Bucherer Quai Général-Guisan 26 Rue du Mont-Blanc 22. Chrono-Time, Rue de la Fontaine 3. Comptoir d'horlogerie de l'Aéroport, Cointrin. Watches of Geneva, Hotel Intercontinental, ch. Petit-Saconnex. **Adelboden:** O. Bruderli, Dorfstr. **Airolo:** R. Grezet, Via S. Gottards. **Arosa:** H. Jäggi & Co., Poststrasse. **Basle:** Bucherer A.G., Freiestrasse 46. Chronométrie Erbe AG., Freiestrasse 15. **Bern:** Rösch & Co. AG., Marktgasse 50 & Bahnhofplatz 7. **Biasca:** A. Grezet. **Biel/Bienne:** O. Brüderli, Collègegasse 12, Av. de la Gare 33. **Burgenstock:** Bucherer AG., Palace Galerie. **Chiasso:** Eredi E. Mariotta, Corso S. Gottardo 20. **Chur:** H. Jäggi & Co., Bahnhofstrasse 42. **Crans s/Sierre:** A. Aeschlimann. **Davos-Platz:** E. Staeuble, Promenade 71. **Gstaad:** O. Brüderli. **Interlaken:** Bucherer AG., Höheweg. **Klosters:** L. Maissen. **Lausanne:** A la Belle Montre, Rue de Bourg 11. Bucherer S.A., 5 Place St. François. **Locarno:** Bucherer S. A., Piazze Grande. Ch. Zenger, Piazzale Stazione. **Lenzerheide:** Jäggi & Co., Hauptstrasse. **Lugano:** Bucherer AG., Via Nassa 56. **Lucerne:** Bucherer AG. Schwanenplatz 5. **Montana:** A. Aeschlimann. **Montreux** : Horlogerie J. C. Schaller, Grand' Rue 100. **Neuchatel:** Ed. Michaud, Place Pury 3. **Ponte Tresa:** P. Jovanovitch. **St. Gallen:** Frischknecht & Co., Engelgasse 2, Marktplatz 18-20. **St. Moritz:** Bucherer AG., Haus Monopol. **Vaduz/FL:** "Quick" Tourist Office. **Visp:** E. Staeuble. **Zermatt:** E. Staeuble **Zurich:** Chronométrie Beyer AG., Bahnhofstrasse 31. S. Brunati Bahnhofstrasse 24. Bucherer AG., Bahnhofstrasse 50.

ROLEX

OF GENEVA

Lausanne

(alt. 372 m. / 643 m.)
On the shores of the Lake of Geneva

Tourist centre: holidays all the year round. A rich programme of cultural and artistic events. Summer and winter sports. A great many possibilities for excursions (lake, vineyards, countryside, forest and mountains).
Easy access by excellent motorway and rail connections. Direct bus service Geneva airport/Lausanne/Geneva.

Congress centre: Palais de Beaulieu — numerous large halls (the largest one for up to 8.000 participants), 1 000 000 sq. ft. of exhibition space. Also available: University and school auditoriums as well as specially equipped halls in several hotels.

Medical and educational centre: University faculties, Federal Institute of Technology, Hotel School, private schools, etc.

All the Sports

In winter, skating, curling, cross-country skiing on the outskirts of the town, Alpine skiing only a few miles away by car in the nearby resorts of the Alps and the Jura.

As soon as spring starts, golf (18-hole course), swimming (beaches and swimming pools), sailing, water skiing and rowing.

All the year round, riding, tennis, private aviation, indoor swimming pool and "Vita" fitness trails, as well as various clubs.

Some dates to remember

October to March — Theatrical season. Big concerts by the "Orchestre de la Suisse romande", the Lausanne Chamber Orchestra and guest orchestras

February — Furniture Fair
Lausanne International Dance Contest

March — International Tourist and Vacations Fair. KID — International Children's and Teenager's Exhibition
Every other year, International Festival of Films for Children and Teenagers.

April — Operatic season

May-June — Lausanne International Festival (concerts, ballets and operas)

June — Festival in the Old Town. Lausanne Fête. Rose Fortnight

June-September — International Biennal of Tapestry alternating with other big exhibitions

July-August — "Pour un Eté" (free concerts and theatrical performances offered to visitors)

September — Swiss Comptoir, national autumn fair

October — Every other year: Flower Show. The Golden Ring — Eurovision sports contest

November — International Antique Dealers Fair

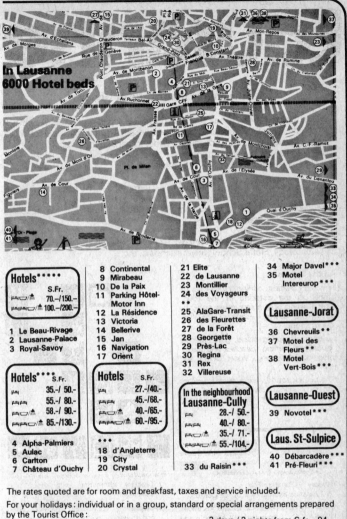

**In Lausanne
6000 Hotel beds**

Hotels *****
S.Fr.

70.–/150.–
100.–/200.–

1 Le Beau-Rivage
2 Lausanne-Palace
3 Royal-Savoy

Hotels ****
S.Fr.

35.–/ 50.–
55.–/ 80.–
58.–/ 90.–
85.–/130.–

4 Alpha-Palmiers
5 Aulac
6 Carlton
7 Château d'Ouchy

Hotels
S.Fr.

27.–/ 40.–
45.–/ 68.–
40.–/ 65.–
60.–/ 95.–

***
18 d'Angleterre
19 City
20 Crystal

8 Continental
9 Mirabeau
10 De la Paix
11 Parking Hôtel-
   Motor Inn
12 La Résidence
13 Victoria
14 Bellerive
15 Jan
16 Navigation
17 Orient

21 Elite
22 de Lausanne
23 Montillier
24 des Voyageurs
**
25 AlaGare-Transit
26 des Fleurettes
27 de la Forêt
28 Georgette
29 Près-Lac
30 Regina
31 Rex
32 Villereuse

In the neighbourhood
Lausanne-Cully

28.–/ 50.–
40.–/ 80.–
35.–/ 71.–
55.–/104.–

33 du Raisin ***

34 Major Davel ***
35 Motel
   Intereurop ***

Lausanne-Jorat

36 Chevreuils **
37 Motel des
   Fleurs **
38 Motel
   Vert-Bois ***

Lausanne-Ouest

39 Novotel ***

Laus. St-Sulpice

40 Débarcadère ***
41 Pré-Fleuri ***

The rates quoted are for room and breakfast, taxes and service included.

For your holidays : individual or in a group, standard or special arrangements prepared by the Tourist Office :

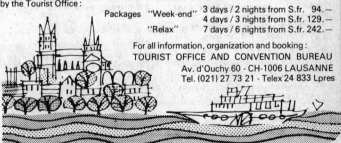

Packages "Week-end" 3 days / 2 nights from S.fr. 94.—
4 days / 3 nights from S.fr. 129.—
"Relax" 7 days / 6 nights from S.fr. 242.—

For all information, organization and booking :
TOURIST OFFICE AND CONVENTION BUREAU
Av. d'Ouchy 60 - CH-1006 LAUSANNE
Tel. (021) 27 73 21 - Telex 24 833 Lpres

So although Swiss prices have risen, they have done so less than in some other countries. However, the continuing strength of the Swiss franc means that you get precious few for your dollar, pound or whatever. And this naturally makes Swiss things that much more expensive for foreigners. Figuring the Swiss franc, then, at *very roughly* two for a dollar, consider that during the winter high season you can pay well over 250 francs a day in fashionable Gstaad for the best accommodation with *full board,* and several of St. Moritz's top hostelries and similar stylish establishments elsewhere can set you back nearly as much.

But away from the big name resorts and jet-set hotels, there are countless places where dependable charm, cleanliness and civilized comfort cost much less than is popularly imagined. Try the small resorts of the Valais, northeastern Switzerland, the Jura, and Ticino's beautiful valleys, where (depending on season and room) bed and breakfast can be had for 20-30 frcs. per person in a double room with bath or shower.

If you hanker after town life, you'll find that Bern, though the capital, is far from being the most expensive city. Or try St. Gallen, in northeastern Switzerland, where bed and breakfast, including tips and taxes, can be found in a good economy hotel for around 30 to 40 frcs.

HOTEL ROOM PER NIGHT

		Major City	Major Resort	Average Town	Budget Resort
Deluxe	S	80-140	80-190	60-120	75-115
	D	100-240	150-350	85-220	135-250
First cl.	S	50-100	50-95	52-65	50-100
	D	70-190	90-180	75-120	90-130
Moderate	S	30-70	35-80	35-55	30-55
	D	50-90	65-150	70-110	60-110
Inexpensive	S	40-75	30-50	30-40	30-45
	D	70-85	50-110	45-80	65-90

Prices in Swiss francs; breakfast, tips, taxes incl.

Hotels in this chapter are listed L, 1, 2, 3 or 4, indicating deluxe, first class, first class reasonable, moderate or inexpensive.

BUDGET ACCOMMODATION. Throughout the country there are numerous pensions, often unpretentious and invariably clean, but with no private baths where bed and breakfast can cost as little as 12 francs. Best get addresses from the local tourist office. Youth Hostel rates vary considerably, from about 5 to 15 frs. per night, plus any resort tax. The Swiss National Tourist Office publishes a free leaflet listing student accommodation and restaurants in university towns. *The Swiss Student Travel Office* has offices in the main university centers and publishes a very useful *Student Guide to Switzerland.* And in most towns and cities the local tourist office is in or very near to the railway station and in addition to maps and advice will have a room-finding service and price lists for you to choose from. There may be a slight change (2 or 3 fr.) for the service.

CHALET RENTAL. *Swiss Chalets,* 10 Sheen Road, Richmond, Surrey, TW9 1AE, or at Buckhauserstrasse 26, 8048 Zurich, have an illustrated brochure describing nearly 2000 chalets of all sizes and at differing price rentals. In the U.S., try *Rent Abroad, Inc.,* 300 Madison Avenue, New York, N.Y. 10017. Within Switzerland, the Swiss National Tourist Office will put you in contact with local real estate agents. If you plan to stay in Switzerland continuously for over three months you will need a visa.

RESTAURANTS. Prices vary widely. In student cafeterias you can get a decent meal for as little as 3 francs; in self-service cafeterias of the *Migros* supermarket chain breakfast is from about 2 frs. and a full meal will run about 5 to 8 frs. Some department stores also have inexpensive cafeterias. A table d'hote meal in a deluxe restaurant may cost ten times as much. Many restaurants span more than one price grade (e.g. the *Mövenpick* chain), so it pays to study the menu usually displayed outside. We list restaurants E, M, or I, indicating expensive, moderate or inexpensive.

CAPITAL. Bern, pop. 152,000.

LANGUAGE. German, French and Italian are the three main tongues. Romansch, derived from ancient Latin, is confined to the Grisons region. English is spoken and understood widely.

CLIMATE. Moderate, changeable, naturally cooler on the mountains, but about 10 degrees warmer south of the Gotthard. In winter, below freezing in a substantial part of Switzerland.

Average maximum daily temperatures in Fahrenheit and centigrade:

Geneva	Jan.	Feb.	Mar.	Apr.	May	June	July	Aug.	Sept.	Oct.	Nov.	Dec.
F°	39	43	50	59	66	73	77	75	70	57	46	39
C°	4	6	10	15	19	23	25	24	21	14	8	4

SEASONS. Summer tourist season from May through Sept. Winter sports season: December through April. Skiing into May and June if you go high enough, and throughout the summer in several places.

 SPECIAL EVENTS. Switzerland has a vast, year-round program of cultural, folklore, sporting and traditional events, often big affairs of international renown, but frequently much smaller, simpler, and relatively local in character. The latter, although drawing fewer spectators, are often the most picturesque. A booklet "Events in Switzerland", published twice yearly, is available free from the Swiss National Tourist Offices.

NATIONAL HOLIDAYS. Jan. 1; Good Friday; Easter Monday; Ascension Day; Whit Monday; Aug. 1 (Swiss Independence Day); Dec. 25 and 26.

CLOSING TIMES. Usual shop hours are from 8 A.M. to 12:15 P.M. and from 1:30 to 6:30 P.M. Banks: hours vary from place to place, but usually 8 A.M. to 4:30 or 5 P.M. Closed for lunch and on Saturdays and Sundays. Foreign currency exchange windows at airports and larger railway stations are open daily until 10 P.M.

SPORTS. During the season you will never be far in Switzerland from *winter sports,* although they are best in the Bernese Oberland, the Grisons and Valais. Skiing, skating, curling, toboganning, horse or car racing on ice—you name it, they have it. Even in mid-summer you can be sure of being able to ski somewhere. There is good trout *fishing,* both lake and river, at many places: permit required; enquire at your hotel or local tourist office. *Golf* is available at thirty courses, two-thirds of them with 18 holes, and most with distractingly lovely scenery. With *mountaineering* you have a choice of everything from a tolerably strenuous hike up a gentle mountain, such as Rigi, to the real thing on the Matterhorn. There are mountaineering schools at Rosenlaui and elsewhere. At lower altitudes *horse riding* is available, and is particularly pleasant in the Jura—for example, at Porrentruy. On the bigger lakes there is *sailing* and *water-skiing,* Lake Thun having a yachting and waterskiing school. On most lakes, too, swimming is excellent, but apt to be chilly. There are signs indicating where pollution is bad.

MONEY. The Swiss monetary unit is the franc, which is divided into 100 centimes, sometimes called Rappen. As rates of exchange fluctuate considerably we suggest that you keep a close eye on the latest figures. As of mid-1978 the deteriorating U.S. dollar was at about $1 = 2 fr. Swiss; the pound sterling at about £1 = 3.65 frs.

Don't change money or travelers checks at "private exchanges" (usually in candy shops or tobacconists near Swiss frontier posts) without ensuring they give the normal rate of exchange. Sometimes they offer a low rate. You may lose 5% or more. It's best to use banks, the larger railway stations, or travel agencies. And when you leave Switzerland for other parts of Europe don't worry about converting those unspent Swiss francs. They will be welcome anywhere, more so than most currencies.

TIPPING. By law, an automatic service charge of 15% is now included in all hotel, restaurant, café and bar bills. This normally covers everything except that some people give the hotel baggage porter 1 franc, two for much baggage. However, if anyone is especially helpful (e.g. the hotel desk porter in saving you money, or giving you advice on tours or nightlife) an appropriate reward would be appreciated. Station and airport porters get 1.50 fr. for each article plus 10%. In a cloakroom where no fixed charge is made give about 50 centimes per person to the attendant. Tip a good 10% in men's barbers and women's hairdressers; for a shampoo and set, 2 frcs. or 15%, whichever is higher. Give 12-15% to cabbies, the larger percentage for shorter rides. In a few resorts you may have to be firm about this. Ushers and washroom attendants may expect 1 fr.; and if you feel that you have had special service from your hotel maid you can leave her about 2 frs. extra. Theatre ushers get 1 fr. if they give you a program.

HOW TO REACH SWITZERLAND. From *North America:* flights go direct to Geneva and Zurich. From *Britain* and *Ireland:* flights connect London with Basel, Bern, Geneva and Zurich, Manchester and Dublin with Geneva and Zurich. Excellent train services connect at Continental ports with cross-Channel ferries.

CUSTOMS. Except for a restriction to 400 cigarettes or 500 grams of tobacco or 100 cigars plus a bottle of spirits (half these quantities for residents of European countries), plus 1 litre of spirits, all of which should be carried in your hand luggage, nothing intended for personal use is barred. As for exports, there are no limits on Swiss products. You may bring in and take out of the country any amount of any currency.

MAIL. Letters: Ordinary mail to most western European countries, up to 20 grams 80 centimes (usually goes air-mail without extra charge); postcards 70 centimes. Surface mail to US and Canada, up to 20 grams 90 centimes; airmail up to 5 grams 1.10 frcs. Aerograms to US one franc. Telephones are fully automatic. Post offices are open 7:30-12:00 and 1:45-6:30 weekdays, Saturdays until 11:00 A.M.

ELECTRICITY. 220 volts, 50 cycles, A.C.

POLLUTION REPORT. Drinking water is as pure and refreshing as the glaciers that supply it. Many lakes, such as Geneva and Zurich, are almost pollution free: others, including Lucerne, Lugano and Maggiore, are a major problem and bathing is prohibited at clearly marked spots. Smog is unknown.

TRAVEL IN SWITZERLAND. By Car. Swiss roads, including the principal mountain passes, are usually well-surfaced although heavy traffic can make driving on some main routes relatively slow. The growing number of motorways are excellent. Major mountain passes, although often steep, can be negotiated without difficulty by an average driver with an average car, but care is needed. Uphill traffic has priority over that coming down. On mountain postal roads (indicated by a sign showing a posthorn against a blue background) the big yellow Swiss postal coaches can demand precedence in any situation. For information by telephone about Alpine road conditions, dial 163. In case of breakdown, dial 140 for road assistance. For police dial 117.

You drive on the right. There is a strictly enforced, absolute speed limit of 100 km. p.h. (62 m.p.h.) on all roads except motorways; latter usually 130 km.p.h (80 m.p.h.). In built-up areas, 60 km.p.h. (37 m.p.h.). *Heavy, on-the-spot fines for infringement.* Except on main roads, vehicles coming from the right have right of way. The international motoring code signs apply. Many towns have parking meters or "Blue Zones": discs for the latter obtainable from tourist offices, automobile clubs, some garages, etc. Motorways are identified by green directional signs.

Special car-carrying trains through Alpine tunnels make year-round transit possible of Albula, St. Gotthard, Simplon and Lötschberg passes. Road tunnels go under the Grand St. Bernard and San Bernardino passes, as well as Mont Blanc (at Chamonix, 50 miles from Geneva).

Third party insurance is compulsory in Switzerland, and motorists are advised to carry an international insurance Green Card. Those without a Green Card have to buy insurance cover at the frontier (about 30 frcs. for 30 days). Safety belts are mandatory in front seats; children under 12 must sit in back.

Gasoline: about 97 centimes to 1.03 francs a liter. Gasoline stations everywhere.

BY TRAIN OR POSTAL COACH. Swiss railroads, perhaps the best in the world, have frequent services. They offer many worthwhile reduced fares including the *Holiday Card* which, except at certain Swiss airports and rail stations, can only be bought in foreign countries. Holders get unlimited travel without further payment on most Swiss trains, postal coaches and boats, as well as 25%-50% reduction on many mountain railways and aerial cableways. A real bargain, it costs, 2nd class, $61.50 for 8 days, $86.50 for 15, and $119.50 for a month. If you want to travel first class it costs $167.00, $119.50 and $86.50 frcs. respectively. Good value, too, are the 7 or 15 day *Regional Holiday Season Tickets* which cover some of the popular tourist areas. They give unlimited free travel on at least five of the days and reduced fares on the rest. There is a special Senior Citizen Travel Card for women over 62 and men over 65 costing $44.50. Children under 6 travel free, from 6 to 16 for half fare.

The sturdy, yellow Swiss Postal Coaches cover routes taking in some of Europe's finest mountain scenery. A special 3-day go-anywhere ticket costs 40 frcs.

CAR HIRE. Most travel agencies and car hire firms, several airlines, and Swiss railroads can arrange to have a self-drive or chauffeur-driven car awaiting your arrival in Switzerland. In Zurich are the head offices of *Budget,* PO Box 84, Scheideggstr. 72; *Europcar/National,* Badenerstr. 812; while *Avis* is at Flughofstr. 61, Glattbrugg. All have offices or agents at Basel, Geneva and Zurich airports and most large towns and resorts. Rates with unlimited free mileage start around 400 frcs. per week for a Mini or Fiat 127.

CAMPING. There are in this small country over 200 camp sites, frequently with superb views, and well equipped (some even have TV and cinemas). Some are open year-round, but the usual season is from May or June through September or October. Rates vary widely and are usually quoted for a family group of two adults, one child, plus car and camper; the range is roughly 6 to 30 frs. a night, with the average around 10-15 frs. A full list is available from the Swiss National Tourist Office. Remember that camping is allowed only on authorized sites.

 USEFUL ADDRESSES. *Embassies:* American, Australian, British, Canadian, South African at Bern. *Consulates:* American and South African at Zurich; Australian and New Zealand at Geneva; British at Basel, Geneva, Lugano, Montreux and Zurich. *Swiss National Tourist Office,* 42 Talacker, Zurich, but local tourist office there at main station. Each locality has its well-run information office, called Verkehrsbüro, Office du Tourisme or Ente Turistico, usually in or very close to the railway station. For police, dial 117; fire brigade, 118.

Geneva and its Lake

Geneva is handsomely situated at the western end of Lake Geneva (in French, Lac Léman), where the river Rhône leaves the lake en route to France and the Mediterranean. The river and lower basin of the lake divide the city into northern and southern sectors, joined by bridges. There are delightful promenades, and famous views across the water towards Mont-Blanc. An ancient city, Geneva was controlled from 58 B.C. to 443 A.D. by the Romans, who had their citadel on the crest of the hill where the Cathedral of St. Peter now dominates the old town. Irrevocably associated with the famous 16th-century French Huguenot reformer, John Calvin, Geneva became a rather staid and melancholy city, thanks to the Protestant sumptuary laws. Understandably, many citizens fled from its drab life, but far more English, French and Italian refugees came in, bringing with them new crafts, trades, and a keen sense of business, a heritage which remains in evidence even today. Today, Geneva has an atmosphere of gaiety and sophistication, and a cosmopolitan one at that. Although the International Red Cross was founded in the city in 1864, it was the establishment of the ill-fated League of Nations there after the First World War which put Geneva firmly on its path as an international center of major importance. Today, with about 165,000 inhabitants, it is the third largest city in Switzerland.

Exploring Geneva

You can see many of the attractions of Geneva in a single walk by starting from the rail station down the Rue du Mont-Blanc. At the lakeside, turn right along the Quai des Bergues flanking the Rhône, crossing the river on the Pont de l'Isle to the Place Bel-Air from which you follow the Rue de la Corraterie to the Place Neuve with its Grand Théâtre, and the Conservatory of Music. From here, you enter the park, which contains the university and Geneva's gigantic international memorial to the Reformation.

Leaving the park, turn left up Rue St. Léger into the charming old Place Bourg-de-Four, and then take any of the narrow streets, ramps and staircases that lead up to St. Peter's Cathedral where you may be stirred or unmoved by the sight of the pulpit from which Calvin preached. But no one can be indifferent to the sweeping view of Geneva and Lac Léman from the top of the North Tower.

The winding, cobbled streets leading down from the cathedral to the modern city have all the picturesque charm of antiquity. The Grand-Rue is the oldest of them; Jean-Jacques Rousseau was born at No. 40 on June 28, 1712. See also in this neighborhood the 12th-century house at No. 6, Rue du Puits-St.-Pierre, and the 17th-century houses built by Italian religious refugees on the Rue de l'Hotel-de-Ville.

For an interesting contrast to these ancient attractions, go back across the Rhône and out to Ariana Park, where the handsome Palais des Nations, begun in 1929 for the League of Nations, is now the European Office of the United Nations Organization: there are guided tours throughout the year.

The Circuit of Lake Geneva

One of the joys of Lake Geneva is that the old road along the northern (Swiss) side is never far from its picturesque shore, although if in a hurry you can take the faster but less interesting motorway almost all the way from Geneva to Villeneuve. If you prefer the prettier but slower road along the lake, you will pass through Coppet, with its lovely château which belonged to Louis XVI's financial adviser Jacques Necker (a Swiss) and his daughter Madame de Staël; attractive Céligny; Nyon, founded by Julius Caesar as a camp for war veterans in 45 B.C. and subsequently (17th and 18th centuries) the center of a flourishing chinaware craft whose flowersprigged productions are still in demand; Morges, a popular yachting and sailing center with a 13th-century castle and a statue of Paderewski, who spent his last years on his beautiful estate at nearby Tolochenaz.

PRACTICAL INFORMATION FOR GENEVA

 WHEN TO GO. Geneva is a summer city, best visited in the usual holiday season, when, of course, it is inevitably crowded. The four-day fête of Geneva, with fireworks, street dancing, parades of flower-covered floats, etc., occurs in the middle of August, and there is much jollification during the mid-December festival of Escalade. For events at the time of your visit, get a copy of *La Semaine à Genève* (This Week in Geneva) from your hotel. Also, all tourist information from Geneva Tourist Office, 2 Rue des Moulins.

 HOTELS. Accommodation used to be a problem in Geneva, particularly during the times of the big conferences, but many new hotels have been built in recent years. However, during the high season there is barely sufficient room for all the visitors. If you arrive without a reservation, the rooming office in Cornavin railway station will place you somewhere, but it may be in only a modest, though comfortable hotel.

NORTH SHORE, the most favored location. All (L) or near deluxe are:
Beau Rivage, 13 Quai du Mont-Blanc. Fine grill room, famous terrace.
Des Bergues, Quai des Bergues, with distinguished atmosphere.
Bristol, 10 Rue du Mont-Blanc, recently much renovated. Top prices.
Inter-Continental, 7 Petit Saconnex, near Palais des Nations. Private suites, pool, smart shops; 16 storeys and 400 rooms.
Mediterrannée, 14 Rue de Lausanne. Modern, opposite rail station.
De la Paix, 11 Quai du Mont-Blanc. Modernized, very attractively furnished. Small but distinguished.
Président, 47 Quai Wilson, tastefully furnished in antique style. Outdoor pool. Expensive.
La Réserve, 301 Rte. de Lausanne. In pleasant park, lakeside terrace. Outdoor pool. Quiet, elegant, luxurious, leisurely, expensive.
Du Rhône, Quai Turrettini, overlooking river. Recently refurbished, brisk, somewhat commercial, but pleasant.
Richemond, Jardin Brunswick. Famous, family-run and owned. Lake view.
On or near the lake, and all (1) are: *California,* 1 Rue Gevray, breakfast only; modern *Du Midi,* Pl. Chevalu, and *Amat-Carlton,* 22 Rue Amat.
Handy for the rail station are: *Royal,* 41 Rue de Lausanne (1); *De Berne* (1), 26 Rue de Berne, starkly modern, designed for package tour groups; *Excelsior,* simple but inexpensive; *Cornavin* (1), *Suisse* and slightly cheaper *Astoria,* both (2) and on Pl. Cornavin; *Alba* (2), 19 Rue du Mont-Blanc; *Rivoli* (2), 6 Rue des Pâquis. All except *De Berne* and *Astoria,* breakfast only.
On Rue des Alpes, *International-Terminus* (3), at No. 20, and *Continental* (3), breakfast only, at No. 17.
In a residential area northwest of station, *Grand Pré* (1), 35 Rue du Grand Pré, breakfast only. Near the Palais des Nations, *Eden* (1), 135 Rue de Lausanne, and slightly cheaper *Mon Repos* at No. 131. In the southern part of the city, the *Centre Universitaire Zofingien,* 6 rue des Voisins, takes non-student overnight guests during July and August. Rooms (M), downstairs restaurant (I).

SOUTH SHORE. Near the Jardin Anglais, *L'Arbalète* (L), 3 Tour Maitresse, has restaurant noted for typical Swiss dishes.
In residential area, *La Résidence* (1), 11 Rte. de Florissant, is highly recommended by readers; easy parking; tennis.

MOTELS within a short drive of the city include *Riviera* at Collonge-Bellerive (off the Thonon road and not to be confused with Collonges); *Le Léman* at Commugny; *de Founex* at Founex; *de la Buna* at Mies; *Perly* at Perly; and *La Tourelle* at Vesenaz.

BUDGET AND YOUTH HOTELS. *Hotel de l'Etoile,* 17 rue des Vieux Grenadiers; *Auberge de Jeunesse,* rue de Plantaporrets; Hotel le Clos Voltaire, 45 rue de Lyon; *Cité Universitaire,* 26 ave. de Miremont, June-November.

RESTAURANTS. Geneva is full of good restaurants, with French cooking dominant, though there are plenty of places that provide the mixed Swiss cuisine, and a number specialize in the dishes of other countries.

There are few pleasanter places to lunch or dine on a fine day than *La Perle du Lac* (E), 128 Rue de Lausanne, where you can dine out of doors in a park right on the lakeside, facing a wonderful panorama. The food—lakefish dishes and other specialties—is tops, and worth the price. The counterpart on the other bank is the restaurant in the *Parc des Eaux-Vives,* slightly less well situated, slightly more expensive, and some say with even better food. Both closed Mons.

One of the best restaurants in town is *Le Gentilhomme* (E), grill of the Hotel Richemond.

The Hôtel du Rhône has the excellent *Le Neptune* (E); outstanding menus and good wine list. Its terrace is a fashionable rendezvous in summer.

At the Inter-Continental Hotel, you can dine by candlelight in their 18th-floor restaurant which has a superb view of the lake. Notable, too, for elegance as well as food are the *Rôtisserie du Chat Botté* of the Hotel Beau Rivage, and the *Amphitryon* of the Hotel des Bergues. All (E).

Among restaurants proper, leaders are the *Béarn* (E), 4 Quai de la Poste, closed Sat. evening and Sun., and *Auberge à la Mère Royaume* (E), 9 Rue des Corps-Saints, old Geneva atmosphere; closed Suns. and second half of June.

First rate and (E) are *Or du Rhône,* at 19 Bd. Georges Favon, and *Au Fin Bec,* 55 Rue de Berne. Further out, about 4 miles southwest, just off the Collonges road, is *L'Auberge de Confignon* (M to E), excellent food and view.

For atmosphere, try *Le Mazot,* 16 Rue du Cendrier, the décor being that of Valais; *Au Pied du Cochon* (M), just off Pl. Bourg-de-Four; *Les Armures* (M), 1 Rue Puits St.-Pierre, close to town hall. For Provençal cuisine go to *L'Aïoli* (I to M), Pl. du Port.

For a nautical touch, *Le Bateau* (M), is an old paddle steamer converted and moored at the south end of Pont du Mont-Blanc.

For anything from a snack to seafood specialties, try the local branches of the *Mövenpick* chain (I to E), one on Place de la Fusterie, and a big, new one on the Right Bank.

In the (I) to (M) bracket are *Chez Bouby,* 1 Rue Grenus (reader-recommended), *Du Centre,* Pl. du Molard, and *Plat d'Argent,* 7 Rue Cherbuliez (said to be the city's oldest eatery).

Budget troubles? Try *La Rochelle* (I), 5 Rue du Commerce, 6th floor; or the self-service *Migros* shop chain and the department stores, (I). Also, *Restaurant Universitaire,* 2 av. du Mail; *Les Amures,* 1 rue du Puits-Saint Pierre; *Zofage,* 6 rue des Voisins; and *Club International des Etudiants,* 6 rue de Saussure; particularly for students, or, younger travelers of all ages.

A short way out is *L'Aéroport Restaurant* (E).

ENTERTAINMENT. Geneva is not Paris, but it comes closer to it than any other city in Switzerland, and can be fairly lively in the evening. There are two theaters, the *Grand Théâtre* and the *Comédie,* where you may see opera, operetta, or plays. You may have a chance to see experimental productions at the *Théâtre de Poche.* In summer, concerts and plays are given in the courtyard of the Hôtel de Ville.

Concert halls are *Victoria Hall,* Rue Général Dufour, where the Orchestre de la Suisse Romande gives its concerts; *Conservatoire de Musique,* Pl. Neuve; *Radio Geneva,* 66 Bd. Carl-Vogt. There are folk dances Tues. and Thurs. at the *American Community House,* 3 Rue de Monthoux.

NIGHTCLUBS. With a good floorshow, entrance will be around 10 francs; a Scotch, rather more. If a "hostess" joins you at your table or at the bar and suggests you buy her a drink, she means champagne (she gets a percentage from the house). Don't be afraid to say no—you won't be the first.

The liveliest are probably the *Ba-Ta-Clan,* 15 Rue de la Fontaine; other lively spots are *Maxim's, Le Grillon,* and *Piccadilly.*

The Pussy Cat Saloon, 15 Rue des Glacis de Rive, puts on two first class international shows and striptease nightly. In the same building, *Club 58* with excellent discotheque and band.

Probably the best spot in town, and the place to go if you want to avoid striptease, is *Maxim's,* Pl. des Alpes. There's neither strip nor floorshow at *La Tour,* 6 Rue Tour-de-Boël, but it always has two bands.

MUSEUMS. Among the best are *Ariana,* Ave. de la Paix (European and Oriental china, and especially that of Nyon and Geneva). *Art and History,* Rue Charles-Galland (archeology; fine arts; Genevese enamels). *Baur Collection,* Rue Munier-Romilly (former private house with fine Chinese and Japanese ceramics; jade; prints; etc.). *Horological Museum,* 15 Rte. de Malagnou (fine collection of timepieces).) *Natural History,* 11 Rte. de Malagnou. *Petit Palais,* 2 Terrasse St.-Victor (modern art, 19th-cent. on). *Rath,* Pl. Neuve (temporary exhibitions, often very good). *Voltaire,* 25 Rue des Délices (relics of Voltaire and his times).

SPORTS. You can *swim* at the Pâquis jetty which projects from the Quai du Mont-Blanc, but you'll probably enjoy it more at Geneva Plage near the yacht harbor on the eastern fringe of the city. There's a fine indoor pool at Quai des Vernets. If you want to hire a *rowboat* you can do so at the Quai du Mont-Blanc and Quai Gustav Ador, and there's *waterskiing,* too. At Château Bessinge, Cologny (on bus route A), there is an 18-hole *golf course.*

SHOPPING. This is still the watchselling center of the world. All the leading Swiss manufacturers have offices and outlets here. When you see the array of jewelry in the shops along the Rue du Rhône du Marché and Rue de la Croix d'Or, or look at the many haute couture boutiques in Rue du Rhône, you'll know that Calvin's sumptuary laws are a dead letter in this town today. If you're looking for antiques, you'll have a field day in those small narrow streets that tumble down from the old quarters clustered around the cathedral.

Lausanne

Lausanne, nearly 40 miles from Geneva on the northern shore of the lake, calls itself "Switzerland's city of the future". A great favorite with such distinguished foreigners as Voltaire and Gibbon in the 18th century, this hilly city, rising in tiers from the lakeside, is the prosperous, civic-minded business center of western Switzerland, and a pleasant resort. With about 136,000 inhabitants, it is Switzerland's fifth largest city.

Sightseeing in Lausanne should include the Cathedral of Notre Dame, a fine example of Burgundian Gothic, restored since vandal Reformation days; the Castle of St. Maire; the 17th-century city hall; and the handsome, modern Federal Palace of Justice. The wooded Jorat heights above the city are ideal for walking tours. Lausanne-Ouchy, an elegant resort, is a good place of embarkation for short, pleasant excursions on those smart white steamers that shuttle across the lake all summer long. Try the half hour trip to St.-Sulpice to see the best-preserved 11th-century Romanesque church in Switzerland. A dozen miles north of Lausanne is La Sarraz, whose castle, on a rocky promontory, is a national monument and contains a splendid furniture collection.

The circuit of Lake Geneva continues east of Lausanne along a beautiful 15-mile stretch past the steep vineyards of Lavaux, which produce excellent vintages, much in demand. Harvest time here in mid-October is very gay on these precipitous slopes where everything must be done by hand. At Pully, five miles east of Lausanne, you have a choice of roads just before entering the village. Take the one which leads away from the lake for the breathtaking Corniche Road that winds through the vineyards to Chexbres, 2,000 feet above sea level, then descends to the lake highway again just before Vevey.

PRACTICAL INFORMATION FOR LAUSANNE

 HOTELS. The Tourist Office at 60 Av. d'Ouchy and its branch in the railway station offer maps of the city and for 2 frs. can reserve you a hotel room. The top (L) hotels are: *Beau-Rivage,* in its own gardens facing the lake at Chemin de Beau-Rivage, Ouchy. *Lausanne-Palace,* in the city center, yet beside pleasant gardens. Superb view from terrace restaurant. *Royal Savoy,* in a private park with outdoor pool; about five minutes walk from the lake and not much more from the town center.

Hotels in class (1), in or near town center are: *Alpha-Palmiers; Continental, Mirabeau, Terminus* and *Victoria,* all near station; *De la Paix;* and *Parking,* adequate private parking, an interesting restaurant.

Down the hill, between the city center and Ouchy is the *Carlton,* with few parking problems, and the recently re-opened *Orient;* both (1).

Close to the lake at Ouchy are the *Château d'Ouchy,* with its 800-year-old Hall of Knights, and *La Résidence;* both (1).

Central and (2) are the *City; de Lausanne; Elite;* and *Regina.* Last two breakfast only.

In same price range are *Angleterre,* at Ouchy, with terrace overlooking lake, and *Montillier* at Pully, on eastern fringe.

For budget, youth and student travelers, there are: the *Salvation Army* (Armée du Salut) at 49 rue Ruchonnet (women) and Place du Vallon (men); *Hotel Select* at 10 rue des Terreaux; the *Youth Hostel* (Auberge de Jeunesse), Chemin du Muguet; and possible student housing through *La Maison de Bellerive,* 64 av. de Rhodanie.

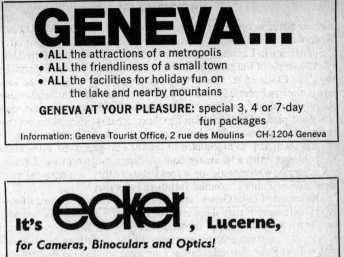

From the creative mind of ...
PIAGET

PIAGET at the world's finest jewellers

2097

WORDS TO THE WISE
A Few Useful Travel Hints

Whether you are on holiday or have important business to do, after a flight through several time zones give your body's clock a chance to catch up. It is easy to underestimate the effects of jet-lag.

Don't carry all your cash, travellers' checks, passport etc. in the same place, spread them around a bit – and never carry your wallet in your hip pocket.

Experienced travellers travel light. Don't forget that the hand luggage you carry with you onto the plane is a vital part of your travel equipment. Make sure you have your essentials in it, not in your other baggage.

With strikes and the cost of excess baggage always in the background, you would be sensible when flying not to take more than you could comfortably carry yourself – in a pinch.

Don't leave already exposed film in your pockets or in any hand luggage while passing through airport X-ray machines. The process can sometimes fog the film and you may find a whole trip's photographs ruined. Put the film on one side while passing through.

Never make long-distance phone calls from your hotel room without checking first on the likely price. Some hotels have been known to mark up the cost of a call as much as 200%.

Several airlines will provide a cardboard carrying box for any loose items you might arrive clutching at the checking-in desk. It saves leaving a trail of last-minute purchases all the way to the plane.

You would be amazed the amount of free information that you can get from National Tourist Offices to help you plan your trip – all the way from brochures to movies.

Put a tag with your name and address on it *inside* your suitcase as well as outside. It will greatly help identification if the case goes astray.

Never leave valuables in your hotel room – put them in the hotel safe.

RESTAURANTS. For fine cuisine and wines in an elegant setting, try the grillrooms of the Lausanne-Palace and Beau-Rivage, the Continental's *Rôtisserie Le Beaujolais,* and *La Grappe d'Or.* In the Alpha-Palmiers Hotel is the steak house *La Calèche* and the typical Swiss cellar *Carnotzet du Petit Chêne,* noted for its cheese specialties and fondue bourguignonne. All the above, fairly expensive. Unpretentious and (M), with excellent food, especially cheese fondue, is reader-recommended *Café du Jorat,* Pl. de l'Ours. Also (M) are *Chez Godio,* 2 Pl. Pépinet; *La Chaumière,* 23 Rue Centrale; *la Pomme de Pin,* Cité Derrière 15; *Chez Charles,* rue des Mousquines; and *Chez Pitch* at Port de Pully. At the lakeside restaurant-club *La Voile d'Or* (E) you can dine with a marvelous view in the excellent French restaurant, or eat at the snack bar (M).

At Signal de Sauvabelin, 500 feet, amid wonderful lake and Alpine views, are the *Swiss Chalet Restaurant* and nearby *Restaurant du Lac.*

The Lausanne *Migros* supermarket-cum-restaurant is on the Place de la Riponne; for a good budget lunch try *Café François,* 38 rue St. Laurent or *Restaurant du Vieux Lausanne,* 6 rue Pierre Vivet.

ENTERTAINMENT. Lausanne's International Festival of Music and Ballet is in May and June. The *Beaulieu* and the *Municipal* theaters present opera, operetta, concerts, plays, etc. all year round. The *Théâtre des Faux-Nez* (120 seats only) gives avant-garde plays in French. Of the nightclubs, the *Tabaris* is one of the most modern in Switzerland (and about the most expensive); the *Brummell,* in the Palace Hotel's building, is very good; the *Metropole* and *Paradou* are more moderately priced. Good places to dance, besides the clubs mentioned, are the *Scotch-Bar, Johnnie's,* the *Paddock* in the Victoria Hotel, the *Château d'Ouchy* and the *Voile d'Or* down by the lakeside.

MUSEUMS. *The Cantonal Fine Arts, Natural History,* and *Botanical* museums are all in the Palais de Rumine. *Museum of Decorative Art,* 4 Rue Villamont. *Olympic Museum. Roman Museum* at nearby Vidy.

SPORTS. There is an 18-hole *golf* links at En Marin, four miles out. *Tennis* at Stade-Lausanne, Lausanne-Sports, or Montchoisi. *Horse racing* at nearby Morges, beginning of June. *Horseback riding,* Centre Equestre Lausannois, Chalet-à-Gobet, 4 miles out. *Swimming* at Bellerive Plage, at Mon-Repos indoor pool in city center, the Vert Bois and Montchoisi pools.

SHOPPING. Lausanne has many well-stocked and temptingly arranged stores, the main shopping areas being around Pl. St.-François, Rue St.-François and Rue de Bourg.

Vevey

Vevey, with its inspiring view across the lake to the lofty peak of Dent d'Oche, has been, with Montreux, a popular resort with the English since the early 19th century. Today, many famous foreigners live hereabouts. At the eastern end of its lovely lakeside promenade is La Tour de Peilz, a resort-suburb named after its 13th-century castle—all of which reminds us that it was in this region that Jean-Jacques Rousseau set his *Nouvelle Héloïse,* that 18th-century European best seller which set the fashion for Swiss travel. In nearby Gruyère you can visit the cheese factory.

PRACTICAL INFORMATION FOR VEVEY

HOTELS. Leader is *Trois Couronnes* (1), with a somewhat Victorian interior but also with a lot of comfort and character; terrace; open-air restaurant overlooking the lake. Next is *Du Lac* (2), followed by the *Comte* (3), both overlooking the lake.

In class (4) are *Vieux-Vevey,* with sauna; *Pavillon & Buffet; Suisse; Touring & Gare.*

On Mont Pèlerin, with splendid Alpine views, are the *Mirador* (L), indoor pool, and *Parc* (2), outdoor pool.

RESTAURANTS. One of the pleasantest places to eat is on top of Mont Pèlerin (funicular from Vevey). There are several restaurants and wonderful views across the lake to the Alps beyond. In town are the *Restaurant-Tearoom Livet* (the best-known spot) and, in the market place, *Chez Pierre Restaurant du Raisin,* an excellent gastronomic rendezvous. *The Buffet de la Gare* is good. By the lake are *Restaurant du Casino* (lakeside terrace and park), *Restaurant du Château* (cheese specialties), and *Voile au Vent* (fish specialties).

Montreux

Even more romantic than Vevey is Montreux, one of Europe's most beautifully situated resorts. A French-style Edwardian town, now much modernized, it caters largely to foreigners, and is famed alike for its mild climate, lush vegetation and well-tended gardens.

There are some wonderful trips to be taken from Montreux. One is by mountain railroad to the Rochers de Naye. Here, at 6,700 feet above sea level, you will have a view over Lake Geneva, the Savoy and the southern Swiss Alps. As late as May you'll be able to enjoy excellent skiing. A second excursion from Montreux is the ride to Glion and Caux with its celebrated "Mountain House", headquarters of the Moral Rearmament movement. Not least, and a mere 1½ miles by trolley bus from Montreux, there is one of Europe's most famous sights, the castle of Chillon. Immortalized by Byron, the island castle (although it's only a few feet from the shore) was built in the 13th century under the direction of Duke Peter of Savoy. The dungeon's most famous prisoner was François Bonivard who, as Prior of St.-Victor in Geneva, had supported the Reformation, conduct which enfuriated the Catholic Duke of Savoy. Bonivard spent six gloomy years here until the Bernese freed him after their liberation of Vaud in 1536.

The Swiss tour of Lake Geneva really ends here at Chillon, though you can continue to Villeneuve and the Rhône estuary, or even strike north to Col du Pillon to take the marvellous cablecar ride up to the perpetual snow of the Diablerets glacier with its panoramic restaurant. But if you cross the Rhône and start back to complete the circuit of the lake, you'll soon find yourself in another country, for much of the southern shore of Lake Geneva is French. If you have a sudden inclination to gamble, you can stop on your way at the popular French thermal resort of Evian.

PRACTICAL INFORMATION FOR MONTREUX

HOTELS. The vast *Montreux-Palace* and its smaller stablemate *Du Cygne* are both (L), under the same management, and with outdoor pool and tennis. Recently refurbished; good lake views.

Top in class (1) are *Eden,* with outdoor pool; *Eurotel,* each room with kitchenette, also has indoor pool, underground garage, located on lakeside; *Excelsior,* freshly and tastefully redecorated, lake views, sauna, indoor pool, good dining room; *National,* in town, but its elevated quiet gardens have fine view, also has pool; *Suisse et Majestic.*

Bonnivard, Bon Accueil, Helvétie, Europe, Hotel de Londres, and Parc et Lac, in town, all (2). At Territet, *Bristol* (2).

RESTAURANTS. *L'Hostellerie de Caux,* outside the city has good steaks and a large wine cellar (E); *Le Montagnard* and *Manoire* are other good places in the same class, and in the hills; *Excelsior* (E), outstanding among hotel restaurants; as is *Eden au Lac. Bavaria,* café type, good beer, excellent for snacks and light meals; *Vieux Montreux,* typical cellar restaurant, good food; *Montreux-Plage* is directly on the water.

ENTERTAINMENT. The *Casino de Montreux* is by the lakeside, next to the Hotel Eden; cabaret, nightclub, gambling (boule). *Museum Club,* typical Swiss restaurant with dancing. *Hungaria* has floorshow and dancing.

MUSEUMS. *Château de Chillon; Old Montreux Museum; Kruger Villa* in Clarens.

SPORTS. There is an 18-hole *golf* course at Aigle, *tennis* at the Montreux Tennis Club, *horses* for hire at the Nouvelle Ecole Montreusienne d'Equitation at Villeneuve, *swimming* at Montreux-Plage which has an Olympic-size pool, *boats* for hire by the hour, and *waterskiing* at Montreux-Plage and Casino de Montreux.

PRACTICAL INFORMATION FOR ELSEWHERE IN THE REGION

CHEXBRES. *Du Signal* (2), indoor pool. *Bellevue* and *Victoria,* both (4).

DIABLERETS, LES. *Grand* and *Eurotel,* both (1) and with indoor pool, sauna. *Mon Abri* (3). *Les Lilas, Alpin,* both (4).

GLION. *Victoria* (1) and *Des Alpes Vaudoises* (2), each with indoor pool. *Mont Fleuri* (4).

NYON. *Clos de Sadex* (1), notable restaurant, lakeside garden. *Beau Rivage* (3).

VILLENEUVE. *Byron* (1). *Aux Vieux Pêcheur* (3). *De l'Aigle, Le Château, Du Port,* all (4).

MOTELS IN THE REGION. At Bussigny, *Novotel Lausanne Ouest.* At Chalet-à-Gobet, *Vert Bois.* At Cully, *Intereurop.* At Etoy, *Lunika* and *des Pêcheurs.* At Grens-sur-Nyon, *du Pressoir.* At Montreux Clarens, *de la Baye.* At Prangins, near

Nyon, *de l'Aérodrome.* At Rennaz, near Villeneuve, *de Rennaz.* At St.-Prex, near Morges, *du Bourg.* At Servion, *des Fleurs.* At St.-Sulpice, *des Pierrettes.* Near Vevey, *des 4 Vents.* At Villars-le-Terroir, near Echallens, *Beauregard.* All open year round except Prangins and Rennaz. For motels near Geneva, see page 671.

Basel

Basel, astride the Rhine, sheltered by the Vosges and the German Black Forest to the north, and the Swiss Jura in the south and west, is the northern gateway of Switzerland. With about 200,000 people, it is Switzerland's second largest city, and an important commercial center. One of Europe's greatest inland ports, it is a lively city rich in interest and culture; one in which elements of quaint medievalism and bustling modernity are commingled. Baselers love fun—their carnival is one of the most uproarious in Europe and they are, perhaps, the friendliest people in Switzerland.

The best way to capture the atmosphere of Basel is to sit at a terrace café beside the Rhine, or stroll along Rheinweg, a pleasant riverside esplanade backed by old houses squeezed one against the other. Overlooking the river is the cathedral (Münster) which has all the charm of Rhenish architecture. And beside it is the exquisite *Munsterplatz,* justly renowned for the perfection of its proportions. Inside are the tombs of Queen Anne (wife of Rudolf of Habsburg) and Erasmus of Rotterdam, one of many brilliant scholars whose names have lent luster to Basel's great university through the centuries. Don't miss the marvelous panorama of the city on both sides of the Rhine from the Wettstein Bridge.

A few paces from Barfusserplatz is the Freie Strasse, Basel's biggest shopping street, leading to the attractive market place and its colorful 16th-century town hall. From the nearby fishmarket, with its Gothic fountain, by climbing up narrow medieval streets, you will come to St. Peter's Place and the New University, hallowed by memories of Erasmus, Burckhardt (historian of the Renaissance), and other great scholars who came here.

There are pleasant daily riverboat excursions in summer, leaving from the embankment behind the Hotel Three Kings. The river is navigable as far as Rheinfelden, about two hours upstream.

PRACTICAL INFORMATION FOR BASEL

HOTELS. Basel now boasts seven (L) hotels, newest being the *Basel,* not far from the town hall. Near the main station is the runner-up, the *Hilton,* with indoor pool. Pride of place in seniority goes to one of Europe's legendary hostelries, the *Three Kings* (*Drei Könige* or *Trois Rois* if you refer to it in German or French). Recently modernized at some cost to its traditional character, today's hotel stands where inns have stood since the 11th century. Its Rhine terrace is as famous as its cuisine.

In the station square are the *Euler,* with elegant luxury and Basel's best food, and the *Schweizerhof* whose rather tatty exterior hides traditional comfort. Both are family owned. About ten minutes walk from the station is the ultra-modern *Alban-Ambassador* and between the station and the city center the recently-rebuilt *International,* with contemporary decor throughout and fine indoor pool.

Others close to the station include the *Victoria-Bahnhof* (2), breakfast only; the *Greub, Jura,* and breakfast only *Bernina,* all (3). *Bristol, Gotthard-Terminus,* the attractively decorated *Alexander,* and the quiet, delightful little *Flugelrad* (an economy snip) are (4).

Not far away are the *City, Drachen* and *Excelsior.* All (2).

In Klein Basel, beside the Mittlere bridge and overlooking the Rhine, is the new *Merian* (2). Also beside the river is the popular *Krafft-am-Rhein* (3). Alongside the Industries Fair buildings is the *Admiral* (3) with heated rooftop pool. The *Alfa* (3) is in the suburb of Birsfelden.

 RESTAURANTS. The finest food in Basel is probably at the Hotel Euler's *Fine Bouche* restaurant, or at the *Bruderholz.*

For Italian food at its best (not just pasta or pizza) go to *Donati.* Top class, too, are *Schutenhaus,* Hilton's *Wettstein Grill,* International Hotel's *Charolaise,* and the Three Kings' *Rôtisserie des Rois.* All the above are (E).

Among the more interesting brasseries are *Fischerstube* (just across the river in Rheingasse) where the doctor-owner brews beer on the premises, and *Braunen Mutz* in busy Barfusserplatz, both (M).

Possibly Basel's best fondue is at cozy *Elizabethenstubli* (M) or the rather more expensive *Taverne Valaisanne.* For typical Basel restaurants with local specialties try the *Basler Keller* (in Hotel Basel), *Goldener Sternen, Safranzunft,* or *Schlusselzunft* restaurants; all (M) or slightly more. *Schloss Binningen* is a redecorated castle in a charming park. (M)

Good spots in a cash crisis are *Schumachernzunft,* Hutgasse (try their 'leberli mit rösti'), and *Gifthuttli* or cheaper *Hasenburg,* both Scheidergasse (latter full of atmosphere but empty of frills). Other cash savers are the department store restaurants and the somewhat basic Migros self-service cafeterias.

 ENTERTAINMENT. *The* fine, new *Stadttheater* produces opera, operetta, musical comedy, and drama. The *Komödie* puts on plays. Cabaret at the *Théâtre Fauteuil.* The many nightspots range from dance bars and nightclubs, with and without floorshows, to striptease. Some stay open to 2 A.M. or later. Best to check all entertainment in *This Week in Basel,* free from hotels, banks, etc.

 MUSEUMS. Basel has an exceptional number of fine and varied museums, art galleries, etc. Pride of place goes to the vast *Kunstmuseum,* one of Switzerland's finest art galleries. Others include *Antiken-Museum* (ancient Greek and Italian art), *Historical Museum, Kunsthalle* (art gallery), *Ethnological and Natural History Museum, Kirschgartenmuseum* (furniture, watches, porcelain, toys), *Gymnastic and Sports Museum.*

SHOPPING. Basel's main shopping area, including elegant Freie Strasse and many other cheaper streets, lies between the market place and central station.

The Swiss Rhineland

Basel is the gateway to the Swiss Rhineland, a beautiful region stretching to Lake Constance and beyond; one in which the river meanders past rich agricultural land, orchards, a sprinkling of castles, medieval towns with the stepped gables typical of the Rhineland, and several resorts and spas. For good measure, near Schaffhausen the river tumbles over the famous Rhine Falls.

PRACTICAL INFORMATION FOR SWISS RHINELAND

BADEN. Hotels: The *Staadhof* (L), *Verenahof* and *Ochsen*, both (1), all under same management, and *Limmathof* (1), have indoor pools. *Bären* (1). The *Adler*, *Hirschen*, and *Parc* are all (3-4). Restaurant: *Kursaal* (E). Boule is played at the Kursaal-Casino, where there is also dancing.

KREUZLINGEN. Hotel: *Plaza* (4). Restaurants: *Schaefli*, family type, open-air dining. *Drachenburg in Gottlieben*, old-fashioned inn on the Rhine.

NEUHAUSEN. Hotel: *Bellevue* (2); looks down on Rhine falls.

OLTEN. Hotels: *Schweizerhof* and *Emmental*, both (4). Restaurants: *Walliser Kanne*, terrace overlooking the Aare, Valais specialties; *Ratskeller*, in a building dating from 1673, weapons collection.

RHEINFELDEN. Hotels: *Eden* (1) has indoor pool, as has *Schützen* (2). *Schwanen* and slightly cheaper *Schiff* are (2). *Ochsen* (3-4).
Restaurants: *Feldschlösschen-Stadt*, Rhine terrace, fish and regional specialties; *Wiedmer*, tearoom with terrace on Rhine.

ROMANSHORN. Hotels: *See-hotel* (3). *Bodan* (4), has fish specialties in its restaurant.

SCHAFFHAUSEN. Hotels: *Bahnhof*, *Park-Villa Garni*, and *Kronenhof*; all (3).
Restaurants: *Fischerzunft*, near the Rhine boat dock, specializing in *Felchen* and *Äschen*, two varieties of Rhine trout; *Brauerei Falken*, beer cellar, bowling alley; *Frieden*, antique décor.

SEENGEN. Hotel: *Schloss Brestenberg* (3), 17th-cent. manor house, converted into small hotel; overlooks lake.

SOLOTHURN. Hotels: *Krone* (3), one of Switzerland's oldest inns, much modernized. *Roter Thurm*, new and bright; *Astoria*; both (4).
Restaurants: *Zunfthaus zu Wirthen* (M), in old guildhall; *Misteli-Gasche*, operated by same family for several decades; *Bahnhofbuffet* (I).

STEIN-AM-RHEIN. Hotel: *Grenstein* (4). Restaurants: *Sonne* (M). *Café Krone* in Rheinfels hotel, terrace over the Rhine.

ZURZACH. Hotels: *Zurzacherhof* (2), indoor pool. *Turmhotel* (2), outdoor pool, has spa water piped in for medicinal baths. *Ochsen* (4).

MOTELS. At Egerkingen, junction on N1 and N2 motorways, *Agip*. At Hauenstein, 3 miles northeast of Olten, *Nord-Sud*. At Itingen, 13 miles southeast of Basel, *Ochsen*. At Solothurn, *Touring*. All open year round.

Zurich
Zurich, with some 410,000 inhabitants, is one of the most beautifully situated cities in Switzerland, and is its largest. It's the industrial heart of the nation, but you'd never know it. There's no smoke, no smog. The industries are all electrified, and the buildings in which they are housed look more like sanatoria or college dormitories than factories. There are no slums. The workers live in pretty little villas with flowers round the

door, or in ultra-modern apartment houses. And beneath the staid pavement of Bahnhofstrasse lie the gold-filled vaults of the banks whose famous numbered accounts have made Zurich a world financial center.

Zurich is Protestant. On a high pedestal beside the Grossmünster, a church said to have been founded by Charlemagne, stands the statue of Ulrich Zwingli. In 1519, defying the Pope, he started preaching the Reformation there, almost splitting the Swiss Confederation in two. His bronze effigy looks out toward the Bellevue Platz, amusement center of the city; even today his spirit tends to live on in Zurich. Ironically, the cathedral's splendid Romanesque architecture dominates the city's most swinging quarter, the Niederdorf. But if the Zurichers have a streak of puritanism, they are also scrupulously honest, fastidiously clean, generous, and truly remarkable for their genuine kindness.

Zurich's weather, to quote James Joyce, who is buried in Zurich and who wrote many pages of his *Ulysses* in the Pfauen Restaurant here, is "as uncertain as a baby's bottom". A rare crystal-clear day providing a wonderful vista of snow-capped mountains rising from the lake is, according to Zurichers, a guarantee that it's going to rain. April and May are almost certain to be rainy and cold, although you may get some blissfully warm, sunny days. From early summer through the fall, the odds are with you.

PRACTICAL INFORMATION FOR ZURICH

HOTELS. If you want the best—and can afford it—Zurich offers you a bewildering choice of superb hotels. In the super-deluxe department the city's top five are:

Atlantis, on southern fringe of city near the 2,800-ft. Uetliberg. Indoor pool; well appointed but somewhat impersonal modern atmosphere. Also has annex (2).

Baur au Lac, stands in its own lakeside minipark near the end of Bahnhofstrasse; an elegant establishment.

Dolder Grand, up among the pinewoods but only about ten mins. from city center. Has a long and distinguish career. Outdoor pool, and superb views.

Eden au Lac, charming, popular; pleasant outlook across lake; tranquil atmosphere, highly recommended restaurant.

Zurich, in the heart of city, beside the river Limmat only a few minutes walk from station. Indoor pool.

Close runners-up and (L) are: *Ascot, Carlton-Elite, Continental, Glarnischhof, Nova Park,* indoor pool, *St. Gotthard, Zum Storchen* and the rebuilt *Waldhaus Dolder.* Also (L) but further out are: *International* at Oerliken, an easily reached district about 3 miles from city center. About a mile from the airport is the *Zurich-Airport Hilton* with all expected Hilton amenities and its own free bus service to the city; spurious Old West theme decor in the public rooms.

Good value are the two *Holiday Inns* (1), each with indoor pool. The larger is beside the airport; the other at Regensdorf. Both are modern, have good food, are convenient, and could just as well be on Miami Beach, or at any airport anywhere, as in Zurich.

Of the other (1) hotels, those handy for the station and Bahnhofstrasse area include the remarkably comfortable little *Kindli,* as well as the *Franziskaner, Glockenhof, Schweizerhof* and *Simplon.* Quietly situated is the *Florhof,* an elegant mansion hotel. Near to the Opera House is the charming, reader-recommended *Europe.*

In the Enge district to the south, *Engamatthof;* and on the Dolder heights, the *Sonnenberg.*

Among numerous class (2-3) establishments are *Bellaria, Du Théâtre, Helmhaus* (breakfast only; reader recommended), *Rigihof, Waldorf,* and *Zurcherhof.*

Outside the city the *Seehotel Meierhof* (indoor pool) at Horgen, halfway along the lake, can be recommended, and at Glattbrugg there's the *Airport Hotel* (not to be confused with the Airport Hilton); both (2).

For *budget* travelers, Zurich is not the place. Except for the *Youth Hostel* (Jugendheberge Zurich, in Mustschallenstrasse) it is nearly impossible to find anything under 20 frs. per person per night. *Glockenhof,* Sihlstrasse 33, is the local YMCA; *Foyer Hottingen* (Hottingerstrasse 31) and *Martahaus* (Zähringerstrasse 36) take only women.

MOTELS. At Adliswil, 4 miles south of Zurich, *Motor-Inn Jolie Ville.* At Brutten, 10 miles northeast *Steighof.* At Rudolfstetten, 10 miles east, *Rudolfstetten.* At Sihlbrugg, 13 miles south, *Sihlbrugg.* At Winterthur, *Wölflingen.* Open all year.

 RESTAURANTS. If cost is no object, the *Veltliner Keller* in the old part of the city (Schlüsselgasse 8, you'll have to ask a half-dozen times before you find it!) is a *must.* Here, served by colorfully costumed waitresses, you have superbly prepared regional specialties (fully described in English on the menu) together with excellent wines. Even if the food weren't magnificent, it would be worth a visit to see the splendid carved-wood décor of the dining rooms.

Next (but no less important) on the gourmet list is the *Baur au Lac Grill* (E), not to be confused with the main dining room of that hotel. The cuisine is French at its best, with an excellent selection of regional dishes.

The *Rôtisserie Côte d'Or* (M-E) in the Goldenes Schwert is excellent, reader-recommended.

Try one of the guildhall restaurants; the *Zunfthaus zur Zimmerleuten* (carpenters), the *Haus zum Rüden* (the attractive Gothic restaurant of the Society of Noblemen), the *Saffran* (spice merchants) and the *Königstuhl, Zunfthaus zur Schneidern* (tailors), or the *Schmieden* (blacksmiths). Good food. Most are (M-E). Highly recommended is *Kronenhalle* (M-E), at the foot of Rämistrasse. The works of famous artists which adorn its walls are originals, and match the restaurant's friendly atmosphere and memorable food. It was James Joyce's favorite restaurant. Maybe you'll sit at the author's table in the corner below his portrait inscribed to the proprietor. Also recommended is the elegant, small restaurant (M-E) of the Florhof hotel.

On a warm evening, try the *Bauschänzli* on its own island in the Limmat river near the Quai Bridge (with concerts) or the *Fischstube Zürichhorn* built on piles over the lake; excellent food. Both (E). Very close is the *Kasino Zürichhorn.* And in suburban, lakeside Küsnacht *Seiler's Ermitage* has garden terraces.

Bellerive au Lac (E), has excellent French cooking and a beautiful terrace overlooking the lake.

On the western shore of the lake, at Thalwil, is the small hotel and restaurant *Alexander am See,* and at Horgen, the *Seehof Meierhof,* both (E) and well known for excellent cooking.

Zurich has many good (M) restaurants. One is *Zeughauskeller,* the old Zurich arsenal, where you can dine decently for about 10 frcs. and order from an English-language menu, too. Only a few paces from the Paradeplatz at Gassenstrasse 16 is the beerhouse-restaurant *Knopf,* another spot where around 10 frcs. will buy a really first-rate meal. The *Bahnhofbuffet* (main rail station restaurant) is apt to be a bit noisy; specialties expensive.

Deserving of special mention is a restaurant chain called *Mövenpick* (the Swiss-German name for the seagulls around Zurich). For addresses, see the phone book. They have a growing number of *Silber Kugel* snack bars, devoid of frills but very popular with the budget conscious.

Outstanding exotic restaurants are: *Hongkong,* Seefeldstr. 60 (oriental); *Emilio,* Müllerstr. 5 and *Bodega Española,* Münstergasse 15 (both Spanish); *Piccoli-Accademia,* Rotwandstr. 48 (excellent), *Chiantiquelle,* Stampfenbachstr. 38, *Ciro's,* Militarstr., and the *Pizzeria Napoli,* Sandstr. 7 are Italian.

For charming atmosphere, entertainment, and good food, try *Töndurys Widder,* Widdergasse 6 (reserve in advance); or *Kindli,* Oberer Rennweg, dinner with outstanding folklore show is (E), lunch (M).

Chässtube (M), Löwenstr. 66, specializes in cheese dishes.

Gleich and *Hiltl,* both vegetarian and (I), are superb of their kind.

Good spots for the budget conscious are the restaurants of the *Migros* chain (self-service), the department stores, the *Zurcher Frauenverein* (Zurich Women's Association), and various university cafeterias such as *The Mensa* (Ramistrasse 71), the *Mensa Polyterrasse* (Leonhardstrasse 34), and *Culmann* (Culmanstrasse 1). *Olivenbaum, Platzli, Fronsinn* and *Restaurant Seidenhof* are all run by a temperance league and offer plain, substantial food, including meatless, at very attractive prices.

ENTERTAINMENT. Zurich nightspots can best be described as undistinguished. Striptease/hostess: *Maxim, La Puce* (in the small bar), *Terrasse,* and *Red House.* Dancing: *Mascotte* (usually, fine jazz), *La Ferme* (rustic style), *Bellerive, Diagonal* of the Baur au Lac (chic), *Hazyland* (good music; western saloon decor). And at *Kindli* (see 'Restaurants', above) there's Swiss folklore and a good, musical stage show.

The *Schauspielhaus* is one of the most progressive serious theaters of Europe. The *Opernhaus* (grand opera, light opera, operetta), produces topnotch performances for the annual June festival. The *Bernhard* theater plays broad farce, the small *Theater am Hechtplatz* is an experimental stage for all sorts of acted entertainment.

MUSEUMS. Just behind the station is the *Swiss National Museum* (*Landesmuseum*), a major collection of Swiss art, culture and history. Many other museums include the *Kunsthaus* (excellent permanent collection of paintings, sculpture, etc., with frequent superb loan exhibitions); *Museum of Applied Arts* (*Kunstgewerbemuseum*), an outstanding exhibition of industrial design, architecture, handicrafts; *Rietberg Museum* (primitive African and Asiatic art, etc.); *Centre Le Corbusier* (the last building designed by the famous Swiss-born architect, now devoted largely to his paintings). For list of museums, art galleries, etc., see 'Zurich Weekly Bulletin', available in most hotels.

SHOPPING. Leading south from the main rail station and Bahnhofplatz (with its subterranean shopping center 'Shop Ville') is the fashionable and elegant Bahnhofstrasse, which the Zurichers call "the Fifth Avenue of Switzerland". Luxurious cars, glittering shops, sleek, well dressed citizens and expensive hotels produce a quietly elegant atmosphere of great wealth and discreet power; leading off each side you'll find the city's handsomest shops and department stores.

The Lake of Zurich and the Northeast

A four-hour trip by boat down this 24-mile-long lake to historic old Rapperswil offers a succession of charming views. Boats leave from the landing at the end of the Bahnhofstrasse. Zug, an ancient walled city with much modern development, can be reached from Zurich by rail. It has an interesting museum of gold and silver work and other handicrafts; also splendid views, from the hill overlooking the town, of the Jungfrau and other great peaks. Einsiedeln, the birthplace of Paracelsus and home of the celebrated Black Madonna of Einsiedeln, performs every 5 years (ending in 5 or 0) *The Great World Theater* by Calderón, a spectacular religious melodrama in which 700 local residents take part. The Abbey Church forms a splendid Baroque backcloth.

Well worth a visit is St. Gallen, a modern little metropolis and ancient seat of culture and learning, famed as a textile center and also for the priceless collection of books and manuscripts—some are 1,000 years old—in the abbey's magnificent rococo library. The town is also a first-rate base for exploring the contrasting delights of the northeast, one of Switzerland's cheapest regions. Within easy striking distance are Lake Constance and a host of smaller lakes, the rolling hills of Appenzell, snow-capped 8,200-feet Mount Säntis, the tiny secluded canton of Glarus, scores of charming unspoiled valleys, villages, townlets and resorts, as well as, for good measure, the pocket principality of Liechtenstein.

PRACTICAL INFORMATION FOR THE NORTHEAST

APPENZELL, folkloric center, ancient town hall. Hotels: *Hecht* and *Säntis,* both (3).

BAD RAGAZ, resort and spa. Hotels: *Quellenhof,* in a park, and the cheaper, adjacent *Hof Ragaz* are (L). Near the station, the smart *Cristal* (1), with indoor pool. *Lattmann, Tamina* and *Sandi* are (2).
Restaurant: *Hotel Wartenstein* (M), high above resort.

BRAUNWALD, quiet mountain plateau resort. No cars. Hotels: *Bellevue (2); Alpina, Alpenblick,* and *Niederschlacht,* all (3).

RAPPERSWIL, pleasant lake resort. Hotels: *Schwanen* (3). *Du Lac* and *Speer* (3-4).

ST. GALLEN (ST. GALL). Hotels: *Walhalla,* near station, and *Hecht* with excellent (M) restaurant, in town center, are both (1). *Metropol* and *Montana* (3). *Ekkehard* and *Continental* are (4), as are the delightful *Dom,* comfortable, quiet, near cathedral, and *Touring,* both breakfast only.
Restaurants: Besides the hotels, *Bahnhof Buffet* (I-M), *Schützengarten,* and *Gaststube Schlössli* are good. The *Baratella* specializes in chicken and Italian food.

UNTERWASSER & WILDHAUS. Adjacent winter and summer resorts, so far "discovered" by relatively few, and thus moderately cheap. At Unterwasser: *Sternen* (2), *Säntis* (4). At Wildhaus, *Acker* (1), *Hirschen* (3), each with indoor pool; *Toggenburg* (4).

ZUG. Hotels: *Ochsen, Rosenberg* and *Guggithal,* all (3); *Löwen* (4).

MOTELS. At Bad Ragaz, *Touring Motel Schloss-Ragaz.* At Wil, *Motel Restaurant Mini-Golf.*

The Bernese Oberland

The Bernese Oberland is a magnificent area of 1,800 square miles, comprising nine valleys, the lovely lakes of Thun and Brienz, and a number of lakelets in the heart of the mountains. Its wild mountain scenery became the rage in the 19th century after its praises had been sung by Jean-Jacques Rousseau. The area derives its name from Bern, Switzerland's capital and fourth largest city (pop. about 155,000), which, the Bernese insist, derives *its* name from the German word for bear, specifically the big black grizzly that Berthold V, Duke of Zähringen, it is said, killed on the spot where he founded the city in 1191. There are living symbols of Bern in the famous bear pit at one end of the capital's Nydegg Bridge, friendly fellows whose clowning delights the carrot-offering kids and tourists. One of Europe's best preserved medieval cities, with arcaded streets, 16th-century fountains, beautiful old buildings and a wealth of towers—this is Bern. Modern art-lovers will find the world's biggest Klee collection here, and music-lovers, too, are well catered for.

PRACTICAL INFORMATION FOR BERN

HOTELS. Bern has two famous (L) hotels. *Bellevue Palace* is high above river Aare with superb views of the Alps; modernized but clearly a hotel in the grand tradition; excellent restaurants. *Schweizerhof,* opposite the new station, is another hotel in the grand tradition; notable for its tastefully displayed antiques, and fine furniture and paintings; memorable cuisine.

Convenient to the station and shops are *Bären, Bristol, Metropole* (relatively new; attractive modern decor), *Savoy* and *Stadthof.* A few minutes west of the station are the *City* (rebuilt 1973) and *Alfa* (new 1973; garage beneath the hotel). All (1).

Among many (2) hotels are *Krebs* (breakfast only; much modernized) and *Wächter,* both within a few paces of the station, and *Continental,* near the Kornhausplatz.

Also near the Kornhausplatz is the *Volkshaus* (3), an old hotel but recently renovated rooms are good; breakfast only, but next door under same management is a group of seven attractive new restaurants and snack bars. *Glocke,* beside the Clock Tower, and *Goldener Adler,* near the Nydegg Bridge, are (4). Simple but inexpensive is the *Nydeck,* in the old section of town.

MOTELS. At Muri, 2 miles southeast of the city, *Krone.* At Münchenbuchsee, 5 miles north, *Bern-Biel.* At Münsingen, *Münsingen.* All open year round.

RESTAURANTS. The standard of Bern's cooking is high. There are many good eateries, and the city has a reputation for giving better than average value for money.

The *Bellevue* and *Schweizerhof* hotels have justly famous grillrooms (E). Slightly cheaper, with notable French cuisine, are the *Ermitage,* Marktgasse 15, *Mistral,* Kramgasse 42 and *Du Théâtre,* Theaterplatz 7. The *Della Casa,* Schauplatzgasse 16, *Räblus,* Zeughausgasse 3, and *Ratskeller,* Gerechtigkeitsgasse 81, are also good and (M-E).

The *Kornhauskeller,* Kornhausplatz, has a large, popular cellar-restaurant with Swiss and local specialties such as Bernerplatte. Another typical cellar-restaurant is the restored, 17th-century *Klötzlikeller,* Gerechtigkeitsgasse 62. Both about (M). If you want to watch a rather noisy but well-presented folklore show while you dine you can do so at the *Swiss Chalet* (M-E), Rathausgasse 75.

A good spot for "fondue," "raclette," and "viande sechée" (mountain dried beef or pork, sliced wafer-thin) is *Taverne Valaisanne* (M), Neuengasse 40. *Le Mazot* (M), Bärenplatz 5, specializes in Swiss cheese dishes. One of the best places for "rösti" in its many varieties is *Zytglogge* (M), Theaterplatz 8.

Pinocchio, Aarbergasse 6, is an attractive small restaurant with excellent Italian food. For paella and other Spanish dishes try *Commerce,* Gerechtigkeitsgasse 74. Both (M-E). Succulent salads and other vegetarian dishes are at *Vegetaris* (I), Neuengasse 15, a first floor restaurant where, surprisingly, you can eat outside in a quiet, first floor garden.

Among Bern's many inexpensive spots are *Spatz, Gfeller,* and *Börse,* all in Bärenplatz, and the new *Siebe Stube* group of restaurant-snackbars at Zeughausgasse 9. The *Mövenpick* restaurant-snackbar chain has four branches in Bern with prices mostly (M). Those with budget problems often make for the department store restaurants. For a fill-up without frills at rockbottom prices try *Migros,* Marktgasse. The morning produce market on Bärenplatz will give you both good sightseeing and the makings for lunch. For students, the *Universität Mensa* is at Gesellschaftstrasse 2, but unfortunately is closed mid-July to mid-October.

ENTERTAINMENT. Unless you understand German, the theater in Bern will be pretty well lost on you, except for the *Municipal Theater* which stages opera, operetta, ballet and plays. Bern is noted for its "cellar-theaters," frequently fascinating, often outstanding. Some are inclined to be ephemeral, but there are usually at least half a dozen. Nightspots in Bern are far from spectacular, but they allow you to while away an evening and get in some dancing. *Mocambo* has two good floorshows and is the most elegant spot in town. *Chikito* also has its *Frisco-Bar* and caters to a very young crowd. You can dance at the *Kursaal* (and, if you wish, fritter away your money at boule). Dance bars include the vast *Babalu* and (mainly for young people) *Happy Light. Restaurant zum Schwert,* Rathausgasse 66, is a popular local drinking place.

 MUSEUMS. There are five, conveniently close to each other on or near Helvetiaplatz square. *Historical Museum* (highlight is the booty captured from Charles the Bold after his defeat by the Confederacy). *Natural History Museum* (noted for collection of stuffed African animals in realistic settings). *Art Museum* (Kunstmuseum, at Hodlerstrasse 12) (Swiss art from 15th cen. and European from 19th and 20th; also world's largest Klee collection). *Swiss Rifle Museum* (weapons, etc). *Alpine Museum* (mountaineering) and *Swiss Postal Museum,* both in the same building.

SHOPPING in Bern, whatever the weather, is always a delight thanks to its arcaded streets. The main shopping area is east of the station.

Interlaken

Gateway to the Bernese Oberland, for generations Interlaken had one purpose only, to attract summer tourists. In winter most of its great hotels, tearooms and bars closed down. But nowadays more and more are open year-round as winter sports enthusiasts begin to realize just how many superb facilities are readily accessible.

Interlaken, as its name implies, is situated 'between the lakes'—those of Thun and Brienz. On a strip of flat, grassy land bisected by the river Aare, it is surrounded by a superb mountain panorama. The west and east sections of the town are connected by the Höheweg, the central boulevard lined with trees, formal gardens, hotels and shops. A quaint touch is given by the fiacres as they clip-clop alongside modern coaches, but it's a nostalgic touch, too, as they are among the few remaining relics of 19th-century and Edwardian Interlaken. The older hotels have been pulled down or modernized, and new ones have arisen such as the skyscraper Hotel Métropole with its breathtaking views from the upper floors.

During the summer, Interlaken has a tradition of open air performances (but the audience sits in a fine covered grandstand) of Schiller's *William Tell,* a drama with many actors which perpetuates the story of the legendary hero and the historic overthrow of the house of Habsburg. The resort also has an outstandingly fine 18-hole golf course, but golfers claim that they are put off by the magnificent scenery!

Obviously Interlaken has many restaurants, cafés, bars, dance halls, cinemas and all the trappings that go to make a successful resort, including a casino standing in beautiful gardens, but first and foremost it is an excursion center, and as such has few rivals throughout Europe.

The Jungfrau

Of Interlaken's many splendid excursions, the most spectacular, given the right weather, is the famous trip to Jungfraujoch (11,333 ft.). From Interlaken east station you go by rail to Lauterbrunnen where, in the green cogwheel train of the Wengernalp railway, the steep climb really begins. The train twists and turns through tunnels and over viaducts, giving a succession of camera-clicking views of mountains, valleys and waterfalls. At Kleine Scheidegg (6,760 ft.) you change to the smart little brown and cream train of the Jungfrau railway which in six miles climbs more than 4,500 feet to the summit station. The line took 16 years to build, was opened as long ago as 1912, and is still one of the world's railway marvels.

Beyond Kleine Scheidegg there are wonderful views of Mönch (13,450 ft.) as well as of the treacherous Eiger North Wall. You do go up it, but in safety and comfort, on the inside! Just beyond Eigergletscher station (7,610 ft.) the train plunges into the 4½ mile long tunnel through the Eiger and Mönch mountains up to Jungfraujoch station. On the way it stops twice: at Eigerwand station (9,400 ft.) just inside the North Wall and at Eismeer (10,370 ft.). At each, enormous windows have been cut in the mountainside, and the train waits long enough for you to get out and peer at the fabulous views.

From the underground Jungfraujoch summit station a free elevator will take you to the 11,720 ft. high Sphinx terrace to gaze at an Alpine panorama that is one of Europe's wonders, and to look down to the 10 mile long Aletsch glacier. You can visit the ice palace, glacier exhibition, souvenir shop or post office, have a sleigh ride or skiing lesson, or eat a meal in the new mountainside restaurant.

On the homeward journey you can descend by the alternative Grindelwald route giving superb views of the North Wall towering above. Back at Interlaken you can reflect that you've been on the highest railway in Europe to the world's highest underground station; stood on Europe's highest mountain observation terrace; looked down on the greatest glacier in the Alps; been on what is almost certainly Europe's finest and most spectacular excursion; and traveled on the world's most expensive railway. But, like some 400,000 people every year, it's a fair bet that you'll think it worth every franc.

PRACTICAL INFORMATION FOR INTERLAKEN

 HOTELS. Small though it is, Interlaken has nearly 100 hotels and can put up 5,000 visitors during the season. The three leaders, all near (L) and with indoor pools, are the *Victoria-Jungfrau;* the slightly cheaper *Beau-Rivage,* recently modernized; and newer, 18-story *Métropole,* superb view from top floor bar.

In class (1) are: the *Bellevue; Bernerhof,* ultra-modern but colorfully charming; and *Royal St.-Georges.* Near Lake Brienz boat landing stage and East station is *Du Lac* (2), very praiseworthy.

The *Bristol-Terminus; Eurotel* (breakfast only); *Merkur; Park-Hotel Mattenhof,* near the Tell theater, outdoor pool; *Weisses Kreuz;* and the exceptionally pleasant *Stella,* one of the best in its class, fine indoor pool, are all (3).

The cheaper (4) hotels include the *Anker, Helvetia, Rugenpark* (breakfast only), *Beyeler, Chalet Swiss, Villa Rio,* and *Hotel Aarburg.*

 RESTAURANTS. Most of the good eating in Interlaken takes place in hotel restaurants. The *Jungfrau Grill-Stube* (E) of the Victoria-Jungfrau hotel, which has an attractive Oberland atmosphere, is noted for charcoal grills and all Swiss dishes including fondue. The *Krebs* hotel has a terrace with a fine view of Jungfrau, and its open-air restaurant (M) specializes in grills and Bernese dishes. Excellent dishes, impeccably prepared and served, rather than lengthy menus, are keynotes of the *Du Lac* (M). The Métropole has several attractive restaurants including the *Charolais* (E), *Raclette Taverne* (M) for Swiss dishes, and *Métrosnack* (I). Near the post office, the *Hotel Bären*'s dining room is well recommended. The enormous *Schuh,* a traditional rendezvous in Interlaken, is both a restaurant (M to E) and a tearoom with memorable patisseries. All the above are in Höheweg. Among other tearooms are *Sigenthaler* and *Deuschle.*

For large, outstandingly good pizzas try *Piz-Paz* (I) in Jungfraustrasse. If cash is a problem, aim for the first floor cafeteria (I) of *Migros,* opposite the west station; also *Gasthof Sternen,* Jungfraustrasse 27.

SHOPPING. Most of Interlaken's shops are located in Bahnhofstrasse and lengthy Höheweg, which together form the resort's backbone.

PRACTICAL INFORMATION FOR THE BERNESE OBERLAND

 SKI CENTERS. The Bernese Oberland is one of the world's most celebrated winter sports areas. The winter season is generally from December through March, but most places double as summer resorts. Each resort has its own tourist office; a postcard request will bring you detailed information.

The main resorts have an abundance of skilifts, cable cars and other winter sports amenities. Among the best are:

Adelboden (4,450 ft.); Beatenberg (3,800 ft.), sunniest; Grindelwald (3,400 ft), a moderately-priced resort; Gstaad (3,450 ft.), one of the most fashionable winter and summer resorts; Jungfraujoch (11,300 ft.); Kandersteg (3,850 ft.); Kleine Scheidegg (6,750 ft.); Lenk (3,600 ft.), unpretentious and relatively inexpensive; Meiringen (1,950 ft.); Mürren (5,400 ft.), no motor traffic; Saanenmöser (4,200 ft.); Wengen (4,200 ft.), long-established, very popular, no road access; Zweisimmen (3,150 ft.), specially good for children and beginners.

HOTELS. The Bernese Oberland has an abundance of hotels that almost invariably give a high standard of service. Whatever the price range you are virtually assured of enjoying good value in the hotel you select. More often than not, of course, in the smaller villages you'll only find relatively modest—although frequently charming—hotels and inns. But remember, some hotels close for varying periods in the year, so check in advance.

ADELBODEN. Best is the *Nevada* (1), indoor pool. The *Bristol, Huldi & Waldhaus, Park-Bellevue* (indoor pool, sauna) and slightly cheaper *Adler* are all (3). *Edelweiss-Schweizerhof* (4).

BEATENBERG. *Blumlisalp-Beatrice* (3).

BÖNINGEN. *Seiler au Lac* (2), lakeside garden.

BRIENZ. *Bären* (3), outdoor pool.

GRINDELWALD. *Grand Hotel Regina* (L), air-conditioned. *Sunstar, Weisses Kreuz, Belvédère, Parkhotel Schönegg* and *Schweizerhof,* each with indoor pool, and *Silberhorn* (kosher), are all (1). The *Spinne* and *Résidence,* are (3).

GSTAAD. *Gstaad Palace* (L), center of society life in Gstaad, has indoor pool, tennis, golf, riding. In class (1) are: *Alpina, Bellevue, Reuteler,* each with outdoor pool. *Alphorn,* rustic-style, with indoor pool, *Olden, Rössli* and *Victoria* are (3). *Chalet Christiania* (breakfast only), *Bernerhof* and *Neueret* are (4).

KANDERSTEG. *Royal-Bellevue* (2), indoor pool. *Victoria, Schweizerhof* and *Parkhotel Gemmi* (indoor pool) are (3). *Adler, Alpenhof* (indoor pool), and *Bernerhof* are (4).

KLEINE SCHEIDEGG. *Scheidegg,* (3).

LENK. *Kurhaus, Bellevue, Kreuz* and *Wildstrubel* are (2-3). *Sternen* (4).

MEIRINGEN. *Sauvage,* and cheaper *Hirschen* and *Weisses Kreuz;* all (4).

MERLIGEN. *Beatus* (L), heated indoor pool, sauna.

MÜRREN. *Mürren Palace* (1), is the center of winter social life. *Eiger* and *Jungfrau Lodge* are both (2). *Alpina, Bellevue, Edelweiss* and *Jungfrau* are all (3). *Belmont* (4).

SAANENMÖSER. *Golf & Sporthotel* (1).

SPIEZ. *Eden,* and *Belvédère,* are (1). *Bahnhof, Des Alpes* and (breakfast only) *Erica* all (3).

THUN. *Holiday Beau Rivage* (indoor pool), and *Bellevue* (outdoor pool) are (3) *Elite* and *Freienhof* (much modernized, 14th-cent. hotel in old town), (4).

WENGEN. *Park-Beausite* (indoor pool) is (1). (2) are *Metropole* (indoor pool), *Lauberhorn* and *Regina. Alpenrose, Belvédère, Falken* and *Silberhorn* are among (3) hotels. *Eiger* is (4).

ZWEISIMMEN. *Rawyl-Sternen, Krone* and *Simmenthal* are (3).

MOTELS. At Einigen, the *Hirschen* and at Faulensee, the *Faulensee* (closed Nov.-Apr.), both near Spiez. At Grindelwald, *Grindelwald* (closed Nov.-Dec.). At Gstaad, *Rütti.* At Interlaken, *Marti-Motel* (closed Nov.-Mar.), the *Golf* and *Golf-Motel Neuhaus* (closed Nov.-Feb.). At Kandersteg, *Kandersteg.* At Meiringen, *Sherlock Holmes.* At Merligen, *Mon Abri.* At Munchenbuchsee, *Bern-Biel.* At Munsingen, near Bern, *Munsingen.* At Wilderswil, *Luna.* At Zweisimmen, *Sport-Motel.* All open year round except where otherwise stated.

Lucerne

Few cities are more beloved by tourists than Lucerne, with its 15th- and 16th-century houses, its medieval covered bridges, and its dreamy old world atmosphere contrasting with the liveliest interest in modern art, music and other expressions of 20th-century culture. April through October is the season here. The August/September music festival is an international event with its topflight orchestras, conductors, singers and soloists. If you want to come for that, it would be wise to make hotel reservations and procure tickets *at least six months in advance.*

You'll have the most fun shamelessly crossing and recrossing those two wonderful 14th- and 15th-century wooden bridges, the Kapell-brücke and the Spreuerbrücke, inspecting the paintings under the roof. The renovated Kapellbrücke, the larger and most famous of the two, leads diagonally across the swiftly-flowing Reuss River from the old St. Peter's chapel, past the picturesque Wasserturm (water tower) to the southern bank. The paintings here depict scenes from Lucerne's history. Those on the Spreuerbrücke portray the Totentanz, grim medieval dance of death. Wander through the picturesque old quarters on the north bank, inspect the ancient city walls, take a look at the quaint Weinmarkt, and you will think you're back in the Middle Ages.

You must, of course, see the famous Lion of Lucerne, designed by Thorwaldsen, carved in stone by Ahorn in the early 19th century, and dedicated to the heroic Swiss Guards of Louis XVI, who defended the Tuileries when the French Revolution broke out in 1792. The Lion lies in a niche hewn out of the cliffside near the celebrated Glacier Gardens, a unique collection of huge potholes created by glacier water during the Ice Age but not unearthed until 1872.

PRACTICAL INFORMATION FOR LUCERNE

HOTELS. Lucerne has three deluxe hotels. The *Grand Hotel National* is superbly situated overlooking the lake. One of the top hostelries of Switzerland, its suites are fit for a king, its ordinary rooms for a crown prince. Service and cuisine are on the same superior level as the appointments.

The *Schweizerhof* looks across busy Schweizerhofquai to the lake. Oldest of the trio, its public rooms have traditional elegance; rooms in the new wing are up-to-date, but parts of the old wing are badly in need of refurbishing.

The most modern is the spacious *Palace,* facing the lake across a tree-lined promenade. It has a fashionable grill and famous bar; public rooms and chambers alike recently redone to advantage.

In class (1), tops is the newly modernized *Carlton-Hotel Tivoli,* which has a view of the water as does the slightly cheaper *Europe Grand.* In the same price bracket as the *Europe* are the *Astoria,* panoramic rooftop terrace and bar, and the *Luzer-nerhof* with a good dining room, and located near the American Express office, as well as the *Montana,* which has a hillside situation with magnificent views, and private funicular.

Other hillside hotels with splendid views are the historic *Château Gütsch* (2-1), where Queen Victoria stayed, and the cheaper *Royal.*

Hotels beside or close to the river include the *Balances & Bellevue* (1), *Des Alpes* (2), with excellent food, reader-recommended, and the *Raben-am-See* and *Schiff,* both (4).

On the south (rail station) side of the river is the long-established *Wilder Mann* (2-1), modernized but retaining its old-world atmosphere and charm; several rooms furnished with antiques; notable restaurant.

Within easy reach of the rail station are: *Monopol* (1); the *Bernerhof, Continental, Diana, Park* and *Schiller,* all (2); *Central* (4).

On Haldenstrasse, close to the lakeside promenade, are *Eden au Lac* (2) and *Beau Séjour au Lac* (4). Not far from the lake is *De la Paix* (2), with pool, reader-recommended, and nearby the *Union* (2-1), with well-known restaurant (M).

At Lucerne-Seeburg, just outside town, the *Seeburg* (1), with a new annex, faces the lake, and offers three restaurants.

RESTAURANTS. Lucerne's most famous restaurant is undoubtedly that of the *Wilden Mann,* mentioned above; it has been operating since 1517. The *Old Swiss House,* near the Lion of Lucerne, is an old converted patrician home. Both (M). Another gourmet favorite is *Zur Gerbern,* built in 1334, at 7 Sternenplatz, in the old city near Kapellplatz. The *Astoria* hotel has pleasant roof-garden dining: cold dishes only. *Li Tai Pe* (Furrengasse 14) (E) is one of Europe's outstanding Chinese restaurants and deservedly popular with discerning citizens.

In a lazy mood choose the *Stadt München* (M), where you may relax at a table on the terrace over the Reuss.

If it's elegance you want, there is the *Schwanen* (E), smack in front of the lake, but you must have a reservation or arrive early to get a table on the small balcony with its view of lake and mountains, the chief reason for coming here. This is no reflection on the food, which is first-rate, and of wide variety.

For Swiss specialties with appropriate Swiss wines, try *Le Mazot,* Eisengasse, or *Walliser Kanne* on Münzgasse. Both (M).

For meals or snacks there's a *Mövenpick* (M-E), in Grendalstrasse. The local *Migros* is at Hertensteinstrasse 46; other budget places include *Café Hofli* at 16 Pfistergasse, and *Joe's Grill Corner* at no. 17, which serves Swiss food despite its disconcerting name.

If you enjoy your swimming at the Strandbad late morning you can lunch at the nearby, open-air *Lido* restaurant.

The *Kunsthaus* (E), near the boat landing stage, has a pleasant garden terrace. Moored the other side of the bridge, beside the Schweizerhofquai, is the former paddle steamer 'Wilhelm Tell' (M-E), with bars and restaurants.

ENTERTAINMENT. Behind the uninspiring exterior of the *Kursaal/Casino* is a large entertainment center with variety shows, concerts, dancing, folklore evenings with flag tossing, yodelling and blowing the Alphorn. You can play *boule* or take tea on the lakeside terrace.

Dancing, sometimes with floorshow, at the Palace Hotel's *Intimo* nightclub, *Hazyland, Du Pont* and elsewhere. For hearty Swiss fun try the *Floragarten* beer garden. In summer there are evening boat trips with dancing and Swiss folklore on board.

MUSEUMS, ETC. Pride of place goes to the outstandingly fine *Swiss Transport Museum* (Verkehrshaus) with its beautifully presented collection of railway carriages and locomotives, cars, ships, aircraft and space rockets—both full size and in model form. There's also an enormous working scale model of the northern side of the Gotthard line and—for good measure—a Planetarium. The paddle steamer 'Rigi', built in London in 1847, which used to ply on Lake Lucerne, has found an honorable resting place high and dry in the large garden courtyard. You can go aboard for a drink or light refreshments in its quaint saloons. The museum is quickly reached by trolley bus from the city center.

Other places to see include the *Kunstmuseum* (fine art), the *Richard Wagner Museum* (in his house at Tribschen, just south of the town), as well as the *Panorama* (a gigantic painting by Castres of the retreat of the French army in 1871), the *Glacier Gardens,* the famous *Lion Monument* ('Löwendenkmal'), and the *Alpineum* (Alpine dioramas), the last four being close together.

SHOPPING. There's an awful lot of souvenir junk in this town, somewhat obscuring the fact that Lucerne has more than its fair share of good shops both in the 'old town' and south of the river.

Excursions from Lucerne

Excursions from Lucerne are delightful. Lake Lucerne, or the Vierwaldstättersee (Lake of the Four Forest Cantons) as the Swiss call it, is the cradle of Swiss history. In addition, it is idyllically beautiful. The classical lake boat tour from Lucerne to Flüelen, stopping en route at many little resorts, is highly recommended, and you should also get up above the lake for one of the sweeping, overall views of this region. See it, for example, from Mount Pilatus south of Lucerne, a 7,000-foot triangular crag accessible by an aerial cableway from Kriens, or by cogwheel railway from Alpnachstad. The Rigi, although only 5,900 feet, will give you further splendid views. It's more gentle, more friendly than Pilatus and has green turf on top. Although the skiing here is excellent, it lasts for only a few weeks in January/February. Two mountain railways go to the summit; one from the pretty little resort of Vitznau, and the other from Arth-Goldau, near Lake Zug and only about 14 miles from Lucerne itself. From Küssnacht, a lakeside resort between Lucerne and Arth-Goldau, to Immensee on Lake Zug, you can take the historic Hohle Gasse or "Sunken Lane", along which the tyrannical Austrian bailiff, Gessler, was riding when William Tell's arrow struck him down. You'll hear much more of this legendary hero at Altdorf, where William Tell shot an arrow through an apple on his little boy's head. At nearby Bürglen (his birthplace) you'll find a vast Wilhelm Tell collection housed in a tower. You can go from Lucerne to Altdorf in one hour by rail; the boat takes about three hours via Flüelen. Schwyz, between Lucerne and Altdorf on the St. Gotthard line, is one of the oldest towns in Switzerland. But its claim to fame lies in the fact that it is the place from which Switzerland (in German, Schweiz) derives both its name and its flag. Here, in the impressive archives building, you may see that precious document, the Oath of Eternal Alliance, which, in 1291, became Switzerland's Declaration of Independence.

The ski resorts in this area are Engelberg (3,500 ft.), but with lifts rising to 9,900 ft.; Stoos (4,200 ft.), with lifts to 6,300 ft., and Andermatt, all old-established and popular.

PRACTICAL INFORMATION FOR CENTRAL SWITZERLAND

ALTDORF. The picturesque capital of the Canton of Uri. Hotel: *Goldener Schlüssel* (4).

ANDERMATT, on the road to the St. Gotthard pass. The road over the pass is closed in winter, but Andermatt can be reached by rail from Göschenen, on the main Gotthard line.

Hotels: *Krone, Helvetia, Monopol-Metropol* and *Kristall* are (3). In class (4) are *Alpenhof, Badus, Bergidyll, Drei Könige, Schweizerhof, Schlüssel,* and *Sonne.*

BRUNNEN, famed for the splendid views from its lakeside gardens. Hotels: All on or near the lake are *Waldstätterhof,* with lido, and *Bellevue,* each with open-air restaurant; *Parkhotel; Schmid;* all (2-3). *Elite* and *Hirschen,* each with dining terrace, are (4).

Restaurants: *Bahnhof,* with garden dining. The *Casino* has concerts, dancing, boule.

BURGENSTOCK, a spectacular mountain ridge jutting into the lake. Hotels: *Grand* and *Palace,* both (L). *Park* (1). *Honegg* and *Waldheim* (4).

ENGELBERG, about an hour by train or car (road is clear year round) from Lucerne.

Hotels: *Bellevue-Terminus, Hess* and *Ring* are (2). The *Crystal, Schweizerhof, Alpina, Central, Edelweiss, Engelberg,* and *Engel* are (3). *Alpenklub, Marguerite,* and marginally cheaper *Schönegg,* are (4).

PILATUS. Hotels: Ultra-modern, circular *Bellevue; Pilatus-Kulm,* traditional décor; both (3-4) and near summit.

RIGI, about 1½ hrs. from Lucerne. Hotels: *Rigi-Kulm* (4), at summit. At Rigi-Kaltbad, *Hostellerie-Rigi* (1), indoor pool, sauna; *Bellevue* (2).

STOOS, a tiny, charming resort, no road traffic. Hotels: *Klingenstock,* recent, and slightly cheaper *Alpstubli,* both (4).

VITZNAU, attractive lakeside resort, fairly small, with all summer sports facilities.

Hotels: *Park* (L), private lido, park, indoor pool, sauna. *Vitznauerhof* (2). *Alpenrose, Kreuz* and *Rigi,* all (3-4).

WEGGIS, one of the biggest lake resorts, popular for its mild, almost sub-tropic climate. Has a June Rose Festival.

Hotels: *Albana, Alexander, Beau-Rivage,* and *Park* are all (3). *Post-Terminus, Rössli* and the slightly cheaper *Bühlegg, Paradies* and *Rigi* are (4).

MOTELS (distances given are from Lucerne). At Giswil, 20 miles south, *Landhaus.* At Kriens, just south, *Luzern-Süd.* At Kussnacht, 8 miles northeast, *Pic-nic.* At Merlischachen, near Kussnacht, *Swiss Chalet.* At Sachseln, 17 miles south, *Kreuz.* At Seewen, *Barcarola.* At Stans, 10 miles south, *Rex.* Some closed Nov.-Mar.

The Grisons (not forgetting the Engadine)

The canton of the Grisons (Graubunden, is its German name) is often spoken of as "Switzerland in miniature" because of its concentration of high Alpine peaks, beautiful lakes and deep valleys. Along with the Bernese Oberland, this is the area most familiar to winter sports devotees. Here are places to which ski enthusiasts flock from all over the world, such as Arosa, Davos, Flims, Klosters, Lenzerheide, Pontresina, and the vast conglomeration of St. Moritz and its winter sports satellites. Here, peppered with all manner of winter and summer resorts, is the famous Engadine—the mountain-bordered valley of the river Inn and its chain of lovely lakes—which cuts a 25 mile long swath across the southern part of the Grisons.

The resort seasons are June to September and December to April. In the winter high season, St. Moritz and other fashionable spots glitter with cosmopolitan sophistication, but you will find countless smaller, less smart resorts as well as unspoiled mountain and valley villages. So don't get the idea you can't enjoy yourself here on a limited budget. You can—and thousands do. However, the Grisons offers much more than winter sports. It is beautiful at most seasons—in the late spring, the summer and fall. Indeed, many consider the best time to be the latter part of June or early July, for then the mountainsides come ablaze with wildflowers.

The variety of the Grisons will provide you with the excitement of many contrasts. Enjoy the medieval streets of Chur; the incomparable ski-runs of Klosters (this place also has a gigantic swimming pool, children's ski school and an 18-hole golf course); the remarkable network of cablecars, chairlifts and ski lifts at nearby Davos, and its famous Parsenn run where, from a height of some 9,000 feet, you can ski down over vast open fields to the town, a drop of 3,500 feet or so; the beautiful village of Guarda (Engadine), under federal protection to ensure that its peasant dwellings with their striking *sgraffiti* ornamentation remain unchanged. Or try the adjoining resorts of Scuol, Vulpera and Tarasp with their healthful waters (good for the liver), worth discovering, especially for the pure white, 11th-century dream castle of Tarasp, perched on top of a sheer cliff some 500 feet above the valley floor.

For two modest resorts, try the charming Engadine villages of Celerina and Samedan, the latter noted for its splendid views of the Bernina mountain chain—Piz Palü (12,900 ft.) and Piz Bernina (13,300 ft.), just a couple of peaks to give you an idea of the scale. Celerina, nearby St. Moritz's kid brother, is first-rate for skiing, with easy access to all of the more celebrated resorts' winter sports facilities. The famous Cresta bobsled run has its terminus here. Not to be missed from either Celerina or Samedan is the trip up the Muottas Muragl funicular with its marvellous view of the upper Inn valley and the chain of lovely lakes starting at St. Moritz.

St. Moritz

St. Moritz itself, at an altitude of 6,000 feet, on the shores of the sky-blue Lake of St. Moritz, has all the cachet of a world capital. Before the rise of Rome, even before the fall of Troy, the healing qualities of its waters were known. Many Europeans still take these waters or soak themselves in baths to cure a wide range of ailments. But the waters are almost forgotten in the flurries of snow and the glitter of international society on the ski slopes. This is the winter playground of the fashionable world, and if you come here to see statesmen, film stars, what remains of European nobility, and Arab oil sheiks worth their weight in diamonds, you won't be disappointed. In summer, when prices are appreciably below winter levels, it is lovely, too, with facilities for swimming, sailing, riding, mountain climbing, golf, tennis and some of the best fishing in Switzerland in the River Inn.

Some of the smart set feel that St. Moritz has become too popular. Their answer is Arosa (5,900 ft.), with every facility for summer and winter sports and a winter specialty of horseracing on the snow and ice. Dressy, smart and elegant, it is less expensive than St. Moritz. It also has a bathing beach on the little lake, one of the largest ski schools in Switzerland (with 100 instructors), heated swimming pool, ice rink and, winter or summer, some of the most magnificent mountain scenery in the world.

 HOTELS. In this region, many hotels close for a month or two during the year; others may open only in summer, or for the winter sports season. Best check in advance.

AROSA. The *Tschuggen* and *Alexandra-Palace,* both ultra-modern, *Arosa Kulm* at top end of town, but well placed for Hörnli gondolas and Carmenna lift, and the *Park,* all with indoor pool, are (L).

In class (1), top are *Eden, Hof Maran, Savoy* (indoor pool), and *Prätschli,* followed by *Bellavista, Excelsior, Valsana* and *Waldorf,* each with indoor pool, and *Bellevue, Raetia* and *Seehof. Des Alpes* and much renovated *Post* are (2).

The *Alpensonne, Belri, Belvédère, Bruggli, Carmenna, Central, Cristallo, Isla, Streiff,* and *Suvretta* are (3). *Alpina, Erzhorn, Hold Merkur,* and *Vetter* are (4).

CELERINA. *Cresta Palace* (1) has indoor pool. *Kulm* (2). *Misani* and *Murail* (3). *Post, Secchi* (4).

CHUR. Best is *Rohan* (2-3), with elegant restaurant, indoor pool, closely followed by *ABC,* breakfast only (both near station), the *Post* and much modernized *Stern,* used and recommended by Fodor editors, both central. The *City,* clinical but comfortable, new, the *Freieck,* renovated throughout, and cheaper *Obertor* are all (4).

DAVOS. In Davos-Platz, leader in (L) class is the *Grand Hotel Belvédère,* closely followed by the slightly cheaper *Central, Europe, Morosani's Post, Sunstar-Park, Schweizerhof* and *Waldhotel-Bellevue.* The *Du Midi, Sunstar* and *Cresta-Victoria* are (1-2). *Angleterre, Bellavista, Terminus,* and the slightly cheaper *Bernina* and *Rinaldi* are (3).

In Davos-Dorf, *Derby, Flüela* and *Seehof* are (L). *Meierhof, Montana* (1). *Bristol, Parsenn* (3). Above Davos, reached by funicular, is the *Berghotel Schatzalp* (L).

FLIMS. Pleasant winter and summer resort. Leader is the *Park-Hotel* (1), in beautiful grounds, but disappointing food reported. Cheaper, delightful, are *Adula,* always full, long advance booking essential, and *Des Alpes. Crap Ner, Schweizerhof* and *Segnes & Post* are (3). All except last with pool.

KLOSTERS. The *Silvretta, Vereina* and *Pardenn,* last 2 with indoor pool, are (L). Top (1) is the chalet-style *Chesa Grischuna,* noted for its cuisine. *Alpina, Weisskreuz-Belvédère,* both (3). *Sporthof, Bünderhof* are (4).

LENZERHEIDE. *Grand Hotel Kurhaus* and *Schweizerhof* are (1). *Sunstar* and rustic *Guarda Val* both (2). The *Lenzerhorn, Post,* and well-run *Park* are (3-4).

At Valbella, on the Chur side of Lenzerheide, the *Post-Hotel* (1), has heated indoor pool, excellent cuisine.

PONTRESINA. The *Schloss* and *Kronenhof-Bellavista* (good food, tasteless decor) are (L). *Walther* (1). The *Parkhotel, Schweizerhof, Sporthotel* and somewhat cheaper *Collina* and *Engadinerhof* are (2-3). *Albris, Steinbock, Weisses Kreuz,* all (4).

ST. MORITZ. Has four of the best, most famous and expensive (L) hotels in Switzerland: the *Palace,* central but with spacious grounds and famous views at the back; the *Kulm,* a little further from center and slightly higher, equally fine views; *Suvretta House,* about 1 mile from town, in park-like grounds which also contain the Shah of Iran's villa; *Carlton,* long famed for its quiet elegance and service (but recently ownership has changed).

Larger (1) hotels include the *Chantarella, Schweizerhof, Crystal, Monopol* and, at St. Moritz-Champfèr, the *Eurotel.* Last 3 have indoor pool, sauna. The *Albana, Bären* with indoor pool, *Calonder, La Margna, Neues Post, Salastrains, Steffani* and *Waldhaus* are (2). *Bernasconi* (4).

At St.Moritz-Bad, *Park-Kurhaus* is (1). All (2) are *San Gian,* new, excellent, the *Bellevue, Chesa sur En, Edelweiss* and *Nolda.*

Many hotels have dancing. The *Hotel Crystal* is a popular spot. For young folk it's the Steffani's recently renovated *Malibu Club* disco.

SAMEDAN, poor man's St.Moritz which is nearby. The *Bernina* and *Quadratscha,* latter with indoor pool, sauna, are (1). *Des Alpes* (2). *Sporthotel* (4).

SCUOL-TARASP-VULPERA, three adjacent summer resorts and spas, gaining winter sports popularity.

At Scuol, best are recently renovated *Belvédère,* lovely views at back, and slightly cheaper *Engadinerhof.* The *Guardaval* and *Post* are (3).

At Bad Tarasp, *Grand Kurhaus* (1). At Vulpera, the *Waldhaus* (L), spacious gardens, pool, tennis. *Schweizerhof* (1). *Silvana* (4).

SILS-MARIA, BASELGIA, quiet village resorts near beautiful lakes and Fex valley.

At Maria, best is *Waldhaus* (L). *Schweizerhof* (2). Full of charm and modern comfort is *Pension Privata* (3).

At Baselgia, *Margna,* near (L). *Chesa Randolina* (2) is a cleverly modernized and enlarged farmhouse.

SILVAPLANA, small resort and lower terminal of cableway to Corvatsch (10,800 ft.) with summer skiing and a panoramic restaurant. *Albana* (1), recent, sauna. *Sonne* (2).

The Valais (Zermatt and the Matterhorn)

Following a roughly L-shaped section of the Rhône between Lake Geneva and the Canton of Ticino, the Valais, or "Wallis" in German, has long been famous as one of Europe's most magnificent regions. The backbone of the canton is the fertile and impressive Rhône Valley, off which an incomparable network of lesser valleys, mostly steep, narrow and often little-known to tourists, leads into superb mountain scenery. Swiss engineers have achieved the near-impossible by building roads up most of these valleys; but you'll see much more, and probably worry less, if you leave the driving to an expert on one of Switzerland's ubiquitous postal buses. The Valais has numerous famous and fashionable resorts, but even more that are quiet, charming and noticeably cheaper than is usual in Switzerland. We list some of the better known resorts, but off-the-beaten-track exploration will bring you rich rewards.

Here's news: *you* can climb the Matterhorn! If you can walk, are tolerably sound in wind and limb, have a few days to spare to get in condition, and can afford to hire one of Zermatt's expert guides, he'll get you to the top of that formidable lump of rock and bring you down again in one piece. The expedition will take about a couple of days and on the way you will come across nothing less than the world's highest (12,000 ft.) public conveniences! You need have no qualms about your guides either; those at Zermatt are famous and many have accompanied scientific expeditions to the Himalayas and other mountain ranges around the world.

With less effort, you can get almost the same sensation (though not the same satisfaction) by taking one of the highest cogwheel railroads in Europe from Zermatt to Gornergrat. Here, at a mere 10,200 feet (the Matterhorn is 14,690), you will have a view over shimmering glaciers and 50 or more king-size peaks.

Zermatt is the leading winter sports center of the Valais, with cogwheel railways, cable cars, chair and ski lifts, skating and curling rinks galore. Skiing often lasts into late spring here, and right through summer in the Theodul Pass area. Saas-Fee, a bit less crowded, is also a first-rate summer and winter resort. Besides ski lifts, there are gondolas and cable cars going to Felskinn, Langefluh and Plattjen, all at dizzy heights. The Sion and Sierre areas, especially the Crans-Montana-Vermala resort complex, are equally lovely in summer and winter. Crans has the distinction of having the first golf course ever installed on the continent. It's still one of the best. Verbier is another well-known winter sports center, while the secluded little Val d'Anniviers is rapidly developing charming winter sports resorts at Grimentz, St. Luc, Chandolin and Zinal, without losing the rustic character of these typical Valaisan mountain villages, with their chalets and raised wooden barns (known locally as *mazots*).

An up-and-coming summer and winter resort is Grächen, a sunny village in the St. Niklaus valley, situated at an altitude of 5,305 feet. You can reach it by car or mail-bus from St. Niklaus Station. It has an aerial cableway which takes you up to the splendid skiing fields on the Hannigalp (6,950 ft.).

PRACTICAL INFORMATION FOR THE VALAIS

HOTELS. Many are closed for varying periods during the year. Best check in advance that they will be open.

ANZÈRE, chic new winter sports resort. *Des Masques* and *Zodiaque,* both (1).

BRIG. *Schloss-Hotel,* breakfast only, new, and *Victoria,* both (3). *Sporting,* breakfast only, and *Europe* are (4).

CHAMPÉRY, winter sports and summer resort (3,500 ft.). *De Champéry* and *Beau Séjour* (3). *Des Alpes* (4), notable cuisine.

CHAMPEX, simple winter sports and beautiful little summer resort. Nearest to chair lift, close to lake are *Crettex* (2) and *Glacier* (4). At quieter end of lake, *Des Alpes* (2) and *Grand Combin* (3).

CRANS. *Du Golf* and *De l'Etrier,* both (L), *Beau Séjour* (1), each with indoor pool. *Alpina & Savoy, Excelsior, Royal,* all (1). *Elite, Beau Site,* both (4).

EVOLENE, noted for traditional costumes and charming old chalets. *Hermitage* (4).

GRÄCHEN. *Beau-Site, Bellevue,* each with pool, and *Elite, Grächerhof, Walliserhof* are (4), as is the comfortable *Hotel zum Zee,* just above village, by a lake.

LEUKERBAD (Loèche-les-Bains), major spa, winter sports resort. Best are *Des Alpes* and *Bristol,* both (1). *Grand Bain* and *Maison Blanche* are but two of many in class (3) and (4). Many hotels have thermal baths on the premises.

MONTANA-VERMALA, on same 5,000-ft. plateau as Crans. Smart, fashionable, rather expensive winter sports and summer resort. *Supercrans* and *Ambassador,* both (1) are leaders. *Mirabeau, Parc* and *Curling,* and cheaper *Valaisia* and *De la Forêt* are (3). *Forest* (4).

SAAS-FEE, important winter sports resort. No motor traffic in village. *Grand* and *Walliserhof,* both (3). *Derby, Dom, Bristol, Elite, Alphubel,* all (4).

SION. *Du Rhone* (3). The *Continental, Cerf, Touring* (good restaurant), and *Treize Etoiles* are (4), the last with small excellent (M) restaurant adjoining.

VERBIER has one of the biggest growth rates in the region; first-class shops, plenty of entertainment. The *Farinet, Parc* and *Rhodania* are (2). *Grand Combin, Poste* (3). *Rosa Blanche* (4).

ZERMATT. One of the newest and best, but not most expensive, is the *Nicoletta* (1), used and recommended by Fodor editors.

Leader of the famous Seiler group is *Mont Cervin* (L), then *Monte Rosa* (2) and, at 8,475 ft., the *Schwarzee* (3).

Owned by Zermatt's burghers and well-known are the *Zermatterhof* (L), and above town, the *Riffelberg* (3) at 8,480 ft., *Kulmhotel Gornergrat* (3) at 10,170 ft., and *Belvédère* (4) at 11,150 ft.

Reader-recommended are the Valais-style *Tenne* (1), the *Couronne* (2), and breakfast only *Dom* (3) and *Albana* (4).

Notable is the traditional-style, atmospheric *Walliserhof* (2).

MOTELS. At Bourge-St.-Pierre, *au Bivouac Napoleon.* At Charrat, near Martigny, *Mon Moulin* (closed Jan.). At Gampel, *Vallesia.* At Lavey, *Idéal.* At Martigny, *La Croisée, des Sports* and *Transalpin* (closed Dec.-Feb.). At Raron, *Simplonblick.* At St.-Leonard, *Auto-Grill du Soleil* and *13 Etoiles.* At St.-Maurice, *Inter Alps.* At Saxon, *de la Tour d'Anselme.* At Sembrancher, *Bristol.*

Ticino, Southernmost Canton

South of St. Gotthard is Ticino, the odd-man-out of the Swiss cantons partly because it is the only Italian-speaking one. It projects like a spearhead into Italy and it is hardly surprising that this part of Switzerland has a distinctly Italian flavor not only in its food, but also in its buildings, people, atmosphere and climate. In the lake district, December and January can admittedly be cold and wet, but the rest of the year is normally blissfully warm and sunny except for occasional stormy spells —usually shortlived. And summer can be downright hot.

But don't be fooled by Ticino's appearance. You are still very much in Switzerland! Like many another Swiss canton it has winter sports, Alpine scenery, lakes, and plenty of mountain transport as well as typical Swiss efficiency and hospitality. But as a free bonus Ticino throws in its almost Mediterranean climate at lower levels, some lovely unspoiled valleys, and three world famous resorts—Lugano, Locarno and Ascona. Prices in Ticino, away from the big resorts, are a trifle below normal Swiss standards.

Just as the three resorts have their distinctive personalities, so do Ticino's many valleys, each vying with the other for scenery and charm. Like many other unsung attractions in Ticino, these lovely valleys are missed by most tourists, although they are nearly all easy to reach, as the canton is endowed with a fine network of public transport. Good, if sometimes narrow, roads lead everywhere, in several cases almost to the summit of fair-sized mountains.

Lugano

Set around a large bay in Lake Lugano, with the green heights of Monte Salvatore and Monte Brè as sentinels at each end, the city of Lugano rises from the shore up the sides of gently rolling hills. Forming, with its suburbs of Paradiso and Castagnola, an almost unbroken line of hotels and elegant villas around the bay, Lugano has a rather opulent air of pleasantly self-conscious sophistication. And not without reason. For with its mild climate and magnificent setting it is virtually a year-round resort; one with everything in the way of entertainment, sport, sidewalk cafés, lakeside promenades, to say nothing of an enviable selection of shops to suit millionaires (and they are frequently around in Lugano) as well as travelers on a shoestring budget.

Art lovers will find much to interest them in Lugano and its neighborhood. In the town itself, the old Franciscan church of Santa Maria degli Angeli has the famous 'Crucifixion' fresco and other smaller ones which Bernardino Luini painted in 1529. The cathedral of San Lorenzo, up the hill to the station, is notable for its 16th-century early Renaissance façade, and for the splendid lake and city view from its terrace. Beside the lake in Castagnola is the beautiful mansion, La Villa Favorita, bought in 1932 by the late Baron Heinrich von Thyssen. In its Pinacoteca—a specially built wing—are over twenty superbly lit and arranged salons containing his priceless art collection as well as additions made by the present Baron. Probably Europe's finest private collection, and a 'must' for all art lovers, the Pinacoteca is normally open April to October, but check exact times and dates locally.

Excursions from Lugano

You can best get your bearings by taking a funicular to the top of Monte San Salvatore (2,995 ft.) or Monte Brè (3,053 ft.). Either will give you an eagle's eye view of Lugano and its irregularly shaped lake, and the hills, valleys and mountains of the region. Better still is the ascent of Monte Generoso (5,590 ft.). Take a boat to Capolago at the southern end of the lake (about 50 minutes from Lugano) where, beside the jetty, the little, red cogwheel-train will take you on its 40-minute climb to the top station. The grassy summit is about 250 feet higher, but there is a prepared path, steep and rough but not too difficult. From the top, on a clear day you'll see the Po valley and Apennines in the south, the snow-capped Alps to the north, and much of Ticino in between. Choose good weather for these ascents and go before the clouds have begun to gather around the peaks as they often do about mid-day.

There are many lake excursions from Lugano. An amusing, 20-minute trip (it's rather less by bus) is to Campione d'Italia on the opposite shore, a square mile of Italian territory entirely surrounded by Switzerland. Campione's chief attraction is a large, glamorous and glittering casino. Being Italian, although Swiss money is used, the maximum stakes are high and you can fritter away your fortune on roulette, baccara and what-have-you in a fraction of the time it takes in Lugano where stakes are limited by Swiss law to a mere 5 francs. Another 20-minute boat trip from Lugano, or better still a delightful half-hour lakeside walk from the Castagnola trolley stop, is to the picturesque village of Gandria whose cottages rise straight from the water's edge.

For contrast, take the lovely drive from Lugano, past a succession of spectacular lake and mountain views, along the high ridge which leads to the village of Carona, then on through the equally charming village of Vico Morcote and steeply down to the waterside townlet of Morcote. If you return to Lugano along the lake shore road, stop for a while at Melide to visit 'Swissminiatur', a vast exhibition of typical or famous Swiss houses, churches, castles, villages, trains, ships, the lot—all at 1/25th life size. But it's in the open air, so don't go if it is raining.

PRACTICAL INFORMATION FOR LUGANO

HOTELS. Lugano's five (L) leaders are the *Admiral,* newest; *Commodore,* combining contemporary comfort with traditional elegance; *Eden,* an outstanding example of almost avant-garde decor; *Europa au Lac,* much renovated and improved; and *Splendide-Royal,* old world elegance in its furnishings but modern in all other respects. All beside or facing lake, and with private pools.

Of numerous (1) and (2) hotels the following have private pools: *Bellevue au Lac, Belmonte, Du Lac Seehof* and *Meister.* Among many (3) hotels, the *Nizza* has a heated outdoor pool. So has *Calypso* (4), one of numerous hotels in and around Lugano, and the resort's largest.

 RESTAURANTS. Cooking in Lugano is good and usually follows Italian inspiration. *Bianchi's,* Via Pessina 3, is regarded by residents as one of the best and most elegant, but other fine ones include *Galleria,* Via G. Vegezzi 4; *Huguenin,* Riva Albertolli 1; and *Orologio,* Via G. Nizzola 2, all (E). Outside Lugano, *La Romantica* (E), at Melide, features nightclub acts. Dinner-dances at Campione's *Casino* (E), where the smart set congregates. *Capo San Martino,* with a good lake view is quiet, moderately priced, popular. For a filling meal from around 5 francs try the *Innovazione* store's self-service, Piazza Dante.

SHOPPING. In this town of fine shops, you'll find the best on Via Nassa.

Locarno

More relaxed than Lugano and only half the size, Locarno, on the shore of Lake Maggiore, is now an international resort, but in the old part of the town, with its attractive, narrow streets of arcaded houses, you will soon realize its age. The 16th century was a bad one for Locarno. First, about 60 of its most distinguished Protestant families were exiled, fleeing to Zurich, where they helped to establish that city's prosperous silk trade. Then the town was struck by the Black Plague, which cut its population from 4,800 to 700. At the beginning of the 20th century, it was still a place of no great note despite its beautiful situation. But in 1925 it suddenly leapt to world fame when Briand, Stresemann, Mussolini and Chamberlain met here to sign the Locarno Pact.

Today, Locarno is a go-ahead resort which has somehow managed to remain almost unspoiled by popularity; it is sunny, spacious, with a subtle air of dignity and sophistication. From the middle of the town itself, and only a few paces from the treeshaded waterfront, you can be whisked by cable railway, cablecar and chair lift up to Cardada (4,050 ft.) and Cimetta (4,950 ft.). Both have magnificent views of Lake Maggiore and the Alps, and in winter you can ski on the snowy slopes while others bask in the sun by the lake below.

Only 2½ miles from Locarno is the small resort-town of Ascona. What gives Ascona a character of its own is its gay and relaxed atmosphere—and more particularly its contrast. For almost hidden behind the lively, colorful cafés which line the treebordered shore promenade is Ascona's other face—an intriguing muddle of quaint old streets and twisting alleys surrounding the eye-catching church tower; streets and alleys filled with boutiques, antique shops, bookbinders, art galleries and other craft shops.

Locarno and Ascona are alike in being first-rate centers for excursions by road, rail or on the lake. From either, smart white boats, and even hydrofoils, give plenty of opportunities to explore the beauties of Lake Maggiore and its islands. You can make the trip of half-an-hour or so to the minuscule Brissago islands with their lovely sub-tropical gardens. Or, if you can spare a day or half-day you can go further afield to the Italian resort of Stresa or the beautiful Borromean Islands. From both Locarno and Ascona, too, it's a quick, easy drive to valleys which are wild and secluded; Valle Verzasca and Valle Maggia are two of the best.

PRACTICAL INFORMATION FOR THE TICINO

ASCONA. Hotels: Leader is the *Eden Roc* (L), followed by the somewhat cheaper *Delta, Sonnenhof* and *Casa Berno,* all (L). *Europe au Lac* and *Monte Verita* are (1). Among class (3) are *Arancio, Bellaria, Moro, Riposo, Seeschloss* and *Schweizerhof.* All the above have indoor or outdoor pools. *Mulino, Pergola* (4).

LOCARNO. Hotels: *La Palma au Lac* (L) has beautiful situation with lakeside gardens, indoor pool. In class (1) are *Park,* with lovely gardens; *Reber au Lac,* on lakeside promenade; *Esplanade,* traditional décor, in huge gardens; *Muralto,* fine lake view. First three have heated outdoor pools.

The *Quisisana, Grand, Schloss* (Renaissance style, noted for its antiques), and *Orselina,* high above town with splendid views, are all (2) and have indoor or outdoor pools. *Beau Rivage* (2). Another fine cliff-hanger is the 4500 ft.-high *Cardada Hotel* (2).

The *Camelia, Carmine* and *Montaldi* are (3-4), as is the comfortable, breakfast only *Remorino,* a few minutes from city center.

Restaurants: *Ristorante du Lac* (hotel), *Chez Alfredo* (Muralto hotel), and *da Emilio* on lakeside, all with excellent cuisine, are (E). *Gambrinus* and *Montaldi,* both (M), have good food, as has *Caverna degli Dei.* Somewhat cheaper are

Verbania au Lac and *Dell'Angelo.* Moderate, and recommended is *Campagna Ristorante and Grotto,* in town.

In Brione, *Los Gatos* and *Da Stefano,* both (E), are excellent.

MORCOTE. Hotel: *Olivella au Lac* (2) has two heated pools.

Note: As some hotels close during the off-season it is best to check in advance.

MOTELS. Around Bellinzona: At Castione, 3 miles north, *Castione;* at Claro, 5 miles north, *San Gottardo* and *Riviera;* at Lumino, 3 miles northeast, *Lumino.*

Around Lugano: At Melano, 6 miles south, *Lido;* at Mezzovico, 6 miles out, *Mezzovico;* at Vezia, 2 miles north, *Vezia.*

Between Lugano and Bellinzona, at Cadenazzo, *Mona Lisa.* Between Locarno and Bellinzona, at Riazzino, *Riazzino,* and *Lago Maggiore.* At Ponte Tresa, *Ponte Tresa.* At Vira-Gambarogno, on Lake Maggiore opposite Locarno, *Touring Motel Bellavista.* At Coldrerio, between Lugano and Chiasso, *Mobil.* As some close in winter, best check in advance.

SPORTS. *Bathing:* Outdoor and hotel pools. Fine indoor pool at Locarno lido (with nursery for 5 to 9 year olds), but bathing forbidden in certain parts of the lake due to pollution. *Boats* for hire. 18-hole *golf course* between Locarno and Ascona. *Wintersports* above Locarno and, of course, in Ticino's mountainous north.

TURKEY

This country spanning two continents offers an abundance of magnificent beaches, exciting historical sites, art treasures and a myriad of exotic mosques. Roughly 296,000 square miles in size, it has a population of 40,000,000. Because it's still relatively undeveloped with regard to hotels and related facilities visitors concentrate mostly on Istanbul, Ankara and the Aegean coast. But the "turquoise coast" farther south has the best beaches and the most interesting archaeological sites; the beautiful Black Sea coast is unspoiled and unpretentious; and the vast highlands of eastern Turkey can still provide free adventure for those less-demanding of the creature comforts. (In the latter region organized travel is the most advantageous way of exploring the widely scattered sites and taking care of the formidable accommodation and language problems.)

In general, the best time of year to visit Turkey is between April and November, and the primary objectives are: Istanbul, one of the most beautifully sited cities in the world; the ancient Greek towns of Pergamum, Ephesus and Side; and the renowned "Seven Churches of Asia" from the journeys of St. Paul and the underground cities and carved churches of Cappadocia.

A Bit of History

From the beginning Turkey has been rich in legend. Noah's Ark is claimed to have come to rest on Mount Ararat, Homer to have been born in Izmir (the ancient Greek Smyrna), and the Virgin Mary to have spent her last days on earth at Ephesus. Turkey as a nation came into existence only in 1923, through the efforts of Mustafa Kemal Atatürk after the collapse of the Ottoman Empire and foreign intervention. After two army coups, democracy returned in 1973 under coalition governments made even more unstable by the indecisive elections in 1977.

Food and Drink

Turkish cuisine isn't all that exotic, as it is based on age-old recipes common to the eastern Mediterranean but far less oily than the Greek, less spicy than the Asian. It's a good idea to remember a few Turkish names for dishes so you won't be limited to eating *shish kebabs* (meat, usually lamb, roasted on a spit together with assorted cooked vegetables): *kiliç* is swordfish with bay leaves, spit-roasted; *çerkes tavugu,* chicken cooked with a red pepper and walnut sauce; *dolmas,* vine leaves stuffed with black currants, pine nuts and rice, cooked in olive oil; these are just a few. The yogurt is superb, but the honey-and-nut pastries are excessively sweet. You can eat safely and deliciously from virtually any street stand.

The Turkish national drink is *raki,* a potent potion which the Turks drink as an apéritif. There are some very drinkable wines and a variety of liqueurs. And of course, Turkish coffee: brewed with the sugar and never to be stirred.

PRACTICAL INFORMATION FOR TURKEY

WHAT WILL IT COST? Despite inflation Turkey ranks as one of the less expensive countries, though comparisons may be deceptive because of lower standards. Outside the three main towns, Istanbul, Ankara and Izmir, there are few first class hotels; many are often downright rock bottom category but prices are correspondingly cheap. The plumbing leaves much to be desired everywhere except in the deluxe places. Hotels are rated luxury (L), first-class reasonable (1), moderate (2), inexpensive (3) and rock bottom (4). It must be considered adventurous, to put it mildly, to go below the moderate category.

Rates below are exclusive of breakfast, 15% service and 10% tax; meal prices in hotels or equivalent restaurants are exclusive of 15% tax, or beverages. Hotel prices depend on category except along the Bosphorous where the lower grades are unusually expensive. Most hotels grant up to 30% reductions off-season (November to April).

Restaurants are rated expensive (E), about 170–270TL; moderate (M), from about 100TL; and inexpensive (I), below 100TL.

	HOTEL ROOM		MEALS	
	Single	Double	Breakfast	Lunch/ dinner
Deluxe	600-1300	700-1500	35-55	170-270
1st class	350-550	400-700	30-45	120-200
Moderate	200-350	250-400	25-35	100-140
Inexpensive	120-200	140-280	20-30	70-120
Rock bottom	60-120	75-140	12-20	40-75
	Prices in Turkish lira			

CAPITAL. Ankara, pop. 1,800,000.

LANGUAGE. Turkish. English, German and French spoken in Istanbul and tourist centers, only rarely in the interior.

CLIMATE. The tourist season is from April to November. Central and southern Turkey are very hot in summer.

Average maximum daily temperatures in Fahrenheit and centigrade:

Istanbul	Jan.	Feb.	Mar.	Apr.	May	June	July	Aug.	Sept.	Oct.	Nov.	Dec.
F°	46	48	52	61	70	77	82	82	75	68	59	52
C°	8	9	11	16	21	25	28	28	24	20	15	11

MONEY. One Turkish *lira* equals 100 *kurus.* At the time of writing, there are about 20 lira to the US dollar, 35 to the £ sterling. Any amount of foreign currency can be brought into Turkey and re-exported. You are allowed to bring in (or take out) only 100 lira in local currency, but can change back your remaining lira into foreign currency on producing your exchange statement.

TIPPING. Except at rock bottom establishments, a service charge of 15% is added to the bill, but does not necessarily find its way to the personnel. Keep this in mind and give a small tip to those who took care of you; 5 to 15 lira per day to the chambermaid. Waiters expect another 5-10 percent. Porters, 5 lira per bag, also bellhops; washroom attendants, movie and theater ushers, 3-5 lira. No need to tip taxi drivers, they overcharge outrageously anyway. Meters are only for show, and though there is a complicated table listing prices to various destinations, best fix the price in advance, after consulting your hotel porter.

HOURS. Shops are open from 8:30 to 18:30 hours, with a break for lunch, daily except Sunday. Banks open Monday to Friday 9-12, 14-17 hours.

HOW TO REACH TURKEY. By Air: *Pan Am* flies daily from New New York to Istanbul and Ankara. Most airlines have regular services from their respective capitals, but *Turkish Airlines* (THY), alone connects several European countries with Izmir.

By Sea: *Turkish Maritime Lines:* weekly service from Barcelona (Spain) to Istanbul (4 days); *Adriatica Line* sails weekly from Trieste or Genoa (Italy); *Truva* and *Istanbul* car ferries from Venice/Brindisi to Istanbul or to Izmir (3 days).

By Rail: *Orient Express* and *Marmara Express* from London via Paris and Milan to Istanbul; *Balkan Express* from Vienna; *Toros Express* from Baghdad; *Lake Van Express* from Tehran.

By Car: if you *must* drive all the way, it's 1,860 miles from Ostend to Istanbul, driving on main routes southeast across Europe via Yugoslavia and Bulgaria: better use a car-sleeper train from London to Ljubljana (Yugoslavia) or London-Milan-Brindisi, connecting with the car ferry. **By Bus.** From London, Brussels and Munich.

CUSTOMS. Turkish custom officials are lenient and rarely look through luggage. You are allowed your personal belongings, sporting, camping, and photographic equipment, and a bottle of alcohol, but only 50 cigarettes. On the way out, you have the right to souvenirs and gifts, silver and carpets up to 2,000 Turkish lira; beyond that, you must have an exchange slip to prove such objects were acquired with foreign currency. There is no duty, however, going out.

Note. Exporting antiquities is strictly prohibited, and the penalties for attempting to do so without prior authorization are severe!

SPECIAL EVENTS. *May,* festivals in the ancient amphitheaters of Ephesus, Pergamum (near Izmir) and Hierapolis (Pamukkale); *June,* Mediterranean Festival, Izmir; *June/July,* Istanbul Festival. *August/September,* International Fair, Izmir, Festival of Antalya/Aspendos.

TRAVEL IN TURKEY. Turkish Airlines operate 32 airports in summer, half this number in winter. Trains offer first and second class accommodation, but take first (fares are quite cheap); most have sleeping and dining or buffet cars, run by Wagons-Lits. The much faster diesel trains (one class only) travel only in daytime.

Faster and more comfortable than buses, the *dolmus* or shared taxi will take you from city to city or on long excursions. Fares are cheap, so be prepared to share the space with lots of other passengers.

GUIDES. The Information Offices of the Ministry of Tourism, as well as travel agencies, have professional interpreter-guides to show travelers around. In large cities like Ankara, Istanbul, and Izmir, guides for small groups are paid from 35-40 TL an hour. Special *Tourist Police,* speaking English, French and German, are on duty in Istanbul, Ankara and Izmir.

MAIL. An airmail letter to the US costs 5 lira for 10 grams, a postcard 4 lira.

ELECTRICITY is 220 volts A.C. in Anatolian (Asiatic) Turkey, and 110 volts in Istanbul. However, all new hotels have 220 volts.

DRINKING WATER. Water is safe to drink in all main cities; in remote areas, best stick to bottled mineral water, such as *Kizilay.*

MOTORING. Fuel costs from 3 to 6.50 TL a liter for regular, 7 to 7.50 TL for super grade. The international insurance (green) card is valid for European Turkey (Thrace) only. You'll have to take out insurance at the border for Anatolian Turkey. There is a good selection of motels along the Mediterranean coast but the unspoiled delights of central and eastern Turkey are starkly primitive.

CAMPING. This is a camping-conscious country where sites cost as little as 15 lira a night, per person. The BP Touring Service has a chain of modern filling stations, some with camping space, and also runs a network of camping sites (Mocamps) that have everything, including lovely locations, all for 20 lira per night, plus 7 lira parking.

CAR HIRE. The Touring-Auto Club offices in the large cities supply information. Istanbul head office is: *Türkiye Turing ve Otomobil Kurumu,* Sisli Meydani 364. *Hertz Rent-a-Car,* Mete Caddesi 26/4 and at the Istanbul Hilton Hotel. *Avis* at the airport, Divan Hotel and Cumhuriyet Cad 107; all in Istanbul. In Ankara: Hertz, Maltepe Bitistiren 1; Avis, Yenisehir Kumrular Sok 6-B.

USEFUL ADDRESSES. In Istanbul: Consulates: *American,* and *British,* Tepebasi. Tourist offices: Mesrutiyet Cad. 57, and Hilton Hotel; *Bayram Tours,* Cumhuriyet Cad 257; *Wagon-Lits/Cook,* Cumhuriyet Cad 22. The *American Hospital* is at Admiral Bristol, Nisantasi. In Ankara: Embassies: *American,* Ataturk Blvd. 110; *British,* Sehit Ersan Caddesi 4-6A, Cankaya; *Canadian,* Nenehatun Caddesi 75, Gazionanpesa. Tourist offices: Mithat Pasa Cadesi 20; *Wagon-Lits/Cook,* Ziya Gökalp Caddesi 20A.

Istanbul

Istanbul is Turkey's traditional gateway from the West, and the traveler in a hurry is bound to concentrate his time here. It's worth fitting a stop at Istanbul into even the tightest of schedules, because few places can offer so much impact in so little time. The Turks rightly claim that you haven't seen Turkey when you've seen Istanbul alone . . . but it's still unique.

With a population of about 2,700,000, Istanbul sprawls over 2,080 square miles. It's been there since 658 B.C., when it was founded by a Megarian Greek named Byzas (hence the name of Byzantium). In 330 A.D., it became the capital of the Roman Empire as Constantinople (from the Roman Emperor Constantine). The Turks then captured it in 1453 and called it Istanbul—a corruption of Islambol, meaning "Many Islams".

All these ups and downs have left their traces on the old section of Istanbul—the walled city between the sea and the Golden Horn is still partially spared by the bulldozers of progress.

Crammed into the old city are its marvelous mosques and palaces, which rise up like a vision from the Arabian Nights. In the center of the sightseeing area stands St. Sophia, built by the Emperor Constantine in 347, destroyed by fire and then rebuilt in the sixth century by Emperor Justinian. The Turks converted the world-famous basilica into a mosque with four minarets instead of tearing it down. It's now a museum so some mosaics can again be seen, giving an idea of the former splendor. Beyond the graceful fountain of Ahmed III stands the Mosque of Sultan Ahmed, known as the Blue Mosque from the colored tilework in its interior, a fascinating lesson in abstract design. Just don the oversized slippers at the door to cover your shoes and you can enter any mosque in Istanbul.

You go back to the Romans at the partly reconstructed imperial stables, now the Museum of Mosaics. But within the Hippodrome are two imported landmarks, the Serpentine Column which came from Delphi and the Obelisk, from Egypt. Something really unusual near St. Sophia is the "sunken palace" of Istanbul, actually a cistern built almost 1450 years ago through whose 336 columns boats can row.

From here, you can go to lunch or to the Grand Bazaar, depending upon your stamina. At any rate, take a breather before visiting the Seraglio, which is really enormous. The old palace of the sultans, now known as the Topkapi Museum, covers the walled town's eastern promontory jutting out into the water. The view of the Bosphorus, the Golden Horn, and Asia beyond is incomparable. The three main sights to see are the treasury with unbelievably enormous emeralds; the harem, through which you must take a guided tour; and the pavilion housing several relics sacred to Islam. At the archaeological museum you can say "sic transit gloria" in front of the supposed sarcophagus of Alexander the Great.

That's enough for any city, but Istanbul isn't just any city. You should visit the Suleymaniye Mosque built in the 16th century by Sinan, the greatest of Turkish architects. From here, you will probably return to your hotel in the new town over the Atatürk Bridge, which gives you a chance to take in the aqueduct built by Valens 1,700 years ago.

On the shores of the Bosphorus is the Dolmabahçe Palace, constructed in the 19th century, where the sultans lived after abandoning the Seraglio but, like the smaller Beylerbey Palace on the Asiatic shore, closed for restoration; check for opening.

The Grand Bazaar

There are some four thousand tiny shops under one roof in a complex that dates back to the 16th century, although it has been partly burned down a goodly number of times since then, the 1954 reconstruction being itself severely damaged in a 1975 fire. The Grand Bazaar of Istanbul offers everything from hair curlers to TV sets, but for the visitor the fine craftwork is more important than the mass-produced junk. No matter what the price asked, you are expected to bargain—even if you think the first price is reasonable. It's not that the bazaar vendors are out to fleece the customer, it's just that bargaining is part of the game. If you don't buy, no one will be offended.

Our best advice to you is to look around and absorb the local color instead of buying in a hurry. Best buys, leather coats and jackets, copper and brass ware, rugs and embroideries, onyx jewelry, and Turkish slippers. Don't get conned into buying any so-called antiques. Remember that because Turkey is considered a developing country, many of the things you buy there may be exempt from U.S. Customs duties under the G.S.P. plan, as explained in the section on Customs in Facts at Your Fingertips, at the beginning of this volume.

PRACTICAL INFORMATION FOR ISTANBUL

HOTELS. Make reservations in advance, especially during the season. All deluxe and most first-class hotels are air-conditioned; though only hotels with private bath or shower are listed below, water is sometimes rationed in summer.

Deluxe

HILTON, 418 rooms; Turkey's only casino; swimming pool; several restaurants.

INTERCONTINENTAL, 432 rooms, heated swimming pool, shopping arcade, all amenities.

SHERATON, in Taksim Park, 460 rooms; Turkey's largest hotel in Istanbul's tallest building, splendid view; all amenities.

First Class

DIVAN, 98 rooms, excellent service, fine restaurant.

ETAP, 200 rooms, newest, only swimming pool in this class.

PARK, has 208 rooms, a reputation for excellent service and is popular with foreigners.

UNVER, 91 rooms, next to the Divan.

MACKA, 188 rooms, away from center.

Moderate

DILSON, 89 rooms; *Siraserviler Cad.,* off Taksim Sq.

KEBAN, 84 rooms, next door, with the added attraction of a garage.

KENNEDY, 60 rooms, same street.

PERA PALAS, declining survivor of the opulent days, 110 rooms.

T.M.T., at Gayreteppe, has 69 rooms; comfortable.

Inexpensive

KONAK, off Cumhuriyet Cad.; 23 rooms.

OPERA, 61 rooms. Off Taksim Square.

SANTRAL, 55 rooms, Central.

OLD TOWN

Büyük Keban, Gençtürk Cad., Lâleli, 148 rooms; *Kalyon,* 39 rooms, on Kennedy Cad. facing the sea; *Olcay* and *Sözmen,* 76 rooms, Millet Cad., Çapa, on the main avenue to the airport. All modern, moderate, with garages.

 RESTAURANTS. The restaurants of the *Hilton, Inter-Continental, Sheraton* and *Divan* hotels provide a home from home for the foreign palate, but also authentic local dishes in their Turkish-style dining rooms; dinner dancing and floorshows too. Below listed are the better-known expensive and moderate spots; there are dozens of inexpensive *lokanta* serving excellent dishes, though the choice is limited.

Expensive

ABDULLAH, Istanbul's most famous restaurant, located on Emirgan hills halfway along the Bosphorous; seafood specialties.

GALATA TOWER is another famous spot; terrific view, floorshow in nightclub.

ÇINAR, in hotel near airport, has smart open-air dinner dancing on terrace and beach-side American bar.

Moderate

007, near Divan Hotel, **Aziz,** Rumeli Han Passage, and **Facoli,** near Hilton Hotel, are all good places.

HACI SALIH, Sakizagaci Sok, Beyoglou, is large and serves no alcohol.

LIMAN LOKANTASI, Rihtim Cad. in Galata district, is a longstanding favorite for seafood; open lunch only.

PANDELI, a hole in the wall in the bazaar of the old city but it's famous for its grills and Turkish desserts; open lunch only, a bit touristy.

KONYA LEZZET, Ankara Cad., at Sirkeci has excellent Turkish fare, plenty of local color.

TOPKAPI SARAYI, in the palace gardens, is a blessing to the hungry sightseer.

BOSPHORUS

The European shore of the Bosphorus teems with restaurants; those below listed are all moderate to expensive. From south to north: the *Batanay* and the *Lido* (small cabaret) at Ortaköy; Russian *Surreya* excels in seafood at Arnavut-köy, where you can also dance at the Bogaziçi, the *Gaskonyali Toma* is at Küçük-bebek and the *Hisar* near Rumeli Hisar fortress. *Façyo's*, *Fidan's* and *Palet 2* are outstanding among the string of seaside terraces at Tarabya. Equally enjoyable are *Mardiros* and *Andon* at Büyükdere. Farthest in the quest for good food is *Canli Balik's* cuisine at Sariyer, worth the journey.

HOTELS IN ISTANBUL ENVIRONS

Cinar, deluxe, on the European shore of the Sea of Marmara, at Yesilköy, near airport. 200 rooms, nightclub, pool. Somewhat closer to town is the largest and best of the numerous beach hotels, *Ataköy Plaj,* 315 rooms; farther along the highway west are the *Yesilköy,* 30 rooms; *Baler,* 64 rooms; *Istanbul,* 82 rooms; *Solu,* 20 rooms; *Otel A,* 48 rooms; *Marin,* 165 rooms.

On the Asian shore of the Sea of Marmara, on their own beach, *Suadiye,* 117 rooms; *Erdim,* 52 rooms; *Marmara Beach,* 72 rooms, *Motel 212,* 28 rooms; *Kare,* 20 rooms.

On the Bosphorus, the *Tarabya,* 262 rooms, is reasonably priced for its deluxe class. Next best is the *Carlton,* 122 rooms; and descending south, as well as in price, the *Bogaziçi,* 26 rooms.

At Kilyos, on the Black Sea: *Kilyos Motel,* 109 rooms, on excellent beach.

ENTERTAINMENT. Theatrical performances are, of course, in Turkish, but seeing a performance in the superb setting of the Rumelihissar castle during the summer festival is an unforgettable experience, no less than the historical plays and sword dances in the Topkapi courtyard; check dates with the tourist office.

Opera and ballet have returned to the opera house on Taksim Square, reopened as the *Atatürk Cultural Center* in 1977. The main concert season runs from October to June but Istanbul's Symphony Orchestra plays too in the open-air theater near the Hilton during the summer festival. There are Sound and Light performances before the Blue Mosque at 9 P.M. in summer (twice weekly in English).

Nightlife. Sorely disappointing by international standards; drinks cost between 60 and 150TL at the better places, most offer floorshows, variety acts and striptease. Apart from those in the major hotels and equally expensive are: *Kervansaray, Oriental* and *Pariziyen* on Cumhuriyet Cad.; *Galata Tower* below and *Kulüp Resat* just off Istiklal Cad. Considerably cheaper are *Kulüp 33, Play Boy* and *Yeni Hydromel* adjoining one another in the beginning of Cumhuriyet Cad., as well as the *Taksim Belediye Gazinosu* on Taksim Square; for just plain dancing try *Abidik Gubedik, Dag Klup* and *Klup A,* all in Rumeli Cad., Nisantas.

TRANSPORTATION. The best means of public transport are the trolleycars, but they are too few. Taxis usually wait at hotel entrances and charge outrageously, as the meters, if any, don't work. To economize, do as the Turks do: take a shared taxi or *dolmus.* At the Sirkeci Rail Station, a signpost shows the way to the dolmus starting-place for Taksim; the cost of the fare is written on the stop sign, so there can be no mistake; you do not tip the driver. Nor do you talk to the other passengers, any more than on a town bus. If you wish to get off before reaching the terminal, just say *dour;* stop. The driver will draw up anywhere, one of the reasons which make driving in town something of a nightmare.

There are several electric train routes of the Turkish Railways (TCDD) for the suburbs. Leaving from the Sirkeci Station, they take you to Ataköy and Florya, beaches on the Sea of Marmara.

Tours. Guided bus tours of the city and outskirts are accompanied by an English-speaking guide; pick-up and delivery from your hotel. Check with your hotel desk, the tourist office or *Bayram Tours,* Cumhuriyet Cad. 257.

Excursions from Istanbul

A good plan is to cruise along the Bosphorus. The ferryboats leave from the Galata Bridge and zigzag between Europe and Asia until they reach the Black Sea (with the Soviet Union across the water beyond the horizon). On this trip, you sail past Rumelihisar castle, under Europe's longest suspension bridge, 3,540 feet, connecting two continents, opened on the 50th anniversary of the Republic in October 1973, and between charming little villages serving delectable seafood. At Sariyer, you can get a bus or a taxi back (the round trip by boat takes three hours).

More relaxing can be done on an excursion by boat, also from Galata Bridge, to the Princes' Islands, six miles from the southern end of the Bosphorus in the Sea of Marmara. There are nine islands, but only four are inhabited. They are pleasant wooded resort spots with open-air restaurants and the easy pace of the horse-and-buggy age (no cars are allowed). The ferry takes you to Büyük Ada, the biggest of the islands.

Bursa, Troy and Thrace

If you want to go farther afield, there are four flights daily to Anatolian Turkey's loveliest town: Bursa, which was the first capital of the Osmanli Turks in the 14th century and still has the Green Mosque and the splendid tombs of the sultans. Bursa is famous for its handmade carpets. 4,000 feet up Mount Uludag are two pleasant Swiss-chalet type hotels where people go in summer to escape the heat and in winter to ski.

Troy itself is disappointing. Familiarity with your Homer might tempt you close to the entrance of the Dardanelles, but only an archeologist would be able to conjure up Priam's mighty palace from the mound of rubble left by nine subsequent cities over a period of some 3,500 years.

If you are driving through Thrace from Greece or Bulgaria, though it means a detour of 65 miles, don't miss Edirne (Adrianople), whose central square is framed by three particularly lovely mosques.

PRACTICAL INFORMATION FOR ENVIRONS

BURSA. *Akdogan; Celik Palas* with thermal pool, and *Gönlü Ferah* with Turkish bath; all (2).
On Mt. Uludag are *Panorama* and *Fahri* inns, both comfortable (3)s.

CANAKKALE, near Troy. *Mola* and *Motel Tusan-Truva.*

EDIRNE. *Kervan,* 48 rooms, and *Sultan,* 51 rooms; both adequate (3)s.

IZMIR
The fire of 1922 destroyed almost all of the old town, only sparing the colorful sprawl of houses on the hillside surrounding the bay. Highlights

are the Agora (ancient Greek marketplace); the fortress of Kadifekale, on Mount Pagos, with its beautiful view over the bay of Izmir; the Archaeological Museum in the Kulturpark; and the caravanserai (old inns). Opposite the Clock Tower, built in the beginning of the century, it is well worth taking a look at the small mosque of Konak, with its fine glazed tiles.

For a rest from sightseeing, you might go for a swim at Inciralti, about seven miles out of town, towards the beach resort of Cesme. A pleasant outing is to take the ferry-boat across the bay, towards Karsikaya. Visit too the acropolis of old Smyrna, dating from the 1st century B.C., near the railway station of Turan.

The Aegean Provinces

Along the eastern shore of the Aegean the wealth and liberality of the Hellenistic kings and Roman emperors were lavished for centuries. The most extensive ruins of Graeco-Roman antiquity, palaces, temples and theaters in magnificent settings bear mute witness to a great past.

Pergamum was the center of the cult of Aesculapius, god of medicine. In his honor, the town built the *Asklepieion,* a temple with a medical library and a theater holding 3,500 spectators, restored for the annual Theatrical Festival held in May.

In the modern town of Bergama, you will come upon the Basilica, whose red brick has given it the name of Kizilavlu (the Red Courtyard). Over the centuries it has housed a succession of religious practices, from those of the Egyptian God Serapis to those of Christ and Mohammed. Across the stream flowing by the basilica is a beautiful Roman bridge with three arches.

After the Basilica, turn to the left—by car if possible, you have two miles to go—and upwards towards the Acropolis. At the end of the road, park your car and take the path leading to the gateway or Royal Door of the town's first wall. Inside and facing you are the remains of the world-renowned library of Pergamum, which once held 200,000 books gathered in the third century B.C. These books were written on parchment, a word deriving from the Greek root, *pergamene,* meaning "of Pergamon"—a paper made here from sheepskin. The whole grandiose complex is fascinating and evokes memories of a long line of empires under the same, timeless sun.

Selçuk (Ephesus)

Throughout its long history, the town has been rebuilt so often and has changed so much that it has lost its very name. On arriving, you stop at a signpost—Selçuk, while the guide says, "You are in Ephesus".

Mounts Pion and Koressos, Greco-Roman remains, a Byzantine basilica, and a Seljuk mosque constitute a hodgepodge of history. The pride of the museum is two splendid marble statues of Artemis, Greek in name but unmistakably Anatolian in appearance, with a triple row of breasts and a strange assortment of monsters on the garments.

For ancient paganism as for the beginnings of Christianity, Ephesus was an important center, second only to Athens, and later, to Jerusalem. The cult of Artemis changed into the cult of the Virgin Mary, as St. Paul and St. John both preached in the town. Up to the Middle Ages, Ephesus kept its standing till the silting up of its port. The world's first bank—run on the lines of today's banks, that is—opened here. A car is essential to visit the scattered sites, which include the water-logged remains of the Temple of Artemis, one of the Seven Wonders of the World, and vast Hellenistic and Roman ruins, many laced with memories of the early Christian church.

Driving out of town, from the Manisa Gate, views over the plain of Selçuk are revealed at every turn of the mountain road to Meryemana. Here is the simple House of Mary, thought to have been the place where St. John brought the mother of Christ after the Crucifixion, and from which, some believe, the Virgin ascended to heaven. Pope Paul VI paid a visit here in 1967, and it has been an increasingly popular target for pilgrimages ever since.

When you have done with the sightseeing, relax on the sea only 12 miles away. Kusadasi lies in the middle of a huge landlocked gulf divided by promontories into a series of fine beaches, each provided with modern hotels. This is an ideal center for excursions not only to nearby Priene, Miletus and Didyma, but also to Bodrum, ancient Halicarnassus further south, and inland to Pamukkale, the hot springs and pools above a petrified Niagara at the ancient city of Hierapolis.

The Turquoise Coast

Few shores can rival the profusion of natural and artistic beauties found along the 400 miles from the Bay of Antalya to the Bay of Mersin.

Antalya is the queen city of this Riviera—it was a summer resort in the days of the Seljuk Turks 800 years ago—and it offers an imposing portal built for the entry of the Emperor Hadrian in A.D. 130, a grooved minaret dating back to 1230, and the Karatay Mosque of 1250. And, best of all, the spectacular view over the gulf to the wild Lycian mountains jutting into the sea beyond the miles of pebbled beach at Konyaalti (where a large part of the province's population spends the summer in ungainly wooden shacks). Eight miles east is the fine sandy beach of Lara in a semi-tropical setting of banana plantations and orange groves. In season, there is a twice-daily plane service from Istanbul to Alanya. It's ideal for early or later sunshine; July and August are advisable only if you really like heat.

When you get tired of sunning and swimming, there is plenty to see. Near Antalya lie the vast ancient ruins of Perge. The best-preserved amphitheater of the ancient world (seating capacity 15,000, still used for performances of classical tragedies during the annual late summer Festival) is at Aspendos, 31 miles to the east. There's an even bigger amphitheater at Side, 19 miles on. To the west an excellent road hugs the gulf for 27 miles to Kemer, but only an atrocious track leads the remaining 67 spectacular miles to Demre, the Myra of old, where you can see the church and the sarcophagus of the fourth-century Saint Nicholas, Bishop of Myra, who later became known as Santa Claus.

Farther east, the 800 foot cliff at Alanya is crowned by an enormous fortress, its outer wall five miles in circumference.

Adana, Turkey's fourth city, lies on the Seyhan River 25 miles inland, in the middle of a fertile plain of cotton fields and orange groves. At the head of the southernmost gulf lies Iskenderun (Alexandretta), a busy port and fishing center as well as a banana-growing region.

Thirty-five miles south is Antakya, the ancient Antioch, where the followers of Jesus were first called Christians in the grotto of St. Peter. The town was founded in 301 B.C. and the first Christian church was established here. The Archaeological Museum contains a collection of magnificent Roman mosaics, but the huge medieval fortifications on the mountain top are crumbling away.

Ankara

In Istanbul or on the shores of the Mediterranean you are on fairly familiar ground, but Anatolia is Asia and Ankara is at its heart. Ankara became the capital in 1923. Atatürk called in leading European town planners, swamps were drained, malaria vanished, huge government buildings were raised and wide, airy boulevards and parks were laid out. Spreading out over a ring of hills commanding the Anatolian plateau, Ankara is still expanding.

The most imposing structure in Ankara is the Atatürk Mausoleum, a vast soaring hall surrounded by colonnades. But the citadel of old Angora still stands, too, with its inner fortress and its white tower. At this crossroads of history, there are the Temple of Augustus, Roman baths and an aqueduct, the Alâeddin and Aslanhane mosques, a model farm founded by Atatürk, the National Opera House and the Turkish National Theater. And last, but not least, the Museum of Anatolian Civilizations adroitly housed in a former *bedesten* (bazaar), where you can admire the most important collection of Hittite art in existence. If you want to know more about these mysterious people and their civilization, take a day-excursion to Bogazkale and Yazilikaya, where the quotations from the ancient testament concerning the Hittites will spring to life.

Cappadocia

Ankara can be your base for excursions into Anatolia, notably to Göreme (center of Cappadocia), Kayseri and Konya.

The Göreme valley is easily accessible, a site unparalled on earth with its fairy chimneys and honeycombed rocks. This was once a monastic center with 365 churches. You can see rupestral "houses" (dwellings of three and four stories, sometimes higher). Nearly all the churches have frescos, most of them amazingly bright and clear, depicting an endless series of biblical scenes, painted in a rather simple, childlike way. Tokali Kilise is the largest of the churches, the Karanlik (Dark) Kilise needs a flashlight, and the newest (13th century) frescos are in the Elmali Kilise. All are worth passing quiet hours inspecting.

Four miles west of Ürgüp, from whose hotel windows you look straight into the cataclysmic landscape, the gigantic rocky needle of Ortahisar thrusts up, bearing a citadel hewn out of its sugarloaf point, which you may climb to the railed-in top, though the cave-dwellers have been removed to ordinary houses on the safer ground below. At Uchisar a serrated escarpment pitted with crumbling dwellings dominates the horizon. It is an extraordinary setting—the village is still inhabited, and if picturesqueness is what you're after, this is it—plus a magnificent view from the citadel out over the countryside.

To complete this visit, don't miss the underground cities, where the ingenuity of persecuted men created in the 8th century an underworld with ominous overtones of the shape of things to come. Eight spacious floors, each offering accommodation for 200 people, were carved into the bowels of the earth. At Kaymakli, 7 miles south of Nevsehir, a central airshaft assures perfect ventilation all the 250 feet down to the bottom, from which a tunnel runs 6 miles south to another self-contained city at Derinkuyu.

Kayseri, the ancient Caesarea, is a 40 minute flight or a 200-mile drive from Ankara and lies at an altitude of 3,270 feet. It offers remains of the civilization of the Seljuk Turks, including the Great Mosque of 1136.

Konya lies 160 miles from Ankara. The monastery round the tomb of the founder of the Whirling Dervishes is now a religious museum. The 13th-century Karatay Medrese is a ceramics museum; and the Ince Minaret Medrese, with its superb portal, is a museum of stone and wood carvings.

The Black Sea

The beach of Sile is within easy reach from Istanbul. The western coastal towns are accessible by paved branches off the Istanbul-Ankara highway. A good road hugs the sea all the way from Sinop via Samsun and Trabzon, through the subtropical tea plantations round Rize and Hopa to the Russian border. The landscape is beautiful, but there is little of historical or archaeological interest except at Trabzon, imperial Byzantine Trebizond, with the nearby Sumela Monastery. The climate is temperate, but skies are often overcast and it may rain for days on end, even in summer. The wet weather prevents the development of beach resorts, but favors the cultivation of hazelnut, maize, tea and tobacco on the lush coastal plains and hills below the Pontine mountain ranges.

The hotel situation being unsatisfactory, make one of the *Denizyollari* Turkish Maritime Line boats your hotel, calling at various ports and then returning to your base by plane from Trabzon.

Eastern Turkey

The big attractions in the eastern part of Turkey are Mount Ararat, the Nemrut Dagh, Antiochus' burial place, and Lake Van. With the exception of this last-mentioned place, which is on the Istanbul-Tehran railway and boasts an airport, getting to these localities implies major discomfort. But if you hanker after more than just the dutifully trodden paths, join one of the organized tours. To attempt these vast empty spaces on your own is frankly, unwise; properly arranged it can be a rewarding experience.

PRACTICAL INFORMATION FOR TURKISH REGIONS

(**Note:** All hotels listed below are in the moderate category and have rooms with shower, unless otherwise stated.)

ADANA. *Büyük Sürmeli,* (1) 80 rooms; *Ipek Palas,* 84 rooms; *Koza,* 66 rooms.

ALANYA. In town: *Kaptan* and *Kent;* good choice of modern motels on the beach: best *Alantur,* followed by *Banana, Internasyonal, Merhaba, Panorama, Selam, Attila.* On successive beaches to the west, *Dinlenme, Turtas, Aspendos, Incekum,* all motels.

ANKARA. *Büyük Ankara,* (L), 210 rooms, 14 suites, three restaurants, night-club, pool. *Marmara,* 50 rooms, on Atatürk's farm; *Dedeman,* 252 rooms, pool, rooftop nightclub; *Bulvar Palas,* good restaurant; *Kent, Mola, Tunali, Roma,* all first class. *Stad,* largest; *Barikan* and *Yeni,* moderate.

Restaurants: *Altin Nal, Hülya* and *Kazan,* all on Cankaya Hill, are fashionable. Excellent kebab at the *Kebapçi Yesil Bursa* and *Kebapçi Bursa Iskender.* Dinner dancing at the deluxe and first-class hotels, also *Gar* and *Kösk* (expensive). Straight nightclubs, moderate, are *Elma Müsikhol, Kulüp Anamur, Sehrazat Gazinosu* and *Tuna.*

ANTAKYA. *Atahan,* 28 rooms; *Divan,* 25 rooms, very modest. Better stay at the cooler Harbiye suburb, 4 miles out: *Hidro,* 20 rooms.

ANTALYA. *Antalya* (1), 150 air-conditioned rooms, on a cliff, pool. *Büyük,* 42 rooms; *Perge,* 20 rooms, in town, are poor. Motels: *Alpay, Antalya, Derya, Sabo,* all rather unsatisfactory.

AYVALIK. Motels *Arci,* 28 rooms, and *Aytas,* 51 rooms, on beach.

BERGAMA (Pergamum). *Tusan Moteli,* adequate, 42 rooms, 2 miles from town.

ÇESME. Seaside resort 53 miles west of Izmir. *Çesme* (1), outstanding modern hotel. Five adequate motels: *Balin, Harem, Hüsam, Motes, Turtes.* A 1,000-bed superior holiday village, *Golden Dolphin,* is nearby.

EDREMIT. Four motels on the beach: *Akçan, Beyaz Saray, Dogan, Öge;* one in town: *Asiyan.*

EPHESUS (EFES). *Tusan,* 12 rooms, near ruins. *Belediye Motel,* 20 rooms; it's better to stay at Kusadasi.

GÜMÜLDÜR. Motels *Pasa,* 106 rooms, and *Sultan,* 110 rooms, on good beach.

ISKENDERUN. Most modern *Hitit,* 41 rooms; *Güney Palas,* 30 rooms, *Atlantik,* have restaurants. 7 miles out of town, on beach: *Mavi Yali Motel,* 30 rooms.

IZMIR. *Büyük Efes,* (L), is alone worth a stay in Izmir. Set in a park, with wonderful views, it has 300 rooms, 24 suites, roof and terrace restaurants, nightclub.

Anba, 54 rooms, *Izmir Palas,* 153 rooms, *Karaca,* 62 rooms, and *Taner,* 127 rooms, all (1) air-conditioned. *Kilim,* 89 rooms, *Kismet,* 68 rooms.

Restaurants: *Imbat* and *Yengeç,* for seafood; *Abdullah* and *Safak,* all in Atatürk Caddesi; *Park,* in the Kultur park; *Kale* in the citadel; *Sato,* in the hills, superb view added to good food. All moderately expensive.

KAYSERI. *Turan,* 72 rooms; *Turist,* 30 rooms, both (3) with restaurant.

KONYA. Three modest (3) hotels on central square: *Saray,* 40 rooms; *Basak Palas,* 40 rooms; *Sahin,* 41 rooms.

KUSADASI. *Imbat,* 139 rooms; *Tusan,* 70 rooms, both on private beach; *Kismet,* 64 rooms, nearer to village.

MARMARIS. Attractive fishing village on good beach; *Lydia,* 220 rooms in self-contained complex. Two adequate motels on the sea; *Altinisik,* 49 rooms; *Marti,* 114 rooms. Simple *Marmaris* holiday village, 224 bungalows.

NEVSEHIR. *Tusan Capadocia,* 80 rooms; *Göreme,* 72 rooms.

SIDE. *Athena,* 55 rooms; *Turtel,* 66 rooms, above average. On a lonely beach *Tusan Akdeniz,* 40 rooms.

ÜRGÜP. *Büyük,* 54 rooms, *Tepe,* 36 rooms, and *Cimenli Tepe Motel,* 6 rooms, on campsite with pool.

VAN. *Bayram,* 64 rooms.

YUGOSLAVIA

This is a good country in which to clear your head in readiness for a large number of confusing impressions, the like of which you will get nowhere else. In every sense the country is a fantastic mixture. Its scenery varies from rich Alpine valleys, superbly fertile vast plains, and rolling green hills to bare, rocky, lowering gorges up to 3,000 feet deep, forests where you can still shoot bears and wolves, and huge expanses of gaunt limestone mountains dropping suddenly down to the coast, where a thousand-odd islands betray the summits of submerged mountain ranges.

Climate varies enormously with altitude and location. You can swelter on the coast in late October while snow lies a foot deep ten miles inland, on the nearest mountains' further slopes. Politically, Yugoslavia is Communist—or so Yugoslavs say. Yet it retains nearly all the incentives for independent initiative that we regard as the West's pride. Thirty years ago it was a frighteningly poor country. Today, thousands of smart villas lining the coasts are Yugoslavs' second homes and rush-hour traffic james in large cities can hold their own with any part of Europe. Yugoslavia is one of the few "developing" countries that are catching up with the West in material prosperity. And this despite a historical, political, and ethnic jumble that only a man of Tito's indomitable personality could have dealt with.

The Country and the People

As the Turks were gradually driven out in the 19th century, the map of Yugoslavia began to change. There emerged the independent kingdoms of Serbia and Montenegro. Bosnia-Hercegovina was transferred to the administration of Austro-Hungary in 1878. Macedonia remained under Turkish domination until the Balkan Wars of 1912/13. Slovenia in the north-west and Croatia, including the entire Dalmatian coast, stayed under Austro-Hungarian rule. It seems impossible that Yugoslavia could ever have become an entity. When the Kingdom of Yugoslavia was formed in 1918, rivalries between the formerly independent principalities remained acute. The complexity of the situation persists even today, with 21,000,000 people, descended from five main and many minor nationalities, dispersed among six republics in an area of 98,725 square miles. Although Yugoslavia's main language is Serbo-Croat, there are two other major ones (Slovenian and Macedonian). There are also two alphabets (Roman and Cyrillic) and three major religions (Orthodox, Catholic and Moslem). In fact, there is unity only in the people's independent spirit.

In the Second World War a fifth of the country's entire population was killed fighting—but one-third of the dead fell at the hands of fellow-Yugoslavs. The country's leader since then, Marshal Tito, commander of the victorious Partisan army, granted autonomy to each major ethnic group after the war. So modern Yugoslavia is a federation made up of six independent republics: Serbia, Slovenia, Croatia, Bosnia-Hercegovina, Macedonia, and Montenegro, with two autonomous regions, the Vojvodina and Kosmet, inside Serbia. Under the federal government in Belgrade, decentralization of political and economic power has continued—not without protest from old-style politicians. Lending powers, for example, have been removed from formerly monopolist State banks and transferred to strictly commercial non-governmental concerns owned and run by their employees. Legislation is controlled as much by chambers representing trades and professions as by politicians, and all representatives are subject to recall by electors. Individual Republics have the right to secede—at least in theory, but they must contribute to the federal economic development plans for poorer regions, which led to argument and even riots in wealthy Croatia in the early 1970s.

A major characteristic of the Yugoslav system is workers' self-management, by which enterprises (with the exception of certain services) are owned and run, not by the State, but by the people who work for them. This gives rise to an unexpected degree of competition, since rival organizations operate bus services, hotels, travel agencies, shops, etc. in opposition to each other in any given area.

Finally, while independence is certainly every Yugoslav's ferociously-held ambition, the country today has become an entity in a way that was unthinkable in its previous history. This is of special importance, considering the age of President Tito, the last survivor of the World War II leaders.

Food and Drink

Yugoslav cooking shows considerable regional differences. Bosnian and Macedonian dishes have the greatest Turkish influence; Slovenian ones have similarities with those of neighboring Austria. Along the Dalmatian coast there is a distinctly Mediterranean flavor. On the whole, meat specialties are better prepared than fish. Here are a few national favorites: *piktije,* jellied pork or duck; *prsut,* smoked ham; *cevapcici,* charcoal-grilled minced meat, and *raznjici,* skewered meat; *sarma* or *japrak,* vine or cabbage leaves stuffed with meat and rice; *Bosanski lonac,* an excellent Bosnian meat and vegetable hot-pot. Desserts are heavy and sweet: *strukli,* nuts and plums stuffed into cheese balls, then boiled; *lokum,* Turkish delight, and *alva,* nuts crushed in honey, are very sweet indeed.

This is a great wine-growing country and wine flows cheaply everywhere. Slovenia's wines are best known: *Ljutomer, Traminer* and *Riesling.* The white *Vugava,* grown in Vis is excellent. Potent *slivovica* (slivovitz), plum brandy is the national liquor, and *maraskino,* made of morello cherries, the tastiest liqueur.

PRACTICAL INFORMATION FOR YUGOSLAVIA

WHAT WILL IT COST. Yugoslavia is no longer outstandingly cheap. Prices have risen steeply in recent years, though they have become more stable since 1977. Hotels are rated, with full board (per person, double occupancy): luxury (L) from $28 a day; first class superior (1) $20-27; first class reasonable (2) $15-20; moderate (3) $12-15; inexpensive (4) under $12. Hotels grant up to 50% reduction off season; quite a few, however, close in winter. Unless you are prepared to take pot luck, book as far ahead as possible if you are visiting the coast at the height of the season. The main new change of emphasis is the development of centers in the very beautiful interior of the country, where prices are mainly lower. Private accommodation is well organized throughout the country and very reasonable; local travel bureaus have information.

Restaurants are reasonably priced and rated expensive (E) 100 dinars up; moderate (M) 50-90 dinars; inexpensive (I) below 50 dinars.

Transportation is cheap: Belgrade to Zagreb (260 miles) costs about 340 dinars by air, 166–206 (depending on train) first class by rail, and 90–100 dinars by bus.

CAPITAL. Belgrade. Population is 1,200,000.

LANGUAGE. Serbo-Croatian. English and German spoken in all better hotels. Simple French is understood.

CLIMATE. Winter temperatures on Dalmatian coast are higher than those of French and Italian Rivieras. Spring and summer delightful. Inland can be torrid in summer and very cold in winter.

Average maximum daily temperatures in Fahrenheit and centigrade:

Belgrade	Jan.	Feb.	Mar.	Apr.	May	June	July	Aug.	Sept.	Oct.	Nov.	Dec.
F°	37	41	52	64	73	79	82	82	75	64	52	41
C°	3	5	11	18	23	26	28	28	24	18	11	5
Split												
F°	50	52	57	64	73	81	86	86	79	68	59	54
C°	10	11	14	18	23	27	30	30	26	20	15	12

SPECIAL EVENTS. Public holidays are *January 1 and 2; May 1 and 2* (Labor Day); *July 4* (Veterans Day); *November 29 and 30* (Republic Day), with the following additional days in each republic: Serbia, *July 7;* Montenegro, *July 13;* Slovenia, *July 22;* Croatia and Bosnia-Hercegovina, *July 27;* Macedonia, *August 2* and *October 11.* Among a crowded calendar of events, the following are some of the major festivals held each year: *May,* Peasant Wedding folklore event,

Ljubljana; *June-August* summer festivals in many centers, notably Split, Ljubljana, Sibenik; *June-October,* Opatija Summer Festival; *July,* Festival of Yugoslav Folk Music in Ilidza, Galicnik Wedding folklore event, International Review of Original Folklore in Zagreb, (27th) Moreska Sword Dance in Korcula (main performance but also held at other times), Peasant Wedding folklore event in Bohinj; *July-August,* Dubrovnik Summer Festival, Ohrid Summer Festival, Festival of Yugoslav Films in Pula; *August,* Sinj Equestrian tournament; *September,* Belgrade International Theatre Festival; *October,* Belgrade Music Festivities; *October-December,* concert and theatre season in all main cities.

SPAS. There are some hundreds of these and about 40 are now well equipped, mainly in Slovenia, Serbia and Croatia.

SPORTS. The Dalmatian coast and the sea around Istria provide wonderful *swimming, skin-diving* and *deep-sea fishing.* The country is teeming with all sorts of game but *hunting* here is really a rich man's sport. Fast flowing mountain rivers offer trout, perch, pike and other fish for *angling.* Yugoslavia is one of the best places for *canoeing.* Slovenia is the finest and nearest *ski* area for the sportsman from the West, though good new resorts are developing fast—for example in the area of Jahorina mountain near Sarajevo, Bosnia. There is a big move to attract more people into the lovely Yugoslav interior with its great mountain ranges, 300 lakes and 1,900 rivers, and possibilities of leisure activities.

MONEY. Monetary unit is the *dinar* divided into 100 *paras.* The rate of exchange is about 18 dinars to the US dollar, 35 to the pound sterling, but check current rates before changing.

SHOPPING. Remember that because Yugoslavia is a developing country, many of the things you buy there may benefit from GSP exemptions when you bring them through U.S. Customs upon your return. For details see under Customs in Facts at Your Fingertips at the beginning of this volume.

TIPPING is a practice that is growing—mainly taxi drivers (10%) and waiters (5–10% for good service).

HOW TO REACH YUGOSLAVIA. By air. From New York by JAT (*Yugoslav Airlines*) to Belgrade and Zagreb, and from Washington and New York by *Pan Am* to Belgrade; from London and European cities by *BA, JAT* and all major airlines.

By train. A number of international expresses starting from London, Paris, and other main cities provide through connections for all major Yugoslav towns; basic second-class return fare, £112.

By car. Via Italy and Austria; also by car-ferry from Italy: Ancona-Zadar, Ancona-Split, Bari-Dubrovnik, Bari-Bar, Ancona-Dubrovnik, Pescara-Split and Pescara-Primosten. There are car-carrying trains from various European towns to Ljubljana, Zagreb, Belgrade and Rijeka.

CUSTOMS. Normally, customs formalities are simple and quick. You may take in duty-free 200 cigarettes or 50 cigars, a bottle of wine and a liter of spirits. Any amount of foreign currency and travelers checks is permissible but you may not import more than 1500 dinars or export more than 1000 dinars in notes not higher than 100 dinars; any leftover or surplus Yugoslav currency can be exchanged at the border.

MAIL. Airmail letters to the U.S. and Canada cost 7.70 dinars up to 20 grams; to the U.K. 5.30 dinars up to 20 grams. Postcards go to all destinations outside Yugoslavia for 3.40 dinars.

ELECTRICITY. 220 volts, 50 cycles, A.C.

DRINKING WATER in main towns and recognized tourist resorts is excellent but don't trust country wells. Bottled mineral water (*mineralna voda*), fruit juices, wines and beer are cheap and good.

 TRAVEL IN YUGOSLAVIA. By air: All main cities, including the chief coast resorts in summer, are linked by domestic air routes.

By sea: The Dalmatian coast can be visited by "Jadrolinija" steamers, very crowded in season, sailing from Venice, Trieste and Rijeka southward, and there are any number of express or slower services linking the main centers and islands along the coast. Hydrofoils are also used for excursions and transfers to and from many points.

By train: Yugoslavia is one of the few countries that is expanding instead of contracting its railway network. The lines to Zadar and Ploce (via Sarajevo and Mostar) on the coast are among those recently developed. Newest of all is the Belgrade-Bar route, one of the most spectacular in Europe.

By Car: No international documents are required for the entry of your car: its registration certificate and your home driving permit are sufficient. Drive on the right hand side of the road. Third party insurance is compulsory; those without must obtain it at frontier posts. Gasoline (petrol) is about 7 dinars per liter, but coupons enabling visitors to buy it at a reduction of 20% are available at the border.

All main roads are surfaced, but the two principal highways, the *autoput* from Austria via Ljubljana-Zagreb-Belgrade-Nis-Skopje to Greece as well as the scenically magnificent Adriatic coastal road known as the *jadranska* from the Italian border to the frontier of Albania, are very narrow and overcrowded. The former is being enlarged at present. Maps are available at Yugoslav National Tourist Offices. In case of emergency, dial 987 throughout the country.

Car hire: *Autotehna* Marticeva 51, Zagreb, represents Avis and *Kompas,* Prazakova 4, Ljubljana, Hertz; branches in major towns. Cars can also be hired from many travel agencies but a fairly large deposit is required. Fly/drive arrangements are available through British Airways.

By bus: A comprehensive network covers the country, and main routes are serviced by modern, comfortable express buses. They can, however, be crowded, especially at public holiday times, so get your ticket in advance and arrive early. In remoter areas or on slower services, buses may well be of older vintage and some of the roads may be less than smooth. But it's a good way to see the countryside and meet the people—and the fares are low.

CAMPING. Sites are now quite numerous in all main tourist areas and growing in number elsewhere. A list is available from the Yugoslav National Tourist Office, indicating the facilities available at each. There are also youth hostels, including some excellent international youth centers (age group 16-31 years), such as at Rovinj, Becici and Dubrovnik.

 USEFUL ADDRESSES. *Embassies:* American, Kneza Milosa 50, British, Generala Zdanova 46, Canadian, Proleterskih Brigada 69, all Belgrade. *Consulates:* American, Zrinjski Trg 13, British, Ilica 12, both Zagreb. *Tourist Association of Yugoslavia,* Mose Pijade 8, Belgrade. Every town and main resort has a tourist information center or bureau. There are also several major Yugoslav travel agencies with offices in many towns and resorts; their services include excursions and various special-interest activities.

Slovenia

Set in Yugoslavia's northwest corner, against Italian and Austrian frontiers, Slovenia is the part of Yugoslavia seen first by most visitors entering the country by road or rail. It is not really typical. Slovenia consists in the north of Alpine territory identical with Austria's. Flatter, rolling hill country begins south of the Julian Alps, and extends to a tiny section of the large Istrian Peninsula's coast south of the Italian border near Trieste.

The thickly-wooded Alpine regions contain many charming lakes, notably Lake Bled, with its 11th-century castle, romantic island and fine modern hotels, and Lake Bohinj, quieter and higher. The outstanding feature of the southern inland area is the Postojna Caves, Europe's most striking series of vast interconnected underground caverns. Also worth visiting is Lipica where the famous stud for Lippizaner horses, founded 400 years ago, was re-established some years ago. As you approach Slovenia's short section of coast, the vegetation changes abruptly to vines, olives and figs and the climate becomes wholly Mediterranean. Here sophisticated, old-established Portoroz rubs shoulders with the newer coast resorts of Koper and Piran, based on old fishing ports. All, however, have many modern hotels and all the facilities that tourists expect.

Ljubljana, Slovenia's capital, is built around its hilltop castle. The city offers fine museums and Baroque churches. Its summer festival, with open-air performances of opera and ballet, is well worth a visit. So is the autumn Wine Fair, when anyone can sample, without charge, hundreds of varieties of Yugoslav wines. From here you can visit Ptuj and Celje, the latter with discoveries of Roman art treasures. Maribor, near the Austrian border, is the main center for the Pohorje mountains.

Slovenia is Yugoslavia's best-known winter sports area, largely because the resorts are easily accessible. There is a ski lift at Kranjska Gora to the best slopes of the Vitranc Mountains and lifts at Bohinj to the vast terrain of the Vogel Plateau. The Pokljuka region provides perfect conditions for beginners. In the Pohorje the ground is even easier—and the prices reasonable. In summer, climbing and walking attract visitors to the same mountains. For kayak enthusiasts Slovenia offers splendid descents from Dravograd to Maribor on the Drava or from Zuzemberk on the Krka River. All forms of water sports are practised on the coast.

PRACTICAL INFORMATION FOR SLOVENIA

 HOTELS AND RESTAURANTS. All establishments have restaurants unless the contrary is noted, and all resorts have at least some hotels open all year, unless seasonal dates are quoted. Most hotels down to category (3) have rooms with bath.

ANKARAN, with a good beach. *Adria* hotel group has several establishments (2) and (3), including one in a restored nunnery.

BLED. *Toplice* (1), good old-established hotel with private beach; annex *Trst* (2). *Golf* (1), on lake, golf course; new *Park* (1/2); *Krim* with new annex (2/3); *Jelovica* (3) with annexes (3) and (4).

BOHINJ. *Bellevue, Jezero, Pod Voglom, Zlatorog,* all (3); *Ski Hotel* (4) on Vogel Plateau above village.

BOVEC. Mountain resort in Julian Alps. *Kanin* (3), *Alp* (4).

CELJE. *Merx; Europa,* both (3).

KOPER. Picturesque port and resort; good yachting. *Triglav* (3) has beautiful terrace overlooking the sea. Motel *Zusterna* (3).

KRANJSKA GORA. Pleasant mountain resort, winter and summer. *Kompas,* near golf course, (1); *Lek, Larix, Alpina* (2); *Prisank, Alpe Adria, Motel Kompas,* all (3).

LIPICA. *Maestoso* (2).

LJUBLJANA. Excellent modern *Lev,* central *Slon* with good restaurant, *Union-Grand Hotel,* all (1). *Turist, Ilirija* farther out, and *Motel Medno* out of town, all (2/3).
Restaurants: *Macek* on river; *Pri Vitezu* and *Zlatorog;* all (M)

MARIBOR. *Slavija* (1), *Orel* (2), *Turist, Habakuk, Zamorec* (3/4). *Motel Jezero* (4), four miles out of town.

OTOCEC. *Grad Otocec* (3), a converted castle on island. *Motel Otocec* (4) on autoput.

PIRAN. Delightful port, half Venetian, half Austrian in atmosphere. *Piran* and *Punta,* both (3).

PORTOROZ. International Mediterranean atmosphere. *Grand Hotel Metropol* (L) and *Grand Hotel Palace* (1), both with private beaches; *Palace* (2) and *Riviera* (3) with modern annexes (2). Also new *Bernardin* holiday village. "*Aquatel*", accommodation in Chris Craft houseboats, has shore base with restaurants, bar, etc.

POSTOJNA. Europe's largest caves. *Jama* (2/3) and *Kras, Sport,* large *Motel Proteus,* all (3).

ROGASKA SLATINA. Slovenia's best-known thermal spa. *Donat* (1/2); *Park, Slovenski Dom, Soca, Zaraviliski Dom,* all (3).

Croatia and its Coasts

In the north the rich rolling farmlands of the Zagorje lie below the Slovenian Alps bordering Austria. South of Zagreb an upland region, the Gorski Kotar, leads into the still remote Lika, separated from the sea by the gaunt 50-mile-long, 5,000-foot-high Velebit Range. Almost all Istria's coastline as well as the 600 miles of the Croatian Littoral and Dalmatia, the narrow beautiful coastal strip and its hundreds of islands extending all the way from Starigrad-Paklenica to Sutorina, south of

Dubrovnik, belong to Croatia, with the exception of the Bosnian port of Ploce.

In Istria, the 400 years of Venetian rule are evident in most coastal towns and villages, while the succeeding century of Austrian dominion shows clearly in the main coastal resort of Opatija. Tourist complexes (villas, chalets, hotels, bars, restaurants, campsites and trailer parks, beaches, etc.) have grown up around many previously tiny villages. Being so accessible, this part of the coast is extremely popular. Its beaches are safe for children and good underwater fishing can be had, as along all Yugoslavia's coast (but check local regulations first.

In Crikvenica, on the Croatian Littoral south from Rijeka, modern development overshadows the older buildings—at least as far as sun-seeking tourists are concerned. The lovely islands of Krk and Losinj are well-provided with accommodation. Beautiful Rab, a popular holiday spot for generations, can boast in its capital (of the same name) one of Yugoslavia's loveliest Venetian towns. In atmosphere it is purely Dalmatian.

Zagreb and Inland Croatia

Zagreb, on the fringe of a fertile plain, is the capital of Croatia and rivals Belgrade in artistic achievements. It is largely central European in appearance due to the fact that during the historical see-saw of past centuries, Croatia formed an autonomous part of Austria and, later, of Hungary. Perched on the summit of a hill lies the old town, known as Gornji Grad; its patrician palaces are dominated by St. Mark's Church. On the outskirts of Zagreb is a cable-car which carries you up to Mount Sljeme, and beyond it there is the whole of the lovely Zagorje region with its old castles and churches, spas and quaint villages, in an unspoiled rural setting. Tito's childhood home at the village of Kumrovec is now a museum.

The most popular inland resort in Croatia is Plitvice, with its 16 lakes lying like terraces, one higher than the other, one of nature's wonders. Shooting is available in inland Croatia, which is extremely rich in deer and game birds. Prices are high. Your travel agent can supply you with full information about hunting parties.

PRACTICAL INFORMATION FOR CROATIA

Most hotels have restaurants and all have rooms with bath available.

CRES. Fishing village. *Kimen* (3).

CRIKVENICA. Family beach resort. *Omorika* (2); *Ad Turres, International, Riviera, Zagreb, Kacjak* tourist settlement, all (3).

KARLOVAC. *Korana* (3).

KRALJEVICA. On coast 15 miles south of Rijeka. Tourist villages *Ostro-villas* (2) and *Uvala Scott* (3).

KRK island. At Malinska, the fine *Haludovo* complex has accommodation in the (1/2) range, as well as villas and apartments. The *Malin* and its annexes are

(3). At Omisalj, *Adriatic* and annexes are mainly (3), as are the *Park* at Punat, and the *Drazica* in Krk town.

LOVRAN. Just south of Opatija. *Park, Miramare, Splendid, Beograd, Jadran* and various annexes, mostly (3).

MALI LOSINJ. On Losinj island. *Alhambra, Bellevue, Helios, Punta, Aurora* and *Vespera* (all 1/2) with annexes).

OPATIJA. Large beach resort with old world atmosphere and very good medical center. *Ambassador* (1) and older *Kvarner* (1) are best. *Adriatic, Kristal,* (2); *Opatija* and *Residenz* (3); *Atlantic, Belvedere* and *Imperial* (4).

PLITVICE. National Park featuring the Plitvice lakes. *Jezero* and *Plitvice,* both (1).

POREC. Lovely old town with famous Byzantine basilica, popular beach resort. *Albatros, Lotos, Materada, Mediteran, Parentium, Diamant, Galeb, Turist, Kristal, Delfin* (2/3), are all modern and very large, mostly some distance from town.

PULA. Remarkable Roman ruins. *Brioni* (1); *Park, Splendid* and annexes (3). Tourist villages nearby: *Zlatne Stijene, Medulin, Premantura, Verudela,* mostly (3).

RABAC. *Apollo, Fortuna, Hedera* and *Lanterna, Mimosa* and the hotel-complexes *Girandela* and *St. Andrea* are all (2/3).

RIJEKA. The country's largest port. *Bonavia* (1) and *Neboder* (3) are in town, *Jadran* (2) and *Park* (3) along the sea in Susak district.
Restaurants: *Gradski Restoran,* on the wharf, or *Zlatna Skoljka,* nearby, both (M).

ROVINJ. *Rovinj* (3) near town and beach. *Eden* (1), *Park, Monte Mulin* and *Lone,* all (3), outside town. Nudist center at Valalta.

UMAG. Major beach resort. *Adriatic, Koral, Umag,* all (2); *Istra* (3) and numerous apartment complexes, including *Stella Maris.*

VARAZDIN. Historic fortress. *Turist* (3) is fairly modern. Half rooms with bath.

VELI LOSINJ. On Losinj island. *Punta* (2). (April-Oct.).

ZAGREB. *Esplanade* and *Zagreb Intercontinental* both (L) with all amenities. *Palace* (1). *International,* near the motorway (1); *Dubrovnik, Central, Beograd,* all (2); *Laguna* and *Sport* (3), in or near center.
Restaurants: *Medulic,* Meduliceva 2. *Drina,* Preradoviceva 11, and *Lovacki Rog,* Ilica 14 (wild game) are best; (M-E). *Savskom Mlinu,* Remetinecka 14, and *Vila Rebar,* on road to Sljeme; both (M).

Dalmatia

This long stretch of coast and its numerous islands forms a separate entity, though administratively and ethnically, it is part of Croatia. The coastal regions present important differences from the interior, due to geography and still more to their separate historical background. While the Turks occupied much of present-day Yugoslavia, Venice ruled the Adriatic coast until the Napoleonic Wars. Only one Dalmatian city remained independent throughout these stormy centuries, namely Ragusa, today Dubrovnik.

The Dalmatian coast possesses not only dozens of seaside resorts, but also many historic towns. The whole of the walled city of Dubrovnik is an exquisite example of late Renaissance architecture. Split's old center lies within the walls of the monumental palace built by the Roman Emperor Diocletian. Trogir is an unspoilt medieval town and the historic city of Zadar contains impressive Roman and Romanesque remains. In addition there are scores of ancient little towns, some on the islands, where Venice left her imprint, such as Rab, Hvar, Ston, Sibenik and Korcula. For peace and quiet, try the islands of Kolocep, Lopud, Brac or Solta. Main centers like Dubrovnik and Split become very crowded in summer. Dalmatia possesses several old colorful traditional ceremonies and customs; if you are in the vicinity, don't miss the Moreska, at Korcula, July 27, or the Alka, at Sinj, in August.

Thanks to the indented coastline and the large number of islands, this part of the Adriatic is of some interest to fishermen. The travel agencies at main centers organize fishing expeditions lasting several days. All kinds of fish are available for underwater sport, under fairly strict regulations. Permits can be obtained locally.

PRACTICAL INFORMATION FOR DALMATIA

BRELA. Resort north of Makarska. *Maestral* (1) with annexes (1); *Berulia* (1/2).

CAVTAT, near Dubrovnik. *Croatia* (L), *Albatros* (1), *Adriatic, Cavtat* and *Epidaurus,* all (3).

DUBROVNIK. Book early for July-Aug. *Argentina* and *Excelsior,* both on sea, indoor pools, private beaches, are (L/1); *Imperial,* by Pile Gate, and *Villa Dubrovnik,* by the sea, both (1).

At nearby Lapad: new hotel complex *President* (L) and *Plakir, Argosy, Tirena* (1), with all amenities. *Park, Adriatic, Neptun, Bellevue, Kompas, Splendid* are (1/2)s, near beaches but away from old town. Nearer town, *Libertas* (L) and *Palace* (1), both overlooking sea. There is an *Aquatel* with Chris Craft houseboat cruisers.

Restaurants: *Gradska Kafana* (E), famous café in the old port; *Jadran* and *Prijeko* (M-E) in the old town; *Labirint* (M), open-air bar near the ramparts.

HVAR. Main town of Hvar island. *Adriatic, Palace,* and *Amfora* (1/2); *Dalmacija, Pharos, Bodul, Sirena, Galeb* and *Delfin,* all (3). Other island centers are Stari Grad, with the *Arkada* (1/2), *Adriatic* (2) and large *Helios* (2/3); Jelsa, with *Jadran, Mina* and tourist complex *Fontana,* all (2).

KORCULA. Enchanting little town on the island of same name. *Marko Polo* (2); *Bon Repos, Park* (2/3)s.

LOPUD. Island off Dubrovnik. *Lafodia* (2), *Lopud* (2/3), *Dubrava-Pracat* (3).

MAKARSKA. Fine old coast town and resort. *Dalmacija* (2); *Riviera* and *Park*, both (3).

OREBIC. On the Peljesac Peninsula, with lovely views to Korcula island. *Bellevue, Orsan* and *Ratheneum,* all (3).

PODGORA. Partisans' wartime naval HQ. *Minerva* (2); *Aurora, Mediteran, Salines* (3)s.

PRIMOSTEN. Charming fishing village near Sibenik, with nearby tourist settlements: *Marina Lucica, Raduca, Slava, Zora,* all (2).

RAB. Delightful capital of lovely island. *International* (2) is best. *Imperial, Istra* (3) are older. Bungalow village *Suha Punta* (3) with *Carolina* hotel (2) are three miles away, and the *San Marino* complex (3) 10 miles away at Lopar.

SIBENIK. Fine old coast town and resort. In town, the *Jadran* and *Krka* are (3/4). Outside town, the large, modern *Solaris Hotels* complex (2/3) has particularly good recreation facilities. This is a good launching point for the little known Kornat islands.

SPLIT. *Marjan* overlooks the harbor, and *Park,* both (1); *Split,* on road to Dubrovnik (3). At nearby Miljevac, *Lev* (1) in most attractive setting. At Trstenik, *Split Tourist Settlement* (3).

TROGIR. Medieval walled island-town. Nearby, on mainland, *Medena* (2), one of the biggest in Dalmatia; *Jadran* (3).

TUCEPI. Beach resort south of Makarska. *Jadran* (1/2); *Alga, Neptun* and annexe *Maslinik* (2/3)s.

VODICE. Resort based on old fishing village near Sibenik. *Olympia, Imperial* (2)s; *Punta* (2/3). Also chalets.

ZADAR. In town, *Kolovare* (2/3) and *Zagreb* (3). At Borik, 3 miles away, *Barbara* (1); *Zadar* and *New Park* (2); *Slavija* (3).

Bosnia-Hercegovina

The domes and slender minarets scattered across the towns of these provinces give them an oriental air, hardly to be wondered at when you recall that they formed part of the Ottoman Empire for four centuries. The Turkish heritage is evident not only in the architecture, for a good many of the inhabitants have kept the faith of their former rulers. Although readily accessible, Bosnia-Hercegovina provides a stimulating contrast to the traveler coming from the Adriatic coast. Between them, they comprise a region of bare rocky hills, deep gorges, and vast game forests. The province offers excellent rock climbing and hunting. The rivers contain trout while trips can be made by kayak or raft down the exciting rapids of the Drina Gorge (several major travel firms arrange excursions). The Sutjeska National Park is a particularly wild and beautiful region.

The capital of the combined province is the picturesquely situated city of Sarajevo, a blend of East and West. Mostar, Hercegovina's principal town, features its hump-backed stone bridge over the Neretva, built by the Turks in 1556, around which are clustered Turkish houses and mosques. Other towns in Bosnia are Banja Luka, Jajce, built around an impressive waterfall, and Travnik, the residence of the Turkish vizirs (governors) from 1700 until 1852.

PRACTICAL INFORMATION FOR BOSNIA-HERCEGOVINA

BANJA LUKA. *Bosna, Slavija* (2); *Palace, Motel International,* both (3).

JAJCE. *Jajce, Turist* and *Motel Plivska Jezera* on nearby lakeside, all (3).

MOSTAR. *Bristol, Neretva, Mostar,* all (3); *Hercegovina* (4).

SARAJEVO. Modern *Bristol, Evropa* (2); *Central, Zagreb, National* (3). At Ilidza, a thermal spa six miles away (where Austrian Archduke Franz-Ferdinand spent the night before his assassination which eventually sparked off World War I), modern *Terme* (2) and Auto-camp *Ilidza* (4).

TJENTISTE. South of Foca, in the beautiful Sutjeska National Park. *Mladost* (4).

TRAVNIK. *Orijent* (4)

TREBINJE. *Leotar* and *Villa Lastva,* both (3).

TUZLA. Useful overnight spot for motorists. *Bristol* (3).

VISEGRAD, with famous Drina bridge of Nobel Prize-winning novel. *Bikavac* and *Visegrad* (4).

Montenegro

Shut in between Bosnia-Hercegovina, Serbia and Albania, this smallest republic of the federation possesses some 60 miles of coastline dotted with rapidly expanding seaside resorts, backed by rocky hills. The interior is dominated by the rugged Black Mountains, the Venetian's Montenegro, which the Yugoslavs call Crna Gora. In the north, there are some green valleys, and the region fringing Lake Skadar is magnificent in spring.

Montenegro's history is one of unceasing struggle ever since the foundation of the medieval Serb state, of which it was a province until 1389. Then, following the Turkish victory at Kosovo, Serbia shrank northwards and finally disappeared. Though isolated, Montenegro resisted all foreign invaders. Even more remote than Bosnia-Hercegovina, this small country offers a large choice for holiday activities.

From walled Kotor, deep within the splendid triple bay, a breathtaking road zigzags up Mount Lovcen, offering one of the most startling panoramas in Europe, over the Dalmatian coast, its far-flung islands and a distant view of Albania. The south of Montenegro abuts onto the northern half of mighty Lake Skadar. The former capital Cetinje, which still preserves its pre-World War I atmosphere, lies in a fertile bowl amid soaring bare mountains. In the mighty Durmitor Range to the northeast is the Tara Canyon—55 miles long—one of the most remarkable in Europe. Raft trips can be arranged. Modern beach resorts stretch from Hercegnovi to Ulcinj, from which 11 miles of continuous sand run to the

Albanian border. Montenegro's developing port of Bar is now linked by a spectacular railway route with Belgrade, boring its way through dramatic mountainscapes and along the rim of precipitous gorges.

PRACTICAL INFORMATION FOR MONTENEGRO

BUDVA. Tiny medieval town, swamped by modern developments. *Adriatic, Bellevue, International, Mediteran, Montenegro, Plaza, Slavija* and *Splendid* on coast outside town, all modern (2)s. *Avala* (2) is older and near town walls. Attractive restaurant *Beden* in fortress of old town (M).

CETINJE. *Park* (3) is reasonably comfortable.

HERCEGNOVI. Montenegro's oldest seaside resort. *Centar* and annexes, *Plaza* (2)s; *Boka, Topla* and *Motel Dubrava* are (2/3). At the nearby spa of Igalo, *Tamaris* and *Igalo,* both (2), are large, modern, but the beach is poor.

KOTOR. Medieval walled town and port at the foot of Mt. Lovcen. *Fjord* (2).

MILOCER. Former residence of the Yugoslav royal family. *Milocer* (L) is the old palace, with annexes, private beach, terrace restaurant. *Maestral* also (L).

MOJKOVAC. On main Serbia/Macedonia-Montenegro route. *Mojkovac* (3), modern.

NIKSIC. Gateway to the wild Durmitor mountains. *Onogost.*

PETROVAC. Very popular beach resort. *Castellastva, Oliva, Riviera* (2)s, *Petrovac* (3).

SVETI STEFAN. Rocky island linked to mainland by a narrow causeway; the entire former fishing village is now a hotel of 36 cottages, modernized, with all comforts, casino, shingle beach, (L). On the mainland is Milocer, see above.

TITOGRAD. *Crna Gora, Podgorica* both (3).

TIVAT. On the bay of Kotor. *Mimoza, Kamelija, Park, Tivat,* all (3)s.

ULCINJ. Southernmost seaside resort. In town, *Galeb* and *Mediteran* (3), *Jadran* (4). By 7-mile sand beach some distance south of town, modern complex includes *Grand Lido* and *Olympic,* both (2). *Bojana* (2), naturalist village, 6 miles away.

VIRPAZAR on shore of Skadar Lake. Hotel *13th July* (3), in attractive local style.

ZABLJAK. Mountain resort in superb setting. New *Jezera* (2); *Durmitor* and *Zablijak* (3).

Serbia

Serbian national history begins with the establishment of a kingdom by Stefan Nemanja at the end of the 12th century. By the time of Dusan, in the first half of the 14th century, Serbia was the dominant power in the Balkans. However, at the Battle of Kosovo in 1389, it was overwhelmed by the greater numbers of the Turks and came under their control for five centuries. Serbia regained semi-independence in 1815 and began to regain its lost territories from a weakening Turkey. In 1912, Montenegro, Greece, Bulgaria and Serbia formed an alliance and in the two Balkan Wars redistributed the former Turkish provinces. Serbia's growing importance, and her influence upon the other Slavs under Habsburg rule, contributed to the sparking off of World War I.

In Belgrade (Beograd), you are really in the heart of the Balkans. Since its near-destruction in 1941, it has grown into a modern city of one million two hundred thousand inhabitants, but few cities boast as romantic a city park as the Kalemegdan, formerly a Turkish fortress built on a still more ancient Roman one. The National Museum is well worth a visit. Belgrade is the seat of the Patriarchate of the Serbian Orthodox Church; its Cathedral of the Holy Archangel Michael contains monuments to many heroes of Serbian history. Across the Sava River from the main part of the city lies Novi Beograd, whose unimaginative blocks of cement have risen out of what was formerly swamp land.

In Topola, just south of Belgrade, is the home of Karageorge, the instigator of the first Serbian Insurrection against the Turks in 1804, and ancestor of the Serbian Karageorge dynasty. In town remain several buildings from Karageorge's time. On Oplenac hill, above the town, is the family mausoleum, walls of which are completely covered with fantastic mosaic reproductions of old Serbian frescos. To the southeast is Kragujevac, where over 7,000 of the inhabitants were shot in one day by the Germans as reprisals in the last war. There is a very moving memorial park.

The Iron Gates

North of the Danube are the plains of the Vojvodina, whose mixed population of Serbs, Hungarians, Croatians, Slovaks, Montenegrins, Ruthenians, Macedonians, Germans, Austrians, Greeks and others testifies to the frequent and drastic political changes and struggles which this valuable farming area has undergone through its history. The Vojvodina offers some good fishing and hunting. Downstream from Belgrade, the Danube flows through a spectacular gorge, the Djerdap (Iron Gates), one of the great natural wonders of Europe. The all-day hydrofoil trip from Belgrade, which takes you through the swirling waters of the Djerdap, is well worth the time. At this point, the Danube forms the frontier between Yugoslavia and Romania, and the two nations jointly have constructed a vast hydroelectric, irrigation and navigation scheme. The dam includes a road bridge.

Hidden away in the interior of Serbia, in the remote areas of the Morava and Ibar valleys, you will come upon beautiful medieval Serb-Orthodox churches and monasteries, containing exquisite frescos that reveal the Byzantine influence. Turkish cities like Novi Pazar have preserved their Eastern character.

The extreme southwestern part of Serbia, known as Kosovo, constitutes an autonomous region administratively. Its cities of Pec, Pristina and Prizren present a Turkish appearance. The majority of the people of Kosovo are Albanians and there is a colorful mixture of costumes and traditions here. With its dramatic mountains, ancient monasteries and mosques, this is a very rewarding off-beat area, which now has several good or reasonable hotels.

PRACTICAL INFORMATION FOR SERBIA

BELGRADE (Beograd). It is essential to reserve rooms in advance. Best are the sumptuous and vast *Jugoslavija,* and the large *Metropol* and *Moskva,* all (L). Category (1) are the *Excelsior* and *Majestic;* the skyscraper *Slavija* is a bargain; others are the *Balkan, National, Palace, Prag, Putnik, Splendid* and *Union.* Among the (2/3)s are *Astorija, Srbija, Sumadija,* and *Toplice.*

On Mt. Avala, 12 miles south (location of the Yugoslav Tomb of the Unknown Soldier, as well as of a 700-foot television-observation tower) is modest *Avala* and at the foot of the mountain, *Motel 1000 Ruza,* both (3).

Restaurants: *Dva Jelena, Ima Dana, Tri Sesira,* all in the bohemian street called Skadarska, and all offering Music. Other good ones are *Dva Ribara,* Narodnog fronta 23; *Sest Topola, Sajmiste,* *Dusanov Grad,* Terazije 4, and *London,* Marsala Tita 28; *Pri Majoki,* Slovenian restaurant in New Belgrade.

Shopping: Plenty of big stores, but look out too for the daily open air markets (open Sundays, too), and several shopping complexes open 24 hours a day, seven days a week. A central one is Drag Stor (pronounced Drug Store !).

DECANI. *Visoki Decani* (4), near monastery, in pine forest.

GROCKA. Restaurant: *Vinogradi* (E), one of the best in Yugoslavia; located on a hill overlooking the Danube it provides a memorable outing from Belgrade.

KLADOVO. Terminus of the "Iron Gates" hydrofoil trip. Have lunch or stay overnight at the *Djerdap* (3/4).

KRAGUJEVAC. *Sumarice, Kragujevac,* both (3).

KRALJEVO. Near Zica monastery. *Turist* (3).

NIS. Highrise *Ambassador* (2), *Park, Nis,* both (2/3)s, less well-equipped, but quieter.

NOVI SAD. Capital of the Vojvodina. Best is *Trydjava Varadin* (1), across the river in ancient fortress. *Park,* (1/2) in town; *Putnik, Vojvodina,* (3s); *Sajam,* (2).

PEC. *Metohija* (2), old style but newly renovated; *Korzo* (3).

PRISTINA. Main center of Kosovo. New *Grand Hotel Pristina* (2); *Kosovski Bozur* (3); *Union* (4).

PRIZREN. A 17th-century mosque, and Church of Our Lady of Ljeviska, built in 1307. *Theranda, Motel Vllazerimi,* both (3).

SMEDEREVO. Ancient fort on the banks of the Danube. *Smederevo,* (2).

SOPOCANI. *Sopocani,* (4) near the monastery.

STUDENICA. *Motel Turist,* near the monastery.

SUBOTICA. Near Lake Palic, almost on the Hungarian frontier. *Patria, Park; Jezero* on the lake; all (3).

SVETOZAREVO. Near Manasija and Ravanica monasteries. *Svetozarevo* and *Srbija* (3).

TOPOLA. *Oplenac* (4) is good value.

VRNJACKA BANJA. Serbia's best thermal spa. Near Ljubostinja monastery. *Pinetta* (2); *Fontana, Funtana, Panorama* (3s). Nudist settlement *Koversada* is (2).

Macedonia

The main attraction of this southernmost province is medieval Ohrid, in its lovely lakeside setting. The Serbian Orthodox Church contains some extraordinary frescos and icons. There are two other great lakes, those of Prespa and Dojran, and the countryside holds countless reminders of Greek and Roman times. As in Serbia, there are a great number of Byzantine monasteries. From the summit of Mt. Solunska Glava, you can see as far as the Aegean and the Greek islands.

The disastrous earthquake of July 1963 destroyed the center of Skopje, a city of 200,000 inhabitants and the capital of Macedonia. However, thanks to the help and cooperation of many nations and organizations, Skopje was rebuilt rapidly; its monuments from Roman times (when it also suffered earthquake destruction) and its medieval treasures were restored, among them the church of the Holy Savior, with its famous woodcarvings, the Turkish Bath of Daut Pasha, now an art gallery, and the vast Turkish caravanserai.

PRACTICAL INFORMATION FOR MACEDONIA

BITOLA. Second largest city of Macedonia. *Epinal* (3).

GEVGELIJA. Principal frontier town between Yugoslavia and Greece. *Inex Hotel Vardar* (2).

OHRID. Beautiful old town with ancient monasteries by Lake Ohrid. In town, *Metropol* (2), *Grand Hotel Palace* and annex, *Slavija* (3s). Most new hotels are some distance out, including *Inex Hotel Gorica, Park* and *Villas,* all (2). At Pestani, *Desaret.*

OTESEVO. Summer resort on Lake Prespa. *Otesevo* (3), very pleasant.

POPOVA SAPKA. Winter sports center. *Planinarski Dom* (3).

SARA-BREZOVICA. Winter sports center. *Breza* (4).

SKOPJE. *Continental, Grand Hotel Skopje,* both (2/3); *Turist, Bellevue* (2). *Vodno* and *Saraj,* out of town, both (3). Also *Turist* motel-camp (3).

STARI DOJRAN. Summer resort on lake with some of the best fishing in Yugoslavia. *Dojran,* (4).

STRUGA. Small town on Lake Ohrid. *Drim* (3); *Biser* (3) in attractive local style.

TETOVO. Starting point for mountaineering and skiing on the Sara mountain. *Makedonija* (3).

TITOV VELES. On the road to Greece. *International* (4); *Hotel Mladost.*

HINTS FOR BUSINESSMEN. Normal Government and commercial office hours are 7 A.M. to 2 P.M., so be prepared to adjust your working hours accordingly. You are likely to be offered small cups of strong, Turkish coffee and, quite likely, small glasses of fiery plum brandy depending on the time of day. Avoid August when many people are away, and certainly holidays such as Labour Day (1st and 2nd May) when the entire country celebrates.

INDEX

(The letters H and R indicate hotel and restaurant listings.)

GENERAL

(See also "Practical Information" sections under each country.)

ALBANIA

WEST GERMANY

EAST GERMANY

GIBRALTAR

GREAT BRITAIN

GREECE

LIECHTENSTEIN

LUXEMBOURG

SPAIN

SWEDEN

SWITZERLAND

FODOR TRAVEL GUIDES

Area Guides

Europe '79	☐ Cloth	$12.95	
	☐ Traveltex	$ 9.95	(Sept. '78)*
Europe On A Budget '79	☐ Cloth	$ 9.95	
	☐ Traveltex	$ 4.95	(Nov.'78)
Caribbean and Bahamas '79	☐ Cloth	$12.95	
	☐ Traveltex	$ 9.95	(Sept.'78)
South America '79	☐ Cloth	$12.95	
	☐ Traveltex	$ 9.95	(Oct.'78)

Country Guides

Mexico '79	☐ Cloth	$12.95	
	☐ Traveltex	$ 9.95	(Oct.'78)
Bermuda '79	☐ Cloth	$ 8.95	
	☐ Traveltex	$ 4.95	(Nov.'78)
Great Britain '79	☐ Cloth	$12.95	
	☐ Traveltex	$ 9.95	(Nov.'78)
Canada '79	☐ Cloth	$12.95	
	☐ Traveltex	$ 9.95	(Sept.'78)
France '79	☐ Cloth	$12.95	
	☐ Traveltex	$ 9.95	(Nov.'78)
Germany '79	☐ Cloth	$12.95	
	☐ Traveltex	$ 9.95	(Nov.'78)

City Guides

Paris '79	☐ Cloth	$ 8.95	
	☐ Traveltex	$ 5.95	(Jan.'79)
London '79	☐ Cloth	$ 8.95	
	☐ Traveltex	$ 5.95	(Dec.'78)

U.S.A. Guides

Hawaii '79	☐ Cloth	$ 9.95	(Sept.'78)
U.S.A. '79	☐ Cloth	$14.95	
	☐ Traveltex	$10.95	(Nov.'78)
Far West '79	☐ Cloth	$ 9.95	
	☐ Paper	$ 4.95	(Dec.'78)
The South '79	☐ Cloth	$ 9.95	
	☐ Paper	$ 4.95	(Oct.'78)

Special Interest Guides

Cruises Everywhere '79	☐ Cloth	$12.95	
	☐ Traveltex	$ 9.95	(Oct.'78)
Seaside America '79	☐ Cloth	$12.95	
	☐ Traveltex	$ 9.95	(Pub.'78)
Animal Parks of Africa '79	☐ Cloth	$12.95	
	☐ Traveltex	$ 9.95	(Sept.'78)

*The 1979 editions will be published during the month listed.
For a complete list of the over 70 Fodor Guides, use the coupon below.

Fodor Guides, Dept. 35, 750 Third Ave., New York, N.Y. 10017

☐ Please send a complete list of Fodor Guides.
☐ Please send me the Guides checked above.

I am enclosing $_____. (Check or money order)
N.Y. and Calif. residents add sales tax. Or charge:
☐ Visa   ☐ Master Charge   ☐ American Express

Acct. # _____   M.C. Interbank # _____

Exp. Date_____ Signature_____

Name_____

Address_____

City_____ State_____ Zip_____

Please allow four weeks for delivery. Offer expires 10/79.   FEC